State Rankings 2019

⑤SAGE stats

Featuring State Stats, Local Stats, and Business Stats

What is **SAGE Stats**? **SAGE Stats** is an exciting online destination for finding, mapping, comparing, and exporting statistics across a number of topics and geographic areas. In its three modules, **SAGE Stats** draws together the statistics from the *State Rankings* series of books by CQ Press (SAGE State Stats); a broad collection of data by county, city, and metro area (SAGE Local Stats); and a collection of highly detailed demographic data (including projections) and industry and labor measures available across geographical areas including ZIP Codes (SAGE Business Stats).

Featuring data from more than 250 different government and nongovernment sources and backed by a rich collection of thousands of historical, current, and projected data series on popular topics of research interest, **SAGE Stats** uniquely allows users to discover, view, and export key information measures for the 50 states and the District of Columbia, over 1,400 cities, over 3,000 counties, over 900 metro areas, and thousands of ZIP Codes.

SAGE Stats makes research easy by providing in one place annual measures dating back decades. Data series are displayed in a clear and consistent format with detailed source information. An intuitive interface lets users easily browse by location or by topic, and then compare across locations or across time.

Users can:

- Analyze data patterns by comparing across locations, data series, and time

- Create and export custom visuals including line charts, scatter plots, and maps

- Generate tables and download data for statistical research

- Toggle user display between interactive visual and tabular data view

- Engage a moveable timeline to discover trends

- Explore interactive maps featuring zoom and hover functions

- Export data across multiple years and data series

Ongoing updates to **SAGE Stats** throughout the year ensure that users have the most current data available.

Check it out online at http://data.sagepub.com/.

State Rankings 2019

A Statistical View of America

Editors

Kathleen O'Leary Morgan
and
Scott Morgan

FOR INFORMATION:

CQ Press
An Imprint of SAGE Publications, Inc.
2455 Teller Road
Thousand Oaks, California 91320
E-mail: order@sagepub.com

SAGE Publications Ltd.
1 Oliver's Yard
55 City Road
London, EC1Y 1SP
United Kingdom

SAGE Publications India Pvt. Ltd.
B 1/I 1 Mohan Cooperative Industrial Area
Mathura Road, New Delhi 110 044
India

SAGE Publications Asia-Pacific Pte. Ltd.
18 Cross Street #10-10/11/12
China Square Central
Singapore 048423

ISBN 978-1-5443-5372-2 (cloth)
ISBN 978-1-5443-5371-5 (paper)
ISSN 1057-3623

Senior Acquisitions Editor: Andrew Boney
Associate Editor: Diana Aleman
Production Editor: Tracy Buyan
Cover Designer: Candice Harman
Marketing Manager: Jennifer Jelinski

19 20 21 22 23 10 9 8 7 6 5 4 3 2 1

Contents

Detailed Table of Contents

XI. HEALTH

XIV. SOCIAL WELFARE

XV. TRANSPORTATION

Introduction and Methodology

State Rankings 2019 provides an easily accessible collection of data in a broad range of quality-of-life factors in the United States. In this latest 2019 edition, *State Rankings* compares data from the fifty states and the District of Columbia in 566 tables in the following fifteen different livability categories: agriculture, crime and law enforcement, defense, economy, education, employment and labor, energy and environment, geography, federal government finances, state and local government finances, health, households and housing, population, social welfare, and transportation.

Purpose of This Book

State Rankings 2019 translates complicated and often convoluted statistics into meaningful, easy-to-understand information. Too often there is an abundance of data but far too little information putting those data into context. This book allows researchers, legislators, policy analysts, journalists, and the general public to access information in a manner that not only provides basic facts about a state's quality of life but also gives a meaningful framework by comparing individual states against the rest of the country.

These data and rankings can be used in a variety of ways, by a variety of audiences, including the following examples:

- Policy makers can use the data to help identify areas warranting further study.
- Journalists can easily find impartial state information that puts stories into context.
- The general public can see how a particular state is faring compared to other states.
- Librarians can use the data as a quick reference to assist patrons in research and offer the sources and websites included as a starting point for finding other related data.

The comparison rankings in *State Rankings 2019* provide an annual snapshot of how the states are doing in the fifteen livability categories mentioned above. There are two principle approaches to using these rankings. The first is to examine how a state is doing compared to all other states via the comparison rankings in this book. The second approach is to compare a state to itself over a given period of time. Both approaches are important to achieving a good understanding of how and whether a state is making progress. It is important to keep in mind that the rankings are not a definitive determination of which state is the "best." However, since so many issues are surrounded by emotions, tracking them by the numbers can help bring the discussion back to a more balanced, unbiased review that in the end leads to better decisions.

Data and Limitations

The data featured in *State Rankings 2019* were chosen specifically by the editors from a variety of government and private sector sources. The statistics presented are intended to cover a broad array of quality-of-life subject areas, giving users of the book a solid collection of state information. Nonetheless, the statistics are not inclusive of all the possible data that might be available. The statistics in the book are the latest available from the sources. In a few cases, we have retained tables that have not been updated for several years because we believe our readers will find the data relevant, even if updates are not available. In other cases, we replaced obsolete data with new tables. Longtime users should note in particular that we have updated Government Finances: Federal with new government spending data from the OMB's USASpending.gov, but differences in methodology make those data difficult to compare with past editions.

Previous editions of the book have used the term *most livable* when describing states with the highest livability ranking. This term is no longer being used because it is purely descriptive—at no time do we attempt to explain *why* a particular state is ranking higher or lower in livability factors than others or against the national average. This explanation—currently sought by social science researchers—is beyond the scope of this book. While our selection of factors clearly affects the rankings, we believe the rankings provide a solid measurement of how the fifty states and Washington, D.C., are faring with regard to quality of life in the United States. Researchers, practitioners, and others can confidently use the data to understand livability issues and guide policy decisions.

Methodology

The comparison rankings for *State Rankings 2019* are determined using the same methodology as we have used for the past twenty-plus years. The editors used the previously mentioned fifteen livability categories to select forty-three quality-of-life factors from a broad range of economic, educational, health-oriented, public safety, and environmental statistics. Overall comparison rankings were determined by averaging each state's ranking for each category. The scale is one to fifty; the higher the number, the higher the state is in the rankings (i.e., 50 is the best score to receive). Data used are for the most recent year for which comparable numbers are available from most states. All factors are given equal weight.

While the 566 tables provided in *State Rankings 2019* are ranked highest to lowest without any subjective determination as to whether a subject is "positive" or "negative," for the state comparison rankings, the editors do make a subjective determination as to whether something is "positive" or "negative." Twenty-five of the forty-three factors were determined to be negative, and the remaining eighteen were viewed as positive.

The reason for this division between positive and negative is that if a state ranks first in crime rate (i.e., it has the highest crime rate), its comparison ranking is reduced, whereas if a state ranks first in per-capita personal income (i.e., it has the highest income), its comparison ranking is increased. To account for this, we subtract the rankings for the positive factors from 51 so that a state with the highest ranking in a positive factor ends up with a 50 for that factor (remember, high numbers are best).

Once we have chosen the factors and divided them into positive and negative groupings, we simply average the ranking for each state in all forty-three factors. If a state is missing data for a given factor, its standing is based on the average ranking for the remaining factors. The book uses the latest available data for each livability factor.

As an example, Maine ranks 48th in crime rate (negative factor), 46th in personal bankruptcy rate (negative factor), and ranks 8th in percent of population graduated from high school (positive factor). The 48th and 46th rankings go straight into the comparison formula, whereas the number eight ranking in 7 percent of population graduated from high school is first subtracted from 51 with the resulting 43 going into the ranking. For these three factors for Maine, we would average 48, 46, and 43 with the result being 46.67. If these three factors were the only ones we used, then the resulting average of 46.67 would be the figure we would use to compare Maine to the other forty-nine states. However, for the *State Rankings* comparison rankings, an additional forty factors are added into the calculations before the final results are determined.

Designed with the researcher in mind, the numbers shown in *State Rankings* require no additional calculations to convert them from millions, thousands, and so on. All states are ranked on a high-to-low basis, with any ties among the states listed alphabetically for a given ranking. Negative numbers are shown in parentheses. For tables displaying national totals (as opposed to rates, per capita, etc.), a separate column is included that shows what percent of the national total each individual state's total represents. This column is headed by "% of USA." This percentage figure is particularly interesting when compared with a state's population in a given year. Rates may be per 10,000 persons, per 100,000 persons, or per some other denominator; these are clearly explained by the text following the national rate and, if necessary, the footnotes.

To further assist readers, source information and footnotes clearly are shown at the bottom of each page, while national totals, rates, and percentages are prominently displayed at the top of each table. Every other line is shaded in gray for easier reading. Numerous information-finding tools are provided: a thorough table of contents, table listings at the beginning of each chapter, and a detailed index. In addition, a roster of sources with addresses, phone numbers, and websites is found in the back of the book.

About the Editors

Kathleen O'Leary Morgan and **Scott Morgan** founded Morgan Quitno Press in 1990. They edited more than 2,700 annual state and city statistical reference publications before selling the titles to CQ Press in 2007. They also edited a monthly journal, *State Statistical Trends*, for six years. They have continued to edit a number of the publications continued by CQ Press, as well as an ever-growing online database.

Kathleen received a BS and a master's in public administration from the University of Kansas. She served in a number of media and legislative positions within the U.S. Department of Transportation, where she also served as deputy director of congressional affairs.

Scott received both a BS and a law degree from the University of Kansas. He previously worked on the staffs of two U.S. senators as well as the Senate Judiciary Committee. He represented the Senate on the Federal Election Commission and served as chief counsel for Senator Bob Dole's presidential campaign in 1988. He was chief counsel for Governor Mike Hayden in Kansas until 1990.

The 2019 State Rankings

ALPHA ORDER

RANK	STATE	AVG	18 RANK	CHANGE
45	Alabama	18.98	44	-1
37	Alaska	22.56	36	-1
41	Arizona	21.02	40	-1
44	Arkansas	19.16	42	-2
25	California	25.42	20	-5
7	Colorado	30.88	11	4
11	Connecticut	29.58	10	-1
23	Delaware	25.58	34	11
33	Florida	23.95	32	-1
38	Georgia	22.30	38	0
20	Hawaii	26.47	15	-5
22	Idaho	25.81	23	1
31	Illinois	24.12	32	1
30	Indiana	24.40	29	-1
11	Iowa	29.58	5	-6
19	Kansas	26.91	17	-2
47	Kentucky	17.81	46	-1
50	Louisiana	15.09	50	0
9	Maine	29.93	9	0
17	Maryland	27.63	12	-5
4	Massachusetts	32.40	4	0
29	Michigan	24.60	27	-2
3	Minnesota	32.49	2	-1
49	Mississippi	15.88	47	-2
36	Missouri	23.37	30	-6
27	Montana	25.28	26	-1
13	Nebraska	29.37	7	-6
39	Nevada	21.81	43	4
1	New Hampshire	37.02	1	0
6	New Jersey	31.37	8	2
48	New Mexico	16.70	48	0
21	New York	25.98	25	4
34	North Carolina	23.77	39	5
16	North Dakota	28.30	18	2
34	Ohio	23.77	35	1
40	Oklahoma	21.07	45	5
28	Oregon	25.14	28	0
26	Pennsylvania	25.35	22	-4
24	Rhode Island	25.52	24	0
43	South Carolina	20.58	41	-2
18	South Dakota	27.51	21	3
42	Tennessee	20.88	37	-5
32	Texas	24.07	31	-1
2	Utah	32.79	3	1
5	Vermont	31.81	6	1
15	Virginia	28.49	19	4
10	Washington	29.60	14	4
46	West Virginia	18.63	49	3
14	Wisconsin	28.60	13	-1
8	Wyoming	30.58	15	7

RANK ORDER

RANK	STATE	AVG	18 RANK	CHANGE
1	New Hampshire	37.02	1	0
2	Utah	32.79	3	1
3	Minnesota	32.49	2	-1
4	Massachusetts	32.40	4	0
5	Vermont	31.81	6	1
6	New Jersey	31.37	8	2
7	Colorado	30.88	11	4
8	Wyoming	30.58	15	7
9	Maine	29.93	9	0
10	Washington	29.60	14	4
11	Connecticut	29.58	10	-1
11	Iowa	29.58	5	-6
13	Nebraska	29.37	7	-6
14	Wisconsin	28.60	13	-1
15	Virginia	28.49	19	4
16	North Dakota	28.30	18	2
17	Maryland	27.63	12	-5
18	South Dakota	27.51	21	3
19	Kansas	26.91	17	-2
20	Hawaii	26.47	15	-5
21	New York	25.98	25	4
22	Idaho	25.81	23	1
23	Delaware	25.58	34	11
24	Rhode Island	25.52	24	0
25	California	25.42	20	-5
26	Pennsylvania	25.35	22	-4
27	Montana	25.28	26	-1
28	Oregon	25.14	28	0
29	Michigan	24.60	27	-2
30	Indiana	24.40	29	-1
31	Illinois	24.12	32	1
32	Texas	24.07	31	-1
33	Florida	23.95	32	-1
34	North Carolina	23.77	39	5
34	Ohio	23.77	35	1
36	Missouri	23.37	30	-6
37	Alaska	22.56	36	-1
38	Georgia	22.30	38	0
39	Nevada	21.81	43	4
40	Oklahoma	21.07	45	5
41	Arizona	21.02	40	-1
42	Tennessee	20.88	37	-5
43	South Carolina	20.58	41	-2
44	Arkansas	19.16	42	-2
45	Alabama	18.98	44	-1
46	West Virginia	18.63	49	3
47	Kentucky	17.81	46	-1
48	New Mexico	16.70	48	0
49	Mississippi	15.88	47	-2
50	Louisiana	15.09	50	0

Date Each State Admitted to Statehood*

ALPHA ORDER

RANK	STATE	DATE OF ADMISSION
22	Alabama	December 14, 1819
49	Alaska	January 3, 1959
48	Arizona	February 14, 1912
25	Arkansas	June 15, 1836
31	California	September 9, 1850
38	Colorado	August 1, 1876
5	Connecticut	January 9, 1788
1	Delaware	December 7, 1787
27	Florida	March 3, 1845
4	Georgia	January 2, 1788
50	Hawaii	August 21, 1959
43	Idaho	July 3, 1890
21	Illinois	December 3, 1818
19	Indiana	December 11, 1816
29	Iowa	December 28, 1846
34	Kansas	January 29, 1861
15	Kentucky	June 1, 1792
18	Louisiana	April 30, 1812
23	Maine	March 15, 1820
7	Maryland	April 28, 1788
6	Massachusetts	February 6, 1788
26	Michigan	January 26, 1837
32	Minnesota	May 11, 1858
20	Mississippi	December 10, 1817
24	Missouri	August 10, 1821
41	Montana	November 8, 1889
37	Nebraska	March 1, 1867
36	Nevada	October 31, 1864
9	New Hampshire	June 21, 1788
3	New Jersey	December 18, 1787
47	New Mexico	January 6, 1912
11	New York	July 26, 1788
12	North Carolina	November 21, 1789
39	North Dakota	November 2, 1889
17	Ohio	March 1, 1803
46	Oklahoma	November 16, 1907
33	Oregon	February 14, 1859
2	Pennsylvania	December 12, 1787
13	Rhode Island	May 29, 1790
8	South Carolina	May 23, 1788
39	South Dakota	November 2, 1889
16	Tennessee	June 1, 1796
28	Texas	December 29, 1845
45	Utah	January 4, 1896
14	Vermont	March 4, 1791
10	Virginia	June 26, 1788
42	Washington	November 11, 1889
35	West Virginia	June 20, 1863
30	Wisconsin	May 29, 1848
44	Wyoming	July 10, 1890

RANK ORDER

RANK	STATE	DATE OF ADMISSION
1	Delaware	December 7, 1787
2	Pennsylvania	December 12, 1787
3	New Jersey	December 18, 1787
4	Georgia	January 2, 1788
5	Connecticut	January 9, 1788
6	Massachusetts	February 6, 1788
7	Maryland	April 28, 1788
8	South Carolina	May 23, 1788
9	New Hampshire	June 21, 1788
10	Virginia	June 26, 1788
11	New York	July 26, 1788
12	North Carolina	November 21, 1789
13	Rhode Island	May 29, 1790
14	Vermont	March 4, 1791
15	Kentucky	June 1, 1792
16	Tennessee	June 1, 1796
17	Ohio	March 1, 1803
18	Louisiana	April 30, 1812
19	Indiana	December 11, 1816
20	Mississippi	December 10, 1817
21	Illinois	December 3, 1818
22	Alabama	December 14, 1819
23	Maine	March 15, 1820
24	Missouri	August 10, 1821
25	Arkansas	June 15, 1836
26	Michigan	January 26, 1837
27	Florida	March 3, 1845
28	Texas	December 29, 1845
29	Iowa	December 28, 1846
30	Wisconsin	May 29, 1848
31	California	September 9, 1850
32	Minnesota	May 11, 1858
33	Oregon	February 14, 1859
34	Kansas	January 29, 1861
35	West Virginia	June 20, 1863
36	Nevada	October 31, 1864
37	Nebraska	March 1, 1867
38	Colorado	August 1, 1876
39	North Dakota	November 2, 1889
39	South Dakota	November 2, 1889
41	Montana	November 8, 1889
42	Washington	November 11, 1889
43	Idaho	July 3, 1890
44	Wyoming	July 10, 1890
45	Utah	January 4, 1896
46	Oklahoma	November 16, 1907
47	New Mexico	January 6, 1912
48	Arizona	February 14, 1912
49	Alaska	January 3, 1959
50	Hawaii	August 21, 1959

Source: U.S. Bureau of the Census
"1980 Census of Population" (vol. 1, part A, PC80-1-A)
*First thirteen states show date of ratification of Constitution.

STATE FAST FACTS

STATE	NICKNAME	CAPITAL	POPULATION*	AREA**
Alabama	Heart of Dixie	Montgomery	4,887,871	52,420
Alaska	The Last Frontier	Juneau	737,438	665,384
Arizona	Grand Canyon State	Phoenix	7,171,646	113,990
Arkansas	The Natural State	Little Rock	3,013,825	53,179
California	Golden State	Sacramento	39,557,045	163,695
Colorado	Centennial State	Denver	5,695,564	104,094
Connecticut	Constitution State	Hartford	3,572,665	5,543
Delaware	First State	Dover	967,171	2,489
Florida	Sunshine State	Tallahassee	21,299,325	65,758
Georgia	Peach State	Atlanta	10,519,475	59,425
Hawaii	Aloha State	Honolulu	1,420,491	10,932
Idaho	Gem State	Boise	1,754,208	83,569
Illinois	Land of Lincoln	Springfield	12,741,080	57,914
Indiana	Hoosier State	Indianapolis	6,691,878	36,420
Iowa	Hawkeye State	Des Moines	3,156,145	56,273
Kansas	Sunflower State	Topeka	2,911,505	82,278
Kentucky	Bluegrass State	Frankfort	4,468,402	40,408
Louisiana	Pelican State	Baton Rouge	4,659,978	52,378
Maine	Pine Tree State	Augusta	1,338,404	35,380
Maryland	Free State	Annapolis	6,042,718	12,406
Massachusetts	Bay State	Boston	6,902,149	10,554
Michigan	Great Lake State	Lansing	9,995,915	96,714
Minnesota	North Star State	St. Paul	5,611,179	86,936
Mississippi	Magnolia State	Jackson	2,986,530	48,432
Missouri	Show Me State	Jefferson City	6,126,452	69,707
Montana	Treasure State	Helena	1,062,305	147,040
Nebraska	Cornhusker State	Lincoln	1,929,268	77,348
Nevada	Silver State	Carson City	3,034,392	110,572
New Hampshire	Granite State	Concord	1,356,458	9,349
New Jersey	Garden State	Trenton	8,908,520	8,723
New Mexico	Land of Enchantment	Santa Fe	2,095,428	121,590
New York	Empire State	Albany	19,542,209	54,555
North Carolina	Tar Heel State	Raleigh	10,383,620	53,819
North Dakota	Peace Garden State	Bismarck	760,077	70,698
Ohio	Buckeye State	Columbus	11,689,442	44,826
Oklahoma	Sooner State	Oklahoma City	3,943,079	69,899
Oregon	Beaver State	Salem	4,190,713	98,379
Pennsylvania	Keystone State	Harrisburg	12,807,060	46,054
Rhode Island	Ocean State	Providence	1,057,315	1,545
South Carolina	Palmetto State	Columbia	5,084,127	32,020
South Dakota	Mount Rushmore State	Pierre	882,235	77,116
Tennessee	Volunteer State	Nashville	6,770,010	42,144
Texas	Lone Star State	Austin	28,701,845	268,596
Utah	Beehive State	Salt Lake City	3,161,105	84,897
Vermont	Green Mountain State	Montpelier	626,299	9,616
Virginia	Old Dominion	Richmond	8,517,685	42,775
Washington	Evergreen State	Olympia	7,535,591	71,298
West Virginia	Mountain State	Charleston	1,805,832	24,230
Wisconsin	Badger State	Madison	5,813,568	65,496
Wyoming	Equality State	Cheyenne	577,737	97,813

*U.S. Bureau of the Census, "Population Estimates" (December 2018, http://www.census.gov/programs-surveys/popest.html)
**Total of land and water area in square miles.

STATE SONG	STATE FLOWER	STATE TREE	STATE BIRD
Alabama	Camellia	Southern Pine	Yellowhammer
Alaska's Flag	Forget-Me-Not	Sitka Spruce	Willow Ptarmigan
Arizona	Saguaro Cactus Blossom	Palo Verde	Cactus Wren
Arkansas	Apple Blossom	Pine	Mockingbird
I Love You, California	Golden Poppy	California Redwood	California Valley Quail
Where the Columbines Grow	Rocky Mountain Columbine	Colorado Blue Spruce	Lark Bunting
Yankee Doodle Dandy	Mountain Laurel	White Oak	American Robin
Our Delaware	Peach Blossom	American Holly	Blue Hen Chicken
Swanee River	Orange Blossom	Sabal Palmetto Palm	Mockingbird
Georgia On My Mind	Cherokee Rose	Live Oak	Brown Thrasher
Hawaii Ponoi	Yellow Hibiscus	Candlenut	Nene
Here We Have Idaho	Syringa	White Pine	Mountain Bluebird
Illinois	Purple Violet	White Oak	Cardinal
On the Banks of the Wabash, Far Away	Peony	Tulip Poplar	Cardinal
The Song of Iowa	Wild Rose	Oak	Eastern Goldfinch
Home on the Range	Sunflower	Cottonwood	Western Meadowlark
My Old Kentucky Home	Goldenrod	Tulip Tree	Cardinal
Give Me Louisiana	Magnolia	Cypress	Eastern Brown Pelican
State of Maine Song	White Pine Cone and Tassel	Eastern White Pine	Chickadee
Maryland, My Maryland	Black-eyed Susan	White Oak	Baltimore Oriole
All Hail to Massachusetts	Mayflower	American Elm	Chickadee
Michigan, My Michigan	Apple Blossom	White Pine	Robin
Hail! Minnesota	Pink and White Lady's Slipper	Red Pine	Common Loon
Go, Mississippi!	Magnolia	Magnolia	Mockingbird
Missouri Waltz	Hawthorn	Dogwood	Bluebird
Montana	Bitterroot	Ponderosa Pine	Western Meadowlark
Beautiful Nebraska	Goldenrod	Cottonwood	Western Meadowlark
Home Means Nevada	Sagebrush	Single-Leaf Pinon	Mountain Bluebird
Old New Hampshire	Purple Lilac	White Birch	Purple Finch
Ode to New Jersey	Purple Violet	Red Oak	Eastern Goldfinch
O Fair New Mexico	Yucca	Pinon	Roadrunner
I Love New York	Rose	Sugar Maple	Bluebird
The Old North State	Dogwood	Pine	Cardinal
North Dakota Hymn	Wild Prairie Rose	American Elm	Western Meadowlark
Beautiful Ohio	Scarlet Carnation	Buckeye	Cardinal
Oklahoma!	Mistletoe	Redbud	Scissortailed Flycatcher
Oregon, My Oregon	Oregon Grape	Douglas Fir	Western Meadowlark
Hail! Pennsylvania	Mountain Laurel	Hemlock	Ruffed Grouse
Rhode Island	Violet	Red Maple	Rhode Island Red
Carolina	Yellow Jessamine	Palmetto	Carolina Wren
Hail, South Dakota	Pasque Flower	Black Hills Spruce	Ringnecked Pheasant
The Tennessee Waltz	Iris	Tulip Poplar	Mockingbird
Texas, Our Texas	Bluebonnet	Pecan	Mockingbird
Utah, We Love Thee	Sego Lily	Blue Spruce	Seagull
Hail, Vermont	Red Clover	Sugar Maple	Hermit Thrush
Carry Me Back to Old Virginia	Dogwood	Dogwood	Cardinal
Washington, My Home	Western Rhododendron	Western Hemlock	Willow Goldfinch
The West Virginia Hills; This Is My West Virginia; and West Virginia, My Home, Sweet Home	Big Rhododendron	Sugar Maple	Cardinal
On Wisconsin!	Wood Violet	Sugar Maple	Robin
Wyoming	Indian Paintbrush	Cottonwood	Meadowlark

I. Agriculture

Number of Farms in 2017

National Total = 2,048,000 Farms*

ALPHA ORDER

RANK	STATE	FARMS	% of USA
20	Alabama	43,600	2.1%
50	Alaska	760	0.0%
36	Arizona	19,600	1.0%
21	Arkansas	42,300	2.1%
5	California	77,100	3.8%
27	Colorado	33,800	1.7%
45	Connecticut	6,000	0.3%
48	Delaware	2,500	0.1%
18	Florida	47,000	2.3%
22	Georgia	40,900	2.0%
44	Hawaii	7,000	0.3%
33	Idaho	24,300	1.2%
9	Illinois	71,000	3.5%
14	Indiana	56,800	2.8%
3	Iowa	86,900	4.2%
12	Kansas	59,600	2.9%
6	Kentucky	75,800	3.7%
31	Louisiana	26,500	1.3%
41	Maine	8,200	0.4%
38	Maryland	12,200	0.6%
42	Massachusetts	7,800	0.4%
15	Michigan	50,900	2.5%
8	Minnesota	73,200	3.6%
23	Mississippi	35,800	1.7%
2	Missouri	97,300	4.8%
30	Montana	27,100	1.3%
17	Nebraska	47,400	2.3%
47	Nevada	4,000	0.2%
46	New Hampshire	4,400	0.2%
40	New Jersey	9,100	0.4%
32	New Mexico	24,700	1.2%
25	New York	35,500	1.7%
16	North Carolina	47,800	2.3%
29	North Dakota	29,900	1.5%
7	Ohio	73,600	3.6%
4	Oklahoma	77,200	3.8%
26	Oregon	34,200	1.7%
13	Pennsylvania	58,000	2.8%
49	Rhode Island	1,240	0.1%
33	South Carolina	24,300	1.2%
28	South Dakota	31,000	1.5%
11	Tennessee	65,900	3.2%
1	Texas	240,000	11.7%
37	Utah	18,200	0.9%
43	Vermont	7,300	0.4%
19	Virginia	44,300	2.2%
24	Washington	35,700	1.7%
35	West Virginia	20,400	1.0%
10	Wisconsin	68,500	3.3%
39	Wyoming	11,400	0.6%

RANK ORDER

RANK	STATE	FARMS	% of USA
1	Texas	240,000	11.7%
2	Missouri	97,300	4.8%
3	Iowa	86,900	4.2%
4	Oklahoma	77,200	3.8%
5	California	77,100	3.8%
6	Kentucky	75,800	3.7%
7	Ohio	73,600	3.6%
8	Minnesota	73,200	3.6%
9	Illinois	71,000	3.5%
10	Wisconsin	68,500	3.3%
11	Tennessee	65,900	3.2%
12	Kansas	59,600	2.9%
13	Pennsylvania	58,000	2.8%
14	Indiana	56,800	2.8%
15	Michigan	50,900	2.5%
16	North Carolina	47,800	2.3%
17	Nebraska	47,400	2.3%
18	Florida	47,000	2.3%
19	Virginia	44,300	2.2%
20	Alabama	43,600	2.1%
21	Arkansas	42,300	2.1%
22	Georgia	40,900	2.0%
23	Mississippi	35,800	1.7%
24	Washington	35,700	1.7%
25	New York	35,500	1.7%
26	Oregon	34,200	1.7%
27	Colorado	33,800	1.7%
28	South Dakota	31,000	1.5%
29	North Dakota	29,900	1.5%
30	Montana	27,100	1.3%
31	Louisiana	26,500	1.3%
32	New Mexico	24,700	1.2%
33	Idaho	24,300	1.2%
33	South Carolina	24,300	1.2%
35	West Virginia	20,400	1.0%
36	Arizona	19,600	1.0%
37	Utah	18,200	0.9%
38	Maryland	12,200	0.6%
39	Wyoming	11,400	0.6%
40	New Jersey	9,100	0.4%
41	Maine	8,200	0.4%
42	Massachusetts	7,800	0.4%
43	Vermont	7,300	0.4%
44	Hawaii	7,000	0.3%
45	Connecticut	6,000	0.3%
46	New Hampshire	4,400	0.2%
47	Nevada	4,000	0.2%
48	Delaware	2,500	0.1%
49	Rhode Island	1,240	0.1%
50	Alaska	760	0.0%
	District of Columbia	0	0.0%

Source: U.S. Department of Agriculture, National Agricultural Statistics Service
   "Farms and Land in Farms" (https://usda.library.cornell.edu/concern/publications/5712m6524)
*A farm is any establishment from which $1,000 or more of agricultural products were sold or would normally be sold during the year. This includes places with five or more horses, except horses in boarding stables or racetracks.

Land in Farms in 2017

National Total = 910,000,000 Acres*

RANK	STATE	ACRES	% of USA
31	Alabama	8,900,000	1.0%
44	Alaska	830,000	0.1%
14	Arizona	25,900,000	2.8%
22	Arkansas	13,600,000	1.5%
16	California	25,300,000	2.8%
9	Colorado	31,800,000	3.5%
49	Connecticut	440,000	0.0%
47	Delaware	500,000	0.1%
29	Florida	9,450,000	1.0%
30	Georgia	9,300,000	1.0%
43	Hawaii	1,120,000	0.1%
24	Idaho	11,900,000	1.3%
13	Illinois	26,600,000	2.9%
18	Indiana	14,700,000	1.6%
10	Iowa	30,500,000	3.4%
3	Kansas	45,900,000	5.0%
23	Kentucky	12,800,000	1.4%
34	Louisiana	7,700,000	0.8%
41	Maine	1,450,000	0.2%
40	Maryland	2,030,000	0.2%
46	Massachusetts	520,000	0.1%
28	Michigan	9,950,000	1.1%
14	Minnesota	25,900,000	2.8%
27	Mississippi	10,700,000	1.2%
12	Missouri	28,500,000	3.1%
2	Montana	59,800,000	6.6%
4	Nebraska	45,200,000	5.0%
37	Nevada	5,970,000	0.7%
48	New Hampshire	470,000	0.1%
45	New Jersey	720,000	0.1%
5	New Mexico	43,300,000	4.8%
36	New York	7,200,000	0.8%
32	North Carolina	8,100,000	0.9%
7	North Dakota	39,100,000	4.3%
21	Ohio	14,000,000	1.5%
8	Oklahoma	34,000,000	3.7%
17	Oregon	16,300,000	1.8%
35	Pennsylvania	7,630,000	0.8%
50	Rhode Island	70,000	0.0%
38	South Carolina	5,000,000	0.5%
5	South Dakota	43,300,000	4.8%
26	Tennessee	10,800,000	1.2%
1	Texas	129,600,000	14.2%
25	Utah	11,000,000	1.2%
42	Vermont	1,250,000	0.1%
32	Virginia	8,100,000	0.9%
18	Washington	14,700,000	1.6%
39	West Virginia	3,600,000	0.4%
20	Wisconsin	14,300,000	1.6%
11	Wyoming	30,200,000	3.3%

RANK ORDER

RANK	STATE	ACRES	% of USA
1	Texas	129,600,000	14.2%
2	Montana	59,800,000	6.6%
3	Kansas	45,900,000	5.0%
4	Nebraska	45,200,000	5.0%
5	New Mexico	43,300,000	4.8%
5	South Dakota	43,300,000	4.8%
7	North Dakota	39,100,000	4.3%
8	Oklahoma	34,000,000	3.7%
9	Colorado	31,800,000	3.5%
10	Iowa	30,500,000	3.4%
11	Wyoming	30,200,000	3.3%
12	Missouri	28,500,000	3.1%
13	Illinois	26,600,000	2.9%
14	Arizona	25,900,000	2.8%
14	Minnesota	25,900,000	2.8%
16	California	25,300,000	2.8%
17	Oregon	16,300,000	1.8%
18	Indiana	14,700,000	1.6%
18	Washington	14,700,000	1.6%
20	Wisconsin	14,300,000	1.6%
21	Ohio	14,000,000	1.5%
22	Arkansas	13,600,000	1.5%
23	Kentucky	12,800,000	1.4%
24	Idaho	11,900,000	1.3%
25	Utah	11,000,000	1.2%
26	Tennessee	10,800,000	1.2%
27	Mississippi	10,700,000	1.2%
28	Michigan	9,950,000	1.1%
29	Florida	9,450,000	1.0%
30	Georgia	9,300,000	1.0%
31	Alabama	8,900,000	1.0%
32	North Carolina	8,100,000	0.9%
32	Virginia	8,100,000	0.9%
34	Louisiana	7,700,000	0.8%
35	Pennsylvania	7,630,000	0.8%
36	New York	7,200,000	0.8%
37	Nevada	5,970,000	0.7%
38	South Carolina	5,000,000	0.5%
39	West Virginia	3,600,000	0.4%
40	Maryland	2,030,000	0.2%
41	Maine	1,450,000	0.2%
42	Vermont	1,250,000	0.1%
43	Hawaii	1,120,000	0.1%
44	Alaska	830,000	0.1%
45	New Jersey	720,000	0.1%
46	Massachusetts	520,000	0.1%
47	Delaware	500,000	0.1%
48	New Hampshire	470,000	0.1%
49	Connecticut	440,000	0.0%
50	Rhode Island	70,000	0.0%
	District of Columbia	0	0.0%

Source: U.S. Department of Agriculture, National Agricultural Statistics Service
"Farms and Land in Farms" (https://usda.library.cornell.edu/concern/publications/5712m6524)
*A farm is any establishment from which $1,000 or more of agricultural products were sold or would normally be sold during the year. This includes places with five or more horses, except horses in boarding stables or racetracks.

Average Number of Acres per Farm in 2017

National Average = 444 Acres*

ALPHA ORDER			RANK ORDER		
RANK	**STATE**	**ACRES**	**RANK**	**STATE**	**ACRES**
30	Alabama	204	1	Wyoming	2,649
8	Alaska	1,092	2	Montana	2,207
6	Arizona	1,321	3	New Mexico	1,753
22	Arkansas	322	4	Nevada	1,493
21	California	328	5	South Dakota	1,397
10	Colorado	941	6	Arizona	1,321
48	Connecticut	73	7	North Dakota	1,308
33	Delaware	200	8	Alaska	1,092
32	Florida	201	9	Nebraska	954
27	Georgia	227	10	Colorado	941
44	Hawaii	160	11	Kansas	770
14	Idaho	490	12	Utah	604
18	Illinois	375	13	Texas	540
26	Indiana	259	14	Idaho	490
20	Iowa	351	15	Oregon	477
11	Kansas	770	16	Oklahoma	440
40	Kentucky	169	17	Washington	412
25	Louisiana	291	18	Illinois	375
37	Maine	177	19	Minnesota	354
42	Maryland	166	20	Iowa	351
49	Massachusetts	67	21	California	328
34	Michigan	195	22	Arkansas	322
19	Minnesota	354	23	Mississippi	299
23	Mississippi	299	24	Missouri	293
24	Missouri	293	25	Louisiana	291
2	Montana	2,207	26	Indiana	259
9	Nebraska	954	27	Georgia	227
4	Nevada	1,493	28	Wisconsin	209
46	New Hampshire	107	29	South Carolina	206
47	New Jersey	79	30	Alabama	204
3	New Mexico	1,753	31	New York	203
31	New York	203	32	Florida	201
40	North Carolina	169	33	Delaware	200
7	North Dakota	1,308	34	Michigan	195
35	Ohio	190	35	Ohio	190
16	Oklahoma	440	36	Virginia	183
15	Oregon	477	37	Maine	177
45	Pennsylvania	132	38	West Virginia	176
50	Rhode Island	56	39	Vermont	171
29	South Carolina	206	40	Kentucky	169
5	South Dakota	1,397	40	North Carolina	169
43	Tennessee	164	42	Maryland	166
13	Texas	540	43	Tennessee	164
12	Utah	604	44	Hawaii	160
39	Vermont	171	45	Pennsylvania	132
36	Virginia	183	46	New Hampshire	107
17	Washington	412	47	New Jersey	79
38	West Virginia	176	48	Connecticut	73
28	Wisconsin	209	49	Massachusetts	67
1	Wyoming	2,649	50	Rhode Island	56
				District of Columbia	0

Source: U.S. Department of Agriculture, National Agricultural Statistics Service
   "Farms and Land in Farms" (https://usda.library.cornell.edu/concern/publications/5712m6524)
*A farm is any establishment from which $1,000 or more of agricultural products were sold or would normally be sold during the year. This includes places with five or more horses, except horses in boarding stables or racetracks.

Average per-Acre Value of Farmland in 2018

National Average = $3,140 per Acre*

ALPHA ORDER

RANK	STATE	PER-ACRE VALUE
32	Alabama	$2,780
NA	Alaska**	NA
20	Arizona	4,200
26	Arkansas	3,250
5	California	9,000
44	Colorado	1,420
3	Connecticut	11,200
6	Delaware	8,600
12	Florida	5,700
23	Georgia	3,500
NA	Hawaii**	NA
33	Idaho	2,700
8	Illinois	7,450
10	Indiana	7,100
7	Iowa	8,080
43	Kansas	1,800
24	Kentucky	3,440
28	Louisiana	3,100
39	Maine	2,150
9	Maryland	7,150
4	Massachusetts	10,400
15	Michigan	4,780
16	Minnesota	4,700
35	Mississippi	2,540
22	Missouri	3,700
46	Montana	920
31	Nebraska	2,850
45	Nevada	1,130
18	New Hampshire	4,450
2	New Jersey	12,700
48	New Mexico	530
30	New York	3,000
17	North Carolina	4,480
42	North Dakota	1,830
11	Ohio	5,740
41	Oklahoma	2,000
36	Oregon	2,370
13	Pennsylvania	5,680
1	Rhode Island	13,800
29	South Carolina	3,010
38	South Dakota	2,170
21	Tennessee	3,800
37	Texas	2,280
40	Utah	2,100
25	Vermont	3,400
19	Virginia	4,330
27	Washington	3,150
34	West Virginia	2,570
14	Wisconsin	5,320
47	Wyoming	660

RANK ORDER

RANK	STATE	PER-ACRE VALUE
1	Rhode Island	$13,800
2	New Jersey	12,700
3	Connecticut	11,200
4	Massachusetts	10,400
5	California	9,000
6	Delaware	8,600
7	Iowa	8,080
8	Illinois	7,450
9	Maryland	7,150
10	Indiana	7,100
11	Ohio	5,740
12	Florida	5,700
13	Pennsylvania	5,680
14	Wisconsin	5,320
15	Michigan	4,780
16	Minnesota	4,700
17	North Carolina	4,480
18	New Hampshire	4,450
19	Virginia	4,330
20	Arizona	4,200
21	Tennessee	3,800
22	Missouri	3,700
23	Georgia	3,500
24	Kentucky	3,440
25	Vermont	3,400
26	Arkansas	3,250
27	Washington	3,150
28	Louisiana	3,100
29	South Carolina	3,010
30	New York	3,000
31	Nebraska	2,850
32	Alabama	2,780
33	Idaho	2,700
34	West Virginia	2,570
35	Mississippi	2,540
36	Oregon	2,370
37	Texas	2,280
38	South Dakota	2,170
39	Maine	2,150
40	Utah	2,100
41	Oklahoma	2,000
42	North Dakota	1,830
43	Kansas	1,800
44	Colorado	1,420
45	Nevada	1,130
46	Montana	920
47	Wyoming	660
48	New Mexico	530
NA	Alaska**	NA
NA	Hawaii**	NA
	District of Columbia**	NA

Source: U.S. Department of Agriculture, National Agricultural Statistics Service
  "Land Values and Cash Rents" (https://usda.library.cornell.edu/concern/publications/pn89d6567)
*Value of farmland and buildings in nominal dollars.
**Not applicable or available.

Percent Change in Average per-Acre Value of Farmland: 2017 to 2018

National Percent Change = 1.9% Increase*

ALPHA ORDER				RANK ORDER		
RANK	STATE	PERCENT CHANGE		RANK	STATE	PERCENT CHANGE
23	Alabama	1.1		1	Missouri	10.4
NA	Alaska**	NA		2	Texas	9.1
9	Arizona	2.4		3	Oklahoma	5.3
12	Arkansas	2.2		4	Washington	5.0
6	California	3.4		5	Idaho	3.8
41	Colorado	(0.7)		6	California	3.4
29	Connecticut	0.0		7	Louisiana	3.3
9	Delaware	2.4		8	Oregon	2.6
29	Florida	0.0		9	Arizona	2.4
45	Georgia	(1.4)		9	Delaware	2.4
NA	Hawaii**	NA		11	Wisconsin	2.3
5	Idaho	3.8		12	Arkansas	2.2
13	Illinois	2.1		13	Illinois	2.1
18	Indiana	1.4		14	Nevada	1.8
24	Iowa	1.0		15	Mississippi	1.6
48	Kansas	(2.7)		15	Ohio	1.6
27	Kentucky	0.6		15	Pennsylvania	1.6
7	Louisiana	3.3		18	Indiana	1.4
47	Maine	(2.3)		18	Utah	1.4
20	Maryland	1.3		20	Maryland	1.3
29	Massachusetts	0.0		20	Tennessee	1.3
37	Michigan	(0.4)		22	Vermont	1.2
43	Minnesota	(1.1)		23	Alabama	1.1
15	Mississippi	1.6		24	Iowa	1.0
1	Missouri	10.4		25	New York	0.7
29	Montana	0.0		25	North Carolina	0.7
46	Nebraska	(1.7)		27	Kentucky	0.6
14	Nevada	1.8		28	South Carolina	0.3
43	New Hampshire	(1.1)		29	Connecticut	0.0
42	New Jersey	(0.8)		29	Florida	0.0
29	New Mexico	0.0		29	Massachusetts	0.0
25	New York	0.7		29	Montana	0.0
25	North Carolina	0.7		29	New Mexico	0.0
38	North Dakota	(0.5)		29	Rhode Island	0.0
15	Ohio	1.6		29	West Virginia	0.0
3	Oklahoma	5.3		29	Wyoming	0.0
8	Oregon	2.6		37	Michigan	(0.4)
15	Pennsylvania	1.6		38	North Dakota	(0.5)
29	Rhode Island	0.0		38	South Dakota	(0.5)
28	South Carolina	0.3		38	Virginia	(0.5)
38	South Dakota	(0.5)		41	Colorado	(0.7)
20	Tennessee	1.3		42	New Jersey	(0.8)
2	Texas	9.1		43	Minnesota	(1.1)
18	Utah	1.4		43	New Hampshire	(1.1)
22	Vermont	1.2		45	Georgia	(1.4)
38	Virginia	(0.5)		46	Nebraska	(1.7)
4	Washington	5.0		47	Maine	(2.3)
29	West Virginia	0.0		48	Kansas	(2.7)
11	Wisconsin	2.3		NA	Alaska**	NA
29	Wyoming	0.0		NA	Hawaii**	NA
					District of Columbia**	NA

Source: U.S. Department of Agriculture, National Agricultural Statistics Service
   "Land Values and Cash Rents" (https://usda.library.cornell.edu/concern/publications/pn89d6567)
*Value of farmland and buildings in nominal dollars.
**Not applicable or available.

Net Farm Income in 2017

National Total = $75,381,252,000*

ALPHA ORDER

RANK	STATE	FARM INCOME	% of USA
15	Alabama	$1,723,675,000	2.3%
50	Alaska	(8,534,000)	0.0%
18	Arizona	1,513,571,000	2.0%
16	Arkansas	1,578,785,000	2.1%
1	California	17,812,502,000	23.6%
26	Colorado	884,428,000	1.2%
44	Connecticut	84,773,000	0.1%
35	Delaware	570,804,000	0.8%
8	Florida	2,635,968,000	3.5%
7	Georgia	2,670,711,000	3.5%
42	Hawaii	103,046,000	0.1%
23	Idaho	1,233,221,000	1.6%
9	Illinois	2,054,841,000	2.7%
17	Indiana	1,576,487,000	2.1%
3	Iowa	3,419,509,000	4.5%
25	Kansas	1,158,777,000	1.5%
14	Kentucky	1,743,216,000	2.3%
27	Louisiana	850,572,000	1.1%
41	Maine	143,530,000	0.2%
30	Maryland	678,734,000	0.9%
48	Massachusetts	5,313,000	0.0%
34	Michigan	611,309,000	0.8%
10	Minnesota	1,851,813,000	2.5%
21	Mississippi	1,262,663,000	1.7%
13	Missouri	1,750,149,000	2.3%
36	Montana	361,896,000	0.5%
6	Nebraska	2,686,139,000	3.6%
49	Nevada	(4,437,000)	0.0%
46	New Hampshire	25,185,000	0.0%
37	New Jersey	355,581,000	0.5%
28	New Mexico	793,831,000	1.1%
24	New York	1,165,548,000	1.5%
4	North Carolina	3,190,628,000	4.2%
31	North Dakota	658,094,000	0.9%
22	Ohio	1,240,299,000	1.6%
20	Oklahoma	1,390,127,000	1.8%
33	Oregon	624,550,000	0.8%
12	Pennsylvania	1,754,938,000	2.3%
47	Rhode Island	20,332,000	0.0%
39	South Carolina	301,881,000	0.4%
19	South Dakota	1,448,109,000	1.9%
32	Tennessee	647,750,000	0.9%
2	Texas	4,440,332,000	5.9%
38	Utah	313,730,000	0.4%
40	Vermont	228,883,000	0.3%
29	Virginia	691,458,000	0.9%
5	Washington	3,189,451,000	4.2%
45	West Virginia	60,367,000	0.1%
11	Wisconsin	1,800,574,000	2.4%
43	Wyoming	86,142,000	0.1%

RANK ORDER

RANK	STATE	FARM INCOME	% of USA
1	California	$17,812,502,000	23.6%
2	Texas	4,440,332,000	5.9%
3	Iowa	3,419,509,000	4.5%
4	North Carolina	3,190,628,000	4.2%
5	Washington	3,189,451,000	4.2%
6	Nebraska	2,686,139,000	3.6%
7	Georgia	2,670,711,000	3.5%
8	Florida	2,635,968,000	3.5%
9	Illinois	2,054,841,000	2.7%
10	Minnesota	1,851,813,000	2.5%
11	Wisconsin	1,800,574,000	2.4%
12	Pennsylvania	1,754,938,000	2.3%
13	Missouri	1,750,149,000	2.3%
14	Kentucky	1,743,216,000	2.3%
15	Alabama	1,723,675,000	2.3%
16	Arkansas	1,578,785,000	2.1%
17	Indiana	1,576,487,000	2.1%
18	Arizona	1,513,571,000	2.0%
19	South Dakota	1,448,109,000	1.9%
20	Oklahoma	1,390,127,000	1.8%
21	Mississippi	1,262,663,000	1.7%
22	Ohio	1,240,299,000	1.6%
23	Idaho	1,233,221,000	1.6%
24	New York	1,165,548,000	1.5%
25	Kansas	1,158,777,000	1.5%
26	Colorado	884,428,000	1.2%
27	Louisiana	850,572,000	1.1%
28	New Mexico	793,831,000	1.1%
29	Virginia	691,458,000	0.9%
30	Maryland	678,734,000	0.9%
31	North Dakota	658,094,000	0.9%
32	Tennessee	647,750,000	0.9%
33	Oregon	624,550,000	0.8%
34	Michigan	611,309,000	0.8%
35	Delaware	570,804,000	0.8%
36	Montana	361,896,000	0.5%
37	New Jersey	355,581,000	0.5%
38	Utah	313,730,000	0.4%
39	South Carolina	301,881,000	0.4%
40	Vermont	228,883,000	0.3%
41	Maine	143,530,000	0.2%
42	Hawaii	103,046,000	0.1%
43	Wyoming	86,142,000	0.1%
44	Connecticut	84,773,000	0.1%
45	West Virginia	60,367,000	0.1%
46	New Hampshire	25,185,000	0.0%
47	Rhode Island	20,332,000	0.0%
48	Massachusetts	5,313,000	0.0%
48	Nevada	(4,437,000)	0.0%
50	Alaska	(8,534,000)	0.0%
	District of Columbia	0	0.0%

Source: U.S. Department of Agriculture, Economic Research Service
"Farm Sector Financial Indicators, State Rankings"
(https://www.ers.usda.gov/data-products/farm-income-and-wealth-statistics.aspx)
*Net farm income is a measure of the net value of production in a given year. It is determined by subtracting total production expenses from gross farm income.

Net Farm Income per Operation in 2017

National Average = $36,852 per Operation*

ALPHA ORDER

RANK	STATE	PER OPERATION
12	Alabama	$39,576
50	Alaska	(10,920)
4	Arizona	76,618
15	Arkansas	37,352
1	California	230,912
24	Colorado	26,348
40	Connecticut	14,089
2	Delaware	228,400
8	Florida	56,079
6	Georgia	65,149
39	Hawaii	14,720
10	Idaho	50,960
22	Illinois	28,875
23	Indiana	27,713
13	Iowa	39,312
29	Kansas	19,250
27	Kentucky	22,984
18	Louisiana	32,010
34	Maine	17,523
9	Maryland	55,444
48	Massachusetts	670
43	Michigan	11,895
26	Minnesota	25,134
16	Mississippi	35,282
33	Missouri	17,873
41	Montana	13,242
7	Nebraska	56,286
49	Nevada	(1,493)
46	New Hampshire	5,778
14	New Jersey	39,026
19	New Mexico	31,554
17	New York	32,886
5	North Carolina	66,586
28	North Dakota	22,236
36	Ohio	16,910
32	Oklahoma	18,040
31	Oregon	18,126
21	Pennsylvania	30,360
37	Rhode Island	16,240
42	South Carolina	12,360
11	South Dakota	46,101
44	Tennessee	9,840
30	Texas	18,360
35	Utah	17,516
20	Vermont	31,293
38	Virginia	15,555
3	Washington	89,404
47	West Virginia	2,992
25	Wisconsin	26,334
45	Wyoming	7,947

RANK ORDER

RANK	STATE	PER OPERATION
1	California	$230,912
2	Delaware	228,400
3	Washington	89,404
4	Arizona	76,618
5	North Carolina	66,586
6	Georgia	65,149
7	Nebraska	56,286
8	Florida	56,079
9	Maryland	55,444
10	Idaho	50,960
11	South Dakota	46,101
12	Alabama	39,576
13	Iowa	39,312
14	New Jersey	39,026
15	Arkansas	37,352
16	Mississippi	35,282
17	New York	32,886
18	Louisiana	32,010
19	New Mexico	31,554
20	Vermont	31,293
21	Pennsylvania	30,360
22	Illinois	28,875
23	Indiana	27,713
24	Colorado	26,348
25	Wisconsin	26,334
26	Minnesota	25,134
27	Kentucky	22,984
28	North Dakota	22,236
29	Kansas	19,250
30	Texas	18,360
31	Oregon	18,126
32	Oklahoma	18,040
33	Missouri	17,873
34	Maine	17,523
35	Utah	17,516
36	Ohio	16,910
37	Rhode Island	16,240
38	Virginia	15,555
39	Hawaii	14,720
40	Connecticut	14,089
41	Montana	13,242
42	South Carolina	12,360
43	Michigan	11,895
44	Tennessee	9,840
45	Wyoming	7,947
46	New Hampshire	5,778
47	West Virginia	2,992
48	Massachusetts	670
49	Nevada	(1,493)
50	Alaska	(10,920)

District of Columbia**   NA

Source: CQ Press using data from U.S. Department of Agriculture, Economic Research Service
"Farm Sector Financial Indicators, State Rankings"
(https://www.ers.usda.gov/data-products/farm-income-and-wealth-statistics.aspx)
*Calculated by multiplying average acres per farm by average net farm income per acre.
**Not applicable.

Net Farm Income per Acre in 2017

National Average = $83 per Acre*

ALPHA ORDER

RANK ORDER

RANK	STATE	PER ACRE
11	Alabama	$194
50	Alaska	(10)
34	Arizona	58
18	Arkansas	116
2	California	704
41	Colorado	28
12	Connecticut	193
1	Delaware	1,142
8	Florida	279
7	Georgia	287
24	Hawaii	92
22	Idaho	104
27	Illinois	77
21	Indiana	107
19	Iowa	112
42	Kansas	25
15	Kentucky	136
20	Louisiana	110
23	Maine	99
5	Maryland	334
46	Massachusetts	10
29	Michigan	61
28	Minnesota	71
17	Mississippi	118
29	Missouri	61
47	Montana	6
33	Nebraska	59
49	Nevada	(1)
35	New Hampshire	54
3	New Jersey	494
43	New Mexico	18
14	New York	162
4	North Carolina	394
44	North Dakota	17
25	Ohio	89
36	Oklahoma	41
37	Oregon	38
9	Pennsylvania	230
6	Rhode Island	290
31	South Carolina	60
39	South Dakota	33
31	Tennessee	60
38	Texas	34
40	Utah	29
13	Vermont	183
26	Virginia	85
10	Washington	217
44	West Virginia	17
16	Wisconsin	126
48	Wyoming	3

RANK	STATE	PER ACRE
1	Delaware	$1,142
2	California	704
3	New Jersey	494
4	North Carolina	394
5	Maryland	334
6	Rhode Island	290
7	Georgia	287
8	Florida	279
9	Pennsylvania	230
10	Washington	217
11	Alabama	194
12	Connecticut	193
13	Vermont	183
14	New York	162
15	Kentucky	136
16	Wisconsin	126
17	Mississippi	118
18	Arkansas	116
19	Iowa	112
20	Louisiana	110
21	Indiana	107
22	Idaho	104
23	Maine	99
24	Hawaii	92
25	Ohio	89
26	Virginia	85
27	Illinois	77
28	Minnesota	71
29	Michigan	61
29	Missouri	61
31	South Carolina	60
31	Tennessee	60
33	Nebraska	59
34	Arizona	58
35	New Hampshire	54
36	Oklahoma	41
37	Oregon	38
38	Texas	34
39	South Dakota	33
40	Utah	29
41	Colorado	28
42	Kansas	25
43	New Mexico	18
44	North Dakota	17
44	West Virginia	17
46	Massachusetts	10
47	Montana	6
48	Wyoming	3
49	Nevada	(1)
50	Alaska	(10)

District of Columbia**   NA

Source: CQ Press using data from U.S. Department of Agriculture, Economic Research Service
   "Farm Sector Financial Indicators, State Rankings"
   (https://www.ers.usda.gov/data-products/farm-income-and-wealth-statistics.aspx)
*Net farm income is a measure of the net value of production in a given year. It is determined by subtracting total production expenses from gross farm income.
**Not applicable.

Farm Income: Cash Receipts from Commodities in 2017

National Total = $372,301,967,000*

ALPHA ORDER					RANK ORDER			
RANK	STATE	FARM INCOME	% of USA		RANK	STATE	FARM INCOME	% of USA
26	Alabama	$5,490,773,000	1.5%		1	California	$50,220,538,000	13.5%
50	Alaska	37,666,000	0.0%		2	Iowa	26,520,949,000	7.1%
29	Arizona	4,741,177,000	1.3%		3	Texas	22,961,304,000	6.2%
14	Arkansas	8,917,844,000	2.4%		4	Nebraska	21,334,419,000	5.7%
1	California	50,220,538,000	13.5%		5	Minnesota	17,121,208,000	4.6%
22	Colorado	6,733,850,000	1.8%		6	Illinois	16,279,598,000	4.4%
46	Connecticut	532,940,000	0.1%		7	Kansas	15,733,655,000	4.2%
39	Delaware	1,348,120,000	0.4%		8	North Carolina	11,468,911,000	3.1%
18	Florida	7,641,993,000	2.1%		9	Wisconsin	11,365,634,000	3.1%
15	Georgia	8,864,188,000	2.4%		10	Indiana	10,612,470,000	2.9%
44	Hawaii	667,060,000	0.2%		11	Washington	10,272,241,000	2.8%
20	Idaho	7,202,442,000	1.9%		12	Missouri	9,942,110,000	2.7%
6	Illinois	16,279,598,000	4.4%		13	South Dakota	8,980,787,000	2.4%
10	Indiana	10,612,470,000	2.9%		14	Arkansas	8,917,844,000	2.4%
2	Iowa	26,520,949,000	7.1%		15	Georgia	8,864,188,000	2.4%
7	Kansas	15,733,655,000	4.2%		16	Ohio	8,547,498,000	2.3%
25	Kentucky	5,594,121,000	1.5%		17	North Dakota	7,868,951,000	2.1%
33	Louisiana	3,067,169,000	0.8%		18	Florida	7,641,993,000	2.1%
43	Maine	703,150,000	0.2%		19	Michigan	7,389,142,000	2.0%
36	Maryland	2,191,455,000	0.6%		20	Idaho	7,202,442,000	1.9%
47	Massachusetts	382,221,000	0.1%		21	Pennsylvania	6,737,417,000	1.8%
19	Michigan	7,389,142,000	2.0%		22	Colorado	6,733,850,000	1.8%
5	Minnesota	17,121,208,000	4.6%		23	Oklahoma	6,684,596,000	1.8%
24	Mississippi	5,651,947,000	1.5%		24	Mississippi	5,651,947,000	1.5%
12	Missouri	9,942,110,000	2.7%		25	Kentucky	5,594,121,000	1.5%
30	Montana	3,545,715,000	1.0%		26	Alabama	5,490,773,000	1.5%
4	Nebraska	21,334,419,000	5.7%		27	New York	5,216,571,000	1.4%
45	Nevada	646,933,000	0.2%		28	Oregon	4,796,842,000	1.3%
48	New Hampshire	208,737,000	0.1%		29	Arizona	4,741,177,000	1.3%
40	New Jersey	1,078,139,000	0.3%		30	Montana	3,545,715,000	1.0%
34	New Mexico	2,953,753,000	0.8%		31	Tennessee	3,494,327,000	0.9%
27	New York	5,216,571,000	1.4%		32	Virginia	3,475,590,000	0.9%
8	North Carolina	11,468,911,000	3.1%		33	Louisiana	3,067,169,000	0.8%
17	North Dakota	7,868,951,000	2.1%		34	New Mexico	2,953,753,000	0.8%
16	Ohio	8,547,498,000	2.3%		35	South Carolina	2,299,683,000	0.6%
23	Oklahoma	6,684,596,000	1.8%		36	Maryland	2,191,455,000	0.6%
28	Oregon	4,796,842,000	1.3%		37	Utah	1,740,172,000	0.5%
21	Pennsylvania	6,737,417,000	1.8%		38	Wyoming	1,438,717,000	0.4%
49	Rhode Island	71,553,000	0.0%		39	Delaware	1,348,120,000	0.4%
35	South Carolina	2,299,683,000	0.6%		40	New Jersey	1,078,139,000	0.3%
13	South Dakota	8,980,787,000	2.4%		41	Vermont	816,159,000	0.2%
31	Tennessee	3,494,327,000	0.9%		42	West Virginia	709,533,000	0.2%
3	Texas	22,961,304,000	6.2%		43	Maine	703,150,000	0.2%
37	Utah	1,740,172,000	0.5%		44	Hawaii	667,060,000	0.2%
41	Vermont	816,159,000	0.2%		45	Nevada	646,933,000	0.2%
32	Virginia	3,475,590,000	0.9%		46	Connecticut	532,940,000	0.1%
11	Washington	10,272,241,000	2.8%		47	Massachusetts	382,221,000	0.1%
42	West Virginia	709,533,000	0.2%		48	New Hampshire	208,737,000	0.1%
9	Wisconsin	11,365,634,000	3.1%		49	Rhode Island	71,553,000	0.0%
38	Wyoming	1,438,717,000	0.4%		50	Alaska	37,666,000	0.0%
						District of Columbia	0	0.0%

Source: U.S. Department of Agriculture, Economic Research Service
"Farm Sector Financial Indicators, State Rankings" (www.ers.usda.gov/data-products/farm-income-and-wealth-statistics.aspx)
*Commodities include crops and livestock.

Farm Income: Crops in 2017

National Total = $196,267,672,000

ALPHA ORDER

RANK	STATE	FARM INCOME	% of USA
33	Alabama	$1,097,452,000	0.6%
50	Alaska	30,316,000	0.0%
21	Arizona	2,990,431,000	1.5%
17	Arkansas	3,601,290,000	1.8%
1	California	39,033,477,000	19.9%
26	Colorado	2,121,475,000	1.1%
41	Connecticut	357,539,000	0.2%
43	Delaware	275,274,000	0.1%
11	Florida	5,881,409,000	3.0%
20	Georgia	3,027,465,000	1.5%
38	Hawaii	505,280,000	0.3%
22	Idaho	2,821,936,000	1.4%
2	Illinois	13,700,598,000	7.0%
8	Indiana	6,884,169,000	3.5%
3	Iowa	13,111,299,000	6.7%
10	Kansas	6,204,181,000	3.2%
24	Kentucky	2,394,800,000	1.2%
28	Louisiana	1,970,953,000	1.0%
40	Maine	390,692,000	0.2%
36	Maryland	853,929,000	0.4%
44	Massachusetts	268,235,000	0.1%
15	Michigan	4,162,235,000	2.1%
4	Minnesota	9,538,401,000	4.9%
25	Mississippi	2,319,569,000	1.2%
12	Missouri	5,405,793,000	2.8%
30	Montana	1,835,905,000	0.9%
5	Nebraska	8,870,608,000	4.5%
46	Nevada	170,724,000	0.1%
48	New Hampshire	94,530,000	0.0%
34	New Jersey	944,520,000	0.5%
37	New Mexico	735,076,000	0.4%
29	New York	1,876,244,000	1.0%
16	North Carolina	3,724,062,000	1.9%
9	North Dakota	6,628,084,000	3.4%
13	Ohio	5,157,754,000	2.6%
31	Oklahoma	1,469,381,000	0.7%
19	Oregon	3,238,375,000	1.6%
23	Pennsylvania	2,420,699,000	1.2%
49	Rhode Island	48,848,000	0.0%
35	South Carolina	932,196,000	0.5%
14	South Dakota	5,073,739,000	2.6%
27	Tennessee	2,088,908,000	1.1%
6	Texas	8,623,903,000	4.4%
39	Utah	415,747,000	0.2%
45	Vermont	199,177,000	0.1%
32	Virginia	1,149,555,000	0.6%
7	Washington	7,735,724,000	3.9%
47	West Virginia	149,065,000	0.1%
18	Wisconsin	3,393,592,000	1.7%
42	Wyoming	343,059,000	0.2%

RANK ORDER

RANK	STATE	FARM INCOME	% of USA
1	California	$39,033,477,000	19.9%
2	Illinois	13,700,598,000	7.0%
3	Iowa	13,111,299,000	6.7%
4	Minnesota	9,538,401,000	4.9%
5	Nebraska	8,870,608,000	4.5%
6	Texas	8,623,903,000	4.4%
7	Washington	7,735,724,000	3.9%
8	Indiana	6,884,169,000	3.5%
9	North Dakota	6,628,084,000	3.4%
10	Kansas	6,204,181,000	3.2%
11	Florida	5,881,409,000	3.0%
12	Missouri	5,405,793,000	2.8%
13	Ohio	5,157,754,000	2.6%
14	South Dakota	5,073,739,000	2.6%
15	Michigan	4,162,235,000	2.1%
16	North Carolina	3,724,062,000	1.9%
17	Arkansas	3,601,290,000	1.8%
18	Wisconsin	3,393,592,000	1.7%
19	Oregon	3,238,375,000	1.6%
20	Georgia	3,027,465,000	1.5%
21	Arizona	2,990,431,000	1.5%
22	Idaho	2,821,936,000	1.4%
23	Pennsylvania	2,420,699,000	1.2%
24	Kentucky	2,394,800,000	1.2%
25	Mississippi	2,319,569,000	1.2%
26	Colorado	2,121,475,000	1.1%
27	Tennessee	2,088,908,000	1.1%
28	Louisiana	1,970,953,000	1.0%
29	New York	1,876,244,000	1.0%
30	Montana	1,835,905,000	0.9%
31	Oklahoma	1,469,381,000	0.7%
32	Virginia	1,149,555,000	0.6%
33	Alabama	1,097,452,000	0.6%
34	New Jersey	944,520,000	0.5%
35	South Carolina	932,196,000	0.5%
36	Maryland	853,929,000	0.4%
37	New Mexico	735,076,000	0.4%
38	Hawaii	505,280,000	0.3%
39	Utah	415,747,000	0.2%
40	Maine	390,692,000	0.2%
41	Connecticut	357,539,000	0.2%
42	Wyoming	343,059,000	0.2%
43	Delaware	275,274,000	0.1%
44	Massachusetts	268,235,000	0.1%
45	Vermont	199,177,000	0.1%
46	Nevada	170,724,000	0.1%
47	West Virginia	149,065,000	0.1%
48	New Hampshire	94,530,000	0.0%
49	Rhode Island	48,848,000	0.0%
50	Alaska	30,316,000	0.0%
	District of Columbia	0	0.0%

Source: U.S. Department of Agriculture, Economic Research Service
"Farm Sector Financial Indicators, State Rankings" (www.ers.usda.gov/data-products/farm-income-and-wealth-statistics.aspx)

Farm Income: Livestock in 2017

National Total = $176,034,295,000*

ALPHA ORDER				RANK ORDER			
RANK	STATE	FARM INCOME	% of USA	RANK	STATE	FARM INCOME	% of USA
14	Alabama	$4,393,321,000	2.5%	1	Texas	$14,337,401,000	8.1%
50	Alaska	7,350,000	0.0%	2	Iowa	13,409,650,000	7.6%
29	Arizona	1,750,746,000	1.0%	3	Nebraska	12,463,811,000	7.1%
10	Arkansas	5,316,554,000	3.0%	4	California	11,187,061,000	6.4%
4	California	11,187,061,000	6.4%	5	Kansas	9,529,474,000	5.4%
12	Colorado	4,612,375,000	2.6%	6	Wisconsin	7,972,042,000	4.5%
44	Connecticut	175,401,000	0.1%	7	North Carolina	7,744,849,000	4.4%
39	Delaware	1,072,846,000	0.6%	8	Minnesota	7,582,807,000	4.3%
28	Florida	1,760,584,000	1.0%	9	Georgia	5,836,723,000	3.3%
9	Georgia	5,836,723,000	3.3%	10	Arkansas	5,316,554,000	3.0%
45	Hawaii	161,780,000	0.1%	11	Oklahoma	5,215,215,000	3.0%
15	Idaho	4,380,506,000	2.5%	12	Colorado	4,612,375,000	2.6%
24	Illinois	2,579,000,000	1.5%	13	Missouri	4,536,317,000	2.6%
18	Indiana	3,728,301,000	2.1%	14	Alabama	4,393,321,000	2.5%
2	Iowa	13,409,650,000	7.6%	15	Idaho	4,380,506,000	2.5%
5	Kansas	9,529,474,000	5.4%	16	Pennsylvania	4,316,718,000	2.5%
23	Kentucky	3,199,321,000	1.8%	17	South Dakota	3,907,048,000	2.2%
37	Louisiana	1,096,216,000	0.6%	18	Indiana	3,728,301,000	2.1%
43	Maine	312,458,000	0.2%	19	Ohio	3,389,744,000	1.9%
34	Maryland	1,337,526,000	0.8%	20	New York	3,340,327,000	1.9%
48	Massachusetts	113,986,000	0.1%	21	Mississippi	3,332,378,000	1.9%
22	Michigan	3,226,907,000	1.8%	22	Michigan	3,226,907,000	1.8%
8	Minnesota	7,582,807,000	4.3%	23	Kentucky	3,199,321,000	1.8%
21	Mississippi	3,332,378,000	1.9%	24	Illinois	2,579,000,000	1.5%
13	Missouri	4,536,317,000	2.6%	25	Washington	2,536,517,000	1.4%
30	Montana	1,709,810,000	1.0%	26	Virginia	2,326,035,000	1.3%
3	Nebraska	12,463,811,000	7.1%	27	New Mexico	2,218,677,000	1.3%
42	Nevada	476,209,000	0.3%	28	Florida	1,760,584,000	1.0%
47	New Hampshire	114,207,000	0.1%	29	Arizona	1,750,746,000	1.0%
46	New Jersey	133,619,000	0.1%	30	Montana	1,709,810,000	1.0%
27	New Mexico	2,218,677,000	1.3%	31	Oregon	1,558,467,000	0.9%
20	New York	3,340,327,000	1.9%	32	Tennessee	1,405,419,000	0.8%
7	North Carolina	7,744,849,000	4.4%	33	South Carolina	1,367,487,000	0.8%
36	North Dakota	1,240,867,000	0.7%	34	Maryland	1,337,526,000	0.8%
19	Ohio	3,389,744,000	1.9%	35	Utah	1,324,425,000	0.8%
11	Oklahoma	5,215,215,000	3.0%	36	North Dakota	1,240,867,000	0.7%
31	Oregon	1,558,467,000	0.9%	37	Louisiana	1,096,216,000	0.6%
16	Pennsylvania	4,316,718,000	2.5%	38	Wyoming	1,095,658,000	0.6%
49	Rhode Island	22,705,000	0.0%	39	Delaware	1,072,846,000	0.6%
33	South Carolina	1,367,487,000	0.8%	40	Vermont	616,982,000	0.4%
17	South Dakota	3,907,048,000	2.2%	41	West Virginia	560,468,000	0.3%
32	Tennessee	1,405,419,000	0.8%	42	Nevada	476,209,000	0.3%
1	Texas	14,337,401,000	8.1%	43	Maine	312,458,000	0.2%
35	Utah	1,324,425,000	0.8%	44	Connecticut	175,401,000	0.1%
40	Vermont	616,982,000	0.4%	45	Hawaii	161,780,000	0.1%
26	Virginia	2,326,035,000	1.3%	46	New Jersey	133,619,000	0.1%
25	Washington	2,536,517,000	1.4%	47	New Hampshire	114,207,000	0.1%
41	West Virginia	560,468,000	0.3%	48	Massachusetts	113,986,000	0.1%
6	Wisconsin	7,972,042,000	4.5%	49	Rhode Island	22,705,000	0.0%
38	Wyoming	1,095,658,000	0.6%	50	Alaska	7,350,000	0.0%
					District of Columbia	0	0.0%

Source: U.S. Department of Agriculture, Economic Research Service
   "Farm Sector Financial Indicators, State Rankings" (www.ers.usda.gov/data-products/farm-income-and-wealth-statistics.aspx)
*Includes livestock products.

Farm Income: Government Payments in 2017

National Total = $11,531,611,000*

ALPHA ORDER

RANK	STATE	FARM INCOME	% of USA
20	Alabama	$204,883,000	1.8%
47	Alaska	6,645,000	0.1%
38	Arizona	34,696,000	0.3%
4	Arkansas	650,186,000	5.6%
22	California	178,679,000	1.5%
18	Colorado	268,658,000	2.3%
49	Connecticut	4,994,000	0.0%
39	Delaware	22,122,000	0.2%
30	Florida	91,819,000	0.8%
11	Georgia	391,707,000	3.4%
43	Hawaii	11,542,000	0.1%
24	Idaho	162,352,000	1.4%
6	Illinois	608,956,000	5.3%
13	Indiana	373,228,000	3.2%
3	Iowa	691,386,000	6.0%
5	Kansas	621,942,000	5.4%
23	Kentucky	169,401,000	1.5%
16	Louisiana	293,366,000	2.5%
41	Maine	13,361,000	0.1%
35	Maryland	58,033,000	0.5%
46	Massachusetts	6,827,000	0.1%
21	Michigan	200,576,000	1.7%
9	Minnesota	460,897,000	4.0%
15	Mississippi	311,938,000	2.7%
10	Missouri	423,209,000	3.7%
12	Montana	374,556,000	3.2%
2	Nebraska	803,448,000	7.0%
45	Nevada	9,282,000	0.1%
48	New Hampshire	6,314,000	0.1%
42	New Jersey	12,278,000	0.1%
29	New Mexico	96,144,000	0.8%
33	New York	76,094,000	0.7%
25	North Carolina	156,298,000	1.4%
7	North Dakota	588,382,000	5.1%
14	Ohio	358,470,000	3.1%
17	Oklahoma	289,132,000	2.5%
28	Oregon	123,562,000	1.1%
31	Pennsylvania	88,401,000	0.8%
50	Rhode Island	2,830,000	0.0%
32	South Carolina	85,012,000	0.7%
8	South Dakota	566,272,000	4.9%
26	Tennessee	149,997,000	1.3%
1	Texas	936,584,000	8.1%
37	Utah	47,045,000	0.4%
44	Vermont	10,722,000	0.1%
34	Virginia	75,943,000	0.7%
19	Washington	212,858,000	1.8%
40	West Virginia	17,835,000	0.2%
27	Wisconsin	134,422,000	1.2%
36	Wyoming	48,328,000	0.4%

RANK ORDER

RANK	STATE	FARM INCOME	% of USA
1	Texas	$936,584,000	8.1%
2	Nebraska	803,448,000	7.0%
3	Iowa	691,386,000	6.0%
4	Arkansas	650,186,000	5.6%
5	Kansas	621,942,000	5.4%
6	Illinois	608,956,000	5.3%
7	North Dakota	588,382,000	5.1%
8	South Dakota	566,272,000	4.9%
9	Minnesota	460,897,000	4.0%
10	Missouri	423,209,000	3.7%
11	Georgia	391,707,000	3.4%
12	Montana	374,556,000	3.2%
13	Indiana	373,228,000	3.2%
14	Ohio	358,470,000	3.1%
15	Mississippi	311,938,000	2.7%
16	Louisiana	293,366,000	2.5%
17	Oklahoma	289,132,000	2.5%
18	Colorado	268,658,000	2.3%
19	Washington	212,858,000	1.8%
20	Alabama	204,883,000	1.8%
21	Michigan	200,576,000	1.7%
22	California	178,679,000	1.5%
23	Kentucky	169,401,000	1.5%
24	Idaho	162,352,000	1.4%
25	North Carolina	156,298,000	1.4%
26	Tennessee	149,997,000	1.3%
27	Wisconsin	134,422,000	1.2%
28	Oregon	123,562,000	1.1%
29	New Mexico	96,144,000	0.8%
30	Florida	91,819,000	0.8%
31	Pennsylvania	88,401,000	0.8%
32	South Carolina	85,012,000	0.7%
33	New York	76,094,000	0.7%
34	Virginia	75,943,000	0.7%
35	Maryland	58,033,000	0.5%
36	Wyoming	48,328,000	0.4%
37	Utah	47,045,000	0.4%
38	Arizona	34,696,000	0.3%
39	Delaware	22,122,000	0.2%
40	West Virginia	17,835,000	0.2%
41	Maine	13,361,000	0.1%
42	New Jersey	12,278,000	0.1%
43	Hawaii	11,542,000	0.1%
44	Vermont	10,722,000	0.1%
45	Nevada	9,282,000	0.1%
46	Massachusetts	6,827,000	0.1%
47	Alaska	6,645,000	0.1%
48	New Hampshire	6,314,000	0.1%
49	Connecticut	4,994,000	0.0%
50	Rhode Island	2,830,000	0.0%
	District of Columbia	0	0.0%

Source: U.S. Department of Agriculture, Economic Research Service
"Farm Sector Financial Indicators, State Rankings" (www.ers.usda.gov/data-products/farm-income-and-wealth-statistics.aspx)
*Government payments made directly to farmers in cash.

Acres Planted in 2018

National Total = 319,587,000 Acres*

ALPHA ORDER					RANK ORDER			
RANK	STATE	ACRES	% of USA		RANK	STATE	ACRES	% of USA
30	Alabama	2,330,000	0.7%		1	Iowa	24,291,000	7.6%
NA	Alaska**	NA	NA		2	North Dakota	24,163,000	7.6%
38	Arizona	647,000	0.2%		3	Kansas	23,465,000	7.3%
15	Arkansas	7,292,000	2.3%		4	Illinois	22,936,000	7.2%
27	California	2,940,000	0.9%		5	Texas	21,830,000	6.8%
17	Colorado	6,148,000	1.9%		6	Nebraska	19,792,000	6.2%
46	Connecticut	70,000	0.0%		7	Minnesota	19,534,000	6.1%
40	Delaware	453,000	0.1%		8	South Dakota	17,300,000	5.4%
35	Florida	1,119,000	0.4%		9	Missouri	13,782,000	4.3%
24	Georgia	3,653,000	1.1%		10	Indiana	12,120,000	3.8%
49	Hawaii	0	0.0%		11	Oklahoma	10,036,000	3.1%
21	Idaho	4,187,000	1.3%		12	Ohio	10,015,000	3.1%
4	Illinois	22,936,000	7.2%		13	Montana	9,835,000	3.1%
10	Indiana	12,120,000	3.8%		14	Wisconsin	7,997,000	2.5%
1	Iowa	24,291,000	7.6%		15	Arkansas	7,292,000	2.3%
3	Kansas	23,465,000	7.3%		16	Michigan	6,410,000	2.0%
18	Kentucky	5,753,000	1.8%		17	Colorado	6,148,000	1.9%
26	Louisiana	3,295,000	1.0%		18	Kentucky	5,753,000	1.8%
44	Maine	229,000	0.1%		19	Tennessee	4,916,000	1.5%
32	Maryland	1,572,000	0.5%		20	North Carolina	4,593,000	1.4%
45	Massachusetts	93,000	0.0%		21	Idaho	4,187,000	1.3%
16	Michigan	6,410,000	2.0%		22	Mississippi	4,144,000	1.3%
7	Minnesota	19,534,000	6.1%		23	Washington	3,702,000	1.2%
22	Mississippi	4,144,000	1.3%		24	Georgia	3,653,000	1.1%
9	Missouri	13,782,000	4.3%		25	Pennsylvania	3,493,000	1.1%
13	Montana	9,835,000	3.1%		26	Louisiana	3,295,000	1.0%
6	Nebraska	19,792,000	6.2%		27	California	2,940,000	0.9%
41	Nevada	401,000	0.1%		28	New York	2,854,000	0.9%
47	New Hampshire	52,000	0.0%		29	Virginia	2,634,000	0.8%
42	New Jersey	311,000	0.1%		30	Alabama	2,330,000	0.7%
37	New Mexico	870,000	0.3%		31	Oregon	2,003,000	0.6%
28	New York	2,854,000	0.9%		32	Maryland	1,572,000	0.5%
20	North Carolina	4,593,000	1.4%		33	South Carolina	1,498,000	0.5%
2	North Dakota	24,163,000	7.6%		34	Wyoming	1,473,000	0.5%
12	Ohio	10,015,000	3.1%		35	Florida	1,119,000	0.4%
11	Oklahoma	10,036,000	3.1%		36	Utah	871,000	0.3%
31	Oregon	2,003,000	0.6%		37	New Mexico	870,000	0.3%
25	Pennsylvania	3,493,000	1.1%		38	Arizona	647,000	0.2%
48	Rhode Island	8,000	0.0%		39	West Virginia	616,000	0.2%
33	South Carolina	1,498,000	0.5%		40	Delaware	453,000	0.1%
8	South Dakota	17,300,000	5.4%		41	Nevada	401,000	0.1%
19	Tennessee	4,916,000	1.5%		42	New Jersey	311,000	0.1%
5	Texas	21,830,000	6.8%		43	Vermont	255,000	0.1%
36	Utah	871,000	0.3%		44	Maine	229,000	0.1%
43	Vermont	255,000	0.1%		45	Massachusetts	93,000	0.0%
29	Virginia	2,634,000	0.8%		46	Connecticut	70,000	0.0%
23	Washington	3,702,000	1.2%		47	New Hampshire	52,000	0.0%
39	West Virginia	616,000	0.2%		48	Rhode Island	8,000	0.0%
14	Wisconsin	7,997,000	2.5%		49	Hawaii	0	0.0%
34	Wyoming	1,473,000	0.5%		NA	Alaska**	NA	NA
						District of Columbia**	NA	NA

Source: U.S. Department of Agriculture, National Agricultural Statistics Service
   "Crop Production: 2018 Summary" (February 2019, https://usda.library.cornell.edu/concern/publications/k3569432s)
*Estimated totals.
**No acreage or not available.

Acres Harvested in 2018

National Total = 300,566,000 Acres*

ALPHA ORDER

RANK	STATE	ACRES	% of USA
30	Alabama	2,232,000	0.7%
NA	Alaska**	NA	NA
37	Arizona	622,000	0.2%
15	Arkansas	7,134,000	2.4%
28	California	2,510,000	0.8%
17	Colorado	5,599,000	1.9%
46	Connecticut	67,000	0.0%
40	Delaware	409,000	0.1%
35	Florida	1,060,000	0.4%
25	Georgia	3,186,000	1.1%
49	Hawaii	0	0.0%
21	Idaho	4,074,000	1.4%
3	Illinois	22,780,000	7.6%
10	Indiana	11,990,000	4.0%
1	Iowa	23,959,000	8.0%
4	Kansas	22,726,000	7.6%
18	Kentucky	5,573,000	1.9%
26	Louisiana	3,134,000	1.0%
44	Maine	222,000	0.1%
34	Maryland	1,371,000	0.5%
45	Massachusetts	91,000	0.0%
16	Michigan	6,283,000	2.1%
6	Minnesota	19,223,000	6.4%
22	Mississippi	4,064,000	1.4%
9	Missouri	13,413,000	4.5%
12	Montana	9,350,000	3.1%
5	Nebraska	19,419,000	6.5%
41	Nevada	380,000	0.1%
47	New Hampshire	51,000	0.0%
42	New Jersey	301,000	0.1%
38	New Mexico	620,000	0.2%
27	New York	2,790,000	0.9%
20	North Carolina	4,343,000	1.4%
2	North Dakota	23,642,000	7.9%
11	Ohio	9,890,000	3.3%
14	Oklahoma	7,575,000	2.5%
31	Oregon	1,940,000	0.6%
24	Pennsylvania	3,381,000	1.1%
48	Rhode Island	8,000	0.0%
32	South Carolina	1,430,000	0.5%
7	South Dakota	16,595,000	5.5%
19	Tennessee	4,774,000	1.6%
8	Texas	15,169,000	5.0%
36	Utah	836,000	0.3%
43	Vermont	249,000	0.1%
29	Virginia	2,502,000	0.8%
23	Washington	3,612,000	1.2%
39	West Virginia	609,000	0.2%
13	Wisconsin	7,731,000	2.6%
33	Wyoming	1,416,000	0.5%

RANK ORDER

RANK	STATE	ACRES	% of USA
1	Iowa	23,959,000	8.0%
2	North Dakota	23,642,000	7.9%
3	Illinois	22,780,000	7.6%
4	Kansas	22,726,000	7.6%
5	Nebraska	19,419,000	6.5%
6	Minnesota	19,223,000	6.4%
7	South Dakota	16,595,000	5.5%
8	Texas	15,169,000	5.0%
9	Missouri	13,413,000	4.5%
10	Indiana	11,990,000	4.0%
11	Ohio	9,890,000	3.3%
12	Montana	9,350,000	3.1%
13	Wisconsin	7,731,000	2.6%
14	Oklahoma	7,575,000	2.5%
15	Arkansas	7,134,000	2.4%
16	Michigan	6,283,000	2.1%
17	Colorado	5,599,000	1.9%
18	Kentucky	5,573,000	1.9%
19	Tennessee	4,774,000	1.6%
20	North Carolina	4,343,000	1.4%
21	Idaho	4,074,000	1.4%
22	Mississippi	4,064,000	1.4%
23	Washington	3,612,000	1.2%
24	Pennsylvania	3,381,000	1.1%
25	Georgia	3,186,000	1.1%
26	Louisiana	3,134,000	1.0%
27	New York	2,790,000	0.9%
28	California	2,510,000	0.8%
29	Virginia	2,502,000	0.8%
30	Alabama	2,232,000	0.7%
31	Oregon	1,940,000	0.6%
32	South Carolina	1,430,000	0.5%
33	Wyoming	1,416,000	0.5%
34	Maryland	1,371,000	0.5%
35	Florida	1,060,000	0.4%
36	Utah	836,000	0.3%
37	Arizona	622,000	0.2%
38	New Mexico	620,000	0.2%
39	West Virginia	609,000	0.2%
40	Delaware	409,000	0.1%
41	Nevada	380,000	0.1%
42	New Jersey	301,000	0.1%
43	Vermont	249,000	0.1%
44	Maine	222,000	0.1%
45	Massachusetts	91,000	0.0%
46	Connecticut	67,000	0.0%
47	New Hampshire	51,000	0.0%
48	Rhode Island	8,000	0.0%
49	Hawaii	0	0.0%
NA	Alaska**	NA	NA
	District of Columbia**	NA	NA

Source: U.S. Department of Agriculture, National Agricultural Statistics Service
"Crop Production: 2018 Summary" (February 2019, https://usda.library.cornell.edu/concern/publications/k3569432s)
*Estimated totals.
**No acreage or not available.

Acres Harvested: Corn in 2018

National Total = 81,740,000 Acres*

ALPHA ORDER

RANK	STATE	ACRES	% of USA
28	Alabama	250,000	0.3%
NA	Alaska**	NA	NA
41	Arizona	15,000	0.0%
19	Arkansas	645,000	0.8%
34	California	65,000	0.1%
15	Colorado	1,200,000	1.5%
NA	Connecticut**	NA	NA
29	Delaware	166,000	0.2%
34	Florida	65,000	0.1%
26	Georgia	285,000	0.3%
NA	Hawaii**	NA	NA
30	Idaho	135,000	0.2%
2	Illinois	10,850,000	13.3%
5	Indiana	5,200,000	6.4%
1	Iowa	12,800,000	15.7%
6	Kansas	5,000,000	6.1%
14	Kentucky	1,230,000	1.5%
22	Louisiana	450,000	0.6%
NA	Maine**	NA	NA
23	Maryland	390,000	0.5%
NA	Massachusetts**	NA	NA
12	Michigan	1,940,000	2.4%
4	Minnesota	7,490,000	9.2%
21	Mississippi	465,000	0.6%
8	Missouri	3,330,000	4.1%
33	Montana	68,000	0.1%
3	Nebraska	9,310,000	11.4%
NA	Nevada**	NA	NA
NA	New Hampshire**	NA	NA
36	New Jersey	61,000	0.1%
38	New Mexico	35,000	0.0%
19	New York	645,000	0.8%
17	North Carolina	830,000	1.0%
11	North Dakota	2,930,000	3.6%
9	Ohio	3,300,000	4.0%
27	Oklahoma	280,000	0.3%
37	Oregon	45,000	0.1%
16	Pennsylvania	950,000	1.2%
NA	Rhode Island**	NA	NA
25	South Carolina	310,000	0.4%
7	South Dakota	4,860,000	5.9%
18	Tennessee	690,000	0.8%
13	Texas	1,750,000	2.1%
40	Utah	22,000	0.0%
NA	Vermont**	NA	NA
24	Virginia	325,000	0.4%
31	Washington	85,000	0.1%
39	West Virginia	33,000	0.0%
10	Wisconsin	3,170,000	3.9%
32	Wyoming	70,000	0.1%

RANK ORDER

RANK	STATE	ACRES	% of USA
1	Iowa	12,800,000	15.7%
2	Illinois	10,850,000	13.3%
3	Nebraska	9,310,000	11.4%
4	Minnesota	7,490,000	9.2%
5	Indiana	5,200,000	6.4%
6	Kansas	5,000,000	6.1%
7	South Dakota	4,860,000	5.9%
8	Missouri	3,330,000	4.1%
9	Ohio	3,300,000	4.0%
10	Wisconsin	3,170,000	3.9%
11	North Dakota	2,930,000	3.6%
12	Michigan	1,940,000	2.4%
13	Texas	1,750,000	2.1%
14	Kentucky	1,230,000	1.5%
15	Colorado	1,200,000	1.5%
16	Pennsylvania	950,000	1.2%
17	North Carolina	830,000	1.0%
18	Tennessee	690,000	0.8%
19	Arkansas	645,000	0.8%
19	New York	645,000	0.8%
21	Mississippi	465,000	0.6%
22	Louisiana	450,000	0.6%
23	Maryland	390,000	0.5%
24	Virginia	325,000	0.4%
25	South Carolina	310,000	0.4%
26	Georgia	285,000	0.3%
27	Oklahoma	280,000	0.3%
28	Alabama	250,000	0.3%
29	Delaware	166,000	0.2%
30	Idaho	135,000	0.2%
31	Washington	85,000	0.1%
32	Wyoming	70,000	0.1%
33	Montana	68,000	0.1%
34	California	65,000	0.1%
34	Florida	65,000	0.1%
36	New Jersey	61,000	0.1%
37	Oregon	45,000	0.1%
38	New Mexico	35,000	0.0%
39	West Virginia	33,000	0.0%
40	Utah	22,000	0.0%
41	Arizona	15,000	0.0%
NA	Alaska**	NA	NA
NA	Connecticut**	NA	NA
NA	Hawaii**	NA	NA
NA	Maine**	NA	NA
NA	Massachusetts**	NA	NA
NA	Nevada**	NA	NA
NA	New Hampshire**	NA	NA
NA	Rhode Island**	NA	NA
NA	Vermont**	NA	NA
	District of Columbia**	NA	NA

Source: U.S. Department of Agriculture, National Agricultural Statistics Service
   "Crop Production: 2018 Summary" (February 2019, https://usda.library.cornell.edu/concern/publications/k3569432s)
*Estimated totals. Acres harvested for grain.
**No acreage or not available.

Acres Harvested: Soybeans in 2018

National Total = 88,110,000 Acres*

ALPHA ORDER

RANK ORDER

RANK	STATE	ACRES	% of USA		RANK	STATE	ACRES	% of USA
24	Alabama	340,000	0.4%		1	Illinois	10,750,000	12.2%
NA	Alaska**	NA	NA		2	Iowa	9,910,000	11.2%
NA	Arizona**	NA	NA		3	Minnesota	7,710,000	8.8%
11	Arkansas	3,240,000	3.7%		4	North Dakota	6,860,000	7.8%
NA	California**	NA	NA		5	Indiana	5,920,000	6.7%
NA	Colorado**	NA	NA		6	Missouri	5,800,000	6.6%
NA	Connecticut**	NA	NA		7	Nebraska	5,650,000	6.4%
26	Delaware	168,000	0.2%		8	South Dakota	5,580,000	6.3%
31	Florida	12,000	0.0%		9	Ohio	4,980,000	5.7%
27	Georgia	135,000	0.2%		10	Kansas	4,700,000	5.3%
NA	Hawaii**	NA	NA		11	Arkansas	3,240,000	3.7%
NA	Idaho**	NA	NA		12	Michigan	2,280,000	2.6%
1	Illinois	10,750,000	12.2%		13	Mississippi	2,190,000	2.5%
5	Indiana	5,920,000	6.7%		14	Wisconsin	2,160,000	2.5%
2	Iowa	9,910,000	11.2%		15	Kentucky	1,990,000	2.3%
10	Kansas	4,700,000	5.3%		16	Tennessee	1,670,000	1.9%
15	Kentucky	1,990,000	2.3%		17	North Carolina	1,570,000	1.8%
18	Louisiana	1,200,000	1.4%		18	Louisiana	1,200,000	1.4%
NA	Maine**	NA	NA		19	Pennsylvania	630,000	0.7%
22	Maryland	515,000	0.6%		20	Oklahoma	600,000	0.7%
NA	Massachusetts**	NA	NA		21	Virginia	590,000	0.7%
12	Michigan	2,280,000	2.6%		22	Maryland	515,000	0.6%
3	Minnesota	7,710,000	8.8%		23	South Carolina	375,000	0.4%
13	Mississippi	2,190,000	2.5%		24	Alabama	340,000	0.4%
6	Missouri	5,800,000	6.6%		25	New York	320,000	0.4%
NA	Montana**	NA	NA		26	Delaware	168,000	0.2%
7	Nebraska	5,650,000	6.4%		27	Georgia	135,000	0.2%
NA	Nevada**	NA	NA		27	Texas	135,000	0.2%
NA	New Hampshire**	NA	NA		29	New Jersey	103,000	0.1%
29	New Jersey	103,000	0.1%		30	West Virginia	27,000	0.0%
NA	New Mexico**	NA	NA		31	Florida	12,000	0.0%
25	New York	320,000	0.4%		NA	Alaska**	NA	NA
17	North Carolina	1,570,000	1.8%		NA	Arizona**	NA	NA
4	North Dakota	6,860,000	7.8%		NA	California**	NA	NA
9	Ohio	4,980,000	5.7%		NA	Colorado**	NA	NA
20	Oklahoma	600,000	0.7%		NA	Connecticut**	NA	NA
NA	Oregon**	NA	NA		NA	Hawaii**	NA	NA
19	Pennsylvania	630,000	0.7%		NA	Idaho**	NA	NA
NA	Rhode Island**	NA	NA		NA	Maine**	NA	NA
23	South Carolina	375,000	0.4%		NA	Massachusetts**	NA	NA
8	South Dakota	5,580,000	6.3%		NA	Montana**	NA	NA
16	Tennessee	1,670,000	1.9%		NA	Nevada**	NA	NA
27	Texas	135,000	0.2%		NA	New Hampshire**	NA	NA
NA	Utah**	NA	NA		NA	New Mexico**	NA	NA
NA	Vermont**	NA	NA		NA	Oregon**	NA	NA
21	Virginia	590,000	0.7%		NA	Rhode Island**	NA	NA
NA	Washington**	NA	NA		NA	Utah**	NA	NA
30	West Virginia	27,000	0.0%		NA	Vermont**	NA	NA
14	Wisconsin	2,160,000	2.5%		NA	Washington**	NA	NA
NA	Wyoming**	NA	NA		NA	Wyoming**	NA	NA
					NA	District of Columbia**	NA	NA

Source: U.S. Department of Agriculture, National Agricultural Statistics Service
"Crop Production: 2018 Summary" (February 2019, https://usda.library.cornell.edu/concern/publications/k3569432s)
*Estimated totals.
**No acreage or not available.

Acres Harvested: Wheat in 2018

National Total = 39,605,000 Acres*

ALPHA ORDER

ALPHA ORDER

RANK	STATE	ACRES	% of USA
27	Alabama	110,000	0.3%
NA	Alaska**	NA	NA
32	Arizona	74,000	0.2%
30	Arkansas	95,000	0.2%
25	California	143,000	0.4%
6	Colorado	1,954,000	4.9%
NA	Connecticut**	NA	NA
35	Delaware	45,000	0.1%
38	Florida	10,000	0.0%
33	Georgia	70,000	0.2%
NA	Hawaii**	NA	NA
10	Idaho	1,136,000	2.9%
13	Illinois	560,000	1.4%
20	Indiana	260,000	0.7%
41	Iowa	6,000	0.0%
2	Kansas	7,300,000	18.4%
18	Kentucky	300,000	0.8%
38	Louisiana	10,000	0.0%
NA	Maine**	NA	NA
21	Maryland	200,000	0.5%
NA	Massachusetts**	NA	NA
15	Michigan	470,000	1.2%
9	Minnesota	1,575,000	4.0%
36	Mississippi	30,000	0.1%
14	Missouri	520,000	1.3%
3	Montana	5,165,000	13.0%
11	Nebraska	1,010,000	2.6%
40	Nevada	8,000	0.0%
NA	New Hampshire**	NA	NA
37	New Jersey	15,000	0.0%
28	New Mexico	105,000	0.3%
30	New York	95,000	0.2%
17	North Carolina	370,000	0.9%
1	North Dakota	7,635,000	19.3%
16	Ohio	450,000	1.1%
4	Oklahoma	2,500,000	6.3%
12	Oregon	770,000	1.9%
24	Pennsylvania	145,000	0.4%
NA	Rhode Island**	NA	NA
34	South Carolina	65,000	0.2%
8	South Dakota	1,628,000	4.1%
19	Tennessee	285,000	0.7%
7	Texas	1,750,000	4.4%
29	Utah	103,000	0.3%
NA	Vermont**	NA	NA
23	Virginia	155,000	0.4%
5	Washington	2,165,000	5.5%
42	West Virginia	3,000	0.0%
21	Wisconsin	200,000	0.5%
26	Wyoming	115,000	0.3%

RANK ORDER

RANK	STATE	ACRES	% of USA
1	North Dakota	7,635,000	19.3%
2	Kansas	7,300,000	18.4%
3	Montana	5,165,000	13.0%
4	Oklahoma	2,500,000	6.3%
5	Washington	2,165,000	5.5%
6	Colorado	1,954,000	4.9%
7	Texas	1,750,000	4.4%
8	South Dakota	1,628,000	4.1%
9	Minnesota	1,575,000	4.0%
10	Idaho	1,136,000	2.9%
11	Nebraska	1,010,000	2.6%
12	Oregon	770,000	1.9%
13	Illinois	560,000	1.4%
14	Missouri	520,000	1.3%
15	Michigan	470,000	1.2%
16	Ohio	450,000	1.1%
17	North Carolina	370,000	0.9%
18	Kentucky	300,000	0.8%
19	Tennessee	285,000	0.7%
20	Indiana	260,000	0.7%
21	Maryland	200,000	0.5%
21	Wisconsin	200,000	0.5%
23	Virginia	155,000	0.4%
24	Pennsylvania	145,000	0.4%
25	California	143,000	0.4%
26	Wyoming	115,000	0.3%
27	Alabama	110,000	0.3%
28	New Mexico	105,000	0.3%
29	Utah	103,000	0.3%
30	Arkansas	95,000	0.2%
30	New York	95,000	0.2%
32	Arizona	74,000	0.2%
33	Georgia	70,000	0.2%
34	South Carolina	65,000	0.2%
35	Delaware	45,000	0.1%
36	Mississippi	30,000	0.1%
37	New Jersey	15,000	0.0%
38	Florida	10,000	0.0%
38	Louisiana	10,000	0.0%
40	Nevada	8,000	0.0%
41	Iowa	6,000	0.0%
42	West Virginia	3,000	0.0%
NA	Alaska**	NA	NA
NA	Connecticut**	NA	NA
NA	Hawaii**	NA	NA
NA	Maine**	NA	NA
NA	Massachusetts**	NA	NA
NA	New Hampshire**	NA	NA
NA	Rhode Island**	NA	NA
NA	Vermont**	NA	NA
	District of Columbia**	NA	NA

Source: U.S. Department of Agriculture, National Agricultural Statistics Service
   "Crop Production: 2018 Summary" (February 2019, https://usda.library.cornell.edu/concern/publications/k3569432s)
*Estimated totals.
**No acreage or not available.

Cattle on Farms in 2018

National Total = 94,399,000 Cattle*

ALPHA ORDER					RANK ORDER			
RANK	STATE	CATTLE	% of USA		RANK	STATE	CATTLE	% of USA
23	Alabama	1,340,000	1.4%		1	Texas	12,500,000	13.2%
49	Alaska	14,000	0.0%		2	Nebraska	6,800,000	7.2%
31	Arizona	1,000,000	1.1%		3	Kansas	6,300,000	6.7%
17	Arkansas	1,760,000	1.9%		4	California	5,200,000	5.5%
4	California	5,200,000	5.5%		5	Oklahoma	5,100,000	5.4%
10	Colorado	2,850,000	3.0%		6	Missouri	4,450,000	4.7%
44	Connecticut	50,000	0.1%		7	Iowa	4,000,000	4.2%
48	Delaware	17,000	0.0%		7	South Dakota	4,000,000	4.2%
18	Florida	1,630,000	1.7%		9	Wisconsin	3,500,000	3.7%
30	Georgia	1,070,000	1.1%		10	Colorado	2,850,000	3.0%
42	Hawaii	144,000	0.2%		11	Montana	2,550,000	2.7%
12	Idaho	2,400,000	2.5%		12	Idaho	2,400,000	2.5%
29	Illinois	1,150,000	1.2%		13	Minnesota	2,350,000	2.5%
33	Indiana	870,000	0.9%		14	Kentucky	2,160,000	2.3%
7	Iowa	4,000,000	4.2%		15	North Dakota	1,860,000	2.0%
3	Kansas	6,300,000	6.7%		16	Tennessee	1,830,000	1.9%
14	Kentucky	2,160,000	2.3%		17	Arkansas	1,760,000	1.9%
34	Louisiana	820,000	0.9%		18	Florida	1,630,000	1.7%
43	Maine	82,000	0.1%		19	Pennsylvania	1,620,000	1.7%
41	Maryland	193,000	0.2%		20	New Mexico	1,510,000	1.6%
45	Massachusetts	38,000	0.0%		21	New York	1,480,000	1.6%
27	Michigan	1,160,000	1.2%		21	Virginia	1,480,000	1.6%
13	Minnesota	2,350,000	2.5%		23	Alabama	1,340,000	1.4%
32	Mississippi	930,000	1.0%		24	Wyoming	1,320,000	1.4%
6	Missouri	4,450,000	4.7%		25	Ohio	1,300,000	1.4%
11	Montana	2,550,000	2.7%		26	Oregon	1,270,000	1.3%
2	Nebraska	6,800,000	7.2%		27	Michigan	1,160,000	1.2%
37	Nevada	465,000	0.5%		27	Washington	1,160,000	1.2%
46	New Hampshire	37,000	0.0%		29	Illinois	1,150,000	1.2%
47	New Jersey	29,000	0.0%		30	Georgia	1,070,000	1.1%
20	New Mexico	1,510,000	1.6%		31	Arizona	1,000,000	1.1%
21	New York	1,480,000	1.6%		32	Mississippi	930,000	1.0%
35	North Carolina	810,000	0.9%		33	Indiana	870,000	0.9%
15	North Dakota	1,860,000	2.0%		34	Louisiana	820,000	0.9%
25	Ohio	1,300,000	1.4%		35	North Carolina	810,000	0.9%
5	Oklahoma	5,100,000	5.4%		36	Utah	800,000	0.8%
26	Oregon	1,270,000	1.3%		37	Nevada	465,000	0.5%
19	Pennsylvania	1,620,000	1.7%		38	West Virginia	395,000	0.4%
50	Rhode Island	5,000	0.0%		39	South Carolina	340,000	0.4%
39	South Carolina	340,000	0.4%		40	Vermont	260,000	0.3%
7	South Dakota	4,000,000	4.2%		41	Maryland	193,000	0.2%
16	Tennessee	1,830,000	1.9%		42	Hawaii	144,000	0.2%
1	Texas	12,500,000	13.2%		43	Maine	82,000	0.1%
36	Utah	800,000	0.8%		44	Connecticut	50,000	0.1%
40	Vermont	260,000	0.3%		45	Massachusetts	38,000	0.0%
21	Virginia	1,480,000	1.6%		46	New Hampshire	37,000	0.0%
27	Washington	1,160,000	1.2%		47	New Jersey	29,000	0.0%
38	West Virginia	395,000	0.4%		48	Delaware	17,000	0.0%
9	Wisconsin	3,500,000	3.7%		49	Alaska	14,000	0.0%
24	Wyoming	1,320,000	1.4%		50	Rhode Island	5,000	0.0%
						District of Columbia	0	0.0%

Source: U.S. Department of Agriculture, National Agricultural Statistics Service
"Cattle" (http://usda.mannlib.cornell.edu/MannUsda/viewDocumentInfo.do?documentID=1017)
*As of January 1, 2018.

Milk Cows on Farms in 2017

National Total = 9,392,000 Milk Cows*

ALPHA ORDER

RANK	STATE	MILK COWS	% of USA
43	Alabama	6,000	0.1%
50	Alaska	300	0.0%
13	Arizona	203,000	2.2%
43	Arkansas	6,000	0.1%
1	California	1,749,000	18.6%
15	Colorado	160,000	1.7%
34	Connecticut	19,000	0.2%
47	Delaware	5,000	0.1%
18	Florida	124,000	1.3%
25	Georgia	84,000	0.9%
48	Hawaii	2,300	0.0%
4	Idaho	600,000	6.4%
22	Illinois	93,000	1.0%
14	Indiana	187,000	2.0%
12	Iowa	218,000	2.3%
16	Kansas	152,000	1.6%
27	Kentucky	56,000	0.6%
39	Louisiana	12,000	0.1%
33	Maine	30,000	0.3%
28	Maryland	48,000	0.5%
39	Massachusetts	12,000	0.1%
8	Michigan	427,000	4.5%
7	Minnesota	458,000	4.9%
41	Mississippi	9,000	0.1%
24	Missouri	85,000	0.9%
37	Montana	13,000	0.1%
26	Nebraska	60,000	0.6%
32	Nevada	32,000	0.3%
37	New Hampshire	13,000	0.1%
43	New Jersey	6,000	0.1%
9	New Mexico	329,000	3.5%
3	New York	623,000	6.6%
29	North Carolina	45,000	0.5%
35	North Dakota	16,000	0.2%
11	Ohio	263,000	2.8%
31	Oklahoma	39,000	0.4%
18	Oregon	124,000	1.3%
5	Pennsylvania	525,000	5.6%
49	Rhode Island	800	0.0%
36	South Carolina	15,000	0.2%
20	South Dakota	117,000	1.2%
30	Tennessee	40,000	0.4%
6	Texas	511,000	5.4%
21	Utah	95,000	1.0%
17	Vermont	129,000	1.4%
23	Virginia	87,000	0.9%
10	Washington	274,000	2.9%
42	West Virginia	8,000	0.1%
2	Wisconsin	1,278,000	13.6%
43	Wyoming	6,000	0.1%

RANK ORDER

RANK	STATE	MILK COWS	% of USA
1	California	1,749,000	18.6%
2	Wisconsin	1,278,000	13.6%
3	New York	623,000	6.6%
4	Idaho	600,000	6.4%
5	Pennsylvania	525,000	5.6%
6	Texas	511,000	5.4%
7	Minnesota	458,000	4.9%
8	Michigan	427,000	4.5%
9	New Mexico	329,000	3.5%
10	Washington	274,000	2.9%
11	Ohio	263,000	2.8%
12	Iowa	218,000	2.3%
13	Arizona	203,000	2.2%
14	Indiana	187,000	2.0%
15	Colorado	160,000	1.7%
16	Kansas	152,000	1.6%
17	Vermont	129,000	1.4%
18	Florida	124,000	1.3%
18	Oregon	124,000	1.3%
20	South Dakota	117,000	1.2%
21	Utah	95,000	1.0%
22	Illinois	93,000	1.0%
23	Virginia	87,000	0.9%
24	Missouri	85,000	0.9%
25	Georgia	84,000	0.9%
26	Nebraska	60,000	0.6%
27	Kentucky	56,000	0.6%
28	Maryland	48,000	0.5%
29	North Carolina	45,000	0.5%
30	Tennessee	40,000	0.4%
31	Oklahoma	39,000	0.4%
32	Nevada	32,000	0.3%
33	Maine	30,000	0.3%
34	Connecticut	19,000	0.2%
35	North Dakota	16,000	0.2%
36	South Carolina	15,000	0.2%
37	Montana	13,000	0.1%
37	New Hampshire	13,000	0.1%
39	Louisiana	12,000	0.1%
39	Massachusetts	12,000	0.1%
41	Mississippi	9,000	0.1%
42	West Virginia	8,000	0.1%
43	Alabama	6,000	0.1%
43	Arkansas	6,000	0.1%
43	New Jersey	6,000	0.1%
43	Wyoming	6,000	0.1%
47	Delaware	5,000	0.1%
48	Hawaii	2,300	0.0%
49	Rhode Island	800	0.0%
50	Alaska	300	0.0%
	District of Columbia	0	0.0%

Source: U.S. Department of Agriculture, National Agricultural Statistics Service
"Milk Production, Disposition and Income: 2017 Summary" (April 2018)
(https://usda.library.cornell.edu/concern/publications/h989r321c)
*Average number during year. Excludes heifers not yet fresh.

Milk Production in 2017

National Total = 215,466,000,000 Pounds of Milk*

ALPHA ORDER

RANK	STATE	POUNDS	% of USA
46	Alabama	89,000,000	0.0%
50	Alaska	2,900,000	0.0%
13	Arizona	5,010,000,000	2.3%
47	Arkansas	79,000,000	0.0%
1	California	39,798,000,000	18.5%
15	Colorado	4,189,000,000	1.9%
34	Connecticut	420,000,000	0.2%
45	Delaware	92,800,000	0.0%
20	Florida	2,496,000,000	1.2%
23	Georgia	1,840,000,000	0.9%
48	Hawaii	38,900,000	0.0%
4	Idaho	14,627,000,000	6.8%
22	Illinois	1,929,000,000	0.9%
14	Indiana	4,264,000,000	2.0%
12	Iowa	5,172,000,000	2.4%
16	Kansas	3,496,000,000	1.6%
27	Kentucky	1,041,000,000	0.5%
40	Louisiana	160,000,000	0.1%
33	Maine	630,000,000	0.3%
28	Maryland	953,000,000	0.4%
39	Massachusetts	211,000,000	0.1%
6	Michigan	11,231,000,000	5.2%
8	Minnesota	9,864,000,000	4.6%
42	Mississippi	137,000,000	0.1%
26	Missouri	1,240,000,000	0.6%
36	Montana	288,000,000	0.1%
25	Nebraska	1,444,000,000	0.7%
31	Nevada	709,000,000	0.3%
37	New Hampshire	273,000,000	0.1%
44	New Jersey	119,000,000	0.1%
9	New Mexico	8,212,000,000	3.8%
3	New York	14,912,000,000	6.9%
29	North Carolina	952,000,000	0.4%
35	North Dakota	345,000,000	0.2%
11	Ohio	5,591,000,000	2.6%
30	Oklahoma	728,000,000	0.3%
19	Oregon	2,529,000,000	1.2%
7	Pennsylvania	10,938,000,000	5.1%
49	Rhode Island	13,000,000	0.0%
38	South Carolina	247,000,000	0.1%
18	South Dakota	2,618,000,000	1.2%
32	Tennessee	693,000,000	0.3%
5	Texas	12,054,000,000	5.6%
21	Utah	2,215,000,000	1.0%
17	Vermont	2,728,000,000	1.3%
24	Virginia	1,736,000,000	0.8%
10	Washington	6,526,000,000	3.0%
43	West Virginia	127,000,000	0.1%
2	Wisconsin	30,320,000,000	14.1%
41	Wyoming	138,200,000	0.1%

RANK ORDER

RANK	STATE	POUNDS	% of USA
1	California	39,798,000,000	18.5%
2	Wisconsin	30,320,000,000	14.1%
3	New York	14,912,000,000	6.9%
4	Idaho	14,627,000,000	6.8%
5	Texas	12,054,000,000	5.6%
6	Michigan	11,231,000,000	5.2%
7	Pennsylvania	10,938,000,000	5.1%
8	Minnesota	9,864,000,000	4.6%
9	New Mexico	8,212,000,000	3.8%
10	Washington	6,526,000,000	3.0%
11	Ohio	5,591,000,000	2.6%
12	Iowa	5,172,000,000	2.4%
13	Arizona	5,010,000,000	2.3%
14	Indiana	4,264,000,000	2.0%
15	Colorado	4,189,000,000	1.9%
16	Kansas	3,496,000,000	1.6%
17	Vermont	2,728,000,000	1.3%
18	South Dakota	2,618,000,000	1.2%
19	Oregon	2,529,000,000	1.2%
20	Florida	2,496,000,000	1.2%
21	Utah	2,215,000,000	1.0%
22	Illinois	1,929,000,000	0.9%
23	Georgia	1,840,000,000	0.9%
24	Virginia	1,736,000,000	0.8%
25	Nebraska	1,444,000,000	0.7%
26	Missouri	1,240,000,000	0.6%
27	Kentucky	1,041,000,000	0.5%
28	Maryland	953,000,000	0.4%
29	North Carolina	952,000,000	0.4%
30	Oklahoma	728,000,000	0.3%
31	Nevada	709,000,000	0.3%
32	Tennessee	693,000,000	0.3%
33	Maine	630,000,000	0.3%
34	Connecticut	420,000,000	0.2%
35	North Dakota	345,000,000	0.2%
36	Montana	288,000,000	0.1%
37	New Hampshire	273,000,000	0.1%
38	South Carolina	247,000,000	0.1%
39	Massachusetts	211,000,000	0.1%
40	Louisiana	160,000,000	0.1%
41	Wyoming	138,200,000	0.1%
42	Mississippi	137,000,000	0.1%
43	West Virginia	127,000,000	0.1%
44	New Jersey	119,000,000	0.1%
45	Delaware	92,800,000	0.0%
46	Alabama	89,000,000	0.0%
47	Arkansas	79,000,000	0.0%
48	Hawaii	38,900,000	0.0%
49	Rhode Island	13,000,000	0.0%
50	Alaska	2,900,000	0.0%
	District of Columbia	0	0.0%

Source: U.S. Department of Agriculture, National Agricultural Statistics Service
"Milk Production, Disposition and Income: 2017 Summary" (April 2018)
(https://usda.library.cornell.edu/concern/publications/h989r321c)
*Excludes milk suckled by calves.

Milk Production per Milk Cow in 2017

National Average = 22,941 Pounds of Milk per Cow*

ALPHA ORDER

RANK	STATE	POUNDS
46	Alabama	14,833
50	Alaska	9,667
4	Arizona	24,680
49	Arkansas	13,167
16	California	22,755
2	Colorado	26,181
20	Connecticut	22,105
38	Delaware	18,560
32	Florida	20,129
21	Georgia	21,905
41	Hawaii	16,913
5	Idaho	24,378
30	Illinois	20,742
15	Indiana	22,802
9	Iowa	23,725
14	Kansas	23,000
37	Kentucky	18,589
48	Louisiana	13,333
27	Maine	21,000
34	Maryland	19,854
39	Massachusetts	17,583
1	Michigan	26,302
23	Minnesota	21,537
45	Mississippi	15,222
47	Missouri	14,588
19	Montana	22,154
6	Nebraska	24,067
18	Nevada	22,156
27	New Hampshire	21,000
35	New Jersey	19,833
3	New Mexico	24,960
7	New York	23,936
25	North Carolina	21,156
22	North Dakota	21,563
24	Ohio	21,259
36	Oklahoma	18,667
31	Oregon	20,395
29	Pennsylvania	20,834
43	Rhode Island	16,250
42	South Carolina	16,467
17	South Dakota	22,376
40	Tennessee	17,325
11	Texas	23,589
12	Utah	23,316
26	Vermont	21,147
33	Virginia	19,954
8	Washington	23,818
44	West Virginia	15,875
9	Wisconsin	23,725
13	Wyoming	23,033

RANK ORDER

RANK	STATE	POUNDS
1	Michigan	26,302
2	Colorado	26,181
3	New Mexico	24,960
4	Arizona	24,680
5	Idaho	24,378
6	Nebraska	24,067
7	New York	23,936
8	Washington	23,818
9	Iowa	23,725
9	Wisconsin	23,725
11	Texas	23,589
12	Utah	23,316
13	Wyoming	23,033
14	Kansas	23,000
15	Indiana	22,802
16	California	22,755
17	South Dakota	22,376
18	Nevada	22,156
19	Montana	22,154
20	Connecticut	22,105
21	Georgia	21,905
22	North Dakota	21,563
23	Minnesota	21,537
24	Ohio	21,259
25	North Carolina	21,156
26	Vermont	21,147
27	Maine	21,000
27	New Hampshire	21,000
29	Pennsylvania	20,834
30	Illinois	20,742
31	Oregon	20,395
32	Florida	20,129
33	Virginia	19,954
34	Maryland	19,854
35	New Jersey	19,833
36	Oklahoma	18,667
37	Kentucky	18,589
38	Delaware	18,560
39	Massachusetts	17,583
40	Tennessee	17,325
41	Hawaii	16,913
42	South Carolina	16,467
43	Rhode Island	16,250
44	West Virginia	15,875
45	Mississippi	15,222
46	Alabama	14,833
47	Missouri	14,588
48	Louisiana	13,333
49	Arkansas	13,167
50	Alaska	9,667
	District of Columbia**	NA

Source: U.S. Department of Agriculture, National Agricultural Statistics Service
  "Milk Production, Disposition and Income: 2017 Summary" (April 2018)
  (https://usda.library.cornell.edu/concern/publications/h989r321c)
*Excludes milk suckled by calves.
**Not applicable.

Hogs and Pigs on Farms in 2018

National Total = 74,550,200 Hogs and Pigs*

<table>
<thead>
<tr><th colspan="4">ALPHA ORDER</th><th colspan="4">RANK ORDER</th></tr>
<tr><th>RANK</th><th>STATE</th><th>HOGS AND PIGS</th><th>% of USA</th><th>RANK</th><th>STATE</th><th>HOGS AND PIGS</th><th>% of USA</th></tr>
</thead>
<tbody>
<tr><td>30</td><td>Alabama</td><td>53,000</td><td>0.1%</td><td>1</td><td>Iowa</td><td>23,300,000</td><td>31.3%</td></tr>
<tr><td>48</td><td>Alaska</td><td>1,900</td><td>0.0%</td><td>2</td><td>North Carolina</td><td>9,100,000</td><td>12.2%</td></tr>
<tr><td>24</td><td>Arizona</td><td>170,000</td><td>0.2%</td><td>3</td><td>Minnesota</td><td>8,900,000</td><td>11.9%</td></tr>
<tr><td>26</td><td>Arkansas</td><td>130,000</td><td>0.2%</td><td>4</td><td>Illinois</td><td>5,300,000</td><td>7.1%</td></tr>
<tr><td>27</td><td>California</td><td>101,000</td><td>0.1%</td><td>5</td><td>Indiana</td><td>4,200,000</td><td>5.6%</td></tr>
<tr><td>15</td><td>Colorado</td><td>750,000</td><td>1.0%</td><td>6</td><td>Missouri</td><td>3,550,000</td><td>4.8%</td></tr>
<tr><td>45</td><td>Connecticut</td><td>3,700</td><td>0.0%</td><td>7</td><td>Nebraska</td><td>3,500,000</td><td>4.7%</td></tr>
<tr><td>40</td><td>Delaware</td><td>6,500</td><td>0.0%</td><td>8</td><td>Ohio</td><td>2,550,000</td><td>3.4%</td></tr>
<tr><td>35</td><td>Florida</td><td>13,000</td><td>0.0%</td><td>9</td><td>Oklahoma</td><td>2,200,000</td><td>3.0%</td></tr>
<tr><td>29</td><td>Georgia</td><td>67,000</td><td>0.1%</td><td>10</td><td>Kansas</td><td>2,050,000</td><td>2.7%</td></tr>
<tr><td>36</td><td>Hawaii</td><td>9,000</td><td>0.0%</td><td>11</td><td>South Dakota</td><td>1,740,000</td><td>2.3%</td></tr>
<tr><td>32</td><td>Idaho</td><td>32,000</td><td>0.0%</td><td>12</td><td>Pennsylvania</td><td>1,310,000</td><td>1.8%</td></tr>
<tr><td>4</td><td>Illinois</td><td>5,300,000</td><td>7.1%</td><td>13</td><td>Michigan</td><td>1,180,000</td><td>1.6%</td></tr>
<tr><td>5</td><td>Indiana</td><td>4,200,000</td><td>5.6%</td><td>14</td><td>Texas</td><td>1,110,000</td><td>1.5%</td></tr>
<tr><td>1</td><td>Iowa</td><td>23,300,000</td><td>31.3%</td><td>15</td><td>Colorado</td><td>750,000</td><td>1.0%</td></tr>
<tr><td>10</td><td>Kansas</td><td>2,050,000</td><td>2.7%</td><td>16</td><td>Utah</td><td>710,000</td><td>1.0%</td></tr>
<tr><td>20</td><td>Kentucky</td><td>285,000</td><td>0.4%</td><td>17</td><td>Mississippi</td><td>575,000</td><td>0.8%</td></tr>
<tr><td>41</td><td>Louisiana</td><td>6,000</td><td>0.0%</td><td>18</td><td>Virginia</td><td>345,000</td><td>0.5%</td></tr>
<tr><td>43</td><td>Maine</td><td>4,400</td><td>0.0%</td><td>19</td><td>Wisconsin</td><td>325,000</td><td>0.4%</td></tr>
<tr><td>33</td><td>Maryland</td><td>19,000</td><td>0.0%</td><td>20</td><td>Kentucky</td><td>285,000</td><td>0.4%</td></tr>
<tr><td>39</td><td>Massachusetts</td><td>8,000</td><td>0.0%</td><td>21</td><td>Tennessee</td><td>220,000</td><td>0.3%</td></tr>
<tr><td>13</td><td>Michigan</td><td>1,180,000</td><td>1.6%</td><td>22</td><td>South Carolina</td><td>200,000</td><td>0.3%</td></tr>
<tr><td>3</td><td>Minnesota</td><td>8,900,000</td><td>11.9%</td><td>23</td><td>Montana</td><td>192,000</td><td>0.3%</td></tr>
<tr><td>17</td><td>Mississippi</td><td>575,000</td><td>0.8%</td><td>24</td><td>Arizona</td><td>170,000</td><td>0.2%</td></tr>
<tr><td>6</td><td>Missouri</td><td>3,550,000</td><td>4.8%</td><td>25</td><td>North Dakota</td><td>145,000</td><td>0.2%</td></tr>
<tr><td>23</td><td>Montana</td><td>192,000</td><td>0.3%</td><td>26</td><td>Arkansas</td><td>130,000</td><td>0.2%</td></tr>
<tr><td>7</td><td>Nebraska</td><td>3,500,000</td><td>4.7%</td><td>27</td><td>California</td><td>101,000</td><td>0.1%</td></tr>
<tr><td>41</td><td>Nevada</td><td>6,000</td><td>0.0%</td><td>28</td><td>Wyoming</td><td>88,000</td><td>0.1%</td></tr>
<tr><td>47</td><td>New Hampshire</td><td>3,500</td><td>0.0%</td><td>29</td><td>Georgia</td><td>67,000</td><td>0.1%</td></tr>
<tr><td>38</td><td>New Jersey</td><td>8,500</td><td>0.0%</td><td>30</td><td>Alabama</td><td>53,000</td><td>0.1%</td></tr>
<tr><td>50</td><td>New Mexico</td><td>1,300</td><td>0.0%</td><td>31</td><td>New York</td><td>46,000</td><td>0.1%</td></tr>
<tr><td>31</td><td>New York</td><td>46,000</td><td>0.1%</td><td>32</td><td>Idaho</td><td>32,000</td><td>0.0%</td></tr>
<tr><td>2</td><td>North Carolina</td><td>9,100,000</td><td>12.2%</td><td>33</td><td>Maryland</td><td>19,000</td><td>0.0%</td></tr>
<tr><td>25</td><td>North Dakota</td><td>145,000</td><td>0.2%</td><td>34</td><td>Washington</td><td>17,000</td><td>0.0%</td></tr>
<tr><td>8</td><td>Ohio</td><td>2,550,000</td><td>3.4%</td><td>35</td><td>Florida</td><td>13,000</td><td>0.0%</td></tr>
<tr><td>9</td><td>Oklahoma</td><td>2,200,000</td><td>3.0%</td><td>36</td><td>Hawaii</td><td>9,000</td><td>0.0%</td></tr>
<tr><td>36</td><td>Oregon</td><td>9,000</td><td>0.0%</td><td>36</td><td>Oregon</td><td>9,000</td><td>0.0%</td></tr>
<tr><td>12</td><td>Pennsylvania</td><td>1,310,000</td><td>1.8%</td><td>38</td><td>New Jersey</td><td>8,500</td><td>0.0%</td></tr>
<tr><td>49</td><td>Rhode Island</td><td>1,700</td><td>0.0%</td><td>39</td><td>Massachusetts</td><td>8,000</td><td>0.0%</td></tr>
<tr><td>22</td><td>South Carolina</td><td>200,000</td><td>0.3%</td><td>40</td><td>Delaware</td><td>6,500</td><td>0.0%</td></tr>
<tr><td>11</td><td>South Dakota</td><td>1,740,000</td><td>2.3%</td><td>41</td><td>Louisiana</td><td>6,000</td><td>0.0%</td></tr>
<tr><td>21</td><td>Tennessee</td><td>220,000</td><td>0.3%</td><td>41</td><td>Nevada</td><td>6,000</td><td>0.0%</td></tr>
<tr><td>14</td><td>Texas</td><td>1,110,000</td><td>1.5%</td><td>43</td><td>Maine</td><td>4,400</td><td>0.0%</td></tr>
<tr><td>16</td><td>Utah</td><td>710,000</td><td>1.0%</td><td>44</td><td>West Virginia</td><td>4,000</td><td>0.0%</td></tr>
<tr><td>45</td><td>Vermont</td><td>3,700</td><td>0.0%</td><td>45</td><td>Connecticut</td><td>3,700</td><td>0.0%</td></tr>
<tr><td>18</td><td>Virginia</td><td>345,000</td><td>0.5%</td><td>45</td><td>Vermont</td><td>3,700</td><td>0.0%</td></tr>
<tr><td>34</td><td>Washington</td><td>17,000</td><td>0.0%</td><td>47</td><td>New Hampshire</td><td>3,500</td><td>0.0%</td></tr>
<tr><td>44</td><td>West Virginia</td><td>4,000</td><td>0.0%</td><td>48</td><td>Alaska</td><td>1,900</td><td>0.0%</td></tr>
<tr><td>19</td><td>Wisconsin</td><td>325,000</td><td>0.4%</td><td>49</td><td>Rhode Island</td><td>1,700</td><td>0.0%</td></tr>
<tr><td>28</td><td>Wyoming</td><td>88,000</td><td>0.1%</td><td>50</td><td>New Mexico</td><td>1,300</td><td>0.0%</td></tr>
<tr><td></td><td></td><td></td><td></td><td></td><td>District of Columbia</td><td>0</td><td>0.0%</td></tr>
</tbody>
</table>

Source: U.S. Department of Agriculture, National Agricultural Statistics Service
   "Quarterly Hogs and Pigs" (https://usda.library.cornell.edu/concern/publications/rj430453j)
*As of December 1, 2018.

Chickens in 2017

National Total = 8,913,000,000 Chickens*

ALPHA ORDER				RANK ORDER			
RANK	STATE	CHICKENS	% of USA	RANK	STATE	CHICKENS	% of USA
2	Alabama	1,095,400,000	12.3%	1	Georgia	1,363,400,000	15.3%
NA	Alaska***	NA	NA	2	Alabama	1,095,400,000	12.3%
NA	Arizona***	NA	NA	3	Arkansas	1,059,000,000	11.9%
3	Arkansas	1,059,000,000	11.9%	4	North Carolina	830,800,000	9.3%
NA	California**	NA	NA	5	Mississippi	741,100,000	8.3%
NA	Colorado***	NA	NA	6	Texas	651,200,000	7.3%
NA	Connecticut***	NA	NA	7	Maryland	306,700,000	3.4%
11	Delaware	259,800,000	2.9%	8	Kentucky	295,800,000	3.3%
18	Florida	65,200,000	0.7%	9	Missouri	291,100,000	3.3%
1	Georgia	1,363,400,000	15.3%	10	Virginia	277,400,000	3.1%
NA	Hawaii***	NA	NA	11	Delaware	259,800,000	2.9%
NA	Idaho***	NA	NA	12	South Carolina	243,100,000	2.7%
NA	Illinois**	NA	NA	13	Oklahoma	204,500,000	2.3%
NA	Indiana**	NA	NA	14	Pennsylvania	185,200,000	2.1%
NA	Iowa**	NA	NA	15	Tennessee	171,500,000	1.9%
NA	Kansas***	NA	NA	16	Ohio	99,300,000	1.1%
8	Kentucky	295,800,000	3.3%	17	West Virginia	86,100,000	1.0%
NA	Louisiana**	NA	NA	18	Florida	65,200,000	0.7%
NA	Maine***	NA	NA	19	Minnesota	59,700,000	0.7%
7	Maryland	306,700,000	3.4%	20	Wisconsin	53,800,000	0.6%
NA	Massachusetts***	NA	NA	NA	Alaska***	NA	NA
NA	Michigan**	NA	NA	NA	Arizona***	NA	NA
19	Minnesota	59,700,000	0.7%	NA	California**	NA	NA
5	Mississippi	741,100,000	8.3%	NA	Colorado***	NA	NA
9	Missouri	291,100,000	3.3%	NA	Connecticut***	NA	NA
NA	Montana***	NA	NA	NA	Hawaii***	NA	NA
NA	Nebraska**	NA	NA	NA	Idaho***	NA	NA
NA	Nevada***	NA	NA	NA	Illinois**	NA	NA
NA	New Hampshire***	NA	NA	NA	Indiana**	NA	NA
NA	New Jersey***	NA	NA	NA	Iowa**	NA	NA
NA	New Mexico***	NA	NA	NA	Kansas***	NA	NA
NA	New York**	NA	NA	NA	Louisiana**	NA	NA
4	North Carolina	830,800,000	9.3%	NA	Maine***	NA	NA
NA	North Dakota***	NA	NA	NA	Massachusetts***	NA	NA
16	Ohio	99,300,000	1.1%	NA	Michigan**	NA	NA
13	Oklahoma	204,500,000	2.3%	NA	Montana***	NA	NA
NA	Oregon**	NA	NA	NA	Nebraska**	NA	NA
14	Pennsylvania	185,200,000	2.1%	NA	Nevada***	NA	NA
NA	Rhode Island***	NA	NA	NA	New Hampshire***	NA	NA
12	South Carolina	243,100,000	2.7%	NA	New Jersey***	NA	NA
NA	South Dakota***	NA	NA	NA	New Mexico***	NA	NA
15	Tennessee	171,500,000	1.9%	NA	New York**	NA	NA
6	Texas	651,200,000	7.3%	NA	North Dakota***	NA	NA
NA	Utah***	NA	NA	NA	Oregon**	NA	NA
NA	Vermont***	NA	NA	NA	Rhode Island***	NA	NA
10	Virginia	277,400,000	3.1%	NA	South Dakota***	NA	NA
NA	Washington**	NA	NA	NA	Utah***	NA	NA
17	West Virginia	86,100,000	1.0%	NA	Vermont***	NA	NA
20	Wisconsin	53,800,000	0.6%	NA	Washington**	NA	NA
NA	Wyoming***	NA	NA	NA	Wyoming***	NA	NA
					District of Columbia***	NA	NA

Source: U.S. Department of Agriculture, National Agricultural Statistics Service
   "Poultry - Production and Value: 2017 Summary" (April 2018, https://usda.library.cornell.edu/concern/publications/m039k491c)
*Broilers. Total includes numbers for states not shown separately but excludes states producing less than 500,000 birds. **These states produced a combined total of 572,900,000 chickens. They are combined to avoid disclosing individual operations.
National total does not include chickens used for egg production. ***Produces fewer than 500,000 chickens or are not available.

Eggs Produced in 2017

National Total = 105,688,700,000 Eggs*

ALPHA ORDER

RANK	STATE	EGGS	% of USA
16	Alabama	2,072,300,000	2.0%
NA	Alaska**	NA	NA
NA	Arizona**	NA	NA
10	Arkansas	3,376,900,000	3.2%
9	California	3,758,500,000	3.6%
21	Colorado	1,394,100,000	1.3%
NA	Connecticut**	NA	NA
NA	Delaware**	NA	NA
15	Florida	2,095,100,000	2.0%
6	Georgia	4,964,100,000	4.7%
NA	Hawaii**	NA	NA
NA	Idaho**	NA	NA
20	Illinois	1,478,100,000	1.4%
2	Indiana	9,581,600,000	9.1%
1	Iowa	15,953,100,000	15.1%
NA	Kansas**	NA	NA
23	Kentucky	1,289,300,000	1.2%
30	Louisiana	480,200,000	0.5%
NA	Maine**	NA	NA
25	Maryland	833,700,000	0.8%
35	Massachusetts	40,200,000	0.0%
7	Michigan	4,224,700,000	4.0%
11	Minnesota	3,103,100,000	2.9%
22	Mississippi	1,392,600,000	1.3%
12	Missouri	3,057,000,000	2.9%
33	Montana	153,800,000	0.1%
13	Nebraska	2,489,200,000	2.4%
NA	Nevada**	NA	NA
NA	New Hampshire**	NA	NA
NA	New Jersey**	NA	NA
NA	New Mexico**	NA	NA
18	New York	1,694,100,000	1.6%
8	North Carolina	3,935,300,000	3.7%
NA	North Dakota**	NA	NA
3	Ohio	8,903,800,000	8.4%
29	Oklahoma	666,500,000	0.6%
27	Oregon	743,900,000	0.7%
4	Pennsylvania	8,212,800,000	7.8%
NA	Rhode Island**	NA	NA
24	South Carolina	1,067,900,000	1.0%
26	South Dakota	785,400,000	0.7%
31	Tennessee	374,600,000	0.4%
5	Texas	5,760,500,000	5.5%
19	Utah	1,512,700,000	1.4%
34	Vermont	43,900,000	0.0%
28	Virginia	691,400,000	0.7%
14	Washington	2,103,700,000	2.0%
32	West Virginia	273,100,000	0.3%
17	Wisconsin	1,759,400,000	1.7%
NA	Wyoming**	NA	NA

RANK ORDER

RANK	STATE	EGGS	% of USA
1	Iowa	15,953,100,000	15.1%
2	Indiana	9,581,600,000	9.1%
3	Ohio	8,903,800,000	8.4%
4	Pennsylvania	8,212,800,000	7.8%
5	Texas	5,760,500,000	5.5%
6	Georgia	4,964,100,000	4.7%
7	Michigan	4,224,700,000	4.0%
8	North Carolina	3,935,300,000	3.7%
9	California	3,758,500,000	3.6%
10	Arkansas	3,376,900,000	3.2%
11	Minnesota	3,103,100,000	2.9%
12	Missouri	3,057,000,000	2.9%
13	Nebraska	2,489,200,000	2.4%
14	Washington	2,103,700,000	2.0%
15	Florida	2,095,100,000	2.0%
16	Alabama	2,072,300,000	2.0%
17	Wisconsin	1,759,400,000	1.7%
18	New York	1,694,100,000	1.6%
19	Utah	1,512,700,000	1.4%
20	Illinois	1,478,100,000	1.4%
21	Colorado	1,394,100,000	1.3%
22	Mississippi	1,392,600,000	1.3%
23	Kentucky	1,289,300,000	1.2%
24	South Carolina	1,067,900,000	1.0%
25	Maryland	833,700,000	0.8%
26	South Dakota	785,400,000	0.7%
27	Oregon	743,900,000	0.7%
28	Virginia	691,400,000	0.7%
29	Oklahoma	666,500,000	0.6%
30	Louisiana	480,200,000	0.5%
31	Tennessee	374,600,000	0.4%
32	West Virginia	273,100,000	0.3%
33	Montana	153,800,000	0.1%
34	Vermont	43,900,000	0.0%
35	Massachusetts	40,200,000	0.0%
NA	Alaska**	NA	NA
NA	Arizona**	NA	NA
NA	Connecticut**	NA	NA
NA	Delaware**	NA	NA
NA	Hawaii**	NA	NA
NA	Idaho**	NA	NA
NA	Kansas**	NA	NA
NA	Maine**	NA	NA
NA	Nevada**	NA	NA
NA	New Hampshire**	NA	NA
NA	New Jersey**	NA	NA
NA	New Mexico**	NA	NA
NA	North Dakota**	NA	NA
NA	Rhode Island**	NA	NA
NA	Wyoming**	NA	NA
	District of Columbia	0	0.0%

Source: U.S. Department of Agriculture, National Agricultural Statistics Service

"Poultry - Production and Value: 2017 Summary" (April 2018, https://usda.library.cornell.edu/concern/publications/m039k491c)
*Includes hatching and market (table) eggs. **These states produced a combined 5,422,100,000 eggs. They are combined to avoid disclosing individual operations.

II. Crime and Law Enforcement

Arrests:

Important Note Regarding Arrest Numbers

The state arrest numbers reported by the FBI and shown on page 55 are only from those law enforcement agencies that submitted complete arrests reports for twelve months in 2017. The arrest rates were calculated by the editors using population totals provided by the FBI for those jurisdictions reporting. Reports from law enforcement agencies in Illinois, Nebraska, New Mexico, and the District of Columbia were insufficient to calculate rates. Reports from Mississippi and New York represented less than 60 percent of their state population. Rates for these states should be interpreted with caution.

Juveniles:

Important Note Regarding Juvenile Arrest Rates

The juvenile arrest rates shown on page 56 were calculated by the editors as follows:

The state arrest numbers reported by the FBI are only from those law enforcement agencies that submitted complete arrest reports for twelve months in 2017. Included in the FBI report are population totals of these reporting jurisdictions by state. Using these FBI population figures, we first determined what percentage the FBI numbers represented of each state's total resident population. Next, using 2017 Census state estimates for ten- to seventeen-year-olds, we multiplied the percentages derived from the FBI population figures into the Census Bureau's total juvenile population counts. The resulting juvenile population is the base that was used to determine juvenile arrests per 100,000 juvenile population. The national rate was calculated in the same manner.

Reports from law enforcement agencies in Illinois, Nebraska, and the District of Columbia were insufficient to calculate rates. Reports from Mississippi, New Mexico, and New York represented less than 60 percent of their state population. Rates for these states should be interpreted with caution.

Crimes (Revised Definition) in 2017

National Total = 8,977,306 Crimes*

ALPHA ORDER

RANK	STATE	CRIMES	% of USA
19	Alabama	169,711	1.9%
40	Alaska	32,337	0.4%
12	Arizona	240,159	2.7%
28	Arkansas	109,160	1.2%
1	California	1,164,741	13.0%
18	Colorado	172,121	1.9%
36	Connecticut	71,689	0.8%
43	Delaware	27,838	0.3%
3	Florida	612,845	6.8%
5	Georgia	335,556	3.7%
38	Hawaii	43,969	0.5%
41	Idaho	31,967	0.4%
7	Illinois	313,677	3.5%
15	Indiana	187,730	2.1%
35	Iowa	76,085	0.8%
33	Kansas	93,623	1.0%
29	Kentucky	104,889	1.2%
17	Louisiana	183,804	2.0%
44	Maine	21,750	0.2%
21	Maryland	164,769	1.8%
27	Massachusetts	123,135	1.4%
13	Michigan	224,144	2.5%
23	Minnesota	135,503	1.5%
34	Mississippi	90,107	1.0%
14	Missouri	205,673	2.3%
42	Montana	31,186	0.3%
37	Nebraska	49,536	0.6%
31	Nevada	94,989	1.1%
45	New Hampshire	21,223	0.2%
22	New Jersey	160,690	1.8%
30	New Mexico	98,665	1.1%
4	New York	371,354	4.1%
8	North Carolina	298,850	3.3%
48	North Dakota	18,727	0.2%
6	Ohio	316,717	3.5%
25	Oklahoma	131,000	1.5%
24	Oregon	135,396	1.5%
10	Pennsylvania	251,340	2.8%
46	Rhode Island	21,021	0.2%
16	South Carolina	186,007	2.1%
47	South Dakota	20,088	0.2%
11	Tennessee	241,243	2.7%
2	Texas	849,566	9.5%
32	Utah	93,648	1.0%
50	Vermont	9,994	0.1%
20	Virginia	169,487	1.9%
9	Washington	257,575	2.9%
39	West Virginia	39,998	0.4%
26	Wisconsin	123,341	1.4%
49	Wyoming	11,980	0.1%

RANK ORDER

RANK	STATE	CRIMES	% of USA
1	California	1,164,741	13.0%
2	Texas	849,566	9.5%
3	Florida	612,845	6.8%
4	New York	371,354	4.1%
5	Georgia	335,556	3.7%
6	Ohio	316,717	3.5%
7	Illinois	313,677	3.5%
8	North Carolina	298,850	3.3%
9	Washington	257,575	2.9%
10	Pennsylvania	251,340	2.8%
11	Tennessee	241,243	2.7%
12	Arizona	240,159	2.7%
13	Michigan	224,144	2.5%
14	Missouri	205,673	2.3%
15	Indiana	187,730	2.1%
16	South Carolina	186,007	2.1%
17	Louisiana	183,804	2.0%
18	Colorado	172,121	1.9%
19	Alabama	169,711	1.9%
20	Virginia	169,487	1.9%
21	Maryland	164,769	1.8%
22	New Jersey	160,690	1.8%
23	Minnesota	135,503	1.5%
24	Oregon	135,396	1.5%
25	Oklahoma	131,000	1.5%
26	Wisconsin	123,341	1.4%
27	Massachusetts	123,135	1.4%
28	Arkansas	109,160	1.2%
29	Kentucky	104,889	1.2%
30	New Mexico	98,665	1.1%
31	Nevada	94,989	1.1%
32	Utah	93,648	1.0%
33	Kansas	93,623	1.0%
34	Mississippi	90,107	1.0%
35	Iowa	76,085	0.8%
36	Connecticut	71,689	0.8%
37	Nebraska	49,536	0.6%
38	Hawaii	43,969	0.5%
39	West Virginia	39,998	0.4%
40	Alaska	32,337	0.4%
41	Idaho	31,967	0.4%
42	Montana	31,186	0.3%
43	Delaware	27,838	0.3%
44	Maine	21,750	0.2%
45	New Hampshire	21,223	0.2%
46	Rhode Island	21,021	0.2%
47	South Dakota	20,088	0.2%
48	North Dakota	18,727	0.2%
49	Wyoming	11,980	0.1%
50	Vermont	9,994	0.1%
	District of Columbia	36,703	0.4%

Source: CQ Press using reported data from the Federal Bureau of Investigation
  "Crime in the United States 2017" (Uniform Crime Reports, September 24, 2018, https://ucr.fbi.gov/)
*Includes murder, rape (revised definition), robbery, aggravated assault, burglary, larceny-theft, and motor vehicle theft.

Crime Rate (Revised Definition) in 2017

National Rate = 2,756.2 Crimes per 100,000 Population*

ALPHA ORDER

RANK	STATE	RATE
7	Alabama	3,481.5
2	Alaska	4,371.1
9	Arizona	3,422.9
5	Arkansas	3,633.5
22	California	2,946.0
17	Colorado	3,069.7
41	Connecticut	1,997.9
25	Delaware	2,894.0
23	Florida	2,920.4
13	Georgia	3,217.4
16	Hawaii	3,080.1
45	Idaho	1,861.8
31	Illinois	2,450.2
26	Indiana	2,815.9
33	Iowa	2,418.7
14	Kansas	3,213.9
34	Kentucky	2,354.9
3	Louisiana	3,923.8
48	Maine	1,628.1
27	Maryland	2,722.5
46	Massachusetts	1,795.0
36	Michigan	2,250.0
32	Minnesota	2,429.8
18	Mississippi	3,019.6
10	Missouri	3,364.2
21	Montana	2,968.7
29	Nebraska	2,579.9
15	Nevada	3,168.3
50	New Hampshire	1,580.5
47	New Jersey	1,784.3
1	New Mexico	4,725.2
44	New York	1,870.9
24	North Carolina	2,909.0
30	North Dakota	2,479.1
28	Ohio	2,716.6
11	Oklahoma	3,332.6
12	Oregon	3,268.3
43	Pennsylvania	1,962.7
42	Rhode Island	1,983.8
4	South Carolina	3,702.1
35	South Dakota	2,309.8
6	Tennessee	3,592.1
20	Texas	3,001.5
19	Utah	3,019.1
49	Vermont	1,602.5
40	Virginia	2,001.1
8	Washington	3,478.1
37	West Virginia	2,202.7
38	Wisconsin	2,128.2
39	Wyoming	2,067.9

RANK ORDER

RANK	STATE	RATE
1	New Mexico	4,725.2
2	Alaska	4,371.1
3	Louisiana	3,923.8
4	South Carolina	3,702.1
5	Arkansas	3,633.5
6	Tennessee	3,592.1
7	Alabama	3,481.5
8	Washington	3,478.1
9	Arizona	3,422.9
10	Missouri	3,364.2
11	Oklahoma	3,332.6
12	Oregon	3,268.3
13	Georgia	3,217.4
14	Kansas	3,213.9
15	Nevada	3,168.3
16	Hawaii	3,080.1
17	Colorado	3,069.7
18	Mississippi	3,019.6
19	Utah	3,019.1
20	Texas	3,001.5
21	Montana	2,968.7
22	California	2,946.0
23	Florida	2,920.4
24	North Carolina	2,909.0
25	Delaware	2,894.0
26	Indiana	2,815.9
27	Maryland	2,722.5
28	Ohio	2,716.6
29	Nebraska	2,579.9
30	North Dakota	2,479.1
31	Illinois	2,450.2
32	Minnesota	2,429.8
33	Iowa	2,418.7
34	Kentucky	2,354.9
35	South Dakota	2,309.8
36	Michigan	2,250.0
37	West Virginia	2,202.7
38	Wisconsin	2,128.2
39	Wyoming	2,067.9
40	Virginia	2,001.1
41	Connecticut	1,997.9
42	Rhode Island	1,983.8
43	Pennsylvania	1,962.7
44	New York	1,870.9
45	Idaho	1,861.8
46	Massachusetts	1,795.0
47	New Jersey	1,784.3
48	Maine	1,628.1
49	Vermont	1,602.5
50	New Hampshire	1,580.5

District of Columbia   5,288.8

Source: CQ Press using reported data from the Federal Bureau of Investigation
"Crime in the United States 2017" (Uniform Crime Reports, September 24, 2018, https://ucr.fbi.gov/)
*Includes murder, rape (revised definition), robbery, aggravated assault, burglary, larceny-theft, and motor vehicle theft.

Percent Change in Crime Rate (Revised Definition): 2016 to 2017

National Percent Change = 3.3% Decrease*

ALPHA ORDER			RANK ORDER		
RANK	**STATE**	**PERCENT CHANGE**	**RANK**	**STATE**	**PERCENT CHANGE**
11	Alabama	0.0	1	Alaska	5.1
1	Alaska	5.1	2	Minnesota	2.4
15	Arizona	(1.4)	3	Tennessee	2.2
35	Arkansas	(5.3)	4	New Mexico	2.1
17	California	(1.6)	5	Louisiana	1.6
13	Colorado	(0.8)	6	Missouri	1.3
19	Connecticut	(1.9)	7	Iowa	0.9
50	Delaware	(11.7)	8	Nebraska	0.7
40	Florida	(6.1)	9	Oregon	0.6
31	Georgia	(4.5)	10	New Jersey	0.2
28	Hawaii	(3.9)	11	Alabama	0.0
38	Idaho	(5.9)	12	Kansas	(0.5)
16	Illinois	(1.5)	13	Colorado	(0.8)
29	Indiana	(4.2)	14	Mississippi	(0.9)
7	Iowa	0.9	15	Arizona	(1.4)
12	Kansas	(0.5)	16	Illinois	(1.5)
25	Kentucky	(3.4)	17	California	(1.6)
5	Louisiana	1.6	17	South Carolina	(1.6)
46	Maine	(8.1)	19	Connecticut	(1.9)
22	Maryland	(2.8)	20	Rhode Island	(2.1)
45	Massachusetts	(7.5)	21	New York	(2.2)
35	Michigan	(5.3)	22	Maryland	(2.8)
2	Minnesota	2.4	22	Nevada	(2.8)
14	Mississippi	(0.9)	24	North Dakota	(3.2)
6	Missouri	1.3	25	Kentucky	(3.4)
26	Montana	(3.8)	26	Montana	(3.8)
8	Nebraska	0.7	26	Oklahoma	(3.8)
22	Nevada	(2.8)	28	Hawaii	(3.9)
47	New Hampshire	(8.2)	29	Indiana	(4.2)
10	New Jersey	0.2	29	Virginia	(4.2)
4	New Mexico	2.1	31	Georgia	(4.5)
21	New York	(2.2)	31	Pennsylvania	(4.5)
44	North Carolina	(6.4)	31	South Dakota	(4.5)
24	North Dakota	(3.2)	34	Wisconsin	(5.2)
41	Ohio	(6.2)	35	Arkansas	(5.3)
26	Oklahoma	(3.8)	35	Michigan	(5.3)
9	Oregon	0.6	37	Vermont	(5.4)
31	Pennsylvania	(4.5)	38	Idaho	(5.9)
20	Rhode Island	(2.1)	39	Texas	(6.0)
17	South Carolina	(1.6)	40	Florida	(6.1)
31	South Dakota	(4.5)	41	Ohio	(6.2)
3	Tennessee	2.2	41	Utah	(6.2)
39	Texas	(6.0)	41	Wyoming	(6.2)
41	Utah	(6.2)	44	North Carolina	(6.4)
37	Vermont	(5.4)	45	Massachusetts	(7.5)
29	Virginia	(4.2)	46	Maine	(8.1)
49	Washington	(8.6)	47	New Hampshire	(8.2)
48	West Virginia	(8.3)	48	West Virginia	(8.3)
34	Wisconsin	(5.2)	49	Washington	(8.6)
41	Wyoming	(6.2)	50	Delaware	(11.7)
				District of Columbia	(10.9)

Source: CQ Press using reported data from the Federal Bureau of Investigation
 "Crime in the United States 2017" (Uniform Crime Reports, September 24, 2018, https://ucr.fbi.gov/)
*Includes murder, rape (revised definition), robbery, aggravated assault, burglary, larceny-theft, and motor vehicle theft.

Violent Crimes (Revised Definition) in 2017

National Total = 1,283,220 Violent Crimes*

ALPHA ORDER					RANK ORDER				

RANK	STATE	CRIMES	% of USA		RANK	STATE	CRIMES	% of USA
17	Alabama	25,551	2.0%		1	California	177,627	13.8%
38	Alaska	6,133	0.5%		2	Texas	124,238	9.7%
11	Arizona	35,644	2.8%		3	Florida	85,625	6.7%
26	Arkansas	16,671	1.3%		4	New York	70,799	5.5%
1	California	177,627	13.8%		5	Illinois	56,180	4.4%
21	Colorado	20,638	1.6%		6	Michigan	44,826	3.5%
35	Connecticut	8,180	0.6%		7	Tennessee	43,755	3.4%
40	Delaware	4,361	0.3%		8	Pennsylvania	40,120	3.1%
3	Florida	85,625	6.7%		9	North Carolina	37,364	2.9%
10	Georgia	37,258	2.9%		10	Georgia	37,258	2.9%
44	Hawaii	3,577	0.3%		11	Arizona	35,644	2.8%
42	Idaho	3,888	0.3%		12	Ohio	34,683	2.7%
5	Illinois	56,180	4.4%		13	Missouri	32,420	2.5%
15	Indiana	26,598	2.1%		14	Maryland	30,273	2.4%
33	Iowa	9,230	0.7%		15	Indiana	26,598	2.1%
30	Kansas	12,030	0.9%		16	Louisiana	26,092	2.0%
32	Kentucky	10,056	0.8%		17	Alabama	25,551	2.0%
16	Louisiana	26,092	2.0%		18	South Carolina	25,432	2.0%
48	Maine	1,617	0.1%		19	Massachusetts	24,560	1.9%
14	Maryland	30,273	2.4%		20	Washington	22,548	1.8%
19	Massachusetts	24,560	1.9%		21	Colorado	20,638	1.6%
6	Michigan	44,826	3.5%		22	New Jersey	20,604	1.6%
29	Minnesota	13,291	1.0%		23	Wisconsin	18,539	1.4%
34	Mississippi	8,526	0.7%		24	Oklahoma	17,934	1.4%
13	Missouri	32,420	2.5%		25	Virginia	17,632	1.4%
41	Montana	3,961	0.3%		26	Arkansas	16,671	1.3%
39	Nebraska	5,873	0.5%		27	Nevada	16,667	1.3%
27	Nevada	16,667	1.3%		28	New Mexico	16,359	1.3%
45	New Hampshire	2,668	0.2%		29	Minnesota	13,291	1.0%
22	New Jersey	20,604	1.6%		30	Kansas	12,030	0.9%
28	New Mexico	16,359	1.3%		31	Oregon	11,674	0.9%
4	New York	70,799	5.5%		32	Kentucky	10,056	0.8%
9	North Carolina	37,364	2.9%		33	Iowa	9,230	0.7%
47	North Dakota	2,125	0.2%		34	Mississippi	8,526	0.7%
12	Ohio	34,683	2.7%		35	Connecticut	8,180	0.6%
24	Oklahoma	17,934	1.4%		36	Utah	7,410	0.6%
31	Oregon	11,674	0.9%		37	West Virginia	6,368	0.5%
8	Pennsylvania	40,120	3.1%		38	Alaska	6,133	0.5%
46	Rhode Island	2,460	0.2%		39	Nebraska	5,873	0.5%
18	South Carolina	25,432	2.0%		40	Delaware	4,361	0.3%
43	South Dakota	3,771	0.3%		41	Montana	3,961	0.3%
7	Tennessee	43,755	3.4%		42	Idaho	3,888	0.3%
2	Texas	124,238	9.7%		43	South Dakota	3,771	0.3%
36	Utah	7,410	0.6%		44	Hawaii	3,577	0.3%
50	Vermont	1,034	0.1%		45	New Hampshire	2,668	0.2%
25	Virginia	17,632	1.4%		46	Rhode Island	2,460	0.2%
20	Washington	22,548	1.8%		47	North Dakota	2,125	0.2%
37	West Virginia	6,368	0.5%		48	Maine	1,617	0.1%
23	Wisconsin	18,539	1.4%		49	Wyoming	1,376	0.1%
49	Wyoming	1,376	0.1%		50	Vermont	1,034	0.1%
						District of Columbia	6,974	0.5%

Source: Reported data from the Federal Bureau of Investigation
"Crime in the United States 2017" (Uniform Crime Reports, September 24, 2018, https://ucr.fbi.gov/)
*Violent crimes are offenses of murder, rape (revised definition), robbery, and aggravated assault.

Violent Crime Rate (Revised Definition) in 2017

National Rate = 394.0 Violent Crimes per 100,000 Population*

ALPHA ORDER

RANK ORDER

RANK	STATE	RATE	RANK	STATE	RATE
8	Alabama	524.2	1	Alaska	829.0
1	Alaska	829.0	2	New Mexico	783.5
9	Arizona	508.0	3	Tennessee	651.5
6	Arkansas	554.9	4	Louisiana	557.0
15	California	449.3	5	Nevada	555.9
23	Colorado	368.1	6	Arkansas	554.9
44	Connecticut	228.0	7	Missouri	530.3
13	Delaware	453.4	8	Alabama	524.2
20	Florida	408.0	9	Arizona	508.0
26	Georgia	357.2	10	South Carolina	506.2
38	Hawaii	250.6	11	Maryland	500.2
45	Idaho	226.4	12	Oklahoma	456.2
17	Illinois	438.8	13	Delaware	453.4
21	Indiana	399.0	14	Michigan	450.0
34	Iowa	293.4	15	California	449.3
19	Kansas	413.0	16	Texas	438.9
46	Kentucky	225.8	17	Illinois	438.8
4	Louisiana	557.0	18	South Dakota	433.6
50	Maine	121.0	19	Kansas	413.0
11	Maryland	500.2	20	Florida	408.0
25	Massachusetts	358.0	21	Indiana	399.0
14	Michigan	450.0	22	Montana	377.1
40	Minnesota	238.3	23	Colorado	368.1
35	Mississippi	285.7	24	North Carolina	363.7
7	Missouri	530.3	25	Massachusetts	358.0
22	Montana	377.1	26	Georgia	357.2
31	Nebraska	305.9	27	New York	356.7
5	Nevada	555.9	28	West Virginia	350.7
48	New Hampshire	198.7	29	Wisconsin	319.9
43	New Jersey	228.8	30	Pennsylvania	313.3
2	New Mexico	783.5	31	Nebraska	305.9
27	New York	356.7	32	Washington	304.5
24	North Carolina	363.7	33	Ohio	297.5
37	North Dakota	281.3	34	Iowa	293.4
33	Ohio	297.5	35	Mississippi	285.7
12	Oklahoma	456.2	36	Oregon	281.8
36	Oregon	281.8	37	North Dakota	281.3
30	Pennsylvania	313.3	38	Hawaii	250.6
42	Rhode Island	232.2	39	Utah	238.9
10	South Carolina	506.2	40	Minnesota	238.3
18	South Dakota	433.6	41	Wyoming	237.5
3	Tennessee	651.5	42	Rhode Island	232.2
16	Texas	438.9	43	New Jersey	228.8
39	Utah	238.9	44	Connecticut	228.0
49	Vermont	165.8	45	Idaho	226.4
47	Virginia	208.2	46	Kentucky	225.8
32	Washington	304.5	47	Virginia	208.2
28	West Virginia	350.7	48	New Hampshire	198.7
29	Wisconsin	319.9	49	Vermont	165.8
41	Wyoming	237.5	50	Maine	121.0
				District of Columbia	1,004.9

Source: Reported data from the Federal Bureau of Investigation
   "Crime in the United States 2017" (Uniform Crime Reports, September 24, 2018, https://ucr.fbi.gov/)
*Violent crimes are offenses of murder, rape (revised definition), robbery, and aggravated assault.

Percent Change in Violent Crime Rate (Revised Definition): 2016 to 2017

National Percent Change = 0.9% Decrease*

ALPHA ORDER			RANK ORDER		
RANK	**STATE**	**PERCENT CHANGE**	**RANK**	**STATE**	**PERCENT CHANGE**
32	Alabama	(1.6)	1	Vermont	21.4
11	Alaska	3.0	2	New Mexico	12.0
4	Arizona	7.9	3	North Dakota	11.6
24	Arkansas	0.1	4	Arizona	7.9
18	California	1.0	5	Colorado	7.0
5	Colorado	7.0	6	Oregon	4.8
24	Connecticut	0.1	7	Wisconsin	4.2
49	Delaware	(11.1)	8	Maryland	3.8
44	Florida	(5.0)	9	Hawaii	3.7
48	Georgia	(8.5)	10	Nebraska	3.1
9	Hawaii	3.7	11	Alaska	3.0
33	Idaho	(1.8)	12	Kansas	2.9
20	Illinois	0.5	13	South Dakota	2.7
27	Indiana	(0.2)	14	Tennessee	2.0
22	Iowa	0.2	15	Missouri	1.8
12	Kansas	2.9	16	Mississippi	1.4
42	Kentucky	(4.2)	17	Texas	1.2
30	Louisiana	(1.4)	18	California	1.0
36	Maine	(2.4)	19	Montana	0.8
8	Maryland	3.8	20	Illinois	0.5
46	Massachusetts	(5.9)	21	Washington	0.3
36	Michigan	(2.4)	22	Iowa	0.2
31	Minnesota	(1.5)	22	Oklahoma	0.2
16	Mississippi	1.4	24	Arkansas	0.1
15	Missouri	1.8	24	Connecticut	0.1
19	Montana	0.8	26	South Carolina	(0.1)
10	Nebraska	3.1	27	Indiana	(0.2)
50	Nevada	(18.0)	28	New Hampshire	(0.6)
28	New Hampshire	(0.6)	29	Pennsylvania	(0.8)
47	New Jersey	(6.0)	30	Louisiana	(1.4)
2	New Mexico	12.0	31	Minnesota	(1.5)
43	New York	(4.8)	32	Alabama	(1.6)
35	North Carolina	(2.2)	33	Idaho	(1.8)
3	North Dakota	11.6	33	Utah	(1.8)
40	Ohio	(3.3)	35	North Carolina	(2.2)
22	Oklahoma	0.2	36	Maine	(2.4)
6	Oregon	4.8	36	Michigan	(2.4)
29	Pennsylvania	(0.8)	38	Rhode Island	(2.9)
38	Rhode Island	(2.9)	38	Wyoming	(2.9)
26	South Carolina	(0.1)	40	Ohio	(3.3)
13	South Dakota	2.7	40	West Virginia	(3.3)
14	Tennessee	2.0	42	Kentucky	(4.2)
17	Texas	1.2	43	New York	(4.8)
33	Utah	(1.8)	44	Florida	(5.0)
1	Vermont	21.4	45	Virginia	(5.3)
45	Virginia	(5.3)	46	Massachusetts	(5.9)
21	Washington	0.3	47	New Jersey	(6.0)
40	West Virginia	(3.3)	48	Georgia	(8.5)
7	Wisconsin	4.2	49	Delaware	(11.1)
38	Wyoming	(2.9)	50	Nevada	(18.0)
				District of Columbia	(16.5)

Source: Reported data from the Federal Bureau of Investigation
"Crime in the United States 2017" (Uniform Crime Reports, September 24, 2018, https://ucr.fbi.gov/)
*Violent crimes are offenses of murder, rape (revised definition), robbery, and aggravated assault.

Murders in 2017

National Total = 17,284 Murders*

ALPHA ORDER

RANK	STATE	MURDERS	% of USA
17	Alabama	404	2.3%
38	Alaska	62	0.4%
16	Arizona	416	2.4%
23	Arkansas	258	1.5%
1	California	1,830	10.6%
27	Colorado	221	1.3%
35	Connecticut	102	0.6%
39	Delaware	54	0.3%
3	Florida	1,057	6.1%
7	Georgia	703	4.1%
42	Hawaii	39	0.2%
43	Idaho	32	0.2%
4	Illinois	997	5.8%
18	Indiana	397	2.3%
33	Iowa	104	0.6%
30	Kansas	160	0.9%
22	Kentucky	263	1.5%
10	Louisiana	582	3.4%
45	Maine	23	0.1%
13	Maryland	546	3.2%
29	Massachusetts	173	1.0%
11	Michigan	569	3.3%
32	Minnesota	113	0.7%
24	Mississippi	245	1.4%
8	Missouri	600	3.5%
41	Montana	41	0.2%
40	Nebraska	43	0.2%
21	Nevada	274	1.6%
48	New Hampshire	14	0.1%
20	New Jersey	324	1.9%
31	New Mexico	148	0.9%
12	New York	548	3.2%
9	North Carolina	591	3.4%
50	North Dakota	10	0.1%
6	Ohio	710	4.1%
25	Oklahoma	242	1.4%
33	Oregon	104	0.6%
5	Pennsylvania	739	4.3%
46	Rhode Island	20	0.1%
19	South Carolina	390	2.3%
44	South Dakota	25	0.1%
14	Tennessee	527	3.0%
2	Texas	1,412	8.2%
37	Utah	73	0.4%
48	Vermont	14	0.1%
15	Virginia	453	2.6%
26	Washington	230	1.3%
36	West Virginia	85	0.5%
28	Wisconsin	186	1.1%
47	Wyoming	15	0.1%

RANK ORDER

RANK	STATE	MURDERS	% of USA
1	California	1,830	10.6%
2	Texas	1,412	8.2%
3	Florida	1,057	6.1%
4	Illinois	997	5.8%
5	Pennsylvania	739	4.3%
6	Ohio	710	4.1%
7	Georgia	703	4.1%
8	Missouri	600	3.5%
9	North Carolina	591	3.4%
10	Louisiana	582	3.4%
11	Michigan	569	3.3%
12	New York	548	3.2%
13	Maryland	546	3.2%
14	Tennessee	527	3.0%
15	Virginia	453	2.6%
16	Arizona	416	2.4%
17	Alabama	404	2.3%
18	Indiana	397	2.3%
19	South Carolina	390	2.3%
20	New Jersey	324	1.9%
21	Nevada	274	1.6%
22	Kentucky	263	1.5%
23	Arkansas	258	1.5%
24	Mississippi	245	1.4%
25	Oklahoma	242	1.4%
26	Washington	230	1.3%
27	Colorado	221	1.3%
28	Wisconsin	186	1.1%
29	Massachusetts	173	1.0%
30	Kansas	160	0.9%
31	New Mexico	148	0.9%
32	Minnesota	113	0.7%
33	Iowa	104	0.6%
33	Oregon	104	0.6%
35	Connecticut	102	0.6%
36	West Virginia	85	0.5%
37	Utah	73	0.4%
38	Alaska	62	0.4%
39	Delaware	54	0.3%
40	Nebraska	43	0.2%
41	Montana	41	0.2%
42	Hawaii	39	0.2%
43	Idaho	32	0.2%
44	South Dakota	25	0.1%
45	Maine	23	0.1%
46	Rhode Island	20	0.1%
47	Wyoming	15	0.1%
48	New Hampshire	14	0.1%
48	Vermont	14	0.1%
50	North Dakota	10	0.1%
	District of Columbia	116	0.7%

Source: Reported data from the Federal Bureau of Investigation
"Crime in the United States 2017" (Uniform Crime Reports, September 24, 2018, https://ucr.fbi.gov/)
*Includes nonnegligent manslaughter.

Murder Rate in 2017

National Rate = 5.3 Murders per 100,000 Population*

RANK	STATE	RATE
7	Alabama	8.3
6	Alaska	8.4
17	Arizona	5.9
5	Arkansas	8.6
28	California	4.6
29	Colorado	3.9
36	Connecticut	2.8
22	Delaware	5.6
25	Florida	5.0
13	Georgia	6.7
38	Hawaii	2.7
46	Idaho	1.9
9	Illinois	7.8
16	Indiana	6.0
32	Iowa	3.3
23	Kansas	5.5
17	Kentucky	5.9
1	Louisiana	12.4
48	Maine	1.7
4	Maryland	9.0
40	Massachusetts	2.5
21	Michigan	5.7
45	Minnesota	2.0
8	Mississippi	8.2
2	Missouri	9.8
29	Montana	3.9
43	Nebraska	2.2
3	Nevada	9.1
50	New Hampshire	1.0
31	New Jersey	3.6
12	New Mexico	7.1
36	New York	2.8
19	North Carolina	5.8
49	North Dakota	1.3
15	Ohio	6.1
14	Oklahoma	6.2
40	Oregon	2.5
19	Pennsylvania	5.8
46	Rhode Island	1.9
9	South Carolina	7.8
35	South Dakota	2.9
9	Tennessee	7.8
25	Texas	5.0
42	Utah	2.4
43	Vermont	2.2
24	Virginia	5.3
34	Washington	3.1
27	West Virginia	4.7
33	Wisconsin	3.2
39	Wyoming	2.6

RANK	STATE	RATE
1	Louisiana	12.4
2	Missouri	9.8
3	Nevada	9.1
4	Maryland	9.0
5	Arkansas	8.6
6	Alaska	8.4
7	Alabama	8.3
8	Mississippi	8.2
9	Illinois	7.8
9	South Carolina	7.8
9	Tennessee	7.8
12	New Mexico	7.1
13	Georgia	6.7
14	Oklahoma	6.2
15	Ohio	6.1
16	Indiana	6.0
17	Arizona	5.9
17	Kentucky	5.9
19	North Carolina	5.8
19	Pennsylvania	5.8
21	Michigan	5.7
22	Delaware	5.6
23	Kansas	5.5
24	Virginia	5.3
25	Florida	5.0
25	Texas	5.0
27	West Virginia	4.7
28	California	4.6
29	Colorado	3.9
29	Montana	3.9
31	New Jersey	3.6
32	Iowa	3.3
33	Wisconsin	3.2
34	Washington	3.1
35	South Dakota	2.9
36	Connecticut	2.8
36	New York	2.8
38	Hawaii	2.7
39	Wyoming	2.6
40	Massachusetts	2.5
40	Oregon	2.5
42	Utah	2.4
43	Nebraska	2.2
43	Vermont	2.2
45	Minnesota	2.0
46	Idaho	1.9
46	Rhode Island	1.9
48	Maine	1.7
49	North Dakota	1.3
50	New Hampshire	1.0

| | District of Columbia | 16.7 |

Source: Reported data from the Federal Bureau of Investigation
"Crime in the United States 2017" (Uniform Crime Reports, September 24, 2018, https://ucr.fbi.gov/)
*Includes nonnegligent manslaughter.

Percent of Murders Involving Firearms in 2017

National Percent = 72.6% of Murders*

RANK	STATE	PERCENT
NA	Alabama**	NA
32	Alaska	59.7
29	Arizona	61.6
24	Arkansas	67.2
22	California	69.6
27	Colorado	62.8
21	Connecticut	70.6
3	Delaware	84.6
NA	Florida**	NA
6	Georgia	80.7
48	Hawaii	10.3
42	Idaho	46.4
2	Illinois	85.1
5	Indiana	80.8
36	Iowa	57.0
30	Kansas	61.2
18	Kentucky	73.0
4	Louisiana	81.3
40	Maine	52.2
9	Maryland	77.9
34	Massachusetts	58.2
24	Michigan	67.2
31	Minnesota	61.1
15	Mississippi	74.5
1	Missouri	86.2
45	Montana	41.5
19	Nebraska	72.1
16	Nevada	74.4
41	New Hampshire	50.0
13	New Jersey	74.7
27	New Mexico	62.8
39	New York	53.4
12	North Carolina	75.5
38	North Dakota	55.6
20	Ohio	71.1
23	Oklahoma	68.2
35	Oregon	58.0
11	Pennsylvania	77.1
46	Rhode Island	40.0
7	South Carolina	80.6
47	South Dakota	38.1
10	Tennessee	77.5
17	Texas	74.2
26	Utah	63.0
43	Vermont	42.9
14	Virginia	74.6
33	Washington	58.8
36	West Virginia	57.0
8	Wisconsin	80.1
43	Wyoming	42.9

RANK	STATE	PERCENT
1	Missouri	86.2
2	Illinois	85.1
3	Delaware	84.6
4	Louisiana	81.3
5	Indiana	80.8
6	Georgia	80.7
7	South Carolina	80.6
8	Wisconsin	80.1
9	Maryland	77.9
10	Tennessee	77.5
11	Pennsylvania	77.1
12	North Carolina	75.5
13	New Jersey	74.7
14	Virginia	74.6
15	Mississippi	74.5
16	Nevada	74.4
17	Texas	74.2
18	Kentucky	73.0
19	Nebraska	72.1
20	Ohio	71.1
21	Connecticut	70.6
22	California	69.6
23	Oklahoma	68.2
24	Arkansas	67.2
24	Michigan	67.2
26	Utah	63.0
27	Colorado	62.8
27	New Mexico	62.8
29	Arizona	61.6
30	Kansas	61.2
31	Minnesota	61.1
32	Alaska	59.7
33	Washington	58.8
34	Massachusetts	58.2
35	Oregon	58.0
36	Iowa	57.0
36	West Virginia	57.0
38	North Dakota	55.6
39	New York	53.4
40	Maine	52.2
41	New Hampshire	50.0
42	Idaho	46.4
43	Vermont	42.9
43	Wyoming	42.9
45	Montana	41.5
46	Rhode Island	40.0
47	South Dakota	38.1
48	Hawaii	10.3
NA	Alabama**	NA
NA	Florida**	NA

| | District of Columbia | 77.6 |

Source: CQ Press using reported data from the Federal Bureau of Investigation
   "Crime in the United States 2017" (Uniform Crime Reports, September 24, 2018, https://ucr.fbi.gov/)
*Of the 15,128 murders in 2017 for which supplemental data were received by the F.B.I. There were an additional 2,156 murders for which the type of murder weapon was not reported to the F.B.I. Includes nonnegligent manslaughter. National and state percents based on reporting jurisdictions only.
**Not available.

Rapes (Revised Definition) in 2017

National Total = 135,755 Rapes*

ALPHA ORDER					RANK ORDER			
RANK	STATE	RAPES	% of USA		RANK	STATE	RAPES	% of USA
24	Alabama	2,028	1.5%		1	California	14,721	10.8%
37	Alaska	863	0.6%		2	Texas	14,470	10.7%
10	Arizona	3,581	2.6%		3	Florida	7,940	5.8%
23	Arkansas	2,053	1.5%		4	Michigan	7,031	5.2%
1	California	14,721	10.8%		5	New York	6,324	4.7%
9	Colorado	3,858	2.8%		6	Ohio	5,859	4.3%
38	Connecticut	837	0.6%		7	Illinois	5,556	4.1%
48	Delaware	334	0.2%		8	Pennsylvania	4,201	3.1%
3	Florida	7,940	5.8%		9	Colorado	3,858	2.8%
15	Georgia	2,718	2.0%		10	Arizona	3,581	2.6%
44	Hawaii	567	0.4%		11	Washington	3,255	2.4%
40	Idaho	707	0.5%		12	Tennessee	2,934	2.2%
7	Illinois	5,556	4.1%		13	Virginia	2,862	2.1%
17	Indiana	2,625	1.9%		14	Missouri	2,729	2.0%
34	Iowa	1,234	0.9%		15	Georgia	2,718	2.0%
31	Kansas	1,627	1.2%		16	North Carolina	2,715	2.0%
30	Kentucky	1,661	1.2%		17	Indiana	2,625	1.9%
27	Louisiana	1,867	1.4%		18	South Carolina	2,504	1.8%
45	Maine	473	0.3%		19	Minnesota	2,385	1.8%
29	Maryland	1,691	1.2%		20	Massachusetts	2,197	1.6%
20	Massachusetts	2,197	1.6%		21	Oklahoma	2,142	1.6%
4	Michigan	7,031	5.2%		22	Wisconsin	2,139	1.6%
19	Minnesota	2,385	1.8%		23	Arkansas	2,053	1.5%
36	Mississippi	1,091	0.8%		24	Alabama	2,028	1.5%
14	Missouri	2,729	2.0%		25	Oregon	1,999	1.5%
42	Montana	613	0.5%		26	Nevada	1,890	1.4%
35	Nebraska	1,191	0.9%		27	Louisiana	1,867	1.4%
26	Nevada	1,890	1.4%		28	Utah	1,697	1.3%
41	New Hampshire	663	0.5%		29	Maryland	1,691	1.2%
32	New Jersey	1,505	1.1%		30	Kentucky	1,661	1.2%
33	New Mexico	1,259	0.9%		31	Kansas	1,627	1.2%
5	New York	6,324	4.7%		32	New Jersey	1,505	1.1%
16	North Carolina	2,715	2.0%		33	New Mexico	1,259	0.9%
47	North Dakota	399	0.3%		34	Iowa	1,234	0.9%
6	Ohio	5,859	4.3%		35	Nebraska	1,191	0.9%
21	Oklahoma	2,142	1.6%		36	Mississippi	1,091	0.8%
25	Oregon	1,999	1.5%		37	Alaska	863	0.6%
8	Pennsylvania	4,201	3.1%		38	Connecticut	837	0.6%
46	Rhode Island	445	0.3%		39	West Virginia	795	0.6%
18	South Carolina	2,504	1.8%		40	Idaho	707	0.5%
43	South Dakota	595	0.4%		41	New Hampshire	663	0.5%
12	Tennessee	2,934	2.2%		42	Montana	613	0.5%
2	Texas	14,470	10.7%		43	South Dakota	595	0.4%
28	Utah	1,697	1.3%		44	Hawaii	567	0.4%
50	Vermont	218	0.2%		45	Maine	473	0.3%
13	Virginia	2,862	2.1%		46	Rhode Island	445	0.3%
11	Washington	3,255	2.4%		47	North Dakota	399	0.3%
39	West Virginia	795	0.6%		48	Delaware	334	0.2%
22	Wisconsin	2,139	1.6%		49	Wyoming	263	0.2%
49	Wyoming	263	0.2%		50	Vermont	218	0.2%
						District of Columbia	444	0.3%

Source: Reported data from the Federal Bureau of Investigation
"Crime in the United States 2017" (Uniform Crime Reports, September 24, 2018, https://ucr.fbi.gov/)
*The definition of rape was revised in 2013 to "Penetration, no matter how slight, of the vagina or anus with any body part or object, or oral penetration by a sex organ of another person, without the consent of the victim. Attempts or assaults to commit rape are also included; however, statutory rape and incest are excluded." This revised definition includes both male and female victims and drops "forcible" from the title.

Rape Rate (Revised Definition) in 2017

National Rate = 41.7 Rapes per 100,000 Population*

ALPHA ORDER			RANK ORDER		
RANK	STATE	RATE	RANK	STATE	RATE
28	Alabama	41.6	1	Alaska	116.7
1	Alaska	116.7	2	Michigan	70.6
15	Arizona	51.0	3	Colorado	68.8
5	Arkansas	68.3	4	South Dakota	68.4
36	California	37.2	5	Arkansas	68.3
3	Colorado	68.8	6	Nevada	63.0
49	Connecticut	23.3	7	Nebraska	62.0
41	Delaware	34.7	8	New Mexico	60.3
34	Florida	37.8	9	Montana	58.4
48	Georgia	26.1	10	Kansas	55.9
31	Hawaii	39.7	11	Utah	54.7
29	Idaho	41.2	12	Oklahoma	54.5
25	Illinois	43.4	13	North Dakota	52.8
32	Indiana	39.4	14	Texas	51.1
33	Iowa	39.2	15	Arizona	51.0
10	Kansas	55.9	16	Ohio	50.3
35	Kentucky	37.3	17	South Carolina	49.8
30	Louisiana	39.9	18	New Hampshire	49.4
39	Maine	35.4	19	Oregon	48.3
46	Maryland	27.9	20	Wyoming	45.4
44	Massachusetts	32.0	21	Missouri	44.6
2	Michigan	70.6	22	Washington	44.0
26	Minnesota	42.8	23	West Virginia	43.8
38	Mississippi	36.6	24	Tennessee	43.7
21	Missouri	44.6	25	Illinois	43.4
9	Montana	58.4	26	Minnesota	42.8
7	Nebraska	62.0	27	Rhode Island	42.0
6	Nevada	63.0	28	Alabama	41.6
18	New Hampshire	49.4	29	Idaho	41.2
50	New Jersey	16.7	30	Louisiana	39.9
8	New Mexico	60.3	31	Hawaii	39.7
45	New York	31.9	32	Indiana	39.4
47	North Carolina	26.4	33	Iowa	39.2
13	North Dakota	52.8	34	Florida	37.8
16	Ohio	50.3	35	Kentucky	37.3
12	Oklahoma	54.5	36	California	37.2
19	Oregon	48.3	37	Wisconsin	36.9
43	Pennsylvania	32.8	38	Mississippi	36.6
27	Rhode Island	42.0	39	Maine	35.4
17	South Carolina	49.8	40	Vermont	35.0
4	South Dakota	68.4	41	Delaware	34.7
24	Tennessee	43.7	42	Virginia	33.8
14	Texas	51.1	43	Pennsylvania	32.8
11	Utah	54.7	44	Massachusetts	32.0
40	Vermont	35.0	45	New York	31.9
42	Virginia	33.8	46	Maryland	27.9
22	Washington	44.0	47	North Carolina	26.4
23	West Virginia	43.8	48	Georgia	26.1
37	Wisconsin	36.9	49	Connecticut	23.3
20	Wyoming	45.4	50	New Jersey	16.7
				District of Columbia	64.0

Source: Reported data from the Federal Bureau of Investigation
 "Crime in the United States 2017" (Uniform Crime Reports, September 24, 2018, https://ucr.fbi.gov/)
*The definition of rape was revised in 2013 to "Penetration, no matter how slight, of the vagina or anus with any body part or object, or oral penetration by a sex organ of another person, without the consent of the victim. Attempts or assaults to commit rape are also included; however, statutory rape and incest are excluded." This revised definition includes both male and female victims and drops "forcible" from the title.

Robberies in 2017

National Total = 319,356 Robberies*

ALPHA ORDER

RANK	STATE	ROBBERIES	% of USA
23	Alabama	4,217	1.3%
40	Alaska	951	0.3%
13	Arizona	7,440	2.3%
33	Arkansas	1,935	0.6%
1	California	56,622	17.7%
25	Colorado	3,838	1.2%
30	Connecticut	2,813	0.9%
37	Delaware	1,082	0.3%
4	Florida	18,597	5.8%
9	Georgia	10,044	3.1%
38	Hawaii	1,077	0.3%
47	Idaho	196	0.1%
5	Illinois	17,567	5.5%
14	Indiana	6,600	2.1%
36	Iowa	1,253	0.4%
34	Kansas	1,785	0.6%
29	Kentucky	2,958	0.9%
18	Louisiana	5,358	1.7%
45	Maine	249	0.1%
8	Maryland	11,200	3.5%
19	Massachusetts	4,871	1.5%
15	Michigan	6,488	2.0%
27	Minnesota	3,621	1.1%
32	Mississippi	2,071	0.6%
16	Missouri	6,351	2.0%
44	Montana	295	0.1%
39	Nebraska	968	0.3%
20	Nevada	4,841	1.5%
43	New Hampshire	419	0.1%
11	New Jersey	7,895	2.5%
26	New Mexico	3,722	1.2%
3	New York	20,108	6.3%
10	North Carolina	9,350	2.9%
48	North Dakota	183	0.1%
7	Ohio	11,605	3.6%
28	Oklahoma	3,000	0.9%
31	Oregon	2,432	0.8%
6	Pennsylvania	11,793	3.7%
42	Rhode Island	474	0.1%
24	South Carolina	3,870	1.2%
46	South Dakota	238	0.1%
12	Tennessee	7,862	2.5%
2	Texas	32,267	10.1%
35	Utah	1,468	0.5%
49	Vermont	92	0.0%
22	Virginia	4,332	1.4%
17	Washington	5,390	1.7%
41	West Virginia	524	0.2%
21	Wisconsin	4,345	1.4%
50	Wyoming	76	0.0%

RANK ORDER

RANK	STATE	ROBBERIES	% of USA
1	California	56,622	17.7%
2	Texas	32,267	10.1%
3	New York	20,108	6.3%
4	Florida	18,597	5.8%
5	Illinois	17,567	5.5%
6	Pennsylvania	11,793	3.7%
7	Ohio	11,605	3.6%
8	Maryland	11,200	3.5%
9	Georgia	10,044	3.1%
10	North Carolina	9,350	2.9%
11	New Jersey	7,895	2.5%
12	Tennessee	7,862	2.5%
13	Arizona	7,440	2.3%
14	Indiana	6,600	2.1%
15	Michigan	6,488	2.0%
16	Missouri	6,351	2.0%
17	Washington	5,390	1.7%
18	Louisiana	5,358	1.7%
19	Massachusetts	4,871	1.5%
20	Nevada	4,841	1.5%
21	Wisconsin	4,345	1.4%
22	Virginia	4,332	1.4%
23	Alabama	4,217	1.3%
24	South Carolina	3,870	1.2%
25	Colorado	3,838	1.2%
26	New Mexico	3,722	1.2%
27	Minnesota	3,621	1.1%
28	Oklahoma	3,000	0.9%
29	Kentucky	2,958	0.9%
30	Connecticut	2,813	0.9%
31	Oregon	2,432	0.8%
32	Mississippi	2,071	0.6%
33	Arkansas	1,935	0.6%
34	Kansas	1,785	0.6%
35	Utah	1,468	0.5%
36	Iowa	1,253	0.4%
37	Delaware	1,082	0.3%
38	Hawaii	1,077	0.3%
39	Nebraska	968	0.3%
40	Alaska	951	0.3%
41	West Virginia	524	0.2%
42	Rhode Island	474	0.1%
43	New Hampshire	419	0.1%
44	Montana	295	0.1%
45	Maine	249	0.1%
46	South Dakota	238	0.1%
47	Idaho	196	0.1%
48	North Dakota	183	0.1%
49	Vermont	92	0.0%
50	Wyoming	76	0.0%
	District of Columbia	2,623	0.8%

Source: Reported data from the Federal Bureau of Investigation
"Crime in the United States 2017" (Uniform Crime Reports, September 24, 2018, https://ucr.fbi.gov/)
*Robbery is the taking or attempting to take anything of value by force or threat of force.

Robbery Rate in 2017

National Rate = 98.0 Robberies per 100,000 Population*

ALPHA ORDER

RANK	STATE	RATE
21	Alabama	86.5
6	Alaska	128.5
11	Arizona	106.0
34	Arkansas	64.4
4	California	143.2
30	Colorado	68.4
22	Connecticut	78.4
10	Delaware	112.5
19	Florida	88.6
16	Georgia	96.3
25	Hawaii	75.4
50	Idaho	11.4
5	Illinois	137.2
15	Indiana	99.0
41	Iowa	39.8
35	Kansas	61.3
31	Kentucky	66.4
8	Louisiana	114.4
47	Maine	18.6
1	Maryland	185.1
28	Massachusetts	71.0
32	Michigan	65.1
33	Minnesota	64.9
29	Mississippi	69.4
12	Missouri	103.9
44	Montana	28.1
38	Nebraska	50.4
3	Nevada	161.5
42	New Hampshire	31.2
20	New Jersey	87.7
2	New Mexico	178.3
13	New York	101.3
18	North Carolina	91.0
46	North Dakota	24.2
14	Ohio	99.5
24	Oklahoma	76.3
36	Oregon	58.7
17	Pennsylvania	92.1
40	Rhode Island	44.7
23	South Carolina	77.0
45	South Dakota	27.4
7	Tennessee	117.1
9	Texas	114.0
39	Utah	47.3
48	Vermont	14.8
37	Virginia	51.1
27	Washington	72.8
43	West Virginia	28.9
26	Wisconsin	75.0
49	Wyoming	13.1

RANK ORDER

RANK	STATE	RATE
1	Maryland	185.1
2	New Mexico	178.3
3	Nevada	161.5
4	California	143.2
5	Illinois	137.2
6	Alaska	128.5
7	Tennessee	117.1
8	Louisiana	114.4
9	Texas	114.0
10	Delaware	112.5
11	Arizona	106.0
12	Missouri	103.9
13	New York	101.3
14	Ohio	99.5
15	Indiana	99.0
16	Georgia	96.3
17	Pennsylvania	92.1
18	North Carolina	91.0
19	Florida	88.6
20	New Jersey	87.7
21	Alabama	86.5
22	Connecticut	78.4
23	South Carolina	77.0
24	Oklahoma	76.3
25	Hawaii	75.4
26	Wisconsin	75.0
27	Washington	72.8
28	Massachusetts	71.0
29	Mississippi	69.4
30	Colorado	68.4
31	Kentucky	66.4
32	Michigan	65.1
33	Minnesota	64.9
34	Arkansas	64.4
35	Kansas	61.3
36	Oregon	58.7
37	Virginia	51.1
38	Nebraska	50.4
39	Utah	47.3
40	Rhode Island	44.7
41	Iowa	39.8
42	New Hampshire	31.2
43	West Virginia	28.9
44	Montana	28.1
45	South Dakota	27.4
46	North Dakota	24.2
47	Maine	18.6
48	Vermont	14.8
49	Wyoming	13.1
50	Idaho	11.4
	District of Columbia	378.0

Source: Reported data from the Federal Bureau of Investigation
   "Crime in the United States 2017" (Uniform Crime Reports, September 24, 2018, https://ucr.fbi.gov/)
*Robbery is the taking or attempting to take anything of value by force or threat of force.

Aggravated Assaults in 2017

National Total = 810,825 Aggravated Assaults*

ALPHA ORDER

RANK ORDER

RANK	STATE	ASSAULTS	% of USA
13	Alabama	18,902	2.3%
37	Alaska	4,257	0.5%
9	Arizona	24,207	3.0%
23	Arkansas	12,425	1.5%
1	California	104,454	12.9%
21	Colorado	12,721	1.6%
36	Connecticut	4,428	0.5%
43	Delaware	2,891	0.4%
3	Florida	58,031	7.2%
10	Georgia	23,793	2.9%
44	Hawaii	1,894	0.2%
41	Idaho	2,953	0.4%
6	Illinois	32,060	4.0%
17	Indiana	16,976	2.1%
32	Iowa	6,639	0.8%
29	Kansas	8,458	1.0%
33	Kentucky	5,174	0.6%
15	Louisiana	18,285	2.3%
49	Maine	872	0.1%
18	Maryland	16,836	2.1%
16	Massachusetts	17,319	2.1%
7	Michigan	30,738	3.8%
30	Minnesota	7,172	0.9%
34	Mississippi	5,119	0.6%
12	Missouri	22,740	2.8%
40	Montana	3,012	0.4%
39	Nebraska	3,671	0.5%
28	Nevada	9,662	1.2%
45	New Hampshire	1,572	0.2%
26	New Jersey	10,880	1.3%
25	New Mexico	11,230	1.4%
4	New York	43,819	5.4%
8	North Carolina	24,708	3.0%
46	North Dakota	1,533	0.2%
19	Ohio	16,509	2.0%
22	Oklahoma	12,550	1.5%
31	Oregon	7,139	0.9%
11	Pennsylvania	23,387	2.9%
47	Rhode Island	1,521	0.2%
14	South Carolina	18,668	2.3%
42	South Dakota	2,913	0.4%
5	Tennessee	32,432	4.0%
2	Texas	76,089	9.4%
38	Utah	4,172	0.5%
50	Vermont	710	0.1%
27	Virginia	9,985	1.2%
20	Washington	13,673	1.7%
35	West Virginia	4,964	0.6%
24	Wisconsin	11,869	1.5%
48	Wyoming	1,022	0.1%

RANK	STATE	ASSAULTS	% of USA
1	California	104,454	12.9%
2	Texas	76,089	9.4%
3	Florida	58,031	7.2%
4	New York	43,819	5.4%
5	Tennessee	32,432	4.0%
6	Illinois	32,060	4.0%
7	Michigan	30,738	3.8%
8	North Carolina	24,708	3.0%
9	Arizona	24,207	3.0%
10	Georgia	23,793	2.9%
11	Pennsylvania	23,387	2.9%
12	Missouri	22,740	2.8%
13	Alabama	18,902	2.3%
14	South Carolina	18,668	2.3%
15	Louisiana	18,285	2.3%
16	Massachusetts	17,319	2.1%
17	Indiana	16,976	2.1%
18	Maryland	16,836	2.1%
19	Ohio	16,509	2.0%
20	Washington	13,673	1.7%
21	Colorado	12,721	1.6%
22	Oklahoma	12,550	1.5%
23	Arkansas	12,425	1.5%
24	Wisconsin	11,869	1.5%
25	New Mexico	11,230	1.4%
26	New Jersey	10,880	1.3%
27	Virginia	9,985	1.2%
28	Nevada	9,662	1.2%
29	Kansas	8,458	1.0%
30	Minnesota	7,172	0.9%
31	Oregon	7,139	0.9%
32	Iowa	6,639	0.8%
33	Kentucky	5,174	0.6%
34	Mississippi	5,119	0.6%
35	West Virginia	4,964	0.6%
36	Connecticut	4,428	0.5%
37	Alaska	4,257	0.5%
38	Utah	4,172	0.5%
39	Nebraska	3,671	0.5%
40	Montana	3,012	0.4%
41	Idaho	2,953	0.4%
42	South Dakota	2,913	0.4%
43	Delaware	2,891	0.4%
44	Hawaii	1,894	0.2%
45	New Hampshire	1,572	0.2%
46	North Dakota	1,533	0.2%
47	Rhode Island	1,521	0.2%
48	Wyoming	1,022	0.1%
49	Maine	872	0.1%
50	Vermont	710	0.1%
	District of Columbia	3,791	0.5%

Source: Reported data from the Federal Bureau of Investigation
"Crime in the United States 2017" (Uniform Crime Reports, September 24, 2018, https://ucr.fbi.gov/)
*Aggravated assault is an attack for the purpose of inflicting severe bodily injury.

Aggravated Assault Rate in 2017

National Rate = 248.9 Aggravated Assaults per 100,000 Population*

ALPHA ORDER

ALPHA ORDER

RANK ORDER

RANK	STATE	RATE		RANK	STATE	RATE
6	Alabama	387.8		1	Alaska	575.4
1	Alaska	575.4		2	New Mexico	537.8
9	Arizona	345.0		3	Tennessee	482.9
4	Arkansas	413.6		4	Arkansas	413.6
21	California	264.2		5	Louisiana	390.3
27	Colorado	226.9		6	Alabama	387.8
44	Connecticut	123.4		7	Missouri	372.0
14	Delaware	300.5		8	South Carolina	371.5
18	Florida	276.5		9	Arizona	345.0
26	Georgia	228.1		10	South Dakota	335.0
42	Hawaii	132.7		11	Nevada	322.3
37	Idaho	172.0		12	Oklahoma	319.3
24	Illinois	250.4		13	Michigan	308.5
22	Indiana	254.6		14	Delaware	300.5
29	Iowa	211.0		15	Kansas	290.3
15	Kansas	290.3		16	Montana	286.7
48	Kentucky	116.2		17	Maryland	278.2
5	Louisiana	390.3		18	Florida	276.5
50	Maine	65.3		19	West Virginia	273.4
17	Maryland	278.2		20	Texas	268.8
23	Massachusetts	252.5		21	California	264.2
13	Michigan	308.5		22	Indiana	254.6
43	Minnesota	128.6		23	Massachusetts	252.5
38	Mississippi	171.5		24	Illinois	250.4
7	Missouri	372.0		25	North Carolina	240.5
16	Montana	286.7		26	Georgia	228.1
32	Nebraska	191.2		27	Colorado	226.9
11	Nevada	322.3		28	New York	220.8
47	New Hampshire	117.1		29	Iowa	211.0
45	New Jersey	120.8		30	Wisconsin	204.8
2	New Mexico	537.8		31	North Dakota	202.9
28	New York	220.8		32	Nebraska	191.2
25	North Carolina	240.5		33	Washington	184.6
31	North Dakota	202.9		34	Pennsylvania	182.6
40	Ohio	141.6		35	Wyoming	176.4
12	Oklahoma	319.3		36	Oregon	172.3
36	Oregon	172.3		37	Idaho	172.0
34	Pennsylvania	182.6		38	Mississippi	171.5
39	Rhode Island	143.5		39	Rhode Island	143.5
8	South Carolina	371.5		40	Ohio	141.6
10	South Dakota	335.0		41	Utah	134.5
3	Tennessee	482.9		42	Hawaii	132.7
20	Texas	268.8		43	Minnesota	128.6
41	Utah	134.5		44	Connecticut	123.4
49	Vermont	113.8		45	New Jersey	120.8
46	Virginia	117.9		46	Virginia	117.9
33	Washington	184.6		47	New Hampshire	117.1
19	West Virginia	273.4		48	Kentucky	116.2
30	Wisconsin	204.8		49	Vermont	113.8
35	Wyoming	176.4		50	Maine	65.3

District of Columbia 546.3

Source: Reported data from the Federal Bureau of Investigation
   "Crime in the United States 2017" (Uniform Crime Reports, September 24, 2018, https://ucr.fbi.gov/)
*Aggravated assault is an attack for the purpose of inflicting severe bodily injury.

Property Crimes in 2017

National Total = 7,694,086 Property Crimes*

ALPHA ORDER

RANK	STATE	CRIMES	% of USA
20	Alabama	144,160	1.9%
42	Alaska	26,204	0.3%
11	Arizona	204,515	2.7%
29	Arkansas	92,489	1.2%
1	California	987,114	12.8%
19	Colorado	151,483	2.0%
36	Connecticut	63,509	0.8%
43	Delaware	23,477	0.3%
3	Florida	527,220	6.9%
5	Georgia	298,298	3.9%
38	Hawaii	40,392	0.5%
40	Idaho	28,079	0.4%
8	Illinois	257,497	3.3%
15	Indiana	161,132	2.1%
35	Iowa	66,855	0.9%
32	Kansas	81,593	1.1%
28	Kentucky	94,833	1.2%
17	Louisiana	157,712	2.0%
44	Maine	20,133	0.3%
22	Maryland	134,496	1.7%
27	Massachusetts	98,575	1.3%
13	Michigan	179,318	2.3%
24	Minnesota	122,212	1.6%
33	Mississippi	81,581	1.1%
14	Missouri	173,253	2.3%
41	Montana	27,225	0.4%
37	Nebraska	43,663	0.6%
34	Nevada	78,322	1.0%
46	New Hampshire	18,555	0.2%
21	New Jersey	140,086	1.8%
31	New Mexico	82,306	1.1%
4	New York	300,555	3.9%
7	North Carolina	261,486	3.4%
47	North Dakota	16,602	0.2%
6	Ohio	282,034	3.7%
25	Oklahoma	113,066	1.5%
23	Oregon	123,722	1.6%
10	Pennsylvania	211,220	2.7%
45	Rhode Island	18,561	0.2%
16	South Carolina	160,575	2.1%
48	South Dakota	16,317	0.2%
12	Tennessee	197,488	2.6%
2	Texas	725,328	9.4%
30	Utah	86,238	1.1%
50	Vermont	8,960	0.1%
18	Virginia	151,855	2.0%
9	Washington	235,027	3.1%
39	West Virginia	33,630	0.4%
26	Wisconsin	104,802	1.4%
49	Wyoming	10,604	0.1%

RANK ORDER

RANK	STATE	CRIMES	% of USA
1	California	987,114	12.8%
2	Texas	725,328	9.4%
3	Florida	527,220	6.9%
4	New York	300,555	3.9%
5	Georgia	298,298	3.9%
6	Ohio	282,034	3.7%
7	North Carolina	261,486	3.4%
8	Illinois	257,497	3.3%
9	Washington	235,027	3.1%
10	Pennsylvania	211,220	2.7%
11	Arizona	204,515	2.7%
12	Tennessee	197,488	2.6%
13	Michigan	179,318	2.3%
14	Missouri	173,253	2.3%
15	Indiana	161,132	2.1%
16	South Carolina	160,575	2.1%
17	Louisiana	157,712	2.0%
18	Virginia	151,855	2.0%
19	Colorado	151,483	2.0%
20	Alabama	144,160	1.9%
21	New Jersey	140,086	1.8%
22	Maryland	134,496	1.7%
23	Oregon	123,722	1.6%
24	Minnesota	122,212	1.6%
25	Oklahoma	113,066	1.5%
26	Wisconsin	104,802	1.4%
27	Massachusetts	98,575	1.3%
28	Kentucky	94,833	1.2%
29	Arkansas	92,489	1.2%
30	Utah	86,238	1.1%
31	New Mexico	82,306	1.1%
32	Kansas	81,593	1.1%
33	Mississippi	81,581	1.1%
34	Nevada	78,322	1.0%
35	Iowa	66,855	0.9%
36	Connecticut	63,509	0.8%
37	Nebraska	43,663	0.6%
38	Hawaii	40,392	0.5%
39	West Virginia	33,630	0.4%
40	Idaho	28,079	0.4%
41	Montana	27,225	0.4%
42	Alaska	26,204	0.3%
43	Delaware	23,477	0.3%
44	Maine	20,133	0.3%
45	Rhode Island	18,561	0.2%
46	New Hampshire	18,555	0.2%
47	North Dakota	16,602	0.2%
48	South Dakota	16,317	0.2%
49	Wyoming	10,604	0.1%
50	Vermont	8,960	0.1%
	District of Columbia	29,729	0.4%

Source: Reported data from the Federal Bureau of Investigation
   "Crime in the United States 2017" (Uniform Crime Reports, September 24, 2018, https://ucr.fbi.gov/)
*Property crimes are offenses of burglary, larceny-theft, and motor vehicle theft.

Property Crime Rate in 2017

National Rate = 2,362.2 Property Crimes per 100,000 Population*

ALPHA ORDER

RANK	STATE	RATE
8	Alabama	2,957.3
2	Alaska	3,542.1
10	Arizona	2,914.9
6	Arkansas	3,078.6
24	California	2,496.7
18	Colorado	2,701.6
41	Connecticut	1,769.9
25	Delaware	2,440.6
23	Florida	2,512.4
12	Georgia	2,860.2
14	Hawaii	2,829.5
44	Idaho	1,635.4
34	Illinois	2,011.4
27	Indiana	2,416.9
33	Iowa	2,125.3
15	Kansas	2,800.9
32	Kentucky	2,129.1
3	Louisiana	3,366.8
47	Maine	1,507.1
29	Maryland	2,222.3
48	Massachusetts	1,437.0
39	Michigan	1,800.0
31	Minnesota	2,191.5
17	Mississippi	2,733.9
13	Missouri	2,833.9
20	Montana	2,591.6
28	Nebraska	2,274.0
19	Nevada	2,612.4
50	New Hampshire	1,381.8
45	New Jersey	1,555.5
1	New Mexico	3,941.7
46	New York	1,514.2
22	North Carolina	2,545.3
30	North Dakota	2,197.8
26	Ohio	2,419.1
11	Oklahoma	2,876.4
7	Oregon	2,986.5
43	Pennsylvania	1,649.4
42	Rhode Island	1,751.6
4	South Carolina	3,195.9
35	South Dakota	1,876.2
9	Tennessee	2,940.6
21	Texas	2,562.6
16	Utah	2,780.2
49	Vermont	1,436.7
40	Virginia	1,792.9
5	Washington	3,173.6
36	West Virginia	1,852.0
38	Wisconsin	1,808.3
37	Wyoming	1,830.4

RANK ORDER

RANK	STATE	RATE
1	New Mexico	3,941.7
2	Alaska	3,542.1
3	Louisiana	3,366.8
4	South Carolina	3,195.9
5	Washington	3,173.6
6	Arkansas	3,078.6
7	Oregon	2,986.5
8	Alabama	2,957.3
9	Tennessee	2,940.6
10	Arizona	2,914.9
11	Oklahoma	2,876.4
12	Georgia	2,860.2
13	Missouri	2,833.9
14	Hawaii	2,829.5
15	Kansas	2,800.9
16	Utah	2,780.2
17	Mississippi	2,733.9
18	Colorado	2,701.6
19	Nevada	2,612.4
20	Montana	2,591.6
21	Texas	2,562.6
22	North Carolina	2,545.3
23	Florida	2,512.4
24	California	2,496.7
25	Delaware	2,440.6
26	Ohio	2,419.1
27	Indiana	2,416.9
28	Nebraska	2,274.0
29	Maryland	2,222.3
30	North Dakota	2,197.8
31	Minnesota	2,191.5
32	Kentucky	2,129.1
33	Iowa	2,125.3
34	Illinois	2,011.4
35	South Dakota	1,876.2
36	West Virginia	1,852.0
37	Wyoming	1,830.4
38	Wisconsin	1,808.3
39	Michigan	1,800.0
40	Virginia	1,792.9
41	Connecticut	1,769.9
42	Rhode Island	1,751.6
43	Pennsylvania	1,649.4
44	Idaho	1,635.4
45	New Jersey	1,555.5
46	New York	1,514.2
47	Maine	1,507.1
48	Massachusetts	1,437.0
49	Vermont	1,436.7
50	New Hampshire	1,381.8
	District of Columbia	4,283.9

Source: Reported data from the Federal Bureau of Investigation
   "Crime in the United States 2017" (Uniform Crime Reports, September 24, 2018, https://ucr.fbi.gov/)
*Property crimes are offenses of burglary, larceny-theft, and motor vehicle theft.

Percent Change in Property Crime Rate: 2016 to 2017

National Percent Change = 3.6% Decrease*

ALPHA ORDER

RANK ORDER

RANK	STATE	PERCENT CHANGE	RANK	STATE	PERCENT CHANGE
10	Alabama	0.3	1	Alaska	5.6
1	Alaska	5.6	2	Minnesota	2.9
22	Arizona	(2.9)	3	Tennessee	2.3
35	Arkansas	(6.2)	4	Louisiana	2.1
20	California	(2.1)	5	New Jersey	1.2
16	Colorado	(1.8)	6	Missouri	1.1
20	Connecticut	(2.1)	6	Nevada	1.1
50	Delaware	(11.8)	8	Iowa	1.0
36	Florida	(6.3)	9	Nebraska	0.4
24	Georgia	(4.0)	10	Alabama	0.3
29	Hawaii	(4.6)	10	New Mexico	0.3
37	Idaho	(6.4)	10	Oregon	0.3
17	Illinois	(1.9)	13	Kansas	(1.0)
30	Indiana	(4.8)	14	Mississippi	(1.1)
8	Iowa	1.0	15	New York	(1.6)
13	Kansas	(1.0)	16	Colorado	(1.8)
23	Kentucky	(3.3)	17	Illinois	(1.9)
4	Louisiana	2.1	17	South Carolina	(1.9)
46	Maine	(8.5)	19	Rhode Island	(2.0)
26	Maryland	(4.2)	20	California	(2.1)
45	Massachusetts	(7.9)	20	Connecticut	(2.1)
33	Michigan	(6.0)	22	Arizona	(2.9)
2	Minnesota	2.9	23	Kentucky	(3.3)
14	Mississippi	(1.1)	24	Georgia	(4.0)
6	Missouri	1.1	25	Virginia	(4.1)
27	Montana	(4.4)	26	Maryland	(4.2)
9	Nebraska	0.4	27	Montana	(4.4)
6	Nevada	1.1	27	Oklahoma	(4.4)
47	New Hampshire	(9.2)	29	Hawaii	(4.6)
5	New Jersey	1.2	30	Indiana	(4.8)
10	New Mexico	0.3	30	North Dakota	(4.8)
15	New York	(1.6)	32	Pennsylvania	(5.2)
42	North Carolina	(6.9)	33	Michigan	(6.0)
30	North Dakota	(4.8)	34	South Dakota	(6.1)
39	Ohio	(6.6)	35	Arkansas	(6.2)
27	Oklahoma	(4.4)	36	Florida	(6.3)
10	Oregon	0.3	37	Idaho	(6.4)
32	Pennsylvania	(5.2)	38	Utah	(6.5)
19	Rhode Island	(2.0)	39	Ohio	(6.6)
17	South Carolina	(1.9)	39	Wyoming	(6.6)
34	South Dakota	(6.1)	41	Wisconsin	(6.7)
3	Tennessee	2.3	42	North Carolina	(6.9)
43	Texas	(7.1)	43	Texas	(7.1)
38	Utah	(6.5)	44	Vermont	(7.7)
44	Vermont	(7.7)	45	Massachusetts	(7.9)
25	Virginia	(4.1)	46	Maine	(8.5)
49	Washington	(9.4)	47	New Hampshire	(9.2)
47	West Virginia	(9.2)	47	West Virginia	(9.2)
41	Wisconsin	(6.7)	49	Washington	(9.4)
39	Wyoming	(6.6)	50	Delaware	(11.8)
				District of Columbia	(9.5)

Source: Reported data from the Federal Bureau of Investigation
"Crime in the United States 2017" (Uniform Crime Reports, September 24, 2018, https://ucr.fbi.gov/)
*Property crimes are offenses of burglary, larceny-theft, and motor vehicle theft.

Burglaries in 2017

National Total = 1,401,840 Burglaries*

ALPHA ORDER

RANK	STATE	BURGLARIES	% of USA
15	Alabama	31,477	2.2%
41	Alaska	4,171	0.3%
10	Arizona	37,627	2.7%
24	Arkansas	21,862	1.6%
1	California	176,690	12.6%
23	Colorado	22,813	1.6%
36	Connecticut	8,890	0.6%
42	Delaware	3,970	0.3%
3	Florida	88,853	6.3%
6	Georgia	55,374	4.0%
40	Hawaii	5,549	0.4%
39	Idaho	5,655	0.4%
8	Illinois	43,459	3.1%
17	Indiana	30,140	2.2%
33	Iowa	15,078	1.1%
34	Kansas	13,931	1.0%
25	Kentucky	20,195	1.4%
13	Louisiana	34,265	2.4%
44	Maine	3,334	0.2%
22	Maryland	23,508	1.7%
32	Massachusetts	17,089	1.2%
11	Michigan	35,641	2.5%
27	Minnesota	18,787	1.3%
20	Mississippi	24,710	1.8%
18	Missouri	30,081	2.1%
43	Montana	3,615	0.3%
38	Nebraska	6,472	0.5%
26	Nevada	20,049	1.4%
48	New Hampshire	2,574	0.2%
21	New Jersey	23,891	1.7%
29	New Mexico	17,917	1.3%
12	New York	35,002	2.5%
4	North Carolina	64,786	4.6%
46	North Dakota	2,942	0.2%
5	Ohio	58,573	4.2%
19	Oklahoma	28,608	2.0%
30	Oregon	17,705	1.3%
14	Pennsylvania	32,057	2.3%
45	Rhode Island	3,217	0.2%
16	South Carolina	31,306	2.2%
47	South Dakota	2,707	0.2%
9	Tennessee	38,716	2.8%
2	Texas	134,066	9.6%
35	Utah	11,817	0.8%
49	Vermont	1,854	0.1%
28	Virginia	18,468	1.3%
7	Washington	43,720	3.1%
37	West Virginia	7,628	0.5%
31	Wisconsin	17,599	1.3%
50	Wyoming	1,593	0.1%

RANK ORDER

RANK	STATE	BURGLARIES	% of USA
1	California	176,690	12.6%
2	Texas	134,066	9.6%
3	Florida	88,853	6.3%
4	North Carolina	64,786	4.6%
5	Ohio	58,573	4.2%
6	Georgia	55,374	4.0%
7	Washington	43,720	3.1%
8	Illinois	43,459	3.1%
9	Tennessee	38,716	2.8%
10	Arizona	37,627	2.7%
11	Michigan	35,641	2.5%
12	New York	35,002	2.5%
13	Louisiana	34,265	2.4%
14	Pennsylvania	32,057	2.3%
15	Alabama	31,477	2.2%
16	South Carolina	31,306	2.2%
17	Indiana	30,140	2.2%
18	Missouri	30,081	2.1%
19	Oklahoma	28,608	2.0%
20	Mississippi	24,710	1.8%
21	New Jersey	23,891	1.7%
22	Maryland	23,508	1.7%
23	Colorado	22,813	1.6%
24	Arkansas	21,862	1.6%
25	Kentucky	20,195	1.4%
26	Nevada	20,049	1.4%
27	Minnesota	18,787	1.3%
28	Virginia	18,468	1.3%
29	New Mexico	17,917	1.3%
30	Oregon	17,705	1.3%
31	Wisconsin	17,599	1.3%
32	Massachusetts	17,089	1.2%
33	Iowa	15,078	1.1%
34	Kansas	13,931	1.0%
35	Utah	11,817	0.8%
36	Connecticut	8,890	0.6%
37	West Virginia	7,628	0.5%
38	Nebraska	6,472	0.5%
39	Idaho	5,655	0.4%
40	Hawaii	5,549	0.4%
41	Alaska	4,171	0.3%
42	Delaware	3,970	0.3%
43	Montana	3,615	0.3%
44	Maine	3,334	0.2%
45	Rhode Island	3,217	0.2%
46	North Dakota	2,942	0.2%
47	South Dakota	2,707	0.2%
48	New Hampshire	2,574	0.2%
49	Vermont	1,854	0.1%
50	Wyoming	1,593	0.1%
	District of Columbia	1,809	0.1%

Source: Reported data from the Federal Bureau of Investigation
"Crime in the United States 2017" (Uniform Crime Reports, September 24, 2018, https://ucr.fbi.gov/)
*Burglary is the unlawful entry of a structure to commit a felony or theft. Attempts are included.

Burglary Rate in 2017

National Rate = 430.4 Burglaries per 100,000 Population*

ALPHA ORDER				RANK ORDER		
RANK	STATE	RATE		RANK	STATE	RATE
7	Alabama	645.7		1	New Mexico	858.1
12	Alaska	563.8		2	Mississippi	828.1
13	Arizona	536.3		3	Louisiana	731.5
5	Arkansas	727.7		4	Oklahoma	727.8
22	California	446.9		5	Arkansas	727.7
27	Colorado	406.9		6	Nevada	668.7
47	Connecticut	247.8		7	Alabama	645.7
26	Delaware	412.7		8	North Carolina	630.6
24	Florida	423.4		9	South Carolina	623.1
14	Georgia	530.9		10	Washington	590.4
29	Hawaii	388.7		11	Tennessee	576.5
37	Idaho	329.4		12	Alaska	563.8
34	Illinois	339.5		13	Arizona	536.3
21	Indiana	452.1		14	Georgia	530.9
17	Iowa	479.3		15	Ohio	502.4
18	Kansas	478.2		16	Missouri	492.0
20	Kentucky	453.4		17	Iowa	479.3
3	Louisiana	731.5		18	Kansas	478.2
45	Maine	249.6		19	Texas	473.7
30	Maryland	388.4		20	Kentucky	453.4
46	Massachusetts	249.1		21	Indiana	452.1
32	Michigan	357.8		22	California	446.9
36	Minnesota	336.9		23	Oregon	427.4
2	Mississippi	828.1		24	Florida	423.4
16	Missouri	492.0		25	West Virginia	420.1
33	Montana	344.1		26	Delaware	412.7
35	Nebraska	337.1		27	Colorado	406.9
6	Nevada	668.7		28	North Dakota	389.5
49	New Hampshire	191.7		29	Hawaii	388.7
43	New Jersey	265.3		30	Maryland	388.4
1	New Mexico	858.1		31	Utah	381.0
50	New York	176.3		32	Michigan	357.8
8	North Carolina	630.6		33	Montana	344.1
28	North Dakota	389.5		34	Illinois	339.5
15	Ohio	502.4		35	Nebraska	337.1
4	Oklahoma	727.8		36	Minnesota	336.9
23	Oregon	427.4		37	Idaho	329.4
44	Pennsylvania	250.3		38	South Dakota	311.3
40	Rhode Island	303.6		39	Wisconsin	303.7
9	South Carolina	623.1		40	Rhode Island	303.6
38	South Dakota	311.3		41	Vermont	297.3
11	Tennessee	576.5		42	Wyoming	275.0
19	Texas	473.7		43	New Jersey	265.3
31	Utah	381.0		44	Pennsylvania	250.3
41	Vermont	297.3		45	Maine	249.6
48	Virginia	218.0		46	Massachusetts	249.1
10	Washington	590.4		47	Connecticut	247.8
25	West Virginia	420.1		48	Virginia	218.0
39	Wisconsin	303.7		49	New Hampshire	191.7
42	Wyoming	275.0		50	New York	176.3
					District of Columbia	260.7

Source: Reported data from the Federal Bureau of Investigation
   "Crime in the United States 2017" (Uniform Crime Reports, September 24, 2018, https://ucr.fbi.gov/)
*Burglary is the unlawful entry of a structure to commit a felony or theft. Attempts are included.

Larceny-Thefts in 2017

National Total = 5,519,107 Larceny-Thefts*

<table>
<tr><td colspan="4">ALPHA ORDER</td><td colspan="4">RANK ORDER</td></tr>
<tr><td>RANK</td><td>STATE</td><td>THEFTS</td><td>% of USA</td><td>RANK</td><td>STATE</td><td>THEFTS</td><td>% of USA</td></tr>
<tr><td>21</td><td>Alabama</td><td>99,842</td><td>1.8%</td><td>1</td><td>California</td><td>642,033</td><td>11.6%</td></tr>
<tr><td>43</td><td>Alaska</td><td>17,775</td><td>0.3%</td><td>2</td><td>Texas</td><td>523,221</td><td>9.5%</td></tr>
<tr><td>11</td><td>Arizona</td><td>147,830</td><td>2.7%</td><td>3</td><td>Florida</td><td>395,453</td><td>7.2%</td></tr>
<tr><td>30</td><td>Arkansas</td><td>63,374</td><td>1.1%</td><td>4</td><td>New York</td><td>252,143</td><td>4.6%</td></tr>
<tr><td>1</td><td>California</td><td>642,033</td><td>11.6%</td><td>5</td><td>Georgia</td><td>216,661</td><td>3.9%</td></tr>
<tr><td>19</td><td>Colorado</td><td>106,809</td><td>1.9%</td><td>6</td><td>Ohio</td><td>203,208</td><td>3.7%</td></tr>
<tr><td>34</td><td>Connecticut</td><td>47,310</td><td>0.9%</td><td>7</td><td>Illinois</td><td>193,157</td><td>3.5%</td></tr>
<tr><td>42</td><td>Delaware</td><td>18,138</td><td>0.3%</td><td>8</td><td>North Carolina</td><td>180,902</td><td>3.3%</td></tr>
<tr><td>3</td><td>Florida</td><td>395,453</td><td>7.2%</td><td>9</td><td>Pennsylvania</td><td>166,178</td><td>3.0%</td></tr>
<tr><td>5</td><td>Georgia</td><td>216,661</td><td>3.9%</td><td>10</td><td>Washington</td><td>162,511</td><td>2.9%</td></tr>
<tr><td>38</td><td>Hawaii</td><td>29,574</td><td>0.5%</td><td>11</td><td>Arizona</td><td>147,830</td><td>2.7%</td></tr>
<tr><td>41</td><td>Idaho</td><td>20,278</td><td>0.4%</td><td>12</td><td>Tennessee</td><td>140,248</td><td>2.5%</td></tr>
<tr><td>7</td><td>Illinois</td><td>193,157</td><td>3.5%</td><td>13</td><td>Michigan</td><td>124,104</td><td>2.2%</td></tr>
<tr><td>16</td><td>Indiana</td><td>115,591</td><td>2.1%</td><td>14</td><td>Missouri</td><td>123,251</td><td>2.2%</td></tr>
<tr><td>35</td><td>Iowa</td><td>46,198</td><td>0.8%</td><td>15</td><td>Virginia</td><td>123,215</td><td>2.2%</td></tr>
<tr><td>31</td><td>Kansas</td><td>59,816</td><td>1.1%</td><td>16</td><td>Indiana</td><td>115,591</td><td>2.1%</td></tr>
<tr><td>29</td><td>Kentucky</td><td>64,394</td><td>1.2%</td><td>17</td><td>South Carolina</td><td>115,012</td><td>2.1%</td></tr>
<tr><td>18</td><td>Louisiana</td><td>112,485</td><td>2.0%</td><td>18</td><td>Louisiana</td><td>112,485</td><td>2.0%</td></tr>
<tr><td>44</td><td>Maine</td><td>16,006</td><td>0.3%</td><td>19</td><td>Colorado</td><td>106,809</td><td>1.9%</td></tr>
<tr><td>22</td><td>Maryland</td><td>97,420</td><td>1.8%</td><td>20</td><td>New Jersey</td><td>104,025</td><td>1.9%</td></tr>
<tr><td>26</td><td>Massachusetts</td><td>73,946</td><td>1.3%</td><td>21</td><td>Alabama</td><td>99,842</td><td>1.8%</td></tr>
<tr><td>13</td><td>Michigan</td><td>124,104</td><td>2.2%</td><td>22</td><td>Maryland</td><td>97,420</td><td>1.8%</td></tr>
<tr><td>23</td><td>Minnesota</td><td>93,446</td><td>1.7%</td><td>23</td><td>Minnesota</td><td>93,446</td><td>1.7%</td></tr>
<tr><td>33</td><td>Mississippi</td><td>52,240</td><td>0.9%</td><td>24</td><td>Oregon</td><td>88,877</td><td>1.6%</td></tr>
<tr><td>14</td><td>Missouri</td><td>123,251</td><td>2.2%</td><td>25</td><td>Wisconsin</td><td>77,735</td><td>1.4%</td></tr>
<tr><td>40</td><td>Montana</td><td>21,018</td><td>0.4%</td><td>26</td><td>Massachusetts</td><td>73,946</td><td>1.3%</td></tr>
<tr><td>37</td><td>Nebraska</td><td>31,988</td><td>0.6%</td><td>27</td><td>Oklahoma</td><td>72,207</td><td>1.3%</td></tr>
<tr><td>36</td><td>Nevada</td><td>45,461</td><td>0.8%</td><td>28</td><td>Utah</td><td>64,892</td><td>1.2%</td></tr>
<tr><td>45</td><td>New Hampshire</td><td>15,066</td><td>0.3%</td><td>29</td><td>Kentucky</td><td>64,394</td><td>1.2%</td></tr>
<tr><td>20</td><td>New Jersey</td><td>104,025</td><td>1.9%</td><td>30</td><td>Arkansas</td><td>63,374</td><td>1.1%</td></tr>
<tr><td>32</td><td>New Mexico</td><td>52,617</td><td>1.0%</td><td>31</td><td>Kansas</td><td>59,816</td><td>1.1%</td></tr>
<tr><td>4</td><td>New York</td><td>252,143</td><td>4.6%</td><td>32</td><td>New Mexico</td><td>52,617</td><td>1.0%</td></tr>
<tr><td>8</td><td>North Carolina</td><td>180,902</td><td>3.3%</td><td>33</td><td>Mississippi</td><td>52,240</td><td>0.9%</td></tr>
<tr><td>48</td><td>North Dakota</td><td>11,887</td><td>0.2%</td><td>34</td><td>Connecticut</td><td>47,310</td><td>0.9%</td></tr>
<tr><td>6</td><td>Ohio</td><td>203,208</td><td>3.7%</td><td>35</td><td>Iowa</td><td>46,198</td><td>0.8%</td></tr>
<tr><td>27</td><td>Oklahoma</td><td>72,207</td><td>1.3%</td><td>36</td><td>Nevada</td><td>45,461</td><td>0.8%</td></tr>
<tr><td>24</td><td>Oregon</td><td>88,877</td><td>1.6%</td><td>37</td><td>Nebraska</td><td>31,988</td><td>0.6%</td></tr>
<tr><td>9</td><td>Pennsylvania</td><td>166,178</td><td>3.0%</td><td>38</td><td>Hawaii</td><td>29,574</td><td>0.5%</td></tr>
<tr><td>46</td><td>Rhode Island</td><td>13,861</td><td>0.3%</td><td>39</td><td>West Virginia</td><td>23,000</td><td>0.4%</td></tr>
<tr><td>17</td><td>South Carolina</td><td>115,012</td><td>2.1%</td><td>40</td><td>Montana</td><td>21,018</td><td>0.4%</td></tr>
<tr><td>47</td><td>South Dakota</td><td>12,227</td><td>0.2%</td><td>41</td><td>Idaho</td><td>20,278</td><td>0.4%</td></tr>
<tr><td>12</td><td>Tennessee</td><td>140,248</td><td>2.5%</td><td>42</td><td>Delaware</td><td>18,138</td><td>0.3%</td></tr>
<tr><td>2</td><td>Texas</td><td>523,221</td><td>9.5%</td><td>43</td><td>Alaska</td><td>17,775</td><td>0.3%</td></tr>
<tr><td>28</td><td>Utah</td><td>64,892</td><td>1.2%</td><td>44</td><td>Maine</td><td>16,006</td><td>0.3%</td></tr>
<tr><td>50</td><td>Vermont</td><td>6,912</td><td>0.1%</td><td>45</td><td>New Hampshire</td><td>15,066</td><td>0.3%</td></tr>
<tr><td>15</td><td>Virginia</td><td>123,215</td><td>2.2%</td><td>46</td><td>Rhode Island</td><td>13,861</td><td>0.3%</td></tr>
<tr><td>10</td><td>Washington</td><td>162,511</td><td>2.9%</td><td>47</td><td>South Dakota</td><td>12,227</td><td>0.2%</td></tr>
<tr><td>39</td><td>West Virginia</td><td>23,000</td><td>0.4%</td><td>48</td><td>North Dakota</td><td>11,887</td><td>0.2%</td></tr>
<tr><td>25</td><td>Wisconsin</td><td>77,735</td><td>1.4%</td><td>49</td><td>Wyoming</td><td>8,232</td><td>0.1%</td></tr>
<tr><td>49</td><td>Wyoming</td><td>8,232</td><td>0.1%</td><td>50</td><td>Vermont</td><td>6,912</td><td>0.1%</td></tr>
<tr><td></td><td></td><td></td><td></td><td></td><td>District of Columbia</td><td>25,333</td><td>0.5%</td></tr>
</table>

Source: Reported data from the Federal Bureau of Investigation
"Crime in the United States 2017" (Uniform Crime Reports, September 24, 2018, https://ucr.fbi.gov/)
*Larceny-theft is the unlawful taking of property without use of force, violence, or fraud. Attempts are included. Motor vehicle thefts are excluded.

Larceny-Theft Rate in 2017

National Rate = 1,694.4 Larceny-Thefts per 100,000 Population*

<table>
<tr><td colspan="3">ALPHA ORDER</td><td colspan="3">RANK ORDER</td></tr>
<tr><td>RANK</td><td>STATE</td><td>RATE</td><td>RANK</td><td>STATE</td><td>RATE</td></tr>
<tr><td>14</td><td>Alabama</td><td>2,048.1</td><td>1</td><td>New Mexico</td><td>2,519.9</td></tr>
<tr><td>2</td><td>Alaska</td><td>2,402.7</td><td>2</td><td>Alaska</td><td>2,402.7</td></tr>
<tr><td>8</td><td>Arizona</td><td>2,107.0</td><td>3</td><td>Louisiana</td><td>2,401.3</td></tr>
<tr><td>7</td><td>Arkansas</td><td>2,109.5</td><td>4</td><td>South Carolina</td><td>2,289.1</td></tr>
<tr><td>28</td><td>California</td><td>1,623.9</td><td>5</td><td>Washington</td><td>2,194.4</td></tr>
<tr><td>17</td><td>Colorado</td><td>1,904.9</td><td>6</td><td>Oregon</td><td>2,145.3</td></tr>
<tr><td>39</td><td>Connecticut</td><td>1,318.5</td><td>7</td><td>Arkansas</td><td>2,109.5</td></tr>
<tr><td>18</td><td>Delaware</td><td>1,885.6</td><td>8</td><td>Arizona</td><td>2,107.0</td></tr>
<tr><td>19</td><td>Florida</td><td>1,884.5</td><td>9</td><td>Utah</td><td>2,092.1</td></tr>
<tr><td>11</td><td>Georgia</td><td>2,077.4</td><td>10</td><td>Tennessee</td><td>2,088.3</td></tr>
<tr><td>12</td><td>Hawaii</td><td>2,071.7</td><td>11</td><td>Georgia</td><td>2,077.4</td></tr>
<tr><td>46</td><td>Idaho</td><td>1,181.1</td><td>12</td><td>Hawaii</td><td>2,071.7</td></tr>
<tr><td>32</td><td>Illinois</td><td>1,508.8</td><td>13</td><td>Kansas</td><td>2,053.3</td></tr>
<tr><td>25</td><td>Indiana</td><td>1,733.8</td><td>14</td><td>Alabama</td><td>2,048.1</td></tr>
<tr><td>33</td><td>Iowa</td><td>1,468.6</td><td>15</td><td>Missouri</td><td>2,016.0</td></tr>
<tr><td>13</td><td>Kansas</td><td>2,053.3</td><td>16</td><td>Montana</td><td>2,000.8</td></tr>
<tr><td>35</td><td>Kentucky</td><td>1,445.7</td><td>17</td><td>Colorado</td><td>1,904.9</td></tr>
<tr><td>3</td><td>Louisiana</td><td>2,401.3</td><td>18</td><td>Delaware</td><td>1,885.6</td></tr>
<tr><td>45</td><td>Maine</td><td>1,198.1</td><td>19</td><td>Florida</td><td>1,884.5</td></tr>
<tr><td>29</td><td>Maryland</td><td>1,609.7</td><td>20</td><td>Texas</td><td>1,848.5</td></tr>
<tr><td>50</td><td>Massachusetts</td><td>1,078.0</td><td>21</td><td>Oklahoma</td><td>1,836.9</td></tr>
<tr><td>44</td><td>Michigan</td><td>1,245.7</td><td>22</td><td>North Carolina</td><td>1,760.9</td></tr>
<tr><td>26</td><td>Minnesota</td><td>1,675.7</td><td>23</td><td>Mississippi</td><td>1,750.6</td></tr>
<tr><td>23</td><td>Mississippi</td><td>1,750.6</td><td>24</td><td>Ohio</td><td>1,743.0</td></tr>
<tr><td>15</td><td>Missouri</td><td>2,016.0</td><td>25</td><td>Indiana</td><td>1,733.8</td></tr>
<tr><td>16</td><td>Montana</td><td>2,000.8</td><td>26</td><td>Minnesota</td><td>1,675.7</td></tr>
<tr><td>27</td><td>Nebraska</td><td>1,666.0</td><td>27</td><td>Nebraska</td><td>1,666.0</td></tr>
<tr><td>31</td><td>Nevada</td><td>1,516.4</td><td>28</td><td>California</td><td>1,623.9</td></tr>
<tr><td>48</td><td>New Hampshire</td><td>1,122.0</td><td>29</td><td>Maryland</td><td>1,609.7</td></tr>
<tr><td>47</td><td>New Jersey</td><td>1,155.1</td><td>30</td><td>North Dakota</td><td>1,573.6</td></tr>
<tr><td>1</td><td>New Mexico</td><td>2,519.9</td><td>31</td><td>Nevada</td><td>1,516.4</td></tr>
<tr><td>42</td><td>New York</td><td>1,270.3</td><td>32</td><td>Illinois</td><td>1,508.8</td></tr>
<tr><td>22</td><td>North Carolina</td><td>1,760.9</td><td>33</td><td>Iowa</td><td>1,468.6</td></tr>
<tr><td>30</td><td>North Dakota</td><td>1,573.6</td><td>34</td><td>Virginia</td><td>1,454.7</td></tr>
<tr><td>24</td><td>Ohio</td><td>1,743.0</td><td>35</td><td>Kentucky</td><td>1,445.7</td></tr>
<tr><td>21</td><td>Oklahoma</td><td>1,836.9</td><td>36</td><td>Wyoming</td><td>1,421.0</td></tr>
<tr><td>6</td><td>Oregon</td><td>2,145.3</td><td>37</td><td>South Dakota</td><td>1,405.9</td></tr>
<tr><td>41</td><td>Pennsylvania</td><td>1,297.7</td><td>38</td><td>Wisconsin</td><td>1,341.3</td></tr>
<tr><td>40</td><td>Rhode Island</td><td>1,308.1</td><td>39</td><td>Connecticut</td><td>1,318.5</td></tr>
<tr><td>4</td><td>South Carolina</td><td>2,289.1</td><td>40</td><td>Rhode Island</td><td>1,308.1</td></tr>
<tr><td>37</td><td>South Dakota</td><td>1,405.9</td><td>41</td><td>Pennsylvania</td><td>1,297.7</td></tr>
<tr><td>10</td><td>Tennessee</td><td>2,088.3</td><td>42</td><td>New York</td><td>1,270.3</td></tr>
<tr><td>20</td><td>Texas</td><td>1,848.5</td><td>43</td><td>West Virginia</td><td>1,266.6</td></tr>
<tr><td>9</td><td>Utah</td><td>2,092.1</td><td>44</td><td>Michigan</td><td>1,245.7</td></tr>
<tr><td>49</td><td>Vermont</td><td>1,108.3</td><td>45</td><td>Maine</td><td>1,198.1</td></tr>
<tr><td>34</td><td>Virginia</td><td>1,454.7</td><td>46</td><td>Idaho</td><td>1,181.1</td></tr>
<tr><td>5</td><td>Washington</td><td>2,194.4</td><td>47</td><td>New Jersey</td><td>1,155.1</td></tr>
<tr><td>43</td><td>West Virginia</td><td>1,266.6</td><td>48</td><td>New Hampshire</td><td>1,122.0</td></tr>
<tr><td>38</td><td>Wisconsin</td><td>1,341.3</td><td>49</td><td>Vermont</td><td>1,108.3</td></tr>
<tr><td>36</td><td>Wyoming</td><td>1,421.0</td><td>50</td><td>Massachusetts</td><td>1,078.0</td></tr>
<tr><td></td><td></td><td></td><td></td><td>District of Columbia</td><td>3,650.4</td></tr>
</table>

Source: Reported data from the Federal Bureau of Investigation
"Crime in the United States 2017" (Uniform Crime Reports, September 24, 2018, https://ucr.fbi.gov/)
*Larceny-theft is the unlawful taking of property without use of force, violence, or fraud. Attempts are included. Motor vehicle thefts are excluded.

Motor Vehicle Thefts in 2017

National Total = 773,139 Motor Vehicle Thefts*

ALPHA ORDER

RANK	STATE	THEFTS	% of USA
20	Alabama	12,841	1.7%
39	Alaska	4,258	0.6%
11	Arizona	19,058	2.5%
34	Arkansas	7,253	0.9%
1	California	168,391	21.8%
6	Colorado	21,861	2.8%
33	Connecticut	7,309	0.9%
46	Delaware	1,369	0.2%
3	Florida	42,914	5.6%
5	Georgia	26,263	3.4%
36	Hawaii	5,269	0.7%
42	Idaho	2,146	0.3%
7	Illinois	20,881	2.7%
15	Indiana	15,401	2.0%
35	Iowa	5,579	0.7%
31	Kansas	7,846	1.0%
26	Kentucky	10,244	1.3%
25	Louisiana	10,962	1.4%
48	Maine	793	0.1%
17	Maryland	13,568	1.8%
32	Massachusetts	7,540	1.0%
10	Michigan	19,573	2.5%
28	Minnesota	9,979	1.3%
38	Mississippi	4,631	0.6%
9	Missouri	19,921	2.6%
41	Montana	2,592	0.3%
37	Nebraska	5,203	0.7%
21	Nevada	12,812	1.7%
47	New Hampshire	915	0.1%
23	New Jersey	12,170	1.6%
24	New Mexico	11,772	1.5%
18	New York	13,410	1.7%
14	North Carolina	15,798	2.0%
43	North Dakota	1,773	0.2%
8	Ohio	20,253	2.6%
22	Oklahoma	12,251	1.6%
13	Oregon	17,140	2.2%
19	Pennsylvania	12,985	1.7%
44	Rhode Island	1,483	0.2%
16	South Carolina	14,257	1.8%
45	South Dakota	1,383	0.2%
12	Tennessee	18,524	2.4%
2	Texas	68,041	8.8%
29	Utah	9,529	1.2%
50	Vermont	194	0.0%
27	Virginia	10,172	1.3%
4	Washington	28,796	3.7%
40	West Virginia	3,002	0.4%
30	Wisconsin	9,468	1.2%
49	Wyoming	779	0.1%

RANK ORDER

RANK	STATE	THEFTS	% of USA
1	California	168,391	21.8%
2	Texas	68,041	8.8%
3	Florida	42,914	5.6%
4	Washington	28,796	3.7%
5	Georgia	26,263	3.4%
6	Colorado	21,861	2.8%
7	Illinois	20,881	2.7%
8	Ohio	20,253	2.6%
9	Missouri	19,921	2.6%
10	Michigan	19,573	2.5%
11	Arizona	19,058	2.5%
12	Tennessee	18,524	2.4%
13	Oregon	17,140	2.2%
14	North Carolina	15,798	2.0%
15	Indiana	15,401	2.0%
16	South Carolina	14,257	1.8%
17	Maryland	13,568	1.8%
18	New York	13,410	1.7%
19	Pennsylvania	12,985	1.7%
20	Alabama	12,841	1.7%
21	Nevada	12,812	1.7%
22	Oklahoma	12,251	1.6%
23	New Jersey	12,170	1.6%
24	New Mexico	11,772	1.5%
25	Louisiana	10,962	1.4%
26	Kentucky	10,244	1.3%
27	Virginia	10,172	1.3%
28	Minnesota	9,979	1.3%
29	Utah	9,529	1.2%
30	Wisconsin	9,468	1.2%
31	Kansas	7,846	1.0%
32	Massachusetts	7,540	1.0%
33	Connecticut	7,309	0.9%
34	Arkansas	7,253	0.9%
35	Iowa	5,579	0.7%
36	Hawaii	5,269	0.7%
37	Nebraska	5,203	0.7%
38	Mississippi	4,631	0.6%
39	Alaska	4,258	0.6%
40	West Virginia	3,002	0.4%
41	Montana	2,592	0.3%
42	Idaho	2,146	0.3%
43	North Dakota	1,773	0.2%
44	Rhode Island	1,483	0.2%
45	South Dakota	1,383	0.2%
46	Delaware	1,369	0.2%
47	New Hampshire	915	0.1%
48	Maine	793	0.1%
49	Wyoming	779	0.1%
50	Vermont	194	0.0%
	District of Columbia	2,587	0.3%

Source: Reported data from the Federal Bureau of Investigation
   "Crime in the United States 2017" (Uniform Crime Reports, September 24, 2018, https://ucr.fbi.gov/)
*Includes the theft or attempted theft of a self-propelled vehicle. Excludes motorboats, construction equipment, airplanes, and farming equipment.

Motor Vehicle Theft Rate in 2017

National Rate = 237.4 Motor Vehicle Thefts per 100,000 Population*

ALPHA ORDER			RANK ORDER		
RANK	STATE	RATE	RANK	STATE	RATE
17	Alabama	263.4	1	Alaska	575.6
1	Alaska	575.6	2	New Mexico	563.8
14	Arizona	271.6	3	Nevada	427.3
20	Arkansas	241.4	4	California	425.9
4	California	425.9	5	Oregon	413.7
6	Colorado	389.9	6	Colorado	389.9
28	Connecticut	203.7	7	Washington	388.8
39	Delaware	142.3	8	Hawaii	369.1
27	Florida	204.5	9	Missouri	325.9
18	Georgia	251.8	10	Oklahoma	311.7
8	Hawaii	369.1	11	Utah	307.2
43	Idaho	125.0	12	South Carolina	283.8
35	Illinois	163.1	13	Tennessee	275.8
24	Indiana	231.0	14	Arizona	271.6
31	Iowa	177.4	15	Nebraska	271.0
16	Kansas	269.3	16	Kansas	269.3
25	Kentucky	230.0	17	Alabama	263.4
23	Louisiana	234.0	18	Georgia	251.8
49	Maine	59.4	19	Montana	246.7
26	Maryland	224.2	20	Arkansas	241.4
45	Massachusetts	109.9	21	Texas	240.4
29	Michigan	196.5	22	North Dakota	234.7
30	Minnesota	178.9	23	Louisiana	234.0
37	Mississippi	155.2	24	Indiana	231.0
9	Missouri	325.9	25	Kentucky	230.0
19	Montana	246.7	26	Maryland	224.2
15	Nebraska	271.0	27	Florida	204.5
3	Nevada	427.3	28	Connecticut	203.7
47	New Hampshire	68.1	29	Michigan	196.5
41	New Jersey	135.1	30	Minnesota	178.9
2	New Mexico	563.8	31	Iowa	177.4
48	New York	67.6	32	Ohio	173.7
38	North Carolina	153.8	33	West Virginia	165.3
22	North Dakota	234.7	34	Wisconsin	163.4
32	Ohio	173.7	35	Illinois	163.1
10	Oklahoma	311.7	36	South Dakota	159.0
5	Oregon	413.7	37	Mississippi	155.2
46	Pennsylvania	101.4	38	North Carolina	153.8
40	Rhode Island	140.0	39	Delaware	142.3
12	South Carolina	283.8	40	Rhode Island	140.0
36	South Dakota	159.0	41	New Jersey	135.1
13	Tennessee	275.8	42	Wyoming	134.5
21	Texas	240.4	43	Idaho	125.0
11	Utah	307.2	44	Virginia	120.1
50	Vermont	31.1	45	Massachusetts	109.9
44	Virginia	120.1	46	Pennsylvania	101.4
7	Washington	388.8	47	New Hampshire	68.1
33	West Virginia	165.3	48	New York	67.6
34	Wisconsin	163.4	49	Maine	59.4
42	Wyoming	134.5	50	Vermont	31.1
				District of Columbia	372.8

Source: Reported data from the Federal Bureau of Investigation
   "Crime in the United States 2017" (Uniform Crime Reports, September 24, 2018, https://ucr.fbi.gov/)
*Includes the theft or attempted theft of a self-propelled vehicle. Excludes motorboats, construction equipment, airplanes, and farming equipment.

Rate of Consumer Fraud Complaints in 2017

National Rate = 709 Complaints per 100,000 Population*

ALPHA ORDER

RANK	STATE	RATE
8	Alabama	687
45	Alaska	406
11	Arizona	644
34	Arkansas	481
18	California	570
19	Colorado	568
23	Connecticut	541
4	Delaware	758
1	Florida	993
2	Georgia	924
41	Hawaii	428
37	Idaho	477
26	Illinois	518
24	Indiana	521
48	Iowa	330
32	Kansas	501
31	Kentucky	502
17	Louisiana	582
42	Maine	423
7	Maryland	694
34	Massachusetts	481
5	Michigan	750
40	Minnesota	434
27	Mississippi	514
12	Missouri	640
38	Montana	473
46	Nebraska	395
3	Nevada	770
30	New Hampshire	509
22	New Jersey	556
15	New Mexico	590
29	New York	510
16	North Carolina	587
50	North Dakota	277
14	Ohio	598
36	Oklahoma	478
28	Oregon	512
21	Pennsylvania	560
20	Rhode Island	561
9	South Carolina	660
49	South Dakota	309
10	Tennessee	649
6	Texas	729
44	Utah	413
47	Vermont	388
13	Virginia	613
24	Washington	521
33	West Virginia	493
39	Wisconsin	452
43	Wyoming	414

RANK ORDER

RANK	STATE	RATE
1	Florida	993
2	Georgia	924
3	Nevada	770
4	Delaware	758
5	Michigan	750
6	Texas	729
7	Maryland	694
8	Alabama	687
9	South Carolina	660
10	Tennessee	649
11	Arizona	644
12	Missouri	640
13	Virginia	613
14	Ohio	598
15	New Mexico	590
16	North Carolina	587
17	Louisiana	582
18	California	570
19	Colorado	568
20	Rhode Island	561
21	Pennsylvania	560
22	New Jersey	556
23	Connecticut	541
24	Indiana	521
24	Washington	521
26	Illinois	518
27	Mississippi	514
28	Oregon	512
29	New York	510
30	New Hampshire	509
31	Kentucky	502
32	Kansas	501
33	West Virginia	493
34	Arkansas	481
34	Massachusetts	481
36	Oklahoma	478
37	Idaho	477
38	Montana	473
39	Wisconsin	452
40	Minnesota	434
41	Hawaii	428
42	Maine	423
43	Wyoming	414
44	Utah	413
45	Alaska	406
46	Nebraska	395
47	Vermont	388
48	Iowa	330
49	South Dakota	309
50	North Dakota	277
	District of Columbia	1,141

Source: Federal Trade Commission, Consumer Sentinel

"Consumer Sentinel Network Data Book for January - December 2017" (March 2018, https://www.ftc.gov/sentinel/)

*National rate includes complaints not shown by state. Rates include "other" complaints but do not include identity theft or "Do Not Call" registry complaints.

Rate of Identity Theft Complaints in 2017

National Rate = 114 Complaints per 100,000 Population*

ALPHA ORDER

RANK	STATE	RATE
32	Alabama	74
39	Alaska	67
10	Arizona	119
36	Arkansas	69
3	California	140
13	Colorado	108
12	Connecticut	114
6	Delaware	126
2	Florida	149
9	Georgia	120
42	Hawaii	62
27	Idaho	79
7	Illinois	124
31	Indiana	75
47	Iowa	59
34	Kansas	72
36	Kentucky	69
35	Louisiana	71
46	Maine	60
4	Maryland	129
23	Massachusetts	88
1	Michigan	151
29	Minnesota	78
36	Mississippi	69
25	Missouri	82
44	Montana	61
44	Nebraska	61
5	Nevada	128
25	New Hampshire	82
14	New Jersey	106
19	New Mexico	91
15	New York	103
18	North Carolina	92
42	North Dakota	62
29	Ohio	78
32	Oklahoma	74
20	Oregon	90
17	Pennsylvania	97
8	Rhode Island	123
20	South Carolina	90
50	South Dakota	46
24	Tennessee	83
11	Texas	118
27	Utah	79
48	Vermont	57
20	Virginia	90
16	Washington	99
49	West Virginia	55
41	Wisconsin	64
39	Wyoming	67

RANK ORDER

RANK	STATE	RATE
1	Michigan	151
2	Florida	149
3	California	140
4	Maryland	129
5	Nevada	128
6	Delaware	126
7	Illinois	124
8	Rhode Island	123
9	Georgia	120
10	Arizona	119
11	Texas	118
12	Connecticut	114
13	Colorado	108
14	New Jersey	106
15	New York	103
16	Washington	99
17	Pennsylvania	97
18	North Carolina	92
19	New Mexico	91
20	Oregon	90
20	South Carolina	90
20	Virginia	90
23	Massachusetts	88
24	Tennessee	83
25	Missouri	82
25	New Hampshire	82
27	Idaho	79
27	Utah	79
29	Minnesota	78
29	Ohio	78
31	Indiana	75
32	Alabama	74
32	Oklahoma	74
34	Kansas	72
35	Louisiana	71
36	Arkansas	69
36	Kentucky	69
36	Mississippi	69
39	Alaska	67
39	Wyoming	67
41	Wisconsin	64
42	Hawaii	62
42	North Dakota	62
44	Montana	61
44	Nebraska	61
46	Maine	60
47	Iowa	59
48	Vermont	57
49	West Virginia	55
50	South Dakota	46

District of Columbia   192

Source: Federal Trade Commission, Consumer Sentinel
"Consumer Sentinel Network Data Book for January - December 2017" (March 2018, https://www.ftc.gov/sentinel/)
*National rate includes complaints not shown by state. Rates do not include consumer fraud or "Do Not Call" registry complaints.

Reported Arrest Rate in 2017

National Rate = 3,262.7 Reported Arrests per 100,000 Population*

ALPHA ORDER

RANK	STATE	RATE
13	Alabama	4,101.1
15	Alaska	3,959.8
11	Arizona	4,338.4
8	Arkansas	4,491.1
38	California	2,776.0
7	Colorado	4,611.0
35	Connecticut	2,832.4
28	Delaware	3,279.7
23	Florida	3,400.3
37	Georgia	2,810.8
43	Hawaii	2,495.1
24	Idaho	3,369.0
NA	Illinois**	NA
21	Indiana	3,449.4
20	Iowa	3,516.5
29	Kansas	3,217.2
6	Kentucky	5,077.9
9	Louisiana	4,453.1
30	Maine	3,044.7
31	Maryland	3,022.0
47	Massachusetts	1,819.6
42	Michigan	2,496.7
39	Minnesota	2,671.5
2	Mississippi	5,645.2
14	Missouri	4,053.3
32	Montana	2,970.7
NA	Nebraska**	NA
12	Nevada	4,178.1
19	New Hampshire	3,675.9
27	New Jersey	3,304.9
NA	New Mexico**	NA
41	New York***	2,561.4
18	North Carolina	3,722.0
4	North Dakota	5,326.3
45	Ohio	2,397.1
36	Oklahoma	2,816.2
25	Oregon	3,333.8
33	Pennsylvania	2,968.1
44	Rhode Island	2,407.7
17	South Carolina	3,917.6
1	South Dakota	8,718.1
3	Tennessee	5,394.4
34	Texas	2,870.3
16	Utah	3,958.5
46	Vermont	2,326.7
26	Virginia	3,326.6
40	Washington	2,595.5
22	West Virginia	3,416.2
10	Wisconsin	4,422.9
5	Wyoming	5,131.4

RANK ORDER

RANK	STATE	RATE
1	South Dakota	8,718.1
2	Mississippi	5,645.2
3	Tennessee	5,394.4
4	North Dakota	5,326.3
5	Wyoming	5,131.4
6	Kentucky	5,077.9
7	Colorado	4,611.0
8	Arkansas	4,491.1
9	Louisiana	4,453.1
10	Wisconsin	4,422.9
11	Arizona	4,338.4
12	Nevada	4,178.1
13	Alabama	4,101.1
14	Missouri	4,053.3
15	Alaska	3,959.8
16	Utah	3,958.5
17	South Carolina	3,917.6
18	North Carolina	3,722.0
19	New Hampshire	3,675.9
20	Iowa	3,516.5
21	Indiana	3,449.4
22	West Virginia	3,416.2
23	Florida	3,400.3
24	Idaho	3,369.0
25	Oregon	3,333.8
26	Virginia	3,326.6
27	New Jersey	3,304.9
28	Delaware	3,279.7
29	Kansas	3,217.2
30	Maine	3,044.7
31	Maryland	3,022.0
32	Montana	2,970.7
33	Pennsylvania	2,968.1
34	Texas	2,870.3
35	Connecticut	2,832.4
36	Oklahoma	2,816.2
37	Georgia	2,810.8
38	California	2,776.0
39	Minnesota	2,671.5
40	Washington	2,595.5
41	New York***	2,561.4
42	Michigan	2,496.7
43	Hawaii	2,495.1
44	Rhode Island	2,407.7
45	Ohio	2,397.1
46	Vermont	2,326.7
47	Massachusetts	1,819.6
NA	Illinois**	NA
NA	Nebraska**	NA
NA	New Mexico**	NA
	District of Columbia**	NA

Source: CQ Press using reported data from the Federal Bureau of Investigation
"Crime in the United States 2017" (Uniform Crime Reports, September 24, 2018, https://ucr.fbi.gov/)
*By law enforcement agencies submitting complete reports to the F.B.I. for 12 months in 2017. These rates based on population estimates for areas under the jurisdiction of those agencies reporting. Arrest rate based on the F.B.I. estimate of total arrests is 3,240.5 reported and unreported arrests per 100,000 population.
**Not available. ***New York's figure does not include New York City.

Reported Juvenile Arrest Rate in 2017

National Rate = 2,417.6 Reported Arrests per 100,000 Juvenile Population*

ALPHA ORDER

RANK	STATE	RATE
45	Alabama	1,210.9
35	Alaska	2,031.0
14	Arizona	3,271.1
22	Arkansas	2,667.2
44	California	1,259.8
7	Colorado	4,006.6
30	Connecticut	2,253.7
9	Delaware	3,638.5
20	Florida	2,869.3
32	Georgia	2,150.8
27	Hawaii	2,374.0
12	Idaho	3,372.2
NA	Illinois**	NA
26	Indiana	2,466.8
10	Iowa	3,610.1
36	Kansas	1,941.4
46	Kentucky	1,182.3
5	Louisiana	4,423.6
24	Maine	2,533.4
16	Maryland	3,153.1
47	Massachusetts	1,098.1
41	Michigan	1,633.8
8	Minnesota	3,730.8
31	Mississippi	2,225.3
18	Missouri	2,993.9
6	Montana	4,198.7
NA	Nebraska**	NA
21	Nevada	2,805.8
19	New Hampshire	2,904.3
39	New Jersey	1,817.2
43	New Mexico	1,451.5
37	New York***	1,916.2
29	North Carolina	2,346.1
3	North Dakota	6,498.4
28	Ohio	2,371.1
33	Oklahoma	2,098.9
25	Oregon	2,490.8
11	Pennsylvania	3,560.6
23	Rhode Island	2,584.4
17	South Carolina	3,132.4
1	South Dakota	8,604.0
13	Tennessee	3,293.6
38	Texas	1,872.9
15	Utah	3,199.3
42	Vermont	1,480.5
34	Virginia	2,088.7
40	Washington	1,805.6
48	West Virginia	955.3
2	Wisconsin	6,708.8
4	Wyoming	5,436.4

RANK ORDER

RANK	STATE	RATE
1	South Dakota	8,604.0
2	Wisconsin	6,708.8
3	North Dakota	6,498.4
4	Wyoming	5,436.4
5	Louisiana	4,423.6
6	Montana	4,198.7
7	Colorado	4,006.6
8	Minnesota	3,730.8
9	Delaware	3,638.5
10	Iowa	3,610.1
11	Pennsylvania	3,560.6
12	Idaho	3,372.2
13	Tennessee	3,293.6
14	Arizona	3,271.1
15	Utah	3,199.3
16	Maryland	3,153.1
17	South Carolina	3,132.4
18	Missouri	2,993.9
19	New Hampshire	2,904.3
20	Florida	2,869.3
21	Nevada	2,805.8
22	Arkansas	2,667.2
23	Rhode Island	2,584.4
24	Maine	2,533.4
25	Oregon	2,490.8
26	Indiana	2,466.8
27	Hawaii	2,374.0
28	Ohio	2,371.1
29	North Carolina	2,346.1
30	Connecticut	2,253.7
31	Mississippi	2,225.3
32	Georgia	2,150.8
33	Oklahoma	2,098.9
34	Virginia	2,088.7
35	Alaska	2,031.0
36	Kansas	1,941.4
37	New York***	1,916.2
38	Texas	1,872.9
39	New Jersey	1,817.2
40	Washington	1,805.6
41	Michigan	1,633.8
42	Vermont	1,480.5
43	New Mexico	1,451.5
44	California	1,259.8
45	Alabama	1,210.9
46	Kentucky	1,182.3
47	Massachusetts	1,098.1
48	West Virginia	955.3
NA	Illinois**	NA
NA	Nebraska**	NA
	District of Columbia**	NA

Source: CQ Press using reported data from the Federal Bureau of Investigation
"Crime in the United States 2017" (Uniform Crime Reports, September 24, 2018, https://ucr.fbi.gov/)
*By law enforcement agencies submitting complete reports to the F.B.I. for 12 months in 2017. Arrests of youths 17 years and younger divided into population of 10 to 17 year olds.
**Not available.
***New York's figure does not include New York City.

Prisoners in State Correctional Institutions: Year End 2016

National Total = 1,316,205 State Prisoners*

ALPHA ORDER

RANK	STATE	PRISONERS	% of USA
15	Alabama	28,883	2.2%
42	Alaska	4,434	0.3%
9	Arizona	42,320	3.2%
27	Arkansas	17,537	1.3%
2	California	130,390	9.9%
23	Colorado	19,981	1.5%
29	Connecticut	14,957	1.1%
38	Delaware	6,585	0.5%
3	Florida	99,974	7.6%
4	Georgia	53,627	4.1%
40	Hawaii	5,602	0.4%
35	Idaho	8,252	0.6%
8	Illinois	43,657	3.3%
18	Indiana	25,546	1.9%
34	Iowa	9,031	0.7%
32	Kansas	9,920	0.8%
20	Kentucky	23,022	1.7%
13	Louisiana	35,682	2.7%
47	Maine	2,404	0.2%
22	Maryland	19,994	1.5%
33	Massachusetts	9,403	0.7%
10	Michigan	41,122	3.1%
31	Minnesota	10,592	0.8%
25	Mississippi	19,192	1.5%
14	Missouri	32,461	2.5%
44	Montana	3,814	0.3%
41	Nebraska	5,302	0.4%
30	Nevada	13,757	1.0%
46	New Hampshire	2,818	0.2%
24	New Jersey	19,786	1.5%
37	New Mexico	7,055	0.5%
6	New York	50,716	3.9%
12	North Carolina	35,697	2.7%
49	North Dakota	1,791	0.1%
5	Ohio	52,175	4.0%
17	Oklahoma	26,871	2.0%
28	Oregon	15,166	1.2%
7	Pennsylvania	49,244	3.7%
45	Rhode Island	3,103	0.2%
21	South Carolina	20,858	1.6%
43	South Dakota	3,831	0.3%
16	Tennessee	28,203	2.1%
1	Texas	163,703	12.4%
39	Utah	6,182	0.5%
50	Vermont	1,735	0.1%
11	Virginia	37,813	2.9%
26	Washington	19,104	1.5%
36	West Virginia	7,162	0.5%
19	Wisconsin	23,377	1.8%
48	Wyoming	2,374	0.2%

RANK ORDER

RANK	STATE	PRISONERS	% of USA
1	Texas	163,703	12.4%
2	California	130,390	9.9%
3	Florida	99,974	7.6%
4	Georgia	53,627	4.1%
5	Ohio	52,175	4.0%
6	New York	50,716	3.9%
7	Pennsylvania	49,244	3.7%
8	Illinois	43,657	3.3%
9	Arizona	42,320	3.2%
10	Michigan	41,122	3.1%
11	Virginia	37,813	2.9%
12	North Carolina	35,697	2.7%
13	Louisiana	35,682	2.7%
14	Missouri	32,461	2.5%
15	Alabama	28,883	2.2%
16	Tennessee	28,203	2.1%
17	Oklahoma	26,871	2.0%
18	Indiana	25,546	1.9%
19	Wisconsin	23,377	1.8%
20	Kentucky	23,022	1.7%
21	South Carolina	20,858	1.6%
22	Maryland	19,994	1.5%
23	Colorado	19,981	1.5%
24	New Jersey	19,786	1.5%
25	Mississippi	19,192	1.5%
26	Washington	19,104	1.5%
27	Arkansas	17,537	1.3%
28	Oregon	15,166	1.2%
29	Connecticut	14,957	1.1%
30	Nevada	13,757	1.0%
31	Minnesota	10,592	0.8%
32	Kansas	9,920	0.8%
33	Massachusetts	9,403	0.7%
34	Iowa	9,031	0.7%
35	Idaho	8,252	0.6%
36	West Virginia	7,162	0.5%
37	New Mexico	7,055	0.5%
38	Delaware	6,585	0.5%
39	Utah	6,182	0.5%
40	Hawaii	5,602	0.4%
41	Nebraska	5,302	0.4%
42	Alaska	4,434	0.3%
43	South Dakota	3,831	0.3%
44	Montana	3,814	0.3%
45	Rhode Island	3,103	0.2%
46	New Hampshire	2,818	0.2%
47	Maine	2,404	0.2%
48	Wyoming	2,374	0.2%
49	North Dakota	1,791	0.1%
50	Vermont	1,735	0.1%
	District of Columbia**	NA	NA

Source: U.S. Department of Justice, Bureau of Justice Statistics
   "Prisoners in 2016" (January 2018, NCJ 251149, http://bjs.ojp.usdoj.gov/)
*As of December 31, 2016. Totals reflect all prisoners, including those sentenced to a year or less and those unsentenced.
National total does not include 189,192 prisoners under federal jurisdiction. State and federal prisoners combined total 1,505,397.
**Responsibility for sentenced felons in D.C. was transferred to the Federal Bureau of Prisons in 2001.

State Prisoner Imprisonment Rate in 2016

National Rate = 397 State Prisoners per 100,000 Population*

ALPHA ORDER

RANK	STATE	RATE
6	Alabama	571
37	Alaska	281
4	Arizona	585
5	Arkansas	583
32	California	331
28	Colorado	356
35	Connecticut	290
17	Delaware	428
11	Florida	481
10	Georgia	512
41	Hawaii	254
16	Idaho	435
29	Illinois	341
23	Indiana	384
36	Iowa	286
32	Kansas	331
9	Kentucky	518
1	Louisiana	760
50	Maine	137
34	Maryland	329
49	Massachusetts	156
19	Michigan	414
48	Minnesota	191
3	Mississippi	624
8	Missouri	532
27	Montana	364
38	Nebraska	274
12	Nevada	460
44	New Hampshire	211
43	New Jersey	221
31	New Mexico	335
40	New York	256
30	North Carolina	339
42	North Dakota	234
13	Ohio	449
2	Oklahoma	673
26	Oregon	367
24	Pennsylvania	383
47	Rhode Island	192
20	South Carolina	408
15	South Dakota	440
18	Tennessee	422
7	Texas	563
45	Utah	201
46	Vermont	197
14	Virginia	448
39	Washington	259
22	West Virginia	392
24	Wisconsin	383
21	Wyoming	406

RANK ORDER

RANK	STATE	RATE
1	Louisiana	760
2	Oklahoma	673
3	Mississippi	624
4	Arizona	585
5	Arkansas	583
6	Alabama	571
7	Texas	563
8	Missouri	532
9	Kentucky	518
10	Georgia	512
11	Florida	481
12	Nevada	460
13	Ohio	449
14	Virginia	448
15	South Dakota	440
16	Idaho	435
17	Delaware	428
18	Tennessee	422
19	Michigan	414
20	South Carolina	408
21	Wyoming	406
22	West Virginia	392
23	Indiana	384
24	Pennsylvania	383
24	Wisconsin	383
26	Oregon	367
27	Montana	364
28	Colorado	356
29	Illinois	341
30	North Carolina	339
31	New Mexico	335
32	California	331
32	Kansas	331
34	Maryland	329
35	Connecticut	290
36	Iowa	286
37	Alaska	281
38	Nebraska	274
39	Washington	259
40	New York	256
41	Hawaii	254
42	North Dakota	234
43	New Jersey	221
44	New Hampshire	211
45	Utah	201
46	Vermont	197
47	Rhode Island	192
48	Minnesota	191
49	Massachusetts	156
50	Maine	137

District of Columbia**		NA

Source: U.S. Department of Justice, Bureau of Justice Statistics
   "Prisoners in 2016" (January 2018, NCJ 251149, http://bjs.ojp.usdoj.gov/)
*Figures as of December 31, 2016. Includes only inmates sentenced to more than one year. Does not include federal imprisonment rate of 53 prisoners per 100,000 population. State and federal combined imprisonment rate is 450 prisoners per 100,000 population.
**Responsibility for sentenced felons in D.C. was transferred to the Federal Bureau of Prisons in 2001.

Percent Change in Number of State Prisoners: 2015 to 2016

National Percent Change = 1.0% Decrease*

ALPHA ORDER			RANK ORDER		
RANK	STATE	PERCENT CHANGE	RANK	STATE	PERCENT CHANGE
45	Alabama	(6.3)	1	South Dakota	7.5
47	Alaska	(16.9)	2	Kentucky	6.1
22	Arizona	(0.9)	3	Maine	5.5
24	Arkansas	(1.0)	4	Washington	4.5
11	California	0.6	5	Montana	3.5
19	Colorado	(0.3)	6	Georgia	2.7
43	Connecticut	(5.4)	7	Idaho	2.5
24	Delaware	(1.0)	8	Iowa	2.1
28	Florida	(1.4)	9	Wisconsin	1.7
6	Georgia	2.7	10	Mississippi	1.5
40	Hawaii	(4.7)	11	California	0.6
7	Idaho	2.5	11	Kansas	0.6
NA	Illinois**	NA	11	West Virginia	0.6
46	Indiana	(6.6)	14	Missouri	0.4
8	Iowa	2.1	15	Tennessee	0.1
11	Kansas	0.6	16	Ohio	(0.1)
2	Kentucky	6.1	16	Texas	(0.1)
30	Louisiana	(1.9)	18	North Dakota	(0.2)
3	Maine	5.5	19	Colorado	(0.3)
38	Maryland	(3.7)	19	South Carolina	(0.3)
42	Massachusetts	(5.2)	21	New Mexico	(0.7)
37	Michigan	(3.5)	22	Arizona	(0.9)
30	Minnesota	(1.9)	22	Vermont	(0.9)
10	Mississippi	1.5	24	Arkansas	(1.0)
14	Missouri	0.4	24	Delaware	(1.0)
5	Montana	3.5	26	Pennsylvania	(1.2)
27	Nebraska	(1.3)	27	Nebraska	(1.3)
NA	Nevada**	NA	28	Florida	(1.4)
35	New Hampshire	(2.7)	29	Virginia	(1.5)
36	New Jersey	(3.4)	30	Louisiana	(1.9)
21	New Mexico	(0.7)	30	Minnesota	(1.9)
32	New York	(2.0)	32	New York	(2.0)
34	North Carolina	(2.5)	33	Wyoming	(2.1)
18	North Dakota	(0.2)	34	North Carolina	(2.5)
16	Ohio	(0.1)	35	New Hampshire	(2.7)
44	Oklahoma	(5.9)	36	New Jersey	(3.4)
NA	Oregon**	NA	37	Michigan	(3.5)
26	Pennsylvania	(1.2)	38	Maryland	(3.7)
39	Rhode Island	(4.5)	39	Rhode Island	(4.5)
19	South Carolina	(0.3)	40	Hawaii	(4.7)
1	South Dakota	7.5	41	Utah	(4.8)
15	Tennessee	0.1	42	Massachusetts	(5.2)
16	Texas	(0.1)	43	Connecticut	(5.4)
41	Utah	(4.8)	44	Oklahoma	(5.9)
22	Vermont	(0.9)	45	Alabama	(6.3)
29	Virginia	(1.5)	46	Indiana	(6.6)
4	Washington	4.5	47	Alaska	(16.9)
11	West Virginia	0.6	NA	Illinois**	NA
9	Wisconsin	1.7	NA	Nevada**	NA
33	Wyoming	(2.1)	NA	Oregon**	NA
				District of Columbia***	NA

Source: U.S. Department of Justice, Bureau of Justice Statistics
   "Prisoners in 2016" (January 2018, NCJ 251149, http://bjs.ojp.usdoj.gov/)
*From December 31, 2015 to December 31, 2016. Includes inmates sentenced to more than one year and those sentenced to a year or less or with no sentence. The percent change in number of prisoners under federal jurisdiction during the same period was an 3.7% decrease. The combined state and federal decrease was 1.4%. **Not available.
***Responsibility for sentenced felons in D.C. was transferred to the Federal Bureau of Prisons in 2001.

Prisoners under Sentence of Death as of July 1, 2018 (NAACP)

National Total = 2,674 State Prisoners*

ALPHA ORDER

RANK ORDER

RANK	STATE	PRISONERS	% of USA		RANK	STATE	PRISONERS	% of USA
4	Alabama	185	6.9%		1	California	740	27.7%
NA	Alaska**	NA	NA		2	Florida	353	13.2%
8	Arizona	121	4.5%		3	Texas	232	8.7%
18	Arkansas	31	1.2%		4	Alabama	185	6.9%
1	California	740	27.7%		5	Pennsylvania	160	6.0%
26	Colorado	3	0.1%		6	North Carolina	144	5.4%
NA	Connecticut**	NA	NA		6	Ohio	144	5.4%
NA	Delaware**	NA	NA		8	Arizona	121	4.5%
2	Florida	353	13.2%		9	Nevada	75	2.8%
12	Georgia	56	2.1%		10	Louisiana	71	2.7%
NA	Hawaii**	NA	NA		11	Tennessee	62	2.3%
23	Idaho	9	0.3%		12	Georgia	56	2.1%
NA	Illinois**	NA	NA		13	Oklahoma	49	1.8%
20	Indiana	12	0.4%		14	Mississippi	47	1.8%
NA	Iowa**	NA	NA		15	South Carolina	39	1.5%
22	Kansas	10	0.4%		16	Oregon	33	1.2%
17	Kentucky	32	1.2%		17	Kentucky	32	1.2%
10	Louisiana	71	2.7%		18	Arkansas	31	1.2%
NA	Maine**	NA	NA		19	Missouri	25	0.9%
NA	Maryland**	NA	NA		20	Indiana	12	0.4%
NA	Massachusetts**	NA	NA		20	Nebraska	12	0.4%
NA	Michigan**	NA	NA		22	Kansas	10	0.4%
NA	Minnesota**	NA	NA		23	Idaho	9	0.3%
14	Mississippi	47	1.8%		23	Utah	9	0.3%
19	Missouri	25	0.9%		25	Washington	8	0.3%
29	Montana	2	0.1%		26	Colorado	3	0.1%
20	Nebraska	12	0.4%		26	South Dakota	3	0.1%
9	Nevada	75	2.8%		26	Virginia	3	0.1%
31	New Hampshire	1	0.0%		29	Montana	2	0.1%
NA	New Jersey**	NA	NA		29	New Mexico	2	0.1%
29	New Mexico	2	0.1%		31	New Hampshire	1	0.0%
NA	New York**	NA	NA		31	Wyoming	1	0.0%
6	North Carolina	144	5.4%		NA	Alaska**	NA	NA
NA	North Dakota**	NA	NA		NA	Connecticut**	NA	NA
6	Ohio	144	5.4%		NA	Delaware**	NA	NA
13	Oklahoma	49	1.8%		NA	Hawaii**	NA	NA
16	Oregon	33	1.2%		NA	Illinois**	NA	NA
5	Pennsylvania	160	6.0%		NA	Iowa**	NA	NA
NA	Rhode Island**	NA	NA		NA	Maine**	NA	NA
15	South Carolina	39	1.5%		NA	Maryland**	NA	NA
26	South Dakota	3	0.1%		NA	Massachusetts**	NA	NA
11	Tennessee	62	2.3%		NA	Michigan**	NA	NA
3	Texas	232	8.7%		NA	Minnesota**	NA	NA
23	Utah	9	0.3%		NA	New Jersey**	NA	NA
NA	Vermont**	NA	NA		NA	New York**	NA	NA
26	Virginia	3	0.1%		NA	North Dakota**	NA	NA
25	Washington	8	0.3%		NA	Rhode Island**	NA	NA
NA	West Virginia**	NA	NA		NA	Vermont**	NA	NA
NA	Wisconsin**	NA	NA		NA	West Virginia**	NA	NA
31	Wyoming	1	0.0%		NA	Wisconsin**	NA	NA
					District of Columbia**		NA	NA

Source: NAACP Legal Defense and Educational Fund, Inc., Criminal Justice Project
   "Death Row USA, Summer 2018" (https://www.naacpldf.org/our-thinking/death-row-usa/)
*Total does not include 63 federal prisoners or five military prisoners under sentence of death. Four prisoners are sentenced to death in more than one state and are counted twice.
**No death penalty as of July 1, 2018.

Rate of State and Local Police Officers in 2017

National Rate = 22 Officers per 10,000 Population*

ALPHA ORDER

RANK	STATE	RATE
9	Alabama	23
40	Alaska	17
23	Arizona	21
13	Arkansas	22
35	California	18
30	Colorado	20
13	Connecticut	22
13	Delaware	22
33	Florida	19
13	Georgia	22
13	Hawaii	22
46	Idaho	16
4	Illinois	26
35	Indiana	18
40	Iowa	17
13	Kansas	22
40	Kentucky	17
3	Louisiana	29
35	Maine	18
9	Maryland	23
8	Massachusetts	24
40	Michigan	17
46	Minnesota	16
6	Mississippi	25
13	Missouri	22
35	Montana	18
30	Nebraska	20
40	Nevada	17
13	New Hampshire	22
2	New Jersey	30
9	New Mexico	23
1	New York	39
9	North Carolina	23
23	North Dakota	21
23	Ohio	21
23	Oklahoma	21
48	Oregon	15
23	Pennsylvania	21
13	Rhode Island	22
13	South Carolina	22
33	South Dakota	19
4	Tennessee	26
30	Texas	20
48	Utah	15
40	Vermont	17
23	Virginia	21
50	Washington	14
35	West Virginia	18
23	Wisconsin	21
6	Wyoming	25

RANK ORDER

RANK	STATE	RATE
1	New York	39
2	New Jersey	30
3	Louisiana	29
4	Illinois	26
4	Tennessee	26
6	Mississippi	25
6	Wyoming	25
8	Massachusetts	24
9	Alabama	23
9	Maryland	23
9	New Mexico	23
9	North Carolina	23
13	Arkansas	22
13	Connecticut	22
13	Delaware	22
13	Georgia	22
13	Hawaii	22
13	Kansas	22
13	Missouri	22
13	New Hampshire	22
13	Rhode Island	22
13	South Carolina	22
23	Arizona	21
23	North Dakota	21
23	Ohio	21
23	Oklahoma	21
23	Pennsylvania	21
23	Virginia	21
23	Wisconsin	21
30	Colorado	20
30	Nebraska	20
30	Texas	20
33	Florida	19
33	South Dakota	19
35	California	18
35	Indiana	18
35	Maine	18
35	Montana	18
35	West Virginia	18
40	Alaska	17
40	Iowa	17
40	Kentucky	17
40	Michigan	17
40	Nevada	17
40	Vermont	17
46	Idaho	16
46	Minnesota	16
48	Oregon	15
48	Utah	15
50	Washington	14

| District of Columbia | | 60 |

Source: CQ Press using data from U.S. Bureau of the Census, Governments Division
"Annual Survey of Public Employment and Payroll" (https://www.census.gov/programs-surveys/apes.html)
*Full-time equivalent as of March 2017. Does not include employees of police departments who are not officers.

Per Capita State and Local Government Expenditures for Police Protection in 2016
National Per Capita = $338*

ALPHA ORDER

ALPHA ORDER

RANK	STATE	PER CAPITA
38	Alabama	$257
2	Alaska	499
19	Arizona	326
45	Arkansas	231
3	California	448
16	Colorado	338
14	Connecticut	346
11	Delaware	367
10	Florida	380
37	Georgia	264
23	Hawaii	321
34	Idaho	272
7	Illinois	407
49	Indiana	189
40	Iowa	249
32	Kansas	274
50	Kentucky	160
15	Louisiana	345
46	Maine	222
4	Maryland	441
11	Massachusetts	367
39	Michigan	252
13	Minnesota	348
41	Mississippi	248
27	Missouri	286
28	Montana	279
42	Nebraska	241
8	Nevada	406
25	New Hampshire	293
9	New Jersey	388
17	New Mexico	335
1	New York	505
21	North Carolina	322
31	North Dakota	276
18	Ohio	334
35	Oklahoma	271
21	Oregon	322
26	Pennsylvania	291
6	Rhode Island	412
42	South Carolina	241
44	South Dakota	233
28	Tennessee	279
33	Texas	273
47	Utah	215
24	Vermont	302
30	Virginia	278
36	Washington	268
48	West Virginia	211
20	Wisconsin	325
5	Wyoming	414

RANK ORDER

RANK	STATE	PER CAPITA
1	New York	$505
2	Alaska	499
3	California	448
4	Maryland	441
5	Wyoming	414
6	Rhode Island	412
7	Illinois	407
8	Nevada	406
9	New Jersey	388
10	Florida	380
11	Delaware	367
11	Massachusetts	367
13	Minnesota	348
14	Connecticut	346
15	Louisiana	345
16	Colorado	338
17	New Mexico	335
18	Ohio	334
19	Arizona	326
20	Wisconsin	325
21	North Carolina	322
21	Oregon	322
23	Hawaii	321
24	Vermont	302
25	New Hampshire	293
26	Pennsylvania	291
27	Missouri	286
28	Montana	279
28	Tennessee	279
30	Virginia	278
31	North Dakota	276
32	Kansas	274
33	Texas	273
34	Idaho	272
35	Oklahoma	271
36	Washington	268
37	Georgia	264
38	Alabama	257
39	Michigan	252
40	Iowa	249
41	Mississippi	248
42	Nebraska	241
42	South Carolina	241
44	South Dakota	233
45	Arkansas	231
46	Maine	222
47	Utah	215
48	West Virginia	211
49	Indiana	189
50	Kentucky	160

District of Columbia	864

Source: CQ Press using data from U.S. Bureau of the Census, Governments Division
"2016 State and Local Government Finances" (https://www.census.gov/programs-surveys/gov-finances.html)
*Direct general expenditures.

Per Capita State and Local Government Expenditures for Corrections in 2016

National Per Capita = $241*

ALPHA ORDER

RANK	STATE	PER CAPITA
47	Alabama	$148
1	Alaska	456
16	Arizona	243
29	Arkansas	199
2	California	395
18	Colorado	237
33	Connecticut	191
6	Delaware	325
26	Florida	206
34	Georgia	186
45	Hawaii	152
27	Idaho	204
49	Illinois	144
39	Indiana	175
50	Iowa	142
37	Kansas	177
27	Kentucky	204
16	Louisiana	243
30	Maine	198
7	Maryland	316
43	Massachusetts	164
13	Michigan	253
35	Minnesota	183
42	Mississippi	167
44	Missouri	158
14	Montana	247
12	Nebraska	262
15	Nevada	244
47	New Hampshire	148
21	New Jersey	230
4	New Mexico	333
5	New York	332
36	North Carolina	180
20	North Dakota	232
41	Ohio	172
32	Oklahoma	192
9	Oregon	297
10	Pennsylvania	274
24	Rhode Island	210
45	South Carolina	152
25	South Dakota	208
37	Tennessee	177
23	Texas	212
40	Utah	173
22	Vermont	220
8	Virginia	304
18	Washington	237
31	West Virginia	193
11	Wisconsin	269
3	Wyoming	367

RANK ORDER

RANK	STATE	PER CAPITA
1	Alaska	$456
2	California	395
3	Wyoming	367
4	New Mexico	333
5	New York	332
6	Delaware	325
7	Maryland	316
8	Virginia	304
9	Oregon	297
10	Pennsylvania	274
11	Wisconsin	269
12	Nebraska	262
13	Michigan	253
14	Montana	247
15	Nevada	244
16	Arizona	243
16	Louisiana	243
18	Colorado	237
18	Washington	237
20	North Dakota	232
21	New Jersey	230
22	Vermont	220
23	Texas	212
24	Rhode Island	210
25	South Dakota	208
26	Florida	206
27	Idaho	204
27	Kentucky	204
29	Arkansas	199
30	Maine	198
31	West Virginia	193
32	Oklahoma	192
33	Connecticut	191
34	Georgia	186
35	Minnesota	183
36	North Carolina	180
37	Kansas	177
37	Tennessee	177
39	Indiana	175
40	Utah	173
41	Ohio	172
42	Mississippi	167
43	Massachusetts	164
44	Missouri	158
45	Hawaii	152
45	South Carolina	152
47	Alabama	148
47	New Hampshire	148
49	Illinois	144
50	Iowa	142

| | District of Columbia | 211 |

Source: CQ Press using data from U.S. Bureau of the Census, Governments Division
"2016 State and Local Government Finances" (https://www.census.gov/programs-surveys/gov-finances.html)
*Direct general expenditures.

Per Capita State and Local Government Expenditures for Judicial and Legal Services in 2016
National Per Capita = $143*

ALPHA ORDER

RANK	STATE	PER CAPITA
48	Alabama	$74
1	Alaska	343
21	Arizona	142
48	Arkansas	74
3	California	221
24	Colorado	136
2	Connecticut	231
4	Delaware	219
31	Florida	115
30	Georgia	118
7	Hawaii	206
29	Idaho	119
28	Illinois	121
45	Indiana	86
36	Iowa	114
37	Kansas	113
21	Kentucky	142
17	Louisiana	153
46	Maine	84
16	Maryland	155
13	Massachusetts	159
31	Michigan	115
25	Minnesota	132
43	Mississippi	92
43	Missouri	92
8	Montana	203
41	Nebraska	97
12	Nevada	163
40	New Hampshire	105
10	New Jersey	173
14	New Mexico	157
6	New York	212
47	North Carolina	75
11	North Dakota	167
19	Ohio	150
42	Oklahoma	96
9	Oregon	190
20	Pennsylvania	149
23	Rhode Island	139
50	South Carolina	72
39	South Dakota	106
31	Tennessee	115
38	Texas	108
31	Utah	115
26	Vermont	129
27	Virginia	123
15	Washington	156
18	West Virginia	152
31	Wisconsin	115
5	Wyoming	216

RANK ORDER

RANK	STATE	PER CAPITA
1	Alaska	$343
2	Connecticut	231
3	California	221
4	Delaware	219
5	Wyoming	216
6	New York	212
7	Hawaii	206
8	Montana	203
9	Oregon	190
10	New Jersey	173
11	North Dakota	167
12	Nevada	163
13	Massachusetts	159
14	New Mexico	157
15	Washington	156
16	Maryland	155
17	Louisiana	153
18	West Virginia	152
19	Ohio	150
20	Pennsylvania	149
21	Arizona	142
21	Kentucky	142
23	Rhode Island	139
24	Colorado	136
25	Minnesota	132
26	Vermont	129
27	Virginia	123
28	Illinois	121
29	Idaho	119
30	Georgia	118
31	Florida	115
31	Michigan	115
31	Tennessee	115
31	Utah	115
31	Wisconsin	115
36	Iowa	114
37	Kansas	113
38	Texas	108
39	South Dakota	106
40	New Hampshire	105
41	Nebraska	97
42	Oklahoma	96
43	Mississippi	92
43	Missouri	92
45	Indiana	86
46	Maine	84
47	North Carolina	75
48	Alabama	74
48	Arkansas	74
50	South Carolina	72

District of Columbia 193

Source: CQ Press using data from U.S. Bureau of the Census, Governments Division
"2016 State and Local Government Finances" (https://www.census.gov/programs-surveys/gov-finances.html)
*Direct general expenditures. Includes courts, prosecution and legal services, and public defense.

Base Salary for Justices of States' Highest Courts in 2019

National Average = $176,714*

ALPHA ORDER		
RANK	STATE	SALARY
27	Alabama	$172,716
7	Alaska	205,176
35	Arizona	159,685
25	Arkansas	174,925
1	California	253,189
17	Colorado	182,671
14	Connecticut	185,610
11	Delaware	196,245
5	Florida	220,600
24	Georgia	175,600
4	Hawaii	227,664
41	Idaho	151,400
2	Illinois	234,391
20	Indiana	177,244
26	Iowa	174,808
45	Kansas	142,089
47	Kentucky	138,890
29	Louisiana	170,325
48	Maine	138,070
18	Maryland	181,433
9	Massachusetts	200,984
33	Michigan	164,610
19	Minnesota	177,697
40	Mississippi	152,250
22	Missouri	176,157
44	Montana	144,061
21	Nebraska	176,299
30	Nevada	170,000
23	New Hampshire	175,837
8	New Jersey	201,842
46	New Mexico	139,819
3	New York	230,200
42	North Carolina	149,115
37	North Dakota	157,009
28	Ohio	172,200
38	Oklahoma	154,174
39	Oregon	154,040
6	Pennsylvania	211,027
15	Rhode Island	183,872
43	South Carolina	148,794
49	South Dakota	136,893
13	Tennessee	188,952
31	Texas	168,000
16	Utah	182,950
34	Vermont	163,757
10	Virginia	197,827
12	Washington	190,415
50	West Virginia	136,000
36	Wisconsin	159,297
32	Wyoming	165,000

RANK ORDER		
RANK	STATE	SALARY
1	California	$253,189
2	Illinois	234,391
3	New York	230,200
4	Hawaii	227,664
5	Florida	220,600
6	Pennsylvania	211,027
7	Alaska	205,176
8	New Jersey	201,842
9	Massachusetts	200,984
10	Virginia	197,827
11	Delaware	196,245
12	Washington	190,415
13	Tennessee	188,952
14	Connecticut	185,610
15	Rhode Island	183,872
16	Utah	182,950
17	Colorado	182,671
18	Maryland	181,433
19	Minnesota	177,697
20	Indiana	177,244
21	Nebraska	176,299
22	Missouri	176,157
23	New Hampshire	175,837
24	Georgia	175,600
25	Arkansas	174,925
26	Iowa	174,808
27	Alabama	172,716
28	Ohio	172,200
29	Louisiana	170,325
30	Nevada	170,000
31	Texas	168,000
32	Wyoming	165,000
33	Michigan	164,610
34	Vermont	163,757
35	Arizona	159,685
36	Wisconsin	159,297
37	North Dakota	157,009
38	Oklahoma	154,174
39	Oregon	154,040
40	Mississippi	152,250
41	Idaho	151,400
42	North Carolina	149,115
43	South Carolina	148,794
44	Montana	144,061
45	Kansas	142,089
46	New Mexico	139,819
47	Kentucky	138,890
48	Maine	138,070
49	South Dakota	136,893
50	West Virginia	136,000
	District of Columbia	220,600

Source: National Center for State Courts
"Survey of Judicial Salaries" (Volume 44, Number 1, https://www.ncsc.org/salarytracker)
*As of January 2019.

Base Salary for Judges of General Trial Courts in 2019

National Average = $158,748*

ALPHA ORDER			RANK ORDER		
RANK	STATE	SALARY	RANK	STATE	SALARY
40	Alabama	$138,991	1	New York	$208,000
5	Alaska	189,720	2	California	207,424
29	Arizona	149,383	3	Hawaii	205,080
15	Arkansas	168,096	4	Illinois	202,433
2	California	207,424	5	Alaska	189,720
14	Colorado	168,202	6	Massachusetts	184,694
16	Connecticut	167,634	7	Delaware	184,444
7	Delaware	184,444	8	Pennsylvania	183,184
21	Florida	160,688	9	New Jersey	181,000
11	Georgia	173,714	10	Tennessee	176,364
3	Hawaii	205,080	11	Georgia	173,714
42	Idaho	135,400	12	Washington	172,571
4	Illinois	202,433	13	Virginia	171,120
33	Indiana	147,164	14	Colorado	168,202
32	Iowa	147,494	15	Arkansas	168,096
50	Kansas	125,499	16	Connecticut	167,634
47	Kentucky	127,733	17	Utah	166,300
26	Louisiana	153,143	18	Rhode Island	165,545
45	Maine	129,397	19	New Hampshire	164,911
23	Maryland	159,433	20	Nebraska	163,077
6	Massachusetts	184,694	21	Florida	160,688
34	Michigan	146,721	22	Nevada	160,000
24	Minnesota	157,179	23	Maryland	159,433
41	Mississippi	136,000	24	Minnesota	157,179
27	Missouri	151,840	25	Vermont	155,677
44	Montana	132,558	26	Louisiana	153,143
20	Nebraska	163,077	27	Missouri	151,840
22	Nevada	160,000	28	Wyoming	150,000
19	New Hampshire	164,911	29	Arizona	149,383
9	New Jersey	181,000	30	Texas	149,000
48	New Mexico	126,187	31	Ohio	147,600
1	New York	208,000	32	Iowa	147,494
43	North Carolina	135,236	33	Indiana	147,164
35	North Dakota	143,869	34	Michigan	146,721
31	Ohio	147,600	35	North Dakota	143,869
39	Oklahoma	139,298	36	Oregon	142,136
36	Oregon	142,136	37	Wisconsin	141,773
8	Pennsylvania	183,184	38	South Carolina	141,354
18	Rhode Island	165,545	39	Oklahoma	139,298
38	South Carolina	141,354	40	Alabama	138,991
46	South Dakota	127,862	41	Mississippi	136,000
10	Tennessee	176,364	42	Idaho	135,400
30	Texas	149,000	43	North Carolina	135,236
17	Utah	166,300	44	Montana	132,558
25	Vermont	155,677	45	Maine	129,397
13	Virginia	171,120	46	South Dakota	127,862
12	Washington	172,571	47	Kentucky	127,733
49	West Virginia	126,000	48	New Mexico	126,187
37	Wisconsin	141,773	49	West Virginia	126,000
28	Wyoming	150,000	50	Kansas	125,499
				District of Columbia	208,000

Source: National Center for State Courts
   "Survey of Judicial Salaries" (Volume 44, Number 1, https://www.ncsc.org/salarytracker)
*As of January 2019.

III. Defense

Homeland Security Grants in 2018

National Total = $982,000,000*

ALPHA ORDER

RANK	STATE	GRANTS	% of USA
23	Alabama	$3,980,000	0.4%
23	Alaska	3,980,000	0.4%
16	Arizona	7,980,000	0.8%
23	Arkansas	3,980,000	0.4%
2	California	181,935,000	18.5%
19	Colorado	6,980,000	0.7%
23	Connecticut	3,980,000	0.4%
23	Delaware	3,980,000	0.4%
8	Florida	21,066,000	2.1%
9	Georgia	12,508,000	1.3%
22	Hawaii	5,480,000	0.6%
23	Idaho	3,980,000	0.4%
3	Illinois	83,712,000	8.5%
23	Indiana	3,980,000	0.4%
23	Iowa	3,980,000	0.4%
23	Kansas	3,980,000	0.4%
23	Kentucky	3,980,000	0.4%
23	Louisiana	3,980,000	0.4%
23	Maine	3,980,000	0.4%
12	Maryland	9,882,000	1.0%
7	Massachusetts	22,895,000	2.3%
10	Michigan	11,368,000	1.2%
13	Minnesota	8,980,000	0.9%
23	Mississippi	3,980,000	0.4%
19	Missouri	6,980,000	0.7%
23	Montana	3,980,000	0.4%
23	Nebraska	3,980,000	0.4%
13	Nevada	8,980,000	0.9%
23	New Hampshire	3,980,000	0.4%
5	New Jersey	30,743,000	3.1%
23	New Mexico	3,980,000	0.4%
1	New York	255,680,000	26.0%
17	North Carolina	7,746,000	0.8%
23	North Dakota	3,980,000	0.4%
18	Ohio	7,364,000	0.7%
23	Oklahoma	3,980,000	0.4%
21	Oregon	6,480,000	0.7%
6	Pennsylvania	29,622,000	3.0%
23	Rhode Island	3,980,000	0.4%
23	South Carolina	3,980,000	0.4%
23	South Dakota	3,980,000	0.4%
23	Tennessee	3,980,000	0.4%
4	Texas	59,641,000	6.1%
50	Utah	1,000,000	0.1%
23	Vermont	3,980,000	0.4%
15	Virginia	8,620,000	0.9%
11	Washington	11,208,000	1.1%
23	West Virginia	3,980,000	0.4%
23	Wisconsin	3,980,000	0.4%
23	Wyoming	3,980,000	0.4%

RANK ORDER

RANK	STATE	GRANTS	% of USA
1	New York	$255,680,000	26.0%
2	California	181,935,000	18.5%
3	Illinois	83,712,000	8.5%
4	Texas	59,641,000	6.1%
5	New Jersey	30,743,000	3.1%
6	Pennsylvania	29,622,000	3.0%
7	Massachusetts	22,895,000	2.3%
8	Florida	21,066,000	2.1%
9	Georgia	12,508,000	1.3%
10	Michigan	11,368,000	1.2%
11	Washington	11,208,000	1.1%
12	Maryland	9,882,000	1.0%
13	Minnesota	8,980,000	0.9%
13	Nevada	8,980,000	0.9%
15	Virginia	8,620,000	0.9%
16	Arizona	7,980,000	0.8%
17	North Carolina	7,746,000	0.8%
18	Ohio	7,364,000	0.7%
19	Colorado	6,980,000	0.7%
19	Missouri	6,980,000	0.7%
21	Oregon	6,480,000	0.7%
22	Hawaii	5,480,000	0.6%
23	Alabama	3,980,000	0.4%
23	Alaska	3,980,000	0.4%
23	Arkansas	3,980,000	0.4%
23	Connecticut	3,980,000	0.4%
23	Delaware	3,980,000	0.4%
23	Idaho	3,980,000	0.4%
23	Indiana	3,980,000	0.4%
23	Iowa	3,980,000	0.4%
23	Kansas	3,980,000	0.4%
23	Kentucky	3,980,000	0.4%
23	Louisiana	3,980,000	0.4%
23	Maine	3,980,000	0.4%
23	Mississippi	3,980,000	0.4%
23	Montana	3,980,000	0.4%
23	Nebraska	3,980,000	0.4%
23	New Hampshire	3,980,000	0.4%
23	New Mexico	3,980,000	0.4%
23	North Dakota	3,980,000	0.4%
23	Oklahoma	3,980,000	0.4%
23	Rhode Island	3,980,000	0.4%
23	South Carolina	3,980,000	0.4%
23	South Dakota	3,980,000	0.4%
23	Tennessee	3,980,000	0.4%
23	Vermont	3,980,000	0.4%
23	West Virginia	3,980,000	0.4%
23	Wisconsin	3,980,000	0.4%
23	Wyoming	3,980,000	0.4%
50	Utah	1,000,000	0.1%
	District of Columbia	56,730,000	5.8%

Source: CQ Press using data from U.S. Department of Homeland Security
"FY 2018 Homeland Security Grant Program (HSGP)" (https://www.fema.gov/media-library/assets/documents/164422)
*For fiscal year 2018. National total includes $10,960,000 in grants to U.S. territories. The Homeland Security Grant Program (HSGP) includes three sub-grant programs: State Homeland Security Program (SHSP), Urban Area Security Initiative (UASI), and Operation Stonegarden (OPSG). Law Enforcement Terrorism Prevention Activities (LETPA) allocations are a 25 percent subset of the SHSP and UASI allocations.

Per Capita Homeland Security Grants in 2018

National Per Capita = $2.97*

ALPHA ORDER			RANK ORDER		
RANK	STATE	PER CAPITA	RANK	STATE	PER CAPITA
43	Alabama	$0.81	1	New York	$13.08
5	Alaska	5.40	2	Wyoming	6.89
36	Arizona	1.11	3	Illinois	6.57
30	Arkansas	1.32	4	Vermont	6.35
7	California	4.60	5	Alaska	5.40
32	Colorado	1.23	6	North Dakota	5.24
36	Connecticut	1.11	7	California	4.60
9	Delaware	4.12	8	South Dakota	4.51
40	Florida	0.99	9	Delaware	4.12
33	Georgia	1.19	10	Hawaii	3.86
10	Hawaii	3.86	11	Rhode Island	3.76
19	Idaho	2.27	12	Montana	3.75
3	Illinois	6.57	13	New Jersey	3.45
48	Indiana	0.59	14	Massachusetts	3.32
31	Iowa	1.26	15	Maine	2.97
28	Kansas	1.37	16	Nevada	2.96
41	Kentucky	0.89	17	New Hampshire	2.93
42	Louisiana	0.85	18	Pennsylvania	2.31
15	Maine	2.97	19	Idaho	2.27
24	Maryland	1.64	20	West Virginia	2.20
14	Massachusetts	3.32	21	Texas	2.08
34	Michigan	1.14	22	Nebraska	2.06
25	Minnesota	1.60	23	New Mexico	1.90
29	Mississippi	1.33	24	Maryland	1.64
34	Missouri	1.14	25	Minnesota	1.60
12	Montana	3.75	26	Oregon	1.55
22	Nebraska	2.06	27	Washington	1.49
16	Nevada	2.96	28	Kansas	1.37
17	New Hampshire	2.93	29	Mississippi	1.33
13	New Jersey	3.45	30	Arkansas	1.32
23	New Mexico	1.90	31	Iowa	1.26
1	New York	13.08	32	Colorado	1.23
45	North Carolina	0.75	33	Georgia	1.19
6	North Dakota	5.24	34	Michigan	1.14
47	Ohio	0.63	34	Missouri	1.14
38	Oklahoma	1.01	36	Arizona	1.11
26	Oregon	1.55	36	Connecticut	1.11
18	Pennsylvania	2.31	38	Oklahoma	1.01
11	Rhode Island	3.76	38	Virginia	1.01
44	South Carolina	0.78	40	Florida	0.99
8	South Dakota	4.51	41	Kentucky	0.89
48	Tennessee	0.59	42	Louisiana	0.85
21	Texas	2.08	43	Alabama	0.81
50	Utah	0.32	44	South Carolina	0.78
4	Vermont	6.35	45	North Carolina	0.75
38	Virginia	1.01	46	Wisconsin	0.68
27	Washington	1.49	47	Ohio	0.63
20	West Virginia	2.20	48	Indiana	0.59
46	Wisconsin	0.68	48	Tennessee	0.59
2	Wyoming	6.89	50	Utah	0.32
				District of Columbia	80.76

Source: CQ Press using data from CQ Press using data from U.S. Department of Homeland Security
"FY 2018 Homeland Security Grant Program (HSGP)" (https://www.fema.gov/media-library/assets/documents/164422)
*For fiscal year 2018. National per capita does not include grants to U.S. territories. The Homeland Security Grant Program (HSGP) includes three sub-grant programs: State Homeland Security Program (SHSP), Urban Area Security Initiative (UASI), and Operation Stonegarden (OPSG). Law Enforcement Terrorism Prevention Activities (LETPA) allocations are a 25 percent subset of the SHSP and UASI allocations.

U.S. Department of Defense Expenditures in 2016

National Total = $304,130,236,000*

ALPHA ORDER

RANK	STATE	EXPENDITURES	% of USA
13	Alabama	$8,803,865,865	2.9%
33	Alaska	1,264,175,606	0.4%
11	Arizona	9,465,055,712	3.1%
43	Arkansas	338,703,740	0.1%
1	California	32,977,026,967	10.8%
17	Colorado	5,674,941,822	1.9%
4	Connecticut	14,222,273,291	4.7%
49	Delaware	167,872,046	0.1%
5	Florida	14,004,642,555	4.6%
12	Georgia	9,288,937,106	3.1%
28	Hawaii	1,938,085,080	0.6%
44	Idaho	242,102,947	0.1%
18	Illinois	5,590,394,480	1.8%
23	Indiana	3,016,864,706	1.0%
36	Iowa	1,163,340,186	0.4%
38	Kansas	807,063,040	0.3%
15	Kentucky	5,794,454,391	1.9%
31	Louisiana	1,593,644,871	0.5%
29	Maine	1,722,848,278	0.6%
6	Maryland	13,423,295,717	4.4%
10	Massachusetts	9,705,444,559	3.2%
24	Michigan	2,910,001,119	1.0%
19	Minnesota	3,799,723,354	1.2%
21	Mississippi	3,686,805,490	1.2%
8	Missouri	10,219,272,694	3.4%
46	Montana	209,379,802	0.1%
41	Nebraska	633,683,163	0.2%
32	Nevada	1,507,974,267	0.5%
37	New Hampshire	1,159,215,300	0.4%
16	New Jersey	5,679,797,165	1.9%
34	New Mexico	1,214,274,173	0.4%
14	New York	5,966,682,617	2.0%
25	North Carolina	2,597,171,717	0.9%
47	North Dakota	203,389,512	0.1%
20	Ohio	3,728,095,837	1.2%
22	Oklahoma	3,116,014,210	1.0%
39	Oregon	676,590,911	0.2%
7	Pennsylvania	11,499,327,993	3.8%
40	Rhode Island	671,310,143	0.2%
26	South Carolina	2,504,786,411	0.8%
48	South Dakota	196,225,175	0.1%
30	Tennessee	1,714,998,616	0.6%
3	Texas	28,533,522,115	9.4%
35	Utah	1,165,742,178	0.4%
42	Vermont	365,412,133	0.1%
2	Virginia	31,857,315,547	10.5%
9	Washington	9,716,487,972	3.2%
45	West Virginia	222,514,242	0.1%
27	Wisconsin	2,474,023,606	0.8%
50	Wyoming	117,900,643	0.0%

RANK ORDER

RANK	STATE	EXPENDITURES	% of USA
1	California	$32,977,026,967	10.8%
2	Virginia	31,857,315,547	10.5%
3	Texas	28,533,522,115	9.4%
4	Connecticut	14,222,273,291	4.7%
5	Florida	14,004,642,555	4.6%
6	Maryland	13,423,295,717	4.4%
7	Pennsylvania	11,499,327,993	3.8%
8	Missouri	10,219,272,694	3.4%
9	Washington	9,716,487,972	3.2%
10	Massachusetts	9,705,444,559	3.2%
11	Arizona	9,465,055,712	3.1%
12	Georgia	9,288,937,106	3.1%
13	Alabama	8,803,865,865	2.9%
14	New York	5,966,682,617	2.0%
15	Kentucky	5,794,454,391	1.9%
16	New Jersey	5,679,797,165	1.9%
17	Colorado	5,674,941,822	1.9%
18	Illinois	5,590,394,480	1.8%
19	Minnesota	3,799,723,354	1.2%
20	Ohio	3,728,095,837	1.2%
21	Mississippi	3,686,805,490	1.2%
22	Oklahoma	3,116,014,210	1.0%
23	Indiana	3,016,864,706	1.0%
24	Michigan	2,910,001,119	1.0%
25	North Carolina	2,597,171,717	0.9%
26	South Carolina	2,504,786,411	0.8%
27	Wisconsin	2,474,023,606	0.8%
28	Hawaii	1,938,085,080	0.6%
29	Maine	1,722,848,278	0.6%
30	Tennessee	1,714,998,616	0.6%
31	Louisiana	1,593,644,871	0.5%
32	Nevada	1,507,974,267	0.5%
33	Alaska	1,264,175,606	0.4%
34	New Mexico	1,214,274,173	0.4%
35	Utah	1,165,742,178	0.4%
36	Iowa	1,163,340,186	0.4%
37	New Hampshire	1,159,215,300	0.4%
38	Kansas	807,063,040	0.3%
39	Oregon	676,590,911	0.2%
40	Rhode Island	671,310,143	0.2%
41	Nebraska	633,683,163	0.2%
42	Vermont	365,412,133	0.1%
43	Arkansas	338,703,740	0.1%
44	Idaho	242,102,947	0.1%
45	West Virginia	222,514,242	0.1%
46	Montana	209,379,802	0.1%
47	North Dakota	203,389,512	0.1%
48	South Dakota	196,225,175	0.1%
49	Delaware	167,872,046	0.1%
50	Wyoming	117,900,643	0.0%
	District of Columbia	3,887,430,578	1.3%

Source: U.S. Office of Management and Budget, USAspending.gov
   "Prime Award Spending Data Summary" (https://www.usaspending.gov/, as of January 26, 2018)
*Total includes $20,690,135,000 in U.S. territories and in expenditures not distributed by state. Expenditures allocated based on place of performance of a contract. Includes Contracts, Grants, Direct Payments, Insurance, and "Other." This source replaces a previous data series, "Atlas/Data Abstract for the United States", and definitions may differ.

Per Capita U.S. Department of Defense Expenditures in 2016

National Per Capita = $876*

RANK	STATE	PER CAPITA
4	Alabama	$1,811
5	Alaska	1,705
8	Arizona	1,370
50	Arkansas	113
19	California	839
15	Colorado	1,026
1	Connecticut	3,964
46	Delaware	176
22	Florida	678
16	Georgia	901
9	Hawaii	1,357
48	Idaho	144
30	Illinois	436
29	Indiana	455
33	Iowa	372
39	Kansas	278
11	Kentucky	1,306
34	Louisiana	340
12	Maine	1,295
3	Maryland	2,228
7	Massachusetts	1,422
38	Michigan	293
21	Minnesota	688
13	Mississippi	1,235
6	Missouri	1,678
44	Montana	202
35	Nebraska	332
27	Nevada	513
18	New Hampshire	868
24	New Jersey	633
26	New Mexico	582
37	New York	301
42	North Carolina	256
40	North Dakota	269
36	Ohio	321
20	Oklahoma	795
47	Oregon	168
17	Pennsylvania	899
23	Rhode Island	636
28	South Carolina	512
43	South Dakota	229
41	Tennessee	260
14	Texas	1,040
32	Utah	390
25	Vermont	584
2	Virginia	3,807
9	Washington	1,357
49	West Virginia	121
31	Wisconsin	429
45	Wyoming	201

RANK	STATE	PER CAPITA
1	Connecticut	$3,964
2	Virginia	3,807
3	Maryland	2,228
4	Alabama	1,811
5	Alaska	1,705
6	Missouri	1,678
7	Massachusetts	1,422
8	Arizona	1,370
9	Hawaii	1,357
9	Washington	1,357
11	Kentucky	1,306
12	Maine	1,295
13	Mississippi	1,235
14	Texas	1,040
15	Colorado	1,026
16	Georgia	901
17	Pennsylvania	899
18	New Hampshire	868
19	California	839
20	Oklahoma	795
21	Minnesota	688
22	Florida	678
23	Rhode Island	636
24	New Jersey	633
25	Vermont	584
26	New Mexico	582
27	Nevada	513
28	South Carolina	512
29	Indiana	455
30	Illinois	436
31	Wisconsin	429
32	Utah	390
33	Iowa	372
34	Louisiana	340
35	Nebraska	332
36	Ohio	321
37	New York	301
38	Michigan	293
39	Kansas	278
40	North Dakota	269
41	Tennessee	260
42	North Carolina	256
43	South Dakota	229
44	Montana	202
45	Wyoming	201
46	Delaware	176
47	Oregon	168
48	Idaho	144
49	West Virginia	121
50	Arkansas	113
	District of Columbia	5,681

Source: CQ Press using data from U.S. Office of Management and Budget, USAspending.gov
"Prime Award Spending Data Summary" (https://www.usaspending.gov/, as of January 26, 2018)
*National per capita excludes expenditures and population for territories and undistributed amounts. Expenditures allocated based on place of performance of a contract. Includes Contracts, Grants, Direct Payments, Insurance, and "Other." This source replaces a previous data series, "Atlas/Data Abstract for the United States", and definitions may differ.

U.S. Department of Defense Expenditures as a Percent of Total Federal Government Expenditures in 2016
National Percent = 9.5%*

ALPHA ORDER			RANK ORDER		
RANK	STATE	PERCENT	RANK	STATE	PERCENT
14	Alabama	13.2	1	Virginia	33.6
8	Alaska	15.8	2	Maryland	20.1
14	Arizona	13.2	3	Missouri	19.3
48	Arkansas	1.5	4	Connecticut	19.1
17	California	11.4	5	Hawaii	17.4
12	Colorado	14.4	6	Texas	16.8
4	Connecticut	19.1	7	Washington	16.7
42	Delaware	2.5	8	Alaska	15.8
21	Florida	8.2	9	Massachusetts	15.6
13	Georgia	14.3	10	Mississippi	15.0
5	Hawaii	17.4	11	Maine	14.8
47	Idaho	2.0	12	Colorado	14.4
24	Illinois	6.9	13	Georgia	14.3
44	Indiana	2.3	14	Alabama	13.2
30	Iowa	5.0	14	Arizona	13.2
30	Kansas	5.0	16	New Hampshire	12.0
26	Kentucky	6.5	17	California	11.4
34	Louisiana	4.5	18	Oklahoma	11.0
11	Maine	14.8	19	New Jersey	9.3
2	Maryland	20.1	20	Nevada	8.5
9	Massachusetts	15.6	21	Florida	8.2
36	Michigan	3.8	22	Utah	8.0
33	Minnesota	4.7	23	Rhode Island	7.5
10	Mississippi	15.0	24	Illinois	6.9
3	Missouri	19.3	25	Vermont	6.7
42	Montana	2.5	26	Kentucky	6.5
29	Nebraska	5.2	27	Pennsylvania	5.9
20	Nevada	8.5	28	New Mexico	5.3
16	New Hampshire	12.0	29	Nebraska	5.2
19	New Jersey	9.3	30	Iowa	5.0
28	New Mexico	5.3	30	Kansas	5.0
36	New York	3.8	32	Ohio	4.9
35	North Carolina	4.1	33	Minnesota	4.7
50	North Dakota	0.3	34	Louisiana	4.5
32	Ohio	4.9	35	North Carolina	4.1
18	Oklahoma	11.0	36	Michigan	3.8
46	Oregon	2.1	36	New York	3.8
27	Pennsylvania	5.9	38	South Carolina	3.2
23	Rhode Island	7.5	39	South Dakota	2.9
38	South Carolina	3.2	39	Wisconsin	2.9
39	South Dakota	2.9	41	Wyoming	2.8
44	Tennessee	2.3	42	Delaware	2.5
6	Texas	16.8	42	Montana	2.5
22	Utah	8.0	44	Indiana	2.3
25	Vermont	6.7	44	Tennessee	2.3
1	Virginia	33.6	46	Oregon	2.1
7	Washington	16.7	47	Idaho	2.0
48	West Virginia	1.5	48	Arkansas	1.5
39	Wisconsin	2.9	48	West Virginia	1.5
41	Wyoming	2.8	50	North Dakota	0.3
				District of Columbia	12.5

Source: CQ Press using data from U.S. Office of Management and Budget, USAspending.gov
"Prime Award Spending Data Summary" (https://www.usaspending.gov/, as of January 26, 2018)
*National percent excludes expenditures and population for territories and undistributed amounts. Expenditures allocated based on place of performance of a contract. Includes Contracts, Grants, Direct Payments, Insurance, and "Other." This source replaces a previous data series, "Atlas/Data Abstract for the United States", and definitions may differ.

U.S. Active Duty Military Personnel Stationed in the United States in 2017

National Total = 1,039,640 Personnel*

RANK	STATE	PERSONNEL	% of USA
24	Alabama	8,022	0.8%
18	Alaska	17,659	1.7%
17	Arizona	18,975	1.8%
31	Arkansas	3,557	0.3%
1	California	127,720	12.3%
10	Colorado	35,192	3.4%
30	Connecticut	3,992	0.4%
32	Delaware	3,446	0.3%
6	Florida	53,559	5.2%
5	Georgia	63,448	6.1%
9	Hawaii	35,796	3.4%
33	Idaho	3,438	0.3%
14	Illinois	20,660	2.0%
42	Indiana	932	0.1%
48	Iowa	216	0.0%
13	Kansas	22,160	2.1%
11	Kentucky	32,933	3.2%
20	Louisiana	14,503	1.4%
47	Maine	239	0.0%
12	Maryland	28,405	2.7%
39	Massachusetts	1,976	0.2%
41	Michigan	987	0.1%
46	Minnesota	470	0.0%
22	Mississippi	11,509	1.1%
19	Missouri	17,145	1.6%
35	Montana	3,328	0.3%
27	Nebraska	6,295	0.6%
23	Nevada	10,892	1.0%
45	New Hampshire	506	0.0%
28	New Jersey	6,084	0.6%
21	New Mexico	12,319	1.2%
16	New York	20,344	2.0%
3	North Carolina	97,025	9.3%
25	North Dakota	7,297	0.7%
26	Ohio	6,551	0.6%
15	Oklahoma	20,433	2.0%
44	Oregon	542	0.1%
38	Pennsylvania	2,279	0.2%
37	Rhode Island	3,053	0.3%
8	South Carolina	37,304	3.6%
34	South Dakota	3,370	0.3%
40	Tennessee	1,952	0.2%
2	Texas	116,810	11.2%
29	Utah	4,206	0.4%
50	Vermont	130	0.0%
4	Virginia	88,045	8.5%
7	Washington	45,793	4.4%
49	West Virginia	132	0.0%
43	Wisconsin	696	0.1%
36	Wyoming	3,147	0.3%

RANK	STATE	PERSONNEL	% of USA
1	California	127,720	12.3%
2	Texas	116,810	11.2%
3	North Carolina	97,025	9.3%
4	Virginia	88,045	8.5%
5	Georgia	63,448	6.1%
6	Florida	53,559	5.2%
7	Washington	45,793	4.4%
8	South Carolina	37,304	3.6%
9	Hawaii	35,796	3.4%
10	Colorado	35,192	3.4%
11	Kentucky	32,933	3.2%
12	Maryland	28,405	2.7%
13	Kansas	22,160	2.1%
14	Illinois	20,660	2.0%
15	Oklahoma	20,433	2.0%
16	New York	20,344	2.0%
17	Arizona	18,975	1.8%
18	Alaska	17,659	1.7%
19	Missouri	17,145	1.6%
20	Louisiana	14,503	1.4%
21	New Mexico	12,319	1.2%
22	Mississippi	11,509	1.1%
23	Nevada	10,892	1.0%
24	Alabama	8,022	0.8%
25	North Dakota	7,297	0.7%
26	Ohio	6,551	0.6%
27	Nebraska	6,295	0.6%
28	New Jersey	6,084	0.6%
29	Utah	4,206	0.4%
30	Connecticut	3,992	0.4%
31	Arkansas	3,557	0.3%
32	Delaware	3,446	0.3%
33	Idaho	3,438	0.3%
34	South Dakota	3,370	0.3%
35	Montana	3,328	0.3%
36	Wyoming	3,147	0.3%
37	Rhode Island	3,053	0.3%
38	Pennsylvania	2,279	0.2%
39	Massachusetts	1,976	0.2%
40	Tennessee	1,952	0.2%
41	Michigan	987	0.1%
42	Indiana	932	0.1%
43	Wisconsin	696	0.1%
44	Oregon	542	0.1%
45	New Hampshire	506	0.0%
46	Minnesota	470	0.0%
47	Maine	239	0.0%
48	Iowa	216	0.0%
49	West Virginia	132	0.0%
50	Vermont	130	0.0%
	District of Columbia	8,269	0.8%

Source: U.S. Department of Defense

"Demographics 2017" (https://www.militaryonesource.mil/reports-and-surveys/demographic-profiles)

*Includes 5,899 not shown by state. Numbers reflect where the personnel are stationed.

U.S. Selected Reserve Personnel Stationed in the United States in 2017

National Total = 790,459 Personnel*

ALPHA ORDER

RANK	STATE	PERSONNEL	% of USA
11	Alabama	19,709	2.5%
43	Alaska	4,664	0.6%
24	Arizona	15,144	1.9%
30	Arkansas	11,177	1.4%
1	California	57,031	7.2%
27	Colorado	13,467	1.7%
37	Connecticut	6,876	0.9%
41	Delaware	5,024	0.6%
3	Florida	36,772	4.7%
7	Georgia	27,184	3.4%
34	Hawaii	9,542	1.2%
39	Idaho	5,457	0.7%
9	Illinois	24,516	3.1%
13	Indiana	19,082	2.4%
31	Iowa	10,905	1.4%
32	Kansas	10,328	1.3%
28	Kentucky	12,786	1.6%
20	Louisiana	17,275	2.2%
48	Maine	3,913	0.5%
14	Maryland	19,012	2.4%
22	Massachusetts	15,334	1.9%
23	Michigan	15,243	1.9%
16	Minnesota	18,796	2.4%
21	Mississippi	16,653	2.1%
12	Missouri	19,566	2.5%
44	Montana	4,459	0.6%
38	Nebraska	6,316	0.8%
36	Nevada	7,740	1.0%
47	New Hampshire	4,239	0.5%
19	New Jersey	17,340	2.2%
40	New Mexico	5,143	0.7%
5	New York	29,271	3.7%
10	North Carolina	22,009	2.8%
45	North Dakota	4,421	0.6%
6	Ohio	28,267	3.6%
26	Oklahoma	13,736	1.7%
33	Oregon	9,602	1.2%
4	Pennsylvania	31,112	3.9%
46	Rhode Island	4,311	0.5%
18	South Carolina	18,120	2.3%
42	South Dakota	4,703	0.6%
17	Tennessee	18,423	2.3%
2	Texas	54,628	6.9%
29	Utah	11,929	1.5%
49	Vermont	3,709	0.5%
8	Virginia	26,747	3.4%
15	Washington	18,909	2.4%
35	West Virginia	8,173	1.0%
25	Wisconsin	14,512	1.8%
50	Wyoming	2,916	0.4%

RANK ORDER

RANK	STATE	PERSONNEL	% of USA
1	California	57,031	7.2%
2	Texas	54,628	6.9%
3	Florida	36,772	4.7%
4	Pennsylvania	31,112	3.9%
5	New York	29,271	3.7%
6	Ohio	28,267	3.6%
7	Georgia	27,184	3.4%
8	Virginia	26,747	3.4%
9	Illinois	24,516	3.1%
10	North Carolina	22,009	2.8%
11	Alabama	19,709	2.5%
12	Missouri	19,566	2.5%
13	Indiana	19,082	2.4%
14	Maryland	19,012	2.4%
15	Washington	18,909	2.4%
16	Minnesota	18,796	2.4%
17	Tennessee	18,423	2.3%
18	South Carolina	18,120	2.3%
19	New Jersey	17,340	2.2%
20	Louisiana	17,275	2.2%
21	Mississippi	16,653	2.1%
22	Massachusetts	15,334	1.9%
23	Michigan	15,243	1.9%
24	Arizona	15,144	1.9%
25	Wisconsin	14,512	1.8%
26	Oklahoma	13,736	1.7%
27	Colorado	13,467	1.7%
28	Kentucky	12,786	1.6%
29	Utah	11,929	1.5%
30	Arkansas	11,177	1.4%
31	Iowa	10,905	1.4%
32	Kansas	10,328	1.3%
33	Oregon	9,602	1.2%
34	Hawaii	9,542	1.2%
35	West Virginia	8,173	1.0%
36	Nevada	7,740	1.0%
37	Connecticut	6,876	0.9%
38	Nebraska	6,316	0.8%
39	Idaho	5,457	0.7%
40	New Mexico	5,143	0.7%
41	Delaware	5,024	0.6%
42	South Dakota	4,703	0.6%
43	Alaska	4,664	0.6%
44	Montana	4,459	0.6%
45	North Dakota	4,421	0.6%
46	Rhode Island	4,311	0.5%
47	New Hampshire	4,239	0.5%
48	Maine	3,913	0.5%
49	Vermont	3,709	0.5%
50	Wyoming	2,916	0.4%
	District of Columbia	4,268	0.5%

Source: U.S. Department of Defense
"Demographics 2017" (https://www.militaryonesource.mil/reports-and-surveys/demographic-profiles)
*Numbers reflect where the personnel are stationed.

Veterans in 2018

National Total = 19,602,316 Veterans*

ALPHA ORDER					RANK ORDER			
RANK	STATE	VETERANS	% of USA		RANK	STATE	VETERANS	% of USA
20	Alabama	365,895	1.9%		1	California	1,629,238	8.3%
45	Alaska	68,847	0.4%		2	Texas	1,574,021	8.0%
13	Arizona	500,133	2.6%		3	Florida	1,491,070	7.6%
29	Arkansas	219,334	1.1%		4	Pennsylvania	793,321	4.0%
1	California	1,629,238	8.3%		5	Ohio	753,809	3.8%
18	Colorado	398,783	2.0%		6	New York	747,146	3.8%
34	Connecticut	177,235	0.9%		7	North Carolina	728,178	3.7%
44	Delaware	70,798	0.4%		8	Virginia	719,916	3.7%
3	Florida	1,491,070	7.6%		9	Georgia	694,168	3.5%
9	Georgia	694,168	3.5%		10	Illinois	609,881	3.1%
40	Hawaii	111,459	0.6%		11	Michigan	570,662	2.9%
39	Idaho	120,903	0.6%		12	Washington	552,291	2.8%
10	Illinois	609,881	3.1%		13	Arizona	500,133	2.6%
16	Indiana	401,070	2.0%		14	Tennessee	465,675	2.4%
31	Iowa	201,353	1.0%		15	Missouri	434,373	2.2%
32	Kansas	191,353	1.0%		16	Indiana	401,070	2.0%
27	Kentucky	291,660	1.5%		17	South Carolina	400,742	2.0%
28	Louisiana	280,549	1.4%		18	Colorado	398,783	2.0%
41	Maine	111,266	0.6%		19	Maryland	380,317	1.9%
19	Maryland	380,317	1.9%		20	Alabama	365,895	1.9%
24	Massachusetts	310,649	1.6%		21	Wisconsin	354,266	1.8%
11	Michigan	570,662	2.9%		22	New Jersey	340,561	1.7%
23	Minnesota	318,062	1.6%		23	Minnesota	318,062	1.6%
33	Mississippi	189,085	1.0%		24	Massachusetts	310,649	1.6%
15	Missouri	434,373	2.2%		25	Oklahoma	300,100	1.5%
43	Montana	90,231	0.5%		26	Oregon	297,039	1.5%
38	Nebraska	127,255	0.6%		27	Kentucky	291,660	1.5%
30	Nevada	214,639	1.1%		28	Louisiana	280,549	1.4%
42	New Hampshire	102,682	0.5%		29	Arkansas	219,334	1.1%
22	New Jersey	340,561	1.7%		30	Nevada	214,639	1.1%
35	New Mexico	156,595	0.8%		31	Iowa	201,353	1.0%
6	New York	747,146	3.8%		32	Kansas	191,353	1.0%
7	North Carolina	728,178	3.7%		33	Mississippi	189,085	1.0%
48	North Dakota	51,265	0.3%		34	Connecticut	177,235	0.9%
5	Ohio	753,809	3.8%		35	New Mexico	156,595	0.8%
25	Oklahoma	300,100	1.5%		36	West Virginia	140,027	0.7%
26	Oregon	297,039	1.5%		37	Utah	132,571	0.7%
4	Pennsylvania	793,321	4.0%		38	Nebraska	127,255	0.6%
47	Rhode Island	61,078	0.3%		39	Idaho	120,903	0.6%
17	South Carolina	400,742	2.0%		40	Hawaii	111,459	0.6%
46	South Dakota	64,733	0.3%		41	Maine	111,266	0.6%
14	Tennessee	465,675	2.4%		42	New Hampshire	102,682	0.5%
2	Texas	1,574,021	8.0%		43	Montana	90,231	0.5%
37	Utah	132,571	0.7%		44	Delaware	70,798	0.4%
50	Vermont	42,120	0.2%		45	Alaska	68,847	0.4%
8	Virginia	719,916	3.7%		46	South Dakota	64,733	0.3%
12	Washington	552,291	2.8%		47	Rhode Island	61,078	0.3%
36	West Virginia	140,027	0.7%		48	North Dakota	51,265	0.3%
21	Wisconsin	354,266	1.8%		49	Wyoming	46,927	0.2%
49	Wyoming	46,927	0.2%		50	Vermont	42,120	0.2%
						District of Columbia	27,356	0.1%

Source: U.S. Department of Veteran Affairs
  "Veteran Data and Information" (https://www.va.gov/vetdata/Veteran_Population.asp)
*Estimates based on 2016 data. Includes 179,622 veterans in U.S. territories or other countries.

Percent of Adult Population Who Are Veterans in 2018

National Percent = 7.7%*

<table>
<tr><td colspan="3">ALPHA ORDER</td><td colspan="3">RANK ORDER</td></tr>
<tr><td>RANK</td><td>STATE</td><td>PERCENT</td><td>RANK</td><td>STATE</td><td>PERCENT</td></tr>
<tr><td>11</td><td>Alabama</td><td>9.7</td><td>1</td><td>Alaska</td><td>12.4</td></tr>
<tr><td>1</td><td>Alaska</td><td>12.4</td><td>2</td><td>Montana</td><td>11.0</td></tr>
<tr><td>17</td><td>Arizona</td><td>9.3</td><td>3</td><td>Virginia</td><td>10.9</td></tr>
<tr><td>14</td><td>Arkansas</td><td>9.5</td><td>4</td><td>Wyoming</td><td>10.6</td></tr>
<tr><td>48</td><td>California</td><td>5.3</td><td>5</td><td>Maine</td><td>10.3</td></tr>
<tr><td>20</td><td>Colorado</td><td>9.2</td><td>6</td><td>South Carolina</td><td>10.2</td></tr>
<tr><td>44</td><td>Connecticut</td><td>6.2</td><td>7</td><td>Oklahoma</td><td>10.1</td></tr>
<tr><td>17</td><td>Delaware</td><td>9.3</td><td>8</td><td>Hawaii</td><td>9.9</td></tr>
<tr><td>24</td><td>Florida</td><td>8.9</td><td>8</td><td>South Dakota</td><td>9.9</td></tr>
<tr><td>26</td><td>Georgia</td><td>8.8</td><td>10</td><td>New Mexico</td><td>9.8</td></tr>
<tr><td>8</td><td>Hawaii</td><td>9.9</td><td>11</td><td>Alabama</td><td>9.7</td></tr>
<tr><td>14</td><td>Idaho</td><td>9.5</td><td>11</td><td>West Virginia</td><td>9.7</td></tr>
<tr><td>44</td><td>Illinois</td><td>6.2</td><td>13</td><td>Washington</td><td>9.6</td></tr>
<tr><td>36</td><td>Indiana</td><td>7.9</td><td>14</td><td>Arkansas</td><td>9.5</td></tr>
<tr><td>31</td><td>Iowa</td><td>8.3</td><td>14</td><td>Idaho</td><td>9.5</td></tr>
<tr><td>29</td><td>Kansas</td><td>8.7</td><td>14</td><td>New Hampshire</td><td>9.5</td></tr>
<tr><td>30</td><td>Kentucky</td><td>8.5</td><td>17</td><td>Arizona</td><td>9.3</td></tr>
<tr><td>38</td><td>Louisiana</td><td>7.8</td><td>17</td><td>Delaware</td><td>9.3</td></tr>
<tr><td>5</td><td>Maine</td><td>10.3</td><td>17</td><td>Nevada</td><td>9.3</td></tr>
<tr><td>35</td><td>Maryland</td><td>8.1</td><td>20</td><td>Colorado</td><td>9.2</td></tr>
<tr><td>47</td><td>Massachusetts</td><td>5.7</td><td>20</td><td>Missouri</td><td>9.2</td></tr>
<tr><td>42</td><td>Michigan</td><td>7.3</td><td>22</td><td>North Carolina</td><td>9.1</td></tr>
<tr><td>41</td><td>Minnesota</td><td>7.4</td><td>22</td><td>Oregon</td><td>9.1</td></tr>
<tr><td>31</td><td>Mississippi</td><td>8.3</td><td>24</td><td>Florida</td><td>8.9</td></tr>
<tr><td>20</td><td>Missouri</td><td>9.2</td><td>24</td><td>Tennessee</td><td>8.9</td></tr>
<tr><td>2</td><td>Montana</td><td>11.0</td><td>26</td><td>Georgia</td><td>8.8</td></tr>
<tr><td>26</td><td>Nebraska</td><td>8.8</td><td>26</td><td>Nebraska</td><td>8.8</td></tr>
<tr><td>17</td><td>Nevada</td><td>9.3</td><td>26</td><td>North Dakota</td><td>8.8</td></tr>
<tr><td>14</td><td>New Hampshire</td><td>9.5</td><td>29</td><td>Kansas</td><td>8.7</td></tr>
<tr><td>49</td><td>New Jersey</td><td>4.8</td><td>30</td><td>Kentucky</td><td>8.5</td></tr>
<tr><td>10</td><td>New Mexico</td><td>9.8</td><td>31</td><td>Iowa</td><td>8.3</td></tr>
<tr><td>49</td><td>New York</td><td>4.8</td><td>31</td><td>Mississippi</td><td>8.3</td></tr>
<tr><td>22</td><td>North Carolina</td><td>9.1</td><td>31</td><td>Ohio</td><td>8.3</td></tr>
<tr><td>26</td><td>North Dakota</td><td>8.8</td><td>31</td><td>Vermont</td><td>8.3</td></tr>
<tr><td>31</td><td>Ohio</td><td>8.3</td><td>35</td><td>Maryland</td><td>8.1</td></tr>
<tr><td>7</td><td>Oklahoma</td><td>10.1</td><td>36</td><td>Indiana</td><td>7.9</td></tr>
<tr><td>22</td><td>Oregon</td><td>9.1</td><td>36</td><td>Wisconsin</td><td>7.9</td></tr>
<tr><td>38</td><td>Pennsylvania</td><td>7.8</td><td>38</td><td>Louisiana</td><td>7.8</td></tr>
<tr><td>43</td><td>Rhode Island</td><td>7.2</td><td>38</td><td>Pennsylvania</td><td>7.8</td></tr>
<tr><td>6</td><td>South Carolina</td><td>10.2</td><td>40</td><td>Texas</td><td>7.5</td></tr>
<tr><td>8</td><td>South Dakota</td><td>9.9</td><td>41</td><td>Minnesota</td><td>7.4</td></tr>
<tr><td>24</td><td>Tennessee</td><td>8.9</td><td>42</td><td>Michigan</td><td>7.3</td></tr>
<tr><td>40</td><td>Texas</td><td>7.5</td><td>43</td><td>Rhode Island</td><td>7.2</td></tr>
<tr><td>46</td><td>Utah</td><td>6.1</td><td>44</td><td>Connecticut</td><td>6.2</td></tr>
<tr><td>31</td><td>Vermont</td><td>8.3</td><td>44</td><td>Illinois</td><td>6.2</td></tr>
<tr><td>3</td><td>Virginia</td><td>10.9</td><td>46</td><td>Utah</td><td>6.1</td></tr>
<tr><td>13</td><td>Washington</td><td>9.6</td><td>47</td><td>Massachusetts</td><td>5.7</td></tr>
<tr><td>11</td><td>West Virginia</td><td>9.7</td><td>48</td><td>California</td><td>5.3</td></tr>
<tr><td>36</td><td>Wisconsin</td><td>7.9</td><td>49</td><td>New Jersey</td><td>4.8</td></tr>
<tr><td>4</td><td>Wyoming</td><td>10.6</td><td>49</td><td>New York</td><td>4.8</td></tr>
<tr><td></td><td></td><td></td><td></td><td>District of Columbia</td><td>4.8</td></tr>
</table>

Source: CQ Press using data from U.S. Department of Veteran Affairs
    "Veteran Data and Information" (https://www.va.gov/vetdata/Veteran_Population.asp)
*Estimates based on 2016 data. National figures does not include veterans in U.S. territories or other countries. Percent
calculated with population 18 years old and older in 2017.

U.S. Military Fatalities in Iraq and Afghanistan as of January 25, 2019

National Total = 6,963 Fatalities*

ALPHA ORDER

RANK	STATE	FATALITIES	% of USA
26	Alabama	105	1.5%
44	Alaska	26	0.4%
13	Arizona	155	2.2%
29	Arkansas	89	1.3%
1	California	749	10.8%
25	Colorado	107	1.5%
39	Connecticut	48	0.7%
49	Delaware	19	0.3%
3	Florida	353	5.1%
9	Georgia	220	3.2%
43	Hawaii	38	0.5%
38	Idaho	49	0.7%
7	Illinois	257	3.7%
12	Indiana	157	2.3%
32	Iowa	73	1.0%
31	Kansas	77	1.1%
23	Kentucky	112	1.6%
20	Louisiana	125	1.8%
36	Maine	51	0.7%
22	Maryland	124	1.8%
17	Massachusetts	128	1.8%
8	Michigan	227	3.3%
28	Minnesota	97	1.4%
30	Mississippi	80	1.1%
15	Missouri	144	2.1%
41	Montana	40	0.6%
33	Nebraska	61	0.9%
35	Nevada	54	0.8%
41	New Hampshire	40	0.6%
20	New Jersey	125	1.8%
34	New Mexico	57	0.8%
4	New York	305	4.4%
11	North Carolina	192	2.8%
48	North Dakota	20	0.3%
6	Ohio	281	4.0%
18	Oklahoma	127	1.8%
24	Oregon	110	1.6%
5	Pennsylvania	298	4.3%
50	Rhode Island	17	0.2%
27	South Carolina	98	1.4%
46	South Dakota	24	0.3%
16	Tennessee	141	2.0%
2	Texas	616	8.8%
37	Utah	50	0.7%
44	Vermont	26	0.4%
10	Virginia	202	2.9%
14	Washington	154	2.2%
40	West Virginia	42	0.6%
18	Wisconsin	127	1.8%
47	Wyoming	22	0.3%

RANK ORDER

RANK	STATE	FATALITIES	% of USA
1	California	749	10.8%
2	Texas	616	8.8%
3	Florida	353	5.1%
4	New York	305	4.4%
5	Pennsylvania	298	4.3%
6	Ohio	281	4.0%
7	Illinois	257	3.7%
8	Michigan	227	3.3%
9	Georgia	220	3.2%
10	Virginia	202	2.9%
11	North Carolina	192	2.8%
12	Indiana	157	2.3%
13	Arizona	155	2.2%
14	Washington	154	2.2%
15	Missouri	144	2.1%
16	Tennessee	141	2.0%
17	Massachusetts	128	1.8%
18	Oklahoma	127	1.8%
18	Wisconsin	127	1.8%
20	Louisiana	125	1.8%
20	New Jersey	125	1.8%
22	Maryland	124	1.8%
23	Kentucky	112	1.6%
24	Oregon	110	1.6%
25	Colorado	107	1.5%
26	Alabama	105	1.5%
27	South Carolina	98	1.4%
28	Minnesota	97	1.4%
29	Arkansas	89	1.3%
30	Mississippi	80	1.1%
31	Kansas	77	1.1%
32	Iowa	73	1.0%
33	Nebraska	61	0.9%
34	New Mexico	57	0.8%
35	Nevada	54	0.8%
36	Maine	51	0.7%
37	Utah	50	0.7%
38	Idaho	49	0.7%
39	Connecticut	48	0.7%
40	West Virginia	42	0.6%
41	Montana	40	0.6%
41	New Hampshire	40	0.6%
43	Hawaii	38	0.5%
44	Alaska	26	0.4%
44	Vermont	26	0.4%
46	South Dakota	24	0.3%
47	Wyoming	22	0.3%
48	North Dakota	20	0.3%
49	Delaware	19	0.3%
50	Rhode Island	17	0.2%
	District of Columbia	10	0.1%

Source: U.S. Department of Defense, Defense Casualty Analysis System
    "U.S. Military Casualties" (https://dcas.dmdc.osd.mil/dcas/pages/report_sum_all.xhtml)
*Total includes 114 deaths of soldiers from U.S. territories. Total does not include deaths of United Kingdom soldiers or other coalition nations. Includes 5,425 combat and 1,538 noncombat deaths. Includes 4,483 deaths in Iraq, 2,409 deaths in Afghanistan, and 71 deaths fighting Islamic State in Syria and Iraq.

Rate of U.S. Military Fatalities in Iraq and Afghanistan as of January 25, 2019

National Rate = 2.1 Fatalities per 100,000 Population*

ALPHA ORDER

RANK	STATE	RATE
30	Alabama	2.1
5	Alaska	3.5
28	Arizona	2.2
8	Arkansas	3.0
38	California	1.9
38	Colorado	1.9
50	Connecticut	1.3
35	Delaware	2.0
44	Florida	1.7
30	Georgia	2.1
11	Hawaii	2.7
10	Idaho	2.8
35	Illinois	2.0
23	Indiana	2.3
23	Iowa	2.3
16	Kansas	2.6
19	Kentucky	2.5
11	Louisiana	2.7
2	Maine	3.8
30	Maryland	2.1
38	Massachusetts	1.9
23	Michigan	2.3
44	Minnesota	1.7
11	Mississippi	2.7
20	Missouri	2.4
2	Montana	3.8
6	Nebraska	3.2
42	Nevada	1.8
9	New Hampshire	2.9
49	New Jersey	1.4
11	New Mexico	2.7
46	New York	1.6
42	North Carolina	1.8
16	North Dakota	2.6
20	Ohio	2.4
6	Oklahoma	3.2
16	Oregon	2.6
23	Pennsylvania	2.3
46	Rhode Island	1.6
38	South Carolina	1.9
11	South Dakota	2.7
30	Tennessee	2.1
30	Texas	2.1
46	Utah	1.6
1	Vermont	4.2
20	Virginia	2.4
35	Washington	2.0
23	West Virginia	2.3
28	Wisconsin	2.2
2	Wyoming	3.8

RANK ORDER

RANK	STATE	RATE
1	Vermont	4.2
2	Maine	3.8
2	Montana	3.8
2	Wyoming	3.8
5	Alaska	3.5
6	Nebraska	3.2
6	Oklahoma	3.2
8	Arkansas	3.0
9	New Hampshire	2.9
10	Idaho	2.8
11	Hawaii	2.7
11	Louisiana	2.7
11	Mississippi	2.7
11	New Mexico	2.7
11	South Dakota	2.7
16	Kansas	2.6
16	North Dakota	2.6
16	Oregon	2.6
19	Kentucky	2.5
20	Missouri	2.4
20	Ohio	2.4
20	Virginia	2.4
23	Indiana	2.3
23	Iowa	2.3
23	Michigan	2.3
23	Pennsylvania	2.3
23	West Virginia	2.3
28	Arizona	2.2
28	Wisconsin	2.2
30	Alabama	2.1
30	Georgia	2.1
30	Maryland	2.1
30	Tennessee	2.1
30	Texas	2.1
35	Delaware	2.0
35	Illinois	2.0
35	Washington	2.0
38	California	1.9
38	Colorado	1.9
38	Massachusetts	1.9
38	South Carolina	1.9
42	Nevada	1.8
42	North Carolina	1.8
44	Florida	1.7
44	Minnesota	1.7
46	New York	1.6
46	Rhode Island	1.6
46	Utah	1.6
49	New Jersey	1.4
50	Connecticut	1.3
	District of Columbia	1.4

Source: CQ Press using data from U.S. Department of Defense, Defense Casualty Analysis System
"U.S. Military Casualties" (https://dcas.dmdc.osd.mil/dcas/pages/report_sum_all.xhtml)
*National rate does not include deaths of soldiers from U.S. territories. Includes combat and noncombat deaths. Calculated with 2018 population estimates.

U.S. Military Wounded in Iraq and Afghanistan as of January 25, 2019

National Total = 52,794 Wounded*

RANK	STATE	WOUNDED	% of USA
18	Alabama	864	1.6%
46	Alaska	162	0.3%
14	Arizona	1,161	2.2%
29	Arkansas	650	1.2%
1	California	4,883	9.2%
22	Colorado	828	1.6%
35	Connecticut	425	0.8%
50	Delaware	85	0.2%
3	Florida	2,514	4.8%
9	Georgia	1,497	2.8%
43	Hawaii	209	0.4%
36	Idaho	392	0.7%
7	Illinois	1,762	3.3%
15	Indiana	1,108	2.1%
31	Iowa	626	1.2%
30	Kansas	629	1.2%
27	Kentucky	748	1.4%
21	Louisiana	834	1.6%
41	Maine	326	0.6%
28	Maryland	683	1.3%
20	Massachusetts	837	1.6%
8	Michigan	1,636	3.1%
26	Minnesota	757	1.4%
33	Mississippi	444	0.8%
13	Missouri	1,191	2.3%
40	Montana	328	0.6%
39	Nebraska	338	0.6%
37	Nevada	380	0.7%
42	New Hampshire	298	0.6%
24	New Jersey	773	1.5%
34	New Mexico	426	0.8%
4	New York	2,333	4.4%
10	North Carolina	1,449	2.7%
49	North Dakota	117	0.2%
5	Ohio	2,047	3.9%
19	Oklahoma	860	1.6%
23	Oregon	797	1.5%
6	Pennsylvania	2,006	3.8%
45	Rhode Island	170	0.3%
25	South Carolina	759	1.4%
44	South Dakota	194	0.4%
16	Tennessee	1,021	1.9%
2	Texas	4,377	8.3%
32	Utah	458	0.9%
47	Vermont	153	0.3%
12	Virginia	1,208	2.3%
11	Washington	1,298	2.5%
38	West Virginia	367	0.7%
17	Wisconsin	919	1.7%
48	Wyoming	150	0.3%

RANK	STATE	WOUNDED	% of USA
1	California	4,883	9.2%
2	Texas	4,377	8.3%
3	Florida	2,514	4.8%
4	New York	2,333	4.4%
5	Ohio	2,047	3.9%
6	Pennsylvania	2,006	3.8%
7	Illinois	1,762	3.3%
8	Michigan	1,636	3.1%
9	Georgia	1,497	2.8%
10	North Carolina	1,449	2.7%
11	Washington	1,298	2.5%
12	Virginia	1,208	2.3%
13	Missouri	1,191	2.3%
14	Arizona	1,161	2.2%
15	Indiana	1,108	2.1%
16	Tennessee	1,021	1.9%
17	Wisconsin	919	1.7%
18	Alabama	864	1.6%
19	Oklahoma	860	1.6%
20	Massachusetts	837	1.6%
21	Louisiana	834	1.6%
22	Colorado	828	1.6%
23	Oregon	797	1.5%
24	New Jersey	773	1.5%
25	South Carolina	759	1.4%
26	Minnesota	757	1.4%
27	Kentucky	748	1.4%
28	Maryland	683	1.3%
29	Arkansas	650	1.2%
30	Kansas	629	1.2%
31	Iowa	626	1.2%
32	Utah	458	0.9%
33	Mississippi	444	0.8%
34	New Mexico	426	0.8%
35	Connecticut	425	0.8%
36	Idaho	392	0.7%
37	Nevada	380	0.7%
38	West Virginia	367	0.7%
39	Nebraska	338	0.6%
40	Montana	328	0.6%
41	Maine	326	0.6%
42	New Hampshire	298	0.6%
43	Hawaii	209	0.4%
44	South Dakota	194	0.4%
45	Rhode Island	170	0.3%
46	Alaska	162	0.3%
47	Vermont	153	0.3%
48	Wyoming	150	0.3%
49	North Dakota	117	0.2%
50	Delaware	85	0.2%
	District of Columbia	30	0.1%

Source: U.S. Department of Defense, Defense Casualty Analysis System
   "U.S. Military Casualties" (https://dcas.dmdc.osd.mil/dcas/pages/report_sum_all.xhtml)
*Total includes 4,287 wounded soldiers from U.S. territories. Total does not include wounded soldiers of United Kingdom or other coalition nations. Only includes wounded in action. Includes 32,253 wounded in Iraq, 20,464 wounded in Afghanistan, and 77 wounded fighting the Islamic State in Syria and Iraq.

IV. Economy

Gross Domestic Product in 2017

National Total = $19,485,394,000,000*

ALPHA ORDER

RANK	STATE	G.D.P.	% of USA
27	Alabama	$211,196,500,000	1.1%
46	Alaska	51,479,000,000	0.3%
20	Arizona	326,445,800,000	1.7%
34	Arkansas	122,703,500,000	0.6%
1	California	2,797,600,900,000	14.4%
19	Colorado	345,233,100,000	1.8%
23	Connecticut	264,509,900,000	1.4%
41	Delaware	72,461,300,000	0.4%
4	Florida	976,385,500,000	5.0%
9	Georgia	563,607,600,000	2.9%
38	Hawaii	88,447,900,000	0.5%
42	Idaho	72,294,200,000	0.4%
5	Illinois	822,539,600,000	4.2%
16	Indiana	352,272,700,000	1.8%
30	Iowa	183,929,800,000	0.9%
32	Kansas	159,108,200,000	0.8%
28	Kentucky	202,174,900,000	1.0%
24	Louisiana	235,960,200,000	1.2%
43	Maine	61,702,800,000	0.3%
15	Maryland	399,537,900,000	2.1%
10	Massachusetts	542,978,800,000	2.8%
14	Michigan	508,904,800,000	2.6%
17	Minnesota	350,178,900,000	1.8%
36	Mississippi	109,375,400,000	0.6%
22	Missouri	303,763,000,000	1.6%
48	Montana	47,079,000,000	0.2%
35	Nebraska	119,587,500,000	0.6%
33	Nevada	158,302,100,000	0.8%
39	New Hampshire	81,649,700,000	0.4%
8	New Jersey	602,069,000,000	3.1%
37	New Mexico	94,210,700,000	0.5%
3	New York	1,606,601,300,000	8.2%
11	North Carolina	540,496,600,000	2.8%
45	North Dakota	52,526,600,000	0.3%
7	Ohio	645,746,900,000	3.3%
29	Oklahoma	188,631,700,000	1.0%
25	Oregon	227,154,500,000	1.2%
6	Pennsylvania	756,268,500,000	3.9%
44	Rhode Island	59,305,700,000	0.3%
26	South Carolina	221,689,600,000	1.1%
47	South Dakota	49,813,100,000	0.3%
18	Tennessee	349,569,200,000	1.8%
2	Texas	1,645,135,900,000	8.4%
31	Utah	164,917,000,000	0.8%
50	Vermont	32,545,200,000	0.2%
13	Virginia	510,586,100,000	2.6%
12	Washington	524,322,700,000	2.7%
40	West Virginia	74,047,400,000	0.4%
21	Wisconsin	321,373,300,000	1.6%
49	Wyoming	38,036,800,000	0.2%

RANK ORDER

RANK	STATE	G.D.P.	% of USA
1	California	$2,797,600,900,000	14.4%
2	Texas	1,645,135,900,000	8.4%
3	New York	1,606,601,300,000	8.2%
4	Florida	976,385,500,000	5.0%
5	Illinois	822,539,600,000	4.2%
6	Pennsylvania	756,268,500,000	3.9%
7	Ohio	645,746,900,000	3.3%
8	New Jersey	602,069,000,000	3.1%
9	Georgia	563,607,600,000	2.9%
10	Massachusetts	542,978,800,000	2.8%
11	North Carolina	540,496,600,000	2.8%
12	Washington	524,322,700,000	2.7%
13	Virginia	510,586,100,000	2.6%
14	Michigan	508,904,800,000	2.6%
15	Maryland	399,537,900,000	2.1%
16	Indiana	352,272,700,000	1.8%
17	Minnesota	350,178,900,000	1.8%
18	Tennessee	349,569,200,000	1.8%
19	Colorado	345,233,100,000	1.8%
20	Arizona	326,445,800,000	1.7%
21	Wisconsin	321,373,300,000	1.6%
22	Missouri	303,763,000,000	1.6%
23	Connecticut	264,509,900,000	1.4%
24	Louisiana	235,960,200,000	1.2%
25	Oregon	227,154,500,000	1.2%
26	South Carolina	221,689,600,000	1.1%
27	Alabama	211,196,500,000	1.1%
28	Kentucky	202,174,900,000	1.0%
29	Oklahoma	188,631,700,000	1.0%
30	Iowa	183,929,800,000	0.9%
31	Utah	164,917,000,000	0.8%
32	Kansas	159,108,200,000	0.8%
33	Nevada	158,302,100,000	0.8%
34	Arkansas	122,703,500,000	0.6%
35	Nebraska	119,587,500,000	0.6%
36	Mississippi	109,375,400,000	0.6%
37	New Mexico	94,210,700,000	0.5%
38	Hawaii	88,447,900,000	0.5%
39	New Hampshire	81,649,700,000	0.4%
40	West Virginia	74,047,400,000	0.4%
41	Delaware	72,461,300,000	0.4%
42	Idaho	72,294,200,000	0.4%
43	Maine	61,702,800,000	0.3%
44	Rhode Island	59,305,700,000	0.3%
45	North Dakota	52,526,600,000	0.3%
46	Alaska	51,479,000,000	0.3%
47	South Dakota	49,813,100,000	0.3%
48	Montana	47,079,000,000	0.2%
49	Wyoming	38,036,800,000	0.2%
50	Vermont	32,545,200,000	0.2%
	District of Columbia	135,768,300,000	0.7%

Source: U.S. Department of Commerce, Bureau of Economic Analysis
    "Gross Domestic Product Data" (https://apps.bea.gov/iTable/index_regional.cfm)
*G.D.P. is the market value of goods and services produced by the labor and property located in a state. It is the state counterpart to the nation's Gross Domestic Product. This was formerly known as Gross State Product (G.S.P.). The difference between the United States and sum-of-states reflects overseas activity, economic activity taking place outside the borders of the United States by the military and associated federal civilian support staff.

Percent Change in Gross Domestic Product: 2013 to 2017
(Adjusted to Constant 2012 Dollars)
National Percent Change = 9.4% Increase*

ALPHA ORDER

RANK	STATE	PERCENT CHANGE
41	Alabama	2.4
50	Alaska	(4.5)
12	Arizona	10.0
42	Arkansas	1.9
3	California	16.0
4	Colorado	14.4
48	Connecticut	(0.9)
19	Delaware	8.0
7	Florida	12.6
6	Georgia	13.3
26	Hawaii	7.0
8	Idaho	12.0
39	Illinois	2.9
30	Indiana	5.7
19	Iowa	8.0
30	Kansas	5.7
38	Kentucky	3.0
47	Louisiana	0.0
28	Maine	5.9
16	Maryland	8.4
11	Massachusetts	10.2
18	Michigan	8.1
23	Minnesota	7.2
45	Mississippi	0.5
43	Missouri	1.3
33	Montana	4.7
27	Nebraska	6.1
9	Nevada	11.4
17	New Hampshire	8.2
34	New Jersey	4.4
32	New Mexico	5.2
23	New York	7.2
15	North Carolina	8.7
49	North Dakota	(3.3)
23	Ohio	7.2
22	Oklahoma	7.5
1	Oregon	18.1
21	Pennsylvania	7.6
40	Rhode Island	2.6
9	South Carolina	11.4
35	South Dakota	4.2
13	Tennessee	9.9
14	Texas	9.7
5	Utah	13.8
37	Vermont	3.7
36	Virginia	3.8
2	Washington	17.0
44	West Virginia	0.6
29	Wisconsin	5.8
45	Wyoming	0.5

RANK ORDER

RANK	STATE	PERCENT CHANGE
1	Oregon	18.1
2	Washington	17.0
3	California	16.0
4	Colorado	14.4
5	Utah	13.8
6	Georgia	13.3
7	Florida	12.6
8	Idaho	12.0
9	Nevada	11.4
9	South Carolina	11.4
11	Massachusetts	10.2
12	Arizona	10.0
13	Tennessee	9.9
14	Texas	9.7
15	North Carolina	8.7
16	Maryland	8.4
17	New Hampshire	8.2
18	Michigan	8.1
19	Delaware	8.0
19	Iowa	8.0
21	Pennsylvania	7.6
22	Oklahoma	7.5
23	Minnesota	7.2
23	New York	7.2
23	Ohio	7.2
26	Hawaii	7.0
27	Nebraska	6.1
28	Maine	5.9
29	Wisconsin	5.8
30	Indiana	5.7
30	Kansas	5.7
32	New Mexico	5.2
33	Montana	4.7
34	New Jersey	4.4
35	South Dakota	4.2
36	Virginia	3.8
37	Vermont	3.7
38	Kentucky	3.0
39	Illinois	2.9
40	Rhode Island	2.6
41	Alabama	2.4
42	Arkansas	1.9
43	Missouri	1.3
44	West Virginia	0.6
45	Mississippi	0.5
45	Wyoming	0.5
47	Louisiana	0.0
48	Connecticut	(0.9)
49	North Dakota	(3.3)
50	Alaska	(4.5)

| | District of Columbia | 8.5 |

Source: CQ Press using data from U.S. Department of Commerce, Bureau of Economic Analysis
  "Gross Domestic Product Data" (https://apps.bea.gov/iTable/index_regional.cfm)
*G.D.P. is the market value of goods and services produced by the labor and property located in a state. It is the state counterpart to the nation's Gross Domestic Product. This was formerly known as Gross State Product (G.S.P.). Adjusted for inflation using chained 2012 dollars.

Average Annual Change in Gross Domestic Product: 2013 to 2017
(Adjusted to Constant 2012 Dollars)
National Annual Percent Change = 1.8% Increase*

RANK	STATE	PERCENT CHANGE
40	Alabama	0.5
50	Alaska	(0.9)
12	Arizona	1.9
42	Arkansas	0.4
3	California	3.0
4	Colorado	2.7
48	Connecticut	(0.2)
16	Delaware	1.6
7	Florida	2.4
6	Georgia	2.5
23	Hawaii	1.4
8	Idaho	2.3
38	Illinois	0.6
29	Indiana	1.1
16	Iowa	1.6
29	Kansas	1.1
38	Kentucky	0.6
47	Louisiana	0.0
27	Maine	1.2
16	Maryland	1.6
11	Massachusetts	2.0
16	Michigan	1.6
23	Minnesota	1.4
44	Mississippi	0.1
43	Missouri	0.3
33	Montana	0.9
27	Nebraska	1.2
9	Nevada	2.2
16	New Hampshire	1.6
33	New Jersey	0.9
32	New Mexico	1.0
23	New York	1.4
15	North Carolina	1.7
49	North Dakota	(0.7)
23	Ohio	1.4
21	Oklahoma	1.5
1	Oregon	3.4
21	Pennsylvania	1.5
40	Rhode Island	0.5
9	South Carolina	2.2
35	South Dakota	0.8
12	Tennessee	1.9
12	Texas	1.9
5	Utah	2.6
37	Vermont	0.7
35	Virginia	0.8
2	Washington	3.2
44	West Virginia	0.1
29	Wisconsin	1.1
44	Wyoming	0.1

RANK	STATE	PERCENT CHANGE
1	Oregon	3.4
2	Washington	3.2
3	California	3.0
4	Colorado	2.7
5	Utah	2.6
6	Georgia	2.5
7	Florida	2.4
8	Idaho	2.3
9	Nevada	2.2
9	South Carolina	2.2
11	Massachusetts	2.0
12	Arizona	1.9
12	Tennessee	1.9
12	Texas	1.9
15	North Carolina	1.7
16	Delaware	1.6
16	Iowa	1.6
16	Maryland	1.6
16	Michigan	1.6
16	New Hampshire	1.6
21	Oklahoma	1.5
21	Pennsylvania	1.5
23	Hawaii	1.4
23	Minnesota	1.4
23	New York	1.4
23	Ohio	1.4
27	Maine	1.2
27	Nebraska	1.2
29	Indiana	1.1
29	Kansas	1.1
29	Wisconsin	1.1
32	New Mexico	1.0
33	Montana	0.9
33	New Jersey	0.9
35	South Dakota	0.8
35	Virginia	0.8
37	Vermont	0.7
38	Illinois	0.6
38	Kentucky	0.6
40	Alabama	0.5
40	Rhode Island	0.5
42	Arkansas	0.4
43	Missouri	0.3
44	Mississippi	0.1
44	West Virginia	0.1
44	Wyoming	0.1
47	Louisiana	0.0
48	Connecticut	(0.2)
49	North Dakota	(0.7)
50	Alaska	(0.9)

District of Columbia	1.6

Source: CQ Press using data from U.S. Department of Commerce, Bureau of Economic Analysis
"Gross Domestic Product Data" (https://apps.bea.gov/iTable/index_regional.cfm)
*G.D.P. is the market value of goods and services produced by the labor and property located in a state. It is the state counterpart to the nation's Gross Domestic Product. This was formerly known as Gross State Product (G.S.P.). Adjusted for inflation using chained 2012 dollars.

Per Capita Gross Domestic Product in 2017

National Per Capita = $59,928*

ALPHA ORDER			RANK ORDER		
RANK	STATE	PER CAPITA	RANK	STATE	PER CAPITA
46	Alabama	$43,321	1	New York	$82,008
7	Alaska	69,586	2	Massachusetts	79,114
40	Arizona	46,312	3	Delaware	75,711
48	Arkansas	40,860	4	Connecticut	74,012
5	California	71,006	5	California	71,006
16	Colorado	61,474	6	Washington	70,612
4	Connecticut	74,012	7	Alaska	69,586
3	Delaware	75,711	8	North Dakota	69,555
39	Florida	46,546	9	New Jersey	67,735
28	Georgia	54,125	10	Maryland	66,315
15	Hawaii	62,103	11	Wyoming	65,701
47	Idaho	42,058	12	Illinois	64,330
12	Illinois	64,330	13	Minnesota	62,890
31	Indiana	52,893	14	Nebraska	62,364
20	Iowa	58,509	15	Hawaii	62,103
27	Kansas	54,663	16	Colorado	61,474
42	Kentucky	45,393	17	New Hampshire	60,492
36	Louisiana	50,518	18	Virginia	60,316
41	Maine	46,217	19	Pennsylvania	59,128
10	Maryland	66,315	20	Iowa	58,509
2	Massachusetts	79,114	21	Texas	58,085
35	Michigan	51,011	22	South Dakota	57,041
13	Minnesota	62,890	23	Rhode Island	56,135
50	Mississippi	36,585	24	Wisconsin	55,485
37	Missouri	49,727	25	Ohio	55,362
44	Montana	44,706	26	Oregon	54,781
14	Nebraska	62,364	27	Kansas	54,663
29	Nevada	53,257	28	Georgia	54,125
17	New Hampshire	60,492	29	Nevada	53,257
9	New Jersey	67,735	30	Utah	53,146
43	New Mexico	45,004	31	Indiana	52,893
1	New York	82,008	32	North Carolina	52,625
32	North Carolina	52,625	33	Vermont	52,112
8	North Dakota	69,555	34	Tennessee	52,106
25	Ohio	55,362	35	Michigan	51,011
38	Oklahoma	47,966	36	Louisiana	50,518
26	Oregon	54,781	37	Missouri	49,727
19	Pennsylvania	59,128	38	Oklahoma	47,966
23	Rhode Island	56,135	39	Florida	46,546
45	South Carolina	44,151	40	Arizona	46,312
22	South Dakota	57,041	41	Maine	46,217
34	Tennessee	52,106	42	Kentucky	45,393
21	Texas	58,085	43	New Mexico	45,004
30	Utah	53,146	44	Montana	44,706
33	Vermont	52,112	45	South Carolina	44,151
18	Virginia	60,316	46	Alabama	43,321
6	Washington	70,612	47	Idaho	42,058
49	West Virginia	40,751	48	Arkansas	40,860
24	Wisconsin	55,485	49	West Virginia	40,751
11	Wyoming	65,701	50	Mississippi	36,585
				District of Columbia	195,156

Source: CQ Press using data from U.S. Department of Commerce, Bureau of Economic Analysis
"Gross Domestic Product Data" (https://apps.bea.gov/iTable/index_regional.cfm)
*G.D.P. is the market value of goods and services produced by the labor and property located in a state. It is the state counterpart to the nation's Gross Domestic Product. This was formerly known as Gross State Product (G.S.P.).

Percent Change in Per Capita Gross Domestic Product: 2013 to 2017
(Adjusted to Constant 2012 Dollars)
National Percent Change = 6.2% Increase*

ALPHA ORDER

RANK	STATE	PERCENT CHANGE
39	Alabama	1.4
49	Alaska	(4.9)
30	Arizona	3.7
45	Arkansas	0.3
1	California	12.5
6	Colorado	7.4
47	Connecticut	(0.5)
29	Delaware	3.9
20	Florida	5.1
4	Georgia	8.5
17	Hawaii	5.5
21	Idaho	5.0
31	Illinois	3.6
26	Indiana	4.1
15	Iowa	6.1
23	Kansas	4.9
38	Kentucky	1.7
48	Louisiana	(1.2)
18	Maine	5.3
13	Maryland	6.2
5	Massachusetts	7.8
6	Michigan	7.4
26	Minnesota	4.1
44	Mississippi	0.6
46	Missouri	0.2
43	Montana	0.8
34	Nebraska	3.2
32	Nevada	3.5
9	New Hampshire	6.5
33	New Jersey	3.4
21	New Mexico	5.0
9	New York	6.5
25	North Carolina	4.3
50	North Dakota	(7.5)
11	Ohio	6.4
18	Oklahoma	5.3
2	Oregon	11.8
6	Pennsylvania	7.4
37	Rhode Island	2.0
16	South Carolina	5.7
42	South Dakota	0.9
13	Tennessee	6.2
35	Texas	2.7
11	Utah	6.4
26	Vermont	4.1
40	Virginia	1.3
3	Washington	10.0
36	West Virginia	2.6
24	Wisconsin	4.7
41	Wyoming	1.0

RANK ORDER

RANK	STATE	PERCENT CHANGE
1	California	12.5
2	Oregon	11.8
3	Washington	10.0
4	Georgia	8.5
5	Massachusetts	7.8
6	Colorado	7.4
6	Michigan	7.4
6	Pennsylvania	7.4
9	New Hampshire	6.5
9	New York	6.5
11	Ohio	6.4
11	Utah	6.4
13	Maryland	6.2
13	Tennessee	6.2
15	Iowa	6.1
16	South Carolina	5.7
17	Hawaii	5.5
18	Maine	5.3
18	Oklahoma	5.3
20	Florida	5.1
21	Idaho	5.0
21	New Mexico	5.0
23	Kansas	4.9
24	Wisconsin	4.7
25	North Carolina	4.3
26	Indiana	4.1
26	Minnesota	4.1
26	Vermont	4.1
29	Delaware	3.9
30	Arizona	3.7
31	Illinois	3.6
32	Nevada	3.5
33	New Jersey	3.4
34	Nebraska	3.2
35	Texas	2.7
36	West Virginia	2.6
37	Rhode Island	2.0
38	Kentucky	1.7
39	Alabama	1.4
40	Virginia	1.3
41	Wyoming	1.0
42	South Dakota	0.9
43	Montana	0.8
44	Mississippi	0.6
45	Arkansas	0.3
46	Missouri	0.2
47	Connecticut	(0.5)
48	Louisiana	(1.2)
49	Alaska	(4.9)
50	North Dakota	(7.5)

	District of Columbia	1.6

Source: CQ Press using data from U.S. Department of Commerce, Bureau of Economic Analysis
    "Gross Domestic Product Data" (https://apps.bea.gov/iTable/index_regional.cfm)
*G.D.P. is the market value of goods and services produced by the labor and property located in a state. It is the state counterpart to the nation's Gross Domestic Product. This was formerly known as Gross State Product (G.S.P.). Adjusted for inflation using chained 2012 dollars.

State Exports in 2017

National Total = $1,451,023,530,000*

ALPHA ORDER

RANK	STATE	EXPORTS	% of USA
22	Alabama	$20,471,180,000	1.4%
41	Alaska	4,350,280,000	0.3%
19	Arizona	22,003,210,000	1.5%
35	Arkansas	5,721,720,000	0.4%
2	California	163,438,920,000	11.3%
33	Colorado	7,580,720,000	0.5%
25	Connecticut	14,393,830,000	1.0%
40	Delaware	4,517,470,000	0.3%
7	Florida	52,031,710,000	3.6%
11	Georgia	35,672,840,000	2.5%
50	Hawaii	795,460,000	0.1%
39	Idaho	4,876,940,000	0.3%
5	Illinois	59,680,980,000	4.1%
12	Indiana	34,650,960,000	2.4%
27	Iowa	12,122,360,000	0.8%
30	Kansas	10,154,440,000	0.7%
17	Kentucky	29,201,010,000	2.0%
9	Louisiana	48,334,630,000	3.3%
45	Maine	2,863,230,000	0.2%
32	Maryland	9,652,840,000	0.7%
18	Massachusetts	25,893,680,000	1.8%
6	Michigan	54,752,200,000	3.8%
23	Minnesota	19,200,340,000	1.3%
29	Mississippi	10,504,700,000	0.7%
26	Missouri	13,934,570,000	1.0%
47	Montana	1,360,040,000	0.1%
34	Nebraska	6,381,340,000	0.4%
31	Nevada	9,765,630,000	0.7%
42	New Hampshire	4,143,670,000	0.3%
15	New Jersey	31,177,530,000	2.1%
43	New Mexico	3,616,160,000	0.2%
4	New York	76,690,180,000	5.3%
16	North Carolina	30,180,140,000	2.1%
36	North Dakota	5,291,550,000	0.4%
8	Ohio	49,330,260,000	3.4%
37	Oklahoma	5,046,080,000	0.3%
20	Oregon	21,771,700,000	1.5%
10	Pennsylvania	36,453,180,000	2.5%
46	Rhode Island	2,278,140,000	0.2%
14	South Carolina	31,323,570,000	2.2%
48	South Dakota	1,218,050,000	0.1%
13	Tennessee	31,494,710,000	2.2%
1	Texas	231,310,080,000	15.9%
28	Utah	12,077,650,000	0.8%
44	Vermont	2,993,020,000	0.2%
24	Virginia	16,310,980,000	1.1%
3	Washington	79,553,460,000	5.5%
38	West Virginia	5,045,350,000	0.3%
21	Wisconsin	21,032,740,000	1.4%
49	Wyoming	1,098,650,000	0.1%

RANK ORDER

RANK	STATE	EXPORTS	% of USA
1	Texas	$231,310,080,000	15.9%
2	California	163,438,920,000	11.3%
3	Washington	79,553,460,000	5.5%
4	New York	76,690,180,000	5.3%
5	Illinois	59,680,980,000	4.1%
6	Michigan	54,752,200,000	3.8%
7	Florida	52,031,710,000	3.6%
8	Ohio	49,330,260,000	3.4%
9	Louisiana	48,334,630,000	3.3%
10	Pennsylvania	36,453,180,000	2.5%
11	Georgia	35,672,840,000	2.5%
12	Indiana	34,650,960,000	2.4%
13	Tennessee	31,494,710,000	2.2%
14	South Carolina	31,323,570,000	2.2%
15	New Jersey	31,177,530,000	2.1%
16	North Carolina	30,180,140,000	2.1%
17	Kentucky	29,201,010,000	2.0%
18	Massachusetts	25,893,680,000	1.8%
19	Arizona	22,003,210,000	1.5%
20	Oregon	21,771,700,000	1.5%
21	Wisconsin	21,032,740,000	1.4%
22	Alabama	20,471,180,000	1.4%
23	Minnesota	19,200,340,000	1.3%
24	Virginia	16,310,980,000	1.1%
25	Connecticut	14,393,830,000	1.0%
26	Missouri	13,934,570,000	1.0%
27	Iowa	12,122,360,000	0.8%
28	Utah	12,077,650,000	0.8%
29	Mississippi	10,504,700,000	0.7%
30	Kansas	10,154,440,000	0.7%
31	Nevada	9,765,630,000	0.7%
32	Maryland	9,652,840,000	0.7%
33	Colorado	7,580,720,000	0.5%
34	Nebraska	6,381,340,000	0.4%
35	Arkansas	5,721,720,000	0.4%
36	North Dakota	5,291,550,000	0.4%
37	Oklahoma	5,046,080,000	0.3%
38	West Virginia	5,045,350,000	0.3%
39	Idaho	4,876,940,000	0.3%
40	Delaware	4,517,470,000	0.3%
41	Alaska	4,350,280,000	0.3%
42	New Hampshire	4,143,670,000	0.3%
43	New Mexico	3,616,160,000	0.2%
44	Vermont	2,993,020,000	0.2%
45	Maine	2,863,230,000	0.2%
46	Rhode Island	2,278,140,000	0.2%
47	Montana	1,360,040,000	0.1%
48	South Dakota	1,218,050,000	0.1%
49	Wyoming	1,098,650,000	0.1%
50	Hawaii	795,460,000	0.1%
	District of Columbia	1,330,670,000	0.1%

Source: U.S. Bureau of the Census
"State Trade Data" (https://www.census.gov/foreign-trade/statistics/state/index.html)
*Based on the state from which the merchandise starts its journey to the port of export; that is, the data reflect the transportation origin of exports. Total includes exports from Puerto Rico, Virgin Islands, and exports with unidentified origin.

Per Capita State Exports in 2017

National Per Capita = $4,260*

ALPHA ORDER			RANK ORDER		
RANK	STATE	PER CAPITA	RANK	STATE	PER CAPITA
16	Alabama	$4,199	1	Washington	$10,714
7	Alaska	5,880	2	Louisiana	10,348
31	Arizona	3,122	3	Texas	8,167
42	Arkansas	1,905	4	North Dakota	7,007
17	California	4,148	5	Kentucky	6,556
47	Colorado	1,350	6	South Carolina	6,238
18	Connecticut	4,028	7	Alaska	5,880
12	Delaware	4,720	8	Michigan	5,488
37	Florida	2,480	9	Oregon	5,251
28	Georgia	3,426	10	Indiana	5,203
50	Hawaii	559	11	Vermont	4,792
35	Idaho	2,837	12	Delaware	4,720
14	Illinois	4,668	13	Tennessee	4,695
10	Indiana	5,203	14	Illinois	4,668
21	Iowa	3,856	15	Ohio	4,229
26	Kansas	3,489	16	Alabama	4,199
5	Kentucky	6,556	17	California	4,148
2	Louisiana	10,348	18	Connecticut	4,028
40	Maine	2,145	19	New York	3,915
45	Maryland	1,602	20	Utah	3,892
22	Massachusetts	3,773	21	Iowa	3,856
8	Michigan	5,488	22	Massachusetts	3,773
27	Minnesota	3,448	23	Wisconsin	3,631
24	Mississippi	3,514	24	Mississippi	3,514
38	Missouri	2,281	25	New Jersey	3,508
48	Montana	1,291	26	Kansas	3,489
29	Nebraska	3,328	27	Minnesota	3,448
30	Nevada	3,285	28	Georgia	3,426
32	New Hampshire	3,070	29	Nebraska	3,328
25	New Jersey	3,508	30	Nevada	3,285
44	New Mexico	1,727	31	Arizona	3,122
19	New York	3,915	32	New Hampshire	3,070
33	North Carolina	2,938	33	North Carolina	2,938
4	North Dakota	7,007	34	Pennsylvania	2,850
15	Ohio	4,229	35	Idaho	2,837
49	Oklahoma	1,283	36	West Virginia	2,777
9	Oregon	5,251	37	Florida	2,480
34	Pennsylvania	2,850	38	Missouri	2,281
39	Rhode Island	2,156	39	Rhode Island	2,156
6	South Carolina	6,238	40	Maine	2,145
46	South Dakota	1,395	41	Virginia	1,927
13	Tennessee	4,695	42	Arkansas	1,905
3	Texas	8,167	43	Wyoming	1,898
20	Utah	3,892	44	New Mexico	1,727
11	Vermont	4,792	45	Maryland	1,602
41	Virginia	1,927	46	South Dakota	1,395
1	Washington	10,714	47	Colorado	1,350
36	West Virginia	2,777	48	Montana	1,291
23	Wisconsin	3,631	49	Oklahoma	1,283
43	Wyoming	1,898	50	Hawaii	559
				District of Columbia	1,913

Source: CQ Press using data from U.S. Bureau of the Census
"State Trade Data" (https://www.census.gov/foreign-trade/statistics/state/index.html)
*Based on the state from which the merchandise starts its journey to the port of export; that is, the data reflect the transportation origin of exports. National figure does not include population or exports from Puerto Rico, Virgin Islands, and exports with unidentified origin.

State Imports in 2017

National Total = $2,341,962,730,000*

ALPHA ORDER

RANK	STATE	IMPORTS	% of USA
23	Alabama	$23,628,660,000	1.0%
48	Alaska	1,731,740,000	0.1%
24	Arizona	20,546,600,000	0.9%
36	Arkansas	9,293,930,000	0.4%
1	California	440,576,220,000	18.8%
30	Colorado	12,953,980,000	0.6%
26	Connecticut	18,673,750,000	0.8%
38	Delaware	7,669,380,000	0.3%
10	Florida	75,360,190,000	3.2%
7	Georgia	91,390,540,000	3.9%
41	Hawaii	3,809,780,000	0.2%
39	Idaho	5,644,410,000	0.2%
4	Illinois	136,098,870,000	5.8%
12	Indiana	54,468,940,000	2.3%
37	Iowa	9,166,060,000	0.4%
33	Kansas	10,789,480,000	0.5%
15	Kentucky	47,065,210,000	2.0%
16	Louisiana	37,691,850,000	1.6%
45	Maine	3,299,320,000	0.1%
19	Maryland	32,302,740,000	1.4%
18	Massachusetts	34,505,210,000	1.5%
3	Michigan	140,222,750,000	6.0%
20	Minnesota	29,679,570,000	1.3%
28	Mississippi	14,989,360,000	0.6%
25	Missouri	18,822,790,000	0.8%
40	Montana	4,288,000,000	0.2%
42	Nebraska	3,754,490,000	0.2%
31	Nevada	12,288,120,000	0.5%
32	New Hampshire	11,355,160,000	0.5%
6	New Jersey	112,639,850,000	4.8%
47	New Mexico	2,278,660,000	0.1%
5	New York	126,622,820,000	5.4%
14	North Carolina	47,352,090,000	2.0%
46	North Dakota	2,732,420,000	0.1%
11	Ohio	67,599,270,000	2.9%
34	Oklahoma	9,697,780,000	0.4%
27	Oregon	18,308,120,000	0.8%
8	Pennsylvania	83,282,830,000	3.6%
35	Rhode Island	9,369,250,000	0.4%
17	South Carolina	37,490,350,000	1.6%
49	South Dakota	1,099,230,000	0.0%
9	Tennessee	78,815,800,000	3.4%
2	Texas	263,238,040,000	11.2%
29	Utah	13,896,940,000	0.6%
43	Vermont	3,590,630,000	0.2%
21	Virginia	29,078,060,000	1.2%
13	Washington	49,846,890,000	2.1%
44	West Virginia	3,396,120,000	0.1%
22	Wisconsin	27,749,870,000	1.2%
50	Wyoming	858,480,000	0.0%

RANK ORDER

RANK	STATE	IMPORTS	% of USA
1	California	$440,576,220,000	18.8%
2	Texas	263,238,040,000	11.2%
3	Michigan	140,222,750,000	6.0%
4	Illinois	136,098,870,000	5.8%
5	New York	126,622,820,000	5.4%
6	New Jersey	112,639,850,000	4.8%
7	Georgia	91,390,540,000	3.9%
8	Pennsylvania	83,282,830,000	3.6%
9	Tennessee	78,815,800,000	3.4%
10	Florida	75,360,190,000	3.2%
11	Ohio	67,599,270,000	2.9%
12	Indiana	54,468,940,000	2.3%
13	Washington	49,846,890,000	2.1%
14	North Carolina	47,352,090,000	2.0%
15	Kentucky	47,065,210,000	2.0%
16	Louisiana	37,691,850,000	1.6%
17	South Carolina	37,490,350,000	1.6%
18	Massachusetts	34,505,210,000	1.5%
19	Maryland	32,302,740,000	1.4%
20	Minnesota	29,679,570,000	1.3%
21	Virginia	29,078,060,000	1.2%
22	Wisconsin	27,749,870,000	1.2%
23	Alabama	23,628,660,000	1.0%
24	Arizona	20,546,600,000	0.9%
25	Missouri	18,822,790,000	0.8%
26	Connecticut	18,673,750,000	0.8%
27	Oregon	18,308,120,000	0.8%
28	Mississippi	14,989,360,000	0.6%
29	Utah	13,896,940,000	0.6%
30	Colorado	12,953,980,000	0.6%
31	Nevada	12,288,120,000	0.5%
32	New Hampshire	11,355,160,000	0.5%
33	Kansas	10,789,480,000	0.5%
34	Oklahoma	9,697,780,000	0.4%
35	Rhode Island	9,369,250,000	0.4%
36	Arkansas	9,293,930,000	0.4%
37	Iowa	9,166,060,000	0.4%
38	Delaware	7,669,380,000	0.3%
39	Idaho	5,644,410,000	0.2%
40	Montana	4,288,000,000	0.2%
41	Hawaii	3,809,780,000	0.2%
42	Nebraska	3,754,490,000	0.2%
43	Vermont	3,590,630,000	0.2%
44	West Virginia	3,396,120,000	0.1%
45	Maine	3,299,320,000	0.1%
46	North Dakota	2,732,420,000	0.1%
47	New Mexico	2,278,660,000	0.1%
48	Alaska	1,731,740,000	0.1%
49	South Dakota	1,099,230,000	0.0%
50	Wyoming	858,480,000	0.0%
	District of Columbia	480,520,000	0.0%

Source: U.S. Bureau of the Census
    "State Trade Data" (https://www.census.gov/foreign-trade/statistics/state/index.html)
*Based on where the merchandise is destined, as known at the time of entry summary filing. If the contents of the shipment are destined to more than one state, territory, or possession, or if the entry summary represents a consolidated shipment, the state of destination is that with the greatest aggregate value.

Per Capita State Imports in 2017

National Per Capita = $7,078*

ALPHA ORDER			RANK ORDER		
RANK	STATE	PER CAPITA	RANK	STATE	PER CAPITA
25	Alabama	$4,847	1	Michigan	$14,055
44	Alaska	2,341	2	New Jersey	12,672
40	Arizona	2,915	3	Tennessee	11,748
37	Arkansas	3,095	4	California	11,182
4	California	11,182	5	Illinois	10,644
45	Colorado	2,307	6	Kentucky	10,567
22	Connecticut	5,225	7	Texas	9,294
13	Delaware	8,013	8	Rhode Island	8,868
34	Florida	3,593	9	Georgia	8,777
9	Georgia	8,777	10	New Hampshire	8,413
41	Hawaii	2,675	11	Indiana	8,178
36	Idaho	3,284	12	Louisiana	8,070
5	Illinois	10,644	13	Delaware	8,013
11	Indiana	8,178	14	South Carolina	7,466
39	Iowa	2,916	15	Washington	6,713
32	Kansas	3,707	16	Pennsylvania	6,511
6	Kentucky	10,567	17	New York	6,463
12	Louisiana	8,070	18	Ohio	5,795
42	Maine	2,471	19	Vermont	5,749
20	Maryland	5,362	20	Maryland	5,362
23	Massachusetts	5,028	21	Minnesota	5,330
1	Michigan	14,055	22	Connecticut	5,225
21	Minnesota	5,330	23	Massachusetts	5,028
24	Mississippi	5,014	24	Mississippi	5,014
38	Missouri	3,081	25	Alabama	4,847
31	Montana	4,072	26	Wisconsin	4,791
46	Nebraska	1,958	27	North Carolina	4,610
30	Nevada	4,134	28	Utah	4,478
10	New Hampshire	8,413	29	Oregon	4,415
2	New Jersey	12,672	30	Nevada	4,134
50	New Mexico	1,088	31	Montana	4,072
17	New York	6,463	32	Kansas	3,707
27	North Carolina	4,610	33	North Dakota	3,618
33	North Dakota	3,618	34	Florida	3,593
18	Ohio	5,795	35	Virginia	3,435
43	Oklahoma	2,466	36	Idaho	3,284
29	Oregon	4,415	37	Arkansas	3,095
16	Pennsylvania	6,511	38	Missouri	3,081
8	Rhode Island	8,868	39	Iowa	2,916
14	South Carolina	7,466	40	Arizona	2,915
49	South Dakota	1,259	41	Hawaii	2,675
3	Tennessee	11,748	42	Maine	2,471
7	Texas	9,294	43	Oklahoma	2,466
28	Utah	4,478	44	Alaska	2,341
19	Vermont	5,749	45	Colorado	2,307
35	Virginia	3,435	46	Nebraska	1,958
15	Washington	6,713	47	West Virginia	1,869
47	West Virginia	1,869	48	Wyoming	1,483
26	Wisconsin	4,791	49	South Dakota	1,259
48	Wyoming	1,483	50	New Mexico	1,088
				District of Columbia	691

Source: CQ Press using data from U.S. Bureau of the Census
    "State Trade Data" (https://www.census.gov/foreign-trade/statistics/state/index.html)
*Based on where the merchandise is destined, as known at the time of entry summary filing. If the contents of the shipment are destined to more than one state, territory, or possession, or if the entry summary represents a consolidated shipment, the state of destination is that with the greatest aggregate value. National figure does not include population or imports from Puerto Rico, Virgin Islands, and imports with unidentified origin.

Personal Income in 2017

National Total = $16,820,250,000,000*

ALPHA ORDER

RANK	STATE	INCOME	% of USA	RANK	STATE	INCOME	% of USA
27	Alabama	$198,916,400,000	1.2%	1	California	$2,364,129,400,000	14.1%
47	Alaska	42,300,900,000	0.3%	2	Texas	1,340,568,400,000	8.0%
20	Arizona	296,648,900,000	1.8%	3	New York	1,281,082,400,000	7.6%
34	Arkansas	123,313,400,000	0.7%	4	Florida	1,000,624,100,000	5.9%
1	California	2,364,129,400,000	14.1%	5	Illinois	693,914,000,000	4.1%
16	Colorado	306,411,100,000	1.8%	6	Pennsylvania	682,533,700,000	4.1%
23	Connecticut	257,713,600,000	1.5%	7	New Jersey	581,198,600,000	3.5%
44	Delaware	47,782,100,000	0.3%	8	Ohio	544,828,500,000	3.2%
4	Florida	1,000,624,100,000	5.9%	9	Virginia	466,743,300,000	2.8%
11	Georgia	460,402,900,000	2.7%	10	Massachusetts	463,930,700,000	2.8%
39	Hawaii	75,355,100,000	0.4%	11	Georgia	460,402,900,000	2.7%
40	Idaho	71,812,900,000	0.4%	12	Michigan	460,270,000,000	2.7%
5	Illinois	693,914,000,000	4.1%	13	North Carolina	454,306,900,000	2.7%
19	Indiana	301,008,200,000	1.8%	14	Washington	428,765,200,000	2.5%
30	Iowa	148,042,700,000	0.9%	15	Maryland	368,258,200,000	2.2%
31	Kansas	141,459,400,000	0.8%	16	Colorado	306,411,100,000	1.8%
28	Kentucky	180,826,500,000	1.1%	17	Tennessee	305,690,600,000	1.8%
25	Louisiana	204,516,800,000	1.2%	18	Minnesota	303,141,300,000	1.8%
42	Maine	62,060,000,000	0.4%	19	Indiana	301,008,200,000	1.8%
15	Maryland	368,258,200,000	2.2%	20	Arizona	296,648,900,000	1.8%
10	Massachusetts	463,930,700,000	2.8%	21	Wisconsin	283,635,800,000	1.7%
12	Michigan	460,270,000,000	2.7%	22	Missouri	274,975,800,000	1.6%
18	Minnesota	303,141,300,000	1.8%	23	Connecticut	257,713,600,000	1.5%
35	Mississippi	109,324,100,000	0.6%	24	South Carolina	209,179,600,000	1.2%
22	Missouri	274,975,800,000	1.6%	25	Louisiana	204,516,800,000	1.2%
45	Montana	47,677,100,000	0.3%	26	Oregon	199,422,200,000	1.2%
36	Nebraska	97,556,500,000	0.6%	27	Alabama	198,916,400,000	1.2%
32	Nevada	138,386,400,000	0.8%	28	Kentucky	180,826,500,000	1.1%
38	New Hampshire	80,122,000,000	0.5%	29	Oklahoma	174,435,400,000	1.0%
7	New Jersey	581,198,600,000	3.5%	30	Iowa	148,042,700,000	0.9%
37	New Mexico	83,127,300,000	0.5%	31	Kansas	141,459,400,000	0.8%
3	New York	1,281,082,400,000	7.6%	32	Nevada	138,386,400,000	0.8%
13	North Carolina	454,306,900,000	2.7%	33	Utah	134,803,800,000	0.8%
48	North Dakota	39,483,600,000	0.2%	34	Arkansas	123,313,400,000	0.7%
8	Ohio	544,828,500,000	3.2%	35	Mississippi	109,324,100,000	0.6%
29	Oklahoma	174,435,400,000	1.0%	36	Nebraska	97,556,500,000	0.6%
26	Oregon	199,422,200,000	1.2%	37	New Mexico	83,127,300,000	0.5%
6	Pennsylvania	682,533,700,000	4.1%	38	New Hampshire	80,122,000,000	0.5%
43	Rhode Island	55,934,000,000	0.3%	39	Hawaii	75,355,100,000	0.4%
24	South Carolina	209,179,600,000	1.2%	40	Idaho	71,812,900,000	0.4%
46	South Dakota	42,455,300,000	0.3%	41	West Virginia	69,872,700,000	0.4%
17	Tennessee	305,690,600,000	1.8%	42	Maine	62,060,000,000	0.4%
2	Texas	1,340,568,400,000	8.0%	43	Rhode Island	55,934,000,000	0.3%
33	Utah	134,803,800,000	0.8%	44	Delaware	47,782,100,000	0.3%
50	Vermont	32,570,400,000	0.2%	45	Montana	47,677,100,000	0.3%
9	Virginia	466,743,300,000	2.8%	46	South Dakota	42,455,300,000	0.3%
14	Washington	428,765,200,000	2.5%	47	Alaska	42,300,900,000	0.3%
41	West Virginia	69,872,700,000	0.4%	48	North Dakota	39,483,600,000	0.2%
21	Wisconsin	283,635,800,000	1.7%	49	Wyoming	33,221,400,000	0.2%
49	Wyoming	33,221,400,000	0.2%	50	Vermont	32,570,400,000	0.2%
					District of Columbia	55,510,400,000	0.3%

Source: U.S. Department of Commerce, Bureau of Economic Analysis
    "Annual State Personal Income" (https://apps.bea.gov/iTable/index_regional.cfm)
*The national total shown here is the sum of the state estimates. It differs from the national income and product accounts
(NIPA) estimate of personal income because it omits the earnings of federal civilian and military personnel stationed abroad and
of U.S. residents employed abroad temporarily by private U.S. firms.

Percent Change in Personal Income: 2016 to 2017

National Percent Change = 4.4% Increase*

<table>
<tr><td colspan="3">ALPHA ORDER</td><td colspan="3">RANK ORDER</td></tr>
<tr><td>RANK</td><td>STATE</td><td>PERCENT CHANGE</td><td>RANK</td><td>STATE</td><td>PERCENT CHANGE</td></tr>
<tr><td>21</td><td>Alabama</td><td>4.1</td><td>1</td><td>Washington</td><td>6.1</td></tr>
<tr><td>47</td><td>Alaska</td><td>2.0</td><td>2</td><td>New York</td><td>6.0</td></tr>
<tr><td>5</td><td>Arizona</td><td>5.6</td><td>3</td><td>Colorado</td><td>5.8</td></tr>
<tr><td>30</td><td>Arkansas</td><td>3.8</td><td>3</td><td>Nevada</td><td>5.8</td></tr>
<tr><td>14</td><td>California</td><td>4.6</td><td>5</td><td>Arizona</td><td>5.6</td></tr>
<tr><td>3</td><td>Colorado</td><td>5.8</td><td>5</td><td>Oklahoma</td><td>5.6</td></tr>
<tr><td>37</td><td>Connecticut</td><td>3.3</td><td>7</td><td>Idaho</td><td>5.5</td></tr>
<tr><td>21</td><td>Delaware</td><td>4.1</td><td>8</td><td>Oregon</td><td>5.2</td></tr>
<tr><td>10</td><td>Florida</td><td>5.0</td><td>9</td><td>New Hampshire</td><td>5.1</td></tr>
<tr><td>12</td><td>Georgia</td><td>4.7</td><td>10</td><td>Florida</td><td>5.0</td></tr>
<tr><td>32</td><td>Hawaii</td><td>3.7</td><td>10</td><td>Utah</td><td>5.0</td></tr>
<tr><td>7</td><td>Idaho</td><td>5.5</td><td>12</td><td>Georgia</td><td>4.7</td></tr>
<tr><td>40</td><td>Illinois</td><td>3.0</td><td>12</td><td>North Carolina</td><td>4.7</td></tr>
<tr><td>21</td><td>Indiana</td><td>4.1</td><td>14</td><td>California</td><td>4.6</td></tr>
<tr><td>47</td><td>Iowa</td><td>2.0</td><td>14</td><td>New Jersey</td><td>4.6</td></tr>
<tr><td>43</td><td>Kansas</td><td>2.4</td><td>14</td><td>South Carolina</td><td>4.6</td></tr>
<tr><td>37</td><td>Kentucky</td><td>3.3</td><td>14</td><td>Tennessee</td><td>4.6</td></tr>
<tr><td>42</td><td>Louisiana</td><td>2.5</td><td>18</td><td>Massachusetts</td><td>4.3</td></tr>
<tr><td>19</td><td>Maine</td><td>4.2</td><td>19</td><td>Maine</td><td>4.2</td></tr>
<tr><td>21</td><td>Maryland</td><td>4.1</td><td>19</td><td>Montana</td><td>4.2</td></tr>
<tr><td>18</td><td>Massachusetts</td><td>4.3</td><td>21</td><td>Alabama</td><td>4.1</td></tr>
<tr><td>35</td><td>Michigan</td><td>3.5</td><td>21</td><td>Delaware</td><td>4.1</td></tr>
<tr><td>27</td><td>Minnesota</td><td>4.0</td><td>21</td><td>Indiana</td><td>4.1</td></tr>
<tr><td>46</td><td>Mississippi</td><td>2.3</td><td>21</td><td>Maryland</td><td>4.1</td></tr>
<tr><td>33</td><td>Missouri</td><td>3.6</td><td>21</td><td>Rhode Island</td><td>4.1</td></tr>
<tr><td>19</td><td>Montana</td><td>4.2</td><td>21</td><td>Texas</td><td>4.1</td></tr>
<tr><td>40</td><td>Nebraska</td><td>3.0</td><td>27</td><td>Minnesota</td><td>4.0</td></tr>
<tr><td>3</td><td>Nevada</td><td>5.8</td><td>27</td><td>Virginia</td><td>4.0</td></tr>
<tr><td>9</td><td>New Hampshire</td><td>5.1</td><td>29</td><td>Pennsylvania</td><td>3.9</td></tr>
<tr><td>14</td><td>New Jersey</td><td>4.6</td><td>30</td><td>Arkansas</td><td>3.8</td></tr>
<tr><td>43</td><td>New Mexico</td><td>2.4</td><td>30</td><td>Ohio</td><td>3.8</td></tr>
<tr><td>2</td><td>New York</td><td>6.0</td><td>32</td><td>Hawaii</td><td>3.7</td></tr>
<tr><td>12</td><td>North Carolina</td><td>4.7</td><td>33</td><td>Missouri</td><td>3.6</td></tr>
<tr><td>50</td><td>North Dakota</td><td>(0.7)</td><td>33</td><td>Wisconsin</td><td>3.6</td></tr>
<tr><td>30</td><td>Ohio</td><td>3.8</td><td>35</td><td>Michigan</td><td>3.5</td></tr>
<tr><td>5</td><td>Oklahoma</td><td>5.6</td><td>36</td><td>West Virginia</td><td>3.4</td></tr>
<tr><td>8</td><td>Oregon</td><td>5.2</td><td>37</td><td>Connecticut</td><td>3.3</td></tr>
<tr><td>29</td><td>Pennsylvania</td><td>3.9</td><td>37</td><td>Kentucky</td><td>3.3</td></tr>
<tr><td>21</td><td>Rhode Island</td><td>4.1</td><td>39</td><td>Vermont</td><td>3.2</td></tr>
<tr><td>14</td><td>South Carolina</td><td>4.6</td><td>40</td><td>Illinois</td><td>3.0</td></tr>
<tr><td>49</td><td>South Dakota</td><td>1.6</td><td>40</td><td>Nebraska</td><td>3.0</td></tr>
<tr><td>14</td><td>Tennessee</td><td>4.6</td><td>42</td><td>Louisiana</td><td>2.5</td></tr>
<tr><td>21</td><td>Texas</td><td>4.1</td><td>43</td><td>Kansas</td><td>2.4</td></tr>
<tr><td>10</td><td>Utah</td><td>5.0</td><td>43</td><td>New Mexico</td><td>2.4</td></tr>
<tr><td>39</td><td>Vermont</td><td>3.2</td><td>43</td><td>Wyoming</td><td>2.4</td></tr>
<tr><td>27</td><td>Virginia</td><td>4.0</td><td>46</td><td>Mississippi</td><td>2.3</td></tr>
<tr><td>1</td><td>Washington</td><td>6.1</td><td>47</td><td>Alaska</td><td>2.0</td></tr>
<tr><td>36</td><td>West Virginia</td><td>3.4</td><td>47</td><td>Iowa</td><td>2.0</td></tr>
<tr><td>33</td><td>Wisconsin</td><td>3.6</td><td>49</td><td>South Dakota</td><td>1.6</td></tr>
<tr><td>43</td><td>Wyoming</td><td>2.4</td><td>50</td><td>North Dakota</td><td>(0.7)</td></tr>
<tr><td></td><td></td><td></td><td></td><td>District of Columbia</td><td>4.7</td></tr>
</table>

Source: U.S. Department of Commerce, Bureau of Economic Analysis
   "Annual State Personal Income" (https://apps.bea.gov/iTable/index_regional.cfm)
*Based on revised 2016 figures.

Per Capita Personal Income in 2017

National Per Capita = $51,640*

ALPHA ORDER

RANK	STATE	PER CAPITA
46	Alabama	$40,805
10	Alaska	57,179
42	Arizona	42,280
45	Arkansas	41,046
6	California	59,796
12	Colorado	54,646
1	Connecticut	71,823
21	Delaware	49,673
26	Florida	47,684
39	Georgia	44,145
16	Hawaii	52,787
43	Idaho	41,826
14	Illinois	54,203
35	Indiana	45,150
28	Iowa	47,062
24	Kansas	48,559
47	Kentucky	40,597
40	Louisiana	43,660
30	Maine	46,455
5	Maryland	60,847
2	Massachusetts	67,630
31	Michigan	46,201
13	Minnesota	54,359
50	Mississippi	36,636
36	Missouri	44,978
34	Montana	45,385
20	Nebraska	50,809
32	Nevada	46,159
7	New Hampshire	59,668
4	New Jersey	64,537
48	New Mexico	39,811
3	New York	64,540
38	North Carolina	44,222
18	North Dakota	52,269
29	Ohio	46,732
37	Oklahoma	44,376
25	Oregon	48,137
15	Pennsylvania	53,300
17	Rhode Island	52,786
44	South Carolina	41,633
23	South Dakota	48,818
33	Tennessee	45,517
27	Texas	47,362
41	Utah	43,459
19	Vermont	52,225
11	Virginia	55,105
8	Washington	57,896
49	West Virginia	38,479
22	Wisconsin	48,941
9	Wyoming	57,346

RANK ORDER

RANK	STATE	PER CAPITA
1	Connecticut	$71,823
2	Massachusetts	67,630
3	New York	64,540
4	New Jersey	64,537
5	Maryland	60,847
6	California	59,796
7	New Hampshire	59,668
8	Washington	57,896
9	Wyoming	57,346
10	Alaska	57,179
11	Virginia	55,105
12	Colorado	54,646
13	Minnesota	54,359
14	Illinois	54,203
15	Pennsylvania	53,300
16	Hawaii	52,787
17	Rhode Island	52,786
18	North Dakota	52,269
19	Vermont	52,225
20	Nebraska	50,809
21	Delaware	49,673
22	Wisconsin	48,941
23	South Dakota	48,818
24	Kansas	48,559
25	Oregon	48,137
26	Florida	47,684
27	Texas	47,362
28	Iowa	47,062
29	Ohio	46,732
30	Maine	46,455
31	Michigan	46,201
32	Nevada	46,159
33	Tennessee	45,517
34	Montana	45,385
35	Indiana	45,150
36	Missouri	44,978
37	Oklahoma	44,376
38	North Carolina	44,222
39	Georgia	44,145
40	Louisiana	43,660
41	Utah	43,459
42	Arizona	42,280
43	Idaho	41,826
44	South Carolina	41,633
45	Arkansas	41,046
46	Alabama	40,805
47	Kentucky	40,597
48	New Mexico	39,811
49	West Virginia	38,479
50	Mississippi	36,636

| | District of Columbia | 79,989 |

Source: U.S. Department of Commerce, Bureau of Economic Analysis
"Annual State Personal Income" (https://apps.bea.gov/iTable/index_regional.cfm)
*The national figure is based on the sum of the state estimates. It differs from the national income and product accounts (NIPA) estimate of personal income because it omits the earnings of federal civilian and military personnel stationed abroad and of U.S. residents employed abroad temporarily by private U.S. firms.

Percent Change in Per Capita Personal Income: 2016 to 2017

National Percent Change = 3.6% Increase*

ALPHA ORDER

RANK	STATE	PERCENT CHANGE
11	Alabama	3.8
43	Alaska	2.3
8	Arizona	4.0
25	Arkansas	3.3
8	California	4.0
4	Colorado	4.3
25	Connecticut	3.3
35	Delaware	3.1
25	Florida	3.3
18	Georgia	3.6
11	Hawaii	3.8
25	Idaho	3.3
25	Illinois	3.3
18	Indiana	3.6
48	Iowa	1.5
47	Kansas	2.2
40	Kentucky	2.9
42	Louisiana	2.5
14	Maine	3.7
18	Maryland	3.6
14	Massachusetts	3.7
32	Michigan	3.2
35	Minnesota	3.1
43	Mississippi	2.3
32	Missouri	3.2
38	Montana	3.0
43	Nebraska	2.3
11	Nevada	3.8
3	New Hampshire	4.5
4	New Jersey	4.3
43	New Mexico	2.3
1	New York	5.9
22	North Carolina	3.5
50	North Dakota	(0.7)
23	Ohio	3.4
2	Oklahoma	5.4
14	Oregon	3.7
14	Pennsylvania	3.7
10	Rhode Island	3.9
25	South Carolina	3.3
49	South Dakota	0.6
18	Tennessee	3.6
41	Texas	2.6
38	Utah	3.0
35	Vermont	3.1
25	Virginia	3.3
4	Washington	4.3
7	West Virginia	4.1
32	Wisconsin	3.2
23	Wyoming	3.4

RANK ORDER

RANK	STATE	PERCENT CHANGE
1	New York	5.9
2	Oklahoma	5.4
3	New Hampshire	4.5
4	Colorado	4.3
4	New Jersey	4.3
4	Washington	4.3
7	West Virginia	4.1
8	Arizona	4.0
8	California	4.0
10	Rhode Island	3.9
11	Alabama	3.8
11	Hawaii	3.8
11	Nevada	3.8
14	Maine	3.7
14	Massachusetts	3.7
14	Oregon	3.7
14	Pennsylvania	3.7
18	Georgia	3.6
18	Indiana	3.6
18	Maryland	3.6
18	Tennessee	3.6
22	North Carolina	3.5
23	Ohio	3.4
23	Wyoming	3.4
25	Arkansas	3.3
25	Connecticut	3.3
25	Florida	3.3
25	Idaho	3.3
25	Illinois	3.3
25	South Carolina	3.3
25	Virginia	3.3
32	Michigan	3.2
32	Missouri	3.2
32	Wisconsin	3.2
35	Delaware	3.1
35	Minnesota	3.1
35	Vermont	3.1
38	Montana	3.0
38	Utah	3.0
40	Kentucky	2.9
41	Texas	2.6
42	Louisiana	2.5
43	Alaska	2.3
43	Mississippi	2.3
43	Nebraska	2.3
43	New Mexico	2.3
47	Kansas	2.2
48	Iowa	1.5
49	South Dakota	0.6
50	North Dakota	(0.7)
	District of Columbia	3.2

Source: U.S. Department of Commerce, Bureau of Economic Analysis
   "Annual State Personal Income" (https://apps.bea.gov/iTable/index_regional.cfm)
*Based on revised 2016 figures.

Disposable Personal Income in 2017

National Total = $14,787,578,000,000*

ALPHA ORDER				RANK ORDER			
RANK	STATE	INCOME	% of USA	RANK	STATE	INCOME	% of USA
26	Alabama	$179,555,200,000	1.2%	1	California	$2,028,335,800,000	13.7%
46	Alaska	38,752,700,000	0.3%	2	Texas	1,214,454,400,000	8.2%
19	Arizona	266,474,000,000	1.8%	3	New York	1,079,714,900,000	7.3%
34	Arkansas	111,109,900,000	0.8%	4	Florida	899,255,800,000	6.1%
1	California	2,028,335,800,000	13.7%	5	Illinois	607,751,400,000	4.1%
18	Colorado	266,887,500,000	1.8%	6	Pennsylvania	602,039,100,000	4.1%
23	Connecticut	218,962,600,000	1.5%	7	New Jersey	501,867,000,000	3.4%
45	Delaware	42,276,300,000	0.3%	8	Ohio	484,543,000,000	3.3%
4	Florida	899,255,800,000	6.1%	9	Georgia	409,428,100,000	2.8%
9	Georgia	409,428,100,000	2.8%	10	Virginia	406,736,400,000	2.8%
39	Hawaii	67,244,200,000	0.5%	11	Michigan	406,342,000,000	2.7%
40	Idaho	64,411,800,000	0.4%	12	North Carolina	402,420,200,000	2.7%
5	Illinois	607,751,400,000	4.1%	13	Massachusetts	392,736,800,000	2.7%
17	Indiana	269,315,000,000	1.8%	14	Washington	380,345,800,000	2.6%
30	Iowa	132,094,500,000	0.9%	15	Maryland	318,952,800,000	2.2%
31	Kansas	126,950,100,000	0.9%	16	Tennessee	278,959,500,000	1.9%
28	Kentucky	161,314,700,000	1.1%	17	Indiana	269,315,000,000	1.8%
25	Louisiana	185,592,300,000	1.3%	18	Colorado	266,887,500,000	1.8%
42	Maine	55,460,300,000	0.4%	19	Arizona	266,474,000,000	1.8%
15	Maryland	318,952,800,000	2.2%	20	Minnesota	261,120,300,000	1.8%
13	Massachusetts	392,736,800,000	2.7%	21	Wisconsin	250,036,000,000	1.7%
11	Michigan	406,342,000,000	2.7%	22	Missouri	244,118,400,000	1.7%
20	Minnesota	261,120,300,000	1.8%	23	Connecticut	218,962,600,000	1.5%
35	Mississippi	100,164,500,000	0.7%	24	South Carolina	187,498,000,000	1.3%
22	Missouri	244,118,400,000	1.7%	25	Louisiana	185,592,300,000	1.3%
44	Montana	42,595,300,000	0.3%	26	Alabama	179,555,200,000	1.2%
36	Nebraska	87,424,500,000	0.6%	27	Oregon	172,857,200,000	1.2%
32	Nevada	123,111,000,000	0.8%	28	Kentucky	161,314,700,000	1.1%
38	New Hampshire	71,603,700,000	0.5%	29	Oklahoma	158,345,000,000	1.1%
7	New Jersey	501,867,000,000	3.4%	30	Iowa	132,094,500,000	0.9%
37	New Mexico	75,754,600,000	0.5%	31	Kansas	126,950,100,000	0.9%
3	New York	1,079,714,900,000	7.3%	32	Nevada	123,111,000,000	0.8%
12	North Carolina	402,420,200,000	2.7%	33	Utah	119,374,700,000	0.8%
48	North Dakota	35,497,400,000	0.2%	34	Arkansas	111,109,900,000	0.8%
8	Ohio	484,543,000,000	3.3%	35	Mississippi	100,164,500,000	0.7%
29	Oklahoma	158,345,000,000	1.1%	36	Nebraska	87,424,500,000	0.6%
27	Oregon	172,857,200,000	1.2%	37	New Mexico	75,754,600,000	0.5%
6	Pennsylvania	602,039,100,000	4.1%	38	New Hampshire	71,603,700,000	0.5%
43	Rhode Island	49,519,300,000	0.3%	39	Hawaii	67,244,200,000	0.5%
24	South Carolina	187,498,000,000	1.3%	40	Idaho	64,411,800,000	0.4%
47	South Dakota	38,538,900,000	0.3%	41	West Virginia	63,285,200,000	0.4%
16	Tennessee	278,959,500,000	1.9%	42	Maine	55,460,300,000	0.4%
2	Texas	1,214,454,400,000	8.2%	43	Rhode Island	49,519,300,000	0.3%
33	Utah	119,374,700,000	0.8%	44	Montana	42,595,300,000	0.3%
50	Vermont	29,175,400,000	0.2%	45	Delaware	42,276,300,000	0.3%
10	Virginia	406,736,400,000	2.8%	46	Alaska	38,752,700,000	0.3%
14	Washington	380,345,800,000	2.6%	47	South Dakota	38,538,900,000	0.3%
41	West Virginia	63,285,200,000	0.4%	48	North Dakota	35,497,400,000	0.2%
21	Wisconsin	250,036,000,000	1.7%	49	Wyoming	30,072,200,000	0.2%
49	Wyoming	30,072,200,000	0.2%	50	Vermont	29,175,400,000	0.2%
					District of Columbia	47,202,500,000	0.3%

Source: U.S. Department of Commerce, Bureau of Economic Analysis
   "Annual State Personal Income" (https://apps.bea.gov/iTable/index_regional.cfm)
*Disposable personal income is personal income less personal tax and nontax payments. It is the income available to persons for spending or saving.

Per Capita Disposable Personal Income in 2017

National Per Capita = $45,400*

ALPHA ORDER

RANK	STATE	PER CAPITA
46	Alabama	$36,834
7	Alaska	52,383
42	Arizona	37,979
45	Arkansas	36,984
10	California	51,303
12	Colorado	47,598
1	Connecticut	61,023
22	Delaware	43,949
26	Florida	42,854
39	Georgia	39,257
14	Hawaii	47,105
43	Idaho	37,515
13	Illinois	47,473
35	Indiana	40,396
27	Iowa	41,992
23	Kansas	43,579
48	Kentucky	36,216
38	Louisiana	39,620
31	Maine	41,515
6	Maryland	52,701
2	Massachusetts	57,252
33	Michigan	40,788
17	Minnesota	46,824
50	Mississippi	33,566
37	Missouri	39,931
34	Montana	40,548
20	Nebraska	45,532
32	Nevada	41,064
5	New Hampshire	53,324
3	New Jersey	55,728
47	New Mexico	36,280
4	New York	54,395
40	North Carolina	39,171
16	North Dakota	46,992
29	Ohio	41,561
36	Oklahoma	40,282
28	Oregon	41,725
15	Pennsylvania	47,014
19	Rhode Island	46,732
44	South Carolina	37,318
21	South Dakota	44,315
30	Tennessee	41,537
25	Texas	42,907
41	Utah	38,485
18	Vermont	46,781
11	Virginia	48,021
9	Washington	51,358
49	West Virginia	34,851
24	Wisconsin	43,143
8	Wyoming	51,910

RANK ORDER

RANK	STATE	PER CAPITA
1	Connecticut	$61,023
2	Massachusetts	57,252
3	New Jersey	55,728
4	New York	54,395
5	New Hampshire	53,324
6	Maryland	52,701
7	Alaska	52,383
8	Wyoming	51,910
9	Washington	51,358
10	California	51,303
11	Virginia	48,021
12	Colorado	47,598
13	Illinois	47,473
14	Hawaii	47,105
15	Pennsylvania	47,014
16	North Dakota	46,992
17	Minnesota	46,824
18	Vermont	46,781
19	Rhode Island	46,732
20	Nebraska	45,532
21	South Dakota	44,315
22	Delaware	43,949
23	Kansas	43,579
24	Wisconsin	43,143
25	Texas	42,907
26	Florida	42,854
27	Iowa	41,992
28	Oregon	41,725
29	Ohio	41,561
30	Tennessee	41,537
31	Maine	41,515
32	Nevada	41,064
33	Michigan	40,788
34	Montana	40,548
35	Indiana	40,396
36	Oklahoma	40,282
37	Missouri	39,931
38	Louisiana	39,620
39	Georgia	39,257
40	North Carolina	39,171
41	Utah	38,485
42	Arizona	37,979
43	Idaho	37,515
44	South Carolina	37,318
45	Arkansas	36,984
46	Alabama	36,834
47	New Mexico	36,280
48	Kentucky	36,216
49	West Virginia	34,851
50	Mississippi	33,566
	District of Columbia	68,018

Source: U.S. Department of Commerce, Bureau of Economic Analysis
   "Annual State Personal Income" (https://apps.bea.gov/iTable/index_regional.cfm)
*Disposable personal income is personal income less personal tax and nontax payments. It is the income available to persons for spending or saving.

Median Household Income in 2017

National Median = $60,052*

ALPHA ORDER			RANK ORDER		
RANK	STATE	INCOME	RANK	STATE	INCOME
44	Alabama	$48,467	1	Maryland	$77,525
3	Alaska	75,766	2	New Hampshire	77,000
28	Arizona	57,838	3	Alaska	75,766
47	Arkansas	46,669	4	Connecticut	75,251
12	California	67,891	5	Massachusetts	72,421
7	Colorado	71,720	6	Washington	72,272
4	Connecticut	75,251	7	Colorado	71,720
23	Delaware	60,457	8	Minnesota	71,587
41	Florida	52,159	9	Hawaii	71,337
37	Georgia	54,741	10	New Jersey	71,222
9	Hawaii	71,337	11	Utah	69,602
32	Idaho	57,134	12	California	67,891
14	Illinois	63,274	13	Virginia	67,597
35	Indiana	56,653	14	Illinois	63,274
19	Iowa	62,270	15	Oregon	62,654
29	Kansas	57,557	16	Pennsylvania	62,649
46	Kentucky	47,183	17	Vermont	62,503
49	Louisiana	44,841	18	Rhode Island	62,291
42	Maine	52,043	19	Iowa	62,270
1	Maryland	77,525	20	New York	61,741
5	Massachusetts	72,421	21	Nebraska	60,947
31	Michigan	57,367	22	Wisconsin	60,633
8	Minnesota	71,587	23	Delaware	60,457
50	Mississippi	42,283	24	North Dakota	60,257
27	Missouri	58,111	25	Wyoming	59,983
33	Montana	56,855	26	Texas	59,041
21	Nebraska	60,947	27	Missouri	58,111
36	Nevada	55,662	28	Arizona	57,838
2	New Hampshire	77,000	29	Kansas	57,557
10	New Jersey	71,222	30	South Dakota	57,518
45	New Mexico	48,010	31	Michigan	57,367
20	New York	61,741	32	Idaho	57,134
39	North Carolina	52,608	33	Montana	56,855
24	North Dakota	60,257	34	Ohio	56,688
34	Ohio	56,688	35	Indiana	56,653
43	Oklahoma	51,918	36	Nevada	55,662
15	Oregon	62,654	37	Georgia	54,741
16	Pennsylvania	62,649	38	South Carolina	52,815
18	Rhode Island	62,291	39	North Carolina	52,608
38	South Carolina	52,815	40	Tennessee	52,220
30	South Dakota	57,518	41	Florida	52,159
40	Tennessee	52,220	42	Maine	52,043
26	Texas	59,041	43	Oklahoma	51,918
11	Utah	69,602	44	Alabama	48,467
17	Vermont	62,503	45	New Mexico	48,010
13	Virginia	67,597	46	Kentucky	47,183
6	Washington	72,272	47	Arkansas	46,669
48	West Virginia	45,003	48	West Virginia	45,003
22	Wisconsin	60,633	49	Louisiana	44,841
25	Wyoming	59,983	50	Mississippi	42,283
				District of Columbia	76,131

Source: U.S. Bureau of the Census

"Historical Income Tables" (www.census.gov/data/tables/time-series/demo/income-poverty/historical-income-households.html)

*This is a 3-year-average of inflation-adjusted single-year medians for the years 2015 through 2017.

Regional Price Parities in 2016

National Index = 100.0*

ALPHA ORDER

RANK	STATE	RATIO
49	Alabama	86.6
10	Alaska	105.4
26	Arizona	95.9
48	Arkansas	86.9
3	California	114.4
11	Colorado	103.0
6	Connecticut	108.7
14	Delaware	100.2
16	Florida	99.7
32	Georgia	92.1
1	Hawaii	118.4
30	Idaho	93.0
18	Illinois	98.9
38	Indiana	90.3
40	Iowa	90.2
35	Kansas	90.5
46	Kentucky	87.8
37	Louisiana	90.4
19	Maine	98.4
5	Maryland	109.5
7	Massachusetts	107.8
29	Michigan	93.3
21	Minnesota	97.5
50	Mississippi	86.4
42	Missouri	89.5
27	Montana	94.1
35	Nebraska	90.5
22	Nevada	97.4
8	New Hampshire	105.9
4	New Jersey	113.2
28	New Mexico	93.6
2	New York	115.6
34	North Carolina	90.9
33	North Dakota	91.5
43	Ohio	89.3
44	Oklahoma	89.0
15	Oregon	99.8
19	Pennsylvania	98.4
17	Rhode Island	99.6
38	South Carolina	90.3
45	South Dakota	88.3
40	Tennessee	90.2
24	Texas	96.9
23	Utah	97.3
13	Vermont	101.6
12	Virginia	102.3
9	Washington	105.5
47	West Virginia	87.6
31	Wisconsin	92.8
25	Wyoming	96.7

RANK ORDER

RANK	STATE	RATIO
1	Hawaii	118.4
2	New York	115.6
3	California	114.4
4	New Jersey	113.2
5	Maryland	109.5
6	Connecticut	108.7
7	Massachusetts	107.8
8	New Hampshire	105.9
9	Washington	105.5
10	Alaska	105.4
11	Colorado	103.0
12	Virginia	102.3
13	Vermont	101.6
14	Delaware	100.2
15	Oregon	99.8
16	Florida	99.7
17	Rhode Island	99.6
18	Illinois	98.9
19	Maine	98.4
19	Pennsylvania	98.4
21	Minnesota	97.5
22	Nevada	97.4
23	Utah	97.3
24	Texas	96.9
25	Wyoming	96.7
26	Arizona	95.9
27	Montana	94.1
28	New Mexico	93.6
29	Michigan	93.3
30	Idaho	93.0
31	Wisconsin	92.8
32	Georgia	92.1
33	North Dakota	91.5
34	North Carolina	90.9
35	Kansas	90.5
35	Nebraska	90.5
37	Louisiana	90.4
38	Indiana	90.3
38	South Carolina	90.3
40	Iowa	90.2
40	Tennessee	90.2
42	Missouri	89.5
43	Ohio	89.3
44	Oklahoma	89.0
45	South Dakota	88.3
46	Kentucky	87.8
47	West Virginia	87.6
48	Arkansas	86.9
49	Alabama	86.6
50	Mississippi	86.4

| | District of Columbia | 115.9 |

Source: U.S. Department of Commerce, Bureau of Economic Analysis
   "Annual State Personal Income" (https://apps.bea.gov/iTable/index_regional.cfm)
*Regional Price Parities (RPPs) are regional price levels expressed as a percentage of the overall national price level for a given year. The price levels are determined by the average prices paid by consumers for the mix of goods and services consumed in each region. Taking the ratio of RPPs shows the difference in price levels across regions.

Real Personal Income in 2016

National Total = $15,460,919,200,000*

ALPHA ORDER

RANK	STATE	INCOME	% of USA
26	Alabama	$212,329,000,000	1.4%
48	Alaska	37,876,400,000	0.2%
21	Arizona	281,969,200,000	1.8%
32	Arkansas	131,534,700,000	0.9%
1	California	1,901,329,100,000	12.3%
22	Colorado	270,768,700,000	1.8%
23	Connecticut	221,000,300,000	1.4%
46	Delaware	44,115,000,000	0.3%
4	Florida	920,066,700,000	6.0%
10	Georgia	459,211,300,000	3.0%
41	Hawaii	59,080,900,000	0.4%
39	Idaho	70,413,500,000	0.5%
5	Illinois	655,520,600,000	4.2%
17	Indiana	308,111,500,000	2.0%
30	Iowa	154,931,600,000	1.0%
31	Kansas	146,852,500,000	0.9%
27	Kentucky	191,962,900,000	1.2%
25	Louisiana	212,579,300,000	1.4%
42	Maine	58,286,800,000	0.4%
16	Maryland	311,147,500,000	2.0%
13	Massachusetts	397,287,000,000	2.6%
11	Michigan	458,789,600,000	3.0%
18	Minnesota	287,715,800,000	1.9%
35	Mississippi	119,120,800,000	0.8%
19	Missouri	285,636,400,000	1.8%
44	Montana	46,782,400,000	0.3%
36	Nebraska	100,783,700,000	0.7%
33	Nevada	129,244,800,000	0.8%
40	New Hampshire	69,325,800,000	0.4%
8	New Jersey	472,723,600,000	3.1%
37	New Mexico	83,520,100,000	0.5%
3	New York	1,005,881,200,000	6.5%
9	North Carolina	459,242,100,000	3.0%
47	North Dakota	41,830,300,000	0.3%
7	Ohio	566,001,000,000	3.7%
29	Oklahoma	178,604,900,000	1.2%
28	Oregon	182,960,400,000	1.2%
6	Pennsylvania	642,880,100,000	4.2%
43	Rhode Island	51,941,800,000	0.3%
24	South Carolina	213,064,300,000	1.4%
45	South Dakota	45,536,600,000	0.3%
15	Tennessee	311,754,500,000	2.0%
2	Texas	1,278,673,500,000	8.3%
34	Utah	126,966,300,000	0.8%
50	Vermont	29,902,700,000	0.2%
12	Virginia	422,263,100,000	2.7%
14	Washington	368,704,900,000	2.4%
38	West Virginia	74,277,700,000	0.5%
20	Wisconsin	284,093,300,000	1.8%
49	Wyoming	32,277,000,000	0.2%

RANK ORDER

RANK	STATE	INCOME	% of USA
1	California	$1,901,329,100,000	12.3%
2	Texas	1,278,673,500,000	8.3%
3	New York	1,005,881,200,000	6.5%
4	Florida	920,066,700,000	6.0%
5	Illinois	655,520,600,000	4.2%
6	Pennsylvania	642,880,100,000	4.2%
7	Ohio	566,001,000,000	3.7%
8	New Jersey	472,723,600,000	3.1%
9	North Carolina	459,242,100,000	3.0%
10	Georgia	459,211,300,000	3.0%
11	Michigan	458,789,600,000	3.0%
12	Virginia	422,263,100,000	2.7%
13	Massachusetts	397,287,000,000	2.6%
14	Washington	368,704,900,000	2.4%
15	Tennessee	311,754,500,000	2.0%
16	Maryland	311,147,500,000	2.0%
17	Indiana	308,111,500,000	2.0%
18	Minnesota	287,715,800,000	1.9%
19	Missouri	285,636,400,000	1.8%
20	Wisconsin	284,093,300,000	1.8%
21	Arizona	281,969,200,000	1.8%
22	Colorado	270,768,700,000	1.8%
23	Connecticut	221,000,300,000	1.4%
24	South Carolina	213,064,300,000	1.4%
25	Louisiana	212,579,300,000	1.4%
26	Alabama	212,329,000,000	1.4%
27	Kentucky	191,962,900,000	1.2%
28	Oregon	182,960,400,000	1.2%
29	Oklahoma	178,604,900,000	1.2%
30	Iowa	154,931,600,000	1.0%
31	Kansas	146,852,500,000	0.9%
32	Arkansas	131,534,700,000	0.9%
33	Nevada	129,244,800,000	0.8%
34	Utah	126,966,300,000	0.8%
35	Mississippi	119,120,800,000	0.8%
36	Nebraska	100,783,700,000	0.7%
37	New Mexico	83,520,100,000	0.5%
38	West Virginia	74,277,700,000	0.5%
39	Idaho	70,413,500,000	0.5%
40	New Hampshire	69,325,800,000	0.4%
41	Hawaii	59,080,900,000	0.4%
42	Maine	58,286,800,000	0.4%
43	Rhode Island	51,941,800,000	0.3%
44	Montana	46,782,400,000	0.3%
45	South Dakota	45,536,600,000	0.3%
46	Delaware	44,115,000,000	0.3%
47	North Dakota	41,830,300,000	0.3%
48	Alaska	37,876,400,000	0.2%
49	Wyoming	32,277,000,000	0.2%
50	Vermont	29,902,700,000	0.2%
	District of Columbia	44,045,900,000	0.3%

Source: U.S. Department of Commerce, Bureau of Economic Analysis
    "Annual State Personal Income" (https://apps.bea.gov/iTable/index_regional.cfm)
*Real personal income is personal income at Regional Price Parities (RPPs) divided by the national Personal Consumption Expenditure price index (a measure of U.S. inflation). RPPs are regional price levels expressed as a percentage of the overall national price level for a given year. The price levels are determined by the average prices paid by consumers for the mix of goods and services consumed in each region. Taking the ratio of RPPs shows the difference in price levels across regions.

Percent Change in Real Personal Income: 2015 to 2016

National Percent Change = 1.5% Increase*

ALPHA ORDER				RANK ORDER		
RANK	STATE	PERCENT CHANGE		RANK	STATE	PERCENT CHANGE
28	Alabama	1.2		1	Utah	3.6
48	Alaska	(2.6)		1	Washington	3.6
7	Arizona	2.8		3	Georgia	3.5
22	Arkansas	1.6		4	Idaho	3.1
14	California	2.3		5	Maryland	2.9
36	Colorado	0.7		5	Oregon	2.9
38	Connecticut	0.5		7	Arizona	2.8
34	Delaware	0.9		7	Hawaii	2.8
11	Florida	2.5		9	Indiana	2.7
3	Georgia	3.5		10	South Carolina	2.6
7	Hawaii	2.8		11	Florida	2.5
4	Idaho	3.1		11	New Hampshire	2.5
35	Illinois	0.8		11	North Carolina	2.5
9	Indiana	2.7		14	California	2.3
41	Iowa	(0.1)		15	Michigan	2.2
42	Kansas	(0.2)		15	Nevada	2.2
25	Kentucky	1.5		17	Maine	2.1
45	Louisiana	(1.0)		17	Montana	2.1
17	Maine	2.1		17	Tennessee	2.1
5	Maryland	2.9		20	Vermont	2.0
22	Massachusetts	1.6		21	New York	1.8
15	Michigan	2.2		22	Arkansas	1.6
27	Minnesota	1.3		22	Massachusetts	1.6
37	Mississippi	0.6		22	Wisconsin	1.6
28	Missouri	1.2		25	Kentucky	1.5
17	Montana	2.1		25	New Jersey	1.5
46	Nebraska	(1.5)		27	Minnesota	1.3
15	Nevada	2.2		28	Alabama	1.2
11	New Hampshire	2.5		28	Missouri	1.2
25	New Jersey	1.5		28	Virginia	1.2
31	New Mexico	1.1		31	New Mexico	1.1
21	New York	1.8		32	Ohio	1.0
11	North Carolina	2.5		32	Pennsylvania	1.0
47	North Dakota	(1.6)		34	Delaware	0.9
32	Ohio	1.0		35	Illinois	0.8
50	Oklahoma	(4.5)		36	Colorado	0.7
5	Oregon	2.9		37	Mississippi	0.6
32	Pennsylvania	1.0		38	Connecticut	0.5
39	Rhode Island	0.3		39	Rhode Island	0.3
10	South Carolina	2.6		40	West Virginia	0.1
43	South Dakota	(0.4)		41	Iowa	(0.1)
17	Tennessee	2.1		42	Kansas	(0.2)
44	Texas	(0.6)		43	South Dakota	(0.4)
1	Utah	3.6		44	Texas	(0.6)
20	Vermont	2.0		45	Louisiana	(1.0)
28	Virginia	1.2		46	Nebraska	(1.5)
1	Washington	3.6		47	North Dakota	(1.6)
40	West Virginia	0.1		48	Alaska	(2.6)
22	Wisconsin	1.6		49	Wyoming	(4.4)
49	Wyoming	(4.4)		50	Oklahoma	(4.5)
					District of Columbia	4.4

Source: U.S. Department of Commerce, Bureau of Economic Analysis
   "Annual State Personal Income" (https://apps.bea.gov/iTable/index_regional.cfm)
*Real personal income is personal income at Regional Price Parities (RPPs) divided by the national Personal Consumption Expenditure price index (a measure of U.S. inflation). RPPs are regional price levels expressed as a percentage of the overall national price level for a given year. The price levels are determined by the average prices paid by consumers for the mix of goods and services consumed in each region. Taking the ratio of RPPs shows the difference in price levels across regions.

Per Capita Real Personal Income in 2016

National Per Capita = $47,807*

ALPHA ORDER

RANK	STATE	PER CAPITA
41	Alabama	$43,684
11	Alaska	51,079
47	Arizona	40,814
38	Arkansas	44,018
23	California	48,384
21	Colorado	48,963
1	Connecticut	61,600
28	Delaware	46,305
36	Florida	44,541
37	Georgia	44,525
46	Hawaii	41,353
44	Idaho	41,912
12	Illinois	51,070
27	Indiana	46,444
18	Iowa	49,485
15	Kansas	50,504
42	Kentucky	43,273
32	Louisiana	45,363
40	Maine	43,817
10	Maryland	51,645
2	Massachusetts	58,221
29	Michigan	46,186
8	Minnesota	52,075
50	Mississippi	39,901
25	Missouri	46,893
34	Montana	45,041
6	Nebraska	52,833
39	Nevada	43,972
9	New Hampshire	51,929
7	New Jersey	52,651
49	New Mexico	40,049
13	New York	50,709
33	North Carolina	45,216
3	North Dakota	55,364
22	Ohio	48,699
31	Oklahoma	45,548
35	Oregon	44,778
16	Pennsylvania	50,276
20	Rhode Island	49,114
43	South Carolina	42,958
5	South Dakota	52,855
26	Tennessee	46,885
30	Texas	45,823
45	Utah	41,706
24	Vermont	47,971
17	Virginia	50,184
14	Washington	50,640
48	West Virginia	40,619
19	Wisconsin	49,211
4	Wyoming	55,183

RANK ORDER

RANK	STATE	PER CAPITA
1	Connecticut	$61,600
2	Massachusetts	58,221
3	North Dakota	55,364
4	Wyoming	55,183
5	South Dakota	52,855
6	Nebraska	52,833
7	New Jersey	52,651
8	Minnesota	52,075
9	New Hampshire	51,929
10	Maryland	51,645
11	Alaska	51,079
12	Illinois	51,070
13	New York	50,709
14	Washington	50,640
15	Kansas	50,504
16	Pennsylvania	50,276
17	Virginia	50,184
18	Iowa	49,485
19	Wisconsin	49,211
20	Rhode Island	49,114
21	Colorado	48,963
22	Ohio	48,699
23	California	48,384
24	Vermont	47,971
25	Missouri	46,893
26	Tennessee	46,885
27	Indiana	46,444
28	Delaware	46,305
29	Michigan	46,186
30	Texas	45,823
31	Oklahoma	45,548
32	Louisiana	45,363
33	North Carolina	45,216
34	Montana	45,041
35	Oregon	44,778
36	Florida	44,541
37	Georgia	44,525
38	Arkansas	44,018
39	Nevada	43,972
40	Maine	43,817
41	Alabama	43,684
42	Kentucky	43,273
43	South Carolina	42,958
44	Idaho	41,912
45	Utah	41,706
46	Hawaii	41,353
47	Arizona	40,814
48	West Virginia	40,619
49	New Mexico	40,049
50	Mississippi	39,901
	District of Columbia	64,363

Source: U.S. Department of Commerce, Bureau of Economic Analysis
"Annual State Personal Income" (https://apps.bea.gov/iTable/index_regional.cfm)
*Real personal income is personal income at Regional Price Parities (RPPs) divided by the national Personal Consumption Expenditure price index (a measure of U.S. inflation). RPPs are regional price levels expressed as a percentage of the overall national price level for a given year. The price levels are determined by the average prices paid by consumers for the mix of goods and services consumed in each region. Taking the ratio of RPPs shows the difference in price levels across regions.

Percent Change in Per Capita Real Personal Income: 2015 to 2016

National Percent Change = 0.7% Increase*

ALPHA ORDER

RANK	STATE	PERCENT CHANGE
25	Alabama	1.0
48	Alaska	(3.1)
17	Arizona	1.2
17	Arkansas	1.2
11	California	1.6
42	Colorado	(1.0)
31	Connecticut	0.7
39	Delaware	0.0
35	Florida	0.5
4	Georgia	2.3
1	Hawaii	2.6
14	Idaho	1.3
25	Illinois	1.0
3	Indiana	2.4
41	Iowa	(0.4)
40	Kansas	(0.3)
22	Kentucky	1.1
44	Louisiana	(1.4)
8	Maine	1.9
2	Maryland	2.5
17	Massachusetts	1.2
7	Michigan	2.0
35	Minnesota	0.5
33	Mississippi	0.6
29	Missouri	0.9
25	Montana	1.0
46	Nebraska	(2.2)
37	Nevada	0.3
6	New Hampshire	2.1
14	New Jersey	1.3
25	New Mexico	1.0
9	New York	1.7
13	North Carolina	1.4
45	North Dakota	(1.7)
30	Ohio	0.8
50	Oklahoma	(4.9)
22	Oregon	1.1
22	Pennsylvania	1.1
38	Rhode Island	0.1
17	South Carolina	1.2
43	South Dakota	(1.3)
17	Tennessee	1.2
46	Texas	(2.2)
11	Utah	1.6
5	Vermont	2.2
33	Virginia	0.6
9	Washington	1.7
31	West Virginia	0.7
14	Wisconsin	1.3
49	Wyoming	(4.2)

RANK ORDER

RANK	STATE	PERCENT CHANGE
1	Hawaii	2.6
2	Maryland	2.5
3	Indiana	2.4
4	Georgia	2.3
5	Vermont	2.2
6	New Hampshire	2.1
7	Michigan	2.0
8	Maine	1.9
9	New York	1.7
9	Washington	1.7
11	California	1.6
11	Utah	1.6
13	North Carolina	1.4
14	Idaho	1.3
14	New Jersey	1.3
14	Wisconsin	1.3
17	Arizona	1.2
17	Arkansas	1.2
17	Massachusetts	1.2
17	South Carolina	1.2
17	Tennessee	1.2
22	Kentucky	1.1
22	Oregon	1.1
22	Pennsylvania	1.1
25	Alabama	1.0
25	Illinois	1.0
25	Montana	1.0
25	New Mexico	1.0
29	Missouri	0.9
30	Ohio	0.8
31	Connecticut	0.7
31	West Virginia	0.7
33	Mississippi	0.6
33	Virginia	0.6
35	Florida	0.5
35	Minnesota	0.5
37	Nevada	0.3
38	Rhode Island	0.1
39	Delaware	0.0
40	Kansas	(0.3)
41	Iowa	(0.4)
42	Colorado	(1.0)
43	South Dakota	(1.3)
44	Louisiana	(1.4)
45	North Dakota	(1.7)
46	Nebraska	(2.2)
46	Texas	(2.2)
48	Alaska	(3.1)
49	Wyoming	(4.2)
50	Oklahoma	(4.9)

District of Columbia	2.6

Source: U.S. Department of Commerce, Bureau of Economic Analysis
"Annual State Personal Income" (https://apps.bea.gov/iTable/index_regional.cfm)
*Real personal income is personal income at Regional Price Parities (RPPs) divided by the national Personal Consumption Expenditure price index (a measure of U.S. inflation). RPPs are regional price levels expressed as a percentage of the overall national price level for a given year. The price levels are determined by the average prices paid by consumers for the mix of goods and services consumed in each region. Taking the ratio of RPPs shows the difference in price levels across regions.

Personal Consumption Expenditures in 2017

National Total = $13,314,862,900,000*

ALPHA ORDER

RANK	STATE	EXPENDITURES	% of USA
27	Alabama	$158,374,900,000	1.2%
47	Alaska	35,537,100,000	0.3%
17	Arizona	242,400,000,000	1.8%
34	Arkansas	98,765,800,000	0.7%
1	California	1,754,083,300,000	13.2%
19	Colorado	236,838,600,000	1.8%
23	Connecticut	181,992,100,000	1.4%
45	Delaware	40,738,800,000	0.3%
4	Florida	829,401,500,000	6.2%
12	Georgia	365,321,200,000	2.7%
39	Hawaii	65,767,900,000	0.5%
41	Idaho	60,675,400,000	0.5%
5	Illinois	549,556,300,000	4.1%
18	Indiana	242,040,600,000	1.8%
31	Iowa	118,443,500,000	0.9%
33	Kansas	106,428,600,000	0.8%
28	Kentucky	150,484,900,000	1.1%
26	Louisiana	161,794,100,000	1.2%
42	Maine	57,930,300,000	0.4%
15	Maryland	272,555,900,000	2.0%
11	Massachusetts	365,404,800,000	2.7%
9	Michigan	390,895,100,000	2.9%
16	Minnesota	252,922,800,000	1.9%
35	Mississippi	89,604,200,000	0.7%
20	Missouri	236,099,700,000	1.8%
44	Montana	43,023,200,000	0.3%
36	Nebraska	77,111,100,000	0.6%
30	Nevada	119,338,900,000	0.9%
38	New Hampshire	67,495,600,000	0.5%
8	New Jersey	449,476,700,000	3.4%
37	New Mexico	72,447,100,000	0.5%
3	New York	978,398,700,000	7.3%
13	North Carolina	350,856,800,000	2.6%
48	North Dakota	35,286,300,000	0.3%
7	Ohio	459,380,900,000	3.5%
29	Oklahoma	129,937,200,000	1.0%
25	Oregon	169,045,600,000	1.3%
6	Pennsylvania	548,320,600,000	4.1%
43	Rhode Island	45,769,500,000	0.3%
24	South Carolina	169,280,600,000	1.3%
46	South Dakota	37,011,500,000	0.3%
22	Tennessee	234,421,900,000	1.8%
2	Texas	1,061,038,200,000	8.0%
32	Utah	111,001,700,000	0.8%
49	Vermont	29,839,100,000	0.2%
10	Virginia	368,875,200,000	2.8%
14	Washington	328,644,500,000	2.5%
40	West Virginia	63,115,200,000	0.5%
21	Wisconsin	235,644,100,000	1.8%
50	Wyoming	23,772,700,000	0.2%

RANK ORDER

RANK	STATE	EXPENDITURES	% of USA
1	California	$1,754,083,300,000	13.2%
2	Texas	1,061,038,200,000	8.0%
3	New York	978,398,700,000	7.3%
4	Florida	829,401,500,000	6.2%
5	Illinois	549,556,300,000	4.1%
6	Pennsylvania	548,320,600,000	4.1%
7	Ohio	459,380,900,000	3.5%
8	New Jersey	449,476,700,000	3.4%
9	Michigan	390,895,100,000	2.9%
10	Virginia	368,875,200,000	2.8%
11	Massachusetts	365,404,800,000	2.7%
12	Georgia	365,321,200,000	2.7%
13	North Carolina	350,856,800,000	2.6%
14	Washington	328,644,500,000	2.5%
15	Maryland	272,555,900,000	2.0%
16	Minnesota	252,922,800,000	1.9%
17	Arizona	242,400,000,000	1.8%
18	Indiana	242,040,600,000	1.8%
19	Colorado	236,838,600,000	1.8%
20	Missouri	236,099,700,000	1.8%
21	Wisconsin	235,644,100,000	1.8%
22	Tennessee	234,421,900,000	1.8%
23	Connecticut	181,992,100,000	1.4%
24	South Carolina	169,280,600,000	1.3%
25	Oregon	169,045,600,000	1.3%
26	Louisiana	161,794,100,000	1.2%
27	Alabama	158,374,900,000	1.2%
28	Kentucky	150,484,900,000	1.1%
29	Oklahoma	129,937,200,000	1.0%
30	Nevada	119,338,900,000	0.9%
31	Iowa	118,443,500,000	0.9%
32	Utah	111,001,700,000	0.8%
33	Kansas	106,428,600,000	0.8%
34	Arkansas	98,765,800,000	0.7%
35	Mississippi	89,604,200,000	0.7%
36	Nebraska	77,111,100,000	0.6%
37	New Mexico	72,447,100,000	0.5%
38	New Hampshire	67,495,600,000	0.5%
39	Hawaii	65,767,900,000	0.5%
40	West Virginia	63,115,200,000	0.5%
41	Idaho	60,675,400,000	0.5%
42	Maine	57,930,300,000	0.4%
43	Rhode Island	45,769,500,000	0.3%
44	Montana	43,023,200,000	0.3%
45	Delaware	40,738,800,000	0.3%
46	South Dakota	37,011,500,000	0.3%
47	Alaska	35,537,100,000	0.3%
48	North Dakota	35,286,300,000	0.3%
49	Vermont	29,839,100,000	0.2%
50	Wyoming	23,772,700,000	0.2%
	District of Columbia	42,272,900,000	0.3%

Source: U.S. Department of Commerce, Bureau of Economic Analysis
    "Personal Consumption Expenditures by State" (https://apps.bea.gov/iTable/index_regional.cfm)
*PCE by state is the state counterpart of the Nation's personal consumption expenditures (PCE). PCE represents the goods and services purchased by or on behalf of households, plus the purchases of nonprofit institutions serving households. For each state and for the District of Columbia, personal consumption expenditures are those expenditures made by or on behalf of residents. These expenditures include expenditures on activities outside of the state.

Per Capita Personal Consumption Expenditures in 2017

National Per Capita = $40,878*

ALPHA ORDER

RANK	STATE	PER CAPITA
49	Alabama	$32,489
6	Alaska	48,036
42	Arizona	34,548
48	Arkansas	32,875
13	California	44,366
21	Colorado	42,239
2	Connecticut	50,720
20	Delaware	42,351
28	Florida	39,525
38	Georgia	35,028
9	Hawaii	46,071
37	Idaho	35,339
17	Illinois	42,927
35	Indiana	36,305
32	Iowa	37,652
34	Kansas	36,534
45	Kentucky	33,785
43	Louisiana	34,539
15	Maine	43,364
11	Maryland	45,034
1	Massachusetts	53,267
30	Michigan	39,237
10	Minnesota	45,354
50	Mississippi	30,027
31	Missouri	38,619
23	Montana	40,955
26	Nebraska	40,160
27	Nevada	39,806
3	New Hampshire	50,265
4	New Jersey	49,911
41	New Mexico	34,696
5	New York	49,291
44	North Carolina	34,152
8	North Dakota	46,713
29	Ohio	39,403
47	Oklahoma	33,056
24	Oregon	40,805
18	Pennsylvania	42,819
16	Rhode Island	43,193
46	South Carolina	33,692
19	South Dakota	42,558
39	Tennessee	34,905
33	Texas	37,486
36	Utah	35,786
7	Vermont	47,845
14	Virginia	43,551
12	Washington	44,377
40	West Virginia	34,758
25	Wisconsin	40,660
22	Wyoming	41,036

RANK ORDER

RANK	STATE	PER CAPITA
1	Massachusetts	$53,267
2	Connecticut	50,720
3	New Hampshire	50,265
4	New Jersey	49,911
5	New York	49,291
6	Alaska	48,036
7	Vermont	47,845
8	North Dakota	46,713
9	Hawaii	46,071
10	Minnesota	45,354
11	Maryland	45,034
12	Washington	44,377
13	California	44,366
14	Virginia	43,551
15	Maine	43,364
16	Rhode Island	43,193
17	Illinois	42,927
18	Pennsylvania	42,819
19	South Dakota	42,558
20	Delaware	42,351
21	Colorado	42,239
22	Wyoming	41,036
23	Montana	40,955
24	Oregon	40,805
25	Wisconsin	40,660
26	Nebraska	40,160
27	Nevada	39,806
28	Florida	39,525
29	Ohio	39,403
30	Michigan	39,237
31	Missouri	38,619
32	Iowa	37,652
33	Texas	37,486
34	Kansas	36,534
35	Indiana	36,305
36	Utah	35,786
37	Idaho	35,339
38	Georgia	35,028
39	Tennessee	34,905
40	West Virginia	34,758
41	New Mexico	34,696
42	Arizona	34,548
43	Louisiana	34,539
44	North Carolina	34,152
45	Kentucky	33,785
46	South Carolina	33,692
47	Oklahoma	33,056
48	Arkansas	32,875
49	Alabama	32,489
50	Mississippi	30,027

District of Columbia — 60,914

Source: U.S. Department of Commerce, Bureau of Economic Analysis
"Personal Consumption Expenditures by State" (https://apps.bea.gov/iTable/index_regional.cfm)
*PCE by state is the state counterpart of the Nation's personal consumption expenditures (PCE). PCE represents the goods and services purchased by or on behalf of households, plus the purchases of nonprofit institutions serving households. For each state and for the District of Columbia, personal consumption expenditures are those expenditures made by or on behalf of residents. These expenditures include expenditures on activities outside of the state.

Percent Change in Personal Consumption Expenditures: 2016 to 2017

National Percent Change = 4.3% Increase*

ALPHA ORDER

RANK	STATE	PERCENT CHANGE
38	Alabama	3.2
35	Alaska	3.5
4	Arizona	5.5
19	Arkansas	4.3
9	California	5.0
5	Colorado	5.4
38	Connecticut	3.2
35	Delaware	3.5
17	Florida	4.4
14	Georgia	4.6
13	Hawaii	4.7
1	Idaho	6.9
28	Illinois	3.8
14	Indiana	4.6
30	Iowa	3.7
38	Kansas	3.2
37	Kentucky	3.3
48	Louisiana	2.5
30	Maine	3.7
24	Maryland	4.0
21	Massachusetts	4.2
33	Michigan	3.6
6	Minnesota	5.3
44	Mississippi	2.8
28	Missouri	3.8
6	Montana	5.3
24	Nebraska	4.0
19	Nevada	4.3
26	New Hampshire	3.9
38	New Jersey	3.2
45	New Mexico	2.7
17	New York	4.4
9	North Carolina	5.0
50	North Dakota	2.0
33	Ohio	3.6
45	Oklahoma	2.7
6	Oregon	5.3
30	Pennsylvania	3.7
38	Rhode Island	3.2
21	South Carolina	4.2
14	South Dakota	4.6
9	Tennessee	5.0
9	Texas	5.0
3	Utah	5.7
43	Vermont	2.9
26	Virginia	3.9
2	Washington	6.1
45	West Virginia	2.7
21	Wisconsin	4.2
48	Wyoming	2.5

RANK ORDER

RANK	STATE	PERCENT CHANGE
1	Idaho	6.9
2	Washington	6.1
3	Utah	5.7
4	Arizona	5.5
5	Colorado	5.4
6	Minnesota	5.3
6	Montana	5.3
6	Oregon	5.3
9	California	5.0
9	North Carolina	5.0
9	Tennessee	5.0
9	Texas	5.0
13	Hawaii	4.7
14	Georgia	4.6
14	Indiana	4.6
14	South Dakota	4.6
17	Florida	4.4
17	New York	4.4
19	Arkansas	4.3
19	Nevada	4.3
21	Massachusetts	4.2
21	South Carolina	4.2
21	Wisconsin	4.2
24	Maryland	4.0
24	Nebraska	4.0
26	New Hampshire	3.9
26	Virginia	3.9
28	Illinois	3.8
28	Missouri	3.8
30	Iowa	3.7
30	Maine	3.7
30	Pennsylvania	3.7
33	Michigan	3.6
33	Ohio	3.6
35	Alaska	3.5
35	Delaware	3.5
37	Kentucky	3.3
38	Alabama	3.2
38	Connecticut	3.2
38	Kansas	3.2
38	New Jersey	3.2
38	Rhode Island	3.2
43	Vermont	2.9
44	Mississippi	2.8
45	New Mexico	2.7
45	Oklahoma	2.7
45	West Virginia	2.7
48	Louisiana	2.5
48	Wyoming	2.5
50	North Dakota	2.0
	District of Columbia	4.5

Source: U.S. Department of Commerce, Bureau of Economic Analysis
"Personal Consumption Expenditures by State" (https://apps.bea.gov/iTable/index_regional.cfm)
*PCE by state is the state counterpart of the Nation's personal consumption expenditures (PCE). PCE represents the goods and services purchased by or on behalf of households, plus the purchases of nonprofit institutions serving households. For each state and for the District of Columbia, personal consumption expenditures are those expenditures made by or on behalf of residents. These expenditures include expenditures on activities outside of the state.

Percent Change in Per Capita
Personal Consumption Expenditures: 2016 to 2017
National Percent Change = 3.6% Increase*

ALPHA ORDER

RANK	STATE	PERCENT CHANGE
38	Alabama	2.9
14	Alaska	3.8
10	Arizona	3.9
17	Arkansas	3.7
4	California	4.3
10	Colorado	3.9
34	Connecticut	3.2
46	Delaware	2.5
43	Florida	2.8
21	Georgia	3.5
1	Hawaii	4.8
2	Idaho	4.6
8	Illinois	4.1
8	Indiana	4.1
34	Iowa	3.2
36	Kansas	3.1
38	Kentucky	2.9
46	Louisiana	2.5
28	Maine	3.3
21	Maryland	3.5
17	Massachusetts	3.7
28	Michigan	3.3
4	Minnesota	4.3
43	Mississippi	2.8
27	Missouri	3.4
7	Montana	4.2
28	Nebraska	3.3
49	Nevada	2.2
28	New Hampshire	3.3
38	New Jersey	2.9
45	New Mexico	2.6
3	New York	4.4
14	North Carolina	3.8
50	North Dakota	2.0
28	Ohio	3.3
46	Oklahoma	2.5
10	Oregon	3.9
21	Pennsylvania	3.5
37	Rhode Island	3.0
38	South Carolina	2.9
20	South Dakota	3.6
10	Tennessee	3.9
21	Texas	3.5
17	Utah	3.7
38	Vermont	2.9
28	Virginia	3.3
4	Washington	4.3
21	West Virginia	3.5
14	Wisconsin	3.8
21	Wyoming	3.5

RANK ORDER

RANK	STATE	PERCENT CHANGE
1	Hawaii	4.8
2	Idaho	4.6
3	New York	4.4
4	California	4.3
4	Minnesota	4.3
4	Washington	4.3
7	Montana	4.2
8	Illinois	4.1
8	Indiana	4.1
10	Arizona	3.9
10	Colorado	3.9
10	Oregon	3.9
10	Tennessee	3.9
14	Alaska	3.8
14	North Carolina	3.8
14	Wisconsin	3.8
17	Arkansas	3.7
17	Massachusetts	3.7
17	Utah	3.7
20	South Dakota	3.6
21	Georgia	3.5
21	Maryland	3.5
21	Pennsylvania	3.5
21	Texas	3.5
21	West Virginia	3.5
21	Wyoming	3.5
27	Missouri	3.4
28	Maine	3.3
28	Michigan	3.3
28	Nebraska	3.3
28	New Hampshire	3.3
28	Ohio	3.3
28	Virginia	3.3
34	Connecticut	3.2
34	Iowa	3.2
36	Kansas	3.1
37	Rhode Island	3.0
38	Alabama	2.9
38	Kentucky	2.9
38	New Jersey	2.9
38	South Carolina	2.9
38	Vermont	2.9
43	Florida	2.8
43	Mississippi	2.8
45	New Mexico	2.6
46	Delaware	2.5
46	Louisiana	2.5
46	Oklahoma	2.5
49	Nevada	2.2
50	North Dakota	2.0
	District of Columbia	3.1

Source: U.S. Department of Commerce, Bureau of Economic Analysis
"Personal Consumption Expenditures by State" (https://apps.bea.gov/iTable/index_regional.cfm)
*PCE by state is the state counterpart of the Nation's personal consumption expenditures (PCE). PCE represents the goods and services purchased by or on behalf of households, plus the purchases of nonprofit institutions serving households. For each state and for the District of Columbia, personal consumption expenditures are those expenditures made by or on behalf of residents. These expenditures include expenditures on activities outside of the state.

Bankruptcy Filings in 2018

National Total = 773,375 Bankruptcies*

ALPHA ORDER

RANK	STATE	BANKRUPTCIES	% of USA
10	Alabama	26,643	3.4%
50	Alaska	452	0.1%
18	Arizona	16,256	2.1%
25	Arkansas	10,642	1.4%
1	California	68,860	8.9%
24	Colorado	11,507	1.5%
34	Connecticut	5,917	0.8%
39	Delaware	3,231	0.4%
4	Florida	42,418	5.5%
3	Georgia	45,720	5.9%
43	Hawaii	1,503	0.2%
37	Idaho	3,709	0.5%
2	Illinois	49,002	6.3%
12	Indiana	22,943	3.0%
35	Iowa	4,566	0.6%
32	Kansas	6,845	0.9%
19	Kentucky	15,110	2.0%
22	Louisiana	13,446	1.7%
44	Maine	1,497	0.2%
16	Maryland	17,556	2.3%
31	Massachusetts	8,556	1.1%
9	Michigan	29,854	3.9%
27	Minnesota	9,880	1.3%
23	Mississippi	12,631	1.6%
15	Missouri	17,583	2.3%
45	Montana	1,279	0.2%
36	Nebraska	4,015	0.5%
29	Nevada	9,258	1.2%
42	New Hampshire	1,812	0.2%
11	New Jersey	26,525	3.4%
38	New Mexico	3,291	0.4%
7	New York	34,457	4.5%
20	North Carolina	14,148	1.8%
48	North Dakota	781	0.1%
5	Ohio	37,500	4.8%
28	Oklahoma	9,636	1.2%
30	Oregon	8,907	1.2%
14	Pennsylvania	21,580	2.8%
41	Rhode Island	2,242	0.3%
33	South Carolina	6,660	0.9%
46	South Dakota	1,075	0.1%
6	Tennessee	34,659	4.5%
8	Texas	33,664	4.4%
26	Utah	9,886	1.3%
49	Vermont	541	0.1%
13	Virginia	22,689	2.9%
21	Washington	13,600	1.8%
40	West Virginia	3,147	0.4%
17	Wisconsin	16,607	2.1%
47	Wyoming	1,070	0.1%

RANK ORDER

RANK	STATE	BANKRUPTCIES	% of USA
1	California	68,860	8.9%
2	Illinois	49,002	6.3%
3	Georgia	45,720	5.9%
4	Florida	42,418	5.5%
5	Ohio	37,500	4.8%
6	Tennessee	34,659	4.5%
7	New York	34,457	4.5%
8	Texas	33,664	4.4%
9	Michigan	29,854	3.9%
10	Alabama	26,643	3.4%
11	New Jersey	26,525	3.4%
12	Indiana	22,943	3.0%
13	Virginia	22,689	2.9%
14	Pennsylvania	21,580	2.8%
15	Missouri	17,583	2.3%
16	Maryland	17,556	2.3%
17	Wisconsin	16,607	2.1%
18	Arizona	16,256	2.1%
19	Kentucky	15,110	2.0%
20	North Carolina	14,148	1.8%
21	Washington	13,600	1.8%
22	Louisiana	13,446	1.7%
23	Mississippi	12,631	1.6%
24	Colorado	11,507	1.5%
25	Arkansas	10,642	1.4%
26	Utah	9,886	1.3%
27	Minnesota	9,880	1.3%
28	Oklahoma	9,636	1.2%
29	Nevada	9,258	1.2%
30	Oregon	8,907	1.2%
31	Massachusetts	8,556	1.1%
32	Kansas	6,845	0.9%
33	South Carolina	6,660	0.9%
34	Connecticut	5,917	0.8%
35	Iowa	4,566	0.6%
36	Nebraska	4,015	0.5%
37	Idaho	3,709	0.5%
38	New Mexico	3,291	0.4%
39	Delaware	3,231	0.4%
40	West Virginia	3,147	0.4%
41	Rhode Island	2,242	0.3%
42	New Hampshire	1,812	0.2%
43	Hawaii	1,503	0.2%
44	Maine	1,497	0.2%
45	Montana	1,279	0.2%
46	South Dakota	1,075	0.1%
47	Wyoming	1,070	0.1%
48	North Dakota	781	0.1%
49	Vermont	541	0.1%
50	Alaska	452	0.1%
	District of Columbia	839	0.1%

Source: CQ Press using data from Administrative Office of the U.S. Courts
"Table F-2, U.S. Bankruptcy Courts" (https://www.uscourts.gov/statistics-reports/caseload-statistics-data-tables)
*For 12 months through September 2018. Includes business (22,103) and non-business (751,272) filings. Includes all chapters of bankruptcy. National total includes 7,180 bankruptcies in U.S. territories.

Personal Bankruptcy Rate in 2018

National Rate = 227 Personal Bankruptcies per 100,000 Population*

ALPHA ORDER

RANK	STATE	RATE
1	Alabama	540
50	Alaska	58
22	Arizona	221
6	Arkansas	346
33	California	167
27	Colorado	195
36	Connecticut	161
20	Delaware	231
28	Florida	191
3	Georgia	427
47	Hawaii	101
24	Idaho	206
5	Illinois	378
7	Indiana	339
38	Iowa	139
21	Kansas	229
8	Kentucky	334
15	Louisiana	282
46	Maine	106
14	Maryland	284
42	Massachusetts	119
12	Michigan	295
31	Minnesota	171
4	Mississippi	416
15	Missouri	282
44	Montana	116
26	Nebraska	202
11	Nevada	296
40	New Hampshire	128
13	New Jersey	290
37	New Mexico	153
34	New York	166
39	North Carolina	132
48	North Dakota	98
9	Ohio	316
19	Oklahoma	239
23	Oregon	207
35	Pennsylvania	163
24	Rhode Island	206
40	South Carolina	128
43	South Dakota	117
2	Tennessee	506
45	Texas	109
10	Utah	308
49	Vermont	80
18	Virginia	261
30	Washington	175
32	West Virginia	168
17	Wisconsin	280
29	Wyoming	176

RANK ORDER

RANK	STATE	RATE
1	Alabama	540
2	Tennessee	506
3	Georgia	427
4	Mississippi	416
5	Illinois	378
6	Arkansas	346
7	Indiana	339
8	Kentucky	334
9	Ohio	316
10	Utah	308
11	Nevada	296
12	Michigan	295
13	New Jersey	290
14	Maryland	284
15	Louisiana	282
15	Missouri	282
17	Wisconsin	280
18	Virginia	261
19	Oklahoma	239
20	Delaware	231
21	Kansas	229
22	Arizona	221
23	Oregon	207
24	Idaho	206
24	Rhode Island	206
26	Nebraska	202
27	Colorado	195
28	Florida	191
29	Wyoming	176
30	Washington	175
31	Minnesota	171
32	West Virginia	168
33	California	167
34	New York	166
35	Pennsylvania	163
36	Connecticut	161
37	New Mexico	153
38	Iowa	139
39	North Carolina	132
40	New Hampshire	128
40	South Carolina	128
42	Massachusetts	119
43	South Dakota	117
44	Montana	116
45	Texas	109
46	Maine	106
47	Hawaii	101
48	North Dakota	98
49	Vermont	80
50	Alaska	58

District of Columbia	114

Source: CQ Press using data from Administrative Office of the U.S. Courts
"Table F-2, U.S. Bankruptcy Courts" (https://www.uscourts.gov/statistics-reports/caseload-statistics-data-tables)
*For 12 months through September 2018. National rate does not include bankruptcies or population in U.S. territories. Includes all nonbusiness bankruptcies.

Percent Change in Personal Bankruptcy Rate: 2017 to 2018

National Percent Change = 2.6% Decrease*

ALPHA ORDER			RANK ORDER		
RANK	STATE	PERCENT CHANGE	RANK	STATE	PERCENT CHANGE
27	Alabama	(2.0)	1	New York	7.8
12	Alaska	1.8	2	Hawaii	6.3
10	Arizona	2.3	3	Wyoming	6.0
21	Arkansas	(0.3)	4	Connecticut	5.9
45	California	(5.1)	5	Iowa	5.3
48	Colorado	(9.3)	6	Mississippi	5.1
4	Connecticut	5.9	7	Nevada	4.6
42	Delaware	(4.1)	8	Maine	3.9
40	Florida	(4.0)	9	Oklahoma	2.6
43	Georgia	(4.3)	10	Arizona	2.3
2	Hawaii	6.3	11	Kansas	2.2
35	Idaho	(3.3)	12	Alaska	1.8
44	Illinois	(4.8)	12	Maryland	1.8
31	Indiana	(2.9)	14	South Carolina	1.6
5	Iowa	5.3	15	Minnesota	1.2
11	Kansas	2.2	16	South Dakota	0.9
38	Kentucky	(3.7)	17	Massachusetts	0.8
18	Louisiana	0.7	18	Louisiana	0.7
8	Maine	3.9	18	New Jersey	0.7
12	Maryland	1.8	20	Rhode Island	0.0
17	Massachusetts	0.8	21	Arkansas	(0.3)
28	Michigan	(2.3)	21	Ohio	(0.3)
15	Minnesota	1.2	23	Virginia	(0.4)
6	Mississippi	5.1	24	New Mexico	(0.6)
36	Missouri	(3.4)	25	North Dakota	(1.0)
30	Montana	(2.5)	26	Nebraska	(1.9)
26	Nebraska	(1.9)	27	Alabama	(2.0)
7	Nevada	4.6	28	Michigan	(2.3)
28	New Hampshire	(2.3)	28	New Hampshire	(2.3)
18	New Jersey	0.7	30	Montana	(2.5)
24	New Mexico	(0.6)	31	Indiana	(2.9)
1	New York	7.8	31	North Carolina	(2.9)
31	North Carolina	(2.9)	31	Tennessee	(2.9)
25	North Dakota	(1.0)	34	Pennsylvania	(3.0)
21	Ohio	(0.3)	35	Idaho	(3.3)
9	Oklahoma	2.6	36	Missouri	(3.4)
38	Oregon	(3.7)	36	Wisconsin	(3.4)
34	Pennsylvania	(3.0)	38	Kentucky	(3.7)
20	Rhode Island	0.0	38	Oregon	(3.7)
14	South Carolina	1.6	40	Florida	(4.0)
16	South Dakota	0.9	40	West Virginia	(4.0)
31	Tennessee	(2.9)	42	Delaware	(4.1)
47	Texas	(6.0)	43	Georgia	(4.3)
50	Utah	(15.8)	44	Illinois	(4.8)
46	Vermont	(5.9)	45	California	(5.1)
23	Virginia	(0.4)	46	Vermont	(5.9)
49	Washington	(11.6)	47	Texas	(6.0)
40	West Virginia	(4.0)	48	Colorado	(9.3)
36	Wisconsin	(3.4)	49	Washington	(11.6)
3	Wyoming	6.0	50	Utah	(15.8)
				District of Columbia	12.9

Source: CQ Press using data from Administrative Office of the U.S. Courts
"Table F-2, U.S. Bankruptcy Courts" (https://www.uscourts.gov/statistics-reports/caseload-statistics-data-tables)
*Twelve months ending in September 2017 to 12 months ending in September 2018. National rate does not include bankruptcies or population in U.S. territories. Includes all nonbusiness bankruptcies.

2019 State Business Tax Climate Index

National Average Score = 5.14*

RANK	STATE	SCORE
39	Alabama	4.61
2	Alaska	7.35
27	Arizona	5.00
46	Arkansas	4.28
49	California	4.00
18	Colorado	5.19
47	Connecticut	4.23
11	Delaware	5.55
4	Florida	6.86
33	Georgia	4.85
38	Hawaii	4.66
21	Idaho	5.12
36	Illinois	4.74
10	Indiana	5.70
45	Iowa	4.33
28	Kansas	4.99
23	Kentucky	5.10
44	Louisiana	4.34
30	Maine	4.95
40	Maryland	4.53
29	Massachusetts	4.98
13	Michigan	5.45
43	Minnesota	4.37
31	Mississippi	4.95
14	Missouri	5.38
5	Montana	6.30
24	Nebraska	5.06
9	Nevada	5.81
6	New Hampshire	6.06
50	New Jersey	3.20
25	New Mexico	5.06
48	New York	4.02
12	North Carolina	5.52
17	North Dakota	5.28
42	Ohio	4.51
26	Oklahoma	5.05
7	Oregon	5.88
34	Pennsylvania	4.85
37	Rhode Island	4.71
35	South Carolina	4.83
3	South Dakota	7.27
16	Tennessee	5.30
15	Texas	5.37
8	Utah	5.83
41	Vermont	4.53
22	Virginia	5.11
20	Washington	5.18
19	West Virginia	5.18
32	Wisconsin	4.87
1	Wyoming	7.62

RANK	STATE	SCORE
1	Wyoming	7.62
2	Alaska	7.35
3	South Dakota	7.27
4	Florida	6.86
5	Montana	6.30
6	New Hampshire	6.06
7	Oregon	5.88
8	Utah	5.83
9	Nevada	5.81
10	Indiana	5.70
11	Delaware	5.55
12	North Carolina	5.52
13	Michigan	5.45
14	Missouri	5.38
15	Texas	5.37
16	Tennessee	5.30
17	North Dakota	5.28
18	Colorado	5.19
19	West Virginia	5.18
20	Washington	5.18
21	Idaho	5.12
22	Virginia	5.11
23	Kentucky	5.10
24	Nebraska	5.06
25	New Mexico	5.06
26	Oklahoma	5.05
27	Arizona	5.00
28	Kansas	4.99
29	Massachusetts	4.98
30	Maine	4.95
31	Mississippi	4.95
32	Wisconsin	4.87
33	Georgia	4.85
34	Pennsylvania	4.85
35	South Carolina	4.83
36	Illinois	4.74
37	Rhode Island	4.71
38	Hawaii	4.66
39	Alabama	4.61
40	Maryland	4.53
41	Vermont	4.53
42	Ohio	4.51
43	Minnesota	4.37
44	Louisiana	4.34
45	Iowa	4.33
46	Arkansas	4.28
47	Connecticut	4.23
48	New York	4.02
49	California	4.00
50	New Jersey	3.20

District of Columbia   4.32

Source: The Tax Foundation
     "State Business Tax Climate Index" (September 2018, https://taxfoundation.org/state-business-tax-climate-index-2019/)
*This index looks at levels of taxation and complexity of compliance to compare the states on how "business friendly" each state is compared to the others. The scale for each factor considered is one to ten, with ten being the "best." Rankings are based on unrounded scores and reflect those of The Tax Foundation.

Fortune 500 Companies in 2017

National Total = 500 Companies*

ALPHA ORDER

RANK	STATE	COMPANIES	% of USA
36	Alabama	1	0.2%
37	Alaska	0	0.0%
24	Arizona	4	0.8%
22	Arkansas	6	1.2%
2	California	53	10.6%
17	Colorado	10	2.0%
9	Connecticut	18	3.6%
30	Delaware	2	0.4%
11	Florida	17	3.4%
11	Georgia	17	3.4%
37	Hawaii	0	0.0%
30	Idaho	2	0.4%
4	Illinois	36	7.2%
21	Indiana	7	1.4%
28	Iowa	3	0.6%
30	Kansas	2	0.4%
28	Kentucky	3	0.6%
30	Louisiana	2	0.4%
37	Maine	0	0.0%
24	Maryland	4	0.8%
14	Massachusetts	13	2.6%
11	Michigan	17	3.4%
9	Minnesota	18	3.6%
37	Mississippi	0	0.0%
17	Missouri	10	2.0%
37	Montana	0	0.0%
24	Nebraska	4	0.8%
30	Nevada	2	0.4%
37	New Hampshire	0	0.0%
7	New Jersey	21	4.2%
37	New Mexico	0	0.0%
1	New York	54	10.8%
15	North Carolina	12	2.4%
37	North Dakota	0	0.0%
5	Ohio	25	5.0%
23	Oklahoma	5	1.0%
30	Oregon	2	0.4%
7	Pennsylvania	21	4.2%
24	Rhode Island	4	0.8%
37	South Carolina	0	0.0%
37	South Dakota	0	0.0%
16	Tennessee	11	2.2%
3	Texas	50	10.0%
37	Utah	0	0.0%
37	Vermont	0	0.0%
6	Virginia	23	4.6%
17	Washington	10	2.0%
37	West Virginia	0	0.0%
20	Wisconsin	9	1.8%
37	Wyoming	0	0.0%

RANK ORDER

RANK	STATE	COMPANIES	% of USA
1	New York	54	10.8%
2	California	53	10.6%
3	Texas	50	10.0%
4	Illinois	36	7.2%
5	Ohio	25	5.0%
6	Virginia	23	4.6%
7	New Jersey	21	4.2%
7	Pennsylvania	21	4.2%
9	Connecticut	18	3.6%
9	Minnesota	18	3.6%
11	Florida	17	3.4%
11	Georgia	17	3.4%
11	Michigan	17	3.4%
14	Massachusetts	13	2.6%
15	North Carolina	12	2.4%
16	Tennessee	11	2.2%
17	Colorado	10	2.0%
17	Missouri	10	2.0%
17	Washington	10	2.0%
20	Wisconsin	9	1.8%
21	Indiana	7	1.4%
22	Arkansas	6	1.2%
23	Oklahoma	5	1.0%
24	Arizona	4	0.8%
24	Maryland	4	0.8%
24	Nebraska	4	0.8%
24	Rhode Island	4	0.8%
28	Iowa	3	0.6%
28	Kentucky	3	0.6%
30	Delaware	2	0.4%
30	Idaho	2	0.4%
30	Kansas	2	0.4%
30	Louisiana	2	0.4%
30	Nevada	2	0.4%
30	Oregon	2	0.4%
36	Alabama	1	0.2%
37	Alaska	0	0.0%
37	Hawaii	0	0.0%
37	Maine	0	0.0%
37	Mississippi	0	0.0%
37	Montana	0	0.0%
37	New Hampshire	0	0.0%
37	New Mexico	0	0.0%
37	North Dakota	0	0.0%
37	South Carolina	0	0.0%
37	South Dakota	0	0.0%
37	Utah	0	0.0%
37	Vermont	0	0.0%
37	West Virginia	0	0.0%
37	Wyoming	0	0.0%
	District of Columbia	2	0.4%

Source: Fortune magazine
    "Fortune 500" (June 15, 2017)
*By state where each company's headquarters is located.

V. Education

(Continued)

(Continued)

Estimated Percent of School-Age Population in Public Schools in 2017

National Percent = 94.2%*

ALPHA ORDER			RANK ORDER		
RANK	STATE	PERCENT	RANK	STATE	PERCENT
29	Alabama	92.9	1	Vermont	101.9
2	Alaska	101.4	2	Alaska	101.4
23	Arizona	93.9	3	West Virginia	101.0
9	Arkansas	96.0	4	Texas	100.5
11	California	95.8	5	Oklahoma	99.8
7	Colorado	97.8	6	Utah	98.3
14	Connecticut	95.5	7	Colorado	97.8
37	Delaware	91.2	8	New Jersey	96.8
32	Florida	91.9	9	Arkansas	96.0
18	Georgia	95.1	10	Maine	95.9
50	Hawaii	84.2	11	California	95.8
40	Idaho	91.0	12	Iowa	95.7
15	Illinois	95.4	13	Massachusetts	95.6
38	Indiana	91.1	14	Connecticut	95.5
12	Iowa	95.7	15	Illinois	95.4
17	Kansas	95.2	16	Michigan	95.3
25	Kentucky	93.2	17	Kansas	95.2
45	Louisiana	89.9	18	Georgia	95.1
10	Maine	95.9	18	South Carolina	95.1
43	Maryland	90.3	20	Nevada	94.8
13	Massachusetts	95.6	20	Virginia	94.8
16	Michigan	95.3	22	Wyoming	94.7
31	Minnesota	92.7	23	Arizona	93.9
33	Mississippi	91.8	24	New Mexico	93.4
42	Missouri	90.7	25	Kentucky	93.2
48	Montana	88.4	25	Rhode Island	93.2
27	Nebraska	93.1	27	Nebraska	93.1
20	Nevada	94.8	27	New Hampshire	93.1
27	New Hampshire	93.1	29	Alabama	92.9
8	New Jersey	96.8	30	Washington	92.8
24	New Mexico	93.4	31	Minnesota	92.7
35	New York	91.3	32	Florida	91.9
34	North Carolina	91.6	33	Mississippi	91.8
44	North Dakota	90.1	34	North Carolina	91.6
46	Ohio	89.7	35	New York	91.3
5	Oklahoma	99.8	35	Wisconsin	91.3
41	Oregon	90.8	37	Delaware	91.2
49	Pennsylvania	88.3	38	Indiana	91.1
25	Rhode Island	93.2	38	Tennessee	91.1
18	South Carolina	95.1	40	Idaho	91.0
47	South Dakota	89.0	41	Oregon	90.8
38	Tennessee	91.1	42	Missouri	90.7
4	Texas	100.5	43	Maryland	90.3
6	Utah	98.3	44	North Dakota	90.1
1	Vermont	101.9	45	Louisiana	89.9
20	Virginia	94.8	46	Ohio	89.7
30	Washington	92.8	47	South Dakota	89.0
3	West Virginia	101.0	48	Montana	88.4
35	Wisconsin	91.3	49	Pennsylvania	88.3
22	Wyoming	94.7	50	Hawaii	84.2
				District of Columbia	108.0

Source: CQ Press using data from U.S. Department of Education, National Center for Education Statistics
"ElSi Table Generator" (https://nces.ed.gov/ccd/elsi/)

*Estimate based on 2017 Census population estimates for 5- to 17-year-olds compared to estimated 2016-2017 school year public school student membership. Student membership figures include counts for pre-kindergarten programs. Figures higher than 100 percent reflect using different sources for population-Age for student membership.

Regular Public Elementary and Secondary School Districts in 2016

National Total = 13,584 Districts*

ALPHA ORDER

RANK	STATE	DISTRICTS	% of USA
34	Alabama	134	1.0%
43	Alaska	53	0.4%
22	Arizona	234	1.7%
23	Arkansas	233	1.7%
1	California	1,058	7.8%
27	Colorado	178	1.3%
30	Connecticut	169	1.2%
48	Delaware	19	0.1%
41	Florida	67	0.5%
24	Georgia	180	1.3%
50	Hawaii	1	0.0%
36	Idaho	115	0.8%
3	Illinois	854	6.3%
17	Indiana	294	2.2%
13	Iowa	336	2.5%
15	Kansas	307	2.3%
29	Kentucky	173	1.3%
40	Louisiana	69	0.5%
19	Maine	248	1.8%
47	Maryland	24	0.2%
21	Massachusetts	239	1.8%
7	Michigan	542	4.0%
14	Minnesota	332	2.4%
33	Mississippi	144	1.1%
8	Missouri	518	3.8%
12	Montana	404	3.0%
20	Nebraska	245	1.8%
49	Nevada	18	0.1%
24	New Hampshire	180	1.3%
6	New Jersey	601	4.4%
38	New Mexico	89	0.7%
4	New York	690	5.1%
36	North Carolina	115	0.8%
28	North Dakota	175	1.3%
5	Ohio	622	4.6%
9	Oklahoma	516	3.8%
26	Oregon	179	1.3%
10	Pennsylvania	500	3.7%
46	Rhode Island	32	0.2%
39	South Carolina	84	0.6%
31	South Dakota	150	1.1%
32	Tennessee	146	1.1%
2	Texas	1,026	7.6%
45	Utah	41	0.3%
18	Vermont	291	2.1%
35	Virginia	130	1.0%
16	Washington	301	2.2%
42	West Virginia	55	0.4%
11	Wisconsin	424	3.1%
44	Wyoming	48	0.4%

RANK ORDER

RANK	STATE	DISTRICTS	% of USA
1	California	1,058	7.8%
2	Texas	1,026	7.6%
3	Illinois	854	6.3%
4	New York	690	5.1%
5	Ohio	622	4.6%
6	New Jersey	601	4.4%
7	Michigan	542	4.0%
8	Missouri	518	3.8%
9	Oklahoma	516	3.8%
10	Pennsylvania	500	3.7%
11	Wisconsin	424	3.1%
12	Montana	404	3.0%
13	Iowa	336	2.5%
14	Minnesota	332	2.4%
15	Kansas	307	2.3%
16	Washington	301	2.2%
17	Indiana	294	2.2%
18	Vermont	291	2.1%
19	Maine	248	1.8%
20	Nebraska	245	1.8%
21	Massachusetts	239	1.8%
22	Arizona	234	1.7%
23	Arkansas	233	1.7%
24	Georgia	180	1.3%
24	New Hampshire	180	1.3%
26	Oregon	179	1.3%
27	Colorado	178	1.3%
28	North Dakota	175	1.3%
29	Kentucky	173	1.3%
30	Connecticut	169	1.2%
31	South Dakota	150	1.1%
32	Tennessee	146	1.1%
33	Mississippi	144	1.1%
34	Alabama	134	1.0%
35	Virginia	130	1.0%
36	Idaho	115	0.8%
36	North Carolina	115	0.8%
38	New Mexico	89	0.7%
39	South Carolina	84	0.6%
40	Louisiana	69	0.5%
41	Florida	67	0.5%
42	West Virginia	55	0.4%
43	Alaska	53	0.4%
44	Wyoming	48	0.4%
45	Utah	41	0.3%
46	Rhode Island	32	0.2%
47	Maryland	24	0.2%
48	Delaware	19	0.1%
49	Nevada	18	0.1%
50	Hawaii	1	0.0%
	District of Columbia	1	0.0%

Source: U.S. Department of Education, National Center for Education Statistics
   "Digest of Education Statistics 2017" (http://nces.ed.gov/programs/digest/index.asp)
*For school year 2015-2016. Regular school districts are agencies responsible for providing free public education for school-age children residing within their jurisdiction. Included in these figures are districts that reported having no students. This can occur when a small district has no pupils or contracts with another district to educate the students under its jurisdiction.

Private Elementary and Secondary Schools in 2016

National Total = 34,576 Schools*

ALPHA ORDER

RANK	STATE	SCHOOLS	% of USA
27	Alabama	352	1.0%
48	Alaska	53	0.2%
31	Arizona	320	0.9%
29	Arkansas	333	1.0%
1	California	3,425	9.9%
19	Colorado	604	1.7%
24	Connecticut	422	1.2%
46	Delaware	97	0.3%
4	Florida	2,201	6.4%
10	Georgia	1,217	3.5%
41	Hawaii	142	0.4%
33	Idaho	255	0.7%
7	Illinois	1,498	4.3%
6	Indiana	1,664	4.8%
21	Iowa	509	1.5%
34	Kansas	210	0.6%
30	Kentucky	329	1.0%
20	Louisiana	578	1.7%
40	Maine	143	0.4%
15	Maryland	764	2.2%
16	Massachusetts	755	2.2%
13	Michigan	886	2.6%
23	Minnesota	473	1.4%
36	Mississippi	182	0.5%
14	Missouri	867	2.5%
44	Montana	122	0.4%
28	Nebraska	346	1.0%
39	Nevada	146	0.4%
32	New Hampshire	259	0.7%
9	New Jersey	1,269	3.7%
37	New Mexico	171	0.5%
5	New York	1,939	5.6%
17	North Carolina	646	1.9%
49	North Dakota	49	0.1%
8	Ohio	1,356	3.9%
35	Oklahoma	183	0.5%
25	Oregon	413	1.2%
2	Pennsylvania	2,741	7.9%
42	Rhode Island	131	0.4%
26	South Carolina	375	1.1%
47	South Dakota	72	0.2%
22	Tennessee	502	1.5%
3	Texas	2,398	6.9%
38	Utah	162	0.5%
45	Vermont	113	0.3%
12	Virginia	951	2.8%
18	Washington	642	1.9%
43	West Virginia	128	0.4%
11	Wisconsin	1,054	3.0%
50	Wyoming	36	0.1%

RANK ORDER

RANK	STATE	SCHOOLS	% of USA
1	California	3,425	9.9%
2	Pennsylvania	2,741	7.9%
3	Texas	2,398	6.9%
4	Florida	2,201	6.4%
5	New York	1,939	5.6%
6	Indiana	1,664	4.8%
7	Illinois	1,498	4.3%
8	Ohio	1,356	3.9%
9	New Jersey	1,269	3.7%
10	Georgia	1,217	3.5%
11	Wisconsin	1,054	3.0%
12	Virginia	951	2.8%
13	Michigan	886	2.6%
14	Missouri	867	2.5%
15	Maryland	764	2.2%
16	Massachusetts	755	2.2%
17	North Carolina	646	1.9%
18	Washington	642	1.9%
19	Colorado	604	1.7%
20	Louisiana	578	1.7%
21	Iowa	509	1.5%
22	Tennessee	502	1.5%
23	Minnesota	473	1.4%
24	Connecticut	422	1.2%
25	Oregon	413	1.2%
26	South Carolina	375	1.1%
27	Alabama	352	1.0%
28	Nebraska	346	1.0%
29	Arkansas	333	1.0%
30	Kentucky	329	1.0%
31	Arizona	320	0.9%
32	New Hampshire	259	0.7%
33	Idaho	255	0.7%
34	Kansas	210	0.6%
35	Oklahoma	183	0.5%
36	Mississippi	182	0.5%
37	New Mexico	171	0.5%
38	Utah	162	0.5%
39	Nevada	146	0.4%
40	Maine	143	0.4%
41	Hawaii	142	0.4%
42	Rhode Island	131	0.4%
43	West Virginia	128	0.4%
44	Montana	122	0.4%
45	Vermont	113	0.3%
46	Delaware	97	0.3%
47	South Dakota	72	0.2%
48	Alaska	53	0.2%
49	North Dakota	49	0.1%
50	Wyoming	36	0.1%
	District of Columbia	93	0.3%

Source: U.S. Department of Education, National Center for Education Statistics
"Characteristics of Private Schools in the United States" (https://nces.ed.gov/pubsearch/pubsinfo.asp?pubid=2017073)
*For school year 2015-2016. Includes private schools that provide instruction for one or more grades kindergarten through 12 (or comparable ungraded levels).

Private Elementary and Secondary School Enrollment in 2016

National Total = 4,903,596 Students*

ALPHA ORDER

RANK	STATE	STUDENTS	% of USA
22	Alabama	63,920	1.3%
49	Alaska	4,518	0.1%
29	Arizona	46,252	0.9%
34	Arkansas	30,607	0.6%
1	California	544,800	11.1%
27	Colorado	47,875	1.0%
24	Connecticut	60,353	1.2%
41	Delaware	17,310	0.4%
3	Florida	325,425	6.6%
9	Georgia	168,718	3.4%
31	Hawaii	41,703	0.9%
43	Idaho	13,901	0.3%
6	Illinois	231,275	4.7%
12	Indiana	149,460	3.0%
25	Iowa	59,419	1.2%
33	Kansas	37,835	0.8%
23	Kentucky	61,766	1.3%
10	Louisiana	152,955	3.1%
42	Maine	17,273	0.4%
14	Maryland	122,189	2.5%
18	Massachusetts	105,960	2.2%
11	Michigan	151,909	3.1%
21	Minnesota	68,496	1.4%
32	Mississippi	38,168	0.8%
16	Missouri	110,040	2.2%
45	Montana	9,604	0.2%
30	Nebraska	43,985	0.9%
38	Nevada	19,166	0.4%
36	New Hampshire	19,993	0.4%
8	New Jersey	172,214	3.5%
37	New Mexico	19,571	0.4%
2	New York	461,297	9.4%
15	North Carolina	110,106	2.2%
48	North Dakota	6,404	0.1%
7	Ohio	222,863	4.5%
35	Oklahoma	26,977	0.6%
28	Oregon	47,127	1.0%
4	Pennsylvania	271,234	5.5%
39	Rhode Island	18,104	0.4%
26	South Carolina	48,393	1.0%
47	South Dakota	8,758	0.2%
20	Tennessee	79,902	1.6%
5	Texas	269,157	5.5%
40	Utah	17,636	0.4%
46	Vermont	9,335	0.2%
17	Virginia	109,991	2.2%
19	Washington	83,322	1.7%
44	West Virginia	12,951	0.3%
13	Wisconsin	126,035	2.6%
50	Wyoming	1,488	0.0%

RANK ORDER

RANK	STATE	STUDENTS	% of USA
1	California	544,800	11.1%
2	New York	461,297	9.4%
3	Florida	325,425	6.6%
4	Pennsylvania	271,234	5.5%
5	Texas	269,157	5.5%
6	Illinois	231,275	4.7%
7	Ohio	222,863	4.5%
8	New Jersey	172,214	3.5%
9	Georgia	168,718	3.4%
10	Louisiana	152,955	3.1%
11	Michigan	151,909	3.1%
12	Indiana	149,460	3.0%
13	Wisconsin	126,035	2.6%
14	Maryland	122,189	2.5%
15	North Carolina	110,106	2.2%
16	Missouri	110,040	2.2%
17	Virginia	109,991	2.2%
18	Massachusetts	105,960	2.2%
19	Washington	83,322	1.7%
20	Tennessee	79,902	1.6%
21	Minnesota	68,496	1.4%
22	Alabama	63,920	1.3%
23	Kentucky	61,766	1.3%
24	Connecticut	60,353	1.2%
25	Iowa	59,419	1.2%
26	South Carolina	48,393	1.0%
27	Colorado	47,875	1.0%
28	Oregon	47,127	1.0%
29	Arizona	46,252	0.9%
30	Nebraska	43,985	0.9%
31	Hawaii	41,703	0.9%
32	Mississippi	38,168	0.8%
33	Kansas	37,835	0.8%
34	Arkansas	30,607	0.6%
35	Oklahoma	26,977	0.6%
36	New Hampshire	19,993	0.4%
37	New Mexico	19,571	0.4%
38	Nevada	19,166	0.4%
39	Rhode Island	18,104	0.4%
40	Utah	17,636	0.4%
41	Delaware	17,310	0.4%
42	Maine	17,273	0.4%
43	Idaho	13,901	0.3%
44	West Virginia	12,951	0.3%
45	Montana	9,604	0.2%
46	Vermont	9,335	0.2%
47	South Dakota	8,758	0.2%
48	North Dakota	6,404	0.1%
49	Alaska	4,518	0.1%
50	Wyoming	1,488	0.0%
	District of Columbia	15,856	0.3%

Source: U.S. Department of Education, National Center for Education Statistics
"Characteristics of Private Schools in the United States" (https://nces.ed.gov/pubsearch/pubsinfo.asp?pubid=2017073)
*For school year 2015-2016. Includes private schools that provide instruction for one or more grades kindergarten through 12 (or comparable ungraded levels).

Public Elementary and Secondary Schools in 2017

National Total = 98,330 Schools*

ALPHA ORDER

RANK	STATE	SCHOOLS	% of USA
24	Alabama	1,513	1.5%
44	Alaska	507	0.5%
14	Arizona	2,308	2.3%
33	Arkansas	1,090	1.1%
1	California	10,291	10.5%
19	Colorado	1,888	1.9%
30	Connecticut	1,250	1.3%
50	Delaware	228	0.2%
4	Florida	4,336	4.4%
15	Georgia	2,300	2.3%
49	Hawaii	290	0.3%
38	Idaho	745	0.8%
5	Illinois	4,173	4.2%
18	Indiana	1,921	2.0%
27	Iowa	1,328	1.4%
28	Kansas	1,318	1.3%
23	Kentucky	1,539	1.6%
26	Louisiana	1,404	1.4%
42	Maine	605	0.6%
25	Maryland	1,424	1.4%
20	Massachusetts	1,856	1.9%
7	Michigan	3,458	3.5%
11	Minnesota	2,513	2.6%
34	Mississippi	1,066	1.1%
13	Missouri	2,424	2.5%
37	Montana	820	0.8%
32	Nebraska	1,095	1.1%
41	Nevada	663	0.7%
45	New Hampshire	490	0.5%
10	New Jersey	2,590	2.6%
36	New Mexico	869	0.9%
3	New York	4,798	4.9%
9	North Carolina	2,624	2.7%
43	North Dakota	518	0.5%
6	Ohio	3,591	3.7%
21	Oklahoma	1,792	1.8%
31	Oregon	1,243	1.3%
8	Pennsylvania	3,004	3.1%
47	Rhode Island	315	0.3%
29	South Carolina	1,252	1.3%
40	South Dakota	697	0.7%
22	Tennessee	1,774	1.8%
2	Texas	8,912	9.1%
35	Utah	1,037	1.1%
48	Vermont	312	0.3%
17	Virginia	2,134	2.2%
12	Washington	2,436	2.5%
39	West Virginia	739	0.8%
16	Wisconsin	2,256	2.3%
46	Wyoming	371	0.4%

RANK ORDER

RANK	STATE	SCHOOLS	% of USA
1	California	10,291	10.5%
2	Texas	8,912	9.1%
3	New York	4,798	4.9%
4	Florida	4,336	4.4%
5	Illinois	4,173	4.2%
6	Ohio	3,591	3.7%
7	Michigan	3,458	3.5%
8	Pennsylvania	3,004	3.1%
9	North Carolina	2,624	2.7%
10	New Jersey	2,590	2.6%
11	Minnesota	2,513	2.6%
12	Washington	2,436	2.5%
13	Missouri	2,424	2.5%
14	Arizona	2,308	2.3%
15	Georgia	2,300	2.3%
16	Wisconsin	2,256	2.3%
17	Virginia	2,134	2.2%
18	Indiana	1,921	2.0%
19	Colorado	1,888	1.9%
20	Massachusetts	1,856	1.9%
21	Oklahoma	1,792	1.8%
22	Tennessee	1,774	1.8%
23	Kentucky	1,539	1.6%
24	Alabama	1,513	1.5%
25	Maryland	1,424	1.4%
26	Louisiana	1,404	1.4%
27	Iowa	1,328	1.4%
28	Kansas	1,318	1.3%
29	South Carolina	1,252	1.3%
30	Connecticut	1,250	1.3%
31	Oregon	1,243	1.3%
32	Nebraska	1,095	1.1%
33	Arkansas	1,090	1.1%
34	Mississippi	1,066	1.1%
35	Utah	1,037	1.1%
36	New Mexico	869	0.9%
37	Montana	820	0.8%
38	Idaho	745	0.8%
39	West Virginia	739	0.8%
40	South Dakota	697	0.7%
41	Nevada	663	0.7%
42	Maine	605	0.6%
43	North Dakota	518	0.5%
44	Alaska	507	0.5%
45	New Hampshire	490	0.5%
46	Wyoming	371	0.4%
47	Rhode Island	315	0.3%
48	Vermont	312	0.3%
49	Hawaii	290	0.3%
50	Delaware	228	0.2%
	District of Columbia	223	0.2%

Source: U.S. Department of Education, National Center for Education Statistics
"ElSi Table Generator" (https://nces.ed.gov/ccd/elsi/)
*For school year 2016-2017.

Enrollment in Public Elementary and Secondary Schools in 2017

National Total = 50,587,859 Students*

ALPHA ORDER

RANK	STATE	STUDENTS	% of USA
24	Alabama	744,930	1.5%
47	Alaska	132,737	0.3%
13	Arizona	1,123,137	2.2%
33	Arkansas	493,447	1.0%
1	California	6,309,138	12.5%
19	Colorado	905,019	1.8%
30	Connecticut	535,118	1.1%
46	Delaware	136,264	0.3%
3	Florida	2,816,791	5.6%
6	Georgia	1,764,346	3.5%
40	Hawaii	181,550	0.4%
38	Idaho	297,200	0.6%
5	Illinois	2,026,718	4.0%
15	Indiana	1,049,547	2.1%
31	Iowa	509,831	1.0%
32	Kansas	494,347	1.0%
27	Kentucky	684,017	1.4%
25	Louisiana	716,293	1.4%
42	Maine	180,512	0.4%
20	Maryland	886,221	1.8%
17	Massachusetts	964,514	1.9%
10	Michigan	1,528,666	3.0%
21	Minnesota	875,021	1.7%
34	Mississippi	483,150	1.0%
18	Missouri	915,040	1.8%
43	Montana	146,375	0.3%
37	Nebraska	319,194	0.6%
35	Nevada	473,744	0.9%
41	New Hampshire	180,888	0.4%
11	New Jersey	1,410,421	2.8%
36	New Mexico	336,263	0.7%
4	New York	2,729,776	5.4%
9	North Carolina	1,550,062	3.1%
48	North Dakota	109,706	0.2%
8	Ohio	1,710,143	3.4%
26	Oklahoma	693,903	1.4%
29	Oregon	578,947	1.1%
7	Pennsylvania	1,727,497	3.4%
44	Rhode Island	142,150	0.3%
23	South Carolina	771,250	1.5%
45	South Dakota	136,302	0.3%
16	Tennessee	1,001,562	2.0%
2	Texas	5,360,849	10.6%
28	Utah	659,801	1.3%
50	Vermont	88,428	0.2%
12	Virginia	1,287,026	2.5%
14	Washington	1,101,711	2.2%
39	West Virginia	273,855	0.5%
22	Wisconsin	864,432	1.7%
49	Wyoming	94,170	0.2%

RANK ORDER

RANK	STATE	STUDENTS	% of USA
1	California	6,309,138	12.5%
2	Texas	5,360,849	10.6%
3	Florida	2,816,791	5.6%
4	New York	2,729,776	5.4%
5	Illinois	2,026,718	4.0%
6	Georgia	1,764,346	3.5%
7	Pennsylvania	1,727,497	3.4%
8	Ohio	1,710,143	3.4%
9	North Carolina	1,550,062	3.1%
10	Michigan	1,528,666	3.0%
11	New Jersey	1,410,421	2.8%
12	Virginia	1,287,026	2.5%
13	Arizona	1,123,137	2.2%
14	Washington	1,101,711	2.2%
15	Indiana	1,049,547	2.1%
16	Tennessee	1,001,562	2.0%
17	Massachusetts	964,514	1.9%
18	Missouri	915,040	1.8%
19	Colorado	905,019	1.8%
20	Maryland	886,221	1.8%
21	Minnesota	875,021	1.7%
22	Wisconsin	864,432	1.7%
23	South Carolina	771,250	1.5%
24	Alabama	744,930	1.5%
25	Louisiana	716,293	1.4%
26	Oklahoma	693,903	1.4%
27	Kentucky	684,017	1.4%
28	Utah	659,801	1.3%
29	Oregon	578,947	1.1%
30	Connecticut	535,118	1.1%
31	Iowa	509,831	1.0%
32	Kansas	494,347	1.0%
33	Arkansas	493,447	1.0%
34	Mississippi	483,150	1.0%
35	Nevada	473,744	0.9%
36	New Mexico	336,263	0.7%
37	Nebraska	319,194	0.6%
38	Idaho	297,200	0.6%
39	West Virginia	273,855	0.5%
40	Hawaii	181,550	0.4%
41	New Hampshire	180,888	0.4%
42	Maine	180,512	0.4%
43	Montana	146,375	0.3%
44	Rhode Island	142,150	0.3%
45	South Dakota	136,302	0.3%
46	Delaware	136,264	0.3%
47	Alaska	132,737	0.3%
48	North Dakota	109,706	0.2%
49	Wyoming	94,170	0.2%
50	Vermont	88,428	0.2%
	District of Columbia	85,850	0.2%

Source: U.S. Department of Education, National Center for Education Statistics
"ElSi Table Generator" (https://nces.ed.gov/ccd/elsi/)
*For school year 2016-2017.

Public Elementary and Secondary School Teachers in 2017

National Total = 3,169,499 Teachers*

ALPHA ORDER

RANK	STATE	TEACHERS	% of USA
25	Alabama	42,533	1.3%
49	Alaska	7,825	0.2%
24	Arizona	48,220	1.5%
31	Arkansas	35,730	1.1%
2	California	271,287	8.6%
21	Colorado	52,014	1.6%
26	Connecticut	42,343	1.3%
47	Delaware	9,208	0.3%
4	Florida	186,339	5.9%
8	Georgia	114,763	3.6%
42	Hawaii	11,782	0.4%
39	Idaho	16,204	0.5%
5	Illinois	128,893	4.1%
16	Indiana	60,162	1.9%
30	Iowa	35,808	1.1%
29	Kansas	36,193	1.1%
27	Kentucky	42,029	1.3%
23	Louisiana	48,408	1.5%
41	Maine	14,750	0.5%
17	Maryland	59,703	1.9%
13	Massachusetts	72,413	2.3%
12	Michigan	83,597	2.6%
20	Minnesota	56,715	1.8%
32	Mississippi	31,924	1.0%
14	Missouri	67,926	2.1%
44	Montana	10,555	0.3%
36	Nebraska	23,611	0.7%
35	Nevada	23,705	0.7%
40	New Hampshire	14,760	0.5%
7	New Jersey	115,729	3.7%
37	New Mexico	21,331	0.7%
3	New York	209,151	6.6%
10	North Carolina	100,220	3.2%
46	North Dakota	9,265	0.3%
9	Ohio	102,600	3.2%
28	Oklahoma	41,090	1.3%
33	Oregon	29,756	0.9%
6	Pennsylvania	122,552	3.9%
43	Rhode Island	10,689	0.3%
22	South Carolina	50,789	1.6%
45	South Dakota	9,777	0.3%
15	Tennessee	64,270	2.0%
1	Texas	352,809	11.1%
34	Utah	28,841	0.9%
48	Vermont	8,187	0.3%
11	Virginia	91,628	2.9%
19	Washington	58,815	1.9%
38	West Virginia	19,356	0.6%
18	Wisconsin	59,011	1.9%
50	Wyoming	7,506	0.2%

RANK ORDER

RANK	STATE	TEACHERS	% of USA
1	Texas	352,809	11.1%
2	California	271,287	8.6%
3	New York	209,151	6.6%
4	Florida	186,339	5.9%
5	Illinois	128,893	4.1%
6	Pennsylvania	122,552	3.9%
7	New Jersey	115,729	3.7%
8	Georgia	114,763	3.6%
9	Ohio	102,600	3.2%
10	North Carolina	100,220	3.2%
11	Virginia	91,628	2.9%
12	Michigan	83,597	2.6%
13	Massachusetts	72,413	2.3%
14	Missouri	67,926	2.1%
15	Tennessee	64,270	2.0%
16	Indiana	60,162	1.9%
17	Maryland	59,703	1.9%
18	Wisconsin	59,011	1.9%
19	Washington	58,815	1.9%
20	Minnesota	56,715	1.8%
21	Colorado	52,014	1.6%
22	South Carolina	50,789	1.6%
23	Louisiana	48,408	1.5%
24	Arizona	48,220	1.5%
25	Alabama	42,533	1.3%
26	Connecticut	42,343	1.3%
27	Kentucky	42,029	1.3%
28	Oklahoma	41,090	1.3%
29	Kansas	36,193	1.1%
30	Iowa	35,808	1.1%
31	Arkansas	35,730	1.1%
32	Mississippi	31,924	1.0%
33	Oregon	29,756	0.9%
34	Utah	28,841	0.9%
35	Nevada	23,705	0.7%
36	Nebraska	23,611	0.7%
37	New Mexico	21,331	0.7%
38	West Virginia	19,356	0.6%
39	Idaho	16,204	0.5%
40	New Hampshire	14,760	0.5%
41	Maine	14,750	0.5%
42	Hawaii	11,782	0.4%
43	Rhode Island	10,689	0.3%
44	Montana	10,555	0.3%
45	South Dakota	9,777	0.3%
46	North Dakota	9,265	0.3%
47	Delaware	9,208	0.3%
48	Vermont	8,187	0.3%
49	Alaska	7,825	0.2%
50	Wyoming	7,506	0.2%
	District of Columbia	6,727	0.2%

Source: U.S. Department of Education, National Center for Education Statistics
"ElSi Table Generator" (https://nces.ed.gov/ccd/elsi/)
*For school year 2016-2017. Counts are full-time equivalent figures.

Pupil-Teacher Ratio in Public Elementary and Secondary Schools in 2017

National Ratio = 16.0 Pupils Per Teacher*

ALPHA ORDER				RANK ORDER		
RANK	STATE	RATIO		RANK	STATE	RATIO
9	Alabama	17.5		1	Arizona	23.3
12	Alaska	17.0		1	California	23.3
1	Arizona	23.3		3	Utah	22.9
37	Arkansas	13.8		4	Nevada	20.0
1	California	23.3		5	Oregon	19.5
11	Colorado	17.4		6	Washington	18.7
44	Connecticut	12.6		7	Idaho	18.3
27	Delaware	14.8		7	Michigan	18.3
25	Florida	15.1		9	Alabama	17.5
20	Georgia	15.4		9	Indiana	17.5
20	Hawaii	15.4		11	Colorado	17.4
7	Idaho	18.3		12	Alaska	17.0
17	Illinois	15.7		13	Oklahoma	16.9
9	Indiana	17.5		14	Ohio	16.7
31	Iowa	14.2		15	Kentucky	16.3
38	Kansas	13.7		16	New Mexico	15.8
15	Kentucky	16.3		17	Illinois	15.7
27	Louisiana	14.8		18	Tennessee	15.6
47	Maine	12.2		19	North Carolina	15.5
27	Maryland	14.8		20	Georgia	15.4
41	Massachusetts	13.3		20	Hawaii	15.4
7	Michigan	18.3		20	Minnesota	15.4
20	Minnesota	15.4		23	South Carolina	15.2
25	Mississippi	15.1		23	Texas	15.2
39	Missouri	13.5		25	Florida	15.1
35	Montana	13.9		25	Mississippi	15.1
39	Nebraska	13.5		27	Delaware	14.8
4	Nevada	20.0		27	Louisiana	14.8
46	New Hampshire	12.3		27	Maryland	14.8
47	New Jersey	12.2		30	Wisconsin	14.7
16	New Mexico	15.8		31	Iowa	14.2
43	New York	13.1		31	West Virginia	14.2
19	North Carolina	15.5		33	Pennsylvania	14.1
49	North Dakota	11.8		33	Virginia	14.1
14	Ohio	16.7		35	Montana	13.9
13	Oklahoma	16.9		35	South Dakota	13.9
5	Oregon	19.5		37	Arkansas	13.8
33	Pennsylvania	14.1		38	Kansas	13.7
41	Rhode Island	13.3		39	Missouri	13.5
23	South Carolina	15.2		39	Nebraska	13.5
35	South Dakota	13.9		41	Massachusetts	13.3
18	Tennessee	15.6		41	Rhode Island	13.3
23	Texas	15.2		43	New York	13.1
3	Utah	22.9		44	Connecticut	12.6
50	Vermont	10.8		44	Wyoming	12.6
33	Virginia	14.1		46	New Hampshire	12.3
6	Washington	18.7		47	Maine	12.2
31	West Virginia	14.2		47	New Jersey	12.2
30	Wisconsin	14.7		49	North Dakota	11.8
44	Wyoming	12.6		50	Vermont	10.8
					District of Columbia	12.8

Source: U.S. Department of Education, National Center for Education Statistics
   "ElSi Table Generator" (https://nces.ed.gov/ccd/elsi/)
*For school year 2016-2017. Based on full-time equivalency counts of teachers.

Estimated Average Salary of Public School Teachers in 2018
(National Education Association)
National Average = $60,483*

ALPHA ORDER

RANK	STATE	SALARY
39	Alabama	$50,239
7	Alaska	69,474
45	Arizona	47,746
42	Arkansas	49,017
2	California	81,126
31	Colorado	52,389
4	Connecticut	73,113
13	Delaware	60,484
46	Florida	47,721
22	Georgia	56,329
17	Hawaii	57,866
40	Idaho	49,225
10	Illinois	65,776
25	Indiana	54,846
21	Iowa	56,790
37	Kansas	50,403
29	Kentucky	52,952
38	Louisiana	50,256
32	Maine	51,663
6	Maryland	69,761
3	Massachusetts	79,710
12	Michigan	62,702
20	Minnesota	57,782
50	Mississippi	43,107
41	Missouri	49,208
30	Montana	52,776
27	Nebraska	53,473
19	Nevada	57,812
18	New Hampshire	57,833
5	New Jersey	69,917
44	New Mexico	47,839
1	New York	83,585
36	North Carolina	50,861
26	North Dakota	54,421
16	Ohio	58,000
48	Oklahoma	45,678
11	Oregon	63,143
8	Pennsylvania	67,398
9	Rhode Island	66,758
34	South Carolina	51,027
43	South Dakota	47,944
35	Tennessee	50,900
28	Texas	53,167
47	Utah	47,604
15	Vermont	58,527
33	Virginia	51,265
24	Washington	55,175
49	West Virginia	45,642
23	Wisconsin	55,895
14	Wyoming	58,578

RANK ORDER

RANK	STATE	SALARY
1	New York	$83,585
2	California	81,126
3	Massachusetts	79,710
4	Connecticut	73,113
5	New Jersey	69,917
6	Maryland	69,761
7	Alaska	69,474
8	Pennsylvania	67,398
9	Rhode Island	66,758
10	Illinois	65,776
11	Oregon	63,143
12	Michigan	62,702
13	Delaware	60,484
14	Wyoming	58,578
15	Vermont	58,527
16	Ohio	58,000
17	Hawaii	57,866
18	New Hampshire	57,833
19	Nevada	57,812
20	Minnesota	57,782
21	Iowa	56,790
22	Georgia	56,329
23	Wisconsin	55,895
24	Washington	55,175
25	Indiana	54,846
26	North Dakota	54,421
27	Nebraska	53,473
28	Texas	53,167
29	Kentucky	52,952
30	Montana	52,776
31	Colorado	52,389
32	Maine	51,663
33	Virginia	51,265
34	South Carolina	51,027
35	Tennessee	50,900
36	North Carolina	50,861
37	Kansas	50,403
38	Louisiana	50,256
39	Alabama	50,239
40	Idaho	49,225
41	Missouri	49,208
42	Arkansas	49,017
43	South Dakota	47,944
44	New Mexico	47,839
45	Arizona	47,746
46	Florida	47,721
47	Utah	47,604
48	Oklahoma	45,678
49	West Virginia	45,642
50	Mississippi	43,107
	District of Columbia	76,486

Source: National Education Association, Washington, D.C.
    "Rankings and Estimates" (Copyright © 2018, NEA, https://www.nea.org/home/44479.htm)
*Estimates for school year 2017-2018 for classroom teachers.

Average Teacher's Salary as a Percent of Average Annual Pay in 2017

National Average = 108.5% of Average Annual Pay*

ALPHA ORDER

ALPHA ORDER

RANK ORDER

RANK	STATE	PERCENT	RANK	STATE	PERCENT
30	Alabama	109.4	1	Alaska	128.1
1	Alaska	128.1	2	Wyoming	126.2
46	Arizona	94.9	3	Rhode Island	126.1
23	Arkansas	113.3	4	Vermont	125.4
9	California	121.7	5	Montana	123.9
48	Colorado	91.5	6	Pennsylvania	123.8
29	Connecticut	109.7	7	Oregon	122.3
33	Delaware	108.1	8	Iowa	122.0
45	Florida	98.0	9	California	121.7
35	Georgia	107.2	10	Nevada	119.7
21	Hawaii	115.3	11	Michigan	119.1
17	Idaho	117.0	12	Indiana	118.2
25	Illinois	112.7	12	Ohio	118.2
12	Indiana	118.2	14	Nebraska	118.0
8	Iowa	122.0	15	Wisconsin	117.4
28	Kansas	110.6	16	New York	117.1
19	Kentucky	116.6	17	Idaho	117.0
34	Louisiana	107.8	17	Maine	117.0
17	Maine	117.0	19	Kentucky	116.6
20	Maryland	115.9	20	Maryland	115.9
24	Massachusetts	112.8	21	Hawaii	115.3
11	Michigan	119.1	22	South Carolina	114.3
42	Minnesota	102.5	23	Arkansas	113.3
27	Mississippi	110.9	24	Massachusetts	112.8
40	Missouri	103.3	25	Illinois	112.7
5	Montana	123.9	26	South Dakota	111.9
14	Nebraska	118.0	27	Mississippi	110.9
10	Nevada	119.7	28	Kansas	110.6
38	New Hampshire	104.6	29	Connecticut	109.7
32	New Jersey	108.9	30	Alabama	109.4
31	New Mexico	109.1	31	New Mexico	109.1
16	New York	117.1	32	New Jersey	108.9
41	North Carolina	103.1	33	Delaware	108.1
36	North Dakota	106.7	34	Louisiana	107.8
12	Ohio	118.2	35	Georgia	107.2
44	Oklahoma	100.8	36	North Dakota	106.7
7	Oregon	122.3	37	West Virginia	105.0
6	Pennsylvania	123.8	38	New Hampshire	104.6
3	Rhode Island	126.1	39	Tennessee	103.4
22	South Carolina	114.3	40	Missouri	103.3
26	South Dakota	111.9	41	North Carolina	103.1
39	Tennessee	103.4	42	Minnesota	102.5
47	Texas	94.8	43	Utah	101.8
43	Utah	101.8	44	Oklahoma	100.8
4	Vermont	125.4	45	Florida	98.0
49	Virginia	90.5	46	Arizona	94.9
50	Washington	88.3	47	Texas	94.8
37	West Virginia	105.0	48	Colorado	91.5
15	Wisconsin	117.4	49	Virginia	90.5
2	Wyoming	126.2	50	Washington	88.3

District of Columbia — 82.2

Source: CQ Press using data from National Education Association, Washington, D.C.
"Rankings and Estimates" (Copyright © 2018, NEA, https://www.nea.org/home/44479.htm) and
"Quarterly Census of Employment and Wages" (https://www.bls.gov/cew/data.htm)
*Average of public elementary and secondary teacher salary for school years 2016-2017 and 2017-2018 compared to each state's 2017 average annual pay for all workers covered by federal unemployment.

Percent of Public School Fourth Graders
Proficient or Better in Reading in 2017
National Percent = 35%*

ALPHA ORDER

RANK	STATE	PERCENT
39	Alabama	31
47	Alaska	28
43	Arizona	30
39	Arkansas	31
39	California	31
11	Colorado	40
3	Connecticut	43
25	Delaware	36
7	Florida	41
30	Georgia	35
36	Hawaii	32
19	Idaho	38
30	Illinois	35
7	Indiana	41
25	Iowa	36
23	Kansas	37
19	Kentucky	38
49	Louisiana	26
25	Maine	36
11	Maryland	40
1	Massachusetts	51
36	Michigan	32
14	Minnesota	39
48	Mississippi	27
23	Missouri	37
19	Montana	38
19	Nebraska	38
39	Nevada	31
3	New Hampshire	43
2	New Jersey	49
50	New Mexico	25
25	New York	36
14	North Carolina	39
33	North Dakota	34
14	Ohio	39
44	Oklahoma	29
34	Oregon	33
11	Pennsylvania	40
14	Rhode Island	39
44	South Carolina	29
25	South Dakota	36
34	Tennessee	33
44	Texas	29
7	Utah	41
3	Vermont	43
3	Virginia	43
14	Washington	39
36	West Virginia	32
30	Wisconsin	35
7	Wyoming	41

RANK ORDER

RANK	STATE	PERCENT
1	Massachusetts	51
2	New Jersey	49
3	Connecticut	43
3	New Hampshire	43
3	Vermont	43
3	Virginia	43
7	Florida	41
7	Indiana	41
7	Utah	41
7	Wyoming	41
11	Colorado	40
11	Maryland	40
11	Pennsylvania	40
14	Minnesota	39
14	North Carolina	39
14	Ohio	39
14	Rhode Island	39
14	Washington	39
19	Idaho	38
19	Kentucky	38
19	Montana	38
19	Nebraska	38
23	Kansas	37
23	Missouri	37
25	Delaware	36
25	Iowa	36
25	Maine	36
25	New York	36
25	South Dakota	36
30	Georgia	35
30	Illinois	35
30	Wisconsin	35
33	North Dakota	34
34	Oregon	33
34	Tennessee	33
36	Hawaii	32
36	Michigan	32
36	West Virginia	32
39	Alabama	31
39	Arkansas	31
39	California	31
39	Nevada	31
43	Arizona	30
44	Oklahoma	29
44	South Carolina	29
44	Texas	29
47	Alaska	28
48	Mississippi	27
49	Louisiana	26
50	New Mexico	25
	District of Columbia	29

Source: U.S. Department of Education, National Center for Education Statistics
"The Nation's Report Card: Reading 2017" (www.nationsreportcard.gov)
*There are four achievement levels: Below Basic, Basic, Proficient, and Advanced. Proficient represents solid academic mastery for 4th graders. Students reaching this level have demonstrated competency over challenging subject matter, including subject matter knowledge, application of such knowledge to real-world situations, and analytical skills appropriate to the subject matter.

Percent of Public School Eighth Graders
Proficient or Better in Reading in 2017
National Percent = 35%*

ALPHA ORDER			RANK ORDER		
RANK	STATE	PERCENT	RANK	STATE	PERCENT
42	Alabama	28	1	Massachusetts	49
47	Alaska	26	2	New Jersey	47
38	Arizona	30	3	New Hampshire	45
41	Arkansas	29	3	Vermont	45
36	California	32	5	Connecticut	44
7	Colorado	41	6	Washington	42
5	Connecticut	44	7	Colorado	41
33	Delaware	33	7	Indiana	41
26	Florida	35	9	Pennsylvania	40
26	Georgia	35	10	Idaho	39
38	Hawaii	30	10	Maine	39
10	Idaho	39	10	Minnesota	39
23	Illinois	36	10	Ohio	39
7	Indiana	41	10	Wisconsin	39
19	Iowa	37	15	Maryland	38
19	Kansas	37	15	Nebraska	38
30	Kentucky	34	15	Utah	38
48	Louisiana	25	15	Wyoming	38
10	Maine	39	19	Iowa	37
15	Maryland	38	19	Kansas	37
1	Massachusetts	49	19	Rhode Island	37
30	Michigan	34	19	Virginia	37
10	Minnesota	39	23	Illinois	36
48	Mississippi	25	23	Oregon	36
26	Missouri	35	23	South Dakota	36
26	Montana	35	26	Florida	35
15	Nebraska	38	26	Georgia	35
42	Nevada	28	26	Missouri	35
3	New Hampshire	45	26	Montana	35
2	New Jersey	47	30	Kentucky	34
50	New Mexico	24	30	Michigan	34
30	New York	34	30	New York	34
33	North Carolina	33	33	Delaware	33
33	North Dakota	33	33	North Carolina	33
10	Ohio	39	33	North Dakota	33
42	Oklahoma	28	36	California	32
23	Oregon	36	37	Tennessee	31
9	Pennsylvania	40	38	Arizona	30
19	Rhode Island	37	38	Hawaii	30
38	South Carolina	30	38	South Carolina	30
23	South Dakota	36	41	Arkansas	29
37	Tennessee	31	42	Alabama	28
42	Texas	28	42	Nevada	28
15	Utah	38	42	Oklahoma	28
3	Vermont	45	42	Texas	28
19	Virginia	37	42	West Virginia	28
6	Washington	42	47	Alaska	26
42	West Virginia	28	48	Louisiana	25
10	Wisconsin	39	48	Mississippi	25
15	Wyoming	38	50	New Mexico	24
				District of Columbia	20

Source: U.S. Department of Education, National Center for Education Statistics
"The Nation's Report Card: Reading 2017" (www.nationsreportcard.gov)
*There are four achievement levels: Below Basic, Basic, Proficient, and Advanced. Proficient represents solid academic mastery for 8th graders. Students reaching this level have demonstrated competency over challenging subject matter, including subject matter knowledge, application of such knowledge to real-world situations, and analytical skills appropriate to the subject matter.

Percent of Public School Fourth Graders Proficient or Better in Mathematics in 2017
National Percent = 40%*

ALPHA ORDER

RANK	STATE	PERCENT
45	Alabama	31
43	Alaska	32
40	Arizona	34
41	Arkansas	33
45	California	31
15	Colorado	42
25	Connecticut	40
33	Delaware	36
7	Florida	48
36	Georgia	35
32	Hawaii	38
25	Idaho	40
30	Illinois	39
7	Indiana	48
10	Iowa	46
15	Kansas	42
25	Kentucky	40
49	Louisiana	27
25	Maine	40
15	Maryland	42
1	Massachusetts	53
33	Michigan	36
1	Minnesota	53
45	Mississippi	31
25	Missouri	40
22	Montana	41
6	Nebraska	49
45	Nevada	31
7	New Hampshire	48
4	New Jersey	50
49	New Mexico	27
36	New York	35
15	North Carolina	42
10	North Dakota	46
22	Ohio	41
36	Oklahoma	35
41	Oregon	33
13	Pennsylvania	44
30	Rhode Island	39
43	South Carolina	32
14	South Dakota	43
33	Tennessee	36
22	Texas	41
12	Utah	45
15	Vermont	42
4	Virginia	50
15	Washington	42
36	West Virginia	35
15	Wisconsin	42
3	Wyoming	51

RANK ORDER

RANK	STATE	PERCENT
1	Massachusetts	53
1	Minnesota	53
3	Wyoming	51
4	New Jersey	50
4	Virginia	50
6	Nebraska	49
7	Florida	48
7	Indiana	48
7	New Hampshire	48
10	Iowa	46
10	North Dakota	46
12	Utah	45
13	Pennsylvania	44
14	South Dakota	43
15	Colorado	42
15	Kansas	42
15	Maryland	42
15	North Carolina	42
15	Vermont	42
15	Washington	42
15	Wisconsin	42
22	Montana	41
22	Ohio	41
22	Texas	41
25	Connecticut	40
25	Idaho	40
25	Kentucky	40
25	Maine	40
25	Missouri	40
30	Illinois	39
30	Rhode Island	39
32	Hawaii	38
33	Delaware	36
33	Michigan	36
33	Tennessee	36
36	Georgia	35
36	New York	35
36	Oklahoma	35
36	West Virginia	35
40	Arizona	34
41	Arkansas	33
41	Oregon	33
43	Alaska	32
43	South Carolina	32
45	Alabama	31
45	California	31
45	Mississippi	31
45	Nevada	31
49	Louisiana	27
49	New Mexico	27
	District of Columbia	32

Source: U.S. Department of Education, National Center for Education Statistics
"The Nation's Report Card: Mathematics 2017" (www.nationsreportcard.gov)
*There are four achievement levels: Below Basic, Basic, Proficient, and Advanced. Proficient represents solid academic mastery for 4th graders. Students reaching this level have demonstrated competency over challenging subject matter, including subject matter knowledge, application of such knowledge to real-world situations, and analytical skills appropriate to the subject matter.

Percent of Public School Eighth Graders Proficient or Better in Mathematics in 2017
National Percent = 33%*

ALPHA ORDER

RANK	STATE	PERCENT
48	Alabama	21
36	Alaska	29
25	Arizona	34
44	Arkansas	25
36	California	29
13	Colorado	38
20	Connecticut	36
40	Delaware	28
36	Florida	29
31	Georgia	31
41	Hawaii	27
22	Idaho	35
30	Illinois	32
13	Indiana	38
18	Iowa	37
22	Kansas	35
36	Kentucky	29
50	Louisiana	19
20	Maine	36
28	Maryland	33
1	Massachusetts	50
31	Michigan	31
2	Minnesota	46
47	Mississippi	22
33	Missouri	30
18	Montana	37
5	Nebraska	41
41	Nevada	27
3	New Hampshire	45
4	New Jersey	44
49	New Mexico	20
25	New York	34
22	North Carolina	35
7	North Dakota	40
7	Ohio	40
45	Oklahoma	24
25	Oregon	34
13	Pennsylvania	38
33	Rhode Island	30
43	South Carolina	26
13	South Dakota	38
33	Tennessee	30
28	Texas	33
10	Utah	39
10	Vermont	39
7	Virginia	40
5	Washington	41
45	West Virginia	24
10	Wisconsin	39
13	Wyoming	38

RANK ORDER

RANK	STATE	PERCENT
1	Massachusetts	50
2	Minnesota	46
3	New Hampshire	45
4	New Jersey	44
5	Nebraska	41
5	Washington	41
7	North Dakota	40
7	Ohio	40
7	Virginia	40
10	Utah	39
10	Vermont	39
10	Wisconsin	39
13	Colorado	38
13	Indiana	38
13	Pennsylvania	38
13	South Dakota	38
13	Wyoming	38
18	Iowa	37
18	Montana	37
20	Connecticut	36
20	Maine	36
22	Idaho	35
22	Kansas	35
22	North Carolina	35
25	Arizona	34
25	New York	34
25	Oregon	34
28	Maryland	33
28	Texas	33
30	Illinois	32
31	Georgia	31
31	Michigan	31
33	Missouri	30
33	Rhode Island	30
33	Tennessee	30
36	Alaska	29
36	California	29
36	Florida	29
36	Kentucky	29
40	Delaware	28
41	Hawaii	27
41	Nevada	27
43	South Carolina	26
44	Arkansas	25
45	Oklahoma	24
45	West Virginia	24
47	Mississippi	22
48	Alabama	21
49	New Mexico	20
50	Louisiana	19
	District of Columbia	21

Source: U.S. Department of Education, National Center for Education Statistics
  "The Nation's Report Card: Mathematics 2017" (www.nationsreportcard.gov)
*There are four achievement levels: Below Basic, Basic, Proficient, and Advanced. Proficient represents solid academic mastery for 8th graders. Students reaching this level have demonstrated competency over challenging subject matter, including subject matter knowledge, application of such knowledge to real-world situations, and analytical skills appropriate to the subject matter.

Percent of Population Graduated from High School in 2017

National Percent = 88.0%*

ALPHA ORDER

RANK	STATE	PERCENT
44	Alabama	86.5
12	Alaska	91.7
38	Arizona	87.2
42	Arkansas	86.7
50	California	83.3
14	Colorado	91.6
24	Connecticut	90.4
22	Delaware	90.6
32	Florida	88.4
40	Georgia	87.0
8	Hawaii	92.3
20	Idaho	90.8
30	Illinois	89.1
31	Indiana	88.6
10	Iowa	92.1
17	Kansas	91.0
45	Kentucky	86.3
47	Louisiana	85.1
8	Maine	92.3
26	Maryland	89.9
20	Massachusetts	90.8
19	Michigan	90.9
1	Minnesota	93.1
48	Mississippi	84.4
28	Missouri	89.7
3	Montana	93.0
15	Nebraska	91.3
41	Nevada	86.8
1	New Hampshire	93.1
26	New Jersey	89.9
46	New Mexico	86.1
43	New York	86.6
35	North Carolina	87.8
4	North Dakota	92.9
25	Ohio	90.3
34	Oklahoma	88.1
17	Oregon	91.0
22	Pennsylvania	90.6
33	Rhode Island	88.3
37	South Carolina	87.4
12	South Dakota	91.7
35	Tennessee	87.8
49	Texas	83.6
10	Utah	92.1
6	Vermont	92.6
28	Virginia	89.7
15	Washington	91.3
39	West Virginia	87.1
7	Wisconsin	92.4
4	Wyoming	92.9

RANK ORDER

RANK	STATE	PERCENT
1	Minnesota	93.1
1	New Hampshire	93.1
3	Montana	93.0
4	North Dakota	92.9
4	Wyoming	92.9
6	Vermont	92.6
7	Wisconsin	92.4
8	Hawaii	92.3
8	Maine	92.3
10	Iowa	92.1
10	Utah	92.1
12	Alaska	91.7
12	South Dakota	91.7
14	Colorado	91.6
15	Nebraska	91.3
15	Washington	91.3
17	Kansas	91.0
17	Oregon	91.0
19	Michigan	90.9
20	Idaho	90.8
20	Massachusetts	90.8
22	Delaware	90.6
22	Pennsylvania	90.6
24	Connecticut	90.4
25	Ohio	90.3
26	Maryland	89.9
26	New Jersey	89.9
28	Missouri	89.7
28	Virginia	89.7
30	Illinois	89.1
31	Indiana	88.6
32	Florida	88.4
33	Rhode Island	88.3
34	Oklahoma	88.1
35	North Carolina	87.8
35	Tennessee	87.8
37	South Carolina	87.4
38	Arizona	87.2
39	West Virginia	87.1
40	Georgia	87.0
41	Nevada	86.8
42	Arkansas	86.7
43	New York	86.6
44	Alabama	86.5
45	Kentucky	86.3
46	New Mexico	86.1
47	Louisiana	85.1
48	Mississippi	84.4
49	Texas	83.6
50	California	83.3
	District of Columbia	90.2

Source: U.S. Bureau of the Census

"2017 American Community Survey-Table CP02" (https://www.census.gov/programs-surveys/acs/)

*Persons age 25 and older. Includes equivalency status.

Projected Public High School Graduates in 2019

National Total = 3,285,250 Graduates*

ALPHA ORDER

ALPHA ORDER

RANK	STATE	GRADUATES	% of USA
25	Alabama	44,480	1.4%
46	Alaska	8,090	0.2%
16	Arizona	67,620	2.1%
33	Arkansas	30,960	0.9%
1	California	417,760	12.7%
22	Colorado	57,040	1.7%
29	Connecticut	35,970	1.1%
45	Delaware	8,720	0.3%
3	Florida	178,560	5.4%
8	Georgia	108,290	3.3%
42	Hawaii	10,370	0.3%
37	Idaho	19,070	0.6%
5	Illinois	138,100	4.2%
14	Indiana	70,820	2.2%
31	Iowa	33,380	1.0%
32	Kansas	33,310	1.0%
24	Kentucky	44,530	1.4%
26	Louisiana	41,340	1.3%
41	Maine	12,290	0.4%
21	Maryland	57,060	1.7%
15	Massachusetts	70,430	2.1%
10	Michigan	100,580	3.1%
20	Minnesota	58,910	1.8%
34	Mississippi	27,070	0.8%
18	Missouri	61,230	1.9%
44	Montana	9,490	0.3%
36	Nebraska	22,360	0.7%
35	Nevada	24,470	0.7%
40	New Hampshire	12,990	0.4%
11	New Jersey	95,020	2.9%
38	New Mexico	18,150	0.6%
4	New York	174,810	5.3%
9	North Carolina	104,920	3.2%
48	North Dakota	7,090	0.2%
6	Ohio	118,750	3.6%
27	Oklahoma	41,060	1.2%
30	Oregon	35,760	1.1%
7	Pennsylvania	116,740	3.6%
43	Rhode Island	9,900	0.3%
23	South Carolina	46,330	1.4%
46	South Dakota	8,090	0.2%
17	Tennessee	64,190	2.0%
2	Texas	349,450	10.6%
28	Utah	38,270	1.2%
49	Vermont	5,790	0.2%
12	Virginia	87,030	2.6%
13	Washington	71,280	2.2%
39	West Virginia	17,350	0.5%
19	Wisconsin	60,100	1.8%
50	Wyoming	5,770	0.2%

RANK ORDER

RANK	STATE	GRADUATES	% of USA
1	California	417,760	12.7%
2	Texas	349,450	10.6%
3	Florida	178,560	5.4%
4	New York	174,810	5.3%
5	Illinois	138,100	4.2%
6	Ohio	118,750	3.6%
7	Pennsylvania	116,740	3.6%
8	Georgia	108,290	3.3%
9	North Carolina	104,920	3.2%
10	Michigan	100,580	3.1%
11	New Jersey	95,020	2.9%
12	Virginia	87,030	2.6%
13	Washington	71,280	2.2%
14	Indiana	70,820	2.2%
15	Massachusetts	70,430	2.1%
16	Arizona	67,620	2.1%
17	Tennessee	64,190	2.0%
18	Missouri	61,230	1.9%
19	Wisconsin	60,100	1.8%
20	Minnesota	58,910	1.8%
21	Maryland	57,060	1.7%
22	Colorado	57,040	1.7%
23	South Carolina	46,330	1.4%
24	Kentucky	44,530	1.4%
25	Alabama	44,480	1.4%
26	Louisiana	41,340	1.3%
27	Oklahoma	41,060	1.2%
28	Utah	38,270	1.2%
29	Connecticut	35,970	1.1%
30	Oregon	35,760	1.1%
31	Iowa	33,380	1.0%
32	Kansas	33,310	1.0%
33	Arkansas	30,960	0.9%
34	Mississippi	27,070	0.8%
35	Nevada	24,470	0.7%
36	Nebraska	22,360	0.7%
37	Idaho	19,070	0.6%
38	New Mexico	18,150	0.6%
39	West Virginia	17,350	0.5%
40	New Hampshire	12,990	0.4%
41	Maine	12,290	0.4%
42	Hawaii	10,370	0.3%
43	Rhode Island	9,900	0.3%
44	Montana	9,490	0.3%
45	Delaware	8,720	0.3%
46	Alaska	8,090	0.2%
46	South Dakota	8,090	0.2%
48	North Dakota	7,090	0.2%
49	Vermont	5,790	0.2%
50	Wyoming	5,770	0.2%
	District of Columbia	4,130	0.1%

Source: U.S. Department of Education, National Center for Education Statistics
  "Digest of Education Statistics" (https://nces.ed.gov/programs/digest/index.asp)
*Projected for school year 2018-2019 as of May 2018. Excludes persons receiving high school equivalency certificates.

Adjusted Cohort Graduation Rate for Public High Schools in 2016

National Average = 84.1%*

ALPHA ORDER			RANK ORDER		
RANK	STATE	PERCENT	RANK	STATE	PERCENT
16	Alabama	87.1	1	Iowa	91.3
47	Alaska	76.1	2	New Jersey	90.1
43	Arizona	79.5	3	West Virginia	89.8
17	Arkansas	87.0	4	Nebraska	89.3
30	California	83.0	5	Texas	89.1
45	Colorado	78.9	6	Missouri	89.0
15	Connecticut	87.4	7	Kentucky	88.6
25	Delaware	85.5	8	Tennessee	88.5
37	Florida	80.7	9	New Hampshire	88.2
44	Georgia	79.4	9	Wisconsin	88.2
32	Hawaii	82.7	11	Vermont	87.7
40	Idaho	79.7	12	Maryland	87.6
25	Illinois	85.5	13	Massachusetts	87.5
19	Indiana	86.8	13	North Dakota	87.5
1	Iowa	91.3	15	Connecticut	87.4
23	Kansas	85.7	16	Alabama	87.1
7	Kentucky	88.6	17	Arkansas	87.0
46	Louisiana	78.6	17	Maine	87.0
17	Maine	87.0	19	Indiana	86.8
12	Maryland	87.6	20	Virginia	86.7
13	Massachusetts	87.5	21	Pennsylvania	86.1
40	Michigan	79.7	22	North Carolina	85.9
35	Minnesota	82.2	23	Kansas	85.7
34	Mississippi	82.3	24	Montana	85.6
6	Missouri	89.0	25	Delaware	85.5
24	Montana	85.6	25	Illinois	85.5
4	Nebraska	89.3	27	Utah	85.2
49	Nevada	73.6	28	South Dakota	83.9
9	New Hampshire	88.2	29	Ohio	83.5
2	New Jersey	90.1	30	California	83.0
50	New Mexico	71.0	31	Rhode Island	82.8
38	New York	80.4	32	Hawaii	82.7
22	North Carolina	85.9	33	South Carolina	82.6
13	North Dakota	87.5	34	Mississippi	82.3
29	Ohio	83.5	35	Minnesota	82.2
36	Oklahoma	81.6	36	Oklahoma	81.6
48	Oregon	74.8	37	Florida	80.7
21	Pennsylvania	86.1	38	New York	80.4
31	Rhode Island	82.8	39	Wyoming	80.0
33	South Carolina	82.6	40	Idaho	79.7
28	South Dakota	83.9	40	Michigan	79.7
8	Tennessee	88.5	40	Washington	79.7
5	Texas	89.1	43	Arizona	79.5
27	Utah	85.2	44	Georgia	79.4
11	Vermont	87.7	45	Colorado	78.9
20	Virginia	86.7	46	Louisiana	78.6
40	Washington	79.7	47	Alaska	76.1
3	West Virginia	89.8	48	Oregon	74.8
9	Wisconsin	88.2	49	Nevada	73.6
39	Wyoming	80.0	50	New Mexico	71.0
				District of Columbia	69.2

Source: U.S. Department of Education, National Center for Education Statistics
   "ED Data Express" (http://eddataexpress.ed.gov/index.cfm)
*The Adjusted Cohort Graduation Rate (ACGR) is the number of students who graduate in four years with a regular high school diploma
divided by the number of students who form the adjusted cohort for the graduating class. From the beginning of 9th grade, students
who are entering that grade for the first time form a cohort that is "adjusted" by adding any students who subsequently transfer into
the cohort and subtracting any students who subsequently transfer out, emigrate to another country, or die.

Adjusted Cohort Graduation Rate for Public High School
Economically Disadvantaged Students in 2016
National Average = 77.6%*

ALPHA ORDER

RANK	STATE	PERCENT
12	Alabama	80.9
43	Alaska	68.4
25	Arizona	76.7
8	Arkansas	83.8
16	California	79.0
46	Colorado	67.8
25	Connecticut	76.7
30	Delaware	76.0
35	Florida	74.4
33	Georgia	75.3
22	Hawaii	77.9
39	Idaho	71.9
25	Illinois	76.7
6	Indiana	85.0
7	Iowa	83.9
23	Kansas	77.5
3	Kentucky	85.6
36	Louisiana	72.9
20	Maine	78.0
15	Maryland	79.2
18	Massachusetts	78.4
47	Michigan	67.1
44	Minnesota	68.2
17	Mississippi	78.8
11	Missouri	82.1
28	Montana	76.4
10	Nebraska	82.2
50	Nevada	66.7
28	New Hampshire	76.4
9	New Jersey	82.7
49	New Mexico	66.9
37	New York	72.8
13	North Carolina	80.6
40	North Dakota	71.0
38	Ohio	72.0
31	Oklahoma	75.9
45	Oregon	68.1
20	Pennsylvania	78.0
34	Rhode Island	74.8
1	South Carolina	87.7
48	South Dakota	67.0
4	Tennessee	85.5
2	Texas	86.0
32	Utah	75.6
14	Vermont	80.0
19	Virginia	78.1
41	Washington	70.2
4	West Virginia	85.5
24	Wisconsin	77.4
42	Wyoming	69.1

RANK ORDER

RANK	STATE	PERCENT
1	South Carolina	87.7
2	Texas	86.0
3	Kentucky	85.6
4	Tennessee	85.5
4	West Virginia	85.5
6	Indiana	85.0
7	Iowa	83.9
8	Arkansas	83.8
9	New Jersey	82.7
10	Nebraska	82.2
11	Missouri	82.1
12	Alabama	80.9
13	North Carolina	80.6
14	Vermont	80.0
15	Maryland	79.2
16	California	79.0
17	Mississippi	78.8
18	Massachusetts	78.4
19	Virginia	78.1
20	Maine	78.0
20	Pennsylvania	78.0
22	Hawaii	77.9
23	Kansas	77.5
24	Wisconsin	77.4
25	Arizona	76.7
25	Connecticut	76.7
25	Illinois	76.7
28	Montana	76.4
28	New Hampshire	76.4
30	Delaware	76.0
31	Oklahoma	75.9
32	Utah	75.6
33	Georgia	75.3
34	Rhode Island	74.8
35	Florida	74.4
36	Louisiana	72.9
37	New York	72.8
38	Ohio	72.0
39	Idaho	71.9
40	North Dakota	71.0
41	Washington	70.2
42	Wyoming	69.1
43	Alaska	68.4
44	Minnesota	68.2
45	Oregon	68.1
46	Colorado	67.8
47	Michigan	67.1
48	South Dakota	67.0
49	New Mexico	66.9
50	Nevada	66.7

	District of Columbia	69.3

Source: U.S. Department of Education, National Center for Education Statistics
   "ED Data Express" (http://eddataexpress.ed.gov/index.cfm)
*The Adjusted Cohort Graduation Rate (ACGR) is the number of students who graduate in four years with a regular high school diploma
divided by the number of students who form the adjusted cohort for the graduating class. From the beginning of 9th grade, students
who are entering that grade for the first time form a cohort that is "adjusted" by adding any students who subsequently transfer into
the cohort and subtracting any students who subsequently transfer out, emigrate to another country, or die.

Adjusted Cohort Graduation Rate for Public High School Students with Limited English Proficiency in 2016
National Average = 66.9%*

ALPHA ORDER

RANK	STATE	PERCENT
30	Alabama	64.0
41	Alaska	55.0
50	Arizona	32.0
2	Arkansas	86.0
14	California	72.0
34	Colorado	61.4
25	Connecticut	67.0
11	Delaware	73.0
33	Florida	62.0
40	Georgia	56.5
19	Hawaii	69.0
11	Idaho	73.0
16	Illinois	71.9
17	Indiana	71.0
3	Iowa	81.0
5	Kansas	77.4
21	Kentucky	68.0
47	Louisiana	43.0
4	Maine	78.0
45	Maryland	48.0
29	Massachusetts	64.1
13	Michigan	72.1
31	Minnesota	63.2
28	Mississippi	65.0
21	Missouri	68.0
35	Montana	59.0
41	Nebraska	55.0
48	Nevada	42.6
14	New Hampshire	72.0
8	New Jersey	74.7
24	New Mexico	67.4
49	New York	37.8
38	North Carolina	57.0
19	North Dakota	69.0
44	Ohio	50.0
36	Oklahoma	58.0
43	Oregon	53.0
32	Pennsylvania	62.7
9	Rhode Island	74.0
6	South Carolina	76.0
38	South Dakota	57.0
6	Tennessee	76.0
10	Texas	73.7
26	Utah	66.0
21	Vermont	68.0
46	Virginia	45.4
37	Washington	57.8
1	West Virginia	93.0
26	Wisconsin	66.0
18	Wyoming	70.0

RANK ORDER

RANK	STATE	PERCENT
1	West Virginia	93.0
2	Arkansas	86.0
3	Iowa	81.0
4	Maine	78.0
5	Kansas	77.4
6	South Carolina	76.0
6	Tennessee	76.0
8	New Jersey	74.7
9	Rhode Island	74.0
10	Texas	73.7
11	Delaware	73.0
11	Idaho	73.0
13	Michigan	72.1
14	California	72.0
14	New Hampshire	72.0
16	Illinois	71.9
17	Indiana	71.0
18	Wyoming	70.0
19	Hawaii	69.0
19	North Dakota	69.0
21	Kentucky	68.0
21	Missouri	68.0
21	Vermont	68.0
24	New Mexico	67.4
25	Connecticut	67.0
26	Utah	66.0
26	Wisconsin	66.0
28	Mississippi	65.0
29	Massachusetts	64.1
30	Alabama	64.0
31	Minnesota	63.2
32	Pennsylvania	62.7
33	Florida	62.0
34	Colorado	61.4
35	Montana	59.0
36	Oklahoma	58.0
37	Washington	57.8
38	North Carolina	57.0
38	South Dakota	57.0
40	Georgia	56.5
41	Alaska	55.0
41	Nebraska	55.0
43	Oregon	53.0
44	Ohio	50.0
45	Maryland	48.0
46	Virginia	45.4
47	Louisiana	43.0
48	Nevada	42.6
49	New York	37.8
50	Arizona	32.0
	District of Columbia	64.0

Source: U.S. Department of Education, National Center for Education Statistics
    "ED Data Express" (http://eddataexpress.ed.gov/index.cfm)
*The Adjusted Cohort Graduation Rate (ACGR) is the number of students who graduate in four years with a regular high school diploma divided by the number of students who form the adjusted cohort for the graduating class. From the beginning of 9th grade, students who are entering that grade for the first time form a cohort that is "adjusted" by adding any students who subsequently transfer into the cohort and subtracting any students who subsequently transfer out, emigrate to another country, or die.

Adjusted Cohort Graduation Rate for Public High School Students with Disabilities in 2016
National Average = 65.5%*

ALPHA ORDER

RANK	STATE	PERCENT
43	Alabama	54.1
44	Alaska	54.0
22	Arizona	69.0
1	Arkansas	84.3
28	California	66.0
39	Colorado	57.2
29	Connecticut	65.2
26	Delaware	67.0
32	Florida	61.6
40	Georgia	56.6
36	Hawaii	59.0
34	Idaho	60.0
17	Illinois	70.5
11	Indiana	72.0
19	Iowa	70.0
5	Kansas	77.5
14	Kentucky	71.9
48	Louisiana	46.6
11	Maine	72.0
27	Maryland	66.9
15	Massachusetts	71.8
42	Michigan	55.4
33	Minnesota	60.8
49	Mississippi	34.7
5	Missouri	77.5
3	Montana	78.0
19	Nebraska	70.0
50	Nevada	29.3
10	New Hampshire	73.0
2	New Jersey	78.8
31	New Mexico	61.9
46	New York	52.6
23	North Carolina	68.9
25	North Dakota	68.0
21	Ohio	69.6
8	Oklahoma	74.4
41	Oregon	55.5
9	Pennsylvania	74.1
36	Rhode Island	59.0
47	South Carolina	52.1
34	South Dakota	60.0
15	Tennessee	71.8
4	Texas	77.9
18	Utah	70.2
11	Vermont	72.0
45	Virginia	53.9
38	Washington	58.7
7	West Virginia	77.0
24	Wisconsin	68.5
30	Wyoming	65.0

RANK ORDER

RANK	STATE	PERCENT
1	Arkansas	84.3
2	New Jersey	78.8
3	Montana	78.0
4	Texas	77.9
5	Kansas	77.5
5	Missouri	77.5
7	West Virginia	77.0
8	Oklahoma	74.4
9	Pennsylvania	74.1
10	New Hampshire	73.0
11	Indiana	72.0
11	Maine	72.0
11	Vermont	72.0
14	Kentucky	71.9
15	Massachusetts	71.8
15	Tennessee	71.8
17	Illinois	70.5
18	Utah	70.2
19	Iowa	70.0
19	Nebraska	70.0
21	Ohio	69.6
22	Arizona	69.0
23	North Carolina	68.9
24	Wisconsin	68.5
25	North Dakota	68.0
26	Delaware	67.0
27	Maryland	66.9
28	California	66.0
29	Connecticut	65.2
30	Wyoming	65.0
31	New Mexico	61.9
32	Florida	61.6
33	Minnesota	60.8
34	Idaho	60.0
34	South Dakota	60.0
36	Hawaii	59.0
36	Rhode Island	59.0
38	Washington	58.7
39	Colorado	57.2
40	Georgia	56.6
41	Oregon	55.5
42	Michigan	55.4
43	Alabama	54.1
44	Alaska	54.0
45	Virginia	53.9
46	New York	52.6
47	South Carolina	52.1
48	Louisiana	46.6
49	Mississippi	34.7
50	Nevada	29.3

| | District of Columbia | 50.0 |

Source: U.S. Department of Education, National Center for Education Statistics
"ED Data Express" (http://eddataexpress.ed.gov/index.cfm)
*The Adjusted Cohort Graduation Rate (ACGR) is the number of students who graduate in four years with a regular high school diploma divided by the number of students who form the adjusted cohort for the graduating class. From the beginning of 9th grade, students who are entering that grade for the first time form a cohort that is "adjusted" by adding any students who subsequently transfer into the cohort and subtracting any students who subsequently transfer out, emigrate to another country, or die.

ACT Average Composite Score in 2018

National Average = 20.8*

ALPHA ORDER				RANK ORDER		
RANK	STATE	AVERAGE SCORE		RANK	STATE	AVERAGE SCORE
45	Alabama	19.1		1	Connecticut	25.6
26	Alaska	20.8		2	Massachusetts	25.5
43	Arizona	19.2		3	New Hampshire	25.1
40	Arkansas	19.4		4	New Mexico	24.5
15	California	22.7		5	Michigan	24.4
9	Colorado	23.9		6	Rhode Island	24.2
1	Connecticut	25.6		7	Vermont	24.1
12	Delaware	23.8		8	Maine	24.0
38	Florida	19.9		9	Colorado	23.9
23	Georgia	21.4		9	Illinois	23.9
47	Hawaii	18.9		9	Virginia	23.9
18	Idaho	22.3		12	Delaware	23.8
9	Illinois	23.9		13	New York	23.7
16	Indiana	22.5		14	Pennsylvania	23.5
21	Iowa	21.8		15	California	22.7
22	Kansas	21.6		16	Indiana	22.5
33	Kentucky	20.2		16	Maryland	22.5
43	Louisiana	19.2		18	Idaho	22.3
8	Maine	24.0		19	Washington	22.2
16	Maryland	22.5		20	South Dakota	21.9
2	Massachusetts	25.5		21	Iowa	21.8
5	Michigan	24.4		22	Kansas	21.6
24	Minnesota	21.3		23	Georgia	21.4
48	Mississippi	18.6		24	Minnesota	21.3
35	Missouri	20.0		24	Oregon	21.3
35	Montana	20.0		26	Alaska	20.8
34	Nebraska	20.1		27	Texas	20.6
50	Nevada	17.7		28	Wisconsin	20.5
3	New Hampshire	25.1		29	Utah	20.4
40	New Jersey	19.4		30	North Dakota	20.3
4	New Mexico	24.5		30	Ohio	20.3
13	New York	23.7		30	West Virginia	20.3
45	North Carolina	19.1		33	Kentucky	20.2
30	North Dakota	20.3		34	Nebraska	20.1
30	Ohio	20.3		35	Missouri	20.0
42	Oklahoma	19.3		35	Montana	20.0
24	Oregon	21.3		35	Wyoming	20.0
14	Pennsylvania	23.5		38	Florida	19.9
6	Rhode Island	24.2		39	Tennessee	19.6
49	South Carolina	18.3		40	Arkansas	19.4
20	South Dakota	21.9		40	New Jersey	19.4
39	Tennessee	19.6		42	Oklahoma	19.3
27	Texas	20.6		43	Arizona	19.2
29	Utah	20.4		43	Louisiana	19.2
7	Vermont	24.1		45	Alabama	19.1
9	Virginia	23.9		45	North Carolina	19.1
19	Washington	22.2		47	Hawaii	18.9
30	West Virginia	20.3		48	Mississippi	18.6
28	Wisconsin	20.5		49	South Carolina	18.3
35	Wyoming	20.0		50	Nevada	17.7
					District of Columbia	23.6

Source: The American College Testing Program (Copyright © 2018)
"Average ACT Scores by State" (http://leadershipblog.act.org/)

*The ACT score range is 1 to 36. Slightly more than two million 2018 U.S. high school graduates took the test. Caution should be used in using ACT scores to compare states. The percentage of high graduates taking the test varies greatly from one state to another. For example, all graduates are required to take the test in seventeen states but, in Maine, only 7 percent of graduates took the test.

Education Expenditures by State and Local Governments in 2016

National Total = $972,905,911,000*

ALPHA ORDER

RANK	STATE	EXPENDITURES	% of USA
25	Alabama	$13,546,877,000	1.4%
41	Alaska	3,541,384,000	0.4%
21	Arizona	14,464,854,000	1.5%
33	Arkansas	8,417,993,000	0.9%
1	California	124,404,187,000	12.8%
19	Colorado	16,074,773,000	1.7%
24	Connecticut	13,563,114,000	1.4%
40	Delaware	3,662,011,000	0.4%
4	Florida	41,519,289,000	4.3%
10	Georgia	26,726,086,000	2.7%
44	Hawaii	3,386,186,000	0.3%
45	Idaho	3,362,735,000	0.3%
6	Illinois	37,732,911,000	3.9%
18	Indiana	17,589,144,000	1.8%
29	Iowa	10,995,599,000	1.1%
32	Kansas	9,388,386,000	1.0%
28	Kentucky	12,550,355,000	1.3%
26	Louisiana	13,043,277,000	1.3%
42	Maine	3,464,923,000	0.4%
15	Maryland	20,006,021,000	2.1%
14	Massachusetts	22,492,815,000	2.3%
9	Michigan	29,997,117,000	3.1%
16	Minnesota	18,291,636,000	1.9%
34	Mississippi	8,321,777,000	0.9%
20	Missouri	15,077,947,000	1.5%
48	Montana	2,893,555,000	0.3%
35	Nebraska	7,279,097,000	0.7%
37	Nevada	6,132,816,000	0.6%
39	New Hampshire	4,130,658,000	0.4%
7	New Jersey	36,108,105,000	3.7%
36	New Mexico	6,647,485,000	0.7%
3	New York	82,511,342,000	8.5%
11	North Carolina	25,446,577,000	2.6%
46	North Dakota	3,186,590,000	0.3%
8	Ohio	34,482,043,000	3.5%
30	Oklahoma	10,629,264,000	1.1%
27	Oregon	12,590,871,000	1.3%
5	Pennsylvania	41,396,950,000	4.3%
43	Rhode Island	3,409,392,000	0.4%
22	South Carolina	14,353,054,000	1.5%
50	South Dakota	2,456,152,000	0.3%
23	Tennessee	13,977,358,000	1.4%
2	Texas	83,062,062,000	8.5%
31	Utah	9,752,423,000	1.0%
49	Vermont	2,678,368,000	0.3%
12	Virginia	25,100,336,000	2.6%
13	Washington	23,786,267,000	2.4%
38	West Virginia	5,358,692,000	0.6%
17	Wisconsin	18,029,866,000	1.9%
47	Wyoming	3,119,419,000	0.3%

RANK ORDER

RANK	STATE	EXPENDITURES	% of USA
1	California	$124,404,187,000	12.8%
2	Texas	83,062,062,000	8.5%
3	New York	82,511,342,000	8.5%
4	Florida	41,519,289,000	4.3%
5	Pennsylvania	41,396,950,000	4.3%
6	Illinois	37,732,911,000	3.9%
7	New Jersey	36,108,105,000	3.7%
8	Ohio	34,482,043,000	3.5%
9	Michigan	29,997,117,000	3.1%
10	Georgia	26,726,086,000	2.7%
11	North Carolina	25,446,577,000	2.6%
12	Virginia	25,100,336,000	2.6%
13	Washington	23,786,267,000	2.4%
14	Massachusetts	22,492,815,000	2.3%
15	Maryland	20,006,021,000	2.1%
16	Minnesota	18,291,636,000	1.9%
17	Wisconsin	18,029,866,000	1.9%
18	Indiana	17,589,144,000	1.8%
19	Colorado	16,074,773,000	1.7%
20	Missouri	15,077,947,000	1.5%
21	Arizona	14,464,854,000	1.5%
22	South Carolina	14,353,054,000	1.5%
23	Tennessee	13,977,358,000	1.4%
24	Connecticut	13,563,114,000	1.4%
25	Alabama	13,546,877,000	1.4%
26	Louisiana	13,043,277,000	1.3%
27	Oregon	12,590,871,000	1.3%
28	Kentucky	12,550,355,000	1.3%
29	Iowa	10,995,599,000	1.1%
30	Oklahoma	10,629,264,000	1.1%
31	Utah	9,752,423,000	1.0%
32	Kansas	9,388,386,000	1.0%
33	Arkansas	8,417,993,000	0.9%
34	Mississippi	8,321,777,000	0.9%
35	Nebraska	7,279,097,000	0.7%
36	New Mexico	6,647,485,000	0.7%
37	Nevada	6,132,816,000	0.6%
38	West Virginia	5,358,692,000	0.6%
39	New Hampshire	4,130,658,000	0.4%
40	Delaware	3,662,011,000	0.4%
41	Alaska	3,541,384,000	0.4%
42	Maine	3,464,923,000	0.4%
43	Rhode Island	3,409,392,000	0.4%
44	Hawaii	3,386,186,000	0.3%
45	Idaho	3,362,735,000	0.3%
46	North Dakota	3,186,590,000	0.3%
47	Wyoming	3,119,419,000	0.3%
48	Montana	2,893,555,000	0.3%
49	Vermont	2,678,368,000	0.3%
50	South Dakota	2,456,152,000	0.3%
	District of Columbia	2,765,772,000	0.3%

Source: U.S. Bureau of the Census, Governments Division
"2016 State and Local Government Finances" (https://www.census.gov/programs-surveys/gov-finances.html)
*Direct general expenditures for higher, secondary, elementary, and, "other" education. Includes capital outlays.

Per Capita State and Local Government Expenditures for Education in 2016

National Per Capita = $3,011*

ALPHA ORDER

RANK	STATE	PER CAPITA
36	Alabama	$2,785
2	Alaska	4,776
48	Arizona	2,083
34	Arkansas	2,815
20	California	3,173
30	Colorado	2,901
9	Connecticut	3,790
7	Delaware	3,858
49	Florida	2,013
42	Georgia	2,594
45	Hawaii	2,371
50	Idaho	1,998
28	Illinois	2,942
40	Indiana	2,652
10	Iowa	3,511
16	Kansas	3,225
33	Kentucky	2,828
35	Louisiana	2,788
41	Maine	2,603
11	Maryland	3,332
13	Massachusetts	3,295
24	Michigan	3,014
12	Minnesota	3,312
36	Mississippi	2,785
44	Missouri	2,477
38	Montana	2,780
8	Nebraska	3,819
47	Nevada	2,100
22	New Hampshire	3,077
6	New Jersey	4,069
19	New Mexico	3,176
5	New York	4,201
43	North Carolina	2,505
4	North Dakota	4,224
27	Ohio	2,964
39	Oklahoma	2,707
22	Oregon	3,077
15	Pennsylvania	3,238
16	Rhode Island	3,225
31	South Carolina	2,895
32	South Dakota	2,846
46	Tennessee	2,103
26	Texas	2,973
18	Utah	3,205
3	Vermont	4,295
25	Virginia	2,984
14	Washington	3,261
29	West Virginia	2,927
21	Wisconsin	3,123
1	Wyoming	5,339

RANK ORDER

RANK	STATE	PER CAPITA
1	Wyoming	$5,339
2	Alaska	4,776
3	Vermont	4,295
4	North Dakota	4,224
5	New York	4,201
6	New Jersey	4,069
7	Delaware	3,858
8	Nebraska	3,819
9	Connecticut	3,790
10	Iowa	3,511
11	Maryland	3,332
12	Minnesota	3,312
13	Massachusetts	3,295
14	Washington	3,261
15	Pennsylvania	3,238
16	Kansas	3,225
16	Rhode Island	3,225
18	Utah	3,205
19	New Mexico	3,176
20	California	3,173
21	Wisconsin	3,123
22	New Hampshire	3,077
22	Oregon	3,077
24	Michigan	3,014
25	Virginia	2,984
26	Texas	2,973
27	Ohio	2,964
28	Illinois	2,942
29	West Virginia	2,927
30	Colorado	2,901
31	South Carolina	2,895
32	South Dakota	2,846
33	Kentucky	2,828
34	Arkansas	2,815
35	Louisiana	2,788
36	Alabama	2,785
36	Mississippi	2,785
38	Montana	2,780
39	Oklahoma	2,707
40	Indiana	2,652
41	Maine	2,603
42	Georgia	2,594
43	North Carolina	2,505
44	Missouri	2,477
45	Hawaii	2,371
46	Tennessee	2,103
47	Nevada	2,100
48	Arizona	2,083
49	Florida	2,013
50	Idaho	1,998

District of Columbia	4,028

Source: CQ Press using data from U.S. Bureau of the Census, Governments Division
   "2016 State and Local Government Finances" (https://www.census.gov/programs-surveys/gov-finances.html)
*Direct general expenditures for higher, secondary, elementary, and, "other" education. Includes capital outlays.

Expenditures for Education as a Percent of
All State and Local Government Expenditures in 2016
National Percent = 33.0%*

ALPHA ORDER

RANK	STATE	PERCENT
13	Alabama	35.5
49	Alaska	25.9
45	Arizona	29.7
20	Arkansas	34.6
47	California	29.0
21	Colorado	34.2
16	Connecticut	35.3
10	Delaware	36.3
48	Florida	28.7
4	Georgia	38.9
50	Hawaii	24.8
41	Idaho	30.5
23	Illinois	33.9
25	Indiana	33.8
12	Iowa	35.6
7	Kansas	37.3
35	Kentucky	32.3
38	Louisiana	31.5
46	Maine	29.4
22	Maryland	34.1
43	Massachusetts	30.1
11	Michigan	36.2
36	Minnesota	32.1
37	Mississippi	31.9
31	Missouri	33.2
32	Montana	33.0
2	Nebraska	41.8
44	Nevada	29.9
8	New Hampshire	37.1
3	New Jersey	39.1
34	New Mexico	32.4
40	New York	30.7
32	North Carolina	33.0
29	North Dakota	33.3
29	Ohio	33.3
9	Oklahoma	36.5
42	Oregon	30.4
23	Pennsylvania	33.9
28	Rhode Island	33.4
18	South Carolina	35.1
18	South Dakota	35.1
39	Tennessee	31.1
5	Texas	38.6
1	Utah	41.9
6	Vermont	38.1
15	Virginia	35.4
26	Washington	33.7
26	West Virginia	33.7
17	Wisconsin	35.2
13	Wyoming	35.5

RANK ORDER

RANK	STATE	PERCENT
1	Utah	41.9
2	Nebraska	41.8
3	New Jersey	39.1
4	Georgia	38.9
5	Texas	38.6
6	Vermont	38.1
7	Kansas	37.3
8	New Hampshire	37.1
9	Oklahoma	36.5
10	Delaware	36.3
11	Michigan	36.2
12	Iowa	35.6
13	Alabama	35.5
13	Wyoming	35.5
15	Virginia	35.4
16	Connecticut	35.3
17	Wisconsin	35.2
18	South Carolina	35.1
18	South Dakota	35.1
20	Arkansas	34.6
21	Colorado	34.2
22	Maryland	34.1
23	Illinois	33.9
23	Pennsylvania	33.9
25	Indiana	33.8
26	Washington	33.7
26	West Virginia	33.7
28	Rhode Island	33.4
29	North Dakota	33.3
29	Ohio	33.3
31	Missouri	33.2
32	Montana	33.0
32	North Carolina	33.0
34	New Mexico	32.4
35	Kentucky	32.3
36	Minnesota	32.1
37	Mississippi	31.9
38	Louisiana	31.5
39	Tennessee	31.1
40	New York	30.7
41	Idaho	30.5
42	Oregon	30.4
43	Massachusetts	30.1
44	Nevada	29.9
45	Arizona	29.7
46	Maine	29.4
47	California	29.0
48	Florida	28.7
49	Alaska	25.9
50	Hawaii	24.8

| | District of Columbia | 21.7 |

Source: CQ Press using data from U.S. Bureau of the Census, Governments Division
"2016 State and Local Government Finances" (https://www.census.gov/programs-surveys/gov-finances.html)
*Direct general expenditures for higher, secondary, elementary, and "other" education as a percent of all direct general expenditures. Includes capital outlays.

State and Local Government Expenditures for Elementary and Secondary Education in 2016
National Total = $632,746,106,000*

ALPHA ORDER

RANK	STATE	EXPENDITURES	% of USA
26	Alabama	$7,638,986,000	1.2%
42	Alaska	2,365,458,000	0.4%
25	Arizona	7,841,674,000	1.2%
32	Arkansas	5,088,236,000	0.8%
1	California	78,530,105,000	12.4%
21	Colorado	9,410,376,000	1.5%
20	Connecticut	9,441,199,000	1.5%
46	Delaware	1,949,722,000	0.3%
5	Florida	27,362,892,000	4.3%
9	Georgia	18,916,855,000	3.0%
43	Hawaii	2,118,410,000	0.3%
44	Idaho	2,046,687,000	0.3%
7	Illinois	26,537,479,000	4.2%
19	Indiana	9,967,447,000	1.6%
29	Iowa	6,584,354,000	1.0%
31	Kansas	5,648,205,000	0.9%
28	Kentucky	7,125,687,000	1.1%
24	Louisiana	7,930,874,000	1.3%
40	Maine	2,424,796,000	0.4%
15	Maryland	12,842,442,000	2.0%
12	Massachusetts	15,460,847,000	2.4%
10	Michigan	16,951,162,000	2.7%
16	Minnesota	12,229,969,000	1.9%
34	Mississippi	4,581,223,000	0.7%
18	Missouri	10,312,395,000	1.6%
48	Montana	1,839,192,000	0.3%
35	Nebraska	4,530,479,000	0.7%
36	Nevada	4,202,930,000	0.7%
39	New Hampshire	2,924,046,000	0.5%
6	New Jersey	26,985,959,000	4.3%
37	New Mexico	3,653,353,000	0.6%
2	New York	66,105,796,000	10.4%
14	North Carolina	13,801,268,000	2.2%
47	North Dakota	1,873,417,000	0.3%
8	Ohio	23,163,315,000	3.7%
30	Oklahoma	5,915,482,000	0.9%
27	Oregon	7,145,470,000	1.1%
4	Pennsylvania	28,231,980,000	4.5%
41	Rhode Island	2,410,811,000	0.4%
23	South Carolina	8,755,862,000	1.4%
50	South Dakota	1,431,042,000	0.2%
22	Tennessee	9,274,112,000	1.5%
3	Texas	52,800,005,000	8.3%
33	Utah	4,817,095,000	0.8%
49	Vermont	1,608,471,000	0.3%
11	Virginia	16,301,534,000	2.6%
13	Washington	14,874,614,000	2.4%
38	West Virginia	3,086,288,000	0.5%
17	Wisconsin	11,084,197,000	1.8%
45	Wyoming	2,015,079,000	0.3%

RANK ORDER

RANK	STATE	EXPENDITURES	% of USA
1	California	$78,530,105,000	12.4%
2	New York	66,105,796,000	10.4%
3	Texas	52,800,005,000	8.3%
4	Pennsylvania	28,231,980,000	4.5%
5	Florida	27,362,892,000	4.3%
6	New Jersey	26,985,959,000	4.3%
7	Illinois	26,537,479,000	4.2%
8	Ohio	23,163,315,000	3.7%
9	Georgia	18,916,855,000	3.0%
10	Michigan	16,951,162,000	2.7%
11	Virginia	16,301,534,000	2.6%
12	Massachusetts	15,460,847,000	2.4%
13	Washington	14,874,614,000	2.4%
14	North Carolina	13,801,268,000	2.2%
15	Maryland	12,842,442,000	2.0%
16	Minnesota	12,229,969,000	1.9%
17	Wisconsin	11,084,197,000	1.8%
18	Missouri	10,312,395,000	1.6%
19	Indiana	9,967,447,000	1.6%
20	Connecticut	9,441,199,000	1.5%
21	Colorado	9,410,376,000	1.5%
22	Tennessee	9,274,112,000	1.5%
23	South Carolina	8,755,862,000	1.4%
24	Louisiana	7,930,874,000	1.3%
25	Arizona	7,841,674,000	1.2%
26	Alabama	7,638,986,000	1.2%
27	Oregon	7,145,470,000	1.1%
28	Kentucky	7,125,687,000	1.1%
29	Iowa	6,584,354,000	1.0%
30	Oklahoma	5,915,482,000	0.9%
31	Kansas	5,648,205,000	0.9%
32	Arkansas	5,088,236,000	0.8%
33	Utah	4,817,095,000	0.8%
34	Mississippi	4,581,223,000	0.7%
35	Nebraska	4,530,479,000	0.7%
36	Nevada	4,202,930,000	0.7%
37	New Mexico	3,653,353,000	0.6%
38	West Virginia	3,086,288,000	0.5%
39	New Hampshire	2,924,046,000	0.5%
40	Maine	2,424,796,000	0.4%
41	Rhode Island	2,410,811,000	0.4%
42	Alaska	2,365,458,000	0.4%
43	Hawaii	2,118,410,000	0.3%
44	Idaho	2,046,687,000	0.3%
45	Wyoming	2,015,079,000	0.3%
46	Delaware	1,949,722,000	0.3%
47	North Dakota	1,873,417,000	0.3%
48	Montana	1,839,192,000	0.3%
49	Vermont	1,608,471,000	0.3%
50	South Dakota	1,431,042,000	0.2%
	District of Columbia	2,606,829,000	0.4%

Source: U.S. Bureau of the Census, Governments Division
"2016 State and Local Government Finances" (https://www.census.gov/programs-surveys/gov-finances.html)
*Direct general expenditures. Includes capital outlays.

Per Capita State and Local Government Expenditures for Elementary and Secondary Education in 2016
National Per Capita = $1,959*

ALPHA ORDER

RANK	STATE	PER CAPITA
40	Alabama	$1,570
3	Alaska	3,190
50	Arizona	1,129
32	Arkansas	1,702
19	California	2,003
33	Colorado	1,698
5	Connecticut	2,638
17	Delaware	2,054
48	Florida	1,326
25	Georgia	1,836
44	Hawaii	1,483
49	Idaho	1,216
16	Illinois	2,069
43	Indiana	1,503
15	Iowa	2,102
21	Kansas	1,940
38	Kentucky	1,606
34	Louisiana	1,695
26	Maine	1,821
14	Maryland	2,139
10	Massachusetts	2,265
31	Michigan	1,703
11	Minnesota	2,214
41	Mississippi	1,533
35	Missouri	1,694
27	Montana	1,767
8	Nebraska	2,377
45	Nevada	1,439
13	New Hampshire	2,178
4	New Jersey	3,041
29	New Mexico	1,746
2	New York	3,366
47	North Carolina	1,359
7	North Dakota	2,483
20	Ohio	1,991
42	Oklahoma	1,506
29	Oregon	1,746
12	Pennsylvania	2,208
9	Rhode Island	2,281
28	South Carolina	1,766
37	South Dakota	1,658
46	Tennessee	1,396
24	Texas	1,890
39	Utah	1,583
6	Vermont	2,579
22	Virginia	1,938
18	Washington	2,039
36	West Virginia	1,686
23	Wisconsin	1,920
1	Wyoming	3,449

RANK ORDER

RANK	STATE	PER CAPITA
1	Wyoming	$3,449
2	New York	3,366
3	Alaska	3,190
4	New Jersey	3,041
5	Connecticut	2,638
6	Vermont	2,579
7	North Dakota	2,483
8	Nebraska	2,377
9	Rhode Island	2,281
10	Massachusetts	2,265
11	Minnesota	2,214
12	Pennsylvania	2,208
13	New Hampshire	2,178
14	Maryland	2,139
15	Iowa	2,102
16	Illinois	2,069
17	Delaware	2,054
18	Washington	2,039
19	California	2,003
20	Ohio	1,991
21	Kansas	1,940
22	Virginia	1,938
23	Wisconsin	1,920
24	Texas	1,890
25	Georgia	1,836
26	Maine	1,821
27	Montana	1,767
28	South Carolina	1,766
29	New Mexico	1,746
29	Oregon	1,746
31	Michigan	1,703
32	Arkansas	1,702
33	Colorado	1,698
34	Louisiana	1,695
35	Missouri	1,694
36	West Virginia	1,686
37	South Dakota	1,658
38	Kentucky	1,606
39	Utah	1,583
40	Alabama	1,570
41	Mississippi	1,533
42	Oklahoma	1,506
43	Indiana	1,503
44	Hawaii	1,483
45	Nevada	1,439
46	Tennessee	1,396
47	North Carolina	1,359
48	Florida	1,326
49	Idaho	1,216
50	Arizona	1,129

	District of Columbia	3,797

Source: CQ Press using data from U.S. Bureau of the Census, Governments Division
"2016 State and Local Government Finances" (https://www.census.gov/programs-surveys/gov-finances.html)
*Direct general expenditures. Includes capital outlays.

Expenditures for Elementary and Secondary Education as a Percent of All State and Local Government Expenditures in 2016

National Percent = 21.5%*

ALPHA ORDER

RANK	STATE	PERCENT
33	Alabama	20.0
47	Alaska	17.3
49	Arizona	16.1
24	Arkansas	20.9
42	California	18.3
33	Colorado	20.0
5	Connecticut	24.6
37	Delaware	19.3
40	Florida	18.9
2	Georgia	27.5
50	Hawaii	15.5
41	Idaho	18.5
8	Illinois	23.8
39	Indiana	19.1
21	Iowa	21.3
15	Kansas	22.4
42	Kentucky	18.3
38	Louisiana	19.2
27	Maine	20.6
17	Maryland	21.9
25	Massachusetts	20.7
29	Michigan	20.5
19	Minnesota	21.5
46	Mississippi	17.5
14	Missouri	22.7
23	Montana	21.0
4	Nebraska	26.0
29	Nevada	20.5
3	New Hampshire	26.3
1	New Jersey	29.2
45	New Mexico	17.8
5	New York	24.6
44	North Carolina	17.9
35	North Dakota	19.6
15	Ohio	22.4
32	Oklahoma	20.3
47	Oregon	17.3
10	Pennsylvania	23.1
9	Rhode Island	23.6
20	South Carolina	21.4
29	South Dakota	20.5
27	Tennessee	20.6
5	Texas	24.6
25	Utah	20.7
13	Vermont	22.9
11	Virginia	23.0
22	Washington	21.1
36	West Virginia	19.4
18	Wisconsin	21.7
11	Wyoming	23.0

RANK ORDER

RANK	STATE	PERCENT
1	New Jersey	29.2
2	Georgia	27.5
3	New Hampshire	26.3
4	Nebraska	26.0
5	Connecticut	24.6
5	New York	24.6
5	Texas	24.6
8	Illinois	23.8
9	Rhode Island	23.6
10	Pennsylvania	23.1
11	Virginia	23.0
11	Wyoming	23.0
13	Vermont	22.9
14	Missouri	22.7
15	Kansas	22.4
15	Ohio	22.4
17	Maryland	21.9
18	Wisconsin	21.7
19	Minnesota	21.5
20	South Carolina	21.4
21	Iowa	21.3
22	Washington	21.1
23	Montana	21.0
24	Arkansas	20.9
25	Massachusetts	20.7
25	Utah	20.7
27	Maine	20.6
27	Tennessee	20.6
29	Michigan	20.5
29	Nevada	20.5
29	South Dakota	20.5
32	Oklahoma	20.3
33	Alabama	20.0
33	Colorado	20.0
35	North Dakota	19.6
36	West Virginia	19.4
37	Delaware	19.3
38	Louisiana	19.2
39	Indiana	19.1
40	Florida	18.9
41	Idaho	18.5
42	California	18.3
42	Kentucky	18.3
44	North Carolina	17.9
45	New Mexico	17.8
46	Mississippi	17.5
47	Alaska	17.3
47	Oregon	17.3
49	Arizona	16.1
50	Hawaii	15.5

District of Columbia   20.4

Source: CQ Press using data from U.S. Bureau of the Census, Governments Division

"2016 State and Local Government Finances" (https://www.census.gov/programs-surveys/gov-finances.html)

*Direct general expenditures as a percent of all direct general expenditures. Includes capital outlays.

Estimated Per Pupil Public Elementary and Secondary School Current Expenditures in 2018
National Per Pupil = $11,934*

ALPHA ORDER

RANK	STATE	PER PUPIL
39	Alabama	$9,354
2	Alaska	22,103
47	Arizona	7,474
36	Arkansas	9,762
32	California	10,420
26	Colorado	11,009
3	Connecticut	21,731
7	Delaware	17,500
40	Florida	9,225
34	Georgia	10,182
17	Hawaii	12,157
49	Idaho	6,849
13	Illinois	14,321
50	Indiana	6,673
25	Iowa	11,198
28	Kansas	10,898
30	Kentucky	10,693
22	Louisiana	11,397
41	Maine	9,035
12	Maryland	14,862
6	Massachusetts	18,072
33	Michigan	10,211
15	Minnesota	12,652
43	Mississippi	8,398
27	Missouri	11,007
24	Montana	11,212
18	Nebraska	12,125
45	Nevada	8,177
9	New Hampshire	16,763
4	New Jersey	21,118
29	New Mexico	10,763
1	New York	23,519
38	North Carolina	9,528
46	North Dakota	8,073
31	Ohio	10,666
44	Oklahoma	8,327
19	Oregon	12,056
11	Pennsylvania	15,338
10	Rhode Island	15,648
20	South Carolina	11,913
42	South Dakota	9,022
37	Tennessee	9,547
35	Texas	9,800
48	Utah	7,058
5	Vermont	19,584
23	Virginia	11,306
16	Washington	12,285
14	West Virginia	13,927
21	Wisconsin	11,592
8	Wyoming	17,127

RANK ORDER

RANK	STATE	PER PUPIL
1	New York	$23,519
2	Alaska	22,103
3	Connecticut	21,731
4	New Jersey	21,118
5	Vermont	19,584
6	Massachusetts	18,072
7	Delaware	17,500
8	Wyoming	17,127
9	New Hampshire	16,763
10	Rhode Island	15,648
11	Pennsylvania	15,338
12	Maryland	14,862
13	Illinois	14,321
14	West Virginia	13,927
15	Minnesota	12,652
16	Washington	12,285
17	Hawaii	12,157
18	Nebraska	12,125
19	Oregon	12,056
20	South Carolina	11,913
21	Wisconsin	11,592
22	Louisiana	11,397
23	Virginia	11,306
24	Montana	11,212
25	Iowa	11,198
26	Colorado	11,009
27	Missouri	11,007
28	Kansas	10,898
29	New Mexico	10,763
30	Kentucky	10,693
31	Ohio	10,666
32	California	10,420
33	Michigan	10,211
34	Georgia	10,182
35	Texas	9,800
36	Arkansas	9,762
37	Tennessee	9,547
38	North Carolina	9,528
39	Alabama	9,354
40	Florida	9,225
41	Maine	9,035
42	South Dakota	9,022
43	Mississippi	8,398
44	Oklahoma	8,327
45	Nevada	8,177
46	North Dakota	8,073
47	Arizona	7,474
48	Utah	7,058
49	Idaho	6,849
50	Indiana	6,673
	District of Columbia	25,323

Source: National Education Association, Washington, D.C.
"Rankings and Estimates" (Copyright © 2018, NEA, https://www.nea.org/home/44479.htm)
*Estimates for school year 2017-2018. Based on student membership.

Higher Education Expenditures by State and Local Governments in 2016

National Total = $287,813,315,000*

RANK	STATE	EXPENDITURES	% of USA
22	Alabama	$4,881,370,000	1.7%
43	Alaska	1,092,961,000	0.4%
17	Arizona	5,910,477,000	2.1%
34	Arkansas	2,711,408,000	0.9%
1	California	39,648,862,000	13.8%
16	Colorado	5,920,949,000	2.1%
32	Connecticut	3,367,320,000	1.2%
39	Delaware	1,248,513,000	0.4%
5	Florida	10,798,564,000	3.8%
18	Georgia	5,721,378,000	2.0%
41	Hawaii	1,110,246,000	0.4%
42	Idaho	1,107,241,000	0.4%
9	Illinois	9,494,824,000	3.3%
13	Indiana	6,434,544,000	2.2%
28	Iowa	3,918,473,000	1.4%
31	Kansas	3,459,326,000	1.2%
24	Kentucky	4,375,744,000	1.5%
30	Louisiana	3,524,192,000	1.2%
49	Maine	813,161,000	0.3%
14	Maryland	6,363,889,000	2.2%
19	Massachusetts	5,371,436,000	1.9%
4	Michigan	11,719,911,000	4.1%
20	Minnesota	5,082,362,000	1.8%
33	Mississippi	3,171,851,000	1.1%
27	Missouri	3,983,189,000	1.4%
45	Montana	940,038,000	0.3%
36	Nebraska	2,431,684,000	0.8%
38	Nevada	1,419,679,000	0.5%
44	New Hampshire	985,188,000	0.3%
12	New Jersey	6,987,420,000	2.4%
35	New Mexico	2,585,618,000	0.9%
3	New York	14,286,762,000	5.0%
7	North Carolina	9,726,786,000	3.4%
40	North Dakota	1,220,090,000	0.4%
8	Ohio	9,585,639,000	3.3%
26	Oklahoma	4,052,903,000	1.4%
21	Oregon	4,943,952,000	1.7%
6	Pennsylvania	10,761,940,000	3.7%
50	Rhode Island	682,812,000	0.2%
25	South Carolina	4,178,957,000	1.5%
47	South Dakota	881,094,000	0.3%
29	Tennessee	3,713,013,000	1.3%
2	Texas	27,959,164,000	9.7%
23	Utah	4,402,104,000	1.5%
48	Vermont	871,891,000	0.3%
10	Virginia	7,759,404,000	2.7%
11	Washington	7,098,530,000	2.5%
37	West Virginia	1,754,454,000	0.6%
15	Wisconsin	6,294,886,000	2.2%
46	Wyoming	898,173,000	0.3%

RANK	STATE	EXPENDITURES	% of USA
1	California	$39,648,862,000	13.8%
2	Texas	27,959,164,000	9.7%
3	New York	14,286,762,000	5.0%
4	Michigan	11,719,911,000	4.1%
5	Florida	10,798,564,000	3.8%
6	Pennsylvania	10,761,940,000	3.7%
7	North Carolina	9,726,786,000	3.4%
8	Ohio	9,585,639,000	3.3%
9	Illinois	9,494,824,000	3.3%
10	Virginia	7,759,404,000	2.7%
11	Washington	7,098,530,000	2.5%
12	New Jersey	6,987,420,000	2.4%
13	Indiana	6,434,544,000	2.2%
14	Maryland	6,363,889,000	2.2%
15	Wisconsin	6,294,886,000	2.2%
16	Colorado	5,920,949,000	2.1%
17	Arizona	5,910,477,000	2.1%
18	Georgia	5,721,378,000	2.0%
19	Massachusetts	5,371,436,000	1.9%
20	Minnesota	5,082,362,000	1.8%
21	Oregon	4,943,952,000	1.7%
22	Alabama	4,881,370,000	1.7%
23	Utah	4,402,104,000	1.5%
24	Kentucky	4,375,744,000	1.5%
25	South Carolina	4,178,957,000	1.5%
26	Oklahoma	4,052,903,000	1.4%
27	Missouri	3,983,189,000	1.4%
28	Iowa	3,918,473,000	1.4%
29	Tennessee	3,713,013,000	1.3%
30	Louisiana	3,524,192,000	1.2%
31	Kansas	3,459,326,000	1.2%
32	Connecticut	3,367,320,000	1.2%
33	Mississippi	3,171,851,000	1.1%
34	Arkansas	2,711,408,000	0.9%
35	New Mexico	2,585,618,000	0.9%
36	Nebraska	2,431,684,000	0.8%
37	West Virginia	1,754,454,000	0.6%
38	Nevada	1,419,679,000	0.5%
39	Delaware	1,248,513,000	0.4%
40	North Dakota	1,220,090,000	0.4%
41	Hawaii	1,110,246,000	0.4%
42	Idaho	1,107,241,000	0.4%
43	Alaska	1,092,961,000	0.4%
44	New Hampshire	985,188,000	0.3%
45	Montana	940,038,000	0.3%
46	Wyoming	898,173,000	0.3%
47	South Dakota	881,094,000	0.3%
48	Vermont	871,891,000	0.3%
49	Maine	813,161,000	0.3%
50	Rhode Island	682,812,000	0.2%
	District of Columbia	158,943,000	0.1%

Source: U.S. Bureau of the Census, Governments Division
   "2016 State and Local Government Finances" (https://www.census.gov/programs-surveys/gov-finances.html)
*Direct general expenditures. Includes capital outlays.

Per Capita State and Local Government Expenditures for Higher Education in 2016
National Per Capita = $891*

ALPHA ORDER

RANK	STATE	PER CAPITA
20	Alabama	$1,003
3	Alaska	1,474
32	Arizona	851
30	Arkansas	907
19	California	1,011
14	Colorado	1,069
27	Connecticut	941
6	Delaware	1,315
49	Florida	523
48	Georgia	555
38	Hawaii	777
43	Idaho	658
40	Illinois	740
24	Indiana	970
8	Iowa	1,251
11	Kansas	1,188
22	Kentucky	986
39	Louisiana	753
46	Maine	611
16	Maryland	1,060
36	Massachusetts	787
12	Michigan	1,178
29	Minnesota	920
15	Mississippi	1,061
44	Missouri	654
31	Montana	903
7	Nebraska	1,276
50	Nevada	486
41	New Hampshire	734
36	New Jersey	787
9	New Mexico	1,235
42	New York	727
25	North Carolina	958
1	North Dakota	1,617
35	Ohio	824
17	Oklahoma	1,032
10	Oregon	1,208
34	Pennsylvania	842
45	Rhode Island	646
33	South Carolina	843
18	South Dakota	1,021
47	Tennessee	559
21	Texas	1,001
4	Utah	1,447
5	Vermont	1,398
28	Virginia	923
23	Washington	973
25	West Virginia	958
13	Wisconsin	1,090
2	Wyoming	1,537

RANK ORDER

RANK	STATE	PER CAPITA
1	North Dakota	$1,617
2	Wyoming	1,537
3	Alaska	1,474
4	Utah	1,447
5	Vermont	1,398
6	Delaware	1,315
7	Nebraska	1,276
8	Iowa	1,251
9	New Mexico	1,235
10	Oregon	1,208
11	Kansas	1,188
12	Michigan	1,178
13	Wisconsin	1,090
14	Colorado	1,069
15	Mississippi	1,061
16	Maryland	1,060
17	Oklahoma	1,032
18	South Dakota	1,021
19	California	1,011
20	Alabama	1,003
21	Texas	1,001
22	Kentucky	986
23	Washington	973
24	Indiana	970
25	North Carolina	958
25	West Virginia	958
27	Connecticut	941
28	Virginia	923
29	Minnesota	920
30	Arkansas	907
31	Montana	903
32	Arizona	851
33	South Carolina	843
34	Pennsylvania	842
35	Ohio	824
36	Massachusetts	787
36	New Jersey	787
38	Hawaii	777
39	Louisiana	753
40	Illinois	740
41	New Hampshire	734
42	New York	727
43	Idaho	658
44	Missouri	654
45	Rhode Island	646
46	Maine	611
47	Tennessee	559
48	Georgia	555
49	Florida	523
50	Nevada	486
	District of Columbia	232

Source: CQ Press using data from U.S. Bureau of the Census, Governments Division
"2016 State and Local Government Finances" (https://www.census.gov/programs-surveys/gov-finances.html)
*Direct general expenditures. Includes capital outlays.

Expenditures for Higher Education as a Percent of All State and Local Government Expenditures in 2016
National Percent = 9.8%*

ALPHA ORDER

RANK	STATE	PERCENT
7	Alabama	12.8
43	Alaska	8.0
19	Arizona	12.1
22	Arkansas	11.2
32	California	9.2
10	Colorado	12.6
35	Connecticut	8.8
14	Delaware	12.4
45	Florida	7.5
40	Georgia	8.3
42	Hawaii	8.1
30	Idaho	10.0
38	Illinois	8.5
14	Indiana	12.4
8	Iowa	12.7
5	Kansas	13.7
21	Kentucky	11.3
38	Louisiana	8.5
47	Maine	6.9
24	Maryland	10.9
46	Massachusetts	7.2
2	Michigan	14.2
33	Minnesota	8.9
18	Mississippi	12.2
35	Missouri	8.8
26	Montana	10.7
3	Nebraska	14.0
47	Nevada	6.9
33	New Hampshire	8.9
44	New Jersey	7.6
10	New Mexico	12.6
50	New York	5.3
10	North Carolina	12.6
8	North Dakota	12.7
31	Ohio	9.3
4	Oklahoma	13.9
20	Oregon	11.9
35	Pennsylvania	8.8
49	Rhode Island	6.7
27	South Carolina	10.2
10	South Dakota	12.6
40	Tennessee	8.3
6	Texas	13.0
1	Utah	18.9
14	Vermont	12.4
24	Virginia	10.9
29	Washington	10.1
23	West Virginia	11.0
17	Wisconsin	12.3
27	Wyoming	10.2

RANK ORDER

RANK	STATE	PERCENT
1	Utah	18.9
2	Michigan	14.2
3	Nebraska	14.0
4	Oklahoma	13.9
5	Kansas	13.7
6	Texas	13.0
7	Alabama	12.8
8	Iowa	12.7
8	North Dakota	12.7
10	Colorado	12.6
10	New Mexico	12.6
10	North Carolina	12.6
10	South Dakota	12.6
14	Delaware	12.4
14	Indiana	12.4
14	Vermont	12.4
17	Wisconsin	12.3
18	Mississippi	12.2
19	Arizona	12.1
20	Oregon	11.9
21	Kentucky	11.3
22	Arkansas	11.2
23	West Virginia	11.0
24	Maryland	10.9
24	Virginia	10.9
26	Montana	10.7
27	South Carolina	10.2
27	Wyoming	10.2
29	Washington	10.1
30	Idaho	10.0
31	Ohio	9.3
32	California	9.2
33	Minnesota	8.9
33	New Hampshire	8.9
35	Connecticut	8.8
35	Missouri	8.8
35	Pennsylvania	8.8
38	Illinois	8.5
38	Louisiana	8.5
40	Georgia	8.3
40	Tennessee	8.3
42	Hawaii	8.1
43	Alaska	8.0
44	New Jersey	7.6
45	Florida	7.5
46	Massachusetts	7.2
47	Maine	6.9
47	Nevada	6.9
49	Rhode Island	6.7
50	New York	5.3

District of Columbia 1.2

Source: CQ Press using data from U.S. Bureau of the Census, Governments Division
"2016 State and Local Government Finances" (https://www.census.gov/programs-surveys/gov-finances.html)
*Direct general expenditures for higher education as a percent of all direct general expenditures. Includes capital outlays.

Average Faculty Salary at Institutions of Higher Education in 2017

National Average = $84,630*

ALPHA ORDER				RANK ORDER		
RANK	STATE	AVERAGE SALARY		RANK	STATE	AVERAGE SALARY
37	Alabama	$70,940		1	Massachusetts	$107,244
17	Alaska	81,735		2	New Jersey	105,422
14	Arizona	83,051		3	Connecticut	105,121
50	Arkansas	61,449		4	California	102,212
4	California	102,212		5	New Hampshire	98,221
16	Colorado	82,031		6	Delaware	97,732
3	Connecticut	105,121		7	Rhode Island	97,284
6	Delaware	97,732		8	New York	94,682
23	Florida	78,984		9	Pennsylvania	90,979
32	Georgia	75,376		10	Michigan	90,365
12	Hawaii	87,788		11	Illinois	89,492
47	Idaho	65,243		12	Hawaii	87,788
11	Illinois	89,492		13	Maryland	83,861
18	Indiana	81,489		14	Arizona	83,051
31	Iowa	76,454		15	Nevada	82,978
40	Kansas	68,384		16	Colorado	82,031
42	Kentucky	66,790		17	Alaska	81,735
44	Louisiana	66,486		18	Indiana	81,489
27	Maine	77,440		19	Minnesota	80,898
13	Maryland	83,861		20	Vermont	80,602
1	Massachusetts	107,244		21	Washington	80,005
10	Michigan	90,365		22	Virginia	79,920
19	Minnesota	80,898		23	Florida	78,984
49	Mississippi	62,237		24	Ohio	78,843
34	Missouri	75,032		25	Oregon	77,613
46	Montana	65,591		26	North Carolina	77,603
36	Nebraska	73,038		27	Maine	77,440
15	Nevada	82,978		28	Texas	77,292
5	New Hampshire	98,221		29	Wisconsin	77,145
2	New Jersey	105,422		30	Utah	76,518
43	New Mexico	66,772		31	Iowa	76,454
8	New York	94,682		32	Georgia	75,376
26	North Carolina	77,603		33	Tennessee	75,051
41	North Dakota	68,263		34	Missouri	75,032
24	Ohio	78,843		35	Wyoming	73,368
39	Oklahoma	68,903		36	Nebraska	73,038
25	Oregon	77,613		37	Alabama	70,940
9	Pennsylvania	90,979		38	South Carolina	69,321
7	Rhode Island	97,284		39	Oklahoma	68,903
38	South Carolina	69,321		40	Kansas	68,384
45	South Dakota	65,660		41	North Dakota	68,263
33	Tennessee	75,051		42	Kentucky	66,790
28	Texas	77,292		43	New Mexico	66,772
30	Utah	76,518		44	Louisiana	66,486
20	Vermont	80,602		45	South Dakota	65,660
22	Virginia	79,920		46	Montana	65,591
21	Washington	80,005		47	Idaho	65,243
48	West Virginia	64,489		48	West Virginia	64,489
29	Wisconsin	77,145		49	Mississippi	62,237
35	Wyoming	73,368		50	Arkansas	61,449
					District of Columbia	106,723

Source: U.S. Department of Education, National Center for Education Statistics
    "Digest of Education Statistics" (http://nces.ed.gov/programs/digest/index.asp)
*For 2016-2017 school year. For full-time instructional faculty on 9-month contracts at four-year and two-year public and private degree-granting institutions.

Average Student Costs at Public Institutions of Higher Education in 2017

National Average = $19,488*

ALPHA ORDER				RANK ORDER		
RANK	STATE	AVERAGE COSTS		RANK	STATE	AVERAGE COSTS
24	Alabama	$19,052		1	New Hampshire	$26,968
34	Alaska	17,370		2	Vermont	26,786
14	Arizona	21,491		3	New Jersey	26,070
38	Arkansas	16,871		4	Pennsylvania	25,331
15	California	21,356		5	Illinois	24,541
19	Colorado	20,943		6	Massachusetts	24,473
7	Connecticut	24,174		7	Connecticut	24,174
12	Delaware	21,698		8	Rhode Island	23,135
47	Florida	14,806		9	Virginia	22,567
35	Georgia	17,353		10	Michigan	21,832
17	Hawaii	21,016		11	New York	21,750
48	Idaho	14,457		12	Delaware	21,698
5	Illinois	24,541		13	South Carolina	21,508
25	Indiana	19,001		14	Arizona	21,491
31	Iowa	17,604		15	California	21,356
32	Kansas	17,560		16	Oregon	21,324
22	Kentucky	19,673		17	Hawaii	21,016
27	Louisiana	18,319		18	Ohio	20,961
23	Maine	19,073		19	Colorado	20,943
20	Maryland	20,647		20	Maryland	20,647
6	Massachusetts	24,473		21	Minnesota	19,727
10	Michigan	21,832		22	Kentucky	19,673
21	Minnesota	19,727		23	Maine	19,073
39	Mississippi	16,843		24	Alabama	19,052
30	Missouri	17,639		25	Indiana	19,001
46	Montana	15,241		26	Tennessee	18,340
33	Nebraska	17,379		27	Louisiana	18,319
36	Nevada	17,145		28	Washington	18,053
1	New Hampshire	26,968		29	Texas	17,799
3	New Jersey	26,070		30	Missouri	17,639
44	New Mexico	15,528		31	Iowa	17,604
11	New York	21,750		32	Kansas	17,560
40	North Carolina	16,635		33	Nebraska	17,379
45	North Dakota	15,388		34	Alaska	17,370
18	Ohio	20,961		35	Georgia	17,353
43	Oklahoma	15,754		36	Nevada	17,145
16	Oregon	21,324		37	West Virginia	17,096
4	Pennsylvania	25,331		38	Arkansas	16,871
8	Rhode Island	23,135		39	Mississippi	16,843
13	South Carolina	21,508		40	North Carolina	16,635
42	South Dakota	16,054		41	Wisconsin	16,246
26	Tennessee	18,340		42	South Dakota	16,054
29	Texas	17,799		43	Oklahoma	15,754
50	Utah	13,709		44	New Mexico	15,528
2	Vermont	26,786		45	North Dakota	15,388
9	Virginia	22,567		46	Montana	15,241
28	Washington	18,053		47	Florida	14,806
37	West Virginia	17,096		48	Idaho	14,457
41	Wisconsin	16,246		49	Wyoming	14,354
49	Wyoming	14,354		50	Utah	13,709
					District of Columbia**	NA

Source: U.S. Department of Education, National Center for Education Statistics
   "Digest of Education Statistics" (http://nces.ed.gov/programs/digest/index.asp)
*Data for 2016-2017 school year. Based on average in-state tuition, room and board, and fees for full-time students in public four-year institutions for an entire academic year.
**Not available.

Average Student Costs at Private Institutions of Higher Education in 2017

National Average = $41,468*

ALPHA ORDER				RANK ORDER		
RANK	STATE	AVERAGE COSTS		RANK	STATE	AVERAGE COSTS
43	Alabama	$24,710		1	Massachusetts	$57,363
41	Alaska	26,132		2	Vermont	54,003
45	Arizona	22,559		3	Maryland	53,775
38	Arkansas	29,804		4	Connecticut	53,198
14	California	44,722		5	Rhode Island	52,874
28	Colorado	34,337		6	Pennsylvania	52,132
4	Connecticut	53,198		7	New York	51,790
42	Delaware	25,996		8	Oregon	48,703
24	Florida	35,876		9	New Jersey	48,439
22	Georgia	39,118		10	Maine	48,107
40	Hawaii	28,393		11	Louisiana	47,559
49	Idaho	13,010		12	Washington	46,746
15	Illinois	43,382		13	New Hampshire	46,533
18	Indiana	41,847		14	California	44,722
25	Iowa	35,780		15	Illinois	43,382
39	Kansas	28,746		16	North Carolina	42,312
27	Kentucky	34,893		17	Texas	41,979
11	Louisiana	47,559		18	Indiana	41,847
10	Maine	48,107		19	Wisconsin	41,503
3	Maryland	53,775		20	Ohio	40,980
1	Massachusetts	57,363		21	Minnesota	40,939
31	Michigan	33,498		22	Georgia	39,118
21	Minnesota	40,939		23	Tennessee	35,929
44	Mississippi	24,698		24	Florida	35,876
32	Missouri	33,433		25	Iowa	35,780
34	Montana	32,375		26	Nevada	35,053
36	Nebraska	32,200		27	Kentucky	34,893
26	Nevada	35,053		28	Colorado	34,337
13	New Hampshire	46,533		29	Oklahoma	33,883
9	New Jersey	48,439		30	South Carolina	33,748
35	New Mexico	32,373		31	Michigan	33,498
7	New York	51,790		32	Missouri	33,433
16	North Carolina	42,312		33	Virginia	32,616
46	North Dakota	20,964		34	Montana	32,375
20	Ohio	40,980		35	New Mexico	32,373
29	Oklahoma	33,883		36	Nebraska	32,200
8	Oregon	48,703		37	South Dakota	30,926
6	Pennsylvania	52,132		38	Arkansas	29,804
5	Rhode Island	52,874		39	Kansas	28,746
30	South Carolina	33,748		40	Hawaii	28,393
37	South Dakota	30,926		41	Alaska	26,132
23	Tennessee	35,929		42	Delaware	25,996
17	Texas	41,979		43	Alabama	24,710
48	Utah	15,212		44	Mississippi	24,698
2	Vermont	54,003		45	Arizona	22,559
33	Virginia	32,616		46	North Dakota	20,964
12	Washington	46,746		47	West Virginia	20,898
47	West Virginia	20,898		48	Utah	15,212
19	Wisconsin	41,503		49	Idaho	13,010
NA	Wyoming**	NA		NA	Wyoming**	NA
					District of Columbia	55,669

Source: U.S. Department of Education, National Center for Education Statistics
    "Digest of Education Statistics" (http://nces.ed.gov/programs/digest/index.asp)
*Data for 2016-2017 school year. Based on average in-state tuition, room and board, and fees for full-time students in private four-year institutions for an entire academic year.
**Not available.

Average College Graduate Debt: Class of 2017

National Average Debt = $28,650*

ALPHA ORDER

RANK	STATE	AVERAGE DEBT
8	Alabama	$31,899
39	Alaska	25,682
43	Arizona	23,967
33	Arkansas	26,799
45	California	22,785
35	Colorado	26,530
1	Connecticut	38,510
5	Delaware	34,144
42	Florida	24,041
24	Georgia	28,653
41	Hawaii	25,125
34	Idaho	26,675
23	Illinois	29,214
21	Indiana	29,561
19	Iowa	29,859
28	Kansas	27,720
26	Kentucky	28,447
30	Louisiana	27,210
10	Maine	31,364
22	Maryland	29,314
7	Massachusetts	32,065
11	Michigan	31,289
9	Minnesota	31,734
17	Mississippi	30,439
31	Missouri	27,108
25	Montana	28,466
38	Nebraska	25,750
47	Nevada	22,064
4	New Hampshire	34,415
6	New Jersey	32,247
48	New Mexico	21,237
13	New York	30,931
36	North Carolina	26,526
NA	North Dakota**	NA
16	Ohio	30,629
37	Oklahoma	25,952
27	Oregon	27,885
2	Pennsylvania	36,854
3	Rhode Island	36,250
14	South Carolina	30,891
12	South Dakota	31,275
40	Tennessee	25,252
32	Texas	26,824
49	Utah	18,838
15	Vermont	30,651
18	Virginia	29,887
44	Washington	23,936
29	West Virginia	27,505
20	Wisconsin	29,569
46	Wyoming	22,524

RANK ORDER

RANK	STATE	AVERAGE DEBT
1	Connecticut	$38,510
2	Pennsylvania	36,854
3	Rhode Island	36,250
4	New Hampshire	34,415
5	Delaware	34,144
6	New Jersey	32,247
7	Massachusetts	32,065
8	Alabama	31,899
9	Minnesota	31,734
10	Maine	31,364
11	Michigan	31,289
12	South Dakota	31,275
13	New York	30,931
14	South Carolina	30,891
15	Vermont	30,651
16	Ohio	30,629
17	Mississippi	30,439
18	Virginia	29,887
19	Iowa	29,859
20	Wisconsin	29,569
21	Indiana	29,561
22	Maryland	29,314
23	Illinois	29,214
24	Georgia	28,653
25	Montana	28,466
26	Kentucky	28,447
27	Oregon	27,885
28	Kansas	27,720
29	West Virginia	27,505
30	Louisiana	27,210
31	Missouri	27,108
32	Texas	26,824
33	Arkansas	26,799
34	Idaho	26,675
35	Colorado	26,530
36	North Carolina	26,526
37	Oklahoma	25,952
38	Nebraska	25,750
39	Alaska	25,682
40	Tennessee	25,252
41	Hawaii	25,125
42	Florida	24,041
43	Arizona	23,967
44	Washington	23,936
45	California	22,785
46	Wyoming	22,524
47	Nevada	22,064
48	New Mexico	21,237
49	Utah	18,838
NA	North Dakota**	NA
	District of Columbia	30,775

Source: The Project on Student Debt
   "Student Debt and The Class of 2017" (September 2018, https://ticas.org/posd/map-state-data)
*For students receiving a bachelor's degree in 2017.
**Not available.

Percent of College Graduates with Debt: Class of 2017

National Percent = 65%*

ALPHA ORDER

ALPHA ORDER

RANK	STATE	PERCENT		RANK	STATE	PERCENT
40	Alabama	50		1	New Hampshire	74
48	Alaska	46		1	South Dakota	74
35	Arizona	54		1	West Virginia	74
33	Arkansas	55		4	Minnesota	68
40	California	50		5	Pennsylvania	67
38	Colorado	52		6	Kentucky	64
24	Connecticut	57		6	Rhode Island	64
10	Delaware	62		6	Wisconsin	64
40	Florida	50		9	Iowa	63
24	Georgia	57		10	Delaware	62
43	Hawaii	49		10	Ohio	62
12	Idaho	61		12	Idaho	61
12	Illinois	61		12	Illinois	61
24	Indiana	57		12	New Jersey	61
9	Iowa	63		15	New York	60
17	Kansas	59		15	Vermont	60
6	Kentucky	64		17	Kansas	59
46	Louisiana	48		17	Massachusetts	59
28	Maine	56		17	Montana	59
28	Maryland	56		20	Michigan	58
17	Massachusetts	59		20	Mississippi	58
20	Michigan	58		20	Missouri	58
4	Minnesota	68		20	South Carolina	58
20	Mississippi	58		24	Connecticut	57
20	Missouri	58		24	Georgia	57
17	Montana	59		24	Indiana	57
35	Nebraska	54		24	North Carolina	57
43	Nevada	49		28	Maine	56
1	New Hampshire	74		28	Maryland	56
12	New Jersey	61		28	Oregon	56
35	New Mexico	54		28	Tennessee	56
15	New York	60		28	Virginia	56
24	North Carolina	57		33	Arkansas	55
NA	North Dakota**	NA		33	Texas	55
10	Ohio	62		35	Arizona	54
43	Oklahoma	49		35	Nebraska	54
28	Oregon	56		35	New Mexico	54
5	Pennsylvania	67		38	Colorado	52
6	Rhode Island	64		38	Washington	52
20	South Carolina	58		40	Alabama	50
1	South Dakota	74		40	California	50
28	Tennessee	56		40	Florida	50
33	Texas	55		43	Hawaii	49
49	Utah	38		43	Nevada	49
15	Vermont	60		43	Oklahoma	49
28	Virginia	56		46	Louisiana	48
38	Washington	52		47	Wyoming	47
1	West Virginia	74		48	Alaska	46
6	Wisconsin	64		49	Utah	38
47	Wyoming	47		NA	North Dakota**	NA
					District of Columbia	46

Source: The Project on Student Debt
    "Student Debt and The Class of 2017" (September 2018, https://ticas.org/posd/map-state-data)
*For students receiving a bachelor's degree in 2017.
**Not available.

Institutions of Higher Education in 2017

National Total = 4,360 Institutions*

ALPHA ORDER

RANK	STATE	INSTITUTIONS	% of USA
22	Alabama	73	1.7%
49	Alaska	8	0.2%
17	Arizona	80	1.8%
31	Arkansas	52	1.2%
1	California	436	10.0%
17	Colorado	80	1.8%
33	Connecticut	43	1.0%
49	Delaware	8	0.2%
5	Florida	208	4.8%
9	Georgia	126	2.9%
44	Hawaii	20	0.5%
46	Idaho	18	0.4%
7	Illinois	177	4.1%
19	Indiana	78	1.8%
27	Iowa	62	1.4%
24	Kansas	70	1.6%
25	Kentucky	65	1.5%
27	Louisiana	62	1.4%
38	Maine	31	0.7%
30	Maryland	56	1.3%
11	Massachusetts	120	2.8%
15	Michigan	92	2.1%
14	Minnesota	100	2.3%
36	Mississippi	39	0.9%
12	Missouri	118	2.7%
41	Montana	23	0.5%
35	Nebraska	41	0.9%
39	Nevada	26	0.6%
40	New Hampshire	25	0.6%
22	New Jersey	73	1.7%
34	New Mexico	42	1.0%
2	New York	298	6.8%
8	North Carolina	144	3.3%
44	North Dakota	20	0.5%
6	Ohio	195	4.5%
26	Oklahoma	63	1.4%
29	Oregon	57	1.3%
4	Pennsylvania	245	5.6%
47	Rhode Island	13	0.3%
20	South Carolina	74	1.7%
43	South Dakota	22	0.5%
13	Tennessee	101	2.3%
3	Texas	262	6.0%
37	Utah	33	0.8%
41	Vermont	23	0.5%
10	Virginia	124	2.8%
16	Washington	81	1.9%
32	West Virginia	45	1.0%
20	Wisconsin	74	1.7%
48	Wyoming	10	0.2%

RANK ORDER

RANK	STATE	INSTITUTIONS	% of USA
1	California	436	10.0%
2	New York	298	6.8%
3	Texas	262	6.0%
4	Pennsylvania	245	5.6%
5	Florida	208	4.8%
6	Ohio	195	4.5%
7	Illinois	177	4.1%
8	North Carolina	144	3.3%
9	Georgia	126	2.9%
10	Virginia	124	2.8%
11	Massachusetts	120	2.8%
12	Missouri	118	2.7%
13	Tennessee	101	2.3%
14	Minnesota	100	2.3%
15	Michigan	92	2.1%
16	Washington	81	1.9%
17	Arizona	80	1.8%
17	Colorado	80	1.8%
19	Indiana	78	1.8%
20	South Carolina	74	1.7%
20	Wisconsin	74	1.7%
22	Alabama	73	1.7%
22	New Jersey	73	1.7%
24	Kansas	70	1.6%
25	Kentucky	65	1.5%
26	Oklahoma	63	1.4%
27	Iowa	62	1.4%
27	Louisiana	62	1.4%
29	Oregon	57	1.3%
30	Maryland	56	1.3%
31	Arkansas	52	1.2%
32	West Virginia	45	1.0%
33	Connecticut	43	1.0%
34	New Mexico	42	1.0%
35	Nebraska	41	0.9%
36	Mississippi	39	0.9%
37	Utah	33	0.8%
38	Maine	31	0.7%
39	Nevada	26	0.6%
40	New Hampshire	25	0.6%
41	Montana	23	0.5%
41	Vermont	23	0.5%
43	South Dakota	22	0.5%
44	Hawaii	20	0.5%
44	North Dakota	20	0.5%
46	Idaho	18	0.4%
47	Rhode Island	13	0.3%
48	Wyoming	10	0.2%
49	Alaska	8	0.2%
49	Delaware	8	0.2%
	District of Columbia	19	0.4%

Source: U.S. Department of Education, National Center for Education Statistics
  "Digest of Education Statistics" (http://nces.ed.gov/programs/digest/index.asp)
*For 2016-2017 school year. Consists of 2,832 four-year and 1,528 two-year public and private (profit and not-for-profit)
degree-granting institutions. Includes five U.S. Service Schools not shown by state.

Enrollment in Institutions of Higher Education in 2016

National Total = 19,841,014 Students*

ALPHA ORDER

RANK	STATE	STUDENTS	% of USA
24	Alabama	304,052	1.5%
50	Alaska	28,446	0.1%
8	Arizona	608,084	3.1%
34	Arkansas	167,320	0.8%
1	California	2,700,106	13.6%
20	Colorado	352,296	1.8%
32	Connecticut	198,011	1.0%
44	Delaware	61,139	0.3%
4	Florida	1,075,496	5.4%
12	Georgia	532,907	2.7%
43	Hawaii	65,858	0.3%
39	Idaho	123,796	0.6%
5	Illinois	777,720	3.9%
16	Indiana	419,203	2.1%
25	Iowa	266,513	1.3%
30	Kansas	214,301	1.1%
26	Kentucky	255,072	1.3%
28	Louisiana	239,287	1.2%
42	Maine	72,116	0.4%
19	Maryland	365,667	1.8%
13	Massachusetts	505,723	2.5%
9	Michigan	583,035	2.9%
14	Minnesota	422,792	2.1%
33	Mississippi	172,712	0.9%
17	Missouri	401,094	2.0%
47	Montana	50,916	0.3%
36	Nebraska	136,102	0.7%
40	Nevada	116,030	0.6%
38	New Hampshire	133,136	0.7%
15	New Jersey	421,377	2.1%
37	New Mexico	134,607	0.7%
3	New York	1,273,651	6.4%
10	North Carolina	561,496	2.8%
45	North Dakota	54,203	0.3%
7	Ohio	658,229	3.3%
31	Oklahoma	208,345	1.1%
29	Oregon	236,235	1.2%
6	Pennsylvania	725,770	3.7%
41	Rhode Island	83,348	0.4%
27	South Carolina	246,563	1.2%
46	South Dakota	53,685	0.3%
22	Tennessee	321,751	1.6%
2	Texas	1,603,259	8.1%
23	Utah	311,534	1.6%
48	Vermont	44,719	0.2%
11	Virginia	557,461	2.8%
18	Washington	366,162	1.8%
35	West Virginia	146,358	0.7%
21	Wisconsin	341,859	1.7%
49	Wyoming	33,365	0.2%

RANK ORDER

RANK	STATE	STUDENTS	% of USA
1	California	2,700,106	13.6%
2	Texas	1,603,259	8.1%
3	New York	1,273,651	6.4%
4	Florida	1,075,496	5.4%
5	Illinois	777,720	3.9%
6	Pennsylvania	725,770	3.7%
7	Ohio	658,229	3.3%
8	Arizona	608,084	3.1%
9	Michigan	583,035	2.9%
10	North Carolina	561,496	2.8%
11	Virginia	557,461	2.8%
12	Georgia	532,907	2.7%
13	Massachusetts	505,723	2.5%
14	Minnesota	422,792	2.1%
15	New Jersey	421,377	2.1%
16	Indiana	419,203	2.1%
17	Missouri	401,094	2.0%
18	Washington	366,162	1.8%
19	Maryland	365,667	1.8%
20	Colorado	352,296	1.8%
21	Wisconsin	341,859	1.7%
22	Tennessee	321,751	1.6%
23	Utah	311,534	1.6%
24	Alabama	304,052	1.5%
25	Iowa	266,513	1.3%
26	Kentucky	255,072	1.3%
27	South Carolina	246,563	1.2%
28	Louisiana	239,287	1.2%
29	Oregon	236,235	1.2%
30	Kansas	214,301	1.1%
31	Oklahoma	208,345	1.1%
32	Connecticut	198,011	1.0%
33	Mississippi	172,712	0.9%
34	Arkansas	167,320	0.8%
35	West Virginia	146,358	0.7%
36	Nebraska	136,102	0.7%
37	New Mexico	134,607	0.7%
38	New Hampshire	133,136	0.7%
39	Idaho	123,796	0.6%
40	Nevada	116,030	0.6%
41	Rhode Island	83,348	0.4%
42	Maine	72,116	0.4%
43	Hawaii	65,858	0.3%
44	Delaware	61,139	0.3%
45	North Dakota	54,203	0.3%
46	South Dakota	53,685	0.3%
47	Montana	50,916	0.3%
48	Vermont	44,719	0.2%
49	Wyoming	33,365	0.2%
50	Alaska	28,446	0.1%
	District of Columbia	93,040	0.5%

Source: U.S. Department of Education, National Center for Education Statistics
"Digest of Education Statistics" (http://nces.ed.gov/programs/digest/index.asp)
*Fall 2016 enrollment. Includes full-time and part-time students at Title IV eligible, degree-granting four-year and two-year institutions. National total includes 15,067 students at U.S. Service Schools not shown by state.

Enrollment Rate in Institutions of Higher Education in 2016

National Rate = 643 Students per 1,000 Population 18 to 24 Years Old*

ALPHA ORDER

RANK	STATE	RATE
19	Alabama	662
50	Alaska	378
3	Arizona	905
35	Arkansas	594
13	California	702
20	Colorado	660
39	Connecticut	562
11	Delaware	714
27	Florida	618
44	Georgia	530
48	Hawaii	511
7	Idaho	791
24	Illinois	640
26	Indiana	634
6	Iowa	827
9	Kansas	721
31	Kentucky	607
42	Louisiana	541
22	Maine	654
17	Maryland	669
10	Massachusetts	718
33	Michigan	598
5	Minnesota	833
36	Mississippi	584
14	Missouri	693
47	Montana	513
12	Nebraska	706
49	Nevada	464
1	New Hampshire	1,044
43	New Jersey	536
16	New Mexico	672
17	New York	669
37	North Carolina	581
34	North Dakota	595
28	Ohio	612
41	Oklahoma	544
23	Oregon	646
29	Pennsylvania	611
8	Rhode Island	729
45	South Carolina	526
25	South Dakota	635
46	Tennessee	521
38	Texas	579
2	Utah	908
20	Vermont	660
15	Virginia	686
40	Washington	554
3	West Virginia	905
30	Wisconsin	608
32	Wyoming	605

RANK ORDER

RANK	STATE	RATE
1	New Hampshire	1,044
2	Utah	908
3	Arizona	905
3	West Virginia	905
5	Minnesota	833
6	Iowa	827
7	Idaho	791
8	Rhode Island	729
9	Kansas	721
10	Massachusetts	718
11	Delaware	714
12	Nebraska	706
13	California	702
14	Missouri	693
15	Virginia	686
16	New Mexico	672
17	Maryland	669
17	New York	669
19	Alabama	662
20	Colorado	660
20	Vermont	660
22	Maine	654
23	Oregon	646
24	Illinois	640
25	South Dakota	635
26	Indiana	634
27	Florida	618
28	Ohio	612
29	Pennsylvania	611
30	Wisconsin	608
31	Kentucky	607
32	Wyoming	605
33	Michigan	598
34	North Dakota	595
35	Arkansas	594
36	Mississippi	584
37	North Carolina	581
38	Texas	579
39	Connecticut	562
40	Washington	554
41	Oklahoma	544
42	Louisiana	541
43	New Jersey	536
44	Georgia	530
45	South Carolina	526
46	Tennessee	521
47	Montana	513
48	Hawaii	511
49	Nevada	464
50	Alaska	378

District of Columbia — 1,161

Source: CQ Press using data from U.S. Department of Education, National Center for Education Statistics
"Digest of Education Statistics" (http://nces.ed.gov/programs/digest/index.asp)
*Based on fall 2016 enrollment and population. National rate includes U.S. Service Schools. Includes students at four-year and two-year public and private degree-granting institutions. Enrollment based on location of institution. Population based on residence.

Enrollment in Public Institutions of Higher Education in 2016

National Total = 14,582,972 Students*

ALPHA ORDER

RANK	STATE	STUDENTS	% of USA
20	Alabama	251,038	1.7%
49	Alaska	27,352	0.2%
12	Arizona	361,400	2.5%
33	Arkansas	149,383	1.0%
1	California	2,228,932	15.3%
18	Colorado	272,667	1.9%
35	Connecticut	117,345	0.8%
45	Delaware	41,816	0.3%
3	Florida	797,048	5.5%
9	Georgia	422,159	2.9%
40	Hawaii	53,418	0.4%
39	Idaho	74,667	0.5%
7	Illinois	492,578	3.4%
14	Indiana	319,581	2.2%
31	Iowa	171,075	1.2%
28	Kansas	180,170	1.2%
25	Kentucky	205,431	1.4%
24	Louisiana	208,254	1.4%
42	Maine	47,763	0.3%
16	Maryland	305,750	2.1%
23	Massachusetts	218,465	1.5%
6	Michigan	492,772	3.4%
19	Minnesota	253,238	1.7%
32	Mississippi	153,205	1.1%
21	Missouri	244,924	1.7%
43	Montana	46,260	0.3%
37	Nebraska	101,032	0.7%
36	Nevada	106,196	0.7%
47	New Hampshire	41,170	0.3%
13	New Jersey	337,090	2.3%
34	New Mexico	129,038	0.9%
4	New York	700,892	4.8%
8	North Carolina	450,162	3.1%
41	North Dakota	47,964	0.3%
5	Ohio	501,474	3.4%
29	Oklahoma	177,641	1.2%
27	Oregon	197,198	1.4%
10	Pennsylvania	406,345	2.8%
46	Rhode Island	41,369	0.3%
26	South Carolina	200,295	1.4%
44	South Dakota	44,305	0.3%
22	Tennessee	221,288	1.5%
2	Texas	1,420,974	9.7%
30	Utah	175,308	1.2%
50	Vermont	25,736	0.2%
11	Virginia	389,446	2.7%
15	Washington	315,356	2.2%
38	West Virginia	85,104	0.6%
17	Wisconsin	278,442	1.9%
48	Wyoming	32,802	0.2%

RANK ORDER

RANK	STATE	STUDENTS	% of USA
1	California	2,228,932	15.3%
2	Texas	1,420,974	9.7%
3	Florida	797,048	5.5%
4	New York	700,892	4.8%
5	Ohio	501,474	3.4%
6	Michigan	492,772	3.4%
7	Illinois	492,578	3.4%
8	North Carolina	450,162	3.1%
9	Georgia	422,159	2.9%
10	Pennsylvania	406,345	2.8%
11	Virginia	389,446	2.7%
12	Arizona	361,400	2.5%
13	New Jersey	337,090	2.3%
14	Indiana	319,581	2.2%
15	Washington	315,356	2.2%
16	Maryland	305,750	2.1%
17	Wisconsin	278,442	1.9%
18	Colorado	272,667	1.9%
19	Minnesota	253,238	1.7%
20	Alabama	251,038	1.7%
21	Missouri	244,924	1.7%
22	Tennessee	221,288	1.5%
23	Massachusetts	218,465	1.5%
24	Louisiana	208,254	1.4%
25	Kentucky	205,431	1.4%
26	South Carolina	200,295	1.4%
27	Oregon	197,198	1.4%
28	Kansas	180,170	1.2%
29	Oklahoma	177,641	1.2%
30	Utah	175,308	1.2%
31	Iowa	171,075	1.2%
32	Mississippi	153,205	1.1%
33	Arkansas	149,383	1.0%
34	New Mexico	129,038	0.9%
35	Connecticut	117,345	0.8%
36	Nevada	106,196	0.7%
37	Nebraska	101,032	0.7%
38	West Virginia	85,104	0.6%
39	Idaho	74,667	0.5%
40	Hawaii	53,418	0.4%
41	North Dakota	47,964	0.3%
42	Maine	47,763	0.3%
43	Montana	46,260	0.3%
44	South Dakota	44,305	0.3%
45	Delaware	41,816	0.3%
46	Rhode Island	41,369	0.3%
47	New Hampshire	41,170	0.3%
48	Wyoming	32,802	0.2%
49	Alaska	27,352	0.2%
50	Vermont	25,736	0.2%
	District of Columbia	4,587	0.0%

Source: U.S. Department of Education, National Center for Education Statistics
"Digest of Education Statistics" (http://nces.ed.gov/programs/digest/index.asp)
*Fall 2016 enrollment. Includes full-time and part-time students at Title IV eligible, degree-granting four-year and two-year institutions. National total includes 15,067 students at U.S. Service Schools not shown by state.

Enrollment in Private Institutions of Higher Education in 2016

National Total = 5,258,042 Students*

ALPHA ORDER

RANK	STATE	STUDENTS	% of USA
27	Alabama	53,014	1.0%
49	Alaska	1,094	0.0%
7	Arizona	246,684	4.7%
42	Arkansas	17,937	0.3%
2	California	471,174	9.0%
23	Colorado	79,629	1.5%
22	Connecticut	80,666	1.5%
40	Delaware	19,323	0.4%
6	Florida	278,448	5.3%
15	Georgia	110,748	2.1%
43	Hawaii	12,440	0.2%
30	Idaho	49,129	0.9%
5	Illinois	285,142	5.4%
17	Indiana	99,622	1.9%
18	Iowa	95,438	1.8%
35	Kansas	34,131	0.6%
29	Kentucky	49,641	0.9%
36	Louisiana	31,033	0.6%
38	Maine	24,353	0.5%
26	Maryland	59,917	1.1%
4	Massachusetts	287,258	5.5%
20	Michigan	90,263	1.7%
9	Minnesota	169,554	3.2%
39	Mississippi	19,507	0.4%
12	Missouri	156,170	3.0%
48	Montana	4,656	0.1%
34	Nebraska	35,070	0.7%
44	Nevada	9,834	0.2%
19	New Hampshire	91,966	1.7%
21	New Jersey	84,287	1.6%
47	New Mexico	5,569	0.1%
1	New York	572,759	10.9%
14	North Carolina	111,334	2.1%
46	North Dakota	6,239	0.1%
11	Ohio	156,755	3.0%
37	Oklahoma	30,704	0.6%
33	Oregon	39,037	0.7%
3	Pennsylvania	319,425	6.1%
32	Rhode Island	41,979	0.8%
31	South Carolina	46,268	0.9%
45	South Dakota	9,380	0.2%
16	Tennessee	100,463	1.9%
8	Texas	182,285	3.5%
13	Utah	136,226	2.6%
41	Vermont	18,983	0.4%
10	Virginia	168,015	3.2%
28	Washington	50,806	1.0%
25	West Virginia	61,254	1.2%
24	Wisconsin	63,417	1.2%
50	Wyoming	563	0.0%

RANK ORDER

RANK	STATE	STUDENTS	% of USA
1	New York	572,759	10.9%
2	California	471,174	9.0%
3	Pennsylvania	319,425	6.1%
4	Massachusetts	287,258	5.5%
5	Illinois	285,142	5.4%
6	Florida	278,448	5.3%
7	Arizona	246,684	4.7%
8	Texas	182,285	3.5%
9	Minnesota	169,554	3.2%
10	Virginia	168,015	3.2%
11	Ohio	156,755	3.0%
12	Missouri	156,170	3.0%
13	Utah	136,226	2.6%
14	North Carolina	111,334	2.1%
15	Georgia	110,748	2.1%
16	Tennessee	100,463	1.9%
17	Indiana	99,622	1.9%
18	Iowa	95,438	1.8%
19	New Hampshire	91,966	1.7%
20	Michigan	90,263	1.7%
21	New Jersey	84,287	1.6%
22	Connecticut	80,666	1.5%
23	Colorado	79,629	1.5%
24	Wisconsin	63,417	1.2%
25	West Virginia	61,254	1.2%
26	Maryland	59,917	1.1%
27	Alabama	53,014	1.0%
28	Washington	50,806	1.0%
29	Kentucky	49,641	0.9%
30	Idaho	49,129	0.9%
31	South Carolina	46,268	0.9%
32	Rhode Island	41,979	0.8%
33	Oregon	39,037	0.7%
34	Nebraska	35,070	0.7%
35	Kansas	34,131	0.6%
36	Louisiana	31,033	0.6%
37	Oklahoma	30,704	0.6%
38	Maine	24,353	0.5%
39	Mississippi	19,507	0.4%
40	Delaware	19,323	0.4%
41	Vermont	18,983	0.4%
42	Arkansas	17,937	0.3%
43	Hawaii	12,440	0.2%
44	Nevada	9,834	0.2%
45	South Dakota	9,380	0.2%
46	North Dakota	6,239	0.1%
47	New Mexico	5,569	0.1%
48	Montana	4,656	0.1%
49	Alaska	1,094	0.0%
50	Wyoming	563	0.0%
	District of Columbia	88,453	1.7%

Source: U.S. Department of Education, National Center for Education Statistics
   "Digest of Education Statistics" (http://nces.ed.gov/programs/digest/index.asp)
*Fall 2016 enrollment. Includes full-time and part-time students at Title IV eligible, degree-granting four-year and two-year institutions.

Percent of Population with a Bachelor's Degree or More in 2017

National Percent = 32.0%*

<table>
<tr><td colspan="3">ALPHA ORDER</td><td colspan="3">RANK ORDER</td></tr>
<tr><td>RANK</td><td>STATE</td><td>PERCENT</td><td>RANK</td><td>STATE</td><td>PERCENT</td></tr>
<tr><td>43</td><td>Alabama</td><td>25.5</td><td>1</td><td>Massachusetts</td><td>43.4</td></tr>
<tr><td>34</td><td>Alaska</td><td>28.8</td><td>2</td><td>Colorado</td><td>41.2</td></tr>
<tr><td>30</td><td>Arizona</td><td>29.4</td><td>3</td><td>Maryland</td><td>39.7</td></tr>
<tr><td>48</td><td>Arkansas</td><td>23.4</td><td>3</td><td>New Jersey</td><td>39.7</td></tr>
<tr><td>16</td><td>California</td><td>33.6</td><td>5</td><td>Connecticut</td><td>38.7</td></tr>
<tr><td>2</td><td>Colorado</td><td>41.2</td><td>5</td><td>Virginia</td><td>38.7</td></tr>
<tr><td>5</td><td>Connecticut</td><td>38.7</td><td>7</td><td>Vermont</td><td>38.3</td></tr>
<tr><td>22</td><td>Delaware</td><td>31.5</td><td>8</td><td>New Hampshire</td><td>36.9</td></tr>
<tr><td>28</td><td>Florida</td><td>29.7</td><td>9</td><td>Minnesota</td><td>36.1</td></tr>
<tr><td>25</td><td>Georgia</td><td>30.9</td><td>10</td><td>New York</td><td>36.0</td></tr>
<tr><td>18</td><td>Hawaii</td><td>32.9</td><td>11</td><td>Washington</td><td>35.5</td></tr>
<tr><td>41</td><td>Idaho</td><td>26.8</td><td>12</td><td>Utah</td><td>34.6</td></tr>
<tr><td>13</td><td>Illinois</td><td>34.4</td><td>13</td><td>Illinois</td><td>34.4</td></tr>
<tr><td>41</td><td>Indiana</td><td>26.8</td><td>14</td><td>Kansas</td><td>33.7</td></tr>
<tr><td>33</td><td>Iowa</td><td>28.9</td><td>14</td><td>Oregon</td><td>33.7</td></tr>
<tr><td>14</td><td>Kansas</td><td>33.7</td><td>16</td><td>California</td><td>33.6</td></tr>
<tr><td>46</td><td>Kentucky</td><td>24.0</td><td>17</td><td>Rhode Island</td><td>33.5</td></tr>
<tr><td>47</td><td>Louisiana</td><td>23.8</td><td>18</td><td>Hawaii</td><td>32.9</td></tr>
<tr><td>20</td><td>Maine</td><td>32.1</td><td>19</td><td>Montana</td><td>32.3</td></tr>
<tr><td>3</td><td>Maryland</td><td>39.7</td><td>20</td><td>Maine</td><td>32.1</td></tr>
<tr><td>1</td><td>Massachusetts</td><td>43.4</td><td>21</td><td>Nebraska</td><td>31.7</td></tr>
<tr><td>31</td><td>Michigan</td><td>29.1</td><td>22</td><td>Delaware</td><td>31.5</td></tr>
<tr><td>9</td><td>Minnesota</td><td>36.1</td><td>23</td><td>Pennsylvania</td><td>31.4</td></tr>
<tr><td>49</td><td>Mississippi</td><td>21.9</td><td>24</td><td>North Carolina</td><td>31.3</td></tr>
<tr><td>31</td><td>Missouri</td><td>29.1</td><td>25</td><td>Georgia</td><td>30.9</td></tr>
<tr><td>19</td><td>Montana</td><td>32.3</td><td>26</td><td>North Dakota</td><td>30.7</td></tr>
<tr><td>21</td><td>Nebraska</td><td>31.7</td><td>27</td><td>Wisconsin</td><td>30.4</td></tr>
<tr><td>45</td><td>Nevada</td><td>24.9</td><td>28</td><td>Florida</td><td>29.7</td></tr>
<tr><td>8</td><td>New Hampshire</td><td>36.9</td><td>29</td><td>Texas</td><td>29.6</td></tr>
<tr><td>3</td><td>New Jersey</td><td>39.7</td><td>30</td><td>Arizona</td><td>29.4</td></tr>
<tr><td>40</td><td>New Mexico</td><td>27.1</td><td>31</td><td>Michigan</td><td>29.1</td></tr>
<tr><td>10</td><td>New York</td><td>36.0</td><td>31</td><td>Missouri</td><td>29.1</td></tr>
<tr><td>24</td><td>North Carolina</td><td>31.3</td><td>33</td><td>Iowa</td><td>28.9</td></tr>
<tr><td>26</td><td>North Dakota</td><td>30.7</td><td>34</td><td>Alaska</td><td>28.8</td></tr>
<tr><td>36</td><td>Ohio</td><td>28.0</td><td>35</td><td>South Dakota</td><td>28.1</td></tr>
<tr><td>43</td><td>Oklahoma</td><td>25.5</td><td>36</td><td>Ohio</td><td>28.0</td></tr>
<tr><td>14</td><td>Oregon</td><td>33.7</td><td>36</td><td>South Carolina</td><td>28.0</td></tr>
<tr><td>23</td><td>Pennsylvania</td><td>31.4</td><td>38</td><td>Wyoming</td><td>27.6</td></tr>
<tr><td>17</td><td>Rhode Island</td><td>33.5</td><td>39</td><td>Tennessee</td><td>27.3</td></tr>
<tr><td>36</td><td>South Carolina</td><td>28.0</td><td>40</td><td>New Mexico</td><td>27.1</td></tr>
<tr><td>35</td><td>South Dakota</td><td>28.1</td><td>41</td><td>Idaho</td><td>26.8</td></tr>
<tr><td>39</td><td>Tennessee</td><td>27.3</td><td>41</td><td>Indiana</td><td>26.8</td></tr>
<tr><td>29</td><td>Texas</td><td>29.6</td><td>43</td><td>Alabama</td><td>25.5</td></tr>
<tr><td>12</td><td>Utah</td><td>34.6</td><td>43</td><td>Oklahoma</td><td>25.5</td></tr>
<tr><td>7</td><td>Vermont</td><td>38.3</td><td>45</td><td>Nevada</td><td>24.9</td></tr>
<tr><td>5</td><td>Virginia</td><td>38.7</td><td>46</td><td>Kentucky</td><td>24.0</td></tr>
<tr><td>11</td><td>Washington</td><td>35.5</td><td>47</td><td>Louisiana</td><td>23.8</td></tr>
<tr><td>50</td><td>West Virginia</td><td>20.2</td><td>48</td><td>Arkansas</td><td>23.4</td></tr>
<tr><td>27</td><td>Wisconsin</td><td>30.4</td><td>49</td><td>Mississippi</td><td>21.9</td></tr>
<tr><td>38</td><td>Wyoming</td><td>27.6</td><td>50</td><td>West Virginia</td><td>20.2</td></tr>
<tr><td></td><td></td><td></td><td></td><td>District of Columbia</td><td>57.3</td></tr>
</table>

Source: U.S. Bureau of the Census
  "2017 American Community Survey-Table CP02" (https://www.census.gov/programs-surveys/acs/)
*Persons age 25 and older.

Percent of Population Who Have Completed an Advanced Degree in 2017

National Percent = 12.3%*

ALPHA ORDER			RANK ORDER		
RANK	STATE	PERCENT	RANK	STATE	PERCENT
40	Alabama	9.6	1	Massachusetts	19.5
28	Alaska	10.8	2	Maryland	18.3
27	Arizona	11.0	3	Connecticut	17.3
46	Arkansas	8.4	4	Virginia	16.7
15	California	12.6	5	New York	15.8
8	Colorado	15.2	5	Vermont	15.8
3	Connecticut	17.3	7	New Jersey	15.6
10	Delaware	13.5	8	Colorado	15.2
28	Florida	10.8	9	New Hampshire	14.3
20	Georgia	11.9	10	Delaware	13.5
24	Hawaii	11.2	11	Illinois	13.4
45	Idaho	8.5	12	Washington	13.3
11	Illinois	13.4	13	Rhode Island	13.1
39	Indiana	9.8	14	Oregon	12.7
41	Iowa	9.5	15	California	12.6
15	Kansas	12.6	15	Kansas	12.6
38	Kentucky	9.9	17	Minnesota	12.5
48	Louisiana	8.3	17	Pennsylvania	12.5
19	Maine	12.1	19	Maine	12.1
2	Maryland	18.3	20	Georgia	11.9
1	Massachusetts	19.5	21	New Mexico	11.8
23	Michigan	11.5	21	Utah	11.8
17	Minnesota	12.5	23	Michigan	11.5
48	Mississippi	8.3	24	Hawaii	11.2
26	Missouri	11.1	24	North Carolina	11.2
31	Montana	10.6	26	Missouri	11.1
28	Nebraska	10.8	27	Arizona	11.0
46	Nevada	8.4	28	Alaska	10.8
9	New Hampshire	14.3	28	Florida	10.8
7	New Jersey	15.6	28	Nebraska	10.8
21	New Mexico	11.8	31	Montana	10.6
5	New York	15.8	31	Ohio	10.6
24	North Carolina	11.2	31	Wisconsin	10.6
42	North Dakota	9.0	34	South Carolina	10.4
31	Ohio	10.6	35	Texas	10.3
44	Oklahoma	8.6	35	Wyoming	10.3
14	Oregon	12.7	37	Tennessee	10.1
17	Pennsylvania	12.5	38	Kentucky	9.9
13	Rhode Island	13.1	39	Indiana	9.8
34	South Carolina	10.4	40	Alabama	9.6
42	South Dakota	9.0	41	Iowa	9.5
37	Tennessee	10.1	42	North Dakota	9.0
35	Texas	10.3	42	South Dakota	9.0
21	Utah	11.8	44	Oklahoma	8.6
5	Vermont	15.8	45	Idaho	8.5
4	Virginia	16.7	46	Arkansas	8.4
12	Washington	13.3	46	Nevada	8.4
50	West Virginia	8.0	48	Louisiana	8.3
31	Wisconsin	10.6	48	Mississippi	8.3
35	Wyoming	10.3	50	West Virginia	8.0
				District of Columbia	33.4

Source: U.S. Bureau of the Census

"2017 American Community Survey-Table CP02" (https://www.census.gov/programs-surveys/acs/)

*Persons age 25 and older who have earned a master's degree or higher.

Public Libraries and Branches in 2016

National Total = 16,568 Libraries and Branches*

ALPHA ORDER

RANK	STATE	LIBRARIES	% of USA
22	Alabama	289	1.7%
44	Alaska	87	0.5%
32	Arizona	221	1.3%
27	Arkansas	231	1.4%
1	California	1,119	6.8%
24	Colorado	261	1.6%
29	Connecticut	229	1.4%
50	Delaware	32	0.2%
9	Florida	533	3.2%
14	Georgia	401	2.4%
49	Hawaii	50	0.3%
39	Idaho	146	0.9%
4	Illinois	779	4.7%
12	Indiana	427	2.6%
8	Iowa	558	3.4%
16	Kansas	368	2.2%
34	Kentucky	205	1.2%
21	Louisiana	338	2.0%
27	Maine	231	1.4%
36	Maryland	190	1.1%
10	Massachusetts	462	2.8%
6	Michigan	645	3.9%
18	Minnesota	356	2.1%
26	Mississippi	236	1.4%
17	Missouri	362	2.2%
42	Montana	117	0.7%
25	Nebraska	256	1.5%
45	Nevada	84	0.5%
30	New Hampshire	227	1.4%
13	New Jersey	425	2.6%
43	New Mexico	116	0.7%
2	New York	1,068	6.4%
15	North Carolina	386	2.3%
46	North Dakota	78	0.5%
5	Ohio	714	4.3%
33	Oklahoma	215	1.3%
30	Oregon	227	1.4%
7	Pennsylvania	620	3.7%
48	Rhode Island	70	0.4%
35	South Carolina	192	1.2%
40	South Dakota	142	0.9%
23	Tennessee	285	1.7%
3	Texas	864	5.2%
41	Utah	128	0.8%
38	Vermont	164	1.0%
18	Virginia	356	2.1%
20	Washington	345	2.1%
37	West Virginia	172	1.0%
11	Wisconsin	459	2.8%
47	Wyoming	76	0.5%

RANK ORDER

RANK	STATE	LIBRARIES	% of USA
1	California	1,119	6.8%
2	New York	1,068	6.4%
3	Texas	864	5.2%
4	Illinois	779	4.7%
5	Ohio	714	4.3%
6	Michigan	645	3.9%
7	Pennsylvania	620	3.7%
8	Iowa	558	3.4%
9	Florida	533	3.2%
10	Massachusetts	462	2.8%
11	Wisconsin	459	2.8%
12	Indiana	427	2.6%
13	New Jersey	425	2.6%
14	Georgia	401	2.4%
15	North Carolina	386	2.3%
16	Kansas	368	2.2%
17	Missouri	362	2.2%
18	Minnesota	356	2.1%
18	Virginia	356	2.1%
20	Washington	345	2.1%
21	Louisiana	338	2.0%
22	Alabama	289	1.7%
23	Tennessee	285	1.7%
24	Colorado	261	1.6%
25	Nebraska	256	1.5%
26	Mississippi	236	1.4%
27	Arkansas	231	1.4%
27	Maine	231	1.4%
29	Connecticut	229	1.4%
30	New Hampshire	227	1.4%
30	Oregon	227	1.4%
32	Arizona	221	1.3%
33	Oklahoma	215	1.3%
34	Kentucky	205	1.2%
35	South Carolina	192	1.2%
36	Maryland	190	1.1%
37	West Virginia	172	1.0%
38	Vermont	164	1.0%
39	Idaho	146	0.9%
40	South Dakota	142	0.9%
41	Utah	128	0.8%
42	Montana	117	0.7%
43	New Mexico	116	0.7%
44	Alaska	87	0.5%
45	Nevada	84	0.5%
46	North Dakota	78	0.5%
47	Wyoming	76	0.5%
48	Rhode Island	70	0.4%
49	Hawaii	50	0.3%
50	Delaware	32	0.2%
	District of Columbia	26	0.2%

Source: Institute of Museum and Library Services
　　"Public Library Survey Fiscal Year 2016" (https://www.imls.gov/research-evaluation)
*For fiscal year 2016. Total of central and branch outlets. Does not include bookmobiles. There are 9,057 public libraries.

Rate of Public Libraries and Branches in 2016

National Average = 19,500 Population per Library*

RANK	STATE	RATE
24	Alabama	16,833
42	Alaska	8,523
6	Arizona	31,427
35	Arkansas	12,945
2	California	35,039
16	Colorado	21,230
28	Connecticut	15,627
7	Delaware	29,663
1	Florida	38,705
11	Georgia	25,698
8	Hawaii	28,562
38	Idaho	11,527
26	Illinois	16,466
29	Indiana	15,535
49	Iowa	5,613
43	Kansas	7,911
15	Kentucky	21,650
34	Louisiana	13,841
48	Maine	5,764
5	Maryland	31,604
33	Massachusetts	14,775
31	Michigan	15,429
30	Minnesota	15,515
36	Mississippi	12,662
25	Missouri	16,815
41	Montana	8,896
45	Nebraska	7,445
3	Nevada	34,759
47	New Hampshire	5,914
18	New Jersey	20,881
22	New Mexico	18,041
20	New York	18,391
9	North Carolina	26,313
40	North Dakota	9,671
27	Ohio	16,296
21	Oklahoma	18,264
23	Oregon	18,024
19	Pennsylvania	20,619
32	Rhode Island	15,101
10	South Carolina	25,824
46	South Dakota	6,077
14	Tennessee	23,316
4	Texas	32,335
12	Utah	23,770
50	Vermont	3,803
13	Virginia	23,626
17	Washington	21,144
39	West Virginia	10,645
37	Wisconsin	12,577
44	Wyoming	7,688

RANK	STATE	RATE
1	Florida	38,705
2	California	35,039
3	Nevada	34,759
4	Texas	32,335
5	Maryland	31,604
6	Arizona	31,427
7	Delaware	29,663
8	Hawaii	28,562
9	North Carolina	26,313
10	South Carolina	25,824
11	Georgia	25,698
12	Utah	23,770
13	Virginia	23,626
14	Tennessee	23,316
15	Kentucky	21,650
16	Colorado	21,230
17	Washington	21,144
18	New Jersey	20,881
19	Pennsylvania	20,619
20	New York	18,391
21	Oklahoma	18,264
22	New Mexico	18,041
23	Oregon	18,024
24	Alabama	16,833
25	Missouri	16,815
26	Illinois	16,466
27	Ohio	16,296
28	Connecticut	15,627
29	Indiana	15,535
30	Minnesota	15,515
31	Michigan	15,429
32	Rhode Island	15,101
33	Massachusetts	14,775
34	Louisiana	13,841
35	Arkansas	12,945
36	Mississippi	12,662
37	Wisconsin	12,577
38	Idaho	11,527
39	West Virginia	10,645
40	North Dakota	9,671
41	Montana	8,896
42	Alaska	8,523
43	Kansas	7,911
44	Wyoming	7,688
45	Nebraska	7,445
46	South Dakota	6,077
47	New Hampshire	5,914
48	Maine	5,764
49	Iowa	5,613
50	Vermont	3,803

| | District of Columbia | 26,407 |

Source: CQ Press using data from Institute of Museum and Library Services
"Public Library Survey Fiscal Year 2016" (https://www.imls.gov/research-evaluation)
*For fiscal year 2016. Based on total of central and branch outlets. Does not include bookmobiles.

Rate of Books in Public Libraries in 2016

National Rate = 2,266 Books per 1,000 Population*

ALPHA ORDER

RANK	STATE	RATE
38	Alabama	1,851
20	Alaska	2,762
50	Arizona	1,103
34	Arkansas	1,913
45	California	1,601
35	Colorado	1,900
7	Connecticut	3,661
44	Delaware	1,614
48	Florida	1,418
43	Georgia	1,634
29	Hawaii	2,078
24	Idaho	2,549
14	Illinois	3,156
10	Indiana	3,421
6	Iowa	3,752
15	Kansas	3,082
30	Kentucky	2,039
26	Louisiana	2,511
2	Maine	4,434
42	Maryland	1,742
1	Massachusetts	4,435
17	Michigan	2,962
23	Minnesota	2,596
36	Mississippi	1,874
22	Missouri	2,632
25	Montana	2,524
18	Nebraska	2,915
47	Nevada	1,421
3	New Hampshire	4,186
16	New Jersey	2,988
32	New Mexico	1,972
8	New York	3,506
46	North Carolina	1,534
19	North Dakota	2,881
9	Ohio	3,443
37	Oklahoma	1,872
27	Oregon	2,321
33	Pennsylvania	1,926
11	Rhode Island	3,369
39	South Carolina	1,807
12	South Dakota	3,193
41	Tennessee	1,753
49	Texas	1,417
28	Utah	2,134
4	Vermont	4,147
31	Virginia	2,033
40	Washington	1,758
21	West Virginia	2,686
13	Wisconsin	3,187
5	Wyoming	3,955

RANK ORDER

RANK	STATE	RATE
1	Massachusetts	4,435
2	Maine	4,434
3	New Hampshire	4,186
4	Vermont	4,147
5	Wyoming	3,955
6	Iowa	3,752
7	Connecticut	3,661
8	New York	3,506
9	Ohio	3,443
10	Indiana	3,421
11	Rhode Island	3,369
12	South Dakota	3,193
13	Wisconsin	3,187
14	Illinois	3,156
15	Kansas	3,082
16	New Jersey	2,988
17	Michigan	2,962
18	Nebraska	2,915
19	North Dakota	2,881
20	Alaska	2,762
21	West Virginia	2,686
22	Missouri	2,632
23	Minnesota	2,596
24	Idaho	2,549
25	Montana	2,524
26	Louisiana	2,511
27	Oregon	2,321
28	Utah	2,134
29	Hawaii	2,078
30	Kentucky	2,039
31	Virginia	2,033
32	New Mexico	1,972
33	Pennsylvania	1,926
34	Arkansas	1,913
35	Colorado	1,900
36	Mississippi	1,874
37	Oklahoma	1,872
38	Alabama	1,851
39	South Carolina	1,807
40	Washington	1,758
41	Tennessee	1,753
42	Maryland	1,742
43	Georgia	1,634
44	Delaware	1,614
45	California	1,601
46	North Carolina	1,534
47	Nevada	1,421
48	Florida	1,418
49	Texas	1,417
50	Arizona	1,103

District of Columbia — 2,713

Source: CQ Press using data from Institute of Museum and Library Services
"Public Library Survey Fiscal Year 2016" (https://www.imls.gov/research-evaluation)
*For fiscal year 2016. Includes serial back files in print.

Rate of Electronic Books in Public Libraries in 2016

National Rate = 1,211 Electronic Books per 1,000 Population*

ALPHA ORDER

RANK	STATE	RATE
24	Alabama	789
23	Alaska	815
36	Arizona	347
44	Arkansas	195
38	California	274
31	Colorado	479
NA	Connecticut**	NA
29	Delaware	499
45	Florida	152
47	Georgia	71
49	Hawaii	41
41	Idaho	217
17	Illinois	1,258
20	Indiana	1,071
7	Iowa	2,729
1	Kansas	9,838
8	Kentucky	2,631
35	Louisiana	371
12	Maine	1,444
40	Maryland	226
4	Massachusetts	4,175
28	Michigan	562
22	Minnesota	870
48	Mississippi	56
27	Missouri	588
15	Montana	1,306
9	Nebraska	2,102
46	Nevada	90
6	New Hampshire	2,933
30	New Jersey	485
43	New Mexico	199
18	New York	1,223
34	North Carolina	412
19	North Dakota	1,080
3	Ohio	6,383
26	Oklahoma	731
14	Oregon	1,355
16	Pennsylvania	1,299
10	Rhode Island	1,870
42	South Carolina	205
13	South Dakota	1,361
5	Tennessee	3,799
39	Texas	243
32	Utah	464
37	Vermont	280
25	Virginia	743
33	Washington	435
10	West Virginia	1,870
2	Wisconsin	9,006
21	Wyoming	912

RANK ORDER

RANK	STATE	RATE
1	Kansas	9,838
2	Wisconsin	9,006
3	Ohio	6,383
4	Massachusetts	4,175
5	Tennessee	3,799
6	New Hampshire	2,933
7	Iowa	2,729
8	Kentucky	2,631
9	Nebraska	2,102
10	Rhode Island	1,870
10	West Virginia	1,870
12	Maine	1,444
13	South Dakota	1,361
14	Oregon	1,355
15	Montana	1,306
16	Pennsylvania	1,299
17	Illinois	1,258
18	New York	1,223
19	North Dakota	1,080
20	Indiana	1,071
21	Wyoming	912
22	Minnesota	870
23	Alaska	815
24	Alabama	789
25	Virginia	743
26	Oklahoma	731
27	Missouri	588
28	Michigan	562
29	Delaware	499
30	New Jersey	485
31	Colorado	479
32	Utah	464
33	Washington	435
34	North Carolina	412
35	Louisiana	371
36	Arizona	347
37	Vermont	280
38	California	274
39	Texas	243
40	Maryland	226
41	Idaho	217
42	South Carolina	205
43	New Mexico	199
44	Arkansas	195
45	Florida	152
46	Nevada	90
47	Georgia	71
48	Mississippi	56
49	Hawaii	41
NA	Connecticut**	NA

District of Columbia 356

Source: CQ Press using data from Institute of Museum and Library Services
"Public Library Survey Fiscal Year 2016" (https://www.imls.gov/research-evaluation)
*For fiscal year 2016.
**Not available.

Internet Terminals in Public Libraries in 2016

National Total = 294,216 Terminals*

RANK	STATE	TERMINALS	% of USA
23	Alabama	5,025	1.7%
47	Alaska	982	0.3%
14	Arizona	7,525	2.6%
34	Arkansas	2,714	0.9%
1	California	22,832	7.8%
15	Colorado	6,537	2.2%
28	Connecticut	4,277	1.5%
45	Delaware	1,108	0.4%
4	Florida	16,874	5.7%
8	Georgia	9,353	3.2%
50	Hawaii	562	0.2%
36	Idaho	1,961	0.7%
5	Illinois	15,529	5.3%
9	Indiana	8,488	2.9%
25	Iowa	4,955	1.7%
29	Kansas	3,718	1.3%
24	Kentucky	4,963	1.7%
20	Louisiana	5,632	1.9%
37	Maine	1,871	0.6%
22	Maryland	5,195	1.8%
16	Massachusetts	6,444	2.2%
7	Michigan	12,248	4.2%
19	Minnesota	5,749	2.0%
32	Mississippi	2,849	1.0%
26	Missouri	4,926	1.7%
43	Montana	1,298	0.4%
33	Nebraska	2,823	1.0%
42	Nevada	1,344	0.5%
40	New Hampshire	1,480	0.5%
10	New Jersey	8,140	2.8%
38	New Mexico	1,727	0.6%
3	New York	19,424	6.6%
13	North Carolina	7,593	2.6%
49	North Dakota	825	0.3%
6	Ohio	13,413	4.6%
30	Oklahoma	3,193	1.1%
31	Oregon	3,042	1.0%
11	Pennsylvania	8,037	2.7%
39	Rhode Island	1,497	0.5%
27	South Carolina	4,278	1.5%
44	South Dakota	1,111	0.4%
21	Tennessee	5,574	1.9%
2	Texas	20,558	7.0%
35	Utah	2,230	0.8%
46	Vermont	1,079	0.4%
12	Virginia	7,653	2.6%
18	Washington	5,877	2.0%
41	West Virginia	1,449	0.5%
17	Wisconsin	6,368	2.2%
48	Wyoming	886	0.3%

RANK ORDER

RANK	STATE	TERMINALS	% of USA
1	California	22,832	7.8%
2	Texas	20,558	7.0%
3	New York	19,424	6.6%
4	Florida	16,874	5.7%
5	Illinois	15,529	5.3%
6	Ohio	13,413	4.6%
7	Michigan	12,248	4.2%
8	Georgia	9,353	3.2%
9	Indiana	8,488	2.9%
10	New Jersey	8,140	2.8%
11	Pennsylvania	8,037	2.7%
12	Virginia	7,653	2.6%
13	North Carolina	7,593	2.6%
14	Arizona	7,525	2.6%
15	Colorado	6,537	2.2%
16	Massachusetts	6,444	2.2%
17	Wisconsin	6,368	2.2%
18	Washington	5,877	2.0%
19	Minnesota	5,749	2.0%
20	Louisiana	5,632	1.9%
21	Tennessee	5,574	1.9%
22	Maryland	5,195	1.8%
23	Alabama	5,025	1.7%
24	Kentucky	4,963	1.7%
25	Iowa	4,955	1.7%
26	Missouri	4,926	1.7%
27	South Carolina	4,278	1.5%
28	Connecticut	4,277	1.5%
29	Kansas	3,718	1.3%
30	Oklahoma	3,193	1.1%
31	Oregon	3,042	1.0%
32	Mississippi	2,849	1.0%
33	Nebraska	2,823	1.0%
34	Arkansas	2,714	0.9%
35	Utah	2,230	0.8%
36	Idaho	1,961	0.7%
37	Maine	1,871	0.6%
38	New Mexico	1,727	0.6%
39	Rhode Island	1,497	0.5%
40	New Hampshire	1,480	0.5%
41	West Virginia	1,449	0.5%
42	Nevada	1,344	0.5%
43	Montana	1,298	0.4%
44	South Dakota	1,111	0.4%
45	Delaware	1,108	0.4%
46	Vermont	1,079	0.4%
47	Alaska	982	0.3%
48	Wyoming	886	0.3%
49	North Dakota	825	0.3%
50	Hawaii	562	0.2%
	District of Columbia	1,000	0.3%

Source: Institute of Museum and Library Services
   "Public Library Survey Fiscal Year 2016" (https://www.imls.gov/research-evaluation)
*For fiscal year 2016. Total of public-use Internet terminals in central and branch outlets.

Rate of Internet Terminals in Public Libraries in 2016

National Rate = 17.8 Terminals per Library*

ALPHA ORDER

RANK	STATE	RATE
22	Alabama	17.4
39	Alaska	11.3
2	Arizona	34.0
37	Arkansas	11.7
12	California	20.4
5	Colorado	25.0
20	Connecticut	18.7
1	Delaware	34.6
3	Florida	31.7
8	Georgia	23.3
40	Hawaii	11.2
33	Idaho	13.4
13	Illinois	19.9
13	Indiana	19.9
45	Iowa	8.9
44	Kansas	10.1
6	Kentucky	24.2
25	Louisiana	16.7
47	Maine	8.1
4	Maryland	27.3
30	Massachusetts	13.9
18	Michigan	19.0
26	Minnesota	16.1
36	Mississippi	12.1
32	Missouri	13.6
41	Montana	11.1
42	Nebraska	11.0
27	Nevada	16.0
50	New Hampshire	6.5
17	New Jersey	19.2
28	New Mexico	14.9
21	New York	18.2
15	North Carolina	19.7
43	North Dakota	10.6
19	Ohio	18.8
28	Oklahoma	14.9
33	Oregon	13.4
35	Pennsylvania	13.0
11	Rhode Island	21.4
9	South Carolina	22.3
48	South Dakota	7.8
16	Tennessee	19.6
7	Texas	23.8
22	Utah	17.4
49	Vermont	6.6
10	Virginia	21.5
24	Washington	17.0
46	West Virginia	8.4
30	Wisconsin	13.9
37	Wyoming	11.7

RANK ORDER

RANK	STATE	RATE
1	Delaware	34.6
2	Arizona	34.0
3	Florida	31.7
4	Maryland	27.3
5	Colorado	25.0
6	Kentucky	24.2
7	Texas	23.8
8	Georgia	23.3
9	South Carolina	22.3
10	Virginia	21.5
11	Rhode Island	21.4
12	California	20.4
13	Illinois	19.9
13	Indiana	19.9
15	North Carolina	19.7
16	Tennessee	19.6
17	New Jersey	19.2
18	Michigan	19.0
19	Ohio	18.8
20	Connecticut	18.7
21	New York	18.2
22	Alabama	17.4
22	Utah	17.4
24	Washington	17.0
25	Louisiana	16.7
26	Minnesota	16.1
27	Nevada	16.0
28	New Mexico	14.9
28	Oklahoma	14.9
30	Massachusetts	13.9
30	Wisconsin	13.9
32	Missouri	13.6
33	Idaho	13.4
33	Oregon	13.4
35	Pennsylvania	13.0
36	Mississippi	12.1
37	Arkansas	11.7
37	Wyoming	11.7
39	Alaska	11.3
40	Hawaii	11.2
41	Montana	11.1
42	Nebraska	11.0
43	North Dakota	10.6
44	Kansas	10.1
45	Iowa	8.9
46	West Virginia	8.4
47	Maine	8.1
48	South Dakota	7.8
49	Vermont	6.6
50	New Hampshire	6.5

District of Columbia — 38.5

Source: CQ Press using data from Institute of Museum and Library Services
"Public Library Survey Fiscal Year 2016" (https://www.imls.gov/research-evaluation)
*For fiscal year 2016. Total of public-use Internet terminals in central and branch outlets divided by the number of outlets.

Per Capita State Art Agencies' Legislative Appropriations in 2019

National Per Capita = $1.08*

ALPHA ORDER				RANK ORDER		
RANK	STATE	PER CAPITA		RANK	STATE	PER CAPITA
13	Alabama	$1.12		1	Minnesota	$7.04
20	Alaska	0.94		2	Hawaii	4.22
45	Arizona	0.29		3	Maryland	3.64
34	Arkansas	0.51		4	Delaware	3.37
28	California	0.68		5	Massachusetts	2.34
39	Colorado	0.42		6	New York	2.06
11	Connecticut	1.20		7	Wyoming	1.91
4	Delaware	3.37		8	Rhode Island	1.88
42	Florida	0.38		9	New Jersey	1.83
49	Georgia	0.12		10	Ohio	1.26
2	Hawaii	4.22		11	Connecticut	1.20
35	Idaho	0.49		12	Vermont	1.15
25	Illinois	0.74		13	Alabama	1.12
32	Indiana	0.60		14	South Dakota	1.09
41	Iowa	0.39		15	Missouri	1.06
50	Kansas	0.06		15	Tennessee	1.06
42	Kentucky	0.38		17	North Dakota	1.04
40	Louisiana	0.41		18	Michigan	1.00
26	Maine	0.71		19	Utah	0.98
3	Maryland	3.64		20	Alaska	0.94
5	Massachusetts	2.34		21	North Carolina	0.89
18	Michigan	1.00		22	South Carolina	0.84
1	Minnesota	7.04		23	Pennsylvania	0.81
33	Mississippi	0.55		24	Nebraska	0.77
15	Missouri	1.06		25	Illinois	0.74
37	Montana	0.44		26	Maine	0.71
24	Nebraska	0.77		26	Oklahoma	0.71
31	Nevada	0.61		28	California	0.68
44	New Hampshire	0.30		29	Oregon	0.65
9	New Jersey	1.83		30	New Mexico	0.64
30	New Mexico	0.64		31	Nevada	0.61
6	New York	2.06		32	Indiana	0.60
21	North Carolina	0.89		33	Mississippi	0.55
17	North Dakota	1.04		34	Arkansas	0.51
10	Ohio	1.26		35	Idaho	0.49
26	Oklahoma	0.71		35	West Virginia	0.49
29	Oregon	0.65		37	Montana	0.44
23	Pennsylvania	0.81		37	Virginia	0.44
8	Rhode Island	1.88		39	Colorado	0.42
22	South Carolina	0.84		40	Louisiana	0.41
14	South Dakota	1.09		41	Iowa	0.39
15	Tennessee	1.06		42	Florida	0.38
47	Texas	0.18		42	Kentucky	0.38
19	Utah	0.98		44	New Hampshire	0.30
12	Vermont	1.15		45	Arizona	0.29
37	Virginia	0.44		46	Washington	0.22
46	Washington	0.22		47	Texas	0.18
35	West Virginia	0.49		48	Wisconsin	0.13
48	Wisconsin	0.13		49	Georgia	0.12
7	Wyoming	1.91		50	Kansas	0.06
					District of Columbia	44.57

Source: National Assembly of State Arts Agencies
"State Arts Agency Legislative Appropriations Preview Fiscal Year 2019" (https://nasaa-arts.org/Research/Funding/)
*Projected figures for fiscal year 2019. Includes line item appropriations. Line items are legislative appropriations that are not controlled by the state art agencies but are passed through their budgets directly to another entity. Calculated using 2017 Census population estimates.

Federal Allocations for Head Start Program in 2017

National Total = $9,224,537,499*

ALPHA ORDER

RANK	STATE	EXPENDITURES	% of USA
20	Alabama	$139,559,876	1.5%
50	Alaska	16,520,308	0.2%
17	Arizona	147,668,314	1.6%
29	Arkansas	90,071,346	1.0%
1	California	1,141,493,769	12.4%
26	Colorado	100,896,672	1.1%
35	Connecticut	65,149,906	0.7%
47	Delaware	18,981,888	0.2%
4	Florida	366,644,876	4.0%
9	Georgia	229,928,415	2.5%
43	Hawaii	28,202,845	0.3%
40	Idaho	32,293,169	0.4%
5	Illinois	353,165,142	3.8%
21	Indiana	134,560,221	1.5%
33	Iowa	67,089,324	0.7%
31	Kansas	69,953,550	0.8%
16	Kentucky	151,698,092	1.6%
12	Louisiana	182,861,782	2.0%
39	Maine	36,450,715	0.4%
28	Maryland	99,919,960	1.1%
19	Massachusetts	139,818,066	1.5%
7	Michigan	313,862,640	3.4%
27	Minnesota	100,504,174	1.1%
11	Mississippi	200,857,179	2.2%
14	Missouri	162,556,555	1.8%
41	Montana	31,167,253	0.3%
37	Nebraska	49,547,684	0.5%
38	Nevada	37,053,862	0.4%
48	New Hampshire	18,311,447	0.2%
13	New Jersey	167,287,070	1.8%
32	New Mexico	67,976,241	0.7%
3	New York	549,935,156	6.0%
10	North Carolina	204,907,482	2.2%
45	North Dakota	22,032,234	0.2%
6	Ohio	331,997,649	3.6%
24	Oklahoma	115,335,976	1.3%
30	Oregon	88,884,019	1.0%
8	Pennsylvania	305,318,439	3.3%
42	Rhode Island	29,737,698	0.3%
25	South Carolina	113,725,844	1.2%
44	South Dakota	24,713,597	0.3%
15	Tennessee	157,404,163	1.7%
2	Texas	623,119,626	6.8%
36	Utah	59,919,954	0.6%
46	Vermont	19,123,591	0.2%
22	Virginia	133,468,488	1.4%
18	Washington	142,530,419	1.5%
34	West Virginia	65,472,936	0.7%
23	Wisconsin	127,252,828	1.4%
49	Wyoming	17,533,594	0.2%

RANK ORDER

RANK	STATE	EXPENDITURES	% of USA
1	California	$1,141,493,769	12.4%
2	Texas	623,119,626	6.8%
3	New York	549,935,156	6.0%
4	Florida	366,644,876	4.0%
5	Illinois	353,165,142	3.8%
6	Ohio	331,997,649	3.6%
7	Michigan	313,862,640	3.4%
8	Pennsylvania	305,318,439	3.3%
9	Georgia	229,928,415	2.5%
10	North Carolina	204,907,482	2.2%
11	Mississippi	200,857,179	2.2%
12	Louisiana	182,861,782	2.0%
13	New Jersey	167,287,070	1.8%
14	Missouri	162,556,555	1.8%
15	Tennessee	157,404,163	1.7%
16	Kentucky	151,698,092	1.6%
17	Arizona	147,668,314	1.6%
18	Washington	142,530,419	1.5%
19	Massachusetts	139,818,066	1.5%
20	Alabama	139,559,876	1.5%
21	Indiana	134,560,221	1.5%
22	Virginia	133,468,488	1.4%
23	Wisconsin	127,252,828	1.4%
24	Oklahoma	115,335,976	1.3%
25	South Carolina	113,725,844	1.2%
26	Colorado	100,896,672	1.1%
27	Minnesota	100,504,174	1.1%
28	Maryland	99,919,960	1.1%
29	Arkansas	90,071,346	1.0%
30	Oregon	88,884,019	1.0%
31	Kansas	69,953,550	0.8%
32	New Mexico	67,976,241	0.7%
33	Iowa	67,089,324	0.7%
34	West Virginia	65,472,936	0.7%
35	Connecticut	65,149,906	0.7%
36	Utah	59,919,954	0.6%
37	Nebraska	49,547,684	0.5%
38	Nevada	37,053,862	0.4%
39	Maine	36,450,715	0.4%
40	Idaho	32,293,169	0.4%
41	Montana	31,167,253	0.3%
42	Rhode Island	29,737,698	0.3%
43	Hawaii	28,202,845	0.3%
44	South Dakota	24,713,597	0.3%
45	North Dakota	22,032,234	0.2%
46	Vermont	19,123,591	0.2%
47	Delaware	18,981,888	0.2%
48	New Hampshire	18,311,447	0.2%
49	Wyoming	17,533,594	0.2%
50	Alaska	16,520,308	0.2%
	District of Columbia	31,039,253	0.3%

Source: U.S. Department of Health and Human Services, Administration for Children and Families
   "Head Start Fact Sheet Fiscal Year 2017" (https://eclkc.ohs.acf.hhs.gov/about-us/article/head-start-program-facts)
*For fiscal year 2017. National total includes $636,745,123 to Migrant and Native American programs not included in state totals, $315,166,280 to U.S. territories, and $348,891,304 in various research, monitoring, training, and support expenditures.

Head Start Program Enrollment in 2017

National Total = 899,374 Children*

ALPHA ORDER

RANK	STATE	ENROLLMENT	% of USA
16	Alabama	15,631	1.7%
49	Alaska	1,506	0.2%
22	Arizona	13,581	1.5%
30	Arkansas	9,983	1.1%
1	California	92,687	10.3%
28	Colorado	10,190	1.1%
35	Connecticut	6,140	0.7%
45	Delaware	2,194	0.2%
4	Florida	39,697	4.4%
9	Georgia	24,597	2.7%
42	Hawaii	2,950	0.3%
41	Idaho	2,986	0.3%
5	Illinois	39,133	4.4%
20	Indiana	14,203	1.6%
33	Iowa	7,449	0.8%
34	Kansas	7,412	0.8%
14	Kentucky	15,984	1.8%
12	Louisiana	21,147	2.4%
38	Maine	3,098	0.3%
29	Maryland	10,069	1.1%
25	Massachusetts	12,008	1.3%
8	Michigan	30,248	3.4%
27	Minnesota	11,338	1.3%
10	Mississippi	23,902	2.7%
17	Missouri	14,997	1.7%
40	Montana	3,079	0.3%
37	Nebraska	4,829	0.5%
39	Nevada	3,096	0.3%
48	New Hampshire	1,563	0.2%
15	New Jersey	15,943	1.8%
32	New Mexico	7,512	0.8%
3	New York	50,432	5.6%
11	North Carolina	21,403	2.4%
46	North Dakota	1,988	0.2%
7	Ohio	35,365	3.9%
18	Oklahoma	14,409	1.6%
23	Oregon	12,913	1.4%
6	Pennsylvania	35,866	4.0%
43	Rhode Island	2,781	0.3%
24	South Carolina	12,604	1.4%
44	South Dakota	2,764	0.3%
13	Tennessee	17,260	1.9%
2	Texas	72,402	8.1%
36	Utah	5,715	0.6%
50	Vermont	1,473	0.2%
19	Virginia	14,264	1.6%
26	Washington	11,962	1.3%
31	West Virginia	7,947	0.9%
21	Wisconsin	13,820	1.5%
47	Wyoming	1,590	0.2%

RANK ORDER

RANK	STATE	ENROLLMENT	% of USA
1	California	92,687	10.3%
2	Texas	72,402	8.1%
3	New York	50,432	5.6%
4	Florida	39,697	4.4%
5	Illinois	39,133	4.4%
6	Pennsylvania	35,866	4.0%
7	Ohio	35,365	3.9%
8	Michigan	30,248	3.4%
9	Georgia	24,597	2.7%
10	Mississippi	23,902	2.7%
11	North Carolina	21,403	2.4%
12	Louisiana	21,147	2.4%
13	Tennessee	17,260	1.9%
14	Kentucky	15,984	1.8%
15	New Jersey	15,943	1.8%
16	Alabama	15,631	1.7%
17	Missouri	14,997	1.7%
18	Oklahoma	14,409	1.6%
19	Virginia	14,264	1.6%
20	Indiana	14,203	1.6%
21	Wisconsin	13,820	1.5%
22	Arizona	13,581	1.5%
23	Oregon	12,913	1.4%
24	South Carolina	12,604	1.4%
25	Massachusetts	12,008	1.3%
26	Washington	11,962	1.3%
27	Minnesota	11,338	1.3%
28	Colorado	10,190	1.1%
29	Maryland	10,069	1.1%
30	Arkansas	9,983	1.1%
31	West Virginia	7,947	0.9%
32	New Mexico	7,512	0.8%
33	Iowa	7,449	0.8%
34	Kansas	7,412	0.8%
35	Connecticut	6,140	0.7%
36	Utah	5,715	0.6%
37	Nebraska	4,829	0.5%
38	Maine	3,098	0.3%
39	Nevada	3,096	0.3%
40	Montana	3,079	0.3%
41	Idaho	2,986	0.3%
42	Hawaii	2,950	0.3%
43	Rhode Island	2,781	0.3%
44	South Dakota	2,764	0.3%
45	Delaware	2,194	0.2%
46	North Dakota	1,988	0.2%
47	Wyoming	1,590	0.2%
48	New Hampshire	1,563	0.2%
49	Alaska	1,506	0.2%
50	Vermont	1,473	0.2%
	District of Columbia	3,533	0.4%

Source: U.S. Department of Health and Human Services, Administration for Children and Families
"Head Start Fact Sheet Fiscal Year 2017" (https://eclkc.ohs.acf.hhs.gov/about-us/article/head-start-program-facts)
*For fiscal year 2017. National total includes 53,752 enrollees not included in state totals enrolled in Migrant and Native American programs and 35,979 enrollees in U.S. territories.

VI. Employment and Labor

Average Annual Pay in 2017

National Average = $55,390*

RANK	STATE	ANNUAL PAY
37	Alabama	$45,997
16	Alaska	53,714
22	Arizona	50,146
46	Arkansas	42,959
4	California	65,857
9	Colorado	56,914
3	Connecticut	66,636
12	Delaware	55,828
27	Florida	48,455
19	Georgia	52,189
23	Hawaii	49,671
49	Idaho	41,345
8	Illinois	57,971
34	Indiana	46,192
36	Iowa	46,074
40	Kansas	45,116
38	Kentucky	45,166
32	Louisiana	46,500
43	Maine	43,911
7	Maryland	59,603
2	Massachusetts	69,929
18	Michigan	52,487
11	Minnesota	56,140
50	Mississippi	38,788
29	Missouri	47,364
48	Montana	42,045
41	Nebraska	44,851
28	Nevada	48,126
14	New Hampshire	55,138
5	New Jersey	64,042
44	New Mexico	43,535
1	New York	70,682
25	North Carolina	48,920
21	North Dakota	50,313
24	Ohio	49,153
39	Oklahoma	45,121
20	Oregon	51,118
15	Pennsylvania	54,000
17	Rhode Island	52,840
42	South Carolina	44,177
47	South Dakota	42,432
26	Tennessee	48,820
13	Texas	55,795
31	Utah	46,575
35	Vermont	46,186
10	Virginia	56,503
6	Washington	62,041
45	West Virginia	43,419
30	Wisconsin	47,238
33	Wyoming	46,270

RANK	STATE	ANNUAL PAY
1	New York	$70,682
2	Massachusetts	69,929
3	Connecticut	66,636
4	California	65,857
5	New Jersey	64,042
6	Washington	62,041
7	Maryland	59,603
8	Illinois	57,971
9	Colorado	56,914
10	Virginia	56,503
11	Minnesota	56,140
12	Delaware	55,828
13	Texas	55,795
14	New Hampshire	55,138
15	Pennsylvania	54,000
16	Alaska	53,714
17	Rhode Island	52,840
18	Michigan	52,487
19	Georgia	52,189
20	Oregon	51,118
21	North Dakota	50,313
22	Arizona	50,146
23	Hawaii	49,671
24	Ohio	49,153
25	North Carolina	48,920
26	Tennessee	48,820
27	Florida	48,455
28	Nevada	48,126
29	Missouri	47,364
30	Wisconsin	47,238
31	Utah	46,575
32	Louisiana	46,500
33	Wyoming	46,270
34	Indiana	46,192
35	Vermont	46,186
36	Iowa	46,074
37	Alabama	45,997
38	Kentucky	45,166
39	Oklahoma	45,121
40	Kansas	45,116
41	Nebraska	44,851
42	South Carolina	44,177
43	Maine	43,911
44	New Mexico	43,535
45	West Virginia	43,419
46	Arkansas	42,959
47	South Dakota	42,432
48	Montana	42,045
49	Idaho	41,345
50	Mississippi	38,788
	District of Columbia	92,544

Source: U.S. Department of Labor, Bureau of Labor Statistics
"Quarterly Census of Employment and Wages" (https://www.bls.gov/cew/data.htm)
*Computed by dividing total annual wages of employees covered by unemployment insurance programs by the average monthly number of these employees. Includes bonuses, cash value of meals and lodging, tips and, in many states, employer contributions to certain deferred compensation plans such as 401(k) plans.

Percent Change in Average Annual Pay: 2016 to 2017

National Percent Change = 3.3% Increase*

<table>
<tr><td colspan="3">ALPHA ORDER</td><td colspan="3">RANK ORDER</td></tr>
<tr><td>RANK</td><td>STATE</td><td>PERCENT CHANGE</td><td>RANK</td><td>STATE</td><td>PERCENT CHANGE</td></tr>
<tr><td>38</td><td>Alabama</td><td>2.6</td><td>1</td><td>Washington</td><td>5.1</td></tr>
<tr><td>50</td><td>Alaska</td><td>0.2</td><td>2</td><td>California</td><td>4.6</td></tr>
<tr><td>12</td><td>Arizona</td><td>3.3</td><td>3</td><td>Idaho</td><td>4.3</td></tr>
<tr><td>12</td><td>Arkansas</td><td>3.3</td><td>4</td><td>West Virginia</td><td>4.2</td></tr>
<tr><td>2</td><td>California</td><td>4.6</td><td>5</td><td>Colorado</td><td>4.1</td></tr>
<tr><td>5</td><td>Colorado</td><td>4.1</td><td>6</td><td>New York</td><td>4.0</td></tr>
<tr><td>49</td><td>Connecticut</td><td>1.2</td><td>7</td><td>Delaware</td><td>3.8</td></tr>
<tr><td>7</td><td>Delaware</td><td>3.8</td><td>8</td><td>Massachusetts</td><td>3.7</td></tr>
<tr><td>18</td><td>Florida</td><td>3.0</td><td>9</td><td>Indiana</td><td>3.6</td></tr>
<tr><td>18</td><td>Georgia</td><td>3.0</td><td>10</td><td>North Carolina</td><td>3.5</td></tr>
<tr><td>16</td><td>Hawaii</td><td>3.1</td><td>11</td><td>Minnesota</td><td>3.4</td></tr>
<tr><td>3</td><td>Idaho</td><td>4.3</td><td>12</td><td>Arizona</td><td>3.3</td></tr>
<tr><td>33</td><td>Illinois</td><td>2.7</td><td>12</td><td>Arkansas</td><td>3.3</td></tr>
<tr><td>9</td><td>Indiana</td><td>3.6</td><td>12</td><td>Montana</td><td>3.3</td></tr>
<tr><td>38</td><td>Iowa</td><td>2.6</td><td>12</td><td>Oregon</td><td>3.3</td></tr>
<tr><td>43</td><td>Kansas</td><td>2.2</td><td>16</td><td>Hawaii</td><td>3.1</td></tr>
<tr><td>42</td><td>Kentucky</td><td>2.4</td><td>16</td><td>Maine</td><td>3.1</td></tr>
<tr><td>47</td><td>Louisiana</td><td>1.9</td><td>18</td><td>Florida</td><td>3.0</td></tr>
<tr><td>16</td><td>Maine</td><td>3.1</td><td>18</td><td>Georgia</td><td>3.0</td></tr>
<tr><td>38</td><td>Maryland</td><td>2.6</td><td>18</td><td>Michigan</td><td>3.0</td></tr>
<tr><td>8</td><td>Massachusetts</td><td>3.7</td><td>18</td><td>Ohio</td><td>3.0</td></tr>
<tr><td>18</td><td>Michigan</td><td>3.0</td><td>18</td><td>South Carolina</td><td>3.0</td></tr>
<tr><td>11</td><td>Minnesota</td><td>3.4</td><td>18</td><td>South Dakota</td><td>3.0</td></tr>
<tr><td>48</td><td>Mississippi</td><td>1.7</td><td>18</td><td>Tennessee</td><td>3.0</td></tr>
<tr><td>33</td><td>Missouri</td><td>2.7</td><td>18</td><td>Virginia</td><td>3.0</td></tr>
<tr><td>12</td><td>Montana</td><td>3.3</td><td>26</td><td>Nebraska</td><td>2.9</td></tr>
<tr><td>26</td><td>Nebraska</td><td>2.9</td><td>26</td><td>New Hampshire</td><td>2.9</td></tr>
<tr><td>45</td><td>Nevada</td><td>2.1</td><td>26</td><td>North Dakota</td><td>2.9</td></tr>
<tr><td>26</td><td>New Hampshire</td><td>2.9</td><td>26</td><td>Pennsylvania</td><td>2.9</td></tr>
<tr><td>46</td><td>New Jersey</td><td>2.0</td><td>26</td><td>Utah</td><td>2.9</td></tr>
<tr><td>43</td><td>New Mexico</td><td>2.2</td><td>26</td><td>Wyoming</td><td>2.9</td></tr>
<tr><td>6</td><td>New York</td><td>4.0</td><td>32</td><td>Oklahoma</td><td>2.8</td></tr>
<tr><td>10</td><td>North Carolina</td><td>3.5</td><td>33</td><td>Illinois</td><td>2.7</td></tr>
<tr><td>26</td><td>North Dakota</td><td>2.9</td><td>33</td><td>Missouri</td><td>2.7</td></tr>
<tr><td>18</td><td>Ohio</td><td>3.0</td><td>33</td><td>Rhode Island</td><td>2.7</td></tr>
<tr><td>32</td><td>Oklahoma</td><td>2.8</td><td>33</td><td>Texas</td><td>2.7</td></tr>
<tr><td>12</td><td>Oregon</td><td>3.3</td><td>33</td><td>Wisconsin</td><td>2.7</td></tr>
<tr><td>26</td><td>Pennsylvania</td><td>2.9</td><td>38</td><td>Alabama</td><td>2.6</td></tr>
<tr><td>33</td><td>Rhode Island</td><td>2.7</td><td>38</td><td>Iowa</td><td>2.6</td></tr>
<tr><td>18</td><td>South Carolina</td><td>3.0</td><td>38</td><td>Maryland</td><td>2.6</td></tr>
<tr><td>18</td><td>South Dakota</td><td>3.0</td><td>38</td><td>Vermont</td><td>2.6</td></tr>
<tr><td>18</td><td>Tennessee</td><td>3.0</td><td>42</td><td>Kentucky</td><td>2.4</td></tr>
<tr><td>33</td><td>Texas</td><td>2.7</td><td>43</td><td>Kansas</td><td>2.2</td></tr>
<tr><td>26</td><td>Utah</td><td>2.9</td><td>43</td><td>New Mexico</td><td>2.2</td></tr>
<tr><td>38</td><td>Vermont</td><td>2.6</td><td>45</td><td>Nevada</td><td>2.1</td></tr>
<tr><td>18</td><td>Virginia</td><td>3.0</td><td>46</td><td>New Jersey</td><td>2.0</td></tr>
<tr><td>1</td><td>Washington</td><td>5.1</td><td>47</td><td>Louisiana</td><td>1.9</td></tr>
<tr><td>4</td><td>West Virginia</td><td>4.2</td><td>48</td><td>Mississippi</td><td>1.7</td></tr>
<tr><td>33</td><td>Wisconsin</td><td>2.7</td><td>49</td><td>Connecticut</td><td>1.2</td></tr>
<tr><td>26</td><td>Wyoming</td><td>2.9</td><td>50</td><td>Alaska</td><td>0.2</td></tr>
<tr><td></td><td></td><td></td><td></td><td>District of Columbia</td><td>3.4</td></tr>
</table>

Source: CQ Press using data from U.S. Department of Labor, Bureau of Labor Statistics
    "Quarterly Census of Employment and Wages" (https://www.bls.gov/cew/data.htm)
*Includes bonuses, cash value of meals and lodging, tips and, in many states, employer contributions to certain deferred compensation plans such as 401(k) plans.

Median Earnings of Male Full-Time Workers in 2017

National Median = $51,284

ALPHA ORDER				RANK ORDER		
RANK	STATE	EARNINGS		RANK	STATE	EARNINGS
33	Alabama	$48,199		1	Massachusetts	$65,939
7	Alaska	57,943		2	New Jersey	64,497
37	Arizona	46,681		3	Connecticut	62,976
47	Arkansas	43,266		4	Maryland	61,263
15	California	52,487		5	Washington	60,893
13	Colorado	54,869		6	New Hampshire	57,966
3	Connecticut	62,976		7	Alaska	57,943
14	Delaware	54,657		8	Virginia	57,690
50	Florida	42,261		9	Minnesota	55,812
36	Georgia	47,114		10	New York	55,636
20	Hawaii	51,594		11	Illinois	55,585
40	Idaho	46,241		12	Rhode Island	55,183
11	Illinois	55,585		13	Colorado	54,869
25	Indiana	50,782		14	Delaware	54,657
27	Iowa	50,295		15	California	52,487
31	Kansas	49,267		16	Utah	52,249
38	Kentucky	46,289		17	Pennsylvania	52,111
26	Louisiana	50,445		18	Wyoming	51,948
29	Maine	49,476		19	Michigan	51,749
4	Maryland	61,263		20	Hawaii	51,594
1	Massachusetts	65,939		21	North Dakota	51,563
19	Michigan	51,749		22	Wisconsin	51,346
9	Minnesota	55,812		23	Ohio	51,000
49	Mississippi	42,287		24	Oregon	50,965
34	Missouri	47,436		25	Indiana	50,782
43	Montana	45,616		26	Louisiana	50,445
28	Nebraska	50,293		27	Iowa	50,295
45	Nevada	45,439		28	Nebraska	50,293
6	New Hampshire	57,966		29	Maine	49,476
2	New Jersey	64,497		30	Texas	49,414
48	New Mexico	42,690		31	Kansas	49,267
10	New York	55,636		32	Vermont	48,924
38	North Carolina	46,289		33	Alabama	48,199
21	North Dakota	51,563		34	Missouri	47,436
23	Ohio	51,000		35	West Virginia	47,425
42	Oklahoma	46,114		36	Georgia	47,114
24	Oregon	50,965		37	Arizona	46,681
17	Pennsylvania	52,111		38	Kentucky	46,289
12	Rhode Island	55,183		38	North Carolina	46,289
44	South Carolina	45,477		40	Idaho	46,241
41	South Dakota	46,170		41	South Dakota	46,170
46	Tennessee	45,032		42	Oklahoma	46,114
30	Texas	49,414		43	Montana	45,616
16	Utah	52,249		44	South Carolina	45,477
32	Vermont	48,924		45	Nevada	45,439
8	Virginia	57,690		46	Tennessee	45,032
5	Washington	60,893		47	Arkansas	43,266
35	West Virginia	47,425		48	New Mexico	42,690
22	Wisconsin	51,346		49	Mississippi	42,287
18	Wyoming	51,948		50	Florida	42,261
					District of Columbia	74,877

Source: U.S. Bureau of the Census
"2017 American Community Survey-Table DP03" (https://www.census.gov/programs-surveys/acs/)

Median Earnings of Female Full-Time Workers in 2017

National Median = $41,453

ALPHA ORDER				RANK ORDER		
RANK	STATE	EARNINGS		RANK	STATE	EARNINGS
44	Alabama	$35,414		1	Massachusetts	$54,646
7	Alaska	47,472		2	Maryland	52,381
27	Arizona	39,675		3	Connecticut	52,120
49	Arkansas	34,154		4	New Jersey	51,538
9	California	46,783		5	New York	48,901
14	Colorado	44,733		6	Washington	47,681
3	Connecticut	52,120		7	Alaska	47,472
8	Delaware	47,052		8	Delaware	47,052
38	Florida	36,746		9	California	46,783
29	Georgia	38,958		10	Rhode Island	46,146
18	Hawaii	41,664		11	New Hampshire	46,044
48	Idaho	34,665		12	Minnesota	45,798
15	Illinois	43,149		13	Virginia	45,692
36	Indiana	37,167		14	Colorado	44,733
28	Iowa	39,658		15	Illinois	43,149
32	Kansas	37,931		16	Vermont	41,976
39	Kentucky	36,487		17	Pennsylvania	41,929
47	Louisiana	34,708		18	Hawaii	41,664
22	Maine	40,618		19	Oregon	41,572
2	Maryland	52,381		20	North Dakota	40,964
1	Massachusetts	54,646		21	Wisconsin	40,930
23	Michigan	40,453		22	Maine	40,618
12	Minnesota	45,798		23	Michigan	40,453
50	Mississippi	32,441		24	Texas	40,236
34	Missouri	37,339		25	Wyoming	40,200
40	Montana	35,964		26	Ohio	39,774
31	Nebraska	38,726		27	Arizona	39,675
33	Nevada	37,880		28	Iowa	39,658
11	New Hampshire	46,044		29	Georgia	38,958
4	New Jersey	51,538		30	North Carolina	38,784
41	New Mexico	35,523		31	Nebraska	38,726
5	New York	48,901		32	Kansas	37,931
30	North Carolina	38,784		33	Nevada	37,880
20	North Dakota	40,964		34	Missouri	37,339
26	Ohio	39,774		35	Utah	37,252
42	Oklahoma	35,488		36	Indiana	37,167
19	Oregon	41,572		37	Tennessee	36,812
17	Pennsylvania	41,929		38	Florida	36,746
10	Rhode Island	46,146		39	Kentucky	36,487
45	South Carolina	35,142		40	Montana	35,964
43	South Dakota	35,424		41	New Mexico	35,523
37	Tennessee	36,812		42	Oklahoma	35,488
24	Texas	40,236		43	South Dakota	35,424
35	Utah	37,252		44	Alabama	35,414
16	Vermont	41,976		45	South Carolina	35,142
13	Virginia	45,692		46	West Virginia	35,078
6	Washington	47,681		47	Louisiana	34,708
46	West Virginia	35,078		48	Idaho	34,665
21	Wisconsin	40,930		49	Arkansas	34,154
25	Wyoming	40,200		50	Mississippi	32,441
					District of Columbia	66,679

Source: U.S. Bureau of the Census
"2017 American Community Survey-Table DP03" (https://www.census.gov/programs-surveys/acs/)

State Minimum Wage Rates in 2019

National Rate = $7.25 per Hour*

ALPHA ORDER

RANK	STATE	MINIMUM WAGE
NA	Alabama**	NA
14	Alaska	9.89
5	Arizona	11.00
16	Arkansas	9.25
5	California	11.00
3	Colorado	11.10
11	Connecticut	10.10
21	Delaware	8.75
26	Florida	8.46
30	Georgia	7.25
11	Hawaii	10.10
30	Idaho	7.25
27	Illinois	8.25
30	Indiana	7.25
30	Iowa	7.25
30	Kansas	7.25
30	Kentucky	7.25
NA	Louisiana**	NA
5	Maine	11.00
11	Maryland	10.10
1	Massachusetts	12.00
16	Michigan	9.25
15	Minnesota	9.86
NA	Mississippi**	NA
23	Missouri	8.60
25	Montana	8.50
19	Nebraska	9.00
27	Nevada	8.25
30	New Hampshire	7.25
20	New Jersey	8.85
29	New Mexico	7.50
3	New York	11.10
30	North Carolina	7.25
30	North Dakota	7.25
24	Ohio	8.55
30	Oklahoma	7.25
9	Oregon	10.75
30	Pennsylvania	7.25
10	Rhode Island	10.50
NA	South Carolina**	NA
18	South Dakota	9.10
NA	Tennessee**	NA
30	Texas	7.25
30	Utah	7.25
8	Vermont	10.78
30	Virginia	7.25
1	Washington	12.00
21	West Virginia	8.75
30	Wisconsin	7.25
30	Wyoming	7.25

RANK ORDER

RANK	STATE	MINIMUM WAGE
1	Massachusetts	$12.00
1	Washington	12.00
3	Colorado	11.10
3	New York	11.10
5	Arizona	11.00
5	California	11.00
5	Maine	11.00
8	Vermont	10.78
9	Oregon	10.75
10	Rhode Island	10.50
11	Connecticut	10.10
11	Hawaii	10.10
11	Maryland	10.10
14	Alaska	9.89
15	Minnesota	9.86
16	Arkansas	9.25
16	Michigan	9.25
18	South Dakota	9.10
19	Nebraska	9.00
20	New Jersey	8.85
21	Delaware	8.75
21	West Virginia	8.75
23	Missouri	8.60
24	Ohio	8.55
25	Montana	8.50
26	Florida	8.46
27	Illinois	8.25
27	Nevada	8.25
29	New Mexico	7.50
30	Georgia	7.25
30	Idaho	7.25
30	Indiana	7.25
30	Iowa	7.25
30	Kansas	7.25
30	Kentucky	7.25
30	New Hampshire	7.25
30	North Carolina	7.25
30	North Dakota	7.25
30	Oklahoma	7.25
30	Pennsylvania	7.25
30	Texas	7.25
30	Utah	7.25
30	Virginia	7.25
30	Wisconsin	7.25
30	Wyoming	7.25
NA	Alabama**	NA
NA	Louisiana**	NA
NA	Mississippi**	NA
NA	South Carolina**	NA
NA	Tennessee**	NA

District of Columbia   13.25

Source: U.S. Department of Labor, Employment Standards Administration
"Minimum Wage Laws in the States" (https://www.dol.gov/whd/minwage/america.htm)
*As of January 1, 2019. State minimum wage rates are for those employers and jobs not covered by the federal program.
**No separate state program.

Average Hourly Earnings of Production Workers on Manufacturing Payrolls in 2018
National Average = $27.30*

ALPHA ORDER

RANK	STATE	HOURLY EARNINGS
38	Alabama	$20.10
3	Alaska	26.91
36	Arizona	20.24
50	Arkansas	18.10
8	California	23.73
2	Colorado	27.13
4	Connecticut	26.90
44	Delaware	19.20
11	Florida	22.46
43	Georgia	19.32
21	Hawaii	21.68
42	Idaho	19.42
19	Illinois	21.73
15	Indiana	21.96
34	Iowa	20.28
32	Kansas	20.60
33	Kentucky	20.31
21	Louisiana	21.68
17	Maine	21.88
28	Maryland	20.86
6	Massachusetts	24.94
19	Michigan	21.73
15	Minnesota	21.96
28	Mississippi	20.86
14	Missouri	22.24
26	Montana	21.12
39	Nebraska	19.99
30	Nevada	20.81
11	New Hampshire	22.46
10	New Jersey	23.14
47	New Mexico	18.59
13	New York	22.40
49	North Carolina	18.36
37	North Dakota	20.21
18	Ohio	21.84
48	Oklahoma	18.49
9	Oregon	23.26
25	Pennsylvania	21.19
46	Rhode Island	18.76
40	South Carolina	19.94
45	South Dakota	18.89
35	Tennessee	20.26
7	Texas	24.25
27	Utah	20.93
23	Vermont	21.30
40	Virginia	19.94
1	Washington	29.54
24	West Virginia	21.28
31	Wisconsin	20.79
5	Wyoming	24.95

RANK ORDER

RANK	STATE	HOURLY EARNINGS
1	Washington	$29.54
2	Colorado	27.13
3	Alaska	26.91
4	Connecticut	26.90
5	Wyoming	24.95
6	Massachusetts	24.94
7	Texas	24.25
8	California	23.73
9	Oregon	23.26
10	New Jersey	23.14
11	Florida	22.46
11	New Hampshire	22.46
13	New York	22.40
14	Missouri	22.24
15	Indiana	21.96
15	Minnesota	21.96
17	Maine	21.88
18	Ohio	21.84
19	Illinois	21.73
19	Michigan	21.73
21	Hawaii	21.68
21	Louisiana	21.68
23	Vermont	21.30
24	West Virginia	21.28
25	Pennsylvania	21.19
26	Montana	21.12
27	Utah	20.93
28	Maryland	20.86
28	Mississippi	20.86
30	Nevada	20.81
31	Wisconsin	20.79
32	Kansas	20.60
33	Kentucky	20.31
34	Iowa	20.28
35	Tennessee	20.26
36	Arizona	20.24
37	North Dakota	20.21
38	Alabama	20.10
39	Nebraska	19.99
40	South Carolina	19.94
40	Virginia	19.94
42	Idaho	19.42
43	Georgia	19.32
44	Delaware	19.20
45	South Dakota	18.89
46	Rhode Island	18.76
47	New Mexico	18.59
48	Oklahoma	18.49
49	North Carolina	18.36
50	Arkansas	18.10

District of Columbia**   NA

Source: U.S. Department of Labor, Bureau of Labor Statistics
"State and Metro Area Employment, Hours and Earnings" (https://www.bls.gov/sae/home.htm)
*Preliminary data for December 2018. Not seasonally adjusted except for national figure.
**Not available.

Average Weekly Earnings of Production Workers
on Manufacturing Payrolls in 2018
National Average = $1,116.57*

ALPHA ORDER				RANK ORDER		
RANK	STATE	WEEKLY EARNINGS		RANK	STATE	WEEKLY EARNINGS
22	Alabama	$900.48		1	Washington	$1,276.13
35	Alaska	855.74		2	Connecticut	1,156.70
33	Arizona	860.20		3	Colorado	1,082.49
46	Arkansas	767.44		4	Massachusetts	1,069.93
9	California	977.68		5	Texas	1,069.43
3	Colorado	1,082.49		6	Wyoming	1,027.94
2	Connecticut	1,156.70		7	New Hampshire	981.50
44	Delaware	794.88		8	Florida	979.26
8	Florida	979.26		9	California	977.68
36	Georgia	848.15		10	Indiana	972.83
43	Hawaii	799.99		11	Louisiana	971.26
40	Idaho	813.70		12	New Jersey	962.62
16	Illinois	943.08		13	Ohio	947.86
10	Indiana	972.83		14	New York	947.52
30	Iowa	872.04		15	Missouri	945.20
25	Kansas	887.86		16	Illinois	943.08
24	Kentucky	891.61		17	Michigan	940.91
11	Louisiana	971.26		18	Oregon	907.14
20	Maine	905.83		19	Minnesota	906.95
21	Maryland	905.32		20	Maine	905.83
4	Massachusetts	1,069.93		21	Maryland	905.32
17	Michigan	940.91		22	Alabama	900.48
19	Minnesota	906.95		23	West Virginia	893.76
26	Mississippi	886.55		24	Kentucky	891.61
15	Missouri	945.20		25	Kansas	887.86
38	Montana	836.35		26	Mississippi	886.55
41	Nebraska	809.60		27	Nevada	884.43
27	Nevada	884.43		28	Pennsylvania	881.50
7	New Hampshire	981.50		29	Wisconsin	873.18
12	New Jersey	962.62		30	Iowa	872.04
50	New Mexico	717.57		31	Vermont	864.78
14	New York	947.52		32	South Carolina	863.40
48	North Carolina	749.09		33	Arizona	860.20
49	North Dakota	745.75		34	Tennessee	857.00
13	Ohio	947.86		35	Alaska	855.74
39	Oklahoma	820.96		36	Georgia	848.15
18	Oregon	907.14		37	Utah	845.57
28	Pennsylvania	881.50		38	Montana	836.35
47	Rhode Island	761.66		39	Oklahoma	820.96
32	South Carolina	863.40		40	Idaho	813.70
42	South Dakota	802.83		41	Nebraska	809.60
34	Tennessee	857.00		42	South Dakota	802.83
5	Texas	1,069.43		43	Hawaii	799.99
37	Utah	845.57		44	Delaware	794.88
31	Vermont	864.78		45	Virginia	789.62
45	Virginia	789.62		46	Arkansas	767.44
1	Washington	1,276.13		47	Rhode Island	761.66
23	West Virginia	893.76		48	North Carolina	749.09
29	Wisconsin	873.18		49	North Dakota	745.75
6	Wyoming	1,027.94		50	New Mexico	717.57
					District of Columbia**	NA

Source: U.S. Department of Labor, Bureau of Labor Statistics
   "State and Metro Area Employment, Hours and Earnings" (https://www.bls.gov/sae/home.htm)
*Preliminary data for December 2018. Not seasonally adjusted except for national figure.
**Not available.

Average Work Week of Production Workers
on Manufacturing Payrolls in 2018
National Average = 40.9 Hours per Week*

ALPHA ORDER

RANK	STATE	WEEKLY HOURS
1	Alabama	44.8
50	Alaska	31.8
20	Arizona	42.5
25	Arkansas	42.4
36	California	41.2
43	Colorado	39.9
17	Connecticut	43.0
33	Delaware	41.4
9	Florida	43.6
6	Georgia	43.9
48	Hawaii	36.9
30	Idaho	41.9
10	Illinois	43.4
4	Indiana	44.3
17	Iowa	43.0
16	Kansas	43.1
6	Kentucky	43.9
1	Louisiana	44.8
33	Maine	41.4
10	Maryland	43.4
19	Massachusetts	42.9
13	Michigan	43.3
35	Minnesota	41.3
20	Mississippi	42.5
20	Missouri	42.5
44	Montana	39.6
41	Nebraska	40.5
20	Nevada	42.5
8	New Hampshire	43.7
31	New Jersey	41.6
47	New Mexico	38.6
26	New York	42.3
38	North Carolina	40.8
48	North Dakota	36.9
10	Ohio	43.4
3	Oklahoma	44.4
46	Oregon	39.0
31	Pennsylvania	41.6
39	Rhode Island	40.6
13	South Carolina	43.3
20	South Dakota	42.5
26	Tennessee	42.3
5	Texas	44.1
42	Utah	40.4
39	Vermont	40.6
44	Virginia	39.6
15	Washington	43.2
28	West Virginia	42.0
28	Wisconsin	42.0
36	Wyoming	41.2

RANK ORDER

RANK	STATE	WEEKLY HOURS
1	Alabama	44.8
1	Louisiana	44.8
3	Oklahoma	44.4
4	Indiana	44.3
5	Texas	44.1
6	Georgia	43.9
6	Kentucky	43.9
8	New Hampshire	43.7
9	Florida	43.6
10	Illinois	43.4
10	Maryland	43.4
10	Ohio	43.4
13	Michigan	43.3
13	South Carolina	43.3
15	Washington	43.2
16	Kansas	43.1
17	Connecticut	43.0
17	Iowa	43.0
19	Massachusetts	42.9
20	Arizona	42.5
20	Mississippi	42.5
20	Missouri	42.5
20	Nevada	42.5
20	South Dakota	42.5
25	Arkansas	42.4
26	New York	42.3
26	Tennessee	42.3
28	West Virginia	42.0
28	Wisconsin	42.0
30	Idaho	41.9
31	New Jersey	41.6
31	Pennsylvania	41.6
33	Delaware	41.4
33	Maine	41.4
35	Minnesota	41.3
36	California	41.2
36	Wyoming	41.2
38	North Carolina	40.8
39	Rhode Island	40.6
39	Vermont	40.6
41	Nebraska	40.5
42	Utah	40.4
43	Colorado	39.9
44	Montana	39.6
44	Virginia	39.6
46	Oregon	39.0
47	New Mexico	38.6
48	Hawaii	36.9
48	North Dakota	36.9
50	Alaska	31.8
	District of Columbia**	NA

Source: U.S. Department of Labor, Bureau of Labor Statistics
"State and Metro Area Employment, Hours and Earnings" (https://www.bls.gov/sae/home.htm)
*Preliminary data for December 2018. Not seasonally adjusted except for national figure.
**Not available.

Average Weekly Unemployment Benefit in 2018

National Average = $355.84 a Week

RANK	STATE	BENEFIT
47	Alabama	$222.85
41	Alaska	264.01
46	Arizona	230.71
39	Arkansas	265.75
31	California	329.00
7	Colorado	430.98
12	Connecticut	390.85
42	Delaware	260.63
45	Florida	247.73
37	Georgia	291.43
2	Hawaii	508.27
32	Idaho	320.16
13	Illinois	379.62
36	Indiana	293.75
11	Iowa	395.20
15	Kansas	376.21
25	Kentucky	341.46
49	Louisiana	212.49
26	Maine	336.36
22	Maryland	346.18
1	Massachusetts	521.71
35	Michigan	307.65
4	Minnesota	457.65
50	Mississippi	208.15
40	Missouri	264.99
24	Montana	342.94
28	Nebraska	334.00
21	Nevada	349.63
27	New Hampshire	335.18
6	New Jersey	451.80
29	New Mexico	332.76
23	New York	344.29
43	North Carolina	257.66
5	North Dakota	455.33
17	Ohio	371.35
18	Oklahoma	364.15
10	Oregon	397.50
14	Pennsylvania	378.83
20	Rhode Island	356.21
44	South Carolina	256.64
30	South Dakota	332.74
48	Tennessee	215.32
9	Texas	401.52
8	Utah	411.26
19	Vermont	361.83
34	Virginia	310.29
3	Washington	466.97
38	West Virginia	290.57
33	Wisconsin	318.34
16	Wyoming	372.11

RANK	STATE	BENEFIT
1	Massachusetts	$521.71
2	Hawaii	508.27
3	Washington	466.97
4	Minnesota	457.65
5	North Dakota	455.33
6	New Jersey	451.80
7	Colorado	430.98
8	Utah	411.26
9	Texas	401.52
10	Oregon	397.50
11	Iowa	395.20
12	Connecticut	390.85
13	Illinois	379.62
14	Pennsylvania	378.83
15	Kansas	376.21
16	Wyoming	372.11
17	Ohio	371.35
18	Oklahoma	364.15
19	Vermont	361.83
20	Rhode Island	356.21
21	Nevada	349.63
22	Maryland	346.18
23	New York	344.29
24	Montana	342.94
25	Kentucky	341.46
26	Maine	336.36
27	New Hampshire	335.18
28	Nebraska	334.00
29	New Mexico	332.76
30	South Dakota	332.74
31	California	329.00
32	Idaho	320.16
33	Wisconsin	318.34
34	Virginia	310.29
35	Michigan	307.65
36	Indiana	293.75
37	Georgia	291.43
38	West Virginia	290.57
39	Arkansas	265.75
40	Missouri	264.99
41	Alaska	264.01
42	Delaware	260.63
43	North Carolina	257.66
44	South Carolina	256.64
45	Florida	247.73
46	Arizona	230.71
47	Alabama	222.85
48	Tennessee	215.32
49	Louisiana	212.49
50	Mississippi	208.15

	District of Columbia	352.15

Source: CQ Press using data from U.S. Department of Labor, Bureau of Labor Statistics
"Unemployment Insurance Data Summary" (https://workforcesecurity.doleta.gov/unemploy/DataDashboard.asp)

Workers' Compensation Benefit Payments in 2016

National Total = $61,918,340,000*

ALPHA ORDER

RANK	STATE	PAYMENTS	% of USA
29	Alabama	$601,283,000	1.0%
42	Alaska	227,630,000	0.4%
23	Arizona	752,452,000	1.2%
44	Arkansas	207,330,000	0.3%
1	California	12,139,445,000	19.6%
21	Colorado	801,148,000	1.3%
20	Connecticut	897,265,000	1.4%
43	Delaware	224,932,000	0.4%
3	Florida	3,175,084,000	5.1%
10	Georgia	1,375,290,000	2.2%
35	Hawaii	306,058,000	0.5%
39	Idaho	268,000,000	0.4%
7	Illinois	2,354,119,000	3.8%
30	Indiana	576,305,000	0.9%
24	Iowa	664,070,000	1.1%
31	Kansas	420,741,000	0.7%
25	Kentucky	652,820,000	1.1%
22	Louisiana	795,040,000	1.3%
41	Maine	240,780,000	0.4%
18	Maryland	908,180,000	1.5%
13	Massachusetts	1,145,216,000	1.8%
16	Michigan	955,311,000	1.5%
14	Minnesota	1,029,149,000	1.7%
36	Mississippi	305,690,000	0.5%
15	Missouri	1,015,523,000	1.6%
40	Montana	261,105,000	0.4%
34	Nebraska	313,531,000	0.5%
33	Nevada	353,544,000	0.6%
45	New Hampshire	205,663,000	0.3%
6	New Jersey	2,356,537,000	3.8%
37	New Mexico	288,206,000	0.5%
2	New York	5,964,217,000	9.6%
11	North Carolina	1,202,888,000	1.9%
47	North Dakota	165,943,000	0.3%
8	Ohio	1,865,750,000	3.0%
28	Oklahoma	617,891,000	1.0%
26	Oregon	632,760,000	1.0%
4	Pennsylvania	3,119,352,000	5.0%
48	Rhode Island	156,642,000	0.3%
19	South Carolina	902,895,000	1.5%
50	South Dakota	103,001,000	0.2%
27	Tennessee	622,459,000	1.0%
9	Texas	1,468,309,000	2.4%
38	Utah	274,913,000	0.4%
49	Vermont	139,893,000	0.2%
17	Virginia	950,570,000	1.5%
5	Washington	2,430,746,000	3.9%
32	West Virginia	413,765,000	0.7%
12	Wisconsin	1,170,936,000	1.9%
46	Wyoming	175,053,000	0.3%

RANK ORDER

RANK	STATE	PAYMENTS	% of USA
1	California	$12,139,445,000	19.6%
2	New York	5,964,217,000	9.6%
3	Florida	3,175,084,000	5.1%
4	Pennsylvania	3,119,352,000	5.0%
5	Washington	2,430,746,000	3.9%
6	New Jersey	2,356,537,000	3.8%
7	Illinois	2,354,119,000	3.8%
8	Ohio	1,865,750,000	3.0%
9	Texas	1,468,309,000	2.4%
10	Georgia	1,375,290,000	2.2%
11	North Carolina	1,202,888,000	1.9%
12	Wisconsin	1,170,936,000	1.9%
13	Massachusetts	1,145,216,000	1.8%
14	Minnesota	1,029,149,000	1.7%
15	Missouri	1,015,523,000	1.6%
16	Michigan	955,311,000	1.5%
17	Virginia	950,570,000	1.5%
18	Maryland	908,180,000	1.5%
19	South Carolina	902,895,000	1.5%
20	Connecticut	897,265,000	1.4%
21	Colorado	801,148,000	1.3%
22	Louisiana	795,040,000	1.3%
23	Arizona	752,452,000	1.2%
24	Iowa	664,070,000	1.1%
25	Kentucky	652,820,000	1.1%
26	Oregon	632,760,000	1.0%
27	Tennessee	622,459,000	1.0%
28	Oklahoma	617,891,000	1.0%
29	Alabama	601,283,000	1.0%
30	Indiana	576,305,000	0.9%
31	Kansas	420,741,000	0.7%
32	West Virginia	413,765,000	0.7%
33	Nevada	353,544,000	0.6%
34	Nebraska	313,531,000	0.5%
35	Hawaii	306,058,000	0.5%
36	Mississippi	305,690,000	0.5%
37	New Mexico	288,206,000	0.5%
38	Utah	274,913,000	0.4%
39	Idaho	268,000,000	0.4%
40	Montana	261,105,000	0.4%
41	Maine	240,780,000	0.4%
42	Alaska	227,630,000	0.4%
43	Delaware	224,932,000	0.4%
44	Arkansas	207,330,000	0.3%
45	New Hampshire	205,663,000	0.3%
46	Wyoming	175,053,000	0.3%
47	North Dakota	165,943,000	0.3%
48	Rhode Island	156,642,000	0.3%
49	Vermont	139,893,000	0.2%
50	South Dakota	103,001,000	0.2%
	District of Columbia	119,645,000	0.2%

Source: National Academy of Social Insurance (Washington, DC)
"Workers' Compensation: Benefits, Coverage, and Costs, 2016" (https://www.nasi.org/research/workers-compensation)
*Estimated payments from private insurance, state and federal funds, and self insurance. National total includes payments for federal civilian employee program, Black Lung Program, and other federal programs.

Workers' Compensation Benefit Payment per Covered Worker in 2016

National Average = $448*

ALPHA ORDER

RANK	STATE	PAYMENTS
33	Alabama	$336
3	Alaska	732
41	Arizona	287
49	Arkansas	181
2	California	737
36	Colorado	322
10	Connecticut	544
11	Delaware	521
21	Florida	406
32	Georgia	337
12	Hawaii	498
23	Idaho	397
21	Illinois	406
48	Indiana	196
15	Iowa	441
38	Kansas	315
28	Kentucky	359
18	Louisiana	424
19	Maine	412
27	Maryland	367
35	Massachusetts	332
45	Michigan	233
26	Minnesota	372
40	Mississippi	291
24	Missouri	394
8	Montana	596
34	Nebraska	334
42	Nevada	280
37	New Hampshire	321
7	New Jersey	603
25	New Mexico	381
5	New York	662
39	North Carolina	294
20	North Dakota	411
29	Ohio	356
17	Oklahoma	425
30	Oregon	349
9	Pennsylvania	555
31	Rhode Island	339
13	South Carolina	474
44	South Dakota	255
46	Tennessee	227
50	Texas	155
47	Utah	204
14	Vermont	469
43	Virginia	268
1	Washington	774
6	West Virginia	638
16	Wisconsin	428
4	Wyoming	663

RANK ORDER

RANK	STATE	PAYMENTS
1	Washington	$774
2	California	737
3	Alaska	732
4	Wyoming	663
5	New York	662
6	West Virginia	638
7	New Jersey	603
8	Montana	596
9	Pennsylvania	555
10	Connecticut	544
11	Delaware	521
12	Hawaii	498
13	South Carolina	474
14	Vermont	469
15	Iowa	441
16	Wisconsin	428
17	Oklahoma	425
18	Louisiana	424
19	Maine	412
20	North Dakota	411
21	Florida	406
21	Illinois	406
23	Idaho	397
24	Missouri	394
25	New Mexico	381
26	Minnesota	372
27	Maryland	367
28	Kentucky	359
29	Ohio	356
30	Oregon	349
31	Rhode Island	339
32	Georgia	337
33	Alabama	336
34	Nebraska	334
35	Massachusetts	332
36	Colorado	322
37	New Hampshire	321
38	Kansas	315
39	North Carolina	294
40	Mississippi	291
41	Arizona	287
42	Nevada	280
43	Virginia	268
44	South Dakota	255
45	Michigan	233
46	Tennessee	227
47	Utah	204
48	Indiana	196
49	Arkansas	181
50	Texas	155

District of Columbia   215

Source: CQ Press using data from National Academy of Social Insurance (Washington, DC)
"Workers' Compensation: Benefits, Coverage, and Costs, 2016" (https://www.nasi.org/research/workers-compensation)
*Estimated payments from private insurance, state and federal funds, and self insurance. National rate includes payments for federal civilian employee program, Black Lung Program, and other federal programs. Total divided by number of workers covered by workers' compensation.

Percent Change in Workers' Compensation Benefit Payments: 2015 to 2016

National Percent Change = 1.2% Decrease*

ALPHA ORDER

RANK	STATE	PERCENT CHANGE
34	Alabama	(2.6)
36	Alaska	(3.3)
16	Arizona	2.1
6	Arkansas	4.0
21	California	0.8
37	Colorado	(3.5)
48	Connecticut	(8.6)
30	Delaware	(1.4)
26	Florida	(0.4)
3	Georgia	4.8
14	Hawaii	2.6
17	Idaho	2.0
31	Illinois	(1.9)
18	Indiana	1.8
1	Iowa	7.6
28	Kansas	(0.7)
40	Kentucky	(4.6)
13	Louisiana	2.8
8	Maine	3.8
44	Maryland	(5.9)
4	Massachusetts	4.4
49	Michigan	(11.4)
26	Minnesota	(0.4)
46	Mississippi	(7.8)
9	Missouri	3.3
9	Montana	3.3
5	Nebraska	4.1
7	Nevada	3.9
38	New Hampshire	(3.9)
22	New Jersey	0.5
41	New Mexico	(5.0)
9	New York	3.3
29	North Carolina	(1.1)
47	North Dakota	(8.0)
43	Ohio	(5.7)
50	Oklahoma	(12.7)
23	Oregon	0.2
2	Pennsylvania	4.9
35	Rhode Island	(3.1)
19	South Carolina	1.4
33	South Dakota	(2.1)
42	Tennessee	(5.6)
39	Texas	(4.4)
15	Utah	2.2
45	Vermont	(6.5)
12	Virginia	3.0
20	Washington	1.1
25	West Virginia	(0.1)
24	Wisconsin	0.1
31	Wyoming	(1.9)

RANK ORDER

RANK	STATE	PERCENT CHANGE
1	Iowa	7.6
2	Pennsylvania	4.9
3	Georgia	4.8
4	Massachusetts	4.4
5	Nebraska	4.1
6	Arkansas	4.0
7	Nevada	3.9
8	Maine	3.8
9	Missouri	3.3
9	Montana	3.3
9	New York	3.3
12	Virginia	3.0
13	Louisiana	2.8
14	Hawaii	2.6
15	Utah	2.2
16	Arizona	2.1
17	Idaho	2.0
18	Indiana	1.8
19	South Carolina	1.4
20	Washington	1.1
21	California	0.8
22	New Jersey	0.5
23	Oregon	0.2
24	Wisconsin	0.1
25	West Virginia	(0.1)
26	Florida	(0.4)
26	Minnesota	(0.4)
28	Kansas	(0.7)
29	North Carolina	(1.1)
30	Delaware	(1.4)
31	Illinois	(1.9)
31	Wyoming	(1.9)
33	South Dakota	(2.1)
34	Alabama	(2.6)
35	Rhode Island	(3.1)
36	Alaska	(3.3)
37	Colorado	(3.5)
38	New Hampshire	(3.9)
39	Texas	(4.4)
40	Kentucky	(4.6)
41	New Mexico	(5.0)
42	Tennessee	(5.6)
43	Ohio	(5.7)
44	Maryland	(5.9)
45	Vermont	(6.5)
46	Mississippi	(7.8)
47	North Dakota	(8.0)
48	Connecticut	(8.6)
49	Michigan	(11.4)
50	Oklahoma	(12.7)

District of Columbia (0.6)

Source: CQ Press using data from National Academy of Social Insurance (Washington, DC)
"Workers' Compensation: Benefits, Coverage, and Costs, 2016" (https://www.nasi.org/research/workers-compensation)
*Estimated payments from private insurance, state and federal funds, and self insurance. National rate includes payments for federal civilian employee program, Black Lung Program, and other federal programs.

Civilian Labor Force in 2018

National Total = 163,240,000 Workers*

ALPHA ORDER

RANK	STATE	LABOR FORCE	% of USA
24	Alabama	2,216,217	1.4%
48	Alaska	355,543	0.2%
15	Arizona	3,446,535	2.1%
34	Arkansas	1,350,399	0.8%
1	California	19,593,041	12.0%
20	Colorado	3,118,212	1.9%
28	Connecticut	1,923,569	1.2%
45	Delaware	487,141	0.3%
3	Florida	10,277,514	6.3%
8	Georgia	5,147,244	3.2%
42	Hawaii	683,405	0.4%
38	Idaho	856,337	0.5%
5	Illinois	6,500,922	4.0%
16	Indiana	3,406,055	2.1%
30	Iowa	1,691,947	1.0%
33	Kansas	1,489,906	0.9%
27	Kentucky	2,074,067	1.3%
26	Louisiana	2,112,783	1.3%
41	Maine	703,363	0.4%
18	Maryland	3,226,938	2.0%
13	Massachusetts	3,842,000	2.4%
10	Michigan	4,898,032	3.0%
21	Minnesota	3,093,361	1.9%
35	Mississippi	1,281,089	0.8%
22	Missouri	3,066,573	1.9%
44	Montana	526,793	0.3%
36	Nebraska	1,024,189	0.6%
32	Nevada	1,524,835	0.9%
40	New Hampshire	763,896	0.5%
11	New Jersey	4,501,043	2.8%
37	New Mexico	949,047	0.6%
4	New York	9,781,522	6.0%
9	North Carolina	4,996,890	3.1%
47	North Dakota	402,143	0.2%
7	Ohio	5,766,953	3.5%
29	Oklahoma	1,849,452	1.1%
25	Oregon	2,116,656	1.3%
6	Pennsylvania	6,461,982	4.0%
43	Rhode Island	561,039	0.3%
23	South Carolina	2,319,627	1.4%
46	South Dakota	459,958	0.3%
17	Tennessee	3,259,991	2.0%
2	Texas	13,902,459	8.5%
31	Utah	1,579,468	1.0%
49	Vermont	344,405	0.2%
12	Virginia	4,359,242	2.7%
14	Washington	3,812,295	2.3%
39	West Virginia	781,846	0.5%
19	Wisconsin	3,149,038	1.9%
50	Wyoming	286,749	0.2%

RANK ORDER

RANK	STATE	LABOR FORCE	% of USA
1	California	19,593,041	12.0%
2	Texas	13,902,459	8.5%
3	Florida	10,277,514	6.3%
4	New York	9,781,522	6.0%
5	Illinois	6,500,922	4.0%
6	Pennsylvania	6,461,982	4.0%
7	Ohio	5,766,953	3.5%
8	Georgia	5,147,244	3.2%
9	North Carolina	4,996,890	3.1%
10	Michigan	4,898,032	3.0%
11	New Jersey	4,501,043	2.8%
12	Virginia	4,359,242	2.7%
13	Massachusetts	3,842,000	2.4%
14	Washington	3,812,295	2.3%
15	Arizona	3,446,535	2.1%
16	Indiana	3,406,055	2.1%
17	Tennessee	3,259,991	2.0%
18	Maryland	3,226,938	2.0%
19	Wisconsin	3,149,038	1.9%
20	Colorado	3,118,212	1.9%
21	Minnesota	3,093,361	1.9%
22	Missouri	3,066,573	1.9%
23	South Carolina	2,319,627	1.4%
24	Alabama	2,216,217	1.4%
25	Oregon	2,116,656	1.3%
26	Louisiana	2,112,783	1.3%
27	Kentucky	2,074,067	1.3%
28	Connecticut	1,923,569	1.2%
29	Oklahoma	1,849,452	1.1%
30	Iowa	1,691,947	1.0%
31	Utah	1,579,468	1.0%
32	Nevada	1,524,835	0.9%
33	Kansas	1,489,906	0.9%
34	Arkansas	1,350,399	0.8%
35	Mississippi	1,281,089	0.8%
36	Nebraska	1,024,189	0.6%
37	New Mexico	949,047	0.6%
38	Idaho	856,337	0.5%
39	West Virginia	781,846	0.5%
40	New Hampshire	763,896	0.5%
41	Maine	703,363	0.4%
42	Hawaii	683,405	0.4%
43	Rhode Island	561,039	0.3%
44	Montana	526,793	0.3%
45	Delaware	487,141	0.3%
46	South Dakota	459,958	0.3%
47	North Dakota	402,143	0.2%
48	Alaska	355,543	0.2%
49	Vermont	344,405	0.2%
50	Wyoming	286,749	0.2%
	District of Columbia	404,563	0.2%

Source: U.S. Department of Labor, Bureau of Labor Statistics
 "State Employment and Unemployment" (press release, January 18, 2019, www.bls.gov/bls/newsrels.htm)
*Seasonally adjusted preliminary data as of December 2018. National total calculated through a different formula.

Employed Civilian Labor Force in 2018

National Total = 156,945,000 Employed Workers*

ALPHA ORDER

RANK	STATE	EMPLOYED	% of USA
24	Alabama	2,130,194	1.4%
49	Alaska	333,153	0.2%
16	Arizona	3,281,027	2.1%
34	Arkansas	1,301,288	0.8%
1	California	18,779,183	12.0%
20	Colorado	3,010,324	1.9%
28	Connecticut	1,847,349	1.2%
45	Delaware	468,966	0.3%
3	Florida	9,942,962	6.3%
8	Georgia	4,962,612	3.2%
42	Hawaii	666,505	0.4%
38	Idaho	833,756	0.5%
5	Illinois	6,223,404	4.0%
15	Indiana	3,284,190	2.1%
30	Iowa	1,651,316	1.1%
33	Kansas	1,440,934	0.9%
27	Kentucky	1,983,080	1.3%
26	Louisiana	2,008,433	1.3%
41	Maine	679,346	0.4%
18	Maryland	3,101,719	2.0%
13	Massachusetts	3,715,785	2.4%
10	Michigan	4,702,352	3.0%
21	Minnesota	3,006,678	1.9%
35	Mississippi	1,220,968	0.8%
22	Missouri	2,971,331	1.9%
44	Montana	507,368	0.3%
36	Nebraska	995,717	0.6%
32	Nevada	1,457,378	0.9%
39	New Hampshire	745,177	0.5%
11	New Jersey	4,322,946	2.8%
37	New Mexico	904,196	0.6%
4	New York	9,403,010	6.0%
9	North Carolina	4,818,454	3.1%
47	North Dakota	391,316	0.2%
7	Ohio	5,502,123	3.5%
29	Oklahoma	1,790,379	1.1%
25	Oregon	2,030,751	1.3%
6	Pennsylvania	6,188,362	3.9%
43	Rhode Island	539,377	0.3%
23	South Carolina	2,242,540	1.4%
46	South Dakota	446,433	0.3%
17	Tennessee	3,143,855	2.0%
2	Texas	13,387,366	8.5%
31	Utah	1,529,522	1.0%
48	Vermont	335,223	0.2%
12	Virginia	4,236,062	2.7%
14	Washington	3,646,568	2.3%
40	West Virginia	741,742	0.5%
19	Wisconsin	3,055,654	1.9%
50	Wyoming	275,130	0.2%

RANK ORDER

RANK	STATE	EMPLOYED	% of USA
1	California	18,779,183	12.0%
2	Texas	13,387,366	8.5%
3	Florida	9,942,962	6.3%
4	New York	9,403,010	6.0%
5	Illinois	6,223,404	4.0%
6	Pennsylvania	6,188,362	3.9%
7	Ohio	5,502,123	3.5%
8	Georgia	4,962,612	3.2%
9	North Carolina	4,818,454	3.1%
10	Michigan	4,702,352	3.0%
11	New Jersey	4,322,946	2.8%
12	Virginia	4,236,062	2.7%
13	Massachusetts	3,715,785	2.4%
14	Washington	3,646,568	2.3%
15	Indiana	3,284,190	2.1%
16	Arizona	3,281,027	2.1%
17	Tennessee	3,143,855	2.0%
18	Maryland	3,101,719	2.0%
19	Wisconsin	3,055,654	1.9%
20	Colorado	3,010,324	1.9%
21	Minnesota	3,006,678	1.9%
22	Missouri	2,971,331	1.9%
23	South Carolina	2,242,540	1.4%
24	Alabama	2,130,194	1.4%
25	Oregon	2,030,751	1.3%
26	Louisiana	2,008,433	1.3%
27	Kentucky	1,983,080	1.3%
28	Connecticut	1,847,349	1.2%
29	Oklahoma	1,790,379	1.1%
30	Iowa	1,651,316	1.1%
31	Utah	1,529,522	1.0%
32	Nevada	1,457,378	0.9%
33	Kansas	1,440,934	0.9%
34	Arkansas	1,301,288	0.8%
35	Mississippi	1,220,968	0.8%
36	Nebraska	995,717	0.6%
37	New Mexico	904,196	0.6%
38	Idaho	833,756	0.5%
39	New Hampshire	745,177	0.5%
40	West Virginia	741,742	0.5%
41	Maine	679,346	0.4%
42	Hawaii	666,505	0.4%
43	Rhode Island	539,377	0.3%
44	Montana	507,368	0.3%
45	Delaware	468,966	0.3%
46	South Dakota	446,433	0.3%
47	North Dakota	391,316	0.2%
48	Vermont	335,223	0.2%
49	Alaska	333,153	0.2%
50	Wyoming	275,130	0.2%
	District of Columbia	382,283	0.2%

Source: U.S. Department of Labor, Bureau of Labor Statistics
   "State Employment and Unemployment" (press release, January 18, 2019, www.bls.gov/bls/newsrels.htm)
*Seasonally adjusted preliminary data as of December 2018. National total calculated through a different formula.

Employment to Population Ratio in 2018

National Percent = 60.2% of Population 16 Years and Older Employed*

ALPHA ORDER

RANK	STATE	PERCENT
47	Alabama	54.5
40	Alaska	58.0
33	Arizona	58.9
45	Arkansas	54.7
30	California	59.6
3	Colorado	67.1
15	Connecticut	62.8
28	Delaware	60.0
42	Florida	57.6
25	Georgia	60.4
41	Hawaii	57.8
14	Idaho	63.0
24	Illinois	60.7
16	Indiana	62.2
6	Iowa	66.1
13	Kansas	63.2
43	Kentucky	55.7
48	Louisiana	54.3
22	Maine	60.9
12	Maryland	63.8
8	Massachusetts	65.7
36	Michigan	58.4
1	Minnesota	68.0
49	Mississippi	51.9
23	Missouri	60.8
29	Montana	59.9
5	Nebraska	66.6
21	Nevada	61.0
4	New Hampshire	66.7
31	New Jersey	59.5
46	New Mexico	54.6
39	New York	58.1
35	North Carolina	58.5
9	North Dakota	65.6
34	Ohio	58.8
38	Oklahoma	58.2
26	Oregon	60.3
32	Pennsylvania	59.2
18	Rhode Island	61.5
44	South Carolina	55.4
7	South Dakota	65.9
36	Tennessee	58.4
18	Texas	61.5
2	Utah	67.2
11	Vermont	64.3
16	Virginia	62.2
20	Washington	61.4
50	West Virginia	49.8
10	Wisconsin	65.5
27	Wyoming	60.2

RANK ORDER

RANK	STATE	PERCENT
1	Minnesota	68.0
2	Utah	67.2
3	Colorado	67.1
4	New Hampshire	66.7
5	Nebraska	66.6
6	Iowa	66.1
7	South Dakota	65.9
8	Massachusetts	65.7
9	North Dakota	65.6
10	Wisconsin	65.5
11	Vermont	64.3
12	Maryland	63.8
13	Kansas	63.2
14	Idaho	63.0
15	Connecticut	62.8
16	Indiana	62.2
16	Virginia	62.2
18	Rhode Island	61.5
18	Texas	61.5
20	Washington	61.4
21	Nevada	61.0
22	Maine	60.9
23	Missouri	60.8
24	Illinois	60.7
25	Georgia	60.4
26	Oregon	60.3
27	Wyoming	60.2
28	Delaware	60.0
29	Montana	59.9
30	California	59.6
31	New Jersey	59.5
32	Pennsylvania	59.2
33	Arizona	58.9
34	Ohio	58.8
35	North Carolina	58.5
36	Michigan	58.4
36	Tennessee	58.4
38	Oklahoma	58.2
39	New York	58.1
40	Alaska	58.0
41	Hawaii	57.8
42	Florida	57.6
43	Kentucky	55.7
44	South Carolina	55.4
45	Arkansas	54.7
46	New Mexico	54.6
47	Alabama	54.5
48	Louisiana	54.3
49	Mississippi	51.9
50	West Virginia	49.8

| | District of Columbia | 65.9 |

Source: CQ Press using data from U.S. Department of Labor, Bureau of Labor Statistics
"State Employment and Unemployment" (press release, January 18, 2019, www.bls.gov/bls/newsrels.htm)
*Seasonally adjusted preliminary data as of December 2018. Calculated with 2017 population data.

Unemployed Civilian Labor Force in 2018

National Total = 6,294,000 Unemployed Workers*

ALPHA ORDER

RANK	STATE	UNEMPLOYED	% of USA
25	Alabama	86,023	1.4%
41	Alaska	22,390	0.4%
13	Arizona	165,508	2.6%
33	Arkansas	49,111	0.8%
1	California	813,858	12.9%
19	Colorado	107,888	1.7%
28	Connecticut	76,220	1.2%
45	Delaware	18,175	0.3%
4	Florida	334,552	5.3%
9	Georgia	184,632	2.9%
46	Hawaii	16,900	0.3%
40	Idaho	22,581	0.4%
5	Illinois	277,518	4.4%
17	Indiana	121,865	1.9%
36	Iowa	40,631	0.6%
34	Kansas	48,972	0.8%
23	Kentucky	90,987	1.4%
20	Louisiana	104,350	1.7%
39	Maine	24,017	0.4%
15	Maryland	125,219	2.0%
14	Massachusetts	126,215	2.0%
8	Michigan	195,680	3.1%
24	Minnesota	86,683	1.4%
30	Mississippi	60,121	1.0%
21	Missouri	95,242	1.5%
43	Montana	19,425	0.3%
38	Nebraska	28,472	0.5%
29	Nevada	67,457	1.1%
44	New Hampshire	18,719	0.3%
11	New Jersey	178,097	2.8%
35	New Mexico	44,851	0.7%
3	New York	378,512	6.0%
10	North Carolina	178,436	2.8%
49	North Dakota	10,827	0.2%
7	Ohio	264,830	4.2%
31	Oklahoma	59,073	0.9%
26	Oregon	85,905	1.4%
6	Pennsylvania	273,620	4.3%
42	Rhode Island	21,662	0.3%
27	South Carolina	77,087	1.2%
47	South Dakota	13,525	0.2%
18	Tennessee	116,136	1.8%
2	Texas	515,093	8.2%
32	Utah	49,946	0.8%
50	Vermont	9,182	0.1%
16	Virginia	123,180	2.0%
12	Washington	165,727	2.6%
37	West Virginia	40,104	0.6%
22	Wisconsin	93,384	1.5%
48	Wyoming	11,619	0.2%

RANK ORDER

RANK	STATE	UNEMPLOYED	% of USA
1	California	813,858	12.9%
2	Texas	515,093	8.2%
3	New York	378,512	6.0%
4	Florida	334,552	5.3%
5	Illinois	277,518	4.4%
6	Pennsylvania	273,620	4.3%
7	Ohio	264,830	4.2%
8	Michigan	195,680	3.1%
9	Georgia	184,632	2.9%
10	North Carolina	178,436	2.8%
11	New Jersey	178,097	2.8%
12	Washington	165,727	2.6%
13	Arizona	165,508	2.6%
14	Massachusetts	126,215	2.0%
15	Maryland	125,219	2.0%
16	Virginia	123,180	2.0%
17	Indiana	121,865	1.9%
18	Tennessee	116,136	1.8%
19	Colorado	107,888	1.7%
20	Louisiana	104,350	1.7%
21	Missouri	95,242	1.5%
22	Wisconsin	93,384	1.5%
23	Kentucky	90,987	1.4%
24	Minnesota	86,683	1.4%
25	Alabama	86,023	1.4%
26	Oregon	85,905	1.4%
27	South Carolina	77,087	1.2%
28	Connecticut	76,220	1.2%
29	Nevada	67,457	1.1%
30	Mississippi	60,121	1.0%
31	Oklahoma	59,073	0.9%
32	Utah	49,946	0.8%
33	Arkansas	49,111	0.8%
34	Kansas	48,972	0.8%
35	New Mexico	44,851	0.7%
36	Iowa	40,631	0.6%
37	West Virginia	40,104	0.6%
38	Nebraska	28,472	0.5%
39	Maine	24,017	0.4%
40	Idaho	22,581	0.4%
41	Alaska	22,390	0.4%
42	Rhode Island	21,662	0.3%
43	Montana	19,425	0.3%
44	New Hampshire	18,719	0.3%
45	Delaware	18,175	0.3%
46	Hawaii	16,900	0.3%
47	South Dakota	13,525	0.2%
48	Wyoming	11,619	0.2%
49	North Dakota	10,827	0.2%
50	Vermont	9,182	0.1%
	District of Columbia	22,280	0.4%

Source: U.S. Department of Labor, Bureau of Labor Statistics
   "State Employment and Unemployment" (press release, January 18, 2019, www.bls.gov/bls/newsrels.htm)
*Seasonally adjusted preliminary data as of December 2018. National total calculated through a different formula.

Unemployment Rate in 2018

National Rate = 3.9% of Labor Force Unemployed*

ALPHA ORDER

RANK	STATE	PERCENT
19	Alabama	3.9
1	Alaska	6.3
4	Arizona	4.8
26	Arkansas	3.6
12	California	4.2
31	Colorado	3.5
16	Connecticut	4.0
23	Delaware	3.7
33	Florida	3.3
26	Georgia	3.6
48	Hawaii	2.5
47	Idaho	2.6
10	Illinois	4.3
26	Indiana	3.6
50	Iowa	2.4
33	Kansas	3.3
8	Kentucky	4.4
3	Louisiana	4.9
32	Maine	3.4
19	Maryland	3.9
33	Massachusetts	3.3
16	Michigan	4.0
42	Minnesota	2.8
5	Mississippi	4.7
39	Missouri	3.1
23	Montana	3.7
42	Nebraska	2.8
8	Nevada	4.4
48	New Hampshire	2.5
16	New Jersey	4.0
5	New Mexico	4.7
19	New York	3.9
26	North Carolina	3.6
45	North Dakota	2.7
7	Ohio	4.6
37	Oklahoma	3.2
14	Oregon	4.1
12	Pennsylvania	4.2
19	Rhode Island	3.9
33	South Carolina	3.3
41	South Dakota	2.9
26	Tennessee	3.6
23	Texas	3.7
37	Utah	3.2
45	Vermont	2.7
42	Virginia	2.8
10	Washington	4.3
2	West Virginia	5.1
40	Wisconsin	3.0
14	Wyoming	4.1

RANK ORDER

RANK	STATE	PERCENT
1	Alaska	6.3
2	West Virginia	5.1
3	Louisiana	4.9
4	Arizona	4.8
5	Mississippi	4.7
5	New Mexico	4.7
7	Ohio	4.6
8	Kentucky	4.4
8	Nevada	4.4
10	Illinois	4.3
10	Washington	4.3
12	California	4.2
12	Pennsylvania	4.2
14	Oregon	4.1
14	Wyoming	4.1
16	Connecticut	4.0
16	Michigan	4.0
16	New Jersey	4.0
19	Alabama	3.9
19	Maryland	3.9
19	New York	3.9
19	Rhode Island	3.9
23	Delaware	3.7
23	Montana	3.7
23	Texas	3.7
26	Arkansas	3.6
26	Georgia	3.6
26	Indiana	3.6
26	North Carolina	3.6
26	Tennessee	3.6
31	Colorado	3.5
32	Maine	3.4
33	Florida	3.3
33	Kansas	3.3
33	Massachusetts	3.3
33	South Carolina	3.3
37	Oklahoma	3.2
37	Utah	3.2
39	Missouri	3.1
40	Wisconsin	3.0
41	South Dakota	2.9
42	Minnesota	2.8
42	Nebraska	2.8
42	Virginia	2.8
45	North Dakota	2.7
45	Vermont	2.7
47	Idaho	2.6
48	Hawaii	2.5
48	New Hampshire	2.5
50	Iowa	2.4

| | District of Columbia | 5.5 |

Source: U.S. Department of Labor, Bureau of Labor Statistics

"State Employment and Unemployment" (press release, January 18, 2019, www.bls.gov/bls/newsrels.htm)

*Seasonally adjusted preliminary data as of December 2018. National figure calculated through a different formula.

Women in Civilian Labor Force in 2017

National Total = 75,175,000 Women*

ALPHA ORDER

RANK	STATE	WOMEN	% of USA
24	Alabama	1,015,000	1.4%
48	Alaska	172,000	0.2%
17	Arizona	1,523,000	2.0%
33	Arkansas	659,000	0.9%
1	California	8,765,000	11.7%
22	Colorado	1,369,000	1.8%
28	Connecticut	928,000	1.2%
45	Delaware	234,000	0.3%
3	Florida	4,817,000	6.4%
8	Georgia	2,433,000	3.2%
42	Hawaii	327,000	0.4%
38	Idaho	380,000	0.5%
5	Illinois	3,064,000	4.1%
16	Indiana	1,563,000	2.1%
30	Iowa	782,000	1.0%
31	Kansas	695,000	0.9%
27	Kentucky	971,000	1.3%
25	Louisiana	1,001,000	1.3%
41	Maine	329,000	0.4%
15	Maryland	1,567,000	2.1%
13	Massachusetts	1,782,000	2.4%
10	Michigan	2,278,000	3.0%
20	Minnesota	1,478,000	2.0%
35	Mississippi	622,000	0.8%
21	Missouri	1,452,000	1.9%
44	Montana	241,000	0.3%
36	Nebraska	471,000	0.6%
34	Nevada	656,000	0.9%
40	New Hampshire	355,000	0.5%
11	New Jersey	2,138,000	2.8%
37	New Mexico	428,000	0.6%
4	New York	4,657,000	6.2%
9	North Carolina	2,373,000	3.2%
47	North Dakota	188,000	0.3%
7	Ohio	2,745,000	3.7%
29	Oklahoma	830,000	1.1%
26	Oregon	996,000	1.3%
6	Pennsylvania	3,039,000	4.0%
43	Rhode Island	268,000	0.4%
23	South Carolina	1,088,000	1.4%
46	South Dakota	215,000	0.3%
18	Tennessee	1,507,000	2.0%
2	Texas	6,069,000	8.1%
32	Utah	693,000	0.9%
49	Vermont	166,000	0.2%
12	Virginia	2,057,000	2.7%
14	Washington	1,709,000	2.3%
39	West Virginia	363,000	0.5%
19	Wisconsin	1,504,000	2.0%
50	Wyoming	133,000	0.2%

RANK ORDER

RANK	STATE	WOMEN	% of USA
1	California	8,765,000	11.7%
2	Texas	6,069,000	8.1%
3	Florida	4,817,000	6.4%
4	New York	4,657,000	6.2%
5	Illinois	3,064,000	4.1%
6	Pennsylvania	3,039,000	4.0%
7	Ohio	2,745,000	3.7%
8	Georgia	2,433,000	3.2%
9	North Carolina	2,373,000	3.2%
10	Michigan	2,278,000	3.0%
11	New Jersey	2,138,000	2.8%
12	Virginia	2,057,000	2.7%
13	Massachusetts	1,782,000	2.4%
14	Washington	1,709,000	2.3%
15	Maryland	1,567,000	2.1%
16	Indiana	1,563,000	2.1%
17	Arizona	1,523,000	2.0%
18	Tennessee	1,507,000	2.0%
19	Wisconsin	1,504,000	2.0%
20	Minnesota	1,478,000	2.0%
21	Missouri	1,452,000	1.9%
22	Colorado	1,369,000	1.8%
23	South Carolina	1,088,000	1.4%
24	Alabama	1,015,000	1.4%
25	Louisiana	1,001,000	1.3%
26	Oregon	996,000	1.3%
27	Kentucky	971,000	1.3%
28	Connecticut	928,000	1.2%
29	Oklahoma	830,000	1.1%
30	Iowa	782,000	1.0%
31	Kansas	695,000	0.9%
32	Utah	693,000	0.9%
33	Arkansas	659,000	0.9%
34	Nevada	656,000	0.9%
35	Mississippi	622,000	0.8%
36	Nebraska	471,000	0.6%
37	New Mexico	428,000	0.6%
38	Idaho	380,000	0.5%
39	West Virginia	363,000	0.5%
40	New Hampshire	355,000	0.5%
41	Maine	329,000	0.4%
42	Hawaii	327,000	0.4%
43	Rhode Island	268,000	0.4%
44	Montana	241,000	0.3%
45	Delaware	234,000	0.3%
46	South Dakota	215,000	0.3%
47	North Dakota	188,000	0.3%
48	Alaska	172,000	0.2%
49	Vermont	166,000	0.2%
50	Wyoming	133,000	0.2%
	District of Columbia	205,000	0.3%

Source: U.S. Department of Labor, Bureau of Labor Statistics
"Geographic Profiles of Employment and Unemployment, 2017" (https://www.bls.gov/lau/ex14tables.htm)
*Annual averages.

Percent of Women in the Civilian Labor Force in 2017

National Percent = 57.0% of Women*

<table>
<tr><td colspan="3">ALPHA ORDER</td><td colspan="3">RANK ORDER</td></tr>
<tr><th>RANK</th><th>STATE</th><th>PERCENT</th><th>RANK</th><th>STATE</th><th>PERCENT</th></tr>
<tr><td>49</td><td>Alabama</td><td>50.2</td><td>1</td><td>Minnesota</td><td>67.0</td></tr>
<tr><td>5</td><td>Alaska</td><td>64.3</td><td>2</td><td>North Dakota</td><td>66.3</td></tr>
<tr><td>42</td><td>Arizona</td><td>54.3</td><td>3</td><td>South Dakota</td><td>65.1</td></tr>
<tr><td>39</td><td>Arkansas</td><td>54.6</td><td>4</td><td>Wisconsin</td><td>64.5</td></tr>
<tr><td>37</td><td>California</td><td>55.3</td><td>5</td><td>Alaska</td><td>64.3</td></tr>
<tr><td>12</td><td>Colorado</td><td>61.8</td><td>6</td><td>New Hampshire</td><td>63.4</td></tr>
<tr><td>11</td><td>Connecticut</td><td>61.9</td><td>7</td><td>Nebraska</td><td>63.3</td></tr>
<tr><td>24</td><td>Delaware</td><td>57.9</td><td>8</td><td>Vermont</td><td>63.0</td></tr>
<tr><td>41</td><td>Florida</td><td>54.5</td><td>9</td><td>Iowa</td><td>62.9</td></tr>
<tr><td>30</td><td>Georgia</td><td>57.6</td><td>10</td><td>Maryland</td><td>62.4</td></tr>
<tr><td>25</td><td>Hawaii</td><td>57.8</td><td>11</td><td>Connecticut</td><td>61.9</td></tr>
<tr><td>25</td><td>Idaho</td><td>57.8</td><td>12</td><td>Colorado</td><td>61.8</td></tr>
<tr><td>19</td><td>Illinois</td><td>58.9</td><td>13</td><td>Utah</td><td>61.5</td></tr>
<tr><td>20</td><td>Indiana</td><td>58.7</td><td>14</td><td>Kansas</td><td>61.3</td></tr>
<tr><td>9</td><td>Iowa</td><td>62.9</td><td>15</td><td>Massachusetts</td><td>61.2</td></tr>
<tr><td>14</td><td>Kansas</td><td>61.3</td><td>16</td><td>Wyoming</td><td>60.0</td></tr>
<tr><td>43</td><td>Kentucky</td><td>54.2</td><td>17</td><td>Virginia</td><td>59.8</td></tr>
<tr><td>45</td><td>Louisiana</td><td>52.9</td><td>18</td><td>Rhode Island</td><td>59.7</td></tr>
<tr><td>23</td><td>Maine</td><td>58.1</td><td>19</td><td>Illinois</td><td>58.9</td></tr>
<tr><td>10</td><td>Maryland</td><td>62.4</td><td>20</td><td>Indiana</td><td>58.7</td></tr>
<tr><td>15</td><td>Massachusetts</td><td>61.2</td><td>20</td><td>Missouri</td><td>58.7</td></tr>
<tr><td>35</td><td>Michigan</td><td>55.7</td><td>22</td><td>Oregon</td><td>58.5</td></tr>
<tr><td>1</td><td>Minnesota</td><td>67.0</td><td>23</td><td>Maine</td><td>58.1</td></tr>
<tr><td>47</td><td>Mississippi</td><td>51.3</td><td>24</td><td>Delaware</td><td>57.9</td></tr>
<tr><td>20</td><td>Missouri</td><td>58.7</td><td>25</td><td>Hawaii</td><td>57.8</td></tr>
<tr><td>25</td><td>Montana</td><td>57.8</td><td>25</td><td>Idaho</td><td>57.8</td></tr>
<tr><td>7</td><td>Nebraska</td><td>63.3</td><td>25</td><td>Montana</td><td>57.8</td></tr>
<tr><td>38</td><td>Nevada</td><td>55.1</td><td>28</td><td>Ohio</td><td>57.7</td></tr>
<tr><td>6</td><td>New Hampshire</td><td>63.4</td><td>28</td><td>Washington</td><td>57.7</td></tr>
<tr><td>30</td><td>New Jersey</td><td>57.6</td><td>30</td><td>Georgia</td><td>57.6</td></tr>
<tr><td>47</td><td>New Mexico</td><td>51.3</td><td>30</td><td>New Jersey</td><td>57.6</td></tr>
<tr><td>34</td><td>New York</td><td>56.0</td><td>32</td><td>Pennsylvania</td><td>57.1</td></tr>
<tr><td>33</td><td>North Carolina</td><td>56.1</td><td>33</td><td>North Carolina</td><td>56.1</td></tr>
<tr><td>2</td><td>North Dakota</td><td>66.3</td><td>34</td><td>New York</td><td>56.0</td></tr>
<tr><td>28</td><td>Ohio</td><td>57.7</td><td>35</td><td>Michigan</td><td>55.7</td></tr>
<tr><td>44</td><td>Oklahoma</td><td>53.7</td><td>36</td><td>Texas</td><td>55.5</td></tr>
<tr><td>22</td><td>Oregon</td><td>58.5</td><td>37</td><td>California</td><td>55.3</td></tr>
<tr><td>32</td><td>Pennsylvania</td><td>57.1</td><td>38</td><td>Nevada</td><td>55.1</td></tr>
<tr><td>18</td><td>Rhode Island</td><td>59.7</td><td>39</td><td>Arkansas</td><td>54.6</td></tr>
<tr><td>46</td><td>South Carolina</td><td>52.2</td><td>39</td><td>Tennessee</td><td>54.6</td></tr>
<tr><td>3</td><td>South Dakota</td><td>65.1</td><td>41</td><td>Florida</td><td>54.5</td></tr>
<tr><td>39</td><td>Tennessee</td><td>54.6</td><td>42</td><td>Arizona</td><td>54.3</td></tr>
<tr><td>36</td><td>Texas</td><td>55.5</td><td>43</td><td>Kentucky</td><td>54.2</td></tr>
<tr><td>13</td><td>Utah</td><td>61.5</td><td>44</td><td>Oklahoma</td><td>53.7</td></tr>
<tr><td>8</td><td>Vermont</td><td>63.0</td><td>45</td><td>Louisiana</td><td>52.9</td></tr>
<tr><td>17</td><td>Virginia</td><td>59.8</td><td>46</td><td>South Carolina</td><td>52.2</td></tr>
<tr><td>28</td><td>Washington</td><td>57.7</td><td>47</td><td>Mississippi</td><td>51.3</td></tr>
<tr><td>50</td><td>West Virginia</td><td>48.5</td><td>47</td><td>New Mexico</td><td>51.3</td></tr>
<tr><td>4</td><td>Wisconsin</td><td>64.5</td><td>49</td><td>Alabama</td><td>50.2</td></tr>
<tr><td>16</td><td>Wyoming</td><td>60.0</td><td>50</td><td>West Virginia</td><td>48.5</td></tr>
<tr><td></td><td></td><td></td><td></td><td>District of Columbia</td><td>67.3</td></tr>
</table>

Source: U.S. Department of Labor, Bureau of Labor Statistics
"Geographic Profiles of Employment and Unemployment, 2017" (https://www.bls.gov/lau/ex14tables.htm)
*Annual averages. Women 16 years and older.

Percent of Civilian Labor Force Comprised of Women in 2017

National Percent = 46.9% of Civilian Labor Force*

ALPHA ORDER

RANK	STATE	PERCENT
28	Alabama	47.0
28	Alaska	47.0
39	Arizona	46.2
5	Arkansas	48.4
42	California	45.5
42	Colorado	45.5
7	Connecticut	48.2
1	Delaware	48.9
16	Florida	47.6
11	Georgia	48.0
12	Hawaii	47.8
42	Idaho	45.5
20	Illinois	47.4
25	Indiana	47.1
35	Iowa	46.7
28	Kansas	47.0
33	Kentucky	46.8
20	Louisiana	47.4
33	Maine	46.8
2	Maryland	48.6
4	Massachusetts	48.5
35	Michigan	46.7
17	Minnesota	47.5
2	Mississippi	48.6
6	Missouri	48.3
38	Montana	46.3
31	Nebraska	46.9
48	Nevada	44.9
14	New Hampshire	47.7
20	New Jersey	47.4
40	New Mexico	45.9
12	New York	47.8
7	North Carolina	48.2
46	North Dakota	45.3
20	Ohio	47.4
46	Oklahoma	45.3
25	Oregon	47.1
17	Pennsylvania	47.5
7	Rhode Island	48.2
17	South Carolina	47.5
31	South Dakota	46.9
25	Tennessee	47.1
48	Texas	44.9
50	Utah	44.2
10	Vermont	48.1
14	Virginia	47.7
40	Washington	45.9
37	West Virginia	46.6
20	Wisconsin	47.4
42	Wyoming	45.5

RANK ORDER

RANK	STATE	PERCENT
1	Delaware	48.9
2	Maryland	48.6
2	Mississippi	48.6
4	Massachusetts	48.5
5	Arkansas	48.4
6	Missouri	48.3
7	Connecticut	48.2
7	North Carolina	48.2
7	Rhode Island	48.2
10	Vermont	48.1
11	Georgia	48.0
12	Hawaii	47.8
12	New York	47.8
14	New Hampshire	47.7
14	Virginia	47.7
16	Florida	47.6
17	Minnesota	47.5
17	Pennsylvania	47.5
17	South Carolina	47.5
20	Illinois	47.4
20	Louisiana	47.4
20	New Jersey	47.4
20	Ohio	47.4
20	Wisconsin	47.4
25	Indiana	47.1
25	Oregon	47.1
25	Tennessee	47.1
28	Alabama	47.0
28	Alaska	47.0
28	Kansas	47.0
31	Nebraska	46.9
31	South Dakota	46.9
33	Kentucky	46.8
33	Maine	46.8
35	Iowa	46.7
35	Michigan	46.7
37	West Virginia	46.6
38	Montana	46.3
39	Arizona	46.2
40	New Mexico	45.9
40	Washington	45.9
42	California	45.5
42	Colorado	45.5
42	Idaho	45.5
42	Wyoming	45.5
46	North Dakota	45.3
46	Oklahoma	45.3
48	Nevada	44.9
48	Texas	44.9
50	Utah	44.2
	District of Columbia	51.0

Source: CQ Press using data from U.S. Department of Labor, Bureau of Labor Statistics
"Geographic Profiles of Employment and Unemployment, 2017" (https://www.bls.gov/lau/ex14tables.htm)
*Annual averages.

Job Growth: 2017 to 2018

National Percent Change = 1.8% Increase*

ALPHA ORDER

RANK	STATE	PERCENT CHANGE	RANK	STATE	PERCENT CHANGE
12	Alabama	2.2	1	Nevada	3.9
49	Alaska	(0.1)	2	Arizona	3.4
2	Arizona	3.4	3	Texas	3.2
29	Arkansas	1.4	4	Utah	3.1
25	California	1.7	4	Washington	3.1
6	Colorado	2.8	6	Colorado	2.8
37	Connecticut	1.2	6	Wyoming	2.8
12	Delaware	2.2	8	Florida	2.7
8	Florida	2.7	8	New Hampshire	2.7
10	Georgia	2.5	10	Georgia	2.5
29	Hawaii	1.4	11	New Mexico	2.4
16	Idaho	2.0	12	Alabama	2.2
37	Illinois	1.2	12	Delaware	2.2
29	Indiana	1.4	14	North Dakota	2.1
44	Iowa	1.0	14	Ohio	2.1
29	Kansas	1.4	16	Idaho	2.0
41	Kentucky	1.1	16	North Carolina	2.0
41	Louisiana	1.1	16	South Carolina	2.0
47	Maine	0.7	16	South Dakota	2.0
21	Maryland	1.9	16	Tennessee	2.0
24	Massachusetts	1.8	21	Maryland	1.9
35	Michigan	1.3	21	Oregon	1.9
41	Minnesota	1.1	21	Virginia	1.9
46	Mississippi	0.9	24	Massachusetts	1.8
29	Missouri	1.4	25	California	1.7
44	Montana	1.0	26	Wisconsin	1.6
37	Nebraska	1.2	27	New Jersey	1.5
1	Nevada	3.9	27	Oklahoma	1.5
8	New Hampshire	2.7	29	Arkansas	1.4
27	New Jersey	1.5	29	Hawaii	1.4
11	New Mexico	2.4	29	Indiana	1.4
35	New York	1.3	29	Kansas	1.4
16	North Carolina	2.0	29	Missouri	1.4
14	North Dakota	2.1	29	Rhode Island	1.4
14	Ohio	2.1	35	Michigan	1.3
27	Oklahoma	1.5	35	New York	1.3
21	Oregon	1.9	37	Connecticut	1.2
37	Pennsylvania	1.2	37	Illinois	1.2
29	Rhode Island	1.4	37	Nebraska	1.2
16	South Carolina	2.0	37	Pennsylvania	1.2
16	South Dakota	2.0	41	Kentucky	1.1
16	Tennessee	2.0	41	Louisiana	1.1
3	Texas	3.2	41	Minnesota	1.1
4	Utah	3.1	44	Iowa	1.0
49	Vermont	(0.1)	44	Montana	1.0
21	Virginia	1.9	46	Mississippi	0.9
4	Washington	3.1	47	Maine	0.7
48	West Virginia	0.6	48	West Virginia	0.6
26	Wisconsin	1.6	49	Alaska	(0.1)
6	Wyoming	2.8	49	Vermont	(0.1)

	District of Columbia	0.3

Source: CQ Press using data from U.S. Department of Labor, Bureau of Labor Statistics

"State Employment and Unemployment" (press release, January 18, 2019, www.bls.gov/bls/newsrels.htm)

*Nonfarm jobs. December 2017 to December 2018, seasonally adjusted. National figure based on nonfarm employment from a different survey.

Employees on Nonfarm Payrolls in 2018

National Total = 150,263,000 Employees*

RANK	STATE	EMPLOYEES	% of USA
24	Alabama	2,063,800	1.4%
48	Alaska	326,100	0.2%
20	Arizona	2,889,200	1.9%
34	Arkansas	1,256,100	0.8%
1	California	17,287,200	11.5%
22	Colorado	2,762,200	1.8%
28	Connecticut	1,705,500	1.1%
45	Delaware	465,700	0.3%
4	Florida	8,891,200	5.9%
8	Georgia	4,601,000	3.1%
41	Hawaii	666,500	0.4%
39	Idaho	742,600	0.5%
5	Illinois	6,152,200	4.1%
15	Indiana	3,159,400	2.1%
30	Iowa	1,598,100	1.1%
32	Kansas	1,431,400	1.0%
26	Kentucky	1,945,300	1.3%
25	Louisiana	1,992,200	1.3%
42	Maine	628,100	0.4%
21	Maryland	2,767,000	1.8%
13	Massachusetts	3,694,400	2.5%
10	Michigan	4,449,800	3.0%
18	Minnesota	2,975,900	2.0%
35	Mississippi	1,173,000	0.8%
19	Missouri	2,919,600	1.9%
44	Montana	481,400	0.3%
36	Nebraska	1,033,800	0.7%
33	Nevada	1,412,200	0.9%
40	New Hampshire	696,000	0.5%
11	New Jersey	4,208,700	2.8%
37	New Mexico	855,700	0.6%
3	New York	9,694,900	6.5%
9	North Carolina	4,536,400	3.0%
47	North Dakota	435,200	0.3%
7	Ohio	5,650,800	3.8%
29	Oklahoma	1,703,400	1.1%
27	Oregon	1,931,900	1.3%
6	Pennsylvania	6,068,400	4.0%
43	Rhode Island	505,000	0.3%
23	South Carolina	2,151,200	1.4%
46	South Dakota	447,000	0.3%
16	Tennessee	3,086,100	2.1%
2	Texas	12,744,100	8.5%
31	Utah	1,536,700	1.0%
49	Vermont	313,300	0.2%
12	Virginia	4,031,100	2.7%
14	Washington	3,474,700	2.3%
38	West Virginia	753,300	0.5%
17	Wisconsin	3,001,600	2.0%
50	Wyoming	291,300	0.2%

RANK	STATE	EMPLOYEES	% of USA
1	California	17,287,200	11.5%
2	Texas	12,744,100	8.5%
3	New York	9,694,900	6.5%
4	Florida	8,891,200	5.9%
5	Illinois	6,152,200	4.1%
6	Pennsylvania	6,068,400	4.0%
7	Ohio	5,650,800	3.8%
8	Georgia	4,601,000	3.1%
9	North Carolina	4,536,400	3.0%
10	Michigan	4,449,800	3.0%
11	New Jersey	4,208,700	2.8%
12	Virginia	4,031,100	2.7%
13	Massachusetts	3,694,400	2.5%
14	Washington	3,474,700	2.3%
15	Indiana	3,159,400	2.1%
16	Tennessee	3,086,100	2.1%
17	Wisconsin	3,001,600	2.0%
18	Minnesota	2,975,900	2.0%
19	Missouri	2,919,600	1.9%
20	Arizona	2,889,200	1.9%
21	Maryland	2,767,000	1.8%
22	Colorado	2,762,200	1.8%
23	South Carolina	2,151,200	1.4%
24	Alabama	2,063,800	1.4%
25	Louisiana	1,992,200	1.3%
26	Kentucky	1,945,300	1.3%
27	Oregon	1,931,900	1.3%
28	Connecticut	1,705,500	1.1%
29	Oklahoma	1,703,400	1.1%
30	Iowa	1,598,100	1.1%
31	Utah	1,536,700	1.0%
32	Kansas	1,431,400	1.0%
33	Nevada	1,412,200	0.9%
34	Arkansas	1,256,100	0.8%
35	Mississippi	1,173,000	0.8%
36	Nebraska	1,033,800	0.7%
37	New Mexico	855,700	0.6%
38	West Virginia	753,300	0.5%
39	Idaho	742,600	0.5%
40	New Hampshire	696,000	0.5%
41	Hawaii	666,500	0.4%
42	Maine	628,100	0.4%
43	Rhode Island	505,000	0.3%
44	Montana	481,400	0.3%
45	Delaware	465,700	0.3%
46	South Dakota	447,000	0.3%
47	North Dakota	435,200	0.3%
48	Alaska	326,100	0.2%
49	Vermont	313,300	0.2%
50	Wyoming	291,300	0.2%
	District of Columbia	796,300	0.5%

Source: U.S. Department of Labor, Bureau of Labor Statistics
"State Employment and Unemployment" (press release, January 18, 2019, www.bls.gov/bls/newsrels.htm)
*Seasonally adjusted preliminary data as of December 2018. National total calculated through a different formula.

Employees in Construction in 2018

National Total = 7,352,000 Employees*

ALPHA ORDER

ALPHA ORDER

RANK	STATE	EMPLOYEES	% of USA
28	Alabama	88,900	1.2%
49	Alaska	15,400	0.2%
13	Arizona	170,200	2.3%
35	Arkansas	53,200	0.7%
1	California	858,400	11.7%
14	Colorado	169,500	2.3%
32	Connecticut	67,000	0.9%
46	Delaware**	24,100	0.3%
3	Florida	554,000	7.5%
10	Georgia	211,100	2.9%
39	Hawaii**	35,500	0.5%
37	Idaho	47,900	0.7%
7	Illinois	227,100	3.1%
17	Indiana	152,600	2.1%
30	Iowa	78,600	1.1%
33	Kansas	60,900	0.8%
31	Kentucky	77,800	1.1%
19	Louisiana	147,500	2.0%
44	Maine	27,400	0.4%
15	Maryland**	164,100	2.2%
16	Massachusetts	160,100	2.2%
12	Michigan	179,200	2.4%
21	Minnesota	128,600	1.7%
38	Mississippi	43,000	0.6%
23	Missouri	120,400	1.6%
42	Montana	28,800	0.4%
34	Nebraska**	54,300	0.7%
27	Nevada	97,100	1.3%
41	New Hampshire	29,400	0.4%
18	New Jersey	151,600	2.1%
36	New Mexico	49,800	0.7%
4	New York	401,500	5.5%
8	North Carolina	216,900	3.0%
43	North Dakota	27,800	0.4%
6	Ohio	228,000	3.1%
29	Oklahoma	79,900	1.1%
24	Oregon	108,000	1.5%
5	Pennsylvania	257,100	3.5%
48	Rhode Island	19,600	0.3%
26	South Carolina	97,700	1.3%
45	South Dakota**	25,800	0.4%
20	Tennessee**	129,000	1.8%
2	Texas	778,600	10.6%
25	Utah	102,800	1.4%
50	Vermont	15,200	0.2%
11	Virginia	205,500	2.8%
9	Washington	216,700	2.9%
40	West Virginia	35,400	0.5%
22	Wisconsin	125,800	1.7%
47	Wyoming	22,400	0.3%

RANK ORDER

RANK	STATE	EMPLOYEES	% of USA
1	California	858,400	11.7%
2	Texas	778,600	10.6%
3	Florida	554,000	7.5%
4	New York	401,500	5.5%
5	Pennsylvania	257,100	3.5%
6	Ohio	228,000	3.1%
7	Illinois	227,100	3.1%
8	North Carolina	216,900	3.0%
9	Washington	216,700	2.9%
10	Georgia	211,100	2.9%
11	Virginia	205,500	2.8%
12	Michigan	179,200	2.4%
13	Arizona	170,200	2.3%
14	Colorado	169,500	2.3%
15	Maryland**	164,100	2.2%
16	Massachusetts	160,100	2.2%
17	Indiana	152,600	2.1%
18	New Jersey	151,600	2.1%
19	Louisiana	147,500	2.0%
20	Tennessee**	129,000	1.8%
21	Minnesota	128,600	1.7%
22	Wisconsin	125,800	1.7%
23	Missouri	120,400	1.6%
24	Oregon	108,000	1.5%
25	Utah	102,800	1.4%
26	South Carolina	97,700	1.3%
27	Nevada	97,100	1.3%
28	Alabama	88,900	1.2%
29	Oklahoma	79,900	1.1%
30	Iowa	78,600	1.1%
31	Kentucky	77,800	1.1%
32	Connecticut	67,000	0.9%
33	Kansas	60,900	0.8%
34	Nebraska**	54,300	0.7%
35	Arkansas	53,200	0.7%
36	New Mexico	49,800	0.7%
37	Idaho	47,900	0.7%
38	Mississippi	43,000	0.6%
39	Hawaii**	35,500	0.5%
40	West Virginia	35,400	0.5%
41	New Hampshire	29,400	0.4%
42	Montana	28,800	0.4%
43	North Dakota	27,800	0.4%
44	Maine	27,400	0.4%
45	South Dakota**	25,800	0.4%
46	Delaware**	24,100	0.3%
47	Wyoming	22,400	0.3%
48	Rhode Island	19,600	0.3%
49	Alaska	15,400	0.2%
50	Vermont	15,200	0.2%
	District of Columbia**	16,200	0.2%

Source: U.S. Department of Labor, Bureau of Labor Statistics
   "State Employment and Unemployment" (press release, January 18, 2019, www.bls.gov/bls/newsrels.htm)
*Seasonally adjusted preliminary data as of December 2018. National total calculated through a different formula.
**Figures for these states include employees in mining and logging.

Percent of Nonfarm Employees in Construction in 2018

National Percent = 4.9% of Employees*

ALPHA ORDER

RANK	STATE	PERCENT
32	Alabama	4.3
26	Alaska	4.7
12	Arizona	5.9
36	Arkansas	4.2
21	California	5.0
9	Colorado	6.1
46	Connecticut	3.9
19	Delaware	5.2
7	Florida	6.2
29	Georgia	4.6
17	Hawaii	5.3
5	Idaho	6.5
48	Illinois	3.7
24	Indiana	4.8
22	Iowa	4.9
32	Kansas	4.3
43	Kentucky	4.0
2	Louisiana	7.4
31	Maine	4.4
12	Maryland	5.9
32	Massachusetts	4.3
43	Michigan	4.0
32	Minnesota	4.3
48	Mississippi	3.7
41	Missouri	4.1
11	Montana	6.0
17	Nebraska	5.3
3	Nevada	6.9
36	New Hampshire	4.2
50	New Jersey	3.6
14	New Mexico	5.8
41	New York	4.1
24	North Carolina	4.8
6	North Dakota	6.4
43	Ohio	4.0
26	Oklahoma	4.7
16	Oregon	5.6
36	Pennsylvania	4.2
46	Rhode Island	3.9
30	South Carolina	4.5
14	South Dakota	5.8
36	Tennessee	4.2
9	Texas	6.1
4	Utah	6.7
22	Vermont	4.9
20	Virginia	5.1
7	Washington	6.2
26	West Virginia	4.7
36	Wisconsin	4.2
1	Wyoming	7.7

RANK ORDER

RANK	STATE	PERCENT
1	Wyoming	7.7
2	Louisiana	7.4
3	Nevada	6.9
4	Utah	6.7
5	Idaho	6.5
6	North Dakota	6.4
7	Florida	6.2
7	Washington	6.2
9	Colorado	6.1
9	Texas	6.1
11	Montana	6.0
12	Arizona	5.9
12	Maryland	5.9
14	New Mexico	5.8
14	South Dakota	5.8
16	Oregon	5.6
17	Hawaii	5.3
17	Nebraska	5.3
19	Delaware	5.2
20	Virginia	5.1
21	California	5.0
22	Iowa	4.9
22	Vermont	4.9
24	Indiana	4.8
24	North Carolina	4.8
26	Alaska	4.7
26	Oklahoma	4.7
26	West Virginia	4.7
29	Georgia	4.6
30	South Carolina	4.5
31	Maine	4.4
32	Alabama	4.3
32	Kansas	4.3
32	Massachusetts	4.3
32	Minnesota	4.3
36	Arkansas	4.2
36	New Hampshire	4.2
36	Pennsylvania	4.2
36	Tennessee	4.2
36	Wisconsin	4.2
41	Missouri	4.1
41	New York	4.1
43	Kentucky	4.0
43	Michigan	4.0
43	Ohio	4.0
46	Connecticut	3.9
46	Rhode Island	3.9
48	Illinois	3.7
48	Mississippi	3.7
50	New Jersey	3.6
	District of Columbia	2.0

Source: CQ Press using data from U.S. Department of Labor, Bureau of Labor Statistics

"State Employment and Unemployment" (press release, January 18, 2019, www.bls.gov/bls/newsrels.htm)

*Seasonally adjusted preliminary data as of December 2018. National figure calculated through a different formula.

**Figures for these states include employees in mining and logging.

Employees in Education and Health Services in 2018

National Total = 23,897,000 Employees*

ALPHA ORDER

RANK	STATE	EMPLOYEES	% of USA
28	Alabama	246,300	1.0%
49	Alaska	50,600	0.2%
20	Arizona	447,500	1.9%
33	Arkansas	189,900	0.8%
1	California	2,743,500	11.5%
23	Colorado	341,400	1.4%
22	Connecticut	343,100	1.4%
44	Delaware	80,100	0.3%
4	Florida	1,333,800	5.6%
12	Georgia	594,600	2.5%
43	Hawaii	87,300	0.4%
42	Idaho	106,100	0.4%
7	Illinois	934,900	3.9%
16	Indiana	483,000	2.0%
30	Iowa	234,200	1.0%
32	Kansas	198,600	0.8%
26	Kentucky	276,000	1.2%
24	Louisiana	321,200	1.3%
39	Maine	129,000	0.5%
17	Maryland	480,900	2.0%
8	Massachusetts	811,200	3.4%
10	Michigan	679,700	2.8%
14	Minnesota	536,500	2.2%
35	Mississippi	146,000	0.6%
18	Missouri	479,300	2.0%
45	Montana	77,100	0.3%
34	Nebraska	156,200	0.7%
37	Nevada	141,000	0.6%
40	New Hampshire	127,500	0.5%
9	New Jersey	713,100	3.0%
36	New Mexico	141,700	0.6%
2	New York	2,086,600	8.7%
11	North Carolina	615,900	2.6%
48	North Dakota	65,100	0.3%
6	Ohio	951,200	4.0%
29	Oklahoma	238,000	1.0%
25	Oregon	299,000	1.3%
5	Pennsylvania	1,295,200	5.4%
41	Rhode Island	109,600	0.5%
27	South Carolina	254,800	1.1%
46	South Dakota	72,800	0.3%
21	Tennessee	438,300	1.8%
3	Texas	1,723,700	7.2%
31	Utah	207,300	0.9%
47	Vermont	66,800	0.3%
13	Virginia	548,500	2.3%
15	Washington	493,400	2.1%
38	West Virginia	133,100	0.6%
19	Wisconsin	461,400	1.9%
50	Wyoming	28,600	0.1%

RANK ORDER

RANK	STATE	EMPLOYEES	% of USA
1	California	2,743,500	11.5%
2	New York	2,086,600	8.7%
3	Texas	1,723,700	7.2%
4	Florida	1,333,800	5.6%
5	Pennsylvania	1,295,200	5.4%
6	Ohio	951,200	4.0%
7	Illinois	934,900	3.9%
8	Massachusetts	811,200	3.4%
9	New Jersey	713,100	3.0%
10	Michigan	679,700	2.8%
11	North Carolina	615,900	2.6%
12	Georgia	594,600	2.5%
13	Virginia	548,500	2.3%
14	Minnesota	536,500	2.2%
15	Washington	493,400	2.1%
16	Indiana	483,000	2.0%
17	Maryland	480,900	2.0%
18	Missouri	479,300	2.0%
19	Wisconsin	461,400	1.9%
20	Arizona	447,500	1.9%
21	Tennessee	438,300	1.8%
22	Connecticut	343,100	1.4%
23	Colorado	341,400	1.4%
24	Louisiana	321,200	1.3%
25	Oregon	299,000	1.3%
26	Kentucky	276,000	1.2%
27	South Carolina	254,800	1.1%
28	Alabama	246,300	1.0%
29	Oklahoma	238,000	1.0%
30	Iowa	234,200	1.0%
31	Utah	207,300	0.9%
32	Kansas	198,600	0.8%
33	Arkansas	189,900	0.8%
34	Nebraska	156,200	0.7%
35	Mississippi	146,000	0.6%
36	New Mexico	141,700	0.6%
37	Nevada	141,000	0.6%
38	West Virginia	133,100	0.6%
39	Maine	129,000	0.5%
40	New Hampshire	127,500	0.5%
41	Rhode Island	109,600	0.5%
42	Idaho	106,100	0.4%
43	Hawaii	87,300	0.4%
44	Delaware	80,100	0.3%
45	Montana	77,100	0.3%
46	South Dakota	72,800	0.3%
47	Vermont	66,800	0.3%
48	North Dakota	65,100	0.3%
49	Alaska	50,600	0.2%
50	Wyoming	28,600	0.1%
	District of Columbia	135,600	0.6%

Source: U.S. Department of Labor, Bureau of Labor Statistics
  "State Employment and Unemployment" (press release, January 18, 2019, www.bls.gov/bls/newsrels.htm)
*Seasonally adjusted preliminary data as of December 2018. National total calculated through a different formula.

Percent of Nonfarm Employees in Education and Health Services in 2018

National Percent = 15.9% of Employees*

ALPHA ORDER

RANK	STATE	PERCENT
47	Alabama	11.9
21	Alaska	15.5
21	Arizona	15.5
28	Arkansas	15.1
20	California	15.9
45	Colorado	12.4
7	Connecticut	20.1
12	Delaware	17.2
30	Florida	15.0
44	Georgia	12.9
43	Hawaii	13.1
33	Idaho	14.3
27	Illinois	15.2
25	Indiana	15.3
32	Iowa	14.7
38	Kansas	13.9
34	Kentucky	14.2
18	Louisiana	16.1
6	Maine	20.5
11	Maryland	17.4
1	Massachusetts	22.0
25	Michigan	15.3
9	Minnesota	18.0
45	Mississippi	12.4
16	Missouri	16.4
19	Montana	16.0
28	Nebraska	15.1
49	Nevada	10.0
8	New Hampshire	18.3
13	New Jersey	16.9
15	New Mexico	16.6
3	New York	21.5
39	North Carolina	13.6
30	North Dakota	15.0
14	Ohio	16.8
37	Oklahoma	14.0
21	Oregon	15.5
4	Pennsylvania	21.3
2	Rhode Island	21.7
48	South Carolina	11.8
17	South Dakota	16.3
34	Tennessee	14.2
41	Texas	13.5
41	Utah	13.5
4	Vermont	21.3
39	Virginia	13.6
34	Washington	14.2
10	West Virginia	17.7
24	Wisconsin	15.4
50	Wyoming	9.8

RANK ORDER

RANK	STATE	PERCENT
1	Massachusetts	22.0
2	Rhode Island	21.7
3	New York	21.5
4	Pennsylvania	21.3
4	Vermont	21.3
6	Maine	20.5
7	Connecticut	20.1
8	New Hampshire	18.3
9	Minnesota	18.0
10	West Virginia	17.7
11	Maryland	17.4
12	Delaware	17.2
13	New Jersey	16.9
14	Ohio	16.8
15	New Mexico	16.6
16	Missouri	16.4
17	South Dakota	16.3
18	Louisiana	16.1
19	Montana	16.0
20	California	15.9
21	Alaska	15.5
21	Arizona	15.5
21	Oregon	15.5
24	Wisconsin	15.4
25	Indiana	15.3
25	Michigan	15.3
27	Illinois	15.2
28	Arkansas	15.1
28	Nebraska	15.1
30	Florida	15.0
30	North Dakota	15.0
32	Iowa	14.7
33	Idaho	14.3
34	Kentucky	14.2
34	Tennessee	14.2
34	Washington	14.2
37	Oklahoma	14.0
38	Kansas	13.9
39	North Carolina	13.6
39	Virginia	13.6
41	Texas	13.5
41	Utah	13.5
43	Hawaii	13.1
44	Georgia	12.9
45	Colorado	12.4
45	Mississippi	12.4
47	Alabama	11.9
48	South Carolina	11.8
49	Nevada	10.0
50	Wyoming	9.8

District of Columbia	17.0

Source: CQ Press using data from U.S. Department of Labor, Bureau of Labor Statistics
   "State Employment and Unemployment" (press release, January 18, 2019, www.bls.gov/bls/newsrels.htm)
*Seasonally adjusted preliminary data as of December 2018. National figure calculated through a different formula.

Employees in Financial Activities in 2018

National Total = 8,621,000 Employees*

ALPHA ORDER

ALPHA ORDER

RANK ORDER

RANK	STATE	EMPLOYEES	% of USA
27	Alabama	97,600	1.1%
50	Alaska	11,100	0.1%
13	Arizona	219,100	2.5%
35	Arkansas	54,100	0.6%
1	California	839,900	9.7%
17	Colorado	168,500	2.0%
23	Connecticut	130,400	1.5%
36	Delaware	47,900	0.6%
4	Florida	591,800	6.9%
10	Georgia	240,800	2.8%
43	Hawaii	30,200	0.4%
39	Idaho	36,400	0.4%
5	Illinois	399,800	4.6%
21	Indiana	140,300	1.6%
24	Iowa	111,800	1.3%
31	Kansas	80,300	0.9%
29	Kentucky	94,000	1.1%
28	Louisiana	94,400	1.1%
42	Maine	32,100	0.4%
22	Maryland	136,400	1.6%
12	Massachusetts	222,500	2.6%
11	Michigan	223,300	2.6%
15	Minnesota	181,400	2.1%
37	Mississippi	44,800	0.5%
16	Missouri	176,100	2.0%
46	Montana	24,900	0.3%
33	Nebraska	75,800	0.9%
34	Nevada	66,900	0.8%
40	New Hampshire	36,000	0.4%
8	New Jersey	247,500	2.9%
41	New Mexico	35,800	0.4%
3	New York	718,800	8.3%
9	North Carolina	242,500	2.8%
47	North Dakota	24,600	0.3%
7	Ohio	311,900	3.6%
32	Oklahoma	79,000	0.9%
26	Oregon	101,100	1.2%
6	Pennsylvania	327,200	3.8%
38	Rhode Island	36,700	0.4%
25	South Carolina	102,100	1.2%
44	South Dakota	29,600	0.3%
19	Tennessee	161,600	1.9%
2	Texas	784,400	9.1%
30	Utah	87,800	1.0%
48	Vermont	12,200	0.1%
14	Virginia	210,200	2.4%
18	Washington	162,500	1.9%
45	West Virginia	26,800	0.3%
20	Wisconsin	151,200	1.8%
49	Wyoming	11,400	0.1%

RANK	STATE	EMPLOYEES	% of USA
1	California	839,900	9.7%
2	Texas	784,400	9.1%
3	New York	718,800	8.3%
4	Florida	591,800	6.9%
5	Illinois	399,800	4.6%
6	Pennsylvania	327,200	3.8%
7	Ohio	311,900	3.6%
8	New Jersey	247,500	2.9%
9	North Carolina	242,500	2.8%
10	Georgia	240,800	2.8%
11	Michigan	223,300	2.6%
12	Massachusetts	222,500	2.6%
13	Arizona	219,100	2.5%
14	Virginia	210,200	2.4%
15	Minnesota	181,400	2.1%
16	Missouri	176,100	2.0%
17	Colorado	168,500	2.0%
18	Washington	162,500	1.9%
19	Tennessee	161,600	1.9%
20	Wisconsin	151,200	1.8%
21	Indiana	140,300	1.6%
22	Maryland	136,400	1.6%
23	Connecticut	130,400	1.5%
24	Iowa	111,800	1.3%
25	South Carolina	102,100	1.2%
26	Oregon	101,100	1.2%
27	Alabama	97,600	1.1%
28	Louisiana	94,400	1.1%
29	Kentucky	94,000	1.1%
30	Utah	87,800	1.0%
31	Kansas	80,300	0.9%
32	Oklahoma	79,000	0.9%
33	Nebraska	75,800	0.9%
34	Nevada	66,900	0.8%
35	Arkansas	54,100	0.6%
36	Delaware	47,900	0.6%
37	Mississippi	44,800	0.5%
38	Rhode Island	36,700	0.4%
39	Idaho	36,400	0.4%
40	New Hampshire	36,000	0.4%
41	New Mexico	35,800	0.4%
42	Maine	32,100	0.4%
43	Hawaii	30,200	0.4%
44	South Dakota	29,600	0.3%
45	West Virginia	26,800	0.3%
46	Montana	24,900	0.3%
47	North Dakota	24,600	0.3%
48	Vermont	12,200	0.1%
49	Wyoming	11,400	0.1%
50	Alaska	11,100	0.1%
	District of Columbia	31,600	0.4%

Source: U.S. Department of Labor, Bureau of Labor Statistics
"State Employment and Unemployment" (press release, January 18, 2019, www.bls.gov/bls/newsrels.htm)
*Seasonally adjusted preliminary data as of December 2018. National total calculated through a different formula. Financial activities include insurance and real estate.

Percent of Nonfarm Employees in Financial Activities in 2018

National Percent = 5.7% of Employees*

ALPHA ORDER				RANK ORDER		
RANK	STATE	PERCENT		RANK	STATE	PERCENT
36	Alabama	4.7		1	Delaware	10.3
50	Alaska	3.4		2	Arizona	7.6
2	Arizona	7.6		2	Connecticut	7.6
44	Arkansas	4.3		4	New York	7.4
32	California	4.9		5	Nebraska	7.3
12	Colorado	6.1		5	Rhode Island	7.3
2	Connecticut	7.6		7	Iowa	7.0
1	Delaware	10.3		8	Florida	6.7
8	Florida	6.7		9	South Dakota	6.6
23	Georgia	5.2		10	Illinois	6.5
42	Hawaii	4.5		11	Texas	6.2
32	Idaho	4.9		12	Colorado	6.1
10	Illinois	6.5		12	Minnesota	6.1
43	Indiana	4.4		14	Massachusetts	6.0
7	Iowa	7.0		14	Missouri	6.0
19	Kansas	5.6		16	New Jersey	5.9
35	Kentucky	4.8		17	North Dakota	5.7
36	Louisiana	4.7		17	Utah	5.7
29	Maine	5.1		19	Kansas	5.6
32	Maryland	4.9		20	Ohio	5.5
14	Massachusetts	6.0		21	Pennsylvania	5.4
30	Michigan	5.0		22	North Carolina	5.3
12	Minnesota	6.1		23	Georgia	5.2
48	Mississippi	3.8		23	Montana	5.2
14	Missouri	6.0		23	New Hampshire	5.2
23	Montana	5.2		23	Oregon	5.2
5	Nebraska	7.3		23	Tennessee	5.2
36	Nevada	4.7		23	Virginia	5.2
23	New Hampshire	5.2		29	Maine	5.1
16	New Jersey	5.9		30	Michigan	5.0
45	New Mexico	4.2		30	Wisconsin	5.0
4	New York	7.4		32	California	4.9
22	North Carolina	5.3		32	Idaho	4.9
17	North Dakota	5.7		32	Maryland	4.9
20	Ohio	5.5		35	Kentucky	4.8
41	Oklahoma	4.6		36	Alabama	4.7
23	Oregon	5.2		36	Louisiana	4.7
21	Pennsylvania	5.4		36	Nevada	4.7
5	Rhode Island	7.3		36	South Carolina	4.7
36	South Carolina	4.7		36	Washington	4.7
9	South Dakota	6.6		41	Oklahoma	4.6
23	Tennessee	5.2		42	Hawaii	4.5
11	Texas	6.2		43	Indiana	4.4
17	Utah	5.7		44	Arkansas	4.3
46	Vermont	3.9		45	New Mexico	4.2
23	Virginia	5.2		46	Vermont	3.9
36	Washington	4.7		46	Wyoming	3.9
49	West Virginia	3.6		48	Mississippi	3.8
30	Wisconsin	5.0		49	West Virginia	3.6
46	Wyoming	3.9		50	Alaska	3.4
					District of Columbia	4.0

Source: CQ Press using data from U.S. Department of Labor, Bureau of Labor Statistics
"State Employment and Unemployment" (press release, January 18, 2019, www.bls.gov/bls/newsrels.htm)
*Seasonally adjusted preliminary data as of December 2018. National figure calculated through a different formula. Financial activities include insurance and real estate.

Employees in Government in 2018

National Total = 22,405,000 Employees*

ALPHA ORDER

RANK	STATE	EMPLOYEES	% of USA
23	Alabama	389,100	1.7%
46	Alaska	80,200	0.4%
21	Arizona	417,000	1.9%
34	Arkansas	211,400	0.9%
1	California	2,609,400	11.6%
16	Colorado	447,000	2.0%
33	Connecticut	227,500	1.0%
48	Delaware	67,200	0.3%
4	Florida	1,101,600	4.9%
10	Georgia	693,700	3.1%
40	Hawaii	126,100	0.6%
39	Idaho	127,800	0.6%
5	Illinois	855,500	3.8%
20	Indiana	427,800	1.9%
29	Iowa	260,300	1.2%
30	Kansas	259,700	1.2%
27	Kentucky	313,900	1.4%
26	Louisiana	323,700	1.4%
41	Maine	100,000	0.4%
14	Maryland	503,300	2.2%
15	Massachusetts	452,600	2.0%
12	Michigan	612,200	2.7%
19	Minnesota	429,800	1.9%
32	Mississippi	244,500	1.1%
17	Missouri	434,500	1.9%
42	Montana	92,900	0.4%
36	Nebraska	173,200	0.8%
37	Nevada	168,700	0.8%
43	New Hampshire	91,000	0.4%
11	New Jersey	614,000	2.7%
35	New Mexico	188,000	0.8%
3	New York	1,451,200	6.5%
7	North Carolina	739,000	3.3%
44	North Dakota	81,000	0.4%
6	Ohio	793,700	3.5%
25	Oklahoma	352,200	1.6%
28	Oregon	298,000	1.3%
8	Pennsylvania	701,800	3.1%
49	Rhode Island	60,800	0.3%
24	South Carolina	369,800	1.7%
45	South Dakota	80,300	0.4%
18	Tennessee	434,100	1.9%
2	Texas	1,945,700	8.7%
31	Utah	251,300	1.1%
50	Vermont	55,800	0.2%
9	Virginia	700,200	3.1%
13	Washington	596,600	2.7%
38	West Virginia	155,700	0.7%
22	Wisconsin	409,700	1.8%
47	Wyoming	69,300	0.3%

RANK ORDER

RANK	STATE	EMPLOYEES	% of USA
1	California	2,609,400	11.6%
2	Texas	1,945,700	8.7%
3	New York	1,451,200	6.5%
4	Florida	1,101,600	4.9%
5	Illinois	855,500	3.8%
6	Ohio	793,700	3.5%
7	North Carolina	739,000	3.3%
8	Pennsylvania	701,800	3.1%
9	Virginia	700,200	3.1%
10	Georgia	693,700	3.1%
11	New Jersey	614,000	2.7%
12	Michigan	612,200	2.7%
13	Washington	596,600	2.7%
14	Maryland	503,300	2.2%
15	Massachusetts	452,600	2.0%
16	Colorado	447,000	2.0%
17	Missouri	434,500	1.9%
18	Tennessee	434,100	1.9%
19	Minnesota	429,800	1.9%
20	Indiana	427,800	1.9%
21	Arizona	417,000	1.9%
22	Wisconsin	409,700	1.8%
23	Alabama	389,100	1.7%
24	South Carolina	369,800	1.7%
25	Oklahoma	352,200	1.6%
26	Louisiana	323,700	1.4%
27	Kentucky	313,900	1.4%
28	Oregon	298,000	1.3%
29	Iowa	260,300	1.2%
30	Kansas	259,700	1.2%
31	Utah	251,300	1.1%
32	Mississippi	244,500	1.1%
33	Connecticut	227,500	1.0%
34	Arkansas	211,400	0.9%
35	New Mexico	188,000	0.8%
36	Nebraska	173,200	0.8%
37	Nevada	168,700	0.8%
38	West Virginia	155,700	0.7%
39	Idaho	127,800	0.6%
40	Hawaii	126,100	0.6%
41	Maine	100,000	0.4%
42	Montana	92,900	0.4%
43	New Hampshire	91,000	0.4%
44	North Dakota	81,000	0.4%
45	South Dakota	80,300	0.4%
46	Alaska	80,200	0.4%
47	Wyoming	69,300	0.3%
48	Delaware	67,200	0.3%
49	Rhode Island	60,800	0.3%
50	Vermont	55,800	0.2%
	District of Columbia	237,000	1.1%

Source: U.S. Department of Labor, Bureau of Labor Statistics
    "State Employment and Unemployment" (press release, January 18, 2019, www.bls.gov/bls/newsrels.htm)
*Seasonally adjusted preliminary data as of December 2018. National total calculated through a different formula.

Percent of Nonfarm Employees in Government in 2018

National Percent = 14.9% of Employees*

ALPHA ORDER

RANK	STATE	PERCENT
8	Alabama	18.9
1	Alaska	24.6
35	Arizona	14.4
19	Arkansas	16.8
30	California	15.1
24	Colorado	16.2
44	Connecticut	13.3
35	Delaware	14.4
46	Florida	12.4
30	Georgia	15.1
8	Hawaii	18.9
16	Idaho	17.2
40	Illinois	13.9
43	Indiana	13.5
22	Iowa	16.3
12	Kansas	18.1
26	Kentucky	16.1
24	Louisiana	16.2
27	Maine	15.9
11	Maryland	18.2
47	Massachusetts	12.3
41	Michigan	13.8
35	Minnesota	14.4
4	Mississippi	20.8
33	Missouri	14.9
7	Montana	19.3
19	Nebraska	16.8
49	Nevada	11.9
45	New Hampshire	13.1
34	New Jersey	14.6
3	New Mexico	22.0
32	New York	15.0
22	North Carolina	16.3
10	North Dakota	18.6
39	Ohio	14.0
5	Oklahoma	20.7
28	Oregon	15.4
50	Pennsylvania	11.6
48	Rhode Island	12.0
16	South Carolina	17.2
13	South Dakota	18.0
38	Tennessee	14.1
29	Texas	15.3
21	Utah	16.4
14	Vermont	17.8
15	Virginia	17.4
16	Washington	17.2
5	West Virginia	20.7
42	Wisconsin	13.6
2	Wyoming	23.8

RANK ORDER

RANK	STATE	PERCENT
1	Alaska	24.6
2	Wyoming	23.8
3	New Mexico	22.0
4	Mississippi	20.8
5	Oklahoma	20.7
5	West Virginia	20.7
7	Montana	19.3
8	Alabama	18.9
8	Hawaii	18.9
10	North Dakota	18.6
11	Maryland	18.2
12	Kansas	18.1
13	South Dakota	18.0
14	Vermont	17.8
15	Virginia	17.4
16	Idaho	17.2
16	South Carolina	17.2
16	Washington	17.2
19	Arkansas	16.8
19	Nebraska	16.8
21	Utah	16.4
22	Iowa	16.3
22	North Carolina	16.3
24	Colorado	16.2
24	Louisiana	16.2
26	Kentucky	16.1
27	Maine	15.9
28	Oregon	15.4
29	Texas	15.3
30	California	15.1
30	Georgia	15.1
32	New York	15.0
33	Missouri	14.9
34	New Jersey	14.6
35	Arizona	14.4
35	Delaware	14.4
35	Minnesota	14.4
38	Tennessee	14.1
39	Ohio	14.0
40	Illinois	13.9
41	Michigan	13.8
42	Wisconsin	13.6
43	Indiana	13.5
44	Connecticut	13.3
45	New Hampshire	13.1
46	Florida	12.4
47	Massachusetts	12.3
48	Rhode Island	12.0
49	Nevada	11.9
50	Pennsylvania	11.6

District of Columbia	29.8

Source: CQ Press using data from U.S. Department of Labor, Bureau of Labor Statistics
"State Employment and Unemployment" (press release, January 18, 2019, www.bls.gov/bls/newsrels.htm)
*Seasonally adjusted preliminary data as of December 2018. National figure calculated through a different formula.

Employees in Leisure and Hospitality in 2018

National Total = 16,513,000 Employees*

ALPHA ORDER

ALPHA ORDER

RANK	STATE	EMPLOYEES	% of USA
27	Alabama	205,700	1.2%
49	Alaska	36,400	0.2%
18	Arizona	334,800	2.0%
36	Arkansas	118,300	0.7%
1	California	2,035,900	12.3%
15	Colorado	352,400	2.1%
30	Connecticut	160,500	1.0%
45	Delaware	50,500	0.3%
3	Florida	1,267,500	7.7%
9	Georgia	498,900	3.0%
35	Hawaii	128,800	0.8%
39	Idaho	77,300	0.5%
5	Illinois	624,100	3.8%
20	Indiana	304,800	1.8%
32	Iowa	143,500	0.9%
34	Kansas	131,300	0.8%
28	Kentucky	193,200	1.2%
25	Louisiana	238,700	1.4%
42	Maine	67,600	0.4%
22	Maryland	284,100	1.7%
13	Massachusetts	375,600	2.3%
10	Michigan	443,400	2.7%
23	Minnesota	281,400	1.7%
33	Mississippi	140,000	0.8%
19	Missouri	320,000	1.9%
43	Montana	66,400	0.4%
38	Nebraska	96,500	0.6%
14	Nevada	357,700	2.2%
40	New Hampshire	76,400	0.5%
12	New Jersey	383,100	2.3%
37	New Mexico	105,800	0.6%
4	New York	964,400	5.8%
8	North Carolina	506,600	3.1%
47	North Dakota	39,000	0.2%
7	Ohio	580,000	3.5%
29	Oklahoma	176,100	1.1%
26	Oregon	220,200	1.3%
6	Pennsylvania	589,400	3.6%
44	Rhode Island	58,600	0.4%
24	South Carolina	268,900	1.6%
46	South Dakota	47,800	0.3%
16	Tennessee	352,100	2.1%
2	Texas	1,385,200	8.4%
31	Utah	153,800	0.9%
50	Vermont	36,000	0.2%
11	Virginia	415,900	2.5%
17	Washington	342,200	2.1%
41	West Virginia	74,900	0.5%
21	Wisconsin	295,200	1.8%
48	Wyoming	38,400	0.2%

RANK ORDER

RANK	STATE	EMPLOYEES	% of USA
1	California	2,035,900	12.3%
2	Texas	1,385,200	8.4%
3	Florida	1,267,500	7.7%
4	New York	964,400	5.8%
5	Illinois	624,100	3.8%
6	Pennsylvania	589,400	3.6%
7	Ohio	580,000	3.5%
8	North Carolina	506,600	3.1%
9	Georgia	498,900	3.0%
10	Michigan	443,400	2.7%
11	Virginia	415,900	2.5%
12	New Jersey	383,100	2.3%
13	Massachusetts	375,600	2.3%
14	Nevada	357,700	2.2%
15	Colorado	352,400	2.1%
16	Tennessee	352,100	2.1%
17	Washington	342,200	2.1%
18	Arizona	334,800	2.0%
19	Missouri	320,000	1.9%
20	Indiana	304,800	1.8%
21	Wisconsin	295,200	1.8%
22	Maryland	284,100	1.7%
23	Minnesota	281,400	1.7%
24	South Carolina	268,900	1.6%
25	Louisiana	238,700	1.4%
26	Oregon	220,200	1.3%
27	Alabama	205,700	1.2%
28	Kentucky	193,200	1.2%
29	Oklahoma	176,100	1.1%
30	Connecticut	160,500	1.0%
31	Utah	153,800	0.9%
32	Iowa	143,500	0.9%
33	Mississippi	140,000	0.8%
34	Kansas	131,300	0.8%
35	Hawaii	128,800	0.8%
36	Arkansas	118,300	0.7%
37	New Mexico	105,800	0.6%
38	Nebraska	96,500	0.6%
39	Idaho	77,300	0.5%
40	New Hampshire	76,400	0.5%
41	West Virginia	74,900	0.5%
42	Maine	67,600	0.4%
43	Montana	66,400	0.4%
44	Rhode Island	58,600	0.4%
45	Delaware	50,500	0.3%
46	South Dakota	47,800	0.3%
47	North Dakota	39,000	0.2%
48	Wyoming	38,400	0.2%
49	Alaska	36,400	0.2%
50	Vermont	36,000	0.2%
	District of Columbia	79,000	0.5%

Source: U.S. Department of Labor, Bureau of Labor Statistics
"State Employment and Unemployment" (press release, January 18, 2019, www.bls.gov/bls/newsrels.htm)
*Seasonally adjusted preliminary data as of December 2018. National total calculated through a different formula.

Percent of Nonfarm Employees in Leisure and Hospitality in 2018

National Percent = 11.0% of Employees*

ALPHA ORDER				RANK ORDER		
RANK	STATE	PERCENT		RANK	STATE	PERCENT
33	Alabama	10.0		1	Nevada	25.3
17	Alaska	11.2		2	Hawaii	19.3
12	Arizona	11.6		3	Florida	14.3
44	Arkansas	9.4		4	Montana	13.8
11	California	11.8		5	Wyoming	13.2
6	Colorado	12.8		6	Colorado	12.8
44	Connecticut	9.4		7	South Carolina	12.5
22	Delaware	10.8		8	New Mexico	12.4
3	Florida	14.3		9	Louisiana	12.0
22	Georgia	10.8		10	Mississippi	11.9
2	Hawaii	19.3		11	California	11.8
26	Idaho	10.4		12	Arizona	11.6
32	Illinois	10.1		12	Rhode Island	11.6
42	Indiana	9.6		14	Vermont	11.5
49	Iowa	9.0		15	Oregon	11.4
47	Kansas	9.2		15	Tennessee	11.4
36	Kentucky	9.9		17	Alaska	11.2
9	Louisiana	12.0		17	North Carolina	11.2
22	Maine	10.8		19	Missouri	11.0
27	Maryland	10.3		19	New Hampshire	11.0
31	Massachusetts	10.2		21	Texas	10.9
33	Michigan	10.0		22	Delaware	10.8
43	Minnesota	9.5		22	Georgia	10.8
10	Mississippi	11.9		22	Maine	10.8
19	Missouri	11.0		25	South Dakota	10.7
4	Montana	13.8		26	Idaho	10.4
46	Nebraska	9.3		27	Maryland	10.3
1	Nevada	25.3		27	Ohio	10.3
19	New Hampshire	11.0		27	Oklahoma	10.3
48	New Jersey	9.1		27	Virginia	10.3
8	New Mexico	12.4		31	Massachusetts	10.2
36	New York	9.9		32	Illinois	10.1
17	North Carolina	11.2		33	Alabama	10.0
49	North Dakota	9.0		33	Michigan	10.0
27	Ohio	10.3		33	Utah	10.0
27	Oklahoma	10.3		36	Kentucky	9.9
15	Oregon	11.4		36	New York	9.9
41	Pennsylvania	9.7		36	West Virginia	9.9
12	Rhode Island	11.6		39	Washington	9.8
7	South Carolina	12.5		39	Wisconsin	9.8
25	South Dakota	10.7		41	Pennsylvania	9.7
15	Tennessee	11.4		42	Indiana	9.6
21	Texas	10.9		43	Minnesota	9.5
33	Utah	10.0		44	Arkansas	9.4
14	Vermont	11.5		44	Connecticut	9.4
27	Virginia	10.3		46	Nebraska	9.3
39	Washington	9.8		47	Kansas	9.2
36	West Virginia	9.9		48	New Jersey	9.1
39	Wisconsin	9.8		49	Iowa	9.0
5	Wyoming	13.2		49	North Dakota	9.0
					District of Columbia	9.9

Source: CQ Press using data from U.S. Department of Labor, Bureau of Labor Statistics
"State Employment and Unemployment" (press release, January 18, 2019, www.bls.gov/bls/newsrels.htm)
*Seasonally adjusted preliminary data as of December 2018. National figure calculated through a different formula.

Employees in Manufacturing in 2018

National Total = 12,842,000 Employees*

ALPHA ORDER

RANK	STATE	EMPLOYEES	% of USA
16	Alabama	276,300	2.2%
49	Alaska	12,500	0.1%
25	Arizona	176,600	1.4%
28	Arkansas	161,700	1.3%
1	California	1,322,200	10.3%
29	Colorado	149,800	1.2%
27	Connecticut	164,100	1.3%
45	Delaware	26,200	0.2%
12	Florida	379,500	3.0%
11	Georgia	404,400	3.1%
48	Hawaii	13,900	0.1%
37	Idaho	70,400	0.5%
5	Illinois	591,500	4.6%
7	Indiana	535,800	4.2%
23	Iowa	230,600	1.8%
26	Kansas	167,000	1.3%
19	Kentucky	253,500	2.0%
31	Louisiana	139,300	1.1%
39	Maine	52,900	0.4%
34	Maryland	108,500	0.8%
21	Massachusetts	247,500	1.9%
4	Michigan	625,300	4.9%
14	Minnesota	325,300	2.5%
30	Mississippi	146,900	1.1%
17	Missouri	273,700	2.1%
47	Montana	20,200	0.2%
35	Nebraska	102,900	0.8%
38	Nevada	58,200	0.5%
36	New Hampshire	72,700	0.6%
18	New Jersey	255,700	2.0%
44	New Mexico	27,000	0.2%
10	New York	445,800	3.5%
9	North Carolina	475,600	3.7%
46	North Dakota	25,200	0.2%
3	Ohio	705,700	5.5%
33	Oklahoma	131,600	1.0%
24	Oregon	195,200	1.5%
6	Pennsylvania	566,200	4.4%
42	Rhode Island	40,900	0.3%
22	South Carolina	246,700	1.9%
41	South Dakota	45,400	0.4%
13	Tennessee	355,600	2.8%
2	Texas	896,700	7.0%
32	Utah	135,100	1.1%
43	Vermont	30,100	0.2%
20	Virginia	248,100	1.9%
15	Washington	296,500	2.3%
40	West Virginia	47,200	0.4%
8	Wisconsin	490,400	3.8%
50	Wyoming	10,000	0.1%

RANK ORDER

RANK	STATE	EMPLOYEES	% of USA
1	California	1,322,200	10.3%
2	Texas	896,700	7.0%
3	Ohio	705,700	5.5%
4	Michigan	625,300	4.9%
5	Illinois	591,500	4.6%
6	Pennsylvania	566,200	4.4%
7	Indiana	535,800	4.2%
8	Wisconsin	490,400	3.8%
9	North Carolina	475,600	3.7%
10	New York	445,800	3.5%
11	Georgia	404,400	3.1%
12	Florida	379,500	3.0%
13	Tennessee	355,600	2.8%
14	Minnesota	325,300	2.5%
15	Washington	296,500	2.3%
16	Alabama	276,300	2.2%
17	Missouri	273,700	2.1%
18	New Jersey	255,700	2.0%
19	Kentucky	253,500	2.0%
20	Virginia	248,100	1.9%
21	Massachusetts	247,500	1.9%
22	South Carolina	246,700	1.9%
23	Iowa	230,600	1.8%
24	Oregon	195,200	1.5%
25	Arizona	176,600	1.4%
26	Kansas	167,000	1.3%
27	Connecticut	164,100	1.3%
28	Arkansas	161,700	1.3%
29	Colorado	149,800	1.2%
30	Mississippi	146,900	1.1%
31	Louisiana	139,300	1.1%
32	Utah	135,100	1.1%
33	Oklahoma	131,600	1.0%
34	Maryland	108,500	0.8%
35	Nebraska	102,900	0.8%
36	New Hampshire	72,700	0.6%
37	Idaho	70,400	0.5%
38	Nevada	58,200	0.5%
39	Maine	52,900	0.4%
40	West Virginia	47,200	0.4%
41	South Dakota	45,400	0.4%
42	Rhode Island	40,900	0.3%
43	Vermont	30,100	0.2%
44	New Mexico	27,000	0.2%
45	Delaware	26,200	0.2%
46	North Dakota	25,200	0.2%
47	Montana	20,200	0.2%
48	Hawaii	13,900	0.1%
49	Alaska	12,500	0.1%
50	Wyoming	10,000	0.1%
	District of Columbia	1,400	0.0%

Source: U.S. Department of Labor, Bureau of Labor Statistics
"State Employment and Unemployment" (press release, January 18, 2019, www.bls.gov/bls/newsrels.htm)
*Seasonally adjusted preliminary data as of December 2018. National total calculated through a different formula.

Percent of Nonfarm Employees in Manufacturing in 2018

National Percent = 8.5% of Employees*

ALPHA ORDER				RANK ORDER		
RANK	STATE	PERCENT		RANK	STATE	PERCENT
5	Alabama	13.4		1	Indiana	17.0
47	Alaska	3.8		2	Wisconsin	16.3
37	Arizona	6.1		3	Iowa	14.4
7	Arkansas	12.9		4	Michigan	14.1
31	California	7.6		5	Alabama	13.4
41	Colorado	5.4		6	Kentucky	13.0
19	Connecticut	9.6		7	Arkansas	12.9
40	Delaware	5.6		8	Mississippi	12.5
43	Florida	4.3		8	Ohio	12.5
25	Georgia	8.8		10	Kansas	11.7
50	Hawaii	2.1		11	South Carolina	11.5
22	Idaho	9.5		11	Tennessee	11.5
19	Illinois	9.6		13	Minnesota	10.9
1	Indiana	17.0		14	North Carolina	10.5
3	Iowa	14.4		15	New Hampshire	10.4
10	Kansas	11.7		16	South Dakota	10.2
6	Kentucky	13.0		17	Oregon	10.1
32	Louisiana	7.0		18	Nebraska	10.0
28	Maine	8.4		19	Connecticut	9.6
46	Maryland	3.9		19	Illinois	9.6
34	Massachusetts	6.7		19	Vermont	9.6
4	Michigan	14.1		22	Idaho	9.5
13	Minnesota	10.9		23	Missouri	9.4
8	Mississippi	12.5		24	Pennsylvania	9.3
23	Missouri	9.4		25	Georgia	8.8
44	Montana	4.2		25	Utah	8.8
18	Nebraska	10.0		27	Washington	8.5
45	Nevada	4.1		28	Maine	8.4
15	New Hampshire	10.4		29	Rhode Island	8.1
37	New Jersey	6.1		30	Oklahoma	7.7
49	New Mexico	3.2		31	California	7.6
42	New York	4.6		32	Louisiana	7.0
14	North Carolina	10.5		32	Texas	7.0
39	North Dakota	5.8		34	Massachusetts	6.7
8	Ohio	12.5		35	West Virginia	6.3
30	Oklahoma	7.7		36	Virginia	6.2
17	Oregon	10.1		37	Arizona	6.1
24	Pennsylvania	9.3		37	New Jersey	6.1
29	Rhode Island	8.1		39	North Dakota	5.8
11	South Carolina	11.5		40	Delaware	5.6
16	South Dakota	10.2		41	Colorado	5.4
11	Tennessee	11.5		42	New York	4.6
32	Texas	7.0		43	Florida	4.3
25	Utah	8.8		44	Montana	4.2
19	Vermont	9.6		45	Nevada	4.1
36	Virginia	6.2		46	Maryland	3.9
27	Washington	8.5		47	Alaska	3.8
35	West Virginia	6.3		48	Wyoming	3.4
2	Wisconsin	16.3		49	New Mexico	3.2
48	Wyoming	3.4		50	Hawaii	2.1
					District of Columbia	0.2

Source: CQ Press using data from U.S. Department of Labor, Bureau of Labor Statistics
   "State Employment and Unemployment" (press release, January 18, 2019, www.bls.gov/bls/newsrels.htm)
*Seasonally adjusted preliminary data as of December 2018. National figure calculated through a different formula.

Employees in Mining and Logging in 2018

National Total = 759,000 Employees*

ALPHA ORDER

RANK	STATE	EMPLOYEES	% of USA
16	Alabama	10,000	1.3%
12	Alaska	13,200	1.7%
14	Arizona	11,800	1.6%
31	Arkansas	5,300	0.7%
6	California	22,100	2.9%
4	Colorado	32,200	4.2%
47	Connecticut	500	0.1%
NA	Delaware**	NA	NA
29	Florida	5,800	0.8%
17	Georgia	9,400	1.2%
NA	Hawaii**	NA	NA
37	Idaho	3,500	0.5%
20	Illinois	7,500	1.0%
26	Indiana	6,300	0.8%
38	Iowa	2,400	0.3%
21	Kansas	7,200	0.9%
15	Kentucky	10,500	1.4%
3	Louisiana	34,800	4.6%
39	Maine	2,300	0.3%
42	Maryland	1,100	0.1%
41	Massachusetts	1,200	0.2%
23	Michigan	6,900	0.9%
27	Minnesota	6,000	0.8%
25	Mississippi	6,500	0.9%
35	Missouri	4,200	0.6%
21	Montana	7,200	0.9%
42	Nebraska	1,100	0.1%
11	Nevada	14,400	1.9%
44	New Hampshire	900	0.1%
40	New Jersey	1,300	0.2%
6	New Mexico	22,100	2.9%
32	New York	4,800	0.6%
30	North Carolina	5,500	0.7%
8	North Dakota	21,700	2.9%
13	Ohio	12,700	1.7%
2	Oklahoma	57,000	7.5%
24	Oregon	6,700	0.9%
5	Pennsylvania	30,600	4.0%
48	Rhode Island	200	0.0%
33	South Carolina	4,500	0.6%
44	South Dakota	900	0.1%
36	Tennessee	4,100	0.5%
1	Texas	271,700	35.8%
19	Utah	8,300	1.1%
46	Vermont	700	0.1%
18	Virginia	8,400	1.1%
27	Washington	6,000	0.8%
8	West Virginia	21,700	2.9%
34	Wisconsin	4,400	0.6%
10	Wyoming	21,200	2.8%

RANK ORDER

RANK	STATE	EMPLOYEES	% of USA
1	Texas	271,700	35.8%
2	Oklahoma	57,000	7.5%
3	Louisiana	34,800	4.6%
4	Colorado	32,200	4.2%
5	Pennsylvania	30,600	4.0%
6	California	22,100	2.9%
6	New Mexico	22,100	2.9%
8	North Dakota	21,700	2.9%
8	West Virginia	21,700	2.9%
10	Wyoming	21,200	2.8%
11	Nevada	14,400	1.9%
12	Alaska	13,200	1.7%
13	Ohio	12,700	1.7%
14	Arizona	11,800	1.6%
15	Kentucky	10,500	1.4%
16	Alabama	10,000	1.3%
17	Georgia	9,400	1.2%
18	Virginia	8,400	1.1%
19	Utah	8,300	1.1%
20	Illinois	7,500	1.0%
21	Kansas	7,200	0.9%
21	Montana	7,200	0.9%
23	Michigan	6,900	0.9%
24	Oregon	6,700	0.9%
25	Mississippi	6,500	0.9%
26	Indiana	6,300	0.8%
27	Minnesota	6,000	0.8%
27	Washington	6,000	0.8%
29	Florida	5,800	0.8%
30	North Carolina	5,500	0.7%
31	Arkansas	5,300	0.7%
32	New York	4,800	0.6%
33	South Carolina	4,500	0.6%
34	Wisconsin	4,400	0.6%
35	Missouri	4,200	0.6%
36	Tennessee	4,100	0.5%
37	Idaho	3,500	0.5%
38	Iowa	2,400	0.3%
39	Maine	2,300	0.3%
40	New Jersey	1,300	0.2%
41	Massachusetts	1,200	0.2%
42	Maryland	1,100	0.1%
42	Nebraska	1,100	0.1%
44	New Hampshire	900	0.1%
44	South Dakota	900	0.1%
46	Vermont	700	0.1%
47	Connecticut	500	0.1%
48	Rhode Island	200	0.0%
NA	Delaware**	NA	NA
NA	Hawaii**	NA	NA
	District of Columbia**	NA	NA

Source: U.S. Department of Labor, Bureau of Labor Statistics
   "State Employment and Unemployment" (press release, January 18, 2019, www.bls.gov/bls/newsrels.htm)
*Not seasonally adjusted preliminary data as of December 2018. National total calculated through a different formula.
**The Bureau of Labor Statistics does not publish figures in this category for these states.

Percent of Nonfarm Employees in Mining and Logging in 2018

National Percent = 0.5% of Employees*

ALPHA ORDER				RANK ORDER		
RANK	STATE	PERCENT		RANK	STATE	PERCENT
13	Alabama	0.5		1	Wyoming	7.3
3	Alaska	4.2		2	North Dakota	5.0
19	Arizona	0.4		3	Alaska	4.2
19	Arkansas	0.4		4	Oklahoma	3.3
33	California	0.1		5	West Virginia	2.8
10	Colorado	1.2		6	New Mexico	2.6
43	Connecticut	0.0		7	Texas	2.1
NA	Delaware**	NA		8	Louisiana	1.7
33	Florida	0.1		9	Montana	1.5
23	Georgia	0.2		10	Colorado	1.2
NA	Hawaii**	NA		11	Nevada	1.0
13	Idaho	0.5		12	Mississippi	0.6
33	Illinois	0.1		13	Alabama	0.5
23	Indiana	0.2		13	Idaho	0.5
33	Iowa	0.1		13	Kansas	0.5
13	Kansas	0.5		13	Kentucky	0.5
13	Kentucky	0.5		13	Pennsylvania	0.5
8	Louisiana	1.7		13	Utah	0.5
19	Maine	0.4		19	Arizona	0.4
43	Maryland	0.0		19	Arkansas	0.4
43	Massachusetts	0.0		19	Maine	0.4
23	Michigan	0.2		22	Oregon	0.3
23	Minnesota	0.2		23	Georgia	0.2
12	Mississippi	0.6		23	Indiana	0.2
33	Missouri	0.1		23	Michigan	0.2
9	Montana	1.5		23	Minnesota	0.2
33	Nebraska	0.1		23	Ohio	0.2
11	Nevada	1.0		23	South Carolina	0.2
33	New Hampshire	0.1		23	South Dakota	0.2
43	New Jersey	0.0		23	Vermont	0.2
6	New Mexico	2.6		23	Virginia	0.2
43	New York	0.0		23	Washington	0.2
33	North Carolina	0.1		33	California	0.1
2	North Dakota	5.0		33	Florida	0.1
23	Ohio	0.2		33	Illinois	0.1
4	Oklahoma	3.3		33	Iowa	0.1
22	Oregon	0.3		33	Missouri	0.1
13	Pennsylvania	0.5		33	Nebraska	0.1
43	Rhode Island	0.0		33	New Hampshire	0.1
23	South Carolina	0.2		33	North Carolina	0.1
23	South Dakota	0.2		33	Tennessee	0.1
33	Tennessee	0.1		33	Wisconsin	0.1
7	Texas	2.1		43	Connecticut	0.0
13	Utah	0.5		43	Maryland	0.0
23	Vermont	0.2		43	Massachusetts	0.0
23	Virginia	0.2		43	New Jersey	0.0
23	Washington	0.2		43	New York	0.0
5	West Virginia	2.8		43	Rhode Island	0.0
33	Wisconsin	0.1		NA	Delaware**	NA
1	Wyoming	7.3		NA	Hawaii**	NA
					District of Columbia**	NA

Source: CQ Press using data from U.S. Department of Labor, Bureau of Labor Statistics

"State Employment and Unemployment" (press release, January 18, 2019, www.bls.gov/bls/newsrels.htm)

*Not seasonally adjusted preliminary data as of December 2018. National figure calculated through a different formula.

**The Bureau of Labor Statistics does not publish seasonally adjusted figures in this category for these states.

Employees in Professional and Business Services in 2018

National Total = 21,260,000 Employees*

ALPHA ORDER

RANK	STATE	EMPLOYEES	% of USA
24	Alabama	253,000	1.2%
49	Alaska	27,600	0.1%
17	Arizona	439,800	2.1%
33	Arkansas	149,700	0.7%
1	California	2,674,300	12.6%
16	Colorado	439,900	2.1%
26	Connecticut	220,800	1.0%
44	Delaware	64,300	0.3%
3	Florida	1,378,800	6.5%
9	Georgia	700,200	3.3%
39	Hawaii	85,300	0.4%
38	Idaho	95,600	0.4%
5	Illinois	944,200	4.4%
21	Indiana	346,500	1.6%
34	Iowa	143,000	0.7%
32	Kansas	186,500	0.9%
27	Kentucky	220,000	1.0%
29	Louisiana	212,300	1.0%
42	Maine	66,900	0.3%
14	Maryland	466,400	2.2%
13	Massachusetts	602,500	2.8%
11	Michigan	659,600	3.1%
20	Minnesota	376,300	1.8%
36	Mississippi	117,700	0.6%
19	Missouri	398,400	1.9%
45	Montana	43,500	0.2%
35	Nebraska	122,300	0.6%
30	Nevada	192,300	0.9%
40	New Hampshire	81,500	0.4%
10	New Jersey	686,800	3.2%
37	New Mexico	108,200	0.5%
4	New York	1,342,600	6.3%
12	North Carolina	646,000	3.0%
46	North Dakota	35,700	0.2%
8	Ohio	727,100	3.4%
31	Oklahoma	191,200	0.9%
25	Oregon	249,100	1.2%
6	Pennsylvania	829,200	3.9%
41	Rhode Island	70,300	0.3%
23	South Carolina	286,800	1.3%
47	South Dakota	34,900	0.2%
18	Tennessee	419,000	2.0%
2	Texas	1,767,500	8.3%
28	Utah	212,500	1.0%
48	Vermont	29,000	0.1%
7	Virginia	750,600	3.5%
15	Washington	440,000	2.1%
43	West Virginia	65,200	0.3%
22	Wisconsin	321,700	1.5%
50	Wyoming	19,200	0.1%

RANK ORDER

RANK	STATE	EMPLOYEES	% of USA
1	California	2,674,300	12.6%
2	Texas	1,767,500	8.3%
3	Florida	1,378,800	6.5%
4	New York	1,342,600	6.3%
5	Illinois	944,200	4.4%
6	Pennsylvania	829,200	3.9%
7	Virginia	750,600	3.5%
8	Ohio	727,100	3.4%
9	Georgia	700,200	3.3%
10	New Jersey	686,800	3.2%
11	Michigan	659,600	3.1%
12	North Carolina	646,000	3.0%
13	Massachusetts	602,500	2.8%
14	Maryland	466,400	2.2%
15	Washington	440,000	2.1%
16	Colorado	439,900	2.1%
17	Arizona	439,800	2.1%
18	Tennessee	419,000	2.0%
19	Missouri	398,400	1.9%
20	Minnesota	376,300	1.8%
21	Indiana	346,500	1.6%
22	Wisconsin	321,700	1.5%
23	South Carolina	286,800	1.3%
24	Alabama	253,000	1.2%
25	Oregon	249,100	1.2%
26	Connecticut	220,800	1.0%
27	Kentucky	220,000	1.0%
28	Utah	212,500	1.0%
29	Louisiana	212,300	1.0%
30	Nevada	192,300	0.9%
31	Oklahoma	191,200	0.9%
32	Kansas	186,500	0.9%
33	Arkansas	149,700	0.7%
34	Iowa	143,000	0.7%
35	Nebraska	122,300	0.6%
36	Mississippi	117,700	0.6%
37	New Mexico	108,200	0.5%
38	Idaho	95,600	0.4%
39	Hawaii	85,300	0.4%
40	New Hampshire	81,500	0.4%
41	Rhode Island	70,300	0.3%
42	Maine	66,900	0.3%
43	West Virginia	65,200	0.3%
44	Delaware	64,300	0.3%
45	Montana	43,500	0.2%
46	North Dakota	35,700	0.2%
47	South Dakota	34,900	0.2%
48	Vermont	29,000	0.1%
49	Alaska	27,600	0.1%
50	Wyoming	19,200	0.1%
	District of Columbia	168,100	0.8%

Source: U.S. Department of Labor, Bureau of Labor Statistics
   "State Employment and Unemployment" (press release, January 18, 2019, www.bls.gov/bls/newsrels.htm)
*Seasonally adjusted preliminary data as of December 2018. National total calculated through a different formula.

Percent of Nonfarm Employees in Professional and Business Services in 2018

National Percent = 14.1% of Employees*

ALPHA ORDER				RANK ORDER		
RANK	STATE	PERCENT		RANK	STATE	PERCENT
32	Alabama	12.3		1	Virginia	18.6
47	Alaska	8.5		2	Maryland	16.9
9	Arizona	15.2		3	Massachusetts	16.3
33	Arkansas	11.9		3	New Jersey	16.3
6	California	15.5		5	Colorado	15.9
5	Colorado	15.9		6	California	15.5
24	Connecticut	12.9		6	Florida	15.5
15	Delaware	13.8		8	Illinois	15.3
6	Florida	15.5		9	Arizona	15.2
9	Georgia	15.2		9	Georgia	15.2
28	Hawaii	12.8		11	Michigan	14.8
24	Idaho	12.9		12	North Carolina	14.2
8	Illinois	15.3		13	Rhode Island	13.9
38	Indiana	11.0		13	Texas	13.9
45	Iowa	8.9		15	Delaware	13.8
23	Kansas	13.0		15	New York	13.8
36	Kentucky	11.3		15	Utah	13.8
39	Louisiana	10.7		18	Pennsylvania	13.7
39	Maine	10.7		19	Missouri	13.6
2	Maryland	16.9		19	Nevada	13.6
3	Massachusetts	16.3		19	Tennessee	13.6
11	Michigan	14.8		22	South Carolina	13.3
30	Minnesota	12.6		23	Kansas	13.0
42	Mississippi	10.0		24	Connecticut	12.9
19	Missouri	13.6		24	Idaho	12.9
44	Montana	9.0		24	Ohio	12.9
34	Nebraska	11.8		24	Oregon	12.9
19	Nevada	13.6		28	Hawaii	12.8
35	New Hampshire	11.7		29	Washington	12.7
3	New Jersey	16.3		30	Minnesota	12.6
30	New Mexico	12.6		30	New Mexico	12.6
15	New York	13.8		32	Alabama	12.3
12	North Carolina	14.2		33	Arkansas	11.9
48	North Dakota	8.2		34	Nebraska	11.8
24	Ohio	12.9		35	New Hampshire	11.7
37	Oklahoma	11.2		36	Kentucky	11.3
24	Oregon	12.9		37	Oklahoma	11.2
18	Pennsylvania	13.7		38	Indiana	11.0
13	Rhode Island	13.9		39	Louisiana	10.7
22	South Carolina	13.3		39	Maine	10.7
49	South Dakota	7.8		39	Wisconsin	10.7
19	Tennessee	13.6		42	Mississippi	10.0
13	Texas	13.9		43	Vermont	9.3
15	Utah	13.8		44	Montana	9.0
43	Vermont	9.3		45	Iowa	8.9
1	Virginia	18.6		46	West Virginia	8.7
29	Washington	12.7		47	Alaska	8.5
46	West Virginia	8.7		48	North Dakota	8.2
39	Wisconsin	10.7		49	South Dakota	7.8
50	Wyoming	6.6		50	Wyoming	6.6
					District of Columbia	21.1

Source: CQ Press using data from U.S. Department of Labor, Bureau of Labor Statistics

"State Employment and Unemployment" (press release, January 18, 2019, www.bls.gov/bls/newsrels.htm)

*Seasonally adjusted preliminary data as of December 2018. National figure calculated through a different formula.

Employees in Trade, Transportation, and Public Utilities in 2018

National Total = 27,963,000 Employees*

ALPHA ORDER

RANK	STATE	EMPLOYEES	% of USA
26	Alabama	380,000	1.4%
48	Alaska	62,600	0.2%
20	Arizona	533,600	1.9%
34	Arkansas	252,200	0.9%
1	California	3,075,800	11.0%
21	Colorado	475,600	1.7%
31	Connecticut	295,000	1.1%
46	Delaware	81,700	0.3%
3	Florida	1,779,900	6.4%
8	Georgia	973,600	3.5%
41	Hawaii	121,600	0.4%
38	Idaho	142,300	0.5%
5	Illinois	1,223,800	4.4%
15	Indiana	609,000	2.2%
28	Iowa	315,700	1.1%
32	Kansas	273,200	1.0%
23	Kentucky	416,700	1.5%
25	Louisiana	380,500	1.4%
42	Maine	120,800	0.4%
22	Maryland	470,300	1.7%
16	Massachusetts	585,600	2.1%
11	Michigan	792,600	2.8%
18	Minnesota	545,300	2.0%
35	Mississippi	231,200	0.8%
17	Missouri	546,400	2.0%
43	Montana	93,700	0.3%
36	Nebraska	199,700	0.7%
33	Nevada	257,700	0.9%
37	New Hampshire	142,700	0.5%
9	New Jersey	908,000	3.2%
39	New Mexico	137,100	0.5%
4	New York	1,585,100	5.7%
10	North Carolina	856,500	3.1%
44	North Dakota	93,200	0.3%
7	Ohio	1,043,800	3.7%
29	Oklahoma	310,400	1.1%
27	Oregon	354,700	1.3%
6	Pennsylvania	1,129,600	4.0%
47	Rhode Island	77,400	0.3%
24	South Carolina	414,400	1.5%
45	South Dakota	87,700	0.3%
14	Tennessee	635,300	2.3%
2	Texas	2,553,100	9.1%
30	Utah	296,000	1.1%
49	Vermont	53,600	0.2%
12	Virginia	670,900	2.4%
13	Washington	658,800	2.4%
40	West Virginia	133,000	0.5%
19	Wisconsin	542,200	1.9%
50	Wyoming	53,300	0.2%

RANK ORDER

RANK	STATE	EMPLOYEES	% of USA
1	California	3,075,800	11.0%
2	Texas	2,553,100	9.1%
3	Florida	1,779,900	6.4%
4	New York	1,585,100	5.7%
5	Illinois	1,223,800	4.4%
6	Pennsylvania	1,129,600	4.0%
7	Ohio	1,043,800	3.7%
8	Georgia	973,600	3.5%
9	New Jersey	908,000	3.2%
10	North Carolina	856,500	3.1%
11	Michigan	792,600	2.8%
12	Virginia	670,900	2.4%
13	Washington	658,800	2.4%
14	Tennessee	635,300	2.3%
15	Indiana	609,000	2.2%
16	Massachusetts	585,600	2.1%
17	Missouri	546,400	2.0%
18	Minnesota	545,300	2.0%
19	Wisconsin	542,200	1.9%
20	Arizona	533,600	1.9%
21	Colorado	475,600	1.7%
22	Maryland	470,300	1.7%
23	Kentucky	416,700	1.5%
24	South Carolina	414,400	1.5%
25	Louisiana	380,500	1.4%
26	Alabama	380,000	1.4%
27	Oregon	354,700	1.3%
28	Iowa	315,700	1.1%
29	Oklahoma	310,400	1.1%
30	Utah	296,000	1.1%
31	Connecticut	295,000	1.1%
32	Kansas	273,200	1.0%
33	Nevada	257,700	0.9%
34	Arkansas	252,200	0.9%
35	Mississippi	231,200	0.8%
36	Nebraska	199,700	0.7%
37	New Hampshire	142,700	0.5%
38	Idaho	142,300	0.5%
39	New Mexico	137,100	0.5%
40	West Virginia	133,000	0.5%
41	Hawaii	121,600	0.4%
42	Maine	120,800	0.4%
43	Montana	93,700	0.3%
44	North Dakota	93,200	0.3%
45	South Dakota	87,700	0.3%
46	Delaware	81,700	0.3%
47	Rhode Island	77,400	0.3%
48	Alaska	62,600	0.2%
49	Vermont	53,600	0.2%
50	Wyoming	53,300	0.2%
	District of Columbia	33,400	0.1%

Source: U.S. Department of Labor, Bureau of Labor Statistics

"State Employment and Unemployment" (press release, January 18, 2019, www.bls.gov/bls/newsrels.htm)

*Seasonally adjusted preliminary data as of December 2018. National total calculated through a different formula.

Percent of Nonfarm Employees in
Trade, Transportation, and Public Utilities in 2018
National Percent = 18.6% of Employees*

ALPHA ORDER

RANK	STATE	PERCENT
30	Alabama	18.4
19	Alaska	19.2
28	Arizona	18.5
7	Arkansas	20.1
38	California	17.8
43	Colorado	17.2
42	Connecticut	17.3
41	Delaware	17.5
8	Florida	20.0
4	Georgia	21.2
34	Hawaii	18.2
19	Idaho	19.2
10	Illinois	19.9
15	Indiana	19.3
11	Iowa	19.8
22	Kansas	19.1
2	Kentucky	21.4
22	Louisiana	19.1
19	Maine	19.2
45	Maryland	17.0
49	Massachusetts	15.9
38	Michigan	17.8
32	Minnesota	18.3
12	Mississippi	19.7
26	Missouri	18.7
14	Montana	19.5
15	Nebraska	19.3
34	Nevada	18.2
6	New Hampshire	20.5
1	New Jersey	21.6
48	New Mexico	16.0
47	New York	16.3
25	North Carolina	18.9
2	North Dakota	21.4
28	Ohio	18.5
34	Oklahoma	18.2
30	Oregon	18.4
27	Pennsylvania	18.6
50	Rhode Island	15.3
15	South Carolina	19.3
13	South Dakota	19.6
5	Tennessee	20.6
8	Texas	20.0
15	Utah	19.3
44	Vermont	17.1
46	Virginia	16.6
24	Washington	19.0
40	West Virginia	17.7
37	Wisconsin	18.1
32	Wyoming	18.3

RANK ORDER

RANK	STATE	PERCENT
1	New Jersey	21.6
2	Kentucky	21.4
2	North Dakota	21.4
4	Georgia	21.2
5	Tennessee	20.6
6	New Hampshire	20.5
7	Arkansas	20.1
8	Florida	20.0
8	Texas	20.0
10	Illinois	19.9
11	Iowa	19.8
12	Mississippi	19.7
13	South Dakota	19.6
14	Montana	19.5
15	Indiana	19.3
15	Nebraska	19.3
15	South Carolina	19.3
15	Utah	19.3
19	Alaska	19.2
19	Idaho	19.2
19	Maine	19.2
22	Kansas	19.1
22	Louisiana	19.1
24	Washington	19.0
25	North Carolina	18.9
26	Missouri	18.7
27	Pennsylvania	18.6
28	Arizona	18.5
28	Ohio	18.5
30	Alabama	18.4
30	Oregon	18.4
32	Minnesota	18.3
32	Wyoming	18.3
34	Hawaii	18.2
34	Nevada	18.2
34	Oklahoma	18.2
37	Wisconsin	18.1
38	California	17.8
38	Michigan	17.8
40	West Virginia	17.7
41	Delaware	17.5
42	Connecticut	17.3
43	Colorado	17.2
44	Vermont	17.1
45	Maryland	17.0
46	Virginia	16.6
47	New York	16.3
48	New Mexico	16.0
49	Massachusetts	15.9
50	Rhode Island	15.3

| | District of Columbia | 4.2 |

Source: CQ Press using data from U.S. Department of Labor, Bureau of Labor Statistics
 "State Employment and Unemployment" (press release, January 18, 2019, www.bls.gov/bls/newsrels.htm)
*Seasonally adjusted preliminary data as of December 2018. National figure calculated through a different formula.

VII. Energy and Environment

Energy Consumption in 2016

National Total = 97,314,700,000,000,000 BTUs*

ALPHA ORDER

ALPHA ORDER

RANK	STATE	BTUs	% of USA
17	Alabama	1,933,600,000,000,000	2.0%
39	Alaska	600,000,000,000,000	0.6%
26	Arizona	1,470,600,000,000,000	1.5%
31	Arkansas	1,056,500,000,000,000	1.1%
2	California	7,830,300,000,000,000	8.0%
25	Colorado	1,484,600,000,000,000	1.5%
36	Connecticut	723,900,000,000,000	0.7%
48	Delaware	273,500,000,000,000	0.3%
3	Florida	4,240,200,000,000,000	4.4%
9	Georgia	2,838,900,000,000,000	2.9%
47	Hawaii	282,900,000,000,000	0.3%
41	Idaho	528,500,000,000,000	0.5%
5	Illinois	3,907,100,000,000,000	4.0%
10	Indiana	2,802,300,000,000,000	2.9%
24	Iowa	1,529,800,000,000,000	1.6%
30	Kansas	1,093,000,000,000,000	1.1%
21	Kentucky	1,702,400,000,000,000	1.7%
4	Louisiana	4,205,300,000,000,000	4.3%
44	Maine	387,800,000,000,000	0.4%
28	Maryland	1,359,300,000,000,000	1.4%
27	Massachusetts	1,422,800,000,000,000	1.5%
11	Michigan	2,751,600,000,000,000	2.8%
18	Minnesota	1,806,900,000,000,000	1.9%
29	Mississippi	1,166,300,000,000,000	1.2%
20	Missouri	1,780,000,000,000,000	1.8%
43	Montana	394,500,000,000,000	0.4%
33	Nebraska	868,300,000,000,000	0.9%
37	Nevada	679,100,000,000,000	0.7%
46	New Hampshire	300,900,000,000,000	0.3%
14	New Jersey	2,219,400,000,000,000	2.3%
38	New Mexico	667,800,000,000,000	0.7%
8	New York	3,661,500,000,000,000	3.8%
12	North Carolina	2,553,800,000,000,000	2.6%
40	North Dakota	586,400,000,000,000	0.6%
7	Ohio	3,684,800,000,000,000	3.8%
23	Oklahoma	1,636,000,000,000,000	1.7%
32	Oregon	977,500,000,000,000	1.0%
6	Pennsylvania	3,755,300,000,000,000	3.9%
49	Rhode Island	186,200,000,000,000	0.2%
22	South Carolina	1,653,300,000,000,000	1.7%
45	South Dakota	383,200,000,000,000	0.4%
15	Tennessee	2,211,300,000,000,000	2.3%
1	Texas	13,183,500,000,000,000	13.5%
34	Utah	810,100,000,000,000	0.8%
50	Vermont	128,700,000,000,000	0.1%
13	Virginia	2,332,000,000,000,000	2.4%
16	Washington	2,058,200,000,000,000	2.1%
35	West Virginia	766,200,000,000,000	0.8%
19	Wisconsin	1,781,100,000,000,000	1.8%
42	Wyoming	502,900,000,000,000	0.5%

RANK ORDER

RANK	STATE	BTUs	% of USA
1	Texas	13,183,500,000,000,000	13.5%
2	California	7,830,300,000,000,000	8.0%
3	Florida	4,240,200,000,000,000	4.4%
4	Louisiana	4,205,300,000,000,000	4.3%
5	Illinois	3,907,100,000,000,000	4.0%
6	Pennsylvania	3,755,300,000,000,000	3.9%
7	Ohio	3,684,800,000,000,000	3.8%
8	New York	3,661,500,000,000,000	3.8%
9	Georgia	2,838,900,000,000,000	2.9%
10	Indiana	2,802,300,000,000,000	2.9%
11	Michigan	2,751,600,000,000,000	2.8%
12	North Carolina	2,553,800,000,000,000	2.6%
13	Virginia	2,332,000,000,000,000	2.4%
14	New Jersey	2,219,400,000,000,000	2.3%
15	Tennessee	2,211,300,000,000,000	2.3%
16	Washington	2,058,200,000,000,000	2.1%
17	Alabama	1,933,600,000,000,000	2.0%
18	Minnesota	1,806,900,000,000,000	1.9%
19	Wisconsin	1,781,100,000,000,000	1.8%
20	Missouri	1,780,000,000,000,000	1.8%
21	Kentucky	1,702,400,000,000,000	1.7%
22	South Carolina	1,653,300,000,000,000	1.7%
23	Oklahoma	1,636,000,000,000,000	1.7%
24	Iowa	1,529,800,000,000,000	1.6%
25	Colorado	1,484,600,000,000,000	1.5%
26	Arizona	1,470,600,000,000,000	1.5%
27	Massachusetts	1,422,800,000,000,000	1.5%
28	Maryland	1,359,300,000,000,000	1.4%
29	Mississippi	1,166,300,000,000,000	1.2%
30	Kansas	1,093,000,000,000,000	1.1%
31	Arkansas	1,056,500,000,000,000	1.1%
32	Oregon	977,500,000,000,000	1.0%
33	Nebraska	868,300,000,000,000	0.9%
34	Utah	810,100,000,000,000	0.8%
35	West Virginia	766,200,000,000,000	0.8%
36	Connecticut	723,900,000,000,000	0.7%
37	Nevada	679,100,000,000,000	0.7%
38	New Mexico	667,800,000,000,000	0.7%
39	Alaska	600,000,000,000,000	0.6%
40	North Dakota	586,400,000,000,000	0.6%
41	Idaho	528,500,000,000,000	0.5%
42	Wyoming	502,900,000,000,000	0.5%
43	Montana	394,500,000,000,000	0.4%
44	Maine	387,800,000,000,000	0.4%
45	South Dakota	383,200,000,000,000	0.4%
46	New Hampshire	300,900,000,000,000	0.3%
47	Hawaii	282,900,000,000,000	0.3%
48	Delaware	273,500,000,000,000	0.3%
49	Rhode Island	186,200,000,000,000	0.2%
50	Vermont	128,700,000,000,000	0.1%
	District of Columbia	174,200,000,000,000	0.2%

Source: U.S. Department of Energy, Energy Information Administration
"State Energy Data 2016: Consumption" (https://www.eia.gov/state/seds/)
*British Thermal Units: The amount of heat required to raise the temperature of one pound of water one degree. National total includes 19.1 trillion Btu of net imports of coal coke that are not allocated to the states.

Per Capita Energy Consumption in 2016

National Per Capita = 301,217,370 BTUs*

RANK	STATE	PER CAPITA	RANK	STATE	PER CAPITA
12	Alabama	397,472,015	1	Louisiana	898,911,230
3	Alaska	809,166,235	2	Wyoming	860,702,733
42	Arizona	211,735,680	3	Alaska	809,166,235
17	Arkansas	353,296,036	4	North Dakota	777,354,899
47	California	199,706,053	5	Iowa	488,475,422
34	Colorado	267,933,797	6	Texas	471,892,753
46	Connecticut	202,281,627	7	Nebraska	455,579,551
29	Delaware	288,132,522	8	South Dakota	444,089,050
45	Florida	205,535,807	9	Indiana	422,456,607
33	Georgia	275,493,963	10	West Virginia	418,476,085
48	Hawaii	198,094,678	11	Oklahoma	416,627,512
23	Idaho	314,035,640	12	Alabama	397,472,015
25	Illinois	304,602,166	13	Mississippi	390,289,054
9	Indiana	422,456,607	14	Kentucky	383,576,422
5	Iowa	488,475,422	15	Montana	379,012,416
16	Kansas	375,438,427	16	Kansas	375,438,427
14	Kentucky	383,576,422	17	Arkansas	353,296,036
1	Louisiana	898,911,230	18	South Carolina	333,445,268
28	Maine	291,278,908	19	Tennessee	332,775,973
40	Maryland	226,372,976	20	Minnesota	327,134,927
43	Massachusetts	208,437,652	21	New Mexico	319,095,714
32	Michigan	276,490,194	22	Ohio	316,699,532
20	Minnesota	327,134,927	23	Idaho	314,035,640
13	Mississippi	390,289,054	24	Wisconsin	308,524,677
27	Missouri	292,416,731	25	Illinois	304,602,166
15	Montana	379,012,416	26	Pennsylvania	293,760,616
7	Nebraska	455,579,551	27	Missouri	292,416,731
39	Nevada	232,586,654	28	Maine	291,278,908
41	New Hampshire	224,155,283	29	Delaware	288,132,522
37	New Jersey	250,086,878	30	Washington	282,150,828
21	New Mexico	319,095,714	31	Virginia	277,257,754
49	New York	186,415,671	32	Michigan	276,490,194
36	North Carolina	251,440,456	33	Georgia	275,493,963
4	North Dakota	777,354,899	34	Colorado	267,933,797
22	Ohio	316,699,532	35	Utah	266,251,410
11	Oklahoma	416,627,512	36	North Carolina	251,440,456
38	Oregon	238,915,541	37	New Jersey	250,086,878
26	Pennsylvania	293,760,616	38	Oregon	238,915,541
50	Rhode Island	176,148,441	39	Nevada	232,586,654
18	South Carolina	333,445,268	40	Maryland	226,372,976
8	South Dakota	444,089,050	41	New Hampshire	224,155,283
19	Tennessee	332,775,973	42	Arizona	211,735,680
6	Texas	471,892,753	43	Massachusetts	208,437,652
35	Utah	266,251,410	44	Vermont	206,367,735
44	Vermont	206,367,735	45	Florida	205,535,807
31	Virginia	277,257,754	46	Connecticut	202,281,627
30	Washington	282,150,828	47	California	199,706,053
10	West Virginia	418,476,085	48	Hawaii	198,094,678
24	Wisconsin	308,524,677	49	New York	186,415,671
2	Wyoming	860,702,733	50	Rhode Island	176,148,441
				District of Columbia	253,723,191

Source: CQ Press using data from U.S. Department of Energy, Energy Information Administration
     "State Energy Data 2016: Consumption" (https://www.eia.gov/state/seds/)
*British Thermal Units: The amount of heat required to raise the temperature of one pound of water one degree. National figure includes 17.8 trillion Btu of net imports of coal coke that are not allocated to the states.

Energy Prices in 2016

National Rate = $15.92 per Million BTUs*

RANK	STATE	RATE		RANK	STATE	RATE
	ALPHA ORDER				RANK ORDER	
39	Alabama	$14.77		1	Hawaii	$25.09
23	Alaska	16.61		2	Connecticut	21.92
5	Arizona	20.70		3	New Hampshire	21.25
43	Arkansas	14.56		4	Rhode Island	21.20
9	California	19.90		5	Arizona	20.70
31	Colorado	15.75		6	Massachusetts	20.67
2	Connecticut	21.92		7	Vermont	20.40
11	Delaware	18.51		8	Maryland	20.17
10	Florida	18.78		9	California	19.90
24	Georgia	16.50		10	Florida	18.78
1	Hawaii	25.09		11	Delaware	18.51
34	Idaho	15.56		12	New York	18.48
42	Illinois	14.57		13	North Carolina	17.95
45	Indiana	13.67		14	Oregon	17.43
47	Iowa	12.89		15	Nevada	17.31
28	Kansas	16.02		16	New Jersey	17.22
36	Kentucky	15.35		17	Missouri	17.18
50	Louisiana	9.12		18	South Carolina	17.09
20	Maine	16.84		19	New Mexico	16.85
8	Maryland	20.17		20	Maine	16.84
6	Massachusetts	20.67		21	Pennsylvania	16.65
33	Michigan	15.70		22	Virginia	16.62
38	Minnesota	14.92		23	Alaska	16.61
41	Mississippi	14.70		24	Georgia	16.50
17	Missouri	17.18		25	West Virginia	16.38
27	Montana	16.07		26	Tennessee	16.17
44	Nebraska	14.26		27	Montana	16.07
15	Nevada	17.31		28	Kansas	16.02
3	New Hampshire	21.25		29	Washington	15.82
16	New Jersey	17.22		30	Wisconsin	15.81
19	New Mexico	16.85		31	Colorado	15.75
12	New York	18.48		32	Utah	15.71
13	North Carolina	17.95		33	Michigan	15.70
49	North Dakota	12.28		34	Idaho	15.56
35	Ohio	15.51		35	Ohio	15.51
40	Oklahoma	14.74		36	Kentucky	15.35
14	Oregon	17.43		37	South Dakota	15.02
21	Pennsylvania	16.65		38	Minnesota	14.92
4	Rhode Island	21.20		39	Alabama	14.77
18	South Carolina	17.09		40	Oklahoma	14.74
37	South Dakota	15.02		41	Mississippi	14.70
26	Tennessee	16.17		42	Illinois	14.57
48	Texas	12.36		43	Arkansas	14.56
32	Utah	15.71		44	Nebraska	14.26
7	Vermont	20.40		45	Indiana	13.67
22	Virginia	16.62		46	Wyoming	13.25
29	Washington	15.82		47	Iowa	12.89
25	West Virginia	16.38		48	Texas	12.36
30	Wisconsin	15.81		49	North Dakota	12.28
46	Wyoming	13.25		50	Louisiana	9.12
					District of Columbia	22.36

Source: U.S. Department of Energy, Energy Information Administration
"State Energy Data 2016: Prices and Expenditures" (https://www.eia.gov/state/seds/)
*British Thermal Units: The amount of heat required to raise the temperature of one pound of water one degree.

Energy Expenditures in 2016

National Total = $1,038,504,200,000*

Source: U.S. Department of Energy, Energy Information Administration
"State Energy Data 2016: Prices and Expenditures" (https://www.eia.gov/state/seds/)
*The national total includes a negative $184 million for coal coke net imports, which is not allocated to the states.

Per Capita Energy Expenditures in 2016

National Per Capita = $3,214

<table>
<tr><td colspan="3">ALPHA ORDER</td><td colspan="3">RANK ORDER</td></tr>
<tr><td>RANK</td><td>STATE</td><td>PER CAPITA</td><td>RANK</td><td>STATE</td><td>PER CAPITA</td></tr>
<tr><td>9</td><td>Alabama</td><td>$3,965</td><td>1</td><td>Wyoming</td><td>$6,820</td></tr>
<tr><td>2</td><td>Alaska</td><td>6,241</td><td>2</td><td>Alaska</td><td>6,241</td></tr>
<tr><td>47</td><td>Arizona</td><td>2,743</td><td>3</td><td>North Dakota</td><td>6,082</td></tr>
<tr><td>22</td><td>Arkansas</td><td>3,445</td><td>4</td><td>Louisiana</td><td>5,647</td></tr>
<tr><td>43</td><td>California</td><td>2,878</td><td>5</td><td>South Dakota</td><td>4,091</td></tr>
<tr><td>48</td><td>Colorado</td><td>2,676</td><td>6</td><td>Iowa</td><td>4,051</td></tr>
<tr><td>28</td><td>Connecticut</td><td>3,290</td><td>7</td><td>Texas</td><td>3,999</td></tr>
<tr><td>27</td><td>Delaware</td><td>3,293</td><td>8</td><td>Nebraska</td><td>3,966</td></tr>
<tr><td>50</td><td>Florida</td><td>2,528</td><td>9</td><td>Alabama</td><td>3,965</td></tr>
<tr><td>37</td><td>Georgia</td><td>3,024</td><td>10</td><td>Maine</td><td>3,964</td></tr>
<tr><td>20</td><td>Hawaii</td><td>3,528</td><td>11</td><td>Mississippi</td><td>3,945</td></tr>
<tr><td>24</td><td>Idaho</td><td>3,368</td><td>12</td><td>West Virginia</td><td>3,905</td></tr>
<tr><td>39</td><td>Illinois</td><td>2,926</td><td>13</td><td>Vermont</td><td>3,828</td></tr>
<tr><td>15</td><td>Indiana</td><td>3,788</td><td>14</td><td>Montana</td><td>3,818</td></tr>
<tr><td>6</td><td>Iowa</td><td>4,051</td><td>15</td><td>Indiana</td><td>3,788</td></tr>
<tr><td>18</td><td>Kansas</td><td>3,617</td><td>16</td><td>Oklahoma</td><td>3,754</td></tr>
<tr><td>17</td><td>Kentucky</td><td>3,648</td><td>17</td><td>Kentucky</td><td>3,648</td></tr>
<tr><td>4</td><td>Louisiana</td><td>5,647</td><td>18</td><td>Kansas</td><td>3,617</td></tr>
<tr><td>10</td><td>Maine</td><td>3,964</td><td>19</td><td>South Carolina</td><td>3,570</td></tr>
<tr><td>38</td><td>Maryland</td><td>2,935</td><td>20</td><td>Hawaii</td><td>3,528</td></tr>
<tr><td>32</td><td>Massachusetts</td><td>3,154</td><td>21</td><td>New Hampshire</td><td>3,496</td></tr>
<tr><td>35</td><td>Michigan</td><td>3,076</td><td>22</td><td>Arkansas</td><td>3,445</td></tr>
<tr><td>25</td><td>Minnesota</td><td>3,320</td><td>23</td><td>Tennessee</td><td>3,376</td></tr>
<tr><td>11</td><td>Mississippi</td><td>3,945</td><td>24</td><td>Idaho</td><td>3,368</td></tr>
<tr><td>29</td><td>Missouri</td><td>3,264</td><td>25</td><td>Minnesota</td><td>3,320</td></tr>
<tr><td>14</td><td>Montana</td><td>3,818</td><td>26</td><td>Wisconsin</td><td>3,313</td></tr>
<tr><td>8</td><td>Nebraska</td><td>3,966</td><td>27</td><td>Delaware</td><td>3,293</td></tr>
<tr><td>45</td><td>Nevada</td><td>2,839</td><td>28</td><td>Connecticut</td><td>3,290</td></tr>
<tr><td>21</td><td>New Hampshire</td><td>3,496</td><td>29</td><td>Missouri</td><td>3,264</td></tr>
<tr><td>31</td><td>New Jersey</td><td>3,160</td><td>30</td><td>Ohio</td><td>3,252</td></tr>
<tr><td>34</td><td>New Mexico</td><td>3,078</td><td>31</td><td>New Jersey</td><td>3,160</td></tr>
<tr><td>49</td><td>New York</td><td>2,549</td><td>32</td><td>Massachusetts</td><td>3,154</td></tr>
<tr><td>41</td><td>North Carolina</td><td>2,888</td><td>33</td><td>Pennsylvania</td><td>3,109</td></tr>
<tr><td>3</td><td>North Dakota</td><td>6,082</td><td>34</td><td>New Mexico</td><td>3,078</td></tr>
<tr><td>30</td><td>Ohio</td><td>3,252</td><td>35</td><td>Michigan</td><td>3,076</td></tr>
<tr><td>16</td><td>Oklahoma</td><td>3,754</td><td>36</td><td>Virginia</td><td>3,025</td></tr>
<tr><td>42</td><td>Oregon</td><td>2,881</td><td>37</td><td>Georgia</td><td>3,024</td></tr>
<tr><td>33</td><td>Pennsylvania</td><td>3,109</td><td>38</td><td>Maryland</td><td>2,935</td></tr>
<tr><td>44</td><td>Rhode Island</td><td>2,867</td><td>39</td><td>Illinois</td><td>2,926</td></tr>
<tr><td>19</td><td>South Carolina</td><td>3,570</td><td>40</td><td>Washington</td><td>2,917</td></tr>
<tr><td>5</td><td>South Dakota</td><td>4,091</td><td>41</td><td>North Carolina</td><td>2,888</td></tr>
<tr><td>23</td><td>Tennessee</td><td>3,376</td><td>42</td><td>Oregon</td><td>2,881</td></tr>
<tr><td>7</td><td>Texas</td><td>3,999</td><td>43</td><td>California</td><td>2,878</td></tr>
<tr><td>46</td><td>Utah</td><td>2,774</td><td>44</td><td>Rhode Island</td><td>2,867</td></tr>
<tr><td>13</td><td>Vermont</td><td>3,828</td><td>45</td><td>Nevada</td><td>2,839</td></tr>
<tr><td>36</td><td>Virginia</td><td>3,025</td><td>46</td><td>Utah</td><td>2,774</td></tr>
<tr><td>40</td><td>Washington</td><td>2,917</td><td>47</td><td>Arizona</td><td>2,743</td></tr>
<tr><td>12</td><td>West Virginia</td><td>3,905</td><td>48</td><td>Colorado</td><td>2,676</td></tr>
<tr><td>26</td><td>Wisconsin</td><td>3,313</td><td>49</td><td>New York</td><td>2,549</td></tr>
<tr><td>1</td><td>Wyoming</td><td>6,820</td><td>50</td><td>Florida</td><td>2,528</td></tr>
<tr><td></td><td></td><td></td><td></td><td>District of Columbia</td><td>2,887</td></tr>
</table>

Source: CQ Press using data from U.S. Department of Energy, Energy Information Administration
"State Energy Data 2016: Prices and Expenditures" (https://www.eia.gov/state/seds/)

Average Monthly Electric Bill for Industrial Customers in 2017

National Average = $6,713 per Month

ALPHA ORDER				RANK ORDER		
RANK	STATE	MONTHLY BILL		RANK	STATE	MONTHLY BILL
9	Alabama	$21,253		1	Tennessee	$100,888
18	Alaska	14,078		2	Hawaii	88,243
22	Arizona	9,060		3	Vermont	64,806
47	Arkansas	2,437		4	Illinois	40,725
42	California	3,491		5	South Carolina	31,922
32	Colorado	5,973		6	Michigan	29,599
24	Connecticut	8,077		7	Wisconsin	26,673
12	Delaware	17,310		8	Virginia	25,228
35	Florida	5,086		9	Alabama	21,253
27	Georgia	6,930		10	Kentucky	19,336
2	Hawaii	88,243		11	Nevada	18,729
49	Idaho	1,705		12	Delaware	17,310
4	Illinois	40,725		13	Ohio	15,641
15	Indiana	15,339		14	Iowa	15,401
14	Iowa	15,401		15	Indiana	15,339
45	Kansas	2,982		16	Minnesota	15,236
10	Kentucky	19,336		17	North Carolina	14,098
23	Louisiana	8,651		18	Alaska	14,078
28	Maine	6,577		19	New York	12,568
44	Maryland	3,026		20	Pennsylvania	11,887
25	Massachusetts	7,662		21	Missouri	9,849
6	Michigan	29,599		22	Arizona	9,060
16	Minnesota	15,236		23	Louisiana	8,651
26	Mississippi	7,216		24	Connecticut	8,077
21	Missouri	9,849		25	Massachusetts	7,662
48	Montana	1,996		26	Mississippi	7,216
50	Nebraska	1,172		27	Georgia	6,930
11	Nevada	18,729		28	Maine	6,577
31	New Hampshire	6,246		29	West Virginia	6,525
34	New Jersey	5,258		30	North Dakota	6,400
41	New Mexico	4,219		31	New Hampshire	6,246
19	New York	12,568		32	Colorado	5,973
17	North Carolina	14,098		33	Wyoming	5,402
30	North Dakota	6,400		34	New Jersey	5,258
13	Ohio	15,641		35	Florida	5,086
40	Oklahoma	4,366		36	Utah	4,943
46	Oregon	2,737		37	Rhode Island	4,938
20	Pennsylvania	11,887		38	South Dakota	4,930
37	Rhode Island	4,938		39	Texas	4,661
5	South Carolina	31,922		40	Oklahoma	4,366
38	South Dakota	4,930		41	New Mexico	4,219
1	Tennessee	100,888		42	California	3,491
39	Texas	4,661		43	Washington	3,426
36	Utah	4,943		44	Maryland	3,026
3	Vermont	64,806		45	Kansas	2,982
8	Virginia	25,228		46	Oregon	2,737
43	Washington	3,426		47	Arkansas	2,437
29	West Virginia	6,525		48	Montana	1,996
7	Wisconsin	26,673		49	Idaho	1,705
33	Wyoming	5,402		50	Nebraska	1,172
					District of Columbia	1,235,475

Source: U.S. Department of Energy, Energy Information Administration
"Electric Sales, Revenue and Average Price 2017" (https://www.eia.gov/electricity/sales_revenue_price/index.cfm)

Average Monthly Electric Bill for Commercial Customers in 2017

National Average = $655 per Month

ALPHA ORDER

RANK	STATE	MONTHLY BILL
27	Alabama	$594
8	Alaska	796
7	Arizona	810
44	Arkansas	440
4	California	912
40	Colorado	459
2	Connecticut	1,080
17	Delaware	637
25	Florida	608
13	Georgia	679
1	Hawaii	1,123
49	Idaho	392
21	Illinois	619
28	Indiana	591
47	Iowa	402
26	Kansas	599
34	Kentucky	520
18	Louisiana	627
48	Maine	398
3	Maryland	1,023
6	Massachusetts	842
16	Michigan	647
12	Minnesota	694
36	Mississippi	513
20	Missouri	624
50	Montana	391
42	Nebraska	452
42	Nevada	452
37	New Hampshire	504
11	New Jersey	751
33	New Mexico	521
5	New York	850
38	North Carolina	495
14	North Dakota	671
22	Ohio	617
39	Oklahoma	492
32	Oregon	523
41	Pennsylvania	457
10	Rhode Island	768
35	South Carolina	514
30	South Dakota	538
23	Tennessee	612
19	Texas	625
15	Utah	665
45	Vermont	427
9	Virginia	794
29	Washington	558
46	West Virginia	419
24	Wisconsin	609
31	Wyoming	525

RANK ORDER

RANK	STATE	MONTHLY BILL
1	Hawaii	$1,123
2	Connecticut	1,080
3	Maryland	1,023
4	California	912
5	New York	850
6	Massachusetts	842
7	Arizona	810
8	Alaska	796
9	Virginia	794
10	Rhode Island	768
11	New Jersey	751
12	Minnesota	694
13	Georgia	679
14	North Dakota	671
15	Utah	665
16	Michigan	647
17	Delaware	637
18	Louisiana	627
19	Texas	625
20	Missouri	624
21	Illinois	619
22	Ohio	617
23	Tennessee	612
24	Wisconsin	609
25	Florida	608
26	Kansas	599
27	Alabama	594
28	Indiana	591
29	Washington	558
30	South Dakota	538
31	Wyoming	525
32	Oregon	523
33	New Mexico	521
34	Kentucky	520
35	South Carolina	514
36	Mississippi	513
37	New Hampshire	504
38	North Carolina	495
39	Oklahoma	492
40	Colorado	459
41	Pennsylvania	457
42	Nebraska	452
42	Nevada	452
44	Arkansas	440
45	Vermont	427
46	West Virginia	419
47	Iowa	402
48	Maine	398
49	Idaho	392
50	Montana	391
	District of Columbia	2,979

Source: U.S. Department of Energy, Energy Information Administration
"Electric Sales, Revenue and Average Price 2017" (https://www.eia.gov/electricity/sales_revenue_price/index.cfm)

Average Monthly Electric Bill for Residential Customers in 2017

National Average = $112 per Month

ALPHA ORDER

RANK	STATE	MONTHLY BILL
2	Alabama	$143
6	Alaska	128
6	Arizona	128
28	Arkansas	106
37	California	101
48	Colorado	82
4	Connecticut	140
13	Delaware	122
8	Florida	126
8	Georgia	126
1	Hawaii	149
38	Idaho	100
46	Illinois	90
22	Indiana	114
32	Iowa	103
19	Kansas	115
22	Kentucky	114
17	Louisiana	116
47	Maine	87
5	Maryland	131
16	Massachusetts	117
41	Michigan	97
40	Minnesota	98
10	Mississippi	125
17	Missouri	116
43	Montana	95
31	Nebraska	105
35	Nevada	102
19	New Hampshire	115
35	New Jersey	102
50	New Mexico	79
32	New York	103
22	North Carolina	114
27	North Dakota	109
28	Ohio	106
26	Oklahoma	110
32	Oregon	103
22	Pennsylvania	114
28	Rhode Island	106
3	South Carolina	141
19	South Dakota	115
12	Tennessee	123
13	Texas	122
48	Utah	82
43	Vermont	95
10	Virginia	125
39	Washington	99
15	West Virginia	119
43	Wisconsin	95
41	Wyoming	97

RANK ORDER

RANK	STATE	MONTHLY BILL
1	Hawaii	$149
2	Alabama	143
3	South Carolina	141
4	Connecticut	140
5	Maryland	131
6	Alaska	128
6	Arizona	128
8	Florida	126
8	Georgia	126
10	Mississippi	125
10	Virginia	125
12	Tennessee	123
13	Delaware	122
13	Texas	122
15	West Virginia	119
16	Massachusetts	117
17	Louisiana	116
17	Missouri	116
19	Kansas	115
19	New Hampshire	115
19	South Dakota	115
22	Indiana	114
22	Kentucky	114
22	North Carolina	114
22	Pennsylvania	114
26	Oklahoma	110
27	North Dakota	109
28	Arkansas	106
28	Ohio	106
28	Rhode Island	106
31	Nebraska	105
32	Iowa	103
32	New York	103
32	Oregon	103
35	Nevada	102
35	New Jersey	102
37	California	101
38	Idaho	100
39	Washington	99
40	Minnesota	98
41	Michigan	97
41	Wyoming	97
43	Montana	95
43	Vermont	95
43	Wisconsin	95
46	Illinois	90
47	Maine	87
48	Colorado	82
48	Utah	82
50	New Mexico	79
	District of Columbia	97

Source: U.S. Department of Energy, Energy Information Administration
"Electric Sales, Revenue and Average Price 2017" (https://www.eia.gov/electricity/sales_revenue_price/index.cfm)

Electricity Generated through Renewable Sources in 2017

National Total = 659,300,328,000 Kilowatthours*

ALPHA ORDER

RANK	STATE	KWH	% of USA
12	Alabama	12,843,671,000	1.9%
45	Alaska	1,856,533,000	0.3%
13	Arizona	12,486,681,000	1.9%
34	Arkansas	4,410,867,000	0.7%
1	California	97,593,148,000	14.8%
14	Colorado	12,438,776,000	1.9%
48	Connecticut	1,177,183,000	0.2%
50	Delaware	118,421,000	0.0%
25	Florida	6,103,925,000	0.9%
20	Georgia	9,414,357,000	1.4%
47	Hawaii	1,494,657,000	0.2%
8	Idaho	14,258,007,000	2.2%
16	Illinois	11,314,770,000	1.7%
26	Indiana	5,956,632,000	0.9%
7	Iowa	21,320,526,000	3.2%
9	Kansas	14,202,542,000	2.2%
32	Kentucky	5,020,593,000	0.8%
36	Louisiana	3,675,524,000	0.6%
24	Maine	7,764,842,000	1.2%
38	Maryland	3,295,941,000	0.5%
39	Massachusetts	3,202,492,000	0.5%
23	Michigan	8,932,161,000	1.4%
10	Minnesota	13,720,297,000	2.1%
46	Mississippi	1,562,971,000	0.2%
41	Missouri	2,503,850,000	0.4%
11	Montana	13,121,467,000	2.0%
29	Nebraska	5,400,065,000	0.8%
19	Nevada	9,651,987,000	1.5%
37	New Hampshire	3,455,905,000	0.5%
44	New Jersey	1,889,248,000	0.3%
31	New Mexico	5,021,862,000	0.8%
5	New York	36,728,299,000	5.6%
15	North Carolina	11,750,738,000	1.8%
17	North Dakota	10,756,025,000	1.6%
42	Ohio	2,354,786,000	0.4%
6	Oklahoma	22,436,616,000	3.4%
4	Oregon	46,625,778,000	7.1%
21	Pennsylvania	9,107,333,000	1.4%
49	Rhode Island	245,971,000	0.0%
35	South Carolina	4,314,279,000	0.7%
22	South Dakota	8,971,835,000	1.4%
18	Tennessee	9,768,898,000	1.5%
3	Texas	62,358,872,000	9.5%
33	Utah	4,885,699,000	0.7%
43	Vermont	2,118,224,000	0.3%
30	Virginia	5,238,455,000	0.8%
2	Washington	92,123,756,000	14.0%
40	West Virginia	3,090,646,000	0.5%
27	Wisconsin	5,654,088,000	0.9%
28	Wyoming	5,512,962,000	0.8%

RANK ORDER

RANK	STATE	KWH	% of USA
1	California	97,593,148,000	14.8%
2	Washington	92,123,756,000	14.0%
3	Texas	62,358,872,000	9.5%
4	Oregon	46,625,778,000	7.1%
5	New York	36,728,299,000	5.6%
6	Oklahoma	22,436,616,000	3.4%
7	Iowa	21,320,526,000	3.2%
8	Idaho	14,258,007,000	2.2%
9	Kansas	14,202,542,000	2.2%
10	Minnesota	13,720,297,000	2.1%
11	Montana	13,121,467,000	2.0%
12	Alabama	12,843,671,000	1.9%
13	Arizona	12,486,681,000	1.9%
14	Colorado	12,438,776,000	1.9%
15	North Carolina	11,750,738,000	1.8%
16	Illinois	11,314,770,000	1.7%
17	North Dakota	10,756,025,000	1.6%
18	Tennessee	9,768,898,000	1.5%
19	Nevada	9,651,987,000	1.5%
20	Georgia	9,414,357,000	1.4%
21	Pennsylvania	9,107,333,000	1.4%
22	South Dakota	8,971,835,000	1.4%
23	Michigan	8,932,161,000	1.4%
24	Maine	7,764,842,000	1.2%
25	Florida	6,103,925,000	0.9%
26	Indiana	5,956,632,000	0.9%
27	Wisconsin	5,654,088,000	0.9%
28	Wyoming	5,512,962,000	0.8%
29	Nebraska	5,400,065,000	0.8%
30	Virginia	5,238,455,000	0.8%
31	New Mexico	5,021,862,000	0.8%
32	Kentucky	5,020,593,000	0.8%
33	Utah	4,885,699,000	0.7%
34	Arkansas	4,410,867,000	0.7%
35	South Carolina	4,314,279,000	0.7%
36	Louisiana	3,675,524,000	0.6%
37	New Hampshire	3,455,905,000	0.5%
38	Maryland	3,295,941,000	0.5%
39	Massachusetts	3,202,492,000	0.5%
40	West Virginia	3,090,646,000	0.5%
41	Missouri	2,503,850,000	0.4%
42	Ohio	2,354,786,000	0.4%
43	Vermont	2,118,224,000	0.3%
44	New Jersey	1,889,248,000	0.3%
45	Alaska	1,856,533,000	0.3%
46	Mississippi	1,562,971,000	0.2%
47	Hawaii	1,494,657,000	0.2%
48	Connecticut	1,177,183,000	0.2%
49	Rhode Island	245,971,000	0.0%
50	Delaware	118,421,000	0.0%
	District of Columbia	47,167,000	0.0%

Source: U.S. Department of Energy, Energy Information Administration
"Electricity" (https://www.eia.gov/electricity/data/state/)
*Includes hydroelectric, geothermal, solar thermal and photovoltaic, wind, wood and wood-derived fuels, and other biomass.

Percent of Electricity Generated through Renewable Sources in 2017

National Percent = 16.3%*

RANK	STATE	PERCENT
29	Alabama	9.2
12	Alaska	28.6
25	Arizona	11.8
34	Arkansas	7.3
7	California	47.3
17	Colorado	23.1
43	Connecticut	3.4
50	Delaware	1.6
46	Florida	2.6
33	Georgia	7.4
20	Hawaii	15.2
2	Idaho	82.0
36	Illinois	6.2
37	Indiana	6.0
9	Iowa	36.8
13	Kansas	27.9
35	Kentucky	6.9
42	Louisiana	3.8
6	Maine	68.9
28	Maryland	9.7
27	Massachusetts	9.9
32	Michigan	8.0
16	Minnesota	23.4
46	Mississippi	2.6
45	Missouri	3.0
8	Montana	46.5
19	Nebraska	15.3
15	Nevada	25.3
18	New Hampshire	19.8
48	New Jersey	2.5
21	New Mexico	14.9
11	New York	28.7
30	North Carolina	9.1
14	North Dakota	25.9
49	Ohio	2.0
10	Oklahoma	30.4
5	Oregon	74.3
40	Pennsylvania	4.3
44	Rhode Island	3.2
39	South Carolina	4.6
2	South Dakota	82.0
24	Tennessee	12.4
22	Texas	13.8
23	Utah	13.1
1	Vermont	98.9
38	Virginia	5.8
4	Washington	79.5
41	West Virginia	4.2
31	Wisconsin	8.7
25	Wyoming	11.8

RANK	STATE	PERCENT
1	Vermont	98.9
2	Idaho	82.0
2	South Dakota	82.0
4	Washington	79.5
5	Oregon	74.3
6	Maine	68.9
7	California	47.3
8	Montana	46.5
9	Iowa	36.8
10	Oklahoma	30.4
11	New York	28.7
12	Alaska	28.6
13	Kansas	27.9
14	North Dakota	25.9
15	Nevada	25.3
16	Minnesota	23.4
17	Colorado	23.1
18	New Hampshire	19.8
19	Nebraska	15.3
20	Hawaii	15.2
21	New Mexico	14.9
22	Texas	13.8
23	Utah	13.1
24	Tennessee	12.4
25	Arizona	11.8
25	Wyoming	11.8
27	Massachusetts	9.9
28	Maryland	9.7
29	Alabama	9.2
30	North Carolina	9.1
31	Wisconsin	8.7
32	Michigan	8.0
33	Georgia	7.4
34	Arkansas	7.3
35	Kentucky	6.9
36	Illinois	6.2
37	Indiana	6.0
38	Virginia	5.8
39	South Carolina	4.6
40	Pennsylvania	4.3
41	West Virginia	4.2
42	Louisiana	3.8
43	Connecticut	3.4
44	Rhode Island	3.2
45	Missouri	3.0
46	Florida	2.6
46	Mississippi	2.6
48	New Jersey	2.5
49	Ohio	2.0
50	Delaware	1.6
	District of Columbia	70.5

Source: CQ Press using data from U.S. Department of Energy, Energy Information Administration
"Electricity" (https://www.eia.gov/electricity/data/state/)
*Includes hydroelectric, geothermal, solar thermal and photovoltaic, wind, wood and wood-derived fuels, and other biomass.

Average Price of Natural Gas Delivered to Industrial Customers in 2017

National Average = $4.10 per Thousand Cubic Feet

ALPHA ORDER

RANK	STATE	RATE
44	Alabama	$4.24
38	Alaska	4.63
18	Arizona	6.47
14	Arkansas	6.67
12	California	7.05
24	Colorado	5.58
17	Connecticut	6.48
2	Delaware	9.91
20	Florida	6.17
37	Georgia	4.68
1	Hawaii	19.62
42	Idaho	4.44
23	Illinois	5.76
21	Indiana	5.99
28	Iowa	5.21
45	Kansas	4.16
41	Kentucky	4.46
46	Louisiana	3.64
7	Maine	8.15
3	Maryland	9.84
8	Massachusetts	8.02
22	Michigan	5.97
40	Minnesota	4.48
30	Mississippi	5.07
15	Missouri	6.64
16	Montana	6.60
39	Nebraska	4.54
31	Nevada	5.06
4	New Hampshire	9.09
9	New Jersey	7.92
31	New Mexico	5.06
11	New York	7.21
19	North Carolina	6.24
50	North Dakota	3.15
13	Ohio	6.71
47	Oklahoma	3.30
27	Oregon	5.31
6	Pennsylvania	8.38
5	Rhode Island	8.48
36	South Carolina	4.86
29	South Dakota	5.09
33	Tennessee	5.04
48	Texas	3.28
25	Utah	5.51
35	Vermont	4.92
33	Virginia	5.04
10	Washington	7.39
49	West Virginia	3.21
26	Wisconsin	5.34
43	Wyoming	4.28

RANK ORDER

RANK	STATE	RATE
1	Hawaii	$19.62
2	Delaware	9.91
3	Maryland	9.84
4	New Hampshire	9.09
5	Rhode Island	8.48
6	Pennsylvania	8.38
7	Maine	8.15
8	Massachusetts	8.02
9	New Jersey	7.92
10	Washington	7.39
11	New York	7.21
12	California	7.05
13	Ohio	6.71
14	Arkansas	6.67
15	Missouri	6.64
16	Montana	6.60
17	Connecticut	6.48
18	Arizona	6.47
19	North Carolina	6.24
20	Florida	6.17
21	Indiana	5.99
22	Michigan	5.97
23	Illinois	5.76
24	Colorado	5.58
25	Utah	5.51
26	Wisconsin	5.34
27	Oregon	5.31
28	Iowa	5.21
29	South Dakota	5.09
30	Mississippi	5.07
31	Nevada	5.06
31	New Mexico	5.06
33	Tennessee	5.04
33	Virginia	5.04
35	Vermont	4.92
36	South Carolina	4.86
37	Georgia	4.68
38	Alaska	4.63
39	Nebraska	4.54
40	Minnesota	4.48
41	Kentucky	4.46
42	Idaho	4.44
43	Wyoming	4.28
44	Alabama	4.24
45	Kansas	4.16
46	Louisiana	3.64
47	Oklahoma	3.30
48	Texas	3.28
49	West Virginia	3.21
50	North Dakota	3.15
	District of Columbia*	NA

Source: U.S. Department of Energy, Energy Information Administration
"Natural Gas" (https://www.eia.gov/naturalgas/annual/)
*Not available.

Average Price of Natural Gas Delivered to Commercial Customers in 2017

National Average = $7.88 per Thousand Cubic Feet

ALPHA ORDER

RANK	STATE	RATE
2	Alabama	$12.03
10	Alaska	9.79
18	Arizona	8.97
27	Arkansas	8.34
22	California	8.76
36	Colorado	7.17
12	Connecticut	9.30
7	Delaware	10.37
6	Florida	10.97
21	Georgia	8.78
1	Hawaii	27.41
43	Idaho	6.62
30	Illinois	7.78
33	Indiana	7.52
40	Iowa	6.87
11	Kansas	9.36
16	Kentucky	9.06
17	Louisiana	8.99
4	Maine	11.33
8	Maryland	10.27
9	Massachusetts	10.16
38	Michigan	7.02
42	Minnesota	6.80
20	Mississippi	8.82
25	Missouri	8.44
34	Montana	7.42
46	Nebraska	6.37
50	Nevada	5.71
3	New Hampshire	11.71
15	New Jersey	9.14
45	New Mexico	6.59
40	New York	6.87
19	North Carolina	8.92
49	North Dakota	6.00
48	Ohio	6.11
25	Oklahoma	8.44
23	Oregon	8.74
14	Pennsylvania	9.16
5	Rhode Island	11.30
12	South Carolina	9.30
47	South Dakota	6.26
23	Tennessee	8.74
31	Texas	7.71
35	Utah	7.40
37	Vermont	7.04
29	Virginia	7.99
28	Washington	8.30
32	West Virginia	7.65
44	Wisconsin	6.60
39	Wyoming	6.92

RANK ORDER

RANK	STATE	RATE
1	Hawaii	$27.41
2	Alabama	12.03
3	New Hampshire	11.71
4	Maine	11.33
5	Rhode Island	11.30
6	Florida	10.97
7	Delaware	10.37
8	Maryland	10.27
9	Massachusetts	10.16
10	Alaska	9.79
11	Kansas	9.36
12	Connecticut	9.30
12	South Carolina	9.30
14	Pennsylvania	9.16
15	New Jersey	9.14
16	Kentucky	9.06
17	Louisiana	8.99
18	Arizona	8.97
19	North Carolina	8.92
20	Mississippi	8.82
21	Georgia	8.78
22	California	8.76
23	Oregon	8.74
23	Tennessee	8.74
25	Missouri	8.44
25	Oklahoma	8.44
27	Arkansas	8.34
28	Washington	8.30
29	Virginia	7.99
30	Illinois	7.78
31	Texas	7.71
32	West Virginia	7.65
33	Indiana	7.52
34	Montana	7.42
35	Utah	7.40
36	Colorado	7.17
37	Vermont	7.04
38	Michigan	7.02
39	Wyoming	6.92
40	Iowa	6.87
40	New York	6.87
42	Minnesota	6.80
43	Idaho	6.62
44	Wisconsin	6.60
45	New Mexico	6.59
46	Nebraska	6.37
47	South Dakota	6.26
48	Ohio	6.11
49	North Dakota	6.00
50	Nevada	5.71

District of Columbia   10.87

Source: U.S. Department of Energy, Energy Information Administration
"Natural Gas" (https://www.eia.gov/naturalgas/annual/)

Average Price of Natural Gas Delivered to Residential Customers in 2017

National Average = $10.91 per Thousand Cubic Feet

ALPHA ORDER

RANK	STATE	RATE
4	Alabama	$16.11
30	Alaska	10.52
5	Arizona	15.78
16	Arkansas	12.97
19	California	12.49
47	Colorado	8.08
11	Connecticut	13.95
18	Delaware	12.84
2	Florida	21.15
3	Georgia	16.93
1	Hawaii	38.88
48	Idaho	7.65
41	Illinois	8.83
40	Indiana	8.94
34	Iowa	9.30
27	Kansas	10.95
24	Kentucky	11.62
15	Louisiana	13.04
6	Maine	14.61
16	Maryland	12.97
13	Massachusetts	13.32
45	Michigan	8.38
43	Minnesota	8.47
22	Mississippi	11.83
23	Missouri	11.78
50	Montana	7.62
38	Nebraska	9.01
42	Nevada	8.82
8	New Hampshire	14.55
36	New Jersey	9.14
35	New Mexico	9.22
21	New York	12.04
14	North Carolina	13.29
49	North Dakota	7.64
32	Ohio	9.72
25	Oklahoma	11.40
29	Oregon	10.59
25	Pennsylvania	11.40
10	Rhode Island	14.02
7	South Carolina	14.57
46	South Dakota	8.18
31	Tennessee	10.31
12	Texas	13.61
37	Utah	9.05
9	Vermont	14.12
20	Virginia	12.34
28	Washington	10.62
33	West Virginia	9.43
44	Wisconsin	8.40
38	Wyoming	9.01

RANK ORDER

RANK	STATE	RATE
1	Hawaii	$38.88
2	Florida	21.15
3	Georgia	16.93
4	Alabama	16.11
5	Arizona	15.78
6	Maine	14.61
7	South Carolina	14.57
8	New Hampshire	14.55
9	Vermont	14.12
10	Rhode Island	14.02
11	Connecticut	13.95
12	Texas	13.61
13	Massachusetts	13.32
14	North Carolina	13.29
15	Louisiana	13.04
16	Arkansas	12.97
16	Maryland	12.97
18	Delaware	12.84
19	California	12.49
20	Virginia	12.34
21	New York	12.04
22	Mississippi	11.83
23	Missouri	11.78
24	Kentucky	11.62
25	Oklahoma	11.40
25	Pennsylvania	11.40
27	Kansas	10.95
28	Washington	10.62
29	Oregon	10.59
30	Alaska	10.52
31	Tennessee	10.31
32	Ohio	9.72
33	West Virginia	9.43
34	Iowa	9.30
35	New Mexico	9.22
36	New Jersey	9.14
37	Utah	9.05
38	Nebraska	9.01
38	Wyoming	9.01
40	Indiana	8.94
41	Illinois	8.83
42	Nevada	8.82
43	Minnesota	8.47
44	Wisconsin	8.40
45	Michigan	8.38
46	South Dakota	8.18
47	Colorado	8.08
48	Idaho	7.65
49	North Dakota	7.64
50	Montana	7.62

| | District of Columbia | 12.53 |

Source: U.S. Department of Energy, Energy Information Administration
"Natural Gas" (https://www.eia.gov/naturalgas/annual/)

Natural Gas Consumption in 2017

National Total = 27,110,271,000,000 Cubic Feet*

ALPHA ORDER

RANK	STATE	CUBIC FEET	% of USA
14	Alabama	669,088,000,000	2.5%
23	Alaska	345,941,000,000	1.3%
26	Arizona	321,638,000,000	1.2%
27	Arkansas	317,684,000,000	1.2%
2	California	2,110,829,000,000	7.8%
21	Colorado	438,697,000,000	1.6%
34	Connecticut	238,151,000,000	0.9%
43	Delaware	99,781,000,000	0.4%
4	Florida	1,394,213,000,000	5.1%
12	Georgia	695,941,000,000	2.6%
50	Hawaii	3,106,000,000	0.0%
42	Idaho	110,737,000,000	0.4%
7	Illinois	992,869,000,000	3.7%
10	Indiana	739,636,000,000	2.7%
22	Iowa	389,462,000,000	1.4%
31	Kansas	272,145,000,000	1.0%
29	Kentucky	287,575,000,000	1.1%
3	Louisiana	1,587,234,000,000	5.9%
48	Maine	49,140,000,000	0.2%
36	Maryland	223,251,000,000	0.8%
20	Massachusetts	449,463,000,000	1.7%
9	Michigan	874,167,000,000	3.2%
19	Minnesota	461,356,000,000	1.7%
16	Mississippi	533,010,000,000	2.0%
32	Missouri	259,993,000,000	1.0%
46	Montana	80,404,000,000	0.3%
39	Nebraska	165,607,000,000	0.6%
28	Nevada	295,001,000,000	1.1%
47	New Hampshire	52,183,000,000	0.2%
11	New Jersey	709,185,000,000	2.6%
33	New Mexico	239,990,000,000	0.9%
6	New York	1,255,344,000,000	4.6%
17	North Carolina	509,440,000,000	1.9%
41	North Dakota	112,230,000,000	0.4%
8	Ohio	946,911,000,000	3.5%
13	Oklahoma	670,777,000,000	2.5%
35	Oregon	231,727,000,000	0.9%
5	Pennsylvania	1,263,972,000,000	4.7%
44	Rhode Island	82,389,000,000	0.3%
30	South Carolina	276,513,000,000	1.0%
45	South Dakota	81,484,000,000	0.3%
24	Tennessee	323,540,000,000	1.2%
1	Texas	3,886,571,000,000	14.3%
37	Utah	222,088,000,000	0.8%
49	Vermont	11,930,000,000	0.0%
15	Virginia	582,394,000,000	2.1%
25	Washington	321,898,000,000	1.2%
38	West Virginia	188,194,000,000	0.7%
18	Wisconsin	484,559,000,000	1.8%
40	Wyoming	126,368,000,000	0.5%

RANK ORDER

RANK	STATE	CUBIC FEET	% of USA
1	Texas	3,886,571,000,000	14.3%
2	California	2,110,829,000,000	7.8%
3	Louisiana	1,587,234,000,000	5.9%
4	Florida	1,394,213,000,000	5.1%
5	Pennsylvania	1,263,972,000,000	4.7%
6	New York	1,255,344,000,000	4.6%
7	Illinois	992,869,000,000	3.7%
8	Ohio	946,911,000,000	3.5%
9	Michigan	874,167,000,000	3.2%
10	Indiana	739,636,000,000	2.7%
11	New Jersey	709,185,000,000	2.6%
12	Georgia	695,941,000,000	2.6%
13	Oklahoma	670,777,000,000	2.5%
14	Alabama	669,088,000,000	2.5%
15	Virginia	582,394,000,000	2.1%
16	Mississippi	533,010,000,000	2.0%
17	North Carolina	509,440,000,000	1.9%
18	Wisconsin	484,559,000,000	1.8%
19	Minnesota	461,356,000,000	1.7%
20	Massachusetts	449,463,000,000	1.7%
21	Colorado	438,697,000,000	1.6%
22	Iowa	389,462,000,000	1.4%
23	Alaska	345,941,000,000	1.3%
24	Tennessee	323,540,000,000	1.2%
25	Washington	321,898,000,000	1.2%
26	Arizona	321,638,000,000	1.2%
27	Arkansas	317,684,000,000	1.2%
28	Nevada	295,001,000,000	1.1%
29	Kentucky	287,575,000,000	1.1%
30	South Carolina	276,513,000,000	1.0%
31	Kansas	272,145,000,000	1.0%
32	Missouri	259,993,000,000	1.0%
33	New Mexico	239,990,000,000	0.9%
34	Connecticut	238,151,000,000	0.9%
35	Oregon	231,727,000,000	0.9%
36	Maryland	223,251,000,000	0.8%
37	Utah	222,088,000,000	0.8%
38	West Virginia	188,194,000,000	0.7%
39	Nebraska	165,607,000,000	0.6%
40	Wyoming	126,368,000,000	0.5%
41	North Dakota	112,230,000,000	0.4%
42	Idaho	110,737,000,000	0.4%
43	Delaware	99,781,000,000	0.4%
44	Rhode Island	82,389,000,000	0.3%
45	South Dakota	81,484,000,000	0.3%
46	Montana	80,404,000,000	0.3%
47	New Hampshire	52,183,000,000	0.2%
48	Maine	49,140,000,000	0.2%
49	Vermont	11,930,000,000	0.0%
50	Hawaii	3,106,000,000	0.0%
	District of Columbia	30,181,000,000	0.1%

Source: U.S. Department of Energy, Energy Information Administration
     "Natural Gas" (https://www.eia.gov/naturalgas/annual/)
*National total includes 94,284,000,000 cubic feet of consumption in the Gulf of Mexico not shown by state.

Coal Mines in 2017

National Total = 680 Mines*

<table>
<tr><td colspan="4">ALPHA ORDER</td><td colspan="4">RANK ORDER</td></tr>
<tr><th>RANK</th><th>STATE</th><th>MINES</th><th>% of USA</th><th>RANK</th><th>STATE</th><th>MINES</th><th>% of USA</th></tr>
<tr><td>5</td><td>Alabama</td><td>30</td><td>4.4%</td><td>1</td><td>Pennsylvania</td><td>153</td><td>22.5%</td></tr>
<tr><td>22</td><td>Alaska</td><td>1</td><td>0.1%</td><td>2</td><td>Kentucky</td><td>151</td><td>22.2%</td></tr>
<tr><td>22</td><td>Arizona</td><td>1</td><td>0.1%</td><td>3</td><td>West Virginia</td><td>140</td><td>20.6%</td></tr>
<tr><td>18</td><td>Arkansas</td><td>3</td><td>0.4%</td><td>4</td><td>Virginia</td><td>52</td><td>7.6%</td></tr>
<tr><td>NA</td><td>California**</td><td>NA</td><td>NA</td><td>5</td><td>Alabama</td><td>30</td><td>4.4%</td></tr>
<tr><td>13</td><td>Colorado</td><td>7</td><td>1.0%</td><td>6</td><td>Illinois</td><td>18</td><td>2.6%</td></tr>
<tr><td>NA</td><td>Connecticut**</td><td>NA</td><td>NA</td><td>6</td><td>Indiana</td><td>18</td><td>2.6%</td></tr>
<tr><td>NA</td><td>Delaware**</td><td>NA</td><td>NA</td><td>6</td><td>Ohio</td><td>18</td><td>2.6%</td></tr>
<tr><td>NA</td><td>Florida**</td><td>NA</td><td>NA</td><td>9</td><td>Wyoming</td><td>17</td><td>2.5%</td></tr>
<tr><td>NA</td><td>Georgia**</td><td>NA</td><td>NA</td><td>10</td><td>Maryland</td><td>14</td><td>2.1%</td></tr>
<tr><td>NA</td><td>Hawaii**</td><td>NA</td><td>NA</td><td>11</td><td>Texas</td><td>10</td><td>1.5%</td></tr>
<tr><td>NA</td><td>Idaho**</td><td>NA</td><td>NA</td><td>12</td><td>Utah</td><td>8</td><td>1.2%</td></tr>
<tr><td>6</td><td>Illinois</td><td>18</td><td>2.6%</td><td>13</td><td>Colorado</td><td>7</td><td>1.0%</td></tr>
<tr><td>6</td><td>Indiana</td><td>18</td><td>2.6%</td><td>14</td><td>Montana</td><td>6</td><td>0.9%</td></tr>
<tr><td>NA</td><td>Iowa**</td><td>NA</td><td>NA</td><td>14</td><td>Tennessee</td><td>6</td><td>0.9%</td></tr>
<tr><td>NA</td><td>Kansas**</td><td>NA</td><td>NA</td><td>16</td><td>North Dakota</td><td>5</td><td>0.7%</td></tr>
<tr><td>2</td><td>Kentucky</td><td>151</td><td>22.2%</td><td>16</td><td>Oklahoma</td><td>5</td><td>0.7%</td></tr>
<tr><td>20</td><td>Louisiana</td><td>2</td><td>0.3%</td><td>18</td><td>Arkansas</td><td>3</td><td>0.4%</td></tr>
<tr><td>NA</td><td>Maine**</td><td>NA</td><td>NA</td><td>18</td><td>New Mexico</td><td>3</td><td>0.4%</td></tr>
<tr><td>10</td><td>Maryland</td><td>14</td><td>2.1%</td><td>20</td><td>Louisiana</td><td>2</td><td>0.3%</td></tr>
<tr><td>NA</td><td>Massachusetts**</td><td>NA</td><td>NA</td><td>20</td><td>Mississippi</td><td>2</td><td>0.3%</td></tr>
<tr><td>NA</td><td>Michigan**</td><td>NA</td><td>NA</td><td>22</td><td>Alaska</td><td>1</td><td>0.1%</td></tr>
<tr><td>NA</td><td>Minnesota**</td><td>NA</td><td>NA</td><td>22</td><td>Arizona</td><td>1</td><td>0.1%</td></tr>
<tr><td>20</td><td>Mississippi</td><td>2</td><td>0.3%</td><td>22</td><td>Missouri</td><td>1</td><td>0.1%</td></tr>
<tr><td>22</td><td>Missouri</td><td>1</td><td>0.1%</td><td>NA</td><td>California**</td><td>NA</td><td>NA</td></tr>
<tr><td>14</td><td>Montana</td><td>6</td><td>0.9%</td><td>NA</td><td>Connecticut**</td><td>NA</td><td>NA</td></tr>
<tr><td>NA</td><td>Nebraska**</td><td>NA</td><td>NA</td><td>NA</td><td>Delaware**</td><td>NA</td><td>NA</td></tr>
<tr><td>NA</td><td>Nevada**</td><td>NA</td><td>NA</td><td>NA</td><td>Florida**</td><td>NA</td><td>NA</td></tr>
<tr><td>NA</td><td>New Hampshire**</td><td>NA</td><td>NA</td><td>NA</td><td>Georgia**</td><td>NA</td><td>NA</td></tr>
<tr><td>NA</td><td>New Jersey**</td><td>NA</td><td>NA</td><td>NA</td><td>Hawaii**</td><td>NA</td><td>NA</td></tr>
<tr><td>18</td><td>New Mexico</td><td>3</td><td>0.4%</td><td>NA</td><td>Idaho**</td><td>NA</td><td>NA</td></tr>
<tr><td>NA</td><td>New York**</td><td>NA</td><td>NA</td><td>NA</td><td>Iowa**</td><td>NA</td><td>NA</td></tr>
<tr><td>NA</td><td>North Carolina**</td><td>NA</td><td>NA</td><td>NA</td><td>Kansas**</td><td>NA</td><td>NA</td></tr>
<tr><td>16</td><td>North Dakota</td><td>5</td><td>0.7%</td><td>NA</td><td>Maine**</td><td>NA</td><td>NA</td></tr>
<tr><td>6</td><td>Ohio</td><td>18</td><td>2.6%</td><td>NA</td><td>Massachusetts**</td><td>NA</td><td>NA</td></tr>
<tr><td>16</td><td>Oklahoma</td><td>5</td><td>0.7%</td><td>NA</td><td>Michigan**</td><td>NA</td><td>NA</td></tr>
<tr><td>NA</td><td>Oregon**</td><td>NA</td><td>NA</td><td>NA</td><td>Minnesota**</td><td>NA</td><td>NA</td></tr>
<tr><td>1</td><td>Pennsylvania</td><td>153</td><td>22.5%</td><td>NA</td><td>Nebraska**</td><td>NA</td><td>NA</td></tr>
<tr><td>NA</td><td>Rhode Island**</td><td>NA</td><td>NA</td><td>NA</td><td>Nevada**</td><td>NA</td><td>NA</td></tr>
<tr><td>NA</td><td>South Carolina**</td><td>NA</td><td>NA</td><td>NA</td><td>New Hampshire**</td><td>NA</td><td>NA</td></tr>
<tr><td>NA</td><td>South Dakota**</td><td>NA</td><td>NA</td><td>NA</td><td>New Jersey**</td><td>NA</td><td>NA</td></tr>
<tr><td>14</td><td>Tennessee</td><td>6</td><td>0.9%</td><td>NA</td><td>New York**</td><td>NA</td><td>NA</td></tr>
<tr><td>11</td><td>Texas</td><td>10</td><td>1.5%</td><td>NA</td><td>North Carolina**</td><td>NA</td><td>NA</td></tr>
<tr><td>12</td><td>Utah</td><td>8</td><td>1.2%</td><td>NA</td><td>Oregon**</td><td>NA</td><td>NA</td></tr>
<tr><td>NA</td><td>Vermont**</td><td>NA</td><td>NA</td><td>NA</td><td>Rhode Island**</td><td>NA</td><td>NA</td></tr>
<tr><td>4</td><td>Virginia</td><td>52</td><td>7.6%</td><td>NA</td><td>South Carolina**</td><td>NA</td><td>NA</td></tr>
<tr><td>NA</td><td>Washington**</td><td>NA</td><td>NA</td><td>NA</td><td>South Dakota**</td><td>NA</td><td>NA</td></tr>
<tr><td>3</td><td>West Virginia</td><td>140</td><td>20.6%</td><td>NA</td><td>Vermont**</td><td>NA</td><td>NA</td></tr>
<tr><td>NA</td><td>Wisconsin**</td><td>NA</td><td>NA</td><td>NA</td><td>Washington**</td><td>NA</td><td>NA</td></tr>
<tr><td>9</td><td>Wyoming</td><td>17</td><td>2.5%</td><td>NA</td><td>Wisconsin**</td><td>NA</td><td>NA</td></tr>
<tr><td></td><td></td><td></td><td></td><td></td><td>District of Columbia**</td><td>NA</td><td>NA</td></tr>
</table>

Source: U.S. Department of Energy, Energy Information Administration
"Annual Coal Report" (https://www.eia.gov/coal/annual/)
*National total includes 9 coal mines in refuse recovery not shown by state.
**Not available or no mines.

Coal Production in 2017

National Total = 774,609,000 Short Tons*

ALPHA ORDER

RANK	STATE	SHORT TONS	% of USA
14	Alabama	12,861,000	1.7%
20	Alaska	959,000	0.1%
16	Arizona	6,221,000	0.8%
24	Arkansas	43,000	0.0%
NA	California**	NA	NA
10	Colorado	15,047,000	1.9%
NA	Connecticut**	NA	NA
NA	Delaware**	NA	NA
NA	Florida**	NA	NA
NA	Georgia**	NA	NA
NA	Hawaii**	NA	NA
NA	Idaho**	NA	NA
4	Illinois	48,204,000	6.2%
8	Indiana	31,472,000	4.1%
NA	Iowa**	NA	NA
NA	Kansas**	NA	NA
5	Kentucky	41,784,000	5.4%
18	Louisiana	2,079,000	0.3%
NA	Maine**	NA	NA
19	Maryland	1,808,000	0.2%
NA	Massachusetts**	NA	NA
NA	Michigan**	NA	NA
NA	Minnesota**	NA	NA
17	Mississippi	2,604,000	0.3%
23	Missouri	244,000	0.0%
7	Montana	35,232,000	4.5%
NA	Nebraska**	NA	NA
NA	Nevada**	NA	NA
NA	New Hampshire**	NA	NA
NA	New Jersey**	NA	NA
12	New Mexico	13,844,000	1.8%
NA	New York**	NA	NA
NA	North Carolina**	NA	NA
9	North Dakota	28,788,000	3.7%
15	Ohio	9,489,000	1.2%
21	Oklahoma	561,000	0.1%
NA	Oregon**	NA	NA
3	Pennsylvania	49,085,000	6.3%
NA	Rhode Island**	NA	NA
NA	South Carolina**	NA	NA
NA	South Dakota**	NA	NA
22	Tennessee	431,000	0.1%
6	Texas	36,382,000	4.7%
11	Utah	14,326,000	1.8%
NA	Vermont**	NA	NA
13	Virginia	13,202,000	1.7%
NA	Washington**	NA	NA
2	West Virginia	92,791,000	12.0%
NA	Wisconsin**	NA	NA
1	Wyoming	316,454,000	40.9%

RANK ORDER

RANK	STATE	SHORT TONS	% of USA
1	Wyoming	316,454,000	40.9%
2	West Virginia	92,791,000	12.0%
3	Pennsylvania	49,085,000	6.3%
4	Illinois	48,204,000	6.2%
5	Kentucky	41,784,000	5.4%
6	Texas	36,382,000	4.7%
7	Montana	35,232,000	4.5%
8	Indiana	31,472,000	4.1%
9	North Dakota	28,788,000	3.7%
10	Colorado	15,047,000	1.9%
11	Utah	14,326,000	1.8%
12	New Mexico	13,844,000	1.8%
13	Virginia	13,202,000	1.7%
14	Alabama	12,861,000	1.7%
15	Ohio	9,489,000	1.2%
16	Arizona	6,221,000	0.8%
17	Mississippi	2,604,000	0.3%
18	Louisiana	2,079,000	0.3%
19	Maryland	1,808,000	0.2%
20	Alaska	959,000	0.1%
21	Oklahoma	561,000	0.1%
22	Tennessee	431,000	0.1%
23	Missouri	244,000	0.0%
24	Arkansas	43,000	0.0%
NA	California**	NA	NA
NA	Connecticut**	NA	NA
NA	Delaware**	NA	NA
NA	Florida**	NA	NA
NA	Georgia**	NA	NA
NA	Hawaii**	NA	NA
NA	Idaho**	NA	NA
NA	Iowa**	NA	NA
NA	Kansas**	NA	NA
NA	Maine**	NA	NA
NA	Massachusetts**	NA	NA
NA	Michigan**	NA	NA
NA	Minnesota**	NA	NA
NA	Nebraska**	NA	NA
NA	Nevada**	NA	NA
NA	New Hampshire**	NA	NA
NA	New Jersey**	NA	NA
NA	New York**	NA	NA
NA	North Carolina**	NA	NA
NA	Oregon**	NA	NA
NA	Rhode Island**	NA	NA
NA	South Carolina**	NA	NA
NA	South Dakota**	NA	NA
NA	Vermont**	NA	NA
NA	Washington**	NA	NA
NA	Wisconsin**	NA	NA
	District of Columbia**	NA	NA

Source: U.S. Department of Energy, Energy Information Administration
"Annual Coal Report" (https://www.eia.gov/coal/annual/)
*National total includes 699,000 short tons from refuse recovery not shown by state.
**Not available or no production.

Gasoline Used in 2016

National Total = 144,846,445,000 Gallons*

ALPHA ORDER

RANK	STATE	GALLONS	% of USA
20	Alabama	2,792,760,000	1.9%
50	Alaska	296,696,000	0.2%
16	Arizona	2,933,404,000	2.0%
31	Arkansas	1,537,354,000	1.1%
1	California	15,507,693,000	10.7%
24	Colorado	2,384,635,000	1.6%
32	Connecticut	1,520,557,000	1.0%
44	Delaware	490,959,000	0.3%
3	Florida	9,063,973,000	6.3%
8	Georgia	4,849,071,000	3.3%
45	Hawaii	476,288,000	0.3%
40	Idaho	798,180,000	0.6%
7	Illinois	4,909,599,000	3.4%
15	Indiana	3,212,071,000	2.2%
29	Iowa	1,749,542,000	1.2%
33	Kansas	1,385,466,000	1.0%
26	Kentucky	2,253,925,000	1.6%
25	Louisiana	2,300,315,000	1.6%
39	Maine	808,179,000	0.6%
21	Maryland	2,766,832,000	1.9%
18	Massachusetts	2,847,702,000	2.0%
9	Michigan	4,818,198,000	3.3%
22	Minnesota	2,718,121,000	1.9%
28	Mississippi	1,772,202,000	1.2%
14	Missouri	3,263,674,000	2.3%
42	Montana	553,280,000	0.4%
37	Nebraska	918,562,000	0.6%
35	Nevada	1,190,679,000	0.8%
41	New Hampshire	724,109,000	0.5%
11	New Jersey	4,242,312,000	2.9%
36	New Mexico	974,583,000	0.7%
4	New York	5,722,043,000	4.0%
10	North Carolina	4,764,796,000	3.3%
46	North Dakota	450,482,000	0.3%
5	Ohio	5,176,318,000	3.6%
27	Oklahoma	1,997,284,000	1.4%
30	Oregon	1,614,113,000	1.1%
6	Pennsylvania	5,005,677,000	3.5%
47	Rhode Island	378,042,000	0.3%
17	South Carolina	2,884,052,000	2.0%
43	South Dakota	491,190,000	0.3%
13	Tennessee	3,465,026,000	2.4%
2	Texas	14,354,583,000	9.9%
34	Utah	1,213,040,000	0.8%
49	Vermont	314,924,000	0.2%
12	Virginia	4,111,964,000	2.8%
19	Washington	2,846,883,000	2.0%
38	West Virginia	835,971,000	0.6%
23	Wisconsin	2,663,044,000	1.8%
48	Wyoming	375,825,000	0.3%

RANK ORDER

RANK	STATE	GALLONS	% of USA
1	California	15,507,693,000	10.7%
2	Texas	14,354,583,000	9.9%
3	Florida	9,063,973,000	6.3%
4	New York	5,722,043,000	4.0%
5	Ohio	5,176,318,000	3.6%
6	Pennsylvania	5,005,677,000	3.5%
7	Illinois	4,909,599,000	3.4%
8	Georgia	4,849,071,000	3.3%
9	Michigan	4,818,198,000	3.3%
10	North Carolina	4,764,796,000	3.3%
11	New Jersey	4,242,312,000	2.9%
12	Virginia	4,111,964,000	2.8%
13	Tennessee	3,465,026,000	2.4%
14	Missouri	3,263,674,000	2.3%
15	Indiana	3,212,071,000	2.2%
16	Arizona	2,933,404,000	2.0%
17	South Carolina	2,884,052,000	2.0%
18	Massachusetts	2,847,702,000	2.0%
19	Washington	2,846,883,000	2.0%
20	Alabama	2,792,760,000	1.9%
21	Maryland	2,766,832,000	1.9%
22	Minnesota	2,718,121,000	1.9%
23	Wisconsin	2,663,044,000	1.8%
24	Colorado	2,384,635,000	1.6%
25	Louisiana	2,300,315,000	1.6%
26	Kentucky	2,253,925,000	1.6%
27	Oklahoma	1,997,284,000	1.4%
28	Mississippi	1,772,202,000	1.2%
29	Iowa	1,749,542,000	1.2%
30	Oregon	1,614,113,000	1.1%
31	Arkansas	1,537,354,000	1.1%
32	Connecticut	1,520,557,000	1.0%
33	Kansas	1,385,466,000	1.0%
34	Utah	1,213,040,000	0.8%
35	Nevada	1,190,679,000	0.8%
36	New Mexico	974,583,000	0.7%
37	Nebraska	918,562,000	0.6%
38	West Virginia	835,971,000	0.6%
39	Maine	808,179,000	0.6%
40	Idaho	798,180,000	0.6%
41	New Hampshire	724,109,000	0.5%
42	Montana	553,280,000	0.4%
43	South Dakota	491,190,000	0.3%
44	Delaware	490,959,000	0.3%
45	Hawaii	476,288,000	0.3%
46	North Dakota	450,482,000	0.3%
47	Rhode Island	378,042,000	0.3%
48	Wyoming	375,825,000	0.3%
49	Vermont	314,924,000	0.2%
50	Alaska	296,696,000	0.2%
	District of Columbia	120,263,000	0.1%

Source: U.S. Department of Transportation, Federal Highway Administration
    "Highway Statistics 2016" (Table MF-21, https://www.fhwa.dot.gov/policyinformation/statistics/2016/)
*Includes gasoline for highway and nonhighway uses as well as for losses allowed for evaporation and handling. "Gasoline" includes gasohol but excludes "special fuels" such as diesel.

Per Capita Gasoline Used in 2016

National Per Capita = 448 Gallons*

ALPHA ORDER

RANK	STATE	PER CAPITA
6	Alabama	574
41	Alaska	400
38	Arizona	422
14	Arkansas	514
43	California	396
36	Colorado	430
37	Connecticut	425
13	Delaware	517
35	Florida	439
28	Georgia	471
49	Hawaii	334
27	Idaho	474
47	Illinois	383
22	Indiana	484
8	Iowa	559
26	Kansas	476
17	Kentucky	508
19	Louisiana	492
2	Maine	607
31	Maryland	461
39	Massachusetts	417
22	Michigan	484
19	Minnesota	492
4	Mississippi	593
10	Missouri	536
11	Montana	532
24	Nebraska	482
40	Nevada	408
9	New Hampshire	539
25	New Jersey	478
30	New Mexico	466
50	New York	291
29	North Carolina	469
3	North Dakota	597
34	Ohio	445
16	Oklahoma	509
44	Oregon	395
45	Pennsylvania	392
48	Rhode Island	358
5	South Carolina	582
7	South Dakota	569
12	Tennessee	521
14	Texas	514
42	Utah	399
18	Vermont	505
21	Virginia	489
46	Washington	390
33	West Virginia	457
31	Wisconsin	461
1	Wyoming	643

RANK ORDER

RANK	STATE	PER CAPITA
1	Wyoming	643
2	Maine	607
3	North Dakota	597
4	Mississippi	593
5	South Carolina	582
6	Alabama	574
7	South Dakota	569
8	Iowa	559
9	New Hampshire	539
10	Missouri	536
11	Montana	532
12	Tennessee	521
13	Delaware	517
14	Arkansas	514
14	Texas	514
16	Oklahoma	509
17	Kentucky	508
18	Vermont	505
19	Louisiana	492
19	Minnesota	492
21	Virginia	489
22	Indiana	484
22	Michigan	484
24	Nebraska	482
25	New Jersey	478
26	Kansas	476
27	Idaho	474
28	Georgia	471
29	North Carolina	469
30	New Mexico	466
31	Maryland	461
31	Wisconsin	461
33	West Virginia	457
34	Ohio	445
35	Florida	439
36	Colorado	430
37	Connecticut	425
38	Arizona	422
39	Massachusetts	417
40	Nevada	408
41	Alaska	400
42	Utah	399
43	California	396
44	Oregon	395
45	Pennsylvania	392
46	Washington	390
47	Illinois	383
48	Rhode Island	358
49	Hawaii	334
50	New York	291
	District of Columbia	175

Source: CQ Press using data from U.S. Department of Transportation, Federal Highway Administration
"Highway Statistics 2016" (Table MF-21, https://www.fhwa.dot.gov/policyinformation/statistics/2016/)
*Includes gasoline for highway and nonhighway uses as well as for losses allowed for evaporation and handling. "Gasoline" includes gasohol but excludes "special fuels" such as diesel.

Daily Production of Crude Oil in 2017

National Total = 9,351,715 Barrels a Day*

ALPHA ORDER

RANK	STATE	BARRELS	% of USA
17	Alabama	18,704	0.2%
3	Alaska	494,430	5.3%
31	Arizona	36	0.0%
20	Arkansas	14,488	0.2%
4	California	477,005	5.1%
7	Colorado	358,170	3.8%
NA	Connecticut**	NA	NA
NA	Delaware**	NA	NA
23	Florida	5,268	0.1%
NA	Georgia**	NA	NA
NA	Hawaii**	NA	NA
30	Idaho	249	0.0%
16	Illinois	22,778	0.2%
24	Indiana	4,874	0.1%
NA	Iowa**	NA	NA
10	Kansas	98,142	1.0%
21	Kentucky	6,786	0.1%
9	Louisiana	142,532	1.5%
NA	Maine**	NA	NA
NA	Maryland**	NA	NA
NA	Massachusetts**	NA	NA
19	Michigan	14,573	0.2%
NA	Minnesota**	NA	NA
14	Mississippi	48,715	0.5%
29	Missouri	310	0.0%
12	Montana	56,729	0.6%
22	Nebraska	5,822	0.1%
26	Nevada	784	0.0%
NA	New Hampshire**	NA	NA
NA	New Jersey**	NA	NA
5	New Mexico	469,699	5.0%
28	New York	504	0.0%
NA	North Carolina**	NA	NA
2	North Dakota	1,074,321	11.5%
13	Ohio	51,896	0.6%
6	Oklahoma	454,575	4.9%
NA	Oregon**	NA	NA
18	Pennsylvania	18,008	0.2%
NA	Rhode Island**	NA	NA
NA	South Carolina**	NA	NA
25	South Dakota	3,575	0.0%
27	Tennessee	742	0.0%
1	Texas	3,486,507	37.3%
11	Utah	93,712	1.0%
NA	Vermont**	NA	NA
32	Virginia	19	0.0%
NA	Washington**	NA	NA
15	West Virginia	25,942	0.3%
NA	Wisconsin**	NA	NA
8	Wyoming	207,312	2.2%

RANK ORDER

RANK	STATE	BARRELS	% of USA
1	Texas	3,486,507	37.3%
2	North Dakota	1,074,321	11.5%
3	Alaska	494,430	5.3%
4	California	477,005	5.1%
5	New Mexico	469,699	5.0%
6	Oklahoma	454,575	4.9%
7	Colorado	358,170	3.8%
8	Wyoming	207,312	2.2%
9	Louisiana	142,532	1.5%
10	Kansas	98,142	1.0%
11	Utah	93,712	1.0%
12	Montana	56,729	0.6%
13	Ohio	51,896	0.6%
14	Mississippi	48,715	0.5%
15	West Virginia	25,942	0.3%
16	Illinois	22,778	0.2%
17	Alabama	18,704	0.2%
18	Pennsylvania	18,008	0.2%
19	Michigan	14,573	0.2%
20	Arkansas	14,488	0.2%
21	Kentucky	6,786	0.1%
22	Nebraska	5,822	0.1%
23	Florida	5,268	0.1%
24	Indiana	4,874	0.1%
25	South Dakota	3,575	0.0%
26	Nevada	784	0.0%
27	Tennessee	742	0.0%
28	New York	504	0.0%
29	Missouri	310	0.0%
30	Idaho	249	0.0%
31	Arizona	36	0.0%
32	Virginia	19	0.0%
NA	Connecticut**	NA	NA
NA	Delaware**	NA	NA
NA	Georgia**	NA	NA
NA	Hawaii**	NA	NA
NA	Iowa**	NA	NA
NA	Maine**	NA	NA
NA	Maryland**	NA	NA
NA	Massachusetts**	NA	NA
NA	Minnesota**	NA	NA
NA	New Hampshire**	NA	NA
NA	New Jersey**	NA	NA
NA	North Carolina**	NA	NA
NA	Oregon**	NA	NA
NA	Rhode Island**	NA	NA
NA	South Carolina**	NA	NA
NA	Vermont**	NA	NA
NA	Washington**	NA	NA
NA	Wisconsin**	NA	NA
	District of Columbia**	NA	NA

Source: CQ Press using data from U.S. Department of Energy, Energy Information Administration

"Petroleum Supply Annual 2017, Volume 1" (https://tonto.eia.doe.gov/dnav/pet/pet_crd_crpdn_adc_mbbl_m.htm)

*National total includes 1,694,504 barrels a day in federal offshore production. Figures for Alaska, California, Louisiana, and Texas include state offshore production.

**No reported production.

Fossil Fuel Emissions in 2016

National Total = 4,966,000,000 Metric Tons of Carbon Dioxide (CO2)*

ALPHA ORDER

RANK	STATE	TONS OF CO2	% of USA
15	Alabama	113,810,000	2.3%
40	Alaska	34,710,000	0.7%
24	Arizona	86,790,000	1.7%
31	Arkansas	62,220,000	1.3%
2	California	366,410,000	7.4%
23	Colorado	88,530,000	1.8%
41	Connecticut	34,400,000	0.7%
47	Delaware	13,960,000	0.3%
3	Florida	229,110,000	4.6%
11	Georgia	135,590,000	2.7%
43	Hawaii	18,500,000	0.4%
44	Idaho	18,420,000	0.4%
7	Illinois	205,530,000	4.1%
8	Indiana	181,340,000	3.7%
26	Iowa	74,390,000	1.5%
30	Kansas	62,310,000	1.3%
12	Kentucky	124,550,000	2.5%
5	Louisiana	213,170,000	4.3%
45	Maine	16,500,000	0.3%
34	Maryland	58,210,000	1.2%
29	Massachusetts	64,390,000	1.3%
10	Michigan	151,690,000	3.1%
22	Minnesota	89,270,000	1.8%
28	Mississippi	69,130,000	1.4%
14	Missouri	117,870,000	2.4%
42	Montana	30,830,000	0.6%
37	Nebraska	48,280,000	1.0%
39	Nevada	36,690,000	0.7%
48	New Hampshire	13,780,000	0.3%
16	New Jersey	111,720,000	2.2%
36	New Mexico	48,660,000	1.0%
9	New York	164,530,000	3.3%
13	North Carolina	119,750,000	2.4%
35	North Dakota	51,120,000	1.0%
6	Ohio	205,730,000	4.1%
19	Oklahoma	97,180,000	2.0%
38	Oregon	37,920,000	0.8%
4	Pennsylvania	216,840,000	4.4%
49	Rhode Island	9,750,000	0.2%
27	South Carolina	72,120,000	1.5%
46	South Dakota	14,920,000	0.3%
18	Tennessee	102,700,000	2.1%
1	Texas	705,460,000	14.2%
33	Utah	58,460,000	1.2%
50	Vermont	5,980,000	0.1%
17	Virginia	103,810,000	2.1%
25	Washington	81,060,000	1.6%
21	West Virginia	92,750,000	1.9%
20	Wisconsin	95,200,000	1.9%
32	Wyoming	60,670,000	1.2%

RANK ORDER

RANK	STATE	TONS OF CO2	% of USA
1	Texas	705,460,000	14.2%
2	California	366,410,000	7.4%
3	Florida	229,110,000	4.6%
4	Pennsylvania	216,840,000	4.4%
5	Louisiana	213,170,000	4.3%
6	Ohio	205,730,000	4.1%
7	Illinois	205,530,000	4.1%
8	Indiana	181,340,000	3.7%
9	New York	164,530,000	3.3%
10	Michigan	151,690,000	3.1%
11	Georgia	135,590,000	2.7%
12	Kentucky	124,550,000	2.5%
13	North Carolina	119,750,000	2.4%
14	Missouri	117,870,000	2.4%
15	Alabama	113,810,000	2.3%
16	New Jersey	111,720,000	2.2%
17	Virginia	103,810,000	2.1%
18	Tennessee	102,700,000	2.1%
19	Oklahoma	97,180,000	2.0%
20	Wisconsin	95,200,000	1.9%
21	West Virginia	92,750,000	1.9%
22	Minnesota	89,270,000	1.8%
23	Colorado	88,530,000	1.8%
24	Arizona	86,790,000	1.7%
25	Washington	81,060,000	1.6%
26	Iowa	74,390,000	1.5%
27	South Carolina	72,120,000	1.5%
28	Mississippi	69,130,000	1.4%
29	Massachusetts	64,390,000	1.3%
30	Kansas	62,310,000	1.3%
31	Arkansas	62,220,000	1.3%
32	Wyoming	60,670,000	1.2%
33	Utah	58,460,000	1.2%
34	Maryland	58,210,000	1.2%
35	North Dakota	51,120,000	1.0%
36	New Mexico	48,660,000	1.0%
37	Nebraska	48,280,000	1.0%
38	Oregon	37,920,000	0.8%
39	Nevada	36,690,000	0.7%
40	Alaska	34,710,000	0.7%
41	Connecticut	34,400,000	0.7%
42	Montana	30,830,000	0.6%
43	Hawaii	18,500,000	0.4%
44	Idaho	18,420,000	0.4%
45	Maine	16,500,000	0.3%
46	South Dakota	14,920,000	0.3%
47	Delaware	13,960,000	0.3%
48	New Hampshire	13,780,000	0.3%
49	Rhode Island	9,750,000	0.2%
50	Vermont	5,980,000	0.1%
	District of Columbia	2,770,000	0.1%

Source: U.S. Environmental Protection Agency
   "Energy CO2 Emissions by State" (https://www.epa.gov/statelocalenergy/state-co2-emissions-fossil-fuel-combustion)
*Carbon dioxide (CO2) emissions from fossil fuel combustion. This represents the largest source (94%) of total CO2 emissions from all emission sources. Emissions are based on the location where fossil fuels are used. Fuels can be used in one state to generate electricity consumed in another. National figure does not include non-energy use of fuels.

Per Capita Fossil Fuel Emissions in 2016

National Per Capita = 15.4 Metric Tons of Carbon Dioxide (CO2)*

ALPHA ORDER

RANK ORDER

RANK	STATE	PER CAPITA		RANK	STATE	PER CAPITA
13	Alabama	23.4		1	Wyoming	103.8
4	Alaska	46.8		2	North Dakota	67.8
35	Arizona	12.5		3	West Virginia	50.7
17	Arkansas	20.8		4	Alaska	46.8
47	California	9.3		5	Louisiana	45.6
25	Colorado	16.0		6	Montana	29.6
44	Connecticut	9.6		7	Kentucky	28.1
29	Delaware	14.7		8	Indiana	27.3
39	Florida	11.1		9	Nebraska	25.3
31	Georgia	13.2		9	Texas	25.3
32	Hawaii	13.0		11	Oklahoma	24.7
41	Idaho	10.9		12	Iowa	23.8
25	Illinois	16.0		13	Alabama	23.4
8	Indiana	27.3		14	New Mexico	23.3
12	Iowa	23.8		15	Mississippi	23.1
16	Kansas	21.4		16	Kansas	21.4
7	Kentucky	28.1		17	Arkansas	20.8
5	Louisiana	45.6		18	Missouri	19.4
36	Maine	12.4		19	Utah	19.2
43	Maryland	9.7		20	Ohio	17.7
46	Massachusetts	9.4		21	South Dakota	17.3
28	Michigan	15.2		22	Pennsylvania	17.0
24	Minnesota	16.2		23	Wisconsin	16.5
15	Mississippi	23.1		24	Minnesota	16.2
18	Missouri	19.4		25	Colorado	16.0
6	Montana	29.6		25	Illinois	16.0
9	Nebraska	25.3		27	Tennessee	15.5
33	Nevada	12.6		28	Michigan	15.2
42	New Hampshire	10.3		29	Delaware	14.7
33	New Jersey	12.6		30	South Carolina	14.5
14	New Mexico	23.3		31	Georgia	13.2
50	New York	8.4		32	Hawaii	13.0
38	North Carolina	11.8		33	Nevada	12.6
2	North Dakota	67.8		33	New Jersey	12.6
20	Ohio	17.7		35	Arizona	12.5
11	Oklahoma	24.7		36	Maine	12.4
47	Oregon	9.3		37	Virginia	12.3
22	Pennsylvania	17.0		38	North Carolina	11.8
49	Rhode Island	9.2		39	Florida	11.1
30	South Carolina	14.5		39	Washington	11.1
21	South Dakota	17.3		41	Idaho	10.9
27	Tennessee	15.5		42	New Hampshire	10.3
9	Texas	25.3		43	Maryland	9.7
19	Utah	19.2		44	Connecticut	9.6
44	Vermont	9.6		44	Vermont	9.6
37	Virginia	12.3		46	Massachusetts	9.4
39	Washington	11.1		47	California	9.3
3	West Virginia	50.7		47	Oregon	9.3
23	Wisconsin	16.5		49	Rhode Island	9.2
1	Wyoming	103.8		50	New York	8.4
					District of Columbia	4.0

Source: CQ Press using data from U.S. Environmental Protection Agency
    "Energy CO2 Emissions by State" (https://www.epa.gov/statelocalenergy/state-co2-emissions-fossil-fuel-combustion)
*Carbon dioxide (CO2) emissions from fossil fuel combustion. This represents the largest source (94%) of total CO2 emissions from all emission sources. Emissions are based on the location where fossil fuels are used. Fuels can be used in one state to generate electricity consumed in another. National figure doe not include non-energy use of fuels.

Percent Change in Fossil Fuel Emissions: 2012 to 2016

National Percent Change = 1.2% Decrease*

ALPHA ORDER				RANK ORDER		
RANK	STATE	PERCENT CHANGE		RANK	STATE	PERCENT CHANGE
41	Alabama	(6.4)		1	Idaho	17.3
47	Alaska	(8.5)		2	Washington	14.2
35	Arizona	(4.7)		3	Mississippi	10.6
37	Arkansas	(5.4)		4	Vermont	8.9
17	California	2.1		5	Virginia	6.5
27	Colorado	(1.6)		6	Nevada	6.3
20	Connecticut	0.4		6	New Jersey	6.3
21	Delaware	(0.1)		8	Wisconsin	5.6
13	Florida	3.2		9	Texas	5.3
21	Georgia	(0.1)		10	Maine	4.0
27	Hawaii	(1.6)		11	Massachusetts	3.9
1	Idaho	17.3		12	Tennessee	3.5
36	Illinois	(5.1)		13	Florida	3.2
40	Indiana	(6.2)		14	Minnesota	2.8
48	Iowa	(8.7)		14	Oregon	2.8
37	Kansas	(5.4)		14	West Virginia	2.8
49	Kentucky	(9.3)		17	California	2.1
26	Louisiana	(1.3)		18	New York	1.5
10	Maine	4.0		19	Montana	1.1
31	Maryland	(3.6)		20	Connecticut	0.4
11	Massachusetts	3.9		21	Delaware	(0.1)
25	Michigan	(0.3)		21	Georgia	(0.1)
14	Minnesota	2.8		23	North Carolina	(0.2)
3	Mississippi	10.6		23	South Dakota	(0.2)
42	Missouri	(7.1)		25	Michigan	(0.3)
19	Montana	1.1		26	Louisiana	(1.3)
32	Nebraska	(3.9)		27	Colorado	(1.6)
6	Nevada	6.3		27	Hawaii	(1.6)
37	New Hampshire	(5.4)		29	South Carolina	(2.0)
6	New Jersey	6.3		30	North Dakota	(2.7)
50	New Mexico	(9.4)		31	Maryland	(3.6)
18	New York	1.5		32	Nebraska	(3.9)
23	North Carolina	(0.2)		33	Utah	(4.3)
30	North Dakota	(2.7)		34	Ohio	(4.5)
34	Ohio	(4.5)		35	Arizona	(4.7)
43	Oklahoma	(7.2)		36	Illinois	(5.1)
14	Oregon	2.8		37	Arkansas	(5.4)
45	Pennsylvania	(7.8)		37	Kansas	(5.4)
44	Rhode Island	(7.7)		37	New Hampshire	(5.4)
29	South Carolina	(2.0)		40	Indiana	(6.2)
23	South Dakota	(0.2)		41	Alabama	(6.4)
12	Tennessee	3.5		42	Missouri	(7.1)
9	Texas	5.3		43	Oklahoma	(7.2)
33	Utah	(4.3)		44	Rhode Island	(7.7)
4	Vermont	8.9		45	Pennsylvania	(7.8)
5	Virginia	6.5		46	Wyoming	(8.1)
2	Washington	14.2		47	Alaska	(8.5)
14	West Virginia	2.8		48	Iowa	(8.7)
8	Wisconsin	5.6		49	Kentucky	(9.3)
46	Wyoming	(8.1)		50	New Mexico	(9.4)
					District of Columbia	4.1

Source: CQ Press using data from U.S. Environmental Protection Agency
"Energy CO2 Emissions by State" (https://www.epa.gov/statelocalenergy/state-co2-emissions-fossil-fuel-combustion)
*Based on metric tons of carbon dioxide (CO2).

Toxic Releases: Total Pollution Released in 2017

National Total = 3,875,362,462 Pounds*

ALPHA ORDER

RANK	STATE	POUNDS	% of USA
12	Alabama	77,303,792	2.0%
1	Alaska	1,174,114,486	30.3%
11	Arizona	77,609,387	2.0%
26	Arkansas	31,980,022	0.8%
32	California	25,685,903	0.7%
27	Colorado	31,718,247	0.8%
47	Connecticut	1,665,614	0.0%
44	Delaware	4,938,801	0.1%
14	Florida	58,883,130	1.5%
19	Georgia	48,037,030	1.2%
46	Hawaii	3,061,992	0.1%
21	Idaho	35,951,281	0.9%
8	Illinois	107,849,708	2.8%
6	Indiana	126,141,894	3.3%
23	Iowa	34,247,271	0.9%
37	Kansas	17,641,430	0.5%
18	Kentucky	49,190,687	1.3%
5	Louisiana	143,916,906	3.7%
40	Maine	11,870,987	0.3%
43	Maryland	4,955,602	0.1%
45	Massachusetts	4,369,358	0.1%
9	Michigan	92,745,979	2.4%
33	Minnesota	23,034,541	0.6%
13	Mississippi	65,979,839	1.7%
15	Missouri	55,384,607	1.4%
20	Montana	39,428,005	1.0%
38	Nebraska	16,528,990	0.4%
2	Nevada	397,742,968	10.3%
50	New Hampshire	304,812	0.0%
41	New Jersey	10,941,759	0.3%
36	New Mexico	17,786,085	0.5%
39	New York	12,762,463	0.3%
16	North Carolina	52,107,974	1.3%
25	North Dakota	32,076,741	0.8%
7	Ohio	111,464,576	2.9%
31	Oklahoma	30,091,306	0.8%
35	Oregon	17,839,373	0.5%
17	Pennsylvania	51,959,853	1.3%
49	Rhode Island	360,320	0.0%
24	South Carolina	32,934,203	0.8%
42	South Dakota	6,407,149	0.2%
10	Tennessee	82,310,995	2.1%
4	Texas	202,986,826	5.2%
3	Utah	304,098,383	7.8%
48	Vermont	406,027	0.0%
22	Virginia	34,468,311	0.9%
28	Washington	31,596,966	0.8%
30	West Virginia	30,139,482	0.8%
29	Wisconsin	30,199,582	0.8%
34	Wyoming	20,113,355	0.5%

RANK ORDER

RANK	STATE	POUNDS	% of USA
1	Alaska	1,174,114,486	30.3%
2	Nevada	397,742,968	10.3%
3	Utah	304,098,383	7.8%
4	Texas	202,986,826	5.2%
5	Louisiana	143,916,906	3.7%
6	Indiana	126,141,894	3.3%
7	Ohio	111,464,576	2.9%
8	Illinois	107,849,708	2.8%
9	Michigan	92,745,979	2.4%
10	Tennessee	82,310,995	2.1%
11	Arizona	77,609,387	2.0%
12	Alabama	77,303,792	2.0%
13	Mississippi	65,979,839	1.7%
14	Florida	58,883,130	1.5%
15	Missouri	55,384,607	1.4%
16	North Carolina	52,107,974	1.3%
17	Pennsylvania	51,959,853	1.3%
18	Kentucky	49,190,687	1.3%
19	Georgia	48,037,030	1.2%
20	Montana	39,428,005	1.0%
21	Idaho	35,951,281	0.9%
22	Virginia	34,468,311	0.9%
23	Iowa	34,247,271	0.9%
24	South Carolina	32,934,203	0.8%
25	North Dakota	32,076,741	0.8%
26	Arkansas	31,980,022	0.8%
27	Colorado	31,718,247	0.8%
28	Washington	31,596,966	0.8%
29	Wisconsin	30,199,582	0.8%
30	West Virginia	30,139,482	0.8%
31	Oklahoma	30,091,306	0.8%
32	California	25,685,903	0.7%
33	Minnesota	23,034,541	0.6%
34	Wyoming	20,113,355	0.5%
35	Oregon	17,839,373	0.5%
36	New Mexico	17,786,085	0.5%
37	Kansas	17,641,430	0.5%
38	Nebraska	16,528,990	0.4%
39	New York	12,762,463	0.3%
40	Maine	11,870,987	0.3%
41	New Jersey	10,941,759	0.3%
42	South Dakota	6,407,149	0.2%
43	Maryland	4,955,602	0.1%
44	Delaware	4,938,801	0.1%
45	Massachusetts	4,369,358	0.1%
46	Hawaii	3,061,992	0.1%
47	Connecticut	1,665,614	0.0%
48	Vermont	406,027	0.0%
49	Rhode Island	360,320	0.0%
50	New Hampshire	304,812	0.0%
	District of Columbia	27,464	0.0%

Source: U.S. Environmental Protection Agency, Office of Pollution Prevention and Toxics Information Management
   "2017 Toxics Release Inventory" (https://iaspub.epa.gov/triexplorer/tri_release.chemical)
*National total does not include 2,190,594 pounds of toxins in U.S. territories. Includes discharges to air, surface water, underground injection, and surface land. Includes both original (or manufacturing) industries and those added by EPA since it began tracking releases.

Toxic Releases: Total Air Emissions in 2017

National Total = 598,900,258 Pounds*

ALPHA ORDER

RANK	STATE	POUNDS	% of USA
5	Alabama	27,194,212	4.5%
47	Alaska	319,720	0.1%
36	Arizona	2,292,704	0.4%
17	Arkansas	15,321,535	2.6%
27	California	7,182,408	1.2%
35	Colorado	2,330,315	0.4%
45	Connecticut	728,217	0.1%
44	Delaware	746,669	0.1%
12	Florida	18,878,636	3.2%
4	Georgia	31,522,319	5.3%
39	Hawaii	2,001,955	0.3%
31	Idaho	5,130,768	0.9%
7	Illinois	25,056,903	4.2%
6	Indiana	25,466,379	4.3%
14	Iowa	17,021,322	2.8%
22	Kansas	9,772,341	1.6%
10	Kentucky	20,545,992	3.4%
1	Louisiana	55,617,952	9.3%
34	Maine	3,212,140	0.5%
33	Maryland	3,305,169	0.6%
41	Massachusetts	1,191,406	0.2%
21	Michigan	11,754,409	2.0%
25	Minnesota	8,535,336	1.4%
13	Mississippi	17,901,790	3.0%
26	Missouri	8,153,657	1.4%
38	Montana	2,067,144	0.3%
30	Nebraska	5,442,021	0.9%
46	Nevada	707,323	0.1%
49	New Hampshire	138,347	0.0%
40	New Jersey	1,720,216	0.3%
43	New Mexico	947,666	0.2%
32	New York	4,502,756	0.8%
9	North Carolina	22,648,693	3.8%
24	North Dakota	8,889,983	1.5%
3	Ohio	35,876,537	6.0%
15	Oklahoma	16,988,451	2.8%
29	Oregon	5,969,552	1.0%
18	Pennsylvania	14,675,650	2.5%
48	Rhode Island	178,697	0.0%
11	South Carolina	19,606,744	3.3%
42	South Dakota	1,173,133	0.2%
8	Tennessee	24,921,691	4.2%
2	Texas	52,260,085	8.7%
20	Utah	12,115,148	2.0%
50	Vermont	27,077	0.0%
16	Virginia	16,504,109	2.8%
28	Washington	6,881,247	1.1%
19	West Virginia	12,227,417	2.0%
23	Wisconsin	9,074,141	1.5%
37	Wyoming	2,171,781	0.4%

RANK ORDER

RANK	STATE	POUNDS	% of USA
1	Louisiana	55,617,952	9.3%
2	Texas	52,260,085	8.7%
3	Ohio	35,876,537	6.0%
4	Georgia	31,522,319	5.3%
5	Alabama	27,194,212	4.5%
6	Indiana	25,466,379	4.3%
7	Illinois	25,056,903	4.2%
8	Tennessee	24,921,691	4.2%
9	North Carolina	22,648,693	3.8%
10	Kentucky	20,545,992	3.4%
11	South Carolina	19,606,744	3.3%
12	Florida	18,878,636	3.2%
13	Mississippi	17,901,790	3.0%
14	Iowa	17,021,322	2.8%
15	Oklahoma	16,988,451	2.8%
16	Virginia	16,504,109	2.8%
17	Arkansas	15,321,535	2.6%
18	Pennsylvania	14,675,650	2.5%
19	West Virginia	12,227,417	2.0%
20	Utah	12,115,148	2.0%
21	Michigan	11,754,409	2.0%
22	Kansas	9,772,341	1.6%
23	Wisconsin	9,074,141	1.5%
24	North Dakota	8,889,983	1.5%
25	Minnesota	8,535,336	1.4%
26	Missouri	8,153,657	1.4%
27	California	7,182,408	1.2%
28	Washington	6,881,247	1.1%
29	Oregon	5,969,552	1.0%
30	Nebraska	5,442,021	0.9%
31	Idaho	5,130,768	0.9%
32	New York	4,502,756	0.8%
33	Maryland	3,305,169	0.6%
34	Maine	3,212,140	0.5%
35	Colorado	2,330,315	0.4%
36	Arizona	2,292,704	0.4%
37	Wyoming	2,171,781	0.4%
38	Montana	2,067,144	0.3%
39	Hawaii	2,001,955	0.3%
40	New Jersey	1,720,216	0.3%
41	Massachusetts	1,191,406	0.2%
42	South Dakota	1,173,133	0.2%
43	New Mexico	947,666	0.2%
44	Delaware	746,669	0.1%
45	Connecticut	728,217	0.1%
46	Nevada	707,323	0.1%
47	Alaska	319,720	0.1%
48	Rhode Island	178,697	0.0%
49	New Hampshire	138,347	0.0%
50	Vermont	27,077	0.0%
	District of Columbia	395	0.0%

Source: U.S. Environmental Protection Agency, Office of Pollution Prevention and Toxics Information Management
"2017 Toxics Release Inventory" (https://iaspub.epa.gov/triexplorer/tri_release.chemical)
*Includes fugitive and point source air emissions. National total does not include 1,668,170 pounds of emissions in U.S. territories. Includes both original (or manufacturing) industries and those added by EPA since it began tracking releases.

Toxic Releases: Total Surface Water Discharges in 2017

National Total = 190,301,436 Pounds*

ALPHA ORDER				RANK ORDER			
RANK	STATE	POUNDS	% of USA	RANK	STATE	POUNDS	% of USA
5	Alabama	11,203,306	5.9%	1	Texas	16,450,023	8.6%
36	Alaska	276,440	0.1%	2	Louisiana	14,208,845	7.5%
48	Arizona	829	0.0%	3	Indiana	14,130,840	7.4%
15	Arkansas	5,300,491	2.8%	4	Virginia	11,297,741	5.9%
28	California	2,514,308	1.3%	5	Alabama	11,203,306	5.9%
33	Colorado	1,421,988	0.7%	6	Mississippi	7,958,374	4.2%
45	Connecticut	30,308	0.0%	7	Georgia	7,316,820	3.8%
21	Delaware	3,823,135	2.0%	8	Illinois	7,296,084	3.8%
32	Florida	1,513,368	0.8%	9	North Carolina	7,195,898	3.8%
7	Georgia	7,316,820	3.8%	10	Ohio	6,887,399	3.6%
35	Hawaii	593,620	0.3%	11	Kentucky	6,487,889	3.4%
26	Idaho	2,728,213	1.4%	12	Iowa	6,388,293	3.4%
8	Illinois	7,296,084	3.8%	13	Pennsylvania	6,161,183	3.2%
3	Indiana	14,130,840	7.4%	14	Maine	5,408,731	2.8%
12	Iowa	6,388,293	3.4%	15	Arkansas	5,300,491	2.8%
37	Kansas	162,884	0.1%	16	New York	5,063,798	2.7%
11	Kentucky	6,487,889	3.4%	17	South Carolina	4,205,578	2.2%
2	Louisiana	14,208,845	7.5%	18	Nebraska	4,082,319	2.1%
14	Maine	5,408,731	2.8%	19	New Jersey	3,939,824	2.1%
41	Maryland	99,687	0.1%	20	Oklahoma	3,911,279	2.1%
46	Massachusetts	9,893	0.0%	21	Delaware	3,823,135	2.0%
25	Michigan	2,762,651	1.5%	22	Tennessee	3,415,678	1.8%
30	Minnesota	1,900,294	1.0%	23	South Dakota	3,208,741	1.7%
6	Mississippi	7,958,374	4.2%	24	Wisconsin	2,997,415	1.6%
29	Missouri	2,170,929	1.1%	25	Michigan	2,762,651	1.5%
42	Montana	76,457	0.0%	26	Idaho	2,728,213	1.4%
18	Nebraska	4,082,319	2.1%	27	Washington	2,527,952	1.3%
43	Nevada	43,575	0.0%	28	California	2,514,308	1.3%
49	New Hampshire	453	0.0%	29	Missouri	2,170,929	1.1%
19	New Jersey	3,939,824	2.1%	30	Minnesota	1,900,294	1.0%
44	New Mexico	36,480	0.0%	31	West Virginia	1,772,113	0.9%
16	New York	5,063,798	2.7%	32	Florida	1,513,368	0.8%
9	North Carolina	7,195,898	3.8%	33	Colorado	1,421,988	0.7%
39	North Dakota	134,845	0.1%	34	Oregon	907,473	0.5%
10	Ohio	6,887,399	3.6%	35	Hawaii	593,620	0.3%
20	Oklahoma	3,911,279	2.1%	36	Alaska	276,440	0.1%
34	Oregon	907,473	0.5%	37	Kansas	162,884	0.1%
13	Pennsylvania	6,161,183	3.2%	38	Vermont	143,046	0.1%
50	Rhode Island	368	0.0%	39	North Dakota	134,845	0.1%
17	South Carolina	4,205,578	2.2%	40	Utah	123,505	0.1%
23	South Dakota	3,208,741	1.7%	41	Maryland	99,687	0.1%
22	Tennessee	3,415,678	1.8%	42	Montana	76,457	0.0%
1	Texas	16,450,023	8.6%	43	Nevada	43,575	0.0%
40	Utah	123,505	0.1%	44	New Mexico	36,480	0.0%
38	Vermont	143,046	0.1%	45	Connecticut	30,308	0.0%
4	Virginia	11,297,741	5.9%	46	Massachusetts	9,893	0.0%
27	Washington	2,527,952	1.3%	47	Wyoming	8,668	0.0%
31	West Virginia	1,772,113	0.9%	48	Arizona	829	0.0%
24	Wisconsin	2,997,415	1.6%	49	New Hampshire	453	0.0%
47	Wyoming	8,668	0.0%	50	Rhode Island	368	0.0%
					District of Columbia	1,405	0.0%

Source: U.S. Environmental Protection Agency, Office of Pollution Prevention and Toxics Information Management
"2017 Toxics Release Inventory" (https://iaspub.epa.gov/triexplorer/tri_release.chemical)
*National total does not include 258,763 pounds of discharges in U.S. territories. Includes both original (or manufacturing) industries and those added by EPA since it began tracking releases.

Hazardous Waste Sites on the National Priority List in 2018

National Total = 1,400 Sites*

ALPHA ORDER				RANK ORDER			
RANK	STATE	SITES	% of USA	RANK	STATE	SITES	% of USA
31	Alabama	14	1.0%	1	New Jersey	115	8.2%
45	Alaska	6	0.4%	2	California	100	7.1%
41	Arizona	9	0.6%	3	Pennsylvania	97	6.9%
41	Arkansas	9	0.6%	4	New York	87	6.2%
2	California	100	7.1%	5	Michigan	67	4.8%
19	Colorado	21	1.5%	6	Texas	56	4.0%
30	Connecticut	15	1.1%	7	Florida	55	3.9%
27	Delaware	16	1.1%	8	Washington	51	3.6%
7	Florida	55	3.9%	9	Illinois	49	3.5%
25	Georgia	17	1.2%	10	Ohio	43	3.1%
46	Hawaii	3	0.2%	11	Indiana	42	3.0%
41	Idaho	9	0.6%	12	North Carolina	39	2.8%
9	Illinois	49	3.5%	13	Wisconsin	38	2.7%
11	Indiana	42	3.0%	14	Massachusetts	33	2.4%
33	Iowa	13	0.9%	14	Missouri	33	2.4%
33	Kansas	13	0.9%	16	Virginia	31	2.2%
33	Kentucky	13	0.9%	17	South Carolina	26	1.9%
27	Louisiana	16	1.1%	18	Minnesota	25	1.8%
33	Maine	13	0.9%	19	Colorado	21	1.5%
19	Maryland	21	1.5%	19	Maryland	21	1.5%
14	Massachusetts	33	2.4%	19	New Hampshire	21	1.5%
5	Michigan	67	4.8%	22	Tennessee	19	1.4%
18	Minnesota	25	1.8%	23	Montana	18	1.3%
39	Mississippi	11	0.8%	23	Utah	18	1.3%
14	Missouri	33	2.4%	25	Georgia	17	1.2%
23	Montana	18	1.3%	25	Nebraska	17	1.2%
25	Nebraska	17	1.2%	27	Delaware	16	1.1%
47	Nevada	2	0.1%	27	Louisiana	16	1.1%
19	New Hampshire	21	1.5%	27	New Mexico	16	1.1%
1	New Jersey	115	8.2%	30	Connecticut	15	1.1%
27	New Mexico	16	1.1%	31	Alabama	14	1.0%
4	New York	87	6.2%	31	Oregon	14	1.0%
12	North Carolina	39	2.8%	33	Iowa	13	0.9%
50	North Dakota	0	0.0%	33	Kansas	13	0.9%
10	Ohio	43	3.1%	33	Kentucky	13	0.9%
41	Oklahoma	9	0.6%	33	Maine	13	0.9%
31	Oregon	14	1.0%	37	Rhode Island	12	0.9%
3	Pennsylvania	97	6.9%	37	Vermont	12	0.9%
37	Rhode Island	12	0.9%	39	Mississippi	11	0.8%
17	South Carolina	26	1.9%	40	West Virginia	10	0.7%
47	South Dakota	2	0.1%	41	Arizona	9	0.6%
22	Tennessee	19	1.4%	41	Arkansas	9	0.6%
6	Texas	56	4.0%	41	Idaho	9	0.6%
23	Utah	18	1.3%	41	Oklahoma	9	0.6%
37	Vermont	12	0.9%	45	Alaska	6	0.4%
16	Virginia	31	2.2%	46	Hawaii	3	0.2%
8	Washington	51	3.6%	47	Nevada	2	0.1%
40	West Virginia	10	0.7%	47	South Dakota	2	0.1%
13	Wisconsin	38	2.7%	47	Wyoming	2	0.1%
47	Wyoming	2	0.1%	50	North Dakota	0	0.0%
					District of Columbia	1	0.1%

Source: U.S. Environmental Protection Agency
    "National Priorities List (NPL) Sites in the United States" (http://www.epa.gov/superfund/sites/npl/)
*As of January 18, 2018. Includes final and proposed General Superfund and Federal Facilities Sites. National total includes 18 sites in Puerto Rico, two in Guam, and one in the U.S. Virgin Islands.

Hazardous Waste Sites on the National Priority List
per 10,000 Square Miles in 2018
National Rate = 3.6 Sites per 10,000 Square Miles*

ALPHA ORDER

RANK	STATE	RATE
30	Alabama	2.7
49	Alaska	0.1
45	Arizona	0.8
38	Arkansas	1.7
20	California	6.1
37	Colorado	2.0
5	Connecticut	27.1
3	Delaware	64.3
14	Florida	8.4
28	Georgia	2.9
30	Hawaii	2.7
44	Idaho	1.1
13	Illinois	8.5
11	Indiana	11.5
32	Iowa	2.3
39	Kansas	1.6
26	Kentucky	3.2
27	Louisiana	3.1
25	Maine	3.7
8	Maryland	16.9
4	Massachusetts	31.3
19	Michigan	6.9
28	Minnesota	2.9
32	Mississippi	2.3
22	Missouri	4.7
43	Montana	1.2
34	Nebraska	2.2
47	Nevada	0.2
6	New Hampshire	22.5
1	New Jersey	131.8
41	New Mexico	1.3
9	New York	15.9
16	North Carolina	7.2
50	North Dakota	0.0
12	Ohio	9.6
41	Oklahoma	1.3
40	Oregon	1.4
7	Pennsylvania	21.1
2	Rhode Island	77.7
15	South Carolina	8.1
46	South Dakota	0.3
23	Tennessee	4.5
35	Texas	2.1
35	Utah	2.1
10	Vermont	12.5
16	Virginia	7.2
16	Washington	7.2
24	West Virginia	4.1
21	Wisconsin	5.8
47	Wyoming	0.2

RANK ORDER

RANK	STATE	RATE
1	New Jersey	131.8
2	Rhode Island	77.7
3	Delaware	64.3
4	Massachusetts	31.3
5	Connecticut	27.1
6	New Hampshire	22.5
7	Pennsylvania	21.1
8	Maryland	16.9
9	New York	15.9
10	Vermont	12.5
11	Indiana	11.5
12	Ohio	9.6
13	Illinois	8.5
14	Florida	8.4
15	South Carolina	8.1
16	North Carolina	7.2
16	Virginia	7.2
16	Washington	7.2
19	Michigan	6.9
20	California	6.1
21	Wisconsin	5.8
22	Missouri	4.7
23	Tennessee	4.5
24	West Virginia	4.1
25	Maine	3.7
26	Kentucky	3.2
27	Louisiana	3.1
28	Georgia	2.9
28	Minnesota	2.9
30	Alabama	2.7
30	Hawaii	2.7
32	Iowa	2.3
32	Mississippi	2.3
34	Nebraska	2.2
35	Texas	2.1
35	Utah	2.1
37	Colorado	2.0
38	Arkansas	1.7
39	Kansas	1.6
40	Oregon	1.4
41	New Mexico	1.3
41	Oklahoma	1.3
43	Montana	1.2
44	Idaho	1.1
45	Arizona	0.8
46	South Dakota	0.3
47	Nevada	0.2
47	Wyoming	0.2
49	Alaska	0.1
50	North Dakota	0.0
	District of Columbia**	NA

Source: CQ Press using data from U.S. Environmental Protection Agency
"National Priorities List (NPL) Sites in the United States" (http://www.epa.gov/superfund/sites/npl/)
*As of January 18, 2018. Includes final and proposed General Superfund and Federal Facilities Sites. National rate excludes
sites and square miles in Puerto Rico, Guam and the Virgin Islands. Based on land and water area of states.
**The District of Columbia has one site in its 68 square miles.

Hazardous Waste Sites Deleted from the National Priorities List as of 2018

National Total = 395 Sites*

ALPHA ORDER

RANK	STATE	SITES	% of USA
31	Alabama	3	0.8%
31	Alaska	3	0.8%
31	Arizona	3	0.8%
13	Arkansas	8	2.0%
8	California	13	3.3%
31	Colorado	3	0.8%
31	Connecticut	3	0.8%
14	Delaware	7	1.8%
4	Florida	26	6.6%
24	Georgia	5	1.3%
44	Hawaii	1	0.3%
31	Idaho	3	0.8%
20	Illinois	6	1.5%
11	Indiana	10	2.5%
11	Iowa	10	2.5%
24	Kansas	5	1.3%
14	Kentucky	7	1.8%
9	Louisiana	12	3.0%
31	Maine	3	0.8%
28	Maryland	4	1.0%
14	Massachusetts	7	1.8%
6	Michigan	20	5.1%
5	Minnesota	22	5.6%
31	Mississippi	3	0.8%
24	Missouri	5	1.3%
49	Montana	0	0.0%
44	Nebraska	1	0.3%
49	Nevada	0	0.0%
44	New Hampshire	1	0.3%
1	New Jersey	35	8.9%
28	New Mexico	4	1.0%
2	New York	32	8.1%
31	North Carolina	3	0.8%
40	North Dakota	2	0.5%
14	Ohio	7	1.8%
14	Oklahoma	7	1.8%
24	Oregon	5	1.3%
3	Pennsylvania	30	7.6%
44	Rhode Island	1	0.3%
20	South Carolina	6	1.5%
40	South Dakota	2	0.5%
20	Tennessee	6	1.5%
9	Texas	12	3.0%
20	Utah	6	1.5%
40	Vermont	2	0.5%
28	Virginia	4	1.0%
7	Washington	17	4.3%
40	West Virginia	2	0.5%
14	Wisconsin	7	1.8%
44	Wyoming	1	0.3%

RANK ORDER

RANK	STATE	SITES	% of USA
1	New Jersey	35	8.9%
2	New York	32	8.1%
3	Pennsylvania	30	7.6%
4	Florida	26	6.6%
5	Minnesota	22	5.6%
6	Michigan	20	5.1%
7	Washington	17	4.3%
8	California	13	3.3%
9	Louisiana	12	3.0%
9	Texas	12	3.0%
11	Indiana	10	2.5%
11	Iowa	10	2.5%
13	Arkansas	8	2.0%
14	Delaware	7	1.8%
14	Kentucky	7	1.8%
14	Massachusetts	7	1.8%
14	Ohio	7	1.8%
14	Oklahoma	7	1.8%
14	Wisconsin	7	1.8%
20	Illinois	6	1.5%
20	South Carolina	6	1.5%
20	Tennessee	6	1.5%
20	Utah	6	1.5%
24	Georgia	5	1.3%
24	Kansas	5	1.3%
24	Missouri	5	1.3%
24	Oregon	5	1.3%
28	Maryland	4	1.0%
28	New Mexico	4	1.0%
28	Virginia	4	1.0%
31	Alabama	3	0.8%
31	Alaska	3	0.8%
31	Arizona	3	0.8%
31	Colorado	3	0.8%
31	Connecticut	3	0.8%
31	Idaho	3	0.8%
31	Maine	3	0.8%
31	Mississippi	3	0.8%
31	North Carolina	3	0.8%
40	North Dakota	2	0.5%
40	South Dakota	2	0.5%
40	Vermont	2	0.5%
40	West Virginia	2	0.5%
44	Hawaii	1	0.3%
44	Nebraska	1	0.3%
44	New Hampshire	1	0.3%
44	Rhode Island	1	0.3%
44	Wyoming	1	0.3%
49	Montana	0	0.0%
49	Nevada	0	0.0%
	District of Columbia	0	0.0%

Source: U.S. Environmental Protection Agency
   "National Priorities List (NPL) Sites in the United States" (http://www.epa.gov/superfund/sites/npl/)
*Cumulative total as of January 18, 2018. National total includes six sites in Puerto Rico and four in other U.S. territories.

VIII. Geography

Total Area of States in Square Miles in 2010

National Total = 3,796,742 Square Miles*

<table>
<tr><td colspan="4">ALPHA ORDER</td><td colspan="4">RANK ORDER</td></tr>
<tr><th>RANK</th><th>STATE</th><th>MILES</th><th>% of USA</th><th>RANK</th><th>STATE</th><th>MILES</th><th>% of USA</th></tr>
<tr><td>30</td><td>Alabama</td><td>52,420</td><td>1.4%</td><td>1</td><td>Alaska</td><td>665,384</td><td>17.5%</td></tr>
<tr><td>1</td><td>Alaska</td><td>665,384</td><td>17.5%</td><td>2</td><td>Texas</td><td>268,596</td><td>7.1%</td></tr>
<tr><td>6</td><td>Arizona</td><td>113,990</td><td>3.0%</td><td>3</td><td>California</td><td>163,695</td><td>4.3%</td></tr>
<tr><td>29</td><td>Arkansas</td><td>53,179</td><td>1.4%</td><td>4</td><td>Montana</td><td>147,040</td><td>3.9%</td></tr>
<tr><td>3</td><td>California</td><td>163,695</td><td>4.3%</td><td>5</td><td>New Mexico</td><td>121,590</td><td>3.2%</td></tr>
<tr><td>8</td><td>Colorado</td><td>104,094</td><td>2.7%</td><td>6</td><td>Arizona</td><td>113,990</td><td>3.0%</td></tr>
<tr><td>48</td><td>Connecticut</td><td>5,543</td><td>0.1%</td><td>7</td><td>Nevada</td><td>110,572</td><td>2.9%</td></tr>
<tr><td>49</td><td>Delaware</td><td>2,489</td><td>0.1%</td><td>8</td><td>Colorado</td><td>104,094</td><td>2.7%</td></tr>
<tr><td>22</td><td>Florida</td><td>65,758</td><td>1.7%</td><td>9</td><td>Oregon</td><td>98,379</td><td>2.6%</td></tr>
<tr><td>24</td><td>Georgia</td><td>59,425</td><td>1.6%</td><td>10</td><td>Wyoming</td><td>97,813</td><td>2.6%</td></tr>
<tr><td>43</td><td>Hawaii</td><td>10,932</td><td>0.3%</td><td>11</td><td>Michigan</td><td>96,714</td><td>2.5%</td></tr>
<tr><td>14</td><td>Idaho</td><td>83,569</td><td>2.2%</td><td>12</td><td>Minnesota</td><td>86,936</td><td>2.3%</td></tr>
<tr><td>25</td><td>Illinois</td><td>57,914</td><td>1.5%</td><td>13</td><td>Utah</td><td>84,897</td><td>2.2%</td></tr>
<tr><td>38</td><td>Indiana</td><td>36,420</td><td>1.0%</td><td>14</td><td>Idaho</td><td>83,569</td><td>2.2%</td></tr>
<tr><td>26</td><td>Iowa</td><td>56,273</td><td>1.5%</td><td>15</td><td>Kansas</td><td>82,278</td><td>2.2%</td></tr>
<tr><td>15</td><td>Kansas</td><td>82,278</td><td>2.2%</td><td>16</td><td>Nebraska</td><td>77,348</td><td>2.0%</td></tr>
<tr><td>37</td><td>Kentucky</td><td>40,408</td><td>1.1%</td><td>17</td><td>South Dakota</td><td>77,116</td><td>2.0%</td></tr>
<tr><td>31</td><td>Louisiana</td><td>52,378</td><td>1.4%</td><td>18</td><td>Washington</td><td>71,298</td><td>1.9%</td></tr>
<tr><td>39</td><td>Maine</td><td>35,380</td><td>0.9%</td><td>19</td><td>North Dakota</td><td>70,698</td><td>1.9%</td></tr>
<tr><td>42</td><td>Maryland</td><td>12,406</td><td>0.3%</td><td>20</td><td>Oklahoma</td><td>69,899</td><td>1.8%</td></tr>
<tr><td>44</td><td>Massachusetts</td><td>10,554</td><td>0.3%</td><td>21</td><td>Missouri</td><td>69,707</td><td>1.8%</td></tr>
<tr><td>11</td><td>Michigan</td><td>96,714</td><td>2.5%</td><td>22</td><td>Florida</td><td>65,758</td><td>1.7%</td></tr>
<tr><td>12</td><td>Minnesota</td><td>86,936</td><td>2.3%</td><td>23</td><td>Wisconsin</td><td>65,496</td><td>1.7%</td></tr>
<tr><td>32</td><td>Mississippi</td><td>48,432</td><td>1.3%</td><td>24</td><td>Georgia</td><td>59,425</td><td>1.6%</td></tr>
<tr><td>21</td><td>Missouri</td><td>69,707</td><td>1.8%</td><td>25</td><td>Illinois</td><td>57,914</td><td>1.5%</td></tr>
<tr><td>4</td><td>Montana</td><td>147,040</td><td>3.9%</td><td>26</td><td>Iowa</td><td>56,273</td><td>1.5%</td></tr>
<tr><td>16</td><td>Nebraska</td><td>77,348</td><td>2.0%</td><td>27</td><td>New York</td><td>54,555</td><td>1.4%</td></tr>
<tr><td>7</td><td>Nevada</td><td>110,572</td><td>2.9%</td><td>28</td><td>North Carolina</td><td>53,819</td><td>1.4%</td></tr>
<tr><td>46</td><td>New Hampshire</td><td>9,349</td><td>0.2%</td><td>29</td><td>Arkansas</td><td>53,179</td><td>1.4%</td></tr>
<tr><td>47</td><td>New Jersey</td><td>8,723</td><td>0.2%</td><td>30</td><td>Alabama</td><td>52,420</td><td>1.4%</td></tr>
<tr><td>5</td><td>New Mexico</td><td>121,590</td><td>3.2%</td><td>31</td><td>Louisiana</td><td>52,378</td><td>1.4%</td></tr>
<tr><td>27</td><td>New York</td><td>54,555</td><td>1.4%</td><td>32</td><td>Mississippi</td><td>48,432</td><td>1.3%</td></tr>
<tr><td>28</td><td>North Carolina</td><td>53,819</td><td>1.4%</td><td>33</td><td>Pennsylvania</td><td>46,054</td><td>1.2%</td></tr>
<tr><td>19</td><td>North Dakota</td><td>70,698</td><td>1.9%</td><td>34</td><td>Ohio</td><td>44,826</td><td>1.2%</td></tr>
<tr><td>34</td><td>Ohio</td><td>44,826</td><td>1.2%</td><td>35</td><td>Virginia</td><td>42,775</td><td>1.1%</td></tr>
<tr><td>20</td><td>Oklahoma</td><td>69,899</td><td>1.8%</td><td>36</td><td>Tennessee</td><td>42,144</td><td>1.1%</td></tr>
<tr><td>9</td><td>Oregon</td><td>98,379</td><td>2.6%</td><td>37</td><td>Kentucky</td><td>40,408</td><td>1.1%</td></tr>
<tr><td>33</td><td>Pennsylvania</td><td>46,054</td><td>1.2%</td><td>38</td><td>Indiana</td><td>36,420</td><td>1.0%</td></tr>
<tr><td>50</td><td>Rhode Island</td><td>1,545</td><td>0.0%</td><td>39</td><td>Maine</td><td>35,380</td><td>0.9%</td></tr>
<tr><td>40</td><td>South Carolina</td><td>32,020</td><td>0.8%</td><td>40</td><td>South Carolina</td><td>32,020</td><td>0.8%</td></tr>
<tr><td>17</td><td>South Dakota</td><td>77,116</td><td>2.0%</td><td>41</td><td>West Virginia</td><td>24,230</td><td>0.6%</td></tr>
<tr><td>36</td><td>Tennessee</td><td>42,144</td><td>1.1%</td><td>42</td><td>Maryland</td><td>12,406</td><td>0.3%</td></tr>
<tr><td>2</td><td>Texas</td><td>268,596</td><td>7.1%</td><td>43</td><td>Hawaii</td><td>10,932</td><td>0.3%</td></tr>
<tr><td>13</td><td>Utah</td><td>84,897</td><td>2.2%</td><td>44</td><td>Massachusetts</td><td>10,554</td><td>0.3%</td></tr>
<tr><td>45</td><td>Vermont</td><td>9,616</td><td>0.3%</td><td>45</td><td>Vermont</td><td>9,616</td><td>0.3%</td></tr>
<tr><td>35</td><td>Virginia</td><td>42,775</td><td>1.1%</td><td>46</td><td>New Hampshire</td><td>9,349</td><td>0.2%</td></tr>
<tr><td>18</td><td>Washington</td><td>71,298</td><td>1.9%</td><td>47</td><td>New Jersey</td><td>8,723</td><td>0.2%</td></tr>
<tr><td>41</td><td>West Virginia</td><td>24,230</td><td>0.6%</td><td>48</td><td>Connecticut</td><td>5,543</td><td>0.1%</td></tr>
<tr><td>23</td><td>Wisconsin</td><td>65,496</td><td>1.7%</td><td>49</td><td>Delaware</td><td>2,489</td><td>0.1%</td></tr>
<tr><td>10</td><td>Wyoming</td><td>97,813</td><td>2.6%</td><td>50</td><td>Rhode Island</td><td>1,545</td><td>0.0%</td></tr>
<tr><td></td><td></td><td></td><td></td><td></td><td>District of Columbia</td><td>68</td><td>0.0%</td></tr>
</table>

Source: U.S. Bureau of the Census
   "State Area Measurements" (http://www.census.gov/geo/reference/state-area.html)
*Total of land and water area. Revised figures as of January 1, 2010

Land Area of States in Square Miles in 2010

National Total = 3,531,905 Square Miles of Land Area*

ALPHA ORDER

RANK	STATE	MILES	% of USA
28	Alabama	50,645	1.4%
1	Alaska	570,641	16.2%
6	Arizona	113,594	3.2%
27	Arkansas	52,035	1.5%
3	California	155,779	4.4%
8	Colorado	103,642	2.9%
48	Connecticut	4,842	0.1%
49	Delaware	1,949	0.1%
26	Florida	53,625	1.5%
21	Georgia	57,513	1.6%
47	Hawaii	6,423	0.2%
11	Idaho	82,643	2.3%
24	Illinois	55,519	1.6%
38	Indiana	35,826	1.0%
23	Iowa	55,857	1.6%
13	Kansas	81,759	2.3%
37	Kentucky	39,486	1.1%
33	Louisiana	43,204	1.2%
39	Maine	30,843	0.9%
42	Maryland	9,707	0.3%
45	Massachusetts	7,800	0.2%
22	Michigan	56,539	1.6%
14	Minnesota	79,627	2.3%
31	Mississippi	46,923	1.3%
18	Missouri	68,742	1.9%
4	Montana	145,546	4.1%
15	Nebraska	76,824	2.2%
7	Nevada	109,781	3.1%
44	New Hampshire	8,953	0.3%
46	New Jersey	7,354	0.2%
5	New Mexico	121,298	3.4%
30	New York	47,126	1.3%
29	North Carolina	48,618	1.4%
17	North Dakota	69,001	2.0%
35	Ohio	40,861	1.2%
19	Oklahoma	68,595	1.9%
10	Oregon	95,988	2.7%
32	Pennsylvania	44,743	1.3%
50	Rhode Island	1,034	0.0%
40	South Carolina	30,061	0.9%
16	South Dakota	75,811	2.1%
34	Tennessee	41,235	1.2%
2	Texas	261,232	7.4%
12	Utah	82,170	2.3%
43	Vermont	9,217	0.3%
36	Virginia	39,490	1.1%
20	Washington	66,456	1.9%
41	West Virginia	24,038	0.7%
25	Wisconsin	54,158	1.5%
9	Wyoming	97,093	2.7%

RANK ORDER

RANK	STATE	MILES	% of USA
1	Alaska	570,641	16.2%
2	Texas	261,232	7.4%
3	California	155,779	4.4%
4	Montana	145,546	4.1%
5	New Mexico	121,298	3.4%
6	Arizona	113,594	3.2%
7	Nevada	109,781	3.1%
8	Colorado	103,642	2.9%
9	Wyoming	97,093	2.7%
10	Oregon	95,988	2.7%
11	Idaho	82,643	2.3%
12	Utah	82,170	2.3%
13	Kansas	81,759	2.3%
14	Minnesota	79,627	2.3%
15	Nebraska	76,824	2.2%
16	South Dakota	75,811	2.1%
17	North Dakota	69,001	2.0%
18	Missouri	68,742	1.9%
19	Oklahoma	68,595	1.9%
20	Washington	66,456	1.9%
21	Georgia	57,513	1.6%
22	Michigan	56,539	1.6%
23	Iowa	55,857	1.6%
24	Illinois	55,519	1.6%
25	Wisconsin	54,158	1.5%
26	Florida	53,625	1.5%
27	Arkansas	52,035	1.5%
28	Alabama	50,645	1.4%
29	North Carolina	48,618	1.4%
30	New York	47,126	1.3%
31	Mississippi	46,923	1.3%
32	Pennsylvania	44,743	1.3%
33	Louisiana	43,204	1.2%
34	Tennessee	41,235	1.2%
35	Ohio	40,861	1.2%
36	Virginia	39,490	1.1%
37	Kentucky	39,486	1.1%
38	Indiana	35,826	1.0%
39	Maine	30,843	0.9%
40	South Carolina	30,061	0.9%
41	West Virginia	24,038	0.7%
42	Maryland	9,707	0.3%
43	Vermont	9,217	0.3%
44	New Hampshire	8,953	0.3%
45	Massachusetts	7,800	0.2%
46	New Jersey	7,354	0.2%
47	Hawaii	6,423	0.2%
48	Connecticut	4,842	0.1%
49	Delaware	1,949	0.1%
50	Rhode Island	1,034	0.0%
	District of Columbia	61	0.0%

Source: U.S. Bureau of the Census
"State Area Measurements" (http://www.census.gov/geo/reference/state-area.html)
*Includes dry land temporarily or partially covered by water, such as marshland, swamps, etc.; streams and canals under one-eighth mile wide; and lakes, reservoirs, and ponds under 40 acres. Revised figures as of August 2010.

Water Area of States in Square Miles in 2010

National Total = 264,837 Square Miles of Water*

ALPHA ORDER				RANK ORDER			
RANK	STATE	MILES	% of USA	RANK	STATE	MILES	% of USA
23	Alabama	1,775	0.7%	1	Alaska	94,743	35.8%
1	Alaska	94,743	35.8%	2	Michigan	40,175	15.2%
48	Arizona	396	0.1%	3	Florida	12,133	4.6%
31	Arkansas	1,143	0.4%	4	Wisconsin	11,339	4.3%
6	California	7,916	3.0%	5	Louisiana	9,174	3.5%
44	Colorado	452	0.2%	6	California	7,916	3.0%
38	Connecticut	701	0.3%	7	New York	7,429	2.8%
40	Delaware	540	0.2%	8	Texas	7,365	2.8%
3	Florida	12,133	4.6%	9	Minnesota	7,309	2.8%
22	Georgia	1,912	0.7%	10	North Carolina	5,201	2.0%
13	Hawaii	4,509	1.7%	11	Washington	4,842	1.8%
33	Idaho	926	0.3%	12	Maine	4,537	1.7%
19	Illinois	2,395	0.9%	13	Hawaii	4,509	1.7%
39	Indiana	593	0.2%	14	Ohio	3,965	1.5%
45	Iowa	416	0.2%	15	Virginia	3,285	1.2%
42	Kansas	520	0.2%	16	Massachusetts	2,754	1.0%
34	Kentucky	921	0.3%	17	Utah	2,727	1.0%
5	Louisiana	9,174	3.5%	18	Maryland	2,699	1.0%
12	Maine	4,537	1.7%	19	Illinois	2,395	0.9%
18	Maryland	2,699	1.0%	20	Oregon	2,391	0.9%
16	Massachusetts	2,754	1.0%	21	South Carolina	1,960	0.7%
2	Michigan	40,175	15.2%	22	Georgia	1,912	0.7%
9	Minnesota	7,309	2.8%	23	Alabama	1,775	0.7%
25	Mississippi	1,509	0.6%	24	North Dakota	1,698	0.6%
32	Missouri	965	0.4%	25	Mississippi	1,509	0.6%
26	Montana	1,494	0.6%	26	Montana	1,494	0.6%
41	Nebraska	524	0.2%	27	New Jersey	1,368	0.5%
36	Nevada	791	0.3%	28	Pennsylvania	1,312	0.5%
47	New Hampshire	397	0.1%	29	South Dakota	1,305	0.5%
27	New Jersey	1,368	0.5%	30	Oklahoma	1,304	0.5%
49	New Mexico	292	0.1%	31	Arkansas	1,143	0.4%
7	New York	7,429	2.8%	32	Missouri	965	0.4%
10	North Carolina	5,201	2.0%	33	Idaho	926	0.3%
24	North Dakota	1,698	0.6%	34	Kentucky	921	0.3%
14	Ohio	3,965	1.5%	35	Tennessee	909	0.3%
30	Oklahoma	1,304	0.5%	36	Nevada	791	0.3%
20	Oregon	2,391	0.9%	37	Wyoming	720	0.3%
28	Pennsylvania	1,312	0.5%	38	Connecticut	701	0.3%
43	Rhode Island	511	0.2%	39	Indiana	593	0.2%
21	South Carolina	1,960	0.7%	40	Delaware	540	0.2%
29	South Dakota	1,305	0.5%	41	Nebraska	524	0.2%
35	Tennessee	909	0.3%	42	Kansas	520	0.2%
8	Texas	7,365	2.8%	43	Rhode Island	511	0.2%
17	Utah	2,727	1.0%	44	Colorado	452	0.2%
46	Vermont	400	0.2%	45	Iowa	416	0.2%
15	Virginia	3,285	1.2%	46	Vermont	400	0.2%
11	Washington	4,842	1.8%	47	New Hampshire	397	0.1%
50	West Virginia	192	0.1%	48	Arizona	396	0.1%
4	Wisconsin	11,339	4.3%	49	New Mexico	292	0.1%
37	Wyoming	720	0.3%	50	West Virginia	192	0.1%
					District of Columbia	7	0.0%

Source: U.S. Bureau of the Census
   "State Area Measurements" (http://www.census.gov/geo/reference/state-area.html)
*Includes permanent inland water surface, such as lakes, reservoirs, and ponds having an area of 40 acres or more, canals one-eighth mile or more in width; coastal waters behind or sheltered by headlands or islands separated by less than 1 nautical mile of water, and islands under 40 acres in area. Excludes areas of oceans, bays, etc., lying within U.S. jurisdiction but not defined as inland water. Revised figures as of August 2010.

Highest Point of Elevation in Feet

National High Point = 20,320 Feet Above Sea Level (Mt. McKinley, Alaska)

ALPHA ORDER

RANK	STATE	HIGHEST POINT
35	Alabama	2,407
1	Alaska	20,320
12	Arizona	12,633
34	Arkansas	2,753
2	California	14,494
3	Colorado	14,433
36	Connecticut	2,380
49	Delaware	448
50	Florida	345
25	Georgia	4,784
6	Hawaii	13,796
11	Idaho	12,662
45	Illinois	1,235
44	Indiana	1,257
42	Iowa	1,670
28	Kansas	4,039
27	Kentucky	4,145
48	Louisiana	535
22	Maine	5,268
32	Maryland	3,360
31	Massachusetts	3,491
38	Michigan	1,979
37	Minnesota	2,301
47	Mississippi	806
41	Missouri	1,772
10	Montana	12,799
20	Nebraska	5,424
9	Nevada	13,140
18	New Hampshire	6,288
40	New Jersey	1,803
8	New Mexico	13,161
21	New York	5,344
16	North Carolina	6,684
30	North Dakota	3,506
43	Ohio	1,550
23	Oklahoma	4,973
13	Oregon	11,239
33	Pennsylvania	3,213
46	Rhode Island	812
29	South Carolina	3,560
15	South Dakota	7,242
17	Tennessee	6,643
14	Texas	8,749
7	Utah	13,528
26	Vermont	4,393
19	Virginia	5,729
4	Washington	14,411
24	West Virginia	4,863
39	Wisconsin	1,951
5	Wyoming	13,804

RANK ORDER

RANK	STATE	HIGHEST POINT
1	Alaska	20,320
2	California	14,494
3	Colorado	14,433
4	Washington	14,411
5	Wyoming	13,804
6	Hawaii	13,796
7	Utah	13,528
8	New Mexico	13,161
9	Nevada	13,140
10	Montana	12,799
11	Idaho	12,662
12	Arizona	12,633
13	Oregon	11,239
14	Texas	8,749
15	South Dakota	7,242
16	North Carolina	6,684
17	Tennessee	6,643
18	New Hampshire	6,288
19	Virginia	5,729
20	Nebraska	5,424
21	New York	5,344
22	Maine	5,268
23	Oklahoma	4,973
24	West Virginia	4,863
25	Georgia	4,784
26	Vermont	4,393
27	Kentucky	4,145
28	Kansas	4,039
29	South Carolina	3,560
30	North Dakota	3,506
31	Massachusetts	3,491
32	Maryland	3,360
33	Pennsylvania	3,213
34	Arkansas	2,753
35	Alabama	2,407
36	Connecticut	2,380
37	Minnesota	2,301
38	Michigan	1,979
39	Wisconsin	1,951
40	New Jersey	1,803
41	Missouri	1,772
42	Iowa	1,670
43	Ohio	1,550
44	Indiana	1,257
45	Illinois	1,235
46	Rhode Island	812
47	Mississippi	806
48	Louisiana	535
49	Delaware	448
50	Florida	345
	District of Columbia	410

Source: U.S. Department of Interior, U.S. Geological Survey
"Elevations and Distances in the United States" (https://pubs.usgs.gov/gip/Elevations-Distances/elvadist.html)

Lowest Point of Elevation in Feet

National Low Point = 282 Feet Below Sea Level (Death Valley, California)*

ALPHA ORDER

ALPHA ORDER

RANK	STATE	LOWEST POINT	RANK	STATE	LOWEST POINT
3	Alabama	0	1	California	(282)
3	Alaska	0	2	Louisiana	(8)
26	Arizona	70	3	Alabama*	0
25	Arkansas	55	3	Alaska	0
1	California	(282)	3	Connecticut	0
50	Colorado	3,315	3	Delaware	0
3	Connecticut	0	3	Florida	0
3	Delaware	0	3	Georgia	0
3	Florida	0	3	Hawaii	0
3	Georgia	0	3	Maine	0
3	Hawaii	0	3	Maryland	0
42	Idaho	710	3	Massachusetts	0
32	Illinois	279	3	Mississippi	0
34	Indiana	320	3	New Hampshire	0
37	Iowa	480	3	New Jersey	0
41	Kansas	679	3	New York	0
31	Kentucky	257	3	North Carolina	0
2	Louisiana	(8)	3	Oregon	0
3	Maine	0	3	Pennsylvania	0
3	Maryland	0	3	Rhode Island	0
3	Massachusetts	0	3	South Carolina	0
38	Michigan	571	3	Texas	0
40	Minnesota	601	3	Virginia	0
3	Mississippi	0	3	Washington	0
29	Missouri	230	25	Arkansas	55
46	Montana	1,800	26	Arizona	70
44	Nebraska	840	27	Vermont	95
36	Nevada	479	28	Tennessee	178
3	New Hampshire	0	29	Missouri	230
3	New Jersey	0	30	West Virginia	240
48	New Mexico	2,842	31	Kentucky	257
3	New York	0	32	Illinois	279
3	North Carolina	0	33	Oklahoma	289
43	North Dakota	750	34	Indiana	320
35	Ohio	455	35	Ohio	455
33	Oklahoma	289	36	Nevada	479
3	Oregon	0	37	Iowa	480
3	Pennsylvania	0	38	Michigan	571
3	Rhode Island	0	39	Wisconsin	579
3	South Carolina	0	40	Minnesota	601
45	South Dakota	966	41	Kansas	679
28	Tennessee	178	42	Idaho	710
3	Texas	0	43	North Dakota	750
47	Utah	2,000	44	Nebraska	840
27	Vermont	95	45	South Dakota	966
3	Virginia	0	46	Montana	1,800
3	Washington	0	47	Utah	2,000
30	West Virginia	240	48	New Mexico	2,842
39	Wisconsin	579	49	Wyoming	3,099
49	Wyoming	3,099	50	Colorado	3,315
				District of Columbia	1

Source: U.S. Department of Interior, U.S. Geological Survey
"Elevations and Distances in the United States" (https://pubs.usgs.gov/gip/Elevations-Distances/elvadist.html)
*States with "0" have sea level as lowest point.

Approximate Mean Elevation in Feet

Approximate National Mean Elevation = 2,500 Feet Above Sea Level

ALPHA ORDER

RANK	STATE	MEAN ELEVATION
40	Alabama	500
15	Alaska	1,900
7	Arizona	4,100
36	Arkansas	650
11	California	2,900
1	Colorado	6,800
40	Connecticut	500
50	Delaware	60
48	Florida	100
37	Georgia	600
10	Hawaii	3,030
6	Idaho	5,000
37	Illinois	600
34	Indiana	700
22	Iowa	1,100
14	Kansas	2,000
33	Kentucky	750
48	Louisiana	100
37	Maine	600
43	Maryland	350
40	Massachusetts	500
29	Michigan	900
21	Minnesota	1,200
45	Mississippi	300
32	Missouri	800
8	Montana	3,400
12	Nebraska	2,600
5	Nevada	5,500
25	New Hampshire	1,000
46	New Jersey	250
4	New Mexico	5,700
25	New York	1,000
34	North Carolina	700
15	North Dakota	1,900
31	Ohio	850
20	Oklahoma	1,300
9	Oregon	3,300
22	Pennsylvania	1,100
47	Rhode Island	200
43	South Carolina	350
13	South Dakota	2,200
29	Tennessee	900
17	Texas	1,700
3	Utah	6,100
25	Vermont	1,000
28	Virginia	950
17	Washington	1,700
19	West Virginia	1,500
24	Wisconsin	1,050
2	Wyoming	6,700

RANK ORDER

RANK	STATE	MEAN ELEVATION
1	Colorado	6,800
2	Wyoming	6,700
3	Utah	6,100
4	New Mexico	5,700
5	Nevada	5,500
6	Idaho	5,000
7	Arizona	4,100
8	Montana	3,400
9	Oregon	3,300
10	Hawaii	3,030
11	California	2,900
12	Nebraska	2,600
13	South Dakota	2,200
14	Kansas	2,000
15	Alaska	1,900
15	North Dakota	1,900
17	Texas	1,700
17	Washington	1,700
19	West Virginia	1,500
20	Oklahoma	1,300
21	Minnesota	1,200
22	Iowa	1,100
22	Pennsylvania	1,100
24	Wisconsin	1,050
25	New Hampshire	1,000
25	New York	1,000
25	Vermont	1,000
28	Virginia	950
29	Michigan	900
29	Tennessee	900
31	Ohio	850
32	Missouri	800
33	Kentucky	750
34	Indiana	700
34	North Carolina	700
36	Arkansas	650
37	Georgia	600
37	Illinois	600
37	Maine	600
40	Alabama	500
40	Connecticut	500
40	Massachusetts	500
43	Maryland	350
43	South Carolina	350
45	Mississippi	300
46	New Jersey	250
47	Rhode Island	200
48	Florida	100
48	Louisiana	100
50	Delaware	60
	District of Columbia	150

Source: U.S. Department of Interior, U.S. Geological Survey
"Elevations and Distances in the United States" (http://erg.usgs.gov/isb/pubs/booklets/elvadist/elvadist.html)

Normal Daily Mean Temperature*

ALPHA ORDER			RANK ORDER		
RANK	STATE	MEAN TEMPERATURE	RANK	STATE	MEAN TEMPERATURE
7	Alabama	63.7	1	Hawaii	75.7
50	Alaska	31.9	2	Florida	72.0
6	Arizona	63.9	3	Louisiana	67.4
10	Arkansas	62.0	4	Texas	66.8
12	California	60.3	5	South Carolina	64.0
38	Colorado	48.4	6	Arizona	63.9
27	Connecticut	51.2	7	Alabama	63.7
20	Delaware**	54.4	8	Georgia	63.6
2	Florida	72.0	9	Mississippi	63.4
8	Georgia	63.6	10	Arkansas	62.0
1	Hawaii	75.7	11	Oklahoma	60.5
31	Idaho	50.3	12	California	60.3
33	Illinois	50.1	13	North Carolina	60.1
24	Indiana	52.0	14	Tennessee	58.7
39	Iowa	48.1	15	Virginia	57.2
22	Kansas	54.0	16	New Mexico	57.0
17	Kentucky	55.8	17	Kentucky	55.8
3	Louisiana	67.4	18	Missouri	55.2
47	Maine	42.5	19	Maryland**	54.6
19	Maryland**	54.6	20	Delaware**	54.4
37	Massachusetts	49.3	20	New Jersey	54.4
45	Michigan	44.7	22	Kansas	54.0
48	Minnesota	41.4	23	West Virginia	52.7
9	Mississippi	63.4	24	Indiana	52.0
18	Missouri	55.2	24	Nevada	52.0
46	Montana	44.0	26	Pennsylvania	51.6
36	Nebraska	49.4	27	Connecticut	51.2
24	Nevada	52.0	28	Oregon	51.1
41	New Hampshire**	45.9	28	Rhode Island**	51.1
20	New Jersey	54.4	28	Utah	51.1
16	New Mexico	57.0	31	Idaho	50.3
32	New York	50.2	32	New York	50.2
13	North Carolina	60.1	33	Illinois	50.1
49	North Dakota	41.3	34	Ohio	50.0
34	Ohio	50.0	34	Washington	50.0
11	Oklahoma	60.5	36	Nebraska	49.4
28	Oregon	51.1	37	Massachusetts	49.3
26	Pennsylvania	51.6	38	Colorado	48.4
28	Rhode Island**	51.1	39	Iowa	48.1
5	South Carolina	64.0	40	Wisconsin	46.3
42	South Dakota	45.2	41	New Hampshire**	45.9
14	Tennessee	58.7	42	South Dakota	45.2
4	Texas	66.8	42	Vermont**	45.2
28	Utah	51.1	44	Wyoming	44.8
42	Vermont**	45.2	45	Michigan	44.7
15	Virginia	57.2	46	Montana	44.0
34	Washington	50.0	47	Maine	42.5
23	West Virginia	52.7	48	Minnesota	41.4
40	Wisconsin	46.3	49	North Dakota	41.3
44	Wyoming	44.8	50	Alaska	31.9
				District of Columbia	55.9

Source: CQ Press using data from U.S. Department of Commerce, National Oceanic and Atmospheric Administration
    "Comparative Climatic Data Through 2012" (ftp://ftp.ncdc.noaa.gov/pub/data/ccd-data/CCD-2012.pdf)
*Based on 30-year averages, 1971-2000.
**Temperatures from these states are from a single location. All other states are from two or more reporting cities within each state, which were averaged to determine each state's average.

Percent of Days That Are Sunny*

ALPHA ORDER

ALPHA ORDER

RANK	STATE	PERCENT OF DAYS SUNNY
26	Alabama	58
50	Alaska	38
1	Arizona	85
8	Arkansas	66
4	California	72
4	Colorado	72
34	Connecticut**	56
36	Delaware**	55
7	Florida	67
16	Georgia	63
8	Hawaii	66
14	Idaho	64
31	Illinois	57
26	Indiana	58
22	Iowa	60
8	Kansas	66
36	Kentucky	55
14	Louisiana	64
31	Maine**	57
31	Maryland**	57
36	Massachusetts	55
44	Michigan	49
36	Minnesota	55
16	Mississippi	63
26	Missouri	58
24	Montana	59
16	Nebraska	63
2	Nevada	76
48	New Hampshire	44
34	New Jersey**	56
3	New Mexico	75
42	New York	51
22	North Carolina	60
24	North Dakota	59
42	Ohio	51
12	Oklahoma	65
46	Oregon**	48
41	Pennsylvania	53
26	Rhode Island**	58
20	South Carolina	62
16	South Dakota	63
26	Tennessee	58
12	Texas	65
6	Utah	68
44	Vermont**	49
21	Virginia	61
47	Washington	45
49	West Virginia**	40
40	Wisconsin	54
8	Wyoming	66

RANK ORDER

RANK	STATE	PERCENT OF DAYS SUNNY
1	Arizona	85
2	Nevada	76
3	New Mexico	75
4	California	72
4	Colorado	72
6	Utah	68
7	Florida	67
8	Arkansas	66
8	Hawaii	66
8	Kansas	66
8	Wyoming	66
12	Oklahoma	65
12	Texas	65
14	Idaho	64
14	Louisiana	64
16	Georgia	63
16	Mississippi	63
16	Nebraska	63
16	South Dakota	63
20	South Carolina	62
21	Virginia	61
22	Iowa	60
22	North Carolina	60
24	Montana	59
24	North Dakota	59
26	Alabama	58
26	Indiana	58
26	Missouri	58
26	Rhode Island**	58
26	Tennessee	58
31	Illinois	57
31	Maine**	57
31	Maryland**	57
34	Connecticut**	56
34	New Jersey**	56
36	Delaware**	55
36	Kentucky	55
36	Massachusetts	55
36	Minnesota	55
40	Wisconsin	54
41	Pennsylvania	53
42	New York	51
42	Ohio	51
44	Michigan	49
44	Vermont**	49
46	Oregon**	48
47	Washington	45
48	New Hampshire	44
49	West Virginia**	40
50	Alaska	38
	District of Columbia**	56

Source: CQ Press using data from U.S. Department of Commerce, National Oceanic and Atmospheric Administration
"Comparative Climatic Data Through 2012" (ftp://ftp.ncdc.noaa.gov/pub/data/ccd-data/CCD-2012.pdf)
*As a percent of possible sunshine updated through 2012.
**Percentages from these states are from a single location. All other states are from two or more reporting cities within each state, which were averaged to determine each state's average.

Average Wind Speed (MPH)*

<table>
<tr><td colspan="3">ALPHA ORDER</td><td colspan="3">RANK ORDER</td></tr>
<tr><td>RANK</td><td>STATE</td><td>MILES PER HOUR</td><td>RANK</td><td>STATE</td><td>MILES PER HOUR</td></tr>
<tr><td>41</td><td>Alabama</td><td>7.6</td><td>1</td><td>Massachusetts</td><td>12.5</td></tr>
<tr><td>24</td><td>Alaska</td><td>9.3</td><td>2</td><td>Kansas</td><td>12.0</td></tr>
<tr><td>42</td><td>Arizona</td><td>7.5</td><td>3</td><td>Oklahoma</td><td>11.2</td></tr>
<tr><td>40</td><td>Arkansas</td><td>7.7</td><td>4</td><td>South Dakota</td><td>11.1</td></tr>
<tr><td>46</td><td>California</td><td>6.9</td><td>5</td><td>Hawaii</td><td>10.9</td></tr>
<tr><td>32</td><td>Colorado</td><td>8.5</td><td>6</td><td>Iowa</td><td>10.7</td></tr>
<tr><td>19</td><td>Connecticut</td><td>9.6</td><td>7</td><td>North Dakota</td><td>10.6</td></tr>
<tr><td>26</td><td>Delaware**</td><td>9.0</td><td>8</td><td>Rhode Island</td><td>10.5</td></tr>
<tr><td>33</td><td>Florida</td><td>8.3</td><td>9</td><td>Nebraska</td><td>10.3</td></tr>
<tr><td>45</td><td>Georgia</td><td>7.4</td><td>9</td><td>Texas</td><td>10.3</td></tr>
<tr><td>5</td><td>Hawaii</td><td>10.9</td><td>11</td><td>Minnesota</td><td>10.2</td></tr>
<tr><td>22</td><td>Idaho</td><td>9.4</td><td>11</td><td>New York</td><td>10.2</td></tr>
<tr><td>18</td><td>Illinois</td><td>9.8</td><td>13</td><td>Missouri</td><td>10.1</td></tr>
<tr><td>22</td><td>Indiana</td><td>9.4</td><td>13</td><td>Wyoming</td><td>10.1</td></tr>
<tr><td>6</td><td>Iowa</td><td>10.7</td><td>15</td><td>New Jersey</td><td>10.0</td></tr>
<tr><td>2</td><td>Kansas</td><td>12.0</td><td>16</td><td>New Mexico</td><td>9.9</td></tr>
<tr><td>39</td><td>Kentucky</td><td>7.8</td><td>16</td><td>Wisconsin</td><td>9.9</td></tr>
<tr><td>36</td><td>Louisiana</td><td>8.1</td><td>18</td><td>Illinois</td><td>9.8</td></tr>
<tr><td>27</td><td>Maine</td><td>8.9</td><td>19</td><td>Connecticut</td><td>9.6</td></tr>
<tr><td>30</td><td>Maryland**</td><td>8.6</td><td>19</td><td>Ohio</td><td>9.6</td></tr>
<tr><td>1</td><td>Massachusetts</td><td>12.5</td><td>21</td><td>Michigan</td><td>9.5</td></tr>
<tr><td>21</td><td>Michigan</td><td>9.5</td><td>22</td><td>Idaho</td><td>9.4</td></tr>
<tr><td>11</td><td>Minnesota</td><td>10.2</td><td>22</td><td>Indiana</td><td>9.4</td></tr>
<tr><td>48</td><td>Mississippi</td><td>6.5</td><td>24</td><td>Alaska</td><td>9.3</td></tr>
<tr><td>13</td><td>Missouri</td><td>10.1</td><td>25</td><td>Montana</td><td>9.2</td></tr>
<tr><td>25</td><td>Montana</td><td>9.2</td><td>26</td><td>Delaware**</td><td>9.0</td></tr>
<tr><td>9</td><td>Nebraska</td><td>10.3</td><td>27</td><td>Maine</td><td>8.9</td></tr>
<tr><td>37</td><td>Nevada</td><td>8.0</td><td>27</td><td>Vermont**</td><td>8.9</td></tr>
<tr><td>47</td><td>New Hampshire**</td><td>6.7</td><td>29</td><td>Utah**</td><td>8.8</td></tr>
<tr><td>15</td><td>New Jersey</td><td>10.0</td><td>30</td><td>Maryland**</td><td>8.6</td></tr>
<tr><td>16</td><td>New Mexico</td><td>9.9</td><td>30</td><td>Pennsylvania</td><td>8.6</td></tr>
<tr><td>11</td><td>New York</td><td>10.2</td><td>32</td><td>Colorado</td><td>8.5</td></tr>
<tr><td>34</td><td>North Carolina</td><td>8.2</td><td>33</td><td>Florida</td><td>8.3</td></tr>
<tr><td>7</td><td>North Dakota</td><td>10.6</td><td>34</td><td>North Carolina</td><td>8.2</td></tr>
<tr><td>19</td><td>Ohio</td><td>9.6</td><td>34</td><td>Virginia</td><td>8.2</td></tr>
<tr><td>3</td><td>Oklahoma</td><td>11.2</td><td>36</td><td>Louisiana</td><td>8.1</td></tr>
<tr><td>38</td><td>Oregon</td><td>7.9</td><td>37</td><td>Nevada</td><td>8.0</td></tr>
<tr><td>30</td><td>Pennsylvania</td><td>8.6</td><td>38</td><td>Oregon</td><td>7.9</td></tr>
<tr><td>8</td><td>Rhode Island</td><td>10.5</td><td>39</td><td>Kentucky</td><td>7.8</td></tr>
<tr><td>42</td><td>South Carolina</td><td>7.5</td><td>40</td><td>Arkansas</td><td>7.7</td></tr>
<tr><td>4</td><td>South Dakota</td><td>11.1</td><td>41</td><td>Alabama</td><td>7.6</td></tr>
<tr><td>48</td><td>Tennessee</td><td>6.5</td><td>42</td><td>Arizona</td><td>7.5</td></tr>
<tr><td>9</td><td>Texas</td><td>10.3</td><td>42</td><td>South Carolina</td><td>7.5</td></tr>
<tr><td>29</td><td>Utah**</td><td>8.8</td><td>42</td><td>Washington</td><td>7.5</td></tr>
<tr><td>27</td><td>Vermont**</td><td>8.9</td><td>45</td><td>Georgia</td><td>7.4</td></tr>
<tr><td>34</td><td>Virginia</td><td>8.2</td><td>46</td><td>California</td><td>6.9</td></tr>
<tr><td>42</td><td>Washington</td><td>7.5</td><td>47</td><td>New Hampshire**</td><td>6.7</td></tr>
<tr><td>48</td><td>West Virginia</td><td>6.5</td><td>48</td><td>Mississippi</td><td>6.5</td></tr>
<tr><td>16</td><td>Wisconsin</td><td>9.9</td><td>48</td><td>Tennessee</td><td>6.5</td></tr>
<tr><td>13</td><td>Wyoming</td><td>10.1</td><td>48</td><td>West Virginia</td><td>6.5</td></tr>
</table>

District of Columbia   8.4

Source: CQ Press using data from U.S. Department of Commerce, National Oceanic and Atmospheric Administration
"Comparative Climatic Data Through 2012" (ftp://ftp.ncdc.noaa.gov/pub/data/ccd-data/CCD-2012.pdf)
*Updated through 2012.
**Averages from these states are from a single location. All other states are from two or more reporting cities within each state, which were averaged to determine each state's average.

Hazardous Weather Fatalities in 2017

National Total = 497 Fatalities*

ALPHA ORDER					RANK ORDER			
RANK	STATE	FATALITIES	% of USA		RANK	STATE	FATALITIES	% of USA
7	Alabama	14	2.8%		1	Texas	138	27.8%
26	Alaska	2	0.4%		2	Nevada	83	16.7%
8	Arizona	13	2.6%		3	California	43	8.7%
12	Arkansas	9	1.8%		4	Florida	32	6.4%
3	California	43	8.7%		5	Georgia	20	4.0%
20	Colorado	4	0.8%		6	North Carolina	16	3.2%
26	Connecticut	2	0.4%		7	Alabama	14	2.8%
42	Delaware	0	0.0%		8	Arizona	13	2.6%
4	Florida	32	6.4%		8	Missouri	13	2.6%
5	Georgia	20	4.0%		10	New Jersey	11	2.2%
26	Hawaii	2	0.4%		11	Wisconsin	10	2.0%
34	Idaho	1	0.2%		12	Arkansas	9	1.8%
12	Illinois	9	1.8%		12	Illinois	9	1.8%
34	Indiana	1	0.2%		12	Mississippi	9	1.8%
34	Iowa	1	0.2%		15	Oregon	8	1.6%
18	Kansas	5	1.0%		16	Louisiana	7	1.4%
34	Kentucky	1	0.2%		17	Michigan	6	1.2%
16	Louisiana	7	1.4%		18	Kansas	5	1.0%
42	Maine	0	0.0%		18	Oklahoma	5	1.0%
34	Maryland	1	0.2%		20	Colorado	4	0.8%
26	Massachusetts	2	0.4%		20	New Mexico	4	0.8%
17	Michigan	6	1.2%		20	Pennsylvania	4	0.8%
24	Minnesota	3	0.6%		20	South Carolina	4	0.8%
12	Mississippi	9	1.8%		24	Minnesota	3	0.6%
8	Missouri	13	2.6%		24	South Dakota	3	0.6%
34	Montana	1	0.2%		26	Alaska	2	0.4%
42	Nebraska	0	0.0%		26	Connecticut	2	0.4%
2	Nevada	83	16.7%		26	Hawaii	2	0.4%
42	New Hampshire	0	0.0%		26	Massachusetts	2	0.4%
10	New Jersey	11	2.2%		26	New York	2	0.4%
20	New Mexico	4	0.8%		26	Ohio	2	0.4%
26	New York	2	0.4%		26	Tennessee	2	0.4%
6	North Carolina	16	3.2%		26	West Virginia	2	0.4%
42	North Dakota	0	0.0%		34	Idaho	1	0.2%
26	Ohio	2	0.4%		34	Indiana	1	0.2%
18	Oklahoma	5	1.0%		34	Iowa	1	0.2%
15	Oregon	8	1.6%		34	Kentucky	1	0.2%
20	Pennsylvania	4	0.8%		34	Maryland	1	0.2%
42	Rhode Island	0	0.0%		34	Montana	1	0.2%
20	South Carolina	4	0.8%		34	Washington	1	0.2%
24	South Dakota	3	0.6%		34	Wyoming	1	0.2%
26	Tennessee	2	0.4%		42	Delaware	0	0.0%
1	Texas	138	27.8%		42	Maine	0	0.0%
42	Utah	0	0.0%		42	Nebraska	0	0.0%
42	Vermont	0	0.0%		42	New Hampshire	0	0.0%
42	Virginia	0	0.0%		42	North Dakota	0	0.0%
34	Washington	1	0.2%		42	Rhode Island	0	0.0%
26	West Virginia	2	0.4%		42	Utah	0	0.0%
11	Wisconsin	10	2.0%		42	Vermont	0	0.0%
34	Wyoming	1	0.2%		42	Virginia	0	0.0%
						District of Columbia	0	0.0%

Source: National Weather Service, Water and Weather Services
"2017 Summary of Hazardous Weather Fatalities" (http://www.nws.noaa.gov/om/hazstats.shtml)
*Includes lightning, tornado, thunderstorm, extreme temperature, flood, coastal storm, rip current, hurricane, winter storm, fog, avalanche, and other weather events. National total does not include 11 fatalities in U.S. waters or territories.

Tornadoes in 2018

National Total = 1,154 Tornadoes*

ALPHA ORDER

RANK	STATE	TORNADOES	% of USA
5	Alabama	52	4.5%
44	Alaska	0	0.0%
35	Arizona	6	0.5%
17	Arkansas	33	2.9%
35	California	6	0.5%
12	Colorado	39	3.4%
33	Connecticut	8	0.7%
44	Delaware	0	0.0%
9	Florida	44	3.8%
22	Georgia	21	1.8%
44	Hawaii	0	0.0%
29	Idaho	11	1.0%
4	Illinois	64	5.5%
27	Indiana	14	1.2%
1	Iowa	84	7.3%
8	Kansas	45	3.9%
10	Kentucky	40	3.5%
1	Louisiana	84	7.3%
44	Maine	0	0.0%
40	Maryland	2	0.2%
34	Massachusetts	7	0.6%
28	Michigan	13	1.1%
14	Minnesota	36	3.1%
3	Mississippi	67	5.8%
7	Missouri	48	4.2%
31	Montana	10	0.9%
13	Nebraska	37	3.2%
37	Nevada	4	0.3%
38	New Hampshire	3	0.3%
44	New Jersey	0	0.0%
31	New Mexico	10	0.9%
29	New York	11	1.0%
10	North Carolina	40	3.5%
18	North Dakota	31	2.7%
25	Ohio	17	1.5%
21	Oklahoma	24	2.1%
38	Oregon	3	0.3%
18	Pennsylvania	31	2.7%
42	Rhode Island	1	0.1%
26	South Carolina	16	1.4%
24	South Dakota	19	1.6%
23	Tennessee	20	1.7%
6	Texas	50	4.3%
40	Utah	2	0.2%
44	Vermont	0	0.0%
16	Virginia	34	2.9%
44	Washington	0	0.0%
42	West Virginia	1	0.1%
15	Wisconsin	35	3.0%
18	Wyoming	31	2.7%

RANK ORDER

RANK	STATE	TORNADOES	% of USA
1	Iowa	84	7.3%
1	Louisiana	84	7.3%
3	Mississippi	67	5.8%
4	Illinois	64	5.5%
5	Alabama	52	4.5%
6	Texas	50	4.3%
7	Missouri	48	4.2%
8	Kansas	45	3.9%
9	Florida	44	3.8%
10	Kentucky	40	3.5%
10	North Carolina	40	3.5%
12	Colorado	39	3.4%
13	Nebraska	37	3.2%
14	Minnesota	36	3.1%
15	Wisconsin	35	3.0%
16	Virginia	34	2.9%
17	Arkansas	33	2.9%
18	North Dakota	31	2.7%
18	Pennsylvania	31	2.7%
18	Wyoming	31	2.7%
21	Oklahoma	24	2.1%
22	Georgia	21	1.8%
23	Tennessee	20	1.7%
24	South Dakota	19	1.6%
25	Ohio	17	1.5%
26	South Carolina	16	1.4%
27	Indiana	14	1.2%
28	Michigan	13	1.1%
29	Idaho	11	1.0%
29	New York	11	1.0%
31	Montana	10	0.9%
31	New Mexico	10	0.9%
33	Connecticut	8	0.7%
34	Massachusetts	7	0.6%
35	Arizona	6	0.5%
35	California	6	0.5%
37	Nevada	4	0.3%
38	New Hampshire	3	0.3%
38	Oregon	3	0.3%
40	Maryland	2	0.2%
40	Utah	2	0.2%
42	Rhode Island	1	0.1%
42	West Virginia	1	0.1%
44	Alaska	0	0.0%
44	Delaware	0	0.0%
44	Hawaii	0	0.0%
44	Maine	0	0.0%
44	New Jersey	0	0.0%
44	Vermont	0	0.0%
44	Washington	0	0.0%
	District of Columbia	0	0.0%

Source: National Weather Service, Storm Prediction Center
"Annual Severe Weather Report Summary - 2018" (https://www.spc.noaa.gov/climo/online/monthly/newm.html)
*Preliminary figures. Tornadoes striking more than one state are counted in each state.

Fatalities Caused by Tornadoes: 2008 to 2018

National Total = 1,014 Fatalities

ALPHA ORDER

RANK	STATE	FATALITIES	% of USA
1	Alabama	261	25.7%
32	Alaska	0	0.0%
32	Arizona	0	0.0%
6	Arkansas	64	6.3%
32	California	0	0.0%
28	Colorado	1	0.1%
32	Connecticut	0	0.0%
32	Delaware	0	0.0%
20	Florida	4	0.4%
7	Georgia	39	3.8%
32	Hawaii	0	0.0%
32	Idaho	0	0.0%
11	Illinois	23	2.3%
12	Indiana	17	1.7%
13	Iowa	16	1.6%
17	Kansas	8	0.8%
8	Kentucky	32	3.2%
16	Louisiana	10	1.0%
32	Maine	0	0.0%
23	Maryland	2	0.2%
22	Massachusetts	3	0.3%
28	Michigan	1	0.1%
19	Minnesota	5	0.5%
3	Mississippi	81	8.0%
2	Missouri	193	19.0%
23	Montana	2	0.2%
23	Nebraska	2	0.2%
32	Nevada	0	0.0%
28	New Hampshire	1	0.1%
32	New Jersey	0	0.0%
32	New Mexico	0	0.0%
18	New York	6	0.6%
9	North Carolina	30	3.0%
23	North Dakota	2	0.2%
14	Ohio	11	1.1%
4	Oklahoma	77	7.6%
32	Oregon	0	0.0%
32	Pennsylvania	0	0.0%
32	Rhode Island	0	0.0%
20	South Carolina	4	0.4%
32	South Dakota	0	0.0%
5	Tennessee	76	7.5%
10	Texas	29	2.9%
32	Utah	0	0.0%
32	Vermont	0	0.0%
14	Virginia	11	1.1%
32	Washington	0	0.0%
28	West Virginia	1	0.1%
23	Wisconsin	2	0.2%
32	Wyoming	0	0.0%

RANK ORDER

RANK	STATE	FATALITIES	% of USA
1	Alabama	261	25.7%
2	Missouri	193	19.0%
3	Mississippi	81	8.0%
4	Oklahoma	77	7.6%
5	Tennessee	76	7.5%
6	Arkansas	64	6.3%
7	Georgia	39	3.8%
8	Kentucky	32	3.2%
9	North Carolina	30	3.0%
10	Texas	29	2.9%
11	Illinois	23	2.3%
12	Indiana	17	1.7%
13	Iowa	16	1.6%
14	Ohio	11	1.1%
14	Virginia	11	1.1%
16	Louisiana	10	1.0%
17	Kansas	8	0.8%
18	New York	6	0.6%
19	Minnesota	5	0.5%
20	Florida	4	0.4%
20	South Carolina	4	0.4%
22	Massachusetts	3	0.3%
23	Maryland	2	0.2%
23	Montana	2	0.2%
23	Nebraska	2	0.2%
23	North Dakota	2	0.2%
23	Wisconsin	2	0.2%
28	Colorado	1	0.1%
28	Michigan	1	0.1%
28	New Hampshire	1	0.1%
28	West Virginia	1	0.1%
32	Alaska	0	0.0%
32	Arizona	0	0.0%
32	California	0	0.0%
32	Connecticut	0	0.0%
32	Delaware	0	0.0%
32	Hawaii	0	0.0%
32	Idaho	0	0.0%
32	Maine	0	0.0%
32	Nevada	0	0.0%
32	New Jersey	0	0.0%
32	New Mexico	0	0.0%
32	Oregon	0	0.0%
32	Pennsylvania	0	0.0%
32	Rhode Island	0	0.0%
32	South Dakota	0	0.0%
32	Utah	0	0.0%
32	Vermont	0	0.0%
32	Washington	0	0.0%
32	Wyoming	0	0.0%
	District of Columbia	0	0.0%

Source: CQ Press using data from National Weather Service, Storm Prediction Center
"Annual U.S. Killer Tornado Statistics" (https://www.spc.noaa.gov/climo/torn/fatalmap.php)

Cost of Damage from Hazardous Weather in 2017

National Total = $74,261,270,000*

ALPHA ORDER

RANK	STATE	DAMAGE	% of USA
24	Alabama	$31,590,000	0.0%
39	Alaska	6,530,000	0.0%
37	Arizona	11,150,000	0.0%
19	Arkansas	61,090,000	0.1%
4	California	867,060,000	1.2%
3	Colorado	1,426,780,000	1.9%
43	Connecticut	1,450,000	0.0%
50	Delaware	0	0.0%
2	Florida	4,557,430,000	6.1%
7	Georgia	680,840,000	0.9%
47	Hawaii	240,000	0.0%
8	Idaho	171,100,000	0.2%
17	Illinois	63,190,000	0.1%
33	Indiana	15,910,000	0.0%
22	Iowa	51,520,000	0.1%
36	Kansas	12,900,000	0.0%
25	Kentucky	28,110,000	0.0%
12	Louisiana	107,640,000	0.1%
46	Maine	340,000	0.0%
45	Maryland	1,100,000	0.0%
40	Massachusetts	4,950,000	0.0%
6	Michigan	742,020,000	1.0%
28	Minnesota	23,620,000	0.0%
18	Mississippi	61,280,000	0.1%
9	Missouri	156,200,000	0.2%
44	Montana	1,170,000	0.0%
15	Nebraska	77,860,000	0.1%
29	Nevada	19,950,000	0.0%
32	New Hampshire	16,970,000	0.0%
42	New Jersey	1,790,000	0.0%
30	New Mexico	18,700,000	0.0%
21	New York	52,240,000	0.1%
20	North Carolina	60,650,000	0.1%
31	North Dakota	17,390,000	0.0%
16	Ohio	71,650,000	0.1%
10	Oklahoma	130,010,000	0.2%
13	Oregon	101,210,000	0.1%
23	Pennsylvania	45,680,000	0.1%
49	Rhode Island	160,000	0.0%
5	South Carolina	755,540,000	1.0%
48	South Dakota	170,000	0.0%
26	Tennessee	27,170,000	0.0%
1	Texas	63,508,160,000	85.5%
27	Utah	25,680,000	0.0%
34	Vermont	14,640,000	0.0%
35	Virginia	13,820,000	0.0%
14	Washington	82,470,000	0.1%
38	West Virginia	6,880,000	0.0%
11	Wisconsin	124,270,000	0.2%
41	Wyoming	3,000,000	0.0%

RANK ORDER

RANK	STATE	DAMAGE	% of USA
1	Texas	$63,508,160,000	85.5%
2	Florida	4,557,430,000	6.1%
3	Colorado	1,426,780,000	1.9%
4	California	867,060,000	1.2%
5	South Carolina	755,540,000	1.0%
6	Michigan	742,020,000	1.0%
7	Georgia	680,840,000	0.9%
8	Idaho	171,100,000	0.2%
9	Missouri	156,200,000	0.2%
10	Oklahoma	130,010,000	0.2%
11	Wisconsin	124,270,000	0.2%
12	Louisiana	107,640,000	0.1%
13	Oregon	101,210,000	0.1%
14	Washington	82,470,000	0.1%
15	Nebraska	77,860,000	0.1%
16	Ohio	71,650,000	0.1%
17	Illinois	63,190,000	0.1%
18	Mississippi	61,280,000	0.1%
19	Arkansas	61,090,000	0.1%
20	North Carolina	60,650,000	0.1%
21	New York	52,240,000	0.1%
22	Iowa	51,520,000	0.1%
23	Pennsylvania	45,680,000	0.1%
24	Alabama	31,590,000	0.0%
25	Kentucky	28,110,000	0.0%
26	Tennessee	27,170,000	0.0%
27	Utah	25,680,000	0.0%
28	Minnesota	23,620,000	0.0%
29	Nevada	19,950,000	0.0%
30	New Mexico	18,700,000	0.0%
31	North Dakota	17,390,000	0.0%
32	New Hampshire	16,970,000	0.0%
33	Indiana	15,910,000	0.0%
34	Vermont	14,640,000	0.0%
35	Virginia	13,820,000	0.0%
36	Kansas	12,900,000	0.0%
37	Arizona	11,150,000	0.0%
38	West Virginia	6,880,000	0.0%
39	Alaska	6,530,000	0.0%
40	Massachusetts	4,950,000	0.0%
41	Wyoming	3,000,000	0.0%
42	New Jersey	1,790,000	0.0%
43	Connecticut	1,450,000	0.0%
44	Montana	1,170,000	0.0%
45	Maryland	1,100,000	0.0%
46	Maine	340,000	0.0%
47	Hawaii	240,000	0.0%
48	South Dakota	170,000	0.0%
49	Rhode Island	160,000	0.0%
50	Delaware	0	0.0%
	District of Columbia	0	0.0%

Source: National Weather Service, Water and Weather Services
   "2017 Summary of Hazardous Weather Fatalities" (http://www.nws.noaa.gov/om/hazstats.shtml)
*Includes property and crop damage from lightning, tornado, thunderstorm, extreme temperature, flood, coastal storm, rip current, hurricane, winter storm, fog, avalanche, and other weather events. National total does not include damage costs in U.S. territories.

National Park Service Land in 2017

National Total = 85,040,323 Acres*

ALPHA ORDER

RANK	STATE	ACRES	% of USA
41	Alabama	22,744	0.0%
1	Alaska	54,653,962	64.3%
3	Arizona	2,947,560	3.5%
26	Arkansas	104,975	0.1%
2	California	8,170,932	9.6%
12	Colorado	738,377	0.9%
46	Connecticut	7,782	0.0%
48	Delaware	904	0.0%
4	Florida	2,638,601	3.1%
35	Georgia	64,835	0.1%
18	Hawaii	369,320	0.4%
10	Idaho	806,298	0.9%
50	Illinois	116	0.0%
43	Indiana	15,573	0.0%
47	Iowa	2,713	0.0%
44	Kansas	11,637	0.0%
29	Kentucky	97,124	0.1%
39	Louisiana	23,545	0.0%
22	Maine	180,964	0.2%
32	Maryland	74,278	0.1%
36	Massachusetts	59,500	0.1%
13	Michigan	718,189	0.8%
19	Minnesota	301,330	0.4%
24	Mississippi	118,557	0.1%
31	Missouri	83,516	0.1%
8	Montana	1,274,133	1.5%
34	Nebraska	66,570	0.1%
11	Nevada	801,172	0.9%
42	New Hampshire	21,190	0.0%
27	New Jersey	99,469	0.1%
14	New Mexico	480,863	0.6%
28	New York	97,411	0.1%
15	North Carolina	409,966	0.5%
33	North Dakota	72,568	0.1%
37	Ohio	34,550	0.0%
45	Oklahoma	10,241	0.0%
21	Oregon	203,385	0.2%
25	Pennsylvania	116,509	0.1%
49	Rhode Island	331	0.0%
38	South Carolina	32,627	0.0%
20	South Dakota	296,584	0.3%
16	Tennessee	387,857	0.5%
9	Texas	1,252,181	1.5%
6	Utah	2,117,683	2.5%
40	Vermont	23,237	0.0%
17	Virginia	371,365	0.4%
7	Washington	1,967,559	2.3%
30	West Virginia	92,684	0.1%
23	Wisconsin	133,757	0.2%
5	Wyoming	2,396,431	2.8%

RANK ORDER

RANK	STATE	ACRES	% of USA
1	Alaska	54,653,962	64.3%
2	California	8,170,932	9.6%
3	Arizona	2,947,560	3.5%
4	Florida	2,638,601	3.1%
5	Wyoming	2,396,431	2.8%
6	Utah	2,117,683	2.5%
7	Washington	1,967,559	2.3%
8	Montana	1,274,133	1.5%
9	Texas	1,252,181	1.5%
10	Idaho	806,298	0.9%
11	Nevada	801,172	0.9%
12	Colorado	738,377	0.9%
13	Michigan	718,189	0.8%
14	New Mexico	480,863	0.6%
15	North Carolina	409,966	0.5%
16	Tennessee	387,857	0.5%
17	Virginia	371,365	0.4%
18	Hawaii	369,320	0.4%
19	Minnesota	301,330	0.4%
20	South Dakota	296,584	0.3%
21	Oregon	203,385	0.2%
22	Maine	180,964	0.2%
23	Wisconsin	133,757	0.2%
24	Mississippi	118,557	0.1%
25	Pennsylvania	116,509	0.1%
26	Arkansas	104,975	0.1%
27	New Jersey	99,469	0.1%
28	New York	97,411	0.1%
29	Kentucky	97,124	0.1%
30	West Virginia	92,684	0.1%
31	Missouri	83,516	0.1%
32	Maryland	74,278	0.1%
33	North Dakota	72,568	0.1%
34	Nebraska	66,570	0.1%
35	Georgia	64,835	0.1%
36	Massachusetts	59,500	0.1%
37	Ohio	34,550	0.0%
38	South Carolina	32,627	0.0%
39	Louisiana	23,545	0.0%
40	Vermont	23,237	0.0%
41	Alabama	22,744	0.0%
42	New Hampshire	21,190	0.0%
43	Indiana	15,573	0.0%
44	Kansas	11,637	0.0%
45	Oklahoma	10,241	0.0%
46	Connecticut	7,782	0.0%
47	Iowa	2,713	0.0%
48	Delaware	904	0.0%
49	Rhode Island	331	0.0%
50	Illinois	116	0.0%
	District of Columbia	8,625	0.0%

Source: National Park Service
   "Listing of Acreage by State" (https://www.nps.gov/subjects/lwcf/acreagereports.htm)
*As of December 31, 2017. Includes federal and nonfederal land in national parks, monuments, historic sites, recreation areas, preserves, battlefields, grasslands, seashores, parkways, trails, and rivers. Does not include land in national forest or wildlife areas. Includes 58,043 acres in U.S. territories.

Recreation Visits to National Park Service Areas in 2017

National Total = 330,882,772 Visits*

ALPHA ORDER

RANK	STATE	VISITS	% of USA
37	Alabama	968,244	0.3%
26	Alaska	2,786,065	0.8%
6	Arizona	13,770,402	4.2%
24	Arkansas	3,512,692	1.1%
1	California	40,497,299	12.2%
12	Colorado	7,617,580	2.3%
48	Connecticut	38,096	0.0%
50	Delaware	0	0.0%
9	Florida	10,297,457	3.1%
14	Georgia	7,394,337	2.2%
18	Hawaii	6,002,950	1.8%
39	Idaho	694,972	0.2%
43	Illinois	232,265	0.1%
29	Indiana	2,419,390	0.7%
44	Iowa	211,625	0.1%
45	Kansas	117,029	0.0%
31	Kentucky	1,855,444	0.6%
41	Louisiana	527,597	0.2%
23	Maine	3,521,143	1.1%
16	Maryland	6,568,805	2.0%
7	Massachusetts	10,477,438	3.2%
27	Michigan	2,742,804	0.8%
36	Minnesota	1,232,761	0.4%
15	Mississippi	6,617,593	2.0%
25	Missouri	2,921,492	0.9%
20	Montana	5,887,047	1.8%
42	Nebraska	388,804	0.1%
17	Nevada	6,079,783	1.8%
49	New Hampshire	37,556	0.0%
21	New Jersey	4,975,864	1.5%
30	New Mexico	2,045,049	0.6%
3	New York	19,343,416	5.8%
4	North Carolina	18,998,050	5.7%
38	North Dakota	732,976	0.2%
28	Ohio	2,590,212	0.8%
34	Oklahoma	1,545,515	0.5%
35	Oregon	1,291,874	0.4%
8	Pennsylvania	10,393,888	3.1%
46	Rhode Island	80,970	0.0%
32	South Carolina	1,727,544	0.5%
22	South Dakota	4,520,117	1.4%
10	Tennessee	9,332,222	2.8%
19	Texas	5,905,067	1.8%
5	Utah	15,152,428	4.6%
47	Vermont	46,523	0.0%
2	Virginia	24,281,546	7.3%
11	Washington	8,445,797	2.6%
33	West Virginia	1,661,954	0.5%
40	Wisconsin	589,661	0.2%
13	Wyoming	7,456,556	2.3%

RANK ORDER

RANK	STATE	VISITS	% of USA
1	California	40,497,299	12.2%
2	Virginia	24,281,546	7.3%
3	New York	19,343,416	5.8%
4	North Carolina	18,998,050	5.7%
5	Utah	15,152,428	4.6%
6	Arizona	13,770,402	4.2%
7	Massachusetts	10,477,438	3.2%
8	Pennsylvania	10,393,888	3.1%
9	Florida	10,297,457	3.1%
10	Tennessee	9,332,222	2.8%
11	Washington	8,445,797	2.6%
12	Colorado	7,617,580	2.3%
13	Wyoming	7,456,556	2.3%
14	Georgia	7,394,337	2.2%
15	Mississippi	6,617,593	2.0%
16	Maryland	6,568,805	2.0%
17	Nevada	6,079,783	1.8%
18	Hawaii	6,002,950	1.8%
19	Texas	5,905,067	1.8%
20	Montana	5,887,047	1.8%
21	New Jersey	4,975,864	1.5%
22	South Dakota	4,520,117	1.4%
23	Maine	3,521,143	1.1%
24	Arkansas	3,512,692	1.1%
25	Missouri	2,921,492	0.9%
26	Alaska	2,786,065	0.8%
27	Michigan	2,742,804	0.8%
28	Ohio	2,590,212	0.8%
29	Indiana	2,419,390	0.7%
30	New Mexico	2,045,049	0.6%
31	Kentucky	1,855,444	0.6%
32	South Carolina	1,727,544	0.5%
33	West Virginia	1,661,954	0.5%
34	Oklahoma	1,545,515	0.5%
35	Oregon	1,291,874	0.4%
36	Minnesota	1,232,761	0.4%
37	Alabama	968,244	0.3%
38	North Dakota	732,976	0.2%
39	Idaho	694,972	0.2%
40	Wisconsin	589,661	0.2%
41	Louisiana	527,597	0.2%
42	Nebraska	388,804	0.1%
43	Illinois	232,265	0.1%
44	Iowa	211,625	0.1%
45	Kansas	117,029	0.0%
46	Rhode Island	80,970	0.0%
47	Vermont	46,523	0.0%
48	Connecticut	38,096	0.0%
49	New Hampshire	37,556	0.0%
50	Delaware	0	0.0%
	District of Columbia	42,259,179	12.8%

Source: National Park Service, Public Use Statistics Office
"National Park Service National Reports" (https://irma.nps.gov/Stats/reports/national)
*National total includes 1,642,858 visits in U.S. territories.

Percent Change in National Park Service Recreation Visits: 2016 to 2017

National Percent Change = 0.0% Change*

ALPHA ORDER

RANK	STATE	PERCENT CHANGE
40	Alabama	(5.3)
26	Alaska	0.1
5	Arizona	14.7
43	Arkansas	(7.2)
37	California	(3.5)
23	Colorado	2.1
34	Connecticut	(2.5)
NA	Delaware**	NA
39	Florida	(5.1)
14	Georgia	5.0
16	Hawaii	3.7
6	Idaho	10.5
36	Illinois	(3.1)
2	Indiana	24.1
44	Iowa	(7.8)
37	Kansas	(3.5)
32	Kentucky	(1.4)
12	Louisiana	5.4
11	Maine	6.1
33	Maryland	(1.5)
17	Massachusetts	3.5
24	Michigan	1.5
4	Minnesota	21.3
27	Mississippi	0.0
18	Missouri	3.4
15	Montana	4.1
1	Nebraska	26.6
7	Nevada	10.0
48	New Hampshire	(11.4)
19	New Jersey	3.0
9	New Mexico	9.2
22	New York	2.3
21	North Carolina	2.7
42	North Dakota	(6.6)
45	Ohio	(8.1)
46	Oklahoma	(8.5)
35	Oregon	(2.8)
41	Pennsylvania	(6.1)
3	Rhode Island	23.5
20	South Carolina	2.8
25	South Dakota	1.3
29	Tennessee	(0.7)
10	Texas	8.7
13	Utah	5.2
49	Vermont	(16.5)
47	Virginia	(10.4)
30	Washington	(0.9)
31	West Virginia	(1.3)
8	Wisconsin	9.6
28	Wyoming	(0.1)

RANK ORDER

RANK	STATE	PERCENT CHANGE
1	Nebraska	26.6
2	Indiana	24.1
3	Rhode Island	23.5
4	Minnesota	21.3
5	Arizona	14.7
6	Idaho	10.5
7	Nevada	10.0
8	Wisconsin	9.6
9	New Mexico	9.2
10	Texas	8.7
11	Maine	6.1
12	Louisiana	5.4
13	Utah	5.2
14	Georgia	5.0
15	Montana	4.1
16	Hawaii	3.7
17	Massachusetts	3.5
18	Missouri	3.4
19	New Jersey	3.0
20	South Carolina	2.8
21	North Carolina	2.7
22	New York	2.3
23	Colorado	2.1
24	Michigan	1.5
25	South Dakota	1.3
26	Alaska	0.1
27	Mississippi	0.0
28	Wyoming	(0.1)
29	Tennessee	(0.7)
30	Washington	(0.9)
31	West Virginia	(1.3)
32	Kentucky	(1.4)
33	Maryland	(1.5)
34	Connecticut	(2.5)
35	Oregon	(2.8)
36	Illinois	(3.1)
37	California	(3.5)
37	Kansas	(3.5)
39	Florida	(5.1)
40	Alabama	(5.3)
41	Pennsylvania	(6.1)
42	North Dakota	(6.6)
43	Arkansas	(7.2)
44	Iowa	(7.8)
45	Ohio	(8.1)
46	Oklahoma	(8.5)
47	Virginia	(10.4)
48	New Hampshire	(11.4)
49	Vermont	(16.5)
NA	Delaware**	NA
	District of Columbia	(1.0)

Source: CQ Press using data from National Park Service, Public Use Statistics Office
"National Park Service National Reports" (https://irma.nps.gov/Stats/reports/national)
*National percent change includes visits in U.S. territories.
**Not applicable.

IX. Government Finances: Federal

Internal Revenue Service Gross Collections in 2017

National Total = $3,416,714,139,000*

ALPHA ORDER

RANK	STATE	COLLECTIONS	% of USA
30	Alabama	$26,583,916,000	0.8%
48	Alaska	5,399,946,000	0.2%
23	Arizona	43,928,177,000	1.3%
26	Arkansas	32,458,328,000	0.9%
1	California	440,475,243,000	12.9%
21	Colorado	56,742,235,000	1.7%
20	Connecticut	57,540,270,000	1.7%
36	Delaware	17,081,357,000	0.5%
4	Florida	192,869,033,000	5.6%
11	Georgia	94,277,375,000	2.8%
41	Hawaii	9,415,214,000	0.3%
40	Idaho	10,386,020,000	0.3%
5	Illinois	162,326,463,000	4.8%
19	Indiana	58,940,989,000	1.7%
33	Iowa	24,642,287,000	0.7%
31	Kansas	25,563,140,000	0.7%
25	Kentucky	35,126,897,000	1.0%
24	Louisiana	42,724,672,000	1.3%
43	Maine	8,083,275,000	0.2%
17	Maryland	71,246,920,000	2.1%
9	Massachusetts	112,996,320,000	3.3%
15	Michigan	82,676,161,000	2.4%
10	Minnesota	104,429,577,000	3.1%
39	Mississippi	11,740,655,000	0.3%
16	Missouri	71,921,135,000	2.1%
47	Montana	6,080,381,000	0.2%
32	Nebraska	25,450,002,000	0.7%
35	Nevada	21,570,670,000	0.6%
38	New Hampshire	12,138,352,000	0.4%
6	New Jersey	143,835,479,000	4.2%
42	New Mexico	8,979,166,000	0.3%
3	New York	268,353,669,000	7.9%
14	North Carolina	82,855,993,000	2.4%
46	North Dakota	6,640,269,000	0.2%
7	Ohio	142,086,312,000	4.2%
28	Oklahoma	27,113,120,000	0.8%
27	Oregon	32,345,824,000	0.9%
8	Pennsylvania	139,797,047,000	4.1%
37	Rhode Island	14,917,462,000	0.4%
29	South Carolina	26,636,069,000	0.8%
44	South Dakota	7,872,916,000	0.2%
18	Tennessee	69,069,233,000	2.0%
2	Texas	270,955,237,000	7.9%
34	Utah	22,485,663,000	0.7%
49	Vermont	4,422,942,000	0.1%
12	Virginia	87,183,756,000	2.6%
13	Washington	85,875,647,000	2.5%
45	West Virginia	6,980,482,000	0.2%
22	Wisconsin	53,089,052,000	1.6%
50	Wyoming	4,393,700,000	0.1%

RANK ORDER

RANK	STATE	COLLECTIONS	% of USA
1	California	$440,475,243,000	12.9%
2	Texas	270,955,237,000	7.9%
3	New York	268,353,669,000	7.9%
4	Florida	192,869,033,000	5.6%
5	Illinois	162,326,463,000	4.8%
6	New Jersey	143,835,479,000	4.2%
7	Ohio	142,086,312,000	4.2%
8	Pennsylvania	139,797,047,000	4.1%
9	Massachusetts	112,996,320,000	3.3%
10	Minnesota	104,429,577,000	3.1%
11	Georgia	94,277,375,000	2.8%
12	Virginia	87,183,756,000	2.6%
13	Washington	85,875,647,000	2.5%
14	North Carolina	82,855,993,000	2.4%
15	Michigan	82,676,161,000	2.4%
16	Missouri	71,921,135,000	2.1%
17	Maryland	71,246,920,000	2.1%
18	Tennessee	69,069,233,000	2.0%
19	Indiana	58,940,989,000	1.7%
20	Connecticut	57,540,270,000	1.7%
21	Colorado	56,742,235,000	1.7%
22	Wisconsin	53,089,052,000	1.6%
23	Arizona	43,928,177,000	1.3%
24	Louisiana	42,724,672,000	1.3%
25	Kentucky	35,126,897,000	1.0%
26	Arkansas	32,458,328,000	0.9%
27	Oregon	32,345,824,000	0.9%
28	Oklahoma	27,113,120,000	0.8%
29	South Carolina	26,636,069,000	0.8%
30	Alabama	26,583,916,000	0.8%
31	Kansas	25,563,140,000	0.7%
32	Nebraska	25,450,002,000	0.7%
33	Iowa	24,642,287,000	0.7%
34	Utah	22,485,663,000	0.7%
35	Nevada	21,570,670,000	0.6%
36	Delaware	17,081,357,000	0.5%
37	Rhode Island	14,917,462,000	0.4%
38	New Hampshire	12,138,352,000	0.4%
39	Mississippi	11,740,655,000	0.3%
40	Idaho	10,386,020,000	0.3%
41	Hawaii	9,415,214,000	0.3%
42	New Mexico	8,979,166,000	0.3%
43	Maine	8,083,275,000	0.2%
44	South Dakota	7,872,916,000	0.2%
45	West Virginia	6,980,482,000	0.2%
46	North Dakota	6,640,269,000	0.2%
47	Montana	6,080,381,000	0.2%
48	Alaska	5,399,946,000	0.2%
49	Vermont	4,422,942,000	0.1%
50	Wyoming	4,393,700,000	0.1%
	District of Columbia	28,302,953,000	0.8%

Source: U.S. Department of the Treasury, Internal Revenue Service
"Fiscal Year 2017 IRS Data Book" (https://www.irs.gov/statistics/soi-tax-stats-irs-data-book)
*Total includes $17,707,138,000 from U.S. citizens abroad and other miscellaneous returns not shown separately.

Per Capita Internal Revenue Service Gross Collections in 2017

National Per Capita = $10,454*

<table>
<tr><td colspan="3">ALPHA ORDER</td><td colspan="3">RANK ORDER</td></tr>
<tr><th>RANK</th><th>STATE</th><th>PER CAPITA</th><th>RANK</th><th>STATE</th><th>PER CAPITA</th></tr>
<tr><td>46</td><td>Alabama</td><td>$5,453</td><td>1</td><td>Minnesota</td><td>$18,755</td></tr>
<tr><td>36</td><td>Alaska</td><td>7,299</td><td>2</td><td>Delaware</td><td>17,847</td></tr>
<tr><td>42</td><td>Arizona</td><td>6,232</td><td>3</td><td>Massachusetts</td><td>16,464</td></tr>
<tr><td>16</td><td>Arkansas</td><td>10,809</td><td>4</td><td>New Jersey</td><td>16,182</td></tr>
<tr><td>14</td><td>California</td><td>11,180</td><td>5</td><td>Connecticut</td><td>16,100</td></tr>
<tr><td>19</td><td>Colorado</td><td>10,104</td><td>6</td><td>Rhode Island</td><td>14,120</td></tr>
<tr><td>5</td><td>Connecticut</td><td>16,100</td><td>7</td><td>New York</td><td>13,698</td></tr>
<tr><td>2</td><td>Delaware</td><td>17,847</td><td>8</td><td>Nebraska</td><td>13,272</td></tr>
<tr><td>21</td><td>Florida</td><td>9,194</td><td>9</td><td>Illinois</td><td>12,695</td></tr>
<tr><td>24</td><td>Georgia</td><td>9,054</td><td>10</td><td>Ohio</td><td>12,181</td></tr>
<tr><td>41</td><td>Hawaii</td><td>6,611</td><td>11</td><td>Maryland</td><td>11,825</td></tr>
<tr><td>44</td><td>Idaho</td><td>6,042</td><td>12</td><td>Missouri</td><td>11,774</td></tr>
<tr><td>9</td><td>Illinois</td><td>12,695</td><td>13</td><td>Washington</td><td>11,565</td></tr>
<tr><td>27</td><td>Indiana</td><td>8,850</td><td>14</td><td>California</td><td>11,180</td></tr>
<tr><td>33</td><td>Iowa</td><td>7,839</td><td>15</td><td>Pennsylvania</td><td>10,930</td></tr>
<tr><td>29</td><td>Kansas</td><td>8,783</td><td>16</td><td>Arkansas</td><td>10,809</td></tr>
<tr><td>32</td><td>Kentucky</td><td>7,887</td><td>17</td><td>Virginia</td><td>10,299</td></tr>
<tr><td>23</td><td>Louisiana</td><td>9,147</td><td>18</td><td>Tennessee</td><td>10,295</td></tr>
<tr><td>43</td><td>Maine</td><td>6,055</td><td>19</td><td>Colorado</td><td>10,104</td></tr>
<tr><td>11</td><td>Maryland</td><td>11,825</td><td>20</td><td>Texas</td><td>9,567</td></tr>
<tr><td>3</td><td>Massachusetts</td><td>16,464</td><td>21</td><td>Florida</td><td>9,194</td></tr>
<tr><td>30</td><td>Michigan</td><td>8,287</td><td>22</td><td>Wisconsin</td><td>9,166</td></tr>
<tr><td>1</td><td>Minnesota</td><td>18,755</td><td>23</td><td>Louisiana</td><td>9,147</td></tr>
<tr><td>49</td><td>Mississippi</td><td>3,927</td><td>24</td><td>Georgia</td><td>9,054</td></tr>
<tr><td>12</td><td>Missouri</td><td>11,774</td><td>25</td><td>South Dakota</td><td>9,015</td></tr>
<tr><td>45</td><td>Montana</td><td>5,774</td><td>26</td><td>New Hampshire</td><td>8,993</td></tr>
<tr><td>8</td><td>Nebraska</td><td>13,272</td><td>27</td><td>Indiana</td><td>8,850</td></tr>
<tr><td>37</td><td>Nevada</td><td>7,257</td><td>28</td><td>North Dakota</td><td>8,793</td></tr>
<tr><td>26</td><td>New Hampshire</td><td>8,993</td><td>29</td><td>Kansas</td><td>8,783</td></tr>
<tr><td>4</td><td>New Jersey</td><td>16,182</td><td>30</td><td>Michigan</td><td>8,287</td></tr>
<tr><td>48</td><td>New Mexico</td><td>4,289</td><td>31</td><td>North Carolina</td><td>8,067</td></tr>
<tr><td>7</td><td>New York</td><td>13,698</td><td>32</td><td>Kentucky</td><td>7,887</td></tr>
<tr><td>31</td><td>North Carolina</td><td>8,067</td><td>33</td><td>Iowa</td><td>7,839</td></tr>
<tr><td>28</td><td>North Dakota</td><td>8,793</td><td>34</td><td>Oregon</td><td>7,801</td></tr>
<tr><td>10</td><td>Ohio</td><td>12,181</td><td>35</td><td>Wyoming</td><td>7,589</td></tr>
<tr><td>40</td><td>Oklahoma</td><td>6,894</td><td>36</td><td>Alaska</td><td>7,299</td></tr>
<tr><td>34</td><td>Oregon</td><td>7,801</td><td>37</td><td>Nevada</td><td>7,257</td></tr>
<tr><td>15</td><td>Pennsylvania</td><td>10,930</td><td>38</td><td>Utah</td><td>7,246</td></tr>
<tr><td>6</td><td>Rhode Island</td><td>14,120</td><td>39</td><td>Vermont</td><td>7,082</td></tr>
<tr><td>47</td><td>South Carolina</td><td>5,305</td><td>40</td><td>Oklahoma</td><td>6,894</td></tr>
<tr><td>25</td><td>South Dakota</td><td>9,015</td><td>41</td><td>Hawaii</td><td>6,611</td></tr>
<tr><td>18</td><td>Tennessee</td><td>10,295</td><td>42</td><td>Arizona</td><td>6,232</td></tr>
<tr><td>20</td><td>Texas</td><td>9,567</td><td>43</td><td>Maine</td><td>6,055</td></tr>
<tr><td>38</td><td>Utah</td><td>7,246</td><td>44</td><td>Idaho</td><td>6,042</td></tr>
<tr><td>39</td><td>Vermont</td><td>7,082</td><td>45</td><td>Montana</td><td>5,774</td></tr>
<tr><td>17</td><td>Virginia</td><td>10,299</td><td>46</td><td>Alabama</td><td>5,453</td></tr>
<tr><td>13</td><td>Washington</td><td>11,565</td><td>47</td><td>South Carolina</td><td>5,305</td></tr>
<tr><td>50</td><td>West Virginia</td><td>3,842</td><td>48</td><td>New Mexico</td><td>4,289</td></tr>
<tr><td>22</td><td>Wisconsin</td><td>9,166</td><td>49</td><td>Mississippi</td><td>3,927</td></tr>
<tr><td>35</td><td>Wyoming</td><td>7,589</td><td>50</td><td>West Virginia</td><td>3,842</td></tr>
<tr><td></td><td></td><td></td><td></td><td>District of Columbia</td><td>40,683</td></tr>
</table>

Source: CQ Press using data from U.S. Department of the Treasury, Internal Revenue Service
"Fiscal Year 2017 IRS Data Book" (https://www.irs.gov/statistics/soi-tax-stats-irs-data-book)
*National per capita does not include collections from U.S. citizens abroad and other miscellaneous returns not shown separately.

Federal Individual Income Tax Collections in 2017

National Total = $2,990,900,934,000*

ALPHA ORDER

RANK	STATE	COLLECTIONS	% of USA
28	Alabama	$24,588,275,000	0.8%
48	Alaska	5,162,206,000	0.2%
24	Arizona	39,115,624,000	1.3%
27	Arkansas	26,612,837,000	0.9%
1	California	383,364,445,000	12.8%
20	Colorado	52,628,874,000	1.8%
21	Connecticut	48,003,315,000	1.6%
36	Delaware	14,184,894,000	0.5%
4	Florida	179,994,031,000	6.0%
11	Georgia	77,559,778,000	2.6%
42	Hawaii	8,442,127,000	0.3%
40	Idaho	9,973,635,000	0.3%
5	Illinois	139,771,317,000	4.7%
19	Indiana	54,576,722,000	1.8%
30	Iowa	22,881,744,000	0.8%
32	Kansas	22,338,379,000	0.7%
25	Kentucky	32,024,957,000	1.1%
23	Louisiana	40,393,499,000	1.4%
43	Maine	7,557,797,000	0.3%
16	Maryland	66,799,522,000	2.2%
9	Massachusetts	102,354,315,000	3.4%
13	Michigan	76,447,688,000	2.6%
10	Minnesota	84,721,896,000	2.8%
39	Mississippi	10,982,784,000	0.4%
18	Missouri	57,068,168,000	1.9%
47	Montana	5,798,150,000	0.2%
35	Nebraska	18,422,480,000	0.6%
34	Nevada	20,147,901,000	0.7%
37	New Hampshire	11,490,567,000	0.4%
8	New Jersey	116,965,715,000	3.9%
41	New Mexico	8,761,758,000	0.3%
2	New York	238,073,823,000	8.0%
14	North Carolina	73,608,708,000	2.5%
46	North Dakota	6,298,565,000	0.2%
6	Ohio	126,293,181,000	4.2%
31	Oklahoma	22,482,322,000	0.8%
26	Oregon	30,750,109,000	1.0%
7	Pennsylvania	122,021,841,000	4.1%
38	Rhode Island	11,293,955,000	0.4%
29	South Carolina	24,284,628,000	0.8%
44	South Dakota	7,268,084,000	0.2%
17	Tennessee	60,650,500,000	2.0%
3	Texas	225,236,761,000	7.5%
33	Utah	20,465,881,000	0.7%
49	Vermont	4,151,408,000	0.1%
15	Virginia	72,647,063,000	2.4%
12	Washington	77,323,289,000	2.6%
45	West Virginia	6,641,350,000	0.2%
22	Wisconsin	47,480,079,000	1.6%
50	Wyoming	4,007,776,000	0.1%

RANK ORDER

RANK	STATE	COLLECTIONS	% of USA
1	California	$383,364,445,000	12.8%
2	New York	238,073,823,000	8.0%
3	Texas	225,236,761,000	7.5%
4	Florida	179,994,031,000	6.0%
5	Illinois	139,771,317,000	4.7%
6	Ohio	126,293,181,000	4.2%
7	Pennsylvania	122,021,841,000	4.1%
8	New Jersey	116,965,715,000	3.9%
9	Massachusetts	102,354,315,000	3.4%
10	Minnesota	84,721,896,000	2.8%
11	Georgia	77,559,778,000	2.6%
12	Washington	77,323,289,000	2.6%
13	Michigan	76,447,688,000	2.6%
14	North Carolina	73,608,708,000	2.5%
15	Virginia	72,647,063,000	2.4%
16	Maryland	66,799,522,000	2.2%
17	Tennessee	60,650,500,000	2.0%
18	Missouri	57,068,168,000	1.9%
19	Indiana	54,576,722,000	1.8%
20	Colorado	52,628,874,000	1.8%
21	Connecticut	48,003,315,000	1.6%
22	Wisconsin	47,480,079,000	1.6%
23	Louisiana	40,393,499,000	1.4%
24	Arizona	39,115,624,000	1.3%
25	Kentucky	32,024,957,000	1.1%
26	Oregon	30,750,109,000	1.0%
27	Arkansas	26,612,837,000	0.9%
28	Alabama	24,588,275,000	0.8%
29	South Carolina	24,284,628,000	0.8%
30	Iowa	22,881,744,000	0.8%
31	Oklahoma	22,482,322,000	0.8%
32	Kansas	22,338,379,000	0.7%
33	Utah	20,465,881,000	0.7%
34	Nevada	20,147,901,000	0.7%
35	Nebraska	18,422,480,000	0.6%
36	Delaware	14,184,894,000	0.5%
37	New Hampshire	11,490,567,000	0.4%
38	Rhode Island	11,293,955,000	0.4%
39	Mississippi	10,982,784,000	0.4%
40	Idaho	9,973,635,000	0.3%
41	New Mexico	8,761,758,000	0.3%
42	Hawaii	8,442,127,000	0.3%
43	Maine	7,557,797,000	0.3%
44	South Dakota	7,268,084,000	0.2%
45	West Virginia	6,641,350,000	0.2%
46	North Dakota	6,298,565,000	0.2%
47	Montana	5,798,150,000	0.2%
48	Alaska	5,162,206,000	0.2%
49	Vermont	4,151,408,000	0.1%
50	Wyoming	4,007,776,000	0.1%
	District of Columbia	26,467,990,000	0.9%

Source: U.S. Department of the Treasury, Internal Revenue Service
   "Fiscal Year 2017 IRS Data Book" (https://www.irs.gov/statistics/soi-tax-stats-irs-data-book)
*Total includes $14,318,221,000 from U.S. citizens abroad and other miscellaneous returns not shown separately.

Average Revenue Collection per Federal Individual Income Tax Return in 2017

National Average = $19,848 per Return*

ALPHA ORDER				RANK ORDER		
RANK	STATE	PER RETURN		RANK	STATE	PER RETURN
44	Alabama	$12,073		1	Delaware	$31,317
36	Alaska	14,926		2	Minnesota	31,025
41	Arizona	13,395		3	Massachusetts	30,029
11	Arkansas	21,867		4	Connecticut	27,346
12	California	21,555		5	New Jersey	26,696
18	Colorado	19,994		6	New York	24,787
4	Connecticut	27,346		7	Illinois	22,857
1	Delaware	31,317		8	Ohio	22,687
22	Florida	18,520		9	Maryland	22,643
24	Georgia	17,522		10	Washington	22,281
43	Hawaii	12,285		11	Arkansas	21,867
40	Idaho	13,629		12	California	21,555
7	Illinois	22,857		13	Rhode Island	21,361
23	Indiana	17,617		14	Louisiana	20,649
35	Iowa	15,823		15	Missouri	20,558
27	Kansas	16,859		16	Nebraska	20,468
28	Kentucky	16,805		17	Tennessee	20,370
14	Louisiana	20,649		18	Colorado	19,994
45	Maine	11,694		19	Pennsylvania	19,723
9	Maryland	22,643		20	Virginia	18,602
3	Massachusetts	30,029		21	Texas	18,580
33	Michigan	16,228		22	Florida	18,520
2	Minnesota	31,025		23	Indiana	17,617
49	Mississippi	8,940		24	Georgia	17,522
15	Missouri	20,558		25	South Dakota	17,468
46	Montana	11,645		26	North Dakota	17,385
16	Nebraska	20,468		27	Kansas	16,859
38	Nevada	14,751		28	Kentucky	16,805
30	New Hampshire	16,519		29	Wisconsin	16,729
5	New Jersey	26,696		30	New Hampshire	16,519
48	New Mexico	9,658		31	North Carolina	16,435
6	New York	24,787		32	Oregon	16,232
31	North Carolina	16,435		33	Michigan	16,228
26	North Dakota	17,385		34	Utah	15,948
8	Ohio	22,687		35	Iowa	15,823
39	Oklahoma	13,924		36	Alaska	14,926
32	Oregon	16,232		37	Wyoming	14,832
19	Pennsylvania	19,723		38	Nevada	14,751
13	Rhode Island	21,361		39	Oklahoma	13,924
47	South Carolina	11,151		40	Idaho	13,629
25	South Dakota	17,468		41	Arizona	13,395
17	Tennessee	20,370		42	Vermont	12,788
21	Texas	18,580		43	Hawaii	12,285
34	Utah	15,948		44	Alabama	12,073
42	Vermont	12,788		45	Maine	11,694
20	Virginia	18,602		46	Montana	11,645
10	Washington	22,281		47	South Carolina	11,151
50	West Virginia	8,659		48	New Mexico	9,658
29	Wisconsin	16,729		49	Mississippi	8,940
37	Wyoming	14,832		50	West Virginia	8,659

District of Columbia   76,472

Source: CQ Press using data from U.S. Department of the Treasury, Internal Revenue Service
"Fiscal Year 2017 IRS Data Book" (https://www.irs.gov/statistics/soi-tax-stats-irs-data-book)
*National Rate includes collections and returns from U.S. citizens abroad and other miscellaneous returns not shown separately.

Adjusted Gross Income in 2016

National Total = $10,200,123,989,000*

ALPHA ORDER

RANK	STATE	A.G.I.	% of USA
26	Alabama	$113,629,123,000	1.1%
48	Alaska	23,528,106,000	0.2%
19	Arizona	177,716,596,000	1.7%
34	Arkansas	67,927,034,000	0.7%
1	California	1,413,475,964,000	13.9%
17	Colorado	194,421,581,000	1.9%
23	Connecticut	162,758,350,000	1.6%
44	Delaware	29,341,589,000	0.3%
4	Florida	599,322,773,000	5.9%
14	Georgia	269,643,927,000	2.6%
39	Hawaii	42,823,217,000	0.4%
40	Idaho	41,690,089,000	0.4%
5	Illinois	436,922,230,000	4.3%
20	Indiana	177,298,049,000	1.7%
31	Iowa	88,263,413,000	0.9%
33	Kansas	82,418,359,000	0.8%
28	Kentucky	103,817,661,000	1.0%
27	Louisiana	111,967,908,000	1.1%
42	Maine	37,066,370,000	0.4%
15	Maryland	224,468,553,000	2.2%
9	Massachusetts	301,415,039,000	3.0%
11	Michigan	286,575,420,000	2.8%
16	Minnesota	195,637,737,000	1.9%
35	Mississippi	59,498,508,000	0.6%
22	Missouri	165,065,984,000	1.6%
45	Montana	27,982,993,000	0.3%
36	Nebraska	55,220,953,000	0.5%
30	Nevada	88,971,139,000	0.9%
37	New Hampshire	51,608,751,000	0.5%
7	New Jersey	370,381,724,000	3.6%
38	New Mexico	46,568,174,000	0.5%
3	New York	769,643,997,000	7.5%
13	North Carolina	270,985,041,000	2.7%
47	North Dakota	23,859,186,000	0.2%
8	Ohio	325,566,075,000	3.2%
29	Oklahoma	92,312,489,000	0.9%
25	Oregon	123,504,362,000	1.2%
6	Pennsylvania	404,790,353,000	4.0%
43	Rhode Island	33,966,155,000	0.3%
24	South Carolina	124,456,207,000	1.2%
46	South Dakota	25,555,384,000	0.3%
21	Tennessee	174,852,280,000	1.7%
2	Texas	779,505,214,000	7.6%
32	Utah	83,702,730,000	0.8%
49	Vermont	19,310,615,000	0.2%
10	Virginia	292,085,431,000	2.9%
12	Washington	276,796,382,000	2.7%
41	West Virginia	38,375,305,000	0.4%
18	Wisconsin	177,941,473,000	1.7%
50	Wyoming	18,718,215,000	0.2%

RANK ORDER

RANK	STATE	A.G.I.	% of USA
1	California	$1,413,475,964,000	13.9%
2	Texas	779,505,214,000	7.6%
3	New York	769,643,997,000	7.5%
4	Florida	599,322,773,000	5.9%
5	Illinois	436,922,230,000	4.3%
6	Pennsylvania	404,790,353,000	4.0%
7	New Jersey	370,381,724,000	3.6%
8	Ohio	325,566,075,000	3.2%
9	Massachusetts	301,415,039,000	3.0%
10	Virginia	292,085,431,000	2.9%
11	Michigan	286,575,420,000	2.8%
12	Washington	276,796,382,000	2.7%
13	North Carolina	270,985,041,000	2.7%
14	Georgia	269,643,927,000	2.6%
15	Maryland	224,468,553,000	2.2%
16	Minnesota	195,637,737,000	1.9%
17	Colorado	194,421,581,000	1.9%
18	Wisconsin	177,941,473,000	1.7%
19	Arizona	177,716,596,000	1.7%
20	Indiana	177,298,049,000	1.7%
21	Tennessee	174,852,280,000	1.7%
22	Missouri	165,065,984,000	1.6%
23	Connecticut	162,758,350,000	1.6%
24	South Carolina	124,456,207,000	1.2%
25	Oregon	123,504,362,000	1.2%
26	Alabama	113,629,123,000	1.1%
27	Louisiana	111,967,908,000	1.1%
28	Kentucky	103,817,661,000	1.0%
29	Oklahoma	92,312,489,000	0.9%
30	Nevada	88,971,139,000	0.9%
31	Iowa	88,263,413,000	0.9%
32	Utah	83,702,730,000	0.8%
33	Kansas	82,418,359,000	0.8%
34	Arkansas	67,927,034,000	0.7%
35	Mississippi	59,498,508,000	0.6%
36	Nebraska	55,220,953,000	0.5%
37	New Hampshire	51,608,751,000	0.5%
38	New Mexico	46,568,174,000	0.5%
39	Hawaii	42,823,217,000	0.4%
40	Idaho	41,690,089,000	0.4%
41	West Virginia	38,375,305,000	0.4%
42	Maine	37,066,370,000	0.4%
43	Rhode Island	33,966,155,000	0.3%
44	Delaware	29,341,589,000	0.3%
45	Montana	27,982,993,000	0.3%
46	South Dakota	25,555,384,000	0.3%
47	North Dakota	23,859,186,000	0.2%
48	Alaska	23,528,106,000	0.2%
49	Vermont	19,310,615,000	0.2%
50	Wyoming	18,718,215,000	0.2%
	District of Columbia	31,910,557,000	0.3%

Source: U.S. Department of the Treasury, Internal Revenue Service
   "Individual Tax Statistics, State Income" (https://www.irs.gov/statistics)
*Total includes $64,859,224,000 from U.S. citizens abroad and other miscellaneous returns not shown separately.

Per Capita Adjusted Gross Income in 2016

National Per Capita = $31,372*

ALPHA ORDER				RANK ORDER		
RANK	STATE	PER CAPITA		RANK	STATE	PER CAPITA
46	Alabama	$23,358		1	Connecticut	$45,480
15	Alaska	31,730		2	Massachusetts	44,157
40	Arizona	25,587		3	New Jersey	41,735
47	Arkansas	22,715		4	New York	39,184
8	California	36,050		5	New Hampshire	38,446
10	Colorado	35,088		6	Washington	37,945
1	Connecticut	45,480		7	Maryland	37,382
19	Delaware	30,911		8	California	36,050
25	Florida	29,051		9	Minnesota	35,420
39	Georgia	26,167		10	Colorado	35,088
23	Hawaii	29,986		11	Virginia	34,727
42	Idaho	24,772		12	Illinois	34,063
12	Illinois	34,063		13	Rhode Island	32,133
36	Indiana	26,728		14	Wyoming	32,036
29	Iowa	28,183		15	Alaska	31,730
28	Kansas	28,310		16	Pennsylvania	31,665
45	Kentucky	23,392		17	North Dakota	31,629
43	Louisiana	23,934		18	Vermont	30,964
32	Maine	27,841		19	Delaware	30,911
7	Maryland	37,382		20	Wisconsin	30,823
2	Massachusetts	44,157		21	Nevada	30,472
27	Michigan	28,796		22	Oregon	30,186
9	Minnesota	35,420		23	Hawaii	29,986
50	Mississippi	19,911		24	South Dakota	29,616
34	Missouri	27,117		25	Florida	29,051
35	Montana	26,884		26	Nebraska	28,973
26	Nebraska	28,973		27	Michigan	28,796
21	Nevada	30,472		28	Kansas	28,310
5	New Hampshire	38,446		29	Iowa	28,183
3	New Jersey	41,735		30	Ohio	27,982
48	New Mexico	22,252		31	Texas	27,902
4	New York	39,184		32	Maine	27,841
37	North Carolina	26,680		33	Utah	27,510
17	North Dakota	31,629		34	Missouri	27,117
30	Ohio	27,982		35	Montana	26,884
44	Oklahoma	23,509		36	Indiana	26,728
22	Oregon	30,186		37	North Carolina	26,680
16	Pennsylvania	31,665		38	Tennessee	26,313
13	Rhode Island	32,133		39	Georgia	26,167
41	South Carolina	25,101		40	Arizona	25,587
24	South Dakota	29,616		41	South Carolina	25,101
38	Tennessee	26,313		42	Idaho	24,772
31	Texas	27,902		43	Louisiana	23,934
33	Utah	27,510		44	Oklahoma	23,509
18	Vermont	30,964		45	Kentucky	23,392
11	Virginia	34,727		46	Alabama	23,358
6	Washington	37,945		47	Arkansas	22,715
49	West Virginia	20,959		48	New Mexico	22,252
20	Wisconsin	30,823		49	West Virginia	20,959
14	Wyoming	32,036		50	Mississippi	19,911
					District of Columbia	46,478

Source: CQ Press using data from U.S. Department of the Treasury, Internal Revenue Service
  "Individual Tax Statistics, State Income" (https://www.irs.gov/statistics)
*National per capita does not include income from U.S. citizens abroad and other miscellaneous returns not shown separately.

Federal Business Income Tax Collections in 2017

National Total = $338,529,154,000*

ALPHA ORDER

RANK	STATE	COLLECTIONS	% of USA
32	Alabama	$1,599,172,000	0.5%
48	Alaska	173,808,000	0.1%
25	Arizona	3,248,089,000	1.0%
20	Arkansas	5,047,349,000	1.5%
1	California	47,274,455,000	14.0%
26	Colorado	2,899,495,000	0.9%
15	Connecticut	8,670,093,000	2.6%
28	Delaware	2,626,429,000	0.8%
13	Florida	9,057,258,000	2.7%
9	Georgia	12,783,900,000	3.8%
38	Hawaii	700,144,000	0.2%
42	Idaho	337,112,000	0.1%
5	Illinois	18,973,607,000	5.6%
23	Indiana	3,624,764,000	1.1%
33	Iowa	1,416,367,000	0.4%
31	Kansas	1,637,121,000	0.5%
27	Kentucky	2,668,995,000	0.8%
30	Louisiana	1,802,698,000	0.5%
41	Maine	382,005,000	0.1%
22	Maryland	4,121,320,000	1.2%
12	Massachusetts	9,081,122,000	2.7%
19	Michigan	5,305,414,000	1.6%
6	Minnesota	18,538,716,000	5.5%
39	Mississippi	570,425,000	0.2%
10	Missouri	12,238,850,000	3.6%
47	Montana	190,980,000	0.1%
18	Nebraska	6,836,388,000	2.0%
36	Nevada	974,505,000	0.3%
44	New Hampshire	261,057,000	0.1%
3	New Jersey	24,521,317,000	7.2%
49	New Mexico	142,271,000	0.0%
2	New York	26,130,226,000	7.7%
14	North Carolina	8,710,521,000	2.6%
43	North Dakota	273,035,000	0.1%
11	Ohio	11,086,446,000	3.3%
37	Oklahoma	846,993,000	0.3%
35	Oregon	1,139,779,000	0.3%
7	Pennsylvania	15,041,827,000	4.4%
24	Rhode Island	3,456,216,000	1.0%
29	South Carolina	1,953,433,000	0.6%
40	South Dakota	538,298,000	0.2%
17	Tennessee	6,894,252,000	2.0%
4	Texas	22,939,596,000	6.8%
34	Utah	1,302,787,000	0.4%
46	Vermont	242,481,000	0.1%
8	Virginia	14,023,486,000	4.1%
16	Washington	6,985,812,000	2.1%
45	West Virginia	243,825,000	0.1%
21	Wisconsin	4,886,946,000	1.4%
50	Wyoming	100,890,000	0.0%

RANK ORDER

RANK	STATE	COLLECTIONS	% of USA
1	California	$47,274,455,000	14.0%
2	New York	26,130,226,000	7.7%
3	New Jersey	24,521,317,000	7.2%
4	Texas	22,939,596,000	6.8%
5	Illinois	18,973,607,000	5.6%
6	Minnesota	18,538,716,000	5.5%
7	Pennsylvania	15,041,827,000	4.4%
8	Virginia	14,023,486,000	4.1%
9	Georgia	12,783,900,000	3.8%
10	Missouri	12,238,850,000	3.6%
11	Ohio	11,086,446,000	3.3%
12	Massachusetts	9,081,122,000	2.7%
13	Florida	9,057,258,000	2.7%
14	North Carolina	8,710,521,000	2.6%
15	Connecticut	8,670,093,000	2.6%
16	Washington	6,985,812,000	2.1%
17	Tennessee	6,894,252,000	2.0%
18	Nebraska	6,836,388,000	2.0%
19	Michigan	5,305,414,000	1.6%
20	Arkansas	5,047,349,000	1.5%
21	Wisconsin	4,886,946,000	1.4%
22	Maryland	4,121,320,000	1.2%
23	Indiana	3,624,764,000	1.1%
24	Rhode Island	3,456,216,000	1.0%
25	Arizona	3,248,089,000	1.0%
26	Colorado	2,899,495,000	0.9%
27	Kentucky	2,668,995,000	0.8%
28	Delaware	2,626,429,000	0.8%
29	South Carolina	1,953,433,000	0.6%
30	Louisiana	1,802,698,000	0.5%
31	Kansas	1,637,121,000	0.5%
32	Alabama	1,599,172,000	0.5%
33	Iowa	1,416,367,000	0.4%
34	Utah	1,302,787,000	0.4%
35	Oregon	1,139,779,000	0.3%
36	Nevada	974,505,000	0.3%
37	Oklahoma	846,993,000	0.3%
38	Hawaii	700,144,000	0.2%
39	Mississippi	570,425,000	0.2%
40	South Dakota	538,298,000	0.2%
41	Maine	382,005,000	0.1%
42	Idaho	337,112,000	0.1%
43	North Dakota	273,035,000	0.1%
44	New Hampshire	261,057,000	0.1%
45	West Virginia	243,825,000	0.1%
46	Vermont	242,481,000	0.1%
47	Montana	190,980,000	0.1%
48	Alaska	173,808,000	0.1%
49	New Mexico	142,271,000	0.0%
50	Wyoming	100,890,000	0.0%
	District of Columbia	1,747,183,000	0.5%

Source: U.S. Department of the Treasury, Internal Revenue Service
   "Fiscal Year 2017 IRS Data Book" (https://www.irs.gov/statistics/soi-tax-stats-irs-data-book)
*Total includes collections and returns from international sources and others not distributed by state. Includes taxes on
corporation income (Form 1120 series) and unrelated business income from tax-exempt organizations.

Average Revenue Collection per Federal Business Income Tax Return in 2017

National Average = $49,133 per Return*

ALPHA ORDER

ALPHA ORDER   RANK ORDER

RANK	STATE	PER CAPITA		RANK	STATE	PER CAPITA
30	Alabama	$23,859		1	Connecticut	$175,497
41	Alaska	13,558		2	Nebraska	153,803
28	Arizona	26,861		3	Rhode Island	150,630
9	Arkansas	95,890		4	Minnesota	149,441
15	California	56,152		5	New Jersey	136,758
34	Colorado	18,186		6	Missouri	126,159
1	Connecticut	175,497		7	Tennessee	108,775
8	Delaware	103,350		8	Delaware	103,350
45	Florida	11,771		9	Arkansas	95,890
14	Georgia	58,377		10	Virginia	84,809
29	Hawaii	26,119		11	Pennsylvania	69,410
47	Idaho	9,176		12	Ohio	65,770
17	Illinois	54,023		13	Massachusetts	62,042
23	Indiana	32,965		14	Georgia	58,377
32	Iowa	22,928		15	California	56,152
24	Kansas	32,412		16	Wisconsin	54,038
21	Kentucky	41,330		17	Illinois	54,023
33	Louisiana	20,737		18	Washington	49,678
42	Maine	12,946		19	Texas	49,645
25	Maryland	31,828		20	North Carolina	44,892
13	Massachusetts	62,042		21	Kentucky	41,330
26	Michigan	27,976		22	New York	39,590
4	Minnesota	149,441		23	Indiana	32,965
39	Mississippi	14,181		24	Kansas	32,412
6	Missouri	126,159		25	Maryland	31,828
48	Montana	5,428		26	Michigan	27,976
2	Nebraska	153,803		27	South Dakota	27,958
40	Nevada	13,909		28	Arizona	26,861
44	New Hampshire	12,490		29	Hawaii	26,119
5	New Jersey	136,758		30	Alabama	23,859
50	New Mexico	4,936		31	South Carolina	23,240
22	New York	39,590		32	Iowa	22,928
20	North Carolina	44,892		33	Louisiana	20,737
36	North Dakota	16,888		34	Colorado	18,186
12	Ohio	65,770		35	Utah	16,911
46	Oklahoma	11,496		36	North Dakota	16,888
38	Oregon	14,911		37	Vermont	16,065
11	Pennsylvania	69,410		38	Oregon	14,911
3	Rhode Island	150,630		39	Mississippi	14,181
31	South Carolina	23,240		40	Nevada	13,909
27	South Dakota	27,958		41	Alaska	13,558
7	Tennessee	108,775		42	Maine	12,946
19	Texas	49,645		43	West Virginia	12,843
35	Utah	16,911		44	New Hampshire	12,490
37	Vermont	16,065		45	Florida	11,771
10	Virginia	84,809		46	Oklahoma	11,496
18	Washington	49,678		47	Idaho	9,176
43	West Virginia	12,843		48	Montana	5,428
16	Wisconsin	54,038		49	Wyoming	5,274
49	Wyoming	5,274		50	New Mexico	4,936

District of Columbia   96,343

Source: CQ Press using data from U.S. Department of the Treasury, Internal Revenue Service
"Fiscal Year 2017 IRS Data Book" (https://www.irs.gov/statistics/soi-tax-stats-irs-data-book)
*National average does not include income from U.S. citizens abroad and other miscellaneous returns not shown separately.
Includes taxes on corporation income (Form 1120 series) and unrelated business income from tax-exempt organizations.

Federal Tax Returns Filed in 2017

National Total = 245,411,588 Returns*

ALPHA ORDER

RANK	STATE	RETURNS	% of USA
26	Alabama	3,082,175	1.3%
49	Alaska	571,130	0.2%
17	Arizona	4,657,633	1.9%
34	Arkansas	1,944,826	0.8%
1	California	29,756,137	12.1%
18	Colorado	4,652,592	1.9%
27	Connecticut	2,931,144	1.2%
45	Delaware	788,036	0.3%
3	Florida	17,092,377	7.0%
10	Georgia	7,032,080	2.9%
39	Hawaii	1,126,627	0.5%
38	Idaho	1,258,134	0.5%
5	Illinois	10,018,880	4.1%
16	Indiana	4,659,347	1.9%
30	Iowa	2,406,076	1.0%
32	Kansas	2,194,635	0.9%
28	Kentucky	2,894,916	1.2%
25	Louisiana	3,161,283	1.3%
42	Maine	1,109,694	0.5%
15	Maryland	4,700,321	1.9%
14	Massachusetts	5,655,160	2.3%
9	Michigan	7,329,617	3.0%
20	Minnesota	4,488,452	1.8%
35	Mississippi	1,834,890	0.7%
19	Missouri	4,562,427	1.9%
43	Montana	965,325	0.4%
36	Nebraska	1,516,789	0.6%
33	Nevada	2,166,914	0.9%
40	New Hampshire	1,125,693	0.5%
8	New Jersey	7,398,401	3.0%
37	New Mexico	1,402,322	0.6%
4	New York	16,083,546	6.6%
11	North Carolina	7,008,764	2.9%
47	North Dakota	664,041	0.3%
7	Ohio	8,456,707	3.4%
29	Oklahoma	2,688,045	1.1%
24	Oregon	3,275,990	1.3%
6	Pennsylvania	9,751,214	4.0%
44	Rhode Island	858,363	0.3%
23	South Carolina	3,351,343	1.4%
46	South Dakota	755,942	0.3%
22	Tennessee	4,394,284	1.8%
2	Texas	19,239,468	7.8%
31	Utah	2,216,179	0.9%
48	Vermont	572,001	0.2%
12	Virginia	6,216,575	2.5%
13	Washington	5,762,155	2.3%
41	West Virginia	1,122,176	0.5%
21	Wisconsin	4,476,209	1.8%
50	Wyoming	519,070	0.2%

RANK ORDER

RANK	STATE	RETURNS	% of USA
1	California	29,756,137	12.1%
2	Texas	19,239,468	7.8%
3	Florida	17,092,377	7.0%
4	New York	16,083,546	6.6%
5	Illinois	10,018,880	4.1%
6	Pennsylvania	9,751,214	4.0%
7	Ohio	8,456,707	3.4%
8	New Jersey	7,398,401	3.0%
9	Michigan	7,329,617	3.0%
10	Georgia	7,032,080	2.9%
11	North Carolina	7,008,764	2.9%
12	Virginia	6,216,575	2.5%
13	Washington	5,762,155	2.3%
14	Massachusetts	5,655,160	2.3%
15	Maryland	4,700,321	1.9%
16	Indiana	4,659,347	1.9%
17	Arizona	4,657,633	1.9%
18	Colorado	4,652,592	1.9%
19	Missouri	4,562,427	1.9%
20	Minnesota	4,488,452	1.8%
21	Wisconsin	4,476,209	1.8%
22	Tennessee	4,394,284	1.8%
23	South Carolina	3,351,343	1.4%
24	Oregon	3,275,990	1.3%
25	Louisiana	3,161,283	1.3%
26	Alabama	3,082,175	1.3%
27	Connecticut	2,931,144	1.2%
28	Kentucky	2,894,916	1.2%
29	Oklahoma	2,688,045	1.1%
30	Iowa	2,406,076	1.0%
31	Utah	2,216,179	0.9%
32	Kansas	2,194,635	0.9%
33	Nevada	2,166,914	0.9%
34	Arkansas	1,944,826	0.8%
35	Mississippi	1,834,890	0.7%
36	Nebraska	1,516,789	0.6%
37	New Mexico	1,402,322	0.6%
38	Idaho	1,258,134	0.5%
39	Hawaii	1,126,627	0.5%
40	New Hampshire	1,125,693	0.5%
41	West Virginia	1,122,176	0.5%
42	Maine	1,109,694	0.5%
43	Montana	965,325	0.4%
44	Rhode Island	858,363	0.3%
45	Delaware	788,036	0.3%
46	South Dakota	755,942	0.3%
47	North Dakota	664,041	0.3%
48	Vermont	572,001	0.2%
49	Alaska	571,130	0.2%
50	Wyoming	519,070	0.2%
	District of Columbia	603,784	0.2%

Source: U.S. Department of the Treasury, Internal Revenue Service

"Fiscal Year 2017 IRS Data Book" (https://www.irs.gov/statistics/soi-tax-stats-irs-data-book)

*Total includes returns from international sources and other miscellaneous returns not shown separately.

Percent of Federal Returns Filed Electronically in 2017

National Percent = 70.5%*

ALPHA ORDER			RANK ORDER		
RANK	STATE	PERCENT	RANK	STATE	PERCENT
7	Alabama	72.6	1	New York	75.6
44	Alaska	67.2	2	Georgia	74.0
22	Arizona	70.5	3	Rhode Island	73.8
16	Arkansas	71.3	4	Utah	73.4
18	California	70.9	5	Mississippi	72.8
41	Colorado	67.7	5	Tennessee	72.8
27	Connecticut	70.2	7	Alabama	72.6
28	Delaware	69.9	7	Massachusetts	72.6
32	Florida	69.3	9	Nevada	72.5
2	Georgia	74.0	10	Ohio	72.2
50	Hawaii	62.0	11	Indiana	72.1
42	Idaho	67.5	11	South Carolina	72.1
29	Illinois	69.7	13	Kentucky	72.0
11	Indiana	72.1	14	New Jersey	71.9
36	Iowa	68.4	15	Texas	71.8
21	Kansas	70.6	16	Arkansas	71.3
13	Kentucky	72.0	16	Louisiana	71.3
16	Louisiana	71.3	18	California	70.9
43	Maine	67.3	18	Michigan	70.9
36	Maryland	68.4	20	North Carolina	70.7
7	Massachusetts	72.6	21	Kansas	70.6
18	Michigan	70.9	22	Arizona	70.5
25	Minnesota	70.3	22	Oklahoma	70.5
5	Mississippi	72.8	22	Wisconsin	70.5
33	Missouri	69.1	25	Minnesota	70.3
48	Montana	64.5	25	Virginia	70.3
31	Nebraska	69.4	27	Connecticut	70.2
9	Nevada	72.5	28	Delaware	69.9
38	New Hampshire	68.3	29	Illinois	69.7
14	New Jersey	71.9	30	Pennsylvania	69.6
34	New Mexico	69.0	31	Nebraska	69.4
1	New York	75.6	32	Florida	69.3
20	North Carolina	70.7	33	Missouri	69.1
49	North Dakota	63.7	34	New Mexico	69.0
10	Ohio	72.2	35	West Virginia	68.8
22	Oklahoma	70.5	36	Iowa	68.4
40	Oregon	68.1	36	Maryland	68.4
30	Pennsylvania	69.6	38	New Hampshire	68.3
3	Rhode Island	73.8	39	Washington	68.2
11	South Carolina	72.1	40	Oregon	68.1
46	South Dakota	65.0	41	Colorado	67.7
5	Tennessee	72.8	42	Idaho	67.5
15	Texas	71.8	43	Maine	67.3
4	Utah	73.4	44	Alaska	67.2
45	Vermont	65.1	45	Vermont	65.1
25	Virginia	70.3	46	South Dakota	65.0
39	Washington	68.2	47	Wyoming	64.9
35	West Virginia	68.8	48	Montana	64.5
22	Wisconsin	70.5	49	North Dakota	63.7
47	Wyoming	64.9	50	Hawaii	62.0

			District of Columbia	68.9

Source: CQ Press using data from U.S. Department of the Treasury, Internal Revenue Service
"Fiscal Year 2017 IRS Data Book" (https://www.irs.gov/statistics/soi-tax-stats-irs-data-book)
*Total includes returns from international sources and other miscellaneous returns. Includes corporate, individual, partnership, estate, employment and other returns. Excludes returns that cannot be filed electronically including informational returns.

Federal Individual Income Tax Returns Filed in 2017

National Total = 150,690,787 Returns*

ALPHA ORDER

RANK	STATE	RETURNS	% of USA
24	Alabama	2,036,561	1.4%
48	Alaska	345,844	0.2%
18	Arizona	2,920,081	1.9%
35	Arkansas	1,217,048	0.8%
1	California	17,785,476	11.8%
22	Colorado	2,632,228	1.7%
28	Connecticut	1,755,409	1.2%
45	Delaware	452,945	0.3%
3	Florida	9,718,680	6.4%
10	Georgia	4,426,518	2.9%
41	Hawaii	687,190	0.5%
39	Idaho	731,783	0.5%
6	Illinois	6,115,106	4.1%
15	Indiana	3,098,002	2.1%
30	Iowa	1,446,074	1.0%
32	Kansas	1,324,975	0.9%
26	Kentucky	1,905,650	1.3%
25	Louisiana	1,956,230	1.3%
42	Maine	646,316	0.4%
17	Maryland	2,950,158	2.0%
14	Massachusetts	3,408,553	2.3%
8	Michigan	4,710,962	3.1%
21	Minnesota	2,730,771	1.8%
34	Mississippi	1,228,448	0.8%
20	Missouri	2,775,981	1.8%
44	Montana	497,922	0.3%
37	Nebraska	900,046	0.6%
31	Nevada	1,365,858	0.9%
40	New Hampshire	695,598	0.5%
11	New Jersey	4,381,347	2.9%
36	New Mexico	907,178	0.6%
4	New York	9,604,848	6.4%
9	North Carolina	4,478,839	3.0%
47	North Dakota	362,295	0.2%
7	Ohio	5,566,813	3.7%
29	Oklahoma	1,614,695	1.1%
27	Oregon	1,894,466	1.3%
5	Pennsylvania	6,186,744	4.1%
43	Rhode Island	528,728	0.4%
23	South Carolina	2,177,779	1.4%
46	South Dakota	416,088	0.3%
16	Tennessee	2,977,375	2.0%
2	Texas	12,122,417	8.0%
33	Utah	1,283,308	0.9%
49	Vermont	324,645	0.2%
12	Virginia	3,905,332	2.6%
13	Washington	3,470,405	2.3%
38	West Virginia	766,984	0.5%
19	Wisconsin	2,838,148	1.9%
50	Wyoming	270,206	0.2%

RANK ORDER

RANK	STATE	RETURNS	% of USA
1	California	17,785,476	11.8%
2	Texas	12,122,417	8.0%
3	Florida	9,718,680	6.4%
4	New York	9,604,848	6.4%
5	Pennsylvania	6,186,744	4.1%
6	Illinois	6,115,106	4.1%
7	Ohio	5,566,813	3.7%
8	Michigan	4,710,962	3.1%
9	North Carolina	4,478,839	3.0%
10	Georgia	4,426,518	2.9%
11	New Jersey	4,381,347	2.9%
12	Virginia	3,905,332	2.6%
13	Washington	3,470,405	2.3%
14	Massachusetts	3,408,553	2.3%
15	Indiana	3,098,002	2.1%
16	Tennessee	2,977,375	2.0%
17	Maryland	2,950,158	2.0%
18	Arizona	2,920,081	1.9%
19	Wisconsin	2,838,148	1.9%
20	Missouri	2,775,981	1.8%
21	Minnesota	2,730,771	1.8%
22	Colorado	2,632,228	1.7%
23	South Carolina	2,177,779	1.4%
24	Alabama	2,036,561	1.4%
25	Louisiana	1,956,230	1.3%
26	Kentucky	1,905,650	1.3%
27	Oregon	1,894,466	1.3%
28	Connecticut	1,755,409	1.2%
29	Oklahoma	1,614,695	1.1%
30	Iowa	1,446,074	1.0%
31	Nevada	1,365,858	0.9%
32	Kansas	1,324,975	0.9%
33	Utah	1,283,308	0.9%
34	Mississippi	1,228,448	0.8%
35	Arkansas	1,217,048	0.8%
36	New Mexico	907,178	0.6%
37	Nebraska	900,046	0.6%
38	West Virginia	766,984	0.5%
39	Idaho	731,783	0.5%
40	New Hampshire	695,598	0.5%
41	Hawaii	687,190	0.5%
42	Maine	646,316	0.4%
43	Rhode Island	528,728	0.4%
44	Montana	497,922	0.3%
45	Delaware	452,945	0.3%
46	South Dakota	416,088	0.3%
47	North Dakota	362,295	0.2%
48	Alaska	345,844	0.2%
49	Vermont	324,645	0.2%
50	Wyoming	270,206	0.2%
	District of Columbia	346,113	0.2%

Source: U.S. Department of the Treasury, Internal Revenue Service
"Fiscal Year 2017 IRS Data Book" (https://www.irs.gov/statistics/soi-tax-stats-irs-data-book)
*Total includes returns from international sources and other miscellaneous returns not shown separately.

Percent of Federal Individual Income Tax Returns Filed Electronically in 2017

National Percent = 87.4%*

RANK	STATE	PERCENT
19	Alabama	89.1
46	Alaska	86.2
42	Arizona	86.7
9	Arkansas	89.8
40	California	86.8
39	Colorado	86.9
29	Connecticut	87.7
38	Delaware	87.0
48	Florida	86.1
22	Georgia	88.8
50	Hawaii	82.6
15	Idaho	89.3
34	Illinois	87.4
8	Indiana	90.1
1	Iowa	92.9
3	Kansas	91.4
7	Kentucky	90.6
32	Louisiana	87.6
46	Maine	86.2
49	Maryland	83.7
29	Massachusetts	87.7
26	Michigan	88.3
13	Minnesota	89.6
10	Mississippi	89.7
25	Missouri	88.5
10	Montana	89.7
2	Nebraska	92.0
42	Nevada	86.7
42	New Hampshire	86.7
29	New Jersey	87.7
37	New Mexico	87.1
4	New York	91.3
24	North Carolina	88.6
6	North Dakota	90.7
23	Ohio	88.7
10	Oklahoma	89.7
33	Oregon	87.5
40	Pennsylvania	86.8
21	Rhode Island	88.9
15	South Carolina	89.3
5	South Dakota	90.8
19	Tennessee	89.1
45	Texas	86.4
18	Utah	89.2
27	Vermont	87.8
35	Virginia	87.3
36	Washington	87.2
27	West Virginia	87.8
14	Wisconsin	89.5
15	Wyoming	89.3

RANK	STATE	PERCENT
1	Iowa	92.9
2	Nebraska	92.0
3	Kansas	91.4
4	New York	91.3
5	South Dakota	90.8
6	North Dakota	90.7
7	Kentucky	90.6
8	Indiana	90.1
9	Arkansas	89.8
10	Mississippi	89.7
10	Montana	89.7
10	Oklahoma	89.7
13	Minnesota	89.6
14	Wisconsin	89.5
15	Idaho	89.3
15	South Carolina	89.3
15	Wyoming	89.3
18	Utah	89.2
19	Alabama	89.1
19	Tennessee	89.1
21	Rhode Island	88.9
22	Georgia	88.8
23	Ohio	88.7
24	North Carolina	88.6
25	Missouri	88.5
26	Michigan	88.3
27	Vermont	87.8
27	West Virginia	87.8
29	Connecticut	87.7
29	Massachusetts	87.7
29	New Jersey	87.7
32	Louisiana	87.6
33	Oregon	87.5
34	Illinois	87.4
35	Virginia	87.3
36	Washington	87.2
37	New Mexico	87.1
38	Delaware	87.0
39	Colorado	86.9
40	California	86.8
40	Pennsylvania	86.8
42	Arizona	86.7
42	Nevada	86.7
42	New Hampshire	86.7
45	Texas	86.4
46	Alaska	86.2
46	Maine	86.2
48	Florida	86.1
49	Maryland	83.7
50	Hawaii	82.6

District of Columbia	84.7

Source: CQ Press using data from U.S. Department of the Treasury, Internal Revenue Service
"Fiscal Year 2017 IRS Data Book" (https://www.irs.gov/statistics/soi-tax-stats-irs-data-book)
*Total includes returns from international sources and other miscellaneous returns. Includes returns filed electronically by practitioners.

Federal Business Income Tax Returns Filed in 2017

National Total = 6,892,888 Returns*

ALPHA ORDER					RANK ORDER			
RANK	STATE	RETURNS	% of USA		RANK	STATE	RETURNS	% of USA
28	Alabama	67,027	1.0%		1	California	841,906	12.2%
50	Alaska	12,820	0.2%		2	Florida	769,450	11.2%
18	Arizona	120,923	1.8%		3	New York	660,025	9.6%
32	Arkansas	52,637	0.8%		4	Texas	462,069	6.7%
1	California	841,906	12.2%		5	Illinois	351,215	5.1%
13	Colorado	159,435	2.3%		6	Georgia	218,987	3.2%
34	Connecticut	49,403	0.7%		7	Pennsylvania	216,711	3.1%
42	Delaware	25,413	0.4%		8	North Carolina	194,034	2.8%
2	Florida	769,450	11.2%		9	Michigan	189,639	2.8%
6	Georgia	218,987	3.2%		10	New Jersey	179,305	2.6%
41	Hawaii	26,806	0.4%		11	Ohio	168,564	2.4%
37	Idaho	36,739	0.5%		12	Virginia	165,353	2.4%
5	Illinois	351,215	5.1%		13	Colorado	159,435	2.3%
19	Indiana	109,958	1.6%		14	Massachusetts	146,371	2.1%
31	Iowa	61,775	0.9%		15	Washington	140,622	2.0%
33	Kansas	50,509	0.7%		16	Maryland	129,489	1.9%
29	Kentucky	64,578	0.9%		17	Minnesota	124,054	1.8%
22	Louisiana	86,932	1.3%		18	Arizona	120,923	1.8%
39	Maine	29,508	0.4%		19	Indiana	109,958	1.6%
16	Maryland	129,489	1.9%		20	Missouri	97,011	1.4%
14	Massachusetts	146,371	2.1%		21	Wisconsin	90,435	1.3%
9	Michigan	189,639	2.8%		22	Louisiana	86,932	1.3%
17	Minnesota	124,054	1.8%		23	South Carolina	84,056	1.2%
36	Mississippi	40,225	0.6%		24	Utah	77,039	1.1%
20	Missouri	97,011	1.4%		25	Oregon	76,440	1.1%
38	Montana	35,187	0.5%		26	Oklahoma	73,675	1.1%
35	Nebraska	44,449	0.6%		27	Nevada	70,062	1.0%
27	Nevada	70,062	1.0%		28	Alabama	67,027	1.0%
44	New Hampshire	20,901	0.3%		29	Kentucky	64,578	0.9%
10	New Jersey	179,305	2.6%		30	Tennessee	63,381	0.9%
40	New Mexico	28,822	0.4%		31	Iowa	61,775	0.9%
3	New York	660,025	9.6%		32	Arkansas	52,637	0.8%
8	North Carolina	194,034	2.8%		33	Kansas	50,509	0.7%
48	North Dakota	16,167	0.2%		34	Connecticut	49,403	0.7%
11	Ohio	168,564	2.4%		35	Nebraska	44,449	0.6%
26	Oklahoma	73,675	1.1%		36	Mississippi	40,225	0.6%
25	Oregon	76,440	1.1%		37	Idaho	36,739	0.5%
7	Pennsylvania	216,711	3.1%		38	Montana	35,187	0.5%
43	Rhode Island	22,945	0.3%		39	Maine	29,508	0.4%
23	South Carolina	84,056	1.2%		40	New Mexico	28,822	0.4%
45	South Dakota	19,254	0.3%		41	Hawaii	26,806	0.4%
30	Tennessee	63,381	0.9%		42	Delaware	25,413	0.4%
4	Texas	462,069	6.7%		43	Rhode Island	22,945	0.3%
24	Utah	77,039	1.1%		44	New Hampshire	20,901	0.3%
49	Vermont	15,094	0.2%		45	South Dakota	19,254	0.3%
12	Virginia	165,353	2.4%		46	Wyoming	19,131	0.3%
15	Washington	140,622	2.0%		47	West Virginia	18,985	0.3%
47	West Virginia	18,985	0.3%		48	North Dakota	16,167	0.2%
21	Wisconsin	90,435	1.3%		49	Vermont	15,094	0.2%
46	Wyoming	19,131	0.3%		50	Alaska	12,820	0.2%
						District of Columbia	18,135	0.3%

Source: U.S. Department of the Treasury, Internal Revenue Service
   "Fiscal Year 2017 IRS Data Book" (https://www.irs.gov/statistics/soi-tax-stats-irs-data-book)
*Total includes returns from international sources and other miscellaneous returns not shown separately.

Federal Tax Refunds in 2017

National Total = 121,991,952 Refunds*

ALPHA ORDER

RANK	STATE	REFUNDS	% of USA
24	Alabama	1,676,151	1.4%
48	Alaska	283,436	0.2%
18	Arizona	2,277,407	1.9%
35	Arkansas	1,007,785	0.8%
1	California	13,846,488	11.4%
22	Colorado	2,051,877	1.7%
28	Connecticut	1,422,410	1.2%
45	Delaware	375,420	0.3%
3	Florida	8,001,295	6.6%
9	Georgia	3,660,309	3.0%
41	Hawaii	545,207	0.4%
39	Idaho	573,741	0.5%
6	Illinois	5,067,372	4.2%
15	Indiana	2,612,413	2.1%
30	Iowa	1,162,882	1.0%
32	Kansas	1,065,305	0.9%
26	Kentucky	1,612,373	1.3%
25	Louisiana	1,640,935	1.3%
42	Maine	518,916	0.4%
17	Maryland	2,363,151	1.9%
14	Massachusetts	2,751,130	2.3%
8	Michigan	3,839,384	3.1%
21	Minnesota	2,149,182	1.8%
34	Mississippi	1,035,489	0.8%
20	Missouri	2,265,900	1.9%
44	Montana	383,966	0.3%
37	Nebraska	726,442	0.6%
31	Nevada	1,129,260	0.9%
40	New Hampshire	568,397	0.5%
11	New Jersey	3,539,771	2.9%
36	New Mexico	736,423	0.6%
4	New York	7,860,621	6.4%
10	North Carolina	3,635,581	3.0%
47	North Dakota	284,554	0.2%
7	Ohio	4,640,883	3.8%
29	Oklahoma	1,325,483	1.1%
27	Oregon	1,459,595	1.2%
5	Pennsylvania	5,145,524	4.2%
43	Rhode Island	445,927	0.4%
23	South Carolina	1,743,517	1.4%
46	South Dakota	330,591	0.3%
16	Tennessee	2,505,451	2.1%
2	Texas	10,286,833	8.4%
33	Utah	1,051,857	0.9%
49	Vermont	259,915	0.2%
12	Virginia	3,177,783	2.6%
13	Washington	2,806,238	2.3%
38	West Virginia	658,380	0.5%
19	Wisconsin	2,274,762	1.9%
50	Wyoming	221,537	0.2%

RANK ORDER

RANK	STATE	REFUNDS	% of USA
1	California	13,846,488	11.4%
2	Texas	10,286,833	8.4%
3	Florida	8,001,295	6.6%
4	New York	7,860,621	6.4%
5	Pennsylvania	5,145,524	4.2%
6	Illinois	5,067,372	4.2%
7	Ohio	4,640,883	3.8%
8	Michigan	3,839,384	3.1%
9	Georgia	3,660,309	3.0%
10	North Carolina	3,635,581	3.0%
11	New Jersey	3,539,771	2.9%
12	Virginia	3,177,783	2.6%
13	Washington	2,806,238	2.3%
14	Massachusetts	2,751,130	2.3%
15	Indiana	2,612,413	2.1%
16	Tennessee	2,505,451	2.1%
17	Maryland	2,363,151	1.9%
18	Arizona	2,277,407	1.9%
19	Wisconsin	2,274,762	1.9%
20	Missouri	2,265,900	1.9%
21	Minnesota	2,149,182	1.8%
22	Colorado	2,051,877	1.7%
23	South Carolina	1,743,517	1.4%
24	Alabama	1,676,151	1.4%
25	Louisiana	1,640,935	1.3%
26	Kentucky	1,612,373	1.3%
27	Oregon	1,459,595	1.2%
28	Connecticut	1,422,410	1.2%
29	Oklahoma	1,325,483	1.1%
30	Iowa	1,162,882	1.0%
31	Nevada	1,129,260	0.9%
32	Kansas	1,065,305	0.9%
33	Utah	1,051,857	0.9%
34	Mississippi	1,035,489	0.8%
35	Arkansas	1,007,785	0.8%
36	New Mexico	736,423	0.6%
37	Nebraska	726,442	0.6%
38	West Virginia	658,380	0.5%
39	Idaho	573,741	0.5%
40	New Hampshire	568,397	0.5%
41	Hawaii	545,207	0.4%
42	Maine	518,916	0.4%
43	Rhode Island	445,927	0.4%
44	Montana	383,966	0.3%
45	Delaware	375,420	0.3%
46	South Dakota	330,591	0.3%
47	North Dakota	284,554	0.2%
48	Alaska	283,436	0.2%
49	Vermont	259,915	0.2%
50	Wyoming	221,537	0.2%
	District of Columbia	283,179	0.2%

Source: U.S. Department of the Treasury, Internal Revenue Service
   "Fiscal Year 2017 IRS Data Book" (https://www.irs.gov/statistics/soi-tax-stats-irs-data-book)
*Total includes refunds to international sources and other miscellaneous refunds not shown separately.

Value of Federal Tax Refunds in 2017

National Total = $436,971,873,000*

ALPHA ORDER

RANK	STATE	REFUNDS	% of USA
27	Alabama	$4,916,924,000	1.1%
48	Alaska	840,585,000	0.2%
20	Arizona	6,262,820,000	1.4%
35	Arkansas	2,935,066,000	0.7%
1	California	44,842,074,000	10.3%
21	Colorado	6,082,626,000	1.4%
23	Connecticut	5,690,878,000	1.3%
39	Delaware	1,668,868,000	0.4%
4	Florida	24,770,258,000	5.7%
9	Georgia	11,539,377,000	2.6%
41	Hawaii	1,462,267,000	0.3%
42	Idaho	1,441,498,000	0.3%
5	Illinois	17,864,830,000	4.1%
16	Indiana	7,399,326,000	1.7%
30	Iowa	3,757,086,000	0.9%
32	Kansas	3,175,384,000	0.7%
28	Kentucky	4,420,558,000	1.0%
24	Louisiana	5,350,605,000	1.2%
44	Maine	1,295,965,000	0.3%
17	Maryland	7,181,581,000	1.6%
14	Massachusetts	8,809,204,000	2.0%
10	Michigan	10,507,569,000	2.4%
15	Minnesota	8,265,813,000	1.9%
34	Mississippi	3,124,203,000	0.7%
19	Missouri	7,035,631,000	1.6%
46	Montana	929,688,000	0.2%
36	Nebraska	2,120,377,000	0.5%
31	Nevada	3,404,334,000	0.8%
40	New Hampshire	1,592,047,000	0.4%
7	New Jersey	14,700,625,000	3.4%
37	New Mexico	1,989,921,000	0.5%
3	New York	27,179,469,000	6.2%
12	North Carolina	9,910,477,000	2.3%
47	North Dakota	903,489,000	0.2%
8	Ohio	12,884,704,000	2.9%
26	Oklahoma	4,922,820,000	1.1%
29	Oregon	3,929,561,000	0.9%
6	Pennsylvania	15,787,448,000	3.6%
43	Rhode Island	1,373,784,000	0.3%
25	South Carolina	4,931,117,000	1.1%
45	South Dakota	984,209,000	0.2%
18	Tennessee	7,165,543,000	1.6%
2	Texas	40,627,689,000	9.3%
33	Utah	3,162,991,000	0.7%
50	Vermont	634,860,000	0.1%
11	Virginia	9,927,175,000	2.3%
13	Washington	9,074,335,000	2.1%
38	West Virginia	1,761,388,000	0.4%
22	Wisconsin	5,961,644,000	1.4%
49	Wyoming	706,845,000	0.2%

RANK ORDER

RANK	STATE	REFUNDS	% of USA
1	California	$44,842,074,000	10.3%
2	Texas	40,627,689,000	9.3%
3	New York	27,179,469,000	6.2%
4	Florida	24,770,258,000	5.7%
5	Illinois	17,864,830,000	4.1%
6	Pennsylvania	15,787,448,000	3.6%
7	New Jersey	14,700,625,000	3.4%
8	Ohio	12,884,704,000	2.9%
9	Georgia	11,539,377,000	2.6%
10	Michigan	10,507,569,000	2.4%
11	Virginia	9,927,175,000	2.3%
12	North Carolina	9,910,477,000	2.3%
13	Washington	9,074,335,000	2.1%
14	Massachusetts	8,809,204,000	2.0%
15	Minnesota	8,265,813,000	1.9%
16	Indiana	7,399,326,000	1.7%
17	Maryland	7,181,581,000	1.6%
18	Tennessee	7,165,543,000	1.6%
19	Missouri	7,035,631,000	1.6%
20	Arizona	6,262,820,000	1.4%
21	Colorado	6,082,626,000	1.4%
22	Wisconsin	5,961,644,000	1.4%
23	Connecticut	5,690,878,000	1.3%
24	Louisiana	5,350,605,000	1.2%
25	South Carolina	4,931,117,000	1.1%
26	Oklahoma	4,922,820,000	1.1%
27	Alabama	4,916,924,000	1.1%
28	Kentucky	4,420,558,000	1.0%
29	Oregon	3,929,561,000	0.9%
30	Iowa	3,757,086,000	0.9%
31	Nevada	3,404,334,000	0.8%
32	Kansas	3,175,384,000	0.7%
33	Utah	3,162,991,000	0.7%
34	Mississippi	3,124,203,000	0.7%
35	Arkansas	2,935,066,000	0.7%
36	Nebraska	2,120,377,000	0.5%
37	New Mexico	1,989,921,000	0.5%
38	West Virginia	1,761,388,000	0.4%
39	Delaware	1,668,868,000	0.4%
40	New Hampshire	1,592,047,000	0.4%
41	Hawaii	1,462,267,000	0.3%
42	Idaho	1,441,498,000	0.3%
43	Rhode Island	1,373,784,000	0.3%
44	Maine	1,295,965,000	0.3%
45	South Dakota	984,209,000	0.2%
46	Montana	929,688,000	0.2%
47	North Dakota	903,489,000	0.2%
48	Alaska	840,585,000	0.2%
49	Wyoming	706,845,000	0.2%
50	Vermont	634,860,000	0.1%
	District of Columbia	943,076,000	0.2%

Source: U.S. Department of the Treasury, Internal Revenue Service
"Fiscal Year 2017 IRS Data Book" (https://www.irs.gov/statistics/soi-tax-stats-irs-data-book)
*Total includes refunds to international sources and other miscellaneous refunds not shown separately.

Average Value of Federal Tax Refunds in 2017

National Average = $3,582*

ALPHA ORDER

RANK	STATE	AVERAGE REFUND
30	Alabama	$2,933
28	Alaska	2,966
38	Arizona	2,750
32	Arkansas	2,912
10	California	3,239
29	Colorado	2,964
3	Connecticut	4,001
1	Delaware	4,445
19	Florida	3,096
16	Georgia	3,153
44	Hawaii	2,682
47	Idaho	2,512
7	Illinois	3,525
34	Indiana	2,832
12	Iowa	3,231
26	Kansas	2,981
39	Kentucky	2,742
9	Louisiana	3,261
48	Maine	2,497
22	Maryland	3,039
13	Massachusetts	3,202
40	Michigan	2,737
5	Minnesota	3,846
23	Mississippi	3,017
18	Missouri	3,105
50	Montana	2,421
31	Nebraska	2,919
24	Nevada	3,015
36	New Hampshire	2,801
2	New Jersey	4,153
42	New Mexico	2,702
8	New York	3,458
41	North Carolina	2,726
15	North Dakota	3,175
37	Ohio	2,776
6	Oklahoma	3,714
43	Oregon	2,692
21	Pennsylvania	3,068
20	Rhode Island	3,081
35	South Carolina	2,828
27	South Dakota	2,977
33	Tennessee	2,860
4	Texas	3,949
25	Utah	3,007
49	Vermont	2,443
17	Virginia	3,124
11	Washington	3,234
45	West Virginia	2,675
46	Wisconsin	2,621
14	Wyoming	3,191

RANK ORDER

RANK	STATE	AVERAGE REFUND
1	Delaware	$4,445
2	New Jersey	4,153
3	Connecticut	4,001
4	Texas	3,949
5	Minnesota	3,846
6	Oklahoma	3,714
7	Illinois	3,525
8	New York	3,458
9	Louisiana	3,261
10	California	3,239
11	Washington	3,234
12	Iowa	3,231
13	Massachusetts	3,202
14	Wyoming	3,191
15	North Dakota	3,175
16	Georgia	3,153
17	Virginia	3,124
18	Missouri	3,105
19	Florida	3,096
20	Rhode Island	3,081
21	Pennsylvania	3,068
22	Maryland	3,039
23	Mississippi	3,017
24	Nevada	3,015
25	Utah	3,007
26	Kansas	2,981
27	South Dakota	2,977
28	Alaska	2,966
29	Colorado	2,964
30	Alabama	2,933
31	Nebraska	2,919
32	Arkansas	2,912
33	Tennessee	2,860
34	Indiana	2,832
35	South Carolina	2,828
36	New Hampshire	2,801
37	Ohio	2,776
38	Arizona	2,750
39	Kentucky	2,742
40	Michigan	2,737
41	North Carolina	2,726
42	New Mexico	2,702
43	Oregon	2,692
44	Hawaii	2,682
45	West Virginia	2,675
46	Wisconsin	2,621
47	Idaho	2,512
48	Maine	2,497
49	Vermont	2,443
50	Montana	2,421
	District of Columbia	3,330

Source: CQ Press using data from U.S. Department of the Treasury, Internal Revenue Service
"Fiscal Year 2017 IRS Data Book" (https://www.irs.gov/statistics/soi-tax-stats-irs-data-book)
*National average includes refunds to international sources and other miscellaneous refunds not shown separately.

Value of Federal Individual Income Tax Refunds in 2017

National Total = $382,865,300,000*

<table>
<tr><td colspan="4">ALPHA ORDER</td><td colspan="4">RANK ORDER</td></tr>
<tr><td>RANK</td><td>STATE</td><td>REFUNDS</td><td>% of USA</td><td>RANK</td><td>STATE</td><td>REFUNDS</td><td>% of USA</td></tr>
<tr><td>24</td><td>Alabama</td><td>$4,624,241,000</td><td>1.2%</td><td>1</td><td>California</td><td>$39,575,207,000</td><td>10.3%</td></tr>
<tr><td>48</td><td>Alaska</td><td>787,178,000</td><td>0.2%</td><td>2</td><td>Texas</td><td>32,337,862,000</td><td>8.4%</td></tr>
<tr><td>18</td><td>Arizona</td><td>5,998,269,000</td><td>1.6%</td><td>3</td><td>New York</td><td>23,595,156,000</td><td>6.2%</td></tr>
<tr><td>35</td><td>Arkansas</td><td>2,729,706,000</td><td>0.7%</td><td>4</td><td>Florida</td><td>23,040,098,000</td><td>6.0%</td></tr>
<tr><td>1</td><td>California</td><td>39,575,207,000</td><td>10.3%</td><td>5</td><td>Illinois</td><td>14,422,099,000</td><td>3.8%</td></tr>
<tr><td>22</td><td>Colorado</td><td>5,309,226,000</td><td>1.4%</td><td>6</td><td>Pennsylvania</td><td>13,400,915,000</td><td>3.5%</td></tr>
<tr><td>26</td><td>Connecticut</td><td>4,327,595,000</td><td>1.1%</td><td>7</td><td>Ohio</td><td>11,502,219,000</td><td>3.0%</td></tr>
<tr><td>44</td><td>Delaware</td><td>968,360,000</td><td>0.3%</td><td>8</td><td>New Jersey</td><td>10,483,167,000</td><td>2.7%</td></tr>
<tr><td>4</td><td>Florida</td><td>23,040,098,000</td><td>6.0%</td><td>9</td><td>Georgia</td><td>10,180,140,000</td><td>2.7%</td></tr>
<tr><td>9</td><td>Georgia</td><td>10,180,140,000</td><td>2.7%</td><td>10</td><td>Michigan</td><td>9,669,038,000</td><td>2.5%</td></tr>
<tr><td>41</td><td>Hawaii</td><td>1,373,545,000</td><td>0.4%</td><td>11</td><td>North Carolina</td><td>9,411,757,000</td><td>2.5%</td></tr>
<tr><td>40</td><td>Idaho</td><td>1,378,598,000</td><td>0.4%</td><td>12</td><td>Virginia</td><td>8,669,293,000</td><td>2.3%</td></tr>
<tr><td>5</td><td>Illinois</td><td>14,422,099,000</td><td>3.8%</td><td>13</td><td>Massachusetts</td><td>7,708,301,000</td><td>2.0%</td></tr>
<tr><td>15</td><td>Indiana</td><td>6,734,108,000</td><td>1.8%</td><td>14</td><td>Washington</td><td>7,371,618,000</td><td>1.9%</td></tr>
<tr><td>32</td><td>Iowa</td><td>2,969,539,000</td><td>0.8%</td><td>15</td><td>Indiana</td><td>6,734,108,000</td><td>1.8%</td></tr>
<tr><td>33</td><td>Kansas</td><td>2,782,989,000</td><td>0.7%</td><td>16</td><td>Tennessee</td><td>6,721,754,000</td><td>1.8%</td></tr>
<tr><td>27</td><td>Kentucky</td><td>4,210,658,000</td><td>1.1%</td><td>17</td><td>Maryland</td><td>6,663,269,000</td><td>1.7%</td></tr>
<tr><td>23</td><td>Louisiana</td><td>5,019,686,000</td><td>1.3%</td><td>18</td><td>Arizona</td><td>5,998,269,000</td><td>1.6%</td></tr>
<tr><td>42</td><td>Maine</td><td>1,191,053,000</td><td>0.3%</td><td>19</td><td>Missouri</td><td>5,774,799,000</td><td>1.5%</td></tr>
<tr><td>17</td><td>Maryland</td><td>6,663,269,000</td><td>1.7%</td><td>20</td><td>Wisconsin</td><td>5,448,096,000</td><td>1.4%</td></tr>
<tr><td>13</td><td>Massachusetts</td><td>7,708,301,000</td><td>2.0%</td><td>21</td><td>Minnesota</td><td>5,315,059,000</td><td>1.4%</td></tr>
<tr><td>10</td><td>Michigan</td><td>9,669,038,000</td><td>2.5%</td><td>22</td><td>Colorado</td><td>5,309,226,000</td><td>1.4%</td></tr>
<tr><td>21</td><td>Minnesota</td><td>5,315,059,000</td><td>1.4%</td><td>23</td><td>Louisiana</td><td>5,019,686,000</td><td>1.3%</td></tr>
<tr><td>31</td><td>Mississippi</td><td>2,976,038,000</td><td>0.8%</td><td>24</td><td>Alabama</td><td>4,624,241,000</td><td>1.2%</td></tr>
<tr><td>19</td><td>Missouri</td><td>5,774,799,000</td><td>1.5%</td><td>25</td><td>South Carolina</td><td>4,417,281,000</td><td>1.2%</td></tr>
<tr><td>45</td><td>Montana</td><td>895,005,000</td><td>0.2%</td><td>26</td><td>Connecticut</td><td>4,327,595,000</td><td>1.1%</td></tr>
<tr><td>37</td><td>Nebraska</td><td>1,859,339,000</td><td>0.5%</td><td>27</td><td>Kentucky</td><td>4,210,658,000</td><td>1.1%</td></tr>
<tr><td>30</td><td>Nevada</td><td>3,146,930,000</td><td>0.8%</td><td>28</td><td>Oklahoma</td><td>4,028,691,000</td><td>1.1%</td></tr>
<tr><td>39</td><td>New Hampshire</td><td>1,452,899,000</td><td>0.4%</td><td>29</td><td>Oregon</td><td>3,433,349,000</td><td>0.9%</td></tr>
<tr><td>8</td><td>New Jersey</td><td>10,483,167,000</td><td>2.7%</td><td>30</td><td>Nevada</td><td>3,146,930,000</td><td>0.8%</td></tr>
<tr><td>36</td><td>New Mexico</td><td>1,924,875,000</td><td>0.5%</td><td>31</td><td>Mississippi</td><td>2,976,038,000</td><td>0.8%</td></tr>
<tr><td>3</td><td>New York</td><td>23,595,156,000</td><td>6.2%</td><td>32</td><td>Iowa</td><td>2,969,539,000</td><td>0.8%</td></tr>
<tr><td>11</td><td>North Carolina</td><td>9,411,757,000</td><td>2.5%</td><td>33</td><td>Kansas</td><td>2,782,989,000</td><td>0.7%</td></tr>
<tr><td>47</td><td>North Dakota</td><td>827,439,000</td><td>0.2%</td><td>34</td><td>Utah</td><td>2,770,142,000</td><td>0.7%</td></tr>
<tr><td>7</td><td>Ohio</td><td>11,502,219,000</td><td>3.0%</td><td>35</td><td>Arkansas</td><td>2,729,706,000</td><td>0.7%</td></tr>
<tr><td>28</td><td>Oklahoma</td><td>4,028,691,000</td><td>1.1%</td><td>36</td><td>New Mexico</td><td>1,924,875,000</td><td>0.5%</td></tr>
<tr><td>29</td><td>Oregon</td><td>3,433,349,000</td><td>0.9%</td><td>37</td><td>Nebraska</td><td>1,859,339,000</td><td>0.5%</td></tr>
<tr><td>6</td><td>Pennsylvania</td><td>13,400,915,000</td><td>3.5%</td><td>38</td><td>West Virginia</td><td>1,719,268,000</td><td>0.4%</td></tr>
<tr><td>43</td><td>Rhode Island</td><td>1,153,583,000</td><td>0.3%</td><td>39</td><td>New Hampshire</td><td>1,452,899,000</td><td>0.4%</td></tr>
<tr><td>25</td><td>South Carolina</td><td>4,417,281,000</td><td>1.2%</td><td>40</td><td>Idaho</td><td>1,378,598,000</td><td>0.4%</td></tr>
<tr><td>46</td><td>South Dakota</td><td>852,115,000</td><td>0.2%</td><td>41</td><td>Hawaii</td><td>1,373,545,000</td><td>0.4%</td></tr>
<tr><td>16</td><td>Tennessee</td><td>6,721,754,000</td><td>1.8%</td><td>42</td><td>Maine</td><td>1,191,053,000</td><td>0.3%</td></tr>
<tr><td>2</td><td>Texas</td><td>32,337,862,000</td><td>8.4%</td><td>43</td><td>Rhode Island</td><td>1,153,583,000</td><td>0.3%</td></tr>
<tr><td>34</td><td>Utah</td><td>2,770,142,000</td><td>0.7%</td><td>44</td><td>Delaware</td><td>968,360,000</td><td>0.3%</td></tr>
<tr><td>50</td><td>Vermont</td><td>607,908,000</td><td>0.2%</td><td>45</td><td>Montana</td><td>895,005,000</td><td>0.2%</td></tr>
<tr><td>12</td><td>Virginia</td><td>8,669,293,000</td><td>2.3%</td><td>46</td><td>South Dakota</td><td>852,115,000</td><td>0.2%</td></tr>
<tr><td>14</td><td>Washington</td><td>7,371,618,000</td><td>1.9%</td><td>47</td><td>North Dakota</td><td>827,439,000</td><td>0.2%</td></tr>
<tr><td>38</td><td>West Virginia</td><td>1,719,268,000</td><td>0.4%</td><td>48</td><td>Alaska</td><td>787,178,000</td><td>0.2%</td></tr>
<tr><td>20</td><td>Wisconsin</td><td>5,448,096,000</td><td>1.4%</td><td>49</td><td>Wyoming</td><td>641,675,000</td><td>0.2%</td></tr>
<tr><td>49</td><td>Wyoming</td><td>641,675,000</td><td>0.2%</td><td>50</td><td>Vermont</td><td>607,908,000</td><td>0.2%</td></tr>
<tr><td></td><td></td><td></td><td></td><td></td><td>District of Columbia</td><td>804,529,000</td><td>0.2%</td></tr>
</table>

Source: U.S. Department of the Treasury, Internal Revenue Service
"Fiscal Year 2017 IRS Data Book" (https://www.irs.gov/statistics/soi-tax-stats-irs-data-book)
*Total includes refunds to international sources and other miscellaneous refunds not shown separately.

Average Value of Federal Individual Income Tax Refunds in 2017

National Average = $3,194*

ALPHA ORDER

RANK	STATE	AVERAGE REFUND
18	Alabama	$2,802
15	Alaska	2,843
24	Arizona	2,672
20	Arkansas	2,759
11	California	2,911
33	Colorado	2,636
3	Connecticut	3,099
29	Delaware	2,648
9	Florida	2,933
17	Georgia	2,823
41	Hawaii	2,564
45	Idaho	2,457
12	Illinois	2,900
36	Indiana	2,612
37	Iowa	2,602
25	Kansas	2,665
29	Kentucky	2,648
2	Louisiana	3,115
50	Maine	2,336
13	Maryland	2,861
14	Massachusetts	2,850
42	Michigan	2,560
44	Minnesota	2,516
10	Mississippi	2,922
39	Missouri	2,601
47	Montana	2,401
35	Nebraska	2,615
16	Nevada	2,830
37	New Hampshire	2,602
6	New Jersey	3,013
26	New Mexico	2,657
5	New York	3,059
34	North Carolina	2,629
8	North Dakota	2,983
43	Ohio	2,517
4	Oklahoma	3,098
48	Oregon	2,398
31	Pennsylvania	2,643
31	Rhode Island	2,643
40	South Carolina	2,569
27	South Dakota	2,651
21	Tennessee	2,726
1	Texas	3,206
22	Utah	2,681
49	Vermont	2,392
19	Virginia	2,771
22	Washington	2,681
28	West Virginia	2,649
46	Wisconsin	2,436
7	Wyoming	2,989

RANK ORDER

RANK	STATE	AVERAGE REFUND
1	Texas	$3,206
2	Louisiana	3,115
3	Connecticut	3,099
4	Oklahoma	3,098
5	New York	3,059
6	New Jersey	3,013
7	Wyoming	2,989
8	North Dakota	2,983
9	Florida	2,933
10	Mississippi	2,922
11	California	2,911
12	Illinois	2,900
13	Maryland	2,861
14	Massachusetts	2,850
15	Alaska	2,843
16	Nevada	2,830
17	Georgia	2,823
18	Alabama	2,802
19	Virginia	2,771
20	Arkansas	2,759
21	Tennessee	2,726
22	Utah	2,681
22	Washington	2,681
24	Arizona	2,672
25	Kansas	2,665
26	New Mexico	2,657
27	South Dakota	2,651
28	West Virginia	2,649
29	Delaware	2,648
29	Kentucky	2,648
31	Pennsylvania	2,643
31	Rhode Island	2,643
33	Colorado	2,636
34	North Carolina	2,629
35	Nebraska	2,615
36	Indiana	2,612
37	Iowa	2,602
37	New Hampshire	2,602
39	Missouri	2,601
40	South Carolina	2,569
41	Hawaii	2,564
42	Michigan	2,560
43	Ohio	2,517
44	Minnesota	2,516
45	Idaho	2,457
46	Wisconsin	2,436
47	Montana	2,401
48	Oregon	2,398
49	Vermont	2,392
50	Maine	2,336
	District of Columbia	2,900

Source: CQ Press using data from U.S. Department of the Treasury, Internal Revenue Service
"Fiscal Year 2017 IRS Data Book" (https://www.irs.gov/statistics/soi-tax-stats-irs-data-book)
*National average includes refunds to international sources and other miscellaneous refunds not shown separately.

Value of Federal Business Income Tax Refunds in 2017

National Total = $44,894,839,000*

ALPHA ORDER

RANK	STATE	REFUNDS	% of USA
31	Alabama	$252,587,000	0.6%
44	Alaska	38,683,000	0.1%
35	Arizona	168,868,000	0.4%
34	Arkansas	172,677,000	0.4%
2	California	4,153,702,000	9.3%
19	Colorado	584,672,000	1.3%
10	Connecticut	1,149,777,000	2.6%
20	Delaware	564,815,000	1.3%
9	Florida	1,190,121,000	2.7%
14	Georgia	1,123,222,000	2.5%
40	Hawaii	65,289,000	0.1%
45	Idaho	38,057,000	0.1%
4	Illinois	2,912,238,000	6.5%
21	Indiana	523,089,000	1.2%
16	Iowa	729,833,000	1.6%
27	Kansas	352,627,000	0.8%
37	Kentucky	151,466,000	0.3%
30	Louisiana	272,941,000	0.6%
39	Maine	90,188,000	0.2%
26	Maryland	374,737,000	0.8%
15	Massachusetts	828,310,000	1.8%
17	Michigan	655,523,000	1.5%
5	Minnesota	2,799,451,000	6.2%
38	Mississippi	115,506,000	0.3%
13	Missouri	1,128,598,000	2.5%
48	Montana	20,215,000	0.0%
32	Nebraska	215,261,000	0.5%
36	Nevada	161,861,000	0.4%
43	New Hampshire	44,548,000	0.1%
3	New Jersey	3,739,484,000	8.3%
42	New Mexico	49,157,000	0.1%
6	New York	2,589,897,000	5.8%
25	North Carolina	375,342,000	0.8%
41	North Dakota	60,633,000	0.1%
12	Ohio	1,132,046,000	2.5%
18	Oklahoma	610,272,000	1.4%
23	Oregon	429,892,000	1.0%
7	Pennsylvania	2,065,143,000	4.6%
33	Rhode Island	192,338,000	0.4%
22	South Carolina	450,837,000	1.0%
46	South Dakota	34,523,000	0.1%
29	Tennessee	326,981,000	0.7%
1	Texas	7,407,227,000	16.5%
28	Utah	347,073,000	0.8%
48	Vermont	20,215,000	0.0%
11	Virginia	1,135,974,000	2.5%
8	Washington	1,569,071,000	3.5%
47	West Virginia	28,754,000	0.1%
24	Wisconsin	376,088,000	0.8%
50	Wyoming	18,694,000	0.0%

RANK ORDER

RANK	STATE	REFUNDS	% of USA
1	Texas	$7,407,227,000	16.5%
2	California	4,153,702,000	9.3%
3	New Jersey	3,739,484,000	8.3%
4	Illinois	2,912,238,000	6.5%
5	Minnesota	2,799,451,000	6.2%
6	New York	2,589,897,000	5.8%
7	Pennsylvania	2,065,143,000	4.6%
8	Washington	1,569,071,000	3.5%
9	Florida	1,190,121,000	2.7%
10	Connecticut	1,149,777,000	2.6%
11	Virginia	1,135,974,000	2.5%
12	Ohio	1,132,046,000	2.5%
13	Missouri	1,128,598,000	2.5%
14	Georgia	1,123,222,000	2.5%
15	Massachusetts	828,310,000	1.8%
16	Iowa	729,833,000	1.6%
17	Michigan	655,523,000	1.5%
18	Oklahoma	610,272,000	1.4%
19	Colorado	584,672,000	1.3%
20	Delaware	564,815,000	1.3%
21	Indiana	523,089,000	1.2%
22	South Carolina	450,837,000	1.0%
23	Oregon	429,892,000	1.0%
24	Wisconsin	376,088,000	0.8%
25	North Carolina	375,342,000	0.8%
26	Maryland	374,737,000	0.8%
27	Kansas	352,627,000	0.8%
28	Utah	347,073,000	0.8%
29	Tennessee	326,981,000	0.7%
30	Louisiana	272,941,000	0.6%
31	Alabama	252,587,000	0.6%
32	Nebraska	215,261,000	0.5%
33	Rhode Island	192,338,000	0.4%
34	Arkansas	172,677,000	0.4%
35	Arizona	168,868,000	0.4%
36	Nevada	161,861,000	0.4%
37	Kentucky	151,466,000	0.3%
38	Mississippi	115,506,000	0.3%
39	Maine	90,188,000	0.2%
40	Hawaii	65,289,000	0.1%
41	North Dakota	60,633,000	0.1%
42	New Mexico	49,157,000	0.1%
43	New Hampshire	44,548,000	0.1%
44	Alaska	38,683,000	0.1%
45	Idaho	38,057,000	0.1%
46	South Dakota	34,523,000	0.1%
47	West Virginia	28,754,000	0.1%
48	Montana	20,215,000	0.0%
48	Vermont	20,215,000	0.0%
50	Wyoming	18,694,000	0.0%
	District of Columbia	103,769,000	0.2%

Source: U.S. Department of the Treasury, Internal Revenue Service
 "Fiscal Year 2017 IRS Data Book" (https://www.irs.gov/statistics/soi-tax-stats-irs-data-book)
*Total includes refunds to international sources and other miscellaneous refunds not shown separately. Includes taxes on corporation income (Form 1120 series) and unrelated business income from tax-exempt organizations.

Average Value of Federal Business Income Tax Refunds in 2017

National Average = $127,861*

ALPHA ORDER

RANK	STATE	AVERAGE REFUND
25	Alabama	$78,712
34	Alaska	49,594
41	Arizona	35,380
26	Arkansas	67,584
23	California	92,278
19	Colorado	102,845
4	Connecticut	327,106
2	Delaware	361,597
33	Florida	50,220
14	Georgia	130,501
42	Hawaii	33,811
45	Idaho	23,377
6	Illinois	209,273
21	Indiana	101,748
15	Iowa	123,995
24	Kansas	81,269
32	Kentucky	53,979
30	Louisiana	62,933
37	Maine	48,698
27	Maryland	67,193
17	Massachusetts	117,574
31	Michigan	60,217
3	Minnesota	348,017
38	Mississippi	46,500
16	Missouri	119,974
50	Montana	6,899
29	Nebraska	65,869
35	Nevada	49,575
43	New Hampshire	29,003
1	New Jersey	406,908
44	New Mexico	28,464
18	New York	107,247
39	North Carolina	44,887
40	North Dakota	42,019
20	Ohio	102,680
10	Oklahoma	145,789
22	Oregon	93,232
9	Pennsylvania	187,111
8	Rhode Island	199,521
13	South Carolina	130,905
47	South Dakota	19,527
28	Tennessee	66,799
5	Texas	250,016
12	Utah	132,775
48	Vermont	18,327
11	Virginia	140,852
7	Washington	208,321
46	West Virginia	22,605
36	Wisconsin	49,355
49	Wyoming	13,786

RANK ORDER

RANK	STATE	AVERAGE REFUND
1	New Jersey	$406,908
2	Delaware	361,597
3	Minnesota	348,017
4	Connecticut	327,106
5	Texas	250,016
6	Illinois	209,273
7	Washington	208,321
8	Rhode Island	199,521
9	Pennsylvania	187,111
10	Oklahoma	145,789
11	Virginia	140,852
12	Utah	132,775
13	South Carolina	130,905
14	Georgia	130,501
15	Iowa	123,995
16	Missouri	119,974
17	Massachusetts	117,574
18	New York	107,247
19	Colorado	102,845
20	Ohio	102,680
21	Indiana	101,748
22	Oregon	93,232
23	California	92,278
24	Kansas	81,269
25	Alabama	78,712
26	Arkansas	67,584
27	Maryland	67,193
28	Tennessee	66,799
29	Nebraska	65,869
30	Louisiana	62,933
31	Michigan	60,217
32	Kentucky	53,979
33	Florida	50,220
34	Alaska	49,594
35	Nevada	49,575
36	Wisconsin	49,355
37	Maine	48,698
38	Mississippi	46,500
39	North Carolina	44,887
40	North Dakota	42,019
41	Arizona	35,380
42	Hawaii	33,811
43	New Hampshire	29,003
44	New Mexico	28,464
45	Idaho	23,377
46	West Virginia	22,605
47	South Dakota	19,527
48	Vermont	18,327
49	Wyoming	13,786
50	Montana	6,899

District of Columbia 98,173

Source: CQ Press using data from U.S. Department of the Treasury, Internal Revenue Service
"Fiscal Year 2017 IRS Data Book" (https://www.irs.gov/statistics/soi-tax-stats-irs-data-book)
*National average includes refunds to international sources and other miscellaneous refunds not shown separately.

Federal Government Expenditures in 2016

National Total = $3,070,911,835,000*

ALPHA ORDER

RANK	STATE	EXPENDITURES	% of USA
19	Alabama	$66,905,396,454	2.2%
46	Alaska	7,988,794,136	0.3%
17	Arizona	71,716,060,266	2.3%
33	Arkansas	22,916,825,538	0.7%
1	California	289,906,001,150	9.4%
27	Colorado	39,503,488,964	1.3%
15	Connecticut	74,566,355,002	2.4%
48	Delaware	6,623,282,899	0.2%
3	Florida	170,930,415,295	5.5%
20	Georgia	65,125,282,549	2.1%
42	Hawaii	11,143,397,423	0.4%
39	Idaho	12,347,632,185	0.4%
11	Illinois	80,484,543,377	2.6%
6	Indiana	128,479,516,092	4.2%
32	Iowa	23,233,563,544	0.8%
36	Kansas	16,230,438,273	0.5%
8	Kentucky	89,350,644,054	2.9%
28	Louisiana	35,379,086,151	1.1%
41	Maine	11,676,642,139	0.4%
18	Maryland	66,930,108,551	2.2%
23	Massachusetts	62,275,579,959	2.0%
13	Michigan	77,419,893,893	2.5%
10	Minnesota	81,541,932,792	2.6%
31	Mississippi	24,510,955,972	0.8%
26	Missouri	52,921,761,250	1.7%
45	Montana	8,344,393,113	0.3%
40	Nebraska	12,302,857,615	0.4%
35	Nevada	17,777,453,540	0.6%
43	New Hampshire	9,695,691,786	0.3%
24	New Jersey	60,855,085,669	2.0%
34	New Mexico	22,829,600,877	0.7%
5	New York	158,593,098,950	5.1%
21	North Carolina	63,965,875,087	2.1%
22	North Dakota	62,598,781,139	2.0%
14	Ohio	76,121,678,221	2.5%
30	Oklahoma	28,207,147,827	0.9%
29	Oregon	32,010,847,969	1.0%
2	Pennsylvania	193,557,462,424	6.3%
44	Rhode Island	8,955,224,152	0.3%
12	South Carolina	77,734,372,433	2.5%
47	South Dakota	6,763,252,911	0.2%
16	Tennessee	73,875,092,624	2.4%
4	Texas	169,537,149,536	5.5%
38	Utah	14,534,864,156	0.5%
49	Vermont	5,482,828,443	0.2%
7	Virginia	94,755,289,501	3.1%
25	Washington	58,150,899,022	1.9%
37	West Virginia	15,262,409,794	0.5%
9	Wisconsin	84,166,564,963	2.7%
50	Wyoming	4,147,619,639	0.1%

RANK ORDER

RANK	STATE	EXPENDITURES	% of USA
1	California	$289,906,001,150	9.4%
2	Pennsylvania	193,557,462,424	6.3%
3	Florida	170,930,415,295	5.5%
4	Texas	169,537,149,536	5.5%
5	New York	158,593,098,950	5.1%
6	Indiana	128,479,516,092	4.2%
7	Virginia	94,755,289,501	3.1%
8	Kentucky	89,350,644,054	2.9%
9	Wisconsin	84,166,564,963	2.7%
10	Minnesota	81,541,932,792	2.6%
11	Illinois	80,484,543,377	2.6%
12	South Carolina	77,734,372,433	2.5%
13	Michigan	77,419,893,893	2.5%
14	Ohio	76,121,678,221	2.5%
15	Connecticut	74,566,355,002	2.4%
16	Tennessee	73,875,092,624	2.4%
17	Arizona	71,716,060,266	2.3%
18	Maryland	66,930,108,551	2.2%
19	Alabama	66,905,396,454	2.2%
20	Georgia	65,125,282,549	2.1%
21	North Carolina	63,965,875,087	2.1%
22	North Dakota	62,598,781,139	2.0%
23	Massachusetts	62,275,579,959	2.0%
24	New Jersey	60,855,085,669	2.0%
25	Washington	58,150,899,022	1.9%
26	Missouri	52,921,761,250	1.7%
27	Colorado	39,503,488,964	1.3%
28	Louisiana	35,379,086,151	1.1%
29	Oregon	32,010,847,969	1.0%
30	Oklahoma	28,207,147,827	0.9%
31	Mississippi	24,510,955,972	0.8%
32	Iowa	23,233,563,544	0.8%
33	Arkansas	22,916,825,538	0.7%
34	New Mexico	22,829,600,877	0.7%
35	Nevada	17,777,453,540	0.6%
36	Kansas	16,230,438,273	0.5%
37	West Virginia	15,262,409,794	0.5%
38	Utah	14,534,864,156	0.5%
39	Idaho	12,347,632,185	0.4%
40	Nebraska	12,302,857,615	0.4%
41	Maine	11,676,642,139	0.4%
42	Hawaii	11,143,397,423	0.4%
43	New Hampshire	9,695,691,786	0.3%
44	Rhode Island	8,955,224,152	0.3%
45	Montana	8,344,393,113	0.3%
46	Alaska	7,988,794,136	0.3%
47	South Dakota	6,763,252,911	0.2%
48	Delaware	6,623,282,899	0.2%
49	Vermont	5,482,828,443	0.2%
50	Wyoming	4,147,619,639	0.1%
	District of Columbia	31,089,311,296	1.0%

Source: U.S. Office of Management and Budget, USAspending.gov
"Prime Award Spending Data Summary" (https://www.usaspending.gov/, as of January 26, 2018)
*Total includes $89,489,384,000 in U.S. territories and internationally as well as expenditures not distributed by state.
Expenditures allocated based on place of performance of a contract. Includes Contracts, Grants, Loans, and "Other Financial
Assistance."

Per Capita Federal Government Expenditures in 2016

National Per Capita = $9,219*

ALPHA ORDER				RANK ORDER		
RANK	STATE	PER CAPITA		RANK	STATE	PER CAPITA
9	Alabama	$13,765		1	North Dakota	$82,852
14	Alaska	10,774		2	Connecticut	20,784
15	Arizona	10,381		3	Kentucky	20,142
31	Arkansas	7,669		4	Indiana	19,367
34	California	7,377		5	South Carolina	15,881
38	Colorado	7,143		6	Pennsylvania	15,131
2	Connecticut	20,784		7	Minnesota	14,759
40	Delaware	6,952		8	Wisconsin	14,592
22	Florida	8,275		9	Alabama	13,765
44	Georgia	6,314		10	Virginia	11,324
29	Hawaii	7,800		11	Tennessee	11,202
35	Idaho	7,350		12	Maryland	11,109
46	Illinois	6,270		13	New Mexico	10,947
4	Indiana	19,367		14	Alaska	10,774
33	Iowa	7,421		15	Arizona	10,381
49	Kansas	5,582		16	Massachusetts	9,126
3	Kentucky	20,142		17	Maine	8,778
32	Louisiana	7,550		18	Vermont	8,757
17	Maine	8,778		19	Missouri	8,688
12	Maryland	11,109		20	Rhode Island	8,483
16	Massachusetts	9,126		21	West Virginia	8,290
30	Michigan	7,794		22	Florida	8,275
7	Minnesota	14,759		23	Mississippi	8,210
23	Mississippi	8,210		24	Washington	8,121
19	Missouri	8,688		25	Montana	8,034
25	Montana	8,034		26	New York	7,995
43	Nebraska	6,449		27	Oregon	7,954
48	Nevada	6,048		28	South Dakota	7,883
36	New Hampshire	7,263		29	Hawaii	7,800
41	New Jersey	6,778		30	Michigan	7,794
13	New Mexico	10,947		31	Arkansas	7,669
26	New York	7,995		32	Louisiana	7,550
45	North Carolina	6,298		33	Iowa	7,421
1	North Dakota	82,852		34	California	7,377
42	Ohio	6,549		35	Idaho	7,350
37	Oklahoma	7,193		36	New Hampshire	7,263
27	Oregon	7,954		37	Oklahoma	7,193
6	Pennsylvania	15,131		38	Colorado	7,143
20	Rhode Island	8,483		39	Wyoming	7,071
5	South Carolina	15,881		40	Delaware	6,952
28	South Dakota	7,883		41	New Jersey	6,778
11	Tennessee	11,202		42	Ohio	6,549
47	Texas	6,181		43	Nebraska	6,449
50	Utah	4,860		44	Georgia	6,314
18	Vermont	8,757		45	North Carolina	6,298
10	Virginia	11,324		46	Illinois	6,270
24	Washington	8,121		47	Texas	6,181
21	West Virginia	8,290		48	Nevada	6,048
8	Wisconsin	14,592		49	Kansas	5,582
39	Wyoming	7,071		50	Utah	4,860

District of Columbia   45,430

Source: CQ Press using data from U.S. Office of Management and Budget, USAspending.gov
"Prime Award Spending Data Summary" (https://www.usaspending.gov/, as of January 26, 2018)
*National per capita excludes expenditures and population for territories and undistributed amounts. Expenditures allocated based on place of performance of a contract. Includes Contracts, Grants, Loans, and "Other Financial Assistance."

Federal Government Contract Awards in 2016

National Total = $473,955,518,000*

ALPHA ORDER

RANK	STATE	EXPENDITURES	% of USA
13	Alabama	$10,868,712,672	2.3%
37	Alaska	1,659,834,306	0.4%
12	Arizona	11,797,602,231	2.5%
43	Arkansas	901,341,705	0.2%
1	California	51,901,993,858	11.0%
14	Colorado	9,702,336,528	2.0%
7	Connecticut	14,492,244,971	3.1%
50	Delaware	253,213,593	0.1%
5	Florida	17,815,617,299	3.8%
11	Georgia	11,925,783,079	2.5%
33	Hawaii	2,193,655,931	0.5%
31	Idaho	2,599,403,716	0.5%
16	Illinois	8,740,882,341	1.8%
27	Indiana	3,946,383,677	0.8%
36	Iowa	1,661,890,047	0.4%
41	Kansas	1,152,923,485	0.2%
19	Kentucky	6,570,187,775	1.4%
30	Louisiana	2,838,173,444	0.6%
35	Maine	1,818,604,203	0.4%
4	Maryland	30,353,875,589	6.4%
9	Massachusetts	12,933,090,546	2.7%
23	Michigan	5,236,529,649	1.1%
24	Minnesota	4,842,358,641	1.0%
26	Mississippi	4,437,654,914	0.9%
10	Missouri	12,280,432,158	2.6%
48	Montana	523,156,523	0.1%
42	Nebraska	960,847,855	0.2%
32	Nevada	2,407,644,289	0.5%
38	New Hampshire	1,401,198,274	0.3%
18	New Jersey	7,222,026,999	1.5%
17	New Mexico	7,994,679,466	1.7%
15	New York	9,127,327,108	1.9%
25	North Carolina	4,636,612,802	1.0%
45	North Dakota	610,114,979	0.1%
21	Ohio	5,436,821,278	1.1%
28	Oklahoma	3,852,754,577	0.8%
40	Oregon	1,322,164,466	0.3%
6	Pennsylvania	15,413,011,555	3.3%
44	Rhode Island	756,487,243	0.2%
22	South Carolina	5,272,423,379	1.1%
46	South Dakota	540,702,710	0.1%
20	Tennessee	5,755,644,374	1.2%
3	Texas	33,003,412,756	7.0%
34	Utah	1,910,704,207	0.4%
47	Vermont	523,974,536	0.1%
2	Virginia	50,592,344,291	10.7%
8	Washington	14,190,612,655	3.0%
39	West Virginia	1,388,890,486	0.3%
29	Wisconsin	3,316,021,479	0.7%
49	Wyoming	317,939,354	0.1%

RANK ORDER

RANK	STATE	EXPENDITURES	% of USA
1	California	$51,901,993,858	11.0%
2	Virginia	50,592,344,291	10.7%
3	Texas	33,003,412,756	7.0%
4	Maryland	30,353,875,589	6.4%
5	Florida	17,815,617,299	3.8%
6	Pennsylvania	15,413,011,555	3.3%
7	Connecticut	14,492,244,971	3.1%
8	Washington	14,190,612,655	3.0%
9	Massachusetts	12,933,090,546	2.7%
10	Missouri	12,280,432,158	2.6%
11	Georgia	11,925,783,079	2.5%
12	Arizona	11,797,602,231	2.5%
13	Alabama	10,868,712,672	2.3%
14	Colorado	9,702,336,528	2.0%
15	New York	9,127,327,108	1.9%
16	Illinois	8,740,882,341	1.8%
17	New Mexico	7,994,679,466	1.7%
18	New Jersey	7,222,026,999	1.5%
19	Kentucky	6,570,187,775	1.4%
20	Tennessee	5,755,644,374	1.2%
21	Ohio	5,436,821,278	1.1%
22	South Carolina	5,272,423,379	1.1%
23	Michigan	5,236,529,649	1.1%
24	Minnesota	4,842,358,641	1.0%
25	North Carolina	4,636,612,802	1.0%
26	Mississippi	4,437,654,914	0.9%
27	Indiana	3,946,383,677	0.8%
28	Oklahoma	3,852,754,577	0.8%
29	Wisconsin	3,316,021,479	0.7%
30	Louisiana	2,838,173,444	0.6%
31	Idaho	2,599,403,716	0.5%
32	Nevada	2,407,644,289	0.5%
33	Hawaii	2,193,655,931	0.5%
34	Utah	1,910,704,207	0.4%
35	Maine	1,818,604,203	0.4%
36	Iowa	1,661,890,047	0.4%
37	Alaska	1,659,834,306	0.4%
38	New Hampshire	1,401,198,274	0.3%
39	West Virginia	1,388,890,486	0.3%
40	Oregon	1,322,164,466	0.3%
41	Kansas	1,152,923,485	0.2%
42	Nebraska	960,847,855	0.2%
43	Arkansas	901,341,705	0.2%
44	Rhode Island	756,487,243	0.2%
45	North Dakota	610,114,979	0.1%
46	South Dakota	540,702,710	0.1%
47	Vermont	523,974,536	0.1%
48	Montana	523,156,523	0.1%
49	Wyoming	317,939,354	0.1%
50	Delaware	253,213,593	0.1%
	District of Columbia	21,130,924,849	4.5%

Source: U.S. Office of Management and Budget, USAspending.gov
"Prime Award Spending Data Summary" (https://www.usaspending.gov/, as of January 26, 2018)
*Total includes $41,422,349,000 in U.S. territories and internationally as well as expenditures not distributed by state.
Expenditures allocated based on place of performance of a contract. Does not include grants, co-operative agreements, or contracts under grants.

Per Capita Expenditures for Federal Government Contract Awards in 2016
National Per Capita = $1,337*

ALPHA ORDER

RANK	STATE	PER CAPITA
6	Alabama	$2,236
5	Alaska	2,238
11	Arizona	1,708
49	Arkansas	302
17	California	1,321
10	Colorado	1,754
3	Connecticut	4,039
50	Delaware	266
26	Florida	862
20	Georgia	1,156
13	Hawaii	1,535
12	Idaho	1,547
33	Illinois	681
37	Indiana	595
40	Iowa	531
47	Kansas	397
15	Kentucky	1,481
36	Louisiana	606
16	Maine	1,367
2	Maryland	5,038
9	Massachusetts	1,895
41	Michigan	527
24	Minnesota	876
14	Mississippi	1,486
7	Missouri	2,016
42	Montana	504
42	Nebraska	504
28	Nevada	819
22	New Hampshire	1,050
30	New Jersey	804
4	New Mexico	3,834
45	New York	460
46	North Carolina	457
29	North Dakota	808
44	Ohio	468
23	Oklahoma	983
48	Oregon	329
18	Pennsylvania	1,205
32	Rhode Island	717
21	South Carolina	1,077
35	South Dakota	630
25	Tennessee	873
19	Texas	1,203
34	Utah	639
27	Vermont	837
1	Virginia	6,046
8	Washington	1,982
31	West Virginia	754
38	Wisconsin	575
39	Wyoming	542

RANK ORDER

RANK	STATE	PER CAPITA
1	Virginia	$6,046
2	Maryland	5,038
3	Connecticut	4,039
4	New Mexico	3,834
5	Alaska	2,238
6	Alabama	2,236
7	Missouri	2,016
8	Washington	1,982
9	Massachusetts	1,895
10	Colorado	1,754
11	Arizona	1,708
12	Idaho	1,547
13	Hawaii	1,535
14	Mississippi	1,486
15	Kentucky	1,481
16	Maine	1,367
17	California	1,321
18	Pennsylvania	1,205
19	Texas	1,203
20	Georgia	1,156
21	South Carolina	1,077
22	New Hampshire	1,050
23	Oklahoma	983
24	Minnesota	876
25	Tennessee	873
26	Florida	862
27	Vermont	837
28	Nevada	819
29	North Dakota	808
30	New Jersey	804
31	West Virginia	754
32	Rhode Island	717
33	Illinois	681
34	Utah	639
35	South Dakota	630
36	Louisiana	606
37	Indiana	595
38	Wisconsin	575
39	Wyoming	542
40	Iowa	531
41	Michigan	527
42	Montana	504
42	Nebraska	504
44	Ohio	468
45	New York	460
46	North Carolina	457
47	Kansas	397
48	Oregon	329
49	Arkansas	302
50	Delaware	266

District of Columbia   30,878

Source: CQ Press using data from U.S. Office of Management and Budget, USAspending.gov
"Prime Award Spending Data Summary" (https://www.usaspending.gov/, as of January 26, 2018)
*National per capita excludes expenditures and population for territories and undistributed amounts. Expenditures allocated based on place of performance of a contract. Does not include grants, co-operative agreements, or contracts under grants.

Federal Government Assistance in 2016

National Total = $2,596,956,318,000*

ALPHA ORDER

RANK	STATE	EXPENDITURES	% of USA
19	Alabama	$56,036,683,782	2.2%
47	Alaska	6,328,959,830	0.2%
17	Arizona	59,918,458,035	2.3%
31	Arkansas	22,015,483,833	0.8%
1	California	238,004,007,292	9.2%
29	Colorado	29,801,152,436	1.1%
16	Connecticut	60,074,110,031	2.3%
46	Delaware	6,370,069,306	0.2%
3	Florida	153,114,797,996	5.9%
21	Georgia	53,199,499,470	2.0%
42	Hawaii	8,949,741,492	0.3%
41	Idaho	9,748,228,469	0.4%
12	Illinois	71,743,661,036	2.8%
6	Indiana	124,533,132,415	4.8%
32	Iowa	21,571,673,497	0.8%
35	Kansas	15,077,514,788	0.6%
7	Kentucky	82,780,456,279	3.2%
27	Louisiana	32,540,912,707	1.3%
40	Maine	9,858,037,936	0.4%
26	Maryland	36,576,232,962	1.4%
22	Massachusetts	49,342,489,413	1.9%
11	Michigan	72,183,364,244	2.8%
9	Minnesota	76,699,574,151	3.0%
33	Mississippi	20,073,301,058	0.8%
25	Missouri	40,641,329,092	1.6%
45	Montana	7,821,236,590	0.3%
39	Nebraska	11,342,009,760	0.4%
34	Nevada	15,369,809,251	0.6%
43	New Hampshire	8,294,493,512	0.3%
20	New Jersey	53,633,058,670	2.1%
36	New Mexico	14,834,921,411	0.6%
4	New York	149,465,771,842	5.8%
18	North Carolina	59,329,262,285	2.3%
15	North Dakota	61,988,666,160	2.4%
13	Ohio	70,684,856,943	2.7%
30	Oklahoma	24,354,393,250	0.9%
28	Oregon	30,688,683,503	1.2%
2	Pennsylvania	178,144,450,869	6.9%
44	Rhode Island	8,198,736,909	0.3%
10	South Carolina	72,461,949,054	2.8%
48	South Dakota	6,222,550,201	0.2%
14	Tennessee	68,119,448,250	2.6%
5	Texas	136,533,736,780	5.3%
38	Utah	12,624,159,949	0.5%
49	Vermont	4,958,853,907	0.2%
23	Virginia	44,162,945,210	1.7%
24	Washington	43,960,286,367	1.7%
37	West Virginia	13,873,519,308	0.5%
8	Wisconsin	80,850,543,484	3.1%
50	Wyoming	3,829,680,285	0.1%

RANK ORDER

RANK	STATE	EXPENDITURES	% of USA
1	California	$238,004,007,292	9.2%
2	Pennsylvania	178,144,450,869	6.9%
3	Florida	153,114,797,996	5.9%
4	New York	149,465,771,842	5.8%
5	Texas	136,533,736,780	5.3%
6	Indiana	124,533,132,415	4.8%
7	Kentucky	82,780,456,279	3.2%
8	Wisconsin	80,850,543,484	3.1%
9	Minnesota	76,699,574,151	3.0%
10	South Carolina	72,461,949,054	2.8%
11	Michigan	72,183,364,244	2.8%
12	Illinois	71,743,661,036	2.8%
13	Ohio	70,684,856,943	2.7%
14	Tennessee	68,119,448,250	2.6%
15	North Dakota	61,988,666,160	2.4%
16	Connecticut	60,074,110,031	2.3%
17	Arizona	59,918,458,035	2.3%
18	North Carolina	59,329,262,285	2.3%
19	Alabama	56,036,683,782	2.2%
20	New Jersey	53,633,058,670	2.1%
21	Georgia	53,199,499,470	2.0%
22	Massachusetts	49,342,489,413	1.9%
23	Virginia	44,162,945,210	1.7%
24	Washington	43,960,286,367	1.7%
25	Missouri	40,641,329,092	1.6%
26	Maryland	36,576,232,962	1.4%
27	Louisiana	32,540,912,707	1.3%
28	Oregon	30,688,683,503	1.2%
29	Colorado	29,801,152,436	1.1%
30	Oklahoma	24,354,393,250	0.9%
31	Arkansas	22,015,483,833	0.8%
32	Iowa	21,571,673,497	0.8%
33	Mississippi	20,073,301,058	0.8%
34	Nevada	15,369,809,251	0.6%
35	Kansas	15,077,514,788	0.6%
36	New Mexico	14,834,921,411	0.6%
37	West Virginia	13,873,519,308	0.5%
38	Utah	12,624,159,949	0.5%
39	Nebraska	11,342,009,760	0.4%
40	Maine	9,858,037,936	0.4%
41	Idaho	9,748,228,469	0.4%
42	Hawaii	8,949,741,492	0.3%
43	New Hampshire	8,294,493,512	0.3%
44	Rhode Island	8,198,736,909	0.3%
45	Montana	7,821,236,590	0.3%
46	Delaware	6,370,069,306	0.2%
47	Alaska	6,328,959,830	0.2%
48	South Dakota	6,222,550,201	0.2%
49	Vermont	4,958,853,907	0.2%
50	Wyoming	3,829,680,285	0.1%
	District of Columbia	9,958,386,447	0.4%

Source: CQ Press using data from U.S. Office of Management and Budget, USAspending.gov
   "Prime Award Spending Data Summary" (https://www.usaspending.gov/, as of January 26, 2018)
*Total includes $48,067,036,000 in U.S. territories and internationally as well as expenditures not distributed by state.
Expenditures allocated based on place of performance of a contract. Includes grants, loans, and other financial assistance.

Per Capita Federal Government Assistance in 2016

National Per Capita = $7,881*

ALPHA ORDER

RANK	STATE	PER CAPITA
9	Alabama	$11,529
12	Alaska	8,535
11	Arizona	8,673
21	Arkansas	7,367
38	California	6,057
44	Colorado	5,389
4	Connecticut	16,745
29	Delaware	6,686
19	Florida	7,412
48	Georgia	5,158
32	Hawaii	6,264
42	Idaho	5,802
43	Illinois	5,589
2	Indiana	18,772
27	Iowa	6,890
47	Kansas	5,185
3	Kentucky	18,661
26	Louisiana	6,944
20	Maine	7,411
37	Maryland	6,071
24	Massachusetts	7,231
22	Michigan	7,267
8	Minnesota	13,882
28	Mississippi	6,724
30	Missouri	6,672
18	Montana	7,530
40	Nebraska	5,946
46	Nevada	5,229
33	New Hampshire	6,213
39	New Jersey	5,974
25	New Mexico	7,114
17	New York	7,535
41	North Carolina	5,841
1	North Dakota	82,045
36	Ohio	6,082
34	Oklahoma	6,211
15	Oregon	7,625
7	Pennsylvania	13,926
14	Rhode Island	7,767
5	South Carolina	14,804
23	South Dakota	7,253
10	Tennessee	10,329
49	Texas	4,978
50	Utah	4,221
13	Vermont	7,920
45	Virginia	5,278
35	Washington	6,139
16	West Virginia	7,536
6	Wisconsin	14,017
31	Wyoming	6,529

RANK ORDER

RANK	STATE	PER CAPITA
1	North Dakota	$82,045
2	Indiana	18,772
3	Kentucky	18,661
4	Connecticut	16,745
5	South Carolina	14,804
6	Wisconsin	14,017
7	Pennsylvania	13,926
8	Minnesota	13,882
9	Alabama	11,529
10	Tennessee	10,329
11	Arizona	8,673
12	Alaska	8,535
13	Vermont	7,920
14	Rhode Island	7,767
15	Oregon	7,625
16	West Virginia	7,536
17	New York	7,535
18	Montana	7,530
19	Florida	7,412
20	Maine	7,411
21	Arkansas	7,367
22	Michigan	7,267
23	South Dakota	7,253
24	Massachusetts	7,231
25	New Mexico	7,114
26	Louisiana	6,944
27	Iowa	6,890
28	Mississippi	6,724
29	Delaware	6,686
30	Missouri	6,672
31	Wyoming	6,529
32	Hawaii	6,264
33	New Hampshire	6,213
34	Oklahoma	6,211
35	Washington	6,139
36	Ohio	6,082
37	Maryland	6,071
38	California	6,057
39	New Jersey	5,974
40	Nebraska	5,946
41	North Carolina	5,841
42	Idaho	5,802
43	Illinois	5,589
44	Colorado	5,389
45	Virginia	5,278
46	Nevada	5,229
47	Kansas	5,185
48	Georgia	5,158
49	Texas	4,978
50	Utah	4,221

District of Columbia   14,552

Source: CQ Press using data from U.S. Office of Management and Budget, USAspending.gov
"Prime Award Spending Data Summary" (https://www.usaspending.gov/, as of January 26, 2018)
*National per capita excludes expenditures and population for territories and undistributed amounts. Expenditures allocated based on place of performance of a contract. Includes grants, loans and other financial assistance.

Federal Government Grants in 2016

National Total = $668,199,244,000*

ALPHA ORDER					RANK ORDER			
RANK	STATE	EXPENDITURES	% of USA		RANK	STATE	EXPENDITURES	% of USA
26	Alabama	$8,447,657,744	1.3%		1	California	$94,149,533,851	14.1%
37	Alaska	3,397,723,535	0.5%		2	New York	61,800,418,784	9.2%
14	Arizona	14,249,468,152	2.1%		3	Texas	44,676,692,941	6.7%
29	Arkansas	7,336,826,829	1.1%		4	Florida	25,904,994,486	3.9%
1	California	94,149,533,851	14.1%		5	Pennsylvania	24,810,004,284	3.7%
22	Colorado	10,251,186,230	1.5%		6	Illinois	22,604,379,016	3.4%
27	Connecticut	8,404,060,852	1.3%		7	Michigan	21,975,743,949	3.3%
45	Delaware	2,286,979,015	0.3%		8	Ohio	20,923,713,441	3.1%
4	Florida	25,904,994,486	3.9%		9	Massachusetts	19,646,683,882	2.9%
12	Georgia	14,992,551,113	2.2%		10	New Jersey	16,992,879,747	2.5%
41	Hawaii	2,953,474,766	0.4%		11	North Carolina	16,679,391,260	2.5%
44	Idaho	2,604,148,220	0.4%		12	Georgia	14,992,551,113	2.2%
6	Illinois	22,604,379,016	3.4%		13	Washington	14,597,827,353	2.2%
15	Indiana	13,128,912,203	2.0%		14	Arizona	14,249,468,152	2.1%
32	Iowa	5,906,064,612	0.9%		15	Indiana	13,128,912,203	2.0%
38	Kansas	3,302,509,590	0.5%		16	Maryland	13,036,921,038	2.0%
18	Kentucky	11,794,841,777	1.8%		17	Louisiana	12,132,807,870	1.8%
17	Louisiana	12,132,807,870	1.8%		18	Kentucky	11,794,841,777	1.8%
39	Maine	3,085,371,399	0.5%		19	Missouri	11,746,210,228	1.8%
16	Maryland	13,036,921,038	2.0%		20	Minnesota	11,036,974,343	1.7%
9	Massachusetts	19,646,683,882	2.9%		21	Tennessee	10,977,643,998	1.6%
7	Michigan	21,975,743,949	3.3%		22	Colorado	10,251,186,230	1.5%
20	Minnesota	11,036,974,343	1.7%		23	Virginia	9,352,443,333	1.4%
31	Mississippi	6,933,952,027	1.0%		24	Oregon	9,170,080,309	1.4%
19	Missouri	11,746,210,228	1.8%		25	Wisconsin	8,595,613,468	1.3%
43	Montana	2,775,046,780	0.4%		26	Alabama	8,447,657,744	1.3%
42	Nebraska	2,835,516,838	0.4%		27	Connecticut	8,404,060,852	1.3%
34	Nevada	4,713,949,854	0.7%		28	South Carolina	7,982,142,953	1.2%
46	New Hampshire	2,240,382,525	0.3%		29	Arkansas	7,336,826,829	1.1%
10	New Jersey	16,992,879,747	2.5%		30	Oklahoma	6,993,952,011	1.0%
33	New Mexico	5,630,141,953	0.8%		31	Mississippi	6,933,952,027	1.0%
2	New York	61,800,418,784	9.2%		32	Iowa	5,906,064,612	0.9%
11	North Carolina	16,679,391,260	2.5%		33	New Mexico	5,630,141,953	0.8%
48	North Dakota	2,004,904,822	0.3%		34	Nevada	4,713,949,854	0.7%
8	Ohio	20,923,713,441	3.1%		35	West Virginia	4,150,901,078	0.6%
30	Oklahoma	6,993,952,011	1.0%		36	Utah	4,061,946,764	0.6%
24	Oregon	9,170,080,309	1.4%		37	Alaska	3,397,723,535	0.5%
5	Pennsylvania	24,810,004,284	3.7%		38	Kansas	3,302,509,590	0.5%
40	Rhode Island	3,032,563,000	0.5%		39	Maine	3,085,371,399	0.5%
28	South Carolina	7,982,142,953	1.2%		40	Rhode Island	3,032,563,000	0.5%
49	South Dakota	1,702,366,285	0.3%		41	Hawaii	2,953,474,766	0.4%
21	Tennessee	10,977,643,998	1.6%		42	Nebraska	2,835,516,838	0.4%
3	Texas	44,676,692,941	6.7%		43	Montana	2,775,046,780	0.4%
36	Utah	4,061,946,764	0.6%		44	Idaho	2,604,148,220	0.4%
47	Vermont	2,137,508,075	0.3%		45	Delaware	2,286,979,015	0.3%
23	Virginia	9,352,443,333	1.4%		46	New Hampshire	2,240,382,525	0.3%
13	Washington	14,597,827,353	2.2%		47	Vermont	2,137,508,075	0.3%
35	West Virginia	4,150,901,078	0.6%		48	North Dakota	2,004,904,822	0.3%
25	Wisconsin	8,595,613,468	1.3%		49	South Dakota	1,702,366,285	0.3%
50	Wyoming	1,460,303,748	0.2%		50	Wyoming	1,460,303,748	0.2%
						District of Columbia	7,389,235,998	1.1%

Source: U.S. Office of Management and Budget, USAspending.gov
  "Prime Award Spending Data Summary" (https://www.usaspending.gov/, as of January 26, 2018)
*Total includes $19,201,695,000 in U.S. territories and internationally as well as expenditures not distributed by state.
Expenditures allocated based on place of performance of a contract. Includes funds awarded to a non-federal entity for a defined
public or private purpose in which services are not rendered to the federal government.

Per Capita Expenditures for Federal Government Grants in 2016

National Per Capita = $2,007*

ALPHA ORDER

RANK	STATE	PER CAPITA
36	Alabama	$1,738
1	Alaska	4,582
23	Arizona	2,063
12	Arkansas	2,455
14	California	2,396
32	Colorado	1,854
15	Connecticut	2,342
13	Delaware	2,401
48	Florida	1,254
46	Georgia	1,454
22	Hawaii	2,067
43	Idaho	1,550
35	Illinois	1,761
27	Indiana	1,979
31	Iowa	1,886
49	Kansas	1,136
8	Kentucky	2,659
10	Louisiana	2,589
17	Maine	2,319
21	Maryland	2,164
4	Massachusetts	2,879
20	Michigan	2,212
25	Minnesota	1,998
16	Mississippi	2,323
29	Missouri	1,928
7	Montana	2,672
45	Nebraska	1,486
42	Nevada	1,604
37	New Hampshire	1,678
30	New Jersey	1,893
6	New Mexico	2,700
3	New York	3,116
39	North Carolina	1,642
9	North Dakota	2,654
33	Ohio	1,800
34	Oklahoma	1,784
18	Oregon	2,278
28	Pennsylvania	1,940
5	Rhode Island	2,873
40	South Carolina	1,631
26	South Dakota	1,984
38	Tennessee	1,665
41	Texas	1,629
47	Utah	1,358
2	Vermont	3,414
50	Virginia	1,118
24	Washington	2,039
19	West Virginia	2,255
44	Wisconsin	1,490
11	Wyoming	2,490

RANK ORDER

RANK	STATE	PER CAPITA
1	Alaska	$4,582
2	Vermont	3,414
3	New York	3,116
4	Massachusetts	2,879
5	Rhode Island	2,873
6	New Mexico	2,700
7	Montana	2,672
8	Kentucky	2,659
9	North Dakota	2,654
10	Louisiana	2,589
11	Wyoming	2,490
12	Arkansas	2,455
13	Delaware	2,401
14	California	2,396
15	Connecticut	2,342
16	Mississippi	2,323
17	Maine	2,319
18	Oregon	2,278
19	West Virginia	2,255
20	Michigan	2,212
21	Maryland	2,164
22	Hawaii	2,067
23	Arizona	2,063
24	Washington	2,039
25	Minnesota	1,998
26	South Dakota	1,984
27	Indiana	1,979
28	Pennsylvania	1,940
29	Missouri	1,928
30	New Jersey	1,893
31	Iowa	1,886
32	Colorado	1,854
33	Ohio	1,800
34	Oklahoma	1,784
35	Illinois	1,761
36	Alabama	1,738
37	New Hampshire	1,678
38	Tennessee	1,665
39	North Carolina	1,642
40	South Carolina	1,631
41	Texas	1,629
42	Nevada	1,604
43	Idaho	1,550
44	Wisconsin	1,490
45	Nebraska	1,486
46	Georgia	1,454
47	Utah	1,358
48	Florida	1,254
49	Kansas	1,136
50	Virginia	1,118

District of Columbia — 10,798

Source: CQ Press using data from U.S. Office of Management and Budget, USAspending.gov
"Prime Award Spending Data Summary" (https://www.usaspending.gov/, as of January 26, 2018)
*National per capita excludes expenditures and population for territories and undistributed amounts. Expenditures allocated based on place of performance of a contract. Includes funds awarded to a non-federal entity for a defined public or private purpose in which services are not rendered to the federal government.

Federal Government Loans in 2016

National Total = $2,431,709,000*

ALPHA ORDER

RANK	STATE	EXPENDITURES	% of USA
26	Alabama	$16,053,720	0.7%
46	Alaska	4,893,006	0.2%
21	Arizona	20,014,079	0.8%
36	Arkansas	10,497,467	0.4%
5	California	101,428,699	4.2%
16	Colorado	25,016,006	1.0%
37	Connecticut	10,398,730	0.4%
48	Delaware	3,133,065	0.1%
9	Florida	53,984,234	2.2%
7	Georgia	63,510,872	2.6%
38	Hawaii	10,151,385	0.4%
43	Idaho	6,572,069	0.3%
3	Illinois	272,999,146	11.2%
39	Indiana	10,124,677	0.4%
15	Iowa	27,075,948	1.1%
27	Kansas	15,501,011	0.6%
12	Kentucky	33,907,071	1.4%
17	Louisiana	23,767,518	1.0%
44	Maine	5,605,749	0.2%
1	Maryland	894,813,400	36.8%
40	Massachusetts	7,504,139	0.3%
18	Michigan	23,429,032	1.0%
28	Minnesota	15,429,125	0.6%
25	Mississippi	16,640,858	0.7%
20	Missouri	21,355,244	0.9%
41	Montana	7,094,312	0.3%
34	Nebraska	10,850,456	0.4%
33	Nevada	11,782,172	0.5%
4	New Hampshire	207,722,155	8.5%
13	New Jersey	32,835,076	1.4%
47	New Mexico	4,643,607	0.2%
6	New York	63,712,700	2.6%
8	North Carolina	57,704,384	2.4%
31	North Dakota	13,805,565	0.6%
19	Ohio	22,904,227	0.9%
30	Oklahoma	14,542,263	0.6%
24	Oregon	17,243,354	0.7%
32	Pennsylvania	13,280,077	0.5%
50	Rhode Island	1,675,540	0.1%
11	South Carolina	41,670,986	1.7%
23	South Dakota	18,965,522	0.8%
22	Tennessee	19,487,457	0.8%
2	Texas	413,045,539	17.0%
35	Utah	10,705,188	0.4%
42	Vermont	6,785,676	0.3%
10	Virginia	49,033,433	2.0%
14	Washington	27,930,534	1.1%
45	West Virginia	5,412,554	0.2%
29	Wisconsin	15,278,908	0.6%
49	Wyoming	3,048,182	0.1%

RANK ORDER

RANK	STATE	EXPENDITURES	% of USA
1	Maryland	$894,813,400	36.8%
2	Texas	413,045,539	17.0%
3	Illinois	272,999,146	11.2%
4	New Hampshire	207,722,155	8.5%
5	California	101,428,699	4.2%
6	New York	63,712,700	2.6%
7	Georgia	63,510,872	2.6%
8	North Carolina	57,704,384	2.4%
9	Florida	53,984,234	2.2%
10	Virginia	49,033,433	2.0%
11	South Carolina	41,670,986	1.7%
12	Kentucky	33,907,071	1.4%
13	New Jersey	32,835,076	1.4%
14	Washington	27,930,534	1.1%
15	Iowa	27,075,948	1.1%
16	Colorado	25,016,006	1.0%
17	Louisiana	23,767,518	1.0%
18	Michigan	23,429,032	1.0%
19	Ohio	22,904,227	0.9%
20	Missouri	21,355,244	0.9%
21	Arizona	20,014,079	0.8%
22	Tennessee	19,487,457	0.8%
23	South Dakota	18,965,522	0.8%
24	Oregon	17,243,354	0.7%
25	Mississippi	16,640,858	0.7%
26	Alabama	16,053,720	0.7%
27	Kansas	15,501,011	0.6%
28	Minnesota	15,429,125	0.6%
29	Wisconsin	15,278,908	0.6%
30	Oklahoma	14,542,263	0.6%
31	North Dakota	13,805,565	0.6%
32	Pennsylvania	13,280,077	0.5%
33	Nevada	11,782,172	0.5%
34	Nebraska	10,850,456	0.4%
35	Utah	10,705,188	0.4%
36	Arkansas	10,497,467	0.4%
37	Connecticut	10,398,730	0.4%
38	Hawaii	10,151,385	0.4%
39	Indiana	10,124,677	0.4%
40	Massachusetts	7,504,139	0.3%
41	Montana	7,094,312	0.3%
42	Vermont	6,785,676	0.3%
43	Idaho	6,572,069	0.3%
44	Maine	5,605,749	0.2%
45	West Virginia	5,412,554	0.2%
46	Alaska	4,893,006	0.2%
47	New Mexico	4,643,607	0.2%
48	Delaware	3,133,065	0.1%
49	Wyoming	3,048,182	0.1%
50	Rhode Island	1,675,540	0.1%
	District of Columbia	1,495,068	0.1%

Source: U.S. Office of Management and Budget, USAspending.gov
   "Prime Award Spending Data Summary" (https://www.usaspending.gov/, as of January 26, 2018)
*Total includes a negative $354,753,000 in U.S. territories and internationally as well as expenditures not distributed by state.
Expenditures allocated based on place of performance of a contract. Includes federal awards that the borrowers will eventually
pay back to the government. Guaranteed loans require the federal government to pay the bank and take over the loan if the
borrower defaults.

Per Capita Federal Government Loans in 2016

National Per Capita = $8.62*

ALPHA ORDER

RANK	STATE	PER CAPITA
33	Alabama	$3.30
13	Alaska	6.60
38	Arizona	2.90
31	Arkansas	3.51
43	California	2.58
22	Colorado	4.52
38	Connecticut	2.90
34	Delaware	3.29
42	Florida	2.61
14	Georgia	6.16
11	Hawaii	7.11
26	Idaho	3.91
4	Illinois	21.27
48	Indiana	1.53
8	Iowa	8.65
19	Kansas	5.33
10	Kentucky	7.64
21	Louisiana	5.07
24	Maine	4.21
2	Maryland	148.52
49	Massachusetts	1.10
44	Michigan	2.36
40	Minnesota	2.79
18	Mississippi	5.57
31	Missouri	3.51
12	Montana	6.83
16	Nebraska	5.69
25	Nevada	4.01
1	New Hampshire	155.60
29	New Jersey	3.66
45	New Mexico	2.23
35	New York	3.21
17	North Carolina	5.68
5	North Dakota	18.27
46	Ohio	1.97
28	Oklahoma	3.71
23	Oregon	4.28
50	Pennsylvania	1.04
47	Rhode Island	1.59
9	South Carolina	8.51
3	South Dakota	22.11
36	Tennessee	2.95
6	Texas	15.06
30	Utah	3.58
7	Vermont	10.84
15	Virginia	5.86
27	Washington	3.90
37	West Virginia	2.94
41	Wisconsin	2.65
20	Wyoming	5.20

RANK ORDER

RANK	STATE	PER CAPITA
1	New Hampshire	$155.60
2	Maryland	148.52
3	South Dakota	22.11
4	Illinois	21.27
5	North Dakota	18.27
6	Texas	15.06
7	Vermont	10.84
8	Iowa	8.65
9	South Carolina	8.51
10	Kentucky	7.64
11	Hawaii	7.11
12	Montana	6.83
13	Alaska	6.60
14	Georgia	6.16
15	Virginia	5.86
16	Nebraska	5.69
17	North Carolina	5.68
18	Mississippi	5.57
19	Kansas	5.33
20	Wyoming	5.20
21	Louisiana	5.07
22	Colorado	4.52
23	Oregon	4.28
24	Maine	4.21
25	Nevada	4.01
26	Idaho	3.91
27	Washington	3.90
28	Oklahoma	3.71
29	New Jersey	3.66
30	Utah	3.58
31	Arkansas	3.51
31	Missouri	3.51
33	Alabama	3.30
34	Delaware	3.29
35	New York	3.21
36	Tennessee	2.95
37	West Virginia	2.94
38	Arizona	2.90
38	Connecticut	2.90
40	Minnesota	2.79
41	Wisconsin	2.65
42	Florida	2.61
43	California	2.58
44	Michigan	2.36
45	New Mexico	2.23
46	Ohio	1.97
47	Rhode Island	1.59
48	Indiana	1.53
49	Massachusetts	1.10
50	Pennsylvania	1.04

District of Columbia   2.18

Source: CQ Press using data from U.S. Office of Management and Budget, USAspending.gov
"Prime Award Spending Data Summary" (https://www.usaspending.gov/, as of January 26, 2018)
*National per capita excludes expenditures and population for territories and undistributed amounts. Expenditures allocated based on place of performance of a contract. Includes Federal awards that the borrowers will eventually pay back to the government. Guaranteed loans require the federal government to pay the bank and take over the loan if the borrower defaults.

Federal Government "Other Financial Assistance" in 2016

National Total = $1,926,325,366,000*

ALPHA ORDER

ALPHA ORDER

RANK	STATE	EXPENDITURES	% of USA
17	Alabama	$47,572,972,318	2.5%
48	Alaska	2,926,343,289	0.2%
18	Arizona	45,648,975,804	2.4%
32	Arkansas	14,668,159,537	0.8%
2	California	143,753,044,742	7.5%
29	Colorado	19,524,950,200	1.0%
13	Connecticut	51,659,650,449	2.7%
47	Delaware	4,079,957,226	0.2%
3	Florida	127,155,819,276	6.6%
20	Georgia	38,143,437,485	2.0%
42	Hawaii	5,986,115,341	0.3%
40	Idaho	7,137,508,180	0.4%
16	Illinois	48,866,282,874	2.5%
4	Indiana	111,394,095,535	5.8%
31	Iowa	15,638,532,937	0.8%
34	Kansas	11,759,504,187	0.6%
8	Kentucky	70,951,707,431	3.7%
28	Louisiana	20,384,337,319	1.1%
41	Maine	6,767,060,788	0.4%
26	Maryland	22,644,498,524	1.2%
23	Massachusetts	29,688,301,392	1.5%
14	Michigan	50,184,191,263	2.6%
9	Minnesota	65,647,170,683	3.4%
33	Mississippi	13,122,708,173	0.7%
25	Missouri	28,873,763,620	1.5%
45	Montana	5,039,095,498	0.3%
39	Nebraska	8,495,642,466	0.4%
35	Nevada	10,644,077,225	0.6%
43	New Hampshire	5,846,388,832	0.3%
21	New Jersey	36,607,343,847	1.9%
37	New Mexico	9,200,135,851	0.5%
6	New York	87,601,640,358	4.5%
19	North Carolina	42,592,166,641	2.2%
11	North Dakota	59,969,955,773	3.1%
15	Ohio	49,738,239,275	2.6%
30	Oklahoma	17,345,898,976	0.9%
27	Oregon	21,501,359,840	1.1%
1	Pennsylvania	153,321,166,508	8.0%
44	Rhode Island	5,164,498,369	0.3%
10	South Carolina	64,438,135,115	3.3%
46	South Dakota	4,501,218,394	0.2%
12	Tennessee	57,122,316,795	3.0%
5	Texas	91,443,998,300	4.7%
38	Utah	8,551,507,997	0.4%
49	Vermont	2,814,560,156	0.1%
22	Virginia	34,761,468,444	1.8%
24	Washington	29,334,528,480	1.5%
36	West Virginia	9,717,205,676	0.5%
7	Wisconsin	72,239,651,108	3.8%
50	Wyoming	2,366,328,355	0.1%

RANK ORDER

RANK	STATE	EXPENDITURES	% of USA
1	Pennsylvania	$153,321,166,508	8.0%
2	California	143,753,044,742	7.5%
3	Florida	127,155,819,276	6.6%
4	Indiana	111,394,095,535	5.8%
5	Texas	91,443,998,300	4.7%
6	New York	87,601,640,358	4.5%
7	Wisconsin	72,239,651,108	3.8%
8	Kentucky	70,951,707,431	3.7%
9	Minnesota	65,647,170,683	3.4%
10	South Carolina	64,438,135,115	3.3%
11	North Dakota	59,969,955,773	3.1%
12	Tennessee	57,122,316,795	3.0%
13	Connecticut	51,659,650,449	2.7%
14	Michigan	50,184,191,263	2.6%
15	Ohio	49,738,239,275	2.6%
16	Illinois	48,866,282,874	2.5%
17	Alabama	47,572,972,318	2.5%
18	Arizona	45,648,975,804	2.4%
19	North Carolina	42,592,166,641	2.2%
20	Georgia	38,143,437,485	2.0%
21	New Jersey	36,607,343,847	1.9%
22	Virginia	34,761,468,444	1.8%
23	Massachusetts	29,688,301,392	1.5%
24	Washington	29,334,528,480	1.5%
25	Missouri	28,873,763,620	1.5%
26	Maryland	22,644,498,524	1.2%
27	Oregon	21,501,359,840	1.1%
28	Louisiana	20,384,337,319	1.1%
29	Colorado	19,524,950,200	1.0%
30	Oklahoma	17,345,898,976	0.9%
31	Iowa	15,638,532,937	0.8%
32	Arkansas	14,668,159,537	0.8%
33	Mississippi	13,122,708,173	0.7%
34	Kansas	11,759,504,187	0.6%
35	Nevada	10,644,077,225	0.6%
36	West Virginia	9,717,205,676	0.5%
37	New Mexico	9,200,135,851	0.5%
38	Utah	8,551,507,997	0.4%
39	Nebraska	8,495,642,466	0.4%
40	Idaho	7,137,508,180	0.4%
41	Maine	6,767,060,788	0.4%
42	Hawaii	5,986,115,341	0.3%
43	New Hampshire	5,846,388,832	0.3%
44	Rhode Island	5,164,498,369	0.3%
45	Montana	5,039,095,498	0.3%
46	South Dakota	4,501,218,394	0.2%
47	Delaware	4,079,957,226	0.2%
48	Alaska	2,926,343,289	0.2%
49	Vermont	2,814,560,156	0.1%
50	Wyoming	2,366,328,355	0.1%
	District of Columbia	2,567,655,381	0.1%

Source: CQ Press using data from U.S. Office of Management and Budget, USAspending.gov
"Prime Award Spending Data Summary" (https://www.usaspending.gov/, as of January 26, 2018)
*Total includes $29,220,093,000 in U.S. territories and internationally as well as expenditures not distributed by state.
Expenditures allocated based on place of performance of a contract. Includes direct payments to individuals (such as Medicare and food stamps), insurance payments (such as, unemployment benefits, flood insurance), and other types of assistance payments (such as, reimbursements for prescriptions for veterans).

Per Capita Federal Government "Other Financial Assistance" in 2016

National Per Capita = $5,866*

<table>
<tr><td colspan="3">ALPHA ORDER</td><td colspan="3">RANK ORDER</td></tr>
<tr><td>RANK</td><td>STATE</td><td>PER CAPITA</td><td>RANK</td><td>STATE</td><td>PER CAPITA</td></tr>
<tr><td>9</td><td>Alabama</td><td>$9,788</td><td>1</td><td>North Dakota</td><td>$79,373</td></tr>
<tr><td>42</td><td>Alaska</td><td>3,946</td><td>2</td><td>Indiana</td><td>16,791</td></tr>
<tr><td>11</td><td>Arizona</td><td>6,608</td><td>3</td><td>Kentucky</td><td>15,994</td></tr>
<tr><td>19</td><td>Arkansas</td><td>4,909</td><td>4</td><td>Connecticut</td><td>14,399</td></tr>
<tr><td>46</td><td>California</td><td>3,658</td><td>5</td><td>South Carolina</td><td>13,165</td></tr>
<tr><td>48</td><td>Colorado</td><td>3,531</td><td>6</td><td>Wisconsin</td><td>12,524</td></tr>
<tr><td>4</td><td>Connecticut</td><td>14,399</td><td>7</td><td>Pennsylvania</td><td>11,986</td></tr>
<tr><td>32</td><td>Delaware</td><td>4,283</td><td>8</td><td>Minnesota</td><td>11,882</td></tr>
<tr><td>12</td><td>Florida</td><td>6,156</td><td>9</td><td>Alabama</td><td>9,788</td></tr>
<tr><td>45</td><td>Georgia</td><td>3,698</td><td>10</td><td>Tennessee</td><td>8,661</td></tr>
<tr><td>36</td><td>Hawaii</td><td>4,190</td><td>11</td><td>Arizona</td><td>6,608</td></tr>
<tr><td>34</td><td>Idaho</td><td>4,248</td><td>12</td><td>Florida</td><td>6,156</td></tr>
<tr><td>43</td><td>Illinois</td><td>3,807</td><td>13</td><td>Oregon</td><td>5,342</td></tr>
<tr><td>2</td><td>Indiana</td><td>16,791</td><td>14</td><td>West Virginia</td><td>5,278</td></tr>
<tr><td>18</td><td>Iowa</td><td>4,995</td><td>15</td><td>South Dakota</td><td>5,247</td></tr>
<tr><td>40</td><td>Kansas</td><td>4,044</td><td>16</td><td>Maine</td><td>5,087</td></tr>
<tr><td>3</td><td>Kentucky</td><td>15,994</td><td>17</td><td>Michigan</td><td>5,052</td></tr>
<tr><td>31</td><td>Louisiana</td><td>4,350</td><td>18</td><td>Iowa</td><td>4,995</td></tr>
<tr><td>16</td><td>Maine</td><td>5,087</td><td>19</td><td>Arkansas</td><td>4,909</td></tr>
<tr><td>44</td><td>Maryland</td><td>3,759</td><td>20</td><td>Rhode Island</td><td>4,892</td></tr>
<tr><td>30</td><td>Massachusetts</td><td>4,351</td><td>21</td><td>Montana</td><td>4,852</td></tr>
<tr><td>17</td><td>Michigan</td><td>5,052</td><td>22</td><td>Missouri</td><td>4,740</td></tr>
<tr><td>8</td><td>Minnesota</td><td>11,882</td><td>23</td><td>Vermont</td><td>4,495</td></tr>
<tr><td>28</td><td>Mississippi</td><td>4,396</td><td>24</td><td>Nebraska</td><td>4,454</td></tr>
<tr><td>22</td><td>Missouri</td><td>4,740</td><td>25</td><td>Oklahoma</td><td>4,424</td></tr>
<tr><td>21</td><td>Montana</td><td>4,852</td><td>26</td><td>New York</td><td>4,416</td></tr>
<tr><td>24</td><td>Nebraska</td><td>4,454</td><td>27</td><td>New Mexico</td><td>4,412</td></tr>
<tr><td>47</td><td>Nevada</td><td>3,621</td><td>28</td><td>Mississippi</td><td>4,396</td></tr>
<tr><td>29</td><td>New Hampshire</td><td>4,379</td><td>29</td><td>New Hampshire</td><td>4,379</td></tr>
<tr><td>39</td><td>New Jersey</td><td>4,077</td><td>30</td><td>Massachusetts</td><td>4,351</td></tr>
<tr><td>27</td><td>New Mexico</td><td>4,412</td><td>31</td><td>Louisiana</td><td>4,350</td></tr>
<tr><td>26</td><td>New York</td><td>4,416</td><td>32</td><td>Delaware</td><td>4,283</td></tr>
<tr><td>35</td><td>North Carolina</td><td>4,194</td><td>33</td><td>Ohio</td><td>4,279</td></tr>
<tr><td>1</td><td>North Dakota</td><td>79,373</td><td>34</td><td>Idaho</td><td>4,248</td></tr>
<tr><td>33</td><td>Ohio</td><td>4,279</td><td>35</td><td>North Carolina</td><td>4,194</td></tr>
<tr><td>25</td><td>Oklahoma</td><td>4,424</td><td>36</td><td>Hawaii</td><td>4,190</td></tr>
<tr><td>13</td><td>Oregon</td><td>5,342</td><td>37</td><td>Virginia</td><td>4,154</td></tr>
<tr><td>7</td><td>Pennsylvania</td><td>11,986</td><td>38</td><td>Washington</td><td>4,097</td></tr>
<tr><td>20</td><td>Rhode Island</td><td>4,892</td><td>39</td><td>New Jersey</td><td>4,077</td></tr>
<tr><td>5</td><td>South Carolina</td><td>13,165</td><td>40</td><td>Kansas</td><td>4,044</td></tr>
<tr><td>15</td><td>South Dakota</td><td>5,247</td><td>41</td><td>Wyoming</td><td>4,034</td></tr>
<tr><td>10</td><td>Tennessee</td><td>8,661</td><td>42</td><td>Alaska</td><td>3,946</td></tr>
<tr><td>49</td><td>Texas</td><td>3,334</td><td>43</td><td>Illinois</td><td>3,807</td></tr>
<tr><td>50</td><td>Utah</td><td>2,859</td><td>44</td><td>Maryland</td><td>3,759</td></tr>
<tr><td>23</td><td>Vermont</td><td>4,495</td><td>45</td><td>Georgia</td><td>3,698</td></tr>
<tr><td>37</td><td>Virginia</td><td>4,154</td><td>46</td><td>California</td><td>3,658</td></tr>
<tr><td>38</td><td>Washington</td><td>4,097</td><td>47</td><td>Nevada</td><td>3,621</td></tr>
<tr><td>14</td><td>West Virginia</td><td>5,278</td><td>48</td><td>Colorado</td><td>3,531</td></tr>
<tr><td>6</td><td>Wisconsin</td><td>12,524</td><td>49</td><td>Texas</td><td>3,334</td></tr>
<tr><td>41</td><td>Wyoming</td><td>4,034</td><td>50</td><td>Utah</td><td>2,859</td></tr>
<tr><td></td><td></td><td></td><td></td><td>District of Columbia</td><td>3,752</td></tr>
</table>

Source: CQ Press using data from U.S. Office of Management and Budget, USAspending.gov
"Prime Award Spending Data Summary" (https://www.usaspending.gov/, as of January 26, 2018)
*National per capita excludes expenditures and population for territories and undistributed amounts. Expenditures allocated based on place of performance of a contract. Includes direct payments to individuals (such as Medicare and food stamps), insurance payments (such as, unemployment benefits, flood insurance), and other types of assistance payments (such as, reimbursements for prescriptions for veterans).

Federal Civilian Employees in 2017

National Total = 1,869,986 Employees*

ALPHA ORDER

RANK	STATE	EMPLOYEES	% of USA
15	Alabama	37,386	2.0%
39	Alaska	10,398	0.6%
13	Arizona	38,087	2.0%
35	Arkansas	12,557	0.7%
1	California	152,466	8.2%
16	Colorado	36,848	2.0%
42	Connecticut	7,998	0.4%
50	Delaware	3,039	0.2%
5	Florida	89,504	4.8%
6	Georgia	71,739	3.8%
23	Hawaii	23,453	1.3%
43	Idaho	7,731	0.4%
11	Illinois	44,760	2.4%
24	Indiana	22,610	1.2%
41	Iowa	8,042	0.4%
33	Kansas	15,672	0.8%
25	Kentucky	22,181	1.2%
28	Louisiana	19,537	1.0%
37	Maine	11,285	0.6%
4	Maryland	120,705	6.5%
21	Massachusetts	25,063	1.3%
18	Michigan	27,405	1.5%
32	Minnesota	16,795	0.9%
30	Mississippi	17,295	0.9%
17	Missouri	33,377	1.8%
40	Montana	8,589	0.5%
38	Nebraska	10,468	0.6%
36	Nevada	12,186	0.7%
49	New Hampshire	4,331	0.2%
22	New Jersey	24,758	1.3%
26	New Mexico	21,954	1.2%
8	New York	60,727	3.2%
12	North Carolina	42,772	2.3%
46	North Dakota	5,460	0.3%
10	Ohio	49,450	2.6%
14	Oklahoma	37,486	2.0%
31	Oregon	17,252	0.9%
7	Pennsylvania	62,366	3.3%
45	Rhode Island	6,864	0.4%
27	South Carolina	21,050	1.1%
44	South Dakota	7,547	0.4%
20	Tennessee	25,099	1.3%
3	Texas	132,952	7.1%
19	Utah	26,109	1.4%
48	Vermont	4,845	0.3%
2	Virginia	144,295	7.7%
9	Washington	53,211	2.8%
29	West Virginia	18,656	1.0%
34	Wisconsin	14,045	0.8%
47	Wyoming	4,977	0.3%

RANK ORDER

RANK	STATE	EMPLOYEES	% of USA
1	California	152,466	8.2%
2	Virginia	144,295	7.7%
3	Texas	132,952	7.1%
4	Maryland	120,705	6.5%
5	Florida	89,504	4.8%
6	Georgia	71,739	3.8%
7	Pennsylvania	62,366	3.3%
8	New York	60,727	3.2%
9	Washington	53,211	2.8%
10	Ohio	49,450	2.6%
11	Illinois	44,760	2.4%
12	North Carolina	42,772	2.3%
13	Arizona	38,087	2.0%
14	Oklahoma	37,486	2.0%
15	Alabama	37,386	2.0%
16	Colorado	36,848	2.0%
17	Missouri	33,377	1.8%
18	Michigan	27,405	1.5%
19	Utah	26,109	1.4%
20	Tennessee	25,099	1.3%
21	Massachusetts	25,063	1.3%
22	New Jersey	24,758	1.3%
23	Hawaii	23,453	1.3%
24	Indiana	22,610	1.2%
25	Kentucky	22,181	1.2%
26	New Mexico	21,954	1.2%
27	South Carolina	21,050	1.1%
28	Louisiana	19,537	1.0%
29	West Virginia	18,656	1.0%
30	Mississippi	17,295	0.9%
31	Oregon	17,252	0.9%
32	Minnesota	16,795	0.9%
33	Kansas	15,672	0.8%
34	Wisconsin	14,045	0.8%
35	Arkansas	12,557	0.7%
36	Nevada	12,186	0.7%
37	Maine	11,285	0.6%
38	Nebraska	10,468	0.6%
39	Alaska	10,398	0.6%
40	Montana	8,589	0.5%
41	Iowa	8,042	0.4%
42	Connecticut	7,998	0.4%
43	Idaho	7,731	0.4%
44	South Dakota	7,547	0.4%
45	Rhode Island	6,864	0.4%
46	North Dakota	5,460	0.3%
47	Wyoming	4,977	0.3%
48	Vermont	4,845	0.3%
49	New Hampshire	4,331	0.2%
50	Delaware	3,039	0.2%
	District of Columbia	141,367	7.6%

Source: U.S. Office of Personnel Management
   "Common Characteristics of the Government" (https://www.opm.gov/feddata/)
*Non-seasonal, full-time, permanent employees as of September. Head count based on place of employment. There were an estimated 2,087,747 federal civilian employees including seasonal and non permanent employees. Total includes 35,237 employees either outside the U.S. or unspecified. Excludes Central Intelligence Agency, Defense Intelligence Agency, and National Security Agency.

Rate of Federal Civilian Employees in 2017

National Rate = 56 Employees per 10,000 Population*

ALPHA ORDER

RANK	STATE	RATE
14	Alabama	77
4	Alaska	141
23	Arizona	54
30	Arkansas	42
37	California	39
18	Colorado	66
50	Connecticut	22
42	Delaware	32
29	Florida	43
17	Georgia	69
3	Hawaii	165
28	Idaho	45
40	Illinois	35
41	Indiana	34
48	Iowa	26
23	Kansas	54
25	Kentucky	50
30	Louisiana	42
10	Maine	85
1	Maryland	200
38	Massachusetts	37
47	Michigan	27
45	Minnesota	30
20	Mississippi	58
21	Missouri	55
12	Montana	82
21	Nebraska	55
36	Nevada	41
42	New Hampshire	32
46	New Jersey	28
5	New Mexico	105
44	New York	31
30	North Carolina	42
15	North Dakota	72
30	Ohio	42
7	Oklahoma	95
30	Oregon	42
26	Pennsylvania	49
19	Rhode Island	65
30	South Carolina	42
8	South Dakota	86
38	Tennessee	37
27	Texas	47
11	Utah	84
13	Vermont	78
2	Virginia	170
15	Washington	72
6	West Virginia	103
49	Wisconsin	24
8	Wyoming	86

RANK ORDER

RANK	STATE	RATE
1	Maryland	200
2	Virginia	170
3	Hawaii	165
4	Alaska	141
5	New Mexico	105
6	West Virginia	103
7	Oklahoma	95
8	South Dakota	86
8	Wyoming	86
10	Maine	85
11	Utah	84
12	Montana	82
13	Vermont	78
14	Alabama	77
15	North Dakota	72
15	Washington	72
17	Georgia	69
18	Colorado	66
19	Rhode Island	65
20	Mississippi	58
21	Missouri	55
21	Nebraska	55
23	Arizona	54
23	Kansas	54
25	Kentucky	50
26	Pennsylvania	49
27	Texas	47
28	Idaho	45
29	Florida	43
30	Arkansas	42
30	Louisiana	42
30	North Carolina	42
30	Ohio	42
30	Oregon	42
30	South Carolina	42
36	Nevada	41
37	California	39
38	Massachusetts	37
38	Tennessee	37
40	Illinois	35
41	Indiana	34
42	Delaware	32
42	New Hampshire	32
44	New York	31
45	Minnesota	30
46	New Jersey	28
47	Michigan	27
48	Iowa	26
49	Wisconsin	24
50	Connecticut	22

District of Columbia	2,032

Source: CQ Press using data from U.S. Office of Personnel Management
"Common Characteristics of the Government" (https://www.opm.gov/feddata/)
*Non-seasonal, full-time, permanent employees as of September. Head count based on place of employment. There were an estimated 2,087,747 federal civilian employees including seasonal and non permanent employees. National rate excludes employees either outside the U.S. or unspecified. Excludes Central Intelligence Agency, Defense Intelligence Agency, and National Security Agency.

X. Government Finances: State and Local

(Continued)

(Continued)

State and Local Government Total Revenue in 2016

National Total = $3,401,687,410,000*

ALPHA ORDER

RANK	STATE	REVENUE	% of USA
24	Alabama	$45,952,641,000	1.4%
44	Alaska	11,642,881,000	0.3%
17	Arizona	58,987,986,000	1.7%
34	Arkansas	26,750,193,000	0.8%
1	California	515,972,637,000	15.2%
20	Colorado	55,237,381,000	1.6%
27	Connecticut	41,963,223,000	1.2%
45	Delaware	10,197,112,000	0.3%
4	Florida	162,751,329,000	4.8%
14	Georgia	78,432,518,000	2.3%
38	Hawaii	17,378,714,000	0.5%
40	Idaho	13,108,121,000	0.4%
6	Illinois	129,388,295,000	3.8%
18	Indiana	58,977,153,000	1.7%
29	Iowa	35,362,888,000	1.0%
32	Kansas	27,710,901,000	0.8%
28	Kentucky	40,309,982,000	1.2%
26	Louisiana	43,113,127,000	1.3%
41	Maine	12,734,039,000	0.4%
15	Maryland	64,145,974,000	1.9%
11	Massachusetts	85,864,568,000	2.5%
9	Michigan	98,851,746,000	2.9%
16	Minnesota	63,721,253,000	1.9%
31	Mississippi	29,311,458,000	0.9%
22	Missouri	52,505,583,000	1.5%
47	Montana	9,431,952,000	0.3%
37	Nebraska	22,804,588,000	0.7%
35	Nevada	26,271,781,000	0.8%
42	New Hampshire	12,646,424,000	0.4%
8	New Jersey	103,773,736,000	3.1%
36	New Mexico	23,394,588,000	0.7%
2	New York	328,217,489,000	9.6%
10	North Carolina	90,340,239,000	2.7%
46	North Dakota	9,926,276,000	0.3%
7	Ohio	117,494,958,000	3.5%
30	Oklahoma	32,831,466,000	1.0%
23	Oregon	47,155,698,000	1.4%
5	Pennsylvania	134,879,470,000	4.0%
43	Rhode Island	11,784,683,000	0.3%
25	South Carolina	45,741,776,000	1.3%
50	South Dakota	7,395,287,000	0.2%
19	Tennessee	56,956,424,000	1.7%
3	Texas	246,157,080,000	7.2%
33	Utah	27,360,010,000	0.8%
49	Vermont	7,728,333,000	0.2%
13	Virginia	78,738,114,000	2.3%
12	Washington	85,067,153,000	2.5%
39	West Virginia	17,311,430,000	0.5%
21	Wisconsin	54,175,477,000	1.6%
48	Wyoming	9,102,101,000	0.3%

RANK ORDER

RANK	STATE	REVENUE	% of USA
1	California	$515,972,637,000	15.2%
2	New York	328,217,489,000	9.6%
3	Texas	246,157,080,000	7.2%
4	Florida	162,751,329,000	4.8%
5	Pennsylvania	134,879,470,000	4.0%
6	Illinois	129,388,295,000	3.8%
7	Ohio	117,494,958,000	3.5%
8	New Jersey	103,773,736,000	3.1%
9	Michigan	98,851,746,000	2.9%
10	North Carolina	90,340,239,000	2.7%
11	Massachusetts	85,864,568,000	2.5%
12	Washington	85,067,153,000	2.5%
13	Virginia	78,738,114,000	2.3%
14	Georgia	78,432,518,000	2.3%
15	Maryland	64,145,974,000	1.9%
16	Minnesota	63,721,253,000	1.9%
17	Arizona	58,987,986,000	1.7%
18	Indiana	58,977,153,000	1.7%
19	Tennessee	56,956,424,000	1.7%
20	Colorado	55,237,381,000	1.6%
21	Wisconsin	54,175,477,000	1.6%
22	Missouri	52,505,583,000	1.5%
23	Oregon	47,155,698,000	1.4%
24	Alabama	45,952,641,000	1.4%
25	South Carolina	45,741,776,000	1.3%
26	Louisiana	43,113,127,000	1.3%
27	Connecticut	41,963,223,000	1.2%
28	Kentucky	40,309,982,000	1.2%
29	Iowa	35,362,888,000	1.0%
30	Oklahoma	32,831,466,000	1.0%
31	Mississippi	29,311,458,000	0.9%
32	Kansas	27,710,901,000	0.8%
33	Utah	27,360,010,000	0.8%
34	Arkansas	26,750,193,000	0.8%
35	Nevada	26,271,781,000	0.8%
36	New Mexico	23,394,588,000	0.7%
37	Nebraska	22,804,588,000	0.7%
38	Hawaii	17,378,714,000	0.5%
39	West Virginia	17,311,430,000	0.5%
40	Idaho	13,108,121,000	0.4%
41	Maine	12,734,039,000	0.4%
42	New Hampshire	12,646,424,000	0.4%
43	Rhode Island	11,784,683,000	0.3%
44	Alaska	11,642,881,000	0.3%
45	Delaware	10,197,112,000	0.3%
46	North Dakota	9,926,276,000	0.3%
47	Montana	9,431,952,000	0.3%
48	Wyoming	9,102,101,000	0.3%
49	Vermont	7,728,333,000	0.2%
50	South Dakota	7,395,287,000	0.2%
	District of Columbia	14,629,174,000	0.4%

Source: U.S. Bureau of the Census, Governments Division
"2016 State and Local Government Finances" (https://www.census.gov/programs-surveys/gov-finances.html)
*Total revenue includes all money received from external sources. This includes taxes, intergovernmental transfers and
insurance trust revenue, and revenue from government owned utilities and other commercial or auxiliary enterprise.

Per Capita State and Local Government Revenue in 2016

National Per Capita = $10,529*

ALPHA ORDER

RANK	STATE	PER CAPITA
29	Alabama	$9,446
2	Alaska	15,702
46	Arizona	8,493
39	Arkansas	8,945
4	California	13,160
23	Colorado	9,969
10	Connecticut	11,726
18	Delaware	10,743
48	Florida	7,889
50	Georgia	7,611
8	Hawaii	12,169
49	Idaho	7,789
22	Illinois	10,087
41	Indiana	8,891
15	Iowa	11,292
27	Kansas	9,519
35	Kentucky	9,082
34	Louisiana	9,216
26	Maine	9,565
19	Maryland	10,683
6	Massachusetts	12,579
24	Michigan	9,933
13	Minnesota	11,537
25	Mississippi	9,809
43	Missouri	8,626
36	Montana	9,062
9	Nebraska	11,965
37	Nevada	8,998
30	New Hampshire	9,421
11	New Jersey	11,693
16	New Mexico	11,179
1	New York	16,710
40	North Carolina	8,895
5	North Dakota	13,159
21	Ohio	10,098
47	Oklahoma	8,361
14	Oregon	11,526
20	Pennsylvania	10,551
17	Rhode Island	11,149
33	South Carolina	9,225
45	South Dakota	8,570
44	Tennessee	8,571
42	Texas	8,811
38	Utah	8,992
7	Vermont	12,392
32	Virginia	9,361
12	Washington	11,662
28	West Virginia	9,455
31	Wisconsin	9,384
3	Wyoming	15,578

RANK ORDER

RANK	STATE	PER CAPITA
1	New York	$16,710
2	Alaska	15,702
3	Wyoming	15,578
4	California	13,160
5	North Dakota	13,159
6	Massachusetts	12,579
7	Vermont	12,392
8	Hawaii	12,169
9	Nebraska	11,965
10	Connecticut	11,726
11	New Jersey	11,693
12	Washington	11,662
13	Minnesota	11,537
14	Oregon	11,526
15	Iowa	11,292
16	New Mexico	11,179
17	Rhode Island	11,149
18	Delaware	10,743
19	Maryland	10,683
20	Pennsylvania	10,551
21	Ohio	10,098
22	Illinois	10,087
23	Colorado	9,969
24	Michigan	9,933
25	Mississippi	9,809
26	Maine	9,565
27	Kansas	9,519
28	West Virginia	9,455
29	Alabama	9,446
30	New Hampshire	9,421
31	Wisconsin	9,384
32	Virginia	9,361
33	South Carolina	9,225
34	Louisiana	9,216
35	Kentucky	9,082
36	Montana	9,062
37	Nevada	8,998
38	Utah	8,992
39	Arkansas	8,945
40	North Carolina	8,895
41	Indiana	8,891
42	Texas	8,811
43	Missouri	8,626
44	Tennessee	8,571
45	South Dakota	8,570
46	Arizona	8,493
47	Oklahoma	8,361
48	Florida	7,889
49	Idaho	7,789
50	Georgia	7,611

	District of Columbia	21,307

Source: CQ Press using data from U.S. Bureau of the Census, Governments Division

"2016 State and Local Government Finances" (https://www.census.gov/programs-surveys/gov-finances.html)

*Total revenue includes all money received from external sources. This includes taxes, intergovernmental transfers and insurance trust revenue, and revenue from government owned utilities and other commercial or auxiliary enterprise.

State and Local Government Revenue from the Federal Government in 2016

National Total = $690,208,739,000

ALPHA ORDER   RANK ORDER

RANK	STATE	REVENUE	% of USA	RANK	STATE	REVENUE	% of USA
24	Alabama	$10,409,596,000	1.5%	1	California	$103,675,750,000	15.0%
40	Alaska	3,128,811,000	0.5%	2	New York	62,347,319,000	9.0%
14	Arizona	14,992,304,000	2.2%	3	Texas	45,162,100,000	6.5%
30	Arkansas	7,673,867,000	1.1%	4	Florida	30,735,624,000	4.5%
1	California	103,675,750,000	15.0%	5	Pennsylvania	28,865,774,000	4.2%
26	Colorado	9,505,845,000	1.4%	6	Ohio	25,816,579,000	3.7%
29	Connecticut	7,872,088,000	1.1%	7	Illinois	23,075,208,000	3.3%
46	Delaware	2,240,114,000	0.3%	8	Michigan	22,389,149,000	3.2%
4	Florida	30,735,624,000	4.5%	9	North Carolina	18,917,600,000	2.7%
12	Georgia	15,655,415,000	2.3%	10	New Jersey	18,313,904,000	2.7%
39	Hawaii	3,326,658,000	0.5%	11	Massachusetts	17,256,715,000	2.5%
42	Idaho	2,853,313,000	0.4%	12	Georgia	15,655,415,000	2.3%
7	Illinois	23,075,208,000	3.3%	13	Washington	15,047,498,000	2.2%
15	Indiana	13,505,772,000	2.0%	14	Arizona	14,992,304,000	2.2%
33	Iowa	7,131,716,000	1.0%	15	Indiana	13,505,772,000	2.0%
37	Kansas	4,059,124,000	0.6%	16	Maryland	13,147,422,000	1.9%
17	Kentucky	12,104,989,000	1.8%	17	Kentucky	12,104,989,000	1.8%
22	Louisiana	11,228,992,000	1.6%	18	Tennessee	11,920,365,000	1.7%
41	Maine	2,972,220,000	0.4%	19	Minnesota	11,843,510,000	1.7%
16	Maryland	13,147,422,000	1.9%	20	Virginia	11,505,307,000	1.7%
11	Massachusetts	17,256,715,000	2.5%	21	Missouri	11,496,480,000	1.7%
8	Michigan	22,389,149,000	3.2%	22	Louisiana	11,228,992,000	1.6%
19	Minnesota	11,843,510,000	1.7%	23	Oregon	10,865,333,000	1.6%
27	Mississippi	8,682,032,000	1.3%	24	Alabama	10,409,596,000	1.5%
21	Missouri	11,496,480,000	1.7%	25	Wisconsin	9,672,383,000	1.4%
43	Montana	2,657,680,000	0.4%	26	Colorado	9,505,845,000	1.4%
38	Nebraska	3,449,087,000	0.5%	27	Mississippi	8,682,032,000	1.3%
35	Nevada	4,929,703,000	0.7%	28	South Carolina	8,184,793,000	1.2%
45	New Hampshire	2,343,086,000	0.3%	29	Connecticut	7,872,088,000	1.1%
10	New Jersey	18,313,904,000	2.7%	30	Arkansas	7,673,867,000	1.1%
32	New Mexico	7,212,620,000	1.0%	31	Oklahoma	7,525,270,000	1.1%
2	New York	62,347,319,000	9.0%	32	New Mexico	7,212,620,000	1.0%
9	North Carolina	18,917,600,000	2.7%	33	Iowa	7,131,716,000	1.0%
49	North Dakota	1,839,133,000	0.3%	34	West Virginia	4,938,092,000	0.7%
6	Ohio	25,816,579,000	3.7%	35	Nevada	4,929,703,000	0.7%
31	Oklahoma	7,525,270,000	1.1%	36	Utah	4,663,128,000	0.7%
23	Oregon	10,865,333,000	1.6%	37	Kansas	4,059,124,000	0.6%
5	Pennsylvania	28,865,774,000	4.2%	38	Nebraska	3,449,087,000	0.5%
44	Rhode Island	2,644,625,000	0.4%	39	Hawaii	3,326,658,000	0.5%
28	South Carolina	8,184,793,000	1.2%	40	Alaska	3,128,811,000	0.5%
50	South Dakota	1,646,794,000	0.2%	41	Maine	2,972,220,000	0.4%
18	Tennessee	11,920,365,000	1.7%	42	Idaho	2,853,313,000	0.4%
3	Texas	45,162,100,000	6.5%	43	Montana	2,657,680,000	0.4%
36	Utah	4,663,128,000	0.7%	44	Rhode Island	2,644,625,000	0.4%
47	Vermont	2,208,635,000	0.3%	45	New Hampshire	2,343,086,000	0.3%
20	Virginia	11,505,307,000	1.7%	46	Delaware	2,240,114,000	0.3%
13	Washington	15,047,498,000	2.2%	47	Vermont	2,208,635,000	0.3%
34	West Virginia	4,938,092,000	0.7%	48	Wyoming	2,085,297,000	0.3%
25	Wisconsin	9,672,383,000	1.4%	49	North Dakota	1,839,133,000	0.3%
48	Wyoming	2,085,297,000	0.3%	50	South Dakota	1,646,794,000	0.2%
					District of Columbia	4,483,920,000	0.6%

Source: U.S. Bureau of the Census, Governments Division
"2016 State and Local Government Finances" (https://www.census.gov/programs-surveys/gov-finances.html)

Per Capita State and Local Government Revenue
from the Federal Government in 2016
National Per Capita = $2,136

ALPHA ORDER

ALPHA ORDER

RANK	STATE	PER CAPITA
28	Alabama	$2,140
1	Alaska	4,220
26	Arizona	2,159
11	Arkansas	2,566
10	California	2,644
40	Colorado	1,716
24	Connecticut	2,200
17	Delaware	2,360
48	Florida	1,490
47	Georgia	1,519
18	Hawaii	2,329
41	Idaho	1,695
37	Illinois	1,799
31	Indiana	2,036
19	Iowa	2,277
49	Kansas	1,394
7	Kentucky	2,727
16	Louisiana	2,400
22	Maine	2,232
25	Maryland	2,190
13	Massachusetts	2,528
21	Michigan	2,250
27	Minnesota	2,144
6	Mississippi	2,905
34	Missouri	1,889
12	Montana	2,553
36	Nebraska	1,810
42	Nevada	1,688
39	New Hampshire	1,745
29	New Jersey	2,064
4	New Mexico	3,446
5	New York	3,174
35	North Carolina	1,863
15	North Dakota	2,438
23	Ohio	2,219
32	Oklahoma	1,916
9	Oregon	2,656
20	Pennsylvania	2,258
14	Rhode Island	2,502
44	South Carolina	1,651
33	South Dakota	1,908
38	Tennessee	1,794
45	Texas	1,617
46	Utah	1,533
3	Vermont	3,541
50	Virginia	1,368
30	Washington	2,063
8	West Virginia	2,697
43	Wisconsin	1,675
2	Wyoming	3,569

RANK ORDER

RANK	STATE	PER CAPITA
1	Alaska	$4,220
2	Wyoming	3,569
3	Vermont	3,541
4	New Mexico	3,446
5	New York	3,174
6	Mississippi	2,905
7	Kentucky	2,727
8	West Virginia	2,697
9	Oregon	2,656
10	California	2,644
11	Arkansas	2,566
12	Montana	2,553
13	Massachusetts	2,528
14	Rhode Island	2,502
15	North Dakota	2,438
16	Louisiana	2,400
17	Delaware	2,360
18	Hawaii	2,329
19	Iowa	2,277
20	Pennsylvania	2,258
21	Michigan	2,250
22	Maine	2,232
23	Ohio	2,219
24	Connecticut	2,200
25	Maryland	2,190
26	Arizona	2,159
27	Minnesota	2,144
28	Alabama	2,140
29	New Jersey	2,064
30	Washington	2,063
31	Indiana	2,036
32	Oklahoma	1,916
33	South Dakota	1,908
34	Missouri	1,889
35	North Carolina	1,863
36	Nebraska	1,810
37	Illinois	1,799
38	Tennessee	1,794
39	New Hampshire	1,745
40	Colorado	1,716
41	Idaho	1,695
42	Nevada	1,688
43	Wisconsin	1,675
44	South Carolina	1,651
45	Texas	1,617
46	Utah	1,533
47	Georgia	1,519
48	Florida	1,490
49	Kansas	1,394
50	Virginia	1,368

District of Columbia — 6,531

Source: CQ Press using data from U.S. Bureau of the Census, Governments Division
"2016 State and Local Government Finances" (https://www.census.gov/programs-surveys/gov-finances.html)

Percent of State and Local Government Revenue from the Federal Government in 2016
National Percent = 20.3%*

RANK	STATE	PERCENT
16	Alabama	22.7
8	Alaska	26.9
10	Arizona	25.4
4	Arkansas	28.7
29	California	20.1
46	Colorado	17.2
35	Connecticut	18.8
20	Delaware	22.0
34	Florida	18.9
31	Georgia	20.0
32	Hawaii	19.1
23	Idaho	21.8
43	Illinois	17.8
13	Indiana	22.9
28	Iowa	20.2
49	Kansas	14.6
2	Kentucky	30.0
9	Louisiana	26.0
11	Maine	23.3
27	Maryland	20.5
29	Massachusetts	20.1
17	Michigan	22.6
37	Minnesota	18.6
3	Mississippi	29.6
22	Missouri	21.9
7	Montana	28.2
48	Nebraska	15.1
35	Nevada	18.8
38	New Hampshire	18.5
45	New Jersey	17.6
1	New Mexico	30.8
33	New York	19.0
25	North Carolina	20.9
38	North Dakota	18.5
20	Ohio	22.0
13	Oklahoma	22.9
12	Oregon	23.0
24	Pennsylvania	21.4
18	Rhode Island	22.4
41	South Carolina	17.9
19	South Dakota	22.3
25	Tennessee	20.9
40	Texas	18.3
47	Utah	17.0
5	Vermont	28.6
49	Virginia	14.6
44	Washington	17.7
6	West Virginia	28.5
41	Wisconsin	17.9
13	Wyoming	22.9

RANK	STATE	PERCENT
1	New Mexico	30.8
2	Kentucky	30.0
3	Mississippi	29.6
4	Arkansas	28.7
5	Vermont	28.6
6	West Virginia	28.5
7	Montana	28.2
8	Alaska	26.9
9	Louisiana	26.0
10	Arizona	25.4
11	Maine	23.3
12	Oregon	23.0
13	Indiana	22.9
13	Oklahoma	22.9
13	Wyoming	22.9
16	Alabama	22.7
17	Michigan	22.6
18	Rhode Island	22.4
19	South Dakota	22.3
20	Delaware	22.0
20	Ohio	22.0
22	Missouri	21.9
23	Idaho	21.8
24	Pennsylvania	21.4
25	North Carolina	20.9
25	Tennessee	20.9
27	Maryland	20.5
28	Iowa	20.2
29	California	20.1
29	Massachusetts	20.1
31	Georgia	20.0
32	Hawaii	19.1
33	New York	19.0
34	Florida	18.9
35	Connecticut	18.8
35	Nevada	18.8
37	Minnesota	18.6
38	New Hampshire	18.5
38	North Dakota	18.5
40	Texas	18.3
41	South Carolina	17.9
41	Wisconsin	17.9
43	Illinois	17.8
44	Washington	17.7
45	New Jersey	17.6
46	Colorado	17.2
47	Utah	17.0
48	Nebraska	15.1
49	Kansas	14.6
49	Virginia	14.6

| | District of Columbia | 30.7 |

Source: CQ Press using data from U.S. Bureau of the Census, Governments Division
"2016 State and Local Government Finances" (https://www.census.gov/programs-surveys/gov-finances.html)
*As a percent of total revenue.

State and Local Government Own Source Revenue in 2016

National Total = $2,318,053,057,000*

<table>
<tr><th colspan="4">ALPHA ORDER</th><th colspan="4">RANK ORDER</th></tr>
<tr><th>RANK</th><th>STATE</th><th>REVENUE</th><th>% of USA</th><th>RANK</th><th>STATE</th><th>REVENUE</th><th>% of USA</th></tr>
<tr><td>27</td><td>Alabama</td><td>$27,633,995,000</td><td>1.2%</td><td>1</td><td>California</td><td>$342,023,090,000</td><td>14.8%</td></tr>
<tr><td>44</td><td>Alaska</td><td>7,660,950,000</td><td>0.3%</td><td>2</td><td>New York</td><td>232,093,048,000</td><td>10.0%</td></tr>
<tr><td>20</td><td>Arizona</td><td>35,392,508,000</td><td>1.5%</td><td>3</td><td>Texas</td><td>166,072,120,000</td><td>7.2%</td></tr>
<tr><td>35</td><td>Arkansas</td><td>16,986,887,000</td><td>0.7%</td><td>4</td><td>Florida</td><td>117,111,171,000</td><td>5.1%</td></tr>
<tr><td>1</td><td>California</td><td>342,023,090,000</td><td>14.8%</td><td>5</td><td>Illinois</td><td>93,479,103,000</td><td>4.0%</td></tr>
<tr><td>19</td><td>Colorado</td><td>39,049,778,000</td><td>1.7%</td><td>6</td><td>Pennsylvania</td><td>90,842,253,000</td><td>3.9%</td></tr>
<tr><td>24</td><td>Connecticut</td><td>31,158,610,000</td><td>1.3%</td><td>7</td><td>New Jersey</td><td>78,387,366,000</td><td>3.4%</td></tr>
<tr><td>45</td><td>Delaware</td><td>7,350,375,000</td><td>0.3%</td><td>8</td><td>Ohio</td><td>77,756,243,000</td><td>3.4%</td></tr>
<tr><td>4</td><td>Florida</td><td>117,111,171,000</td><td>5.1%</td><td>9</td><td>Michigan</td><td>63,403,599,000</td><td>2.7%</td></tr>
<tr><td>14</td><td>Georgia</td><td>54,252,238,000</td><td>2.3%</td><td>10</td><td>North Carolina</td><td>62,051,134,000</td><td>2.7%</td></tr>
<tr><td>38</td><td>Hawaii</td><td>13,113,050,000</td><td>0.6%</td><td>11</td><td>Massachusetts</td><td>59,253,538,000</td><td>2.6%</td></tr>
<tr><td>42</td><td>Idaho</td><td>8,759,094,000</td><td>0.4%</td><td>12</td><td>Virginia</td><td>58,893,547,000</td><td>2.5%</td></tr>
<tr><td>5</td><td>Illinois</td><td>93,479,103,000</td><td>4.0%</td><td>13</td><td>Washington</td><td>55,975,786,000</td><td>2.4%</td></tr>
<tr><td>17</td><td>Indiana</td><td>40,289,555,000</td><td>1.7%</td><td>14</td><td>Georgia</td><td>54,252,238,000</td><td>2.3%</td></tr>
<tr><td>29</td><td>Iowa</td><td>24,447,988,000</td><td>1.1%</td><td>15</td><td>Maryland</td><td>46,687,794,000</td><td>2.0%</td></tr>
<tr><td>31</td><td>Kansas</td><td>20,936,040,000</td><td>0.9%</td><td>16</td><td>Minnesota</td><td>46,201,485,000</td><td>2.0%</td></tr>
<tr><td>28</td><td>Kentucky</td><td>24,660,629,000</td><td>1.1%</td><td>17</td><td>Indiana</td><td>40,289,555,000</td><td>1.7%</td></tr>
<tr><td>26</td><td>Louisiana</td><td>27,934,648,000</td><td>1.2%</td><td>18</td><td>Wisconsin</td><td>39,885,373,000</td><td>1.7%</td></tr>
<tr><td>40</td><td>Maine</td><td>8,952,056,000</td><td>0.4%</td><td>19</td><td>Colorado</td><td>39,049,778,000</td><td>1.7%</td></tr>
<tr><td>15</td><td>Maryland</td><td>46,687,794,000</td><td>2.0%</td><td>20</td><td>Arizona</td><td>35,392,508,000</td><td>1.5%</td></tr>
<tr><td>11</td><td>Massachusetts</td><td>59,253,538,000</td><td>2.6%</td><td>21</td><td>Missouri</td><td>34,183,366,000</td><td>1.5%</td></tr>
<tr><td>9</td><td>Michigan</td><td>63,403,599,000</td><td>2.7%</td><td>22</td><td>Tennessee</td><td>33,528,164,000</td><td>1.4%</td></tr>
<tr><td>16</td><td>Minnesota</td><td>46,201,485,000</td><td>2.0%</td><td>23</td><td>South Carolina</td><td>31,695,411,000</td><td>1.4%</td></tr>
<tr><td>33</td><td>Mississippi</td><td>17,838,168,000</td><td>0.8%</td><td>24</td><td>Connecticut</td><td>31,158,610,000</td><td>1.3%</td></tr>
<tr><td>21</td><td>Missouri</td><td>34,183,366,000</td><td>1.5%</td><td>25</td><td>Oregon</td><td>30,034,664,000</td><td>1.3%</td></tr>
<tr><td>48</td><td>Montana</td><td>5,781,315,000</td><td>0.2%</td><td>26</td><td>Louisiana</td><td>27,934,648,000</td><td>1.2%</td></tr>
<tr><td>36</td><td>Nebraska</td><td>13,991,467,000</td><td>0.6%</td><td>27</td><td>Alabama</td><td>27,633,995,000</td><td>1.2%</td></tr>
<tr><td>34</td><td>Nevada</td><td>17,209,661,000</td><td>0.7%</td><td>28</td><td>Kentucky</td><td>24,660,629,000</td><td>1.1%</td></tr>
<tr><td>41</td><td>New Hampshire</td><td>8,850,493,000</td><td>0.4%</td><td>29</td><td>Iowa</td><td>24,447,988,000</td><td>1.1%</td></tr>
<tr><td>7</td><td>New Jersey</td><td>78,387,366,000</td><td>3.4%</td><td>30</td><td>Oklahoma</td><td>22,081,714,000</td><td>1.0%</td></tr>
<tr><td>37</td><td>New Mexico</td><td>13,541,113,000</td><td>0.6%</td><td>31</td><td>Kansas</td><td>20,936,040,000</td><td>0.9%</td></tr>
<tr><td>2</td><td>New York</td><td>232,093,048,000</td><td>10.0%</td><td>32</td><td>Utah</td><td>18,942,237,000</td><td>0.8%</td></tr>
<tr><td>10</td><td>North Carolina</td><td>62,051,134,000</td><td>2.7%</td><td>33</td><td>Mississippi</td><td>17,838,168,000</td><td>0.8%</td></tr>
<tr><td>46</td><td>North Dakota</td><td>7,216,598,000</td><td>0.3%</td><td>34</td><td>Nevada</td><td>17,209,661,000</td><td>0.7%</td></tr>
<tr><td>8</td><td>Ohio</td><td>77,756,243,000</td><td>3.4%</td><td>35</td><td>Arkansas</td><td>16,986,887,000</td><td>0.7%</td></tr>
<tr><td>30</td><td>Oklahoma</td><td>22,081,714,000</td><td>1.0%</td><td>36</td><td>Nebraska</td><td>13,991,467,000</td><td>0.6%</td></tr>
<tr><td>25</td><td>Oregon</td><td>30,034,664,000</td><td>1.3%</td><td>37</td><td>New Mexico</td><td>13,541,113,000</td><td>0.6%</td></tr>
<tr><td>6</td><td>Pennsylvania</td><td>90,842,253,000</td><td>3.9%</td><td>38</td><td>Hawaii</td><td>13,113,050,000</td><td>0.6%</td></tr>
<tr><td>43</td><td>Rhode Island</td><td>8,098,006,000</td><td>0.3%</td><td>39</td><td>West Virginia</td><td>11,304,789,000</td><td>0.5%</td></tr>
<tr><td>23</td><td>South Carolina</td><td>31,695,411,000</td><td>1.4%</td><td>40</td><td>Maine</td><td>8,952,056,000</td><td>0.4%</td></tr>
<tr><td>49</td><td>South Dakota</td><td>5,071,928,000</td><td>0.2%</td><td>41</td><td>New Hampshire</td><td>8,850,493,000</td><td>0.4%</td></tr>
<tr><td>22</td><td>Tennessee</td><td>33,528,164,000</td><td>1.4%</td><td>42</td><td>Idaho</td><td>8,759,094,000</td><td>0.4%</td></tr>
<tr><td>3</td><td>Texas</td><td>166,072,120,000</td><td>7.2%</td><td>43</td><td>Rhode Island</td><td>8,098,006,000</td><td>0.3%</td></tr>
<tr><td>32</td><td>Utah</td><td>18,942,237,000</td><td>0.8%</td><td>44</td><td>Alaska</td><td>7,660,950,000</td><td>0.3%</td></tr>
<tr><td>50</td><td>Vermont</td><td>4,901,981,000</td><td>0.2%</td><td>45</td><td>Delaware</td><td>7,350,375,000</td><td>0.3%</td></tr>
<tr><td>12</td><td>Virginia</td><td>58,893,547,000</td><td>2.5%</td><td>46</td><td>North Dakota</td><td>7,216,598,000</td><td>0.3%</td></tr>
<tr><td>13</td><td>Washington</td><td>55,975,786,000</td><td>2.4%</td><td>47</td><td>Wyoming</td><td>5,957,103,000</td><td>0.3%</td></tr>
<tr><td>39</td><td>West Virginia</td><td>11,304,789,000</td><td>0.5%</td><td>48</td><td>Montana</td><td>5,781,315,000</td><td>0.2%</td></tr>
<tr><td>18</td><td>Wisconsin</td><td>39,885,373,000</td><td>1.7%</td><td>49</td><td>South Dakota</td><td>5,071,928,000</td><td>0.2%</td></tr>
<tr><td>47</td><td>Wyoming</td><td>5,957,103,000</td><td>0.3%</td><td>50</td><td>Vermont</td><td>4,901,981,000</td><td>0.2%</td></tr>
<tr><td></td><td></td><td></td><td></td><td></td><td>District of Columbia</td><td>9,129,828,000</td><td>0.4%</td></tr>
</table>

Source: U.S. Bureau of the Census, Governments Division
"2016 State and Local Government Finances" (https://www.census.gov/programs-surveys/gov-finances.html)
*Own source revenue includes taxes, current charges, and miscellaneous general revenue. Excluded are intergovernmental transfers, insurance trust revenue, and revenue from government owned utilities and other commercial or auxiliary enterprise.

Per Capita State and Local Government Own Source Revenue in 2016

National Per Capita = $7,175*

ALPHA ORDER

RANK	STATE	PER CAPITA
40	Alabama	$5,680
2	Alaska	10,332
49	Arizona	5,096
40	Arkansas	5,680
7	California	8,723
22	Colorado	7,048
8	Connecticut	8,707
14	Delaware	7,744
42	Florida	5,677
47	Georgia	5,265
5	Hawaii	9,182
48	Idaho	5,205
19	Illinois	7,288
34	Indiana	6,074
12	Iowa	7,806
20	Kansas	7,191
45	Kentucky	5,556
35	Louisiana	5,971
25	Maine	6,724
13	Maryland	7,775
9	Massachusetts	8,681
30	Michigan	6,371
10	Minnesota	8,365
36	Mississippi	5,969
44	Missouri	5,616
46	Montana	5,554
17	Nebraska	7,341
38	Nevada	5,894
27	New Hampshire	6,593
6	New Jersey	8,833
28	New Mexico	6,470
1	New York	11,816
33	North Carolina	6,109
4	North Dakota	9,567
26	Ohio	6,683
43	Oklahoma	5,623
17	Oregon	7,341
21	Pennsylvania	7,106
16	Rhode Island	7,661
29	South Carolina	6,392
39	South Dakota	5,878
50	Tennessee	5,046
37	Texas	5,944
31	Utah	6,226
11	Vermont	7,860
23	Virginia	7,002
15	Washington	7,674
32	West Virginia	6,174
24	Wisconsin	6,909
3	Wyoming	10,195

RANK ORDER

RANK	STATE	PER CAPITA
1	New York	$11,816
2	Alaska	10,332
3	Wyoming	10,195
4	North Dakota	9,567
5	Hawaii	9,182
6	New Jersey	8,833
7	California	8,723
8	Connecticut	8,707
9	Massachusetts	8,681
10	Minnesota	8,365
11	Vermont	7,860
12	Iowa	7,806
13	Maryland	7,775
14	Delaware	7,744
15	Washington	7,674
16	Rhode Island	7,661
17	Nebraska	7,341
17	Oregon	7,341
19	Illinois	7,288
20	Kansas	7,191
21	Pennsylvania	7,106
22	Colorado	7,048
23	Virginia	7,002
24	Wisconsin	6,909
25	Maine	6,724
26	Ohio	6,683
27	New Hampshire	6,593
28	New Mexico	6,470
29	South Carolina	6,392
30	Michigan	6,371
31	Utah	6,226
32	West Virginia	6,174
33	North Carolina	6,109
34	Indiana	6,074
35	Louisiana	5,971
36	Mississippi	5,969
37	Texas	5,944
38	Nevada	5,894
39	South Dakota	5,878
40	Alabama	5,680
40	Arkansas	5,680
42	Florida	5,677
43	Oklahoma	5,623
44	Missouri	5,616
45	Kentucky	5,556
46	Montana	5,554
47	Georgia	5,265
48	Idaho	5,205
49	Arizona	5,096
50	Tennessee	5,046

District of Columbia 13,298

Source: CQ Press using data from U.S. Bureau of the Census, Governments Division
"2016 State and Local Government Finances" (https://www.census.gov/programs-surveys/gov-finances.html)
*Own source revenue includes taxes, current charges, and miscellaneous general revenue. Excluded are intergovernmental transfers, insurance trust revenue, and revenue from government owned utilities and other commercial or auxiliary enterprise.

State and Local Government Tax Revenue in 2016

National Total = $1,599,513,900,000

ALPHA ORDER

RANK	STATE	REVENUE	% of USA
28	Alabama	$15,584,922,000	1.0%
50	Alaska	2,827,027,000	0.2%
21	Arizona	24,743,711,000	1.5%
33	Arkansas	11,826,467,000	0.7%
1	California	238,805,116,000	14.9%
20	Colorado	25,556,460,000	1.6%
18	Connecticut	25,904,645,000	1.6%
45	Delaware	4,532,143,000	0.3%
5	Florida	71,847,399,000	4.5%
13	Georgia	37,743,701,000	2.4%
37	Hawaii	9,239,417,000	0.6%
42	Idaho	5,902,944,000	0.4%
4	Illinois	72,574,959,000	4.5%
19	Indiana	25,689,873,000	1.6%
29	Iowa	15,291,346,000	1.0%
31	Kansas	13,077,707,000	0.8%
27	Kentucky	16,958,063,000	1.1%
25	Louisiana	18,218,729,000	1.1%
40	Maine	6,924,560,000	0.4%
15	Maryland	36,310,235,000	2.3%
9	Massachusetts	44,142,186,000	2.8%
10	Michigan	40,549,215,000	2.5%
16	Minnesota	33,650,134,000	2.1%
35	Mississippi	10,785,451,000	0.7%
22	Missouri	22,429,511,000	1.4%
46	Montana	3,974,456,000	0.2%
36	Nebraska	9,704,585,000	0.6%
32	Nevada	12,571,202,000	0.8%
41	New Hampshire	6,431,537,000	0.4%
7	New Jersey	60,237,873,000	3.8%
38	New Mexico	8,114,437,000	0.5%
2	New York	177,667,289,000	11.1%
11	North Carolina	39,805,449,000	2.5%
44	North Dakota	5,009,263,000	0.3%
8	Ohio	51,993,411,000	3.3%
30	Oklahoma	13,558,709,000	0.8%
24	Oregon	18,420,002,000	1.2%
6	Pennsylvania	64,680,716,000	4.0%
43	Rhode Island	5,882,267,000	0.4%
26	South Carolina	17,037,643,000	1.1%
48	South Dakota	3,392,779,000	0.2%
23	Tennessee	22,089,758,000	1.4%
3	Texas	112,176,589,000	7.0%
34	Utah	11,395,728,000	0.7%
47	Vermont	3,680,191,000	0.2%
12	Virginia	38,372,579,000	2.4%
14	Washington	36,770,738,000	2.3%
39	West Virginia	7,161,887,000	0.4%
17	Wisconsin	27,607,145,000	1.7%
49	Wyoming	3,243,067,000	0.2%

RANK ORDER

RANK	STATE	REVENUE	% of USA
1	California	$238,805,116,000	14.9%
2	New York	177,667,289,000	11.1%
3	Texas	112,176,589,000	7.0%
4	Illinois	72,574,959,000	4.5%
5	Florida	71,847,399,000	4.5%
6	Pennsylvania	64,680,716,000	4.0%
7	New Jersey	60,237,873,000	3.8%
8	Ohio	51,993,411,000	3.3%
9	Massachusetts	44,142,186,000	2.8%
10	Michigan	40,549,215,000	2.5%
11	North Carolina	39,805,449,000	2.5%
12	Virginia	38,372,579,000	2.4%
13	Georgia	37,743,701,000	2.4%
14	Washington	36,770,738,000	2.3%
15	Maryland	36,310,235,000	2.3%
16	Minnesota	33,650,134,000	2.1%
17	Wisconsin	27,607,145,000	1.7%
18	Connecticut	25,904,645,000	1.6%
19	Indiana	25,689,873,000	1.6%
20	Colorado	25,556,460,000	1.6%
21	Arizona	24,743,711,000	1.5%
22	Missouri	22,429,511,000	1.4%
23	Tennessee	22,089,758,000	1.4%
24	Oregon	18,420,002,000	1.2%
25	Louisiana	18,218,729,000	1.1%
26	South Carolina	17,037,643,000	1.1%
27	Kentucky	16,958,063,000	1.1%
28	Alabama	15,584,922,000	1.0%
29	Iowa	15,291,346,000	1.0%
30	Oklahoma	13,558,709,000	0.8%
31	Kansas	13,077,707,000	0.8%
32	Nevada	12,571,202,000	0.8%
33	Arkansas	11,826,467,000	0.7%
34	Utah	11,395,728,000	0.7%
35	Mississippi	10,785,451,000	0.7%
36	Nebraska	9,704,585,000	0.6%
37	Hawaii	9,239,417,000	0.6%
38	New Mexico	8,114,437,000	0.5%
39	West Virginia	7,161,887,000	0.4%
40	Maine	6,924,560,000	0.4%
41	New Hampshire	6,431,537,000	0.4%
42	Idaho	5,902,944,000	0.4%
43	Rhode Island	5,882,267,000	0.4%
44	North Dakota	5,009,263,000	0.3%
45	Delaware	4,532,143,000	0.3%
46	Montana	3,974,456,000	0.2%
47	Vermont	3,680,191,000	0.2%
48	South Dakota	3,392,779,000	0.2%
49	Wyoming	3,243,067,000	0.2%
50	Alaska	2,827,027,000	0.2%
	District of Columbia	7,418,679,000	0.5%

Source: U.S. Bureau of the Census, Governments Division
"2016 State and Local Government Finances" (https://www.census.gov/programs-surveys/gov-finances.html)

Per Capita State and Local Government Tax Revenue in 2016

National Per Capita = $4,951

ALPHA ORDER

RANK	STATE	PER CAPITA
50	Alabama	$3,204
39	Alaska	3,813
44	Arizona	3,563
30	Arkansas	3,955
8	California	6,091
22	Colorado	4,612
2	Connecticut	7,239
21	Delaware	4,775
46	Florida	3,483
42	Georgia	3,663
5	Hawaii	6,470
45	Idaho	3,508
11	Illinois	5,658
36	Indiana	3,873
18	Iowa	4,883
25	Kansas	4,492
37	Kentucky	3,821
34	Louisiana	3,894
14	Maine	5,201
9	Maryland	6,047
6	Massachusetts	6,467
28	Michigan	4,075
7	Minnesota	6,092
43	Mississippi	3,609
41	Missouri	3,685
38	Montana	3,818
15	Nebraska	5,092
27	Nevada	4,306
19	New Hampshire	4,791
3	New Jersey	6,788
35	New Mexico	3,877
1	New York	9,045
32	North Carolina	3,919
4	North Dakota	6,640
26	Ohio	4,469
47	Oklahoma	3,453
24	Oregon	4,502
16	Pennsylvania	5,060
12	Rhode Island	5,565
48	South Carolina	3,436
31	South Dakota	3,932
49	Tennessee	3,324
29	Texas	4,015
40	Utah	3,745
10	Vermont	5,901
23	Virginia	4,562
17	Washington	5,041
33	West Virginia	3,912
20	Wisconsin	4,782
13	Wyoming	5,550

RANK ORDER

RANK	STATE	PER CAPITA
1	New York	$9,045
2	Connecticut	7,239
3	New Jersey	6,788
4	North Dakota	6,640
5	Hawaii	6,470
6	Massachusetts	6,467
7	Minnesota	6,092
8	California	6,091
9	Maryland	6,047
10	Vermont	5,901
11	Illinois	5,658
12	Rhode Island	5,565
13	Wyoming	5,550
14	Maine	5,201
15	Nebraska	5,092
16	Pennsylvania	5,060
17	Washington	5,041
18	Iowa	4,883
19	New Hampshire	4,791
20	Wisconsin	4,782
21	Delaware	4,775
22	Colorado	4,612
23	Virginia	4,562
24	Oregon	4,502
25	Kansas	4,492
26	Ohio	4,469
27	Nevada	4,306
28	Michigan	4,075
29	Texas	4,015
30	Arkansas	3,955
31	South Dakota	3,932
32	North Carolina	3,919
33	West Virginia	3,912
34	Louisiana	3,894
35	New Mexico	3,877
36	Indiana	3,873
37	Kentucky	3,821
38	Montana	3,818
39	Alaska	3,813
40	Utah	3,745
41	Missouri	3,685
42	Georgia	3,663
43	Mississippi	3,609
44	Arizona	3,563
45	Idaho	3,508
46	Florida	3,483
47	Oklahoma	3,453
48	South Carolina	3,436
49	Tennessee	3,324
50	Alabama	3,204
	District of Columbia	10,805

Source: CQ Press using data from U.S. Bureau of the Census, Governments Division
"2016 State and Local Government Finances" (https://www.census.gov/programs-surveys/gov-finances.html)

Percent of State and Local Government Revenue from Taxes in 2016

National Percent = 47.0%

<table>
<tr><td colspan="3">ALPHA ORDER</td><td colspan="3">RANK ORDER</td></tr>
<tr><td>RANK</td><td>STATE</td><td>PERCENT</td><td>RANK</td><td>STATE</td><td>PERCENT</td></tr>
<tr><td>49</td><td>Alabama</td><td>33.9</td><td>1</td><td>Connecticut</td><td>61.7</td></tr>
<tr><td>50</td><td>Alaska</td><td>24.3</td><td>2</td><td>New Jersey</td><td>58.0</td></tr>
<tr><td>38</td><td>Arizona</td><td>41.9</td><td>3</td><td>Maryland</td><td>56.6</td></tr>
<tr><td>27</td><td>Arkansas</td><td>44.2</td><td>4</td><td>Illinois</td><td>56.1</td></tr>
<tr><td>20</td><td>California</td><td>46.3</td><td>5</td><td>Maine</td><td>54.4</td></tr>
<tr><td>20</td><td>Colorado</td><td>46.3</td><td>6</td><td>New York</td><td>54.1</td></tr>
<tr><td>1</td><td>Connecticut</td><td>61.7</td><td>7</td><td>Hawaii</td><td>53.2</td></tr>
<tr><td>25</td><td>Delaware</td><td>44.4</td><td>8</td><td>Minnesota</td><td>52.8</td></tr>
<tr><td>28</td><td>Florida</td><td>44.1</td><td>9</td><td>Massachusetts</td><td>51.4</td></tr>
<tr><td>15</td><td>Georgia</td><td>48.1</td><td>10</td><td>Wisconsin</td><td>51.0</td></tr>
<tr><td>7</td><td>Hawaii</td><td>53.2</td><td>11</td><td>New Hampshire</td><td>50.9</td></tr>
<tr><td>24</td><td>Idaho</td><td>45.0</td><td>12</td><td>North Dakota</td><td>50.5</td></tr>
<tr><td>4</td><td>Illinois</td><td>56.1</td><td>13</td><td>Rhode Island</td><td>49.9</td></tr>
<tr><td>30</td><td>Indiana</td><td>43.6</td><td>14</td><td>Virginia</td><td>48.7</td></tr>
<tr><td>31</td><td>Iowa</td><td>43.2</td><td>15</td><td>Georgia</td><td>48.1</td></tr>
<tr><td>19</td><td>Kansas</td><td>47.2</td><td>16</td><td>Pennsylvania</td><td>48.0</td></tr>
<tr><td>36</td><td>Kentucky</td><td>42.1</td><td>17</td><td>Nevada</td><td>47.9</td></tr>
<tr><td>35</td><td>Louisiana</td><td>42.3</td><td>18</td><td>Vermont</td><td>47.6</td></tr>
<tr><td>5</td><td>Maine</td><td>54.4</td><td>19</td><td>Kansas</td><td>47.2</td></tr>
<tr><td>3</td><td>Maryland</td><td>56.6</td><td>20</td><td>California</td><td>46.3</td></tr>
<tr><td>9</td><td>Massachusetts</td><td>51.4</td><td>20</td><td>Colorado</td><td>46.3</td></tr>
<tr><td>42</td><td>Michigan</td><td>41.0</td><td>22</td><td>South Dakota</td><td>45.9</td></tr>
<tr><td>8</td><td>Minnesota</td><td>52.8</td><td>23</td><td>Texas</td><td>45.6</td></tr>
<tr><td>46</td><td>Mississippi</td><td>36.8</td><td>24</td><td>Idaho</td><td>45.0</td></tr>
<tr><td>33</td><td>Missouri</td><td>42.7</td><td>25</td><td>Delaware</td><td>44.4</td></tr>
<tr><td>36</td><td>Montana</td><td>42.1</td><td>26</td><td>Ohio</td><td>44.3</td></tr>
<tr><td>34</td><td>Nebraska</td><td>42.6</td><td>27</td><td>Arkansas</td><td>44.2</td></tr>
<tr><td>17</td><td>Nevada</td><td>47.9</td><td>28</td><td>Florida</td><td>44.1</td></tr>
<tr><td>11</td><td>New Hampshire</td><td>50.9</td><td>28</td><td>North Carolina</td><td>44.1</td></tr>
<tr><td>2</td><td>New Jersey</td><td>58.0</td><td>30</td><td>Indiana</td><td>43.6</td></tr>
<tr><td>48</td><td>New Mexico</td><td>34.7</td><td>31</td><td>Iowa</td><td>43.2</td></tr>
<tr><td>6</td><td>New York</td><td>54.1</td><td>31</td><td>Washington</td><td>43.2</td></tr>
<tr><td>28</td><td>North Carolina</td><td>44.1</td><td>33</td><td>Missouri</td><td>42.7</td></tr>
<tr><td>12</td><td>North Dakota</td><td>50.5</td><td>34</td><td>Nebraska</td><td>42.6</td></tr>
<tr><td>26</td><td>Ohio</td><td>44.3</td><td>35</td><td>Louisiana</td><td>42.3</td></tr>
<tr><td>41</td><td>Oklahoma</td><td>41.3</td><td>36</td><td>Kentucky</td><td>42.1</td></tr>
<tr><td>43</td><td>Oregon</td><td>39.1</td><td>36</td><td>Montana</td><td>42.1</td></tr>
<tr><td>16</td><td>Pennsylvania</td><td>48.0</td><td>38</td><td>Arizona</td><td>41.9</td></tr>
<tr><td>13</td><td>Rhode Island</td><td>49.9</td><td>39</td><td>Utah</td><td>41.7</td></tr>
<tr><td>45</td><td>South Carolina</td><td>37.2</td><td>40</td><td>West Virginia</td><td>41.4</td></tr>
<tr><td>22</td><td>South Dakota</td><td>45.9</td><td>41</td><td>Oklahoma</td><td>41.3</td></tr>
<tr><td>44</td><td>Tennessee</td><td>38.8</td><td>42</td><td>Michigan</td><td>41.0</td></tr>
<tr><td>23</td><td>Texas</td><td>45.6</td><td>43</td><td>Oregon</td><td>39.1</td></tr>
<tr><td>39</td><td>Utah</td><td>41.7</td><td>44</td><td>Tennessee</td><td>38.8</td></tr>
<tr><td>18</td><td>Vermont</td><td>47.6</td><td>45</td><td>South Carolina</td><td>37.2</td></tr>
<tr><td>14</td><td>Virginia</td><td>48.7</td><td>46</td><td>Mississippi</td><td>36.8</td></tr>
<tr><td>31</td><td>Washington</td><td>43.2</td><td>47</td><td>Wyoming</td><td>35.6</td></tr>
<tr><td>40</td><td>West Virginia</td><td>41.4</td><td>48</td><td>New Mexico</td><td>34.7</td></tr>
<tr><td>10</td><td>Wisconsin</td><td>51.0</td><td>49</td><td>Alabama</td><td>33.9</td></tr>
<tr><td>47</td><td>Wyoming</td><td>35.6</td><td>50</td><td>Alaska</td><td>24.3</td></tr>
<tr><td></td><td></td><td></td><td></td><td>District of Columbia</td><td>50.7</td></tr>
</table>

Source: CQ Press using data from U.S. Bureau of the Census, Governments Division
"2016 State and Local Government Finances" (https://www.census.gov/programs-surveys/gov-finances.html)

State and Local Government Tax Revenue as a Percent of Personal Income in 2016
National Percent = 9.9% of Personal Income*

ALPHA ORDER

RANK	STATE	PERCENT
45	Alabama	8.2
50	Alaska	6.8
35	Arizona	8.8
18	Arkansas	10.0
10	California	10.6
35	Colorado	8.8
13	Connecticut	10.4
21	Delaware	9.9
49	Florida	7.5
40	Georgia	8.6
2	Hawaii	12.7
37	Idaho	8.7
8	Illinois	10.8
33	Indiana	8.9
12	Iowa	10.5
28	Kansas	9.5
25	Kentucky	9.7
30	Louisiana	9.1
5	Maine	11.6
14	Maryland	10.3
21	Massachusetts	9.9
30	Michigan	9.1
6	Minnesota	11.5
16	Mississippi	10.1
43	Missouri	8.4
37	Montana	8.7
15	Nebraska	10.2
27	Nevada	9.6
43	New Hampshire	8.4
8	New Jersey	10.8
18	New Mexico	10.0
1	New York	14.7
29	North Carolina	9.2
3	North Dakota	12.6
21	Ohio	9.9
45	Oklahoma	8.2
25	Oregon	9.7
24	Pennsylvania	9.8
7	Rhode Island	10.9
42	South Carolina	8.5
47	South Dakota	8.1
48	Tennessee	7.6
37	Texas	8.7
33	Utah	8.9
4	Vermont	11.7
40	Virginia	8.6
30	Washington	9.1
10	West Virginia	10.6
16	Wisconsin	10.1
18	Wyoming	10.0

RANK ORDER

RANK	STATE	PERCENT
1	New York	14.7
2	Hawaii	12.7
3	North Dakota	12.6
4	Vermont	11.7
5	Maine	11.6
6	Minnesota	11.5
7	Rhode Island	10.9
8	Illinois	10.8
8	New Jersey	10.8
10	California	10.6
10	West Virginia	10.6
12	Iowa	10.5
13	Connecticut	10.4
14	Maryland	10.3
15	Nebraska	10.2
16	Mississippi	10.1
16	Wisconsin	10.1
18	Arkansas	10.0
18	New Mexico	10.0
18	Wyoming	10.0
21	Delaware	9.9
21	Massachusetts	9.9
21	Ohio	9.9
24	Pennsylvania	9.8
25	Kentucky	9.7
25	Oregon	9.7
27	Nevada	9.6
28	Kansas	9.5
29	North Carolina	9.2
30	Louisiana	9.1
30	Michigan	9.1
30	Washington	9.1
33	Indiana	8.9
33	Utah	8.9
35	Arizona	8.8
35	Colorado	8.8
37	Idaho	8.7
37	Montana	8.7
37	Texas	8.7
40	Georgia	8.6
40	Virginia	8.6
42	South Carolina	8.5
43	Missouri	8.4
43	New Hampshire	8.4
45	Alabama	8.2
45	Oklahoma	8.2
47	South Dakota	8.1
48	Tennessee	7.6
49	Florida	7.5
50	Alaska	6.8

| | District of Columbia | 14.0 |

Source: CQ Press using data from U.S. Bureau of the Census, Governments Division
"Annual State Personal Income" (https://apps.bea.gov/iTable/index_regional.cfm) and
"2016 State and Local Government Finances" (https://www.census.gov/programs-surveys/gov-finances.html)
*The personal income total used for this table is the sum of state estimates. This total differs from the national income and product accounts (NIPA) estimate of personal income because it omits the earnings of federal civilian and military personnel stationed abroad and of U.S. residents employed abroad temporarily by private U.S. firms.

State and Local Government General Sales Tax Revenue in 2016

National Total = $376,980,434,000*

ALPHA ORDER					RANK ORDER			
RANK	STATE	REVENUE	% of USA		RANK	STATE	REVENUE	% of USA
24	Alabama	$4,784,981,000	1.3%		1	California	$52,355,605,000	13.9%
46	Alaska	234,526,000	0.1%		2	Texas	39,750,736,000	10.5%
10	Arizona	9,587,284,000	2.5%		3	New York	29,754,771,000	7.9%
27	Arkansas	4,432,850,000	1.2%		4	Florida	24,521,655,000	6.5%
1	California	52,355,605,000	13.9%		5	Washington	17,068,353,000	4.5%
17	Colorado	6,770,833,000	1.8%		6	Ohio	14,636,239,000	3.9%
30	Connecticut	3,752,793,000	1.0%		7	Illinois	14,008,593,000	3.7%
47	Delaware	0	0.0%		8	Pennsylvania	11,135,202,000	3.0%
4	Florida	24,521,655,000	6.5%		9	North Carolina	9,964,550,000	2.6%
14	Georgia	9,077,701,000	2.4%		10	Arizona	9,587,284,000	2.5%
33	Hawaii	3,439,477,000	0.9%		11	New Jersey	9,267,703,000	2.5%
38	Idaho	1,562,111,000	0.4%		12	Tennessee	9,170,847,000	2.4%
7	Illinois	14,008,593,000	3.7%		13	Michigan	9,163,542,000	2.4%
16	Indiana	7,306,331,000	1.9%		14	Georgia	9,077,701,000	2.4%
31	Iowa	3,480,691,000	0.9%		15	Louisiana	7,468,561,000	2.0%
28	Kansas	4,198,462,000	1.1%		16	Indiana	7,306,331,000	1.9%
32	Kentucky	3,462,704,000	0.9%		17	Colorado	6,770,833,000	1.8%
15	Louisiana	7,468,561,000	2.0%		18	Missouri	6,127,314,000	1.6%
39	Maine	1,359,190,000	0.4%		19	Massachusetts	6,089,860,000	1.6%
26	Maryland	4,504,242,000	1.2%		20	Minnesota	5,743,795,000	1.5%
19	Massachusetts	6,089,860,000	1.6%		21	Wisconsin	5,461,241,000	1.4%
13	Michigan	9,163,542,000	2.4%		22	Virginia	5,286,082,000	1.4%
20	Minnesota	5,743,795,000	1.5%		23	Nevada	4,947,528,000	1.3%
34	Mississippi	3,297,760,000	0.9%		24	Alabama	4,784,981,000	1.3%
18	Missouri	6,127,314,000	1.6%		25	Oklahoma	4,509,859,000	1.2%
47	Montana	0	0.0%		26	Maryland	4,504,242,000	1.2%
37	Nebraska	2,173,027,000	0.6%		27	Arkansas	4,432,850,000	1.2%
23	Nevada	4,947,528,000	1.3%		28	Kansas	4,198,462,000	1.1%
47	New Hampshire	0	0.0%		29	South Carolina	3,767,174,000	1.0%
11	New Jersey	9,267,703,000	2.5%		30	Connecticut	3,752,793,000	1.0%
35	New Mexico	3,066,700,000	0.8%		31	Iowa	3,480,691,000	0.9%
3	New York	29,754,771,000	7.9%		32	Kentucky	3,462,704,000	0.9%
9	North Carolina	9,964,550,000	2.6%		33	Hawaii	3,439,477,000	0.9%
42	North Dakota	1,282,114,000	0.3%		34	Mississippi	3,297,760,000	0.9%
6	Ohio	14,636,239,000	3.9%		35	New Mexico	3,066,700,000	0.8%
25	Oklahoma	4,509,859,000	1.2%		36	Utah	2,826,292,000	0.7%
47	Oregon	0	0.0%		37	Nebraska	2,173,027,000	0.6%
8	Pennsylvania	11,135,202,000	3.0%		38	Idaho	1,562,111,000	0.4%
43	Rhode Island	973,585,000	0.3%		39	Maine	1,359,190,000	0.4%
29	South Carolina	3,767,174,000	1.0%		40	South Dakota	1,342,390,000	0.4%
40	South Dakota	1,342,390,000	0.4%		41	West Virginia	1,320,903,000	0.4%
12	Tennessee	9,170,847,000	2.4%		42	North Dakota	1,282,114,000	0.3%
2	Texas	39,750,736,000	10.5%		43	Rhode Island	973,585,000	0.3%
36	Utah	2,826,292,000	0.7%		44	Wyoming	816,550,000	0.2%
45	Vermont	384,535,000	0.1%		45	Vermont	384,535,000	0.1%
22	Virginia	5,286,082,000	1.4%		46	Alaska	234,526,000	0.1%
5	Washington	17,068,353,000	4.5%		47	Delaware	0	0.0%
41	West Virginia	1,320,903,000	0.4%		47	Montana	0	0.0%
21	Wisconsin	5,461,241,000	1.4%		47	New Hampshire	0	0.0%
44	Wyoming	816,550,000	0.2%		47	Oregon	0	0.0%
						District of Columbia	1,343,192,000	0.4%

Source: U.S. Bureau of the Census, Governments Division
   "2016 State and Local Government Finances" (https://www.census.gov/programs-surveys/gov-finances.html)
*Does not include special sales taxes such as those on sale of alcohol, gasoline, or tobacco.

Per Capita State and Local Government General Sales Tax Revenue in 2016

National Per Capita = $1,167*

ALPHA ORDER			RANK ORDER		
RANK	STATE	PER CAPITA	RANK	STATE	PER CAPITA
30	Alabama	$984	1	Hawaii	$2,408
46	Alaska	316	2	Washington	2,340
13	Arizona	1,380	3	North Dakota	1,700
8	Arkansas	1,482	4	Nevada	1,694
15	California	1,335	5	Louisiana	1,596
17	Colorado	1,222	6	South Dakota	1,556
25	Connecticut	1,049	7	New York	1,515
47	Delaware	0	8	Arkansas	1,482
18	Florida	1,189	9	New Mexico	1,465
38	Georgia	881	10	Kansas	1,442
1	Hawaii	2,408	11	Texas	1,423
34	Idaho	928	12	Wyoming	1,398
24	Illinois	1,092	13	Arizona	1,380
23	Indiana	1,101	13	Tennessee	1,380
21	Iowa	1,111	15	California	1,335
10	Kansas	1,442	16	Ohio	1,258
40	Kentucky	780	17	Colorado	1,222
5	Louisiana	1,596	18	Florida	1,189
28	Maine	1,021	19	Oklahoma	1,148
42	Maryland	750	20	Nebraska	1,140
37	Massachusetts	892	21	Iowa	1,111
35	Michigan	921	22	Mississippi	1,104
27	Minnesota	1,040	23	Indiana	1,101
22	Mississippi	1,104	24	Illinois	1,092
29	Missouri	1,007	25	Connecticut	1,049
47	Montana	0	26	New Jersey	1,044
20	Nebraska	1,140	27	Minnesota	1,040
4	Nevada	1,694	28	Maine	1,021
47	New Hampshire	0	29	Missouri	1,007
26	New Jersey	1,044	30	Alabama	984
9	New Mexico	1,465	31	North Carolina	981
7	New York	1,515	32	Wisconsin	946
31	North Carolina	981	33	Utah	929
3	North Dakota	1,700	34	Idaho	928
16	Ohio	1,258	35	Michigan	921
19	Oklahoma	1,148	35	Rhode Island	921
47	Oregon	0	37	Massachusetts	892
39	Pennsylvania	871	38	Georgia	881
35	Rhode Island	921	39	Pennsylvania	871
41	South Carolina	760	40	Kentucky	780
6	South Dakota	1,556	41	South Carolina	760
13	Tennessee	1,380	42	Maryland	750
11	Texas	1,423	43	West Virginia	721
33	Utah	929	44	Virginia	628
45	Vermont	617	45	Vermont	617
44	Virginia	628	46	Alaska	316
2	Washington	2,340	47	Delaware	0
43	West Virginia	721	47	Montana	0
32	Wisconsin	946	47	New Hampshire	0
12	Wyoming	1,398	47	Oregon	0
				District of Columbia	1,956

Source: CQ Press using data from U.S. Bureau of the Census, Governments Division

"2016 State and Local Government Finances" (https://www.census.gov/programs-surveys/gov-finances.html)

*Does not include special sales taxes such as those on sale of alcohol, gasoline, or tobacco.

State and Local Government General Retail Sales Tax Rates in 2018

National Median = 6.80 Percent*

ALPHA ORDER

RANK	STATE	PERCENT
5	Alabama	9.10
46	Alaska	1.76
11	Arizona	8.33
3	Arkansas	9.41
9	California	8.54
16	Colorado	7.52
33	Connecticut	6.35
47	Delaware	0.00
26	Florida	6.80
19	Georgia	7.15
45	Hawaii	4.35
37	Idaho	6.03
7	Illinois	8.70
22	Indiana	7.00
26	Iowa	6.80
8	Kansas	8.68
38	Kentucky	6.00
1	Louisiana	10.02
42	Maine	5.50
38	Maryland	6.00
35	Massachusetts	6.25
38	Michigan	6.00
17	Minnesota	7.42
21	Mississippi	7.07
14	Missouri	8.03
47	Montana	0.00
25	Nebraska	6.89
13	Nevada	8.14
47	New Hampshire	0.00
30	New Jersey	6.60
15	New Mexico	7.66
10	New York	8.49
24	North Carolina	6.95
26	North Dakota	6.80
19	Ohio	7.15
6	Oklahoma	8.91
47	Oregon	0.00
34	Pennsylvania	6.34
22	Rhode Island	7.00
18	South Carolina	7.37
31	South Dakota	6.40
2	Tennessee	9.46
12	Texas	8.17
29	Utah	6.77
36	Vermont	6.18
41	Virginia	5.63
4	Washington	9.18
32	West Virginia	6.37
44	Wisconsin	5.42
43	Wyoming	5.46

RANK ORDER

RANK	STATE	PERCENT
1	Louisiana	10.02
2	Tennessee	9.46
3	Arkansas	9.41
4	Washington	9.18
5	Alabama	9.10
6	Oklahoma	8.91
7	Illinois	8.70
8	Kansas	8.68
9	California	8.54
10	New York	8.49
11	Arizona	8.33
12	Texas	8.17
13	Nevada	8.14
14	Missouri	8.03
15	New Mexico	7.66
16	Colorado	7.52
17	Minnesota	7.42
18	South Carolina	7.37
19	Georgia	7.15
19	Ohio	7.15
21	Mississippi	7.07
22	Indiana	7.00
22	Rhode Island	7.00
24	North Carolina	6.95
25	Nebraska	6.89
26	Florida	6.80
26	Iowa	6.80
26	North Dakota	6.80
29	Utah	6.77
30	New Jersey	6.60
31	South Dakota	6.40
32	West Virginia	6.37
33	Connecticut	6.35
34	Pennsylvania	6.34
35	Massachusetts	6.25
36	Vermont	6.18
37	Idaho	6.03
38	Kentucky	6.00
38	Maryland	6.00
38	Michigan	6.00
41	Virginia	5.63
42	Maine	5.50
43	Wyoming	5.46
44	Wisconsin	5.42
45	Hawaii	4.35
46	Alaska	1.76
47	Delaware	0.00
47	Montana	0.00
47	New Hampshire	0.00
47	Oregon	0.00

District of Columbia	5.75

Source: The Tax Foundation

"State and Local Sales Tax Rates in 2018" (https://taxfoundation.org/state-and-local-sales-tax-rates-2018/)

*As of January 1, 2018. There are great differences on what states exempt from sales taxes. These rates are based on average local rates where local governments can set different tax rates.

State and Local Government Property Tax Revenue in 2016

National Total = $503,262,149,000

ALPHA ORDER

RANK	STATE	REVENUE	% of USA
37	Alabama	$2,664,939,000	0.5%
46	Alaska	1,517,902,000	0.3%
20	Arizona	7,335,486,000	1.5%
39	Arkansas	2,126,572,000	0.4%
1	California	61,266,035,000	12.2%
19	Colorado	7,879,825,000	1.6%
13	Connecticut	10,501,407,000	2.1%
50	Delaware	819,763,000	0.2%
6	Florida	26,098,485,000	5.2%
12	Georgia	11,957,637,000	2.4%
41	Hawaii	1,629,213,000	0.3%
44	Idaho	1,586,295,000	0.3%
5	Illinois	27,210,946,000	5.4%
21	Indiana	6,417,679,000	1.3%
26	Iowa	4,953,594,000	1.0%
27	Kansas	4,331,278,000	0.9%
31	Kentucky	3,437,591,000	0.7%
29	Louisiana	4,154,951,000	0.8%
35	Maine	2,799,804,000	0.6%
17	Maryland	9,319,099,000	1.9%
8	Massachusetts	16,085,279,000	3.2%
10	Michigan	14,039,225,000	2.8%
18	Minnesota	8,658,731,000	1.7%
33	Mississippi	2,949,828,000	0.6%
22	Missouri	5,916,722,000	1.2%
45	Montana	1,578,300,000	0.3%
30	Nebraska	3,642,245,000	0.7%
34	Nevada	2,923,029,000	0.6%
28	New Hampshire	4,159,186,000	0.8%
4	New Jersey	28,078,904,000	5.6%
43	New Mexico	1,602,481,000	0.3%
2	New York	55,176,119,000	11.0%
15	North Carolina	9,906,032,000	2.0%
49	North Dakota	979,445,000	0.2%
9	Ohio	14,689,729,000	2.9%
36	Oklahoma	2,741,393,000	0.5%
23	Oregon	5,901,314,000	1.2%
7	Pennsylvania	18,894,224,000	3.8%
38	Rhode Island	2,554,186,000	0.5%
24	South Carolina	5,772,550,000	1.1%
48	South Dakota	1,201,255,000	0.2%
25	Tennessee	5,559,994,000	1.1%
3	Texas	49,167,498,000	9.8%
32	Utah	3,100,857,000	0.6%
42	Vermont	1,616,283,000	0.3%
11	Virginia	13,001,233,000	2.6%
14	Washington	10,458,113,000	2.1%
40	West Virginia	1,673,725,000	0.3%
16	Wisconsin	9,406,961,000	1.9%
47	Wyoming	1,399,911,000	0.3%

RANK ORDER

RANK	STATE	REVENUE	% of USA
1	California	$61,266,035,000	12.2%
2	New York	55,176,119,000	11.0%
3	Texas	49,167,498,000	9.8%
4	New Jersey	28,078,904,000	5.6%
5	Illinois	27,210,946,000	5.4%
6	Florida	26,098,485,000	5.2%
7	Pennsylvania	18,894,224,000	3.8%
8	Massachusetts	16,085,279,000	3.2%
9	Ohio	14,689,729,000	2.9%
10	Michigan	14,039,225,000	2.8%
11	Virginia	13,001,233,000	2.6%
12	Georgia	11,957,637,000	2.4%
13	Connecticut	10,501,407,000	2.1%
14	Washington	10,458,113,000	2.1%
15	North Carolina	9,906,032,000	2.0%
16	Wisconsin	9,406,961,000	1.9%
17	Maryland	9,319,099,000	1.9%
18	Minnesota	8,658,731,000	1.7%
19	Colorado	7,879,825,000	1.6%
20	Arizona	7,335,486,000	1.5%
21	Indiana	6,417,679,000	1.3%
22	Missouri	5,916,722,000	1.2%
23	Oregon	5,901,314,000	1.2%
24	South Carolina	5,772,550,000	1.1%
25	Tennessee	5,559,994,000	1.1%
26	Iowa	4,953,594,000	1.0%
27	Kansas	4,331,278,000	0.9%
28	New Hampshire	4,159,186,000	0.8%
29	Louisiana	4,154,951,000	0.8%
30	Nebraska	3,642,245,000	0.7%
31	Kentucky	3,437,591,000	0.7%
32	Utah	3,100,857,000	0.6%
33	Mississippi	2,949,828,000	0.6%
34	Nevada	2,923,029,000	0.6%
35	Maine	2,799,804,000	0.6%
36	Oklahoma	2,741,393,000	0.5%
37	Alabama	2,664,939,000	0.5%
38	Rhode Island	2,554,186,000	0.5%
39	Arkansas	2,126,572,000	0.4%
40	West Virginia	1,673,725,000	0.3%
41	Hawaii	1,629,213,000	0.3%
42	Vermont	1,616,283,000	0.3%
43	New Mexico	1,602,481,000	0.3%
44	Idaho	1,586,295,000	0.3%
45	Montana	1,578,300,000	0.3%
46	Alaska	1,517,902,000	0.3%
47	Wyoming	1,399,911,000	0.3%
48	South Dakota	1,201,255,000	0.2%
49	North Dakota	979,445,000	0.2%
50	Delaware	819,763,000	0.2%
	District of Columbia	2,418,896,000	0.5%

Source: U.S. Bureau of the Census, Governments Division
"2016 State and Local Government Finances" (https://www.census.gov/programs-surveys/gov-finances.html)

Per Capita State and Local Government Property Tax Revenue in 2016

National Per Capita = $1,558

ALPHA ORDER

RANK	STATE	PER CAPITA
50	Alabama	$548
11	Alaska	2,047
34	Arizona	1,056
48	Arkansas	711
17	California	1,563
25	Colorado	1,422
3	Connecticut	2,934
44	Delaware	864
29	Florida	1,265
32	Georgia	1,160
33	Hawaii	1,141
41	Idaho	943
9	Illinois	2,121
40	Indiana	967
15	Iowa	1,582
21	Kansas	1,488
46	Kentucky	775
43	Louisiana	888
10	Maine	2,103
18	Maryland	1,552
8	Massachusetts	2,356
26	Michigan	1,411
16	Minnesota	1,568
37	Mississippi	987
39	Missouri	972
20	Montana	1,516
12	Nebraska	1,911
36	Nevada	1,001
2	New Hampshire	3,098
1	New Jersey	3,164
47	New Mexico	766
4	New York	2,809
38	North Carolina	975
28	North Dakota	1,298
30	Ohio	1,263
49	Oklahoma	698
23	Oregon	1,442
22	Pennsylvania	1,478
6	Rhode Island	2,416
31	South Carolina	1,164
27	South Dakota	1,392
45	Tennessee	837
13	Texas	1,760
35	Utah	1,019
5	Vermont	2,592
19	Virginia	1,546
24	Washington	1,434
42	West Virginia	914
14	Wisconsin	1,629
7	Wyoming	2,396

RANK ORDER

RANK	STATE	PER CAPITA
1	New Jersey	$3,164
2	New Hampshire	3,098
3	Connecticut	2,934
4	New York	2,809
5	Vermont	2,592
6	Rhode Island	2,416
7	Wyoming	2,396
8	Massachusetts	2,356
9	Illinois	2,121
10	Maine	2,103
11	Alaska	2,047
12	Nebraska	1,911
13	Texas	1,760
14	Wisconsin	1,629
15	Iowa	1,582
16	Minnesota	1,568
17	California	1,563
18	Maryland	1,552
19	Virginia	1,546
20	Montana	1,516
21	Kansas	1,488
22	Pennsylvania	1,478
23	Oregon	1,442
24	Washington	1,434
25	Colorado	1,422
26	Michigan	1,411
27	South Dakota	1,392
28	North Dakota	1,298
29	Florida	1,265
30	Ohio	1,263
31	South Carolina	1,164
32	Georgia	1,160
33	Hawaii	1,141
34	Arizona	1,056
35	Utah	1,019
36	Nevada	1,001
37	Mississippi	987
38	North Carolina	975
39	Missouri	972
40	Indiana	967
41	Idaho	943
42	West Virginia	914
43	Louisiana	888
44	Delaware	864
45	Tennessee	837
46	Kentucky	775
47	New Mexico	766
48	Arkansas	711
49	Oklahoma	698
50	Alabama	548

District of Columbia   3,523

Source: CQ Press using data from U.S. Bureau of the Census, Governments Division
"2016 State and Local Government Finances" (https://www.census.gov/programs-surveys/gov-finances.html)

State and Local Government Property Tax as a Percent of State and Local Government Total Revenue in 2016
National Percent = 14.8%

ALPHA ORDER

RANK	STATE	PERCENT
50	Alabama	5.8
26	Alaska	13.0
30	Arizona	12.4
48	Arkansas	7.9
33	California	11.9
21	Colorado	14.3
3	Connecticut	25.0
47	Delaware	8.0
15	Florida	16.0
19	Georgia	15.2
44	Hawaii	9.4
32	Idaho	12.1
6	Illinois	21.0
38	Indiana	10.9
23	Iowa	14.0
17	Kansas	15.6
45	Kentucky	8.5
43	Louisiana	9.6
4	Maine	22.0
20	Maryland	14.5
9	Massachusetts	18.7
22	Michigan	14.2
25	Minnesota	13.6
39	Mississippi	10.1
34	Missouri	11.3
12	Montana	16.7
15	Nebraska	16.0
36	Nevada	11.1
1	New Hampshire	32.9
2	New Jersey	27.1
49	New Mexico	6.8
11	New York	16.8
37	North Carolina	11.0
40	North Dakota	9.9
28	Ohio	12.5
46	Oklahoma	8.3
28	Oregon	12.5
23	Pennsylvania	14.0
5	Rhode Island	21.7
27	South Carolina	12.6
14	South Dakota	16.2
41	Tennessee	9.8
8	Texas	20.0
34	Utah	11.3
7	Vermont	20.9
13	Virginia	16.5
31	Washington	12.3
42	West Virginia	9.7
10	Wisconsin	17.4
18	Wyoming	15.4

RANK ORDER

RANK	STATE	PERCENT
1	New Hampshire	32.9
2	New Jersey	27.1
3	Connecticut	25.0
4	Maine	22.0
5	Rhode Island	21.7
6	Illinois	21.0
7	Vermont	20.9
8	Texas	20.0
9	Massachusetts	18.7
10	Wisconsin	17.4
11	New York	16.8
12	Montana	16.7
13	Virginia	16.5
14	South Dakota	16.2
15	Florida	16.0
15	Nebraska	16.0
17	Kansas	15.6
18	Wyoming	15.4
19	Georgia	15.2
20	Maryland	14.5
21	Colorado	14.3
22	Michigan	14.2
23	Iowa	14.0
23	Pennsylvania	14.0
25	Minnesota	13.6
26	Alaska	13.0
27	South Carolina	12.6
28	Ohio	12.5
28	Oregon	12.5
30	Arizona	12.4
31	Washington	12.3
32	Idaho	12.1
33	California	11.9
34	Missouri	11.3
34	Utah	11.3
36	Nevada	11.1
37	North Carolina	11.0
38	Indiana	10.9
39	Mississippi	10.1
40	North Dakota	9.9
41	Tennessee	9.8
42	West Virginia	9.7
43	Louisiana	9.6
44	Hawaii	9.4
45	Kentucky	8.5
46	Oklahoma	8.3
47	Delaware	8.0
48	Arkansas	7.9
49	New Mexico	6.8
50	Alabama	5.8
	District of Columbia	16.5

Source: CQ Press using data from U.S. Bureau of the Census, Governments Division
"2016 State and Local Government Finances" (https://www.census.gov/programs-surveys/gov-finances.html)

State and Local Government Property Tax Revenue as a Percent of State and Local Government Own Source Revenue in 2016
National Percent = 21.7%*

ALPHA ORDER				RANK ORDER		
RANK	STATE	PERCENT		RANK	STATE	PERCENT
50	Alabama	9.6		1	New Hampshire	47.0
26	Alaska	19.8		2	New Jersey	35.8
21	Arizona	20.7		3	Connecticut	33.7
45	Arkansas	12.5		4	Vermont	33.0
33	California	17.9		5	Rhode Island	31.5
24	Colorado	20.2		6	Maine	31.3
3	Connecticut	33.7		7	Texas	29.6
49	Delaware	11.2		8	Illinois	29.1
16	Florida	22.3		9	Montana	27.3
19	Georgia	22.0		10	Massachusetts	27.1
46	Hawaii	12.4		11	Nebraska	26.0
32	Idaho	18.1		12	New York	23.8
8	Illinois	29.1		13	South Dakota	23.7
40	Indiana	15.9		14	Wisconsin	23.6
23	Iowa	20.3		15	Wyoming	23.5
21	Kansas	20.7		16	Florida	22.3
43	Kentucky	13.9		17	Michigan	22.1
41	Louisiana	14.9		17	Virginia	22.1
6	Maine	31.3		19	Georgia	22.0
25	Maryland	20.0		20	Pennsylvania	20.8
10	Massachusetts	27.1		21	Arizona	20.7
17	Michigan	22.1		21	Kansas	20.7
29	Minnesota	18.7		23	Iowa	20.3
37	Mississippi	16.5		24	Colorado	20.2
34	Missouri	17.3		25	Maryland	20.0
9	Montana	27.3		26	Alaska	19.8
11	Nebraska	26.0		27	Oregon	19.6
35	Nevada	17.0		28	Ohio	18.9
1	New Hampshire	47.0		29	Minnesota	18.7
2	New Jersey	35.8		29	Washington	18.7
48	New Mexico	11.8		31	South Carolina	18.2
12	New York	23.8		32	Idaho	18.1
39	North Carolina	16.0		33	California	17.9
44	North Dakota	13.6		34	Missouri	17.3
28	Ohio	18.9		35	Nevada	17.0
46	Oklahoma	12.4		36	Tennessee	16.6
27	Oregon	19.6		37	Mississippi	16.5
20	Pennsylvania	20.8		38	Utah	16.4
5	Rhode Island	31.5		39	North Carolina	16.0
31	South Carolina	18.2		40	Indiana	15.9
13	South Dakota	23.7		41	Louisiana	14.9
36	Tennessee	16.6		42	West Virginia	14.8
7	Texas	29.6		43	Kentucky	13.9
38	Utah	16.4		44	North Dakota	13.6
4	Vermont	33.0		45	Arkansas	12.5
17	Virginia	22.1		46	Hawaii	12.4
29	Washington	18.7		46	Oklahoma	12.4
42	West Virginia	14.8		48	New Mexico	11.8
14	Wisconsin	23.6		49	Delaware	11.2
15	Wyoming	23.5		50	Alabama	9.6

District of Columbia 26.5

Source: CQ Press using data from U.S. Bureau of the Census, Governments Division
"2016 State and Local Government Finances" (https://www.census.gov/programs-surveys/gov-finances.html)
*Own source revenue includes taxes, current charges, and miscellaneous general revenue. Excluded are intergovernmental transfers, insurance trust revenue, and revenue from government owned utilities and other commercial or auxiliary enterprise.

State and Local Tax Burden as a Percent of Income in 2016

National Percent = 8.9% of Income*

ALPHA ORDER

RANK	STATE	PERCENT
42	Alabama	7.3
50	Alaska	5.1
28	Arizona	8.2
16	Arkansas	9.1
10	California	9.5
34	Colorado	8.1
8	Connecticut	9.7
49	Delaware	5.5
47	Florida	6.5
34	Georgia	8.1
2	Hawaii	11.7
39	Idaho	7.7
9	Illinois	9.6
28	Indiana	8.2
10	Iowa	9.5
21	Kansas	8.7
19	Kentucky	8.8
24	Louisiana	8.5
3	Maine	10.8
12	Maryland	9.3
19	Massachusetts	8.8
25	Michigan	8.4
5	Minnesota	10.3
16	Mississippi	9.1
37	Missouri	7.8
42	Montana	7.3
14	Nebraska	9.2
28	Nevada	8.2
46	New Hampshire	6.9
7	New Jersey	9.9
22	New Mexico	8.6
1	New York	13.0
25	North Carolina	8.4
36	North Dakota	7.9
12	Ohio	9.3
45	Oklahoma	7.1
27	Oregon	8.3
22	Pennsylvania	8.6
5	Rhode Island	10.3
40	South Carolina	7.5
42	South Dakota	7.3
48	Tennessee	6.3
28	Texas	8.2
28	Utah	8.2
4	Vermont	10.7
37	Virginia	7.8
28	Washington	8.2
14	West Virginia	9.2
16	Wisconsin	9.1
40	Wyoming	7.5

RANK ORDER

RANK	STATE	PERCENT
1	New York	13.0
2	Hawaii	11.7
3	Maine	10.8
4	Vermont	10.7
5	Minnesota	10.3
5	Rhode Island	10.3
7	New Jersey	9.9
8	Connecticut	9.7
9	Illinois	9.6
10	California	9.5
10	Iowa	9.5
12	Maryland	9.3
12	Ohio	9.3
14	Nebraska	9.2
14	West Virginia	9.2
16	Arkansas	9.1
16	Mississippi	9.1
16	Wisconsin	9.1
19	Kentucky	8.8
19	Massachusetts	8.8
21	Kansas	8.7
22	New Mexico	8.6
22	Pennsylvania	8.6
24	Louisiana	8.5
25	Michigan	8.4
25	North Carolina	8.4
27	Oregon	8.3
28	Arizona	8.2
28	Indiana	8.2
28	Nevada	8.2
28	Texas	8.2
28	Utah	8.2
28	Washington	8.2
34	Colorado	8.1
34	Georgia	8.1
36	North Dakota	7.9
37	Missouri	7.8
37	Virginia	7.8
39	Idaho	7.7
40	South Carolina	7.5
40	Wyoming	7.5
42	Alabama	7.3
42	Montana	7.3
42	South Dakota	7.3
45	Oklahoma	7.1
46	New Hampshire	6.9
47	Florida	6.5
48	Tennessee	6.3
49	Delaware	5.5
50	Alaska	5.1

District of Columbia 11.6

Source: CQ Press using data from U.S. Bureau of the Census, Governments Division
"Annual State Personal Income" (http://www.bea.gov/iTable/index_regional.cfm) and
"2016 State and Local Government Finances" (https://www.census.gov/programs-surveys/gov-finances.html)
*Calculated using property taxes, personal income taxes, and sales and gross receipts taxes.

State and Local Government Total Expenditures in 2016

National Total = $3,517,971,479,000*

<table>
<tr><td colspan="4"><u>ALPHA ORDER</u></td><td colspan="4"><u>RANK ORDER</u></td></tr>
<tr><td>RANK</td><td>STATE</td><td>EXPENDITURES</td><td>% of USA</td><td>RANK</td><td>STATE</td><td>EXPENDITURES</td><td>% of USA</td></tr>
<tr><td>28</td><td>Alabama</td><td>$45,277,563,000</td><td>1.3%</td><td>1</td><td>California</td><td>$535,759,667,000</td><td>15.2%</td></tr>
<tr><td>40</td><td>Alaska</td><td>15,808,697,000</td><td>0.4%</td><td>2</td><td>New York</td><td>331,281,858,000</td><td>9.4%</td></tr>
<tr><td>18</td><td>Arizona</td><td>58,975,013,000</td><td>1.7%</td><td>3</td><td>Texas</td><td>252,400,912,000</td><td>7.2%</td></tr>
<tr><td>34</td><td>Arkansas</td><td>27,300,171,000</td><td>0.8%</td><td>4</td><td>Florida</td><td>167,229,459,000</td><td>4.8%</td></tr>
<tr><td>1</td><td>California</td><td>535,759,667,000</td><td>15.2%</td><td>5</td><td>Pennsylvania</td><td>143,554,132,000</td><td>4.1%</td></tr>
<tr><td>21</td><td>Colorado</td><td>57,298,776,000</td><td>1.6%</td><td>6</td><td>Illinois</td><td>139,837,137,000</td><td>4.0%</td></tr>
<tr><td>26</td><td>Connecticut</td><td>45,649,898,000</td><td>1.3%</td><td>7</td><td>Ohio</td><td>125,579,570,000</td><td>3.6%</td></tr>
<tr><td>45</td><td>Delaware</td><td>11,413,963,000</td><td>0.3%</td><td>8</td><td>New Jersey</td><td>109,767,828,000</td><td>3.1%</td></tr>
<tr><td>4</td><td>Florida</td><td>167,229,459,000</td><td>4.8%</td><td>9</td><td>Michigan</td><td>96,622,086,000</td><td>2.7%</td></tr>
<tr><td>13</td><td>Georgia</td><td>82,188,266,000</td><td>2.3%</td><td>10</td><td>Massachusetts</td><td>89,563,251,000</td><td>2.5%</td></tr>
<tr><td>39</td><td>Hawaii</td><td>16,217,724,000</td><td>0.5%</td><td>11</td><td>North Carolina</td><td>88,950,464,000</td><td>2.5%</td></tr>
<tr><td>43</td><td>Idaho</td><td>12,506,304,000</td><td>0.4%</td><td>12</td><td>Washington</td><td>86,881,984,000</td><td>2.5%</td></tr>
<tr><td>6</td><td>Illinois</td><td>139,837,137,000</td><td>4.0%</td><td>13</td><td>Georgia</td><td>82,188,266,000</td><td>2.3%</td></tr>
<tr><td>19</td><td>Indiana</td><td>57,921,968,000</td><td>1.6%</td><td>14</td><td>Virginia</td><td>80,156,488,000</td><td>2.3%</td></tr>
<tr><td>29</td><td>Iowa</td><td>34,916,262,000</td><td>1.0%</td><td>15</td><td>Maryland</td><td>67,447,139,000</td><td>1.9%</td></tr>
<tr><td>32</td><td>Kansas</td><td>28,791,130,000</td><td>0.8%</td><td>16</td><td>Minnesota</td><td>65,611,257,000</td><td>1.9%</td></tr>
<tr><td>27</td><td>Kentucky</td><td>45,455,165,000</td><td>1.3%</td><td>17</td><td>Wisconsin</td><td>59,534,828,000</td><td>1.7%</td></tr>
<tr><td>25</td><td>Louisiana</td><td>47,492,664,000</td><td>1.4%</td><td>18</td><td>Arizona</td><td>58,975,013,000</td><td>1.7%</td></tr>
<tr><td>41</td><td>Maine</td><td>12,973,463,000</td><td>0.4%</td><td>19</td><td>Indiana</td><td>57,921,968,000</td><td>1.6%</td></tr>
<tr><td>15</td><td>Maryland</td><td>67,447,139,000</td><td>1.9%</td><td>20</td><td>Tennessee</td><td>57,758,388,000</td><td>1.6%</td></tr>
<tr><td>10</td><td>Massachusetts</td><td>89,563,251,000</td><td>2.5%</td><td>21</td><td>Colorado</td><td>57,298,776,000</td><td>1.6%</td></tr>
<tr><td>9</td><td>Michigan</td><td>96,622,086,000</td><td>2.7%</td><td>22</td><td>Missouri</td><td>53,642,230,000</td><td>1.5%</td></tr>
<tr><td>16</td><td>Minnesota</td><td>65,611,257,000</td><td>1.9%</td><td>23</td><td>Oregon</td><td>49,654,207,000</td><td>1.4%</td></tr>
<tr><td>31</td><td>Mississippi</td><td>29,930,149,000</td><td>0.9%</td><td>24</td><td>South Carolina</td><td>47,533,649,000</td><td>1.4%</td></tr>
<tr><td>22</td><td>Missouri</td><td>53,642,230,000</td><td>1.5%</td><td>25</td><td>Louisiana</td><td>47,492,664,000</td><td>1.4%</td></tr>
<tr><td>48</td><td>Montana</td><td>10,007,594,000</td><td>0.3%</td><td>26</td><td>Connecticut</td><td>45,649,898,000</td><td>1.3%</td></tr>
<tr><td>37</td><td>Nebraska</td><td>23,071,752,000</td><td>0.7%</td><td>27</td><td>Kentucky</td><td>45,455,165,000</td><td>1.3%</td></tr>
<tr><td>35</td><td>Nevada</td><td>24,541,020,000</td><td>0.7%</td><td>28</td><td>Alabama</td><td>45,277,563,000</td><td>1.3%</td></tr>
<tr><td>42</td><td>New Hampshire</td><td>12,586,531,000</td><td>0.4%</td><td>29</td><td>Iowa</td><td>34,916,262,000</td><td>1.0%</td></tr>
<tr><td>8</td><td>New Jersey</td><td>109,767,828,000</td><td>3.1%</td><td>30</td><td>Oklahoma</td><td>34,528,657,000</td><td>1.0%</td></tr>
<tr><td>36</td><td>New Mexico</td><td>23,590,658,000</td><td>0.7%</td><td>31</td><td>Mississippi</td><td>29,930,149,000</td><td>0.9%</td></tr>
<tr><td>2</td><td>New York</td><td>331,281,858,000</td><td>9.4%</td><td>32</td><td>Kansas</td><td>28,791,130,000</td><td>0.8%</td></tr>
<tr><td>11</td><td>North Carolina</td><td>88,950,464,000</td><td>2.5%</td><td>33</td><td>Utah</td><td>27,324,285,000</td><td>0.8%</td></tr>
<tr><td>46</td><td>North Dakota</td><td>10,793,163,000</td><td>0.3%</td><td>34</td><td>Arkansas</td><td>27,300,171,000</td><td>0.8%</td></tr>
<tr><td>7</td><td>Ohio</td><td>125,579,570,000</td><td>3.6%</td><td>35</td><td>Nevada</td><td>24,541,020,000</td><td>0.7%</td></tr>
<tr><td>30</td><td>Oklahoma</td><td>34,528,657,000</td><td>1.0%</td><td>36</td><td>New Mexico</td><td>23,590,658,000</td><td>0.7%</td></tr>
<tr><td>23</td><td>Oregon</td><td>49,654,207,000</td><td>1.4%</td><td>37</td><td>Nebraska</td><td>23,071,752,000</td><td>0.7%</td></tr>
<tr><td>5</td><td>Pennsylvania</td><td>143,554,132,000</td><td>4.1%</td><td>38</td><td>West Virginia</td><td>18,054,885,000</td><td>0.5%</td></tr>
<tr><td>44</td><td>Rhode Island</td><td>12,184,375,000</td><td>0.3%</td><td>39</td><td>Hawaii</td><td>16,217,724,000</td><td>0.5%</td></tr>
<tr><td>24</td><td>South Carolina</td><td>47,533,649,000</td><td>1.4%</td><td>40</td><td>Alaska</td><td>15,808,697,000</td><td>0.4%</td></tr>
<tr><td>49</td><td>South Dakota</td><td>7,968,273,000</td><td>0.2%</td><td>41</td><td>Maine</td><td>12,973,463,000</td><td>0.4%</td></tr>
<tr><td>20</td><td>Tennessee</td><td>57,758,388,000</td><td>1.6%</td><td>42</td><td>New Hampshire</td><td>12,586,531,000</td><td>0.4%</td></tr>
<tr><td>3</td><td>Texas</td><td>252,400,912,000</td><td>7.2%</td><td>43</td><td>Idaho</td><td>12,506,304,000</td><td>0.4%</td></tr>
<tr><td>33</td><td>Utah</td><td>27,324,285,000</td><td>0.8%</td><td>44</td><td>Rhode Island</td><td>12,184,375,000</td><td>0.3%</td></tr>
<tr><td>50</td><td>Vermont</td><td>7,774,956,000</td><td>0.2%</td><td>45</td><td>Delaware</td><td>11,413,963,000</td><td>0.3%</td></tr>
<tr><td>14</td><td>Virginia</td><td>80,156,488,000</td><td>2.3%</td><td>46</td><td>North Dakota</td><td>10,793,163,000</td><td>0.3%</td></tr>
<tr><td>12</td><td>Washington</td><td>86,881,984,000</td><td>2.5%</td><td>47</td><td>Wyoming</td><td>10,067,959,000</td><td>0.3%</td></tr>
<tr><td>38</td><td>West Virginia</td><td>18,054,885,000</td><td>0.5%</td><td>48</td><td>Montana</td><td>10,007,594,000</td><td>0.3%</td></tr>
<tr><td>17</td><td>Wisconsin</td><td>59,534,828,000</td><td>1.7%</td><td>49</td><td>South Dakota</td><td>7,968,273,000</td><td>0.2%</td></tr>
<tr><td>47</td><td>Wyoming</td><td>10,067,959,000</td><td>0.3%</td><td>50</td><td>Vermont</td><td>7,774,956,000</td><td>0.2%</td></tr>
<tr><td></td><td></td><td></td><td></td><td></td><td>District of Columbia</td><td>16,593,661,000</td><td>0.5%</td></tr>
</table>

Source: U.S. Bureau of the Census, Governments Division

"2016 State and Local Government Finances" (https://www.census.gov/programs-surveys/gov-finances.html)

*Total expenditures includes all money paid other than for retirement of debt and extension of loans. Includes payments from all sources of funds including current revenues and proceeds from borrowing and prior year fund balances. Includes intergovernmental transfers and expenditures for government owned utilities and other commercial or auxiliary enterprise, and insurance trust expenditures.

Per Capita State and Local Government Total Expenditures in 2016

National Per Capita = $10,889*

<table>
<tr><td colspan="3">ALPHA ORDER</td><td colspan="3">RANK ORDER</td></tr>
<tr><td>RANK</td><td>STATE</td><td>PER CAPITA</td><td>RANK</td><td>STATE</td><td>PER CAPITA</td></tr>
<tr><td>36</td><td>Alabama</td><td>$9,307</td><td>1</td><td>Alaska</td><td>$21,320</td></tr>
<tr><td>1</td><td>Alaska</td><td>21,320</td><td>2</td><td>Wyoming</td><td>17,231</td></tr>
<tr><td>46</td><td>Arizona</td><td>8,491</td><td>3</td><td>New York</td><td>16,866</td></tr>
<tr><td>38</td><td>Arkansas</td><td>9,129</td><td>4</td><td>North Dakota</td><td>14,308</td></tr>
<tr><td>5</td><td>California</td><td>13,664</td><td>5</td><td>California</td><td>13,664</td></tr>
<tr><td>23</td><td>Colorado</td><td>10,341</td><td>6</td><td>Massachusetts</td><td>13,121</td></tr>
<tr><td>7</td><td>Connecticut</td><td>12,756</td><td>7</td><td>Connecticut</td><td>12,756</td></tr>
<tr><td>12</td><td>Delaware</td><td>12,025</td><td>8</td><td>Vermont</td><td>12,467</td></tr>
<tr><td>48</td><td>Florida</td><td>8,106</td><td>9</td><td>New Jersey</td><td>12,369</td></tr>
<tr><td>49</td><td>Georgia</td><td>7,976</td><td>10</td><td>Oregon</td><td>12,136</td></tr>
<tr><td>16</td><td>Hawaii</td><td>11,356</td><td>11</td><td>Nebraska</td><td>12,105</td></tr>
<tr><td>50</td><td>Idaho</td><td>7,431</td><td>12</td><td>Delaware</td><td>12,025</td></tr>
<tr><td>21</td><td>Illinois</td><td>10,902</td><td>13</td><td>Washington</td><td>11,910</td></tr>
<tr><td>44</td><td>Indiana</td><td>8,732</td><td>14</td><td>Minnesota</td><td>11,879</td></tr>
<tr><td>20</td><td>Iowa</td><td>11,149</td><td>15</td><td>Rhode Island</td><td>11,527</td></tr>
<tr><td>28</td><td>Kansas</td><td>9,890</td><td>16</td><td>Hawaii</td><td>11,356</td></tr>
<tr><td>25</td><td>Kentucky</td><td>10,242</td><td>17</td><td>New Mexico</td><td>11,272</td></tr>
<tr><td>26</td><td>Louisiana</td><td>10,152</td><td>18</td><td>Maryland</td><td>11,232</td></tr>
<tr><td>30</td><td>Maine</td><td>9,744</td><td>19</td><td>Pennsylvania</td><td>11,230</td></tr>
<tr><td>18</td><td>Maryland</td><td>11,232</td><td>20</td><td>Iowa</td><td>11,149</td></tr>
<tr><td>6</td><td>Massachusetts</td><td>13,121</td><td>21</td><td>Illinois</td><td>10,902</td></tr>
<tr><td>31</td><td>Michigan</td><td>9,709</td><td>22</td><td>Ohio</td><td>10,793</td></tr>
<tr><td>14</td><td>Minnesota</td><td>11,879</td><td>23</td><td>Colorado</td><td>10,341</td></tr>
<tr><td>27</td><td>Mississippi</td><td>10,016</td><td>24</td><td>Wisconsin</td><td>10,313</td></tr>
<tr><td>41</td><td>Missouri</td><td>8,812</td><td>25</td><td>Kentucky</td><td>10,242</td></tr>
<tr><td>32</td><td>Montana</td><td>9,615</td><td>26</td><td>Louisiana</td><td>10,152</td></tr>
<tr><td>11</td><td>Nebraska</td><td>12,105</td><td>27</td><td>Mississippi</td><td>10,016</td></tr>
<tr><td>47</td><td>Nevada</td><td>8,405</td><td>28</td><td>Kansas</td><td>9,890</td></tr>
<tr><td>35</td><td>New Hampshire</td><td>9,376</td><td>29</td><td>West Virginia</td><td>9,861</td></tr>
<tr><td>9</td><td>New Jersey</td><td>12,369</td><td>30</td><td>Maine</td><td>9,744</td></tr>
<tr><td>17</td><td>New Mexico</td><td>11,272</td><td>31</td><td>Michigan</td><td>9,709</td></tr>
<tr><td>3</td><td>New York</td><td>16,866</td><td>32</td><td>Montana</td><td>9,615</td></tr>
<tr><td>43</td><td>North Carolina</td><td>8,758</td><td>33</td><td>South Carolina</td><td>9,587</td></tr>
<tr><td>4</td><td>North Dakota</td><td>14,308</td><td>34</td><td>Virginia</td><td>9,530</td></tr>
<tr><td>22</td><td>Ohio</td><td>10,793</td><td>35</td><td>New Hampshire</td><td>9,376</td></tr>
<tr><td>42</td><td>Oklahoma</td><td>8,793</td><td>36</td><td>Alabama</td><td>9,307</td></tr>
<tr><td>10</td><td>Oregon</td><td>12,136</td><td>37</td><td>South Dakota</td><td>9,234</td></tr>
<tr><td>19</td><td>Pennsylvania</td><td>11,230</td><td>38</td><td>Arkansas</td><td>9,129</td></tr>
<tr><td>15</td><td>Rhode Island</td><td>11,527</td><td>39</td><td>Texas</td><td>9,034</td></tr>
<tr><td>33</td><td>South Carolina</td><td>9,587</td><td>40</td><td>Utah</td><td>8,981</td></tr>
<tr><td>37</td><td>South Dakota</td><td>9,234</td><td>41</td><td>Missouri</td><td>8,812</td></tr>
<tr><td>45</td><td>Tennessee</td><td>8,692</td><td>42</td><td>Oklahoma</td><td>8,793</td></tr>
<tr><td>39</td><td>Texas</td><td>9,034</td><td>43</td><td>North Carolina</td><td>8,758</td></tr>
<tr><td>40</td><td>Utah</td><td>8,981</td><td>44</td><td>Indiana</td><td>8,732</td></tr>
<tr><td>8</td><td>Vermont</td><td>12,467</td><td>45</td><td>Tennessee</td><td>8,692</td></tr>
<tr><td>34</td><td>Virginia</td><td>9,530</td><td>46</td><td>Arizona</td><td>8,491</td></tr>
<tr><td>13</td><td>Washington</td><td>11,910</td><td>47</td><td>Nevada</td><td>8,405</td></tr>
<tr><td>29</td><td>West Virginia</td><td>9,861</td><td>48</td><td>Florida</td><td>8,106</td></tr>
<tr><td>24</td><td>Wisconsin</td><td>10,313</td><td>49</td><td>Georgia</td><td>7,976</td></tr>
<tr><td>2</td><td>Wyoming</td><td>17,231</td><td>50</td><td>Idaho</td><td>7,431</td></tr>
<tr><td></td><td></td><td></td><td></td><td>District of Columbia</td><td>24,169</td></tr>
</table>

Source: CQ Press using data from U.S. Bureau of the Census, Governments Division

"2016 State and Local Government Finances" (https://www.census.gov/programs-surveys/gov-finances.html)

*Total expenditures includes all money paid other than for retirement of debt and extension of loans. Includes payments from all sources of funds including current revenues and proceeds from borrowing and prior year fund balances. Includes intergovernmental transfers and expenditures for government owned utilities and other commercial or auxiliary enterprise, and insurance trust expenditures.

State and Local Government Direct General Expenditures in 2016

National Total = $2,944,651,388,000*

ALPHA ORDER

ALPHA ORDER

RANK	STATE	EXPENDITURES	% of USA
28	Alabama	$38,202,826,000	1.3%
39	Alaska	13,665,100,000	0.5%
19	Arizona	48,726,033,000	1.7%
33	Arkansas	24,315,231,000	0.8%
1	California	428,900,021,000	14.6%
20	Colorado	46,980,948,000	1.6%
27	Connecticut	38,424,945,000	1.3%
45	Delaware	10,092,031,000	0.3%
4	Florida	144,860,827,000	4.9%
14	Georgia	68,696,712,000	2.3%
40	Hawaii	13,627,195,000	0.5%
43	Idaho	11,039,406,000	0.4%
6	Illinois	111,433,768,000	3.8%
17	Indiana	52,073,775,000	1.8%
29	Iowa	30,893,618,000	1.0%
32	Kansas	25,200,117,000	0.9%
26	Kentucky	38,879,227,000	1.3%
24	Louisiana	41,342,876,000	1.4%
41	Maine	11,770,620,000	0.4%
15	Maryland	58,617,967,000	2.0%
11	Massachusetts	74,786,172,000	2.5%
9	Michigan	82,785,998,000	2.8%
16	Minnesota	56,956,351,000	1.9%
31	Mississippi	26,104,979,000	0.9%
21	Missouri	45,483,238,000	1.5%
48	Montana	8,774,994,000	0.3%
37	Nebraska	17,426,285,000	0.6%
36	Nevada	20,499,945,000	0.7%
42	New Hampshire	11,127,429,000	0.4%
8	New Jersey	92,449,735,000	3.1%
35	New Mexico	20,521,083,000	0.7%
2	New York	268,376,396,000	9.1%
10	North Carolina	77,208,640,000	2.6%
46	North Dakota	9,576,859,000	0.3%
7	Ohio	103,575,215,000	3.5%
30	Oklahoma	29,145,709,000	1.0%
23	Oregon	41,372,696,000	1.4%
5	Pennsylvania	122,179,360,000	4.1%
44	Rhode Island	10,220,342,000	0.3%
25	South Carolina	40,888,043,000	1.4%
50	South Dakota	6,991,455,000	0.2%
22	Tennessee	44,974,379,000	1.5%
3	Texas	215,064,375,000	7.3%
34	Utah	23,284,863,000	0.8%
49	Vermont	7,031,170,000	0.2%
12	Virginia	70,866,665,000	2.4%
13	Washington	70,595,670,000	2.4%
38	West Virginia	15,915,217,000	0.5%
18	Wisconsin	51,177,365,000	1.7%
47	Wyoming	8,776,997,000	0.3%

RANK ORDER

RANK	STATE	EXPENDITURES	% of USA
1	California	$428,900,021,000	14.6%
2	New York	268,376,396,000	9.1%
3	Texas	215,064,375,000	7.3%
4	Florida	144,860,827,000	4.9%
5	Pennsylvania	122,179,360,000	4.1%
6	Illinois	111,433,768,000	3.8%
7	Ohio	103,575,215,000	3.5%
8	New Jersey	92,449,735,000	3.1%
9	Michigan	82,785,998,000	2.8%
10	North Carolina	77,208,640,000	2.6%
11	Massachusetts	74,786,172,000	2.5%
12	Virginia	70,866,665,000	2.4%
13	Washington	70,595,670,000	2.4%
14	Georgia	68,696,712,000	2.3%
15	Maryland	58,617,967,000	2.0%
16	Minnesota	56,956,351,000	1.9%
17	Indiana	52,073,775,000	1.8%
18	Wisconsin	51,177,365,000	1.7%
19	Arizona	48,726,033,000	1.7%
20	Colorado	46,980,948,000	1.6%
21	Missouri	45,483,238,000	1.5%
22	Tennessee	44,974,379,000	1.5%
23	Oregon	41,372,696,000	1.4%
24	Louisiana	41,342,876,000	1.4%
25	South Carolina	40,888,043,000	1.4%
26	Kentucky	38,879,227,000	1.3%
27	Connecticut	38,424,945,000	1.3%
28	Alabama	38,202,826,000	1.3%
29	Iowa	30,893,618,000	1.0%
30	Oklahoma	29,145,709,000	1.0%
31	Mississippi	26,104,979,000	0.9%
32	Kansas	25,200,117,000	0.9%
33	Arkansas	24,315,231,000	0.8%
34	Utah	23,284,863,000	0.8%
35	New Mexico	20,521,083,000	0.7%
36	Nevada	20,499,945,000	0.7%
37	Nebraska	17,426,285,000	0.6%
38	West Virginia	15,915,217,000	0.5%
39	Alaska	13,665,100,000	0.5%
40	Hawaii	13,627,195,000	0.5%
41	Maine	11,770,620,000	0.4%
42	New Hampshire	11,127,429,000	0.4%
43	Idaho	11,039,406,000	0.4%
44	Rhode Island	10,220,342,000	0.3%
45	Delaware	10,092,031,000	0.3%
46	North Dakota	9,576,859,000	0.3%
47	Wyoming	8,776,997,000	0.3%
48	Montana	8,774,994,000	0.3%
49	Vermont	7,031,170,000	0.2%
50	South Dakota	6,991,455,000	0.2%
	District of Columbia	12,770,520,000	0.4%

Source: U.S. Bureau of the Census, Governments Division
"2016 State and Local Government Finances" (https://www.census.gov/programs-surveys/gov-finances.html)
*Direct general expenditures include expenditures for current operations, assistance and subsidies, interest on debt, and capital outlay. Excludes intergovernmental transfers, expenditures for government owned utilities and other commercial or auxiliary enterprise, and insurance trust expenditures.

Per Capita State and Local Government Direct General Expenditures in 2016

National Per Capita = $9,115*

ALPHA ORDER

RANK	STATE	PER CAPITA
38	Alabama	$7,853
1	Alaska	18,429
47	Arizona	7,016
36	Arkansas	8,131
7	California	10,939
30	Colorado	8,479
8	Connecticut	10,737
9	Delaware	10,632
45	Florida	7,022
49	Georgia	6,667
19	Hawaii	9,542
50	Idaho	6,560
28	Illinois	8,688
39	Indiana	7,850
13	Iowa	9,865
29	Kansas	8,656
25	Kentucky	8,760
24	Louisiana	8,837
23	Maine	8,841
15	Maryland	9,762
6	Massachusetts	10,956
33	Michigan	8,319
11	Minnesota	10,312
26	Mississippi	8,736
43	Missouri	7,472
31	Montana	8,430
20	Nebraska	9,143
46	Nevada	7,021
34	New Hampshire	8,289
10	New Jersey	10,417
14	New Mexico	9,806
3	New York	13,664
42	North Carolina	7,602
4	North Dakota	12,695
21	Ohio	8,902
44	Oklahoma	7,422
12	Oregon	10,112
18	Pennsylvania	9,558
17	Rhode Island	9,669
35	South Carolina	8,246
37	South Dakota	8,102
48	Tennessee	6,768
40	Texas	7,698
41	Utah	7,653
5	Vermont	11,274
32	Virginia	8,426
16	Washington	9,678
27	West Virginia	8,692
22	Wisconsin	8,865
2	Wyoming	15,022

RANK ORDER

RANK	STATE	PER CAPITA
1	Alaska	$18,429
2	Wyoming	15,022
3	New York	13,664
4	North Dakota	12,695
5	Vermont	11,274
6	Massachusetts	10,956
7	California	10,939
8	Connecticut	10,737
9	Delaware	10,632
10	New Jersey	10,417
11	Minnesota	10,312
12	Oregon	10,112
13	Iowa	9,865
14	New Mexico	9,806
15	Maryland	9,762
16	Washington	9,678
17	Rhode Island	9,669
18	Pennsylvania	9,558
19	Hawaii	9,542
20	Nebraska	9,143
21	Ohio	8,902
22	Wisconsin	8,865
23	Maine	8,841
24	Louisiana	8,837
25	Kentucky	8,760
26	Mississippi	8,736
27	West Virginia	8,692
28	Illinois	8,688
29	Kansas	8,656
30	Colorado	8,479
31	Montana	8,430
32	Virginia	8,426
33	Michigan	8,319
34	New Hampshire	8,289
35	South Carolina	8,246
36	Arkansas	8,131
37	South Dakota	8,102
38	Alabama	7,853
39	Indiana	7,850
40	Texas	7,698
41	Utah	7,653
42	North Carolina	7,602
43	Missouri	7,472
44	Oklahoma	7,422
45	Florida	7,022
46	Nevada	7,021
47	Arizona	7,016
48	Tennessee	6,768
49	Georgia	6,667
50	Idaho	6,560

District of Columbia   18,600

Source: CQ Press using data from U.S. Bureau of the Census, Governments Division
"2016 State and Local Government Finances" (https://www.census.gov/programs-surveys/gov-finances.html)
*Direct general expenditures include expenditures for current operations, assistance and subsidies, interest on debt, and capital outlay. Excludes intergovernmental transfers, expenditures for government owned utilities and other commercial or auxiliary enterprise, and insurance trust expenditures.

State and Local Government Debt Outstanding in 2016

National Total = $3,002,061,759,000*

ALPHA ORDER

RANK	STATE	DEBT	% of USA
29	Alabama	$28,868,246,000	1.0%
42	Alaska	9,349,996,000	0.3%
18	Arizona	48,794,673,000	1.6%
34	Arkansas	15,886,520,000	0.5%
1	California	433,916,743,000	14.5%
14	Colorado	52,924,295,000	1.8%
19	Connecticut	48,338,809,000	1.6%
44	Delaware	7,587,916,000	0.3%
5	Florida	139,084,205,000	4.6%
13	Georgia	57,938,369,000	1.9%
35	Hawaii	15,383,314,000	0.5%
46	Idaho	5,973,178,000	0.2%
4	Illinois	151,665,910,000	5.1%
16	Indiana	50,845,405,000	1.7%
32	Iowa	18,524,415,000	0.6%
28	Kansas	29,234,162,000	1.0%
25	Kentucky	38,829,771,000	1.3%
26	Louisiana	37,079,855,000	1.2%
43	Maine	7,802,612,000	0.3%
15	Maryland	52,893,714,000	1.8%
8	Massachusetts	95,033,587,000	3.2%
11	Michigan	72,506,815,000	2.4%
17	Minnesota	50,821,610,000	1.7%
38	Mississippi	14,041,530,000	0.5%
21	Missouri	45,884,302,000	1.5%
48	Montana	5,269,547,000	0.2%
37	Nebraska	15,281,470,000	0.5%
30	Nevada	28,726,202,000	1.0%
41	New Hampshire	10,436,475,000	0.3%
7	New Jersey	100,132,665,000	3.3%
36	New Mexico	15,316,148,000	0.5%
2	New York	356,519,187,000	11.9%
20	North Carolina	47,251,977,000	1.6%
45	North Dakota	6,783,386,000	0.2%
9	Ohio	85,209,881,000	2.8%
31	Oklahoma	18,711,149,000	0.6%
27	Oregon	33,904,603,000	1.1%
6	Pennsylvania	121,863,876,000	4.1%
39	Rhode Island	11,730,991,000	0.4%
23	South Carolina	43,613,571,000	1.5%
47	South Dakota	5,768,487,000	0.2%
24	Tennessee	42,270,933,000	1.4%
3	Texas	279,348,691,000	9.3%
33	Utah	18,423,457,000	0.6%
49	Vermont	3,630,283,000	0.1%
12	Virginia	66,095,159,000	2.2%
10	Washington	85,085,198,000	2.8%
40	West Virginia	10,702,688,000	0.4%
22	Wisconsin	44,341,272,000	1.5%
50	Wyoming	1,914,004,000	0.1%

RANK ORDER

RANK	STATE	DEBT	% of USA
1	California	$433,916,743,000	14.5%
2	New York	356,519,187,000	11.9%
3	Texas	279,348,691,000	9.3%
4	Illinois	151,665,910,000	5.1%
5	Florida	139,084,205,000	4.6%
6	Pennsylvania	121,863,876,000	4.1%
7	New Jersey	100,132,665,000	3.3%
8	Massachusetts	95,033,587,000	3.2%
9	Ohio	85,209,881,000	2.8%
10	Washington	85,085,198,000	2.8%
11	Michigan	72,506,815,000	2.4%
12	Virginia	66,095,159,000	2.2%
13	Georgia	57,938,369,000	1.9%
14	Colorado	52,924,295,000	1.8%
15	Maryland	52,893,714,000	1.8%
16	Indiana	50,845,405,000	1.7%
17	Minnesota	50,821,610,000	1.7%
18	Arizona	48,794,673,000	1.6%
19	Connecticut	48,338,809,000	1.6%
20	North Carolina	47,251,977,000	1.6%
21	Missouri	45,884,302,000	1.5%
22	Wisconsin	44,341,272,000	1.5%
23	South Carolina	43,613,571,000	1.5%
24	Tennessee	42,270,933,000	1.4%
25	Kentucky	38,829,771,000	1.3%
26	Louisiana	37,079,855,000	1.2%
27	Oregon	33,904,603,000	1.1%
28	Kansas	29,234,162,000	1.0%
29	Alabama	28,868,246,000	1.0%
30	Nevada	28,726,202,000	1.0%
31	Oklahoma	18,711,149,000	0.6%
32	Iowa	18,524,415,000	0.6%
33	Utah	18,423,457,000	0.6%
34	Arkansas	15,886,520,000	0.5%
35	Hawaii	15,383,314,000	0.5%
36	New Mexico	15,316,148,000	0.5%
37	Nebraska	15,281,470,000	0.5%
38	Mississippi	14,041,530,000	0.5%
39	Rhode Island	11,730,991,000	0.4%
40	West Virginia	10,702,688,000	0.4%
41	New Hampshire	10,436,475,000	0.3%
42	Alaska	9,349,996,000	0.3%
43	Maine	7,802,612,000	0.3%
44	Delaware	7,587,916,000	0.3%
45	North Dakota	6,783,386,000	0.2%
46	Idaho	5,973,178,000	0.2%
47	South Dakota	5,768,487,000	0.2%
48	Montana	5,269,547,000	0.2%
49	Vermont	3,630,283,000	0.1%
50	Wyoming	1,914,004,000	0.1%
	District of Columbia	14,520,507,000	0.5%

Source: U.S. Bureau of the Census, Governments Division
"2016 State and Local Government Finances" (https://www.census.gov/programs-surveys/gov-finances.html)
*Includes short-term, long-term, full faith and credit, nonguaranteed, and public debt for private purposes.

Per Capita State and Local Government Debt Outstanding in 2016

National Per Capita = $9,292*

ALPHA ORDER

RANK	STATE	PER CAPITA
38	Alabama	$5,934
4	Alaska	12,610
33	Arizona	7,025
44	Arkansas	5,312
9	California	11,067
14	Colorado	9,552
3	Connecticut	13,507
23	Delaware	7,994
34	Florida	6,742
43	Georgia	5,622
10	Hawaii	10,772
49	Idaho	3,549
5	Illinois	11,824
28	Indiana	7,665
39	Iowa	5,915
11	Kansas	10,042
20	Kentucky	8,749
24	Louisiana	7,926
40	Maine	5,861
18	Maryland	8,809
2	Massachusetts	13,922
32	Michigan	7,286
16	Minnesota	9,201
47	Mississippi	4,699
29	Missouri	7,538
45	Montana	5,063
22	Nebraska	8,018
13	Nevada	9,839
26	New Hampshire	7,775
7	New Jersey	11,283
31	New Mexico	7,319
1	New York	18,151
48	North Carolina	4,652
17	North Dakota	8,992
30	Ohio	7,324
46	Oklahoma	4,765
21	Oregon	8,287
15	Pennsylvania	9,533
8	Rhode Island	11,098
19	South Carolina	8,796
35	South Dakota	6,685
36	Tennessee	6,361
12	Texas	9,999
37	Utah	6,055
42	Vermont	5,821
25	Virginia	7,858
6	Washington	11,664
41	West Virginia	5,845
27	Wisconsin	7,681
50	Wyoming	3,276

RANK ORDER

RANK	STATE	PER CAPITA
1	New York	$18,151
2	Massachusetts	13,922
3	Connecticut	13,507
4	Alaska	12,610
5	Illinois	11,824
6	Washington	11,664
7	New Jersey	11,283
8	Rhode Island	11,098
9	California	11,067
10	Hawaii	10,772
11	Kansas	10,042
12	Texas	9,999
13	Nevada	9,839
14	Colorado	9,552
15	Pennsylvania	9,533
16	Minnesota	9,201
17	North Dakota	8,992
18	Maryland	8,809
19	South Carolina	8,796
20	Kentucky	8,749
21	Oregon	8,287
22	Nebraska	8,018
23	Delaware	7,994
24	Louisiana	7,926
25	Virginia	7,858
26	New Hampshire	7,775
27	Wisconsin	7,681
28	Indiana	7,665
29	Missouri	7,538
30	Ohio	7,324
31	New Mexico	7,319
32	Michigan	7,286
33	Arizona	7,025
34	Florida	6,742
35	South Dakota	6,685
36	Tennessee	6,361
37	Utah	6,055
38	Alabama	5,934
39	Iowa	5,915
40	Maine	5,861
41	West Virginia	5,845
42	Vermont	5,821
43	Georgia	5,622
44	Arkansas	5,312
45	Montana	5,063
46	Oklahoma	4,765
47	Mississippi	4,699
48	North Carolina	4,652
49	Idaho	3,549
50	Wyoming	3,276
	District of Columbia	21,149

Source: CQ Press using data from U.S. Bureau of the Census, Governments Division
"2016 State and Local Government Finances" (https://www.census.gov/programs-surveys/gov-finances.html)
*Includes short-term, long-term, full faith and credit, nonguaranteed, and public debt for private purposes.

State and Local Government Full-Time Equivalent Employees in 2017

National Total = 16,584,617 FTE Employees*

RANK	STATE	EMPLOYEES	% of USA
22	Alabama	281,490	1.7%
44	Alaska	51,843	0.3%
23	Arizona	281,188	1.7%
33	Arkansas	168,344	1.0%
1	California	1,861,274	11.2%
19	Colorado	299,168	1.8%
32	Connecticut	186,362	1.1%
46	Delaware	49,757	0.3%
4	Florida	890,784	5.4%
9	Georgia	520,907	3.1%
40	Hawaii	75,958	0.5%
39	Idaho	84,584	0.5%
5	Illinois	618,377	3.7%
16	Indiana	324,678	2.0%
31	Iowa	186,539	1.1%
28	Kansas	201,209	1.2%
26	Kentucky	243,100	1.5%
25	Louisiana	259,348	1.6%
42	Maine	69,527	0.4%
18	Maryland	306,799	1.8%
14	Massachusetts	328,534	2.0%
12	Michigan	433,801	2.6%
20	Minnesota	294,085	1.8%
30	Mississippi	188,616	1.1%
17	Missouri	319,206	1.9%
43	Montana	57,296	0.3%
36	Nebraska	121,477	0.7%
37	Nevada	115,575	0.7%
41	New Hampshire	71,360	0.4%
10	New Jersey	477,619	2.9%
35	New Mexico	123,517	0.7%
3	New York	1,200,144	7.2%
8	North Carolina	562,411	3.4%
48	North Dakota	47,309	0.3%
6	Ohio	588,784	3.6%
27	Oklahoma	211,127	1.3%
29	Oregon	200,962	1.2%
7	Pennsylvania	566,129	3.4%
47	Rhode Island	47,509	0.3%
24	South Carolina	265,525	1.6%
49	South Dakota	47,014	0.3%
15	Tennessee	327,864	2.0%
2	Texas	1,513,358	9.1%
34	Utah	154,507	0.9%
50	Vermont	40,965	0.2%
11	Virginia	448,838	2.7%
13	Washington	382,426	2.3%
38	West Virginia	101,952	0.6%
21	Wisconsin	284,715	1.7%
45	Wyoming	50,084	0.3%

RANK	STATE	EMPLOYEES	% of USA
1	California	1,861,274	11.2%
2	Texas	1,513,358	9.1%
3	New York	1,200,144	7.2%
4	Florida	890,784	5.4%
5	Illinois	618,377	3.7%
6	Ohio	588,784	3.6%
7	Pennsylvania	566,129	3.4%
8	North Carolina	562,411	3.4%
9	Georgia	520,907	3.1%
10	New Jersey	477,619	2.9%
11	Virginia	448,838	2.7%
12	Michigan	433,801	2.6%
13	Washington	382,426	2.3%
14	Massachusetts	328,534	2.0%
15	Tennessee	327,864	2.0%
16	Indiana	324,678	2.0%
17	Missouri	319,206	1.9%
18	Maryland	306,799	1.8%
19	Colorado	299,168	1.8%
20	Minnesota	294,085	1.8%
21	Wisconsin	284,715	1.7%
22	Alabama	281,490	1.7%
23	Arizona	281,188	1.7%
24	South Carolina	265,525	1.6%
25	Louisiana	259,348	1.6%
26	Kentucky	243,100	1.5%
27	Oklahoma	211,127	1.3%
28	Kansas	201,209	1.2%
29	Oregon	200,962	1.2%
30	Mississippi	188,616	1.1%
31	Iowa	186,539	1.1%
32	Connecticut	186,362	1.1%
33	Arkansas	168,344	1.0%
34	Utah	154,507	0.9%
35	New Mexico	123,517	0.7%
36	Nebraska	121,477	0.7%
37	Nevada	115,575	0.7%
38	West Virginia	101,952	0.6%
39	Idaho	84,584	0.5%
40	Hawaii	75,958	0.5%
41	New Hampshire	71,360	0.4%
42	Maine	69,527	0.4%
43	Montana	57,296	0.3%
44	Alaska	51,843	0.3%
45	Wyoming	50,084	0.3%
46	Delaware	49,757	0.3%
47	Rhode Island	47,509	0.3%
48	North Dakota	47,309	0.3%
49	South Dakota	47,014	0.3%
50	Vermont	40,965	0.2%
	District of Columbia	50,672	0.3%

Source: U.S. Bureau of the Census, Governments Division
  "Annual Survey of Public Employment and Payroll" (https://www.census.gov/programs-surveys/apes.html)
*Full-time equivalent as of March 2017.

Rate of State and Local Government Full-Time Equivalent Employees in 2017

National Rate = 510 FTE Employees per 10,000 Population*

ALPHA ORDER

RANK	STATE	RATE
11	Alabama	577
2	Alaska	701
49	Arizona	399
12	Arkansas	561
44	California	472
22	Colorado	533
29	Connecticut	521
31	Delaware	520
48	Florida	425
35	Georgia	500
22	Hawaii	533
37	Idaho	492
42	Illinois	484
40	Indiana	487
9	Iowa	593
3	Kansas	691
16	Kentucky	546
14	Louisiana	555
29	Maine	521
33	Maryland	509
43	Massachusetts	479
47	Michigan	435
27	Minnesota	528
6	Mississippi	631
28	Missouri	523
17	Montana	544
5	Nebraska	633
50	Nevada	389
25	New Hampshire	529
19	New Jersey	537
10	New Mexico	590
8	New York	613
15	North Carolina	548
7	North Dakota	626
34	Ohio	505
19	Oklahoma	537
41	Oregon	485
46	Pennsylvania	443
45	Rhode Island	450
25	South Carolina	529
18	South Dakota	538
39	Tennessee	489
21	Texas	534
36	Utah	498
4	Vermont	656
24	Virginia	530
32	Washington	515
12	West Virginia	561
37	Wisconsin	492
1	Wyoming	865

RANK ORDER

RANK	STATE	RATE
1	Wyoming	865
2	Alaska	701
3	Kansas	691
4	Vermont	656
5	Nebraska	633
6	Mississippi	631
7	North Dakota	626
8	New York	613
9	Iowa	593
10	New Mexico	590
11	Alabama	577
12	Arkansas	561
12	West Virginia	561
14	Louisiana	555
15	North Carolina	548
16	Kentucky	546
17	Montana	544
18	South Dakota	538
19	New Jersey	537
19	Oklahoma	537
21	Texas	534
22	Colorado	533
22	Hawaii	533
24	Virginia	530
25	New Hampshire	529
25	South Carolina	529
27	Minnesota	528
28	Missouri	523
29	Connecticut	521
29	Maine	521
31	Delaware	520
32	Washington	515
33	Maryland	509
34	Ohio	505
35	Georgia	500
36	Utah	498
37	Idaho	492
37	Wisconsin	492
39	Tennessee	489
40	Indiana	487
41	Oregon	485
42	Illinois	484
43	Massachusetts	479
44	California	472
45	Rhode Island	450
46	Pennsylvania	443
47	Michigan	435
48	Florida	425
49	Arizona	399
50	Nevada	389
	District of Columbia	728

Source: CQ Press using data from U.S. Bureau of the Census, Governments Division
"Annual Survey of Public Employment and Payroll" (https://www.census.gov/programs-surveys/apes.html)
*Full-time equivalent as of March 2017.

Average Annual Earnings of Full-Time State and Local Government Employees in 2017
National Average = $60,508*

ALPHA ORDER

RANK ORDER

RANK	STATE	SALARY	RANK	STATE	SALARY
41	Alabama	$48,349	1	California	$83,370
6	Alaska	70,216	2	New Jersey	74,702
27	Arizona	55,640	3	New York	73,312
48	Arkansas	43,554	4	Washington	73,065
1	California	83,370	5	Connecticut	72,311
15	Colorado	61,408	6	Alaska	70,216
5	Connecticut	72,311	7	Rhode Island	70,150
20	Delaware	58,539	8	Massachusetts	68,516
32	Florida	52,249	9	Maryland	68,012
40	Georgia	48,559	10	Illinois	65,787
18	Hawaii	60,577	11	Nevada	65,263
36	Idaho	50,139	12	Oregon	64,738
10	Illinois	65,787	13	Minnesota	64,359
37	Indiana	49,395	14	Michigan	61,857
17	Iowa	60,714	15	Colorado	61,408
38	Kansas	48,726	16	Pennsylvania	61,087
44	Kentucky	47,665	17	Iowa	60,714
45	Louisiana	47,247	18	Hawaii	60,577
35	Maine	50,246	19	Wisconsin	59,337
9	Maryland	68,012	20	Delaware	58,539
8	Massachusetts	68,516	21	New Hampshire	57,864
14	Michigan	61,857	22	Vermont	57,109
13	Minnesota	64,359	23	Virginia	56,902
50	Mississippi	42,312	24	Ohio	56,819
46	Missouri	47,084	25	Wyoming	56,652
30	Montana	52,901	26	North Dakota	56,087
29	Nebraska	54,713	27	Arizona	55,640
11	Nevada	65,263	28	Utah	55,533
21	New Hampshire	57,864	29	Nebraska	54,713
2	New Jersey	74,702	30	Montana	52,901
34	New Mexico	50,381	31	Texas	52,271
3	New York	73,312	32	Florida	52,249
33	North Carolina	51,742	33	North Carolina	51,742
26	North Dakota	56,087	34	New Mexico	50,381
24	Ohio	56,819	35	Maine	50,246
47	Oklahoma	45,162	36	Idaho	50,139
12	Oregon	64,738	37	Indiana	49,395
16	Pennsylvania	61,087	38	Kansas	48,726
7	Rhode Island	70,150	39	South Dakota	48,665
42	South Carolina	48,299	40	Georgia	48,559
39	South Dakota	48,665	41	Alabama	48,349
43	Tennessee	48,192	42	South Carolina	48,299
31	Texas	52,271	43	Tennessee	48,192
28	Utah	55,533	44	Kentucky	47,665
22	Vermont	57,109	45	Louisiana	47,247
23	Virginia	56,902	46	Missouri	47,084
4	Washington	73,065	47	Oklahoma	45,162
49	West Virginia	43,248	48	Arkansas	43,554
19	Wisconsin	59,337	49	West Virginia	43,248
25	Wyoming	56,652	50	Mississippi	42,312

District of Columbia   85,767

Source: CQ Press using data from U.S. Bureau of the Census, Governments Division
"Annual Survey of Public Employment and Payroll" (https://www.census.gov/programs-surveys/apes.html)
*March 2017 full-time payroll (multiplied by 12) divided by full-time employees.

State Government Total Revenue in 2016

National Total = $2,136,454,470,000*

ALPHA ORDER

ALPHA ORDER

RANK	STATE	REVENUE	% of USA
24	Alabama	$30,172,490,000	1.4%
45	Alaska	8,060,170,000	0.4%
18	Arizona	38,241,052,000	1.8%
31	Arkansas	21,431,620,000	1.0%
1	California	322,332,307,000	15.1%
23	Colorado	31,420,496,000	1.5%
27	Connecticut	28,131,478,000	1.3%
44	Delaware	8,083,659,000	0.4%
5	Florida	85,094,000,000	4.0%
14	Georgia	45,859,766,000	2.1%
38	Hawaii	13,417,567,000	0.6%
40	Idaho	9,401,987,000	0.4%
7	Illinois	75,492,133,000	3.5%
17	Indiana	38,687,720,000	1.8%
29	Iowa	23,715,459,000	1.1%
35	Kansas	17,609,012,000	0.8%
25	Kentucky	29,917,300,000	1.4%
28	Louisiana	26,819,360,000	1.3%
41	Maine	8,987,038,000	0.4%
16	Maryland	42,026,293,000	2.0%
10	Massachusetts	60,353,489,000	2.8%
8	Michigan	71,179,575,000	3.3%
15	Minnesota	44,247,753,000	2.1%
32	Mississippi	20,880,788,000	1.0%
20	Missouri	33,012,463,000	1.5%
47	Montana	6,862,804,000	0.3%
39	Nebraska	10,881,575,000	0.5%
36	Nevada	16,808,682,000	0.8%
42	New Hampshire	8,329,009,000	0.4%
9	New Jersey	66,894,648,000	3.1%
33	New Mexico	18,553,383,000	0.9%
2	New York	185,619,993,000	8.7%
11	North Carolina	55,216,832,000	2.6%
46	North Dakota	7,303,271,000	0.3%
6	Ohio	78,250,125,000	3.7%
30	Oklahoma	22,858,117,000	1.1%
21	Oregon	32,763,887,000	1.5%
4	Pennsylvania	90,792,145,000	4.2%
43	Rhode Island	8,201,456,000	0.4%
26	South Carolina	28,937,622,000	1.4%
50	South Dakota	4,535,024,000	0.2%
22	Tennessee	31,425,681,000	1.5%
3	Texas	143,831,737,000	6.7%
34	Utah	18,162,218,000	0.9%
48	Vermont	6,488,122,000	0.3%
12	Virginia	51,655,912,000	2.4%
13	Washington	51,094,731,000	2.4%
37	West Virginia	13,645,274,000	0.6%
19	Wisconsin	36,853,220,000	1.7%
49	Wyoming	5,914,027,000	0.3%

RANK ORDER

RANK	STATE	REVENUE	% of USA
1	California	$322,332,307,000	15.1%
2	New York	185,619,993,000	8.7%
3	Texas	143,831,737,000	6.7%
4	Pennsylvania	90,792,145,000	4.2%
5	Florida	85,094,000,000	4.0%
6	Ohio	78,250,125,000	3.7%
7	Illinois	75,492,133,000	3.5%
8	Michigan	71,179,575,000	3.3%
9	New Jersey	66,894,648,000	3.1%
10	Massachusetts	60,353,489,000	2.8%
11	North Carolina	55,216,832,000	2.6%
12	Virginia	51,655,912,000	2.4%
13	Washington	51,094,731,000	2.4%
14	Georgia	45,859,766,000	2.1%
15	Minnesota	44,247,753,000	2.1%
16	Maryland	42,026,293,000	2.0%
17	Indiana	38,687,720,000	1.8%
18	Arizona	38,241,052,000	1.8%
19	Wisconsin	36,853,220,000	1.7%
20	Missouri	33,012,463,000	1.5%
21	Oregon	32,763,887,000	1.5%
22	Tennessee	31,425,681,000	1.5%
23	Colorado	31,420,496,000	1.5%
24	Alabama	30,172,490,000	1.4%
25	Kentucky	29,917,300,000	1.4%
26	South Carolina	28,937,622,000	1.4%
27	Connecticut	28,131,478,000	1.3%
28	Louisiana	26,819,360,000	1.3%
29	Iowa	23,715,459,000	1.1%
30	Oklahoma	22,858,117,000	1.1%
31	Arkansas	21,431,620,000	1.0%
32	Mississippi	20,880,788,000	1.0%
33	New Mexico	18,553,383,000	0.9%
34	Utah	18,162,218,000	0.9%
35	Kansas	17,609,012,000	0.8%
36	Nevada	16,808,682,000	0.8%
37	West Virginia	13,645,274,000	0.6%
38	Hawaii	13,417,567,000	0.6%
39	Nebraska	10,881,575,000	0.5%
40	Idaho	9,401,987,000	0.4%
41	Maine	8,987,038,000	0.4%
42	New Hampshire	8,329,009,000	0.4%
43	Rhode Island	8,201,456,000	0.4%
44	Delaware	8,083,659,000	0.4%
45	Alaska	8,060,170,000	0.4%
46	North Dakota	7,303,271,000	0.3%
47	Montana	6,862,804,000	0.3%
48	Vermont	6,488,122,000	0.3%
49	Wyoming	5,914,027,000	0.3%
50	South Dakota	4,535,024,000	0.2%
	District of Columbia**	NA	NA

Source: U.S. Bureau of the Census, Governments Division
   "2016 State and Local Government Finances" (https://www.census.gov/programs-surveys/gov-finances.html)
*Total revenue includes all money received from external sources. This includes taxes, intergovernmental transfers and insurance trust revenue, and revenue from government owned utilities and other commercial or auxiliary enterprise.
**Not applicable.

Per Capita State Government Total Revenue in 2016

National Per Capita = $6,627*

RANK	STATE	PER CAPITA		RANK	STATE	PER CAPITA
ALPHA ORDER				RANK ORDER		
30	Alabama	$6,202		1	Alaska	$10,870
1	Alaska	10,870		2	Vermont	10,404
43	Arizona	5,506		3	Wyoming	10,122
18	Arkansas	7,167		4	North Dakota	9,682
10	California	8,221		5	New York	9,450
41	Colorado	5,671		6	Hawaii	9,395
13	Connecticut	7,861		7	New Mexico	8,865
9	Delaware	8,516		8	Massachusetts	8,842
50	Florida	4,125		9	Delaware	8,516
49	Georgia	4,450		10	California	8,221
6	Hawaii	9,395		11	Minnesota	8,011
42	Idaho	5,587		12	Oregon	8,008
34	Illinois	5,885		13	Connecticut	7,861
36	Indiana	5,832		14	Rhode Island	7,759
15	Iowa	7,573		15	Iowa	7,573
32	Kansas	6,049		16	New Jersey	7,538
25	Kentucky	6,741		17	West Virginia	7,453
39	Louisiana	5,733		18	Arkansas	7,167
24	Maine	6,750		19	Michigan	7,152
22	Maryland	6,999		20	Pennsylvania	7,102
8	Massachusetts	8,842		21	Washington	7,004
19	Michigan	7,152		22	Maryland	6,999
11	Minnesota	8,011		23	Mississippi	6,988
23	Mississippi	6,988		24	Maine	6,750
45	Missouri	5,423		25	Kentucky	6,741
27	Montana	6,593		26	Ohio	6,725
40	Nebraska	5,709		27	Montana	6,593
38	Nevada	5,757		28	Wisconsin	6,384
29	New Hampshire	6,205		29	New Hampshire	6,205
16	New Jersey	7,538		30	Alabama	6,202
7	New Mexico	8,865		31	Virginia	6,142
5	New York	9,450		32	Kansas	6,049
44	North Carolina	5,437		33	Utah	5,969
4	North Dakota	9,682		34	Illinois	5,885
26	Ohio	6,725		35	South Carolina	5,836
37	Oklahoma	5,821		36	Indiana	5,832
12	Oregon	8,008		37	Oklahoma	5,821
20	Pennsylvania	7,102		38	Nevada	5,757
14	Rhode Island	7,759		39	Louisiana	5,733
35	South Carolina	5,836		40	Nebraska	5,709
46	South Dakota	5,256		41	Colorado	5,671
48	Tennessee	4,729		42	Idaho	5,587
47	Texas	5,148		43	Arizona	5,506
33	Utah	5,969		44	North Carolina	5,437
2	Vermont	10,404		45	Missouri	5,423
31	Virginia	6,142		46	South Dakota	5,256
21	Washington	7,004		47	Texas	5,148
17	West Virginia	7,453		48	Tennessee	4,729
28	Wisconsin	6,384		49	Georgia	4,450
3	Wyoming	10,122		50	Florida	4,125

District of Columbia** NA

Source: CQ Press using data from U.S. Bureau of the Census, Governments Division
"2016 State and Local Government Finances" (https://www.census.gov/programs-surveys/gov-finances.html)
*Total revenue includes all money received from external sources. This includes taxes, intergovernmental transfers and insurance trust revenue, and revenue from government owned utilities and other commercial or auxiliary enterprise.
**Not applicable.

State Government Intergovernmental Revenue in 2016

National Total = $637,167,820,000*

ALPHA ORDER

RANK	STATE	REVENUE	% of USA
24	Alabama	$9,521,969,000	1.5%
41	Alaska	2,853,202,000	0.4%
13	Arizona	14,540,462,000	2.3%
29	Arkansas	7,431,541,000	1.2%
1	California	94,336,283,000	14.8%
26	Colorado	8,703,745,000	1.4%
30	Connecticut	7,320,793,000	1.1%
46	Delaware	2,231,253,000	0.4%
4	Florida	27,390,107,000	4.3%
12	Georgia	14,571,741,000	2.3%
39	Hawaii	2,943,334,000	0.5%
42	Idaho	2,721,730,000	0.4%
8	Illinois	20,264,895,000	3.2%
15	Indiana	13,041,760,000	2.0%
33	Iowa	6,645,791,000	1.0%
37	Kansas	3,828,203,000	0.6%
17	Kentucky	11,563,609,000	1.8%
21	Louisiana	10,361,925,000	1.6%
40	Maine	2,893,648,000	0.5%
16	Maryland	12,290,258,000	1.9%
10	Massachusetts	16,401,221,000	2.6%
7	Michigan	20,908,261,000	3.3%
18	Minnesota	11,321,336,000	1.8%
27	Mississippi	8,299,349,000	1.3%
20	Missouri	10,987,857,000	1.7%
45	Montana	2,445,647,000	0.4%
38	Nebraska	3,162,157,000	0.5%
35	Nevada	4,558,408,000	0.7%
43	New Hampshire	2,609,075,000	0.4%
9	New Jersey	17,976,242,000	2.8%
32	New Mexico	7,030,082,000	1.1%
2	New York	56,822,852,000	8.9%
11	North Carolina	15,908,501,000	2.5%
49	North Dakota	1,641,468,000	0.3%
6	Ohio	24,257,560,000	3.8%
31	Oklahoma	7,246,312,000	1.1%
23	Oregon	10,027,193,000	1.6%
5	Pennsylvania	26,240,030,000	4.1%
44	Rhode Island	2,518,206,000	0.4%
28	South Carolina	8,272,305,000	1.3%
50	South Dakota	1,475,385,000	0.2%
19	Tennessee	11,238,782,000	1.8%
3	Texas	43,750,542,000	6.9%
36	Utah	4,233,941,000	0.7%
48	Vermont	2,139,158,000	0.3%
22	Virginia	10,227,735,000	1.6%
14	Washington	13,704,988,000	2.2%
34	West Virginia	4,845,755,000	0.8%
25	Wisconsin	9,317,942,000	1.5%
47	Wyoming	2,143,281,000	0.3%

RANK ORDER

RANK	STATE	REVENUE	% of USA
1	California	$94,336,283,000	14.8%
2	New York	56,822,852,000	8.9%
3	Texas	43,750,542,000	6.9%
4	Florida	27,390,107,000	4.3%
5	Pennsylvania	26,240,030,000	4.1%
6	Ohio	24,257,560,000	3.8%
7	Michigan	20,908,261,000	3.3%
8	Illinois	20,264,895,000	3.2%
9	New Jersey	17,976,242,000	2.8%
10	Massachusetts	16,401,221,000	2.6%
11	North Carolina	15,908,501,000	2.5%
12	Georgia	14,571,741,000	2.3%
13	Arizona	14,540,462,000	2.3%
14	Washington	13,704,988,000	2.2%
15	Indiana	13,041,760,000	2.0%
16	Maryland	12,290,258,000	1.9%
17	Kentucky	11,563,609,000	1.8%
18	Minnesota	11,321,336,000	1.8%
19	Tennessee	11,238,782,000	1.8%
20	Missouri	10,987,857,000	1.7%
21	Louisiana	10,361,925,000	1.6%
22	Virginia	10,227,735,000	1.6%
23	Oregon	10,027,193,000	1.6%
24	Alabama	9,521,969,000	1.5%
25	Wisconsin	9,317,942,000	1.5%
26	Colorado	8,703,745,000	1.4%
27	Mississippi	8,299,349,000	1.3%
28	South Carolina	8,272,305,000	1.3%
29	Arkansas	7,431,541,000	1.2%
30	Connecticut	7,320,793,000	1.1%
31	Oklahoma	7,246,312,000	1.1%
32	New Mexico	7,030,082,000	1.1%
33	Iowa	6,645,791,000	1.0%
34	West Virginia	4,845,755,000	0.8%
35	Nevada	4,558,408,000	0.7%
36	Utah	4,233,941,000	0.7%
37	Kansas	3,828,203,000	0.6%
38	Nebraska	3,162,157,000	0.5%
39	Hawaii	2,943,334,000	0.5%
40	Maine	2,893,648,000	0.5%
41	Alaska	2,853,202,000	0.4%
42	Idaho	2,721,730,000	0.4%
43	New Hampshire	2,609,075,000	0.4%
44	Rhode Island	2,518,206,000	0.4%
45	Montana	2,445,647,000	0.4%
46	Delaware	2,231,253,000	0.4%
47	Wyoming	2,143,281,000	0.3%
48	Vermont	2,139,158,000	0.3%
49	North Dakota	1,641,468,000	0.3%
50	South Dakota	1,475,385,000	0.2%
	District of Columbia**	NA	NA

Source: U.S. Bureau of the Census, Governments Division
   "2016 State and Local Government Finances" (https://www.census.gov/programs-surveys/gov-finances.html)
*Includes revenue from federal and local government sources.
**Not applicable.

Per Capita State Government Intergovernmental Revenue in 2016

National Per Capita = $1,976*

ALPHA ORDER

RANK ORDER

RANK	STATE	PER CAPITA		RANK	STATE	PER CAPITA
30	Alabama	$1,957		1	Alaska	$3,848
1	Alaska	3,848		2	Wyoming	3,668
21	Arizona	2,094		3	Vermont	3,430
9	Arkansas	2,485		4	New Mexico	3,359
11	California	2,406		5	New York	2,893
42	Colorado	1,571		6	Mississippi	2,777
27	Connecticut	2,046		7	West Virginia	2,647
14	Delaware	2,351		8	Kentucky	2,605
48	Florida	1,328		9	Arkansas	2,485
46	Georgia	1,414		10	Oregon	2,451
23	Hawaii	2,061		11	California	2,406
39	Idaho	1,617		12	Massachusetts	2,403
41	Illinois	1,580		13	Rhode Island	2,382
29	Indiana	1,966		14	Delaware	2,351
19	Iowa	2,122		15	Montana	2,350
49	Kansas	1,315		16	Louisiana	2,215
8	Kentucky	2,605		17	North Dakota	2,176
16	Louisiana	2,215		18	Maine	2,173
18	Maine	2,173		19	Iowa	2,122
26	Maryland	2,047		20	Michigan	2,101
12	Massachusetts	2,403		21	Arizona	2,094
20	Michigan	2,101		22	Ohio	2,085
25	Minnesota	2,050		23	Hawaii	2,061
6	Mississippi	2,777		24	Pennsylvania	2,053
34	Missouri	1,805		25	Minnesota	2,050
15	Montana	2,350		26	Maryland	2,047
38	Nebraska	1,659		27	Connecticut	2,046
45	Nevada	1,561		28	New Jersey	2,026
31	New Hampshire	1,944		29	Indiana	1,966
28	New Jersey	2,026		30	Alabama	1,957
4	New Mexico	3,359		31	New Hampshire	1,944
5	New York	2,893		32	Washington	1,879
43	North Carolina	1,566		33	Oklahoma	1,845
17	North Dakota	2,176		34	Missouri	1,805
22	Ohio	2,085		35	South Dakota	1,710
33	Oklahoma	1,845		36	Tennessee	1,691
10	Oregon	2,451		37	South Carolina	1,668
24	Pennsylvania	2,053		38	Nebraska	1,659
13	Rhode Island	2,382		39	Idaho	1,617
37	South Carolina	1,668		40	Wisconsin	1,614
35	South Dakota	1,710		41	Illinois	1,580
36	Tennessee	1,691		42	Colorado	1,571
43	Texas	1,566		43	North Carolina	1,566
47	Utah	1,392		43	Texas	1,566
3	Vermont	3,430		45	Nevada	1,561
50	Virginia	1,216		46	Georgia	1,414
32	Washington	1,879		47	Utah	1,392
7	West Virginia	2,647		48	Florida	1,328
40	Wisconsin	1,614		49	Kansas	1,315
2	Wyoming	3,668		50	Virginia	1,216

District of Columbia**   NA

Source: CQ Press using data from U.S. Bureau of the Census, Governments Division

"2016 State and Local Government Finances" (https://www.census.gov/programs-surveys/gov-finances.html)

*Includes revenue from federal and local government sources.

**Not applicable.

State Government Own Source Revenue in 2016

National Total = $1,272,154,019,000*

<table>
<tr><td colspan="4">ALPHA ORDER</td><td colspan="4">RANK ORDER</td></tr>
<tr><td>RANK</td><td>STATE</td><td>REVENUE</td><td>% of USA</td><td>RANK</td><td>STATE</td><td>REVENUE</td><td>% of USA</td></tr>
<tr><td>27</td><td>Alabama</td><td>$15,766,917,000</td><td>1.2%</td><td>1</td><td>California</td><td>$188,571,643,000</td><td>14.8%</td></tr>
<tr><td>45</td><td>Alaska</td><td>4,775,449,000</td><td>0.4%</td><td>2</td><td>New York</td><td>107,576,041,000</td><td>8.5%</td></tr>
<tr><td>19</td><td>Arizona</td><td>20,042,499,000</td><td>1.6%</td><td>3</td><td>Texas</td><td>79,044,196,000</td><td>6.2%</td></tr>
<tr><td>31</td><td>Arkansas</td><td>12,914,555,000</td><td>1.0%</td><td>4</td><td>Pennsylvania</td><td>53,497,864,000</td><td>4.2%</td></tr>
<tr><td>1</td><td>California</td><td>188,571,643,000</td><td>14.8%</td><td>5</td><td>Florida</td><td>52,871,217,000</td><td>4.2%</td></tr>
<tr><td>21</td><td>Colorado</td><td>18,850,879,000</td><td>1.5%</td><td>6</td><td>Illinois</td><td>48,582,302,000</td><td>3.8%</td></tr>
<tr><td>20</td><td>Connecticut</td><td>18,850,911,000</td><td>1.5%</td><td>7</td><td>Ohio</td><td>43,208,882,000</td><td>3.4%</td></tr>
<tr><td>40</td><td>Delaware</td><td>5,731,632,000</td><td>0.5%</td><td>8</td><td>New Jersey</td><td>42,976,639,000</td><td>3.4%</td></tr>
<tr><td>5</td><td>Florida</td><td>52,871,217,000</td><td>4.2%</td><td>9</td><td>Michigan</td><td>40,337,842,000</td><td>3.2%</td></tr>
<tr><td>15</td><td>Georgia</td><td>27,707,810,000</td><td>2.2%</td><td>10</td><td>Massachusetts</td><td>38,300,174,000</td><td>3.0%</td></tr>
<tr><td>35</td><td>Hawaii</td><td>9,975,962,000</td><td>0.8%</td><td>11</td><td>North Carolina</td><td>35,201,941,000</td><td>2.8%</td></tr>
<tr><td>41</td><td>Idaho</td><td>5,429,041,000</td><td>0.4%</td><td>12</td><td>Virginia</td><td>35,197,852,000</td><td>2.8%</td></tr>
<tr><td>6</td><td>Illinois</td><td>48,582,302,000</td><td>3.8%</td><td>13</td><td>Washington</td><td>30,272,143,000</td><td>2.4%</td></tr>
<tr><td>18</td><td>Indiana</td><td>23,217,973,000</td><td>1.8%</td><td>14</td><td>Minnesota</td><td>29,891,876,000</td><td>2.3%</td></tr>
<tr><td>28</td><td>Iowa</td><td>14,428,599,000</td><td>1.1%</td><td>15</td><td>Georgia</td><td>27,707,810,000</td><td>2.2%</td></tr>
<tr><td>32</td><td>Kansas</td><td>12,631,494,000</td><td>1.0%</td><td>16</td><td>Maryland</td><td>26,869,413,000</td><td>2.1%</td></tr>
<tr><td>25</td><td>Kentucky</td><td>16,634,840,000</td><td>1.3%</td><td>17</td><td>Wisconsin</td><td>25,324,588,000</td><td>2.0%</td></tr>
<tr><td>29</td><td>Louisiana</td><td>13,748,472,000</td><td>1.1%</td><td>18</td><td>Indiana</td><td>23,217,973,000</td><td>1.8%</td></tr>
<tr><td>42</td><td>Maine</td><td>5,416,760,000</td><td>0.4%</td><td>19</td><td>Arizona</td><td>20,042,499,000</td><td>1.6%</td></tr>
<tr><td>16</td><td>Maryland</td><td>26,869,413,000</td><td>2.1%</td><td>20</td><td>Connecticut</td><td>18,850,911,000</td><td>1.5%</td></tr>
<tr><td>10</td><td>Massachusetts</td><td>38,300,174,000</td><td>3.0%</td><td>21</td><td>Colorado</td><td>18,850,879,000</td><td>1.5%</td></tr>
<tr><td>9</td><td>Michigan</td><td>40,337,842,000</td><td>3.2%</td><td>22</td><td>Oregon</td><td>18,081,421,000</td><td>1.4%</td></tr>
<tr><td>14</td><td>Minnesota</td><td>29,891,876,000</td><td>2.3%</td><td>23</td><td>Missouri</td><td>17,862,564,000</td><td>1.4%</td></tr>
<tr><td>34</td><td>Mississippi</td><td>10,654,583,000</td><td>0.8%</td><td>24</td><td>Tennessee</td><td>17,745,636,000</td><td>1.4%</td></tr>
<tr><td>23</td><td>Missouri</td><td>17,862,564,000</td><td>1.4%</td><td>25</td><td>Kentucky</td><td>16,634,840,000</td><td>1.3%</td></tr>
<tr><td>48</td><td>Montana</td><td>3,565,576,000</td><td>0.3%</td><td>26</td><td>South Carolina</td><td>16,632,600,000</td><td>1.3%</td></tr>
<tr><td>39</td><td>Nebraska</td><td>6,967,600,000</td><td>0.5%</td><td>27</td><td>Alabama</td><td>15,766,917,000</td><td>1.2%</td></tr>
<tr><td>37</td><td>Nevada</td><td>9,346,066,000</td><td>0.7%</td><td>28</td><td>Iowa</td><td>14,428,599,000</td><td>1.1%</td></tr>
<tr><td>46</td><td>New Hampshire</td><td>4,387,611,000</td><td>0.3%</td><td>29</td><td>Louisiana</td><td>13,748,472,000</td><td>1.1%</td></tr>
<tr><td>8</td><td>New Jersey</td><td>42,976,639,000</td><td>3.4%</td><td>30</td><td>Oklahoma</td><td>13,674,269,000</td><td>1.1%</td></tr>
<tr><td>36</td><td>New Mexico</td><td>9,506,657,000</td><td>0.7%</td><td>31</td><td>Arkansas</td><td>12,914,555,000</td><td>1.0%</td></tr>
<tr><td>2</td><td>New York</td><td>107,576,041,000</td><td>8.5%</td><td>32</td><td>Kansas</td><td>12,631,494,000</td><td>1.0%</td></tr>
<tr><td>11</td><td>North Carolina</td><td>35,201,941,000</td><td>2.8%</td><td>33</td><td>Utah</td><td>12,207,081,000</td><td>1.0%</td></tr>
<tr><td>43</td><td>North Dakota</td><td>5,057,975,000</td><td>0.4%</td><td>34</td><td>Mississippi</td><td>10,654,583,000</td><td>0.8%</td></tr>
<tr><td>7</td><td>Ohio</td><td>43,208,882,000</td><td>3.4%</td><td>35</td><td>Hawaii</td><td>9,975,962,000</td><td>0.8%</td></tr>
<tr><td>30</td><td>Oklahoma</td><td>13,674,269,000</td><td>1.1%</td><td>36</td><td>New Mexico</td><td>9,506,657,000</td><td>0.7%</td></tr>
<tr><td>22</td><td>Oregon</td><td>18,081,421,000</td><td>1.4%</td><td>37</td><td>Nevada</td><td>9,346,066,000</td><td>0.7%</td></tr>
<tr><td>4</td><td>Pennsylvania</td><td>53,497,864,000</td><td>4.2%</td><td>38</td><td>West Virginia</td><td>7,999,274,000</td><td>0.6%</td></tr>
<tr><td>44</td><td>Rhode Island</td><td>4,912,034,000</td><td>0.4%</td><td>39</td><td>Nebraska</td><td>6,967,600,000</td><td>0.5%</td></tr>
<tr><td>26</td><td>South Carolina</td><td>16,632,600,000</td><td>1.3%</td><td>40</td><td>Delaware</td><td>5,731,632,000</td><td>0.5%</td></tr>
<tr><td>50</td><td>South Dakota</td><td>2,775,334,000</td><td>0.2%</td><td>41</td><td>Idaho</td><td>5,429,041,000</td><td>0.4%</td></tr>
<tr><td>24</td><td>Tennessee</td><td>17,745,636,000</td><td>1.4%</td><td>42</td><td>Maine</td><td>5,416,760,000</td><td>0.4%</td></tr>
<tr><td>3</td><td>Texas</td><td>79,044,196,000</td><td>6.2%</td><td>43</td><td>North Dakota</td><td>5,057,975,000</td><td>0.4%</td></tr>
<tr><td>33</td><td>Utah</td><td>12,207,081,000</td><td>1.0%</td><td>44</td><td>Rhode Island</td><td>4,912,034,000</td><td>0.4%</td></tr>
<tr><td>47</td><td>Vermont</td><td>3,982,160,000</td><td>0.3%</td><td>45</td><td>Alaska</td><td>4,775,449,000</td><td>0.4%</td></tr>
<tr><td>12</td><td>Virginia</td><td>35,197,852,000</td><td>2.8%</td><td>46</td><td>New Hampshire</td><td>4,387,611,000</td><td>0.3%</td></tr>
<tr><td>13</td><td>Washington</td><td>30,272,143,000</td><td>2.4%</td><td>47</td><td>Vermont</td><td>3,982,160,000</td><td>0.3%</td></tr>
<tr><td>38</td><td>West Virginia</td><td>7,999,274,000</td><td>0.6%</td><td>48</td><td>Montana</td><td>3,565,576,000</td><td>0.3%</td></tr>
<tr><td>17</td><td>Wisconsin</td><td>25,324,588,000</td><td>2.0%</td><td>49</td><td>Wyoming</td><td>2,947,172,000</td><td>0.2%</td></tr>
<tr><td>49</td><td>Wyoming</td><td>2,947,172,000</td><td>0.2%</td><td>50</td><td>South Dakota</td><td>2,775,334,000</td><td>0.2%</td></tr>
<tr><td></td><td></td><td></td><td></td><td></td><td>District of Columbia**</td><td>NA</td><td>NA</td></tr>
</table>

Source: U.S. Bureau of the Census, Governments Division
"2016 State and Local Government Finances" (https://www.census.gov/programs-surveys/gov-finances.html)
*Own source revenue includes taxes, current charges, and miscellaneous general revenue. Excluded are intergovernmental transfers, insurance trust revenue, and revenue from government owned utilities and other commercial or auxiliary enterprise.
**Not applicable.

Per Capita State Government Own Source Revenue in 2016

National Per Capita = $3,946*

ALPHA ORDER			RANK ORDER		
RANK	STATE	PER CAPITA	RANK	STATE	PER CAPITA
40	Alabama	$3,241	1	Hawaii	$6,985
3	Alaska	6,440	2	North Dakota	6,705
46	Arizona	2,886	3	Alaska	6,440
21	Arkansas	4,319	4	Vermont	6,385
12	California	4,809	5	Delaware	6,038
37	Colorado	3,402	6	Massachusetts	5,611
9	Connecticut	5,268	7	New York	5,477
5	Delaware	6,038	8	Minnesota	5,412
50	Florida	2,563	9	Connecticut	5,268
48	Georgia	2,689	10	Wyoming	5,044
1	Hawaii	6,985	11	New Jersey	4,843
41	Idaho	3,226	12	California	4,809
28	Illinois	3,788	13	Rhode Island	4,647
33	Indiana	3,500	14	Iowa	4,607
14	Iowa	4,607	15	New Mexico	4,543
20	Kansas	4,339	16	Maryland	4,475
29	Kentucky	3,748	17	Oregon	4,419
44	Louisiana	2,939	18	Wisconsin	4,387
25	Maine	4,069	19	West Virginia	4,369
16	Maryland	4,475	20	Kansas	4,339
6	Massachusetts	5,611	21	Arkansas	4,319
26	Michigan	4,053	22	Pennsylvania	4,185
8	Minnesota	5,412	22	Virginia	4,185
32	Mississippi	3,565	24	Washington	4,150
45	Missouri	2,934	25	Maine	4,069
36	Montana	3,426	26	Michigan	4,053
31	Nebraska	3,656	27	Utah	4,012
43	Nevada	3,201	28	Illinois	3,788
39	New Hampshire	3,269	29	Kentucky	3,748
11	New Jersey	4,843	30	Ohio	3,714
15	New Mexico	4,543	31	Nebraska	3,656
7	New York	5,477	32	Mississippi	3,565
35	North Carolina	3,466	33	Indiana	3,500
2	North Dakota	6,705	34	Oklahoma	3,482
30	Ohio	3,714	35	North Carolina	3,466
34	Oklahoma	3,482	36	Montana	3,426
17	Oregon	4,419	37	Colorado	3,402
22	Pennsylvania	4,185	38	South Carolina	3,355
13	Rhode Island	4,647	39	New Hampshire	3,269
38	South Carolina	3,355	40	Alabama	3,241
42	South Dakota	3,216	41	Idaho	3,226
49	Tennessee	2,671	42	South Dakota	3,216
47	Texas	2,829	43	Nevada	3,201
27	Utah	4,012	44	Louisiana	2,939
4	Vermont	6,385	45	Missouri	2,934
22	Virginia	4,185	46	Arizona	2,886
24	Washington	4,150	47	Texas	2,829
19	West Virginia	4,369	48	Georgia	2,689
18	Wisconsin	4,387	49	Tennessee	2,671
10	Wyoming	5,044	50	Florida	2,563

District of Columbia**   NA

Source: CQ Press using data from U.S. Bureau of the Census, Governments Division

"2016 State and Local Government Finances" (https://www.census.gov/programs-surveys/gov-finances.html)

*Own source revenue includes taxes, current charges, and miscellaneous general revenue. Excluded are intergovernmental transfers, insurance trust revenue, and revenue from government owned utilities and other commercial or auxiliary enterprise.

**Not applicable.

Projected vs. Actual State Tax Collections in 2018

National Percent = 102.8% of Projected Taxes*

ALPHA ORDER				RANK ORDER		
RANK	STATE	PERCENT		RANK	STATE	PERCENT
22	Alabama	102.8		1	New Hampshire	116.3
50	Alaska	93.5		2	New Mexico	115.3
19	Arizona	103.3		3	Kentucky	112.1
46	Arkansas	99.1		4	Oklahoma	110.4
17	California	103.6		5	Connecticut	110.2
10	Colorado	105.7		6	Texas	109.6
5	Connecticut	110.2		7	Oregon	109.3
23	Delaware	102.5		8	Idaho	106.8
36	Florida	100.5		9	North Dakota	105.8
30	Georgia	101.3		10	Colorado	105.7
24	Hawaii	102.0		11	Kansas	105.0
8	Idaho	106.8		12	Massachusetts	104.9
28	Illinois	101.7		13	Nebraska	104.5
45	Indiana	99.3		14	Vermont	104.1
41	Iowa	100.0		15	Utah	104.0
11	Kansas	105.0		15	Washington	104.0
3	Kentucky	112.1		17	California	103.6
24	Louisiana	102.0		17	New Jersey	103.6
48	Maine	98.8		19	Arizona	103.3
39	Maryland	100.1		20	Ohio	103.0
12	Massachusetts	104.9		20	Wyoming	103.0
35	Michigan	100.6		22	Alabama	102.8
37	Minnesota	100.4		23	Delaware	102.5
32	Mississippi	101.1		24	Hawaii	102.0
39	Missouri	100.1		24	Louisiana	102.0
49	Montana	98.3		24	South Carolina	102.0
13	Nebraska	104.5		27	New York	101.8
46	Nevada	99.1		28	Illinois	101.7
1	New Hampshire	116.3		28	West Virginia	101.7
17	New Jersey	103.6		30	Georgia	101.3
2	New Mexico	115.3		31	Virginia	101.2
27	New York	101.8		32	Mississippi	101.1
33	North Carolina	100.9		33	North Carolina	100.9
9	North Dakota	105.8		34	Wisconsin	100.7
20	Ohio	103.0		35	Michigan	100.6
4	Oklahoma	110.4		36	Florida	100.5
7	Oregon	109.3		37	Minnesota	100.4
44	Pennsylvania	99.6		37	Rhode Island	100.4
37	Rhode Island	100.4		39	Maryland	100.1
24	South Carolina	102.0		39	Missouri	100.1
41	South Dakota	100.0		41	Iowa	100.0
41	Tennessee	100.0		41	South Dakota	100.0
6	Texas	109.6		41	Tennessee	100.0
15	Utah	104.0		44	Pennsylvania	99.6
14	Vermont	104.1		45	Indiana	99.3
31	Virginia	101.2		46	Arkansas	99.1
15	Washington	104.0		46	Nevada	99.1
28	West Virginia	101.7		48	Maine	98.8
34	Wisconsin	100.7		49	Montana	98.3
20	Wyoming	103.0		50	Alaska	93.5
					District of Columbia**	NA

Source: CQ Press using data from National Association of State Budget Officers
   "The Fiscal Survey of States" (Fall 2018, https://www.nasbo.org)
*For fiscal year 2018. This table compares sales, personal, and corporate income tax collections projected in adopting budgets
with the amount collected.
**Not available.

State Government Tax Revenue in 2017

National Total = $950,532,820,000

<table>
<tr><td colspan="4">ALPHA ORDER</td><td colspan="4">RANK ORDER</td></tr>
<tr><td>RANK</td><td>STATE</td><td>REVENUE</td><td>% of USA</td><td>RANK</td><td>STATE</td><td>REVENUE</td><td>% of USA</td></tr>
<tr><td>27</td><td>Alabama</td><td>$10,418,152,000</td><td>1.1%</td><td>1</td><td>California</td><td>$155,632,088,000</td><td>16.4%</td></tr>
<tr><td>50</td><td>Alaska</td><td>1,189,786,000</td><td>0.1%</td><td>2</td><td>New York</td><td>79,678,037,000</td><td>8.4%</td></tr>
<tr><td>21</td><td>Arizona</td><td>13,888,611,000</td><td>1.5%</td><td>3</td><td>Texas</td><td>53,612,926,000</td><td>5.6%</td></tr>
<tr><td>30</td><td>Arkansas</td><td>9,516,281,000</td><td>1.0%</td><td>4</td><td>Florida</td><td>40,218,365,000</td><td>4.2%</td></tr>
<tr><td>1</td><td>California</td><td>155,632,088,000</td><td>16.4%</td><td>5</td><td>Illinois</td><td>37,978,923,000</td><td>4.0%</td></tr>
<tr><td>22</td><td>Colorado</td><td>13,197,606,000</td><td>1.4%</td><td>6</td><td>Pennsylvania</td><td>37,853,091,000</td><td>4.0%</td></tr>
<tr><td>19</td><td>Connecticut</td><td>16,345,525,000</td><td>1.7%</td><td>7</td><td>New Jersey</td><td>32,325,850,000</td><td>3.4%</td></tr>
<tr><td>42</td><td>Delaware</td><td>3,588,905,000</td><td>0.4%</td><td>8</td><td>Ohio</td><td>30,306,468,000</td><td>3.2%</td></tr>
<tr><td>4</td><td>Florida</td><td>40,218,365,000</td><td>4.2%</td><td>9</td><td>Michigan</td><td>28,628,517,000</td><td>3.0%</td></tr>
<tr><td>14</td><td>Georgia</td><td>22,419,440,000</td><td>2.4%</td><td>10</td><td>Massachusetts</td><td>27,518,360,000</td><td>2.9%</td></tr>
<tr><td>36</td><td>Hawaii</td><td>7,029,026,000</td><td>0.7%</td><td>11</td><td>North Carolina</td><td>26,855,304,000</td><td>2.8%</td></tr>
<tr><td>40</td><td>Idaho</td><td>4,511,208,000</td><td>0.5%</td><td>12</td><td>Minnesota</td><td>25,594,522,000</td><td>2.7%</td></tr>
<tr><td>5</td><td>Illinois</td><td>37,978,923,000</td><td>4.0%</td><td>13</td><td>Washington</td><td>23,997,592,000</td><td>2.5%</td></tr>
<tr><td>18</td><td>Indiana</td><td>18,051,598,000</td><td>1.9%</td><td>14</td><td>Georgia</td><td>22,419,440,000</td><td>2.4%</td></tr>
<tr><td>29</td><td>Iowa</td><td>9,755,430,000</td><td>1.0%</td><td>15</td><td>Virginia</td><td>22,213,025,000</td><td>2.3%</td></tr>
<tr><td>33</td><td>Kansas</td><td>8,173,821,000</td><td>0.9%</td><td>16</td><td>Maryland</td><td>21,599,795,000</td><td>2.3%</td></tr>
<tr><td>25</td><td>Kentucky</td><td>11,907,759,000</td><td>1.3%</td><td>17</td><td>Wisconsin</td><td>18,133,496,000</td><td>1.9%</td></tr>
<tr><td>26</td><td>Louisiana</td><td>11,104,720,000</td><td>1.2%</td><td>18</td><td>Indiana</td><td>18,051,598,000</td><td>1.9%</td></tr>
<tr><td>41</td><td>Maine</td><td>4,232,556,000</td><td>0.4%</td><td>19</td><td>Connecticut</td><td>16,345,525,000</td><td>1.7%</td></tr>
<tr><td>16</td><td>Maryland</td><td>21,599,795,000</td><td>2.3%</td><td>20</td><td>Tennessee</td><td>13,893,728,000</td><td>1.5%</td></tr>
<tr><td>10</td><td>Massachusetts</td><td>27,518,360,000</td><td>2.9%</td><td>21</td><td>Arizona</td><td>13,888,611,000</td><td>1.5%</td></tr>
<tr><td>9</td><td>Michigan</td><td>28,628,517,000</td><td>3.0%</td><td>22</td><td>Colorado</td><td>13,197,606,000</td><td>1.4%</td></tr>
<tr><td>12</td><td>Minnesota</td><td>25,594,522,000</td><td>2.7%</td><td>23</td><td>Missouri</td><td>12,495,505,000</td><td>1.3%</td></tr>
<tr><td>35</td><td>Mississippi</td><td>7,783,031,000</td><td>0.8%</td><td>24</td><td>Oregon</td><td>11,914,567,000</td><td>1.3%</td></tr>
<tr><td>23</td><td>Missouri</td><td>12,495,505,000</td><td>1.3%</td><td>25</td><td>Kentucky</td><td>11,907,759,000</td><td>1.3%</td></tr>
<tr><td>46</td><td>Montana</td><td>2,654,444,000</td><td>0.3%</td><td>26</td><td>Louisiana</td><td>11,104,720,000</td><td>1.2%</td></tr>
<tr><td>38</td><td>Nebraska</td><td>5,103,105,000</td><td>0.5%</td><td>27</td><td>Alabama</td><td>10,418,152,000</td><td>1.1%</td></tr>
<tr><td>31</td><td>Nevada</td><td>8,624,618,000</td><td>0.9%</td><td>28</td><td>South Carolina</td><td>9,828,825,000</td><td>1.0%</td></tr>
<tr><td>47</td><td>New Hampshire</td><td>2,496,719,000</td><td>0.3%</td><td>29</td><td>Iowa</td><td>9,755,430,000</td><td>1.0%</td></tr>
<tr><td>7</td><td>New Jersey</td><td>32,325,850,000</td><td>3.4%</td><td>30</td><td>Arkansas</td><td>9,516,281,000</td><td>1.0%</td></tr>
<tr><td>37</td><td>New Mexico</td><td>5,776,271,000</td><td>0.6%</td><td>31</td><td>Nevada</td><td>8,624,618,000</td><td>0.9%</td></tr>
<tr><td>2</td><td>New York</td><td>79,678,037,000</td><td>8.4%</td><td>32</td><td>Oklahoma</td><td>8,569,402,000</td><td>0.9%</td></tr>
<tr><td>11</td><td>North Carolina</td><td>26,855,304,000</td><td>2.8%</td><td>33</td><td>Kansas</td><td>8,173,821,000</td><td>0.9%</td></tr>
<tr><td>43</td><td>North Dakota</td><td>3,465,326,000</td><td>0.4%</td><td>34</td><td>Utah</td><td>7,832,889,000</td><td>0.8%</td></tr>
<tr><td>8</td><td>Ohio</td><td>30,306,468,000</td><td>3.2%</td><td>35</td><td>Mississippi</td><td>7,783,031,000</td><td>0.8%</td></tr>
<tr><td>32</td><td>Oklahoma</td><td>8,569,402,000</td><td>0.9%</td><td>36</td><td>Hawaii</td><td>7,029,026,000</td><td>0.7%</td></tr>
<tr><td>24</td><td>Oregon</td><td>11,914,567,000</td><td>1.3%</td><td>37</td><td>New Mexico</td><td>5,776,271,000</td><td>0.6%</td></tr>
<tr><td>6</td><td>Pennsylvania</td><td>37,853,091,000</td><td>4.0%</td><td>38</td><td>Nebraska</td><td>5,103,105,000</td><td>0.5%</td></tr>
<tr><td>44</td><td>Rhode Island</td><td>3,266,663,000</td><td>0.3%</td><td>39</td><td>West Virginia</td><td>5,092,275,000</td><td>0.5%</td></tr>
<tr><td>28</td><td>South Carolina</td><td>9,828,825,000</td><td>1.0%</td><td>40</td><td>Idaho</td><td>4,511,208,000</td><td>0.5%</td></tr>
<tr><td>48</td><td>South Dakota</td><td>1,828,543,000</td><td>0.2%</td><td>41</td><td>Maine</td><td>4,232,556,000</td><td>0.4%</td></tr>
<tr><td>20</td><td>Tennessee</td><td>13,893,728,000</td><td>1.5%</td><td>42</td><td>Delaware</td><td>3,588,905,000</td><td>0.4%</td></tr>
<tr><td>3</td><td>Texas</td><td>53,612,926,000</td><td>5.6%</td><td>43</td><td>North Dakota</td><td>3,465,326,000</td><td>0.4%</td></tr>
<tr><td>34</td><td>Utah</td><td>7,832,889,000</td><td>0.8%</td><td>44</td><td>Rhode Island</td><td>3,266,663,000</td><td>0.3%</td></tr>
<tr><td>45</td><td>Vermont</td><td>3,127,523,000</td><td>0.3%</td><td>45</td><td>Vermont</td><td>3,127,523,000</td><td>0.3%</td></tr>
<tr><td>15</td><td>Virginia</td><td>22,213,025,000</td><td>2.3%</td><td>46</td><td>Montana</td><td>2,654,444,000</td><td>0.3%</td></tr>
<tr><td>13</td><td>Washington</td><td>23,997,592,000</td><td>2.5%</td><td>47</td><td>New Hampshire</td><td>2,496,719,000</td><td>0.3%</td></tr>
<tr><td>39</td><td>West Virginia</td><td>5,092,275,000</td><td>0.5%</td><td>48</td><td>South Dakota</td><td>1,828,543,000</td><td>0.2%</td></tr>
<tr><td>17</td><td>Wisconsin</td><td>18,133,496,000</td><td>1.9%</td><td>49</td><td>Wyoming</td><td>1,649,550,000</td><td>0.2%</td></tr>
<tr><td>49</td><td>Wyoming</td><td>1,649,550,000</td><td>0.2%</td><td>50</td><td>Alaska</td><td>1,189,786,000</td><td>0.1%</td></tr>
<tr><td></td><td></td><td></td><td></td><td></td><td>District of Columbia</td><td>7,653,053,000</td><td>0.8%</td></tr>
</table>

Source: U.S. Bureau of the Census, Governments Division
"2017 State Government Tax Collections" (https://www.census.gov/programs-surveys/stc.html)

Per Capita State Government Tax Revenue in 2017

National Per Capita = $2,923

ALPHA ORDER

RANK	STATE	PER CAPITA
41	Alabama	$2,137
50	Alaska	1,608
45	Arizona	1,970
14	Arkansas	3,169
8	California	3,950
38	Colorado	2,350
5	Connecticut	4,574
9	Delaware	3,750
47	Florida	1,917
40	Georgia	2,153
2	Hawaii	4,935
30	Idaho	2,624
18	Illinois	2,970
27	Indiana	2,710
16	Iowa	3,103
24	Kansas	2,808
28	Kentucky	2,674
37	Louisiana	2,377
13	Maine	3,170
11	Maryland	3,585
7	Massachusetts	4,010
22	Michigan	2,870
3	Minnesota	4,597
33	Mississippi	2,603
44	Missouri	2,046
36	Montana	2,521
29	Nebraska	2,661
20	Nevada	2,902
49	New Hampshire	1,850
10	New Jersey	3,637
26	New Mexico	2,759
6	New York	4,067
32	North Carolina	2,615
4	North Dakota	4,589
34	Ohio	2,598
39	Oklahoma	2,179
21	Oregon	2,873
19	Pennsylvania	2,959
17	Rhode Island	3,092
46	South Carolina	1,957
42	South Dakota	2,094
43	Tennessee	2,071
48	Texas	1,893
35	Utah	2,524
1	Vermont	5,008
30	Virginia	2,624
12	Washington	3,232
25	West Virginia	2,802
15	Wisconsin	3,131
23	Wyoming	2,849

RANK ORDER

RANK	STATE	PER CAPITA
1	Vermont	$5,008
2	Hawaii	4,935
3	Minnesota	4,597
4	North Dakota	4,589
5	Connecticut	4,574
6	New York	4,067
7	Massachusetts	4,010
8	California	3,950
9	Delaware	3,750
10	New Jersey	3,637
11	Maryland	3,585
12	Washington	3,232
13	Maine	3,170
14	Arkansas	3,169
15	Wisconsin	3,131
16	Iowa	3,103
17	Rhode Island	3,092
18	Illinois	2,970
19	Pennsylvania	2,959
20	Nevada	2,902
21	Oregon	2,873
22	Michigan	2,870
23	Wyoming	2,849
24	Kansas	2,808
25	West Virginia	2,802
26	New Mexico	2,759
27	Indiana	2,710
28	Kentucky	2,674
29	Nebraska	2,661
30	Idaho	2,624
30	Virginia	2,624
32	North Carolina	2,615
33	Mississippi	2,603
34	Ohio	2,598
35	Utah	2,524
36	Montana	2,521
37	Louisiana	2,377
38	Colorado	2,350
39	Oklahoma	2,179
40	Georgia	2,153
41	Alabama	2,137
42	South Dakota	2,094
43	Tennessee	2,071
44	Missouri	2,046
45	Arizona	1,970
46	South Carolina	1,957
47	Florida	1,917
48	Texas	1,893
49	New Hampshire	1,850
50	Alaska	1,608
	District of Columbia	11,001

Source: CQ Press using data from U.S. Bureau of the Census, Governments Division
"2017 State Government Tax Collections" (https://www.census.gov/programs-surveys/stc.html)

State Government Tax Revenue as a Percent of Personal Income in 2017

National Percent = 5.7% of Personal Income

ALPHA ORDER

RANK	STATE	PERCENT
35	Alabama	5.2
50	Alaska	2.8
41	Arizona	4.7
5	Arkansas	7.7
11	California	6.6
45	Colorado	4.3
15	Connecticut	6.3
6	Delaware	7.5
47	Florida	4.0
38	Georgia	4.9
2	Hawaii	9.3
15	Idaho	6.3
32	Illinois	5.5
20	Indiana	6.0
11	Iowa	6.6
25	Kansas	5.8
11	Kentucky	6.6
34	Louisiana	5.4
10	Maine	6.8
22	Maryland	5.9
22	Massachusetts	5.9
17	Michigan	6.2
4	Minnesota	8.4
8	Mississippi	7.1
43	Missouri	4.5
28	Montana	5.6
35	Nebraska	5.2
17	Nevada	6.2
49	New Hampshire	3.1
28	New Jersey	5.6
9	New Mexico	6.9
17	New York	6.2
22	North Carolina	5.9
3	North Dakota	8.8
28	Ohio	5.6
38	Oklahoma	4.9
20	Oregon	6.0
32	Pennsylvania	5.5
25	Rhode Island	5.8
41	South Carolina	4.7
45	South Dakota	4.3
43	Tennessee	4.5
47	Texas	4.0
25	Utah	5.8
1	Vermont	9.6
40	Virginia	4.8
28	Washington	5.6
7	West Virginia	7.3
14	Wisconsin	6.4
37	Wyoming	5.0

RANK ORDER

RANK	STATE	PERCENT
1	Vermont	9.6
2	Hawaii	9.3
3	North Dakota	8.8
4	Minnesota	8.4
5	Arkansas	7.7
6	Delaware	7.5
7	West Virginia	7.3
8	Mississippi	7.1
9	New Mexico	6.9
10	Maine	6.8
11	California	6.6
11	Iowa	6.6
11	Kentucky	6.6
14	Wisconsin	6.4
15	Connecticut	6.3
15	Idaho	6.3
17	Michigan	6.2
17	Nevada	6.2
17	New York	6.2
20	Indiana	6.0
20	Oregon	6.0
22	Maryland	5.9
22	Massachusetts	5.9
22	North Carolina	5.9
25	Kansas	5.8
25	Rhode Island	5.8
25	Utah	5.8
28	Montana	5.6
28	New Jersey	5.6
28	Ohio	5.6
28	Washington	5.6
32	Illinois	5.5
32	Pennsylvania	5.5
34	Louisiana	5.4
35	Alabama	5.2
35	Nebraska	5.2
37	Wyoming	5.0
38	Georgia	4.9
38	Oklahoma	4.9
40	Virginia	4.8
41	Arizona	4.7
41	South Carolina	4.7
43	Missouri	4.5
43	Tennessee	4.5
45	Colorado	4.3
45	South Dakota	4.3
47	Florida	4.0
47	Texas	4.0
49	New Hampshire	3.1
50	Alaska	2.8

	District of Columbia	13.8

Source: CQ Press using data from U.S. Bureau of the Census, Governments Division
"2017 State Government Tax Collections" (https://www.census.gov/programs-surveys/stc.html) and
U.S. Department of Commerce, Bureau of Economic Analysis
"Annual State Personal Income" (https://apps.bea.gov/iTable/index_regional.cfm)

State Government Individual Income Tax Revenue in 2017

National Total = $352,834,534,000

ALPHA ORDER

RANK	STATE	REVENUE	% of USA
23	Alabama	$3,624,543,000	1.0%
44	Alaska	0	0.0%
25	Arizona	3,445,650,000	1.0%
28	Arkansas	2,767,767,000	0.8%
1	California	84,196,751,000	23.9%
17	Colorado	6,791,929,000	1.9%
15	Connecticut	7,959,492,000	2.3%
38	Delaware	1,180,975,000	0.3%
44	Florida	0	0.0%
9	Georgia	10,977,693,000	3.1%
31	Hawaii	2,095,601,000	0.6%
34	Idaho	1,660,248,000	0.5%
5	Illinois	13,256,769,000	3.8%
19	Indiana	5,435,292,000	1.5%
22	Iowa	3,655,462,000	1.0%
29	Kansas	2,327,652,000	0.7%
20	Kentucky	4,394,185,000	1.2%
27	Louisiana	2,949,939,000	0.8%
35	Maine	1,534,866,000	0.4%
12	Maryland	9,066,709,000	2.6%
3	Massachusetts	14,724,277,000	4.2%
11	Michigan	9,485,325,000	2.7%
10	Minnesota	10,956,205,000	3.1%
32	Mississippi	1,834,688,000	0.5%
18	Missouri	6,149,468,000	1.7%
39	Montana	1,177,958,000	0.3%
30	Nebraska	2,228,486,000	0.6%
44	Nevada	0	0.0%
43	New Hampshire	65,467,000	0.0%
4	New Jersey	13,958,119,000	4.0%
36	New Mexico	1,338,768,000	0.4%
2	New York	44,631,769,000	12.6%
7	North Carolina	12,086,332,000	3.4%
41	North Dakota	319,507,000	0.1%
14	Ohio	8,377,450,000	2.4%
26	Oklahoma	3,122,602,000	0.9%
13	Oregon	8,379,225,000	2.4%
8	Pennsylvania	12,063,782,000	3.4%
37	Rhode Island	1,238,928,000	0.4%
21	South Carolina	4,142,276,000	1.2%
44	South Dakota	0	0.0%
42	Tennessee	249,977,000	0.1%
44	Texas	0	0.0%
24	Utah	3,621,199,000	1.0%
40	Vermont	743,630,000	0.2%
6	Virginia	13,052,887,000	3.7%
44	Washington	0	0.0%
33	West Virginia	1,813,866,000	0.5%
16	Wisconsin	7,792,543,000	2.2%
44	Wyoming	0	0.0%

RANK ORDER

RANK	STATE	REVENUE	% of USA
1	California	$84,196,751,000	23.9%
2	New York	44,631,769,000	12.6%
3	Massachusetts	14,724,277,000	4.2%
4	New Jersey	13,958,119,000	4.0%
5	Illinois	13,256,769,000	3.8%
6	Virginia	13,052,887,000	3.7%
7	North Carolina	12,086,332,000	3.4%
8	Pennsylvania	12,063,782,000	3.4%
9	Georgia	10,977,693,000	3.1%
10	Minnesota	10,956,205,000	3.1%
11	Michigan	9,485,325,000	2.7%
12	Maryland	9,066,709,000	2.6%
13	Oregon	8,379,225,000	2.4%
14	Ohio	8,377,450,000	2.4%
15	Connecticut	7,959,492,000	2.3%
16	Wisconsin	7,792,543,000	2.2%
17	Colorado	6,791,929,000	1.9%
18	Missouri	6,149,468,000	1.7%
19	Indiana	5,435,292,000	1.5%
20	Kentucky	4,394,185,000	1.2%
21	South Carolina	4,142,276,000	1.2%
22	Iowa	3,655,462,000	1.0%
23	Alabama	3,624,543,000	1.0%
24	Utah	3,621,199,000	1.0%
25	Arizona	3,445,650,000	1.0%
26	Oklahoma	3,122,602,000	0.9%
27	Louisiana	2,949,939,000	0.8%
28	Arkansas	2,767,767,000	0.8%
29	Kansas	2,327,652,000	0.7%
30	Nebraska	2,228,486,000	0.6%
31	Hawaii	2,095,601,000	0.6%
32	Mississippi	1,834,688,000	0.5%
33	West Virginia	1,813,866,000	0.5%
34	Idaho	1,660,248,000	0.5%
35	Maine	1,534,866,000	0.4%
36	New Mexico	1,338,768,000	0.4%
37	Rhode Island	1,238,928,000	0.4%
38	Delaware	1,180,975,000	0.3%
39	Montana	1,177,958,000	0.3%
40	Vermont	743,630,000	0.2%
41	North Dakota	319,507,000	0.1%
42	Tennessee	249,977,000	0.1%
43	New Hampshire	65,467,000	0.0%
44	Alaska	0	0.0%
44	Florida	0	0.0%
44	Nevada	0	0.0%
44	South Dakota	0	0.0%
44	Texas	0	0.0%
44	Washington	0	0.0%
44	Wyoming	0	0.0%
	District of Columbia	1,958,277,000	0.6%

Source: U.S. Bureau of the Census, Governments Division
"2017 State Government Tax Collections" (https://www.census.gov/programs-surveys/stc.html)

Per Capita State Government Individual Income Tax Revenue in 2017

National Per Capita = $1,085

ALPHA ORDER

RANK	STATE	PER CAPITA
35	Alabama	$743
44	Alaska	0
40	Arizona	489
30	Arkansas	922
4	California	2,137
13	Colorado	1,209
2	Connecticut	2,227
12	Delaware	1,234
44	Florida	0
22	Georgia	1,054
10	Hawaii	1,471
27	Idaho	966
23	Illinois	1,037
32	Indiana	816
18	Iowa	1,163
33	Kansas	800
26	Kentucky	987
38	Louisiana	632
20	Maine	1,150
9	Maryland	1,505
3	Massachusetts	2,145
28	Michigan	951
6	Minnesota	1,968
39	Mississippi	614
24	Missouri	1,007
21	Montana	1,119
19	Nebraska	1,162
44	Nevada	0
42	New Hampshire	49
7	New Jersey	1,570
37	New Mexico	640
1	New York	2,278
15	North Carolina	1,177
41	North Dakota	423
36	Ohio	718
34	Oklahoma	794
5	Oregon	2,021
29	Pennsylvania	943
16	Rhode Island	1,173
31	South Carolina	825
44	South Dakota	0
43	Tennessee	37
44	Texas	0
17	Utah	1,167
14	Vermont	1,191
8	Virginia	1,542
44	Washington	0
25	West Virginia	998
11	Wisconsin	1,345
44	Wyoming	0

RANK ORDER

RANK	STATE	PER CAPITA
1	New York	$2,278
2	Connecticut	2,227
3	Massachusetts	2,145
4	California	2,137
5	Oregon	2,021
6	Minnesota	1,968
7	New Jersey	1,570
8	Virginia	1,542
9	Maryland	1,505
10	Hawaii	1,471
11	Wisconsin	1,345
12	Delaware	1,234
13	Colorado	1,209
14	Vermont	1,191
15	North Carolina	1,177
16	Rhode Island	1,173
17	Utah	1,167
18	Iowa	1,163
19	Nebraska	1,162
20	Maine	1,150
21	Montana	1,119
22	Georgia	1,054
23	Illinois	1,037
24	Missouri	1,007
25	West Virginia	998
26	Kentucky	987
27	Idaho	966
28	Michigan	951
29	Pennsylvania	943
30	Arkansas	922
31	South Carolina	825
32	Indiana	816
33	Kansas	800
34	Oklahoma	794
35	Alabama	743
36	Ohio	718
37	New Mexico	640
38	Louisiana	632
39	Mississippi	614
40	Arizona	489
41	North Dakota	423
42	New Hampshire	49
43	Tennessee	37
44	Alaska	0
44	Florida	0
44	Nevada	0
44	South Dakota	0
44	Texas	0
44	Washington	0
44	Wyoming	0
	District of Columbia	2,815

Source: CQ Press using data from U.S. Bureau of the Census, Governments Division
"2017 State Government Tax Collections" (https://www.census.gov/programs-surveys/stc.html)

State Government Corporation Net Income Tax Revenue in 2017

National Total = $45,181,846,000

ALPHA ORDER

RANK	STATE	REVENUE	% of USA
21	Alabama	$520,113,000	1.2%
42	Alaska	87,775,000	0.2%
28	Arizona	368,136,000	0.8%
25	Arkansas	396,989,000	0.9%
1	California	10,112,520,000	22.4%
20	Colorado	528,541,000	1.2%
15	Connecticut	897,247,000	2.0%
33	Delaware	246,175,000	0.5%
4	Florida	2,383,783,000	5.3%
13	Georgia	971,898,000	2.2%
35	Hawaii	184,840,000	0.4%
34	Idaho	216,641,000	0.5%
3	Illinois	2,877,499,000	6.4%
11	Indiana	1,025,498,000	2.3%
23	Iowa	432,020,000	1.0%
26	Kansas	386,966,000	0.9%
22	Kentucky	458,650,000	1.0%
31	Louisiana	291,321,000	0.6%
36	Maine	175,239,000	0.4%
12	Maryland	1,001,934,000	2.2%
6	Massachusetts	2,196,474,000	4.9%
10	Michigan	1,195,399,000	2.6%
9	Minnesota	1,227,028,000	2.7%
24	Mississippi	407,913,000	0.9%
30	Missouri	307,443,000	0.7%
39	Montana	125,003,000	0.3%
32	Nebraska	264,440,000	0.6%
47	Nevada	0	0.0%
19	New Hampshire	573,653,000	1.3%
7	New Jersey	2,109,930,000	4.7%
41	New Mexico	91,876,000	0.2%
2	New York	4,026,353,000	8.9%
17	North Carolina	757,041,000	1.7%
44	North Dakota	60,871,000	0.1%
46	Ohio	8,833,000	0.0%
37	Oklahoma	157,894,000	0.3%
18	Oregon	633,046,000	1.4%
5	Pennsylvania	2,344,344,000	5.2%
38	Rhode Island	129,732,000	0.3%
27	South Carolina	375,655,000	0.8%
45	South Dakota	30,728,000	0.1%
8	Tennessee	1,726,223,000	3.8%
47	Texas	0	0.0%
29	Utah	329,577,000	0.7%
43	Vermont	81,395,000	0.2%
16	Virginia	826,961,000	1.8%
47	Washington	0	0.0%
40	West Virginia	116,305,000	0.3%
14	Wisconsin	959,699,000	2.1%
47	Wyoming	0	0.0%

RANK ORDER

RANK	STATE	REVENUE	% of USA
1	California	$10,112,520,000	22.4%
2	New York	4,026,353,000	8.9%
3	Illinois	2,877,499,000	6.4%
4	Florida	2,383,783,000	5.3%
5	Pennsylvania	2,344,344,000	5.2%
6	Massachusetts	2,196,474,000	4.9%
7	New Jersey	2,109,930,000	4.7%
8	Tennessee	1,726,223,000	3.8%
9	Minnesota	1,227,028,000	2.7%
10	Michigan	1,195,399,000	2.6%
11	Indiana	1,025,498,000	2.3%
12	Maryland	1,001,934,000	2.2%
13	Georgia	971,898,000	2.2%
14	Wisconsin	959,699,000	2.1%
15	Connecticut	897,247,000	2.0%
16	Virginia	826,961,000	1.8%
17	North Carolina	757,041,000	1.7%
18	Oregon	633,046,000	1.4%
19	New Hampshire	573,653,000	1.3%
20	Colorado	528,541,000	1.2%
21	Alabama	520,113,000	1.2%
22	Kentucky	458,650,000	1.0%
23	Iowa	432,020,000	1.0%
24	Mississippi	407,913,000	0.9%
25	Arkansas	396,989,000	0.9%
26	Kansas	386,966,000	0.9%
27	South Carolina	375,655,000	0.8%
28	Arizona	368,136,000	0.8%
29	Utah	329,577,000	0.7%
30	Missouri	307,443,000	0.7%
31	Louisiana	291,321,000	0.6%
32	Nebraska	264,440,000	0.6%
33	Delaware	246,175,000	0.5%
34	Idaho	216,641,000	0.5%
35	Hawaii	184,840,000	0.4%
36	Maine	175,239,000	0.4%
37	Oklahoma	157,894,000	0.3%
38	Rhode Island	129,732,000	0.3%
39	Montana	125,003,000	0.3%
40	West Virginia	116,305,000	0.3%
41	New Mexico	91,876,000	0.2%
42	Alaska	87,775,000	0.2%
43	Vermont	81,395,000	0.2%
44	North Dakota	60,871,000	0.1%
45	South Dakota	30,728,000	0.1%
46	Ohio	8,833,000	0.0%
47	Nevada	0	0.0%
47	Texas	0	0.0%
47	Washington	0	0.0%
47	Wyoming	0	0.0%
	District of Columbia	554,245,000	1.2%

Source: U.S. Bureau of the Census, Governments Division
"2017 State Government Tax Collections" (https://www.census.gov/programs-surveys/stc.html)

Per Capita State Government Corporation Net Income Tax Revenue in 2017

National Per Capita = $139

ALPHA ORDER

RANK	STATE	PER CAPITA
30	Alabama	$107
27	Alaska	119
41	Arizona	52
20	Arkansas	132
3	California	257
34	Colorado	94
6	Connecticut	251
3	Delaware	257
29	Florida	114
35	Georgia	93
22	Hawaii	130
24	Idaho	126
8	Illinois	225
14	Indiana	154
17	Iowa	137
19	Kansas	133
32	Kentucky	103
40	Louisiana	62
21	Maine	131
12	Maryland	166
2	Massachusetts	320
26	Michigan	120
9	Minnesota	220
18	Mississippi	136
42	Missouri	50
27	Montana	119
16	Nebraska	138
47	Nevada	0
1	New Hampshire	425
7	New Jersey	237
43	New Mexico	44
10	New York	206
38	North Carolina	74
36	North Dakota	81
46	Ohio	1
44	Oklahoma	40
15	Oregon	153
11	Pennsylvania	183
25	Rhode Island	123
37	South Carolina	75
45	South Dakota	35
3	Tennessee	257
47	Texas	0
31	Utah	106
22	Vermont	130
33	Virginia	98
47	Washington	0
39	West Virginia	64
12	Wisconsin	166
47	Wyoming	0

RANK ORDER

RANK	STATE	PER CAPITA
1	New Hampshire	$425
2	Massachusetts	320
3	California	257
3	Delaware	257
3	Tennessee	257
6	Connecticut	251
7	New Jersey	237
8	Illinois	225
9	Minnesota	220
10	New York	206
11	Pennsylvania	183
12	Maryland	166
12	Wisconsin	166
14	Indiana	154
15	Oregon	153
16	Nebraska	138
17	Iowa	137
18	Mississippi	136
19	Kansas	133
20	Arkansas	132
21	Maine	131
22	Hawaii	130
22	Vermont	130
24	Idaho	126
25	Rhode Island	123
26	Michigan	120
27	Alaska	119
27	Montana	119
29	Florida	114
30	Alabama	107
31	Utah	106
32	Kentucky	103
33	Virginia	98
34	Colorado	94
35	Georgia	93
36	North Dakota	81
37	South Carolina	75
38	North Carolina	74
39	West Virginia	64
40	Louisiana	62
41	Arizona	52
42	Missouri	50
43	New Mexico	44
44	Oklahoma	40
45	South Dakota	35
46	Ohio	1
47	Nevada	0
47	Texas	0
47	Washington	0
47	Wyoming	0

District of Columbia	797

Source: CQ Press using data from U.S. Bureau of the Census, Governments Division
   "2017 State Government Tax Collections" (https://www.census.gov/programs-surveys/stc.html)

State Government General Sales Tax Revenue in 2017

National Total = $301,195,952,000*

ALPHA ORDER					RANK ORDER			
RANK	STATE	REVENUE	% of USA		RANK	STATE	REVENUE	% of USA
33	Alabama	$2,654,883,000	0.9%		1	California	$35,357,699,000	11.7%
46	Alaska	0	0.0%		2	Texas	32,490,144,000	10.8%
14	Arizona	6,566,503,000	2.2%		3	Florida	25,346,166,000	8.4%
27	Arkansas	3,384,394,000	1.1%		4	Washington	14,509,841,000	4.8%
1	California	35,357,699,000	11.7%		5	New York	14,132,141,000	4.7%
32	Colorado	2,978,382,000	1.0%		6	Ohio	13,343,149,000	4.4%
21	Connecticut	4,236,619,000	1.4%		7	Illinois	11,363,366,000	3.8%
46	Delaware	0	0.0%		8	Pennsylvania	10,509,734,000	3.5%
3	Florida	25,346,166,000	8.4%		9	New Jersey	9,591,881,000	3.2%
17	Georgia	5,729,916,000	1.9%		10	Michigan	9,223,737,000	3.1%
29	Hawaii	3,239,225,000	1.1%		11	North Carolina	7,656,898,000	2.5%
38	Idaho	1,650,498,000	0.5%		12	Indiana	7,556,326,000	2.5%
7	Illinois	11,363,366,000	3.8%		13	Tennessee	7,260,193,000	2.4%
12	Indiana	7,556,326,000	2.5%		14	Arizona	6,566,503,000	2.2%
31	Iowa	3,205,997,000	1.1%		15	Massachusetts	6,240,822,000	2.1%
30	Kansas	3,209,506,000	1.1%		16	Minnesota	5,888,795,000	2.0%
26	Kentucky	3,490,639,000	1.2%		17	Georgia	5,729,916,000	1.9%
22	Louisiana	4,215,378,000	1.4%		18	Wisconsin	5,223,935,000	1.7%
39	Maine	1,441,867,000	0.5%		19	Nevada	4,756,243,000	1.6%
20	Maryland	4,609,538,000	1.5%		20	Maryland	4,609,538,000	1.5%
15	Massachusetts	6,240,822,000	2.1%		21	Connecticut	4,236,619,000	1.4%
10	Michigan	9,223,737,000	3.1%		22	Louisiana	4,215,378,000	1.4%
16	Minnesota	5,888,795,000	2.0%		23	Virginia	3,970,133,000	1.3%
25	Mississippi	3,526,913,000	1.2%		24	Missouri	3,604,570,000	1.2%
24	Missouri	3,604,570,000	1.2%		25	Mississippi	3,526,913,000	1.2%
46	Montana	0	0.0%		26	Kentucky	3,490,639,000	1.2%
37	Nebraska	1,835,037,000	0.6%		27	Arkansas	3,384,394,000	1.1%
19	Nevada	4,756,243,000	1.6%		28	South Carolina	3,285,007,000	1.1%
46	New Hampshire	0	0.0%		29	Hawaii	3,239,225,000	1.1%
9	New Jersey	9,591,881,000	3.2%		30	Kansas	3,209,506,000	1.1%
36	New Mexico	2,258,767,000	0.7%		31	Iowa	3,205,997,000	1.1%
5	New York	14,132,141,000	4.7%		32	Colorado	2,978,382,000	1.0%
11	North Carolina	7,656,898,000	2.5%		33	Alabama	2,654,883,000	0.9%
43	North Dakota	872,176,000	0.3%		34	Utah	2,533,961,000	0.8%
6	Ohio	13,343,149,000	4.4%		35	Oklahoma	2,465,383,000	0.8%
35	Oklahoma	2,465,383,000	0.8%		36	New Mexico	2,258,767,000	0.7%
46	Oregon	0	0.0%		37	Nebraska	1,835,037,000	0.6%
8	Pennsylvania	10,509,734,000	3.5%		38	Idaho	1,650,498,000	0.5%
42	Rhode Island	996,390,000	0.3%		39	Maine	1,441,867,000	0.5%
28	South Carolina	3,285,007,000	1.1%		40	West Virginia	1,334,168,000	0.4%
41	South Dakota	1,065,361,000	0.4%		41	South Dakota	1,065,361,000	0.4%
13	Tennessee	7,260,193,000	2.4%		42	Rhode Island	996,390,000	0.3%
2	Texas	32,490,144,000	10.8%		43	North Dakota	872,176,000	0.3%
34	Utah	2,533,961,000	0.8%		44	Wyoming	588,866,000	0.2%
45	Vermont	375,870,000	0.1%		45	Vermont	375,870,000	0.1%
23	Virginia	3,970,133,000	1.3%		46	Alaska	0	0.0%
4	Washington	14,509,841,000	4.8%		46	Delaware	0	0.0%
40	West Virginia	1,334,168,000	0.4%		46	Montana	0	0.0%
18	Wisconsin	5,223,935,000	1.7%		46	New Hampshire	0	0.0%
44	Wyoming	588,866,000	0.2%		46	Oregon	0	0.0%
						District of Columbia	1,418,935,000	0.5%

Source: U.S. Bureau of the Census, Governments Division
"2017 State Government Tax Collections" (https://www.census.gov/programs-surveys/stc.html)
*Does not include special sales taxes such as those on sale of alcohol, gasoline, or tobacco.

Per Capita State Government General Sales Tax Revenue in 2017

National Per Capita = $926*

ALPHA ORDER

RANK	STATE	PER CAPITA
43	Alabama	$545
46	Alaska	0
24	Arizona	932
12	Arkansas	1,127
29	California	897
44	Colorado	530
6	Connecticut	1,185
46	Delaware	0
5	Florida	1,208
42	Georgia	550
1	Hawaii	2,274
21	Idaho	960
30	Illinois	889
11	Indiana	1,135
19	Iowa	1,020
13	Kansas	1,103
33	Kentucky	784
27	Louisiana	902
15	Maine	1,080
34	Maryland	765
26	Massachusetts	909
25	Michigan	925
18	Minnesota	1,058
7	Mississippi	1,180
41	Missouri	590
46	Montana	0
22	Nebraska	957
3	Nevada	1,600
46	New Hampshire	0
16	New Jersey	1,079
16	New Mexico	1,079
37	New York	721
35	North Carolina	746
8	North Dakota	1,155
10	Ohio	1,144
39	Oklahoma	627
46	Oregon	0
31	Pennsylvania	822
23	Rhode Island	943
38	South Carolina	654
4	South Dakota	1,220
14	Tennessee	1,082
9	Texas	1,147
32	Utah	817
40	Vermont	602
45	Virginia	469
2	Washington	1,954
36	West Virginia	734
27	Wisconsin	902
20	Wyoming	1,017

RANK ORDER

RANK	STATE	PER CAPITA
1	Hawaii	$2,274
2	Washington	1,954
3	Nevada	1,600
4	South Dakota	1,220
5	Florida	1,208
6	Connecticut	1,185
7	Mississippi	1,180
8	North Dakota	1,155
9	Texas	1,147
10	Ohio	1,144
11	Indiana	1,135
12	Arkansas	1,127
13	Kansas	1,103
14	Tennessee	1,082
15	Maine	1,080
16	New Jersey	1,079
16	New Mexico	1,079
18	Minnesota	1,058
19	Iowa	1,020
20	Wyoming	1,017
21	Idaho	960
22	Nebraska	957
23	Rhode Island	943
24	Arizona	932
25	Michigan	925
26	Massachusetts	909
27	Louisiana	902
27	Wisconsin	902
29	California	897
30	Illinois	889
31	Pennsylvania	822
32	Utah	817
33	Kentucky	784
34	Maryland	765
35	North Carolina	746
36	West Virginia	734
37	New York	721
38	South Carolina	654
39	Oklahoma	627
40	Vermont	602
41	Missouri	590
42	Georgia	550
43	Alabama	545
44	Colorado	530
45	Virginia	469
46	Alaska	0
46	Delaware	0
46	Montana	0
46	New Hampshire	0
46	Oregon	0

District of Columbia	2,040

Source: CQ Press using data from U.S. Bureau of the Census, Governments Division
   "2017 State Government Tax Collections" (https://www.census.gov/programs-surveys/stc.html)
*Does not include special sales taxes such as those on sale of alcohol, gasoline, or tobacco.

State Government Motor Fuels Sales Tax Revenue in 2017

National Total = $45,060,523,000

ALPHA ORDER				RANK ORDER			
RANK	STATE	REVENUE	% of USA	RANK	STATE	REVENUE	% of USA
25	Alabama	$588,992,000	1.3%	1	California	$4,842,749,000	10.7%
50	Alaska	45,944,000	0.1%	2	Texas	3,585,179,000	8.0%
17	Arizona	856,495,000	1.9%	3	Pennsylvania	3,143,576,000	7.0%
30	Arkansas	487,517,000	1.1%	4	Florida	2,727,802,000	6.1%
1	California	4,842,749,000	10.7%	5	Ohio	1,984,392,000	4.4%
23	Colorado	653,790,000	1.5%	6	North Carolina	1,922,400,000	4.3%
31	Connecticut	484,479,000	1.1%	7	Washington	1,812,646,000	4.0%
45	Delaware	129,487,000	0.3%	8	Georgia	1,741,092,000	3.9%
4	Florida	2,727,802,000	6.1%	9	New York	1,647,240,000	3.7%
8	Georgia	1,741,092,000	3.9%	10	Illinois	1,348,414,000	3.0%
48	Hawaii	87,026,000	0.2%	11	Michigan	1,210,628,000	2.7%
37	Idaho	353,548,000	0.8%	12	Maryland	1,078,313,000	2.4%
10	Illinois	1,348,414,000	3.0%	13	Wisconsin	1,044,996,000	2.3%
18	Indiana	854,529,000	1.9%	14	Virginia	997,561,000	2.2%
22	Iowa	674,603,000	1.5%	15	Tennessee	915,858,000	2.0%
33	Kansas	458,008,000	1.0%	16	Minnesota	912,644,000	2.0%
21	Kentucky	701,440,000	1.6%	17	Arizona	856,495,000	1.9%
24	Louisiana	634,883,000	1.4%	18	Indiana	854,529,000	1.9%
39	Maine	252,870,000	0.6%	19	Massachusetts	769,442,000	1.7%
12	Maryland	1,078,313,000	2.4%	20	Missouri	720,849,000	1.6%
19	Massachusetts	769,442,000	1.7%	21	Kentucky	701,440,000	1.6%
11	Michigan	1,210,628,000	2.7%	22	Iowa	674,603,000	1.5%
16	Minnesota	912,644,000	2.0%	23	Colorado	653,790,000	1.5%
34	Mississippi	443,522,000	1.0%	24	Louisiana	634,883,000	1.4%
20	Missouri	720,849,000	1.6%	25	Alabama	588,992,000	1.3%
42	Montana	189,561,000	0.4%	26	South Carolina	583,476,000	1.3%
36	Nebraska	354,234,000	0.8%	27	New Jersey	532,878,000	1.2%
38	Nevada	326,425,000	0.7%	28	Oregon	529,658,000	1.2%
44	New Hampshire	152,086,000	0.3%	29	Utah	487,731,000	1.1%
27	New Jersey	532,878,000	1.2%	30	Arkansas	487,517,000	1.1%
40	New Mexico	242,627,000	0.5%	31	Connecticut	484,479,000	1.1%
9	New York	1,647,240,000	3.7%	32	Oklahoma	473,960,000	1.1%
6	North Carolina	1,922,400,000	4.3%	33	Kansas	458,008,000	1.0%
41	North Dakota	189,718,000	0.4%	34	Mississippi	443,522,000	1.0%
5	Ohio	1,984,392,000	4.4%	35	West Virginia	383,874,000	0.9%
32	Oklahoma	473,960,000	1.1%	36	Nebraska	354,234,000	0.8%
28	Oregon	529,658,000	1.2%	37	Idaho	353,548,000	0.8%
3	Pennsylvania	3,143,576,000	7.0%	38	Nevada	326,425,000	0.7%
47	Rhode Island	90,990,000	0.2%	39	Maine	252,870,000	0.6%
26	South Carolina	583,476,000	1.3%	40	New Mexico	242,627,000	0.5%
43	South Dakota	189,133,000	0.4%	41	North Dakota	189,718,000	0.4%
15	Tennessee	915,858,000	2.0%	42	Montana	189,561,000	0.4%
2	Texas	3,585,179,000	8.0%	43	South Dakota	189,133,000	0.4%
29	Utah	487,731,000	1.1%	44	New Hampshire	152,086,000	0.3%
49	Vermont	81,020,000	0.2%	45	Delaware	129,487,000	0.3%
14	Virginia	997,561,000	2.2%	46	Wyoming	114,140,000	0.3%
7	Washington	1,812,646,000	4.0%	47	Rhode Island	90,990,000	0.2%
35	West Virginia	383,874,000	0.9%	48	Hawaii	87,026,000	0.2%
13	Wisconsin	1,044,996,000	2.3%	49	Vermont	81,020,000	0.2%
46	Wyoming	114,140,000	0.3%	50	Alaska	45,944,000	0.1%
					District of Columbia	26,098,000	0.1%

Source: U.S. Bureau of the Census, Governments Division
"2017 State Government Tax Collections" (https://www.census.gov/programs-surveys/stc.html)

Per Capita State Government Motor Fuel Sales Tax Revenue in 2017

National Per Capita = $139

ALPHA ORDER

RANK	STATE	PER CAPITA
34	Alabama	$121
48	Alaska	62
33	Arizona	122
18	Arkansas	162
32	California	123
39	Colorado	116
24	Connecticut	136
26	Delaware	135
27	Florida	130
16	Georgia	167
49	Hawaii	61
7	Idaho	206
45	Illinois	105
29	Indiana	128
5	Iowa	215
19	Kansas	157
19	Kentucky	157
24	Louisiana	136
9	Maine	189
14	Maryland	179
43	Massachusetts	112
34	Michigan	121
17	Minnesota	164
22	Mississippi	148
37	Missouri	118
12	Montana	180
11	Nebraska	185
44	Nevada	110
42	New Hampshire	113
50	New Jersey	60
39	New Mexico	116
47	New York	84
10	North Carolina	187
1	North Dakota	251
15	Ohio	170
34	Oklahoma	121
29	Oregon	128
2	Pennsylvania	246
46	Rhode Island	86
39	South Carolina	116
4	South Dakota	217
23	Tennessee	137
31	Texas	127
19	Utah	157
27	Vermont	130
37	Virginia	118
3	Washington	244
6	West Virginia	211
12	Wisconsin	180
8	Wyoming	197

RANK ORDER

RANK	STATE	PER CAPITA
1	North Dakota	$251
2	Pennsylvania	246
3	Washington	244
4	South Dakota	217
5	Iowa	215
6	West Virginia	211
7	Idaho	206
8	Wyoming	197
9	Maine	189
10	North Carolina	187
11	Nebraska	185
12	Montana	180
12	Wisconsin	180
14	Maryland	179
15	Ohio	170
16	Georgia	167
17	Minnesota	164
18	Arkansas	162
19	Kansas	157
19	Kentucky	157
19	Utah	157
22	Mississippi	148
23	Tennessee	137
24	Connecticut	136
24	Louisiana	136
26	Delaware	135
27	Florida	130
27	Vermont	130
29	Indiana	128
29	Oregon	128
31	Texas	127
32	California	123
33	Arizona	122
34	Alabama	121
34	Michigan	121
34	Oklahoma	121
37	Missouri	118
37	Virginia	118
39	Colorado	116
39	New Mexico	116
39	South Carolina	116
42	New Hampshire	113
43	Massachusetts	112
44	Nevada	110
45	Illinois	105
46	Rhode Island	86
47	New York	84
48	Alaska	62
49	Hawaii	61
50	New Jersey	60
	District of Columbia	38

Source: CQ Press using data from U.S. Bureau of the Census, Governments Division
"2017 State Government Tax Collections" (https://www.census.gov/programs-surveys/stc.html)

State Tax Rates on Gasoline in 2018

National Median = 25.40 Cents per Gallon*

<table>
<tr><td colspan="3">ALPHA ORDER</td><td colspan="3">RANK ORDER</td></tr>
<tr><th>RANK</th><th>STATE</th><th>CENTS PER GALLON</th><th>RANK</th><th>STATE</th><th>CENTS PER GALLON</th></tr>
<tr><td>44</td><td>Alabama</td><td>18.00</td><td>1</td><td>Pennsylvania</td><td>57.60</td></tr>
<tr><td>50</td><td>Alaska</td><td>8.95</td><td>2</td><td>Washington</td><td>49.40</td></tr>
<tr><td>41</td><td>Arizona</td><td>19.00</td><td>3</td><td>California</td><td>46.70</td></tr>
<tr><td>37</td><td>Arkansas</td><td>21.80</td><td>4</td><td>New Jersey</td><td>37.10</td></tr>
<tr><td>3</td><td>California</td><td>46.70</td><td>5</td><td>West Virginia</td><td>35.70</td></tr>
<tr><td>36</td><td>Colorado</td><td>22.00</td><td>6</td><td>North Carolina</td><td>35.35</td></tr>
<tr><td>28</td><td>Connecticut</td><td>25.00</td><td>7</td><td>Oregon</td><td>34.00</td></tr>
<tr><td>34</td><td>Delaware</td><td>23.00</td><td>7</td><td>Rhode Island</td><td>34.00</td></tr>
<tr><td>13</td><td>Florida</td><td>31.43</td><td>9</td><td>Maryland</td><td>33.80</td></tr>
<tr><td>23</td><td>Georgia</td><td>26.80</td><td>10</td><td>Idaho</td><td>33.00</td></tr>
<tr><td>49</td><td>Hawaii</td><td>16.00</td><td>11</td><td>Wisconsin</td><td>32.90</td></tr>
<tr><td>10</td><td>Idaho</td><td>33.00</td><td>12</td><td>Montana</td><td>31.50</td></tr>
<tr><td>39</td><td>Illinois</td><td>20.10</td><td>13</td><td>Florida</td><td>31.43</td></tr>
<tr><td>21</td><td>Indiana</td><td>28.00</td><td>14</td><td>Vermont</td><td>30.72</td></tr>
<tr><td>15</td><td>Iowa</td><td>30.50</td><td>15</td><td>Iowa</td><td>30.50</td></tr>
<tr><td>27</td><td>Kansas</td><td>25.03</td><td>16</td><td>Maine</td><td>30.00</td></tr>
<tr><td>25</td><td>Kentucky</td><td>26.00</td><td>16</td><td>South Dakota</td><td>30.00</td></tr>
<tr><td>38</td><td>Louisiana</td><td>20.13</td><td>18</td><td>Utah</td><td>29.40</td></tr>
<tr><td>16</td><td>Maine</td><td>30.00</td><td>19</td><td>Nebraska</td><td>29.30</td></tr>
<tr><td>9</td><td>Maryland</td><td>33.80</td><td>20</td><td>Minnesota</td><td>28.60</td></tr>
<tr><td>30</td><td>Massachusetts</td><td>24.00</td><td>21</td><td>Indiana</td><td>28.00</td></tr>
<tr><td>24</td><td>Michigan</td><td>26.30</td><td>21</td><td>Ohio</td><td>28.00</td></tr>
<tr><td>20</td><td>Minnesota</td><td>28.60</td><td>23</td><td>Georgia</td><td>26.80</td></tr>
<tr><td>43</td><td>Mississippi</td><td>18.40</td><td>24</td><td>Michigan</td><td>26.30</td></tr>
<tr><td>45</td><td>Missouri</td><td>17.30</td><td>25</td><td>Kentucky</td><td>26.00</td></tr>
<tr><td>12</td><td>Montana</td><td>31.50</td><td>26</td><td>Tennessee</td><td>25.40</td></tr>
<tr><td>19</td><td>Nebraska</td><td>29.30</td><td>27</td><td>Kansas</td><td>25.03</td></tr>
<tr><td>33</td><td>Nevada</td><td>23.81</td><td>28</td><td>Connecticut</td><td>25.00</td></tr>
<tr><td>32</td><td>New Hampshire</td><td>23.83</td><td>29</td><td>New York</td><td>24.90</td></tr>
<tr><td>4</td><td>New Jersey</td><td>37.10</td><td>30</td><td>Massachusetts</td><td>24.00</td></tr>
<tr><td>42</td><td>New Mexico</td><td>18.88</td><td>30</td><td>Wyoming</td><td>24.00</td></tr>
<tr><td>29</td><td>New York</td><td>24.90</td><td>32</td><td>New Hampshire</td><td>23.83</td></tr>
<tr><td>6</td><td>North Carolina</td><td>35.35</td><td>33</td><td>Nevada</td><td>23.81</td></tr>
<tr><td>34</td><td>North Dakota</td><td>23.00</td><td>34</td><td>Delaware</td><td>23.00</td></tr>
<tr><td>21</td><td>Ohio</td><td>28.00</td><td>34</td><td>North Dakota</td><td>23.00</td></tr>
<tr><td>46</td><td>Oklahoma</td><td>17.00</td><td>36</td><td>Colorado</td><td>22.00</td></tr>
<tr><td>7</td><td>Oregon</td><td>34.00</td><td>37</td><td>Arkansas</td><td>21.80</td></tr>
<tr><td>1</td><td>Pennsylvania</td><td>57.60</td><td>38</td><td>Louisiana</td><td>20.13</td></tr>
<tr><td>7</td><td>Rhode Island</td><td>34.00</td><td>39</td><td>Illinois</td><td>20.10</td></tr>
<tr><td>47</td><td>South Carolina</td><td>16.75</td><td>40</td><td>Texas</td><td>20.00</td></tr>
<tr><td>16</td><td>South Dakota</td><td>30.00</td><td>41</td><td>Arizona</td><td>19.00</td></tr>
<tr><td>26</td><td>Tennessee</td><td>25.40</td><td>42</td><td>New Mexico</td><td>18.88</td></tr>
<tr><td>40</td><td>Texas</td><td>20.00</td><td>43</td><td>Mississippi</td><td>18.40</td></tr>
<tr><td>18</td><td>Utah</td><td>29.40</td><td>44</td><td>Alabama</td><td>18.00</td></tr>
<tr><td>14</td><td>Vermont</td><td>30.72</td><td>45</td><td>Missouri</td><td>17.30</td></tr>
<tr><td>48</td><td>Virginia</td><td>16.20</td><td>46</td><td>Oklahoma</td><td>17.00</td></tr>
<tr><td>2</td><td>Washington</td><td>49.40</td><td>47</td><td>South Carolina</td><td>16.75</td></tr>
<tr><td>5</td><td>West Virginia</td><td>35.70</td><td>48</td><td>Virginia</td><td>16.20</td></tr>
<tr><td>11</td><td>Wisconsin</td><td>32.90</td><td>49</td><td>Hawaii</td><td>16.00</td></tr>
<tr><td>30</td><td>Wyoming</td><td>24.00</td><td>50</td><td>Alaska</td><td>8.95</td></tr>
<tr><td></td><td></td><td></td><td></td><td>District of Columbia</td><td>23.50</td></tr>
</table>

Source: Federation of Tax Administrators
"Motor Fuel Excise Tax Rates" (http://www.taxadmin.org/current-tax-rates)
*As of January 1, 2018. Federal gasoline tax rate is an additional 18.4 cents per gallon. Many states also allow additional local option taxes on gasoline.

State Government Motor Vehicle and Operators' License Tax Revenue in 2017

National Total = $28,724,979,000

ALPHA ORDER

RANK	STATE	REVENUE	% of USA
27	Alabama	$253,123,000	0.9%
49	Alaska	38,900,000	0.1%
28	Arizona	247,065,000	0.9%
36	Arkansas	183,967,000	0.6%
1	California	4,483,295,000	15.6%
15	Colorado	578,477,000	2.0%
25	Connecticut	281,910,000	1.0%
48	Delaware	64,753,000	0.2%
5	Florida	1,538,953,000	5.4%
22	Georgia	476,674,000	1.7%
35	Hawaii	188,302,000	0.7%
34	Idaho	198,616,000	0.7%
3	Illinois	1,842,780,000	6.4%
21	Indiana	513,891,000	1.8%
14	Iowa	652,377,000	2.3%
26	Kansas	256,955,000	0.9%
31	Kentucky	225,216,000	0.8%
44	Louisiana	96,989,000	0.3%
41	Maine	120,748,000	0.4%
17	Maryland	538,976,000	1.9%
19	Massachusetts	535,760,000	1.9%
6	Michigan	1,250,765,000	4.4%
10	Minnesota	836,605,000	2.9%
37	Mississippi	170,557,000	0.6%
24	Missouri	304,098,000	1.1%
38	Montana	152,631,000	0.5%
40	Nebraska	121,513,000	0.4%
29	Nevada	243,976,000	0.8%
43	New Hampshire	110,743,000	0.4%
12	New Jersey	725,061,000	2.5%
33	New Mexico	201,677,000	0.7%
4	New York	1,542,251,000	5.4%
8	North Carolina	960,964,000	3.3%
39	North Dakota	123,954,000	0.4%
9	Ohio	927,986,000	3.2%
11	Oklahoma	780,943,000	2.7%
16	Oregon	578,325,000	2.0%
7	Pennsylvania	998,579,000	3.5%
50	Rhode Island	31,377,000	0.1%
30	South Carolina	236,668,000	0.8%
45	South Dakota	88,357,000	0.3%
23	Tennessee	367,315,000	1.3%
2	Texas	2,377,905,000	8.3%
32	Utah	220,582,000	0.8%
46	Vermont	85,819,000	0.3%
20	Virginia	522,332,000	1.8%
13	Washington	672,470,000	2.3%
42	West Virginia	118,334,000	0.4%
18	Wisconsin	536,348,000	1.9%
47	Wyoming	73,975,000	0.3%

RANK ORDER

RANK	STATE	REVENUE	% of USA
1	California	$4,483,295,000	15.6%
2	Texas	2,377,905,000	8.3%
3	Illinois	1,842,780,000	6.4%
4	New York	1,542,251,000	5.4%
5	Florida	1,538,953,000	5.4%
6	Michigan	1,250,765,000	4.4%
7	Pennsylvania	998,579,000	3.5%
8	North Carolina	960,964,000	3.3%
9	Ohio	927,986,000	3.2%
10	Minnesota	836,605,000	2.9%
11	Oklahoma	780,943,000	2.7%
12	New Jersey	725,061,000	2.5%
13	Washington	672,470,000	2.3%
14	Iowa	652,377,000	2.3%
15	Colorado	578,477,000	2.0%
16	Oregon	578,325,000	2.0%
17	Maryland	538,976,000	1.9%
18	Wisconsin	536,348,000	1.9%
19	Massachusetts	535,760,000	1.9%
20	Virginia	522,332,000	1.8%
21	Indiana	513,891,000	1.8%
22	Georgia	476,674,000	1.7%
23	Tennessee	367,315,000	1.3%
24	Missouri	304,098,000	1.1%
25	Connecticut	281,910,000	1.0%
26	Kansas	256,955,000	0.9%
27	Alabama	253,123,000	0.9%
28	Arizona	247,065,000	0.9%
29	Nevada	243,976,000	0.8%
30	South Carolina	236,668,000	0.8%
31	Kentucky	225,216,000	0.8%
32	Utah	220,582,000	0.8%
33	New Mexico	201,677,000	0.7%
34	Idaho	198,616,000	0.7%
35	Hawaii	188,302,000	0.7%
36	Arkansas	183,967,000	0.6%
37	Mississippi	170,557,000	0.6%
38	Montana	152,631,000	0.5%
39	North Dakota	123,954,000	0.4%
40	Nebraska	121,513,000	0.4%
41	Maine	120,748,000	0.4%
42	West Virginia	118,334,000	0.4%
43	New Hampshire	110,743,000	0.4%
44	Louisiana	96,989,000	0.3%
45	South Dakota	88,357,000	0.3%
46	Vermont	85,819,000	0.3%
47	Wyoming	73,975,000	0.3%
48	Delaware	64,753,000	0.2%
49	Alaska	38,900,000	0.1%
50	Rhode Island	31,377,000	0.1%
	District of Columbia	45,142,000	0.2%

Source: U.S. Bureau of the Census, Governments Division
"2017 State Government Tax Collections" (https://www.census.gov/programs-surveys/stc.html)

Per Capita State Government Motor Vehicle and Operators' License Tax Revenue in 2017
National Per Capita = $88

ALPHA ORDER				RANK ORDER		
RANK	STATE	PER CAPITA		RANK	STATE	PER CAPITA
43	Alabama	$52		1	Iowa	$208
42	Alaska	53		2	Oklahoma	199
48	Arizona	35		3	North Dakota	164
39	Arkansas	61		4	Minnesota	150
13	California	114		5	Montana	145
14	Colorado	103		6	Illinois	144
28	Connecticut	79		7	Oregon	139
35	Delaware	68		8	Vermont	137
33	Florida	73		9	Hawaii	132
47	Georgia	46		10	Wyoming	128
9	Hawaii	132		11	Michigan	125
12	Idaho	116		12	Idaho	116
6	Illinois	144		13	California	114
32	Indiana	77		14	Colorado	103
1	Iowa	208		15	South Dakota	101
22	Kansas	88		16	New Mexico	96
44	Kentucky	51		17	North Carolina	94
50	Louisiana	21		18	Wisconsin	93
20	Maine	90		19	Washington	91
21	Maryland	89		20	Maine	90
30	Massachusetts	78		21	Maryland	89
11	Michigan	125		22	Kansas	88
4	Minnesota	150		23	Texas	84
40	Mississippi	57		24	Nevada	82
45	Missouri	50		24	New Hampshire	82
5	Montana	145		24	New Jersey	82
37	Nebraska	63		27	Ohio	80
24	Nevada	82		28	Connecticut	79
24	New Hampshire	82		28	New York	79
24	New Jersey	82		30	Massachusetts	78
16	New Mexico	96		30	Pennsylvania	78
28	New York	79		32	Indiana	77
17	North Carolina	94		33	Florida	73
3	North Dakota	164		34	Utah	71
27	Ohio	80		35	Delaware	68
2	Oklahoma	199		36	West Virginia	65
7	Oregon	139		37	Nebraska	63
30	Pennsylvania	78		38	Virginia	62
49	Rhode Island	30		39	Arkansas	61
46	South Carolina	47		40	Mississippi	57
15	South Dakota	101		41	Tennessee	55
41	Tennessee	55		42	Alaska	53
23	Texas	84		43	Alabama	52
34	Utah	71		44	Kentucky	51
8	Vermont	137		45	Missouri	50
38	Virginia	62		46	South Carolina	47
19	Washington	91		47	Georgia	46
36	West Virginia	65		48	Arizona	35
18	Wisconsin	93		49	Rhode Island	30
10	Wyoming	128		50	Louisiana	21
					District of Columbia	65

Source: CQ Press using data from U.S. Bureau of the Census, Governments Division
"2017 State Government Tax Collections" (https://www.census.gov/programs-surveys/stc.html)

State Government Tobacco Product Sales Tax Revenue in 2017

National Total = $18,673,887,000

ALPHA ORDER

RANK	STATE	REVENUE	% of USA
30	Alabama	$188,783,000	1.0%
44	Alaska	67,555,000	0.4%
18	Arizona	310,706,000	1.7%
23	Arkansas	228,540,000	1.2%
7	California	852,894,000	4.6%
27	Colorado	199,989,000	1.1%
16	Connecticut	381,778,000	2.0%
39	Delaware	112,349,000	0.6%
4	Florida	1,197,666,000	6.4%
25	Georgia	220,774,000	1.2%
37	Hawaii	124,160,000	0.7%
47	Idaho	50,883,000	0.3%
8	Illinois	781,528,000	4.2%
13	Indiana	434,351,000	2.3%
24	Iowa	220,938,000	1.2%
36	Kansas	138,504,000	0.7%
22	Kentucky	243,096,000	1.3%
31	Louisiana	174,001,000	0.9%
34	Maine	144,243,000	0.8%
15	Maryland	386,965,000	2.1%
12	Massachusetts	619,437,000	3.3%
6	Michigan	1,038,594,000	5.6%
10	Minnesota	681,018,000	3.6%
33	Mississippi	145,059,000	0.8%
40	Missouri	100,391,000	0.5%
42	Montana	83,606,000	0.4%
46	Nebraska	56,954,000	0.3%
28	Nevada	195,371,000	1.0%
26	New Hampshire	203,102,000	1.1%
9	New Jersey	697,577,000	3.7%
41	New Mexico	89,703,000	0.5%
3	New York	1,265,699,000	6.8%
19	North Carolina	292,138,000	1.6%
48	North Dakota	28,977,000	0.2%
5	Ohio	1,109,777,000	5.9%
17	Oklahoma	320,200,000	1.7%
21	Oregon	247,406,000	1.3%
2	Pennsylvania	1,401,259,000	7.5%
35	Rhode Island	140,074,000	0.8%
49	South Carolina	26,383,000	0.1%
45	South Dakota	61,809,000	0.3%
20	Tennessee	256,762,000	1.4%
1	Texas	1,467,486,000	7.9%
38	Utah	116,158,000	0.6%
43	Vermont	76,686,000	0.4%
32	Virginia	171,198,000	0.9%
14	Washington	430,022,000	2.3%
29	West Virginia	194,647,000	1.0%
11	Wisconsin	644,478,000	3.5%
50	Wyoming	22,683,000	0.1%

RANK ORDER

RANK	STATE	REVENUE	% of USA
1	Texas	$1,467,486,000	7.9%
2	Pennsylvania	1,401,259,000	7.5%
3	New York	1,265,699,000	6.8%
4	Florida	1,197,666,000	6.4%
5	Ohio	1,109,777,000	5.9%
6	Michigan	1,038,594,000	5.6%
7	California	852,894,000	4.6%
8	Illinois	781,528,000	4.2%
9	New Jersey	697,577,000	3.7%
10	Minnesota	681,018,000	3.6%
11	Wisconsin	644,478,000	3.5%
12	Massachusetts	619,437,000	3.3%
13	Indiana	434,351,000	2.3%
14	Washington	430,022,000	2.3%
15	Maryland	386,965,000	2.1%
16	Connecticut	381,778,000	2.0%
17	Oklahoma	320,200,000	1.7%
18	Arizona	310,706,000	1.7%
19	North Carolina	292,138,000	1.6%
20	Tennessee	256,762,000	1.4%
21	Oregon	247,406,000	1.3%
22	Kentucky	243,096,000	1.3%
23	Arkansas	228,540,000	1.2%
24	Iowa	220,938,000	1.2%
25	Georgia	220,774,000	1.2%
26	New Hampshire	203,102,000	1.1%
27	Colorado	199,989,000	1.1%
28	Nevada	195,371,000	1.0%
29	West Virginia	194,647,000	1.0%
30	Alabama	188,783,000	1.0%
31	Louisiana	174,001,000	0.9%
32	Virginia	171,198,000	0.9%
33	Mississippi	145,059,000	0.8%
34	Maine	144,243,000	0.8%
35	Rhode Island	140,074,000	0.8%
36	Kansas	138,504,000	0.7%
37	Hawaii	124,160,000	0.7%
38	Utah	116,158,000	0.6%
39	Delaware	112,349,000	0.6%
40	Missouri	100,391,000	0.5%
41	New Mexico	89,703,000	0.5%
42	Montana	83,606,000	0.4%
43	Vermont	76,686,000	0.4%
44	Alaska	67,555,000	0.4%
45	South Dakota	61,809,000	0.3%
46	Nebraska	56,954,000	0.3%
47	Idaho	50,883,000	0.3%
48	North Dakota	28,977,000	0.2%
49	South Carolina	26,383,000	0.1%
50	Wyoming	22,683,000	0.1%
	District of Columbia	29,530,000	0.2%

Source: U.S. Bureau of the Census, Governments Division
"2017 State Government Tax Collections" (https://www.census.gov/programs-surveys/stc.html)

Per Capita State Government Tobacco Sales Tax Revenue in 2017

National Per Capita = $57

ALPHA ORDER

RANK	STATE	PER CAPITA
36	Alabama	$39
13	Alaska	91
34	Arizona	44
19	Arkansas	76
46	California	22
42	Colorado	36
9	Connecticut	107
5	Delaware	117
29	Florida	57
47	Georgia	21
15	Hawaii	87
43	Idaho	30
26	Illinois	61
23	Indiana	65
21	Iowa	70
33	Kansas	48
30	Kentucky	55
40	Louisiana	37
8	Maine	108
25	Maryland	64
14	Massachusetts	90
11	Michigan	104
4	Minnesota	122
32	Mississippi	49
49	Missouri	16
17	Montana	79
43	Nebraska	30
22	Nevada	66
1	New Hampshire	150
18	New Jersey	78
35	New Mexico	43
23	New York	65
45	North Carolina	28
38	North Dakota	38
12	Ohio	95
16	Oklahoma	81
27	Oregon	60
7	Pennsylvania	110
2	Rhode Island	133
50	South Carolina	5
20	South Dakota	71
38	Tennessee	38
31	Texas	52
40	Utah	37
3	Vermont	123
48	Virginia	20
28	Washington	58
9	West Virginia	107
6	Wisconsin	111
36	Wyoming	39

RANK ORDER

RANK	STATE	PER CAPITA
1	New Hampshire	$150
2	Rhode Island	133
3	Vermont	123
4	Minnesota	122
5	Delaware	117
6	Wisconsin	111
7	Pennsylvania	110
8	Maine	108
9	Connecticut	107
9	West Virginia	107
11	Michigan	104
12	Ohio	95
13	Alaska	91
14	Massachusetts	90
15	Hawaii	87
16	Oklahoma	81
17	Montana	79
18	New Jersey	78
19	Arkansas	76
20	South Dakota	71
21	Iowa	70
22	Nevada	66
23	Indiana	65
23	New York	65
25	Maryland	64
26	Illinois	61
27	Oregon	60
28	Washington	58
29	Florida	57
30	Kentucky	55
31	Texas	52
32	Mississippi	49
33	Kansas	48
34	Arizona	44
35	New Mexico	43
36	Alabama	39
36	Wyoming	39
38	North Dakota	38
38	Tennessee	38
40	Louisiana	37
40	Utah	37
42	Colorado	36
43	Idaho	30
43	Nebraska	30
45	North Carolina	28
46	California	22
47	Georgia	21
48	Virginia	20
49	Missouri	16
50	South Carolina	5

District of Columbia — 42

Source: CQ Press using data from U.S. Bureau of the Census, Governments Division
"2017 State Government Tax Collections" (https://www.census.gov/programs-surveys/stc.html)

State Tax on a Pack of Cigarettes in 2019

National Median = $1.66 per Pack*

<table>
<tr><td colspan="3">ALPHA ORDER</td><td colspan="3">RANK ORDER</td></tr>
<tr><td>RANK</td><td>STATE</td><td>TAX PER PACK</td><td>RANK</td><td>STATE</td><td>TAX PER PACK</td></tr>
<tr><td>39</td><td>Alabama</td><td>$0.68</td><td>1</td><td>Connecticut</td><td>$4.35</td></tr>
<tr><td>15</td><td>Alaska</td><td>2.00</td><td>1</td><td>New York</td><td>4.35</td></tr>
<tr><td>15</td><td>Arizona</td><td>2.00</td><td>3</td><td>Rhode Island</td><td>4.25</td></tr>
<tr><td>34</td><td>Arkansas</td><td>1.15</td><td>4</td><td>Massachusetts</td><td>3.51</td></tr>
<tr><td>9</td><td>California</td><td>2.87</td><td>5</td><td>Hawaii</td><td>3.20</td></tr>
<tr><td>38</td><td>Colorado</td><td>0.84</td><td>6</td><td>Vermont</td><td>3.08</td></tr>
<tr><td>1</td><td>Connecticut</td><td>4.35</td><td>7</td><td>Minnesota</td><td>3.04</td></tr>
<tr><td>13</td><td>Delaware</td><td>2.10</td><td>8</td><td>Washington</td><td>3.03</td></tr>
<tr><td>30</td><td>Florida</td><td>1.34</td><td>9</td><td>California</td><td>2.87</td></tr>
<tr><td>48</td><td>Georgia</td><td>0.37</td><td>10</td><td>New Jersey</td><td>2.70</td></tr>
<tr><td>5</td><td>Hawaii</td><td>3.20</td><td>11</td><td>Pennsylvania</td><td>2.60</td></tr>
<tr><td>44</td><td>Idaho</td><td>0.57</td><td>12</td><td>Wisconsin</td><td>2.52</td></tr>
<tr><td>20</td><td>Illinois</td><td>1.98</td><td>13</td><td>Delaware</td><td>2.10</td></tr>
<tr><td>37</td><td>Indiana</td><td>1.00</td><td>14</td><td>Oklahoma</td><td>2.03</td></tr>
<tr><td>29</td><td>Iowa</td><td>1.36</td><td>15</td><td>Alaska</td><td>2.00</td></tr>
<tr><td>32</td><td>Kansas</td><td>1.29</td><td>15</td><td>Arizona</td><td>2.00</td></tr>
<tr><td>35</td><td>Kentucky</td><td>1.10</td><td>15</td><td>Maine</td><td>2.00</td></tr>
<tr><td>36</td><td>Louisiana</td><td>1.08</td><td>15</td><td>Maryland</td><td>2.00</td></tr>
<tr><td>15</td><td>Maine</td><td>2.00</td><td>15</td><td>Michigan</td><td>2.00</td></tr>
<tr><td>15</td><td>Maryland</td><td>2.00</td><td>20</td><td>Illinois</td><td>1.98</td></tr>
<tr><td>4</td><td>Massachusetts</td><td>3.51</td><td>21</td><td>Nevada</td><td>1.80</td></tr>
<tr><td>15</td><td>Michigan</td><td>2.00</td><td>22</td><td>New Hampshire</td><td>1.78</td></tr>
<tr><td>7</td><td>Minnesota</td><td>3.04</td><td>23</td><td>Montana</td><td>1.70</td></tr>
<tr><td>39</td><td>Mississippi</td><td>0.68</td><td>23</td><td>Utah</td><td>1.70</td></tr>
<tr><td>50</td><td>Missouri</td><td>0.17</td><td>25</td><td>New Mexico</td><td>1.66</td></tr>
<tr><td>23</td><td>Montana</td><td>1.70</td><td>26</td><td>Ohio</td><td>1.60</td></tr>
<tr><td>41</td><td>Nebraska</td><td>0.64</td><td>27</td><td>South Dakota</td><td>1.53</td></tr>
<tr><td>21</td><td>Nevada</td><td>1.80</td><td>28</td><td>Texas</td><td>1.41</td></tr>
<tr><td>22</td><td>New Hampshire</td><td>1.78</td><td>29</td><td>Iowa</td><td>1.36</td></tr>
<tr><td>10</td><td>New Jersey</td><td>2.70</td><td>30</td><td>Florida</td><td>1.34</td></tr>
<tr><td>25</td><td>New Mexico</td><td>1.66</td><td>31</td><td>Oregon</td><td>1.33</td></tr>
<tr><td>1</td><td>New York</td><td>4.35</td><td>32</td><td>Kansas</td><td>1.29</td></tr>
<tr><td>46</td><td>North Carolina</td><td>0.45</td><td>33</td><td>West Virginia</td><td>1.20</td></tr>
<tr><td>47</td><td>North Dakota</td><td>0.44</td><td>34</td><td>Arkansas</td><td>1.15</td></tr>
<tr><td>26</td><td>Ohio</td><td>1.60</td><td>35</td><td>Kentucky</td><td>1.10</td></tr>
<tr><td>14</td><td>Oklahoma</td><td>2.03</td><td>36</td><td>Louisiana</td><td>1.08</td></tr>
<tr><td>31</td><td>Oregon</td><td>1.33</td><td>37</td><td>Indiana</td><td>1.00</td></tr>
<tr><td>11</td><td>Pennsylvania</td><td>2.60</td><td>38</td><td>Colorado</td><td>0.84</td></tr>
<tr><td>3</td><td>Rhode Island</td><td>4.25</td><td>39</td><td>Alabama</td><td>0.68</td></tr>
<tr><td>44</td><td>South Carolina</td><td>0.57</td><td>39</td><td>Mississippi</td><td>0.68</td></tr>
<tr><td>27</td><td>South Dakota</td><td>1.53</td><td>41</td><td>Nebraska</td><td>0.64</td></tr>
<tr><td>42</td><td>Tennessee</td><td>0.62</td><td>42</td><td>Tennessee</td><td>0.62</td></tr>
<tr><td>28</td><td>Texas</td><td>1.41</td><td>43</td><td>Wyoming</td><td>0.60</td></tr>
<tr><td>23</td><td>Utah</td><td>1.70</td><td>44</td><td>Idaho</td><td>0.57</td></tr>
<tr><td>6</td><td>Vermont</td><td>3.08</td><td>44</td><td>South Carolina</td><td>0.57</td></tr>
<tr><td>49</td><td>Virginia</td><td>0.30</td><td>46</td><td>North Carolina</td><td>0.45</td></tr>
<tr><td>8</td><td>Washington</td><td>3.03</td><td>47</td><td>North Dakota</td><td>0.44</td></tr>
<tr><td>33</td><td>West Virginia</td><td>1.20</td><td>48</td><td>Georgia</td><td>0.37</td></tr>
<tr><td>12</td><td>Wisconsin</td><td>2.52</td><td>49</td><td>Virginia</td><td>0.30</td></tr>
<tr><td>43</td><td>Wyoming</td><td>0.60</td><td>50</td><td>Missouri</td><td>0.17</td></tr>
<tr><td></td><td></td><td></td><td></td><td>District of Columbia</td><td>4.50</td></tr>
</table>

Source: Federation of Tax Administrators
   "State Excise Tax Rates on Cigarettes" (https://www.taxadmin.org/current-tax-rates)
*As of January 1, 2019. Many states also allow additional local option taxes on cigarettes.

State Government Alcoholic Beverage Sales Tax Revenue in 2017

National Total = $6,626,430,000

ALPHA ORDER

RANK	STATE	REVENUE	% of USA
10	Alabama	$217,790,000	3.3%
34	Alaska	40,097,000	0.6%
23	Arizona	74,126,000	1.1%
26	Arkansas	55,831,000	0.8%
4	California	370,714,000	5.6%
32	Colorado	44,866,000	0.7%
24	Connecticut	63,155,000	1.0%
42	Delaware	20,577,000	0.3%
6	Florida	323,393,000	4.9%
11	Georgia	193,438,000	2.9%
27	Hawaii	51,167,000	0.8%
48	Idaho	9,468,000	0.1%
7	Illinois	294,304,000	4.4%
29	Indiana	49,403,000	0.7%
40	Iowa	22,535,000	0.3%
16	Kansas	137,801,000	2.1%
15	Kentucky	146,227,000	2.2%
22	Louisiana	77,107,000	1.2%
43	Maine	19,266,000	0.3%
37	Maryland	32,151,000	0.5%
21	Massachusetts	85,397,000	1.3%
14	Michigan	159,378,000	2.4%
20	Minnesota	88,222,000	1.3%
33	Mississippi	41,835,000	0.6%
35	Missouri	37,863,000	0.6%
36	Montana	32,926,000	0.5%
38	Nebraska	30,911,000	0.5%
30	Nevada	45,011,000	0.7%
47	New Hampshire	12,678,000	0.2%
17	New Jersey	137,757,000	2.1%
31	New Mexico	44,916,000	0.7%
8	New York	257,690,000	3.9%
2	North Carolina	394,838,000	6.0%
49	North Dakota	8,872,000	0.1%
19	Ohio	107,060,000	1.6%
18	Oklahoma	118,260,000	1.8%
44	Oregon	18,796,000	0.3%
3	Pennsylvania	386,816,000	5.8%
41	Rhode Island	20,873,000	0.3%
13	South Carolina	177,317,000	2.7%
46	South Dakota	16,933,000	0.3%
12	Tennessee	187,125,000	2.8%
1	Texas	1,228,641,000	18.5%
28	Utah	50,002,000	0.8%
39	Vermont	26,028,000	0.4%
9	Virginia	224,426,000	3.4%
5	Washington	354,939,000	5.4%
45	West Virginia	17,782,000	0.3%
25	Wisconsin	61,203,000	0.9%
50	Wyoming	1,878,000	0.0%

RANK ORDER

RANK	STATE	REVENUE	% of USA
1	Texas	$1,228,641,000	18.5%
2	North Carolina	394,838,000	6.0%
3	Pennsylvania	386,816,000	5.8%
4	California	370,714,000	5.6%
5	Washington	354,939,000	5.4%
6	Florida	323,393,000	4.9%
7	Illinois	294,304,000	4.4%
8	New York	257,690,000	3.9%
9	Virginia	224,426,000	3.4%
10	Alabama	217,790,000	3.3%
11	Georgia	193,438,000	2.9%
12	Tennessee	187,125,000	2.8%
13	South Carolina	177,317,000	2.7%
14	Michigan	159,378,000	2.4%
15	Kentucky	146,227,000	2.2%
16	Kansas	137,801,000	2.1%
17	New Jersey	137,757,000	2.1%
18	Oklahoma	118,260,000	1.8%
19	Ohio	107,060,000	1.6%
20	Minnesota	88,222,000	1.3%
21	Massachusetts	85,397,000	1.3%
22	Louisiana	77,107,000	1.2%
23	Arizona	74,126,000	1.1%
24	Connecticut	63,155,000	1.0%
25	Wisconsin	61,203,000	0.9%
26	Arkansas	55,831,000	0.8%
27	Hawaii	51,167,000	0.8%
28	Utah	50,002,000	0.8%
29	Indiana	49,403,000	0.7%
30	Nevada	45,011,000	0.7%
31	New Mexico	44,916,000	0.7%
32	Colorado	44,866,000	0.7%
33	Mississippi	41,835,000	0.6%
34	Alaska	40,097,000	0.6%
35	Missouri	37,863,000	0.6%
36	Montana	32,926,000	0.5%
37	Maryland	32,151,000	0.5%
38	Nebraska	30,911,000	0.5%
39	Vermont	26,028,000	0.4%
40	Iowa	22,535,000	0.3%
41	Rhode Island	20,873,000	0.3%
42	Delaware	20,577,000	0.3%
43	Maine	19,266,000	0.3%
44	Oregon	18,796,000	0.3%
45	West Virginia	17,782,000	0.3%
46	South Dakota	16,933,000	0.3%
47	New Hampshire	12,678,000	0.2%
48	Idaho	9,468,000	0.1%
49	North Dakota	8,872,000	0.1%
50	Wyoming	1,878,000	0.0%
	District of Columbia	6,641,000	0.1%

Source: U.S. Bureau of the Census, Governments Division
"2017 State Government Tax Collections" (https://www.census.gov/programs-surveys/stc.html)

Per Capita State Government Alcoholic Beverage Sales Tax Revenue in 2017

National Per Capita = $20

ALPHA ORDER

ALPHA ORDER

RANK ORDER

RANK	STATE	PER CAPITA	RANK	STATE	PER CAPITA
4	Alabama	$45	1	Alaska	$54
1	Alaska	54	2	Washington	48
37	Arizona	11	3	Kansas	47
20	Arkansas	19	4	Alabama	45
40	California	9	5	Texas	43
43	Colorado	8	6	Vermont	42
23	Connecticut	18	7	North Carolina	38
17	Delaware	21	8	Hawaii	36
29	Florida	15	9	South Carolina	35
20	Georgia	19	10	Kentucky	33
8	Hawaii	36	11	Montana	31
46	Idaho	6	12	Oklahoma	30
16	Illinois	23	12	Pennsylvania	30
44	Indiana	7	14	Tennessee	28
44	Iowa	7	15	Virginia	27
3	Kansas	47	16	Illinois	23
10	Kentucky	33	17	Delaware	21
24	Louisiana	17	17	New Mexico	21
32	Maine	14	19	Rhode Island	20
48	Maryland	5	20	Arkansas	19
35	Massachusetts	12	20	Georgia	19
25	Michigan	16	20	South Dakota	19
25	Minnesota	16	23	Connecticut	18
32	Mississippi	14	24	Louisiana	17
46	Missouri	6	25	Michigan	16
11	Montana	31	25	Minnesota	16
25	Nebraska	16	25	Nebraska	16
29	Nevada	15	25	Utah	16
40	New Hampshire	9	29	Florida	15
29	New Jersey	15	29	Nevada	15
17	New Mexico	21	29	New Jersey	15
34	New York	13	32	Maine	14
7	North Carolina	38	32	Mississippi	14
35	North Dakota	12	34	New York	13
40	Ohio	9	35	Massachusetts	12
12	Oklahoma	30	35	North Dakota	12
48	Oregon	5	37	Arizona	11
12	Pennsylvania	30	37	Wisconsin	11
19	Rhode Island	20	39	West Virginia	10
9	South Carolina	35	40	California	9
20	South Dakota	19	40	New Hampshire	9
14	Tennessee	28	40	Ohio	9
5	Texas	43	43	Colorado	8
25	Utah	16	44	Indiana	7
6	Vermont	42	44	Iowa	7
15	Virginia	27	46	Idaho	6
2	Washington	48	46	Missouri	6
39	West Virginia	10	48	Maryland	5
37	Wisconsin	11	48	Oregon	5
50	Wyoming	3	50	Wyoming	3
				District of Columbia	10

Source: CQ Press using data from U.S. Bureau of the Census, Governments Division
"2017 State Government Tax Collections" (https://www.census.gov/programs-surveys/stc.html)

State Government Total Expenditures in 2016

National Total = $2,225,106,823,000*

ALPHA ORDER

ALPHA ORDER

RANK ORDER

RANK	STATE	EXPENDITURES	% of USA
28	Alabama	$29,747,318,000	1.3%
38	Alaska	12,359,938,000	0.6%
17	Arizona	41,770,242,000	1.9%
31	Arkansas	22,881,728,000	1.0%
1	California	327,898,213,000	14.7%
21	Colorado	34,282,697,000	1.5%
25	Connecticut	31,918,825,000	1.4%
41	Delaware	9,400,299,000	0.4%
5	Florida	87,924,052,000	4.0%
14	Georgia	47,487,009,000	2.1%
39	Hawaii	12,191,854,000	0.5%
43	Idaho	9,225,494,000	0.4%
7	Illinois	77,826,113,000	3.5%
18	Indiana	39,222,656,000	1.8%
30	Iowa	23,381,086,000	1.1%
35	Kansas	18,664,920,000	0.8%
20	Kentucky	35,147,233,000	1.6%
27	Louisiana	31,218,602,000	1.4%
42	Maine	9,330,098,000	0.4%
16	Maryland	43,758,668,000	2.0%
10	Massachusetts	63,568,628,000	2.9%
9	Michigan	70,110,424,000	3.2%
15	Minnesota	46,594,683,000	2.1%
32	Mississippi	22,108,192,000	1.0%
23	Missouri	32,402,563,000	1.5%
47	Montana	7,083,842,000	0.3%
40	Nebraska	10,941,892,000	0.5%
36	Nevada	15,229,381,000	0.7%
46	New Hampshire	7,610,619,000	0.3%
8	New Jersey	72,064,882,000	3.2%
33	New Mexico	20,029,868,000	0.9%
2	New York	194,242,569,000	8.7%
11	North Carolina	53,398,099,000	2.4%
45	North Dakota	8,153,778,000	0.4%
6	Ohio	86,698,956,000	3.9%
29	Oklahoma	24,746,006,000	1.1%
22	Oregon	33,938,756,000	1.5%
4	Pennsylvania	96,292,444,000	4.3%
44	Rhode Island	8,566,490,000	0.4%
26	South Carolina	31,606,505,000	1.4%
50	South Dakota	5,071,455,000	0.2%
24	Tennessee	32,336,553,000	1.5%
3	Texas	145,589,993,000	6.5%
34	Utah	19,284,874,000	0.9%
48	Vermont	6,728,460,000	0.3%
12	Virginia	52,932,360,000	2.4%
13	Washington	52,909,566,000	2.4%
37	West Virginia	14,542,974,000	0.7%
19	Wisconsin	38,230,825,000	1.7%
49	Wyoming	6,454,141,000	0.3%

RANK	STATE	EXPENDITURES	% of USA
1	California	$327,898,213,000	14.7%
2	New York	194,242,569,000	8.7%
3	Texas	145,589,993,000	6.5%
4	Pennsylvania	96,292,444,000	4.3%
5	Florida	87,924,052,000	4.0%
6	Ohio	86,698,956,000	3.9%
7	Illinois	77,826,113,000	3.5%
8	New Jersey	72,064,882,000	3.2%
9	Michigan	70,110,424,000	3.2%
10	Massachusetts	63,568,628,000	2.9%
11	North Carolina	53,398,099,000	2.4%
12	Virginia	52,932,360,000	2.4%
13	Washington	52,909,566,000	2.4%
14	Georgia	47,487,009,000	2.1%
15	Minnesota	46,594,683,000	2.1%
16	Maryland	43,758,668,000	2.0%
17	Arizona	41,770,242,000	1.9%
18	Indiana	39,222,656,000	1.8%
19	Wisconsin	38,230,825,000	1.7%
20	Kentucky	35,147,233,000	1.6%
21	Colorado	34,282,697,000	1.5%
22	Oregon	33,938,756,000	1.5%
23	Missouri	32,402,563,000	1.5%
24	Tennessee	32,336,553,000	1.5%
25	Connecticut	31,918,825,000	1.4%
26	South Carolina	31,606,505,000	1.4%
27	Louisiana	31,218,602,000	1.4%
28	Alabama	29,747,318,000	1.3%
29	Oklahoma	24,746,006,000	1.1%
30	Iowa	23,381,086,000	1.1%
31	Arkansas	22,881,728,000	1.0%
32	Mississippi	22,108,192,000	1.0%
33	New Mexico	20,029,868,000	0.9%
34	Utah	19,284,874,000	0.9%
35	Kansas	18,664,920,000	0.8%
36	Nevada	15,229,381,000	0.7%
37	West Virginia	14,542,974,000	0.7%
38	Alaska	12,359,938,000	0.6%
39	Hawaii	12,191,854,000	0.5%
40	Nebraska	10,941,892,000	0.5%
41	Delaware	9,400,299,000	0.4%
42	Maine	9,330,098,000	0.4%
43	Idaho	9,225,494,000	0.4%
44	Rhode Island	8,566,490,000	0.4%
45	North Dakota	8,153,778,000	0.4%
46	New Hampshire	7,610,619,000	0.3%
47	Montana	7,083,842,000	0.3%
48	Vermont	6,728,460,000	0.3%
49	Wyoming	6,454,141,000	0.3%
50	South Dakota	5,071,455,000	0.2%
	District of Columbia**	NA	NA

Source: U.S. Bureau of the Census, Governments Division
"2016 State and Local Government Finances" (https://www.census.gov/programs-surveys/gov-finances.html)
*Total expenditures includes all money paid other than for retirement of debt and extension of loans. Includes payments from all sources of funds including current revenues and proceeds from borrowing and prior year fund balances. Includes intergovernmental transfers and expenditures for government owned utilities and other commercial or auxiliary enterprise, and insurance trust expenditures. **Not applicable.

Per Capita State Government Total Expenditures in 2016

National Per Capita = $6,902*

ALPHA ORDER

RANK	STATE	PER CAPITA
36	Alabama	$6,115
1	Alaska	16,669
38	Arizona	6,014
18	Arkansas	7,652
12	California	8,363
35	Colorado	6,187
9	Connecticut	8,919
5	Delaware	9,903
50	Florida	4,262
49	Georgia	4,608
10	Hawaii	8,537
43	Idaho	5,482
37	Illinois	6,067
39	Indiana	5,913
20	Iowa	7,466
30	Kansas	6,411
17	Kentucky	7,919
28	Louisiana	6,673
26	Maine	7,008
23	Maryland	7,287
8	Massachusetts	9,313
25	Michigan	7,045
11	Minnesota	8,436
22	Mississippi	7,398
44	Missouri	5,323
27	Montana	6,806
41	Nebraska	5,741
46	Nevada	5,216
42	New Hampshire	5,670
14	New Jersey	8,120
7	New Mexico	9,571
6	New York	9,889
45	North Carolina	5,257
3	North Dakota	10,809
21	Ohio	7,452
33	Oklahoma	6,302
13	Oregon	8,295
19	Pennsylvania	7,533
15	Rhode Island	8,104
31	South Carolina	6,375
40	South Dakota	5,877
48	Tennessee	4,866
47	Texas	5,211
32	Utah	6,338
4	Vermont	10,789
34	Virginia	6,293
24	Washington	7,253
16	West Virginia	7,943
29	Wisconsin	6,622
2	Wyoming	11,046

RANK ORDER

RANK	STATE	PER CAPITA
1	Alaska	$16,669
2	Wyoming	11,046
3	North Dakota	10,809
4	Vermont	10,789
5	Delaware	9,903
6	New York	9,889
7	New Mexico	9,571
8	Massachusetts	9,313
9	Connecticut	8,919
10	Hawaii	8,537
11	Minnesota	8,436
12	California	8,363
13	Oregon	8,295
14	New Jersey	8,120
15	Rhode Island	8,104
16	West Virginia	7,943
17	Kentucky	7,919
18	Arkansas	7,652
19	Pennsylvania	7,533
20	Iowa	7,466
21	Ohio	7,452
22	Mississippi	7,398
23	Maryland	7,287
24	Washington	7,253
25	Michigan	7,045
26	Maine	7,008
27	Montana	6,806
28	Louisiana	6,673
29	Wisconsin	6,622
30	Kansas	6,411
31	South Carolina	6,375
32	Utah	6,338
33	Oklahoma	6,302
34	Virginia	6,293
35	Colorado	6,187
36	Alabama	6,115
37	Illinois	6,067
38	Arizona	6,014
39	Indiana	5,913
40	South Dakota	5,877
41	Nebraska	5,741
42	New Hampshire	5,670
43	Idaho	5,482
44	Missouri	5,323
45	North Carolina	5,257
46	Nevada	5,216
47	Texas	5,211
48	Tennessee	4,866
49	Georgia	4,608
50	Florida	4,262

District of Columbia** NA

Source: CQ Press using data from U.S. Bureau of the Census, Governments Division

"2016 State and Local Government Finances" (https://www.census.gov/programs-surveys/gov-finances.html)

*Total expenditures includes all money paid other than for retirement of debt and extension of loans. Includes payments from all sources of funds including current revenues and proceeds from borrowing and prior year fund balances. Includes intergovernmental transfers and expenditures for government owned utilities and other commercial or auxiliary enterprise, and insurance trust expenditures. **Not applicable.

State Government Direct General Expenditures in 2016

National Total = $1,373,167,217,000*

ALPHA ORDER

RANK	STATE	EXPENDITURES	% of USA
28	Alabama	$19,212,442,000	1.4%
38	Alaska	8,759,170,000	0.6%
18	Arizona	26,569,275,000	1.9%
31	Arkansas	15,062,783,000	1.1%
1	California	173,735,477,000	12.7%
24	Colorado	21,475,428,000	1.6%
25	Connecticut	21,207,569,000	1.5%
41	Delaware	7,050,055,000	0.5%
5	Florida	58,361,618,000	4.3%
14	Georgia	29,192,547,000	2.1%
36	Hawaii	10,671,728,000	0.8%
45	Idaho	5,734,304,000	0.4%
7	Illinois	45,341,139,000	3.3%
17	Indiana	26,628,696,000	1.9%
30	Iowa	15,189,556,000	1.1%
35	Kansas	11,972,832,000	0.9%
19	Kentucky	25,938,973,000	1.9%
26	Louisiana	20,990,011,000	1.5%
42	Maine	7,020,352,000	0.5%
15	Maryland	29,027,345,000	2.1%
8	Massachusetts	44,567,894,000	3.2%
10	Michigan	40,698,013,000	3.0%
16	Minnesota	27,626,605,000	2.0%
32	Mississippi	13,931,090,000	1.0%
23	Missouri	21,699,634,000	1.6%
47	Montana	4,945,248,000	0.4%
40	Nebraska	7,783,934,000	0.6%
39	Nevada	8,170,795,000	0.6%
44	New Hampshire	5,852,540,000	0.4%
9	New Jersey	44,261,778,000	3.2%
34	New Mexico	12,734,813,000	0.9%
2	New York	97,887,516,000	7.1%
12	North Carolina	34,441,408,000	2.5%
46	North Dakota	5,204,750,000	0.4%
6	Ohio	50,132,805,000	3.7%
29	Oklahoma	16,564,633,000	1.2%
21	Oregon	22,593,601,000	1.6%
4	Pennsylvania	62,259,356,000	4.5%
43	Rhode Island	5,894,500,000	0.4%
27	South Carolina	20,221,898,000	1.5%
49	South Dakota	3,757,827,000	0.3%
22	Tennessee	22,098,888,000	1.6%
3	Texas	95,917,162,000	7.0%
33	Utah	13,727,739,000	1.0%
48	Vermont	4,517,952,000	0.3%
11	Virginia	34,881,991,000	2.5%
13	Washington	33,809,714,000	2.5%
37	West Virginia	10,400,931,000	0.8%
20	Wisconsin	23,832,293,000	1.7%
50	Wyoming	3,608,609,000	0.3%

RANK ORDER

RANK	STATE	EXPENDITURES	% of USA
1	California	$173,735,477,000	12.7%
2	New York	97,887,516,000	7.1%
3	Texas	95,917,162,000	7.0%
4	Pennsylvania	62,259,356,000	4.5%
5	Florida	58,361,618,000	4.3%
6	Ohio	50,132,805,000	3.7%
7	Illinois	45,341,139,000	3.3%
8	Massachusetts	44,567,894,000	3.2%
9	New Jersey	44,261,778,000	3.2%
10	Michigan	40,698,013,000	3.0%
11	Virginia	34,881,991,000	2.5%
12	North Carolina	34,441,408,000	2.5%
13	Washington	33,809,714,000	2.5%
14	Georgia	29,192,547,000	2.1%
15	Maryland	29,027,345,000	2.1%
16	Minnesota	27,626,605,000	2.0%
17	Indiana	26,628,696,000	1.9%
18	Arizona	26,569,275,000	1.9%
19	Kentucky	25,938,973,000	1.9%
20	Wisconsin	23,832,293,000	1.7%
21	Oregon	22,593,601,000	1.6%
22	Tennessee	22,098,888,000	1.6%
23	Missouri	21,699,634,000	1.6%
24	Colorado	21,475,428,000	1.6%
25	Connecticut	21,207,569,000	1.5%
26	Louisiana	20,990,011,000	1.5%
27	South Carolina	20,221,898,000	1.5%
28	Alabama	19,212,442,000	1.4%
29	Oklahoma	16,564,633,000	1.2%
30	Iowa	15,189,556,000	1.1%
31	Arkansas	15,062,783,000	1.1%
32	Mississippi	13,931,090,000	1.0%
33	Utah	13,727,739,000	1.0%
34	New Mexico	12,734,813,000	0.9%
35	Kansas	11,972,832,000	0.9%
36	Hawaii	10,671,728,000	0.8%
37	West Virginia	10,400,931,000	0.8%
38	Alaska	8,759,170,000	0.6%
39	Nevada	8,170,795,000	0.6%
40	Nebraska	7,783,934,000	0.6%
41	Delaware	7,050,055,000	0.5%
42	Maine	7,020,352,000	0.5%
43	Rhode Island	5,894,500,000	0.4%
44	New Hampshire	5,852,540,000	0.4%
45	Idaho	5,734,304,000	0.4%
46	North Dakota	5,204,750,000	0.4%
47	Montana	4,945,248,000	0.4%
48	Vermont	4,517,952,000	0.3%
49	South Dakota	3,757,827,000	0.3%
50	Wyoming	3,608,609,000	0.3%
	District of Columbia**	NA	NA

Source: U.S. Bureau of the Census, Governments Division
   "2016 State and Local Government Finances" (https://www.census.gov/programs-surveys/gov-finances.html)
*Direct general expenditures include expenditures for current operations, assistance and subsidies, interest on debt, and capital outlay. Excludes intergovernmental transfers, expenditures for government owned utilities and other commercial or auxiliary enterprise, and insurance trust expenditures.
**Not applicable.

Per Capita State Government Direct General Expenditures in 2016

National Per Capita = $4,259*

ALPHA ORDER

RANK	STATE	PER CAPITA
39	Alabama	$3,949
1	Alaska	11,813
41	Arizona	3,825
15	Arkansas	5,037
27	California	4,431
40	Colorado	3,876
9	Connecticut	5,926
3	Delaware	7,427
49	Florida	2,829
48	Georgia	2,833
2	Hawaii	7,473
45	Idaho	3,407
43	Illinois	3,535
38	Indiana	4,014
20	Iowa	4,850
34	Kansas	4,113
10	Kentucky	5,844
26	Louisiana	4,487
14	Maine	5,273
21	Maryland	4,834
6	Massachusetts	6,529
35	Michigan	4,089
16	Minnesota	5,002
23	Mississippi	4,662
42	Missouri	3,565
22	Montana	4,751
36	Nebraska	4,084
50	Nevada	2,798
28	New Hampshire	4,360
17	New Jersey	4,988
8	New Mexico	6,085
18	New York	4,984
46	North Carolina	3,391
5	North Dakota	6,900
30	Ohio	4,309
31	Oklahoma	4,218
13	Oregon	5,522
19	Pennsylvania	4,870
12	Rhode Island	5,576
37	South Carolina	4,078
29	South Dakota	4,355
47	Tennessee	3,326
44	Texas	3,433
25	Utah	4,512
4	Vermont	7,244
32	Virginia	4,147
24	Washington	4,635
11	West Virginia	5,681
33	Wisconsin	4,128
7	Wyoming	6,176

RANK ORDER

RANK	STATE	PER CAPITA
1	Alaska	$11,813
2	Hawaii	7,473
3	Delaware	7,427
4	Vermont	7,244
5	North Dakota	6,900
6	Massachusetts	6,529
7	Wyoming	6,176
8	New Mexico	6,085
9	Connecticut	5,926
10	Kentucky	5,844
11	West Virginia	5,681
12	Rhode Island	5,576
13	Oregon	5,522
14	Maine	5,273
15	Arkansas	5,037
16	Minnesota	5,002
17	New Jersey	4,988
18	New York	4,984
19	Pennsylvania	4,870
20	Iowa	4,850
21	Maryland	4,834
22	Montana	4,751
23	Mississippi	4,662
24	Washington	4,635
25	Utah	4,512
26	Louisiana	4,487
27	California	4,431
28	New Hampshire	4,360
29	South Dakota	4,355
30	Ohio	4,309
31	Oklahoma	4,218
32	Virginia	4,147
33	Wisconsin	4,128
34	Kansas	4,113
35	Michigan	4,089
36	Nebraska	4,084
37	South Carolina	4,078
38	Indiana	4,014
39	Alabama	3,949
40	Colorado	3,876
41	Arizona	3,825
42	Missouri	3,565
43	Illinois	3,535
44	Texas	3,433
45	Idaho	3,407
46	North Carolina	3,391
47	Tennessee	3,326
48	Georgia	2,833
49	Florida	2,829
50	Nevada	2,798

District of Columbia**   NA

Source: CQ Press using data from U.S. Bureau of the Census, Governments Division

"2016 State and Local Government Finances" (https://www.census.gov/programs-surveys/gov-finances.html)

*Direct general expenditures include expenditures for current operations, assistance and subsidies, interest on debt, and capital outlay. Excludes intergovernmental transfers, expenditures for government owned utilities and other commercial or auxiliary enterprise, and insurance trust expenditures.

**Not applicable.

State Government Debt Outstanding in 2016

National Total = $1,160,488,556,000*

<table>
<tr><td colspan="4">ALPHA ORDER</td><td colspan="4">RANK ORDER</td></tr>
<tr><td>RANK</td><td>STATE</td><td>DEBT</td><td>% of USA</td><td>RANK</td><td>STATE</td><td>DEBT</td><td>% of USA</td></tr>
<tr><td>31</td><td>Alabama</td><td>$8,667,105,000</td><td>0.7%</td><td>1</td><td>California</td><td>$151,307,658,000</td><td>13.0%</td></tr>
<tr><td>39</td><td>Alaska</td><td>5,953,933,000</td><td>0.5%</td><td>2</td><td>New York</td><td>137,479,990,000</td><td>11.8%</td></tr>
<tr><td>24</td><td>Arizona</td><td>14,400,191,000</td><td>1.2%</td><td>3</td><td>Massachusetts</td><td>76,861,071,000</td><td>6.6%</td></tr>
<tr><td>42</td><td>Arkansas</td><td>4,828,756,000</td><td>0.4%</td><td>4</td><td>New Jersey</td><td>66,721,791,000</td><td>5.7%</td></tr>
<tr><td>1</td><td>California</td><td>151,307,658,000</td><td>13.0%</td><td>5</td><td>Illinois</td><td>65,791,900,000</td><td>5.7%</td></tr>
<tr><td>20</td><td>Colorado</td><td>16,686,588,000</td><td>1.4%</td><td>6</td><td>Texas</td><td>49,357,183,000</td><td>4.3%</td></tr>
<tr><td>8</td><td>Connecticut</td><td>37,024,731,000</td><td>3.2%</td><td>7</td><td>Pennsylvania</td><td>47,099,314,000</td><td>4.1%</td></tr>
<tr><td>40</td><td>Delaware</td><td>5,045,161,000</td><td>0.4%</td><td>8</td><td>Connecticut</td><td>37,024,731,000</td><td>3.2%</td></tr>
<tr><td>10</td><td>Florida</td><td>33,469,117,000</td><td>2.9%</td><td>9</td><td>Michigan</td><td>33,744,508,000</td><td>2.9%</td></tr>
<tr><td>26</td><td>Georgia</td><td>13,130,551,000</td><td>1.1%</td><td>10</td><td>Florida</td><td>33,469,117,000</td><td>2.9%</td></tr>
<tr><td>28</td><td>Hawaii</td><td>9,216,583,000</td><td>0.8%</td><td>11</td><td>Ohio</td><td>33,164,507,000</td><td>2.9%</td></tr>
<tr><td>43</td><td>Idaho</td><td>3,542,856,000</td><td>0.3%</td><td>12</td><td>Washington</td><td>33,059,765,000</td><td>2.8%</td></tr>
<tr><td>5</td><td>Illinois</td><td>65,791,900,000</td><td>5.7%</td><td>13</td><td>Virginia</td><td>28,628,254,000</td><td>2.5%</td></tr>
<tr><td>16</td><td>Indiana</td><td>22,470,543,000</td><td>1.9%</td><td>14</td><td>Maryland</td><td>27,871,287,000</td><td>2.4%</td></tr>
<tr><td>38</td><td>Iowa</td><td>5,956,424,000</td><td>0.5%</td><td>15</td><td>Wisconsin</td><td>23,052,389,000</td><td>2.0%</td></tr>
<tr><td>27</td><td>Kansas</td><td>9,537,833,000</td><td>0.8%</td><td>16</td><td>Indiana</td><td>22,470,543,000</td><td>1.9%</td></tr>
<tr><td>23</td><td>Kentucky</td><td>14,453,423,000</td><td>1.2%</td><td>17</td><td>Missouri</td><td>19,103,212,000</td><td>1.6%</td></tr>
<tr><td>18</td><td>Louisiana</td><td>17,913,229,000</td><td>1.5%</td><td>18</td><td>Louisiana</td><td>17,913,229,000</td><td>1.5%</td></tr>
<tr><td>41</td><td>Maine</td><td>4,845,408,000</td><td>0.4%</td><td>19</td><td>North Carolina</td><td>16,919,235,000</td><td>1.5%</td></tr>
<tr><td>14</td><td>Maryland</td><td>27,871,287,000</td><td>2.4%</td><td>20</td><td>Colorado</td><td>16,686,588,000</td><td>1.4%</td></tr>
<tr><td>3</td><td>Massachusetts</td><td>76,861,071,000</td><td>6.6%</td><td>21</td><td>South Carolina</td><td>16,228,097,000</td><td>1.4%</td></tr>
<tr><td>9</td><td>Michigan</td><td>33,744,508,000</td><td>2.9%</td><td>22</td><td>Minnesota</td><td>16,213,046,000</td><td>1.4%</td></tr>
<tr><td>22</td><td>Minnesota</td><td>16,213,046,000</td><td>1.4%</td><td>23</td><td>Kentucky</td><td>14,453,423,000</td><td>1.2%</td></tr>
<tr><td>33</td><td>Mississippi</td><td>7,283,371,000</td><td>0.6%</td><td>24</td><td>Arizona</td><td>14,400,191,000</td><td>1.2%</td></tr>
<tr><td>17</td><td>Missouri</td><td>19,103,212,000</td><td>1.6%</td><td>25</td><td>Oregon</td><td>13,355,878,000</td><td>1.2%</td></tr>
<tr><td>46</td><td>Montana</td><td>3,052,423,000</td><td>0.3%</td><td>26</td><td>Georgia</td><td>13,130,551,000</td><td>1.1%</td></tr>
<tr><td>49</td><td>Nebraska</td><td>1,950,506,000</td><td>0.2%</td><td>27</td><td>Kansas</td><td>9,537,833,000</td><td>0.8%</td></tr>
<tr><td>45</td><td>Nevada</td><td>3,222,367,000</td><td>0.3%</td><td>28</td><td>Hawaii</td><td>9,216,583,000</td><td>0.8%</td></tr>
<tr><td>32</td><td>New Hampshire</td><td>7,869,122,000</td><td>0.7%</td><td>29</td><td>Rhode Island</td><td>9,052,017,000</td><td>0.8%</td></tr>
<tr><td>4</td><td>New Jersey</td><td>66,721,791,000</td><td>5.7%</td><td>30</td><td>Oklahoma</td><td>8,702,914,000</td><td>0.7%</td></tr>
<tr><td>36</td><td>New Mexico</td><td>6,951,535,000</td><td>0.6%</td><td>31</td><td>Alabama</td><td>8,667,105,000</td><td>0.7%</td></tr>
<tr><td>2</td><td>New York</td><td>137,479,990,000</td><td>11.8%</td><td>32</td><td>New Hampshire</td><td>7,869,122,000</td><td>0.7%</td></tr>
<tr><td>19</td><td>North Carolina</td><td>16,919,235,000</td><td>1.5%</td><td>33</td><td>Mississippi</td><td>7,283,371,000</td><td>0.6%</td></tr>
<tr><td>48</td><td>North Dakota</td><td>2,355,700,000</td><td>0.2%</td><td>34</td><td>West Virginia</td><td>7,223,531,000</td><td>0.6%</td></tr>
<tr><td>11</td><td>Ohio</td><td>33,164,507,000</td><td>2.9%</td><td>35</td><td>Utah</td><td>7,013,698,000</td><td>0.6%</td></tr>
<tr><td>30</td><td>Oklahoma</td><td>8,702,914,000</td><td>0.7%</td><td>36</td><td>New Mexico</td><td>6,951,535,000</td><td>0.6%</td></tr>
<tr><td>25</td><td>Oregon</td><td>13,355,878,000</td><td>1.2%</td><td>37</td><td>Tennessee</td><td>6,075,745,000</td><td>0.5%</td></tr>
<tr><td>7</td><td>Pennsylvania</td><td>47,099,314,000</td><td>4.1%</td><td>38</td><td>Iowa</td><td>5,956,424,000</td><td>0.5%</td></tr>
<tr><td>29</td><td>Rhode Island</td><td>9,052,017,000</td><td>0.8%</td><td>39</td><td>Alaska</td><td>5,953,933,000</td><td>0.5%</td></tr>
<tr><td>21</td><td>South Carolina</td><td>16,228,097,000</td><td>1.4%</td><td>40</td><td>Delaware</td><td>5,045,161,000</td><td>0.4%</td></tr>
<tr><td>44</td><td>South Dakota</td><td>3,366,459,000</td><td>0.3%</td><td>41</td><td>Maine</td><td>4,845,408,000</td><td>0.4%</td></tr>
<tr><td>37</td><td>Tennessee</td><td>6,075,745,000</td><td>0.5%</td><td>42</td><td>Arkansas</td><td>4,828,756,000</td><td>0.4%</td></tr>
<tr><td>6</td><td>Texas</td><td>49,357,183,000</td><td>4.3%</td><td>43</td><td>Idaho</td><td>3,542,856,000</td><td>0.3%</td></tr>
<tr><td>35</td><td>Utah</td><td>7,013,698,000</td><td>0.6%</td><td>44</td><td>South Dakota</td><td>3,366,459,000</td><td>0.3%</td></tr>
<tr><td>47</td><td>Vermont</td><td>2,492,083,000</td><td>0.2%</td><td>45</td><td>Nevada</td><td>3,222,367,000</td><td>0.3%</td></tr>
<tr><td>13</td><td>Virginia</td><td>28,628,254,000</td><td>2.5%</td><td>46</td><td>Montana</td><td>3,052,423,000</td><td>0.3%</td></tr>
<tr><td>12</td><td>Washington</td><td>33,059,765,000</td><td>2.8%</td><td>47</td><td>Vermont</td><td>2,492,083,000</td><td>0.2%</td></tr>
<tr><td>34</td><td>West Virginia</td><td>7,223,531,000</td><td>0.6%</td><td>48</td><td>North Dakota</td><td>2,355,700,000</td><td>0.2%</td></tr>
<tr><td>15</td><td>Wisconsin</td><td>23,052,389,000</td><td>2.0%</td><td>49</td><td>Nebraska</td><td>1,950,506,000</td><td>0.2%</td></tr>
<tr><td>50</td><td>Wyoming</td><td>775,568,000</td><td>0.1%</td><td>50</td><td>Wyoming</td><td>775,568,000</td><td>0.1%</td></tr>
<tr><td></td><td></td><td></td><td></td><td></td><td>District of Columbia**</td><td>NA</td><td>NA</td></tr>
</table>

Source: U.S. Bureau of the Census, Governments Division
    "2016 State and Local Government Finances" (https://www.census.gov/programs-surveys/gov-finances.html)
*Includes short-term, long-term, full faith and credit, nonguaranteed, and public debt for private purposes.
**Not applicable.

Per Capita State Government Debt Outstanding in 2016

National Per Capita = $3,600*

ALPHA ORDER

RANK	STATE	PER CAPITA
41	Alabama	$1,782
4	Alaska	8,030
39	Arizona	2,073
45	Arkansas	1,615
17	California	3,859
31	Colorado	3,012
2	Connecticut	10,346
9	Delaware	5,315
44	Florida	1,622
47	Georgia	1,274
7	Hawaii	6,454
38	Idaho	2,105
10	Illinois	5,129
23	Indiana	3,388
40	Iowa	1,902
25	Kansas	3,276
28	Kentucky	3,257
18	Louisiana	3,829
20	Maine	3,639
11	Maryland	4,642
1	Massachusetts	11,260
22	Michigan	3,391
32	Minnesota	2,935
35	Mississippi	2,437
29	Missouri	3,138
33	Montana	2,933
49	Nebraska	1,023
48	Nevada	1,104
8	New Hampshire	5,862
5	New Jersey	7,518
24	New Mexico	3,322
6	New York	6,999
43	North Carolina	1,666
30	North Dakota	3,123
34	Ohio	2,850
37	Oklahoma	2,216
27	Oregon	3,264
19	Pennsylvania	3,684
3	Rhode Island	8,563
26	South Carolina	3,273
16	South Dakota	3,901
50	Tennessee	914
42	Texas	1,767
36	Utah	2,305
13	Vermont	3,996
21	Virginia	3,404
12	Washington	4,532
15	West Virginia	3,945
14	Wisconsin	3,993
46	Wyoming	1,327

RANK ORDER

RANK	STATE	PER CAPITA
1	Massachusetts	$11,260
2	Connecticut	10,346
3	Rhode Island	8,563
4	Alaska	8,030
5	New Jersey	7,518
6	New York	6,999
7	Hawaii	6,454
8	New Hampshire	5,862
9	Delaware	5,315
10	Illinois	5,129
11	Maryland	4,642
12	Washington	4,532
13	Vermont	3,996
14	Wisconsin	3,993
15	West Virginia	3,945
16	South Dakota	3,901
17	California	3,859
18	Louisiana	3,829
19	Pennsylvania	3,684
20	Maine	3,639
21	Virginia	3,404
22	Michigan	3,391
23	Indiana	3,388
24	New Mexico	3,322
25	Kansas	3,276
26	South Carolina	3,273
27	Oregon	3,264
28	Kentucky	3,257
29	Missouri	3,138
30	North Dakota	3,123
31	Colorado	3,012
32	Minnesota	2,935
33	Montana	2,933
34	Ohio	2,850
35	Mississippi	2,437
36	Utah	2,305
37	Oklahoma	2,216
38	Idaho	2,105
39	Arizona	2,073
40	Iowa	1,902
41	Alabama	1,782
42	Texas	1,767
43	North Carolina	1,666
44	Florida	1,622
45	Arkansas	1,615
46	Wyoming	1,327
47	Georgia	1,274
48	Nevada	1,104
49	Nebraska	1,023
50	Tennessee	914
	District of Columbia**	NA

Source: CQ Press using data from U.S. Bureau of the Census, Governments Division
  "2016 State and Local Government Finances" (https://www.census.gov/programs-surveys/gov-finances.html)
*Includes short-term, long-term, full faith and credit, nonguaranteed, and public debt for private purposes.
**Not applicable.

State Government Full-Time Equivalent Employees in 2017

National Total = 4,381,768 FTE Employees*

ALPHA ORDER				RANK ORDER			
RANK	STATE	EMPLOYEES	% of USA	RANK	STATE	EMPLOYEES	% of USA
15	Alabama	90,729	2.1%	1	California	424,359	9.7%
41	Alaska	24,357	0.6%	2	Texas	313,065	7.1%
26	Arizona	72,850	1.7%	3	New York	247,580	5.7%
29	Arkansas	62,066	1.4%	4	Florida	179,738	4.1%
1	California	424,359	9.7%	5	Pennsylvania	164,285	3.7%
17	Colorado	88,130	2.0%	6	Michigan	146,697	3.3%
32	Connecticut	58,803	1.3%	7	North Carolina	144,993	3.3%
40	Delaware	25,872	0.6%	8	New Jersey	139,048	3.2%
4	Florida	179,738	4.1%	9	Ohio	137,560	3.1%
10	Georgia	129,828	3.0%	10	Georgia	129,828	3.0%
31	Hawaii	58,966	1.3%	11	Washington	127,234	2.9%
42	Idaho	24,176	0.6%	12	Virginia	125,605	2.9%
13	Illinois	121,795	2.8%	13	Illinois	121,795	2.8%
16	Indiana	90,341	2.1%	14	Massachusetts	98,206	2.2%
35	Iowa	51,176	1.2%	15	Alabama	90,729	2.1%
34	Kansas	53,820	1.2%	16	Indiana	90,341	2.1%
20	Kentucky	84,042	1.9%	17	Colorado	88,130	2.0%
24	Louisiana	73,488	1.7%	18	Missouri	86,498	2.0%
44	Maine	20,172	0.5%	19	Maryland	85,163	1.9%
19	Maryland	85,163	1.9%	20	Kentucky	84,042	1.9%
14	Massachusetts	98,206	2.2%	21	Minnesota	83,359	1.9%
6	Michigan	146,697	3.3%	22	South Carolina	79,834	1.8%
21	Minnesota	83,359	1.9%	23	Tennessee	78,746	1.8%
33	Mississippi	55,539	1.3%	24	Louisiana	73,488	1.7%
18	Missouri	86,498	2.0%	25	Wisconsin	72,899	1.7%
43	Montana	20,870	0.5%	26	Arizona	72,850	1.7%
38	Nebraska	31,655	0.7%	27	Oregon	70,153	1.6%
39	Nevada	28,936	0.7%	28	Oklahoma	66,128	1.5%
46	New Hampshire	18,931	0.4%	29	Arkansas	62,066	1.4%
8	New Jersey	139,048	3.2%	30	Utah	60,507	1.4%
36	New Mexico	45,194	1.0%	31	Hawaii	58,966	1.3%
3	New York	247,580	5.7%	32	Connecticut	58,803	1.3%
7	North Carolina	144,993	3.3%	33	Mississippi	55,539	1.3%
45	North Dakota	19,026	0.4%	34	Kansas	53,820	1.2%
9	Ohio	137,560	3.1%	35	Iowa	51,176	1.2%
28	Oklahoma	66,128	1.5%	36	New Mexico	45,194	1.0%
27	Oregon	70,153	1.6%	37	West Virginia	39,394	0.9%
5	Pennsylvania	164,285	3.7%	38	Nebraska	31,655	0.7%
47	Rhode Island	18,151	0.4%	39	Nevada	28,936	0.7%
22	South Carolina	79,834	1.8%	40	Delaware	25,872	0.6%
48	South Dakota	14,449	0.3%	41	Alaska	24,357	0.6%
23	Tennessee	78,746	1.8%	42	Idaho	24,176	0.6%
2	Texas	313,065	7.1%	43	Montana	20,870	0.5%
30	Utah	60,507	1.4%	44	Maine	20,172	0.5%
49	Vermont	14,267	0.3%	45	North Dakota	19,026	0.4%
12	Virginia	125,605	2.9%	46	New Hampshire	18,931	0.4%
11	Washington	127,234	2.9%	47	Rhode Island	18,151	0.4%
37	West Virginia	39,394	0.9%	48	South Dakota	14,449	0.3%
25	Wisconsin	72,899	1.7%	49	Vermont	14,267	0.3%
50	Wyoming	13,088	0.3%	50	Wyoming	13,088	0.3%
					District of Columbia**	NA	NA

Source: U.S. Bureau of the Census, Governments Division
"Annual Survey of Public Employment and Payroll" (https://www.census.gov/programs-surveys/apes.html)
*Full-time equivalent as of March 2017.
**Not applicable.

Rate of State Government Full-Time Equivalent Employees in 2017

National Rate = 135 FTE Employees per 10,000 Population*

ALPHA ORDER

RANK	STATE	RATE
13	Alabama	186
2	Alaska	329
47	Arizona	103
9	Arkansas	207
46	California	108
25	Colorado	157
20	Connecticut	165
3	Delaware	270
50	Florida	86
42	Georgia	125
1	Hawaii	414
34	Idaho	141
49	Illinois	95
38	Indiana	136
23	Iowa	163
15	Kansas	185
12	Kentucky	189
25	Louisiana	157
28	Maine	151
34	Maryland	141
32	Massachusetts	143
31	Michigan	147
29	Minnesota	150
13	Mississippi	186
33	Missouri	142
10	Montana	198
20	Nebraska	165
48	Nevada	97
37	New Hampshire	140
27	New Jersey	156
8	New Mexico	216
40	New York	126
34	North Carolina	141
4	North Dakota	252
43	Ohio	118
19	Oklahoma	168
18	Oregon	169
39	Pennsylvania	128
16	Rhode Island	172
24	South Carolina	159
20	South Dakota	165
44	Tennessee	117
45	Texas	111
11	Utah	195
5	Vermont	228
30	Virginia	148
17	Washington	171
7	West Virginia	217
40	Wisconsin	126
6	Wyoming	226

RANK ORDER

RANK	STATE	RATE
1	Hawaii	414
2	Alaska	329
3	Delaware	270
4	North Dakota	252
5	Vermont	228
6	Wyoming	226
7	West Virginia	217
8	New Mexico	216
9	Arkansas	207
10	Montana	198
11	Utah	195
12	Kentucky	189
13	Alabama	186
13	Mississippi	186
15	Kansas	185
16	Rhode Island	172
17	Washington	171
18	Oregon	169
19	Oklahoma	168
20	Connecticut	165
20	Nebraska	165
20	South Dakota	165
23	Iowa	163
24	South Carolina	159
25	Colorado	157
25	Louisiana	157
27	New Jersey	156
28	Maine	151
29	Minnesota	150
30	Virginia	148
31	Michigan	147
32	Massachusetts	143
33	Missouri	142
34	Idaho	141
34	Maryland	141
34	North Carolina	141
37	New Hampshire	140
38	Indiana	136
39	Pennsylvania	128
40	New York	126
40	Wisconsin	126
42	Georgia	125
43	Ohio	118
44	Tennessee	117
45	Texas	111
46	California	108
47	Arizona	103
48	Nevada	97
49	Illinois	95
50	Florida	86

District of Columbia**   NA

Source: CQ Press using data from U.S. Bureau of the Census, Governments Division
    "Annual Survey of Public Employment and Payroll" (https://www.census.gov/programs-surveys/apes.html)
*Full-time equivalent as of March 2017.
**Not applicable.

Average Annual Earnings of Full-Time State Government Employees in 2017

National Average = $65,046*

RANK	STATE	SALARY
35	Alabama	$56,511
9	Alaska	72,314
26	Arizona	60,344
47	Arkansas	50,255
1	California	87,093
12	Colorado	70,027
2	Connecticut	80,300
34	Delaware	56,592
44	Florida	53,165
43	Georgia	53,458
28	Hawaii	58,339
21	Idaho	63,786
11	Illinois	70,530
39	Indiana	54,506
3	Iowa	78,950
36	Kansas	56,327
38	Kentucky	55,547
31	Louisiana	57,202
41	Maine	54,249
17	Maryland	65,418
7	Massachusetts	73,359
10	Michigan	71,431
8	Minnesota	72,472
49	Mississippi	47,969
48	Missouri	48,092
30	Montana	57,718
40	Nebraska	54,415
25	Nevada	61,823
18	New Hampshire	65,336
5	New Jersey	75,481
32	New Mexico	57,134
4	New York	75,791
29	North Carolina	58,261
27	North Dakota	59,705
15	Ohio	66,711
46	Oklahoma	52,152
13	Oregon	67,857
22	Pennsylvania	63,582
6	Rhode Island	73,702
45	South Carolina	52,165
33	South Dakota	56,978
42	Tennessee	53,785
23	Texas	62,470
24	Utah	61,911
14	Vermont	67,070
20	Virginia	64,428
16	Washington	66,355
50	West Virginia	46,680
19	Wisconsin	65,031
37	Wyoming	55,965

RANK	STATE	SALARY
1	California	$87,093
2	Connecticut	80,300
3	Iowa	78,950
4	New York	75,791
5	New Jersey	75,481
6	Rhode Island	73,702
7	Massachusetts	73,359
8	Minnesota	72,472
9	Alaska	72,314
10	Michigan	71,431
11	Illinois	70,530
12	Colorado	70,027
13	Oregon	67,857
14	Vermont	67,070
15	Ohio	66,711
16	Washington	66,355
17	Maryland	65,418
18	New Hampshire	65,336
19	Wisconsin	65,031
20	Virginia	64,428
21	Idaho	63,786
22	Pennsylvania	63,582
23	Texas	62,470
24	Utah	61,911
25	Nevada	61,823
26	Arizona	60,344
27	North Dakota	59,705
28	Hawaii	58,339
29	North Carolina	58,261
30	Montana	57,718
31	Louisiana	57,202
32	New Mexico	57,134
33	South Dakota	56,978
34	Delaware	56,592
35	Alabama	56,511
36	Kansas	56,327
37	Wyoming	55,965
38	Kentucky	55,547
39	Indiana	54,506
40	Nebraska	54,415
41	Maine	54,249
42	Tennessee	53,785
43	Georgia	53,458
44	Florida	53,165
45	South Carolina	52,165
46	Oklahoma	52,152
47	Arkansas	50,255
48	Missouri	48,092
49	Mississippi	47,969
50	West Virginia	46,680
	District of Columbia**	NA

Source: CQ Press using data from U.S. Bureau of the Census, Governments Division
    "Annual Survey of Public Employment and Payroll" (https://www.census.gov/programs-surveys/apes.html)
*March 2017 full-time payroll (multiplied by 12) divided by full-time employees.
**Not applicable.

Local Government Total Revenue in 2016

National Total = $1,805,682,720,000*

ALPHA ORDER

ALPHA ORDER

RANK ORDER

RANK	STATE	REVENUE	% of USA
25	Alabama	$21,776,958,000	1.2%
40	Alaska	5,597,734,000	0.3%
20	Arizona	29,402,701,000	1.6%
36	Arkansas	10,343,182,000	0.6%
1	California	306,847,335,000	17.0%
17	Colorado	30,705,063,000	1.7%
27	Connecticut	18,765,232,000	1.0%
49	Delaware	3,554,455,000	0.2%
4	Florida	98,286,087,000	5.4%
12	Georgia	44,146,207,000	2.4%
46	Hawaii	4,190,598,000	0.2%
39	Idaho	5,918,090,000	0.3%
5	Illinois	73,285,181,000	4.1%
18	Indiana	30,572,837,000	1.7%
28	Iowa	17,203,162,000	1.0%
30	Kansas	14,990,974,000	0.8%
29	Kentucky	15,038,491,000	0.8%
24	Louisiana	22,209,996,000	1.2%
43	Maine	5,132,434,000	0.3%
19	Maryland	30,387,576,000	1.7%
14	Massachusetts	35,058,456,000	1.9%
11	Michigan	46,942,002,000	2.6%
16	Minnesota	31,871,872,000	1.8%
34	Mississippi	13,100,079,000	0.7%
22	Missouri	26,107,728,000	1.4%
47	Montana	3,902,761,000	0.2%
32	Nebraska	14,387,121,000	0.8%
31	Nevada	14,810,477,000	0.8%
38	New Hampshire	6,133,774,000	0.3%
8	New Jersey	49,772,544,000	2.8%
37	New Mexico	8,961,579,000	0.5%
2	New York	196,060,833,000	10.9%
9	North Carolina	49,277,265,000	2.7%
44	North Dakota	4,840,340,000	0.3%
7	Ohio	56,789,781,000	3.1%
33	Oklahoma	13,909,759,000	0.8%
26	Oregon	21,124,247,000	1.2%
6	Pennsylvania	66,157,907,000	3.7%
45	Rhode Island	4,821,742,000	0.3%
23	South Carolina	23,270,476,000	1.3%
48	South Dakota	3,675,012,000	0.2%
15	Tennessee	32,863,434,000	1.8%
3	Texas	137,238,278,000	7.6%
35	Utah	12,456,548,000	0.7%
50	Vermont	2,986,348,000	0.2%
13	Virginia	39,234,937,000	2.2%
10	Washington	47,100,665,000	2.6%
41	West Virginia	5,498,382,000	0.3%
21	Wisconsin	28,845,226,000	1.6%
42	Wyoming	5,386,106,000	0.3%

RANK	STATE	REVENUE	% of USA
1	California	$306,847,335,000	17.0%
2	New York	196,060,833,000	10.9%
3	Texas	137,238,278,000	7.6%
4	Florida	98,286,087,000	5.4%
5	Illinois	73,285,181,000	4.1%
6	Pennsylvania	66,157,907,000	3.7%
7	Ohio	56,789,781,000	3.1%
8	New Jersey	49,772,544,000	2.8%
9	North Carolina	49,277,265,000	2.7%
10	Washington	47,100,665,000	2.6%
11	Michigan	46,942,002,000	2.6%
12	Georgia	44,146,207,000	2.4%
13	Virginia	39,234,937,000	2.2%
14	Massachusetts	35,058,456,000	1.9%
15	Tennessee	32,863,434,000	1.8%
16	Minnesota	31,871,872,000	1.8%
17	Colorado	30,705,063,000	1.7%
18	Indiana	30,572,837,000	1.7%
19	Maryland	30,387,576,000	1.7%
20	Arizona	29,402,701,000	1.6%
21	Wisconsin	28,845,226,000	1.6%
22	Missouri	26,107,728,000	1.4%
23	South Carolina	23,270,476,000	1.3%
24	Louisiana	22,209,996,000	1.2%
25	Alabama	21,776,958,000	1.2%
26	Oregon	21,124,247,000	1.2%
27	Connecticut	18,765,232,000	1.0%
28	Iowa	17,203,162,000	1.0%
29	Kentucky	15,038,491,000	0.8%
30	Kansas	14,990,974,000	0.8%
31	Nevada	14,810,477,000	0.8%
32	Nebraska	14,387,121,000	0.8%
33	Oklahoma	13,909,759,000	0.8%
34	Mississippi	13,100,079,000	0.7%
35	Utah	12,456,548,000	0.7%
36	Arkansas	10,343,182,000	0.6%
37	New Mexico	8,961,579,000	0.5%
38	New Hampshire	6,133,774,000	0.3%
39	Idaho	5,918,090,000	0.3%
40	Alaska	5,597,734,000	0.3%
41	West Virginia	5,498,382,000	0.3%
42	Wyoming	5,386,106,000	0.3%
43	Maine	5,132,434,000	0.3%
44	North Dakota	4,840,340,000	0.3%
45	Rhode Island	4,821,742,000	0.3%
46	Hawaii	4,190,598,000	0.2%
47	Montana	3,902,761,000	0.2%
48	South Dakota	3,675,012,000	0.2%
49	Delaware	3,554,455,000	0.2%
50	Vermont	2,986,348,000	0.2%
	District of Columbia	14,742,748,000	0.8%

Source: U.S. Bureau of the Census, Governments Division
"2016 State and Local Government Finances" (https://www.census.gov/programs-surveys/gov-finances.html)
*Total revenue includes all money received from external sources. This includes taxes, intergovernmental transfers and insurance trust revenue, and revenue from government owned utilities and other commercial or auxiliary enterprise.

Per Capita Local Government Total Revenue in 2016

National Per Capita = $5,589*

<table>
<tr><td colspan="3">ALPHA ORDER</td><td colspan="3">RANK ORDER</td></tr>
<tr><td>RANK</td><td>STATE</td><td>PER CAPITA</td><td>RANK</td><td>STATE</td><td>PER CAPITA</td></tr>
<tr><td>34</td><td>Alabama</td><td>$4,476</td><td>1</td><td>New York</td><td>$9,982</td></tr>
<tr><td>4</td><td>Alaska</td><td>7,549</td><td>2</td><td>Wyoming</td><td>9,218</td></tr>
<tr><td>40</td><td>Arizona</td><td>4,233</td><td>3</td><td>California</td><td>7,826</td></tr>
<tr><td>47</td><td>Arkansas</td><td>3,459</td><td>4</td><td>Alaska</td><td>7,549</td></tr>
<tr><td>3</td><td>California</td><td>7,826</td><td>4</td><td>Nebraska</td><td>7,549</td></tr>
<tr><td>11</td><td>Colorado</td><td>5,542</td><td>6</td><td>Washington</td><td>6,457</td></tr>
<tr><td>13</td><td>Connecticut</td><td>5,244</td><td>7</td><td>North Dakota</td><td>6,417</td></tr>
<tr><td>44</td><td>Delaware</td><td>3,745</td><td>8</td><td>Minnesota</td><td>5,770</td></tr>
<tr><td>26</td><td>Florida</td><td>4,764</td><td>9</td><td>Illinois</td><td>5,713</td></tr>
<tr><td>37</td><td>Georgia</td><td>4,284</td><td>10</td><td>New Jersey</td><td>5,608</td></tr>
<tr><td>50</td><td>Hawaii</td><td>2,934</td><td>11</td><td>Colorado</td><td>5,542</td></tr>
<tr><td>46</td><td>Idaho</td><td>3,517</td><td>12</td><td>Iowa</td><td>5,493</td></tr>
<tr><td>9</td><td>Illinois</td><td>5,713</td><td>13</td><td>Connecticut</td><td>5,244</td></tr>
<tr><td>31</td><td>Indiana</td><td>4,609</td><td>14</td><td>Pennsylvania</td><td>5,175</td></tr>
<tr><td>12</td><td>Iowa</td><td>5,493</td><td>15</td><td>Oregon</td><td>5,163</td></tr>
<tr><td>16</td><td>Kansas</td><td>5,149</td><td>16</td><td>Kansas</td><td>5,149</td></tr>
<tr><td>48</td><td>Kentucky</td><td>3,388</td><td>17</td><td>Massachusetts</td><td>5,136</td></tr>
<tr><td>27</td><td>Louisiana</td><td>4,748</td><td>18</td><td>Nevada</td><td>5,072</td></tr>
<tr><td>42</td><td>Maine</td><td>3,855</td><td>19</td><td>Maryland</td><td>5,061</td></tr>
<tr><td>19</td><td>Maryland</td><td>5,061</td><td>20</td><td>Wisconsin</td><td>4,997</td></tr>
<tr><td>17</td><td>Massachusetts</td><td>5,136</td><td>21</td><td>Tennessee</td><td>4,946</td></tr>
<tr><td>28</td><td>Michigan</td><td>4,717</td><td>22</td><td>Texas</td><td>4,912</td></tr>
<tr><td>8</td><td>Minnesota</td><td>5,770</td><td>23</td><td>Ohio</td><td>4,881</td></tr>
<tr><td>35</td><td>Mississippi</td><td>4,384</td><td>24</td><td>North Carolina</td><td>4,852</td></tr>
<tr><td>36</td><td>Missouri</td><td>4,289</td><td>25</td><td>Vermont</td><td>4,789</td></tr>
<tr><td>43</td><td>Montana</td><td>3,750</td><td>26</td><td>Florida</td><td>4,764</td></tr>
<tr><td>4</td><td>Nebraska</td><td>7,549</td><td>27</td><td>Louisiana</td><td>4,748</td></tr>
<tr><td>18</td><td>Nevada</td><td>5,072</td><td>28</td><td>Michigan</td><td>4,717</td></tr>
<tr><td>32</td><td>New Hampshire</td><td>4,569</td><td>29</td><td>South Carolina</td><td>4,693</td></tr>
<tr><td>10</td><td>New Jersey</td><td>5,608</td><td>30</td><td>Virginia</td><td>4,665</td></tr>
<tr><td>38</td><td>New Mexico</td><td>4,282</td><td>31</td><td>Indiana</td><td>4,609</td></tr>
<tr><td>1</td><td>New York</td><td>9,982</td><td>32</td><td>New Hampshire</td><td>4,569</td></tr>
<tr><td>24</td><td>North Carolina</td><td>4,852</td><td>33</td><td>Rhode Island</td><td>4,561</td></tr>
<tr><td>7</td><td>North Dakota</td><td>6,417</td><td>34</td><td>Alabama</td><td>4,476</td></tr>
<tr><td>23</td><td>Ohio</td><td>4,881</td><td>35</td><td>Mississippi</td><td>4,384</td></tr>
<tr><td>45</td><td>Oklahoma</td><td>3,542</td><td>36</td><td>Missouri</td><td>4,289</td></tr>
<tr><td>15</td><td>Oregon</td><td>5,163</td><td>37</td><td>Georgia</td><td>4,284</td></tr>
<tr><td>14</td><td>Pennsylvania</td><td>5,175</td><td>38</td><td>New Mexico</td><td>4,282</td></tr>
<tr><td>33</td><td>Rhode Island</td><td>4,561</td><td>39</td><td>South Dakota</td><td>4,259</td></tr>
<tr><td>29</td><td>South Carolina</td><td>4,693</td><td>40</td><td>Arizona</td><td>4,233</td></tr>
<tr><td>39</td><td>South Dakota</td><td>4,259</td><td>41</td><td>Utah</td><td>4,094</td></tr>
<tr><td>21</td><td>Tennessee</td><td>4,946</td><td>42</td><td>Maine</td><td>3,855</td></tr>
<tr><td>22</td><td>Texas</td><td>4,912</td><td>43</td><td>Montana</td><td>3,750</td></tr>
<tr><td>41</td><td>Utah</td><td>4,094</td><td>44</td><td>Delaware</td><td>3,745</td></tr>
<tr><td>25</td><td>Vermont</td><td>4,789</td><td>45</td><td>Oklahoma</td><td>3,542</td></tr>
<tr><td>30</td><td>Virginia</td><td>4,665</td><td>46</td><td>Idaho</td><td>3,517</td></tr>
<tr><td>6</td><td>Washington</td><td>6,457</td><td>47</td><td>Arkansas</td><td>3,459</td></tr>
<tr><td>49</td><td>West Virginia</td><td>3,003</td><td>48</td><td>Kentucky</td><td>3,388</td></tr>
<tr><td>20</td><td>Wisconsin</td><td>4,997</td><td>49</td><td>West Virginia</td><td>3,003</td></tr>
<tr><td>2</td><td>Wyoming</td><td>9,218</td><td>50</td><td>Hawaii</td><td>2,934</td></tr>
<tr><td></td><td></td><td></td><td></td><td>District of Columbia</td><td>21,473</td></tr>
</table>

Source: CQ Press using data from U.S. Bureau of the Census, Governments Division
"2016 State and Local Government Finances" (https://www.census.gov/programs-surveys/gov-finances.html)
*Total revenue includes all money received from external sources. This includes taxes, intergovernmental transfers and insurance trust revenue, and revenue from government owned utilities and other commercial or auxiliary enterprise.

Local Government Revenue from the Federal Government in 2016

National Total = $68,699,817,000

ALPHA ORDER

RANK	STATE	REVENUE	% of USA
16	Alabama	$1,018,899,000	1.5%
38	Alaska	283,030,000	0.4%
21	Arizona	760,087,000	1.1%
37	Arkansas	286,486,000	0.4%
1	California	12,470,848,000	18.2%
15	Colorado	1,066,325,000	1.6%
27	Connecticut	569,284,000	0.8%
49	Delaware	76,862,000	0.1%
4	Florida	3,664,184,000	5.3%
14	Georgia	1,138,664,000	1.7%
35	Hawaii	390,667,000	0.6%
45	Idaho	156,568,000	0.2%
5	Illinois	3,250,064,000	4.7%
28	Indiana	533,280,000	0.8%
29	Iowa	511,702,000	0.7%
39	Kansas	269,190,000	0.4%
24	Kentucky	578,782,000	0.8%
18	Louisiana	937,828,000	1.4%
47	Maine	137,864,000	0.2%
13	Maryland	1,236,763,000	1.8%
12	Massachusetts	1,443,770,000	2.1%
11	Michigan	1,663,057,000	2.4%
20	Minnesota	835,324,000	1.2%
31	Mississippi	472,476,000	0.7%
22	Missouri	745,533,000	1.1%
41	Montana	217,537,000	0.3%
36	Nebraska	359,692,000	0.5%
26	Nevada	571,299,000	0.8%
48	New Hampshire	111,901,000	0.2%
17	New Jersey	1,010,516,000	1.5%
34	New Mexico	396,628,000	0.6%
2	New York	6,613,695,000	9.6%
6	North Carolina	3,212,497,000	4.7%
40	North Dakota	246,875,000	0.4%
8	Ohio	2,166,106,000	3.2%
33	Oklahoma	423,515,000	0.6%
19	Oregon	859,496,000	1.3%
7	Pennsylvania	2,835,225,000	4.1%
43	Rhode Island	179,284,000	0.3%
30	South Carolina	491,669,000	0.7%
42	South Dakota	203,613,000	0.3%
23	Tennessee	741,561,000	1.1%
3	Texas	3,987,509,000	5.8%
32	Utah	437,727,000	0.6%
50	Vermont	71,732,000	0.1%
9	Virginia	1,923,064,000	2.8%
10	Washington	1,758,290,000	2.6%
44	West Virginia	177,523,000	0.3%
25	Wisconsin	574,465,000	0.8%
46	Wyoming	146,941,000	0.2%

RANK ORDER

RANK	STATE	REVENUE	% of USA
1	California	$12,470,848,000	18.2%
2	New York	6,613,695,000	9.6%
3	Texas	3,987,509,000	5.8%
4	Florida	3,664,184,000	5.3%
5	Illinois	3,250,064,000	4.7%
6	North Carolina	3,212,497,000	4.7%
7	Pennsylvania	2,835,225,000	4.1%
8	Ohio	2,166,106,000	3.2%
9	Virginia	1,923,064,000	2.8%
10	Washington	1,758,290,000	2.6%
11	Michigan	1,663,057,000	2.4%
12	Massachusetts	1,443,770,000	2.1%
13	Maryland	1,236,763,000	1.8%
14	Georgia	1,138,664,000	1.7%
15	Colorado	1,066,325,000	1.6%
16	Alabama	1,018,899,000	1.5%
17	New Jersey	1,010,516,000	1.5%
18	Louisiana	937,828,000	1.4%
19	Oregon	859,496,000	1.3%
20	Minnesota	835,324,000	1.2%
21	Arizona	760,087,000	1.1%
22	Missouri	745,533,000	1.1%
23	Tennessee	741,561,000	1.1%
24	Kentucky	578,782,000	0.8%
25	Wisconsin	574,465,000	0.8%
26	Nevada	571,299,000	0.8%
27	Connecticut	569,284,000	0.8%
28	Indiana	533,280,000	0.8%
29	Iowa	511,702,000	0.7%
30	South Carolina	491,669,000	0.7%
31	Mississippi	472,476,000	0.7%
32	Utah	437,727,000	0.6%
33	Oklahoma	423,515,000	0.6%
34	New Mexico	396,628,000	0.6%
35	Hawaii	390,667,000	0.6%
36	Nebraska	359,692,000	0.5%
37	Arkansas	286,486,000	0.4%
38	Alaska	283,030,000	0.4%
39	Kansas	269,190,000	0.4%
40	North Dakota	246,875,000	0.4%
41	Montana	217,537,000	0.3%
42	South Dakota	203,613,000	0.3%
43	Rhode Island	179,284,000	0.3%
44	West Virginia	177,523,000	0.3%
45	Idaho	156,568,000	0.2%
46	Wyoming	146,941,000	0.2%
47	Maine	137,864,000	0.2%
48	New Hampshire	111,901,000	0.2%
49	Delaware	76,862,000	0.1%
50	Vermont	71,732,000	0.1%
	District of Columbia	4,483,920,000	6.5%

Source: U.S. Bureau of the Census, Governments Division
"2016 State and Local Government Finances" (https://www.census.gov/programs-surveys/gov-finances.html)

Per Capita Local Government Revenue from the Federal Government in 2016

National Per Capita = $213

ALPHA ORDER

RANK	STATE	PER CAPITA
15	Alabama	$209
1	Alaska	382
39	Arizona	109
45	Arkansas	96
4	California	318
20	Colorado	192
28	Connecticut	159
49	Delaware	81
24	Florida	178
38	Georgia	110
6	Hawaii	274
46	Idaho	93
7	Illinois	253
50	Indiana	80
27	Iowa	163
47	Kansas	92
33	Kentucky	130
18	Louisiana	200
41	Maine	104
17	Maryland	206
13	Massachusetts	212
26	Michigan	167
30	Minnesota	151
29	Mississippi	158
34	Missouri	122
15	Montana	209
22	Nebraska	189
19	Nevada	196
48	New Hampshire	83
36	New Jersey	114
21	New Mexico	190
2	New York	337
5	North Carolina	316
3	North Dakota	327
23	Ohio	186
40	Oklahoma	108
14	Oregon	210
12	Pennsylvania	222
25	Rhode Island	170
43	South Carolina	99
10	South Dakota	236
37	Tennessee	112
32	Texas	143
31	Utah	144
35	Vermont	115
11	Virginia	229
9	Washington	241
44	West Virginia	97
42	Wisconsin	100
8	Wyoming	251

RANK ORDER

RANK	STATE	PER CAPITA
1	Alaska	$382
2	New York	337
3	North Dakota	327
4	California	318
5	North Carolina	316
6	Hawaii	274
7	Illinois	253
8	Wyoming	251
9	Washington	241
10	South Dakota	236
11	Virginia	229
12	Pennsylvania	222
13	Massachusetts	212
14	Oregon	210
15	Alabama	209
15	Montana	209
17	Maryland	206
18	Louisiana	200
19	Nevada	196
20	Colorado	192
21	New Mexico	190
22	Nebraska	189
23	Ohio	186
24	Florida	178
25	Rhode Island	170
26	Michigan	167
27	Iowa	163
28	Connecticut	159
29	Mississippi	158
30	Minnesota	151
31	Utah	144
32	Texas	143
33	Kentucky	130
34	Missouri	122
35	Vermont	115
36	New Jersey	114
37	Tennessee	112
38	Georgia	110
39	Arizona	109
40	Oklahoma	108
41	Maine	104
42	Wisconsin	100
43	South Carolina	99
44	West Virginia	97
45	Arkansas	96
46	Idaho	93
47	Kansas	92
48	New Hampshire	83
49	Delaware	81
50	Indiana	80

District of Columbia   6,531

Source: CQ Press using data from U.S. Bureau of the Census, Governments Division
"2016 State and Local Government Finances" (https://www.census.gov/programs-surveys/gov-finances.html)

Local Government Own Source Revenue in 2016

National Total = $1,045,899,038,000*

ALPHA ORDER

RANK	STATE	REVENUE	% of USA
27	Alabama	$11,867,078,000	1.1%
45	Alaska	2,885,501,000	0.3%
21	Arizona	15,350,009,000	1.5%
37	Arkansas	4,072,332,000	0.4%
1	California	153,451,447,000	14.7%
15	Colorado	20,198,899,000	1.9%
25	Connecticut	12,307,699,000	1.2%
49	Delaware	1,618,743,000	0.2%
4	Florida	64,239,954,000	6.1%
10	Georgia	26,544,428,000	2.5%
43	Hawaii	3,137,088,000	0.3%
40	Idaho	3,330,053,000	0.3%
5	Illinois	44,896,801,000	4.3%
17	Indiana	17,071,582,000	1.6%
28	Iowa	10,019,389,000	1.0%
30	Kansas	8,304,546,000	0.8%
31	Kentucky	8,025,789,000	0.8%
24	Louisiana	14,186,176,000	1.4%
39	Maine	3,535,296,000	0.3%
16	Maryland	19,818,381,000	1.9%
14	Massachusetts	20,953,364,000	2.0%
13	Michigan	23,065,757,000	2.2%
19	Minnesota	16,309,609,000	1.6%
33	Mississippi	7,183,585,000	0.7%
18	Missouri	16,320,802,000	1.6%
47	Montana	2,215,739,000	0.2%
34	Nebraska	7,023,867,000	0.7%
32	Nevada	7,863,595,000	0.8%
36	New Hampshire	4,462,882,000	0.4%
7	New Jersey	35,410,727,000	3.4%
38	New Mexico	4,034,456,000	0.4%
2	New York	124,517,007,000	11.9%
9	North Carolina	26,849,193,000	2.6%
48	North Dakota	2,158,623,000	0.2%
8	Ohio	34,547,361,000	3.3%
29	Oklahoma	8,407,445,000	0.8%
26	Oregon	11,953,243,000	1.1%
6	Pennsylvania	37,344,389,000	3.6%
42	Rhode Island	3,185,972,000	0.3%
22	South Carolina	15,062,811,000	1.4%
46	South Dakota	2,296,594,000	0.2%
20	Tennessee	15,782,528,000	1.5%
3	Texas	87,027,924,000	8.3%
35	Utah	6,735,156,000	0.6%
50	Vermont	919,821,000	0.1%
12	Virginia	23,695,695,000	2.3%
11	Washington	25,703,643,000	2.5%
41	West Virginia	3,305,515,000	0.3%
23	Wisconsin	14,560,785,000	1.4%
44	Wyoming	3,009,931,000	0.3%

RANK ORDER

RANK	STATE	REVENUE	% of USA
1	California	$153,451,447,000	14.7%
2	New York	124,517,007,000	11.9%
3	Texas	87,027,924,000	8.3%
4	Florida	64,239,954,000	6.1%
5	Illinois	44,896,801,000	4.3%
6	Pennsylvania	37,344,389,000	3.6%
7	New Jersey	35,410,727,000	3.4%
8	Ohio	34,547,361,000	3.3%
9	North Carolina	26,849,193,000	2.6%
10	Georgia	26,544,428,000	2.5%
11	Washington	25,703,643,000	2.5%
12	Virginia	23,695,695,000	2.3%
13	Michigan	23,065,757,000	2.2%
14	Massachusetts	20,953,364,000	2.0%
15	Colorado	20,198,899,000	1.9%
16	Maryland	19,818,381,000	1.9%
17	Indiana	17,071,582,000	1.6%
18	Missouri	16,320,802,000	1.6%
19	Minnesota	16,309,609,000	1.6%
20	Tennessee	15,782,528,000	1.5%
21	Arizona	15,350,009,000	1.5%
22	South Carolina	15,062,811,000	1.4%
23	Wisconsin	14,560,785,000	1.4%
24	Louisiana	14,186,176,000	1.4%
25	Connecticut	12,307,699,000	1.2%
26	Oregon	11,953,243,000	1.1%
27	Alabama	11,867,078,000	1.1%
28	Iowa	10,019,389,000	1.0%
29	Oklahoma	8,407,445,000	0.8%
30	Kansas	8,304,546,000	0.8%
31	Kentucky	8,025,789,000	0.8%
32	Nevada	7,863,595,000	0.8%
33	Mississippi	7,183,585,000	0.7%
34	Nebraska	7,023,867,000	0.7%
35	Utah	6,735,156,000	0.6%
36	New Hampshire	4,462,882,000	0.4%
37	Arkansas	4,072,332,000	0.4%
38	New Mexico	4,034,456,000	0.4%
39	Maine	3,535,296,000	0.3%
40	Idaho	3,330,053,000	0.3%
41	West Virginia	3,305,515,000	0.3%
42	Rhode Island	3,185,972,000	0.3%
43	Hawaii	3,137,088,000	0.3%
44	Wyoming	3,009,931,000	0.3%
45	Alaska	2,885,501,000	0.3%
46	South Dakota	2,296,594,000	0.2%
47	Montana	2,215,739,000	0.2%
48	North Dakota	2,158,623,000	0.2%
49	Delaware	1,618,743,000	0.2%
50	Vermont	919,821,000	0.1%
	District of Columbia	9,129,828,000	0.9%

Source: U.S. Bureau of the Census, Governments Division
"2016 State and Local Government Finances" (https://www.census.gov/programs-surveys/gov-finances.html)
*Own source revenue includes taxes, current charges, and miscellaneous general revenue. Excluded are intergovernmental transfers, insurance trust revenue, and revenue from government owned utilities and other commercial or auxiliary enterprise.

Per Capita Local Government Own Source Revenue in 2016

National Per Capita = $3,237*

ALPHA ORDER

RANK	STATE	PER CAPITA
35	Alabama	$2,439
5	Alaska	3,891
40	Arizona	2,210
50	Arkansas	1,362
4	California	3,914
7	Colorado	3,645
10	Connecticut	3,439
48	Delaware	1,705
15	Florida	3,114
32	Georgia	2,576
41	Hawaii	2,197
44	Idaho	1,979
9	Illinois	3,500
33	Indiana	2,574
13	Iowa	3,199
25	Kansas	2,853
46	Kentucky	1,808
18	Louisiana	3,032
30	Maine	2,655
12	Maryland	3,300
16	Massachusetts	3,070
38	Michigan	2,318
21	Minnesota	2,953
36	Mississippi	2,404
28	Missouri	2,681
43	Montana	2,129
6	Nebraska	3,685
27	Nevada	2,693
11	New Hampshire	3,325
3	New Jersey	3,990
45	New Mexico	1,928
1	New York	6,339
31	North Carolina	2,644
24	North Dakota	2,862
20	Ohio	2,969
42	Oklahoma	2,141
22	Oregon	2,922
23	Pennsylvania	2,921
19	Rhode Island	3,014
17	South Carolina	3,038
29	South Dakota	2,662
37	Tennessee	2,375
14	Texas	3,115
39	Utah	2,214
49	Vermont	1,475
26	Virginia	2,817
8	Washington	3,524
47	West Virginia	1,805
34	Wisconsin	2,522
2	Wyoming	5,151

RANK ORDER

RANK	STATE	PER CAPITA
1	New York	$6,339
2	Wyoming	5,151
3	New Jersey	3,990
4	California	3,914
5	Alaska	3,891
6	Nebraska	3,685
7	Colorado	3,645
8	Washington	3,524
9	Illinois	3,500
10	Connecticut	3,439
11	New Hampshire	3,325
12	Maryland	3,300
13	Iowa	3,199
14	Texas	3,115
15	Florida	3,114
16	Massachusetts	3,070
17	South Carolina	3,038
18	Louisiana	3,032
19	Rhode Island	3,014
20	Ohio	2,969
21	Minnesota	2,953
22	Oregon	2,922
23	Pennsylvania	2,921
24	North Dakota	2,862
25	Kansas	2,853
26	Virginia	2,817
27	Nevada	2,693
28	Missouri	2,681
29	South Dakota	2,662
30	Maine	2,655
31	North Carolina	2,644
32	Georgia	2,576
33	Indiana	2,574
34	Wisconsin	2,522
35	Alabama	2,439
36	Mississippi	2,404
37	Tennessee	2,375
38	Michigan	2,318
39	Utah	2,214
40	Arizona	2,210
41	Hawaii	2,197
42	Oklahoma	2,141
43	Montana	2,129
44	Idaho	1,979
45	New Mexico	1,928
46	Kentucky	1,808
47	West Virginia	1,805
48	Delaware	1,705
49	Vermont	1,475
50	Arkansas	1,362
	District of Columbia	13,298

Source: CQ Press using data from U.S. Bureau of the Census, Governments Division
"2016 State and Local Government Finances" (https://www.census.gov/programs-surveys/gov-finances.html)
*Own source revenue includes taxes, current charges, and miscellaneous general revenue. Excluded are intergovernmental transfers, insurance trust revenue, and revenue from government owned utilities and other commercial or auxiliary enterprise.

Local Government Tax Revenue in 2016

National Total = $676,658,061,000

ALPHA ORDER

RANK	STATE	REVENUE	% of USA
28	Alabama	$5,665,128,000	0.8%
43	Alaska	1,784,863,000	0.3%
19	Arizona	10,067,336,000	1.5%
40	Arkansas	2,373,584,000	0.4%
2	California	83,573,864,000	12.4%
16	Colorado	12,761,142,000	1.9%
17	Connecticut	10,659,698,000	1.6%
49	Delaware	1,009,842,000	0.1%
4	Florida	34,206,979,000	5.1%
11	Georgia	16,288,841,000	2.4%
41	Hawaii	2,320,382,000	0.3%
44	Idaho	1,697,096,000	0.3%
5	Illinois	33,667,739,000	5.0%
24	Indiana	8,101,915,000	1.2%
27	Iowa	5,732,288,000	0.8%
31	Kansas	5,018,758,000	0.7%
29	Kentucky	5,179,197,000	0.8%
21	Louisiana	8,909,056,000	1.3%
37	Maine	2,794,318,000	0.4%
12	Maryland	15,416,036,000	2.3%
10	Massachusetts	16,864,902,000	2.5%
15	Michigan	13,112,608,000	1.9%
23	Minnesota	8,461,006,000	1.3%
36	Mississippi	3,125,060,000	0.5%
18	Missouri	10,184,342,000	1.5%
46	Montana	1,346,513,000	0.2%
32	Nebraska	4,587,452,000	0.7%
33	Nevada	4,546,159,000	0.7%
35	New Hampshire	3,789,591,000	0.6%
6	New Jersey	28,691,153,000	4.2%
38	New Mexico	2,652,332,000	0.4%
1	New York	96,313,326,000	14.2%
14	North Carolina	13,603,623,000	2.0%
48	North Dakota	1,300,158,000	0.2%
8	Ohio	23,298,528,000	3.4%
30	Oklahoma	5,067,522,000	0.7%
26	Oregon	7,376,691,000	1.1%
7	Pennsylvania	27,286,127,000	4.0%
39	Rhode Island	2,616,540,000	0.4%
25	South Carolina	7,481,743,000	1.1%
45	South Dakota	1,645,229,000	0.2%
22	Tennessee	8,703,589,000	1.3%
3	Texas	60,043,772,000	8.9%
34	Utah	4,312,767,000	0.6%
50	Vermont	594,326,000	0.1%
9	Virginia	17,152,822,000	2.5%
13	Washington	14,490,650,000	2.1%
42	West Virginia	2,033,917,000	0.3%
20	Wisconsin	9,999,412,000	1.5%
47	Wyoming	1,329,460,000	0.2%

RANK ORDER

RANK	STATE	REVENUE	% of USA
1	New York	$96,313,326,000	14.2%
2	California	83,573,864,000	12.4%
3	Texas	60,043,772,000	8.9%
4	Florida	34,206,979,000	5.1%
5	Illinois	33,667,739,000	5.0%
6	New Jersey	28,691,153,000	4.2%
7	Pennsylvania	27,286,127,000	4.0%
8	Ohio	23,298,528,000	3.4%
9	Virginia	17,152,822,000	2.5%
10	Massachusetts	16,864,902,000	2.5%
11	Georgia	16,288,841,000	2.4%
12	Maryland	15,416,036,000	2.3%
13	Washington	14,490,650,000	2.1%
14	North Carolina	13,603,623,000	2.0%
15	Michigan	13,112,608,000	1.9%
16	Colorado	12,761,142,000	1.9%
17	Connecticut	10,659,698,000	1.6%
18	Missouri	10,184,342,000	1.5%
19	Arizona	10,067,336,000	1.5%
20	Wisconsin	9,999,412,000	1.5%
21	Louisiana	8,909,056,000	1.3%
22	Tennessee	8,703,589,000	1.3%
23	Minnesota	8,461,006,000	1.3%
24	Indiana	8,101,915,000	1.2%
25	South Carolina	7,481,743,000	1.1%
26	Oregon	7,376,691,000	1.1%
27	Iowa	5,732,288,000	0.8%
28	Alabama	5,665,128,000	0.8%
29	Kentucky	5,179,197,000	0.8%
30	Oklahoma	5,067,522,000	0.7%
31	Kansas	5,018,758,000	0.7%
32	Nebraska	4,587,452,000	0.7%
33	Nevada	4,546,159,000	0.7%
34	Utah	4,312,767,000	0.6%
35	New Hampshire	3,789,591,000	0.6%
36	Mississippi	3,125,060,000	0.5%
37	Maine	2,794,318,000	0.4%
38	New Mexico	2,652,332,000	0.4%
39	Rhode Island	2,616,540,000	0.4%
40	Arkansas	2,373,584,000	0.4%
41	Hawaii	2,320,382,000	0.3%
42	West Virginia	2,033,917,000	0.3%
43	Alaska	1,784,863,000	0.3%
44	Idaho	1,697,096,000	0.3%
45	South Dakota	1,645,229,000	0.2%
46	Montana	1,346,513,000	0.2%
47	Wyoming	1,329,460,000	0.2%
48	North Dakota	1,300,158,000	0.2%
49	Delaware	1,009,842,000	0.1%
50	Vermont	594,326,000	0.1%
	District of Columbia	7,418,679,000	1.1%

Source: U.S. Bureau of the Census, Governments Division
"2016 State and Local Government Finances" (https://www.census.gov/programs-surveys/gov-finances.html)

Per Capita Local Government Tax Revenue in 2016

National Per Capita = $2,094

ALPHA ORDER

RANK	STATE	PER CAPITA
44	Alabama	$1,165
9	Alaska	2,407
34	Arizona	1,449
50	Arkansas	794
15	California	2,131
11	Colorado	2,303
3	Connecticut	2,979
46	Delaware	1,064
28	Florida	1,658
30	Georgia	1,581
29	Hawaii	1,625
48	Idaho	1,008
5	Illinois	2,625
42	Indiana	1,221
22	Iowa	1,830
25	Kansas	1,724
43	Kentucky	1,167
21	Louisiana	1,904
16	Maine	2,099
6	Maryland	2,567
8	Massachusetts	2,471
37	Michigan	1,318
32	Minnesota	1,532
47	Mississippi	1,046
27	Missouri	1,673
39	Montana	1,294
9	Nebraska	2,407
31	Nevada	1,557
4	New Hampshire	2,823
2	New Jersey	3,233
41	New Mexico	1,267
1	New York	4,904
36	North Carolina	1,339
25	North Dakota	1,724
18	Ohio	2,002
40	Oklahoma	1,291
23	Oregon	1,803
14	Pennsylvania	2,134
7	Rhode Island	2,475
33	South Carolina	1,509
20	South Dakota	1,907
38	Tennessee	1,310
13	Texas	2,149
35	Utah	1,417
49	Vermont	953
17	Virginia	2,039
19	Washington	1,986
45	West Virginia	1,111
24	Wisconsin	1,732
12	Wyoming	2,275

RANK ORDER

RANK	STATE	PER CAPITA
1	New York	$4,904
2	New Jersey	3,233
3	Connecticut	2,979
4	New Hampshire	2,823
5	Illinois	2,625
6	Maryland	2,567
7	Rhode Island	2,475
8	Massachusetts	2,471
9	Alaska	2,407
9	Nebraska	2,407
11	Colorado	2,303
12	Wyoming	2,275
13	Texas	2,149
14	Pennsylvania	2,134
15	California	2,131
16	Maine	2,099
17	Virginia	2,039
18	Ohio	2,002
19	Washington	1,986
20	South Dakota	1,907
21	Louisiana	1,904
22	Iowa	1,830
23	Oregon	1,803
24	Wisconsin	1,732
25	Kansas	1,724
25	North Dakota	1,724
27	Missouri	1,673
28	Florida	1,658
29	Hawaii	1,625
30	Georgia	1,581
31	Nevada	1,557
32	Minnesota	1,532
33	South Carolina	1,509
34	Arizona	1,449
35	Utah	1,417
36	North Carolina	1,339
37	Michigan	1,318
38	Tennessee	1,310
39	Montana	1,294
40	Oklahoma	1,291
41	New Mexico	1,267
42	Indiana	1,221
43	Kentucky	1,167
44	Alabama	1,165
45	West Virginia	1,111
46	Delaware	1,064
47	Mississippi	1,046
48	Idaho	1,008
49	Vermont	953
50	Arkansas	794
	District of Columbia	10,805

Source: CQ Press using data from U.S. Bureau of the Census, Governments Division
"2016 State and Local Government Finances" (https://www.census.gov/programs-surveys/gov-finances.html)

Local Government Total Expenditures in 2016

National Total = $1,838,514,959,000*

ALPHA ORDER

RANK	STATE	EXPENDITURES	% of USA
24	Alabama	$22,225,069,000	1.2%
41	Alaska	5,487,277,000	0.3%
21	Arizona	28,356,659,000	1.5%
36	Arkansas	10,320,799,000	0.6%
1	California	309,231,926,000	16.8%
19	Colorado	30,354,929,000	1.7%
27	Connecticut	19,175,080,000	1.0%
49	Delaware	3,526,682,000	0.2%
4	Florida	99,991,823,000	5.4%
11	Georgia	46,577,603,000	2.5%
46	Hawaii	4,160,421,000	0.2%
39	Idaho	5,560,301,000	0.3%
5	Illinois	80,116,071,000	4.4%
20	Indiana	28,412,407,000	1.5%
28	Iowa	17,051,032,000	0.9%
30	Kansas	14,927,038,000	0.8%
29	Kentucky	15,098,630,000	0.8%
25	Louisiana	22,063,643,000	1.2%
43	Maine	4,935,430,000	0.3%
15	Maryland	33,092,750,000	1.8%
14	Massachusetts	35,689,811,000	1.9%
10	Michigan	47,605,959,000	2.6%
17	Minnesota	32,231,637,000	1.8%
34	Mississippi	13,074,962,000	0.7%
22	Missouri	27,372,046,000	1.5%
47	Montana	4,018,753,000	0.2%
31	Nebraska	14,507,935,000	0.8%
33	Nevada	13,746,247,000	0.7%
40	New Hampshire	5,512,838,000	0.3%
8	New Jersey	49,814,712,000	2.7%
37	New Mexico	8,558,947,000	0.5%
2	New York	209,200,799,000	11.4%
9	North Carolina	48,542,926,000	2.6%
45	North Dakota	4,764,457,000	0.3%
7	Ohio	57,837,022,000	3.1%
32	Oklahoma	14,196,478,000	0.8%
26	Oregon	21,271,690,000	1.2%
6	Pennsylvania	67,196,545,000	3.7%
44	Rhode Island	4,836,300,000	0.3%
23	South Carolina	22,371,638,000	1.2%
48	South Dakota	3,672,252,000	0.2%
16	Tennessee	33,039,924,000	1.8%
3	Texas	140,299,131,000	7.6%
35	Utah	11,558,437,000	0.6%
50	Vermont	2,819,295,000	0.2%
13	Virginia	39,716,888,000	2.2%
12	Washington	46,030,968,000	2.5%
38	West Virginia	5,901,755,000	0.3%
18	Wisconsin	30,389,806,000	1.7%
42	Wyoming	5,475,570,000	0.3%

RANK ORDER

RANK	STATE	EXPENDITURES	% of USA
1	California	$309,231,926,000	16.8%
2	New York	209,200,799,000	11.4%
3	Texas	140,299,131,000	7.6%
4	Florida	99,991,823,000	5.4%
5	Illinois	80,116,071,000	4.4%
6	Pennsylvania	67,196,545,000	3.7%
7	Ohio	57,837,022,000	3.1%
8	New Jersey	49,814,712,000	2.7%
9	North Carolina	48,542,926,000	2.6%
10	Michigan	47,605,959,000	2.6%
11	Georgia	46,577,603,000	2.5%
12	Washington	46,030,968,000	2.5%
13	Virginia	39,716,888,000	2.2%
14	Massachusetts	35,689,811,000	1.9%
15	Maryland	33,092,750,000	1.8%
16	Tennessee	33,039,924,000	1.8%
17	Minnesota	32,231,637,000	1.8%
18	Wisconsin	30,389,806,000	1.7%
19	Colorado	30,354,929,000	1.7%
20	Indiana	28,412,407,000	1.5%
21	Arizona	28,356,659,000	1.5%
22	Missouri	27,372,046,000	1.5%
23	South Carolina	22,371,638,000	1.2%
24	Alabama	22,225,069,000	1.2%
25	Louisiana	22,063,643,000	1.2%
26	Oregon	21,271,690,000	1.2%
27	Connecticut	19,175,080,000	1.0%
28	Iowa	17,051,032,000	0.9%
29	Kentucky	15,098,630,000	0.8%
30	Kansas	14,927,038,000	0.8%
31	Nebraska	14,507,935,000	0.8%
32	Oklahoma	14,196,478,000	0.8%
33	Nevada	13,746,247,000	0.7%
34	Mississippi	13,074,962,000	0.7%
35	Utah	11,558,437,000	0.6%
36	Arkansas	10,320,799,000	0.6%
37	New Mexico	8,558,947,000	0.5%
38	West Virginia	5,901,755,000	0.3%
39	Idaho	5,560,301,000	0.3%
40	New Hampshire	5,512,838,000	0.3%
41	Alaska	5,487,277,000	0.3%
42	Wyoming	5,475,570,000	0.3%
43	Maine	4,935,430,000	0.3%
44	Rhode Island	4,836,300,000	0.3%
45	North Dakota	4,764,457,000	0.3%
46	Hawaii	4,160,421,000	0.2%
47	Montana	4,018,753,000	0.2%
48	South Dakota	3,672,252,000	0.2%
49	Delaware	3,526,682,000	0.2%
50	Vermont	2,819,295,000	0.2%
	District of Columbia	16,593,661,000	0.9%

Source: U.S. Bureau of the Census, Governments Division

"2016 State and Local Government Finances" (https://www.census.gov/programs-surveys/gov-finances.html)
*Total expenditures includes all money paid other than for retirement of debt and extension of loans. Includes payments from all sources of funds including current revenues and proceeds from borrowing and prior year fund balances. Includes intergovernmental transfers and expenditures for government owned utilities and other commercial or auxiliary enterprise and insurance trust expenditures.

Per Capita Local Government Total Expenditures in 2016

National Per Capita = $5,691*

ALPHA ORDER			RANK ORDER		
RANK	STATE	PER CAPITA	RANK	STATE	PER CAPITA
30	Alabama	$4,569	1	New York	$10,651
5	Alaska	7,400	2	Wyoming	9,371
40	Arizona	4,083	3	California	7,887
46	Arkansas	3,451	4	Nebraska	7,612
3	California	7,887	5	Alaska	7,400
12	Colorado	5,478	6	North Dakota	6,316
14	Connecticut	5,358	7	Washington	6,310
43	Delaware	3,715	8	Illinois	6,246
23	Florida	4,847	9	Minnesota	5,835
32	Georgia	4,520	10	New Jersey	5,613
50	Hawaii	2,913	11	Maryland	5,511
48	Idaho	3,304	12	Colorado	5,478
8	Illinois	6,246	13	Iowa	5,445
36	Indiana	4,283	14	Connecticut	5,358
13	Iowa	5,445	15	Wisconsin	5,264
19	Kansas	5,127	16	Pennsylvania	5,256
47	Kentucky	3,402	17	Massachusetts	5,228
27	Louisiana	4,716	18	Oregon	5,199
44	Maine	3,707	19	Kansas	5,127
11	Maryland	5,511	20	Texas	5,022
17	Massachusetts	5,228	21	Tennessee	4,972
24	Michigan	4,784	22	Ohio	4,971
9	Minnesota	5,835	23	Florida	4,847
35	Mississippi	4,375	24	Michigan	4,784
34	Missouri	4,497	25	North Carolina	4,779
41	Montana	3,861	26	Virginia	4,722
4	Nebraska	7,612	27	Louisiana	4,716
28	Nevada	4,708	28	Nevada	4,708
38	New Hampshire	4,107	29	Rhode Island	4,575
10	New Jersey	5,613	30	Alabama	4,569
39	New Mexico	4,090	31	Vermont	4,521
1	New York	10,651	32	Georgia	4,520
25	North Carolina	4,779	33	South Carolina	4,512
6	North Dakota	6,316	34	Missouri	4,497
22	Ohio	4,971	35	Mississippi	4,375
45	Oklahoma	3,615	36	Indiana	4,283
18	Oregon	5,199	37	South Dakota	4,256
16	Pennsylvania	5,256	38	New Hampshire	4,107
29	Rhode Island	4,575	39	New Mexico	4,090
33	South Carolina	4,512	40	Arizona	4,083
37	South Dakota	4,256	41	Montana	3,861
21	Tennessee	4,972	42	Utah	3,799
20	Texas	5,022	43	Delaware	3,715
42	Utah	3,799	44	Maine	3,707
31	Vermont	4,521	45	Oklahoma	3,615
26	Virginia	4,722	46	Arkansas	3,451
7	Washington	6,310	47	Kentucky	3,402
49	West Virginia	3,223	48	Idaho	3,304
15	Wisconsin	5,264	49	West Virginia	3,223
2	Wyoming	9,371	50	Hawaii	2,913

District of Columbia 24,169

Source: CQ Press using data from U.S. Bureau of the Census, Governments Division

"2016 State and Local Government Finances" (https://www.census.gov/programs-surveys/gov-finances.html)

*Total expenditures includes all money paid other than for retirement of debt and extension of loans. Includes payments from all sources of funds including current revenues and proceeds from borrowing and prior year fund balances. Includes intergovernmental transfers and expenditures for government owned utilities and other commercial or auxiliary enterprise and insurance trust expenditures.

Local Government Direct General Expenditures in 2016

National Total = $1,571,484,171,000*

ALPHA ORDER

RANK	STATE	EXPENDITURES	% of USA
25	Alabama	$18,990,384,000	1.2%
42	Alaska	4,905,930,000	0.3%
22	Arizona	22,156,758,000	1.4%
36	Arkansas	9,252,448,000	0.6%
1	California	255,164,544,000	16.2%
18	Colorado	25,505,520,000	1.6%
27	Connecticut	17,217,376,000	1.1%
48	Delaware	3,041,976,000	0.2%
4	Florida	86,499,209,000	5.5%
11	Georgia	39,504,165,000	2.5%
49	Hawaii	2,955,467,000	0.2%
39	Idaho	5,305,102,000	0.3%
5	Illinois	66,092,629,000	4.2%
19	Indiana	25,445,079,000	1.6%
28	Iowa	15,704,062,000	1.0%
29	Kansas	13,227,285,000	0.8%
30	Kentucky	12,940,254,000	0.8%
24	Louisiana	20,352,865,000	1.3%
43	Maine	4,750,268,000	0.3%
15	Maryland	29,590,622,000	1.9%
14	Massachusetts	30,218,278,000	1.9%
10	Michigan	42,087,985,000	2.7%
16	Minnesota	29,329,746,000	1.9%
33	Mississippi	12,173,889,000	0.8%
20	Missouri	23,783,604,000	1.5%
46	Montana	3,829,746,000	0.2%
34	Nebraska	9,642,351,000	0.6%
32	Nevada	12,329,150,000	0.8%
40	New Hampshire	5,274,889,000	0.3%
8	New Jersey	48,187,957,000	3.1%
37	New Mexico	7,786,270,000	0.5%
2	New York	170,488,880,000	10.8%
9	North Carolina	42,767,232,000	2.7%
44	North Dakota	4,372,109,000	0.3%
7	Ohio	53,442,410,000	3.4%
31	Oklahoma	12,581,076,000	0.8%
26	Oregon	18,779,095,000	1.2%
6	Pennsylvania	59,920,004,000	3.8%
45	Rhode Island	4,325,842,000	0.3%
23	South Carolina	20,666,145,000	1.3%
47	South Dakota	3,233,628,000	0.2%
21	Tennessee	22,875,491,000	1.5%
3	Texas	119,147,213,000	7.6%
35	Utah	9,557,124,000	0.6%
50	Vermont	2,513,218,000	0.2%
13	Virginia	35,984,674,000	2.3%
12	Washington	36,785,956,000	2.3%
38	West Virginia	5,514,286,000	0.4%
17	Wisconsin	27,345,072,000	1.7%
41	Wyoming	5,168,388,000	0.3%

RANK ORDER

RANK	STATE	EXPENDITURES	% of USA
1	California	$255,164,544,000	16.2%
2	New York	170,488,880,000	10.8%
3	Texas	119,147,213,000	7.6%
4	Florida	86,499,209,000	5.5%
5	Illinois	66,092,629,000	4.2%
6	Pennsylvania	59,920,004,000	3.8%
7	Ohio	53,442,410,000	3.4%
8	New Jersey	48,187,957,000	3.1%
9	North Carolina	42,767,232,000	2.7%
10	Michigan	42,087,985,000	2.7%
11	Georgia	39,504,165,000	2.5%
12	Washington	36,785,956,000	2.3%
13	Virginia	35,984,674,000	2.3%
14	Massachusetts	30,218,278,000	1.9%
15	Maryland	29,590,622,000	1.9%
16	Minnesota	29,329,746,000	1.9%
17	Wisconsin	27,345,072,000	1.7%
18	Colorado	25,505,520,000	1.6%
19	Indiana	25,445,079,000	1.6%
20	Missouri	23,783,604,000	1.5%
21	Tennessee	22,875,491,000	1.5%
22	Arizona	22,156,758,000	1.4%
23	South Carolina	20,666,145,000	1.3%
24	Louisiana	20,352,865,000	1.3%
25	Alabama	18,990,384,000	1.2%
26	Oregon	18,779,095,000	1.2%
27	Connecticut	17,217,376,000	1.1%
28	Iowa	15,704,062,000	1.0%
29	Kansas	13,227,285,000	0.8%
30	Kentucky	12,940,254,000	0.8%
31	Oklahoma	12,581,076,000	0.8%
32	Nevada	12,329,150,000	0.8%
33	Mississippi	12,173,889,000	0.8%
34	Nebraska	9,642,351,000	0.6%
35	Utah	9,557,124,000	0.6%
36	Arkansas	9,252,448,000	0.6%
37	New Mexico	7,786,270,000	0.5%
38	West Virginia	5,514,286,000	0.4%
39	Idaho	5,305,102,000	0.3%
40	New Hampshire	5,274,889,000	0.3%
41	Wyoming	5,168,388,000	0.3%
42	Alaska	4,905,930,000	0.3%
43	Maine	4,750,268,000	0.3%
44	North Dakota	4,372,109,000	0.3%
45	Rhode Island	4,325,842,000	0.3%
46	Montana	3,829,746,000	0.2%
47	South Dakota	3,233,628,000	0.2%
48	Delaware	3,041,976,000	0.2%
49	Hawaii	2,955,467,000	0.2%
50	Vermont	2,513,218,000	0.2%
	District of Columbia	12,770,520,000	0.8%

Source: U.S. Bureau of the Census, Governments Division
   "2016 State and Local Government Finances" (https://www.census.gov/programs-surveys/gov-finances.html)
*Direct general expenditures include expenditures for current operations, assistance and subsidies, interest on debt, and capital outlay. Excludes intergovernmental transfers, expenditures for government owned utilities and other commercial or auxiliary enterprise, and insurance trust expenditures.

Per Capita Local Government Direct General Expenditures in 2016

National Per Capita = $4,864*

ALPHA ORDER

RANK	STATE	PER CAPITA
34	Alabama	$3,904
3	Alaska	6,616
44	Arizona	3,190
47	Arkansas	3,094
4	California	6,508
16	Colorado	4,603
13	Connecticut	4,811
42	Delaware	3,205
27	Florida	4,193
36	Georgia	3,834
50	Hawaii	2,070
45	Idaho	3,152
8	Illinois	5,153
35	Indiana	3,836
11	Iowa	5,014
19	Kansas	4,543
49	Kentucky	2,916
21	Louisiana	4,351
40	Maine	3,568
12	Maryland	4,928
20	Massachusetts	4,427
24	Michigan	4,229
7	Minnesota	5,310
30	Mississippi	4,074
33	Missouri	3,907
39	Montana	3,679
9	Nebraska	5,059
25	Nevada	4,223
32	New Hampshire	3,930
6	New Jersey	5,430
38	New Mexico	3,721
2	New York	8,680
26	North Carolina	4,211
5	North Dakota	5,796
17	Ohio	4,593
43	Oklahoma	3,204
18	Oregon	4,590
15	Pennsylvania	4,687
29	Rhode Island	4,092
28	South Carolina	4,168
37	South Dakota	3,747
41	Tennessee	3,443
23	Texas	4,265
46	Utah	3,141
31	Vermont	4,030
22	Virginia	4,278
10	Washington	5,043
48	West Virginia	3,012
14	Wisconsin	4,737
1	Wyoming	8,846

RANK ORDER

RANK	STATE	PER CAPITA
1	Wyoming	$8,846
2	New York	8,680
3	Alaska	6,616
4	California	6,508
5	North Dakota	5,796
6	New Jersey	5,430
7	Minnesota	5,310
8	Illinois	5,153
9	Nebraska	5,059
10	Washington	5,043
11	Iowa	5,014
12	Maryland	4,928
13	Connecticut	4,811
14	Wisconsin	4,737
15	Pennsylvania	4,687
16	Colorado	4,603
17	Ohio	4,593
18	Oregon	4,590
19	Kansas	4,543
20	Massachusetts	4,427
21	Louisiana	4,351
22	Virginia	4,278
23	Texas	4,265
24	Michigan	4,229
25	Nevada	4,223
26	North Carolina	4,211
27	Florida	4,193
28	South Carolina	4,168
29	Rhode Island	4,092
30	Mississippi	4,074
31	Vermont	4,030
32	New Hampshire	3,930
33	Missouri	3,907
34	Alabama	3,904
35	Indiana	3,836
36	Georgia	3,834
37	South Dakota	3,747
38	New Mexico	3,721
39	Montana	3,679
40	Maine	3,568
41	Tennessee	3,443
42	Delaware	3,205
43	Oklahoma	3,204
44	Arizona	3,190
45	Idaho	3,152
46	Utah	3,141
47	Arkansas	3,094
48	West Virginia	3,012
49	Kentucky	2,916
50	Hawaii	2,070

District of Columbia 18,600

Source: CQ Press using data from U.S. Bureau of the Census, Governments Division
"2016 State and Local Government Finances" (https://www.census.gov/programs-surveys/gov-finances.html)
*Direct general expenditures include expenditures for current operations, assistance and subsidies, interest on debt, and capital outlay. Excludes intergovernmental transfers, expenditures for government owned utilities and other commercial or auxiliary enterprise, and insurance trust expenditures.

Local Government Debt Outstanding in 2016

National Total = $1,841,573,203,000*

ALPHA ORDER

RANK	STATE	DEBT	% of USA
26	Alabama	$20,201,141,000	1.1%
41	Alaska	3,396,063,000	0.2%
15	Arizona	34,394,482,000	1.9%
34	Arkansas	11,057,764,000	0.6%
1	California	282,609,085,000	15.3%
12	Colorado	36,237,707,000	2.0%
33	Connecticut	11,314,078,000	0.6%
45	Delaware	2,542,755,000	0.1%
4	Florida	105,615,088,000	5.7%
9	Georgia	44,807,818,000	2.4%
38	Hawaii	6,166,731,000	0.3%
46	Idaho	2,430,322,000	0.1%
5	Illinois	85,874,010,000	4.7%
18	Indiana	28,374,862,000	1.5%
31	Iowa	12,567,991,000	0.7%
27	Kansas	19,696,329,000	1.1%
23	Kentucky	24,376,348,000	1.3%
28	Louisiana	19,166,626,000	1.0%
42	Maine	2,957,204,000	0.2%
22	Maryland	25,022,427,000	1.4%
29	Massachusetts	18,172,516,000	1.0%
10	Michigan	38,762,307,000	2.1%
14	Minnesota	34,608,564,000	1.9%
37	Mississippi	6,758,159,000	0.4%
20	Missouri	26,781,090,000	1.5%
48	Montana	2,217,124,000	0.1%
30	Nebraska	13,330,964,000	0.7%
21	Nevada	25,503,835,000	1.4%
44	New Hampshire	2,567,353,000	0.1%
16	New Jersey	33,410,874,000	1.8%
36	New Mexico	8,364,613,000	0.5%
3	New York	219,039,197,000	11.9%
17	North Carolina	30,332,742,000	1.6%
39	North Dakota	4,427,686,000	0.2%
7	Ohio	52,045,374,000	2.8%
35	Oklahoma	10,008,235,000	0.5%
25	Oregon	20,548,725,000	1.1%
6	Pennsylvania	74,764,562,000	4.1%
43	Rhode Island	2,678,974,000	0.1%
19	South Carolina	27,385,474,000	1.5%
47	South Dakota	2,402,028,000	0.1%
13	Tennessee	36,195,188,000	2.0%
2	Texas	229,991,508,000	12.5%
32	Utah	11,409,759,000	0.6%
50	Vermont	1,138,200,000	0.1%
11	Virginia	37,466,905,000	2.0%
8	Washington	52,025,433,000	2.8%
40	West Virginia	3,479,157,000	0.2%
24	Wisconsin	21,288,883,000	1.2%
49	Wyoming	1,138,436,000	0.1%

RANK ORDER

RANK	STATE	DEBT	% of USA
1	California	$282,609,085,000	15.3%
2	Texas	229,991,508,000	12.5%
3	New York	219,039,197,000	11.9%
4	Florida	105,615,088,000	5.7%
5	Illinois	85,874,010,000	4.7%
6	Pennsylvania	74,764,562,000	4.1%
7	Ohio	52,045,374,000	2.8%
8	Washington	52,025,433,000	2.8%
9	Georgia	44,807,818,000	2.4%
10	Michigan	38,762,307,000	2.1%
11	Virginia	37,466,905,000	2.0%
12	Colorado	36,237,707,000	2.0%
13	Tennessee	36,195,188,000	2.0%
14	Minnesota	34,608,564,000	1.9%
15	Arizona	34,394,482,000	1.9%
16	New Jersey	33,410,874,000	1.8%
17	North Carolina	30,332,742,000	1.6%
18	Indiana	28,374,862,000	1.5%
19	South Carolina	27,385,474,000	1.5%
20	Missouri	26,781,090,000	1.5%
21	Nevada	25,503,835,000	1.4%
22	Maryland	25,022,427,000	1.4%
23	Kentucky	24,376,348,000	1.3%
24	Wisconsin	21,288,883,000	1.2%
25	Oregon	20,548,725,000	1.1%
26	Alabama	20,201,141,000	1.1%
27	Kansas	19,696,329,000	1.1%
28	Louisiana	19,166,626,000	1.0%
29	Massachusetts	18,172,516,000	1.0%
30	Nebraska	13,330,964,000	0.7%
31	Iowa	12,567,991,000	0.7%
32	Utah	11,409,759,000	0.6%
33	Connecticut	11,314,078,000	0.6%
34	Arkansas	11,057,764,000	0.6%
35	Oklahoma	10,008,235,000	0.5%
36	New Mexico	8,364,613,000	0.5%
37	Mississippi	6,758,159,000	0.4%
38	Hawaii	6,166,731,000	0.3%
39	North Dakota	4,427,686,000	0.2%
40	West Virginia	3,479,157,000	0.2%
41	Alaska	3,396,063,000	0.2%
42	Maine	2,957,204,000	0.2%
43	Rhode Island	2,678,974,000	0.1%
44	New Hampshire	2,567,353,000	0.1%
45	Delaware	2,542,755,000	0.1%
46	Idaho	2,430,322,000	0.1%
47	South Dakota	2,402,028,000	0.1%
48	Montana	2,217,124,000	0.1%
49	Wyoming	1,138,436,000	0.1%
50	Vermont	1,138,200,000	0.1%
	District of Columbia	14,520,507,000	0.8%

Source: U.S. Bureau of the Census, Governments Division
   "2016 State and Local Government Finances" (https://www.census.gov/programs-surveys/gov-finances.html)
*Includes short-term, long-term, full faith and credit, nonguaranteed, and public debt for private purposes.

Per Capita Local Government Debt Outstanding in 2016

National Per Capita = $5,700*

ALPHA ORDER

RANK	STATE	PER CAPITA
27	Alabama	$4,153
19	Alaska	4,580
18	Arizona	4,952
34	Arkansas	3,698
4	California	7,208
9	Colorado	6,540
36	Connecticut	3,162
39	Delaware	2,679
16	Florida	5,119
23	Georgia	4,348
24	Hawaii	4,318
50	Idaho	1,444
8	Illinois	6,695
25	Indiana	4,278
29	Iowa	4,013
7	Kansas	6,766
14	Kentucky	5,492
28	Louisiana	4,097
44	Maine	2,221
26	Maryland	4,167
40	Massachusetts	2,662
31	Michigan	3,895
10	Minnesota	6,266
43	Mississippi	2,262
22	Missouri	4,400
45	Montana	2,130
6	Nebraska	6,994
2	Nevada	8,735
47	New Hampshire	1,913
32	New Jersey	3,765
30	New Mexico	3,997
1	New York	11,152
37	North Carolina	2,986
11	North Dakota	5,870
20	Ohio	4,473
41	Oklahoma	2,549
17	Oregon	5,022
12	Pennsylvania	5,849
42	Rhode Island	2,534
13	South Carolina	5,523
38	South Dakota	2,784
15	Tennessee	5,447
3	Texas	8,232
33	Utah	3,750
49	Vermont	1,825
21	Virginia	4,455
5	Washington	7,132
48	West Virginia	1,900
35	Wisconsin	3,688
46	Wyoming	1,948

RANK ORDER

RANK	STATE	PER CAPITA
1	New York	$11,152
2	Nevada	8,735
3	Texas	8,232
4	California	7,208
5	Washington	7,132
6	Nebraska	6,994
7	Kansas	6,766
8	Illinois	6,695
9	Colorado	6,540
10	Minnesota	6,266
11	North Dakota	5,870
12	Pennsylvania	5,849
13	South Carolina	5,523
14	Kentucky	5,492
15	Tennessee	5,447
16	Florida	5,119
17	Oregon	5,022
18	Arizona	4,952
19	Alaska	4,580
20	Ohio	4,473
21	Virginia	4,455
22	Missouri	4,400
23	Georgia	4,348
24	Hawaii	4,318
25	Indiana	4,278
26	Maryland	4,167
27	Alabama	4,153
28	Louisiana	4,097
29	Iowa	4,013
30	New Mexico	3,997
31	Michigan	3,895
32	New Jersey	3,765
33	Utah	3,750
34	Arkansas	3,698
35	Wisconsin	3,688
36	Connecticut	3,162
37	North Carolina	2,986
38	South Dakota	2,784
39	Delaware	2,679
40	Massachusetts	2,662
41	Oklahoma	2,549
42	Rhode Island	2,534
43	Mississippi	2,262
44	Maine	2,221
45	Montana	2,130
46	Wyoming	1,948
47	New Hampshire	1,913
48	West Virginia	1,900
49	Vermont	1,825
50	Idaho	1,444

District of Columbia 21,149

Source: CQ Press using data from U.S. Bureau of the Census, Governments Division
"2016 State and Local Government Finances" (https://www.census.gov/programs-surveys/gov-finances.html)
*Includes short-term, long-term, full faith and credit, nonguaranteed, and public debt for private purposes.

Local Government Full-Time Equivalent Employees in 2017

National Total = 12,202,849 FTE Employees*

ALPHA ORDER

RANK	STATE	EMPLOYEES	% of USA
23	Alabama	190,761	1.6%
47	Alaska	27,486	0.2%
22	Arizona	208,338	1.7%
33	Arkansas	106,278	0.9%
1	California	1,436,915	11.8%
20	Colorado	211,038	1.7%
32	Connecticut	127,559	1.0%
49	Delaware	23,885	0.2%
4	Florida	711,046	5.8%
9	Georgia	391,079	3.2%
50	Hawaii	16,992	0.1%
39	Idaho	60,408	0.5%
5	Illinois	496,582	4.1%
15	Indiana	234,337	1.9%
29	Iowa	135,363	1.1%
27	Kansas	147,389	1.2%
26	Kentucky	159,058	1.3%
24	Louisiana	185,860	1.5%
41	Maine	49,355	0.4%
18	Maryland	221,636	1.8%
17	Massachusetts	230,328	1.9%
12	Michigan	287,104	2.4%
21	Minnesota	210,726	1.7%
30	Mississippi	133,077	1.1%
16	Missouri	232,708	1.9%
43	Montana	36,426	0.3%
35	Nebraska	89,822	0.7%
36	Nevada	86,639	0.7%
40	New Hampshire	52,429	0.4%
10	New Jersey	338,571	2.8%
37	New Mexico	78,323	0.6%
3	New York	952,564	7.8%
7	North Carolina	417,418	3.4%
46	North Dakota	28,283	0.2%
6	Ohio	451,224	3.7%
28	Oklahoma	144,999	1.2%
31	Oregon	130,809	1.1%
8	Pennsylvania	401,844	3.3%
45	Rhode Island	29,358	0.2%
25	South Carolina	185,691	1.5%
44	South Dakota	32,565	0.3%
14	Tennessee	249,118	2.0%
2	Texas	1,200,293	9.8%
34	Utah	94,000	0.8%
48	Vermont	26,698	0.2%
11	Virginia	323,233	2.6%
13	Washington	255,192	2.1%
38	West Virginia	62,558	0.5%
19	Wisconsin	211,816	1.7%
42	Wyoming	36,996	0.3%

RANK ORDER

RANK	STATE	EMPLOYEES	% of USA
1	California	1,436,915	11.8%
2	Texas	1,200,293	9.8%
3	New York	952,564	7.8%
4	Florida	711,046	5.8%
5	Illinois	496,582	4.1%
6	Ohio	451,224	3.7%
7	North Carolina	417,418	3.4%
8	Pennsylvania	401,844	3.3%
9	Georgia	391,079	3.2%
10	New Jersey	338,571	2.8%
11	Virginia	323,233	2.6%
12	Michigan	287,104	2.4%
13	Washington	255,192	2.1%
14	Tennessee	249,118	2.0%
15	Indiana	234,337	1.9%
16	Missouri	232,708	1.9%
17	Massachusetts	230,328	1.9%
18	Maryland	221,636	1.8%
19	Wisconsin	211,816	1.7%
20	Colorado	211,038	1.7%
21	Minnesota	210,726	1.7%
22	Arizona	208,338	1.7%
23	Alabama	190,761	1.6%
24	Louisiana	185,860	1.5%
25	South Carolina	185,691	1.5%
26	Kentucky	159,058	1.3%
27	Kansas	147,389	1.2%
28	Oklahoma	144,999	1.2%
29	Iowa	135,363	1.1%
30	Mississippi	133,077	1.1%
31	Oregon	130,809	1.1%
32	Connecticut	127,559	1.0%
33	Arkansas	106,278	0.9%
34	Utah	94,000	0.8%
35	Nebraska	89,822	0.7%
36	Nevada	86,639	0.7%
37	New Mexico	78,323	0.6%
38	West Virginia	62,558	0.5%
39	Idaho	60,408	0.5%
40	New Hampshire	52,429	0.4%
41	Maine	49,355	0.4%
42	Wyoming	36,996	0.3%
43	Montana	36,426	0.3%
44	South Dakota	32,565	0.3%
45	Rhode Island	29,358	0.2%
46	North Dakota	28,283	0.2%
47	Alaska	27,486	0.2%
48	Vermont	26,698	0.2%
49	Delaware	23,885	0.2%
50	Hawaii	16,992	0.1%
	District of Columbia	50,672	0.4%

Source: U.S. Bureau of the Census, Governments Division
   "Annual Survey of Public Employment and Payroll" (https://www.census.gov/programs-surveys/apes.html)
*As of March 2017.

Rate of Local Government Full-Time Equivalent Employees in 2017

National Rate = 375 FTE Employees per 10,000 Population*

ALPHA ORDER

RANK ORDER

RANK	STATE	RATE		RANK	STATE	RATE
11	Alabama	391		1	Wyoming	639
24	Alaska	372		2	Kansas	506
45	Arizona	296		3	New York	486
34	Arkansas	354		4	Nebraska	468
31	California	365		5	Mississippi	445
19	Colorado	376		6	Iowa	431
32	Connecticut	357		7	Vermont	427
49	Delaware	250		8	Texas	424
40	Florida	339		9	North Carolina	406
19	Georgia	376		10	Louisiana	398
50	Hawaii	119		11	Alabama	391
36	Idaho	351		12	Illinois	388
12	Illinois	388		12	New Hampshire	388
35	Indiana	352		14	Ohio	387
6	Iowa	431		15	Virginia	382
2	Kansas	506		16	Missouri	381
32	Kentucky	357		16	New Jersey	381
10	Louisiana	398		18	Minnesota	378
26	Maine	370		19	Colorado	376
29	Maryland	368		19	Georgia	376
41	Massachusetts	336		21	North Dakota	375
47	Michigan	288		22	New Mexico	374
18	Minnesota	378		23	South Dakota	373
5	Mississippi	445		24	Alaska	372
16	Missouri	381		25	Tennessee	371
37	Montana	346		26	Maine	370
4	Nebraska	468		26	South Carolina	370
46	Nevada	291		28	Oklahoma	369
12	New Hampshire	388		29	Maryland	368
16	New Jersey	381		30	Wisconsin	366
22	New Mexico	374		31	California	365
3	New York	486		32	Connecticut	357
9	North Carolina	406		32	Kentucky	357
21	North Dakota	375		34	Arkansas	354
14	Ohio	387		35	Indiana	352
28	Oklahoma	369		36	Idaho	351
42	Oregon	315		37	Montana	346
43	Pennsylvania	314		38	Washington	344
48	Rhode Island	278		38	West Virginia	344
26	South Carolina	370		40	Florida	339
23	South Dakota	373		41	Massachusetts	336
25	Tennessee	371		42	Oregon	315
8	Texas	424		43	Pennsylvania	314
44	Utah	303		44	Utah	303
7	Vermont	427		45	Arizona	296
15	Virginia	382		46	Nevada	291
38	Washington	344		47	Michigan	288
38	West Virginia	344		48	Rhode Island	278
30	Wisconsin	366		49	Delaware	250
1	Wyoming	639		50	Hawaii	119

District of Columbia 728

Source: CQ Press using data from U.S. Bureau of the Census, Governments Division
"Annual Survey of Public Employment and Payroll" (https://www.census.gov/programs-surveys/apes.html)
*Full-time equivalent as of March 2017.

Average Annual Earnings of Full-Time Local Government Employees in 2017

National Average = $58,919*

<table>
<tr><td colspan="3">ALPHA ORDER</td><td colspan="3">RANK ORDER</td></tr>
<tr><td>RANK</td><td>STATE</td><td>SALARY</td><td>RANK</td><td>STATE</td><td>SALARY</td></tr>
<tr><td>44</td><td>Alabama</td><td>$44,718</td><td>1</td><td>California</td><td>$82,266</td></tr>
<tr><td>7</td><td>Alaska</td><td>68,314</td><td>2</td><td>Washington</td><td>76,659</td></tr>
<tr><td>24</td><td>Arizona</td><td>54,110</td><td>3</td><td>New Jersey</td><td>74,372</td></tr>
<tr><td>50</td><td>Arkansas</td><td>39,777</td><td>4</td><td>New York</td><td>72,658</td></tr>
<tr><td>1</td><td>California</td><td>82,266</td><td>5</td><td>Maryland</td><td>69,054</td></tr>
<tr><td>17</td><td>Colorado</td><td>58,484</td><td>6</td><td>Connecticut</td><td>68,761</td></tr>
<tr><td>6</td><td>Connecticut</td><td>68,761</td><td>7</td><td>Alaska</td><td>68,314</td></tr>
<tr><td>15</td><td>Delaware</td><td>60,619</td><td>8</td><td>Rhode Island</td><td>67,896</td></tr>
<tr><td>28</td><td>Florida</td><td>52,024</td><td>9</td><td>Hawaii</td><td>67,726</td></tr>
<tr><td>36</td><td>Georgia</td><td>47,036</td><td>10</td><td>Nevada</td><td>66,485</td></tr>
<tr><td>9</td><td>Hawaii</td><td>67,726</td><td>11</td><td>Massachusetts</td><td>66,445</td></tr>
<tr><td>43</td><td>Idaho</td><td>44,802</td><td>12</td><td>Illinois</td><td>64,689</td></tr>
<tr><td>12</td><td>Illinois</td><td>64,689</td><td>13</td><td>Oregon</td><td>62,949</td></tr>
<tr><td>35</td><td>Indiana</td><td>47,472</td><td>14</td><td>Minnesota</td><td>61,123</td></tr>
<tr><td>26</td><td>Iowa</td><td>54,061</td><td>15</td><td>Delaware</td><td>60,619</td></tr>
<tr><td>41</td><td>Kansas</td><td>45,921</td><td>16</td><td>Pennsylvania</td><td>60,088</td></tr>
<tr><td>45</td><td>Kentucky</td><td>43,757</td><td>17</td><td>Colorado</td><td>58,484</td></tr>
<tr><td>46</td><td>Louisiana</td><td>43,397</td><td>18</td><td>Wisconsin</td><td>57,479</td></tr>
<tr><td>34</td><td>Maine</td><td>48,591</td><td>19</td><td>Michigan</td><td>57,152</td></tr>
<tr><td>5</td><td>Maryland</td><td>69,054</td><td>20</td><td>Wyoming</td><td>56,911</td></tr>
<tr><td>11</td><td>Massachusetts</td><td>66,445</td><td>21</td><td>New Hampshire</td><td>55,202</td></tr>
<tr><td>19</td><td>Michigan</td><td>57,152</td><td>22</td><td>Nebraska</td><td>54,813</td></tr>
<tr><td>14</td><td>Minnesota</td><td>61,123</td><td>23</td><td>Virginia</td><td>54,168</td></tr>
<tr><td>49</td><td>Mississippi</td><td>39,998</td><td>24</td><td>Arizona</td><td>54,110</td></tr>
<tr><td>37</td><td>Missouri</td><td>46,714</td><td>25</td><td>Ohio</td><td>54,081</td></tr>
<tr><td>31</td><td>Montana</td><td>50,117</td><td>26</td><td>Iowa</td><td>54,061</td></tr>
<tr><td>22</td><td>Nebraska</td><td>54,813</td><td>27</td><td>North Dakota</td><td>53,647</td></tr>
<tr><td>10</td><td>Nevada</td><td>66,485</td><td>28</td><td>Florida</td><td>52,024</td></tr>
<tr><td>21</td><td>New Hampshire</td><td>55,202</td><td>29</td><td>Vermont</td><td>51,370</td></tr>
<tr><td>3</td><td>New Jersey</td><td>74,372</td><td>30</td><td>Utah</td><td>51,192</td></tr>
<tr><td>39</td><td>New Mexico</td><td>46,582</td><td>31</td><td>Montana</td><td>50,117</td></tr>
<tr><td>4</td><td>New York</td><td>72,658</td><td>32</td><td>Texas</td><td>49,760</td></tr>
<tr><td>33</td><td>North Carolina</td><td>49,519</td><td>33</td><td>North Carolina</td><td>49,519</td></tr>
<tr><td>27</td><td>North Dakota</td><td>53,647</td><td>34</td><td>Maine</td><td>48,591</td></tr>
<tr><td>25</td><td>Ohio</td><td>54,081</td><td>35</td><td>Indiana</td><td>47,472</td></tr>
<tr><td>47</td><td>Oklahoma</td><td>42,186</td><td>36</td><td>Georgia</td><td>47,036</td></tr>
<tr><td>13</td><td>Oregon</td><td>62,949</td><td>37</td><td>Missouri</td><td>46,714</td></tr>
<tr><td>16</td><td>Pennsylvania</td><td>60,088</td><td>38</td><td>South Carolina</td><td>46,690</td></tr>
<tr><td>8</td><td>Rhode Island</td><td>67,896</td><td>39</td><td>New Mexico</td><td>46,582</td></tr>
<tr><td>38</td><td>South Carolina</td><td>46,690</td><td>40</td><td>Tennessee</td><td>46,456</td></tr>
<tr><td>42</td><td>South Dakota</td><td>44,979</td><td>41</td><td>Kansas</td><td>45,921</td></tr>
<tr><td>40</td><td>Tennessee</td><td>46,456</td><td>42</td><td>South Dakota</td><td>44,979</td></tr>
<tr><td>32</td><td>Texas</td><td>49,760</td><td>43</td><td>Idaho</td><td>44,802</td></tr>
<tr><td>30</td><td>Utah</td><td>51,192</td><td>44</td><td>Alabama</td><td>44,718</td></tr>
<tr><td>29</td><td>Vermont</td><td>51,370</td><td>45</td><td>Kentucky</td><td>43,757</td></tr>
<tr><td>23</td><td>Virginia</td><td>54,168</td><td>46</td><td>Louisiana</td><td>43,397</td></tr>
<tr><td>2</td><td>Washington</td><td>76,659</td><td>47</td><td>Oklahoma</td><td>42,186</td></tr>
<tr><td>48</td><td>West Virginia</td><td>41,105</td><td>48</td><td>West Virginia</td><td>41,105</td></tr>
<tr><td>18</td><td>Wisconsin</td><td>57,479</td><td>49</td><td>Mississippi</td><td>39,998</td></tr>
<tr><td>20</td><td>Wyoming</td><td>56,911</td><td>50</td><td>Arkansas</td><td>39,777</td></tr>
<tr><td></td><td></td><td></td><td></td><td>District of Columbia</td><td>85,767</td></tr>
</table>

Source: CQ Press using data from U.S. Bureau of the Census, Governments Division
   "Annual Survey of Public Employment and Payroll" (https://www.census.gov/programs-surveys/apes.html)
*March 2017 full-time payroll (multiplied by 12) divided by full-time employees.

XI. Health

Average Annual Single Coverage Health Insurance Premium per Enrolled Employee in 2017
National Average = $6,368*

ALPHA ORDER

RANK	STATE	PREMIUM
40	Alabama	$6,075
1	Alaska	7,964
31	Arizona	6,217
49	Arkansas	5,722
26	California	6,295
18	Colorado	6,456
8	Connecticut	7,012
6	Delaware	7,046
41	Florida	6,068
47	Georgia	5,849
42	Hawaii	6,039
46	Idaho	5,858
17	Illinois	6,493
33	Indiana	6,162
35	Iowa	6,128
36	Kansas	6,107
37	Kentucky	6,101
43	Louisiana	6,026
34	Maine	6,132
11	Maryland	6,577
7	Massachusetts	7,031
20	Michigan	6,388
28	Minnesota	6,268
45	Mississippi	5,878
21	Missouri	6,354
9	Montana	6,763
24	Nebraska	6,305
48	Nevada	5,756
10	New Hampshire	6,670
4	New Jersey	7,074
27	New Mexico	6,275
2	New York	7,309
22	North Carolina	6,348
23	North Dakota	6,341
29	Ohio	6,247
30	Oklahoma	6,236
38	Oregon	6,081
15	Pennsylvania	6,522
5	Rhode Island	7,048
39	South Carolina	6,079
14	South Dakota	6,533
44	Tennessee	6,006
32	Texas	6,202
50	Utah	5,568
13	Vermont	6,551
25	Virginia	6,299
16	Washington	6,495
12	West Virginia	6,574
19	Wisconsin	6,437
3	Wyoming	7,257

RANK ORDER

RANK	STATE	PREMIUM
1	Alaska	$7,964
2	New York	7,309
3	Wyoming	7,257
4	New Jersey	7,074
5	Rhode Island	7,048
6	Delaware	7,046
7	Massachusetts	7,031
8	Connecticut	7,012
9	Montana	6,763
10	New Hampshire	6,670
11	Maryland	6,577
12	West Virginia	6,574
13	Vermont	6,551
14	South Dakota	6,533
15	Pennsylvania	6,522
16	Washington	6,495
17	Illinois	6,493
18	Colorado	6,456
19	Wisconsin	6,437
20	Michigan	6,388
21	Missouri	6,354
22	North Carolina	6,348
23	North Dakota	6,341
24	Nebraska	6,305
25	Virginia	6,299
26	California	6,295
27	New Mexico	6,275
28	Minnesota	6,268
29	Ohio	6,247
30	Oklahoma	6,236
31	Arizona	6,217
32	Texas	6,202
33	Indiana	6,162
34	Maine	6,132
35	Iowa	6,128
36	Kansas	6,107
37	Kentucky	6,101
38	Oregon	6,081
39	South Carolina	6,079
40	Alabama	6,075
41	Florida	6,068
42	Hawaii	6,039
43	Louisiana	6,026
44	Tennessee	6,006
45	Mississippi	5,878
46	Idaho	5,858
47	Georgia	5,849
48	Nevada	5,756
49	Arkansas	5,722
50	Utah	5,568
	District of Columbia	6,704

Source: U.S. Department of Health and Human Services, Agency for Healthcare Research and Quality
"Private-Sector Data by Firm Size and State" (Table II Series, Medical Expenditures Panel Survey)
(https://www.meps.ahrq.gov/mepsweb/survey_comp/Insurance.jsp)
*Enrolled employees at private-sector establishments that offer health insurance coverage.

Average Annual Family Coverage Health Insurance Premium per Enrolled Employee in 2017
National Average = $18,687*

ALPHA ORDER				RANK ORDER		
RANK	STATE	PREMIUM		RANK	STATE	PREMIUM
48	Alabama	$16,902		1	Alaska	$22,417
1	Alaska	22,417		2	Wyoming	21,355
23	Arizona	18,432		3	New York	21,317
49	Arkansas	16,663		4	Massachusetts	21,053
18	California	18,730		5	New Jersey	20,669
11	Colorado	19,339		6	West Virginia	20,252
7	Connecticut	20,020		7	Connecticut	20,020
10	Delaware	19,407		8	Illinois	19,656
44	Florida	17,189		9	Washington	19,472
37	Georgia	17,703		10	Delaware	19,407
21	Hawaii	18,512		11	Colorado	19,339
45	Idaho	17,168		12	New Hampshire	19,230
8	Illinois	19,656		13	Michigan	18,929
26	Indiana	18,253		14	Maryland	18,915
46	Iowa	17,086		15	Wisconsin	18,785
30	Kansas	18,229		16	Missouri	18,763
47	Kentucky	16,948		17	New Mexico	18,738
40	Louisiana	17,400		18	California	18,730
39	Maine	17,422		19	Pennsylvania	18,589
14	Maryland	18,915		20	Vermont	18,552
4	Massachusetts	21,053		21	Hawaii	18,512
13	Michigan	18,929		22	Minnesota	18,507
22	Minnesota	18,507		23	Arizona	18,432
42	Mississippi	17,343		24	Rhode Island	18,387
16	Missouri	18,763		25	Virginia	18,264
35	Montana	17,932		26	Indiana	18,253
31	Nebraska	18,199		27	Oklahoma	18,252
43	Nevada	17,221		27	Texas	18,252
12	New Hampshire	19,230		29	South Carolina	18,241
5	New Jersey	20,669		30	Kansas	18,229
17	New Mexico	18,738		31	Nebraska	18,199
3	New York	21,317		32	Ohio	18,185
33	North Carolina	18,101		33	North Carolina	18,101
36	North Dakota	17,886		34	Oregon	17,953
32	Ohio	18,185		35	Montana	17,932
27	Oklahoma	18,252		36	North Dakota	17,886
34	Oregon	17,953		37	Georgia	17,703
19	Pennsylvania	18,589		38	South Dakota	17,695
24	Rhode Island	18,387		39	Maine	17,422
29	South Carolina	18,241		40	Louisiana	17,400
38	South Dakota	17,695		41	Tennessee	17,349
41	Tennessee	17,349		42	Mississippi	17,343
27	Texas	18,252		43	Nevada	17,221
50	Utah	16,350		44	Florida	17,189
20	Vermont	18,552		45	Idaho	17,168
25	Virginia	18,264		46	Iowa	17,086
9	Washington	19,472		47	Kentucky	16,948
6	West Virginia	20,252		48	Alabama	16,902
15	Wisconsin	18,785		49	Arkansas	16,663
2	Wyoming	21,355		50	Utah	16,350
					District of Columbia	20,960

Source: U.S. Department of Health and Human Services, Agency for Healthcare Research and Quality
"Private-Sector Data by Firm Size and State" (Table II Series, Medical Expenditures Panel Survey)
(https://www.meps.ahrq.gov/mepsweb/survey_comp/Insurance.jsp)
*Enrolled employees at private-sector establishments that offer health insurance coverage.

Percent of Private-Sector Establishments That Offer Health Insurance: 2017

National Percent = 46.9%

RANK	STATE	PERCENT
17	Alabama	49.9
50	Alaska	32.5
19	Arizona	49.4
37	Arkansas	43.2
31	California	45.9
35	Colorado	43.8
18	Connecticut	49.7
5	Delaware	53.3
49	Florida	35.5
41	Georgia	41.2
1	Hawaii	81.8
47	Idaho	36.2
33	Illinois	44.4
26	Indiana	47.8
29	Iowa	47.3
16	Kansas	50.3
15	Kentucky	50.4
11	Louisiana	51.0
39	Maine	41.6
4	Maryland	54.2
2	Massachusetts	64.4
20	Michigan	49.3
22	Minnesota	48.8
9	Mississippi	52.4
23	Missouri	48.5
46	Montana	37.4
38	Nebraska	42.6
14	Nevada	50.6
21	New Hampshire	49.0
11	New Jersey	51.0
13	New Mexico	50.8
30	New York	46.0
41	North Carolina	41.2
25	North Dakota	48.0
6	Ohio	53.1
27	Oklahoma	47.5
44	Oregon	39.4
3	Pennsylvania	54.5
8	Rhode Island	52.6
36	South Carolina	43.7
40	South Dakota	41.4
10	Tennessee	51.8
27	Texas	47.5
47	Utah	36.2
43	Vermont	40.9
7	Virginia	52.9
34	Washington	44.0
23	West Virginia	48.5
32	Wisconsin	44.7
44	Wyoming	39.4

RANK	STATE	PERCENT
1	Hawaii	81.8
2	Massachusetts	64.4
3	Pennsylvania	54.5
4	Maryland	54.2
5	Delaware	53.3
6	Ohio	53.1
7	Virginia	52.9
8	Rhode Island	52.6
9	Mississippi	52.4
10	Tennessee	51.8
11	Louisiana	51.0
11	New Jersey	51.0
13	New Mexico	50.8
14	Nevada	50.6
15	Kentucky	50.4
16	Kansas	50.3
17	Alabama	49.9
18	Connecticut	49.7
19	Arizona	49.4
20	Michigan	49.3
21	New Hampshire	49.0
22	Minnesota	48.8
23	Missouri	48.5
23	West Virginia	48.5
25	North Dakota	48.0
26	Indiana	47.8
27	Oklahoma	47.5
27	Texas	47.5
29	Iowa	47.3
30	New York	46.0
31	California	45.9
32	Wisconsin	44.7
33	Illinois	44.4
34	Washington	44.0
35	Colorado	43.8
36	South Carolina	43.7
37	Arkansas	43.2
38	Nebraska	42.6
39	Maine	41.6
40	South Dakota	41.4
41	Georgia	41.2
41	North Carolina	41.2
43	Vermont	40.9
44	Oregon	39.4
44	Wyoming	39.4
46	Montana	37.4
47	Idaho	36.2
47	Utah	36.2
49	Florida	35.5
50	Alaska	32.5

District of Columbia	68.7

Source: U.S. Department of Health and Human Services, Agency for Healthcare Research and Quality
"Private-Sector Data by Firm Size and State" (Table II Series, Medical Expenditures Panel Survey)
(https://www.meps.ahrq.gov/mepsweb/survey_comp/Insurance.jsp)

Persons Not Covered by Health Insurance in 2017

National Total = 28,019,263 Uninsured

ALPHA ORDER				RANK ORDER			
RANK	STATE	UNINSURED	% of USA	RANK	STATE	UNINSURED	% of USA
19	Alabama	448,926	1.6%	1	Texas	4,816,968	17.2%
41	Alaska	97,796	0.3%	2	California	2,796,589	10.0%
9	Arizona	694,790	2.5%	3	Florida	2,676,147	9.6%
32	Arkansas	231,802	0.8%	4	Georgia	1,375,176	4.9%
2	California	2,796,589	10.0%	5	New York	1,112,942	4.0%
21	Colorado	414,077	1.5%	6	North Carolina	1,075,983	3.8%
33	Connecticut	193,796	0.7%	7	Illinois	859,257	3.1%
48	Delaware	51,243	0.2%	8	Virginia	729,179	2.6%
3	Florida	2,676,147	9.6%	9	Arizona	694,790	2.5%
4	Georgia	1,375,176	4.9%	10	Pennsylvania	692,203	2.5%
47	Hawaii	52,827	0.2%	11	New Jersey	688,068	2.5%
36	Idaho	172,013	0.6%	12	Ohio	686,014	2.4%
7	Illinois	859,257	3.1%	13	Tennessee	629,142	2.2%
17	Indiana	536,399	1.9%	14	Missouri	548,271	2.0%
38	Iowa	146,017	0.5%	15	Oklahoma	545,483	1.9%
29	Kansas	249,392	0.9%	16	South Carolina	541,533	1.9%
31	Kentucky	235,227	0.8%	17	Indiana	536,399	1.9%
22	Louisiana	382,649	1.4%	18	Michigan	509,539	1.8%
40	Maine	107,067	0.4%	19	Alabama	448,926	1.6%
23	Maryland	365,597	1.3%	20	Washington	446,106	1.6%
34	Massachusetts	189,801	0.7%	21	Colorado	414,077	1.5%
18	Michigan	509,539	1.8%	22	Louisiana	382,649	1.4%
30	Minnesota	242,509	0.9%	23	Maryland	365,597	1.3%
24	Mississippi	351,754	1.3%	24	Mississippi	351,754	1.3%
14	Missouri	548,271	2.0%	25	Nevada	332,624	1.2%
42	Montana	87,709	0.3%	26	Wisconsin	309,404	1.1%
37	Nebraska	156,784	0.6%	27	Utah	281,753	1.0%
25	Nevada	332,624	1.2%	28	Oregon	280,816	1.0%
44	New Hampshire	77,059	0.3%	29	Kansas	249,392	0.9%
11	New Jersey	688,068	2.5%	30	Minnesota	242,509	0.9%
35	New Mexico	186,996	0.7%	31	Kentucky	235,227	0.8%
5	New York	1,112,942	4.0%	32	Arkansas	231,802	0.8%
6	North Carolina	1,075,983	3.8%	33	Connecticut	193,796	0.7%
46	North Dakota	55,582	0.2%	34	Massachusetts	189,801	0.7%
12	Ohio	686,014	2.4%	35	New Mexico	186,996	0.7%
15	Oklahoma	545,483	1.9%	36	Idaho	172,013	0.6%
28	Oregon	280,816	1.0%	37	Nebraska	156,784	0.6%
10	Pennsylvania	692,203	2.5%	38	Iowa	146,017	0.5%
49	Rhode Island	48,190	0.2%	39	West Virginia	108,889	0.4%
16	South Carolina	541,533	1.9%	40	Maine	107,067	0.4%
43	South Dakota	77,338	0.3%	41	Alaska	97,796	0.3%
13	Tennessee	629,142	2.2%	42	Montana	87,709	0.3%
1	Texas	4,816,968	17.2%	43	South Dakota	77,338	0.3%
27	Utah	281,753	1.0%	44	New Hampshire	77,059	0.3%
50	Vermont	28,111	0.1%	45	Wyoming	69,715	0.2%
8	Virginia	729,179	2.6%	46	North Dakota	55,582	0.2%
20	Washington	446,106	1.6%	47	Hawaii	52,827	0.2%
39	West Virginia	108,889	0.4%	48	Delaware	51,243	0.2%
26	Wisconsin	309,404	1.1%	49	Rhode Island	48,190	0.2%
45	Wyoming	69,715	0.2%	50	Vermont	28,111	0.1%
					District of Columbia	26,011	0.1%

Source: U.S. Bureau of the Census
"2017 American Community Survey-Table DP03" (https://www.census.gov/programs-surveys/acs/)

Percent of Population Not Covered by Health Insurance in 2017

National Percent = 8.7% of Population*

RANK	STATE	PERCENT
14	Alabama	9.4
3	Alaska	13.7
11	Arizona	10.1
26	Arkansas	7.9
30	California	7.2
28	Colorado	7.5
39	Connecticut	5.5
41	Delaware	5.4
5	Florida	12.9
4	Georgia	13.4
49	Hawaii	3.8
11	Idaho	10.1
31	Illinois	6.8
24	Indiana	8.2
45	Iowa	4.7
20	Kansas	8.7
41	Kentucky	5.4
22	Louisiana	8.4
25	Maine	8.1
33	Maryland	6.1
50	Massachusetts	2.8
44	Michigan	5.2
48	Minnesota	4.4
7	Mississippi	12.0
16	Missouri	9.1
21	Montana	8.5
23	Nebraska	8.3
8	Nevada	11.2
37	New Hampshire	5.8
27	New Jersey	7.7
16	New Mexico	9.1
38	New York	5.7
10	North Carolina	10.7
28	North Dakota	7.5
36	Ohio	6.0
2	Oklahoma	14.2
31	Oregon	6.8
39	Pennsylvania	5.5
46	Rhode Island	4.6
9	South Carolina	11.0
16	South Dakota	9.1
13	Tennessee	9.5
1	Texas	17.3
15	Utah	9.2
46	Vermont	4.6
19	Virginia	8.8
33	Washington	6.1
33	West Virginia	6.1
41	Wisconsin	5.4
6	Wyoming	12.3

RANK	STATE	PERCENT
1	Texas	17.3
2	Oklahoma	14.2
3	Alaska	13.7
4	Georgia	13.4
5	Florida	12.9
6	Wyoming	12.3
7	Mississippi	12.0
8	Nevada	11.2
9	South Carolina	11.0
10	North Carolina	10.7
11	Arizona	10.1
11	Idaho	10.1
13	Tennessee	9.5
14	Alabama	9.4
15	Utah	9.2
16	Missouri	9.1
16	New Mexico	9.1
16	South Dakota	9.1
19	Virginia	8.8
20	Kansas	8.7
21	Montana	8.5
22	Louisiana	8.4
23	Nebraska	8.3
24	Indiana	8.2
25	Maine	8.1
26	Arkansas	7.9
27	New Jersey	7.7
28	Colorado	7.5
28	North Dakota	7.5
30	California	7.2
31	Illinois	6.8
31	Oregon	6.8
33	Maryland	6.1
33	Washington	6.1
33	West Virginia	6.1
36	Ohio	6.0
37	New Hampshire	5.8
38	New York	5.7
39	Connecticut	5.5
39	Pennsylvania	5.5
41	Delaware	5.4
41	Kentucky	5.4
41	Wisconsin	5.4
44	Michigan	5.2
45	Iowa	4.7
46	Rhode Island	4.6
46	Vermont	4.6
48	Minnesota	4.4
49	Hawaii	3.8
50	Massachusetts	2.8
	District of Columbia	3.8

Source: U.S. Bureau of the Census
   "2017 American Community Survey-Table DP03" (https://www.census.gov/programs-surveys/acs/)
*This is a one-year figure. Census has discontinued three-year averages that had been used previously.

Percent of Population Lacking Access to Primary Care in 2019

National Percent = 13.0% of Population*

ALPHA ORDER

RANK	STATE	PERCENT
9	Alabama	21.6
31	Alaska	10.5
5	Arizona	24.2
36	Arkansas	8.3
28	California	11.1
22	Colorado	12.8
23	Connecticut	12.4
15	Delaware	16.6
6	Florida	22.4
13	Georgia	17.5
45	Hawaii	3.5
20	Idaho	14.2
26	Illinois	11.6
38	Indiana	7.4
34	Iowa	9.2
12	Kansas	18.9
24	Kentucky	12.1
14	Louisiana	16.8
44	Maine	3.7
29	Maryland	10.7
42	Massachusetts	4.6
10	Michigan	19.5
43	Minnesota	4.3
2	Mississippi	34.4
4	Missouri	24.9
3	Montana	25.1
49	Nebraska	0.6
17	Nevada	16.3
46	New Hampshire	2.8
50	New Jersey	0.1
1	New Mexico	38.5
7	New York	21.9
32	North Carolina	10.1
16	North Dakota	16.4
40	Ohio	5.5
21	Oklahoma	13.9
30	Oregon	10.6
47	Pennsylvania	2.4
41	Rhode Island	5.4
25	South Carolina	11.9
18	South Dakota	15.8
27	Tennessee	11.3
35	Texas	8.7
33	Utah	9.5
48	Vermont	1.2
39	Virginia	7.2
7	Washington	21.9
11	West Virginia	19.3
37	Wisconsin	8.1
19	Wyoming	15.0

RANK ORDER

RANK	STATE	PERCENT
1	New Mexico	38.5
2	Mississippi	34.4
3	Montana	25.1
4	Missouri	24.9
5	Arizona	24.2
6	Florida	22.4
7	New York	21.9
7	Washington	21.9
9	Alabama	21.6
10	Michigan	19.5
11	West Virginia	19.3
12	Kansas	18.9
13	Georgia	17.5
14	Louisiana	16.8
15	Delaware	16.6
16	North Dakota	16.4
17	Nevada	16.3
18	South Dakota	15.8
19	Wyoming	15.0
20	Idaho	14.2
21	Oklahoma	13.9
22	Colorado	12.8
23	Connecticut	12.4
24	Kentucky	12.1
25	South Carolina	11.9
26	Illinois	11.6
27	Tennessee	11.3
28	California	11.1
29	Maryland	10.7
30	Oregon	10.6
31	Alaska	10.5
32	North Carolina	10.1
33	Utah	9.5
34	Iowa	9.2
35	Texas	8.7
36	Arkansas	8.3
37	Wisconsin	8.1
38	Indiana	7.4
39	Virginia	7.2
40	Ohio	5.5
41	Rhode Island	5.4
42	Massachusetts	4.6
43	Minnesota	4.3
44	Maine	3.7
45	Hawaii	3.5
46	New Hampshire	2.8
47	Pennsylvania	2.4
48	Vermont	1.2
49	Nebraska	0.6
50	New Jersey	0.1

District of Columbia	25.4

Source: CQ Press using data from U.S. Department of Health and Human Services, Division of Shortage Designation
  "State Population and HPSA Designation Population Statistics" (as of January 15, 2019)
    (https://datawarehouse.hrsa.gov/tools/hdwreports/Reports.aspx)
*Percent of population considered under-served by primary medical practitioners (Family and General Practice doctors, Internists, Ob/Gyns, and Pediatricians). An under-served population does not have primary medical care within reasonable economic and geographic bounds.

Professionally Active Physicians in 2018

National Total = 990,688 Physicians*

ALPHA ORDER					RANK ORDER			
RANK	STATE	PHYSICIANS	% of USA		RANK	STATE	PHYSICIANS	% of USA
26	Alabama	11,953	1.2%		1	California	110,602	11.2%
49	Alaska	1,863	0.2%		2	New York	88,419	8.9%
19	Arizona	17,703	1.8%		3	Texas	63,926	6.5%
32	Arkansas	7,082	0.7%		4	Florida	56,002	5.7%
1	California	110,602	11.2%		5	Pennsylvania	50,076	5.1%
23	Colorado	14,347	1.4%		6	Illinois	42,876	4.3%
22	Connecticut	15,276	1.5%		7	Ohio	41,781	4.2%
43	Delaware	3,059	0.3%		8	Michigan	38,366	3.9%
4	Florida	56,002	5.7%		9	Massachusetts	35,956	3.6%
12	Georgia	24,911	2.5%		10	New Jersey	30,069	3.0%
42	Hawaii	3,607	0.4%		11	North Carolina	27,942	2.8%
44	Idaho	2,924	0.3%		12	Georgia	24,911	2.5%
6	Illinois	42,876	4.3%		13	Maryland	24,301	2.5%
21	Indiana	16,707	1.7%		14	Virginia	22,873	2.3%
30	Iowa	8,458	0.9%		15	Washington	21,418	2.2%
31	Kansas	7,825	0.8%		16	Missouri	20,079	2.0%
28	Kentucky	11,670	1.2%		17	Tennessee	18,873	1.9%
24	Louisiana	13,608	1.4%		18	Minnesota	17,858	1.8%
40	Maine	4,666	0.5%		19	Arizona	17,703	1.8%
13	Maryland	24,301	2.5%		20	Wisconsin	17,350	1.8%
9	Massachusetts	35,956	3.6%		21	Indiana	16,707	1.7%
8	Michigan	38,366	3.9%		22	Connecticut	15,276	1.5%
18	Minnesota	17,858	1.8%		23	Colorado	14,347	1.4%
34	Mississippi	6,567	0.7%		24	Louisiana	13,608	1.4%
16	Missouri	20,079	2.0%		25	South Carolina	12,796	1.3%
45	Montana	2,310	0.2%		26	Alabama	11,953	1.2%
38	Nebraska	5,593	0.6%		27	Oregon	11,920	1.2%
35	Nevada	6,080	0.6%		28	Kentucky	11,670	1.2%
41	New Hampshire	4,167	0.4%		29	Oklahoma	9,365	0.9%
10	New Jersey	30,069	3.0%		30	Iowa	8,458	0.9%
36	New Mexico	5,664	0.6%		31	Kansas	7,825	0.8%
2	New York	88,419	8.9%		32	Arkansas	7,082	0.7%
11	North Carolina	27,942	2.8%		33	Utah	6,609	0.7%
48	North Dakota	1,993	0.2%		34	Mississippi	6,567	0.7%
7	Ohio	41,781	4.2%		35	Nevada	6,080	0.6%
29	Oklahoma	9,365	0.9%		36	New Mexico	5,664	0.6%
27	Oregon	11,920	1.2%		37	West Virginia	5,635	0.6%
5	Pennsylvania	50,076	5.1%		38	Nebraska	5,593	0.6%
39	Rhode Island	4,950	0.5%		39	Rhode Island	4,950	0.5%
25	South Carolina	12,796	1.3%		40	Maine	4,666	0.5%
47	South Dakota	2,033	0.2%		41	New Hampshire	4,167	0.4%
17	Tennessee	18,873	1.9%		42	Hawaii	3,607	0.4%
3	Texas	63,926	6.5%		43	Delaware	3,059	0.3%
33	Utah	6,609	0.7%		44	Idaho	2,924	0.3%
46	Vermont	2,267	0.2%		45	Montana	2,310	0.2%
14	Virginia	22,873	2.3%		46	Vermont	2,267	0.2%
15	Washington	21,418	2.2%		47	South Dakota	2,033	0.2%
37	West Virginia	5,635	0.6%		48	North Dakota	1,993	0.2%
20	Wisconsin	17,350	1.8%		49	Alaska	1,863	0.2%
50	Wyoming	1,172	0.1%		50	Wyoming	1,172	0.1%
						District of Columbia	7,141	0.7%

Source: The Henry J. Kaiser Family Foundation
"Professionally Active Dentists" (https://www.kff.org/state-category/providers-service-use/physicians/)
*Includes MDs (medical doctors) and DOs (osteopathic physicians). Includes primary care physicians and specialist physicians.

Rate of Professionally Active Physicians in 2018

National Rate = 303 Physicians per 100,000 Population*

RANK	STATE	RATE
39	Alabama	245
34	Alaska	253
38	Arizona	247
42	Arkansas	235
23	California	280
35	Colorado	252
4	Connecticut	428
15	Delaware	316
30	Florida	263
41	Georgia	237
33	Hawaii	254
50	Idaho	167
12	Illinois	337
37	Indiana	250
29	Iowa	268
26	Kansas	269
32	Kentucky	261
19	Louisiana	292
10	Maine	349
5	Maryland	402
1	Massachusetts	521
7	Michigan	384
14	Minnesota	318
45	Mississippi	220
13	Missouri	328
46	Montana	217
20	Nebraska	290
49	Nevada	200
17	New Hampshire	307
11	New Jersey	338
25	New Mexico	270
3	New York	452
26	North Carolina	269
31	North Dakota	262
9	Ohio	357
40	Oklahoma	238
21	Oregon	284
6	Pennsylvania	391
2	Rhode Island	468
35	South Carolina	252
43	South Dakota	230
24	Tennessee	279
44	Texas	223
47	Utah	209
8	Vermont	362
26	Virginia	269
21	Washington	284
16	West Virginia	312
18	Wisconsin	298
48	Wyoming	203

RANK	STATE	RATE
1	Massachusetts	521
2	Rhode Island	468
3	New York	452
4	Connecticut	428
5	Maryland	402
6	Pennsylvania	391
7	Michigan	384
8	Vermont	362
9	Ohio	357
10	Maine	349
11	New Jersey	338
12	Illinois	337
13	Missouri	328
14	Minnesota	318
15	Delaware	316
16	West Virginia	312
17	New Hampshire	307
18	Wisconsin	298
19	Louisiana	292
20	Nebraska	290
21	Oregon	284
21	Washington	284
23	California	280
24	Tennessee	279
25	New Mexico	270
26	Kansas	269
26	North Carolina	269
26	Virginia	269
29	Iowa	268
30	Florida	263
31	North Dakota	262
32	Kentucky	261
33	Hawaii	254
34	Alaska	253
35	Colorado	252
35	South Carolina	252
37	Indiana	250
38	Arizona	247
39	Alabama	245
40	Oklahoma	238
41	Georgia	237
42	Arkansas	235
43	South Dakota	230
44	Texas	223
45	Mississippi	220
46	Montana	217
47	Utah	209
48	Wyoming	203
49	Nevada	200
50	Idaho	167

District of Columbia	1,017

Source: CQ Press using data from The Henry J. Kaiser Family Foundation
"Professionally Active Dentists" (https://www.kff.org/state-category/providers-service-use/physicians/)
*Includes MDs (medical doctors) and DOs (osteopathic physicians). Includes primary care physicians and specialist physicians.

Rate of Registered Nurses in 2017

National Rate = 892 Nurses per 100,000 Population*

ALPHA ORDER				RANK ORDER		
RANK	STATE	RATE		RANK	STATE	RATE
15	Alabama	1,011		1	South Dakota	1,441
44	Alaska	753		2	Delaware	1,208
39	Arizona	779		2	Massachusetts	1,208
37	Arkansas	812		4	North Dakota	1,194
47	California	714		5	Nebraska	1,191
32	Colorado	880		6	Missouri	1,179
26	Connecticut	956		7	Minnesota	1,157
2	Delaware	1,208		8	West Virginia	1,124
34	Florida	850		9	Pennsylvania	1,118
46	Georgia	719		10	Rhode Island	1,115
43	Hawaii	757		11	Ohio	1,069
40	Idaho	776		12	Maine	1,063
24	Illinois	962		13	Iowa	1,058
14	Indiana	1,028		14	Indiana	1,028
13	Iowa	1,058		15	Alabama	1,011
18	Kansas	992		16	Vermont	1,005
17	Kentucky	997		17	Kentucky	997
20	Louisiana	981		18	Kansas	992
12	Maine	1,063		19	New Hampshire	982
30	Maryland	887		20	Louisiana	981
2	Massachusetts	1,208		21	North Carolina	966
27	Michigan	944		22	Wisconsin	965
7	Minnesota	1,157		23	Mississippi	964
23	Mississippi	964		24	Illinois	962
6	Missouri	1,179		24	Montana	962
24	Montana	962		26	Connecticut	956
5	Nebraska	1,191		27	Michigan	944
49	Nevada	702		28	New York	908
19	New Hampshire	982		29	New Jersey	895
29	New Jersey	895		30	Maryland	887
38	New Mexico	780		31	Tennessee	884
28	New York	908		32	Colorado	880
21	North Carolina	966		33	South Carolina	860
4	North Dakota	1,194		34	Florida	850
11	Ohio	1,069		35	Oregon	848
48	Oklahoma	712		35	Wyoming	848
35	Oregon	848		37	Arkansas	812
9	Pennsylvania	1,118		38	New Mexico	780
10	Rhode Island	1,115		39	Arizona	779
33	South Carolina	860		40	Idaho	776
1	South Dakota	1,441		41	Washington	768
31	Tennessee	884		42	Virginia	759
45	Texas	750		43	Hawaii	757
50	Utah	688		44	Alaska	753
16	Vermont	1,005		45	Texas	750
42	Virginia	759		46	Georgia	719
41	Washington	768		47	California	714
8	West Virginia	1,124		48	Oklahoma	712
22	Wisconsin	965		49	Nevada	702
35	Wyoming	848		50	Utah	688
					District of Columbia	1,585

Source: CQ Press using data from U.S. Department of Labor, Bureau of Labor Statistics
"Occupational Employment and Wages, 2017" (http://www.bls.gov/oes/)
*Does not include self-employed.

Rate of Dentists in 2018

National Rate = 58 Dentists per 100,000 Population*

<table>
<tr><td colspan="3">ALPHA ORDER</td><td colspan="3">RANK ORDER</td></tr>
<tr><td>RANK</td><td>STATE</td><td>RATE</td><td>RANK</td><td>STATE</td><td>RATE</td></tr>
<tr><td>48</td><td>Alabama</td><td>39</td><td>1</td><td>Massachusetts</td><td>79</td></tr>
<tr><td>8</td><td>Alaska</td><td>68</td><td>2</td><td>New Jersey</td><td>78</td></tr>
<tr><td>23</td><td>Arizona</td><td>51</td><td>3</td><td>California</td><td>75</td></tr>
<tr><td>48</td><td>Arkansas</td><td>39</td><td>4</td><td>New York</td><td>74</td></tr>
<tr><td>3</td><td>California</td><td>75</td><td>5</td><td>Connecticut</td><td>70</td></tr>
<tr><td>9</td><td>Colorado</td><td>67</td><td>6</td><td>Hawaii</td><td>69</td></tr>
<tr><td>5</td><td>Connecticut</td><td>70</td><td>6</td><td>Maryland</td><td>69</td></tr>
<tr><td>47</td><td>Delaware</td><td>42</td><td>8</td><td>Alaska</td><td>68</td></tr>
<tr><td>24</td><td>Florida</td><td>50</td><td>9</td><td>Colorado</td><td>67</td></tr>
<tr><td>46</td><td>Georgia</td><td>43</td><td>10</td><td>Washington</td><td>66</td></tr>
<tr><td>6</td><td>Hawaii</td><td>69</td><td>11</td><td>Illinois</td><td>65</td></tr>
<tr><td>28</td><td>Idaho</td><td>49</td><td>12</td><td>Nebraska</td><td>61</td></tr>
<tr><td>11</td><td>Illinois</td><td>65</td><td>12</td><td>Virginia</td><td>61</td></tr>
<tr><td>42</td><td>Indiana</td><td>45</td><td>14</td><td>Pennsylvania</td><td>59</td></tr>
<tr><td>28</td><td>Iowa</td><td>49</td><td>15</td><td>Michigan</td><td>58</td></tr>
<tr><td>34</td><td>Kansas</td><td>48</td><td>15</td><td>New Hampshire</td><td>58</td></tr>
<tr><td>19</td><td>Kentucky</td><td>56</td><td>15</td><td>Utah</td><td>58</td></tr>
<tr><td>40</td><td>Louisiana</td><td>46</td><td>18</td><td>Vermont</td><td>57</td></tr>
<tr><td>34</td><td>Maine</td><td>48</td><td>19</td><td>Kentucky</td><td>56</td></tr>
<tr><td>6</td><td>Maryland</td><td>69</td><td>19</td><td>Montana</td><td>56</td></tr>
<tr><td>1</td><td>Massachusetts</td><td>79</td><td>21</td><td>Minnesota</td><td>54</td></tr>
<tr><td>15</td><td>Michigan</td><td>58</td><td>21</td><td>Wisconsin</td><td>54</td></tr>
<tr><td>21</td><td>Minnesota</td><td>54</td><td>23</td><td>Arizona</td><td>51</td></tr>
<tr><td>48</td><td>Mississippi</td><td>39</td><td>24</td><td>Florida</td><td>50</td></tr>
<tr><td>38</td><td>Missouri</td><td>47</td><td>24</td><td>Nevada</td><td>50</td></tr>
<tr><td>19</td><td>Montana</td><td>56</td><td>24</td><td>Ohio</td><td>50</td></tr>
<tr><td>12</td><td>Nebraska</td><td>61</td><td>24</td><td>Texas</td><td>50</td></tr>
<tr><td>24</td><td>Nevada</td><td>50</td><td>28</td><td>Idaho</td><td>49</td></tr>
<tr><td>15</td><td>New Hampshire</td><td>58</td><td>28</td><td>Iowa</td><td>49</td></tr>
<tr><td>2</td><td>New Jersey</td><td>78</td><td>28</td><td>North Carolina</td><td>49</td></tr>
<tr><td>34</td><td>New Mexico</td><td>48</td><td>28</td><td>North Dakota</td><td>49</td></tr>
<tr><td>4</td><td>New York</td><td>74</td><td>28</td><td>Rhode Island</td><td>49</td></tr>
<tr><td>28</td><td>North Carolina</td><td>49</td><td>28</td><td>Wyoming</td><td>49</td></tr>
<tr><td>28</td><td>North Dakota</td><td>49</td><td>34</td><td>Kansas</td><td>48</td></tr>
<tr><td>24</td><td>Ohio</td><td>50</td><td>34</td><td>Maine</td><td>48</td></tr>
<tr><td>40</td><td>Oklahoma</td><td>46</td><td>34</td><td>New Mexico</td><td>48</td></tr>
<tr><td>45</td><td>Oregon</td><td>44</td><td>34</td><td>Tennessee</td><td>48</td></tr>
<tr><td>14</td><td>Pennsylvania</td><td>59</td><td>38</td><td>Missouri</td><td>47</td></tr>
<tr><td>28</td><td>Rhode Island</td><td>49</td><td>38</td><td>South Dakota</td><td>47</td></tr>
<tr><td>42</td><td>South Carolina</td><td>45</td><td>40</td><td>Louisiana</td><td>46</td></tr>
<tr><td>38</td><td>South Dakota</td><td>47</td><td>40</td><td>Oklahoma</td><td>46</td></tr>
<tr><td>34</td><td>Tennessee</td><td>48</td><td>42</td><td>Indiana</td><td>45</td></tr>
<tr><td>24</td><td>Texas</td><td>50</td><td>42</td><td>South Carolina</td><td>45</td></tr>
<tr><td>15</td><td>Utah</td><td>58</td><td>42</td><td>West Virginia</td><td>45</td></tr>
<tr><td>18</td><td>Vermont</td><td>57</td><td>45</td><td>Oregon</td><td>44</td></tr>
<tr><td>12</td><td>Virginia</td><td>61</td><td>46</td><td>Georgia</td><td>43</td></tr>
<tr><td>10</td><td>Washington</td><td>66</td><td>47</td><td>Delaware</td><td>42</td></tr>
<tr><td>42</td><td>West Virginia</td><td>45</td><td>48</td><td>Alabama</td><td>39</td></tr>
<tr><td>21</td><td>Wisconsin</td><td>54</td><td>48</td><td>Arkansas</td><td>39</td></tr>
<tr><td>28</td><td>Wyoming</td><td>49</td><td>48</td><td>Mississippi</td><td>39</td></tr>
<tr><td colspan="3"></td><td colspan="2">District of Columbia</td><td>89</td></tr>
</table>

Source: CQ Press using data from American Dental Association as reported by The Henry J. Kaiser Family Foundation
"Professionally Active Dentists" (https://www.kff.org/state-category/providers-service-use/dentists/)
*Professionally active dentists. Rates calculated using 2018 Census population estimates.

Community Hospitals in 2016

National Total = 4,840 Hospitals*

ALPHA ORDER

RANK	STATE	HOSPITALS	% of USA
21	Alabama	95	2.0%
47	Alaska	21	0.4%
30	Arizona	70	1.4%
26	Arkansas	80	1.7%
2	California	341	7.0%
27	Colorado	79	1.6%
43	Connecticut	32	0.7%
50	Delaware	7	0.1%
3	Florida	210	4.3%
9	Georgia	141	2.9%
45	Hawaii	23	0.5%
38	Idaho	40	0.8%
4	Illinois	188	3.9%
14	Indiana	119	2.5%
17	Iowa	117	2.4%
10	Kansas	131	2.7%
20	Kentucky	103	2.1%
16	Louisiana	118	2.4%
42	Maine	34	0.7%
35	Maryland	50	1.0%
28	Massachusetts	75	1.5%
8	Michigan	146	3.0%
11	Minnesota	129	2.7%
22	Mississippi	93	1.9%
14	Missouri	119	2.5%
35	Montana	50	1.0%
25	Nebraska	88	1.8%
40	Nevada	36	0.7%
44	New Hampshire	28	0.6%
28	New Jersey	75	1.5%
40	New Mexico	36	0.7%
7	New York	169	3.5%
18	North Carolina	112	2.3%
38	North Dakota	40	0.8%
6	Ohio	179	3.7%
19	Oklahoma	110	2.3%
32	Oregon	59	1.2%
5	Pennsylvania	184	3.8%
49	Rhode Island	11	0.2%
31	South Carolina	68	1.4%
34	South Dakota	53	1.1%
13	Tennessee	120	2.5%
1	Texas	403	8.3%
37	Utah	47	1.0%
48	Vermont	14	0.3%
23	Virginia	92	1.9%
24	Washington	90	1.9%
33	West Virginia	54	1.1%
12	Wisconsin	127	2.6%
45	Wyoming	23	0.5%

RANK ORDER

RANK	STATE	HOSPITALS	% of USA
1	Texas	403	8.3%
2	California	341	7.0%
3	Florida	210	4.3%
4	Illinois	188	3.9%
5	Pennsylvania	184	3.8%
6	Ohio	179	3.7%
7	New York	169	3.5%
8	Michigan	146	3.0%
9	Georgia	141	2.9%
10	Kansas	131	2.7%
11	Minnesota	129	2.7%
12	Wisconsin	127	2.6%
13	Tennessee	120	2.5%
14	Indiana	119	2.5%
14	Missouri	119	2.5%
16	Louisiana	118	2.4%
17	Iowa	117	2.4%
18	North Carolina	112	2.3%
19	Oklahoma	110	2.3%
20	Kentucky	103	2.1%
21	Alabama	95	2.0%
22	Mississippi	93	1.9%
23	Virginia	92	1.9%
24	Washington	90	1.9%
25	Nebraska	88	1.8%
26	Arkansas	80	1.7%
27	Colorado	79	1.6%
28	Massachusetts	75	1.5%
28	New Jersey	75	1.5%
30	Arizona	70	1.4%
31	South Carolina	68	1.4%
32	Oregon	59	1.2%
33	West Virginia	54	1.1%
34	South Dakota	53	1.1%
35	Maryland	50	1.0%
35	Montana	50	1.0%
37	Utah	47	1.0%
38	Idaho	40	0.8%
38	North Dakota	40	0.8%
40	Nevada	36	0.7%
40	New Mexico	36	0.7%
42	Maine	34	0.7%
43	Connecticut	32	0.7%
44	New Hampshire	28	0.6%
45	Hawaii	23	0.5%
45	Wyoming	23	0.5%
47	Alaska	21	0.4%
48	Vermont	14	0.3%
49	Rhode Island	11	0.2%
50	Delaware	7	0.1%
	District of Columbia	11	0.2%

Source: American Hospital Association (Chicago, IL)
    "Hospital Statistics" (2018 edition)
*Community hospitals are all nonfederal, short-term general, and special hospitals whose facilities and services are available to the public.

Rate of Community Hospitals in 2016

National Rate = 1.5 Community Hospitals per 100,000 Population*

ALPHA ORDER

RANK	STATE	RATE
21	Alabama	2.0
10	Alaska	2.8
42	Arizona	1.0
12	Arkansas	2.7
45	California	0.9
31	Colorado	1.4
45	Connecticut	0.9
50	Delaware	0.7
42	Florida	1.0
31	Georgia	1.4
26	Hawaii	1.6
15	Idaho	2.4
27	Illinois	1.5
23	Indiana	1.8
7	Iowa	3.7
5	Kansas	4.5
16	Kentucky	2.3
14	Louisiana	2.5
13	Maine	2.6
48	Maryland	0.8
39	Massachusetts	1.1
27	Michigan	1.5
16	Minnesota	2.3
8	Mississippi	3.1
21	Missouri	2.0
3	Montana	4.8
4	Nebraska	4.6
37	Nevada	1.2
20	New Hampshire	2.1
48	New Jersey	0.8
25	New Mexico	1.7
45	New York	0.9
39	North Carolina	1.1
2	North Dakota	5.3
27	Ohio	1.5
10	Oklahoma	2.8
31	Oregon	1.4
31	Pennsylvania	1.4
42	Rhode Island	1.0
31	South Carolina	1.4
1	South Dakota	6.2
23	Tennessee	1.8
31	Texas	1.4
27	Utah	1.5
18	Vermont	2.2
39	Virginia	1.1
37	Washington	1.2
9	West Virginia	3.0
18	Wisconsin	2.2
6	Wyoming	3.9

RANK ORDER

RANK	STATE	RATE
1	South Dakota	6.2
2	North Dakota	5.3
3	Montana	4.8
4	Nebraska	4.6
5	Kansas	4.5
6	Wyoming	3.9
7	Iowa	3.7
8	Mississippi	3.1
9	West Virginia	3.0
10	Alaska	2.8
10	Oklahoma	2.8
12	Arkansas	2.7
13	Maine	2.6
14	Louisiana	2.5
15	Idaho	2.4
16	Kentucky	2.3
16	Minnesota	2.3
18	Vermont	2.2
18	Wisconsin	2.2
20	New Hampshire	2.1
21	Alabama	2.0
21	Missouri	2.0
23	Indiana	1.8
23	Tennessee	1.8
25	New Mexico	1.7
26	Hawaii	1.6
27	Illinois	1.5
27	Michigan	1.5
27	Ohio	1.5
27	Utah	1.5
31	Colorado	1.4
31	Georgia	1.4
31	Oregon	1.4
31	Pennsylvania	1.4
31	South Carolina	1.4
31	Texas	1.4
37	Nevada	1.2
37	Washington	1.2
39	Massachusetts	1.1
39	North Carolina	1.1
39	Virginia	1.1
42	Arizona	1.0
42	Florida	1.0
42	Rhode Island	1.0
45	California	0.9
45	Connecticut	0.9
45	New York	0.9
48	Maryland	0.8
48	New Jersey	0.8
50	Delaware	0.7
	District of Columbia	1.6

Source: CQ Press using data from American Hospital Association (Chicago, IL)
"Hospital Statistics" (2018 edition)

*Community hospitals are all nonfederal, short-term general, and special hospitals whose facilities and services are available to the public.

Births in 2017

National Total = 3,855,500 Live Births*

ALPHA ORDER

RANK	STATE	BIRTHS	% of USA
24	Alabama	58,941	1.5%
48	Alaska	10,445	0.3%
15	Arizona	81,872	2.1%
31	Arkansas	37,520	1.0%
1	California	471,658	12.2%
22	Colorado	64,382	1.7%
35	Connecticut	35,221	0.9%
45	Delaware	10,855	0.3%
4	Florida	223,630	5.8%
8	Georgia	129,243	3.4%
40	Hawaii	17,517	0.5%
38	Idaho	22,181	0.6%
5	Illinois	149,390	3.9%
14	Indiana	82,170	2.1%
30	Iowa	38,430	1.0%
33	Kansas	36,519	0.9%
26	Kentucky	54,752	1.4%
23	Louisiana	61,018	1.6%
41	Maine	12,298	0.3%
18	Maryland	71,641	1.9%
19	Massachusetts	70,702	1.8%
10	Michigan	111,426	2.9%
20	Minnesota	68,595	1.8%
32	Mississippi	37,357	1.0%
17	Missouri	73,034	1.9%
44	Montana	11,799	0.3%
36	Nebraska	25,821	0.7%
34	Nevada	35,756	0.9%
43	New Hampshire	12,116	0.3%
11	New Jersey	101,250	2.6%
37	New Mexico	23,767	0.6%
3	New York	229,737	6.0%
9	North Carolina	120,125	3.1%
46	North Dakota	10,737	0.3%
7	Ohio	136,832	3.5%
27	Oklahoma	50,214	1.3%
29	Oregon	43,631	1.1%
6	Pennsylvania	137,745	3.6%
47	Rhode Island	10,638	0.3%
25	South Carolina	57,029	1.5%
42	South Dakota	12,134	0.3%
16	Tennessee	81,016	2.1%
2	Texas	382,050	9.9%
28	Utah	48,585	1.3%
50	Vermont	5,655	0.1%
12	Virginia	100,391	2.6%
13	Washington	87,562	2.3%
39	West Virginia	18,675	0.5%
21	Wisconsin	64,975	1.7%
49	Wyoming	6,903	0.2%

RANK ORDER

RANK	STATE	BIRTHS	% of USA
1	California	471,658	12.2%
2	Texas	382,050	9.9%
3	New York	229,737	6.0%
4	Florida	223,630	5.8%
5	Illinois	149,390	3.9%
6	Pennsylvania	137,745	3.6%
7	Ohio	136,832	3.5%
8	Georgia	129,243	3.4%
9	North Carolina	120,125	3.1%
10	Michigan	111,426	2.9%
11	New Jersey	101,250	2.6%
12	Virginia	100,391	2.6%
13	Washington	87,562	2.3%
14	Indiana	82,170	2.1%
15	Arizona	81,872	2.1%
16	Tennessee	81,016	2.1%
17	Missouri	73,034	1.9%
18	Maryland	71,641	1.9%
19	Massachusetts	70,702	1.8%
20	Minnesota	68,595	1.8%
21	Wisconsin	64,975	1.7%
22	Colorado	64,382	1.7%
23	Louisiana	61,018	1.6%
24	Alabama	58,941	1.5%
25	South Carolina	57,029	1.5%
26	Kentucky	54,752	1.4%
27	Oklahoma	50,214	1.3%
28	Utah	48,585	1.3%
29	Oregon	43,631	1.1%
30	Iowa	38,430	1.0%
31	Arkansas	37,520	1.0%
32	Mississippi	37,357	1.0%
33	Kansas	36,519	0.9%
34	Nevada	35,756	0.9%
35	Connecticut	35,221	0.9%
36	Nebraska	25,821	0.7%
37	New Mexico	23,767	0.6%
38	Idaho	22,181	0.6%
39	West Virginia	18,675	0.5%
40	Hawaii	17,517	0.5%
41	Maine	12,298	0.3%
42	South Dakota	12,134	0.3%
43	New Hampshire	12,116	0.3%
44	Montana	11,799	0.3%
45	Delaware	10,855	0.3%
46	North Dakota	10,737	0.3%
47	Rhode Island	10,638	0.3%
48	Alaska	10,445	0.3%
49	Wyoming	6,903	0.2%
50	Vermont	5,655	0.1%
	District of Columbia	9,560	0.2%

Source: U.S. Department of Health and Human Services, National Center for Health Statistics
"National Vital Statistics Reports" (Vol. 67, No. 8, November 7, 2018, https://www.cdc.gov/nchs/nvss/births.htm)
*Final data by state of residence.

Birth Rate in 2017

National Rate = 11.8 Live Births per 1,000 Population*

ALPHA ORDER

RANK ORDER

RANK	STATE	RATE		RANK	STATE	RATE
19	Alabama	12.1		1	Utah	15.7
3	Alaska	14.1		2	North Dakota	14.2
28	Arizona	11.7		3	Alaska	14.1
10	Arkansas	12.5		4	South Dakota	14.0
21	California	11.9		5	Texas	13.5
33	Colorado	11.5		6	Nebraska	13.4
47	Connecticut	9.8		7	Louisiana	13.0
36	Delaware	11.3		8	Idaho	12.9
42	Florida	10.7		9	Oklahoma	12.8
13	Georgia	12.4		10	Arkansas	12.5
14	Hawaii	12.3		10	Kansas	12.5
8	Idaho	12.9		10	Mississippi	12.5
28	Illinois	11.7		13	Georgia	12.4
14	Indiana	12.3		14	Hawaii	12.3
18	Iowa	12.2		14	Indiana	12.3
10	Kansas	12.5		14	Kentucky	12.3
14	Kentucky	12.3		14	Minnesota	12.3
7	Louisiana	13.0		18	Iowa	12.2
48	Maine	9.2		19	Alabama	12.1
26	Maryland	11.8		19	Tennessee	12.1
44	Massachusetts	10.3		21	California	11.9
37	Michigan	11.2		21	Missouri	11.9
14	Minnesota	12.3		21	Nevada	11.9
10	Mississippi	12.5		21	Virginia	11.9
21	Missouri	11.9		21	Wyoming	11.9
37	Montana	11.2		26	Maryland	11.8
6	Nebraska	13.4		26	Washington	11.8
21	Nevada	11.9		28	Arizona	11.7
50	New Hampshire	9.0		28	Illinois	11.7
37	New Jersey	11.2		28	North Carolina	11.7
34	New Mexico	11.4		28	Ohio	11.7
32	New York	11.6		32	New York	11.6
28	North Carolina	11.7		33	Colorado	11.5
2	North Dakota	14.2		34	New Mexico	11.4
28	Ohio	11.7		34	South Carolina	11.4
9	Oklahoma	12.8		36	Delaware	11.3
43	Oregon	10.5		37	Michigan	11.2
41	Pennsylvania	10.8		37	Montana	11.2
46	Rhode Island	10.0		37	New Jersey	11.2
34	South Carolina	11.4		37	Wisconsin	11.2
4	South Dakota	14.0		41	Pennsylvania	10.8
19	Tennessee	12.1		42	Florida	10.7
5	Texas	13.5		43	Oregon	10.5
1	Utah	15.7		44	Massachusetts	10.3
49	Vermont	9.1		44	West Virginia	10.3
21	Virginia	11.9		46	Rhode Island	10.0
26	Washington	11.8		47	Connecticut	9.8
44	West Virginia	10.3		48	Maine	9.2
37	Wisconsin	11.2		49	Vermont	9.1
21	Wyoming	11.9		50	New Hampshire	9.0
					District of Columbia	13.8

Source: U.S. Department of Health and Human Services, National Center for Health Statistics
"National Vital Statistics Reports" (Vol. 67, No. 8, November 7, 2018, https://www.cdc.gov/nchs/nvss/births.htm)
*Final data by state of residence.

Births of Low Birthweight as a Percent of All Births in 2017

National Percent = 8.3% of Live Births*

ALPHA ORDER

RANK	STATE	PERCENT
3	Alabama	10.3
50	Alaska	6.2
33	Arizona	7.5
9	Arkansas	9.3
41	California	6.9
11	Colorado	9.1
27	Connecticut	8.1
13	Delaware	9.0
15	Florida	8.8
4	Georgia	9.9
21	Hawaii	8.5
40	Idaho	7.0
21	Illinois	8.5
26	Indiana	8.3
48	Iowa	6.6
37	Kansas	7.4
15	Kentucky	8.8
2	Louisiana	10.7
39	Maine	7.1
14	Maryland	8.9
33	Massachusetts	7.5
15	Michigan	8.8
45	Minnesota	6.7
1	Mississippi	11.6
18	Missouri	8.7
30	Montana	8.0
33	Nebraska	7.5
11	Nevada	9.1
41	New Hampshire	6.9
31	New Jersey	7.9
6	New Mexico	9.5
27	New York	8.1
8	North Carolina	9.4
45	North Dakota	6.7
18	Ohio	8.7
27	Oklahoma	8.1
44	Oregon	6.8
23	Pennsylvania	8.4
33	Rhode Island	7.5
5	South Carolina	9.7
41	South Dakota	6.9
10	Tennessee	9.2
23	Texas	8.4
38	Utah	7.2
45	Vermont	6.7
23	Virginia	8.4
48	Washington	6.6
6	West Virginia	9.5
32	Wisconsin	7.7
18	Wyoming	8.7

RANK ORDER

RANK	STATE	PERCENT
1	Mississippi	11.6
2	Louisiana	10.7
3	Alabama	10.3
4	Georgia	9.9
5	South Carolina	9.7
6	New Mexico	9.5
6	West Virginia	9.5
8	North Carolina	9.4
9	Arkansas	9.3
10	Tennessee	9.2
11	Colorado	9.1
11	Nevada	9.1
13	Delaware	9.0
14	Maryland	8.9
15	Florida	8.8
15	Kentucky	8.8
15	Michigan	8.8
18	Missouri	8.7
18	Ohio	8.7
18	Wyoming	8.7
21	Hawaii	8.5
21	Illinois	8.5
23	Pennsylvania	8.4
23	Texas	8.4
23	Virginia	8.4
26	Indiana	8.3
27	Connecticut	8.1
27	New York	8.1
27	Oklahoma	8.1
30	Montana	8.0
31	New Jersey	7.9
32	Wisconsin	7.7
33	Arizona	7.5
33	Massachusetts	7.5
33	Nebraska	7.5
33	Rhode Island	7.5
37	Kansas	7.4
38	Utah	7.2
39	Maine	7.1
40	Idaho	7.0
41	California	6.9
41	New Hampshire	6.9
41	South Dakota	6.9
44	Oregon	6.8
45	Minnesota	6.7
45	North Dakota	6.7
45	Vermont	6.7
48	Iowa	6.6
48	Washington	6.6
50	Alaska	6.2

District of Columbia	10.5

Source: U.S. Department of Health and Human Services, National Center for Health Statistics
"National Vital Statistics Reports" (Vol. 67, No. 8, November 7, 2018, https://www.cdc.gov/nchs/nvss/births.htm)
*Final data by state of residence. Births of less than 2,500 grams (5 pounds 8 ounces).

Births to Teenage Mothers as a Percent of All Births in 2016

National Percent = 5.3% of Live Births*

ALPHA ORDER

RANK	STATE	PERCENT
7	Alabama	7.6
24	Alaska	5.2
12	Arizona	6.3
1	Arkansas	8.8
34	California	4.4
29	Colorado	4.6
46	Connecticut	3.2
23	Delaware	5.3
27	Florida	5.0
12	Georgia	6.3
40	Hawaii	4.0
24	Idaho	5.2
27	Illinois	5.0
12	Indiana	6.3
29	Iowa	4.6
21	Kansas	5.6
6	Kentucky	7.8
9	Louisiana	7.2
33	Maine	4.5
38	Maryland	4.1
50	Massachusetts	2.7
26	Michigan	5.1
46	Minnesota	3.2
1	Mississippi	8.8
16	Missouri	6.0
18	Montana	5.9
29	Nebraska	4.6
20	Nevada	5.7
46	New Hampshire	3.2
49	New Jersey	3.0
3	New Mexico	8.2
45	New York	3.4
16	North Carolina	6.0
38	North Dakota	4.1
18	Ohio	5.9
5	Oklahoma	8.1
34	Oregon	4.4
29	Pennsylvania	4.6
34	Rhode Island	4.4
11	South Carolina	6.4
22	South Dakota	5.5
10	Tennessee	7.1
8	Texas	7.5
44	Utah	3.6
43	Vermont	3.7
40	Virginia	4.0
40	Washington	4.0
3	West Virginia	8.2
37	Wisconsin	4.2
12	Wyoming	6.3

RANK ORDER

RANK	STATE	PERCENT
1	Arkansas	8.8
1	Mississippi	8.8
3	New Mexico	8.2
3	West Virginia	8.2
5	Oklahoma	8.1
6	Kentucky	7.8
7	Alabama	7.6
8	Texas	7.5
9	Louisiana	7.2
10	Tennessee	7.1
11	South Carolina	6.4
12	Arizona	6.3
12	Georgia	6.3
12	Indiana	6.3
12	Wyoming	6.3
16	Missouri	6.0
16	North Carolina	6.0
18	Montana	5.9
18	Ohio	5.9
20	Nevada	5.7
21	Kansas	5.6
22	South Dakota	5.5
23	Delaware	5.3
24	Alaska	5.2
24	Idaho	5.2
26	Michigan	5.1
27	Florida	5.0
27	Illinois	5.0
29	Colorado	4.6
29	Iowa	4.6
29	Nebraska	4.6
29	Pennsylvania	4.6
33	Maine	4.5
34	California	4.4
34	Oregon	4.4
34	Rhode Island	4.4
37	Wisconsin	4.2
38	Maryland	4.1
38	North Dakota	4.1
40	Hawaii	4.0
40	Virginia	4.0
40	Washington	4.0
43	Vermont	3.7
44	Utah	3.6
45	New York	3.4
46	Connecticut	3.2
46	Minnesota	3.2
46	New Hampshire	3.2
49	New Jersey	3.0
50	Massachusetts	2.7

	District of Columbia	4.7

Source: CQ Press using data from U.S. Department of Health and Human Services, Centers for Disease Control and Prevention "CDC Wonder" (http://wonder.cdc.gov)

*Final data. Live births to women 15 to 19 years old by state of residence.

Births to Unmarried Women as a Percent of All Births in 2017

National Percent = 39.8% of Live Births*

ALPHA ORDER				RANK ORDER		
RANK	STATE	PERCENT		RANK	STATE	PERCENT
6	Alabama	47.1		1	Mississippi	53.5
38	Alaska	35.3		2	Louisiana	52.7
12	Arizona	44.8		3	New Mexico	51.7
10	Arkansas	45.5		4	Nevada	48.4
31	California	37.5		5	Delaware	47.6
49	Colorado	22.5		6	Alabama	47.1
33	Connecticut	36.6		7	Florida	47.0
5	Delaware	47.6		8	South Carolina	46.1
7	Florida	47.0		9	West Virginia	45.6
11	Georgia	44.9		10	Arkansas	45.5
28	Hawaii	38.6		11	Georgia	44.9
48	Idaho	28.1		12	Arizona	44.8
25	Illinois	39.8		13	Rhode Island	43.9
16	Indiana	42.8		14	Tennessee	43.6
37	Iowa	35.4		15	Ohio	43.2
36	Kansas	35.7		16	Indiana	42.8
18	Kentucky	41.6		17	Oklahoma	42.0
2	Louisiana	52.7		18	Kentucky	41.6
27	Maine	39.0		19	Michigan	41.1
26	Maryland	39.6		20	Pennsylvania	41.0
43	Massachusetts	33.0		20	Texas	41.0
19	Michigan	41.1		22	North Carolina	40.9
45	Minnesota	32.0		23	Vermont	40.1
1	Mississippi	53.5		24	Missouri	39.9
24	Missouri	39.9		25	Illinois	39.8
35	Montana	35.9		26	Maryland	39.6
42	Nebraska	33.2		27	Maine	39.0
4	Nevada	48.4		28	Hawaii	38.6
44	New Hampshire	32.6		29	New York	38.0
40	New Jersey	33.9		30	Wisconsin	37.7
3	New Mexico	51.7		31	California	37.5
29	New York	38.0		32	South Dakota	37.2
22	North Carolina	40.9		33	Connecticut	36.6
47	North Dakota	31.5		34	Oregon	36.2
15	Ohio	43.2		35	Montana	35.9
17	Oklahoma	42.0		36	Kansas	35.7
34	Oregon	36.2		37	Iowa	35.4
20	Pennsylvania	41.0		38	Alaska	35.3
13	Rhode Island	43.9		39	Virginia	34.6
8	South Carolina	46.1		40	New Jersey	33.9
32	South Dakota	37.2		41	Wyoming	33.5
14	Tennessee	43.6		42	Nebraska	33.2
20	Texas	41.0		43	Massachusetts	33.0
50	Utah	18.5		44	New Hampshire	32.6
23	Vermont	40.1		45	Minnesota	32.0
39	Virginia	34.6		46	Washington	31.6
46	Washington	31.6		47	North Dakota	31.5
9	West Virginia	45.6		48	Idaho	28.1
30	Wisconsin	37.7		49	Colorado	22.5
41	Wyoming	33.5		50	Utah	18.5
					District of Columbia	47.8

Source: U.S. Department of Health and Human Services, National Center for Health Statistics
   "National Vital Statistics Reports" (Vol. 67, No. 8, November 7, 2018, https://www.cdc.gov/nchs/nvss/births.htm)
*Final data by state of residence.

Percent of Women Receiving Late or No Prenatal Care in 2016

National Percent = 6.2% of Women*

ALPHA ORDER				RANK ORDER		
RANK	STATE	PERCENT		RANK	STATE	PERCENT
10	Alabama	7.2		1	Arkansas	10.9
24	Alaska	5.8		2	New Mexico	10.8
4	Arizona	8.6		3	Texas	10.4
1	Arkansas	10.9		4	Arizona	8.6
44	California	3.8		5	Georgia	8.2
19	Colorado	6.1		5	Nevada	8.2
47	Connecticut	3.5		7	Maryland	7.8
15	Delaware	6.4		8	Hawaii	7.7
13	Florida	6.8		9	Oklahoma	7.3
5	Georgia	8.2		10	Alabama	7.2
8	Hawaii	7.7		10	South Carolina	7.2
36	Idaho	4.5		12	Louisiana	7.0
24	Illinois	5.8		13	Florida	6.8
21	Indiana	6.0		14	Montana	6.5
40	Iowa	4.3		15	Delaware	6.4
44	Kansas	3.8		15	Ohio	6.4
29	Kentucky	5.6		17	Washington	6.3
12	Louisiana	7.0		18	Pennsylvania	6.2
48	Maine	3.3		19	Colorado	6.1
7	Maryland	7.8		19	Tennessee	6.1
36	Massachusetts	4.5		21	Indiana	6.0
34	Michigan	4.7		21	North Carolina	6.0
42	Minnesota	3.9		23	North Dakota	5.9
34	Mississippi	4.7		24	Alaska	5.8
30	Missouri	5.4		24	Illinois	5.8
14	Montana	6.5		24	New Jersey	5.8
30	Nebraska	5.4		27	South Dakota	5.7
5	Nevada	8.2		27	West Virginia	5.7
46	New Hampshire	3.6		29	Kentucky	5.6
24	New Jersey	5.8		30	Missouri	5.4
2	New Mexico	10.8		30	Nebraska	5.4
32	New York	5.1		32	New York	5.1
21	North Carolina	6.0		33	Wyoming	4.9
23	North Dakota	5.9		34	Michigan	4.7
15	Ohio	6.4		34	Mississippi	4.7
9	Oklahoma	7.3		36	Idaho	4.5
38	Oregon	4.4		36	Massachusetts	4.5
18	Pennsylvania	6.2		38	Oregon	4.4
49	Rhode Island	1.7		38	Virginia	4.4
10	South Carolina	7.2		40	Iowa	4.3
27	South Dakota	5.7		41	Wisconsin	4.1
19	Tennessee	6.1		42	Minnesota	3.9
3	Texas	10.4		42	Utah	3.9
42	Utah	3.9		44	California	3.8
50	Vermont	1.5		44	Kansas	3.8
38	Virginia	4.4		46	New Hampshire	3.6
17	Washington	6.3		47	Connecticut	3.5
27	West Virginia	5.7		48	Maine	3.3
41	Wisconsin	4.1		49	Rhode Island	1.7
33	Wyoming	4.9		50	Vermont	1.5
					District of Columbia	9.4

Source: CQ Press using data from U.S. Department of Health and Human Services, Centers for Disease Control and Prevention "CDC Wonder" (http://wonder.cdc.gov)

*Final data by state of residence. "Late" means care begun in third trimester.

Reported Legal Abortions in 2015

Reporting States' Total = 638,169 Abortions*

ALPHA ORDER				RANK ORDER			
RANK	STATE	ABORTIONS	% of USA	RANK	STATE	ABORTIONS	% of USA
24	Alabama	5,899	0.9%	1	New York	93,096	14.6%
42	Alaska	1,334	0.2%	2	Florida	72,023	11.3%
14	Arizona	12,655	2.0%	3	Texas	53,940	8.5%
31	Arkansas	3,771	0.6%	4	Illinois	39,856	6.2%
NA	California**	NA	NA	5	Pennsylvania	31,818	5.0%
16	Colorado	10,114	1.6%	6	Georgia	31,009	4.9%
17	Connecticut	9,938	1.6%	7	North Carolina	27,631	4.3%
34	Delaware	2,785	0.4%	8	Michigan	27,151	4.3%
2	Florida	72,023	11.3%	9	New Jersey	22,991	3.6%
6	Georgia	31,009	4.9%	10	Ohio	20,976	3.3%
37	Hawaii	2,026	0.3%	11	Virginia	18,663	2.9%
43	Idaho	1,272	0.2%	12	Massachusetts	18,570	2.9%
4	Illinois	39,856	6.2%	13	Washington	17,098	2.7%
21	Indiana	7,957	1.2%	14	Arizona	12,655	2.0%
30	Iowa	3,989	0.6%	15	Tennessee	11,411	1.8%
23	Kansas	6,931	1.1%	16	Colorado	10,114	1.6%
32	Kentucky	3,188	0.5%	17	Connecticut	9,938	1.6%
19	Louisiana	9,362	1.5%	18	Minnesota	9,861	1.5%
39	Maine	1,836	0.3%	19	Louisiana	9,362	1.5%
NA	Maryland**	NA	NA	20	Oregon	8,610	1.3%
12	Massachusetts	18,570	2.9%	21	Indiana	7,957	1.2%
8	Michigan	27,151	4.3%	22	Nevada	7,116	1.1%
18	Minnesota	9,861	1.5%	23	Kansas	6,931	1.1%
36	Mississippi	2,613	0.4%	24	Alabama	5,899	0.9%
27	Missouri	4,765	0.7%	25	South Carolina	5,778	0.9%
40	Montana	1,611	0.3%	26	Wisconsin	5,660	0.9%
38	Nebraska	2,004	0.3%	27	Missouri	4,765	0.7%
22	Nevada	7,116	1.1%	28	Oklahoma	4,709	0.7%
NA	New Hampshire**	NA	NA	29	New Mexico	4,669	0.7%
9	New Jersey	22,991	3.6%	30	Iowa	3,989	0.6%
29	New Mexico	4,669	0.7%	31	Arkansas	3,771	0.6%
1	New York	93,096	14.6%	32	Kentucky	3,188	0.5%
7	North Carolina	27,631	4.3%	33	Utah	3,176	0.5%
45	North Dakota	1,166	0.2%	34	Delaware	2,785	0.4%
10	Ohio	20,976	3.3%	35	Rhode Island	2,649	0.4%
28	Oklahoma	4,709	0.7%	36	Mississippi	2,613	0.4%
20	Oregon	8,610	1.3%	37	Hawaii	2,026	0.3%
5	Pennsylvania	31,818	5.0%	38	Nebraska	2,004	0.3%
35	Rhode Island	2,649	0.4%	39	Maine	1,836	0.3%
25	South Carolina	5,778	0.9%	40	Montana	1,611	0.3%
46	South Dakota	444	0.1%	41	West Virginia	1,516	0.2%
15	Tennessee	11,411	1.8%	42	Alaska	1,334	0.2%
3	Texas	53,940	8.5%	43	Idaho	1,272	0.2%
33	Utah	3,176	0.5%	44	Vermont	1,265	0.2%
44	Vermont	1,265	0.2%	45	North Dakota	1,166	0.2%
11	Virginia	18,663	2.9%	46	South Dakota	444	0.1%
13	Washington	17,098	2.7%	NA	California**	NA	NA
41	West Virginia	1,516	0.2%	NA	Maryland**	NA	NA
26	Wisconsin	5,660	0.9%	NA	New Hampshire**	NA	NA
NA	Wyoming**	NA	NA	NA	Wyoming**	NA	NA
					District of Columbia	1,267	0.2%

Source: U.S. Department of Health and Human Services, Centers for Disease Control and Prevention
   "Abortion Surveillance-United States, 2015" (MMWR, Vol. 67, No. SS-13, 11/23/18, www.cdc.gov/mmwr/mmwr_ss/ss_pvol.html)
*By state of occurrence. Total is for reporting states only.
**Not reported.

Reported Legal Abortions per 1,000 Live Births in 2015

Reporting States' Ratio = 188 Abortions per 1,000 Live Births*

ALPHA ORDER				RANK ORDER		
RANK	STATE	RATIO		RANK	STATE	RATIO
33	Alabama	99		1	New York	392
29	Alaska	118		2	Florida	321
22	Arizona	148		3	Connecticut	278
35	Arkansas	97		4	Massachusetts	260
NA	California**	NA		5	Illinois	252
20	Colorado	152		6	Delaware	249
3	Connecticut	278		7	Rhode Island	241
6	Delaware	249		8	Michigan	240
2	Florida	321		9	Georgia	236
9	Georgia	236		10	North Carolina	229
30	Hawaii	110		11	Pennsylvania	226
45	Idaho	56		12	New Jersey	223
5	Illinois	252		13	Vermont	214
36	Indiana	95		14	Nevada	196
32	Iowa	101		15	Washington	192
19	Kansas	177		16	Oregon	189
44	Kentucky	57		17	New Mexico	181
24	Louisiana	145		17	Virginia	181
23	Maine	146		19	Kansas	177
NA	Maryland**	NA		20	Colorado	152
4	Massachusetts	260		21	Ohio	151
8	Michigan	240		22	Arizona	148
25	Minnesota	141		23	Maine	146
41	Mississippi	68		24	Louisiana	145
42	Missouri	63		25	Minnesota	141
28	Montana	128		26	Tennessee	140
40	Nebraska	75		27	Texas	134
14	Nevada	196		28	Montana	128
NA	New Hampshire**	NA		29	Alaska	118
12	New Jersey	223		30	Hawaii	110
17	New Mexico	181		31	North Dakota	103
1	New York	392		32	Iowa	101
10	North Carolina	229		33	Alabama	99
31	North Dakota	103		33	South Carolina	99
21	Ohio	151		35	Arkansas	97
37	Oklahoma	89		36	Indiana	95
16	Oregon	189		37	Oklahoma	89
11	Pennsylvania	226		38	Wisconsin	84
7	Rhode Island	241		39	West Virginia	77
33	South Carolina	99		40	Nebraska	75
46	South Dakota	36		41	Mississippi	68
26	Tennessee	140		42	Missouri	63
27	Texas	134		42	Utah	63
42	Utah	63		44	Kentucky	57
13	Vermont	214		45	Idaho	56
17	Virginia	181		46	South Dakota	36
15	Washington	192		NA	California**	NA
39	West Virginia	77		NA	Maryland**	NA
38	Wisconsin	84		NA	New Hampshire**	NA
NA	Wyoming**	NA		NA	Wyoming**	NA
					District of Columbia	132

Source: U.S. Department of Health and Human Services, Centers for Disease Control and Prevention

"Abortion Surveillance-United States, 2015" (MMWR, Vol. 67, No. SS-13, 11/23/18, www.cdc.gov/mmwr/mmwr_ss/ss_pvol.html)

*By state of occurrence. National figure is for reporting states only.

**Not reported.

Infant Deaths in 2016

National Total = 23,161 Infant Deaths*

ALPHA ORDER

RANK	STATE	DEATHS	% of USA
14	Alabama	537	2.3%
46	Alaska	60	0.3%
18	Arizona	456	2.0%
28	Arkansas	309	1.3%
2	California	2,057	8.9%
27	Colorado	319	1.4%
35	Connecticut	174	0.8%
41	Delaware	87	0.4%
3	Florida	1,381	6.0%
7	Georgia	976	4.2%
40	Hawaii	110	0.5%
39	Idaho	137	0.6%
6	Illinois	980	4.2%
11	Indiana	620	2.7%
31	Iowa	240	1.0%
32	Kansas	225	1.0%
24	Kentucky	370	1.6%
15	Louisiana	503	2.2%
42	Maine	74	0.3%
17	Maryland	480	2.1%
29	Massachusetts	279	1.2%
10	Michigan	730	3.2%
25	Minnesota	356	1.5%
26	Mississippi	325	1.4%
16	Missouri	488	2.1%
44	Montana	72	0.3%
36	Nebraska	164	0.7%
34	Nevada	207	0.9%
48	New Hampshire	45	0.2%
20	New Jersey	421	1.8%
37	New Mexico	154	0.7%
4	New York	1,047	4.5%
8	North Carolina	870	3.8%
42	North Dakota	74	0.3%
5	Ohio	1,023	4.4%
22	Oklahoma	391	1.7%
33	Oregon	211	0.9%
9	Pennsylvania	857	3.7%
45	Rhode Island	62	0.3%
21	South Carolina	401	1.7%
47	South Dakota	59	0.3%
12	Tennessee	597	2.6%
1	Texas	2,287	9.9%
30	Utah	274	1.2%
50	Vermont	19	0.1%
13	Virginia	595	2.6%
23	Washington	390	1.7%
38	West Virginia	139	0.6%
19	Wisconsin	422	1.8%
49	Wyoming	37	0.2%

RANK ORDER

RANK	STATE	DEATHS	% of USA
1	Texas	2,287	9.9%
2	California	2,057	8.9%
3	Florida	1,381	6.0%
4	New York	1,047	4.5%
5	Ohio	1,023	4.4%
6	Illinois	980	4.2%
7	Georgia	976	4.2%
8	North Carolina	870	3.8%
9	Pennsylvania	857	3.7%
10	Michigan	730	3.2%
11	Indiana	620	2.7%
12	Tennessee	597	2.6%
13	Virginia	595	2.6%
14	Alabama	537	2.3%
15	Louisiana	503	2.2%
16	Missouri	488	2.1%
17	Maryland	480	2.1%
18	Arizona	456	2.0%
19	Wisconsin	422	1.8%
20	New Jersey	421	1.8%
21	South Carolina	401	1.7%
22	Oklahoma	391	1.7%
23	Washington	390	1.7%
24	Kentucky	370	1.6%
25	Minnesota	356	1.5%
26	Mississippi	325	1.4%
27	Colorado	319	1.4%
28	Arkansas	309	1.3%
29	Massachusetts	279	1.2%
30	Utah	274	1.2%
31	Iowa	240	1.0%
32	Kansas	225	1.0%
33	Oregon	211	0.9%
34	Nevada	207	0.9%
35	Connecticut	174	0.8%
36	Nebraska	164	0.7%
37	New Mexico	154	0.7%
38	West Virginia	139	0.6%
39	Idaho	137	0.6%
40	Hawaii	110	0.5%
41	Delaware	87	0.4%
42	Maine	74	0.3%
42	North Dakota	74	0.3%
44	Montana	72	0.3%
45	Rhode Island	62	0.3%
46	Alaska	60	0.3%
47	South Dakota	59	0.3%
48	New Hampshire	45	0.2%
49	Wyoming	37	0.2%
50	Vermont	19	0.1%
	District of Columbia	70	0.3%

Source: U.S. Department of Health and Human Services, National Center for Health Statistics
      "National Vital Statistics Reports" (Vol. 67, No. 5, 2018, http://www.cdc.gov/nchs/deaths.htm)
*Final data. Deaths of infants under 1 year old by state of residence.

Infant Mortality Rate in 2016

National Rate = 5.9 Infant Deaths per 1,000 Live Births*

ALPHA ORDER

RANK	STATE	RATE
1	Alabama	9.1
35	Alaska	5.4
35	Arizona	5.4
3	Arkansas	8.1
46	California	4.2
40	Colorado	4.8
40	Connecticut	4.8
5	Delaware	7.9
24	Florida	6.1
6	Georgia	7.5
24	Hawaii	6.1
24	Idaho	6.1
18	Illinois	6.4
6	Indiana	7.5
24	Iowa	6.1
28	Kansas	5.9
14	Kentucky	6.7
4	Louisiana	8.0
30	Maine	5.8
15	Maryland	6.6
48	Massachusetts	3.9
18	Michigan	6.4
38	Minnesota	5.1
2	Mississippi	8.6
16	Missouri	6.5
28	Montana	5.9
21	Nebraska	6.2
33	Nevada	5.7
49	New Hampshire	3.7
47	New Jersey	4.1
21	New Mexico	6.2
44	New York	4.5
12	North Carolina	7.2
16	North Dakota	6.5
8	Ohio	7.4
8	Oklahoma	7.4
43	Oregon	4.6
21	Pennsylvania	6.2
33	Rhode Island	5.7
13	South Carolina	7.0
40	South Dakota	4.8
8	Tennessee	7.4
30	Texas	5.8
35	Utah	5.4
NA	Vermont**	NA
30	Virginia	5.8
45	Washington	4.3
11	West Virginia	7.3
20	Wisconsin	6.3
39	Wyoming	5.0

RANK ORDER

RANK	STATE	RATE
1	Alabama	9.1
2	Mississippi	8.6
3	Arkansas	8.1
4	Louisiana	8.0
5	Delaware	7.9
6	Georgia	7.5
6	Indiana	7.5
8	Ohio	7.4
8	Oklahoma	7.4
8	Tennessee	7.4
11	West Virginia	7.3
12	North Carolina	7.2
13	South Carolina	7.0
14	Kentucky	6.7
15	Maryland	6.6
16	Missouri	6.5
16	North Dakota	6.5
18	Illinois	6.4
18	Michigan	6.4
20	Wisconsin	6.3
21	Nebraska	6.2
21	New Mexico	6.2
21	Pennsylvania	6.2
24	Florida	6.1
24	Hawaii	6.1
24	Idaho	6.1
24	Iowa	6.1
28	Kansas	5.9
28	Montana	5.9
30	Maine	5.8
30	Texas	5.8
30	Virginia	5.8
33	Nevada	5.7
33	Rhode Island	5.7
35	Alaska	5.4
35	Arizona	5.4
35	Utah	5.4
38	Minnesota	5.1
39	Wyoming	5.0
40	Colorado	4.8
40	Connecticut	4.8
40	South Dakota	4.8
43	Oregon	4.6
44	New York	4.5
45	Washington	4.3
46	California	4.2
47	New Jersey	4.1
48	Massachusetts	3.9
49	New Hampshire	3.7
NA	Vermont**	NA

	District of Columbia	7.1

Source: U.S. Department of Health and Human Services, National Center for Health Statistics
   "National Vital Statistics Reports" (Vol. 67, No. 5, 2018, http://www.cdc.gov/nchs/deaths.htm)
*Final data. Deaths of infants under 1 year old by state of residence.
**Insufficient data to determine a reliable rate.

Deaths in 2016

National Total = 2,744,248 Deaths*

ALPHA ORDER

RANK	STATE	DEATHS	% of USA
19	Alabama	52,466	1.9%
50	Alaska	4,494	0.2%
17	Arizona	56,645	2.1%
29	Arkansas	31,756	1.2%
1	California	262,240	9.6%
27	Colorado	37,530	1.4%
31	Connecticut	30,543	1.1%
45	Delaware	8,874	0.3%
2	Florida	197,313	7.2%
10	Georgia	81,428	3.0%
42	Hawaii	10,913	0.4%
40	Idaho	13,366	0.5%
7	Illinois	107,020	3.9%
14	Indiana	63,473	2.3%
32	Iowa	29,538	1.1%
33	Kansas	26,245	1.0%
23	Kentucky	47,827	1.7%
24	Louisiana	44,306	1.6%
39	Maine	14,182	0.5%
21	Maryland	48,824	1.8%
16	Massachusetts	56,961	2.1%
8	Michigan	96,231	3.5%
25	Minnesota	43,078	1.6%
30	Mississippi	31,741	1.2%
15	Missouri	59,873	2.2%
43	Montana	9,905	0.4%
38	Nebraska	16,217	0.6%
34	Nevada	23,902	0.9%
41	New Hampshire	12,203	0.4%
11	New Jersey	73,155	2.7%
36	New Mexico	18,365	0.7%
4	New York	154,358	5.6%
9	North Carolina	90,465	3.3%
47	North Dakota	6,242	0.2%
6	Ohio	119,572	4.4%
26	Oklahoma	39,276	1.4%
28	Oregon	35,778	1.3%
5	Pennsylvania	133,040	4.8%
44	Rhode Island	9,735	0.4%
22	South Carolina	48,130	1.8%
46	South Dakota	7,845	0.3%
12	Tennessee	67,857	2.5%
3	Texas	191,966	7.0%
37	Utah	17,913	0.7%
48	Vermont	5,909	0.2%
13	Virginia	66,473	2.4%
18	Washington	54,769	2.0%
35	West Virginia	22,732	0.8%
20	Wisconsin	51,815	1.9%
49	Wyoming	4,722	0.2%

RANK ORDER

RANK	STATE	DEATHS	% of USA
1	California	262,240	9.6%
2	Florida	197,313	7.2%
3	Texas	191,966	7.0%
4	New York	154,358	5.6%
5	Pennsylvania	133,040	4.8%
6	Ohio	119,572	4.4%
7	Illinois	107,020	3.9%
8	Michigan	96,231	3.5%
9	North Carolina	90,465	3.3%
10	Georgia	81,428	3.0%
11	New Jersey	73,155	2.7%
12	Tennessee	67,857	2.5%
13	Virginia	66,473	2.4%
14	Indiana	63,473	2.3%
15	Missouri	59,873	2.2%
16	Massachusetts	56,961	2.1%
17	Arizona	56,645	2.1%
18	Washington	54,769	2.0%
19	Alabama	52,466	1.9%
20	Wisconsin	51,815	1.9%
21	Maryland	48,824	1.8%
22	South Carolina	48,130	1.8%
23	Kentucky	47,827	1.7%
24	Louisiana	44,306	1.6%
25	Minnesota	43,078	1.6%
26	Oklahoma	39,276	1.4%
27	Colorado	37,530	1.4%
28	Oregon	35,778	1.3%
29	Arkansas	31,756	1.2%
30	Mississippi	31,741	1.2%
31	Connecticut	30,543	1.1%
32	Iowa	29,538	1.1%
33	Kansas	26,245	1.0%
34	Nevada	23,902	0.9%
35	West Virginia	22,732	0.8%
36	New Mexico	18,365	0.7%
37	Utah	17,913	0.7%
38	Nebraska	16,217	0.6%
39	Maine	14,182	0.5%
40	Idaho	13,366	0.5%
41	New Hampshire	12,203	0.4%
42	Hawaii	10,913	0.4%
43	Montana	9,905	0.4%
44	Rhode Island	9,735	0.4%
45	Delaware	8,874	0.3%
46	South Dakota	7,845	0.3%
47	North Dakota	6,242	0.2%
48	Vermont	5,909	0.2%
49	Wyoming	4,722	0.2%
50	Alaska	4,494	0.2%
	District of Columbia	5,037	0.2%

Source: U.S. Department of Health and Human Services, National Center for Health Statistics
"National Vital Statistics Reports" (Vol. 67, No. 5, 2018, http://www.cdc.gov/nchs/deaths.htm)
*Final data by state of residence.

Age-Adjusted Death Rate in 2016

National Rate = 728.8 Deaths per 100,000 Population*

RANK	STATE	RATE		RANK	STATE	RATE
4	Alabama	920.4		1	Mississippi	948.9
22	Alaska	745.6		2	West Virginia	943.3
40	Arizona	675.8		3	Kentucky	938.4
5	Arkansas	893.2		4	Alabama	920.4
49	California	616.9		5	Arkansas	893.2
42	Colorado	669.5		6	Oklahoma	888.4
46	Connecticut	654.0		7	Tennessee	886.3
21	Delaware	746.2		8	Louisiana	870.5
45	Florida	666.6		9	Indiana	835.0
13	Georgia	800.4		10	Ohio	832.3
50	Hawaii	572.0		11	South Carolina	829.8
25	Idaho	725.0		12	Missouri	808.2
26	Illinois	724.3		13	Georgia	800.4
9	Indiana	835.0		14	Michigan	785.4
28	Iowa	721.1		15	North Carolina	782.4
19	Kansas	756.8		16	Pennsylvania	770.1
3	Kentucky	938.4		17	Nevada	762.6
8	Louisiana	870.5		18	Maine	759.0
18	Maine	759.0		19	Kansas	756.8
32	Maryland	717.6		20	New Mexico	753.4
43	Massachusetts	669.0		21	Delaware	746.2
14	Michigan	785.4		22	Alaska	745.6
47	Minnesota	648.1		23	Montana	743.2
1	Mississippi	948.9		24	Texas	730.6
12	Missouri	808.2		25	Idaho	725.0
23	Montana	743.2		26	Illinois	724.3
36	Nebraska	707.0		27	New Hampshire	721.5
17	Nevada	762.6		28	Iowa	721.1
27	New Hampshire	721.5		29	Wyoming	720.9
44	New Jersey	668.5		30	South Dakota	719.5
20	New Mexico	753.4		31	Wisconsin	717.9
48	New York	640.7		32	Maryland	717.6
15	North Carolina	782.4		33	Virginia	715.5
39	North Dakota	688.4		34	Utah	714.7
10	Ohio	832.3		35	Vermont	712.8
6	Oklahoma	888.4		36	Nebraska	707.0
37	Oregon	705.9		37	Oregon	705.9
16	Pennsylvania	770.1		38	Rhode Island	690.1
38	Rhode Island	690.1		39	North Dakota	688.4
11	South Carolina	829.8		40	Arizona	675.8
30	South Dakota	719.5		41	Washington	672.0
7	Tennessee	886.3		42	Colorado	669.5
24	Texas	730.6		43	Massachusetts	669.0
34	Utah	714.7		44	New Jersey	668.5
35	Vermont	712.8		45	Florida	666.6
33	Virginia	715.5		46	Connecticut	654.0
41	Washington	672.0		47	Minnesota	648.1
2	West Virginia	943.3		48	New York	640.7
31	Wisconsin	717.9		49	California	616.9
29	Wyoming	720.9		50	Hawaii	572.0
					District of Columbia	766.0

Source: U.S. Department of Health and Human Services, National Center for Health Statistics
   "National Vital Statistics Reports" (Vol. 67, No. 5, 2018, http://www.cdc.gov/nchs/deaths.htm)
*Final data by state of residence. Age-adjusted rates eliminate the distorting effects of the aging of the population. Rates based on the year 2000 standard population.

Estimated Deaths by Cancer in 2019

National Estimated Total = 606,880 Deaths

ALPHA ORDER

RANK	STATE	DEATHS	% of USA
22	Alabama	10,630	1.8%
49	Alaska	1,120	0.2%
17	Arizona	12,470	2.1%
29	Arkansas	6,800	1.1%
1	California	60,590	10.0%
28	Colorado	8,120	1.3%
32	Connecticut	6,470	1.1%
43	Delaware	2,140	0.4%
2	Florida	45,000	7.4%
10	Georgia	17,880	2.9%
42	Hawaii	2,560	0.4%
40	Idaho	3,040	0.5%
7	Illinois	24,410	4.0%
14	Indiana	13,690	2.3%
31	Iowa	6,480	1.1%
33	Kansas	5,550	0.9%
23	Kentucky	10,580	1.7%
25	Louisiana	9,260	1.5%
38	Maine	3,310	0.5%
20	Maryland	10,780	1.8%
18	Massachusetts	12,420	2.0%
8	Michigan	21,150	3.5%
24	Minnesota	10,020	1.7%
30	Mississippi	6,720	1.1%
15	Missouri	13,080	2.2%
45	Montana	2,100	0.3%
37	Nebraska	3,520	0.6%
34	Nevada	5,390	0.9%
41	New Hampshire	2,820	0.5%
11	New Jersey	15,860	2.6%
36	New Mexico	3,720	0.6%
4	New York	35,010	5.8%
9	North Carolina	20,410	3.4%
48	North Dakota	1,280	0.2%
6	Ohio	25,440	4.2%
26	Oklahoma	8,420	1.4%
27	Oregon	8,270	1.4%
5	Pennsylvania	28,170	4.6%
43	Rhode Island	2,140	0.4%
21	South Carolina	10,720	1.8%
46	South Dakota	1,680	0.3%
13	Tennessee	14,840	2.4%
3	Texas	41,300	6.8%
38	Utah	3,310	0.5%
47	Vermont	1,440	0.2%
12	Virginia	15,200	2.5%
16	Washington	13,010	2.1%
35	West Virginia	4,820	0.8%
19	Wisconsin	11,730	1.9%
50	Wyoming	980	0.2%

RANK ORDER

RANK	STATE	DEATHS	% of USA
1	California	60,590	10.0%
2	Florida	45,000	7.4%
3	Texas	41,300	6.8%
4	New York	35,010	5.8%
5	Pennsylvania	28,170	4.6%
6	Ohio	25,440	4.2%
7	Illinois	24,410	4.0%
8	Michigan	21,150	3.5%
9	North Carolina	20,410	3.4%
10	Georgia	17,880	2.9%
11	New Jersey	15,860	2.6%
12	Virginia	15,200	2.5%
13	Tennessee	14,840	2.4%
14	Indiana	13,690	2.3%
15	Missouri	13,080	2.2%
16	Washington	13,010	2.1%
17	Arizona	12,470	2.1%
18	Massachusetts	12,420	2.0%
19	Wisconsin	11,730	1.9%
20	Maryland	10,780	1.8%
21	South Carolina	10,720	1.8%
22	Alabama	10,630	1.8%
23	Kentucky	10,580	1.7%
24	Minnesota	10,020	1.7%
25	Louisiana	9,260	1.5%
26	Oklahoma	8,420	1.4%
27	Oregon	8,270	1.4%
28	Colorado	8,120	1.3%
29	Arkansas	6,800	1.1%
30	Mississippi	6,720	1.1%
31	Iowa	6,480	1.1%
32	Connecticut	6,470	1.1%
33	Kansas	5,550	0.9%
34	Nevada	5,390	0.9%
35	West Virginia	4,820	0.8%
36	New Mexico	3,720	0.6%
37	Nebraska	3,520	0.6%
38	Maine	3,310	0.5%
38	Utah	3,310	0.5%
40	Idaho	3,040	0.5%
41	New Hampshire	2,820	0.5%
42	Hawaii	2,560	0.4%
43	Delaware	2,140	0.4%
43	Rhode Island	2,140	0.4%
45	Montana	2,100	0.3%
46	South Dakota	1,680	0.3%
47	Vermont	1,440	0.2%
48	North Dakota	1,280	0.2%
49	Alaska	1,120	0.2%
50	Wyoming	980	0.2%
	District of Columbia	1,020	0.2%

Source: American Cancer Society
"Cancer Facts & Figures 2019" (Copyright 2019, American Cancer Society, www.cancer.org/research/cancer-facts-statistics.html)

Estimated Death Rate by Cancer in 2019

National Estimated Rate = 185.5 Deaths per 100,000 Population*

<u>ALPHA ORDER</u>

RANK	STATE	RATE
11	Alabama	217.5
47	Alaska	151.9
40	Arizona	173.9
5	Arkansas	225.6
46	California	153.2
49	Colorado	142.6
30	Connecticut	181.1
7	Delaware	221.3
15	Florida	211.3
43	Georgia	170.0
31	Hawaii	180.2
41	Idaho	173.3
26	Illinois	191.6
19	Indiana	204.6
18	Iowa	205.3
27	Kansas	190.6
3	Kentucky	236.8
22	Louisiana	198.7
2	Maine	247.3
36	Maryland	178.4
32	Massachusetts	179.9
14	Michigan	211.6
34	Minnesota	178.6
6	Mississippi	225.0
12	Missouri	213.5
23	Montana	197.7
29	Nebraska	182.5
38	Nevada	177.6
17	New Hampshire	207.9
37	New Jersey	178.0
39	New Mexico	177.5
33	New York	179.2
25	North Carolina	196.6
45	North Dakota	168.4
10	Ohio	217.6
12	Oklahoma	213.5
24	Oregon	197.3
8	Pennsylvania	220.0
20	Rhode Island	202.4
16	South Carolina	210.9
28	South Dakota	190.4
9	Tennessee	219.2
48	Texas	143.9
50	Utah	104.7
4	Vermont	229.9
35	Virginia	178.5
42	Washington	172.6
1	West Virginia	266.9
21	Wisconsin	201.8
44	Wyoming	169.6

<u>RANK ORDER</u>

RANK	STATE	RATE
1	West Virginia	266.9
2	Maine	247.3
3	Kentucky	236.8
4	Vermont	229.9
5	Arkansas	225.6
6	Mississippi	225.0
7	Delaware	221.3
8	Pennsylvania	220.0
9	Tennessee	219.2
10	Ohio	217.6
11	Alabama	217.5
12	Missouri	213.5
12	Oklahoma	213.5
14	Michigan	211.6
15	Florida	211.3
16	South Carolina	210.9
17	New Hampshire	207.9
18	Iowa	205.3
19	Indiana	204.6
20	Rhode Island	202.4
21	Wisconsin	201.8
22	Louisiana	198.7
23	Montana	197.7
24	Oregon	197.3
25	North Carolina	196.6
26	Illinois	191.6
27	Kansas	190.6
28	South Dakota	190.4
29	Nebraska	182.5
30	Connecticut	181.1
31	Hawaii	180.2
32	Massachusetts	179.9
33	New York	179.2
34	Minnesota	178.6
35	Virginia	178.5
36	Maryland	178.4
37	New Jersey	178.0
38	Nevada	177.6
39	New Mexico	177.5
40	Arizona	173.9
41	Idaho	173.3
42	Washington	172.6
43	Georgia	170.0
44	Wyoming	169.6
45	North Dakota	168.4
46	California	153.2
47	Alaska	151.9
48	Texas	143.9
49	Colorado	142.6
50	Utah	104.7
	District of Columbia	145.2

Source: CQ Press using data from American Cancer Society
"Cancer Facts & Figures 2019" (Copyright 2019, American Cancer Society, www.cancer.org/research/cancer-facts-statistics.html)
*Rates calculated using 2018 Census resident population estimates. Not age-adjusted.

Estimated New Cancer Cases in 2019

National Estimated Total = 1,762,450 New Cases*

ALPHA ORDER

RANK	STATE	CASES	% of USA
23	Alabama	28,950	1.6%
49	Alaska	3,090	0.2%
15	Arizona	37,490	2.1%
32	Arkansas	16,580	0.9%
1	California	186,920	10.6%
24	Colorado	26,800	1.5%
28	Connecticut	21,950	1.2%
45	Delaware	5,870	0.3%
2	Florida	131,470	7.5%
11	Georgia	50,450	2.9%
42	Hawaii	7,120	0.4%
41	Idaho	8,390	0.5%
6	Illinois	68,560	3.9%
18	Indiana	35,280	2.0%
30	Iowa	17,810	1.0%
33	Kansas	15,340	0.9%
26	Kentucky	26,400	1.5%
24	Louisiana	26,800	1.5%
39	Maine	8,920	0.5%
20	Maryland	33,140	1.9%
13	Massachusetts	40,020	2.3%
9	Michigan	58,360	3.3%
21	Minnesota	30,560	1.7%
31	Mississippi	17,050	1.0%
17	Missouri	35,480	2.0%
44	Montana	5,920	0.3%
37	Nebraska	9,780	0.6%
34	Nevada	14,810	0.8%
40	New Hampshire	8,610	0.5%
10	New Jersey	53,400	3.0%
38	New Mexico	9,460	0.5%
4	New York	111,870	6.3%
8	North Carolina	58,690	3.3%
47	North Dakota	3,940	0.2%
7	Ohio	67,150	3.8%
29	Oklahoma	20,540	1.2%
27	Oregon	23,320	1.3%
5	Pennsylvania	79,890	4.5%
43	Rhode Island	6,540	0.4%
22	South Carolina	29,830	1.7%
46	South Dakota	4,770	0.3%
16	Tennessee	37,350	2.1%
3	Texas	124,890	7.1%
36	Utah	11,620	0.7%
48	Vermont	3,920	0.2%
12	Virginia	45,440	2.6%
14	Washington	39,160	2.2%
35	West Virginia	12,440	0.7%
19	Wisconsin	34,220	1.9%
50	Wyoming	2,930	0.2%

RANK ORDER

RANK	STATE	CASES	% of USA
1	California	186,920	10.6%
2	Florida	131,470	7.5%
3	Texas	124,890	7.1%
4	New York	111,870	6.3%
5	Pennsylvania	79,890	4.5%
6	Illinois	68,560	3.9%
7	Ohio	67,150	3.8%
8	North Carolina	58,690	3.3%
9	Michigan	58,360	3.3%
10	New Jersey	53,400	3.0%
11	Georgia	50,450	2.9%
12	Virginia	45,440	2.6%
13	Massachusetts	40,020	2.3%
14	Washington	39,160	2.2%
15	Arizona	37,490	2.1%
16	Tennessee	37,350	2.1%
17	Missouri	35,480	2.0%
18	Indiana	35,280	2.0%
19	Wisconsin	34,220	1.9%
20	Maryland	33,140	1.9%
21	Minnesota	30,560	1.7%
22	South Carolina	29,830	1.7%
23	Alabama	28,950	1.6%
24	Colorado	26,800	1.5%
24	Louisiana	26,800	1.5%
26	Kentucky	26,400	1.5%
27	Oregon	23,320	1.3%
28	Connecticut	21,950	1.2%
29	Oklahoma	20,540	1.2%
30	Iowa	17,810	1.0%
31	Mississippi	17,050	1.0%
32	Arkansas	16,580	0.9%
33	Kansas	15,340	0.9%
34	Nevada	14,810	0.8%
35	West Virginia	12,440	0.7%
36	Utah	11,620	0.7%
37	Nebraska	9,780	0.6%
38	New Mexico	9,460	0.5%
39	Maine	8,920	0.5%
40	New Hampshire	8,610	0.5%
41	Idaho	8,390	0.5%
42	Hawaii	7,120	0.4%
43	Rhode Island	6,540	0.4%
44	Montana	5,920	0.3%
45	Delaware	5,870	0.3%
46	South Dakota	4,770	0.3%
47	North Dakota	3,940	0.2%
48	Vermont	3,920	0.2%
49	Alaska	3,090	0.2%
50	Wyoming	2,930	0.2%
	District of Columbia	3,190	0.2%

Source: American Cancer Society
"Cancer Facts & Figures 2019" (Copyright 2019, American Cancer Society, www.cancer.org/research/cancer-facts-statistics.html)
*These estimates are offered as a rough guide and should not be regarded as definitive. They are calculated by the American Cancer Society using a model based on 2001-2015 incidence data. Totals do not include basal and squamous cell skin cancers or in situ carcinomas except urinary bladder.

Estimated Rate of New Cancer Cases in 2019

National Estimated Rate = 538.7 New Cases per 100,000 Population*

ALPHA ORDER

RANK	STATE	RATE	RANK	STATE	RATE
11	Alabama	592.3	1	West Virginia	688.9
49	Alaska	419.0	2	Maine	666.5
35	Arizona	522.8	3	New Hampshire	634.7
27	Arkansas	550.1	4	Vermont	625.9
45	California	472.5	5	Pennsylvania	623.8
46	Colorado	470.5	6	Rhode Island	618.5
8	Connecticut	614.4	7	Florida	617.2
9	Delaware	606.9	8	Connecticut	614.4
7	Florida	617.2	9	Delaware	606.9
43	Georgia	479.6	10	New Jersey	599.4
41	Hawaii	501.2	11	Alabama	592.3
44	Idaho	478.3	12	Kentucky	590.8
31	Illinois	538.1	13	Wisconsin	588.6
33	Indiana	527.2	14	South Carolina	586.7
23	Iowa	564.3	15	Michigan	583.8
34	Kansas	526.9	16	Massachusetts	579.8
12	Kentucky	590.8	17	Missouri	579.1
18	Louisiana	575.1	18	Louisiana	575.1
2	Maine	666.5	19	Ohio	574.5
28	Maryland	548.4	20	New York	572.5
16	Massachusetts	579.8	21	Mississippi	570.9
15	Michigan	583.8	22	North Carolina	565.2
29	Minnesota	544.6	23	Iowa	564.3
21	Mississippi	570.9	24	Montana	557.3
17	Missouri	579.1	25	Oregon	556.5
24	Montana	557.3	26	Tennessee	551.7
40	Nebraska	506.9	27	Arkansas	550.1
42	Nevada	488.1	28	Maryland	548.4
3	New Hampshire	634.7	29	Minnesota	544.6
10	New Jersey	599.4	30	South Dakota	540.7
47	New Mexico	451.5	31	Illinois	538.1
20	New York	572.5	32	Virginia	533.5
22	North Carolina	565.2	33	Indiana	527.2
38	North Dakota	518.4	34	Kansas	526.9
19	Ohio	574.5	35	Arizona	522.8
36	Oklahoma	520.9	36	Oklahoma	520.9
25	Oregon	556.5	37	Washington	519.7
5	Pennsylvania	623.8	38	North Dakota	518.4
6	Rhode Island	618.5	39	Wyoming	507.2
14	South Carolina	586.7	40	Nebraska	506.9
30	South Dakota	540.7	41	Hawaii	501.2
26	Tennessee	551.7	42	Nevada	488.1
48	Texas	435.1	43	Georgia	479.6
50	Utah	367.6	44	Idaho	478.3
4	Vermont	625.9	45	California	472.5
32	Virginia	533.5	46	Colorado	470.5
37	Washington	519.7	47	New Mexico	451.5
1	West Virginia	688.9	48	Texas	435.1
13	Wisconsin	588.6	49	Alaska	419.0
39	Wyoming	507.2	50	Utah	367.6
				District of Columbia	454.1

Source: CQ Press using data from American Cancer Society
"Cancer Facts & Figures 2019" (Copyright 2019, American Cancer Society, www.cancer.org/research/cancer-facts-statistics.html)
*These estimates are offered as a rough guide and should not be regarded as definitive. They are calculated by the American Cancer Society using a model based on 2001-2015 incidence data. Totals do not include basal and squamous cell skin cancers or in situ carcinomas except urinary bladder. Rates calculated using 2018 Census resident population estimates.

Deaths by Accidents in 2016

National Total = 161,374 Deaths*

<table>
<tr><td colspan="4">ALPHA ORDER</td><td colspan="4">RANK ORDER</td></tr>
<tr><td>RANK</td><td>STATE</td><td>DEATHS</td><td>% of USA</td><td>RANK</td><td>STATE</td><td>DEATHS</td><td>% of USA</td></tr>
<tr><td>23</td><td>Alabama</td><td>2,755</td><td>1.7%</td><td>1</td><td>California</td><td>13,213</td><td>8.2%</td></tr>
<tr><td>47</td><td>Alaska</td><td>439</td><td>0.3%</td><td>2</td><td>Florida</td><td>12,561</td><td>7.8%</td></tr>
<tr><td>12</td><td>Arizona</td><td>4,010</td><td>2.5%</td><td>3</td><td>Texas</td><td>10,536</td><td>6.5%</td></tr>
<tr><td>33</td><td>Arkansas</td><td>1,604</td><td>1.0%</td><td>4</td><td>Pennsylvania</td><td>8,410</td><td>5.2%</td></tr>
<tr><td>1</td><td>California</td><td>13,213</td><td>8.2%</td><td>5</td><td>Ohio</td><td>7,999</td><td>5.0%</td></tr>
<tr><td>22</td><td>Colorado</td><td>2,880</td><td>1.8%</td><td>6</td><td>New York</td><td>7,354</td><td>4.6%</td></tr>
<tr><td>29</td><td>Connecticut</td><td>1,978</td><td>1.2%</td><td>7</td><td>Illinois</td><td>5,508</td><td>3.4%</td></tr>
<tr><td>45</td><td>Delaware</td><td>516</td><td>0.3%</td><td>8</td><td>North Carolina</td><td>5,476</td><td>3.4%</td></tr>
<tr><td>2</td><td>Florida</td><td>12,561</td><td>7.8%</td><td>9</td><td>Michigan</td><td>5,313</td><td>3.3%</td></tr>
<tr><td>10</td><td>Georgia</td><td>4,701</td><td>2.9%</td><td>10</td><td>Georgia</td><td>4,701</td><td>2.9%</td></tr>
<tr><td>44</td><td>Hawaii</td><td>577</td><td>0.4%</td><td>11</td><td>Tennessee</td><td>4,238</td><td>2.6%</td></tr>
<tr><td>40</td><td>Idaho</td><td>849</td><td>0.5%</td><td>12</td><td>Arizona</td><td>4,010</td><td>2.5%</td></tr>
<tr><td>7</td><td>Illinois</td><td>5,508</td><td>3.4%</td><td>13</td><td>New Jersey</td><td>3,839</td><td>2.4%</td></tr>
<tr><td>18</td><td>Indiana</td><td>3,496</td><td>2.2%</td><td>14</td><td>Massachusetts</td><td>3,831</td><td>2.4%</td></tr>
<tr><td>32</td><td>Iowa</td><td>1,608</td><td>1.0%</td><td>15</td><td>Virginia</td><td>3,710</td><td>2.3%</td></tr>
<tr><td>35</td><td>Kansas</td><td>1,444</td><td>0.9%</td><td>16</td><td>Missouri</td><td>3,625</td><td>2.2%</td></tr>
<tr><td>20</td><td>Kentucky</td><td>3,194</td><td>2.0%</td><td>17</td><td>Wisconsin</td><td>3,575</td><td>2.2%</td></tr>
<tr><td>24</td><td>Louisiana</td><td>2,710</td><td>1.7%</td><td>18</td><td>Indiana</td><td>3,496</td><td>2.2%</td></tr>
<tr><td>39</td><td>Maine</td><td>909</td><td>0.6%</td><td>19</td><td>Washington</td><td>3,221</td><td>2.0%</td></tr>
<tr><td>27</td><td>Maryland</td><td>2,271</td><td>1.4%</td><td>20</td><td>Kentucky</td><td>3,194</td><td>2.0%</td></tr>
<tr><td>14</td><td>Massachusetts</td><td>3,831</td><td>2.4%</td><td>21</td><td>South Carolina</td><td>3,012</td><td>1.9%</td></tr>
<tr><td>9</td><td>Michigan</td><td>5,313</td><td>3.3%</td><td>22</td><td>Colorado</td><td>2,880</td><td>1.8%</td></tr>
<tr><td>25</td><td>Minnesota</td><td>2,697</td><td>1.7%</td><td>23</td><td>Alabama</td><td>2,755</td><td>1.7%</td></tr>
<tr><td>30</td><td>Mississippi</td><td>1,803</td><td>1.1%</td><td>24</td><td>Louisiana</td><td>2,710</td><td>1.7%</td></tr>
<tr><td>16</td><td>Missouri</td><td>3,625</td><td>2.2%</td><td>25</td><td>Minnesota</td><td>2,697</td><td>1.7%</td></tr>
<tr><td>43</td><td>Montana</td><td>626</td><td>0.4%</td><td>26</td><td>Oklahoma</td><td>2,592</td><td>1.6%</td></tr>
<tr><td>41</td><td>Nebraska</td><td>772</td><td>0.5%</td><td>27</td><td>Maryland</td><td>2,271</td><td>1.4%</td></tr>
<tr><td>36</td><td>Nevada</td><td>1,395</td><td>0.9%</td><td>28</td><td>Oregon</td><td>2,105</td><td>1.3%</td></tr>
<tr><td>38</td><td>New Hampshire</td><td>924</td><td>0.6%</td><td>29</td><td>Connecticut</td><td>1,978</td><td>1.2%</td></tr>
<tr><td>13</td><td>New Jersey</td><td>3,839</td><td>2.4%</td><td>30</td><td>Mississippi</td><td>1,803</td><td>1.1%</td></tr>
<tr><td>34</td><td>New Mexico</td><td>1,487</td><td>0.9%</td><td>31</td><td>West Virginia</td><td>1,705</td><td>1.1%</td></tr>
<tr><td>6</td><td>New York</td><td>7,354</td><td>4.6%</td><td>32</td><td>Iowa</td><td>1,608</td><td>1.0%</td></tr>
<tr><td>8</td><td>North Carolina</td><td>5,476</td><td>3.4%</td><td>33</td><td>Arkansas</td><td>1,604</td><td>1.0%</td></tr>
<tr><td>49</td><td>North Dakota</td><td>371</td><td>0.2%</td><td>34</td><td>New Mexico</td><td>1,487</td><td>0.9%</td></tr>
<tr><td>5</td><td>Ohio</td><td>7,999</td><td>5.0%</td><td>35</td><td>Kansas</td><td>1,444</td><td>0.9%</td></tr>
<tr><td>26</td><td>Oklahoma</td><td>2,592</td><td>1.6%</td><td>36</td><td>Nevada</td><td>1,395</td><td>0.9%</td></tr>
<tr><td>28</td><td>Oregon</td><td>2,105</td><td>1.3%</td><td>37</td><td>Utah</td><td>1,211</td><td>0.8%</td></tr>
<tr><td>4</td><td>Pennsylvania</td><td>8,410</td><td>5.2%</td><td>38</td><td>New Hampshire</td><td>924</td><td>0.6%</td></tr>
<tr><td>42</td><td>Rhode Island</td><td>675</td><td>0.4%</td><td>39</td><td>Maine</td><td>909</td><td>0.6%</td></tr>
<tr><td>21</td><td>South Carolina</td><td>3,012</td><td>1.9%</td><td>40</td><td>Idaho</td><td>849</td><td>0.5%</td></tr>
<tr><td>46</td><td>South Dakota</td><td>505</td><td>0.3%</td><td>41</td><td>Nebraska</td><td>772</td><td>0.5%</td></tr>
<tr><td>11</td><td>Tennessee</td><td>4,238</td><td>2.6%</td><td>42</td><td>Rhode Island</td><td>675</td><td>0.4%</td></tr>
<tr><td>3</td><td>Texas</td><td>10,536</td><td>6.5%</td><td>43</td><td>Montana</td><td>626</td><td>0.4%</td></tr>
<tr><td>37</td><td>Utah</td><td>1,211</td><td>0.8%</td><td>44</td><td>Hawaii</td><td>577</td><td>0.4%</td></tr>
<tr><td>48</td><td>Vermont</td><td>372</td><td>0.2%</td><td>45</td><td>Delaware</td><td>516</td><td>0.3%</td></tr>
<tr><td>15</td><td>Virginia</td><td>3,710</td><td>2.3%</td><td>46</td><td>South Dakota</td><td>505</td><td>0.3%</td></tr>
<tr><td>19</td><td>Washington</td><td>3,221</td><td>2.0%</td><td>47</td><td>Alaska</td><td>439</td><td>0.3%</td></tr>
<tr><td>31</td><td>West Virginia</td><td>1,705</td><td>1.1%</td><td>48</td><td>Vermont</td><td>372</td><td>0.2%</td></tr>
<tr><td>17</td><td>Wisconsin</td><td>3,575</td><td>2.2%</td><td>49</td><td>North Dakota</td><td>371</td><td>0.2%</td></tr>
<tr><td>49</td><td>Wyoming</td><td>371</td><td>0.2%</td><td>49</td><td>Wyoming</td><td>371</td><td>0.2%</td></tr>
<tr><td></td><td></td><td></td><td></td><td></td><td>District of Columbia</td><td>401</td><td>0.2%</td></tr>
</table>

Source: U.S. Department of Health and Human Services, National Center for Health Statistics
"National Vital Statistics Reports" (Vol. 67, No. 5, 2018, http://www.cdc.gov/nchs/deaths.htm)
*Final data by state of residence. Includes motor vehicle deaths, poisoning, falls, drowning, and other accidents.

Age-Adjusted Death Rate by Accidents in 2016

National Rate = 47.4 Deaths per 100,000 Population*

ALPHA ORDER

RANK	STATE	RATE
18	Alabama	55.5
7	Alaska	63.1
21	Arizona	54.2
27	Arkansas	51.8
50	California	32.0
29	Colorado	51.2
31	Connecticut	50.3
25	Delaware	52.4
19	Florida	54.9
35	Georgia	45.8
48	Hawaii	35.3
32	Idaho	49.5
43	Illinois	41.0
28	Indiana	51.6
35	Iowa	45.8
37	Kansas	45.7
2	Kentucky	71.0
14	Louisiana	57.4
8	Maine	62.4
47	Maryland	35.7
24	Massachusetts	52.8
30	Michigan	50.5
39	Minnesota	43.8
12	Mississippi	59.2
15	Missouri	57.0
22	Montana	54.1
46	Nebraska	37.0
33	Nevada	46.0
4	New Hampshire	66.6
44	New Jersey	40.8
3	New Mexico	69.5
49	New York	34.2
26	North Carolina	52.2
38	North Dakota	45.4
4	Ohio	66.6
6	Oklahoma	64.1
33	Oregon	46.0
10	Pennsylvania	61.8
16	Rhode Island	56.6
13	South Carolina	58.9
23	South Dakota	53.4
11	Tennessee	61.1
45	Texas	38.6
39	Utah	43.8
20	Vermont	54.8
41	Virginia	42.4
42	Washington	41.4
1	West Virginia	89.7
17	Wisconsin	55.6
9	Wyoming	61.9

RANK ORDER

RANK	STATE	RATE
1	West Virginia	89.7
2	Kentucky	71.0
3	New Mexico	69.5
4	New Hampshire	66.6
4	Ohio	66.6
6	Oklahoma	64.1
7	Alaska	63.1
8	Maine	62.4
9	Wyoming	61.9
10	Pennsylvania	61.8
11	Tennessee	61.1
12	Mississippi	59.2
13	South Carolina	58.9
14	Louisiana	57.4
15	Missouri	57.0
16	Rhode Island	56.6
17	Wisconsin	55.6
18	Alabama	55.5
19	Florida	54.9
20	Vermont	54.8
21	Arizona	54.2
22	Montana	54.1
23	South Dakota	53.4
24	Massachusetts	52.8
25	Delaware	52.4
26	North Carolina	52.2
27	Arkansas	51.8
28	Indiana	51.6
29	Colorado	51.2
30	Michigan	50.5
31	Connecticut	50.3
32	Idaho	49.5
33	Nevada	46.0
33	Oregon	46.0
35	Georgia	45.8
35	Iowa	45.8
37	Kansas	45.7
38	North Dakota	45.4
39	Minnesota	43.8
39	Utah	43.8
41	Virginia	42.4
42	Washington	41.4
43	Illinois	41.0
44	New Jersey	40.8
45	Texas	38.6
46	Nebraska	37.0
47	Maryland	35.7
48	Hawaii	35.3
49	New York	34.2
50	California	32.0

	District of Columbia	58.3

Source: U.S. Department of Health and Human Services, National Center for Health Statistics
    "National Vital Statistics Reports" (Vol. 67, No. 5, 2018, http://www.cdc.gov/nchs/deaths.htm)
*Final data by state of residence. Includes motor vehicle deaths, poisoning, falls, drowning, and other accidents. Age-adjusted rates based on the year 2000 standard population.

Deaths by Cerebrovascular Diseases in 2016

National Total = 142,142 Deaths*

ALPHA ORDER

RANK ORDER

RANK	STATE	DEATHS	% of USA	RANK	STATE	DEATHS	% of USA
16	Alabama	2,967	2.1%	1	California	15,680	11.0%
50	Alaska	196	0.1%	2	Florida	11,854	8.3%
20	Arizona	2,556	1.8%	3	Texas	10,673	7.5%
30	Arkansas	1,643	1.2%	4	Pennsylvania	6,730	4.7%
1	California	15,680	11.0%	5	New York	6,258	4.4%
27	Colorado	1,927	1.4%	6	Ohio	5,987	4.2%
33	Connecticut	1,269	0.9%	7	Illinois	5,658	4.0%
42	Delaware	506	0.4%	8	North Carolina	4,940	3.5%
2	Florida	11,854	8.3%	9	Michigan	4,874	3.4%
10	Georgia	4,349	3.1%	10	Georgia	4,349	3.1%
40	Hawaii	675	0.5%	11	Tennessee	3,508	2.5%
39	Idaho	682	0.5%	12	Virginia	3,502	2.5%
7	Illinois	5,658	4.0%	13	New Jersey	3,401	2.4%
15	Indiana	3,040	2.1%	14	Missouri	3,069	2.2%
31	Iowa	1,388	1.0%	15	Indiana	3,040	2.1%
32	Kansas	1,363	1.0%	16	Alabama	2,967	2.1%
25	Kentucky	2,057	1.4%	17	Washington	2,910	2.0%
23	Louisiana	2,322	1.6%	18	Maryland	2,709	1.9%
41	Maine	663	0.5%	19	South Carolina	2,627	1.8%
18	Maryland	2,709	1.9%	20	Arizona	2,556	1.8%
22	Massachusetts	2,468	1.7%	21	Wisconsin	2,481	1.7%
9	Michigan	4,874	3.4%	22	Massachusetts	2,468	1.7%
24	Minnesota	2,197	1.5%	23	Louisiana	2,322	1.6%
29	Mississippi	1,705	1.2%	24	Minnesota	2,197	1.5%
14	Missouri	3,069	2.2%	25	Kentucky	2,057	1.4%
44	Montana	440	0.3%	26	Oregon	1,943	1.4%
38	Nebraska	787	0.6%	27	Colorado	1,927	1.4%
34	Nevada	1,096	0.8%	28	Oklahoma	1,859	1.3%
43	New Hampshire	490	0.3%	29	Mississippi	1,705	1.2%
13	New Jersey	3,401	2.4%	30	Arkansas	1,643	1.2%
37	New Mexico	885	0.6%	31	Iowa	1,388	1.0%
5	New York	6,258	4.4%	32	Kansas	1,363	1.0%
8	North Carolina	4,940	3.5%	33	Connecticut	1,269	0.9%
47	North Dakota	311	0.2%	34	Nevada	1,096	0.8%
6	Ohio	5,987	4.2%	35	West Virginia	1,039	0.7%
28	Oklahoma	1,859	1.3%	36	Utah	932	0.7%
26	Oregon	1,943	1.4%	37	New Mexico	885	0.6%
4	Pennsylvania	6,730	4.7%	38	Nebraska	787	0.6%
46	Rhode Island	399	0.3%	39	Idaho	682	0.5%
19	South Carolina	2,627	1.8%	40	Hawaii	675	0.5%
45	South Dakota	420	0.3%	41	Maine	663	0.5%
11	Tennessee	3,508	2.5%	42	Delaware	506	0.4%
3	Texas	10,673	7.5%	43	New Hampshire	490	0.3%
36	Utah	932	0.7%	44	Montana	440	0.3%
48	Vermont	247	0.2%	45	South Dakota	420	0.3%
12	Virginia	3,502	2.5%	46	Rhode Island	399	0.3%
17	Washington	2,910	2.0%	47	North Dakota	311	0.2%
35	West Virginia	1,039	0.7%	48	Vermont	247	0.2%
21	Wisconsin	2,481	1.7%	49	Wyoming	208	0.1%
49	Wyoming	208	0.1%	50	Alaska	196	0.1%
					District of Columbia	252	0.2%

Source: U.S. Department of Health and Human Services, National Center for Health Statistics
   "National Vital Statistics Reports" (Vol. 67, No. 5, 2018, http://www.cdc.gov/nchs/deaths.htm)
*Final data by state of residence. Cerebrovascular diseases include stroke and other disorders of the blood vessels of the brain.

Age-Adjusted Death Rate by Cerebrovascular Diseases in 2016

National Rate = 37.3 Deaths per 100,000 Population*

ALPHA ORDER

RANK	STATE	RATE
1	Alabama	51.6
18	Alaska	39.0
44	Arizona	29.8
5	Arkansas	45.6
28	California	36.9
33	Colorado	35.2
49	Connecticut	26.3
12	Delaware	41.6
25	Florida	37.3
7	Georgia	44.3
35	Hawaii	34.3
26	Idaho	37.2
23	Illinois	37.8
17	Indiana	39.5
41	Iowa	32.3
21	Kansas	38.6
14	Kentucky	40.4
3	Louisiana	46.0
34	Maine	34.4
16	Maryland	39.7
47	Massachusetts	27.9
18	Michigan	39.0
39	Minnesota	32.5
2	Mississippi	50.6
14	Missouri	40.4
39	Montana	32.5
37	Nebraska	33.2
29	Nevada	35.9
46	New Hampshire	28.0
43	New Jersey	30.4
32	New Mexico	35.5
50	New York	25.5
8	North Carolina	43.0
38	North Dakota	32.7
13	Ohio	40.6
10	Oklahoma	41.8
23	Oregon	37.8
27	Pennsylvania	37.0
48	Rhode Island	26.8
6	South Carolina	45.5
30	South Dakota	35.8
3	Tennessee	46.0
9	Texas	42.0
20	Utah	38.8
45	Vermont	29.2
22	Virginia	38.2
30	Washington	35.8
11	West Virginia	41.7
36	Wisconsin	33.3
42	Wyoming	31.7

RANK ORDER

RANK	STATE	RATE
1	Alabama	51.6
2	Mississippi	50.6
3	Louisiana	46.0
3	Tennessee	46.0
5	Arkansas	45.6
6	South Carolina	45.5
7	Georgia	44.3
8	North Carolina	43.0
9	Texas	42.0
10	Oklahoma	41.8
11	West Virginia	41.7
12	Delaware	41.6
13	Ohio	40.6
14	Kentucky	40.4
14	Missouri	40.4
16	Maryland	39.7
17	Indiana	39.5
18	Alaska	39.0
18	Michigan	39.0
20	Utah	38.8
21	Kansas	38.6
22	Virginia	38.2
23	Illinois	37.8
23	Oregon	37.8
25	Florida	37.3
26	Idaho	37.2
27	Pennsylvania	37.0
28	California	36.9
29	Nevada	35.9
30	South Dakota	35.8
30	Washington	35.8
32	New Mexico	35.5
33	Colorado	35.2
34	Maine	34.4
35	Hawaii	34.3
36	Wisconsin	33.3
37	Nebraska	33.2
38	North Dakota	32.7
39	Minnesota	32.5
39	Montana	32.5
41	Iowa	32.3
42	Wyoming	31.7
43	New Jersey	30.4
44	Arizona	29.8
45	Vermont	29.2
46	New Hampshire	28.0
47	Massachusetts	27.9
48	Rhode Island	26.8
49	Connecticut	26.3
50	New York	25.5
	District of Columbia	38.4

Source: U.S. Department of Health and Human Services, National Center for Health Statistics
"National Vital Statistics Reports" (Vol. 67, No. 5, 2018, http://www.cdc.gov/nchs/deaths.htm)
*Final data by state of residence. Cerebrovascular diseases include stroke and other disorders of the blood vessels of the brain.
Age-adjusted rates based on the year 2000 standard population.

Deaths by Diseases of the Heart in 2016

National Total = 635,260 Deaths*

ALPHA ORDER

RANK	STATE	DEATHS	% of USA
16	Alabama	12,832	2.0%
50	Alaska	831	0.1%
17	Arizona	11,957	1.9%
26	Arkansas	8,090	1.3%
1	California	61,573	9.7%
29	Colorado	7,277	1.1%
30	Connecticut	7,051	1.1%
45	Delaware	1,974	0.3%
2	Florida	45,659	7.2%
11	Georgia	18,143	2.9%
42	Hawaii	2,488	0.4%
39	Idaho	2,969	0.5%
8	Illinois	25,013	3.9%
15	Indiana	13,952	2.2%
32	Iowa	6,937	1.1%
34	Kansas	5,672	0.9%
23	Kentucky	10,519	1.7%
22	Louisiana	10,943	1.7%
40	Maine	2,907	0.5%
20	Maryland	11,390	1.8%
18	Massachusetts	11,921	1.9%
7	Michigan	25,304	4.0%
28	Minnesota	7,825	1.2%
27	Mississippi	7,865	1.2%
13	Missouri	14,579	2.3%
44	Montana	2,138	0.3%
38	Nebraska	3,322	0.5%
33	Nevada	6,457	1.0%
41	New Hampshire	2,631	0.4%
9	New Jersey	18,597	2.9%
36	New Mexico	3,800	0.6%
3	New York	44,076	6.9%
10	North Carolina	18,266	2.9%
48	North Dakota	1,338	0.2%
6	Ohio	27,410	4.3%
24	Oklahoma	10,209	1.6%
31	Oregon	6,968	1.1%
5	Pennsylvania	31,990	5.0%
43	Rhode Island	2,256	0.4%
25	South Carolina	10,195	1.6%
46	South Dakota	1,729	0.3%
12	Tennessee	15,429	2.4%
4	Texas	43,772	6.9%
37	Utah	3,636	0.6%
47	Vermont	1,366	0.2%
14	Virginia	14,124	2.2%
21	Washington	11,161	1.8%
35	West Virginia	4,767	0.8%
19	Wisconsin	11,526	1.8%
49	Wyoming	1,051	0.2%

RANK ORDER

RANK	STATE	DEATHS	% of USA
1	California	61,573	9.7%
2	Florida	45,659	7.2%
3	New York	44,076	6.9%
4	Texas	43,772	6.9%
5	Pennsylvania	31,990	5.0%
6	Ohio	27,410	4.3%
7	Michigan	25,304	4.0%
8	Illinois	25,013	3.9%
9	New Jersey	18,597	2.9%
10	North Carolina	18,266	2.9%
11	Georgia	18,143	2.9%
12	Tennessee	15,429	2.4%
13	Missouri	14,579	2.3%
14	Virginia	14,124	2.2%
15	Indiana	13,952	2.2%
16	Alabama	12,832	2.0%
17	Arizona	11,957	1.9%
18	Massachusetts	11,921	1.9%
19	Wisconsin	11,526	1.8%
20	Maryland	11,390	1.8%
21	Washington	11,161	1.8%
22	Louisiana	10,943	1.7%
23	Kentucky	10,519	1.7%
24	Oklahoma	10,209	1.6%
25	South Carolina	10,195	1.6%
26	Arkansas	8,090	1.3%
27	Mississippi	7,865	1.2%
28	Minnesota	7,825	1.2%
29	Colorado	7,277	1.1%
30	Connecticut	7,051	1.1%
31	Oregon	6,968	1.1%
32	Iowa	6,937	1.1%
33	Nevada	6,457	1.0%
34	Kansas	5,672	0.9%
35	West Virginia	4,767	0.8%
36	New Mexico	3,800	0.6%
37	Utah	3,636	0.6%
38	Nebraska	3,322	0.5%
39	Idaho	2,969	0.5%
40	Maine	2,907	0.5%
41	New Hampshire	2,631	0.4%
42	Hawaii	2,488	0.4%
43	Rhode Island	2,256	0.4%
44	Montana	2,138	0.3%
45	Delaware	1,974	0.3%
46	South Dakota	1,729	0.3%
47	Vermont	1,366	0.2%
48	North Dakota	1,338	0.2%
49	Wyoming	1,051	0.2%
50	Alaska	831	0.1%
	District of Columbia	1,375	0.2%

Source: U.S. Department of Health and Human Services, National Center for Health Statistics
  "National Vital Statistics Reports" (Vol. 67, No. 5, 2018, http://www.cdc.gov/nchs/deaths.htm)
*Final data by state of residence.

Age-Adjusted Death Rate by Diseases of the Heart in 2016

National Rate = 165.5 Deaths per 100,000 Population*

ALPHA ORDER

RANK ORDER

RANK	STATE	RATE	RANK	STATE	RATE
4	Alabama	222.5	1	Mississippi	233.1
41	Alaska	141.0	2	Oklahoma	228.2
44	Arizona	138.9	3	Arkansas	223.7
3	Arkansas	223.7	4	Alabama	222.5
40	California	143.1	5	Louisiana	213.1
48	Colorado	129.8	6	Nevada	205.9
39	Connecticut	144.3	7	Kentucky	203.0
22	Delaware	163.2	8	Michigan	200.6
38	Florida	146.2	9	Tennessee	198.8
14	Georgia	179.0	10	Missouri	192.1
49	Hawaii	127.0	11	West Virginia	191.0
24	Idaho	160.0	12	Ohio	185.1
19	Illinois	165.7	13	Indiana	180.6
13	Indiana	180.6	14	Georgia	179.0
23	Iowa	162.8	15	New York	177.8
25	Kansas	159.2	16	Pennsylvania	176.2
7	Kentucky	203.0	17	South Carolina	173.8
5	Louisiana	213.1	18	Texas	167.7
37	Maine	149.5	19	Illinois	165.7
21	Maryland	164.3	20	New Jersey	164.7
47	Massachusetts	134.8	21	Maryland	164.3
8	Michigan	200.6	22	Delaware	163.2
50	Minnesota	114.9	23	Iowa	162.8
1	Mississippi	233.1	24	Idaho	160.0
10	Missouri	192.1	25	Kansas	159.2
30	Montana	154.4	26	Vermont	158.8
43	Nebraska	140.3	27	Wyoming	157.8
6	Nevada	205.9	28	North Carolina	155.8
33	New Hampshire	151.1	29	Wisconsin	154.9
20	New Jersey	164.7	30	Montana	154.4
35	New Mexico	150.6	31	South Dakota	153.4
15	New York	177.8	32	Rhode Island	152.4
28	North Carolina	155.8	33	New Hampshire	151.1
42	North Dakota	140.9	34	Virginia	150.7
12	Ohio	185.1	35	New Mexico	150.6
2	Oklahoma	228.2	36	Utah	150.0
46	Oregon	135.0	37	Maine	149.5
16	Pennsylvania	176.2	38	Florida	146.2
32	Rhode Island	152.4	39	Connecticut	144.3
17	South Carolina	173.8	40	California	143.1
31	South Dakota	153.4	41	Alaska	141.0
9	Tennessee	198.8	42	North Dakota	140.9
18	Texas	167.7	43	Nebraska	140.3
36	Utah	150.0	44	Arizona	138.9
26	Vermont	158.8	45	Washington	136.1
34	Virginia	150.7	46	Oregon	135.0
45	Washington	136.1	47	Massachusetts	134.8
11	West Virginia	191.0	48	Colorado	129.8
29	Wisconsin	154.9	49	Hawaii	127.0
27	Wyoming	157.8	50	Minnesota	114.9
				District of Columbia	211.7

Source: U.S. Department of Health and Human Services, National Center for Health Statistics
"National Vital Statistics Reports" (Vol. 67, No. 5, 2018, http://www.cdc.gov/nchs/deaths.htm)
*Final data by state of residence. Age-adjusted rates based on the year 2000 standard population.

Deaths by Suicide in 2016

National Total = 44,965 Suicides*

ALPHA ORDER				RANK ORDER			
RANK	STATE	DEATHS	% of USA	RANK	STATE	DEATHS	% of USA
21	Alabama	788	1.8%	1	California	4,294	9.5%
43	Alaska	193	0.4%	2	Texas	3,488	7.8%
11	Arizona	1,271	2.8%	3	Florida	3,143	7.0%
31	Arkansas	555	1.2%	4	Pennsylvania	1,970	4.4%
1	California	4,294	9.5%	5	Ohio	1,707	3.8%
12	Colorado	1,168	2.6%	6	New York	1,679	3.7%
35	Connecticut	397	0.9%	7	Illinois	1,415	3.1%
49	Delaware	119	0.3%	8	Georgia	1,409	3.1%
3	Florida	3,143	7.0%	9	North Carolina	1,373	3.1%
8	Georgia	1,409	3.1%	10	Michigan	1,364	3.0%
44	Hawaii	174	0.4%	11	Arizona	1,271	2.8%
38	Idaho	351	0.8%	12	Colorado	1,168	2.6%
7	Illinois	1,415	3.1%	13	Virginia	1,166	2.6%
17	Indiana	1,034	2.3%	14	Washington	1,141	2.5%
34	Iowa	451	1.0%	15	Missouri	1,133	2.5%
32	Kansas	514	1.1%	16	Tennessee	1,111	2.5%
23	Kentucky	756	1.7%	17	Indiana	1,034	2.3%
26	Louisiana	677	1.5%	18	Wisconsin	866	1.9%
42	Maine	226	0.5%	19	Oklahoma	822	1.8%
30	Maryland	586	1.3%	20	South Carolina	815	1.8%
28	Massachusetts	631	1.4%	21	Alabama	788	1.8%
10	Michigan	1,364	3.0%	22	Oregon	772	1.7%
24	Minnesota	745	1.7%	23	Kentucky	756	1.7%
36	Mississippi	383	0.9%	24	Minnesota	745	1.7%
15	Missouri	1,133	2.5%	25	New Jersey	687	1.5%
39	Montana	267	0.6%	26	Louisiana	677	1.5%
40	Nebraska	246	0.5%	27	Nevada	650	1.4%
27	Nevada	650	1.4%	28	Massachusetts	631	1.4%
41	New Hampshire	244	0.5%	29	Utah	620	1.4%
25	New Jersey	687	1.5%	30	Maryland	586	1.3%
33	New Mexico	471	1.0%	31	Arkansas	555	1.2%
6	New York	1,679	3.7%	32	Kansas	514	1.1%
9	North Carolina	1,373	3.1%	33	New Mexico	471	1.0%
47	North Dakota	140	0.3%	34	Iowa	451	1.0%
5	Ohio	1,707	3.8%	35	Connecticut	397	0.9%
19	Oklahoma	822	1.8%	36	Mississippi	383	0.9%
22	Oregon	772	1.7%	37	West Virginia	362	0.8%
4	Pennsylvania	1,970	4.4%	38	Idaho	351	0.8%
48	Rhode Island	126	0.3%	39	Montana	267	0.6%
20	South Carolina	815	1.8%	40	Nebraska	246	0.5%
45	South Dakota	163	0.4%	41	New Hampshire	244	0.5%
16	Tennessee	1,111	2.5%	42	Maine	226	0.5%
2	Texas	3,488	7.8%	43	Alaska	193	0.4%
29	Utah	620	1.4%	44	Hawaii	174	0.4%
50	Vermont	118	0.3%	45	South Dakota	163	0.4%
13	Virginia	1,166	2.6%	46	Wyoming	144	0.3%
14	Washington	1,141	2.5%	47	North Dakota	140	0.3%
37	West Virginia	362	0.8%	48	Rhode Island	126	0.3%
18	Wisconsin	866	1.9%	49	Delaware	119	0.3%
46	Wyoming	144	0.3%	50	Vermont	118	0.3%
					District of Columbia	40	0.1%

Source: U.S. Department of Health and Human Services, National Center for Health Statistics
   "National Vital Statistics Reports" (Vol. 67, No. 5, 2018, http://www.cdc.gov/nchs/deaths.htm)
*Final data by state of residence. Also referred to as "Intentional self-harm."

Age-Adjusted Death Rate by Suicide in 2016

National Rate = 13.5 Deaths per 100,000 Population*

ALPHA ORDER

RANK	STATE	RATE
23	Alabama	15.7
2	Alaska	25.8
17	Arizona	17.7
14	Arkansas	18.2
45	California	10.5
9	Colorado	20.5
46	Connecticut	10.1
42	Delaware	11.5
32	Florida	14.0
33	Georgia	13.3
41	Hawaii	12.1
6	Idaho	21.4
44	Illinois	10.7
25	Indiana	15.4
29	Iowa	14.6
15	Kansas	17.9
20	Kentucky	16.8
30	Louisiana	14.2
22	Maine	15.9
47	Maryland	9.4
48	Massachusetts	8.8
33	Michigan	13.3
35	Minnesota	13.2
39	Mississippi	12.7
13	Missouri	18.4
1	Montana	25.9
37	Nebraska	13.1
6	Nevada	21.4
19	New Hampshire	17.2
50	New Jersey	7.2
4	New Mexico	22.5
49	New York	8.1
38	North Carolina	13.0
12	North Dakota	19.0
30	Ohio	14.2
8	Oklahoma	21.0
16	Oregon	17.8
27	Pennsylvania	14.7
43	Rhode Island	11.2
23	South Carolina	15.7
10	South Dakota	20.2
21	Tennessee	16.3
40	Texas	12.6
5	Utah	21.8
18	Vermont	17.3
35	Virginia	13.2
26	Washington	14.9
11	West Virginia	19.3
27	Wisconsin	14.7
3	Wyoming	25.2

RANK ORDER

RANK	STATE	RATE
1	Montana	25.9
2	Alaska	25.8
3	Wyoming	25.2
4	New Mexico	22.5
5	Utah	21.8
6	Idaho	21.4
6	Nevada	21.4
8	Oklahoma	21.0
9	Colorado	20.5
10	South Dakota	20.2
11	West Virginia	19.3
12	North Dakota	19.0
13	Missouri	18.4
14	Arkansas	18.2
15	Kansas	17.9
16	Oregon	17.8
17	Arizona	17.7
18	Vermont	17.3
19	New Hampshire	17.2
20	Kentucky	16.8
21	Tennessee	16.3
22	Maine	15.9
23	Alabama	15.7
23	South Carolina	15.7
25	Indiana	15.4
26	Washington	14.9
27	Pennsylvania	14.7
27	Wisconsin	14.7
29	Iowa	14.6
30	Louisiana	14.2
30	Ohio	14.2
32	Florida	14.0
33	Georgia	13.3
33	Michigan	13.3
35	Minnesota	13.2
35	Virginia	13.2
37	Nebraska	13.1
38	North Carolina	13.0
39	Mississippi	12.7
40	Texas	12.6
41	Hawaii	12.1
42	Delaware	11.5
43	Rhode Island	11.2
44	Illinois	10.7
45	California	10.5
46	Connecticut	10.1
47	Maryland	9.4
48	Massachusetts	8.8
49	New York	8.1
50	New Jersey	7.2
	District of Columbia	5.2

Source: U.S. Department of Health and Human Services, National Center for Health Statistics
   "National Vital Statistics Reports" (Vol. 67, No. 5, 2018, http://www.cdc.gov/nchs/deaths.htm)
*Final data by state of residence. Also referred to as "Intentional self-harm." Age-adjusted rates based on the year 2000 standard population.

Deaths by AIDS in 2016

National Total = 6,160 Deaths*

ALPHA ORDER

RANK	STATE	DEATHS	% of USA
16	Alabama	106	1.7%
43	Alaska	7	0.1%
17	Arizona	97	1.6%
27	Arkansas	48	0.8%
2	California	734	11.9%
29	Colorado	45	0.7%
24	Connecticut	61	1.0%
35	Delaware	17	0.3%
1	Florida	865	14.0%
5	Georgia	348	5.6%
39	Hawaii	14	0.2%
44	Idaho	6	0.1%
10	Illinois	172	2.8%
18	Indiana	95	1.5%
39	Iowa	14	0.2%
37	Kansas	16	0.3%
27	Kentucky	48	0.8%
9	Louisiana	182	3.0%
44	Maine	6	0.1%
8	Maryland	190	3.1%
21	Massachusetts	75	1.2%
19	Michigan	93	1.5%
31	Minnesota	35	0.6%
20	Mississippi	77	1.3%
23	Missouri	65	1.1%
49	Montana	3	0.0%
35	Nebraska	17	0.3%
22	Nevada	68	1.1%
42	New Hampshire	8	0.1%
6	New Jersey	236	3.8%
34	New Mexico	18	0.3%
4	New York	560	9.1%
7	North Carolina	209	3.4%
47	North Dakota	4	0.1%
13	Ohio	120	1.9%
26	Oklahoma	54	0.9%
30	Oregon	38	0.6%
11	Pennsylvania	170	2.8%
41	Rhode Island	13	0.2%
12	South Carolina	152	2.5%
44	South Dakota	6	0.1%
15	Tennessee	112	1.8%
3	Texas	625	10.1%
33	Utah	19	0.3%
47	Vermont	4	0.1%
13	Virginia	120	1.9%
25	Washington	60	1.0%
38	West Virginia	15	0.2%
32	Wisconsin	30	0.5%
50	Wyoming	1	0.0%

RANK ORDER

RANK	STATE	DEATHS	% of USA
1	Florida	865	14.0%
2	California	734	11.9%
3	Texas	625	10.1%
4	New York	560	9.1%
5	Georgia	348	5.6%
6	New Jersey	236	3.8%
7	North Carolina	209	3.4%
8	Maryland	190	3.1%
9	Louisiana	182	3.0%
10	Illinois	172	2.8%
11	Pennsylvania	170	2.8%
12	South Carolina	152	2.5%
13	Ohio	120	1.9%
13	Virginia	120	1.9%
15	Tennessee	112	1.8%
16	Alabama	106	1.7%
17	Arizona	97	1.6%
18	Indiana	95	1.5%
19	Michigan	93	1.5%
20	Mississippi	77	1.3%
21	Massachusetts	75	1.2%
22	Nevada	68	1.1%
23	Missouri	65	1.1%
24	Connecticut	61	1.0%
25	Washington	60	1.0%
26	Oklahoma	54	0.9%
27	Arkansas	48	0.8%
27	Kentucky	48	0.8%
29	Colorado	45	0.7%
30	Oregon	38	0.6%
31	Minnesota	35	0.6%
32	Wisconsin	30	0.5%
33	Utah	19	0.3%
34	New Mexico	18	0.3%
35	Delaware	17	0.3%
35	Nebraska	17	0.3%
37	Kansas	16	0.3%
38	West Virginia	15	0.2%
39	Hawaii	14	0.2%
39	Iowa	14	0.2%
41	Rhode Island	13	0.2%
42	New Hampshire	8	0.1%
43	Alaska	7	0.1%
44	Idaho	6	0.1%
44	Maine	6	0.1%
44	South Dakota	6	0.1%
47	North Dakota	4	0.1%
47	Vermont	4	0.1%
49	Montana	3	0.0%
50	Wyoming	1	0.0%
	District of Columbia	82	1.3%

Source: U.S. Department of Health and Human Services, National Center for Health Statistics
   "National Vital Statistics Reports" (Vol. 67, No. 5, 2018, http://www.cdc.gov/nchs/deaths.htm)
*Final data by state of residence. AIDS is Acquired Immunodeficiency Syndrome. It is a specific group of diseases or
conditions which are indicative of severe immunosuppression related to infection with the Human Immunodeficiency Virus (HIV).

Age-Adjusted Death Rate by AIDS in 2016

National Rate = 1.8 Deaths per 100,000 Population*

ALPHA ORDER			RANK ORDER		
RANK	STATE	RATE	RANK	STATE	RATE
11	Alabama	2.1	1	Louisiana	3.9
NA	Alaska**	NA	2	Florida	3.8
16	Arizona	1.4	3	Georgia	3.2
14	Arkansas	1.6	4	South Carolina	2.9
13	California	1.8	5	Maryland	2.8
28	Colorado	0.8	6	Mississippi	2.7
16	Connecticut	1.4	7	New York	2.5
NA	Delaware**	NA	8	Nevada	2.2
2	Florida	3.8	8	New Jersey	2.2
3	Georgia	3.2	8	Texas	2.2
NA	Hawaii**	NA	11	Alabama	2.1
NA	Idaho**	NA	12	North Carolina	1.9
21	Illinois	1.2	13	California	1.8
16	Indiana	1.4	14	Arkansas	1.6
NA	Iowa**	NA	14	Tennessee	1.6
NA	Kansas**	NA	16	Arizona	1.4
23	Kentucky	1.1	16	Connecticut	1.4
1	Louisiana	3.9	16	Indiana	1.4
NA	Maine**	NA	19	Oklahoma	1.3
5	Maryland	2.8	19	Virginia	1.3
25	Massachusetts	0.9	21	Illinois	1.2
25	Michigan	0.9	21	Pennsylvania	1.2
31	Minnesota	0.6	23	Kentucky	1.1
6	Mississippi	2.7	24	Ohio	1.0
25	Missouri	0.9	25	Massachusetts	0.9
NA	Montana**	NA	25	Michigan	0.9
NA	Nebraska**	NA	25	Missouri	0.9
8	Nevada	2.2	28	Colorado	0.8
NA	New Hampshire**	NA	28	Oregon	0.8
8	New Jersey	2.2	30	Washington	0.7
NA	New Mexico**	NA	31	Minnesota	0.6
7	New York	2.5	32	Wisconsin	0.4
12	North Carolina	1.9	NA	Alaska**	NA
NA	North Dakota**	NA	NA	Delaware**	NA
24	Ohio	1.0	NA	Hawaii**	NA
19	Oklahoma	1.3	NA	Idaho**	NA
28	Oregon	0.8	NA	Iowa**	NA
21	Pennsylvania	1.2	NA	Kansas**	NA
NA	Rhode Island**	NA	NA	Maine**	NA
4	South Carolina	2.9	NA	Montana**	NA
NA	South Dakota**	NA	NA	Nebraska**	NA
14	Tennessee	1.6	NA	New Hampshire**	NA
8	Texas	2.2	NA	New Mexico**	NA
NA	Utah**	NA	NA	North Dakota**	NA
NA	Vermont**	NA	NA	Rhode Island**	NA
19	Virginia	1.3	NA	South Dakota**	NA
30	Washington	0.7	NA	Utah**	NA
NA	West Virginia**	NA	NA	Vermont**	NA
32	Wisconsin	0.4	NA	West Virginia**	NA
NA	Wyoming**	NA	NA	Wyoming**	NA

District of Columbia	12.3

Source: U.S. Department of Health and Human Services, National Center for Health Statistics
"National Vital Statistics Reports" (Vol. 67, No. 5, 2018, http://www.cdc.gov/nchs/deaths.htm)
*Final data by state of residence. AIDS is Acquired Immunodeficiency Syndrome. It is a specific group of diseases or conditions which are indicative of severe immunosuppression related to infection with the Human Immunodeficiency Virus (HIV). Age-adjusted rates based on the year 2000 standard population.
**Insufficient data to determine a reliable rate.

Adult Per Capita Alcohol Consumption in 2016

National Per Capita = 2.6 Gallons Consumed per Adult 21 Years and Older*

ALPHA ORDER

RANK	STATE	PER CAPITA
42	Alabama	2.3
8	Alaska	3.3
25	Arizona	2.6
48	Arkansas	2.0
25	California	2.6
10	Colorado	3.2
21	Connecticut	2.8
2	Delaware	4.2
16	Florida	2.9
44	Georgia	2.2
16	Hawaii	2.9
8	Idaho	3.3
25	Illinois	2.6
32	Indiana	2.5
23	Iowa	2.7
44	Kansas	2.2
44	Kentucky	2.2
16	Louisiana	2.9
12	Maine	3.1
38	Maryland	2.4
16	Massachusetts	2.9
25	Michigan	2.6
12	Minnesota	3.1
32	Mississippi	2.5
21	Missouri	2.8
5	Montana	3.5
32	Nebraska	2.5
3	Nevada	3.9
1	New Hampshire	5.3
25	New Jersey	2.6
25	New Mexico	2.6
32	New York	2.5
38	North Carolina	2.4
4	North Dakota	3.7
42	Ohio	2.3
47	Oklahoma	2.1
12	Oregon	3.1
25	Pennsylvania	2.6
16	Rhode Island	2.9
32	South Carolina	2.5
10	South Dakota	3.2
38	Tennessee	2.4
23	Texas	2.7
50	Utah	1.6
5	Vermont	3.5
38	Virginia	2.4
32	Washington	2.5
48	West Virginia	2.0
7	Wisconsin	3.4
15	Wyoming	3.0

RANK ORDER

RANK	STATE	PER CAPITA
1	New Hampshire	5.3
2	Delaware	4.2
3	Nevada	3.9
4	North Dakota	3.7
5	Montana	3.5
5	Vermont	3.5
7	Wisconsin	3.4
8	Alaska	3.3
8	Idaho	3.3
10	Colorado	3.2
10	South Dakota	3.2
12	Maine	3.1
12	Minnesota	3.1
12	Oregon	3.1
15	Wyoming	3.0
16	Florida	2.9
16	Hawaii	2.9
16	Louisiana	2.9
16	Massachusetts	2.9
16	Rhode Island	2.9
21	Connecticut	2.8
21	Missouri	2.8
23	Iowa	2.7
23	Texas	2.7
25	Arizona	2.6
25	California	2.6
25	Illinois	2.6
25	Michigan	2.6
25	New Jersey	2.6
25	New Mexico	2.6
25	Pennsylvania	2.6
32	Indiana	2.5
32	Mississippi	2.5
32	Nebraska	2.5
32	New York	2.5
32	South Carolina	2.5
32	Washington	2.5
38	Maryland	2.4
38	North Carolina	2.4
38	Tennessee	2.4
38	Virginia	2.4
42	Alabama	2.3
42	Ohio	2.3
44	Georgia	2.2
44	Kansas	2.2
44	Kentucky	2.2
47	Oklahoma	2.1
48	Arkansas	2.0
48	West Virginia	2.0
50	Utah	1.6

| | District of Columbia | 4.2 |

Source: CQ Press using data from U.S. Dept of Health and Human Services, National Institute on Alcohol Abuse and Alcoholism "Apparent Per Capita Alcohol Consumption, 1977-2016" (https://pubs.niaaa.nih.gov/publications/surveillance.htm)

*This is apparent consumption of actual alcohol, not entire volume of an alcoholic beverage (for example, wine is roughly 11% absolute alcohol content). Apparent consumption is based on several sources which together approximate sales but do not actually measure consumption. Accordingly, figures for some states may be skewed by purchases by nonresidents.

Percent of Adults Who Smoke: 2017

National Median = 17.1% of Adults*

ALPHA ORDER

RANK	STATE	PERCENT
10	Alabama	20.9
9	Alaska	21.0
35	Arizona	15.6
5	Arkansas	22.3
49	California	11.3
39	Colorado	14.6
48	Connecticut	12.7
27	Delaware	17.0
29	Florida	16.1
20	Georgia	17.5
47	Hawaii	12.8
41	Idaho	14.4
36	Illinois	15.5
7	Indiana	21.8
26	Iowa	17.1
22	Kansas	17.4
2	Kentucky	24.6
3	Louisiana	23.1
23	Maine	17.3
43	Maryland	13.9
44	Massachusetts	13.7
13	Michigan	19.3
40	Minnesota	14.5
6	Mississippi	22.2
11	Missouri	20.8
24	Montana	17.2
37	Nebraska	15.4
19	Nevada	17.6
33	New Hampshire	15.7
44	New Jersey	13.7
20	New Mexico	17.5
42	New York	14.1
24	North Carolina	17.2
18	North Dakota	18.3
8	Ohio	21.1
12	Oklahoma	20.2
29	Oregon	16.1
15	Pennsylvania	18.8
38	Rhode Island	15.0
15	South Carolina	18.8
13	South Dakota	19.3
4	Tennessee	22.6
33	Texas	15.7
50	Utah	8.9
32	Vermont	15.8
28	Virginia	16.4
46	Washington	13.5
1	West Virginia	26.0
31	Wisconsin	16.0
17	Wyoming	18.7

RANK ORDER

RANK	STATE	PERCENT
1	West Virginia	26.0
2	Kentucky	24.6
3	Louisiana	23.1
4	Tennessee	22.6
5	Arkansas	22.3
6	Mississippi	22.2
7	Indiana	21.8
8	Ohio	21.1
9	Alaska	21.0
10	Alabama	20.9
11	Missouri	20.8
12	Oklahoma	20.2
13	Michigan	19.3
13	South Dakota	19.3
15	Pennsylvania	18.8
15	South Carolina	18.8
17	Wyoming	18.7
18	North Dakota	18.3
19	Nevada	17.6
20	Georgia	17.5
20	New Mexico	17.5
22	Kansas	17.4
23	Maine	17.3
24	Montana	17.2
24	North Carolina	17.2
26	Iowa	17.1
27	Delaware	17.0
28	Virginia	16.4
29	Florida	16.1
29	Oregon	16.1
31	Wisconsin	16.0
32	Vermont	15.8
33	New Hampshire	15.7
33	Texas	15.7
35	Arizona	15.6
36	Illinois	15.5
37	Nebraska	15.4
38	Rhode Island	15.0
39	Colorado	14.6
40	Minnesota	14.5
41	Idaho	14.4
42	New York	14.1
43	Maryland	13.9
44	Massachusetts	13.7
44	New Jersey	13.7
46	Washington	13.5
47	Hawaii	12.8
48	Connecticut	12.7
49	California	11.3
50	Utah	8.9
	District of Columbia	14.4

Source: U.S. Department of Health and Human Services, Centers for Disease Control and Prevention
   "Behavioral Risk Factor Surveillance Summary Prevalence Data" (https://www.cdc.gov/brfss/brfssprevalence/index.html)
*Persons 18 and older who have smoked more than 100 cigarettes during their lifetime and who currently smoke every day or some days.

Percent of Adults Overweight or Obese: 2017

National Median = 66.6% of Adults*

ALPHA ORDER				RANK ORDER		
RANK	STATE	PERCENT		RANK	STATE	PERCENT
4	Alabama	70.2		1	West Virginia	71.7
24	Alaska	66.8		2	Oklahoma	70.6
36	Arizona	64.8		3	Arkansas	70.4
3	Arkansas	70.4		4	Alabama	70.2
47	California	60.9		5	Iowa	70.1
50	Colorado	58.7		6	Louisiana	70.0
40	Connecticut	63.3		7	Mississippi	69.9
11	Delaware	68.5		8	North Dakota	69.4
39	Florida	64.0		8	Texas	69.4
30	Georgia	65.3		10	Nebraska	69.0
49	Hawaii	58.8		11	Delaware	68.5
27	Idaho	65.9		12	Tennessee	68.2
28	Illinois	65.8		13	South Carolina	68.1
14	Indiana	68.0		14	Indiana	68.0
5	Iowa	70.1		14	Ohio	68.0
19	Kansas	67.3		16	Missouri	67.9
17	Kentucky	67.8		17	Kentucky	67.8
6	Louisiana	70.0		17	South Dakota	67.8
32	Maine	65.0		19	Kansas	67.3
26	Maryland	66.2		19	Wisconsin	67.3
45	Massachusetts	61.5		21	Michigan	67.2
21	Michigan	67.2		22	Pennsylvania	67.1
33	Minnesota	64.9		23	North Carolina	66.9
7	Mississippi	69.9		24	Alaska	66.8
16	Missouri	67.9		25	Virginia	66.4
43	Montana	62.3		26	Maryland	66.2
10	Nebraska	69.0		27	Idaho	65.9
29	Nevada	65.7		28	Illinois	65.8
33	New Hampshire	64.9		29	Nevada	65.7
42	New Jersey	62.6		30	Georgia	65.3
31	New Mexico	65.2		31	New Mexico	65.2
46	New York	61.3		32	Maine	65.0
23	North Carolina	66.9		33	Minnesota	64.9
8	North Dakota	69.4		33	New Hampshire	64.9
14	Ohio	68.0		33	Rhode Island	64.9
2	Oklahoma	70.6		36	Arizona	64.8
38	Oregon	64.5		37	Wyoming	64.7
22	Pennsylvania	67.1		38	Oregon	64.5
33	Rhode Island	64.9		39	Florida	64.0
13	South Carolina	68.1		40	Connecticut	63.3
17	South Dakota	67.8		41	Vermont	62.7
12	Tennessee	68.2		42	New Jersey	62.6
8	Texas	69.4		43	Montana	62.3
48	Utah	60.6		44	Washington	62.2
41	Vermont	62.7		45	Massachusetts	61.5
25	Virginia	66.4		46	New York	61.3
44	Washington	62.2		47	California	60.9
1	West Virginia	71.7		48	Utah	60.6
19	Wisconsin	67.3		49	Hawaii	58.8
37	Wyoming	64.7		50	Colorado	58.7

District of Columbia   54.1

Source: CQ Press using data from U.S. Department of Health and Human Services, Centers for Disease Control and Prevention "Behavioral Risk Factor Surveillance Summary Prevalence Data" (https://www.cdc.gov/brfss/brfssprevalence/index.html)
*Persons 18 and older. Overweight is defined as a Body Mass Index (BMI) of 25.0 to 29.9 regardless of sex. Obese is a BMI of 30.0 or greater. BMI is a ratio of height to weight. As an example, a person 5' 8" and weighing 165 pounds has a BMI of 25. The same height at 197 pounds has a BMI of 30.

Percent of Children Aged 19 to 35 Months Fully Immunized in 2017

National Percent = 70.4%*

ALPHA ORDER				RANK ORDER		
RANK	STATE	PERCENT		RANK	STATE	PERCENT
21	Alabama	71.2		1	Massachusetts	82.1
32	Alaska	69.5		2	Tennessee	79.3
44	Arizona	66.5		3	New Hampshire	78.9
34	Arkansas	69.4		4	North Dakota	78.8
39	California	68.6		5	Nebraska	77.9
23	Colorado	71.0		6	Delaware	77.1
10	Connecticut	75.3		6	Virginia	77.1
6	Delaware	77.1		8	Florida	76.2
8	Florida	76.2		9	Illinois	75.4
50	Georgia	65.6		10	Connecticut	75.3
31	Hawaii	69.8		11	Maryland	75.2
36	Idaho	69.2		12	South Dakota	74.7
9	Illinois	75.4		12	West Virginia	74.7
46	Indiana	66.3		14	Rhode Island	74.4
16	Iowa	72.8		15	Vermont	74.0
32	Kansas	69.5		16	Iowa	72.8
23	Kentucky	71.0		17	Maine	72.7
28	Louisiana	70.0		18	Wyoming	72.0
17	Maine	72.7		19	New Mexico	71.9
11	Maryland	75.2		20	Nevada	71.3
1	Massachusetts	82.1		21	Alabama	71.2
29	Michigan	69.9		21	Missouri	71.2
48	Minnesota	66.1		23	Colorado	71.0
38	Mississippi	68.7		23	Kentucky	71.0
21	Missouri	71.2		25	North Carolina	70.9
47	Montana	66.2		26	Pennsylvania	70.4
5	Nebraska	77.9		27	Oregon	70.3
20	Nevada	71.3		28	Louisiana	70.0
3	New Hampshire	78.9		29	Michigan	69.9
35	New Jersey	69.3		29	Washington	69.9
19	New Mexico	71.9		31	Hawaii	69.8
42	New York	67.5		32	Alaska	69.5
25	North Carolina	70.9		32	Kansas	69.5
4	North Dakota	78.8		34	Arkansas	69.4
45	Ohio	66.4		35	New Jersey	69.3
43	Oklahoma	67.3		36	Idaho	69.2
27	Oregon	70.3		36	Wisconsin	69.2
26	Pennsylvania	70.4		38	Mississippi	68.7
14	Rhode Island	74.4		39	California	68.6
49	South Carolina	66.0		40	Utah	67.9
12	South Dakota	74.7		41	Texas	67.8
2	Tennessee	79.3		42	New York	67.5
41	Texas	67.8		43	Oklahoma	67.3
40	Utah	67.9		44	Arizona	66.5
15	Vermont	74.0		45	Ohio	66.4
6	Virginia	77.1		46	Indiana	66.3
29	Washington	69.9		47	Montana	66.2
12	West Virginia	74.7		48	Minnesota	66.1
36	Wisconsin	69.2		49	South Carolina	66.0
18	Wyoming	72.0		50	Georgia	65.6

District of Columbia   74.0

Source: U.S. Department of Health and Human Services, Centers for Disease Control and Prevention
"Vaccination Coverage Among Children" (MMWR, Vol. 67, No. 40, October 12, 2018, https://www.cdc.gov/mmwr/)
*Fully immunized (4:3:1:3:3:1:4 series) children received four doses of DTaP (Diphtheria, Tetanus Toxoids, Pertussis [Whooping Cough]), three doses of Poliovirus Vaccine, one dose of MCV (Measles-Containing Vaccine), full series (3 or 4 doses depending on product type) of Hib (Haemophilus influenzae type b), three doses of Hepatitis B vaccine, one dose of Varicella (chickenpox) vaccine, and four doses of PCV (pneumococcal conjugate vaccine).

XII. Households and Housing

Households in 2017

National Total = 120,062,818 Households*

ALPHA ORDER

RANK	STATE	HOUSEHOLDS	% of USA
24	Alabama	1,841,665	1.5%
49	Alaska	250,741	0.2%
17	Arizona	2,552,972	2.1%
31	Arkansas	1,153,082	1.0%
1	California	13,005,097	10.8%
22	Colorado	2,139,207	1.8%
29	Connecticut	1,356,762	1.1%
45	Delaware	357,937	0.3%
3	Florida	7,689,964	6.4%
10	Georgia	3,745,074	3.1%
42	Hawaii	458,078	0.4%
39	Idaho	625,135	0.5%
6	Illinois	4,808,672	4.0%
16	Indiana	2,557,299	2.1%
30	Iowa	1,257,505	1.0%
32	Kansas	1,128,983	0.9%
26	Kentucky	1,725,034	1.4%
25	Louisiana	1,737,123	1.4%
40	Maine	540,959	0.5%
20	Maryland	2,207,343	1.8%
14	Massachusetts	2,604,954	2.2%
9	Michigan	3,930,017	3.3%
21	Minnesota	2,162,211	1.8%
34	Mississippi	1,091,980	0.9%
18	Missouri	2,385,135	2.0%
43	Montana	423,091	0.4%
37	Nebraska	754,490	0.6%
33	Nevada	1,094,613	0.9%
41	New Hampshire	528,700	0.4%
11	New Jersey	3,218,798	2.7%
36	New Mexico	767,705	0.6%
4	New York	7,304,332	6.1%
8	North Carolina	3,955,069	3.3%
47	North Dakota	316,306	0.3%
7	Ohio	4,667,192	3.9%
28	Oklahoma	1,470,364	1.2%
27	Oregon	1,603,635	1.3%
5	Pennsylvania	5,008,751	4.2%
44	Rhode Island	408,748	0.3%
23	South Carolina	1,905,100	1.6%
46	South Dakota	344,260	0.3%
15	Tennessee	2,588,655	2.2%
2	Texas	9,623,874	8.0%
35	Utah	975,448	0.8%
48	Vermont	256,629	0.2%
12	Virginia	3,120,880	2.6%
13	Washington	2,840,377	2.4%
38	West Virginia	715,308	0.6%
19	Wisconsin	2,350,293	2.0%
50	Wyoming	225,796	0.2%

RANK ORDER

RANK	STATE	HOUSEHOLDS	% of USA
1	California	13,005,097	10.8%
2	Texas	9,623,874	8.0%
3	Florida	7,689,964	6.4%
4	New York	7,304,332	6.1%
5	Pennsylvania	5,008,751	4.2%
6	Illinois	4,808,672	4.0%
7	Ohio	4,667,192	3.9%
8	North Carolina	3,955,069	3.3%
9	Michigan	3,930,017	3.3%
10	Georgia	3,745,074	3.1%
11	New Jersey	3,218,798	2.7%
12	Virginia	3,120,880	2.6%
13	Washington	2,840,377	2.4%
14	Massachusetts	2,604,954	2.2%
15	Tennessee	2,588,655	2.2%
16	Indiana	2,557,299	2.1%
17	Arizona	2,552,972	2.1%
18	Missouri	2,385,135	2.0%
19	Wisconsin	2,350,293	2.0%
20	Maryland	2,207,343	1.8%
21	Minnesota	2,162,211	1.8%
22	Colorado	2,139,207	1.8%
23	South Carolina	1,905,100	1.6%
24	Alabama	1,841,665	1.5%
25	Louisiana	1,737,123	1.4%
26	Kentucky	1,725,034	1.4%
27	Oregon	1,603,635	1.3%
28	Oklahoma	1,470,364	1.2%
29	Connecticut	1,356,762	1.1%
30	Iowa	1,257,505	1.0%
31	Arkansas	1,153,082	1.0%
32	Kansas	1,128,983	0.9%
33	Nevada	1,094,613	0.9%
34	Mississippi	1,091,980	0.9%
35	Utah	975,448	0.8%
36	New Mexico	767,705	0.6%
37	Nebraska	754,490	0.6%
38	West Virginia	715,308	0.6%
39	Idaho	625,135	0.5%
40	Maine	540,959	0.5%
41	New Hampshire	528,700	0.4%
42	Hawaii	458,078	0.4%
43	Montana	423,091	0.4%
44	Rhode Island	408,748	0.3%
45	Delaware	357,937	0.3%
46	South Dakota	344,260	0.3%
47	North Dakota	316,306	0.3%
48	Vermont	256,629	0.2%
49	Alaska	250,741	0.2%
50	Wyoming	225,796	0.2%
	District of Columbia	281,475	0.2%

Source: U.S. Bureau of the Census
   "2017 American Community Survey-Table CP02" (https://www.census.gov/programs-surveys/acs/)
*A household includes all persons who occupy a housing unit. A household consists of a single family, one person living alone,
two or more families living together, or any other group of related or unrelated persons who share living arrangements.

Persons per Household in 2017

National Rate = 2.65 Persons per Household*

ALPHA ORDER			RANK ORDER		
RANK	STATE	PERSONS	RANK	STATE	PERSONS
21	Alabama	2.58	1	Utah	3.13
5	Alaska	2.84	2	Hawaii	3.02
10	Arizona	2.69	3	California	2.98
27	Arkansas	2.53	4	Texas	2.88
3	California	2.98	5	Alaska	2.84
22	Colorado	2.57	6	New Jersey	2.74
24	Connecticut	2.56	7	Georgia	2.72
17	Delaware	2.62	8	Idaho	2.70
12	Florida	2.67	8	Nevada	2.70
7	Georgia	2.72	10	Arizona	2.69
2	Hawaii	3.02	11	Maryland	2.68
8	Idaho	2.70	12	Florida	2.67
19	Illinois	2.60	13	New Mexico	2.66
27	Indiana	2.53	14	Mississippi	2.65
45	Iowa	2.42	15	New York	2.64
33	Kansas	2.51	15	Virginia	2.64
33	Kentucky	2.51	17	Delaware	2.62
17	Louisiana	2.62	17	Louisiana	2.62
47	Maine	2.40	19	Illinois	2.60
11	Maryland	2.68	19	Oklahoma	2.60
26	Massachusetts	2.54	21	Alabama	2.58
38	Michigan	2.48	22	Colorado	2.57
32	Minnesota	2.52	22	South Carolina	2.57
14	Mississippi	2.65	24	Connecticut	2.56
36	Missouri	2.49	24	Washington	2.56
46	Montana	2.41	26	Massachusetts	2.54
38	Nebraska	2.48	27	Arkansas	2.53
8	Nevada	2.70	27	Indiana	2.53
42	New Hampshire	2.46	27	North Carolina	2.53
6	New Jersey	2.74	27	Oregon	2.53
13	New Mexico	2.66	27	Tennessee	2.53
15	New York	2.64	32	Minnesota	2.52
27	North Carolina	2.53	33	Kansas	2.51
50	North Dakota	2.31	33	Kentucky	2.51
43	Ohio	2.43	35	Wyoming	2.50
19	Oklahoma	2.60	36	Missouri	2.49
27	Oregon	2.53	36	Rhode Island	2.49
40	Pennsylvania	2.47	38	Michigan	2.48
36	Rhode Island	2.49	38	Nebraska	2.48
22	South Carolina	2.57	40	Pennsylvania	2.47
43	South Dakota	2.43	40	West Virginia	2.47
27	Tennessee	2.53	42	New Hampshire	2.46
4	Texas	2.88	43	Ohio	2.43
1	Utah	3.13	43	South Dakota	2.43
49	Vermont	2.33	45	Iowa	2.42
15	Virginia	2.64	46	Montana	2.41
24	Washington	2.56	47	Maine	2.40
40	West Virginia	2.47	47	Wisconsin	2.40
47	Wisconsin	2.40	49	Vermont	2.33
35	Wyoming	2.50	50	North Dakota	2.31
				District of Columbia	2.32

Source: U.S. Bureau of the Census
  "2017 American Community Survey-Table CP02" (https://www.census.gov/programs-surveys/acs/)
*A household includes all persons who occupy a housing unit. A household consists of a single family, one person living alone, two or more families living together, or any other group of related or unrelated persons who share living arrangements.

Percent of Households with One Person in 2017

National Percent = 27.9% of Households*

<table>
<tr><td colspan="3">ALPHA ORDER</td><td colspan="3">RANK ORDER</td></tr>
<tr><th>RANK</th><th>STATE</th><th>PERCENT</th><th>RANK</th><th>STATE</th><th>PERCENT</th></tr>
<tr><td>12</td><td>Alabama</td><td>29.9</td><td>1</td><td>Rhode Island</td><td>32.3</td></tr>
<tr><td>46</td><td>Alaska</td><td>25.3</td><td>2</td><td>New Mexico</td><td>32.0</td></tr>
<tr><td>35</td><td>Arizona</td><td>27.8</td><td>3</td><td>North Dakota</td><td>31.7</td></tr>
<tr><td>21</td><td>Arkansas</td><td>29.1</td><td>4</td><td>South Dakota</td><td>31.5</td></tr>
<tr><td>49</td><td>California</td><td>24.0</td><td>5</td><td>Vermont</td><td>31.0</td></tr>
<tr><td>40</td><td>Colorado</td><td>27.1</td><td>6</td><td>Louisiana</td><td>30.7</td></tr>
<tr><td>22</td><td>Connecticut</td><td>29.0</td><td>7</td><td>Maine</td><td>30.5</td></tr>
<tr><td>36</td><td>Delaware</td><td>27.7</td><td>8</td><td>Montana</td><td>30.4</td></tr>
<tr><td>26</td><td>Florida</td><td>28.8</td><td>8</td><td>Pennsylvania</td><td>30.4</td></tr>
<tr><td>41</td><td>Georgia</td><td>26.7</td><td>10</td><td>Ohio</td><td>30.3</td></tr>
<tr><td>48</td><td>Hawaii</td><td>24.4</td><td>11</td><td>Mississippi</td><td>30.0</td></tr>
<tr><td>38</td><td>Idaho</td><td>27.5</td><td>12</td><td>Alabama</td><td>29.9</td></tr>
<tr><td>14</td><td>Illinois</td><td>29.7</td><td>12</td><td>West Virginia</td><td>29.9</td></tr>
<tr><td>24</td><td>Indiana</td><td>28.9</td><td>14</td><td>Illinois</td><td>29.7</td></tr>
<tr><td>19</td><td>Iowa</td><td>29.2</td><td>14</td><td>New York</td><td>29.7</td></tr>
<tr><td>22</td><td>Kansas</td><td>29.0</td><td>16</td><td>Michigan</td><td>29.6</td></tr>
<tr><td>27</td><td>Kentucky</td><td>28.6</td><td>17</td><td>Missouri</td><td>29.5</td></tr>
<tr><td>6</td><td>Louisiana</td><td>30.7</td><td>17</td><td>Wisconsin</td><td>29.5</td></tr>
<tr><td>7</td><td>Maine</td><td>30.5</td><td>19</td><td>Iowa</td><td>29.2</td></tr>
<tr><td>39</td><td>Maryland</td><td>27.4</td><td>19</td><td>Nebraska</td><td>29.2</td></tr>
<tr><td>27</td><td>Massachusetts</td><td>28.6</td><td>21</td><td>Arkansas</td><td>29.1</td></tr>
<tr><td>16</td><td>Michigan</td><td>29.6</td><td>22</td><td>Connecticut</td><td>29.0</td></tr>
<tr><td>32</td><td>Minnesota</td><td>28.4</td><td>22</td><td>Kansas</td><td>29.0</td></tr>
<tr><td>11</td><td>Mississippi</td><td>30.0</td><td>24</td><td>Indiana</td><td>28.9</td></tr>
<tr><td>17</td><td>Missouri</td><td>29.5</td><td>24</td><td>South Carolina</td><td>28.9</td></tr>
<tr><td>8</td><td>Montana</td><td>30.4</td><td>26</td><td>Florida</td><td>28.8</td></tr>
<tr><td>19</td><td>Nebraska</td><td>29.2</td><td>27</td><td>Kentucky</td><td>28.6</td></tr>
<tr><td>34</td><td>Nevada</td><td>28.1</td><td>27</td><td>Massachusetts</td><td>28.6</td></tr>
<tr><td>44</td><td>New Hampshire</td><td>26.2</td><td>27</td><td>North Carolina</td><td>28.6</td></tr>
<tr><td>45</td><td>New Jersey</td><td>25.4</td><td>30</td><td>Oklahoma</td><td>28.5</td></tr>
<tr><td>2</td><td>New Mexico</td><td>32.0</td><td>30</td><td>Wyoming</td><td>28.5</td></tr>
<tr><td>14</td><td>New York</td><td>29.7</td><td>32</td><td>Minnesota</td><td>28.4</td></tr>
<tr><td>27</td><td>North Carolina</td><td>28.6</td><td>33</td><td>Tennessee</td><td>28.3</td></tr>
<tr><td>3</td><td>North Dakota</td><td>31.7</td><td>34</td><td>Nevada</td><td>28.1</td></tr>
<tr><td>10</td><td>Ohio</td><td>30.3</td><td>35</td><td>Arizona</td><td>27.8</td></tr>
<tr><td>30</td><td>Oklahoma</td><td>28.5</td><td>36</td><td>Delaware</td><td>27.7</td></tr>
<tr><td>36</td><td>Oregon</td><td>27.7</td><td>36</td><td>Oregon</td><td>27.7</td></tr>
<tr><td>8</td><td>Pennsylvania</td><td>30.4</td><td>38</td><td>Idaho</td><td>27.5</td></tr>
<tr><td>1</td><td>Rhode Island</td><td>32.3</td><td>39</td><td>Maryland</td><td>27.4</td></tr>
<tr><td>24</td><td>South Carolina</td><td>28.9</td><td>40</td><td>Colorado</td><td>27.1</td></tr>
<tr><td>4</td><td>South Dakota</td><td>31.5</td><td>41</td><td>Georgia</td><td>26.7</td></tr>
<tr><td>33</td><td>Tennessee</td><td>28.3</td><td>42</td><td>Virginia</td><td>26.6</td></tr>
<tr><td>47</td><td>Texas</td><td>25.0</td><td>43</td><td>Washington</td><td>26.5</td></tr>
<tr><td>50</td><td>Utah</td><td>19.6</td><td>44</td><td>New Hampshire</td><td>26.2</td></tr>
<tr><td>5</td><td>Vermont</td><td>31.0</td><td>45</td><td>New Jersey</td><td>25.4</td></tr>
<tr><td>42</td><td>Virginia</td><td>26.6</td><td>46</td><td>Alaska</td><td>25.3</td></tr>
<tr><td>43</td><td>Washington</td><td>26.5</td><td>47</td><td>Texas</td><td>25.0</td></tr>
<tr><td>12</td><td>West Virginia</td><td>29.9</td><td>48</td><td>Hawaii</td><td>24.4</td></tr>
<tr><td>17</td><td>Wisconsin</td><td>29.5</td><td>49</td><td>California</td><td>24.0</td></tr>
<tr><td>30</td><td>Wyoming</td><td>28.5</td><td>50</td><td>Utah</td><td>19.6</td></tr>
<tr><td></td><td></td><td></td><td></td><td>District of Columbia</td><td>45.2</td></tr>
</table>

Source: U.S. Bureau of the Census
    "2017 American Community Survey-Table CP02" (https://www.census.gov/programs-surveys/acs/)
*A household includes all persons who occupy a housing unit. A household consists of a single family, one person living alone, two or more families living together, or any other group of related or unrelated persons who share living arrangements.

Percent of Households Headed by Married Couples in 2017

National Percent = 48.2% of Households*

ALPHA ORDER

RANK	STATE	PERCENT
43	Alabama	46.5
17	Alaska	49.4
37	Arizona	47.3
30	Arkansas	47.9
16	California	49.6
15	Colorado	49.7
30	Connecticut	47.9
17	Delaware	49.4
41	Florida	46.7
32	Georgia	47.8
7	Hawaii	50.9
2	Idaho	54.1
36	Illinois	47.4
27	Indiana	48.2
12	Iowa	50.5
10	Kansas	50.7
22	Kentucky	48.6
50	Louisiana	42.8
19	Maine	48.8
33	Maryland	47.7
40	Massachusetts	47.0
39	Michigan	47.2
6	Minnesota	51.2
47	Mississippi	44.2
33	Missouri	47.7
13	Montana	50.4
7	Nebraska	50.9
46	Nevada	44.9
3	New Hampshire	52.1
5	New Jersey	51.4
49	New Mexico	42.9
48	New York	44.0
27	North Carolina	48.2
26	North Dakota	48.3
44	Ohio	45.8
29	Oklahoma	48.0
20	Oregon	48.7
35	Pennsylvania	47.5
45	Rhode Island	45.5
37	South Carolina	47.3
20	South Dakota	48.7
23	Tennessee	48.5
10	Texas	50.7
1	Utah	60.7
41	Vermont	46.7
7	Virginia	50.9
14	Washington	49.9
25	West Virginia	48.4
23	Wisconsin	48.5
4	Wyoming	51.6

RANK ORDER

RANK	STATE	PERCENT
1	Utah	60.7
2	Idaho	54.1
3	New Hampshire	52.1
4	Wyoming	51.6
5	New Jersey	51.4
6	Minnesota	51.2
7	Hawaii	50.9
7	Nebraska	50.9
7	Virginia	50.9
10	Kansas	50.7
10	Texas	50.7
12	Iowa	50.5
13	Montana	50.4
14	Washington	49.9
15	Colorado	49.7
16	California	49.6
17	Alaska	49.4
17	Delaware	49.4
19	Maine	48.8
20	Oregon	48.7
20	South Dakota	48.7
22	Kentucky	48.6
23	Tennessee	48.5
23	Wisconsin	48.5
25	West Virginia	48.4
26	North Dakota	48.3
27	Indiana	48.2
27	North Carolina	48.2
29	Oklahoma	48.0
30	Arkansas	47.9
30	Connecticut	47.9
32	Georgia	47.8
33	Maryland	47.7
33	Missouri	47.7
35	Pennsylvania	47.5
36	Illinois	47.4
37	Arizona	47.3
37	South Carolina	47.3
39	Michigan	47.2
40	Massachusetts	47.0
41	Florida	46.7
41	Vermont	46.7
43	Alabama	46.5
44	Ohio	45.8
45	Rhode Island	45.5
46	Nevada	44.9
47	Mississippi	44.2
48	New York	44.0
49	New Mexico	42.9
50	Louisiana	42.8
	District of Columbia	25.1

Source: U.S. Bureau of the Census

"2017 American Community Survey-Table CP02" (https://www.census.gov/programs-surveys/acs/)

*A household includes all persons who occupy a housing unit. A household consists of a single family, one person living alone, two or more families living together, or any other group of related or unrelated persons who share living arrangements. Includes married same-sex couple households.

Percent of Households Headed by Single Mothers in 2017

National Percent = 6.5% of Households*

ALPHA ORDER

RANK	STATE	PERCENT
4	Alabama	7.8
17	Alaska	6.6
19	Arizona	6.4
8	Arkansas	7.1
24	California	6.2
43	Colorado	5.0
24	Connecticut	6.2
28	Delaware	6.1
28	Florida	6.1
3	Georgia	8.2
45	Hawaii	4.9
40	Idaho	5.3
19	Illinois	6.4
10	Indiana	6.9
37	Iowa	5.5
28	Kansas	6.1
21	Kentucky	6.3
2	Louisiana	8.3
48	Maine	4.6
14	Maryland	6.7
24	Massachusetts	6.2
21	Michigan	6.3
39	Minnesota	5.4
1	Mississippi	8.8
18	Missouri	6.5
50	Montana	4.0
34	Nebraska	5.9
10	Nevada	6.9
47	New Hampshire	4.7
24	New Jersey	6.2
7	New Mexico	7.3
14	New York	6.7
13	North Carolina	6.8
48	North Dakota	4.6
10	Ohio	6.9
8	Oklahoma	7.1
37	Oregon	5.5
32	Pennsylvania	6.0
21	Rhode Island	6.3
6	South Carolina	7.6
36	South Dakota	5.6
14	Tennessee	6.7
5	Texas	7.7
43	Utah	5.0
45	Vermont	4.9
32	Virginia	6.0
41	Washington	5.2
42	West Virginia	5.1
28	Wisconsin	6.1
35	Wyoming	5.8

RANK ORDER

RANK	STATE	PERCENT
1	Mississippi	8.8
2	Louisiana	8.3
3	Georgia	8.2
4	Alabama	7.8
5	Texas	7.7
6	South Carolina	7.6
7	New Mexico	7.3
8	Arkansas	7.1
8	Oklahoma	7.1
10	Indiana	6.9
10	Nevada	6.9
10	Ohio	6.9
13	North Carolina	6.8
14	Maryland	6.7
14	New York	6.7
14	Tennessee	6.7
17	Alaska	6.6
18	Missouri	6.5
19	Arizona	6.4
19	Illinois	6.4
21	Kentucky	6.3
21	Michigan	6.3
21	Rhode Island	6.3
24	California	6.2
24	Connecticut	6.2
24	Massachusetts	6.2
24	New Jersey	6.2
28	Delaware	6.1
28	Florida	6.1
28	Kansas	6.1
28	Wisconsin	6.1
32	Pennsylvania	6.0
32	Virginia	6.0
34	Nebraska	5.9
35	Wyoming	5.8
36	South Dakota	5.6
37	Iowa	5.5
37	Oregon	5.5
39	Minnesota	5.4
40	Idaho	5.3
41	Washington	5.2
42	West Virginia	5.1
43	Colorado	5.0
43	Utah	5.0
45	Hawaii	4.9
45	Vermont	4.9
47	New Hampshire	4.7
48	Maine	4.6
48	North Dakota	4.6
50	Montana	4.0
	District of Columbia	6.1

Source: U.S. Bureau of the Census
   "2017 American Community Survey-Table CP02" (https://www.census.gov/programs-surveys/acs/)
*No spouse present in household with children under 18 years old. A household includes all persons who occupy a housing unit.
A household consists of a single family, one person living alone, two or more families living together, or any other group of
related or unrelated persons who share living arrangements.

Percent of Households Headed by Single Fathers in 2017

National Percent = 2.3% of Households*

RANK	STATE	PERCENT
49	Alabama	1.7
1	Alaska	3.3
9	Arizona	2.5
21	Arkansas	2.3
4	California	2.6
12	Colorado	2.4
38	Connecticut	2.1
32	Delaware	2.2
32	Florida	2.2
42	Georgia	2.0
38	Hawaii	2.1
21	Idaho	2.3
38	Illinois	2.1
4	Indiana	2.6
4	Iowa	2.6
12	Kansas	2.4
12	Kentucky	2.4
12	Louisiana	2.4
12	Maine	2.4
42	Maryland	2.0
50	Massachusetts	1.6
12	Michigan	2.4
21	Minnesota	2.3
32	Mississippi	2.2
21	Missouri	2.3
32	Montana	2.2
9	Nebraska	2.5
3	Nevada	2.7
12	New Hampshire	2.4
42	New Jersey	2.0
2	New Mexico	2.9
42	New York	2.0
21	North Carolina	2.3
12	North Dakota	2.4
12	Ohio	2.4
4	Oklahoma	2.6
32	Oregon	2.2
38	Pennsylvania	2.1
48	Rhode Island	1.8
46	South Carolina	1.9
21	South Dakota	2.3
21	Tennessee	2.3
21	Texas	2.3
21	Utah	2.3
32	Vermont	2.2
46	Virginia	1.9
21	Washington	2.3
9	West Virginia	2.5
4	Wisconsin	2.6
21	Wyoming	2.3

RANK	STATE	PERCENT
1	Alaska	3.3
2	New Mexico	2.9
3	Nevada	2.7
4	California	2.6
4	Indiana	2.6
4	Iowa	2.6
4	Oklahoma	2.6
4	Wisconsin	2.6
9	Arizona	2.5
9	Nebraska	2.5
9	West Virginia	2.5
12	Colorado	2.4
12	Kansas	2.4
12	Kentucky	2.4
12	Louisiana	2.4
12	Maine	2.4
12	Michigan	2.4
12	New Hampshire	2.4
12	North Dakota	2.4
12	Ohio	2.4
21	Arkansas	2.3
21	Idaho	2.3
21	Minnesota	2.3
21	Missouri	2.3
21	North Carolina	2.3
21	South Dakota	2.3
21	Tennessee	2.3
21	Texas	2.3
21	Utah	2.3
21	Washington	2.3
21	Wyoming	2.3
32	Delaware	2.2
32	Florida	2.2
32	Mississippi	2.2
32	Montana	2.2
32	Oregon	2.2
32	Vermont	2.2
38	Connecticut	2.1
38	Hawaii	2.1
38	Illinois	2.1
38	Pennsylvania	2.1
42	Georgia	2.0
42	Maryland	2.0
42	New Jersey	2.0
42	New York	2.0
46	South Carolina	1.9
46	Virginia	1.9
48	Rhode Island	1.8
49	Alabama	1.7
50	Massachusetts	1.6
	District of Columbia	1.4

Source: U.S. Bureau of the Census

"2017 American Community Survey-Table CP02" (https://www.census.gov/programs-surveys/acs/)

*No spouse present in household with children under 18 years old. A household includes all persons who occupy a housing unit. A household consists of a single family, one person living alone, two or more families living together, or any other group of related or unrelated persons who share living arrangements.

Same-Sex Couple Households in 2017

National Total = 935,229 Households*

RANK	STATE	HOUSEHOLDS	% of USA		RANK	STATE	HOUSEHOLDS	% of USA
30	Alabama	9,208	1.0%		1	California	128,935	13.8%
48	Alaska	1,130	0.1%		2	Texas	71,742	7.7%
12	Arizona	23,892	2.6%		3	Florida	68,857	7.4%
35	Arkansas	6,233	0.7%		4	New York	67,085	7.2%
1	California	128,935	13.8%		5	Pennsylvania	32,719	3.5%
15	Colorado	21,889	2.3%		6	Illinois	31,772	3.4%
25	Connecticut	11,058	1.2%		7	Ohio	31,386	3.4%
43	Delaware	3,133	0.3%		8	Washington	29,723	3.2%
3	Florida	68,857	7.4%		9	Massachusetts	29,132	3.1%
10	Georgia	28,908	3.1%		10	Georgia	28,908	3.1%
37	Hawaii	5,070	0.5%		11	North Carolina	27,366	2.9%
46	Idaho	2,168	0.2%		12	Arizona	23,892	2.6%
6	Illinois	31,772	3.4%		13	Michigan	23,190	2.5%
17	Indiana	17,745	1.9%		14	New Jersey	22,054	2.4%
34	Iowa	6,454	0.7%		15	Colorado	21,889	2.3%
33	Kansas	6,519	0.7%		16	Virginia	21,839	2.3%
26	Kentucky	10,709	1.1%		17	Indiana	17,745	1.9%
27	Louisiana	10,067	1.1%		18	Minnesota	17,454	1.9%
38	Maine	5,016	0.5%		19	Oregon	16,816	1.8%
20	Maryland	16,666	1.8%		20	Maryland	16,666	1.8%
9	Massachusetts	29,132	3.1%		21	Tennessee	15,081	1.6%
13	Michigan	23,190	2.5%		22	Missouri	14,537	1.6%
18	Minnesota	17,454	1.9%		23	Wisconsin	14,275	1.5%
36	Mississippi	5,093	0.5%		24	South Carolina	12,478	1.3%
22	Missouri	14,537	1.6%		25	Connecticut	11,058	1.2%
45	Montana	2,648	0.3%		26	Kentucky	10,709	1.1%
42	Nebraska	3,262	0.3%		27	Louisiana	10,067	1.1%
28	Nevada	9,911	1.1%		28	Nevada	9,911	1.1%
39	New Hampshire	4,559	0.5%		29	Oklahoma	9,730	1.0%
14	New Jersey	22,054	2.4%		30	Alabama	9,208	1.0%
32	New Mexico	6,880	0.7%		31	Utah	8,750	0.9%
4	New York	67,085	7.2%		32	New Mexico	6,880	0.7%
11	North Carolina	27,366	2.9%		33	Kansas	6,519	0.7%
49	North Dakota	1,071	0.1%		34	Iowa	6,454	0.7%
7	Ohio	31,386	3.4%		35	Arkansas	6,233	0.7%
29	Oklahoma	9,730	1.0%		36	Mississippi	5,093	0.5%
19	Oregon	16,816	1.8%		37	Hawaii	5,070	0.5%
5	Pennsylvania	32,719	3.5%		38	Maine	5,016	0.5%
41	Rhode Island	3,685	0.4%		39	New Hampshire	4,559	0.5%
24	South Carolina	12,478	1.3%		40	West Virginia	3,743	0.4%
47	South Dakota	1,602	0.2%		41	Rhode Island	3,685	0.4%
21	Tennessee	15,081	1.6%		42	Nebraska	3,262	0.3%
2	Texas	71,742	7.7%		43	Delaware	3,133	0.3%
31	Utah	8,750	0.9%		44	Vermont	2,898	0.3%
44	Vermont	2,898	0.3%		45	Montana	2,648	0.3%
16	Virginia	21,839	2.3%		46	Idaho	2,168	0.2%
8	Washington	29,723	3.2%		47	South Dakota	1,602	0.2%
40	West Virginia	3,743	0.4%		48	Alaska	1,130	0.1%
23	Wisconsin	14,275	1.5%		49	North Dakota	1,071	0.1%
50	Wyoming	1,058	0.1%		50	Wyoming	1,058	0.1%
						District of Columbia	8,033	0.9%

ALPHA ORDER

RANK ORDER

Source: U.S. Bureau of the Census
   "Same Sex Couples Main" (https://www.census.gov/topics/families/same-sex-couples.html)
*The total is comprised of 555,492 married couples and 379,737 unmarried couples. Male couples are 451,494 of the households.
Female couples are 483,735 of the households.

Percent of Same-Sex Household Couples Who Are Married: 2017

National Percent = 59.4% of Same-Sex Households*

ALPHA ORDER

RANK	STATE	PERCENT
28	Alabama	60.2
2	Alaska	74.3
42	Arizona	55.4
24	Arkansas	60.7
20	California	61.7
37	Colorado	56.9
13	Connecticut	63.2
24	Delaware	60.7
15	Florida	62.8
36	Georgia	57.2
9	Hawaii	65.4
30	Idaho	59.4
31	Illinois	59.2
40	Indiana	56.1
48	Iowa	49.6
47	Kansas	51.5
18	Kentucky	61.9
50	Louisiana	47.6
21	Maine	61.1
7	Maryland	66.5
6	Massachusetts	66.7
41	Michigan	55.5
15	Minnesota	62.8
8	Mississippi	65.6
22	Missouri	60.9
3	Montana	70.7
14	Nebraska	63.1
23	Nevada	60.8
17	New Hampshire	62.7
19	New Jersey	61.8
27	New Mexico	60.3
26	New York	60.4
35	North Carolina	57.3
45	North Dakota	53.3
49	Ohio	48.2
34	Oklahoma	57.7
32	Oregon	59.1
33	Pennsylvania	58.6
12	Rhode Island	63.8
38	South Carolina	56.6
1	South Dakota	80.6
43	Tennessee	55.0
44	Texas	54.4
11	Utah	64.3
4	Vermont	69.4
29	Virginia	59.5
9	Washington	65.4
46	West Virginia	52.7
39	Wisconsin	56.4
5	Wyoming	68.3

RANK ORDER

RANK	STATE	PERCENT
1	South Dakota	80.6
2	Alaska	74.3
3	Montana	70.7
4	Vermont	69.4
5	Wyoming	68.3
6	Massachusetts	66.7
7	Maryland	66.5
8	Mississippi	65.6
9	Hawaii	65.4
9	Washington	65.4
11	Utah	64.3
12	Rhode Island	63.8
13	Connecticut	63.2
14	Nebraska	63.1
15	Florida	62.8
15	Minnesota	62.8
17	New Hampshire	62.7
18	Kentucky	61.9
19	New Jersey	61.8
20	California	61.7
21	Maine	61.1
22	Missouri	60.9
23	Nevada	60.8
24	Arkansas	60.7
24	Delaware	60.7
26	New York	60.4
27	New Mexico	60.3
28	Alabama	60.2
29	Virginia	59.5
30	Idaho	59.4
31	Illinois	59.2
32	Oregon	59.1
33	Pennsylvania	58.6
34	Oklahoma	57.7
35	North Carolina	57.3
36	Georgia	57.2
37	Colorado	56.9
38	South Carolina	56.6
39	Wisconsin	56.4
40	Indiana	56.1
41	Michigan	55.5
42	Arizona	55.4
43	Tennessee	55.0
44	Texas	54.4
45	North Dakota	53.3
46	West Virginia	52.7
47	Kansas	51.5
48	Iowa	49.6
49	Ohio	48.2
50	Louisiana	47.6
	District of Columbia	55.4

Source: U.S. Bureau of the Census

"Same Sex Couples Main" (https://www.census.gov/topics/families/same-sex-couples.html)

*Male-couple households are 58 percent married. Female couple households are 61 percent married.

Housing Units in 2017

National Total = 137,407,308 Housing Units*

ALPHA ORDER

ALPHA ORDER

RANK	STATE	HOUSING UNITS	% of USA
24	Alabama	2,258,669	1.6%
49	Alaska	316,968	0.2%
14	Arizona	2,999,185	2.2%
31	Arkansas	1,370,109	1.0%
1	California	14,177,270	10.3%
22	Colorado	2,385,495	1.7%
29	Connecticut	1,517,495	1.1%
45	Delaware	432,853	0.3%
3	Florida	9,441,585	6.9%
10	Georgia	4,282,254	3.1%
42	Hawaii	542,955	0.4%
40	Idaho	721,818	0.5%
6	Illinois	5,359,416	3.9%
17	Indiana	2,885,342	2.1%
30	Iowa	1,397,739	1.0%
33	Kansas	1,273,776	0.9%
26	Kentucky	1,984,235	1.4%
25	Louisiana	2,061,582	1.5%
39	Maine	742,644	0.5%
20	Maryland	2,449,123	1.8%
16	Massachusetts	2,894,590	2.1%
9	Michigan	4,595,274	3.3%
21	Minnesota	2,437,726	1.8%
32	Mississippi	1,323,754	1.0%
18	Missouri	2,792,445	2.0%
43	Montana	510,408	0.4%
38	Nebraska	837,540	0.6%
34	Nevada	1,249,733	0.9%
41	New Hampshire	634,689	0.5%
11	New Jersey	3,615,891	2.6%
36	New Mexico	937,976	0.7%
4	New York	8,327,621	6.1%
8	North Carolina	4,622,656	3.4%
47	North Dakota	374,591	0.3%
7	Ohio	5,201,701	3.8%
28	Oklahoma	1,734,074	1.3%
27	Oregon	1,768,582	1.3%
5	Pennsylvania	5,694,402	4.1%
44	Rhode Island	468,266	0.3%
23	South Carolina	2,284,820	1.7%
46	South Dakota	392,650	0.3%
15	Tennessee	2,958,799	2.2%
2	Texas	10,933,375	8.0%
35	Utah	1,084,685	0.8%
48	Vermont	335,248	0.2%
12	Virginia	3,512,917	2.6%
13	Washington	3,103,263	2.3%
37	West Virginia	892,240	0.6%
19	Wisconsin	2,695,303	2.0%
50	Wyoming	276,733	0.2%

RANK ORDER

RANK	STATE	HOUSING UNITS	% of USA
1	California	14,177,270	10.3%
2	Texas	10,933,375	8.0%
3	Florida	9,441,585	6.9%
4	New York	8,327,621	6.1%
5	Pennsylvania	5,694,402	4.1%
6	Illinois	5,359,416	3.9%
7	Ohio	5,201,701	3.8%
8	North Carolina	4,622,656	3.4%
9	Michigan	4,595,274	3.3%
10	Georgia	4,282,254	3.1%
11	New Jersey	3,615,891	2.6%
12	Virginia	3,512,917	2.6%
13	Washington	3,103,263	2.3%
14	Arizona	2,999,185	2.2%
15	Tennessee	2,958,799	2.2%
16	Massachusetts	2,894,590	2.1%
17	Indiana	2,885,342	2.1%
18	Missouri	2,792,445	2.0%
19	Wisconsin	2,695,303	2.0%
20	Maryland	2,449,123	1.8%
21	Minnesota	2,437,726	1.8%
22	Colorado	2,385,495	1.7%
23	South Carolina	2,284,820	1.7%
24	Alabama	2,258,669	1.6%
25	Louisiana	2,061,582	1.5%
26	Kentucky	1,984,235	1.4%
27	Oregon	1,768,582	1.3%
28	Oklahoma	1,734,074	1.3%
29	Connecticut	1,517,495	1.1%
30	Iowa	1,397,739	1.0%
31	Arkansas	1,370,109	1.0%
32	Mississippi	1,323,754	1.0%
33	Kansas	1,273,776	0.9%
34	Nevada	1,249,733	0.9%
35	Utah	1,084,685	0.8%
36	New Mexico	937,976	0.7%
37	West Virginia	892,240	0.6%
38	Nebraska	837,540	0.6%
39	Maine	742,644	0.5%
40	Idaho	721,818	0.5%
41	New Hampshire	634,689	0.5%
42	Hawaii	542,955	0.4%
43	Montana	510,408	0.4%
44	Rhode Island	468,266	0.3%
45	Delaware	432,853	0.3%
46	South Dakota	392,650	0.3%
47	North Dakota	374,591	0.3%
48	Vermont	335,248	0.2%
49	Alaska	316,968	0.2%
50	Wyoming	276,733	0.2%
	District of Columbia	314,843	0.2%

Source: U.S. Bureau of the Census
   "2017 American Community Survey-Table CP04" (https://www.census.gov/programs-surveys/acs/)
*A housing unit is a house, an apartment, a mobile home, a group of rooms, or a single room that is occupied (or if vacant, is intended for occupancy) as separate living quarters. Separate living quarters are those in which the occupants live and eat separately from any other persons in the building and which have direct access from the outside of the building or through a common hall.

Housing Units per Square Mile in 2017

National Average = 38.8 Housing Units*

ALPHA ORDER

RANK	STATE	RATE
26	Alabama	44.5
50	Alaska	0.6
33	Arizona	26.4
34	Arkansas	26.3
13	California	90.9
38	Colorado	23.0
4	Connecticut	313.2
6	Delaware	221.5
8	Florida	175.1
19	Georgia	74.0
15	Hawaii	84.5
44	Idaho	8.7
11	Illinois	96.4
17	Indiana	80.4
36	Iowa	25.0
40	Kansas	15.6
22	Kentucky	49.9
24	Louisiana	47.3
37	Maine	24.1
5	Maryland	250.6
3	Massachusetts	369.2
16	Michigan	80.9
31	Minnesota	30.6
32	Mississippi	28.2
28	Missouri	40.5
48	Montana	3.5
43	Nebraska	10.9
42	Nevada	11.4
21	New Hampshire	70.8
1	New Jersey	487.5
45	New Mexico	7.7
7	New York	176.4
12	North Carolina	94.9
46	North Dakota	5.4
10	Ohio	127.0
35	Oklahoma	25.3
39	Oregon	18.4
9	Pennsylvania	127.1
2	Rhode Island	448.1
18	South Carolina	75.9
47	South Dakota	5.2
20	Tennessee	71.8
27	Texas	41.8
41	Utah	13.2
30	Vermont	36.2
14	Virginia	88.7
25	Washington	46.6
29	West Virginia	37.1
23	Wisconsin	49.6
49	Wyoming	2.8

RANK ORDER

RANK	STATE	RATE
1	New Jersey	487.5
2	Rhode Island	448.1
3	Massachusetts	369.2
4	Connecticut	313.2
5	Maryland	250.6
6	Delaware	221.5
7	New York	176.4
8	Florida	175.1
9	Pennsylvania	127.1
10	Ohio	127.0
11	Illinois	96.4
12	North Carolina	94.9
13	California	90.9
14	Virginia	88.7
15	Hawaii	84.5
16	Michigan	80.9
17	Indiana	80.4
18	South Carolina	75.9
19	Georgia	74.0
20	Tennessee	71.8
21	New Hampshire	70.8
22	Kentucky	49.9
23	Wisconsin	49.6
24	Louisiana	47.3
25	Washington	46.6
26	Alabama	44.5
27	Texas	41.8
28	Missouri	40.5
29	West Virginia	37.1
30	Vermont	36.2
31	Minnesota	30.6
32	Mississippi	28.2
33	Arizona	26.4
34	Arkansas	26.3
35	Oklahoma	25.3
36	Iowa	25.0
37	Maine	24.1
38	Colorado	23.0
39	Oregon	18.4
40	Kansas	15.6
41	Utah	13.2
42	Nevada	11.4
43	Nebraska	10.9
44	Idaho	8.7
45	New Mexico	7.7
46	North Dakota	5.4
47	South Dakota	5.2
48	Montana	3.5
49	Wyoming	2.8
50	Alaska	0.6

District of Columbia — 5,161.4

Source: CQ Press using data from U.S. Bureau of the Census
    "2017 American Community Survey-Table CP04" (https://www.census.gov/programs-surveys/acs/)
*Based on land area. A housing unit is a house, an apartment, a mobile home, a group of rooms, or a single room that is occupied (or if vacant, is intended for occupancy) as separate living quarters. Separate living quarters are those in which the occupants live and eat separately from any other persons in the building and which have direct access from the outside of the building or through a common hall.

Percent of Housing Units That Are Owner-Occupied in 2017

National Percent = 63.9% of Housing Units*

ALPHA ORDER

RANK	STATE	PERCENT
17	Alabama	68.0
39	Alaska	63.5
37	Arizona	64.7
33	Arkansas	65.3
49	California	54.8
34	Colorado	65.2
26	Connecticut	66.2
6	Delaware	70.9
34	Florida	65.2
41	Georgia	62.9
47	Hawaii	58.5
10	Idaho	69.7
26	Illinois	66.2
13	Indiana	69.0
3	Iowa	71.6
28	Kansas	65.9
24	Kentucky	66.5
34	Louisiana	65.2
1	Maine	73.2
21	Maryland	66.7
44	Massachusetts	62.3
5	Michigan	71.3
3	Minnesota	71.6
15	Mississippi	68.5
20	Missouri	67.0
12	Montana	69.2
25	Nebraska	66.3
48	Nevada	56.6
9	New Hampshire	69.8
38	New Jersey	63.8
18	New Mexico	67.9
50	New York	53.8
31	North Carolina	65.4
40	North Dakota	63.4
29	Ohio	65.8
30	Oklahoma	65.5
42	Oregon	62.8
16	Pennsylvania	68.3
46	Rhode Island	60.8
14	South Carolina	68.7
19	South Dakota	67.7
31	Tennessee	65.4
45	Texas	62.0
8	Utah	69.9
11	Vermont	69.5
22	Virginia	66.6
42	Washington	62.8
2	West Virginia	72.5
22	Wisconsin	66.6
7	Wyoming	70.8

RANK ORDER

RANK	STATE	PERCENT
1	Maine	73.2
2	West Virginia	72.5
3	Iowa	71.6
3	Minnesota	71.6
5	Michigan	71.3
6	Delaware	70.9
7	Wyoming	70.8
8	Utah	69.9
9	New Hampshire	69.8
10	Idaho	69.7
11	Vermont	69.5
12	Montana	69.2
13	Indiana	69.0
14	South Carolina	68.7
15	Mississippi	68.5
16	Pennsylvania	68.3
17	Alabama	68.0
18	New Mexico	67.9
19	South Dakota	67.7
20	Missouri	67.0
21	Maryland	66.7
22	Virginia	66.6
22	Wisconsin	66.6
24	Kentucky	66.5
25	Nebraska	66.3
26	Connecticut	66.2
26	Illinois	66.2
28	Kansas	65.9
29	Ohio	65.8
30	Oklahoma	65.5
31	North Carolina	65.4
31	Tennessee	65.4
33	Arkansas	65.3
34	Colorado	65.2
34	Florida	65.2
34	Louisiana	65.2
37	Arizona	64.7
38	New Jersey	63.8
39	Alaska	63.5
40	North Dakota	63.4
41	Georgia	62.9
42	Oregon	62.8
42	Washington	62.8
44	Massachusetts	62.3
45	Texas	62.0
46	Rhode Island	60.8
47	Hawaii	58.5
48	Nevada	56.6
49	California	54.8
50	New York	53.8
	District of Columbia	42.2

Source: U.S. Bureau of the Census
    "2017 American Community Survey-Table CP04" (https://www.census.gov/programs-surveys/acs/)
*For occupied housing units.

New Housing Units Authorized in 2017

National Total = 1,264,051 Units*

ALPHA ORDER

RANK	STATE	UNITS	% of USA
28	Alabama	14,497	1.1%
49	Alaska	1,553	0.1%
10	Arizona	37,981	3.0%
33	Arkansas	11,021	0.9%
3	California	113,320	9.0%
7	Colorado	41,911	3.3%
41	Connecticut	4,606	0.4%
37	Delaware	6,735	0.5%
2	Florida	118,548	9.4%
5	Georgia	49,591	3.9%
43	Hawaii	4,035	0.3%
29	Idaho	13,348	1.1%
14	Illinois	25,313	2.0%
20	Indiana	20,115	1.6%
30	Iowa	13,233	1.0%
35	Kansas	8,636	0.7%
31	Kentucky	13,055	1.0%
27	Louisiana	15,232	1.2%
40	Maine	4,607	0.4%
26	Maryland	16,008	1.3%
25	Massachusetts	17,230	1.4%
15	Michigan	24,518	1.9%
18	Minnesota	22,927	1.8%
36	Mississippi	7,881	0.6%
24	Missouri	17,852	1.4%
42	Montana	4,424	0.3%
34	Nebraska	8,919	0.7%
22	Nevada	19,376	1.5%
44	New Hampshire	3,395	0.3%
13	New Jersey	28,893	2.3%
39	New Mexico	4,755	0.4%
8	New York	40,772	3.2%
4	North Carolina	65,009	5.1%
45	North Dakota	3,375	0.3%
17	Ohio	23,755	1.9%
32	Oklahoma	11,168	0.9%
21	Oregon	19,886	1.6%
19	Pennsylvania	22,509	1.8%
50	Rhode Island	1,156	0.1%
11	South Carolina	34,730	2.7%
38	South Dakota	5,364	0.4%
9	Tennessee	38,470	3.0%
1	Texas	169,885	13.4%
16	Utah	24,386	1.9%
48	Vermont	1,727	0.1%
12	Virginia	33,417	2.6%
6	Washington	45,780	3.6%
46	West Virginia	2,700	0.2%
23	Wisconsin	18,511	1.5%
47	Wyoming	1,899	0.2%

RANK ORDER

RANK	STATE	UNITS	% of USA
1	Texas	169,885	13.4%
2	Florida	118,548	9.4%
3	California	113,320	9.0%
4	North Carolina	65,009	5.1%
5	Georgia	49,591	3.9%
6	Washington	45,780	3.6%
7	Colorado	41,911	3.3%
8	New York	40,772	3.2%
9	Tennessee	38,470	3.0%
10	Arizona	37,981	3.0%
11	South Carolina	34,730	2.7%
12	Virginia	33,417	2.6%
13	New Jersey	28,893	2.3%
14	Illinois	25,313	2.0%
15	Michigan	24,518	1.9%
16	Utah	24,386	1.9%
17	Ohio	23,755	1.9%
18	Minnesota	22,927	1.8%
19	Pennsylvania	22,509	1.8%
20	Indiana	20,115	1.6%
21	Oregon	19,886	1.6%
22	Nevada	19,376	1.5%
23	Wisconsin	18,511	1.5%
24	Missouri	17,852	1.4%
25	Massachusetts	17,230	1.4%
26	Maryland	16,008	1.3%
27	Louisiana	15,232	1.2%
28	Alabama	14,497	1.1%
29	Idaho	13,348	1.1%
30	Iowa	13,233	1.0%
31	Kentucky	13,055	1.0%
32	Oklahoma	11,168	0.9%
33	Arkansas	11,021	0.9%
34	Nebraska	8,919	0.7%
35	Kansas	8,636	0.7%
36	Mississippi	7,881	0.6%
37	Delaware	6,735	0.5%
38	South Dakota	5,364	0.4%
39	New Mexico	4,755	0.4%
40	Maine	4,607	0.4%
41	Connecticut	4,606	0.4%
42	Montana	4,424	0.3%
43	Hawaii	4,035	0.3%
44	New Hampshire	3,395	0.3%
45	North Dakota	3,375	0.3%
46	West Virginia	2,700	0.2%
47	Wyoming	1,899	0.2%
48	Vermont	1,727	0.1%
49	Alaska	1,553	0.1%
50	Rhode Island	1,156	0.1%
	District of Columbia	6,037	0.5%

Source: U.S. Bureau of the Census
"Building Permits Survey" (https://www.census.gov/construction/bps/stateannual.html)
*Preliminary and unadjusted year-to-date monthly data as of December 2017. Includes single and multifamily privately owned units. All places issuing building permits for privately owned residential structures. More than 98 percent of all privately owned residential buildings constructed are in permit-issuing places.

Value of New Housing Units Authorized in 2017

National Total = $254,605,033,000*

ALPHA ORDER

RANK	STATE	VALUE	% of USA
28	Alabama	$2,728,080,000	1.1%
48	Alaska	401,752,000	0.2%
8	Arizona	8,322,680,000	3.3%
33	Arkansas	1,764,771,000	0.7%
2	California	27,048,354,000	10.6%
7	Colorado	9,255,053,000	3.6%
37	Connecticut	1,170,409,000	0.5%
43	Delaware	818,053,000	0.3%
3	Florida	26,888,015,000	10.6%
6	Georgia	9,730,898,000	3.8%
38	Hawaii	1,132,364,000	0.4%
29	Idaho	2,530,075,000	1.0%
17	Illinois	4,662,939,000	1.8%
19	Indiana	4,324,752,000	1.7%
30	Iowa	2,489,575,000	1.0%
34	Kansas	1,705,287,000	0.7%
32	Kentucky	2,134,515,000	0.8%
27	Louisiana	2,960,474,000	1.2%
41	Maine	853,578,000	0.3%
26	Maryland	3,236,665,000	1.3%
22	Massachusetts	3,943,824,000	1.5%
15	Michigan	5,036,259,000	2.0%
16	Minnesota	5,006,506,000	2.0%
36	Mississippi	1,334,565,000	0.5%
25	Missouri	3,267,283,000	1.3%
42	Montana	844,812,000	0.3%
35	Nebraska	1,489,682,000	0.6%
24	Nevada	3,310,283,000	1.3%
44	New Hampshire	693,077,000	0.3%
20	New Jersey	4,150,146,000	1.6%
39	New Mexico	945,003,000	0.4%
10	New York	7,094,816,000	2.8%
4	North Carolina	12,353,457,000	4.9%
45	North Dakota	606,088,000	0.2%
14	Ohio	5,059,703,000	2.0%
31	Oklahoma	2,199,267,000	0.9%
21	Oregon	4,125,989,000	1.6%
18	Pennsylvania	4,379,442,000	1.7%
50	Rhode Island	251,186,000	0.1%
9	South Carolina	7,763,489,000	3.0%
40	South Dakota	878,028,000	0.3%
11	Tennessee	7,066,820,000	2.8%
1	Texas	31,879,563,000	12.5%
13	Utah	5,312,600,000	2.1%
49	Vermont	394,976,000	0.2%
12	Virginia	5,721,333,000	2.2%
5	Washington	9,843,132,000	3.9%
47	West Virginia	457,261,000	0.2%
23	Wisconsin	3,822,509,000	1.5%
46	Wyoming	526,106,000	0.2%

RANK ORDER

RANK	STATE	VALUE	% of USA
1	Texas	$31,879,563,000	12.5%
2	California	27,048,354,000	10.6%
3	Florida	26,888,015,000	10.6%
4	North Carolina	12,353,457,000	4.9%
5	Washington	9,843,132,000	3.9%
6	Georgia	9,730,898,000	3.8%
7	Colorado	9,255,053,000	3.6%
8	Arizona	8,322,680,000	3.3%
9	South Carolina	7,763,489,000	3.0%
10	New York	7,094,816,000	2.8%
11	Tennessee	7,066,820,000	2.8%
12	Virginia	5,721,333,000	2.2%
13	Utah	5,312,600,000	2.1%
14	Ohio	5,059,703,000	2.0%
15	Michigan	5,036,259,000	2.0%
16	Minnesota	5,006,506,000	2.0%
17	Illinois	4,662,939,000	1.8%
18	Pennsylvania	4,379,442,000	1.7%
19	Indiana	4,324,752,000	1.7%
20	New Jersey	4,150,146,000	1.6%
21	Oregon	4,125,989,000	1.6%
22	Massachusetts	3,943,824,000	1.5%
23	Wisconsin	3,822,509,000	1.5%
24	Nevada	3,310,283,000	1.3%
25	Missouri	3,267,283,000	1.3%
26	Maryland	3,236,665,000	1.3%
27	Louisiana	2,960,474,000	1.2%
28	Alabama	2,728,080,000	1.1%
29	Idaho	2,530,075,000	1.0%
30	Iowa	2,489,575,000	1.0%
31	Oklahoma	2,199,267,000	0.9%
32	Kentucky	2,134,515,000	0.8%
33	Arkansas	1,764,771,000	0.7%
34	Kansas	1,705,287,000	0.7%
35	Nebraska	1,489,682,000	0.6%
36	Mississippi	1,334,565,000	0.5%
37	Connecticut	1,170,409,000	0.5%
38	Hawaii	1,132,364,000	0.4%
39	New Mexico	945,003,000	0.4%
40	South Dakota	878,028,000	0.3%
41	Maine	853,578,000	0.3%
42	Montana	844,812,000	0.3%
43	Delaware	818,053,000	0.3%
44	New Hampshire	693,077,000	0.3%
45	North Dakota	606,088,000	0.2%
46	Wyoming	526,106,000	0.2%
47	West Virginia	457,261,000	0.2%
48	Alaska	401,752,000	0.2%
49	Vermont	394,976,000	0.2%
50	Rhode Island	251,186,000	0.1%
	District of Columbia	689,537,000	0.3%

Source: U.S. Bureau of the Census
   "Building Permits Survey" (https://www.census.gov/construction/bps/stateannual.html)
*Preliminary and unadjusted year-to-date monthly data as of December 2017. Includes single and multifamily privately owned units. All places issuing building permits for privately owned residential structures. More than 98 percent of all privately owned residential buildings constructed are in permit-issuing places.

Average Value of New Housing Units in 2017

National Average = $201,420 per Unit*

ALPHA ORDER

RANK	STATE	VALUE
32	Alabama	$188,182
3	Alaska	258,694
11	Arizona	219,127
48	Arkansas	160,128
5	California	238,690
10	Colorado	220,826
4	Connecticut	254,105
50	Delaware	121,463
8	Florida	226,811
26	Georgia	196,223
1	Hawaii	280,635
31	Idaho	189,547
36	Illinois	184,211
16	Indiana	215,001
33	Iowa	188,134
24	Kansas	197,463
47	Kentucky	163,502
28	Louisiana	194,359
35	Maine	185,278
22	Maryland	202,190
6	Massachusetts	228,893
20	Michigan	205,411
12	Minnesota	218,367
44	Mississippi	169,340
38	Missouri	183,021
29	Montana	190,961
45	Nebraska	167,023
42	Nevada	170,844
21	New Hampshire	204,146
49	New Jersey	143,638
23	New Mexico	198,739
40	New York	174,012
30	North Carolina	190,027
39	North Dakota	179,582
17	Ohio	212,995
25	Oklahoma	196,926
18	Oregon	207,482
27	Pennsylvania	194,564
14	Rhode Island	217,289
9	South Carolina	223,538
46	South Dakota	163,689
37	Tennessee	183,697
34	Texas	187,654
13	Utah	217,855
7	Vermont	228,706
41	Virginia	171,210
15	Washington	215,009
43	West Virginia	169,356
19	Wisconsin	206,499
2	Wyoming	277,044

RANK ORDER

RANK	STATE	VALUE
1	Hawaii	$280,635
2	Wyoming	277,044
3	Alaska	258,694
4	Connecticut	254,105
5	California	238,690
6	Massachusetts	228,893
7	Vermont	228,706
8	Florida	226,811
9	South Carolina	223,538
10	Colorado	220,826
11	Arizona	219,127
12	Minnesota	218,367
13	Utah	217,855
14	Rhode Island	217,289
15	Washington	215,009
16	Indiana	215,001
17	Ohio	212,995
18	Oregon	207,482
19	Wisconsin	206,499
20	Michigan	205,411
21	New Hampshire	204,146
22	Maryland	202,190
23	New Mexico	198,739
24	Kansas	197,463
25	Oklahoma	196,926
26	Georgia	196,223
27	Pennsylvania	194,564
28	Louisiana	194,359
29	Montana	190,961
30	North Carolina	190,027
31	Idaho	189,547
32	Alabama	188,182
33	Iowa	188,134
34	Texas	187,654
35	Maine	185,278
36	Illinois	184,211
37	Tennessee	183,697
38	Missouri	183,021
39	North Dakota	179,582
40	New York	174,012
41	Virginia	171,210
42	Nevada	170,844
43	West Virginia	169,356
44	Mississippi	169,340
45	Nebraska	167,023
46	South Dakota	163,689
47	Kentucky	163,502
48	Arkansas	160,128
49	New Jersey	143,638
50	Delaware	121,463
	District of Columbia	114,218

Source: CQ Press using data from U.S. Bureau of the Census
   "Building Permits Survey" (https://www.census.gov/construction/bps/stateannual.html)
*Preliminary and unadjusted year-to-date monthly data as of December 2017. Includes single and multifamily privately owned units. All places issuing building permits for privately owned residential structures. More than 98 percent of all privately owned residential buildings constructed are in permit-issuing places.

Median Value of Owner-Occupied Housing in 2017

National Median = $217,600*

ALPHA ORDER				RANK ORDER		
RANK	STATE	MEDIAN		RANK	STATE	MEDIAN
44	Alabama	$141,300		1	Hawaii	$617,400
12	Alaska	273,100		2	California	509,400
21	Arizona	223,400		3	Massachusetts	385,400
48	Arkansas	128,500		4	Colorado	348,900
2	California	509,400		5	Washington	339,000
4	Colorado	348,900		6	New Jersey	334,900
12	Connecticut	273,100		7	Oregon	319,200
17	Delaware	252,800		8	New York	314,500
23	Florida	214,000		9	Maryland	312,500
30	Georgia	173,700		10	Utah	275,100
1	Hawaii	617,400		11	Virginia	273,400
24	Idaho	207,100		12	Alaska	273,100
25	Illinois	195,300		12	Connecticut	273,100
45	Indiana	141,100		14	New Hampshire	263,600
42	Iowa	149,100		15	Nevada	258,200
41	Kansas	150,600		16	Rhode Island	257,800
46	Kentucky	141,000		17	Delaware	252,800
36	Louisiana	162,500		18	Montana	231,300
27	Maine	191,200		19	Vermont	226,300
9	Maryland	312,500		20	Minnesota	224,000
3	Massachusetts	385,400		21	Arizona	223,400
40	Michigan	155,700		22	Wyoming	214,300
20	Minnesota	224,000		23	Florida	214,000
49	Mississippi	120,200		24	Idaho	207,100
38	Missouri	156,700		25	Illinois	195,300
18	Montana	231,300		26	North Dakota	194,700
39	Nebraska	155,800		27	Maine	191,200
15	Nevada	258,200		28	Pennsylvania	181,200
14	New Hampshire	263,600		29	Wisconsin	178,900
6	New Jersey	334,900		30	Georgia	173,700
32	New Mexico	171,300		31	Texas	172,200
8	New York	314,500		32	New Mexico	171,300
33	North Carolina	171,200		33	North Carolina	171,200
26	North Dakota	194,700		34	South Dakota	167,600
43	Ohio	144,200		35	Tennessee	167,500
47	Oklahoma	137,400		36	Louisiana	162,500
7	Oregon	319,200		37	South Carolina	161,800
28	Pennsylvania	181,200		38	Missouri	156,700
16	Rhode Island	257,800		39	Nebraska	155,800
37	South Carolina	161,800		40	Michigan	155,700
34	South Dakota	167,600		41	Kansas	150,600
35	Tennessee	167,500		42	Iowa	149,100
31	Texas	172,200		43	Ohio	144,200
10	Utah	275,100		44	Alabama	141,300
19	Vermont	226,300		45	Indiana	141,100
11	Virginia	273,400		46	Kentucky	141,000
5	Washington	339,000		47	Oklahoma	137,400
50	West Virginia	119,800		48	Arkansas	128,500
29	Wisconsin	178,900		49	Mississippi	120,200
22	Wyoming	214,300		50	West Virginia	119,800
					District of Columbia	607,200

Source: U.S. Bureau of the Census
   "2017 American Community Survey-Table CP04" (https://www.census.gov/programs-surveys/acs/)
*Housing units with a mortgage.

Percent Change in House Prices: 2017 to 2018

National Percent Change = 6.3% Increase*

ALPHA ORDER			RANK ORDER		
RANK	STATE	PERCENT CHANGE	RANK	STATE	PERCENT CHANGE
23	Alabama	6.4	1	Idaho	15.1
50	Alaska	0.2	2	Nevada	15.0
16	Arizona	7.1	3	Washington	10.6
34	Arkansas	4.5	4	Utah	10.0
22	California	6.5	5	Colorado	9.2
5	Colorado	9.2	6	Florida	8.9
47	Connecticut	2.2	7	Rhode Island	8.6
24	Delaware	6.2	8	Georgia	8.4
6	Florida	8.9	9	Indiana	7.9
8	Georgia	8.4	10	North Carolina	7.7
44	Hawaii	3.0	11	Michigan	7.6
1	Idaho	15.1	12	Tennessee	7.5
41	Illinois	3.5	13	Nebraska	7.4
9	Indiana	7.9	14	Oregon	7.3
33	Iowa	5.0	14	South Carolina	7.3
29	Kansas	5.5	16	Arizona	7.1
34	Kentucky	4.5	17	South Dakota	7.0
48	Louisiana	1.5	18	Minnesota	6.9
32	Maine	5.2	18	Missouri	6.9
45	Maryland	2.8	18	Wisconsin	6.9
31	Massachusetts	5.3	21	Ohio	6.6
11	Michigan	7.6	22	California	6.5
18	Minnesota	6.9	23	Alabama	6.4
46	Mississippi	2.7	24	Delaware	6.2
18	Missouri	6.9	24	New Hampshire	6.2
28	Montana	5.6	26	New York	5.9
13	Nebraska	7.4	27	Texas	5.7
2	Nevada	15.0	28	Montana	5.6
24	New Hampshire	6.2	29	Kansas	5.5
39	New Jersey	3.9	29	Vermont	5.5
42	New Mexico	3.4	31	Massachusetts	5.3
26	New York	5.9	32	Maine	5.2
10	North Carolina	7.7	33	Iowa	5.0
49	North Dakota	1.0	34	Arkansas	4.5
21	Ohio	6.6	34	Kentucky	4.5
40	Oklahoma	3.7	36	Pennsylvania	4.4
14	Oregon	7.3	36	Virginia	4.4
36	Pennsylvania	4.4	36	Wyoming	4.4
7	Rhode Island	8.6	39	New Jersey	3.9
14	South Carolina	7.3	40	Oklahoma	3.7
17	South Dakota	7.0	41	Illinois	3.5
12	Tennessee	7.5	42	New Mexico	3.4
27	Texas	5.7	42	West Virginia	3.4
4	Utah	10.0	44	Hawaii	3.0
29	Vermont	5.5	45	Maryland	2.8
36	Virginia	4.4	46	Mississippi	2.7
3	Washington	10.6	47	Connecticut	2.2
42	West Virginia	3.4	48	Louisiana	1.5
18	Wisconsin	6.9	49	North Dakota	1.0
36	Wyoming	4.4	50	Alaska	0.2
				District of Columbia	1.6

Source: Federal Housing Finance Agency
"State HPI Summary" (www.fhfa.gov/DataTools/Tools/Pages/House-Price-Index-%28HPI%29.aspx)
*Single-family house prices. As of September 30, 2018.

Percent Change in House Prices: 2014 to 2018

National Percent Change = 32.7% Increase*

ALPHA ORDER				RANK ORDER		
RANK	STATE	PERCENT CHANGE		RANK	STATE	PERCENT CHANGE
31	Alabama	22.4		1	Nevada	69.5
49	Alaska	10.6		2	Colorado	58.8
8	Arizona	43.7		3	Washington	56.8
39	Arkansas	17.7		4	Florida	53.8
9	California	43.3		5	Idaho	53.1
2	Colorado	58.8		6	Oregon	51.9
50	Connecticut	7.1		7	Utah	44.8
46	Delaware	14.1		8	Arizona	43.7
4	Florida	53.8		9	California	43.3
10	Georgia	42.6		10	Georgia	42.6
16	Hawaii	32.3		11	Texas	40.2
5	Idaho	53.1		12	Michigan	40.1
36	Illinois	19.0		13	Tennessee	37.7
27	Indiana	27.7		14	South Carolina	33.9
32	Iowa	22.0		15	North Carolina	33.5
28	Kansas	25.9		16	Hawaii	32.3
29	Kentucky	24.5		17	Rhode Island	31.3
38	Louisiana	18.0		18	Minnesota	30.7
30	Maine	24.1		19	Nebraska	30.6
43	Maryland	15.9		20	Massachusetts	29.4
20	Massachusetts	29.4		21	Montana	29.2
12	Michigan	40.1		22	Ohio	29.0
18	Minnesota	30.7		23	Wisconsin	28.3
42	Mississippi	16.0		24	Missouri	28.2
24	Missouri	28.2		25	New Hampshire	28.0
21	Montana	29.2		26	South Dakota	27.8
19	Nebraska	30.6		27	Indiana	27.7
1	Nevada	69.5		28	Kansas	25.9
25	New Hampshire	28.0		29	Kentucky	24.5
43	New Jersey	15.9		30	Maine	24.1
41	New Mexico	16.6		31	Alabama	22.4
33	New York	21.8		32	Iowa	22.0
15	North Carolina	33.5		33	New York	21.8
40	North Dakota	17.1		34	Oklahoma	19.8
22	Ohio	29.0		35	Virginia	19.2
34	Oklahoma	19.8		36	Illinois	19.0
6	Oregon	51.9		37	Pennsylvania	18.8
37	Pennsylvania	18.8		38	Louisiana	18.0
17	Rhode Island	31.3		39	Arkansas	17.7
14	South Carolina	33.9		40	North Dakota	17.1
26	South Dakota	27.8		41	New Mexico	16.6
13	Tennessee	37.7		42	Mississippi	16.0
11	Texas	40.2		43	Maryland	15.9
7	Utah	44.8		43	New Jersey	15.9
47	Vermont	12.8		45	Wyoming	15.5
35	Virginia	19.2		46	Delaware	14.1
3	Washington	56.8		47	Vermont	12.8
48	West Virginia	12.3		48	West Virginia	12.3
23	Wisconsin	28.3		49	Alaska	10.6
45	Wyoming	15.5		50	Connecticut	7.1
					District of Columbia	30.6

Source: Federal Housing Finance Agency

"State HPI Summary" (www.fhfa.gov/DataTools/Tools/Pages/House-Price-Index-%28HPI%29.aspx)

*Single-family house prices. As of September 30, 2018.

Percent of Owner-Occupied Housing Units with a Mortgage in 2017

National Percent = 62.8% with Mortgages

ALPHA ORDER

RANK	STATE	PERCENT
42	Alabama	56.4
20	Alaska	64.2
18	Arizona	64.4
44	Arkansas	55.3
4	California	70.5
2	Colorado	71.3
10	Connecticut	68.0
17	Delaware	64.6
41	Florida	56.9
16	Georgia	65.0
20	Hawaii	64.2
18	Idaho	64.4
23	Illinois	63.1
15	Indiana	65.5
28	Iowa	61.6
34	Kansas	59.0
36	Kentucky	58.3
48	Louisiana	52.7
29	Maine	61.5
1	Maryland	72.9
5	Massachusetts	69.9
33	Michigan	60.2
11	Minnesota	67.1
49	Mississippi	49.1
26	Missouri	61.9
40	Montana	57.1
30	Nebraska	61.0
7	Nevada	69.0
14	New Hampshire	65.8
12	New Jersey	67.0
47	New Mexico	53.6
31	New York	60.9
23	North Carolina	63.1
46	North Dakota	54.5
25	Ohio	62.8
45	Oklahoma	54.8
13	Oregon	66.8
32	Pennsylvania	60.3
6	Rhode Island	69.3
39	South Carolina	57.6
43	South Dakota	55.4
35	Tennessee	58.9
38	Texas	57.7
3	Utah	71.1
27	Vermont	61.8
8	Virginia	68.9
9	Washington	68.8
50	West Virginia	45.9
22	Wisconsin	64.1
37	Wyoming	58.1

RANK ORDER

RANK	STATE	PERCENT
1	Maryland	72.9
2	Colorado	71.3
3	Utah	71.1
4	California	70.5
5	Massachusetts	69.9
6	Rhode Island	69.3
7	Nevada	69.0
8	Virginia	68.9
9	Washington	68.8
10	Connecticut	68.0
11	Minnesota	67.1
12	New Jersey	67.0
13	Oregon	66.8
14	New Hampshire	65.8
15	Indiana	65.5
16	Georgia	65.0
17	Delaware	64.6
18	Arizona	64.4
18	Idaho	64.4
20	Alaska	64.2
20	Hawaii	64.2
22	Wisconsin	64.1
23	Illinois	63.1
23	North Carolina	63.1
25	Ohio	62.8
26	Missouri	61.9
27	Vermont	61.8
28	Iowa	61.6
29	Maine	61.5
30	Nebraska	61.0
31	New York	60.9
32	Pennsylvania	60.3
33	Michigan	60.2
34	Kansas	59.0
35	Tennessee	58.9
36	Kentucky	58.3
37	Wyoming	58.1
38	Texas	57.7
39	South Carolina	57.6
40	Montana	57.1
41	Florida	56.9
42	Alabama	56.4
43	South Dakota	55.4
44	Arkansas	55.3
45	Oklahoma	54.8
46	North Dakota	54.5
47	New Mexico	53.6
48	Louisiana	52.7
49	Mississippi	49.1
50	West Virginia	45.9
	District of Columbia	76.0

Source: U.S. Bureau of the Census

"2017 American Community Survey-Table CP04" (https://www.census.gov/programs-surveys/acs/)

Median Monthly Mortgage Payment in 2017

National Median = $1,513*

ALPHA ORDER

RANK	STATE	MEDIAN
45	Alabama	$1,123
9	Alaska	1,844
26	Arizona	1,365
49	Arkansas	1,025
3	California	2,269
13	Colorado	1,681
6	Connecticut	1,976
18	Delaware	1,507
23	Florida	1,423
29	Georgia	1,341
2	Hawaii	2,337
39	Idaho	1,213
15	Illinois	1,603
48	Indiana	1,089
41	Iowa	1,205
31	Kansas	1,314
45	Kentucky	1,123
36	Louisiana	1,233
32	Maine	1,313
7	Maryland	1,915
4	Massachusetts	2,108
37	Michigan	1,231
19	Minnesota	1,500
47	Mississippi	1,090
40	Missouri	1,207
25	Montana	1,367
30	Nebraska	1,334
22	Nevada	1,428
8	New Hampshire	1,874
1	New Jersey	2,348
34	New Mexico	1,244
5	New York	2,036
35	North Carolina	1,242
28	North Dakota	1,356
38	Ohio	1,214
44	Oklahoma	1,183
14	Oregon	1,629
21	Pennsylvania	1,438
11	Rhode Island	1,782
42	South Carolina	1,195
33	South Dakota	1,283
43	Tennessee	1,184
17	Texas	1,513
20	Utah	1,467
16	Vermont	1,527
12	Virginia	1,718
10	Washington	1,806
50	West Virginia	984
27	Wisconsin	1,358
24	Wyoming	1,386

RANK ORDER

RANK	STATE	MEDIAN
1	New Jersey	$2,348
2	Hawaii	2,337
3	California	2,269
4	Massachusetts	2,108
5	New York	2,036
6	Connecticut	1,976
7	Maryland	1,915
8	New Hampshire	1,874
9	Alaska	1,844
10	Washington	1,806
11	Rhode Island	1,782
12	Virginia	1,718
13	Colorado	1,681
14	Oregon	1,629
15	Illinois	1,603
16	Vermont	1,527
17	Texas	1,513
18	Delaware	1,507
19	Minnesota	1,500
20	Utah	1,467
21	Pennsylvania	1,438
22	Nevada	1,428
23	Florida	1,423
24	Wyoming	1,386
25	Montana	1,367
26	Arizona	1,365
27	Wisconsin	1,358
28	North Dakota	1,356
29	Georgia	1,341
30	Nebraska	1,334
31	Kansas	1,314
32	Maine	1,313
33	South Dakota	1,283
34	New Mexico	1,244
35	North Carolina	1,242
36	Louisiana	1,233
37	Michigan	1,231
38	Ohio	1,214
39	Idaho	1,213
40	Missouri	1,207
41	Iowa	1,205
42	South Carolina	1,195
43	Tennessee	1,184
44	Oklahoma	1,183
45	Alabama	1,123
45	Kentucky	1,123
47	Mississippi	1,090
48	Indiana	1,089
49	Arkansas	1,025
50	West Virginia	984
	District of Columbia	2,432

Source: U.S. Bureau of the Census
   "2017 American Community Survey-Table CP04" (https://www.census.gov/programs-surveys/acs/)
*Monthly housing costs for owner-occupied housing.

Percent of Home Owners Spending 30 Percent or More of Household Income on Housing Costs in 2017
National Percent = 27.5% of Home Owners*

ALPHA ORDER

RANK	STATE	PERCENT	RANK	STATE	PERCENT
36	Alabama	23.2	1	Hawaii	39.0
13	Alaska	29.2	2	California	38.4
15	Arizona	28.1	3	New Jersey	34.4
43	Arkansas	21.2	4	New York	33.2
2	California	38.4	5	Florida	32.9
19	Colorado	27.2	6	Vermont	32.1
9	Connecticut	30.9	7	Oregon	31.7
16	Delaware	27.9	8	Rhode Island	31.6
5	Florida	32.9	9	Connecticut	30.9
28	Georgia	25.2	10	Nevada	30.0
1	Hawaii	39.0	11	New Mexico	29.9
23	Idaho	26.1	12	Massachusetts	29.4
18	Illinois	27.3	13	Alaska	29.2
48	Indiana	19.0	14	Washington	28.9
48	Iowa	19.0	15	Arizona	28.1
46	Kansas	19.9	16	Delaware	27.9
40	Kentucky	21.8	17	Montana	27.5
27	Louisiana	25.4	18	Illinois	27.3
22	Maine	26.3	19	Colorado	27.2
20	Maryland	27.1	20	Maryland	27.1
12	Massachusetts	29.4	21	New Hampshire	26.9
37	Michigan	22.8	22	Maine	26.3
41	Minnesota	21.7	23	Idaho	26.1
26	Mississippi	25.5	23	Virginia	26.1
42	Missouri	21.6	25	Texas	25.7
17	Montana	27.5	26	Mississippi	25.5
44	Nebraska	21.0	27	Louisiana	25.4
10	Nevada	30.0	28	Georgia	25.2
21	New Hampshire	26.9	29	South Carolina	25.1
3	New Jersey	34.4	30	Pennsylvania	24.4
11	New Mexico	29.9	31	North Carolina	24.1
4	New York	33.2	32	Wyoming	24.0
31	North Carolina	24.1	33	Oklahoma	23.9
50	North Dakota	16.9	33	Tennessee	23.9
45	Ohio	20.6	33	Utah	23.9
33	Oklahoma	23.9	36	Alabama	23.2
7	Oregon	31.7	37	Michigan	22.8
30	Pennsylvania	24.4	38	Wisconsin	22.4
8	Rhode Island	31.6	39	West Virginia	22.1
29	South Carolina	25.1	40	Kentucky	21.8
47	South Dakota	19.1	41	Minnesota	21.7
33	Tennessee	23.9	42	Missouri	21.6
25	Texas	25.7	43	Arkansas	21.2
33	Utah	23.9	44	Nebraska	21.0
6	Vermont	32.1	45	Ohio	20.6
23	Virginia	26.1	46	Kansas	19.9
14	Washington	28.9	47	South Dakota	19.1
39	West Virginia	22.1	48	Indiana	19.0
38	Wisconsin	22.4	48	Iowa	19.0
32	Wyoming	24.0	50	North Dakota	16.9
				District of Columbia	26.7

Source: U.S. Bureau of the Census

"2017 American Community Survey-Table CP04" (https://www.census.gov/programs-surveys/acs/)

*For owner-occupied housing units with a mortgage.

Median Annual Real Estate Taxes in 2017

National Median = $2,428*

ALPHA ORDER			RANK ORDER		
RANK	STATE	MEDIAN	RANK	STATE	MEDIAN
50	Alabama	$571	1	New Jersey	$8,124
12	Alaska	3,232	2	Connecticut	5,710
35	Arizona	1,456	3	New Hampshire	5,624
48	Arkansas	780	4	New York	5,308
9	California	3,729	5	Massachusetts	4,561
29	Colorado	1,736	6	Illinois	4,328
2	Connecticut	5,710	7	Vermont	4,210
36	Delaware	1,440	8	Rhode Island	4,173
27	Florida	1,861	9	California	3,729
32	Georgia	1,584	10	Maryland	3,336
30	Hawaii	1,716	11	Wisconsin	3,257
38	Idaho	1,408	12	Alaska	3,232
6	Illinois	4,328	13	Washington	3,226
43	Indiana	1,181	14	Texas	3,020
21	Iowa	2,302	15	Oregon	2,978
25	Kansas	2,075	16	Pennsylvania	2,855
42	Kentucky	1,203	17	Nebraska	2,642
47	Louisiana	849	18	Maine	2,562
18	Maine	2,562	19	Minnesota	2,445
10	Maryland	3,336	20	Michigan	2,358
5	Massachusetts	4,561	21	Iowa	2,302
20	Michigan	2,358	22	Ohio	2,217
19	Minnesota	2,445	23	Virginia	2,194
45	Mississippi	942	24	South Dakota	2,119
34	Missouri	1,492	25	Kansas	2,075
26	Montana	1,865	26	Montana	1,865
17	Nebraska	2,642	27	Florida	1,861
33	Nevada	1,499	28	North Dakota	1,838
3	New Hampshire	5,624	29	Colorado	1,736
1	New Jersey	8,124	30	Hawaii	1,716
39	New Mexico	1,361	31	Utah	1,699
4	New York	5,308	32	Georgia	1,584
36	North Carolina	1,440	33	Nevada	1,499
28	North Dakota	1,838	34	Missouri	1,492
22	Ohio	2,217	35	Arizona	1,456
41	Oklahoma	1,225	36	Delaware	1,440
15	Oregon	2,978	36	North Carolina	1,440
16	Pennsylvania	2,855	38	Idaho	1,408
8	Rhode Island	4,173	39	New Mexico	1,361
46	South Carolina	893	40	Wyoming	1,301
24	South Dakota	2,119	41	Oklahoma	1,225
44	Tennessee	1,165	42	Kentucky	1,203
14	Texas	3,020	43	Indiana	1,181
31	Utah	1,699	44	Tennessee	1,165
7	Vermont	4,210	45	Mississippi	942
23	Virginia	2,194	46	South Carolina	893
13	Washington	3,226	47	Louisiana	849
49	West Virginia	686	48	Arkansas	780
11	Wisconsin	3,257	49	West Virginia	686
40	Wyoming	1,301	50	Alabama	571
				District of Columbia	3,238

Source: U.S. Bureau of the Census
   "2017 American Community Survey-Table B25103" (https://www.census.gov/programs-surveys/acs/)
*For owner-occupied housing units with or without mortgages.

Homeownership Rate in 2017

National Rate = 63.9%*

ALPHA ORDER

RANK	STATE	RATE
12	Alabama	70.0
33	Alaska	65.5
36	Arizona	64.4
35	Arkansas	65.0
49	California	54.4
39	Colorado	63.7
28	Connecticut	66.1
12	Delaware	70.0
37	Florida	64.1
41	Georgia	62.8
47	Hawaii	55.9
16	Idaho	69.9
34	Illinois	65.4
12	Indiana	70.0
12	Iowa	70.0
31	Kansas	66.0
11	Kentucky	70.1
28	Louisiana	66.1
7	Maine	71.0
25	Maryland	66.9
45	Massachusetts	60.0
2	Michigan	72.9
4	Minnesota	72.7
7	Mississippi	71.0
21	Missouri	67.6
21	Montana	67.6
28	Nebraska	66.1
48	Nevada	55.0
5	New Hampshire	71.6
37	New Jersey	64.1
26	New Mexico	66.6
50	New York	51.1
27	North Carolina	66.3
42	North Dakota	62.6
31	Ohio	66.0
17	Oklahoma	68.9
43	Oregon	61.8
18	Pennsylvania	68.6
46	Rhode Island	56.6
3	South Carolina	72.8
20	South Dakota	67.8
24	Tennessee	67.2
44	Texas	61.7
7	Utah	71.0
6	Vermont	71.1
23	Virginia	67.5
40	Washington	63.6
1	West Virginia	75.1
19	Wisconsin	68.0
10	Wyoming	70.4

RANK ORDER

RANK	STATE	RATE
1	West Virginia	75.1
2	Michigan	72.9
3	South Carolina	72.8
4	Minnesota	72.7
5	New Hampshire	71.6
6	Vermont	71.1
7	Maine	71.0
7	Mississippi	71.0
7	Utah	71.0
10	Wyoming	70.4
11	Kentucky	70.1
12	Alabama	70.0
12	Delaware	70.0
12	Indiana	70.0
12	Iowa	70.0
16	Idaho	69.9
17	Oklahoma	68.9
18	Pennsylvania	68.6
19	Wisconsin	68.0
20	South Dakota	67.8
21	Missouri	67.6
21	Montana	67.6
23	Virginia	67.5
24	Tennessee	67.2
25	Maryland	66.9
26	New Mexico	66.6
27	North Carolina	66.3
28	Connecticut	66.1
28	Louisiana	66.1
28	Nebraska	66.1
31	Kansas	66.0
31	Ohio	66.0
33	Alaska	65.5
34	Illinois	65.4
35	Arkansas	65.0
36	Arizona	64.4
37	Florida	64.1
37	New Jersey	64.1
39	Colorado	63.7
40	Washington	63.6
41	Georgia	62.8
42	North Dakota	62.6
43	Oregon	61.8
44	Texas	61.7
45	Massachusetts	60.0
46	Rhode Island	56.6
47	Hawaii	55.9
48	Nevada	55.0
49	California	54.4
50	New York	51.1
	District of Columbia	40.3

Source: U.S. Bureau of the Census
 "Housing Vacancies and Homeownership, Annual Statistics: 2017" (https://www.census.gov/housing/hvs/index.html)
*Percent of households occupied by the owner.

Percent of Housing Units That Are Renter-Occupied in 2017

National Percent = 36.1% of Housing Units*

ALPHA ORDER

RANK	STATE	PERCENT
34	Alabama	32.0
12	Alaska	36.5
14	Arizona	35.3
18	Arkansas	34.7
2	California	45.2
15	Colorado	34.8
24	Connecticut	33.8
45	Delaware	29.1
15	Florida	34.8
10	Georgia	37.1
4	Hawaii	41.5
41	Idaho	30.3
24	Illinois	33.8
38	Indiana	31.0
47	Iowa	28.4
23	Kansas	34.1
27	Kentucky	33.5
15	Louisiana	34.8
50	Maine	26.8
30	Maryland	33.3
7	Massachusetts	37.7
46	Michigan	28.7
47	Minnesota	28.4
36	Mississippi	31.5
31	Missouri	33.0
39	Montana	30.8
26	Nebraska	33.7
3	Nevada	43.4
42	New Hampshire	30.2
13	New Jersey	36.2
33	New Mexico	32.1
1	New York	46.2
19	North Carolina	34.6
11	North Dakota	36.6
22	Ohio	34.2
21	Oklahoma	34.5
8	Oregon	37.2
35	Pennsylvania	31.7
5	Rhode Island	39.2
37	South Carolina	31.3
32	South Dakota	32.3
19	Tennessee	34.6
6	Texas	38.0
43	Utah	30.1
40	Vermont	30.5
28	Virginia	33.4
8	Washington	37.2
49	West Virginia	27.5
28	Wisconsin	33.4
44	Wyoming	29.2

RANK ORDER

RANK	STATE	PERCENT
1	New York	46.2
2	California	45.2
3	Nevada	43.4
4	Hawaii	41.5
5	Rhode Island	39.2
6	Texas	38.0
7	Massachusetts	37.7
8	Oregon	37.2
8	Washington	37.2
10	Georgia	37.1
11	North Dakota	36.6
12	Alaska	36.5
13	New Jersey	36.2
14	Arizona	35.3
15	Colorado	34.8
15	Florida	34.8
15	Louisiana	34.8
18	Arkansas	34.7
19	North Carolina	34.6
19	Tennessee	34.6
21	Oklahoma	34.5
22	Ohio	34.2
23	Kansas	34.1
24	Connecticut	33.8
24	Illinois	33.8
26	Nebraska	33.7
27	Kentucky	33.5
28	Virginia	33.4
28	Wisconsin	33.4
30	Maryland	33.3
31	Missouri	33.0
32	South Dakota	32.3
33	New Mexico	32.1
34	Alabama	32.0
35	Pennsylvania	31.7
36	Mississippi	31.5
37	South Carolina	31.3
38	Indiana	31.0
39	Montana	30.8
40	Vermont	30.5
41	Idaho	30.3
42	New Hampshire	30.2
43	Utah	30.1
44	Wyoming	29.2
45	Delaware	29.1
46	Michigan	28.7
47	Iowa	28.4
47	Minnesota	28.4
49	West Virginia	27.5
50	Maine	26.8
	District of Columbia	57.8

Source: U.S. Bureau of the Census
"2017 American Community Survey-Table CP04" (https://www.census.gov/programs-surveys/acs/)
*For occupied housing units.

Median Monthly Rental Payment in 2017

National Median = $1,012*

RANK ORDER

ALPHA ORDER			RANK ORDER		
RANK	STATE	MEDIAN	RANK	STATE	MEDIAN
45	Alabama	$750	1	Hawaii	$1,573
9	Alaska	1,201	2	California	1,447
17	Arizona	1,020	3	Maryland	1,337
49	Arkansas	711	4	New Jersey	1,284
2	California	1,447	5	Colorado	1,240
5	Colorado	1,240	6	New York	1,226
12	Connecticut	1,125	7	Washington	1,216
13	Delaware	1,086	8	Massachusetts	1,208
11	Florida	1,128	9	Alaska	1,201
21	Georgia	958	10	Virginia	1,179
1	Hawaii	1,573	11	Florida	1,128
32	Idaho	822	12	Connecticut	1,125
20	Illinois	974	13	Delaware	1,086
39	Indiana	793	14	Oregon	1,079
43	Iowa	760	15	New Hampshire	1,072
34	Kansas	815	16	Nevada	1,051
47	Kentucky	724	17	Arizona	1,020
28	Louisiana	836	18	Texas	987
36	Maine	806	19	Utah	986
3	Maryland	1,337	20	Illinois	974
8	Massachusetts	1,208	21	Georgia	958
29	Michigan	835	22	Vermont	950
24	Minnesota	939	23	Rhode Island	941
46	Mississippi	742	24	Minnesota	939
38	Missouri	800	25	Pennsylvania	893
44	Montana	759	26	North Carolina	861
37	Nebraska	801	27	South Carolina	848
16	Nevada	1,051	28	Louisiana	836
15	New Hampshire	1,072	29	Michigan	835
4	New Jersey	1,284	30	Tennessee	833
35	New Mexico	813	31	Wyoming	832
6	New York	1,226	32	Idaho	822
26	North Carolina	861	33	Wisconsin	819
40	North Dakota	785	34	Kansas	815
42	Ohio	772	35	New Mexico	813
41	Oklahoma	780	36	Maine	806
14	Oregon	1,079	37	Nebraska	801
25	Pennsylvania	893	38	Missouri	800
23	Rhode Island	941	39	Indiana	793
27	South Carolina	848	40	North Dakota	785
48	South Dakota	722	41	Oklahoma	780
30	Tennessee	833	42	Ohio	772
18	Texas	987	43	Iowa	760
19	Utah	986	44	Montana	759
22	Vermont	950	45	Alabama	750
10	Virginia	1,179	46	Mississippi	742
7	Washington	1,216	47	Kentucky	724
50	West Virginia	690	48	South Dakota	722
33	Wisconsin	819	49	Arkansas	711
31	Wyoming	832	50	West Virginia	690
				District of Columbia	1,499

Source: U.S. Bureau of the Census
   "2017 American Community Survey-Table CP04" (https://www.census.gov/programs-surveys/acs/)
*Monthly housing costs for renter-occupied housing.

Percent of Renters Spending 30 Percent or More of Household Income on Rent and Utilities in 2017
National Percent = 49.5% of Renters

ALPHA ORDER

ALPHA ORDER

RANK ORDER

RANK	STATE	PERCENT	RANK	STATE	PERCENT
25	Alabama	47.4	1	Florida	56.4
31	Alaska	45.8	2	Hawaii	56.1
18	Arizona	48.3	3	Louisiana	55.4
39	Arkansas	44.5	4	California	55.3
4	California	55.3	5	New York	52.7
6	Colorado	52.0	6	Colorado	52.0
9	Connecticut	51.4	7	New Jersey	51.7
15	Delaware	48.7	8	Oregon	51.6
1	Florida	56.4	9	Connecticut	51.4
20	Georgia	48.0	10	Vermont	50.7
2	Hawaii	56.1	11	South Carolina	50.3
31	Idaho	45.8	12	Maryland	50.0
17	Illinois	48.5	13	Massachusetts	49.1
33	Indiana	45.7	14	New Mexico	49.0
47	Iowa	42.2	15	Delaware	48.7
43	Kansas	44.0	16	West Virginia	48.6
45	Kentucky	43.5	17	Illinois	48.5
3	Louisiana	55.4	18	Arizona	48.3
38	Maine	44.6	19	Michigan	48.2
12	Maryland	50.0	20	Georgia	48.0
13	Massachusetts	49.1	21	Mississippi	47.9
19	Michigan	48.2	21	Nevada	47.9
30	Minnesota	46.0	21	Texas	47.9
21	Mississippi	47.9	24	Washington	47.8
37	Missouri	44.7	25	Alabama	47.4
40	Montana	44.4	26	Pennsylvania	47.3
49	Nebraska	40.0	27	Virginia	46.9
21	Nevada	47.9	28	New Hampshire	46.7
28	New Hampshire	46.7	29	North Carolina	46.4
7	New Jersey	51.7	30	Minnesota	46.0
14	New Mexico	49.0	31	Alaska	45.8
5	New York	52.7	31	Idaho	45.8
29	North Carolina	46.4	33	Indiana	45.7
50	North Dakota	39.9	34	Rhode Island	45.6
40	Ohio	44.4	35	Oklahoma	45.5
35	Oklahoma	45.5	36	Tennessee	45.4
8	Oregon	51.6	37	Missouri	44.7
26	Pennsylvania	47.3	38	Maine	44.6
34	Rhode Island	45.6	39	Arkansas	44.5
11	South Carolina	50.3	40	Montana	44.4
48	South Dakota	40.8	40	Ohio	44.4
36	Tennessee	45.4	40	Utah	44.4
21	Texas	47.9	43	Kansas	44.0
40	Utah	44.4	44	Wisconsin	43.7
10	Vermont	50.7	45	Kentucky	43.5
27	Virginia	46.9	46	Wyoming	42.6
24	Washington	47.8	47	Iowa	42.2
16	West Virginia	48.6	48	South Dakota	40.8
44	Wisconsin	43.7	49	Nebraska	40.0
46	Wyoming	42.6	50	North Dakota	39.9
				District of Columbia	47.9

Source: U.S. Bureau of the Census

"2017 American Community Survey-Table CP04" (https://www.census.gov/programs-surveys/acs/)

State and Local Government Expenditures
for Housing and Community Development in 2016
National Total = $50,172,861,000*

ALPHA ORDER

RANK	STATE	EXPENDITURES	% of USA
24	Alabama	$501,056,000	1.0%
29	Alaska	346,095,000	0.7%
27	Arizona	447,925,000	0.9%
40	Arkansas	186,139,000	0.4%
1	California	8,162,757,000	16.3%
18	Colorado	892,783,000	1.8%
17	Connecticut	970,427,000	1.9%
43	Delaware	147,749,000	0.3%
4	Florida	2,273,269,000	4.5%
13	Georgia	1,234,564,000	2.5%
37	Hawaii	247,168,000	0.5%
44	Idaho	147,049,000	0.3%
7	Illinois	1,968,791,000	3.9%
19	Indiana	877,838,000	1.7%
41	Iowa	165,043,000	0.3%
32	Kansas	293,502,000	0.6%
26	Kentucky	452,186,000	0.9%
21	Louisiana	754,482,000	1.5%
35	Maine	284,032,000	0.6%
10	Maryland	1,450,301,000	2.9%
3	Massachusetts	2,761,487,000	5.5%
14	Michigan	1,137,670,000	2.3%
16	Minnesota	1,021,298,000	2.0%
36	Mississippi	273,178,000	0.5%
23	Missouri	637,837,000	1.3%
49	Montana	82,730,000	0.2%
38	Nebraska	216,815,000	0.4%
33	Nevada	292,543,000	0.6%
39	New Hampshire	212,811,000	0.4%
11	New Jersey	1,365,900,000	2.7%
45	New Mexico	144,697,000	0.3%
2	New York	5,901,424,000	11.8%
9	North Carolina	1,465,543,000	2.9%
48	North Dakota	92,555,000	0.2%
5	Ohio	2,134,667,000	4.3%
28	Oklahoma	444,995,000	0.9%
22	Oregon	650,397,000	1.3%
8	Pennsylvania	1,839,406,000	3.7%
34	Rhode Island	291,758,000	0.6%
25	South Carolina	493,741,000	1.0%
47	South Dakota	100,514,000	0.2%
20	Tennessee	805,081,000	1.6%
6	Texas	1,987,036,000	4.0%
30	Utah	338,034,000	0.7%
42	Vermont	149,831,000	0.3%
15	Virginia	1,032,236,000	2.1%
12	Washington	1,355,913,000	2.7%
46	West Virginia	138,779,000	0.3%
31	Wisconsin	306,706,000	0.6%
50	Wyoming	15,151,000	0.0%

RANK ORDER

RANK	STATE	EXPENDITURES	% of USA
1	California	$8,162,757,000	16.3%
2	New York	5,901,424,000	11.8%
3	Massachusetts	2,761,487,000	5.5%
4	Florida	2,273,269,000	4.5%
5	Ohio	2,134,667,000	4.3%
6	Texas	1,987,036,000	4.0%
7	Illinois	1,968,791,000	3.9%
8	Pennsylvania	1,839,406,000	3.7%
9	North Carolina	1,465,543,000	2.9%
10	Maryland	1,450,301,000	2.9%
11	New Jersey	1,365,900,000	2.7%
12	Washington	1,355,913,000	2.7%
13	Georgia	1,234,564,000	2.5%
14	Michigan	1,137,670,000	2.3%
15	Virginia	1,032,236,000	2.1%
16	Minnesota	1,021,298,000	2.0%
17	Connecticut	970,427,000	1.9%
18	Colorado	892,783,000	1.8%
19	Indiana	877,838,000	1.7%
20	Tennessee	805,081,000	1.6%
21	Louisiana	754,482,000	1.5%
22	Oregon	650,397,000	1.3%
23	Missouri	637,837,000	1.3%
24	Alabama	501,056,000	1.0%
25	South Carolina	493,741,000	1.0%
26	Kentucky	452,186,000	0.9%
27	Arizona	447,925,000	0.9%
28	Oklahoma	444,995,000	0.9%
29	Alaska	346,095,000	0.7%
30	Utah	338,034,000	0.7%
31	Wisconsin	306,706,000	0.6%
32	Kansas	293,502,000	0.6%
33	Nevada	292,543,000	0.6%
34	Rhode Island	291,758,000	0.6%
35	Maine	284,032,000	0.6%
36	Mississippi	273,178,000	0.5%
37	Hawaii	247,168,000	0.5%
38	Nebraska	216,815,000	0.4%
39	New Hampshire	212,811,000	0.4%
40	Arkansas	186,139,000	0.4%
41	Iowa	165,043,000	0.3%
42	Vermont	149,831,000	0.3%
43	Delaware	147,749,000	0.3%
44	Idaho	147,049,000	0.3%
45	New Mexico	144,697,000	0.3%
46	West Virginia	138,779,000	0.3%
47	South Dakota	100,514,000	0.2%
48	North Dakota	92,555,000	0.2%
49	Montana	82,730,000	0.2%
50	Wyoming	15,151,000	0.0%
	District of Columbia	678,972,000	1.4%

Source: U.S. Bureau of the Census, Governments Division
   "2016 State and Local Government Finances" (https://www.census.gov/programs-surveys/gov-finances.html)
*Direct general expenditures.

Per Capita State and Local Government Expenditures for Housing and Community Development in 2016
National Per Capita = $155*

ALPHA ORDER

RANK	STATE	PER CAPITA
35	Alabama	$103
1	Alaska	467
46	Arizona	64
47	Arkansas	62
9	California	208
14	Colorado	161
5	Connecticut	271
18	Delaware	156
33	Florida	110
27	Georgia	120
13	Hawaii	173
41	Idaho	87
20	Illinois	153
23	Indiana	132
48	Iowa	53
37	Kansas	101
36	Kentucky	102
14	Louisiana	161
8	Maine	213
6	Maryland	242
2	Massachusetts	405
29	Michigan	114
11	Minnesota	185
40	Mississippi	91
34	Missouri	105
42	Montana	79
29	Nebraska	114
38	Nevada	100
16	New Hampshire	159
19	New Jersey	154
45	New Mexico	69
3	New York	300
21	North Carolina	144
24	North Dakota	123
12	Ohio	183
31	Oklahoma	113
16	Oregon	159
21	Pennsylvania	144
4	Rhode Island	276
38	South Carolina	100
28	South Dakota	116
26	Tennessee	121
44	Texas	71
32	Utah	111
7	Vermont	240
24	Virginia	123
10	Washington	186
43	West Virginia	76
48	Wisconsin	53
50	Wyoming	26

RANK ORDER

RANK	STATE	PER CAPITA
1	Alaska	$467
2	Massachusetts	405
3	New York	300
4	Rhode Island	276
5	Connecticut	271
6	Maryland	242
7	Vermont	240
8	Maine	213
9	California	208
10	Washington	186
11	Minnesota	185
12	Ohio	183
13	Hawaii	173
14	Colorado	161
14	Louisiana	161
16	New Hampshire	159
16	Oregon	159
18	Delaware	156
19	New Jersey	154
20	Illinois	153
21	North Carolina	144
21	Pennsylvania	144
23	Indiana	132
24	North Dakota	123
24	Virginia	123
26	Tennessee	121
27	Georgia	120
28	South Dakota	116
29	Michigan	114
29	Nebraska	114
31	Oklahoma	113
32	Utah	111
33	Florida	110
34	Missouri	105
35	Alabama	103
36	Kentucky	102
37	Kansas	101
38	Nevada	100
38	South Carolina	100
40	Mississippi	91
41	Idaho	87
42	Montana	79
43	West Virginia	76
44	Texas	71
45	New Mexico	69
46	Arizona	64
47	Arkansas	62
48	Iowa	53
48	Wisconsin	53
50	Wyoming	26
	District of Columbia	989

Source: CQ Press using data from U.S. Bureau of the Census, Governments Division
"2016 State and Local Government Finances" (https://www.census.gov/programs-surveys/gov-finances.html)
*Direct general expenditures.

State & Local Government Spending for Housing and Community Development as a Percent of All State and Local Government Expenditures in 2016
National Percent = 1.7%*

ALPHA ORDER

RANK	STATE	PERCENT
34	Alabama	1.3
3	Alaska	2.5
42	Arizona	0.9
46	Arkansas	0.8
10	California	1.9
10	Colorado	1.9
3	Connecticut	2.5
24	Delaware	1.5
22	Florida	1.6
15	Georgia	1.8
15	Hawaii	1.8
34	Idaho	1.3
15	Illinois	1.8
21	Indiana	1.7
49	Iowa	0.5
36	Kansas	1.2
36	Kentucky	1.2
15	Louisiana	1.8
6	Maine	2.4
3	Maryland	2.5
1	Massachusetts	3.7
30	Michigan	1.4
15	Minnesota	1.8
40	Mississippi	1.0
30	Missouri	1.4
42	Montana	0.9
36	Nebraska	1.2
30	Nevada	1.4
10	New Hampshire	1.9
24	New Jersey	1.5
47	New Mexico	0.7
7	New York	2.2
10	North Carolina	1.9
40	North Dakota	1.0
8	Ohio	2.1
24	Oklahoma	1.5
22	Oregon	1.6
24	Pennsylvania	1.5
2	Rhode Island	2.9
36	South Carolina	1.2
30	South Dakota	1.4
15	Tennessee	1.8
42	Texas	0.9
24	Utah	1.5
8	Vermont	2.1
24	Virginia	1.5
10	Washington	1.9
42	West Virginia	0.9
48	Wisconsin	0.6
50	Wyoming	0.2

RANK ORDER

RANK	STATE	PERCENT
1	Massachusetts	3.7
2	Rhode Island	2.9
3	Alaska	2.5
3	Connecticut	2.5
3	Maryland	2.5
6	Maine	2.4
7	New York	2.2
8	Ohio	2.1
8	Vermont	2.1
10	California	1.9
10	Colorado	1.9
10	New Hampshire	1.9
10	North Carolina	1.9
10	Washington	1.9
15	Georgia	1.8
15	Hawaii	1.8
15	Illinois	1.8
15	Louisiana	1.8
15	Minnesota	1.8
15	Tennessee	1.8
21	Indiana	1.7
22	Florida	1.6
22	Oregon	1.6
24	Delaware	1.5
24	New Jersey	1.5
24	Oklahoma	1.5
24	Pennsylvania	1.5
24	Utah	1.5
24	Virginia	1.5
30	Michigan	1.4
30	Missouri	1.4
30	Nevada	1.4
30	South Dakota	1.4
34	Alabama	1.3
34	Idaho	1.3
36	Kansas	1.2
36	Kentucky	1.2
36	Nebraska	1.2
36	South Carolina	1.2
40	Mississippi	1.0
40	North Dakota	1.0
42	Arizona	0.9
42	Montana	0.9
42	Texas	0.9
42	West Virginia	0.9
46	Arkansas	0.8
47	New Mexico	0.7
48	Wisconsin	0.6
49	Iowa	0.5
50	Wyoming	0.2

| | District of Columbia | 5.3 |

Source: CQ Press using data from U.S. Bureau of the Census, Governments Division

"2016 State and Local Government Finances" (https://www.census.gov/programs-surveys/gov-finances.html)

*As a percent of direct general expenditures.

XIII. Population

Population in 2018

National Total = 327,167,434*

ALPHA ORDER

RANK	STATE	POPULATION	% of USA
24	Alabama	4,887,871	1.5%
48	Alaska	737,438	0.2%
14	Arizona	7,171,646	2.2%
33	Arkansas	3,013,825	0.9%
1	California	39,557,045	12.1%
21	Colorado	5,695,564	1.7%
29	Connecticut	3,572,665	1.1%
45	Delaware	967,171	0.3%
3	Florida	21,299,325	6.5%
8	Georgia	10,519,475	3.2%
40	Hawaii	1,420,491	0.4%
39	Idaho	1,754,208	0.5%
6	Illinois	12,741,080	3.9%
17	Indiana	6,691,878	2.0%
31	Iowa	3,156,145	1.0%
35	Kansas	2,911,505	0.9%
26	Kentucky	4,468,402	1.4%
25	Louisiana	4,659,978	1.4%
42	Maine	1,338,404	0.4%
19	Maryland	6,042,718	1.8%
15	Massachusetts	6,902,149	2.1%
10	Michigan	9,995,915	3.1%
22	Minnesota	5,611,179	1.7%
34	Mississippi	2,986,530	0.9%
18	Missouri	6,126,452	1.9%
43	Montana	1,062,305	0.3%
37	Nebraska	1,929,268	0.6%
32	Nevada	3,034,392	0.9%
41	New Hampshire	1,356,458	0.4%
11	New Jersey	8,908,520	2.7%
36	New Mexico	2,095,428	0.6%
4	New York	19,542,209	6.0%
9	North Carolina	10,383,620	3.2%
47	North Dakota	760,077	0.2%
7	Ohio	11,689,442	3.6%
28	Oklahoma	3,943,079	1.2%
27	Oregon	4,190,713	1.3%
5	Pennsylvania	12,807,060	3.9%
44	Rhode Island	1,057,315	0.3%
23	South Carolina	5,084,127	1.6%
46	South Dakota	882,235	0.3%
16	Tennessee	6,770,010	2.1%
2	Texas	28,701,845	8.8%
30	Utah	3,161,105	1.0%
49	Vermont	626,299	0.2%
12	Virginia	8,517,685	2.6%
13	Washington	7,535,591	2.3%
38	West Virginia	1,805,832	0.6%
20	Wisconsin	5,813,568	1.8%
50	Wyoming	577,737	0.2%

RANK ORDER

RANK	STATE	POPULATION	% of USA
1	California	39,557,045	12.1%
2	Texas	28,701,845	8.8%
3	Florida	21,299,325	6.5%
4	New York	19,542,209	6.0%
5	Pennsylvania	12,807,060	3.9%
6	Illinois	12,741,080	3.9%
7	Ohio	11,689,442	3.6%
8	Georgia	10,519,475	3.2%
9	North Carolina	10,383,620	3.2%
10	Michigan	9,995,915	3.1%
11	New Jersey	8,908,520	2.7%
12	Virginia	8,517,685	2.6%
13	Washington	7,535,591	2.3%
14	Arizona	7,171,646	2.2%
15	Massachusetts	6,902,149	2.1%
16	Tennessee	6,770,010	2.1%
17	Indiana	6,691,878	2.0%
18	Missouri	6,126,452	1.9%
19	Maryland	6,042,718	1.8%
20	Wisconsin	5,813,568	1.8%
21	Colorado	5,695,564	1.7%
22	Minnesota	5,611,179	1.7%
23	South Carolina	5,084,127	1.6%
24	Alabama	4,887,871	1.5%
25	Louisiana	4,659,978	1.4%
26	Kentucky	4,468,402	1.4%
27	Oregon	4,190,713	1.3%
28	Oklahoma	3,943,079	1.2%
29	Connecticut	3,572,665	1.1%
30	Utah	3,161,105	1.0%
31	Iowa	3,156,145	1.0%
32	Nevada	3,034,392	0.9%
33	Arkansas	3,013,825	0.9%
34	Mississippi	2,986,530	0.9%
35	Kansas	2,911,505	0.9%
36	New Mexico	2,095,428	0.6%
37	Nebraska	1,929,268	0.6%
38	West Virginia	1,805,832	0.6%
39	Idaho	1,754,208	0.5%
40	Hawaii	1,420,491	0.4%
41	New Hampshire	1,356,458	0.4%
42	Maine	1,338,404	0.4%
43	Montana	1,062,305	0.3%
44	Rhode Island	1,057,315	0.3%
45	Delaware	967,171	0.3%
46	South Dakota	882,235	0.3%
47	North Dakota	760,077	0.2%
48	Alaska	737,438	0.2%
49	Vermont	626,299	0.2%
50	Wyoming	577,737	0.2%
	District of Columbia	702,455	0.2%

Source: U.S. Bureau of the Census
"Population Estimates" (December 2018, http://www.census.gov/programs-surveys/popest.html)
*Resident population estimate as of July 1, 2018.

Population in 2017

National Total = 325,147,121*

ALPHA ORDER

ALPHA ORDER

RANK	STATE	POPULATION	% of USA
24	Alabama	4,875,120	1.5%
48	Alaska	739,786	0.2%
14	Arizona	7,048,876	2.2%
32	Arkansas	3,002,997	0.9%
1	California	39,399,349	12.1%
21	Colorado	5,615,902	1.7%
29	Connecticut	3,573,880	1.1%
45	Delaware	957,078	0.3%
3	Florida	20,976,812	6.5%
8	Georgia	10,413,055	3.2%
40	Hawaii	1,424,203	0.4%
39	Idaho	1,718,904	0.5%
6	Illinois	12,786,196	3.9%
17	Indiana	6,660,082	2.0%
30	Iowa	3,143,637	1.0%
35	Kansas	2,910,689	0.9%
26	Kentucky	4,453,874	1.4%
25	Louisiana	4,670,818	1.4%
42	Maine	1,335,063	0.4%
19	Maryland	6,024,891	1.9%
15	Massachusetts	6,863,246	2.1%
10	Michigan	9,976,447	3.1%
22	Minnesota	5,568,155	1.7%
33	Mississippi	2,989,663	0.9%
18	Missouri	6,108,612	1.9%
44	Montana	1,053,090	0.3%
37	Nebraska	1,917,575	0.6%
34	Nevada	2,972,405	0.9%
41	New Hampshire	1,349,767	0.4%
11	New Jersey	8,888,543	2.7%
36	New Mexico	2,093,395	0.6%
4	New York	19,590,719	6.0%
9	North Carolina	10,270,800	3.2%
47	North Dakota	755,176	0.2%
7	Ohio	11,664,129	3.6%
28	Oklahoma	3,932,640	1.2%
27	Oregon	4,146,592	1.3%
5	Pennsylvania	12,790,447	3.9%
43	Rhode Island	1,056,486	0.3%
23	South Carolina	5,021,219	1.5%
46	South Dakota	873,286	0.3%
16	Tennessee	6,708,794	2.1%
2	Texas	28,322,717	8.7%
31	Utah	3,103,118	1.0%
49	Vermont	624,525	0.2%
12	Virginia	8,465,207	2.6%
13	Washington	7,425,432	2.3%
38	West Virginia	1,817,048	0.6%
20	Wisconsin	5,792,051	1.8%
50	Wyoming	578,934	0.2%

RANK ORDER

RANK	STATE	POPULATION	% of USA
1	California	39,399,349	12.1%
2	Texas	28,322,717	8.7%
3	Florida	20,976,812	6.5%
4	New York	19,590,719	6.0%
5	Pennsylvania	12,790,447	3.9%
6	Illinois	12,786,196	3.9%
7	Ohio	11,664,129	3.6%
8	Georgia	10,413,055	3.2%
9	North Carolina	10,270,800	3.2%
10	Michigan	9,976,447	3.1%
11	New Jersey	8,888,543	2.7%
12	Virginia	8,465,207	2.6%
13	Washington	7,425,432	2.3%
14	Arizona	7,048,876	2.2%
15	Massachusetts	6,863,246	2.1%
16	Tennessee	6,708,794	2.1%
17	Indiana	6,660,082	2.0%
18	Missouri	6,108,612	1.9%
19	Maryland	6,024,891	1.9%
20	Wisconsin	5,792,051	1.8%
21	Colorado	5,615,902	1.7%
22	Minnesota	5,568,155	1.7%
23	South Carolina	5,021,219	1.5%
24	Alabama	4,875,120	1.5%
25	Louisiana	4,670,818	1.4%
26	Kentucky	4,453,874	1.4%
27	Oregon	4,146,592	1.3%
28	Oklahoma	3,932,640	1.2%
29	Connecticut	3,573,880	1.1%
30	Iowa	3,143,637	1.0%
31	Utah	3,103,118	1.0%
32	Arkansas	3,002,997	0.9%
33	Mississippi	2,989,663	0.9%
34	Nevada	2,972,405	0.9%
35	Kansas	2,910,689	0.9%
36	New Mexico	2,093,395	0.6%
37	Nebraska	1,917,575	0.6%
38	West Virginia	1,817,048	0.6%
39	Idaho	1,718,904	0.5%
40	Hawaii	1,424,203	0.4%
41	New Hampshire	1,349,767	0.4%
42	Maine	1,335,063	0.4%
43	Rhode Island	1,056,486	0.3%
44	Montana	1,053,090	0.3%
45	Delaware	957,078	0.3%
46	South Dakota	873,286	0.3%
47	North Dakota	755,176	0.2%
48	Alaska	739,786	0.2%
49	Vermont	624,525	0.2%
50	Wyoming	578,934	0.2%
	District of Columbia	695,691	0.2%

Source: U.S. Bureau of the Census

"Population Estimates" (December 2018, http://www.census.gov/programs-surveys/popest.html)

*Resident population. Revised estimates of July 1, 2018.

Numerical Population Change: 2017 to 2018

National Total = 2,020,313 Increase*

ALPHA ORDER			RANK ORDER		
RANK	STATE	GAIN/LOSS	RANK	STATE	GAIN/LOSS
27	Alabama	12,751	1	Texas	379,128
44	Alaska	(2,348)	2	Florida	322,513
4	Arizona	122,770	3	California	157,696
30	Arkansas	10,828	4	Arizona	122,770
3	California	157,696	5	North Carolina	112,820
8	Colorado	79,662	6	Washington	110,159
43	Connecticut	(1,215)	7	Georgia	106,420
32	Delaware	10,093	8	Colorado	79,662
2	Florida	322,513	9	South Carolina	62,908
7	Georgia	106,420	10	Nevada	61,987
46	Hawaii	(3,712)	11	Tennessee	61,216
17	Idaho	35,304	12	Utah	57,987
49	Illinois	(45,116)	13	Virginia	52,478
18	Indiana	31,796	14	Oregon	44,121
28	Iowa	12,508	15	Minnesota	43,024
41	Kansas	816	16	Massachusetts	38,903
26	Kentucky	14,528	17	Idaho	35,304
47	Louisiana	(10,840)	18	Indiana	31,796
37	Maine	3,341	19	Ohio	25,313
24	Maryland	17,827	20	Wisconsin	21,517
16	Massachusetts	38,903	21	New Jersey	19,977
22	Michigan	19,468	22	Michigan	19,468
15	Minnesota	43,024	23	Missouri	17,840
45	Mississippi	(3,133)	24	Maryland	17,827
23	Missouri	17,840	25	Pennsylvania	16,613
33	Montana	9,215	26	Kentucky	14,528
29	Nebraska	11,693	27	Alabama	12,751
10	Nevada	61,987	28	Iowa	12,508
35	New Hampshire	6,691	29	Nebraska	11,693
21	New Jersey	19,977	30	Arkansas	10,828
38	New Mexico	2,033	31	Oklahoma	10,439
50	New York	(48,510)	32	Delaware	10,093
5	North Carolina	112,820	33	Montana	9,215
36	North Dakota	4,901	34	South Dakota	8,949
19	Ohio	25,313	35	New Hampshire	6,691
31	Oklahoma	10,439	36	North Dakota	4,901
14	Oregon	44,121	37	Maine	3,341
25	Pennsylvania	16,613	38	New Mexico	2,033
40	Rhode Island	829	39	Vermont	1,774
9	South Carolina	62,908	40	Rhode Island	829
34	South Dakota	8,949	41	Kansas	816
11	Tennessee	61,216	42	Wyoming	(1,197)
1	Texas	379,128	43	Connecticut	(1,215)
12	Utah	57,987	44	Alaska	(2,348)
39	Vermont	1,774	45	Mississippi	(3,133)
13	Virginia	52,478	46	Hawaii	(3,712)
6	Washington	110,159	47	Louisiana	(10,840)
48	West Virginia	(11,216)	48	West Virginia	(11,216)
20	Wisconsin	21,517	49	Illinois	(45,116)
42	Wyoming	(1,197)	50	New York	(48,510)
				District of Columbia	6,764

Source: CQ Press using data from U.S. Bureau of the Census
"Population Estimates" (December 2018, http://www.census.gov/programs-surveys/popest.html)
*Resident population from July 1, 2017 to July 1, 2018.

Percent Change in Population: 2017 to 2018

National Percent Change = 0.6% Increase*

ALPHA ORDER			RANK ORDER		
RANK	STATE	PERCENT CHANGE	RANK	STATE	PERCENT CHANGE
28	Alabama	0.3	1	Idaho	2.1
47	Alaska	(0.3)	1	Nevada	2.1
4	Arizona	1.7	3	Utah	1.9
24	Arkansas	0.4	4	Arizona	1.7
24	California	0.4	5	Florida	1.5
7	Colorado	1.4	5	Washington	1.5
41	Connecticut	0.0	7	Colorado	1.4
10	Delaware	1.1	8	South Carolina	1.3
5	Florida	1.5	8	Texas	1.3
13	Georgia	1.0	10	Delaware	1.1
47	Hawaii	(0.3)	10	North Carolina	1.1
1	Idaho	2.1	10	Oregon	1.1
49	Illinois	(0.4)	13	Georgia	1.0
22	Indiana	0.5	13	South Dakota	1.0
24	Iowa	0.4	15	Montana	0.9
41	Kansas	0.0	15	Tennessee	0.9
28	Kentucky	0.3	17	Minnesota	0.8
44	Louisiana	(0.2)	18	Massachusetts	0.6
28	Maine	0.3	18	Nebraska	0.6
28	Maryland	0.3	18	North Dakota	0.6
18	Massachusetts	0.6	18	Virginia	0.6
35	Michigan	0.2	22	Indiana	0.5
17	Minnesota	0.8	22	New Hampshire	0.5
43	Mississippi	(0.1)	24	Arkansas	0.4
28	Missouri	0.3	24	California	0.4
15	Montana	0.9	24	Iowa	0.4
18	Nebraska	0.6	24	Wisconsin	0.4
1	Nevada	2.1	28	Alabama	0.3
22	New Hampshire	0.5	28	Kentucky	0.3
35	New Jersey	0.2	28	Maine	0.3
38	New Mexico	0.1	28	Maryland	0.3
44	New York	(0.2)	28	Missouri	0.3
10	North Carolina	1.1	28	Oklahoma	0.3
18	North Dakota	0.6	28	Vermont	0.3
35	Ohio	0.2	35	Michigan	0.2
28	Oklahoma	0.3	35	New Jersey	0.2
10	Oregon	1.1	35	Ohio	0.2
38	Pennsylvania	0.1	38	New Mexico	0.1
38	Rhode Island	0.1	38	Pennsylvania	0.1
8	South Carolina	1.3	38	Rhode Island	0.1
13	South Dakota	1.0	41	Connecticut	0.0
15	Tennessee	0.9	41	Kansas	0.0
8	Texas	1.3	43	Mississippi	(0.1)
3	Utah	1.9	44	Louisiana	(0.2)
28	Vermont	0.3	44	New York	(0.2)
18	Virginia	0.6	44	Wyoming	(0.2)
5	Washington	1.5	47	Alaska	(0.3)
50	West Virginia	(0.6)	47	Hawaii	(0.3)
24	Wisconsin	0.4	49	Illinois	(0.4)
44	Wyoming	(0.2)	50	West Virginia	(0.6)
				District of Columbia	1.0

Source: CQ Press using data from U.S. Bureau of the Census
"Population Estimates" (December 2018, http://www.census.gov/programs-surveys/popest.html)
*Resident population from July 1, 2017 to July 1, 2018.

Population per Square Mile in 2018

National Rate = 92.6 Persons per Square Mile*

ALPHA ORDER

RANK	STATE	RATE
27	Alabama	96.5
50	Alaska	1.3
33	Arizona	63.1
34	Arkansas	57.9
11	California	253.9
37	Colorado	55.0
4	Connecticut	737.8
6	Delaware	496.2
8	Florida	397.2
17	Georgia	182.9
13	Hawaii	221.2
44	Idaho	21.2
12	Illinois	229.5
16	Indiana	186.8
36	Iowa	56.5
41	Kansas	35.6
23	Kentucky	113.2
25	Louisiana	107.9
39	Maine	43.4
5	Maryland	622.5
3	Massachusetts	884.9
18	Michigan	176.8
30	Minnesota	70.5
32	Mississippi	63.6
28	Missouri	89.1
48	Montana	7.3
43	Nebraska	25.1
42	Nevada	27.6
21	New Hampshire	151.5
1	New Jersey	1,211.4
45	New Mexico	17.3
7	New York	414.7
15	North Carolina	213.6
47	North Dakota	11.0
10	Ohio	286.1
35	Oklahoma	57.5
38	Oregon	43.7
9	Pennsylvania	286.2
2	Rhode Island	1,022.5
19	South Carolina	169.1
46	South Dakota	11.6
20	Tennessee	164.2
24	Texas	109.9
40	Utah	38.5
31	Vermont	68.0
14	Virginia	215.7
22	Washington	113.4
29	West Virginia	75.1
26	Wisconsin	107.3
49	Wyoming	6.0

RANK ORDER

RANK	STATE	RATE
1	New Jersey	1,211.4
2	Rhode Island	1,022.5
3	Massachusetts	884.9
4	Connecticut	737.8
5	Maryland	622.5
6	Delaware	496.2
7	New York	414.7
8	Florida	397.2
9	Pennsylvania	286.2
10	Ohio	286.1
11	California	253.9
12	Illinois	229.5
13	Hawaii	221.2
14	Virginia	215.7
15	North Carolina	213.6
16	Indiana	186.8
17	Georgia	182.9
18	Michigan	176.8
19	South Carolina	169.1
20	Tennessee	164.2
21	New Hampshire	151.5
22	Washington	113.4
23	Kentucky	113.2
24	Texas	109.9
25	Louisiana	107.9
26	Wisconsin	107.3
27	Alabama	96.5
28	Missouri	89.1
29	West Virginia	75.1
30	Minnesota	70.5
31	Vermont	68.0
32	Mississippi	63.6
33	Arizona	63.1
34	Arkansas	57.9
35	Oklahoma	57.5
36	Iowa	56.5
37	Colorado	55.0
38	Oregon	43.7
39	Maine	43.4
40	Utah	38.5
41	Kansas	35.6
42	Nevada	27.6
43	Nebraska	25.1
44	Idaho	21.2
45	New Mexico	17.3
46	South Dakota	11.6
47	North Dakota	11.0
48	Montana	7.3
49	Wyoming	6.0
50	Alaska	1.3
	District of Columbia	11,515.7

Source: CQ Press using data from U.S. Bureau of the Census
"Population Estimates" (December 2018, http://www.census.gov/programs-surveys/popest.html)
*Resident population. Based on land area of states.

Male Population in 2017

National Total = 160,408,119 Males

ALPHA ORDER

ALPHA ORDER

RANK	STATE	MALES	% of USA
24	Alabama	2,359,836	1.5%
48	Alaska	386,792	0.2%
14	Arizona	3,488,301	2.2%
33	Arkansas	1,476,064	0.9%
1	California	19,647,553	12.2%
21	Colorado	2,822,333	1.8%
29	Connecticut	1,751,800	1.1%
45	Delaware	465,514	0.3%
3	Florida	10,256,819	6.4%
8	Georgia	5,075,507	3.2%
40	Hawaii	716,087	0.4%
39	Idaho	860,458	0.5%
5	Illinois	6,292,478	3.9%
16	Indiana	3,287,095	2.0%
30	Iowa	1,564,733	1.0%
34	Kansas	1,451,956	0.9%
26	Kentucky	2,194,318	1.4%
25	Louisiana	2,289,446	1.4%
42	Maine	654,520	0.4%
19	Maryland	2,934,154	1.8%
15	Massachusetts	3,330,365	2.1%
10	Michigan	4,903,752	3.1%
22	Minnesota	2,776,846	1.7%
35	Mississippi	1,445,878	0.9%
18	Missouri	3,002,236	1.9%
43	Montana	528,956	0.3%
37	Nebraska	958,131	0.6%
32	Nevada	1,503,749	0.9%
41	New Hampshire	665,009	0.4%
11	New Jersey	4,396,574	2.7%
36	New Mexico	1,034,144	0.6%
4	New York	9,637,462	6.0%
9	North Carolina	5,001,438	3.1%
47	North Dakota	387,299	0.2%
7	Ohio	5,713,100	3.6%
28	Oklahoma	1,947,562	1.2%
27	Oregon	2,052,989	1.3%
6	Pennsylvania	6,271,329	3.9%
44	Rhode Island	514,991	0.3%
23	South Carolina	2,437,687	1.5%
46	South Dakota	438,960	0.3%
17	Tennessee	3,275,966	2.0%
2	Texas	14,061,793	8.8%
31	Utah	1,561,688	1.0%
49	Vermont	308,256	0.2%
12	Virginia	4,166,727	2.6%
13	Washington	3,703,473	2.3%
38	West Virginia	898,620	0.6%
20	Wisconsin	2,882,738	1.8%
50	Wyoming	295,438	0.2%

RANK ORDER

RANK	STATE	MALES	% of USA
1	California	19,647,553	12.2%
2	Texas	14,061,793	8.8%
3	Florida	10,256,819	6.4%
4	New York	9,637,462	6.0%
5	Illinois	6,292,478	3.9%
6	Pennsylvania	6,271,329	3.9%
7	Ohio	5,713,100	3.6%
8	Georgia	5,075,507	3.2%
9	North Carolina	5,001,438	3.1%
10	Michigan	4,903,752	3.1%
11	New Jersey	4,396,574	2.7%
12	Virginia	4,166,727	2.6%
13	Washington	3,703,473	2.3%
14	Arizona	3,488,301	2.2%
15	Massachusetts	3,330,365	2.1%
16	Indiana	3,287,095	2.0%
17	Tennessee	3,275,966	2.0%
18	Missouri	3,002,236	1.9%
19	Maryland	2,934,154	1.8%
20	Wisconsin	2,882,738	1.8%
21	Colorado	2,822,333	1.8%
22	Minnesota	2,776,846	1.7%
23	South Carolina	2,437,687	1.5%
24	Alabama	2,359,836	1.5%
25	Louisiana	2,289,446	1.4%
26	Kentucky	2,194,318	1.4%
27	Oregon	2,052,989	1.3%
28	Oklahoma	1,947,562	1.2%
29	Connecticut	1,751,800	1.1%
30	Iowa	1,564,733	1.0%
31	Utah	1,561,688	1.0%
32	Nevada	1,503,749	0.9%
33	Arkansas	1,476,064	0.9%
34	Kansas	1,451,956	0.9%
35	Mississippi	1,445,878	0.9%
36	New Mexico	1,034,144	0.6%
37	Nebraska	958,131	0.6%
38	West Virginia	898,620	0.6%
39	Idaho	860,458	0.5%
40	Hawaii	716,087	0.4%
41	New Hampshire	665,009	0.4%
42	Maine	654,520	0.4%
43	Montana	528,956	0.3%
44	Rhode Island	514,991	0.3%
45	Delaware	465,514	0.3%
46	South Dakota	438,960	0.3%
47	North Dakota	387,299	0.2%
48	Alaska	386,792	0.2%
49	Vermont	308,256	0.2%
50	Wyoming	295,438	0.2%
	District of Columbia	329,199	0.2%

Source: U.S. Bureau of the Census
"State Characteristics: Vintage 2017" (https://www.census.gov/programs-surveys/popest/data/data-sets.html)

Female Population in 2017

National Total = 165,311,059 Females

ALPHA ORDER

RANK	STATE	FEMALES	% of USA
24	Alabama	2,514,911	1.5%
48	Alaska	353,003	0.2%
15	Arizona	3,527,969	2.1%
33	Arkansas	1,528,215	0.9%
1	California	19,889,100	12.0%
22	Colorado	2,784,821	1.7%
29	Connecticut	1,836,384	1.1%
45	Delaware	496,425	0.3%
3	Florida	10,727,581	6.5%
8	Georgia	5,353,872	3.2%
40	Hawaii	711,451	0.4%
39	Idaho	856,485	0.5%
6	Illinois	6,509,545	3.9%
17	Indiana	3,379,723	2.0%
30	Iowa	1,580,978	1.0%
35	Kansas	1,461,167	0.9%
26	Kentucky	2,259,871	1.4%
25	Louisiana	2,394,887	1.4%
41	Maine	681,387	0.4%
18	Maryland	3,118,023	1.9%
14	Massachusetts	3,529,454	2.1%
10	Michigan	5,058,559	3.1%
21	Minnesota	2,799,760	1.7%
32	Mississippi	1,538,222	0.9%
19	Missouri	3,111,296	1.9%
44	Montana	521,537	0.3%
37	Nebraska	961,945	0.6%
34	Nevada	1,494,290	0.9%
42	New Hampshire	677,786	0.4%
11	New Jersey	4,609,070	2.8%
36	New Mexico	1,053,926	0.6%
4	New York	10,211,937	6.2%
9	North Carolina	5,271,981	3.2%
47	North Dakota	368,094	0.2%
7	Ohio	5,945,509	3.6%
28	Oklahoma	1,983,302	1.2%
27	Oregon	2,089,787	1.3%
5	Pennsylvania	6,534,208	4.0%
43	Rhode Island	544,648	0.3%
23	South Carolina	2,586,682	1.6%
46	South Dakota	430,706	0.3%
16	Tennessee	3,440,018	2.1%
2	Texas	14,242,803	8.6%
31	Utah	1,540,145	0.9%
49	Vermont	315,401	0.2%
12	Virginia	4,303,293	2.6%
13	Washington	3,702,270	2.2%
38	West Virginia	917,237	0.6%
20	Wisconsin	2,912,745	1.8%
50	Wyoming	283,877	0.2%

RANK ORDER

RANK	STATE	FEMALES	% of USA
1	California	19,889,100	12.0%
2	Texas	14,242,803	8.6%
3	Florida	10,727,581	6.5%
4	New York	10,211,937	6.2%
5	Pennsylvania	6,534,208	4.0%
6	Illinois	6,509,545	3.9%
7	Ohio	5,945,509	3.6%
8	Georgia	5,353,872	3.2%
9	North Carolina	5,271,981	3.2%
10	Michigan	5,058,559	3.1%
11	New Jersey	4,609,070	2.8%
12	Virginia	4,303,293	2.6%
13	Washington	3,702,270	2.2%
14	Massachusetts	3,529,454	2.1%
15	Arizona	3,527,969	2.1%
16	Tennessee	3,440,018	2.1%
17	Indiana	3,379,723	2.0%
18	Maryland	3,118,023	1.9%
19	Missouri	3,111,296	1.9%
20	Wisconsin	2,912,745	1.8%
21	Minnesota	2,799,760	1.7%
22	Colorado	2,784,821	1.7%
23	South Carolina	2,586,682	1.6%
24	Alabama	2,514,911	1.5%
25	Louisiana	2,394,887	1.4%
26	Kentucky	2,259,871	1.4%
27	Oregon	2,089,787	1.3%
28	Oklahoma	1,983,302	1.2%
29	Connecticut	1,836,384	1.1%
30	Iowa	1,580,978	1.0%
31	Utah	1,540,145	0.9%
32	Mississippi	1,538,222	0.9%
33	Arkansas	1,528,215	0.9%
34	Nevada	1,494,290	0.9%
35	Kansas	1,461,167	0.9%
36	New Mexico	1,053,926	0.6%
37	Nebraska	961,945	0.6%
38	West Virginia	917,237	0.6%
39	Idaho	856,485	0.5%
40	Hawaii	711,451	0.4%
41	Maine	681,387	0.4%
42	New Hampshire	677,786	0.4%
43	Rhode Island	544,648	0.3%
44	Montana	521,537	0.3%
45	Delaware	496,425	0.3%
46	South Dakota	430,706	0.3%
47	North Dakota	368,094	0.2%
48	Alaska	353,003	0.2%
49	Vermont	315,401	0.2%
50	Wyoming	283,877	0.2%
	District of Columbia	364,773	0.2%

Source: U.S. Bureau of the Census
"State Characteristics: Vintage 2017" (https://www.census.gov/programs-surveys/popest/data/data-sets.html)

Male to Female Ratio in 2017

National Ratio = 97.0 Males per 100 Females

ALPHA ORDER

RANK	STATE	RATIO
49	Alabama	93.8
1	Alaska	109.6
17	Arizona	98.9
31	Arkansas	96.6
18	California	98.8
7	Colorado	101.3
38	Connecticut	95.4
49	Delaware	93.8
36	Florida	95.6
42	Georgia	94.8
8	Hawaii	100.7
10	Idaho	100.5
30	Illinois	96.7
26	Indiana	97.3
15	Iowa	99.0
13	Kansas	99.4
27	Kentucky	97.1
36	Louisiana	95.6
33	Maine	96.1
47	Maryland	94.1
44	Massachusetts	94.4
28	Michigan	96.9
14	Minnesota	99.2
48	Mississippi	94.0
32	Missouri	96.5
5	Montana	101.4
12	Nebraska	99.6
9	Nevada	100.6
22	New Hampshire	98.1
38	New Jersey	95.4
22	New Mexico	98.1
44	New York	94.4
41	North Carolina	94.9
2	North Dakota	105.2
33	Ohio	96.1
20	Oklahoma	98.2
20	Oregon	98.2
35	Pennsylvania	96.0
43	Rhode Island	94.6
46	South Carolina	94.2
4	South Dakota	101.9
40	Tennessee	95.2
19	Texas	98.7
5	Utah	101.4
25	Vermont	97.7
29	Virginia	96.8
11	Washington	100.0
24	West Virginia	98.0
15	Wisconsin	99.0
3	Wyoming	104.1

RANK ORDER

RANK	STATE	RATIO
1	Alaska	109.6
2	North Dakota	105.2
3	Wyoming	104.1
4	South Dakota	101.9
5	Montana	101.4
5	Utah	101.4
7	Colorado	101.3
8	Hawaii	100.7
9	Nevada	100.6
10	Idaho	100.5
11	Washington	100.0
12	Nebraska	99.6
13	Kansas	99.4
14	Minnesota	99.2
15	Iowa	99.0
15	Wisconsin	99.0
17	Arizona	98.9
18	California	98.8
19	Texas	98.7
20	Oklahoma	98.2
20	Oregon	98.2
22	New Hampshire	98.1
22	New Mexico	98.1
24	West Virginia	98.0
25	Vermont	97.7
26	Indiana	97.3
27	Kentucky	97.1
28	Michigan	96.9
29	Virginia	96.8
30	Illinois	96.7
31	Arkansas	96.6
32	Missouri	96.5
33	Maine	96.1
33	Ohio	96.1
35	Pennsylvania	96.0
36	Florida	95.6
36	Louisiana	95.6
38	Connecticut	95.4
38	New Jersey	95.4
40	Tennessee	95.2
41	North Carolina	94.9
42	Georgia	94.8
43	Rhode Island	94.6
44	Massachusetts	94.4
44	New York	94.4
46	South Carolina	94.2
47	Maryland	94.1
48	Mississippi	94.0
49	Alabama	93.8
49	Delaware	93.8
	District of Columbia	90.2

Source: CQ Press using data from U.S. Bureau of the Census
"State Characteristics: Vintage 2017" (https://www.census.gov/programs-surveys/popest/data/data-sets.html)

Median Age in 2017

National Median = 38.0 Years Old

<table>
<tr><th colspan="3">ALPHA ORDER</th><th colspan="3">RANK ORDER</th></tr>
<tr><th>RANK</th><th>STATE</th><th>MEDIAN AGE</th><th>RANK</th><th>STATE</th><th>MEDIAN AGE</th></tr>
<tr><td>18</td><td>Alabama</td><td>39.0</td><td>1</td><td>Maine</td><td>44.7</td></tr>
<tr><td>49</td><td>Alaska</td><td>34.3</td><td>2</td><td>New Hampshire</td><td>43.1</td></tr>
<tr><td>33</td><td>Arizona</td><td>37.7</td><td>3</td><td>Vermont</td><td>42.9</td></tr>
<tr><td>27</td><td>Arkansas</td><td>38.1</td><td>4</td><td>West Virginia</td><td>42.5</td></tr>
<tr><td>42</td><td>California</td><td>36.6</td><td>5</td><td>Florida</td><td>42.1</td></tr>
<tr><td>39</td><td>Colorado</td><td>36.8</td><td>6</td><td>Connecticut</td><td>40.9</td></tr>
<tr><td>6</td><td>Connecticut</td><td>40.9</td><td>7</td><td>Pennsylvania</td><td>40.7</td></tr>
<tr><td>8</td><td>Delaware</td><td>40.4</td><td>8</td><td>Delaware</td><td>40.4</td></tr>
<tr><td>5</td><td>Florida</td><td>42.1</td><td>9</td><td>Rhode Island</td><td>39.9</td></tr>
<tr><td>41</td><td>Georgia</td><td>36.7</td><td>10</td><td>Michigan</td><td>39.8</td></tr>
<tr><td>18</td><td>Hawaii</td><td>39.0</td><td>10</td><td>Montana</td><td>39.8</td></tr>
<tr><td>46</td><td>Idaho</td><td>36.3</td><td>10</td><td>New Jersey</td><td>39.8</td></tr>
<tr><td>27</td><td>Illinois</td><td>38.1</td><td>13</td><td>Massachusetts</td><td>39.5</td></tr>
<tr><td>33</td><td>Indiana</td><td>37.7</td><td>14</td><td>Ohio</td><td>39.4</td></tr>
<tr><td>27</td><td>Iowa</td><td>38.1</td><td>14</td><td>South Carolina</td><td>39.4</td></tr>
<tr><td>42</td><td>Kansas</td><td>36.6</td><td>14</td><td>Wisconsin</td><td>39.4</td></tr>
<tr><td>20</td><td>Kentucky</td><td>38.8</td><td>17</td><td>Oregon</td><td>39.3</td></tr>
<tr><td>39</td><td>Louisiana</td><td>36.8</td><td>18</td><td>Alabama</td><td>39.0</td></tr>
<tr><td>1</td><td>Maine</td><td>44.7</td><td>18</td><td>Hawaii</td><td>39.0</td></tr>
<tr><td>21</td><td>Maryland</td><td>38.7</td><td>20</td><td>Kentucky</td><td>38.8</td></tr>
<tr><td>13</td><td>Massachusetts</td><td>39.5</td><td>21</td><td>Maryland</td><td>38.7</td></tr>
<tr><td>10</td><td>Michigan</td><td>39.8</td><td>21</td><td>New York</td><td>38.7</td></tr>
<tr><td>30</td><td>Minnesota</td><td>37.9</td><td>21</td><td>North Carolina</td><td>38.7</td></tr>
<tr><td>37</td><td>Mississippi</td><td>37.4</td><td>21</td><td>Tennessee</td><td>38.7</td></tr>
<tr><td>25</td><td>Missouri</td><td>38.6</td><td>25</td><td>Missouri</td><td>38.6</td></tr>
<tr><td>10</td><td>Montana</td><td>39.8</td><td>26</td><td>Virginia</td><td>38.2</td></tr>
<tr><td>45</td><td>Nebraska</td><td>36.4</td><td>27</td><td>Arkansas</td><td>38.1</td></tr>
<tr><td>30</td><td>Nevada</td><td>37.9</td><td>27</td><td>Illinois</td><td>38.1</td></tr>
<tr><td>2</td><td>New Hampshire</td><td>43.1</td><td>27</td><td>Iowa</td><td>38.1</td></tr>
<tr><td>10</td><td>New Jersey</td><td>39.8</td><td>30</td><td>Minnesota</td><td>37.9</td></tr>
<tr><td>32</td><td>New Mexico</td><td>37.8</td><td>30</td><td>Nevada</td><td>37.9</td></tr>
<tr><td>21</td><td>New York</td><td>38.7</td><td>32</td><td>New Mexico</td><td>37.8</td></tr>
<tr><td>21</td><td>North Carolina</td><td>38.7</td><td>33</td><td>Arizona</td><td>37.7</td></tr>
<tr><td>47</td><td>North Dakota</td><td>35.1</td><td>33</td><td>Indiana</td><td>37.7</td></tr>
<tr><td>14</td><td>Ohio</td><td>39.4</td><td>33</td><td>Washington</td><td>37.7</td></tr>
<tr><td>44</td><td>Oklahoma</td><td>36.5</td><td>33</td><td>Wyoming</td><td>37.7</td></tr>
<tr><td>17</td><td>Oregon</td><td>39.3</td><td>37</td><td>Mississippi</td><td>37.4</td></tr>
<tr><td>7</td><td>Pennsylvania</td><td>40.7</td><td>38</td><td>South Dakota</td><td>37.1</td></tr>
<tr><td>9</td><td>Rhode Island</td><td>39.9</td><td>39</td><td>Colorado</td><td>36.8</td></tr>
<tr><td>14</td><td>South Carolina</td><td>39.4</td><td>39</td><td>Louisiana</td><td>36.8</td></tr>
<tr><td>38</td><td>South Dakota</td><td>37.1</td><td>41</td><td>Georgia</td><td>36.7</td></tr>
<tr><td>21</td><td>Tennessee</td><td>38.7</td><td>42</td><td>California</td><td>36.6</td></tr>
<tr><td>48</td><td>Texas</td><td>34.6</td><td>42</td><td>Kansas</td><td>36.6</td></tr>
<tr><td>50</td><td>Utah</td><td>30.9</td><td>44</td><td>Oklahoma</td><td>36.5</td></tr>
<tr><td>3</td><td>Vermont</td><td>42.9</td><td>45</td><td>Nebraska</td><td>36.4</td></tr>
<tr><td>26</td><td>Virginia</td><td>38.2</td><td>46</td><td>Idaho</td><td>36.3</td></tr>
<tr><td>33</td><td>Washington</td><td>37.7</td><td>47</td><td>North Dakota</td><td>35.1</td></tr>
<tr><td>4</td><td>West Virginia</td><td>42.5</td><td>48</td><td>Texas</td><td>34.6</td></tr>
<tr><td>14</td><td>Wisconsin</td><td>39.4</td><td>49</td><td>Alaska</td><td>34.3</td></tr>
<tr><td>33</td><td>Wyoming</td><td>37.7</td><td>50</td><td>Utah</td><td>30.9</td></tr>
<tr><td></td><td></td><td></td><td></td><td>District of Columbia</td><td>34.0</td></tr>
</table>

Source: U.S. Bureau of the Census
"State Characteristics: Vintage 2017" (https://www.census.gov/programs-surveys/popest/data/data-sets.html)

Male Median Age in 2017

National Median = 36.8 Years Old

ALPHA ORDER

RANK	STATE	MEDIAN AGE
18	Alabama	37.5
48	Alaska	33.9
35	Arizona	36.4
31	Arkansas	36.8
41	California	35.5
38	Colorado	35.9
6	Connecticut	39.1
8	Delaware	38.7
5	Florida	40.5
43	Georgia	35.4
18	Hawaii	37.5
41	Idaho	35.5
31	Illinois	36.8
34	Indiana	36.5
30	Iowa	36.9
43	Kansas	35.4
20	Kentucky	37.4
40	Louisiana	35.6
1	Maine	43.3
23	Maryland	37.2
15	Massachusetts	37.9
11	Michigan	38.3
27	Minnesota	37.1
38	Mississippi	35.9
23	Missouri	37.2
8	Montana	38.7
43	Nebraska	35.4
22	Nevada	37.3
2	New Hampshire	41.7
13	New Jersey	38.2
35	New Mexico	36.4
23	New York	37.2
23	North Carolina	37.2
47	North Dakota	34.2
15	Ohio	37.9
46	Oklahoma	35.3
11	Oregon	38.3
6	Pennsylvania	39.1
13	Rhode Island	38.2
17	South Carolina	37.8
37	South Dakota	36.1
20	Tennessee	37.4
49	Texas	33.7
50	Utah	30.3
3	Vermont	41.4
28	Virginia	37.0
33	Washington	36.7
4	West Virginia	41.1
10	Wisconsin	38.4
28	Wyoming	37.0

RANK ORDER

RANK	STATE	MEDIAN AGE
1	Maine	43.3
2	New Hampshire	41.7
3	Vermont	41.4
4	West Virginia	41.1
5	Florida	40.5
6	Connecticut	39.1
6	Pennsylvania	39.1
8	Delaware	38.7
8	Montana	38.7
10	Wisconsin	38.4
11	Michigan	38.3
11	Oregon	38.3
13	New Jersey	38.2
13	Rhode Island	38.2
15	Massachusetts	37.9
15	Ohio	37.9
17	South Carolina	37.8
18	Alabama	37.5
18	Hawaii	37.5
20	Kentucky	37.4
20	Tennessee	37.4
22	Nevada	37.3
23	Maryland	37.2
23	Missouri	37.2
23	New York	37.2
23	North Carolina	37.2
27	Minnesota	37.1
28	Virginia	37.0
28	Wyoming	37.0
30	Iowa	36.9
31	Arkansas	36.8
31	Illinois	36.8
33	Washington	36.7
34	Indiana	36.5
35	Arizona	36.4
35	New Mexico	36.4
37	South Dakota	36.1
38	Colorado	35.9
38	Mississippi	35.9
40	Louisiana	35.6
41	California	35.5
41	Idaho	35.5
43	Georgia	35.4
43	Kansas	35.4
43	Nebraska	35.4
46	Oklahoma	35.3
47	North Dakota	34.2
48	Alaska	33.9
49	Texas	33.7
50	Utah	30.3
	District of Columbia	33.8

Source: U.S. Bureau of the Census
  "State Characteristics: Vintage 2017" (https://www.census.gov/programs-surveys/popest/data/data-sets.html)

Female Median Age in 2017

National Median = 39.4 Years Old

ALPHA ORDER

RANK	STATE	MEDIAN AGE
17	Alabama	40.5
49	Alaska	34.8
31	Arizona	39.1
27	Arkansas	39.5
43	California	37.7
42	Colorado	37.8
6	Connecticut	42.7
8	Delaware	42.1
5	Florida	43.7
40	Georgia	38.0
16	Hawaii	40.6
46	Idaho	37.1
28	Illinois	39.4
32	Indiana	39.0
29	Iowa	39.3
41	Kansas	37.9
20	Kentucky	40.2
38	Louisiana	38.1
1	Maine	46.0
20	Maryland	40.2
12	Massachusetts	40.9
11	Michigan	41.2
33	Minnesota	38.9
33	Mississippi	38.9
25	Missouri	40.0
12	Montana	40.9
45	Nebraska	37.5
36	Nevada	38.6
2	New Hampshire	44.3
10	New Jersey	41.4
29	New Mexico	39.3
20	New York	40.2
20	North Carolina	40.2
47	North Dakota	36.2
15	Ohio	40.8
43	Oklahoma	37.7
19	Oregon	40.3
7	Pennsylvania	42.4
9	Rhode Island	41.7
12	South Carolina	40.9
38	South Dakota	38.1
24	Tennessee	40.1
48	Texas	35.6
50	Utah	31.6
2	Vermont	44.3
26	Virginia	39.6
35	Washington	38.7
4	West Virginia	43.9
17	Wisconsin	40.5
37	Wyoming	38.4

RANK ORDER

RANK	STATE	MEDIAN AGE
1	Maine	46.0
2	New Hampshire	44.3
2	Vermont	44.3
4	West Virginia	43.9
5	Florida	43.7
6	Connecticut	42.7
7	Pennsylvania	42.4
8	Delaware	42.1
9	Rhode Island	41.7
10	New Jersey	41.4
11	Michigan	41.2
12	Massachusetts	40.9
12	Montana	40.9
12	South Carolina	40.9
15	Ohio	40.8
16	Hawaii	40.6
17	Alabama	40.5
17	Wisconsin	40.5
19	Oregon	40.3
20	Kentucky	40.2
20	Maryland	40.2
20	New York	40.2
20	North Carolina	40.2
24	Tennessee	40.1
25	Missouri	40.0
26	Virginia	39.6
27	Arkansas	39.5
28	Illinois	39.4
29	Iowa	39.3
29	New Mexico	39.3
31	Arizona	39.1
32	Indiana	39.0
33	Minnesota	38.9
33	Mississippi	38.9
35	Washington	38.7
36	Nevada	38.6
37	Wyoming	38.4
38	Louisiana	38.1
38	South Dakota	38.1
40	Georgia	38.0
41	Kansas	37.9
42	Colorado	37.8
43	California	37.7
43	Oklahoma	37.7
45	Nebraska	37.5
46	Idaho	37.1
47	North Dakota	36.2
48	Texas	35.6
49	Alaska	34.8
50	Utah	31.6
	District of Columbia	34.2

Source: U.S. Bureau of the Census
"State Characteristics: Vintage 2017" (https://www.census.gov/programs-surveys/popest/data/data-sets.html)

White Population in 2017

National Total = 249,619,493*

ALPHA ORDER

RANK	STATE	POPULATION	% of USA
26	Alabama	3,374,131	1.4%
49	Alaska	486,724	0.2%
14	Arizona	5,827,866	2.3%
33	Arkansas	2,381,662	1.0%
1	California	28,611,160	11.5%
20	Colorado	4,894,372	2.0%
29	Connecticut	2,879,759	1.2%
45	Delaware	670,512	0.3%
3	Florida	16,247,613	6.5%
11	Georgia	6,341,768	2.5%
50	Hawaii	366,546	0.1%
39	Idaho	1,599,814	0.6%
6	Illinois	9,864,942	4.0%
15	Indiana	5,690,929	2.3%
30	Iowa	2,864,664	1.1%
32	Kansas	2,519,176	1.0%
22	Kentucky	3,908,964	1.6%
27	Louisiana	2,951,003	1.2%
40	Maine	1,264,744	0.5%
24	Maryland	3,568,679	1.4%
16	Massachusetts	5,576,725	2.2%
8	Michigan	7,914,418	3.2%
21	Minnesota	4,708,215	1.9%
35	Mississippi	1,766,950	0.7%
18	Missouri	5,080,444	2.0%
42	Montana	935,792	0.4%
37	Nebraska	1,700,881	0.7%
34	Nevada	2,235,657	0.9%
41	New Hampshire	1,256,807	0.5%
10	New Jersey	6,489,409	2.6%
36	New Mexico	1,715,623	0.7%
4	New York	13,807,127	5.5%
9	North Carolina	7,276,995	2.9%
46	North Dakota	661,217	0.3%
7	Ohio	9,579,207	3.8%
28	Oklahoma	2,921,390	1.2%
23	Oregon	3,607,515	1.4%
5	Pennsylvania	10,507,780	4.2%
43	Rhode Island	890,883	0.4%
25	South Carolina	3,440,141	1.4%
44	South Dakota	738,554	0.3%
17	Tennessee	5,276,748	2.1%
2	Texas	22,404,118	9.0%
31	Utah	2,820,387	1.1%
47	Vermont	589,163	0.2%
12	Virginia	5,904,472	2.4%
13	Washington	5,887,060	2.4%
38	West Virginia	1,699,266	0.7%
19	Wisconsin	5,060,891	2.0%
48	Wyoming	537,396	0.2%

RANK ORDER

RANK	STATE	POPULATION	% of USA
1	California	28,611,160	11.5%
2	Texas	22,404,118	9.0%
3	Florida	16,247,613	6.5%
4	New York	13,807,127	5.5%
5	Pennsylvania	10,507,780	4.2%
6	Illinois	9,864,942	4.0%
7	Ohio	9,579,207	3.8%
8	Michigan	7,914,418	3.2%
9	North Carolina	7,276,995	2.9%
10	New Jersey	6,489,409	2.6%
11	Georgia	6,341,768	2.5%
12	Virginia	5,904,472	2.4%
13	Washington	5,887,060	2.4%
14	Arizona	5,827,866	2.3%
15	Indiana	5,690,929	2.3%
16	Massachusetts	5,576,725	2.2%
17	Tennessee	5,276,748	2.1%
18	Missouri	5,080,444	2.0%
19	Wisconsin	5,060,891	2.0%
20	Colorado	4,894,372	2.0%
21	Minnesota	4,708,215	1.9%
22	Kentucky	3,908,964	1.6%
23	Oregon	3,607,515	1.4%
24	Maryland	3,568,679	1.4%
25	South Carolina	3,440,141	1.4%
26	Alabama	3,374,131	1.4%
27	Louisiana	2,951,003	1.2%
28	Oklahoma	2,921,390	1.2%
29	Connecticut	2,879,759	1.2%
30	Iowa	2,864,664	1.1%
31	Utah	2,820,387	1.1%
32	Kansas	2,519,176	1.0%
33	Arkansas	2,381,662	1.0%
34	Nevada	2,235,657	0.9%
35	Mississippi	1,766,950	0.7%
36	New Mexico	1,715,623	0.7%
37	Nebraska	1,700,881	0.7%
38	West Virginia	1,699,266	0.7%
39	Idaho	1,599,814	0.6%
40	Maine	1,264,744	0.5%
41	New Hampshire	1,256,807	0.5%
42	Montana	935,792	0.4%
43	Rhode Island	890,883	0.4%
44	South Dakota	738,554	0.3%
45	Delaware	670,512	0.3%
46	North Dakota	661,217	0.3%
47	Vermont	589,163	0.2%
48	Wyoming	537,396	0.2%
49	Alaska	486,724	0.2%
50	Hawaii	366,546	0.1%
	District of Columbia	313,234	0.1%

Source: U.S. Bureau of the Census

"State Characteristics: Vintage 2017" (https://www.census.gov/programs-surveys/popest/data/data-sets.html)
*Those who identified themselves as one race. "White" is defined by Census as a person having origins in any of the original peoples of Europe, North Africa, or the Middle East. There are 197,803,083 non-Hispanic whites. Census states "Race is a self-identification data item in which respondents choose the race or races with which they most closely identify."

Percent of Population White in 2017

National Percent = 76.6%*

ALPHA ORDER			RANK ORDER		
RANK	STATE	PERCENT	RANK	STATE	PERCENT
43	Alabama	69.2	1	Maine	94.7
45	Alaska	65.8	2	Vermont	94.5
21	Arizona	83.1	3	New Hampshire	93.6
30	Arkansas	79.3	3	West Virginia	93.6
37	California	72.4	5	Idaho	93.2
13	Colorado	87.3	6	Wyoming	92.8
27	Connecticut	80.3	7	Iowa	91.1
40	Delaware	69.7	8	Utah	90.9
33	Florida	77.4	9	Montana	89.1
47	Georgia	60.8	10	Nebraska	88.6
50	Hawaii	25.7	11	Kentucky	87.8
5	Idaho	93.2	12	North Dakota	87.5
34	Illinois	77.1	13	Colorado	87.3
17	Indiana	85.4	13	Wisconsin	87.3
7	Iowa	91.1	15	Oregon	87.1
16	Kansas	86.5	16	Kansas	86.5
11	Kentucky	87.8	17	Indiana	85.4
46	Louisiana	63.0	18	South Dakota	84.9
1	Maine	94.7	19	Minnesota	84.4
49	Maryland	59.0	20	Rhode Island	84.1
26	Massachusetts	81.3	21	Arizona	83.1
29	Michigan	79.4	21	Missouri	83.1
19	Minnesota	84.4	23	New Mexico	82.2
48	Mississippi	59.2	23	Ohio	82.2
21	Missouri	83.1	25	Pennsylvania	82.1
9	Montana	89.1	26	Massachusetts	81.3
10	Nebraska	88.6	27	Connecticut	80.3
35	Nevada	74.6	28	Washington	79.5
3	New Hampshire	93.6	29	Michigan	79.4
38	New Jersey	72.1	30	Arkansas	79.3
23	New Mexico	82.2	31	Texas	79.2
42	New York	69.6	32	Tennessee	78.6
39	North Carolina	70.8	33	Florida	77.4
12	North Dakota	87.5	34	Illinois	77.1
23	Ohio	82.2	35	Nevada	74.6
36	Oklahoma	74.3	36	Oklahoma	74.3
15	Oregon	87.1	37	California	72.4
25	Pennsylvania	82.1	38	New Jersey	72.1
20	Rhode Island	84.1	39	North Carolina	70.8
44	South Carolina	68.5	40	Delaware	69.7
18	South Dakota	84.9	40	Virginia	69.7
32	Tennessee	78.6	42	New York	69.6
31	Texas	79.2	43	Alabama	69.2
8	Utah	90.9	44	South Carolina	68.5
2	Vermont	94.5	45	Alaska	65.8
40	Virginia	69.7	46	Louisiana	63.0
28	Washington	79.5	47	Georgia	60.8
3	West Virginia	93.6	48	Mississippi	59.2
13	Wisconsin	87.3	49	Maryland	59.0
6	Wyoming	92.8	50	Hawaii	25.7
				District of Columbia	45.1

Source: CQ Press using data from U.S. Bureau of the Census
   "State Characteristics: Vintage 2017" (https://www.census.gov/programs-surveys/popest/data/data-sets.html)
*Those who identified themselves as one race. "White" is defined by Census as a person having origins in any of the original peoples of Europe, North Africa, or the Middle East. Non-Hispanic whites comprise 60.7% of the total population. Census states "Race is a self-identification data item in which respondents choose the race or races with which they most closely identify."

Black Population in 2017

National Total = 43,499,874*

ALPHA ORDER

RANK	STATE	POPULATION	% of USA
16	Alabama	1,308,214	3.0%
42	Alaska	27,595	0.1%
27	Arizona	349,944	0.8%
22	Arkansas	471,145	1.1%
5	California	2,553,498	5.9%
31	Colorado	253,666	0.6%
23	Connecticut	426,851	1.0%
32	Delaware	219,310	0.5%
2	Florida	3,547,464	8.2%
4	Georgia	3,361,924	7.7%
41	Hawaii	31,147	0.1%
47	Idaho	15,052	0.0%
7	Illinois	1,872,275	4.3%
20	Indiana	649,813	1.5%
34	Iowa	120,218	0.3%
33	Kansas	179,569	0.4%
25	Kentucky	372,839	0.9%
10	Louisiana	1,528,167	3.5%
45	Maine	21,093	0.0%
8	Maryland	1,862,566	4.3%
21	Massachusetts	603,433	1.4%
13	Michigan	1,408,605	3.2%
26	Minnesota	365,225	0.8%
18	Mississippi	1,126,498	2.6%
19	Missouri	723,029	1.7%
50	Montana	6,114	0.0%
35	Nebraska	97,078	0.2%
30	Nevada	294,676	0.7%
44	New Hampshire	21,239	0.0%
15	New Jersey	1,346,893	3.1%
39	New Mexico	52,622	0.1%
3	New York	3,510,933	8.1%
6	North Carolina	2,279,895	5.2%
43	North Dakota	23,533	0.1%
12	Ohio	1,504,482	3.5%
29	Oklahoma	306,089	0.7%
36	Oregon	90,128	0.2%
11	Pennsylvania	1,520,035	3.5%
37	Rhode Island	87,261	0.2%
14	South Carolina	1,372,547	3.2%
46	South Dakota	18,479	0.0%
17	Tennessee	1,148,218	2.6%
1	Texas	3,593,048	8.3%
40	Utah	43,230	0.1%
48	Vermont	8,475	0.0%
9	Virginia	1,680,680	3.9%
28	Washington	310,425	0.7%
38	West Virginia	64,951	0.1%
24	Wisconsin	385,451	0.9%
49	Wyoming	7,445	0.0%

RANK ORDER

RANK	STATE	POPULATION	% of USA
1	Texas	3,593,048	8.3%
2	Florida	3,547,464	8.2%
3	New York	3,510,933	8.1%
4	Georgia	3,361,924	7.7%
5	California	2,553,498	5.9%
6	North Carolina	2,279,895	5.2%
7	Illinois	1,872,275	4.3%
8	Maryland	1,862,566	4.3%
9	Virginia	1,680,680	3.9%
10	Louisiana	1,528,167	3.5%
11	Pennsylvania	1,520,035	3.5%
12	Ohio	1,504,482	3.5%
13	Michigan	1,408,605	3.2%
14	South Carolina	1,372,547	3.2%
15	New Jersey	1,346,893	3.1%
16	Alabama	1,308,214	3.0%
17	Tennessee	1,148,218	2.6%
18	Mississippi	1,126,498	2.6%
19	Missouri	723,029	1.7%
20	Indiana	649,813	1.5%
21	Massachusetts	603,433	1.4%
22	Arkansas	471,145	1.1%
23	Connecticut	426,851	1.0%
24	Wisconsin	385,451	0.9%
25	Kentucky	372,839	0.9%
26	Minnesota	365,225	0.8%
27	Arizona	349,944	0.8%
28	Washington	310,425	0.7%
29	Oklahoma	306,089	0.7%
30	Nevada	294,676	0.7%
31	Colorado	253,666	0.6%
32	Delaware	219,310	0.5%
33	Kansas	179,569	0.4%
34	Iowa	120,218	0.3%
35	Nebraska	97,078	0.2%
36	Oregon	90,128	0.2%
37	Rhode Island	87,261	0.2%
38	West Virginia	64,951	0.1%
39	New Mexico	52,622	0.1%
40	Utah	43,230	0.1%
41	Hawaii	31,147	0.1%
42	Alaska	27,595	0.1%
43	North Dakota	23,533	0.1%
44	New Hampshire	21,239	0.0%
45	Maine	21,093	0.0%
46	South Dakota	18,479	0.0%
47	Idaho	15,052	0.0%
48	Vermont	8,475	0.0%
49	Wyoming	7,445	0.0%
50	Montana	6,114	0.0%
	District of Columbia	326,807	0.8%

Source: U.S. Bureau of the Census

"State Characteristics: Vintage 2017" (https://www.census.gov/programs-surveys/popest/data/data-sets.html)

*Those who identified themselves as one race. "Black" is defined by Census as a person having origins in any of the Black racial groups of Africa. Census states "Race is a self-identification data item in which respondents choose the race or races with which they most closely identify."

Percent of Population Black in 2017

National Percent = 13.4%*

ALPHA ORDER

ALPHA ORDER

RANK	STATE	PERCENT
6	Alabama	26.8
37	Alaska	3.7
33	Arizona	5.0
13	Arkansas	15.7
29	California	6.5
34	Colorado	4.5
19	Connecticut	11.9
7	Delaware	22.8
12	Florida	16.9
3	Georgia	32.2
41	Hawaii	2.2
49	Idaho	0.9
15	Illinois	14.6
23	Indiana	9.7
36	Iowa	3.8
31	Kansas	6.2
25	Kentucky	8.4
2	Louisiana	32.6
44	Maine	1.6
4	Maryland	30.8
24	Massachusetts	8.8
16	Michigan	14.1
29	Minnesota	6.5
1	Mississippi	37.8
21	Missouri	11.8
50	Montana	0.6
32	Nebraska	5.1
22	Nevada	9.8
44	New Hampshire	1.6
14	New Jersey	15.0
40	New Mexico	2.5
10	New York	17.7
8	North Carolina	22.2
39	North Dakota	3.1
17	Ohio	12.9
27	Oklahoma	7.8
41	Oregon	2.2
19	Pennsylvania	11.9
26	Rhode Island	8.2
5	South Carolina	27.3
43	South Dakota	2.1
11	Tennessee	17.1
18	Texas	12.7
46	Utah	1.4
46	Vermont	1.4
9	Virginia	19.8
35	Washington	4.2
38	West Virginia	3.6
28	Wisconsin	6.7
48	Wyoming	1.3

RANK ORDER

RANK	STATE	PERCENT
1	Mississippi	37.8
2	Louisiana	32.6
3	Georgia	32.2
4	Maryland	30.8
5	South Carolina	27.3
6	Alabama	26.8
7	Delaware	22.8
8	North Carolina	22.2
9	Virginia	19.8
10	New York	17.7
11	Tennessee	17.1
12	Florida	16.9
13	Arkansas	15.7
14	New Jersey	15.0
15	Illinois	14.6
16	Michigan	14.1
17	Ohio	12.9
18	Texas	12.7
19	Connecticut	11.9
19	Pennsylvania	11.9
21	Missouri	11.8
22	Nevada	9.8
23	Indiana	9.7
24	Massachusetts	8.8
25	Kentucky	8.4
26	Rhode Island	8.2
27	Oklahoma	7.8
28	Wisconsin	6.7
29	California	6.5
29	Minnesota	6.5
31	Kansas	6.2
32	Nebraska	5.1
33	Arizona	5.0
34	Colorado	4.5
35	Washington	4.2
36	Iowa	3.8
37	Alaska	3.7
38	West Virginia	3.6
39	North Dakota	3.1
40	New Mexico	2.5
41	Hawaii	2.2
41	Oregon	2.2
43	South Dakota	2.1
44	Maine	1.6
44	New Hampshire	1.6
46	Utah	1.4
46	Vermont	1.4
48	Wyoming	1.3
49	Idaho	0.9
50	Montana	0.6

District of Columbia   47.1

Source: CQ Press using data from U.S. Bureau of the Census
"State Characteristics: Vintage 2017" (https://www.census.gov/programs-surveys/popest/data/data-sets.html)
*Those who identified themselves as one race. "Black" is defined by Census as a person having origins in any of the Black racial groups of Africa. Census states "Race is a self-identification data item in which respondents choose the race or races with which they most closely identify."

Hispanic Population in 2017

National Total = 58,946,729*

ALPHA ORDER

RANK	STATE	POPULATION	% of USA
34	Alabama	211,058	0.4%
43	Alaska	52,250	0.1%
6	Arizona	2,202,172	3.7%
32	Arkansas	227,673	0.4%
1	California	15,477,304	26.3%
8	Colorado	1,206,724	2.0%
18	Connecticut	578,833	1.0%
41	Delaware	89,539	0.2%
3	Florida	5,371,385	9.1%
10	Georgia	1,005,959	1.7%
39	Hawaii	150,125	0.3%
33	Idaho	215,392	0.4%
5	Illinois	2,209,337	3.7%
21	Indiana	466,453	0.8%
36	Iowa	189,818	0.3%
27	Kansas	347,459	0.6%
38	Kentucky	163,489	0.3%
31	Louisiana	245,135	0.4%
49	Maine	22,042	0.0%
17	Maryland	614,248	1.0%
15	Massachusetts	813,359	1.4%
20	Michigan	504,857	0.9%
28	Minnesota	301,407	0.5%
40	Mississippi	94,385	0.2%
30	Missouri	259,154	0.4%
45	Montana	39,633	0.1%
35	Nebraska	210,911	0.4%
14	Nevada	864,665	1.5%
44	New Hampshire	49,567	0.1%
7	New Jersey	1,840,433	3.1%
9	New Mexico	1,018,349	1.7%
4	New York	3,811,945	6.5%
11	North Carolina	972,288	1.6%
48	North Dakota	28,006	0.0%
22	Ohio	440,886	0.7%
24	Oklahoma	417,710	0.7%
19	Oregon	540,923	0.9%
13	Pennsylvania	940,635	1.6%
37	Rhode Island	164,004	0.3%
29	South Carolina	286,382	0.5%
46	South Dakota	32,811	0.1%
26	Tennessee	366,554	0.6%
2	Texas	11,156,514	18.9%
23	Utah	434,288	0.7%
50	Vermont	12,060	0.0%
16	Virginia	795,323	1.3%
12	Washington	940,792	1.6%
47	West Virginia	29,065	0.0%
25	Wisconsin	398,780	0.7%
42	Wyoming	58,122	0.1%

RANK ORDER

RANK	STATE	POPULATION	% of USA
1	California	15,477,304	26.3%
2	Texas	11,156,514	18.9%
3	Florida	5,371,385	9.1%
4	New York	3,811,945	6.5%
5	Illinois	2,209,337	3.7%
6	Arizona	2,202,172	3.7%
7	New Jersey	1,840,433	3.1%
8	Colorado	1,206,724	2.0%
9	New Mexico	1,018,349	1.7%
10	Georgia	1,005,959	1.7%
11	North Carolina	972,288	1.6%
12	Washington	940,792	1.6%
13	Pennsylvania	940,635	1.6%
14	Nevada	864,665	1.5%
15	Massachusetts	813,359	1.4%
16	Virginia	795,323	1.3%
17	Maryland	614,248	1.0%
18	Connecticut	578,833	1.0%
19	Oregon	540,923	0.9%
20	Michigan	504,857	0.9%
21	Indiana	466,453	0.8%
22	Ohio	440,886	0.7%
23	Utah	434,288	0.7%
24	Oklahoma	417,710	0.7%
25	Wisconsin	398,780	0.7%
26	Tennessee	366,554	0.6%
27	Kansas	347,459	0.6%
28	Minnesota	301,407	0.5%
29	South Carolina	286,382	0.5%
30	Missouri	259,154	0.4%
31	Louisiana	245,135	0.4%
32	Arkansas	227,673	0.4%
33	Idaho	215,392	0.4%
34	Alabama	211,058	0.4%
35	Nebraska	210,911	0.4%
36	Iowa	189,818	0.3%
37	Rhode Island	164,004	0.3%
38	Kentucky	163,489	0.3%
39	Hawaii	150,125	0.3%
40	Mississippi	94,385	0.2%
41	Delaware	89,539	0.2%
42	Wyoming	58,122	0.1%
43	Alaska	52,250	0.1%
44	New Hampshire	49,567	0.1%
45	Montana	39,633	0.1%
46	South Dakota	32,811	0.1%
47	West Virginia	29,065	0.0%
48	North Dakota	28,006	0.0%
49	Maine	22,042	0.0%
50	Vermont	12,060	0.0%
	District of Columbia	76,526	0.1%

Source: U.S. Bureau of the Census
   "State Characteristics: Vintage 2017" (https://www.census.gov/programs-surveys/popest/data/data-sets.html)
*Persons of Hispanic origin may be of any race. Census states "Race is a self-identification data item in which respondents choose the race or races with which they most closely identify."

Percent of Population Hispanic in 2017

National Percent = 18.1%*

ALPHA ORDER

RANK	STATE	PERCENT
39	Alabama	4.3
30	Alaska	7.1
4	Arizona	31.4
28	Arkansas	7.6
3	California	39.1
7	Colorado	21.5
11	Connecticut	16.1
27	Delaware	9.3
6	Florida	25.6
24	Georgia	9.6
21	Hawaii	10.5
16	Idaho	12.5
10	Illinois	17.3
31	Indiana	7.0
33	Iowa	6.0
17	Kansas	11.9
44	Kentucky	3.7
37	Louisiana	5.2
49	Maine	1.6
22	Maryland	10.1
17	Massachusetts	11.9
38	Michigan	5.1
36	Minnesota	5.4
47	Mississippi	3.2
40	Missouri	4.2
41	Montana	3.8
19	Nebraska	11.0
44	New Hampshire	3.7
8	New Jersey	20.4
1	New Mexico	48.8
9	New York	19.2
25	North Carolina	9.5
44	North Dakota	3.7
41	Ohio	3.8
20	Oklahoma	10.6
14	Oregon	13.1
29	Pennsylvania	7.3
12	Rhode Island	15.5
34	South Carolina	5.7
41	South Dakota	3.8
35	Tennessee	5.5
2	Texas	39.4
13	Utah	14.0
48	Vermont	1.9
26	Virginia	9.4
15	Washington	12.7
49	West Virginia	1.6
32	Wisconsin	6.9
23	Wyoming	10.0

RANK ORDER

RANK	STATE	PERCENT
1	New Mexico	48.8
2	Texas	39.4
3	California	39.1
4	Arizona	31.4
5	Nevada	28.8
6	Florida	25.6
7	Colorado	21.5
8	New Jersey	20.4
9	New York	19.2
10	Illinois	17.3
11	Connecticut	16.1
12	Rhode Island	15.5
13	Utah	14.0
14	Oregon	13.1
15	Washington	12.7
16	Idaho	12.5
17	Kansas	11.9
17	Massachusetts	11.9
19	Nebraska	11.0
20	Oklahoma	10.6
21	Hawaii	10.5
22	Maryland	10.1
23	Wyoming	10.0
24	Georgia	9.6
25	North Carolina	9.5
26	Virginia	9.4
27	Delaware	9.3
28	Arkansas	7.6
29	Pennsylvania	7.3
30	Alaska	7.1
31	Indiana	7.0
32	Wisconsin	6.9
33	Iowa	6.0
34	South Carolina	5.7
35	Tennessee	5.5
36	Minnesota	5.4
37	Louisiana	5.2
38	Michigan	5.1
39	Alabama	4.3
40	Missouri	4.2
41	Montana	3.8
41	Ohio	3.8
41	South Dakota	3.8
44	Kentucky	3.7
44	New Hampshire	3.7
44	North Dakota	3.7
47	Mississippi	3.2
48	Vermont	1.9
49	Maine	1.6
49	West Virginia	1.6

District of Columbia   11.0

Source: CQ Press using data from U.S. Bureau of the Census
"State Characteristics: Vintage 2017" (https://www.census.gov/programs-surveys/popest/data/data-sets.html)
*Persons of Hispanic origin may be of any race. Census states "Race is a self-identification data item in which respondents choose the race or races with which they most closely identify."

Asian Population in 2017

National Total = 18,989,059*

ALPHA ORDER

RANK	STATE	POPULATION	% of USA
33	Alabama	71,338	0.4%
37	Alaska	47,754	0.3%
19	Arizona	247,790	1.3%
36	Arkansas	49,292	0.3%
1	California	5,993,089	31.6%
21	Colorado	188,635	1.0%
22	Connecticut	173,633	0.9%
38	Delaware	39,768	0.2%
7	Florida	613,880	3.2%
12	Georgia	440,104	2.3%
9	Hawaii	539,280	2.8%
43	Idaho	26,359	0.1%
5	Illinois	729,694	3.8%
24	Indiana	157,668	0.8%
31	Iowa	82,346	0.4%
28	Kansas	89,908	0.5%
34	Kentucky	69,734	0.4%
29	Louisiana	87,305	0.5%
44	Maine	16,643	0.1%
13	Maryland	407,369	2.1%
10	Massachusetts	473,001	2.5%
14	Michigan	319,772	1.7%
16	Minnesota	284,643	1.5%
42	Mississippi	32,515	0.2%
25	Missouri	126,443	0.7%
49	Montana	8,842	0.0%
35	Nebraska	49,912	0.3%
18	Nevada	264,533	1.4%
40	New Hampshire	37,202	0.2%
4	New Jersey	906,671	4.8%
41	New Mexico	36,222	0.2%
2	New York	1,806,646	9.5%
15	North Carolina	313,997	1.7%
47	North Dakota	12,269	0.1%
17	Ohio	271,531	1.4%
27	Oklahoma	91,288	0.5%
20	Oregon	192,917	1.0%
11	Pennsylvania	462,768	2.4%
39	Rhode Island	39,014	0.2%
30	South Carolina	85,665	0.5%
46	South Dakota	12,901	0.1%
26	Tennessee	125,244	0.7%
3	Texas	1,417,555	7.5%
32	Utah	79,393	0.4%
48	Vermont	11,348	0.1%
8	Virginia	575,117	3.0%
6	Washington	660,928	3.5%
45	West Virginia	15,071	0.1%
23	Wisconsin	168,435	0.9%
50	Wyoming	5,880	0.0%

RANK ORDER

RANK	STATE	POPULATION	% of USA
1	California	5,993,089	31.6%
2	New York	1,806,646	9.5%
3	Texas	1,417,555	7.5%
4	New Jersey	906,671	4.8%
5	Illinois	729,694	3.8%
6	Washington	660,928	3.5%
7	Florida	613,880	3.2%
8	Virginia	575,117	3.0%
9	Hawaii	539,280	2.8%
10	Massachusetts	473,001	2.5%
11	Pennsylvania	462,768	2.4%
12	Georgia	440,104	2.3%
13	Maryland	407,369	2.1%
14	Michigan	319,772	1.7%
15	North Carolina	313,997	1.7%
16	Minnesota	284,643	1.5%
17	Ohio	271,531	1.4%
18	Nevada	264,533	1.4%
19	Arizona	247,790	1.3%
20	Oregon	192,917	1.0%
21	Colorado	188,635	1.0%
22	Connecticut	173,633	0.9%
23	Wisconsin	168,435	0.9%
24	Indiana	157,668	0.8%
25	Missouri	126,443	0.7%
26	Tennessee	125,244	0.7%
27	Oklahoma	91,288	0.5%
28	Kansas	89,908	0.5%
29	Louisiana	87,305	0.5%
30	South Carolina	85,665	0.5%
31	Iowa	82,346	0.4%
32	Utah	79,393	0.4%
33	Alabama	71,338	0.4%
34	Kentucky	69,734	0.4%
35	Nebraska	49,912	0.3%
36	Arkansas	49,292	0.3%
37	Alaska	47,754	0.3%
38	Delaware	39,768	0.2%
39	Rhode Island	39,014	0.2%
40	New Hampshire	37,202	0.2%
41	New Mexico	36,222	0.2%
42	Mississippi	32,515	0.2%
43	Idaho	26,359	0.1%
44	Maine	16,643	0.1%
45	West Virginia	15,071	0.1%
46	South Dakota	12,901	0.1%
47	North Dakota	12,269	0.1%
48	Vermont	11,348	0.1%
49	Montana	8,842	0.0%
50	Wyoming	5,880	0.0%
	District of Columbia	29,747	0.2%

Source: U.S. Bureau of the Census
   "State Characteristics: Vintage 2017" (https://www.census.gov/programs-surveys/popest/data/data-sets.html)
*Those who identified themselves as one race. Census states "Race is a self-identification data item in which respondents choose the race or races with which they most closely identify."

Percent of Population Asian in 2017

National Percent = 5.8%*

<table>
<tr><td colspan="3">ALPHA ORDER</td><td colspan="3">RANK ORDER</td></tr>
<tr><td>RANK</td><td>STATE</td><td>PERCENT</td><td>RANK</td><td>STATE</td><td>PERCENT</td></tr>
<tr><td>43</td><td>Alabama</td><td>1.5</td><td>1</td><td>Hawaii</td><td>37.8</td></tr>
<tr><td>10</td><td>Alaska</td><td>6.5</td><td>2</td><td>California</td><td>15.2</td></tr>
<tr><td>20</td><td>Arizona</td><td>3.5</td><td>3</td><td>New Jersey</td><td>10.1</td></tr>
<tr><td>40</td><td>Arkansas</td><td>1.6</td><td>4</td><td>New York</td><td>9.1</td></tr>
<tr><td>2</td><td>California</td><td>15.2</td><td>5</td><td>Washington</td><td>8.9</td></tr>
<tr><td>21</td><td>Colorado</td><td>3.4</td><td>6</td><td>Nevada</td><td>8.8</td></tr>
<tr><td>14</td><td>Connecticut</td><td>4.8</td><td>7</td><td>Massachusetts</td><td>6.9</td></tr>
<tr><td>17</td><td>Delaware</td><td>4.1</td><td>8</td><td>Virginia</td><td>6.8</td></tr>
<tr><td>25</td><td>Florida</td><td>2.9</td><td>9</td><td>Maryland</td><td>6.7</td></tr>
<tr><td>16</td><td>Georgia</td><td>4.2</td><td>10</td><td>Alaska</td><td>6.5</td></tr>
<tr><td>1</td><td>Hawaii</td><td>37.8</td><td>11</td><td>Illinois</td><td>5.7</td></tr>
<tr><td>43</td><td>Idaho</td><td>1.5</td><td>12</td><td>Minnesota</td><td>5.1</td></tr>
<tr><td>11</td><td>Illinois</td><td>5.7</td><td>13</td><td>Texas</td><td>5.0</td></tr>
<tr><td>31</td><td>Indiana</td><td>2.4</td><td>14</td><td>Connecticut</td><td>4.8</td></tr>
<tr><td>28</td><td>Iowa</td><td>2.6</td><td>15</td><td>Oregon</td><td>4.7</td></tr>
<tr><td>23</td><td>Kansas</td><td>3.1</td><td>16</td><td>Georgia</td><td>4.2</td></tr>
<tr><td>40</td><td>Kentucky</td><td>1.6</td><td>17</td><td>Delaware</td><td>4.1</td></tr>
<tr><td>35</td><td>Louisiana</td><td>1.9</td><td>18</td><td>Rhode Island</td><td>3.7</td></tr>
<tr><td>46</td><td>Maine</td><td>1.2</td><td>19</td><td>Pennsylvania</td><td>3.6</td></tr>
<tr><td>9</td><td>Maryland</td><td>6.7</td><td>20</td><td>Arizona</td><td>3.5</td></tr>
<tr><td>7</td><td>Massachusetts</td><td>6.9</td><td>21</td><td>Colorado</td><td>3.4</td></tr>
<tr><td>22</td><td>Michigan</td><td>3.2</td><td>22</td><td>Michigan</td><td>3.2</td></tr>
<tr><td>12</td><td>Minnesota</td><td>5.1</td><td>23</td><td>Kansas</td><td>3.1</td></tr>
<tr><td>47</td><td>Mississippi</td><td>1.1</td><td>23</td><td>North Carolina</td><td>3.1</td></tr>
<tr><td>34</td><td>Missouri</td><td>2.1</td><td>25</td><td>Florida</td><td>2.9</td></tr>
<tr><td>49</td><td>Montana</td><td>0.8</td><td>25</td><td>Wisconsin</td><td>2.9</td></tr>
<tr><td>28</td><td>Nebraska</td><td>2.6</td><td>27</td><td>New Hampshire</td><td>2.8</td></tr>
<tr><td>6</td><td>Nevada</td><td>8.8</td><td>28</td><td>Iowa</td><td>2.6</td></tr>
<tr><td>27</td><td>New Hampshire</td><td>2.8</td><td>28</td><td>Nebraska</td><td>2.6</td></tr>
<tr><td>3</td><td>New Jersey</td><td>10.1</td><td>28</td><td>Utah</td><td>2.6</td></tr>
<tr><td>38</td><td>New Mexico</td><td>1.7</td><td>31</td><td>Indiana</td><td>2.4</td></tr>
<tr><td>4</td><td>New York</td><td>9.1</td><td>32</td><td>Ohio</td><td>2.3</td></tr>
<tr><td>23</td><td>North Carolina</td><td>3.1</td><td>32</td><td>Oklahoma</td><td>2.3</td></tr>
<tr><td>40</td><td>North Dakota</td><td>1.6</td><td>34</td><td>Missouri</td><td>2.1</td></tr>
<tr><td>32</td><td>Ohio</td><td>2.3</td><td>35</td><td>Louisiana</td><td>1.9</td></tr>
<tr><td>32</td><td>Oklahoma</td><td>2.3</td><td>35</td><td>Tennessee</td><td>1.9</td></tr>
<tr><td>15</td><td>Oregon</td><td>4.7</td><td>37</td><td>Vermont</td><td>1.8</td></tr>
<tr><td>19</td><td>Pennsylvania</td><td>3.6</td><td>38</td><td>New Mexico</td><td>1.7</td></tr>
<tr><td>18</td><td>Rhode Island</td><td>3.7</td><td>38</td><td>South Carolina</td><td>1.7</td></tr>
<tr><td>38</td><td>South Carolina</td><td>1.7</td><td>40</td><td>Arkansas</td><td>1.6</td></tr>
<tr><td>43</td><td>South Dakota</td><td>1.5</td><td>40</td><td>Kentucky</td><td>1.6</td></tr>
<tr><td>35</td><td>Tennessee</td><td>1.9</td><td>40</td><td>North Dakota</td><td>1.6</td></tr>
<tr><td>13</td><td>Texas</td><td>5.0</td><td>43</td><td>Alabama</td><td>1.5</td></tr>
<tr><td>28</td><td>Utah</td><td>2.6</td><td>43</td><td>Idaho</td><td>1.5</td></tr>
<tr><td>37</td><td>Vermont</td><td>1.8</td><td>43</td><td>South Dakota</td><td>1.5</td></tr>
<tr><td>8</td><td>Virginia</td><td>6.8</td><td>46</td><td>Maine</td><td>1.2</td></tr>
<tr><td>5</td><td>Washington</td><td>8.9</td><td>47</td><td>Mississippi</td><td>1.1</td></tr>
<tr><td>49</td><td>West Virginia</td><td>0.8</td><td>48</td><td>Wyoming</td><td>1.0</td></tr>
<tr><td>25</td><td>Wisconsin</td><td>2.9</td><td>49</td><td>Montana</td><td>0.8</td></tr>
<tr><td>48</td><td>Wyoming</td><td>1.0</td><td>49</td><td>West Virginia</td><td>0.8</td></tr>
<tr><td></td><td></td><td></td><td></td><td>District of Columbia</td><td>4.3</td></tr>
</table>

Source: CQ Press using data from U.S. Bureau of the Census
"State Characteristics: Vintage 2017" (https://www.census.gov/programs-surveys/popest/data/data-sets.html)
*Those who identified themselves as one race. Census states "Race is a self-identification data item in which respondents choose the race or races with which they most closely identify."

American Indian Population in 2017

National Total = 4,104,295*

RANK	STATE	POPULATION	% of USA
30	Alabama	34,108	0.8%
9	Alaska	112,994	2.8%
2	Arizona	373,532	9.1%
35	Arkansas	29,722	0.7%
1	California	650,250	15.8%
11	Colorado	89,116	2.2%
39	Connecticut	19,480	0.5%
46	Delaware	6,228	0.2%
10	Florida	104,511	2.5%
20	Georgia	53,646	1.3%
47	Hawaii	5,574	0.1%
34	Idaho	29,973	0.7%
13	Illinois	75,867	1.8%
38	Indiana	27,274	0.7%
41	Iowa	16,222	0.4%
28	Kansas	34,664	0.8%
43	Kentucky	13,263	0.3%
26	Louisiana	36,526	0.9%
45	Maine	9,511	0.2%
27	Maryland	35,386	0.9%
31	Massachusetts	33,341	0.8%
16	Michigan	73,124	1.8%
14	Minnesota	75,402	1.8%
40	Mississippi	18,179	0.4%
29	Missouri	34,635	0.8%
17	Montana	69,913	1.7%
36	Nebraska	27,965	0.7%
21	Nevada	49,722	1.2%
49	New Hampshire	3,978	0.1%
19	New Jersey	54,683	1.3%
5	New Mexico	227,132	5.5%
6	New York	193,229	4.7%
7	North Carolina	160,909	3.9%
25	North Dakota	41,588	1.0%
32	Ohio	32,991	0.8%
3	Oklahoma	363,551	8.9%
15	Oregon	74,655	1.8%
22	Pennsylvania	47,983	1.2%
44	Rhode Island	10,948	0.3%
37	South Carolina	27,373	0.7%
12	South Dakota	78,456	1.9%
33	Tennessee	30,876	0.8%
4	Texas	287,312	7.0%
23	Utah	47,581	1.2%
50	Vermont	2,413	0.1%
24	Virginia	45,889	1.1%
8	Washington	141,535	3.4%
48	West Virginia	4,451	0.1%
18	Wisconsin	66,752	1.6%
42	Wyoming	15,743	0.4%

RANK	STATE	POPULATION	% of USA
1	California	650,250	15.8%
2	Arizona	373,532	9.1%
3	Oklahoma	363,551	8.9%
4	Texas	287,312	7.0%
5	New Mexico	227,132	5.5%
6	New York	193,229	4.7%
7	North Carolina	160,909	3.9%
8	Washington	141,535	3.4%
9	Alaska	112,994	2.8%
10	Florida	104,511	2.5%
11	Colorado	89,116	2.2%
12	South Dakota	78,456	1.9%
13	Illinois	75,867	1.8%
14	Minnesota	75,402	1.8%
15	Oregon	74,655	1.8%
16	Michigan	73,124	1.8%
17	Montana	69,913	1.7%
18	Wisconsin	66,752	1.6%
19	New Jersey	54,683	1.3%
20	Georgia	53,646	1.3%
21	Nevada	49,722	1.2%
22	Pennsylvania	47,983	1.2%
23	Utah	47,581	1.2%
24	Virginia	45,889	1.1%
25	North Dakota	41,588	1.0%
26	Louisiana	36,526	0.9%
27	Maryland	35,386	0.9%
28	Kansas	34,664	0.8%
29	Missouri	34,635	0.8%
30	Alabama	34,108	0.8%
31	Massachusetts	33,341	0.8%
32	Ohio	32,991	0.8%
33	Tennessee	30,876	0.8%
34	Idaho	29,973	0.7%
35	Arkansas	29,722	0.7%
36	Nebraska	27,965	0.7%
37	South Carolina	27,373	0.7%
38	Indiana	27,274	0.7%
39	Connecticut	19,480	0.5%
40	Mississippi	18,179	0.4%
41	Iowa	16,222	0.4%
42	Wyoming	15,743	0.4%
43	Kentucky	13,263	0.3%
44	Rhode Island	10,948	0.3%
45	Maine	9,511	0.2%
46	Delaware	6,228	0.2%
47	Hawaii	5,574	0.1%
48	West Virginia	4,451	0.1%
49	New Hampshire	3,978	0.1%
50	Vermont	2,413	0.1%
	District of Columbia	4,139	0.1%

Source: U.S. Bureau of the Census
"State Characteristics: Vintage 2017" (https://www.census.gov/programs-surveys/popest/data/data-sets.html)
*Those who identified themselves as one race. Includes Alaska Native populations. Census states "Race is a self-identification data item in which respondents choose the race or races with which they most closely identify."

Percent of Population American Indian in 2017

National Percent = 1.3%*

ALPHA ORDER

RANK	STATE	PERCENT
26	Alabama	0.7
1	Alaska	15.3
7	Arizona	5.3
21	Arkansas	1.0
13	California	1.6
13	Colorado	1.6
35	Connecticut	0.5
29	Delaware	0.6
35	Florida	0.5
35	Georgia	0.5
43	Hawaii	0.4
11	Idaho	1.7
29	Illinois	0.6
43	Indiana	0.4
35	Iowa	0.5
19	Kansas	1.2
47	Kentucky	0.3
25	Louisiana	0.8
26	Maine	0.7
29	Maryland	0.6
35	Massachusetts	0.5
26	Michigan	0.7
18	Minnesota	1.4
29	Mississippi	0.6
29	Missouri	0.6
5	Montana	6.7
16	Nebraska	1.5
11	Nevada	1.7
47	New Hampshire	0.3
29	New Jersey	0.6
2	New Mexico	10.9
21	New York	1.0
13	North Carolina	1.6
6	North Dakota	5.5
47	Ohio	0.3
3	Oklahoma	9.2
10	Oregon	1.8
43	Pennsylvania	0.4
21	Rhode Island	1.0
35	South Carolina	0.5
4	South Dakota	9.0
35	Tennessee	0.5
21	Texas	1.0
16	Utah	1.5
43	Vermont	0.4
35	Virginia	0.5
9	Washington	1.9
50	West Virginia	0.2
19	Wisconsin	1.2
8	Wyoming	2.7

RANK ORDER

RANK	STATE	PERCENT
1	Alaska	15.3
2	New Mexico	10.9
3	Oklahoma	9.2
4	South Dakota	9.0
5	Montana	6.7
6	North Dakota	5.5
7	Arizona	5.3
8	Wyoming	2.7
9	Washington	1.9
10	Oregon	1.8
11	Idaho	1.7
11	Nevada	1.7
13	California	1.6
13	Colorado	1.6
13	North Carolina	1.6
16	Nebraska	1.5
16	Utah	1.5
18	Minnesota	1.4
19	Kansas	1.2
19	Wisconsin	1.2
21	Arkansas	1.0
21	New York	1.0
21	Rhode Island	1.0
21	Texas	1.0
25	Louisiana	0.8
26	Alabama	0.7
26	Maine	0.7
26	Michigan	0.7
29	Delaware	0.6
29	Illinois	0.6
29	Maryland	0.6
29	Mississippi	0.6
29	Missouri	0.6
29	New Jersey	0.6
35	Connecticut	0.5
35	Florida	0.5
35	Georgia	0.5
35	Iowa	0.5
35	Massachusetts	0.5
35	South Carolina	0.5
35	Tennessee	0.5
35	Virginia	0.5
43	Hawaii	0.4
43	Indiana	0.4
43	Pennsylvania	0.4
43	Vermont	0.4
47	Kentucky	0.3
47	New Hampshire	0.3
47	Ohio	0.3
50	West Virginia	0.2
	District of Columbia	0.6

Source: CQ Press using data from U.S. Bureau of the Census

"State Characteristics: Vintage 2017" (https://www.census.gov/programs-surveys/popest/data/data-sets.html)

*Those who identified themselves as one race. Includes Alaska Native populations. Census states "Race is a self-identification data item in which respondents choose the race or races with which they most closely identify."

Native Hawaiian or Other Pacific Islander Population in 2017

National Total = 785,471*

Source: U.S. Bureau of the Census
   "State Characteristics: Vintage 2017" (https://www.census.gov/programs-surveys/popest/data/data-sets.html)
*Those who identified themselves as one race. Census states "Race is a self-identification data item in which respondents choose the race or races with which they most closely identify."

Percent of Population Native Hawaiian or Other Pacific Islander in 2017

National Percent = 0.2%*

	ALPHA ORDER			RANK ORDER	
RANK	STATE	PERCENT	RANK	STATE	PERCENT
15	Alabama	0.1	1	Hawaii	10.2
2	Alaska	1.4	2	Alaska	1.4
8	Arizona	0.3	3	Utah	1.0
8	Arkansas	0.3	4	Nevada	0.8
6	California	0.5	4	Washington	0.8
10	Colorado	0.2	6	California	0.5
15	Connecticut	0.1	7	Oregon	0.4
15	Delaware	0.1	8	Arizona	0.3
15	Florida	0.1	8	Arkansas	0.3
15	Georgia	0.1	10	Colorado	0.2
1	Hawaii	10.2	10	Idaho	0.2
10	Idaho	0.2	10	New Mexico	0.2
15	Illinois	0.1	10	Oklahoma	0.2
15	Indiana	0.1	10	Rhode Island	0.2
15	Iowa	0.1	15	Alabama	0.1
15	Kansas	0.1	15	Connecticut	0.1
15	Kentucky	0.1	15	Delaware	0.1
15	Louisiana	0.1	15	Florida	0.1
46	Maine	0.0	15	Georgia	0.1
15	Maryland	0.1	15	Illinois	0.1
15	Massachusetts	0.1	15	Indiana	0.1
46	Michigan	0.0	15	Iowa	0.1
15	Minnesota	0.1	15	Kansas	0.1
15	Mississippi	0.1	15	Kentucky	0.1
15	Missouri	0.1	15	Louisiana	0.1
15	Montana	0.1	15	Maryland	0.1
15	Nebraska	0.1	15	Massachusetts	0.1
4	Nevada	0.8	15	Minnesota	0.1
46	New Hampshire	0.0	15	Mississippi	0.1
15	New Jersey	0.1	15	Missouri	0.1
10	New Mexico	0.2	15	Montana	0.1
15	New York	0.1	15	Nebraska	0.1
15	North Carolina	0.1	15	New Jersey	0.1
15	North Dakota	0.1	15	New York	0.1
15	Ohio	0.1	15	North Carolina	0.1
10	Oklahoma	0.2	15	North Dakota	0.1
7	Oregon	0.4	15	Ohio	0.1
15	Pennsylvania	0.1	15	Pennsylvania	0.1
10	Rhode Island	0.2	15	South Carolina	0.1
15	South Carolina	0.1	15	South Dakota	0.1
15	South Dakota	0.1	15	Tennessee	0.1
15	Tennessee	0.1	15	Texas	0.1
15	Texas	0.1	15	Virginia	0.1
3	Utah	1.0	15	Wisconsin	0.1
46	Vermont	0.0	15	Wyoming	0.1
15	Virginia	0.1	46	Maine	0.0
4	Washington	0.8	46	Michigan	0.0
46	West Virginia	0.0	46	New Hampshire	0.0
15	Wisconsin	0.1	46	Vermont	0.0
15	Wyoming	0.1	46	West Virginia	0.0
				District of Columbia	0.1

Source: CQ Press using data from U.S. Bureau of the Census
"State Characteristics: Vintage 2017" (https://www.census.gov/programs-surveys/popest/data/data-sets.html)
*Those who identified themselves as one race. Census states "Race is a self-identification data item in which respondents choose the race or races with which they most closely identify."

Non-Hispanic White Population in 2017

National Total = 197,803,083*

ALPHA ORDER

RANK	STATE	POPULATION	% of USA
24	Alabama	3,196,852	1.6%
49	Alaska	449,776	0.2%
20	Arizona	3,849,130	1.9%
33	Arkansas	2,177,809	1.1%
1	California	14,696,754	7.4%
21	Colorado	3,827,750	1.9%
31	Connecticut	2,404,792	1.2%
46	Delaware	599,260	0.3%
3	Florida	11,343,977	5.7%
10	Georgia	5,507,334	2.8%
50	Hawaii	312,492	0.2%
38	Idaho	1,408,294	0.7%
7	Illinois	7,849,887	4.0%
11	Indiana	5,280,420	2.7%
28	Iowa	2,695,962	1.4%
32	Kansas	2,209,748	1.1%
22	Kentucky	3,768,891	1.9%
27	Louisiana	2,747,730	1.4%
39	Maine	1,246,478	0.6%
26	Maryland	3,077,907	1.6%
16	Massachusetts	4,953,695	2.5%
8	Michigan	7,488,326	3.8%
19	Minnesota	4,455,605	2.3%
34	Mississippi	1,691,566	0.9%
17	Missouri	4,859,227	2.5%
41	Montana	905,811	0.5%
36	Nebraska	1,516,962	0.8%
37	Nevada	1,470,855	0.7%
40	New Hampshire	1,215,447	0.6%
15	New Jersey	4,962,470	2.5%
42	New Mexico	783,064	0.4%
4	New York	10,972,959	5.5%
9	North Carolina	6,486,100	3.3%
45	North Dakota	639,029	0.3%
6	Ohio	9,219,577	4.7%
29	Oklahoma	2,581,568	1.3%
25	Oregon	3,139,685	1.6%
5	Pennsylvania	9,796,510	5.0%
43	Rhode Island	768,229	0.4%
23	South Carolina	3,203,045	1.6%
44	South Dakota	714,881	0.4%
14	Tennessee	4,963,780	2.5%
2	Texas	11,886,381	6.0%
30	Utah	2,434,785	1.2%
47	Vermont	579,149	0.3%
12	Virginia	5,241,262	2.6%
13	Washington	5,091,370	2.6%
35	West Virginia	1,674,557	0.8%
18	Wisconsin	4,713,993	2.4%
48	Wyoming	486,565	0.2%

RANK ORDER

RANK	STATE	POPULATION	% of USA
1	California	14,696,754	7.4%
2	Texas	11,886,381	6.0%
3	Florida	11,343,977	5.7%
4	New York	10,972,959	5.5%
5	Pennsylvania	9,796,510	5.0%
6	Ohio	9,219,577	4.7%
7	Illinois	7,849,887	4.0%
8	Michigan	7,488,326	3.8%
9	North Carolina	6,486,100	3.3%
10	Georgia	5,507,334	2.8%
11	Indiana	5,280,420	2.7%
12	Virginia	5,241,262	2.6%
13	Washington	5,091,370	2.6%
14	Tennessee	4,963,780	2.5%
15	New Jersey	4,962,470	2.5%
16	Massachusetts	4,953,695	2.5%
17	Missouri	4,859,227	2.5%
18	Wisconsin	4,713,993	2.4%
19	Minnesota	4,455,605	2.3%
20	Arizona	3,849,130	1.9%
21	Colorado	3,827,750	1.9%
22	Kentucky	3,768,891	1.9%
23	South Carolina	3,203,045	1.6%
24	Alabama	3,196,852	1.6%
25	Oregon	3,139,685	1.6%
26	Maryland	3,077,907	1.6%
27	Louisiana	2,747,730	1.4%
28	Iowa	2,695,962	1.4%
29	Oklahoma	2,581,568	1.3%
30	Utah	2,434,785	1.2%
31	Connecticut	2,404,792	1.2%
32	Kansas	2,209,748	1.1%
33	Arkansas	2,177,809	1.1%
34	Mississippi	1,691,566	0.9%
35	West Virginia	1,674,557	0.8%
36	Nebraska	1,516,962	0.8%
37	Nevada	1,470,855	0.7%
38	Idaho	1,408,294	0.7%
39	Maine	1,246,478	0.6%
40	New Hampshire	1,215,447	0.6%
41	Montana	905,811	0.5%
42	New Mexico	783,064	0.4%
43	Rhode Island	768,229	0.4%
44	South Dakota	714,881	0.4%
45	North Dakota	639,029	0.3%
46	Delaware	599,260	0.3%
47	Vermont	579,149	0.3%
48	Wyoming	486,565	0.2%
49	Alaska	449,776	0.2%
50	Hawaii	312,492	0.2%
	District of Columbia	255,387	0.1%

Source: U.S. Bureau of the Census
   "State Characteristics: Vintage 2017" (https://www.census.gov/programs-surveys/popest/data/data-sets.html)
*Those who identified themselves as one race. "White" is defined by Census as a person having origins in any of the original peoples of Europe, North Africa, or the Middle East. This is a subset of the 249,619,493 white population. Persons of Hispanic origin may be of any race. Census states "Race is a self-identification data item in which respondents choose the race or races with which they most closely identify."

Percent of Population Non-Hispanic White in 2017

National Percent = 60.7%*

<table>
<tr><td colspan="3">ALPHA ORDER</td><td colspan="3">RANK ORDER</td></tr>
<tr><td>RANK</td><td>STATE</td><td>PERCENT</td><td>RANK</td><td>STATE</td><td>PERCENT</td></tr>
<tr><td>31</td><td>Alabama</td><td>65.6</td><td>1</td><td>Maine</td><td>93.3</td></tr>
<tr><td>37</td><td>Alaska</td><td>60.8</td><td>2</td><td>Vermont</td><td>92.9</td></tr>
<tr><td>42</td><td>Arizona</td><td>54.9</td><td>3</td><td>West Virginia</td><td>92.2</td></tr>
<tr><td>24</td><td>Arkansas</td><td>72.5</td><td>4</td><td>New Hampshire</td><td>90.5</td></tr>
<tr><td>49</td><td>California</td><td>37.2</td><td>5</td><td>Montana</td><td>86.2</td></tr>
<tr><td>28</td><td>Colorado</td><td>68.3</td><td>6</td><td>Iowa</td><td>85.7</td></tr>
<tr><td>29</td><td>Connecticut</td><td>67.0</td><td>7</td><td>Kentucky</td><td>84.6</td></tr>
<tr><td>34</td><td>Delaware</td><td>62.3</td><td>7</td><td>North Dakota</td><td>84.6</td></tr>
<tr><td>43</td><td>Florida</td><td>54.1</td><td>9</td><td>Wyoming</td><td>84.0</td></tr>
<tr><td>44</td><td>Georgia</td><td>52.8</td><td>10</td><td>South Dakota</td><td>82.2</td></tr>
<tr><td>50</td><td>Hawaii</td><td>21.9</td><td>11</td><td>Idaho</td><td>82.0</td></tr>
<tr><td>11</td><td>Idaho</td><td>82.0</td><td>12</td><td>Wisconsin</td><td>81.3</td></tr>
<tr><td>36</td><td>Illinois</td><td>61.3</td><td>13</td><td>Minnesota</td><td>79.9</td></tr>
<tr><td>15</td><td>Indiana</td><td>79.2</td><td>14</td><td>Missouri</td><td>79.5</td></tr>
<tr><td>6</td><td>Iowa</td><td>85.7</td><td>15</td><td>Indiana</td><td>79.2</td></tr>
<tr><td>20</td><td>Kansas</td><td>75.9</td><td>16</td><td>Ohio</td><td>79.1</td></tr>
<tr><td>7</td><td>Kentucky</td><td>84.6</td><td>17</td><td>Nebraska</td><td>79.0</td></tr>
<tr><td>38</td><td>Louisiana</td><td>58.7</td><td>18</td><td>Utah</td><td>78.5</td></tr>
<tr><td>1</td><td>Maine</td><td>93.3</td><td>19</td><td>Pennsylvania</td><td>76.5</td></tr>
<tr><td>45</td><td>Maryland</td><td>50.9</td><td>20</td><td>Kansas</td><td>75.9</td></tr>
<tr><td>26</td><td>Massachusetts</td><td>72.2</td><td>21</td><td>Oregon</td><td>75.8</td></tr>
<tr><td>22</td><td>Michigan</td><td>75.2</td><td>22</td><td>Michigan</td><td>75.2</td></tr>
<tr><td>13</td><td>Minnesota</td><td>79.9</td><td>23</td><td>Tennessee</td><td>73.9</td></tr>
<tr><td>39</td><td>Mississippi</td><td>56.7</td><td>24</td><td>Arkansas</td><td>72.5</td></tr>
<tr><td>14</td><td>Missouri</td><td>79.5</td><td>24</td><td>Rhode Island</td><td>72.5</td></tr>
<tr><td>5</td><td>Montana</td><td>86.2</td><td>26</td><td>Massachusetts</td><td>72.2</td></tr>
<tr><td>17</td><td>Nebraska</td><td>79.0</td><td>27</td><td>Washington</td><td>68.7</td></tr>
<tr><td>46</td><td>Nevada</td><td>49.1</td><td>28</td><td>Colorado</td><td>68.3</td></tr>
<tr><td>4</td><td>New Hampshire</td><td>90.5</td><td>29</td><td>Connecticut</td><td>67.0</td></tr>
<tr><td>41</td><td>New Jersey</td><td>55.1</td><td>30</td><td>Oklahoma</td><td>65.7</td></tr>
<tr><td>48</td><td>New Mexico</td><td>37.5</td><td>31</td><td>Alabama</td><td>65.6</td></tr>
<tr><td>40</td><td>New York</td><td>55.3</td><td>32</td><td>South Carolina</td><td>63.8</td></tr>
<tr><td>33</td><td>North Carolina</td><td>63.1</td><td>33</td><td>North Carolina</td><td>63.1</td></tr>
<tr><td>7</td><td>North Dakota</td><td>84.6</td><td>34</td><td>Delaware</td><td>62.3</td></tr>
<tr><td>16</td><td>Ohio</td><td>79.1</td><td>35</td><td>Virginia</td><td>61.9</td></tr>
<tr><td>30</td><td>Oklahoma</td><td>65.7</td><td>36</td><td>Illinois</td><td>61.3</td></tr>
<tr><td>21</td><td>Oregon</td><td>75.8</td><td>37</td><td>Alaska</td><td>60.8</td></tr>
<tr><td>19</td><td>Pennsylvania</td><td>76.5</td><td>38</td><td>Louisiana</td><td>58.7</td></tr>
<tr><td>24</td><td>Rhode Island</td><td>72.5</td><td>39</td><td>Mississippi</td><td>56.7</td></tr>
<tr><td>32</td><td>South Carolina</td><td>63.8</td><td>40</td><td>New York</td><td>55.3</td></tr>
<tr><td>10</td><td>South Dakota</td><td>82.2</td><td>41</td><td>New Jersey</td><td>55.1</td></tr>
<tr><td>23</td><td>Tennessee</td><td>73.9</td><td>42</td><td>Arizona</td><td>54.9</td></tr>
<tr><td>47</td><td>Texas</td><td>42.0</td><td>43</td><td>Florida</td><td>54.1</td></tr>
<tr><td>18</td><td>Utah</td><td>78.5</td><td>44</td><td>Georgia</td><td>52.8</td></tr>
<tr><td>2</td><td>Vermont</td><td>92.9</td><td>45</td><td>Maryland</td><td>50.9</td></tr>
<tr><td>35</td><td>Virginia</td><td>61.9</td><td>46</td><td>Nevada</td><td>49.1</td></tr>
<tr><td>27</td><td>Washington</td><td>68.7</td><td>47</td><td>Texas</td><td>42.0</td></tr>
<tr><td>3</td><td>West Virginia</td><td>92.2</td><td>48</td><td>New Mexico</td><td>37.5</td></tr>
<tr><td>12</td><td>Wisconsin</td><td>81.3</td><td>49</td><td>California</td><td>37.2</td></tr>
<tr><td>9</td><td>Wyoming</td><td>84.0</td><td>50</td><td>Hawaii</td><td>21.9</td></tr>
<tr><td></td><td></td><td></td><td></td><td>District of Columbia</td><td>36.8</td></tr>
</table>

Source: CQ Press using data from U.S. Bureau of the Census
"State Characteristics: Vintage 2017" (https://www.census.gov/programs-surveys/popest/data/data-sets.html)
*Those who identified themselves as one race. "White" is defined by Census as a person having origins in any of the original peoples of Europe, North Africa, or the Middle East. This non-Hispanic white subset is 79.2% of the total white population. Persons of Hispanic origin may be of any race. Census states "Race is a self-identification data item in which respondents choose the race or races with which they most closely identify."

Multiple Race Population in 2017

National Total = 8,720,986*

ALPHA ORDER

RANK	STATE	POPULATION	% of USA
31	Alabama	81,717	0.9%
36	Alaska	54,644	0.6%
16	Arizona	198,047	2.3%
34	Arkansas	62,805	0.7%
1	California	1,529,207	17.5%
18	Colorado	170,819	2.0%
30	Connecticut	84,616	1.0%
44	Delaware	25,243	0.3%
4	Florida	447,272	5.1%
14	Georgia	219,739	2.5%
6	Hawaii	339,437	3.9%
38	Idaho	42,045	0.5%
10	Illinois	250,871	2.9%
23	Indiana	136,695	1.6%
35	Iowa	58,549	0.7%
28	Kansas	86,376	1.0%
29	Kentucky	85,541	1.0%
33	Louisiana	78,395	0.9%
45	Maine	23,442	0.3%
17	Maryland	171,596	2.0%
19	Massachusetts	166,254	1.9%
11	Michigan	242,305	2.8%
22	Minnesota	139,151	1.6%
40	Mississippi	38,171	0.4%
21	Missouri	139,859	1.6%
43	Montana	28,922	0.3%
39	Nebraska	41,927	0.5%
24	Nevada	130,150	1.5%
46	New Hampshire	22,954	0.3%
15	New Jersey	198,330	2.3%
37	New Mexico	53,099	0.6%
3	New York	504,521	5.8%
13	North Carolina	228,871	2.6%
48	North Dakota	16,264	0.2%
7	Ohio	263,765	3.0%
12	Oklahoma	241,123	2.8%
20	Oregon	159,225	1.8%
8	Pennsylvania	257,365	3.0%
42	Rhode Island	29,518	0.3%
27	South Carolina	93,694	1.1%
47	South Dakota	20,557	0.2%
25	Tennessee	128,470	1.5%
2	Texas	561,823	6.4%
32	Utah	78,813	0.9%
50	Vermont	12,025	0.1%
9	Virginia	254,261	2.9%
5	Washington	348,842	4.0%
41	West Virginia	31,585	0.4%
26	Wisconsin	110,745	1.3%
49	Wyoming	12,272	0.1%

RANK ORDER

RANK	STATE	POPULATION	% of USA
1	California	1,529,207	17.5%
2	Texas	561,823	6.4%
3	New York	504,521	5.8%
4	Florida	447,272	5.1%
5	Washington	348,842	4.0%
6	Hawaii	339,437	3.9%
7	Ohio	263,765	3.0%
8	Pennsylvania	257,365	3.0%
9	Virginia	254,261	2.9%
10	Illinois	250,871	2.9%
11	Michigan	242,305	2.8%
12	Oklahoma	241,123	2.8%
13	North Carolina	228,871	2.6%
14	Georgia	219,739	2.5%
15	New Jersey	198,330	2.3%
16	Arizona	198,047	2.3%
17	Maryland	171,596	2.0%
18	Colorado	170,819	2.0%
19	Massachusetts	166,254	1.9%
20	Oregon	159,225	1.8%
21	Missouri	139,859	1.6%
22	Minnesota	139,151	1.6%
23	Indiana	136,695	1.6%
24	Nevada	130,150	1.5%
25	Tennessee	128,470	1.5%
26	Wisconsin	110,745	1.3%
27	South Carolina	93,694	1.1%
28	Kansas	86,376	1.0%
29	Kentucky	85,541	1.0%
30	Connecticut	84,616	1.0%
31	Alabama	81,717	0.9%
32	Utah	78,813	0.9%
33	Louisiana	78,395	0.9%
34	Arkansas	62,805	0.7%
35	Iowa	58,549	0.7%
36	Alaska	54,644	0.6%
37	New Mexico	53,099	0.6%
38	Idaho	42,045	0.5%
39	Nebraska	41,927	0.5%
40	Mississippi	38,171	0.4%
41	West Virginia	31,585	0.4%
42	Rhode Island	29,518	0.3%
43	Montana	28,922	0.3%
44	Delaware	25,243	0.3%
45	Maine	23,442	0.3%
46	New Hampshire	22,954	0.3%
47	South Dakota	20,557	0.2%
48	North Dakota	16,264	0.2%
49	Wyoming	12,272	0.1%
50	Vermont	12,025	0.1%
	District of Columbia	19,069	0.2%

Source: U.S. Bureau of the Census
   "State Characteristics: Vintage 2017" (https://www.census.gov/programs-surveys/popest/data/data-sets.html)
*This includes those who identified themselves as two or more races. This is the population who did not identify themselves as one race (White, Black, American Indian/Native Alaska Native, Asian, or Native Hawaiian or Other Pacific Islander) but as a member of multiple racial groups. Census states "Race is a self-identification data item in which respondents choose the race or races with which they most closely identify."

Percent of Population Multiple Races in 2017

National Percent = 2.7%*

ALPHA ORDER

RANK	STATE	PERCENT
46	Alabama	1.7
2	Alaska	7.4
11	Arizona	2.8
31	Arkansas	2.1
6	California	3.9
8	Colorado	3.0
20	Connecticut	2.4
15	Delaware	2.6
31	Florida	2.1
31	Georgia	2.1
1	Hawaii	23.8
20	Idaho	2.4
36	Illinois	2.0
31	Indiana	2.1
39	Iowa	1.9
8	Kansas	3.0
39	Kentucky	1.9
46	Louisiana	1.7
45	Maine	1.8
11	Maryland	2.8
20	Massachusetts	2.4
20	Michigan	2.4
16	Minnesota	2.5
50	Mississippi	1.3
25	Missouri	2.3
11	Montana	2.8
27	Nebraska	2.2
5	Nevada	4.3
46	New Hampshire	1.7
27	New Jersey	2.2
16	New Mexico	2.5
16	New York	2.5
27	North Carolina	2.2
27	North Dakota	2.2
25	Ohio	2.3
3	Oklahoma	6.1
7	Oregon	3.8
36	Pennsylvania	2.0
11	Rhode Island	2.8
39	South Carolina	1.9
20	South Dakota	2.4
39	Tennessee	1.9
36	Texas	2.0
16	Utah	2.5
39	Vermont	1.9
8	Virginia	3.0
4	Washington	4.7
46	West Virginia	1.7
39	Wisconsin	1.9
31	Wyoming	2.1

RANK ORDER

RANK	STATE	PERCENT
1	Hawaii	23.8
2	Alaska	7.4
3	Oklahoma	6.1
4	Washington	4.7
5	Nevada	4.3
6	California	3.9
7	Oregon	3.8
8	Colorado	3.0
8	Kansas	3.0
8	Virginia	3.0
11	Arizona	2.8
11	Maryland	2.8
11	Montana	2.8
11	Rhode Island	2.8
15	Delaware	2.6
16	Minnesota	2.5
16	New Mexico	2.5
16	New York	2.5
16	Utah	2.5
20	Connecticut	2.4
20	Idaho	2.4
20	Massachusetts	2.4
20	Michigan	2.4
20	South Dakota	2.4
25	Missouri	2.3
25	Ohio	2.3
27	Nebraska	2.2
27	New Jersey	2.2
27	North Carolina	2.2
27	North Dakota	2.2
31	Arkansas	2.1
31	Florida	2.1
31	Georgia	2.1
31	Indiana	2.1
31	Wyoming	2.1
36	Illinois	2.0
36	Pennsylvania	2.0
36	Texas	2.0
39	Iowa	1.9
39	Kentucky	1.9
39	South Carolina	1.9
39	Tennessee	1.9
39	Vermont	1.9
39	Wisconsin	1.9
45	Maine	1.8
46	Alabama	1.7
46	Louisiana	1.7
46	New Hampshire	1.7
46	West Virginia	1.7
50	Mississippi	1.3

	District of Columbia	2.7

Source: CQ Press using data from U.S. Bureau of the Census
"State Characteristics: Vintage 2017" (https://www.census.gov/programs-surveys/popest/data/data-sets.html)
*This includes those who identified themselves as two or more races. This is the population who did not identify themselves as one race (White, Black, American Indian/Native Alaska Native, Asian, or Native Hawaiian or Other Pacific Islander) but as a member of multiple racial groups. Census states "Race is a self-identification data item in which respondents choose the race or races with which they most closely identify."

Population under 5 Years Old in 2017

National Total = 19,938,860

Source: U.S. Bureau of the Census
"State Characteristics: Vintage 2017" (https://www.census.gov/programs-surveys/popest/data/data-sets.html)

Percent of Population under 5 Years Old in 2017

National Percent = 6.1% of Population

ALPHA ORDER				RANK ORDER		
RANK	STATE	PERCENT		RANK	STATE	PERCENT
28	Alabama	6.0		1	Utah	8.2
2	Alaska	7.3		2	Alaska	7.3
20	Arizona	6.2		3	North Dakota	7.2
11	Arkansas	6.4		3	Texas	7.2
14	California	6.3		5	South Dakota	7.1
28	Colorado	6.0		6	Nebraska	6.9
47	Connecticut	5.1		7	Idaho	6.8
40	Delaware	5.7		8	Louisiana	6.7
43	Florida	5.4		8	Oklahoma	6.7
14	Georgia	6.3		10	Kansas	6.6
14	Hawaii	6.3		11	Arkansas	6.4
7	Idaho	6.8		11	Minnesota	6.4
28	Illinois	6.0		11	Wyoming	6.4
14	Indiana	6.3		14	California	6.3
14	Iowa	6.3		14	Georgia	6.3
10	Kansas	6.6		14	Hawaii	6.3
20	Kentucky	6.2		14	Indiana	6.3
8	Louisiana	6.7		14	Iowa	6.3
48	Maine	4.8		14	Mississippi	6.3
24	Maryland	6.1		20	Arizona	6.2
45	Massachusetts	5.3		20	Kentucky	6.2
36	Michigan	5.8		20	Nevada	6.2
11	Minnesota	6.4		20	Washington	6.2
14	Mississippi	6.3		24	Maryland	6.1
24	Missouri	6.1		24	Missouri	6.1
28	Montana	6.0		24	New Mexico	6.1
6	Nebraska	6.9		24	Tennessee	6.1
20	Nevada	6.2		28	Alabama	6.0
48	New Hampshire	4.8		28	Colorado	6.0
36	New Jersey	5.8		28	Illinois	6.0
24	New Mexico	6.1		28	Montana	6.0
34	New York	5.9		28	Ohio	6.0
34	North Carolina	5.9		28	Virginia	6.0
3	North Dakota	7.2		34	New York	5.9
28	Ohio	6.0		34	North Carolina	5.9
8	Oklahoma	6.7		36	Michigan	5.8
40	Oregon	5.7		36	New Jersey	5.8
42	Pennsylvania	5.5		36	South Carolina	5.8
46	Rhode Island	5.2		36	Wisconsin	5.8
36	South Carolina	5.8		40	Delaware	5.7
5	South Dakota	7.1		40	Oregon	5.7
24	Tennessee	6.1		42	Pennsylvania	5.5
3	Texas	7.2		43	Florida	5.4
1	Utah	8.2		43	West Virginia	5.4
48	Vermont	4.8		45	Massachusetts	5.3
28	Virginia	6.0		46	Rhode Island	5.2
20	Washington	6.2		47	Connecticut	5.1
43	West Virginia	5.4		48	Maine	4.8
36	Wisconsin	5.8		48	New Hampshire	4.8
11	Wyoming	6.4		48	Vermont	4.8
					District of Columbia	6.5

Source: CQ Press using data from U.S. Bureau of the Census
"State Characteristics: Vintage 2017" (https://www.census.gov/programs-surveys/popest/data/data-sets.html)

Population 5 to 17 Years Old in 2017

National Total = 53,716,518

ALPHA ORDER

ALPHA ORDER

RANK	STATE	POPULATION	% of USA
24	Alabama	801,919	1.5%
47	Alaska	130,845	0.2%
13	Arizona	1,196,228	2.2%
34	Arkansas	514,105	1.0%
1	California	6,588,623	12.3%
22	Colorado	925,626	1.7%
30	Connecticut	560,505	1.0%
46	Delaware	149,492	0.3%
3	Florida	3,063,888	5.7%
8	Georgia	1,854,385	3.5%
40	Hawaii	215,635	0.4%
38	Idaho	326,755	0.6%
5	Illinois	2,124,136	4.0%
15	Indiana	1,152,233	2.1%
31	Iowa	532,951	1.0%
33	Kansas	519,399	1.0%
26	Kentucky	733,656	1.4%
25	Louisiana	796,365	1.5%
42	Maine	188,132	0.4%
19	Maryland	981,121	1.8%
17	Massachusetts	1,009,367	1.9%
10	Michigan	1,603,367	3.0%
21	Minnesota	943,426	1.8%
32	Mississippi	526,390	1.0%
18	Missouri	1,008,492	1.9%
43	Montana	165,598	0.3%
37	Nebraska	342,672	0.6%
35	Nevada	499,626	0.9%
41	New Hampshire	194,292	0.4%
11	New Jersey	1,457,300	2.7%
36	New Mexico	359,945	0.7%
4	New York	2,990,091	5.6%
9	North Carolina	1,692,633	3.2%
48	North Dakota	121,729	0.2%
7	Ohio	1,906,455	3.5%
27	Oklahoma	695,545	1.3%
29	Oregon	637,651	1.2%
6	Pennsylvania	1,955,686	3.6%
45	Rhode Island	152,571	0.3%
23	South Carolina	811,021	1.5%
44	South Dakota	153,097	0.3%
16	Tennessee	1,098,858	2.0%
2	Texas	5,334,414	9.9%
28	Utah	671,499	1.3%
50	Vermont	86,790	0.2%
12	Virginia	1,357,502	2.5%
14	Washington	1,187,603	2.2%
39	West Virginia	271,234	0.5%
20	Wisconsin	946,756	1.8%
49	Wyoming	99,452	0.2%

RANK ORDER

RANK	STATE	POPULATION	% of USA
1	California	6,588,623	12.3%
2	Texas	5,334,414	9.9%
3	Florida	3,063,888	5.7%
4	New York	2,990,091	5.6%
5	Illinois	2,124,136	4.0%
6	Pennsylvania	1,955,686	3.6%
7	Ohio	1,906,455	3.5%
8	Georgia	1,854,385	3.5%
9	North Carolina	1,692,633	3.2%
10	Michigan	1,603,367	3.0%
11	New Jersey	1,457,300	2.7%
12	Virginia	1,357,502	2.5%
13	Arizona	1,196,228	2.2%
14	Washington	1,187,603	2.2%
15	Indiana	1,152,233	2.1%
16	Tennessee	1,098,858	2.0%
17	Massachusetts	1,009,367	1.9%
18	Missouri	1,008,492	1.9%
19	Maryland	981,121	1.8%
20	Wisconsin	946,756	1.8%
21	Minnesota	943,426	1.8%
22	Colorado	925,626	1.7%
23	South Carolina	811,021	1.5%
24	Alabama	801,919	1.5%
25	Louisiana	796,365	1.5%
26	Kentucky	733,656	1.4%
27	Oklahoma	695,545	1.3%
28	Utah	671,499	1.3%
29	Oregon	637,651	1.2%
30	Connecticut	560,505	1.0%
31	Iowa	532,951	1.0%
32	Mississippi	526,390	1.0%
33	Kansas	519,399	1.0%
34	Arkansas	514,105	1.0%
35	Nevada	499,626	0.9%
36	New Mexico	359,945	0.7%
37	Nebraska	342,672	0.6%
38	Idaho	326,755	0.6%
39	West Virginia	271,234	0.5%
40	Hawaii	215,635	0.4%
41	New Hampshire	194,292	0.4%
42	Maine	188,132	0.4%
43	Montana	165,598	0.3%
44	South Dakota	153,097	0.3%
45	Rhode Island	152,571	0.3%
46	Delaware	149,492	0.3%
47	Alaska	130,845	0.2%
48	North Dakota	121,729	0.2%
49	Wyoming	99,452	0.2%
50	Vermont	86,790	0.2%
	District of Columbia	79,457	0.1%

Source: CQ Press using data from U.S. Bureau of the Census
"State Characteristics: Vintage 2017" (https://www.census.gov/programs-surveys/popest/data/data-sets.html)

Percent of Population 5 to 17 Years Old in 2017

National Percent = 16.5% of Population

ALPHA ORDER

RANK	STATE	PERCENT
22	Alabama	16.5
7	Alaska	17.7
15	Arizona	17.0
14	Arkansas	17.1
19	California	16.7
22	Colorado	16.5
38	Connecticut	15.6
39	Delaware	15.5
46	Florida	14.6
4	Georgia	17.8
42	Hawaii	15.1
2	Idaho	19.0
21	Illinois	16.6
11	Indiana	17.3
17	Iowa	16.9
4	Kansas	17.8
22	Kentucky	16.5
15	Louisiana	17.0
49	Maine	14.1
30	Maryland	16.2
45	Massachusetts	14.7
32	Michigan	16.1
17	Minnesota	16.9
9	Mississippi	17.6
22	Missouri	16.5
37	Montana	15.8
4	Nebraska	17.8
19	Nevada	16.7
47	New Hampshire	14.5
30	New Jersey	16.2
12	New Mexico	17.2
42	New York	15.1
22	North Carolina	16.5
32	North Dakota	16.1
27	Ohio	16.4
7	Oklahoma	17.7
40	Oregon	15.4
41	Pennsylvania	15.3
48	Rhode Island	14.4
32	South Carolina	16.1
9	South Dakota	17.6
27	Tennessee	16.4
3	Texas	18.8
1	Utah	21.6
50	Vermont	13.9
35	Virginia	16.0
35	Washington	16.0
44	West Virginia	14.9
29	Wisconsin	16.3
12	Wyoming	17.2

RANK ORDER

RANK	STATE	PERCENT
1	Utah	21.6
2	Idaho	19.0
3	Texas	18.8
4	Georgia	17.8
4	Kansas	17.8
4	Nebraska	17.8
7	Alaska	17.7
7	Oklahoma	17.7
9	Mississippi	17.6
9	South Dakota	17.6
11	Indiana	17.3
12	New Mexico	17.2
12	Wyoming	17.2
14	Arkansas	17.1
15	Arizona	17.0
15	Louisiana	17.0
17	Iowa	16.9
17	Minnesota	16.9
19	California	16.7
19	Nevada	16.7
21	Illinois	16.6
22	Alabama	16.5
22	Colorado	16.5
22	Kentucky	16.5
22	Missouri	16.5
22	North Carolina	16.5
27	Ohio	16.4
27	Tennessee	16.4
29	Wisconsin	16.3
30	Maryland	16.2
30	New Jersey	16.2
32	Michigan	16.1
32	North Dakota	16.1
32	South Carolina	16.1
35	Virginia	16.0
35	Washington	16.0
37	Montana	15.8
38	Connecticut	15.6
39	Delaware	15.5
40	Oregon	15.4
41	Pennsylvania	15.3
42	Hawaii	15.1
42	New York	15.1
44	West Virginia	14.9
45	Massachusetts	14.7
46	Florida	14.6
47	New Hampshire	14.5
48	Rhode Island	14.4
49	Maine	14.1
50	Vermont	13.9

District of Columbia — 11.4

Source: CQ Press using data from U.S. Bureau of the Census
"State Characteristics: Vintage 2017" (https://www.census.gov/programs-surveys/popest/data/data-sets.html)

Population 18 Years Old and Older in 2017

National Total = 252,063,800

ALPHA ORDER

RANK	STATE	POPULATION	% of USA
24	Alabama	3,779,274	1.5%
48	Alaska	554,867	0.2%
15	Arizona	5,382,780	2.1%
32	Arkansas	2,298,739	0.9%
1	California	30,476,517	12.1%
21	Colorado	4,345,321	1.7%
29	Connecticut	2,844,358	1.1%
45	Delaware	757,455	0.3%
3	Florida	16,782,417	6.7%
9	Georgia	7,914,681	3.1%
40	Hawaii	1,121,794	0.4%
39	Idaho	1,273,151	0.5%
6	Illinois	9,904,838	3.9%
17	Indiana	5,093,409	2.0%
30	Iowa	2,413,764	1.0%
34	Kansas	2,200,585	0.9%
26	Kentucky	3,443,650	1.4%
25	Louisiana	3,575,930	1.4%
42	Maine	1,083,273	0.4%
19	Maryland	4,704,671	1.9%
14	Massachusetts	5,489,864	2.2%
10	Michigan	7,785,662	3.1%
22	Minnesota	4,277,949	1.7%
33	Mississippi	2,270,533	0.9%
18	Missouri	4,730,561	1.9%
44	Montana	821,604	0.3%
38	Nebraska	1,444,343	0.6%
31	Nevada	2,312,576	0.9%
41	New Hampshire	1,084,022	0.4%
11	New Jersey	7,026,626	2.8%
36	New Mexico	1,599,980	0.6%
4	New York	15,694,902	6.2%
8	North Carolina	7,971,073	3.2%
47	North Dakota	579,621	0.2%
7	Ohio	9,053,374	3.6%
28	Oklahoma	2,971,579	1.2%
27	Oregon	3,269,157	1.3%
5	Pennsylvania	10,141,022	4.0%
43	Rhode Island	852,307	0.3%
23	South Carolina	3,919,695	1.6%
46	South Dakota	654,810	0.3%
16	Tennessee	5,208,482	2.1%
2	Texas	20,938,557	8.3%
35	Utah	2,175,134	0.9%
49	Vermont	506,832	0.2%
12	Virginia	6,600,844	2.6%
13	Washington	5,759,927	2.3%
37	West Virginia	1,446,139	0.6%
20	Wisconsin	4,512,839	1.8%
50	Wyoming	442,832	0.2%

RANK ORDER

RANK	STATE	POPULATION	% of USA
1	California	30,476,517	12.1%
2	Texas	20,938,557	8.3%
3	Florida	16,782,417	6.7%
4	New York	15,694,902	6.2%
5	Pennsylvania	10,141,022	4.0%
6	Illinois	9,904,838	3.9%
7	Ohio	9,053,374	3.6%
8	North Carolina	7,971,073	3.2%
9	Georgia	7,914,681	3.1%
10	Michigan	7,785,662	3.1%
11	New Jersey	7,026,626	2.8%
12	Virginia	6,600,844	2.6%
13	Washington	5,759,927	2.3%
14	Massachusetts	5,489,864	2.2%
15	Arizona	5,382,780	2.1%
16	Tennessee	5,208,482	2.1%
17	Indiana	5,093,409	2.0%
18	Missouri	4,730,561	1.9%
19	Maryland	4,704,671	1.9%
20	Wisconsin	4,512,839	1.8%
21	Colorado	4,345,321	1.7%
22	Minnesota	4,277,949	1.7%
23	South Carolina	3,919,695	1.6%
24	Alabama	3,779,274	1.5%
25	Louisiana	3,575,930	1.4%
26	Kentucky	3,443,650	1.4%
27	Oregon	3,269,157	1.3%
28	Oklahoma	2,971,579	1.2%
29	Connecticut	2,844,358	1.1%
30	Iowa	2,413,764	1.0%
31	Nevada	2,312,576	0.9%
32	Arkansas	2,298,739	0.9%
33	Mississippi	2,270,533	0.9%
34	Kansas	2,200,585	0.9%
35	Utah	2,175,134	0.9%
36	New Mexico	1,599,980	0.6%
37	West Virginia	1,446,139	0.6%
38	Nebraska	1,444,343	0.6%
39	Idaho	1,273,151	0.5%
40	Hawaii	1,121,794	0.4%
41	New Hampshire	1,084,022	0.4%
42	Maine	1,083,273	0.4%
43	Rhode Island	852,307	0.3%
44	Montana	821,604	0.3%
45	Delaware	757,455	0.3%
46	South Dakota	654,810	0.3%
47	North Dakota	579,621	0.2%
48	Alaska	554,867	0.2%
49	Vermont	506,832	0.2%
50	Wyoming	442,832	0.2%
	District of Columbia	569,480	0.2%

Source: U.S. Bureau of the Census
"State Characteristics: Vintage 2017" (https://www.census.gov/programs-surveys/popest/data/data-sets.html)

Percent of Population 18 Years Old and Older in 2017

National Percent = 77.4% of Population

ALPHA ORDER

RANK	STATE	PERCENT
25	Alabama	77.5
47	Alaska	75.0
32	Arizona	76.7
37	Arkansas	76.5
30	California	77.1
25	Colorado	77.5
8	Connecticut	79.3
12	Delaware	78.7
5	Florida	80.0
42	Georgia	75.9
13	Hawaii	78.6
48	Idaho	74.2
27	Illinois	77.4
38	Indiana	76.4
32	Iowa	76.7
44	Kansas	75.5
29	Kentucky	77.3
40	Louisiana	76.3
2	Maine	81.1
21	Maryland	77.7
5	Massachusetts	80.0
14	Michigan	78.2
32	Minnesota	76.7
41	Mississippi	76.1
27	Missouri	77.4
14	Montana	78.2
46	Nebraska	75.2
30	Nevada	77.1
3	New Hampshire	80.7
16	New Jersey	78.0
36	New Mexico	76.6
10	New York	79.1
23	North Carolina	77.6
32	North Dakota	76.7
21	Ohio	77.7
43	Oklahoma	75.6
11	Oregon	78.9
9	Pennsylvania	79.2
4	Rhode Island	80.4
16	South Carolina	78.0
45	South Dakota	75.3
23	Tennessee	77.6
49	Texas	74.0
50	Utah	70.1
1	Vermont	81.3
18	Virginia	77.9
20	Washington	77.8
7	West Virginia	79.6
18	Wisconsin	77.9
38	Wyoming	76.4

RANK ORDER

RANK	STATE	PERCENT
1	Vermont	81.3
2	Maine	81.1
3	New Hampshire	80.7
4	Rhode Island	80.4
5	Florida	80.0
5	Massachusetts	80.0
7	West Virginia	79.6
8	Connecticut	79.3
9	Pennsylvania	79.2
10	New York	79.1
11	Oregon	78.9
12	Delaware	78.7
13	Hawaii	78.6
14	Michigan	78.2
14	Montana	78.2
16	New Jersey	78.0
16	South Carolina	78.0
18	Virginia	77.9
18	Wisconsin	77.9
20	Washington	77.8
21	Maryland	77.7
21	Ohio	77.7
23	North Carolina	77.6
23	Tennessee	77.6
25	Alabama	77.5
25	Colorado	77.5
27	Illinois	77.4
27	Missouri	77.4
29	Kentucky	77.3
30	California	77.1
30	Nevada	77.1
32	Arizona	76.7
32	Iowa	76.7
32	Minnesota	76.7
32	North Dakota	76.7
36	New Mexico	76.6
37	Arkansas	76.5
38	Indiana	76.4
38	Wyoming	76.4
40	Louisiana	76.3
41	Mississippi	76.1
42	Georgia	75.9
43	Oklahoma	75.6
44	Kansas	75.5
45	South Dakota	75.3
46	Nebraska	75.2
47	Alaska	75.0
48	Idaho	74.2
49	Texas	74.0
50	Utah	70.1

District of Columbia — 82.1

Source: CQ Press using data from U.S. Bureau of the Census
"State Characteristics: Vintage 2017" (https://www.census.gov/programs-surveys/popest/data/data-sets.html)

Population 18 to 24 Years Old in 2017

National Total = 30,616,469

ALPHA ORDER

RANK	STATE	POPULATION	% of USA
24	Alabama	456,229	1.5%
48	Alaska	72,209	0.2%
14	Arizona	672,443	2.2%
34	Arkansas	281,348	0.9%
1	California	3,798,952	12.4%
21	Colorado	521,230	1.7%
29	Connecticut	352,183	1.2%
46	Delaware	84,974	0.3%
4	Florida	1,741,788	5.7%
8	Georgia	1,003,431	3.3%
41	Hawaii	124,183	0.4%
38	Idaho	158,794	0.5%
5	Illinois	1,195,103	3.9%
15	Indiana	657,874	2.1%
31	Iowa	320,538	1.0%
32	Kansas	296,269	1.0%
26	Kentucky	418,416	1.4%
25	Louisiana	435,147	1.4%
43	Maine	109,662	0.4%
20	Maryland	540,688	1.8%
13	Massachusetts	700,399	2.3%
10	Michigan	970,807	3.2%
22	Minnesota	505,388	1.7%
33	Mississippi	292,380	1.0%
18	Missouri	570,952	1.9%
44	Montana	98,346	0.3%
37	Nebraska	191,018	0.6%
35	Nevada	249,027	0.8%
40	New Hampshire	127,059	0.4%
12	New Jersey	787,218	2.6%
36	New Mexico	199,146	0.7%
3	New York	1,872,542	6.1%
9	North Carolina	972,516	3.2%
45	North Dakota	86,439	0.3%
7	Ohio	1,073,568	3.5%
27	Oklahoma	379,876	1.2%
28	Oregon	363,082	1.2%
6	Pennsylvania	1,176,379	3.8%
42	Rhode Island	113,736	0.4%
23	South Carolina	467,788	1.5%
47	South Dakota	82,803	0.3%
17	Tennessee	612,673	2.0%
2	Texas	2,768,427	9.0%
30	Utah	345,661	1.1%
49	Vermont	66,853	0.2%
11	Virginia	804,935	2.6%
16	Washington	652,869	2.1%
39	West Virginia	158,605	0.5%
19	Wisconsin	557,213	1.8%
50	Wyoming	52,539	0.2%

RANK ORDER

RANK	STATE	POPULATION	% of USA
1	California	3,798,952	12.4%
2	Texas	2,768,427	9.0%
3	New York	1,872,542	6.1%
4	Florida	1,741,788	5.7%
5	Illinois	1,195,103	3.9%
6	Pennsylvania	1,176,379	3.8%
7	Ohio	1,073,568	3.5%
8	Georgia	1,003,431	3.3%
9	North Carolina	972,516	3.2%
10	Michigan	970,807	3.2%
11	Virginia	804,935	2.6%
12	New Jersey	787,218	2.6%
13	Massachusetts	700,399	2.3%
14	Arizona	672,443	2.2%
15	Indiana	657,874	2.1%
16	Washington	652,869	2.1%
17	Tennessee	612,673	2.0%
18	Missouri	570,952	1.9%
19	Wisconsin	557,213	1.8%
20	Maryland	540,688	1.8%
21	Colorado	521,230	1.7%
22	Minnesota	505,388	1.7%
23	South Carolina	467,788	1.5%
24	Alabama	456,229	1.5%
25	Louisiana	435,147	1.4%
26	Kentucky	418,416	1.4%
27	Oklahoma	379,876	1.2%
28	Oregon	363,082	1.2%
29	Connecticut	352,183	1.2%
30	Utah	345,661	1.1%
31	Iowa	320,538	1.0%
32	Kansas	296,269	1.0%
33	Mississippi	292,380	1.0%
34	Arkansas	281,348	0.9%
35	Nevada	249,027	0.8%
36	New Mexico	199,146	0.7%
37	Nebraska	191,018	0.6%
38	Idaho	158,794	0.5%
39	West Virginia	158,605	0.5%
40	New Hampshire	127,059	0.4%
41	Hawaii	124,183	0.4%
42	Rhode Island	113,736	0.4%
43	Maine	109,662	0.4%
44	Montana	98,346	0.3%
45	North Dakota	86,439	0.3%
46	Delaware	84,974	0.3%
47	South Dakota	82,803	0.3%
48	Alaska	72,209	0.2%
49	Vermont	66,853	0.2%
50	Wyoming	52,539	0.2%
	District of Columbia	74,764	0.2%

Source: U.S. Bureau of the Census
   "State Characteristics: Vintage 2017" (https://www.census.gov/programs-surveys/popest/data/data-sets.html)

Percent of Population 18 to 24 Years Old in 2017

National Percent = 9.4% of Population

ALPHA ORDER

RANK	STATE	PERCENT
25	Alabama	9.4
10	Alaska	9.8
16	Arizona	9.6
25	Arkansas	9.4
16	California	9.6
30	Colorado	9.3
10	Connecticut	9.8
42	Delaware	8.8
48	Florida	8.3
16	Georgia	9.6
45	Hawaii	8.7
35	Idaho	9.2
30	Illinois	9.3
8	Indiana	9.9
5	Iowa	10.2
5	Kansas	10.2
25	Kentucky	9.4
30	Louisiana	9.3
50	Maine	8.2
41	Maryland	8.9
5	Massachusetts	10.2
14	Michigan	9.7
38	Minnesota	9.1
10	Mississippi	9.8
30	Missouri	9.3
25	Montana	9.4
8	Nebraska	9.9
48	Nevada	8.3
20	New Hampshire	9.5
45	New Jersey	8.7
20	New Mexico	9.5
25	New York	9.4
20	North Carolina	9.5
1	North Dakota	11.4
35	Ohio	9.2
14	Oklahoma	9.7
42	Oregon	8.8
35	Pennsylvania	9.2
3	Rhode Island	10.7
30	South Carolina	9.3
20	South Dakota	9.5
38	Tennessee	9.1
10	Texas	9.8
2	Utah	11.1
3	Vermont	10.7
20	Virginia	9.5
42	Washington	8.8
45	West Virginia	8.7
16	Wisconsin	9.6
38	Wyoming	9.1

RANK ORDER

RANK	STATE	PERCENT
1	North Dakota	11.4
2	Utah	11.1
3	Rhode Island	10.7
3	Vermont	10.7
5	Iowa	10.2
5	Kansas	10.2
5	Massachusetts	10.2
8	Indiana	9.9
8	Nebraska	9.9
10	Alaska	9.8
10	Connecticut	9.8
10	Mississippi	9.8
10	Texas	9.8
14	Michigan	9.7
14	Oklahoma	9.7
16	Arizona	9.6
16	California	9.6
16	Georgia	9.6
16	Wisconsin	9.6
20	New Hampshire	9.5
20	New Mexico	9.5
20	North Carolina	9.5
20	South Dakota	9.5
20	Virginia	9.5
25	Alabama	9.4
25	Arkansas	9.4
25	Kentucky	9.4
25	Montana	9.4
25	New York	9.4
30	Colorado	9.3
30	Illinois	9.3
30	Louisiana	9.3
30	Missouri	9.3
30	South Carolina	9.3
35	Idaho	9.2
35	Ohio	9.2
35	Pennsylvania	9.2
38	Minnesota	9.1
38	Tennessee	9.1
38	Wyoming	9.1
41	Maryland	8.9
42	Delaware	8.8
42	Oregon	8.8
42	Washington	8.8
45	Hawaii	8.7
45	New Jersey	8.7
45	West Virginia	8.7
48	Florida	8.3
48	Nevada	8.3
50	Maine	8.2
	District of Columbia	10.8

Source: CQ Press using data from U.S. Bureau of the Census
"State Characteristics: Vintage 2017" (https://www.census.gov/programs-surveys/popest/data/data-sets.html)

Population 25 to 44 Years Old in 2017

National Total = 86,218,042

ALPHA ORDER				RANK ORDER			
RANK	STATE	POPULATION	% of USA	RANK	STATE	POPULATION	% of USA
25	Alabama	1,232,097	1.4%	1	California	11,246,841	13.0%
47	Alaska	213,427	0.2%	2	Texas	7,966,789	9.2%
14	Arizona	1,814,574	2.1%	3	New York	5,402,756	6.3%
33	Arkansas	761,740	0.9%	4	Florida	5,260,531	6.1%
1	California	11,246,841	13.0%	5	Illinois	3,415,241	4.0%
18	Colorado	1,630,436	1.9%	6	Pennsylvania	3,174,030	3.7%
30	Connecticut	866,929	1.0%	7	Ohio	2,904,979	3.4%
45	Delaware	239,594	0.3%	8	Georgia	2,820,792	3.3%
4	Florida	5,260,531	6.1%	9	North Carolina	2,660,925	3.1%
8	Georgia	2,820,792	3.3%	10	Michigan	2,424,937	2.8%
40	Hawaii	385,962	0.4%	11	New Jersey	2,324,767	2.7%
38	Idaho	438,337	0.5%	12	Virginia	2,279,002	2.6%
5	Illinois	3,415,241	4.0%	13	Washington	2,090,428	2.4%
17	Indiana	1,685,582	2.0%	14	Arizona	1,814,574	2.1%
32	Iowa	768,731	0.9%	15	Massachusetts	1,804,432	2.1%
35	Kansas	735,554	0.9%	16	Tennessee	1,750,560	2.0%
27	Kentucky	1,131,236	1.3%	17	Indiana	1,685,582	2.0%
24	Louisiana	1,258,135	1.5%	18	Colorado	1,630,436	1.9%
42	Maine	309,747	0.4%	19	Maryland	1,607,328	1.9%
19	Maryland	1,607,328	1.9%	20	Missouri	1,556,437	1.8%
15	Massachusetts	1,804,432	2.1%	21	Minnesota	1,451,638	1.7%
10	Michigan	2,424,937	2.8%	22	Wisconsin	1,425,496	1.7%
21	Minnesota	1,451,638	1.7%	23	South Carolina	1,269,660	1.5%
34	Mississippi	757,687	0.9%	24	Louisiana	1,258,135	1.5%
20	Missouri	1,556,437	1.8%	25	Alabama	1,232,097	1.4%
44	Montana	257,819	0.3%	26	Oregon	1,134,206	1.3%
37	Nebraska	490,188	0.6%	27	Kentucky	1,131,236	1.3%
31	Nevada	837,426	1.0%	28	Oklahoma	1,028,804	1.2%
41	New Hampshire	315,451	0.4%	29	Utah	879,970	1.0%
11	New Jersey	2,324,767	2.7%	30	Connecticut	866,929	1.0%
36	New Mexico	527,887	0.6%	31	Nevada	837,426	1.0%
3	New York	5,402,756	6.3%	32	Iowa	768,731	0.9%
9	North Carolina	2,660,925	3.1%	33	Arkansas	761,740	0.9%
48	North Dakota	202,399	0.2%	34	Mississippi	757,687	0.9%
7	Ohio	2,904,979	3.4%	35	Kansas	735,554	0.9%
28	Oklahoma	1,028,804	1.2%	36	New Mexico	527,887	0.6%
26	Oregon	1,134,206	1.3%	37	Nebraska	490,188	0.6%
6	Pennsylvania	3,174,030	3.7%	38	Idaho	438,337	0.5%
43	Rhode Island	268,638	0.3%	39	West Virginia	434,914	0.5%
23	South Carolina	1,269,660	1.5%	40	Hawaii	385,962	0.4%
46	South Dakota	214,599	0.2%	41	New Hampshire	315,451	0.4%
16	Tennessee	1,750,560	2.0%	42	Maine	309,747	0.4%
2	Texas	7,966,789	9.2%	43	Rhode Island	268,638	0.3%
29	Utah	879,970	1.0%	44	Montana	257,819	0.3%
50	Vermont	142,631	0.2%	45	Delaware	239,594	0.3%
12	Virginia	2,279,002	2.6%	46	South Dakota	214,599	0.2%
13	Washington	2,090,428	2.4%	47	Alaska	213,427	0.2%
39	West Virginia	434,914	0.5%	48	North Dakota	202,399	0.2%
22	Wisconsin	1,425,496	1.7%	49	Wyoming	151,133	0.2%
49	Wyoming	151,133	0.2%	50	Vermont	142,631	0.2%
					District of Columbia	264,640	0.3%

Source: U.S. Bureau of the Census
"State Characteristics: Vintage 2017" (https://www.census.gov/programs-surveys/popest/data/data-sets.html)

Percent of Population 25 to 44 Years Old in 2017

National Percent = 26.5% of Population

ALPHA ORDER				RANK ORDER		
RANK	**STATE**	**PERCENT**		**RANK**	**STATE**	**PERCENT**
32	Alabama	25.3		1	Colorado	29.1
2	Alaska	28.8		2	Alaska	28.8
22	Arizona	25.9		3	California	28.4
28	Arkansas	25.4		3	Utah	28.4
3	California	28.4		5	Washington	28.2
1	Colorado	29.1		6	Texas	28.1
46	Connecticut	24.2		7	Nevada	27.9
38	Delaware	24.9		8	Oregon	27.4
37	Florida	25.1		9	New York	27.2
10	Georgia	27.0		10	Georgia	27.0
10	Hawaii	27.0		10	Hawaii	27.0
25	Idaho	25.5		12	Louisiana	26.9
15	Illinois	26.7		12	Virginia	26.9
32	Indiana	25.3		14	North Dakota	26.8
44	Iowa	24.4		15	Illinois	26.7
36	Kansas	25.2		16	Maryland	26.6
28	Kentucky	25.4		17	Massachusetts	26.3
12	Louisiana	26.9		18	Oklahoma	26.2
49	Maine	23.2		19	Tennessee	26.1
16	Maryland	26.6		19	Wyoming	26.1
17	Massachusetts	26.3		21	Minnesota	26.0
45	Michigan	24.3		22	Arizona	25.9
21	Minnesota	26.0		22	North Carolina	25.9
28	Mississippi	25.4		24	New Jersey	25.8
25	Missouri	25.5		25	Idaho	25.5
43	Montana	24.5		25	Missouri	25.5
25	Nebraska	25.5		25	Nebraska	25.5
7	Nevada	27.9		28	Arkansas	25.4
48	New Hampshire	23.5		28	Kentucky	25.4
24	New Jersey	25.8		28	Mississippi	25.4
32	New Mexico	25.3		28	Rhode Island	25.4
9	New York	27.2		32	Alabama	25.3
22	North Carolina	25.9		32	Indiana	25.3
14	North Dakota	26.8		32	New Mexico	25.3
38	Ohio	24.9		32	South Carolina	25.3
18	Oklahoma	26.2		36	Kansas	25.2
8	Oregon	27.4		37	Florida	25.1
40	Pennsylvania	24.8		38	Delaware	24.9
28	Rhode Island	25.4		38	Ohio	24.9
32	South Carolina	25.3		40	Pennsylvania	24.8
41	South Dakota	24.7		41	South Dakota	24.7
19	Tennessee	26.1		42	Wisconsin	24.6
6	Texas	28.1		43	Montana	24.5
3	Utah	28.4		44	Iowa	24.4
50	Vermont	22.9		45	Michigan	24.3
12	Virginia	26.9		46	Connecticut	24.2
5	Washington	28.2		47	West Virginia	24.0
47	West Virginia	24.0		48	New Hampshire	23.5
42	Wisconsin	24.6		49	Maine	23.2
19	Wyoming	26.1		50	Vermont	22.9
					District of Columbia	38.1

Source: CQ Press using data from U.S. Bureau of the Census
"State Characteristics: Vintage 2017" (https://www.census.gov/programs-surveys/popest/data/data-sets.html)

Population 45 to 64 Years Old in 2017

National Total = 84,370,610

ALPHA ORDER

RANK	STATE	POPULATION	% of USA
24	Alabama	1,287,177	1.5%
47	Alaska	186,651	0.2%
17	Arizona	1,694,017	2.0%
33	Arkansas	756,507	0.9%
1	California	9,925,366	11.8%
22	Colorado	1,421,613	1.7%
28	Connecticut	1,022,836	1.2%
45	Delaware	258,759	0.3%
3	Florida	5,565,463	6.6%
10	Georgia	2,682,648	3.2%
42	Hawaii	358,089	0.4%
39	Idaho	411,119	0.5%
6	Illinois	3,349,096	4.0%
16	Indiana	1,725,063	2.0%
30	Iowa	798,438	0.9%
34	Kansas	719,199	0.9%
26	Kentucky	1,182,649	1.4%
25	Louisiana	1,185,265	1.4%
41	Maine	397,650	0.5%
18	Maryland	1,651,984	2.0%
14	Massachusetts	1,876,424	2.2%
8	Michigan	2,722,722	3.2%
21	Minnesota	1,460,714	1.7%
32	Mississippi	758,947	0.9%
19	Missouri	1,596,139	1.9%
44	Montana	274,916	0.3%
38	Nebraska	467,764	0.6%
31	Nevada	767,064	0.9%
40	New Hampshire	405,355	0.5%
11	New Jersey	2,496,038	3.0%
36	New Mexico	520,346	0.6%
4	New York	5,257,411	6.2%
9	North Carolina	2,707,187	3.2%
49	North Dakota	177,575	0.2%
7	Ohio	3,131,691	3.7%
29	Oklahoma	960,076	1.1%
27	Oregon	1,063,052	1.3%
5	Pennsylvania	3,510,926	4.2%
43	Rhode Island	291,978	0.3%
23	South Carolina	1,317,670	1.6%
46	South Dakota	215,784	0.3%
15	Tennessee	1,768,647	2.1%
2	Texas	6,730,629	8.0%
35	Utah	613,931	0.7%
48	Vermont	180,479	0.2%
12	Virginia	2,245,479	2.7%
13	Washington	1,901,588	2.3%
37	West Virginia	501,021	0.6%
20	Wisconsin	1,575,573	1.9%
50	Wyoming	147,553	0.2%

RANK ORDER

RANK	STATE	POPULATION	% of USA
1	California	9,925,366	11.8%
2	Texas	6,730,629	8.0%
3	Florida	5,565,463	6.6%
4	New York	5,257,411	6.2%
5	Pennsylvania	3,510,926	4.2%
6	Illinois	3,349,096	4.0%
7	Ohio	3,131,691	3.7%
8	Michigan	2,722,722	3.2%
9	North Carolina	2,707,187	3.2%
10	Georgia	2,682,648	3.2%
11	New Jersey	2,496,038	3.0%
12	Virginia	2,245,479	2.7%
13	Washington	1,901,588	2.3%
14	Massachusetts	1,876,424	2.2%
15	Tennessee	1,768,647	2.1%
16	Indiana	1,725,063	2.0%
17	Arizona	1,694,017	2.0%
18	Maryland	1,651,984	2.0%
19	Missouri	1,596,139	1.9%
20	Wisconsin	1,575,573	1.9%
21	Minnesota	1,460,714	1.7%
22	Colorado	1,421,613	1.7%
23	South Carolina	1,317,670	1.6%
24	Alabama	1,287,177	1.5%
25	Louisiana	1,185,265	1.4%
26	Kentucky	1,182,649	1.4%
27	Oregon	1,063,052	1.3%
28	Connecticut	1,022,836	1.2%
29	Oklahoma	960,076	1.1%
30	Iowa	798,438	0.9%
31	Nevada	767,064	0.9%
32	Mississippi	758,947	0.9%
33	Arkansas	756,507	0.9%
34	Kansas	719,199	0.9%
35	Utah	613,931	0.7%
36	New Mexico	520,346	0.6%
37	West Virginia	501,021	0.6%
38	Nebraska	467,764	0.6%
39	Idaho	411,119	0.5%
40	New Hampshire	405,355	0.5%
41	Maine	397,650	0.5%
42	Hawaii	358,089	0.4%
43	Rhode Island	291,978	0.3%
44	Montana	274,916	0.3%
45	Delaware	258,759	0.3%
46	South Dakota	215,784	0.3%
47	Alaska	186,651	0.2%
48	Vermont	180,479	0.2%
49	North Dakota	177,575	0.2%
50	Wyoming	147,553	0.2%
	District of Columbia	146,342	0.2%

Source: U.S. Bureau of the Census
"State Characteristics: Vintage 2017" (https://www.census.gov/programs-surveys/popest/data/data-sets.html)

Percent of Population 45 to 64 Years Old in 2017

National Percent = 25.9% of Population

<table>
<tr><td colspan="3">ALPHA ORDER</td><td colspan="3">RANK ORDER</td></tr>
<tr><th>RANK</th><th>STATE</th><th>PERCENT</th><th>RANK</th><th>STATE</th><th>PERCENT</th></tr>
<tr><td>19</td><td>Alabama</td><td>26.4</td><td>1</td><td>New Hampshire</td><td>30.2</td></tr>
<tr><td>37</td><td>Alaska</td><td>25.2</td><td>2</td><td>Maine</td><td>29.8</td></tr>
<tr><td>46</td><td>Arizona</td><td>24.1</td><td>3</td><td>Vermont</td><td>28.9</td></tr>
<tr><td>37</td><td>Arkansas</td><td>25.2</td><td>4</td><td>Connecticut</td><td>28.5</td></tr>
<tr><td>39</td><td>California</td><td>25.1</td><td>5</td><td>New Jersey</td><td>27.7</td></tr>
<tr><td>33</td><td>Colorado</td><td>25.4</td><td>6</td><td>Rhode Island</td><td>27.6</td></tr>
<tr><td>4</td><td>Connecticut</td><td>28.5</td><td>6</td><td>West Virginia</td><td>27.6</td></tr>
<tr><td>13</td><td>Delaware</td><td>26.9</td><td>8</td><td>Massachusetts</td><td>27.4</td></tr>
<tr><td>16</td><td>Florida</td><td>26.5</td><td>8</td><td>Pennsylvania</td><td>27.4</td></tr>
<tr><td>28</td><td>Georgia</td><td>25.7</td><td>10</td><td>Maryland</td><td>27.3</td></tr>
<tr><td>39</td><td>Hawaii</td><td>25.1</td><td>10</td><td>Michigan</td><td>27.3</td></tr>
<tr><td>47</td><td>Idaho</td><td>23.9</td><td>12</td><td>Wisconsin</td><td>27.2</td></tr>
<tr><td>22</td><td>Illinois</td><td>26.2</td><td>13</td><td>Delaware</td><td>26.9</td></tr>
<tr><td>27</td><td>Indiana</td><td>25.9</td><td>13</td><td>Ohio</td><td>26.9</td></tr>
<tr><td>33</td><td>Iowa</td><td>25.4</td><td>15</td><td>Kentucky</td><td>26.6</td></tr>
<tr><td>43</td><td>Kansas</td><td>24.7</td><td>16</td><td>Florida</td><td>26.5</td></tr>
<tr><td>15</td><td>Kentucky</td><td>26.6</td><td>16</td><td>New York</td><td>26.5</td></tr>
<tr><td>36</td><td>Louisiana</td><td>25.3</td><td>16</td><td>Virginia</td><td>26.5</td></tr>
<tr><td>2</td><td>Maine</td><td>29.8</td><td>19</td><td>Alabama</td><td>26.4</td></tr>
<tr><td>10</td><td>Maryland</td><td>27.3</td><td>19</td><td>North Carolina</td><td>26.4</td></tr>
<tr><td>8</td><td>Massachusetts</td><td>27.4</td><td>21</td><td>Tennessee</td><td>26.3</td></tr>
<tr><td>10</td><td>Michigan</td><td>27.3</td><td>22</td><td>Illinois</td><td>26.2</td></tr>
<tr><td>22</td><td>Minnesota</td><td>26.2</td><td>22</td><td>Minnesota</td><td>26.2</td></tr>
<tr><td>33</td><td>Mississippi</td><td>25.4</td><td>22</td><td>Montana</td><td>26.2</td></tr>
<tr><td>26</td><td>Missouri</td><td>26.1</td><td>22</td><td>South Carolina</td><td>26.2</td></tr>
<tr><td>22</td><td>Montana</td><td>26.2</td><td>26</td><td>Missouri</td><td>26.1</td></tr>
<tr><td>44</td><td>Nebraska</td><td>24.4</td><td>27</td><td>Indiana</td><td>25.9</td></tr>
<tr><td>31</td><td>Nevada</td><td>25.6</td><td>28</td><td>Georgia</td><td>25.7</td></tr>
<tr><td>1</td><td>New Hampshire</td><td>30.2</td><td>28</td><td>Oregon</td><td>25.7</td></tr>
<tr><td>5</td><td>New Jersey</td><td>27.7</td><td>28</td><td>Washington</td><td>25.7</td></tr>
<tr><td>41</td><td>New Mexico</td><td>24.9</td><td>31</td><td>Nevada</td><td>25.6</td></tr>
<tr><td>16</td><td>New York</td><td>26.5</td><td>32</td><td>Wyoming</td><td>25.5</td></tr>
<tr><td>19</td><td>North Carolina</td><td>26.4</td><td>33</td><td>Colorado</td><td>25.4</td></tr>
<tr><td>49</td><td>North Dakota</td><td>23.5</td><td>33</td><td>Iowa</td><td>25.4</td></tr>
<tr><td>13</td><td>Ohio</td><td>26.9</td><td>33</td><td>Mississippi</td><td>25.4</td></tr>
<tr><td>44</td><td>Oklahoma</td><td>24.4</td><td>36</td><td>Louisiana</td><td>25.3</td></tr>
<tr><td>28</td><td>Oregon</td><td>25.7</td><td>37</td><td>Alaska</td><td>25.2</td></tr>
<tr><td>8</td><td>Pennsylvania</td><td>27.4</td><td>37</td><td>Arkansas</td><td>25.2</td></tr>
<tr><td>6</td><td>Rhode Island</td><td>27.6</td><td>39</td><td>California</td><td>25.1</td></tr>
<tr><td>22</td><td>South Carolina</td><td>26.2</td><td>39</td><td>Hawaii</td><td>25.1</td></tr>
<tr><td>42</td><td>South Dakota</td><td>24.8</td><td>41</td><td>New Mexico</td><td>24.9</td></tr>
<tr><td>21</td><td>Tennessee</td><td>26.3</td><td>42</td><td>South Dakota</td><td>24.8</td></tr>
<tr><td>48</td><td>Texas</td><td>23.8</td><td>43</td><td>Kansas</td><td>24.7</td></tr>
<tr><td>50</td><td>Utah</td><td>19.8</td><td>44</td><td>Nebraska</td><td>24.4</td></tr>
<tr><td>3</td><td>Vermont</td><td>28.9</td><td>44</td><td>Oklahoma</td><td>24.4</td></tr>
<tr><td>16</td><td>Virginia</td><td>26.5</td><td>46</td><td>Arizona</td><td>24.1</td></tr>
<tr><td>28</td><td>Washington</td><td>25.7</td><td>47</td><td>Idaho</td><td>23.9</td></tr>
<tr><td>6</td><td>West Virginia</td><td>27.6</td><td>48</td><td>Texas</td><td>23.8</td></tr>
<tr><td>12</td><td>Wisconsin</td><td>27.2</td><td>49</td><td>North Dakota</td><td>23.5</td></tr>
<tr><td>32</td><td>Wyoming</td><td>25.5</td><td>50</td><td>Utah</td><td>19.8</td></tr>
<tr><td></td><td></td><td></td><td></td><td>District of Columbia</td><td>21.1</td></tr>
</table>

Source: CQ Press using data from U.S. Bureau of the Census
"State Characteristics: Vintage 2017" (https://www.census.gov/programs-surveys/popest/data/data-sets.html)

Population 65 Years Old and Older in 2017

National Total = 50,858,679

RANK	STATE	POPULATION	% of USA
23	Alabama	803,771	1.6%
50	Alaska	82,580	0.2%
13	Arizona	1,201,746	2.4%
31	Arkansas	499,144	1.0%
1	California	5,505,358	10.8%
24	Colorado	772,042	1.5%
29	Connecticut	602,410	1.2%
45	Delaware	174,128	0.3%
2	Florida	4,214,635	8.3%
11	Georgia	1,407,810	2.8%
41	Hawaii	253,560	0.5%
40	Idaho	264,901	0.5%
6	Illinois	1,945,398	3.8%
17	Indiana	1,024,890	2.0%
30	Iowa	526,057	1.0%
34	Kansas	449,563	0.9%
25	Kentucky	711,349	1.4%
27	Louisiana	697,383	1.4%
39	Maine	266,214	0.5%
20	Maryland	904,671	1.8%
15	Massachusetts	1,108,609	2.2%
8	Michigan	1,667,196	3.3%
22	Minnesota	860,209	1.7%
32	Mississippi	461,519	0.9%
18	Missouri	1,007,033	2.0%
43	Montana	190,523	0.4%
38	Nebraska	295,373	0.6%
33	Nevada	459,059	0.9%
42	New Hampshire	236,157	0.5%
10	New Jersey	1,418,603	2.8%
35	New Mexico	352,601	0.7%
4	New York	3,162,193	6.2%
9	North Carolina	1,630,445	3.2%
48	North Dakota	113,208	0.2%
7	Ohio	1,943,136	3.8%
28	Oklahoma	602,823	1.2%
26	Oregon	708,817	1.4%
5	Pennsylvania	2,279,687	4.5%
44	Rhode Island	177,955	0.3%
21	South Carolina	864,577	1.7%
46	South Dakota	141,624	0.3%
16	Tennessee	1,076,602	2.1%
3	Texas	3,472,712	6.8%
37	Utah	335,572	0.7%
47	Vermont	116,869	0.2%
12	Virginia	1,271,428	2.5%
14	Washington	1,115,042	2.2%
36	West Virginia	351,599	0.7%
19	Wisconsin	954,557	1.9%
49	Wyoming	91,607	0.2%

RANK	STATE	POPULATION	% of USA
1	California	5,505,358	10.8%
2	Florida	4,214,635	8.3%
3	Texas	3,472,712	6.8%
4	New York	3,162,193	6.2%
5	Pennsylvania	2,279,687	4.5%
6	Illinois	1,945,398	3.8%
7	Ohio	1,943,136	3.8%
8	Michigan	1,667,196	3.3%
9	North Carolina	1,630,445	3.2%
10	New Jersey	1,418,603	2.8%
11	Georgia	1,407,810	2.8%
12	Virginia	1,271,428	2.5%
13	Arizona	1,201,746	2.4%
14	Washington	1,115,042	2.2%
15	Massachusetts	1,108,609	2.2%
16	Tennessee	1,076,602	2.1%
17	Indiana	1,024,890	2.0%
18	Missouri	1,007,033	2.0%
19	Wisconsin	954,557	1.9%
20	Maryland	904,671	1.8%
21	South Carolina	864,577	1.7%
22	Minnesota	860,209	1.7%
23	Alabama	803,771	1.6%
24	Colorado	772,042	1.5%
25	Kentucky	711,349	1.4%
26	Oregon	708,817	1.4%
27	Louisiana	697,383	1.4%
28	Oklahoma	602,823	1.2%
29	Connecticut	602,410	1.2%
30	Iowa	526,057	1.0%
31	Arkansas	499,144	1.0%
32	Mississippi	461,519	0.9%
33	Nevada	459,059	0.9%
34	Kansas	449,563	0.9%
35	New Mexico	352,601	0.7%
36	West Virginia	351,599	0.7%
37	Utah	335,572	0.7%
38	Nebraska	295,373	0.6%
39	Maine	266,214	0.5%
40	Idaho	264,901	0.5%
41	Hawaii	253,560	0.5%
42	New Hampshire	236,157	0.5%
43	Montana	190,523	0.4%
44	Rhode Island	177,955	0.3%
45	Delaware	174,128	0.3%
46	South Dakota	141,624	0.3%
47	Vermont	116,869	0.2%
48	North Dakota	113,208	0.2%
49	Wyoming	91,607	0.2%
50	Alaska	82,580	0.2%
	District of Columbia	83,734	0.2%

Source: U.S. Bureau of the Census
"State Characteristics: Vintage 2017" (https://www.census.gov/programs-surveys/popest/data/data-sets.html)

Percent of Population 65 Years Old and Older in 2017

National Percent = 15.6% of Population

ALPHA ORDER

RANK	STATE	PERCENT
20	Alabama	16.5
49	Alaska	11.2
11	Arizona	17.1
19	Arkansas	16.6
45	California	13.9
46	Colorado	13.8
14	Connecticut	16.8
5	Delaware	18.1
1	Florida	20.1
47	Georgia	13.5
7	Hawaii	17.8
32	Idaho	15.4
39	Illinois	15.2
32	Indiana	15.4
16	Iowa	16.7
32	Kansas	15.4
25	Kentucky	16.0
43	Louisiana	14.9
2	Maine	19.9
43	Maryland	14.9
24	Massachusetts	16.2
16	Michigan	16.7
32	Minnesota	15.4
31	Mississippi	15.5
20	Missouri	16.5
5	Montana	18.1
32	Nebraska	15.4
37	Nevada	15.3
9	New Hampshire	17.6
29	New Jersey	15.8
13	New Mexico	16.9
27	New York	15.9
27	North Carolina	15.9
41	North Dakota	15.0
16	Ohio	16.7
37	Oklahoma	15.3
11	Oregon	17.1
7	Pennsylvania	17.8
14	Rhode Island	16.8
10	South Carolina	17.2
23	South Dakota	16.3
25	Tennessee	16.0
48	Texas	12.3
50	Utah	10.8
4	Vermont	18.7
41	Virginia	15.0
40	Washington	15.1
3	West Virginia	19.4
20	Wisconsin	16.5
29	Wyoming	15.8

RANK ORDER

RANK	STATE	PERCENT
1	Florida	20.1
2	Maine	19.9
3	West Virginia	19.4
4	Vermont	18.7
5	Delaware	18.1
5	Montana	18.1
7	Hawaii	17.8
7	Pennsylvania	17.8
9	New Hampshire	17.6
10	South Carolina	17.2
11	Arizona	17.1
11	Oregon	17.1
13	New Mexico	16.9
14	Connecticut	16.8
14	Rhode Island	16.8
16	Iowa	16.7
16	Michigan	16.7
16	Ohio	16.7
19	Arkansas	16.6
20	Alabama	16.5
20	Missouri	16.5
20	Wisconsin	16.5
23	South Dakota	16.3
24	Massachusetts	16.2
25	Kentucky	16.0
25	Tennessee	16.0
27	New York	15.9
27	North Carolina	15.9
29	New Jersey	15.8
29	Wyoming	15.8
31	Mississippi	15.5
32	Idaho	15.4
32	Indiana	15.4
32	Kansas	15.4
32	Minnesota	15.4
32	Nebraska	15.4
37	Nevada	15.3
37	Oklahoma	15.3
39	Illinois	15.2
40	Washington	15.1
41	North Dakota	15.0
41	Virginia	15.0
43	Louisiana	14.9
43	Maryland	14.9
45	California	13.9
46	Colorado	13.8
47	Georgia	13.5
48	Texas	12.3
49	Alaska	11.2
50	Utah	10.8
	District of Columbia	12.1

Source: CQ Press using data from U.S. Bureau of the Census
"State Characteristics: Vintage 2017" (https://www.census.gov/programs-surveys/popest/data/data-sets.html)

Population 85 Years Old and Older in 2017

National Total = 6,468,682

ALPHA ORDER

ALPHA ORDER

RANK ORDER

RANK	STATE	POPULATION	% of USA
23	Alabama	88,179	1.4%
50	Alaska	6,554	0.1%
14	Arizona	136,727	2.1%
32	Arkansas	57,882	0.9%
1	California	732,793	11.3%
25	Colorado	86,268	1.3%
22	Connecticut	92,655	1.4%
46	Delaware	19,516	0.3%
2	Florida	555,552	8.6%
13	Georgia	142,597	2.2%
36	Hawaii	40,341	0.6%
42	Idaho	28,607	0.4%
6	Illinois	265,897	4.1%
16	Indiana	130,060	2.0%
29	Iowa	79,337	1.2%
31	Kansas	64,942	1.0%
28	Kentucky	79,613	1.2%
27	Louisiana	79,928	1.2%
40	Maine	32,728	0.5%
21	Maryland	116,498	1.8%
11	Massachusetts	160,490	2.5%
8	Michigan	213,758	3.3%
19	Minnesota	120,570	1.9%
33	Mississippi	51,461	0.8%
17	Missouri	130,000	2.0%
44	Montana	22,384	0.3%
34	Nebraska	42,996	0.7%
35	Nevada	41,528	0.6%
41	New Hampshire	30,054	0.5%
9	New Jersey	204,068	3.2%
37	New Mexico	39,991	0.6%
3	New York	456,343	7.1%
10	North Carolina	181,945	2.8%
47	North Dakota	18,649	0.3%
7	Ohio	256,430	4.0%
30	Oklahoma	71,367	1.1%
26	Oregon	83,435	1.3%
5	Pennsylvania	335,429	5.2%
43	Rhode Island	27,864	0.4%
24	South Carolina	86,373	1.3%
45	South Dakota	20,781	0.3%
20	Tennessee	117,903	1.8%
4	Texas	395,391	6.1%
39	Utah	37,275	0.6%
48	Vermont	14,272	0.2%
12	Virginia	148,534	2.3%
15	Washington	131,417	2.0%
38	West Virginia	39,810	0.6%
18	Wisconsin	128,848	2.0%
49	Wyoming	10,509	0.2%

RANK	STATE	POPULATION	% of USA
1	California	732,793	11.3%
2	Florida	555,552	8.6%
3	New York	456,343	7.1%
4	Texas	395,391	6.1%
5	Pennsylvania	335,429	5.2%
6	Illinois	265,897	4.1%
7	Ohio	256,430	4.0%
8	Michigan	213,758	3.3%
9	New Jersey	204,068	3.2%
10	North Carolina	181,945	2.8%
11	Massachusetts	160,490	2.5%
12	Virginia	148,534	2.3%
13	Georgia	142,597	2.2%
14	Arizona	136,727	2.1%
15	Washington	131,417	2.0%
16	Indiana	130,060	2.0%
17	Missouri	130,000	2.0%
18	Wisconsin	128,848	2.0%
19	Minnesota	120,570	1.9%
20	Tennessee	117,903	1.8%
21	Maryland	116,498	1.8%
22	Connecticut	92,655	1.4%
23	Alabama	88,179	1.4%
24	South Carolina	86,373	1.3%
25	Colorado	86,268	1.3%
26	Oregon	83,435	1.3%
27	Louisiana	79,928	1.2%
28	Kentucky	79,613	1.2%
29	Iowa	79,337	1.2%
30	Oklahoma	71,367	1.1%
31	Kansas	64,942	1.0%
32	Arkansas	57,882	0.9%
33	Mississippi	51,461	0.8%
34	Nebraska	42,996	0.7%
35	Nevada	41,528	0.6%
36	Hawaii	40,341	0.6%
37	New Mexico	39,991	0.6%
38	West Virginia	39,810	0.6%
39	Utah	37,275	0.6%
40	Maine	32,728	0.5%
41	New Hampshire	30,054	0.5%
42	Idaho	28,607	0.4%
43	Rhode Island	27,864	0.4%
44	Montana	22,384	0.3%
45	South Dakota	20,781	0.3%
46	Delaware	19,516	0.3%
47	North Dakota	18,649	0.3%
48	Vermont	14,272	0.2%
49	Wyoming	10,509	0.2%
50	Alaska	6,554	0.1%
	District of Columbia	12,133	0.2%

Source: U.S. Bureau of the Census
"State Characteristics: Vintage 2017" (https://www.census.gov/programs-surveys/popest/data/data-sets.html)

Percent of Population 85 Years Old and Older in 2017

National Percent = 2.0% of Population

ALPHA ORDER

RANK	STATE	PERCENT
33	Alabama	1.8
50	Alaska	0.9
28	Arizona	1.9
28	Arkansas	1.9
28	California	1.9
45	Colorado	1.5
2	Connecticut	2.6
25	Delaware	2.0
2	Florida	2.6
46	Georgia	1.4
1	Hawaii	2.8
41	Idaho	1.7
21	Illinois	2.1
25	Indiana	2.0
6	Iowa	2.5
14	Kansas	2.2
33	Kentucky	1.8
41	Louisiana	1.7
8	Maine	2.4
28	Maryland	1.9
10	Massachusetts	2.3
21	Michigan	2.1
14	Minnesota	2.2
41	Mississippi	1.7
21	Missouri	2.1
21	Montana	2.1
14	Nebraska	2.2
46	Nevada	1.4
14	New Hampshire	2.2
10	New Jersey	2.3
28	New Mexico	1.9
10	New York	2.3
33	North Carolina	1.8
6	North Dakota	2.5
14	Ohio	2.2
33	Oklahoma	1.8
25	Oregon	2.0
2	Pennsylvania	2.6
2	Rhode Island	2.6
41	South Carolina	1.7
8	South Dakota	2.4
33	Tennessee	1.8
46	Texas	1.4
49	Utah	1.2
10	Vermont	2.3
33	Virginia	1.8
33	Washington	1.8
14	West Virginia	2.2
14	Wisconsin	2.2
33	Wyoming	1.8

RANK ORDER

RANK	STATE	PERCENT
1	Hawaii	2.8
2	Connecticut	2.6
2	Florida	2.6
2	Pennsylvania	2.6
2	Rhode Island	2.6
6	Iowa	2.5
6	North Dakota	2.5
8	Maine	2.4
8	South Dakota	2.4
10	Massachusetts	2.3
10	New Jersey	2.3
10	New York	2.3
10	Vermont	2.3
14	Kansas	2.2
14	Minnesota	2.2
14	Nebraska	2.2
14	New Hampshire	2.2
14	Ohio	2.2
14	West Virginia	2.2
14	Wisconsin	2.2
21	Illinois	2.1
21	Michigan	2.1
21	Missouri	2.1
21	Montana	2.1
25	Delaware	2.0
25	Indiana	2.0
25	Oregon	2.0
28	Arizona	1.9
28	Arkansas	1.9
28	California	1.9
28	Maryland	1.9
28	New Mexico	1.9
33	Alabama	1.8
33	Kentucky	1.8
33	North Carolina	1.8
33	Oklahoma	1.8
33	Tennessee	1.8
33	Virginia	1.8
33	Washington	1.8
33	Wyoming	1.8
41	Idaho	1.7
41	Louisiana	1.7
41	Mississippi	1.7
41	South Carolina	1.7
45	Colorado	1.5
46	Georgia	1.4
46	Nevada	1.4
46	Texas	1.4
49	Utah	1.2
50	Alaska	0.9
	District of Columbia	1.7

Source: CQ Press using data from U.S. Bureau of the Census
"State Characteristics: Vintage 2017" (https://www.census.gov/programs-surveys/popest/data/data-sets.html)

Percent of Native Population Born in Their State of Residence in 2017

National Percent = 67.5%

ALPHA ORDER				RANK ORDER		
RANK	STATE	PERCENT		RANK	STATE	PERCENT
12	Alabama	72.4		1	Michigan	81.9
45	Alaska	46.1		2	Louisiana	81.7
46	Arizona	45.7		3	New York	81.6
29	Arkansas	63.6		4	Ohio	78.3
7	California	76.1		5	Illinois	78.1
44	Colorado	46.7		6	Pennsylvania	77.6
29	Connecticut	63.6		7	California	76.1
43	Delaware	48.1		8	Wisconsin	75.1
47	Florida	45.4		9	Iowa	74.2
32	Georgia	61.4		10	Minnesota	73.8
24	Hawaii	65.2		11	Mississippi	73.6
42	Idaho	50.6		12	Alabama	72.4
5	Illinois	78.1		13	Massachusetts	72.3
16	Indiana	71.8		14	Kentucky	72.0
9	Iowa	74.2		14	Texas	72.0
28	Kansas	64.0		16	Indiana	71.8
14	Kentucky	72.0		17	West Virginia	71.2
2	Louisiana	81.7		18	Nebraska	69.7
23	Maine	65.7		19	Missouri	68.9
37	Maryland	55.7		20	Utah	67.8
13	Massachusetts	72.3		21	New Jersey	67.3
1	Michigan	81.9		22	South Dakota	67.1
10	Minnesota	73.8		23	Maine	65.7
11	Mississippi	73.6		24	Hawaii	65.2
19	Missouri	68.9		25	Oklahoma	64.9
39	Montana	54.3		26	North Dakota	64.8
18	Nebraska	69.7		27	Rhode Island	64.5
50	Nevada	32.3		28	Kansas	64.0
49	New Hampshire	44.5		29	Arkansas	63.6
21	New Jersey	67.3		29	Connecticut	63.6
34	New Mexico	59.9		31	Tennessee	63.0
3	New York	81.6		32	Georgia	61.4
32	North Carolina	61.4		32	North Carolina	61.4
26	North Dakota	64.8		34	New Mexico	59.9
4	Ohio	78.3		35	South Carolina	59.0
25	Oklahoma	64.9		36	Virginia	56.2
41	Oregon	51.1		37	Maryland	55.7
6	Pennsylvania	77.6		38	Washington	54.7
27	Rhode Island	64.5		39	Montana	54.3
35	South Carolina	59.0		40	Vermont	54.0
22	South Dakota	67.1		41	Oregon	51.1
31	Tennessee	63.0		42	Idaho	50.6
14	Texas	72.0		43	Delaware	48.1
20	Utah	67.8		44	Colorado	46.7
40	Vermont	54.0		45	Alaska	46.1
36	Virginia	56.2		46	Arizona	45.7
38	Washington	54.7		47	Florida	45.4
17	West Virginia	71.2		48	Wyoming	44.6
8	Wisconsin	75.1		49	New Hampshire	44.5
48	Wyoming	44.6		50	Nevada	32.3
					District of Columbia	43.8

Source: U.S. Bureau of the Census

"2017 American Community Survey-Table R0601" (https://www.census.gov/programs-surveys/acs/)

Domestic Migration of Population: 2017 to 2018

National Net Migration = 0 People*

ALPHA ORDER

RANK	STATE	NET MIGRATION
17	Alabama	5,718
36	Alaska	(10,752)
2	Arizona	83,240
21	Arkansas	2,475
49	California	(156,068)
8	Colorado	43,293
43	Connecticut	(21,509)
14	Delaware	6,858
1	Florida	132,602
9	Georgia	41,914
39	Hawaii	(12,430)
12	Idaho	24,095
48	Illinois	(114,154)
20	Indiana	3,555
29	Iowa	(2,886)
40	Kansas	(12,564)
22	Kentucky	798
46	Louisiana	(27,914)
18	Maine	4,469
44	Maryland	(24,518)
45	Massachusetts	(25,755)
41	Michigan	(16,766)
15	Minnesota	6,769
37	Mississippi	(10,818)
28	Missouri	(2,790)
16	Montana	5,987
30	Nebraska	(3,314)
6	Nevada	47,596
19	New Hampshire	3,928
47	New Jersey	(50,591)
33	New Mexico	(5,851)
50	New York	(180,306)
4	North Carolina	66,991
26	North Dakota	(2,379)
38	Ohio	(12,146)
32	Oklahoma	(4,474)
11	Oregon	26,819
42	Pennsylvania	(20,463)
27	Rhode Island	(2,639)
5	South Carolina	50,775
23	South Dakota	638
10	Tennessee	39,952
3	Texas	82,569
13	Utah	16,052
24	Vermont	(62)
35	Virginia	(9,831)
7	Washington	46,549
34	West Virginia	(7,029)
25	Wisconsin	(1,011)
31	Wyoming	(3,686)

RANK ORDER

RANK	STATE	NET MIGRATION
1	Florida	132,602
2	Arizona	83,240
3	Texas	82,569
4	North Carolina	66,991
5	South Carolina	50,775
6	Nevada	47,596
7	Washington	46,549
8	Colorado	43,293
9	Georgia	41,914
10	Tennessee	39,952
11	Oregon	26,819
12	Idaho	24,095
13	Utah	16,052
14	Delaware	6,858
15	Minnesota	6,769
16	Montana	5,987
17	Alabama	5,718
18	Maine	4,469
19	New Hampshire	3,928
20	Indiana	3,555
21	Arkansas	2,475
22	Kentucky	798
23	South Dakota	638
24	Vermont	(62)
25	Wisconsin	(1,011)
26	North Dakota	(2,379)
27	Rhode Island	(2,639)
28	Missouri	(2,790)
29	Iowa	(2,886)
30	Nebraska	(3,314)
31	Wyoming	(3,686)
32	Oklahoma	(4,474)
33	New Mexico	(5,851)
34	West Virginia	(7,029)
35	Virginia	(9,831)
36	Alaska	(10,752)
37	Mississippi	(10,818)
38	Ohio	(12,146)
39	Hawaii	(12,430)
40	Kansas	(12,564)
41	Michigan	(16,766)
42	Pennsylvania	(20,463)
43	Connecticut	(21,509)
44	Maryland	(24,518)
45	Massachusetts	(25,755)
46	Louisiana	(27,914)
47	New Jersey	(50,591)
48	Illinois	(114,154)
49	California	(156,068)
50	New York	(180,306)
	District of Columbia	(936)

Source: U.S. Bureau of the Census

"State Population Totals Tables" (https://www.census.gov/programs-surveys/popest/data/data-sets.html)
*From July 1, 2017 to June 30, 2018. Includes armed forces residing in each state. Net Domestic Migration is the difference between domestic inmigration to an area and domestic outmigration from it during the period. Domestic inmigration and outmigration consist of moves where both the origins and destinations are within the United States (excluding Puerto Rico).

Net International Migration: 2017 to 2018

National Net = 978,826 Immigrants*

ALPHA ORDER

RANK	STATE	IMMIGRANTS	% of USA
33	Alabama	3,344	0.3%
40	Alaska	2,401	0.2%
17	Arizona	14,335	1.5%
42	Arkansas	2,260	0.2%
2	California	117,797	12.0%
22	Colorado	8,207	0.8%
16	Connecticut	16,494	1.7%
45	Delaware	1,820	0.2%
1	Florida	175,670	17.9%
12	Georgia	21,786	2.2%
31	Hawaii	4,075	0.4%
46	Idaho	1,681	0.2%
9	Illinois	30,735	3.1%
19	Indiana	9,227	0.9%
26	Iowa	5,828	0.6%
43	Kansas	2,057	0.2%
27	Kentucky	5,816	0.6%
35	Louisiana	3,012	0.3%
49	Maine	570	0.1%
11	Maryland	22,575	2.3%
5	Massachusetts	53,013	5.4%
13	Michigan	21,415	2.2%
18	Minnesota	10,718	1.1%
37	Mississippi	2,749	0.3%
24	Missouri	8,077	0.8%
47	Montana	889	0.1%
29	Nebraska	4,705	0.5%
34	Nevada	3,100	0.3%
38	New Hampshire	2,606	0.3%
6	New Jersey	46,660	4.8%
41	New Mexico	2,342	0.2%
4	New York	70,375	7.2%
15	North Carolina	20,035	2.0%
39	North Dakota	2,597	0.3%
14	Ohio	20,514	2.1%
30	Oklahoma	4,272	0.4%
23	Oregon	8,177	0.8%
7	Pennsylvania	35,377	3.6%
36	Rhode Island	2,755	0.3%
28	South Carolina	5,490	0.6%
32	South Dakota	3,659	0.4%
20	Tennessee	8,994	0.9%
3	Texas	104,976	10.7%
21	Utah	8,967	0.9%
44	Vermont	1,850	0.2%
8	Virginia	31,641	3.2%
10	Washington	30,557	3.1%
50	West Virginia	386	0.0%
25	Wisconsin	8,051	0.8%
48	Wyoming	597	0.1%

RANK ORDER

RANK	STATE	IMMIGRANTS	% of USA
1	Florida	175,670	17.9%
2	California	117,797	12.0%
3	Texas	104,976	10.7%
4	New York	70,375	7.2%
5	Massachusetts	53,013	5.4%
6	New Jersey	46,660	4.8%
7	Pennsylvania	35,377	3.6%
8	Virginia	31,641	3.2%
9	Illinois	30,735	3.1%
10	Washington	30,557	3.1%
11	Maryland	22,575	2.3%
12	Georgia	21,786	2.2%
13	Michigan	21,415	2.2%
14	Ohio	20,514	2.1%
15	North Carolina	20,035	2.0%
16	Connecticut	16,494	1.7%
17	Arizona	14,335	1.5%
18	Minnesota	10,718	1.1%
19	Indiana	9,227	0.9%
20	Tennessee	8,994	0.9%
21	Utah	8,967	0.9%
22	Colorado	8,207	0.8%
23	Oregon	8,177	0.8%
24	Missouri	8,077	0.8%
25	Wisconsin	8,051	0.8%
26	Iowa	5,828	0.6%
27	Kentucky	5,816	0.6%
28	South Carolina	5,490	0.6%
29	Nebraska	4,705	0.5%
30	Oklahoma	4,272	0.4%
31	Hawaii	4,075	0.4%
32	South Dakota	3,659	0.4%
33	Alabama	3,344	0.3%
34	Nevada	3,100	0.3%
35	Louisiana	3,012	0.3%
36	Rhode Island	2,755	0.3%
37	Mississippi	2,749	0.3%
38	New Hampshire	2,606	0.3%
39	North Dakota	2,597	0.3%
40	Alaska	2,401	0.2%
41	New Mexico	2,342	0.2%
42	Arkansas	2,260	0.2%
43	Kansas	2,057	0.2%
44	Vermont	1,850	0.2%
45	Delaware	1,820	0.2%
46	Idaho	1,681	0.2%
47	Montana	889	0.1%
48	Wyoming	597	0.1%
49	Maine	570	0.1%
50	West Virginia	386	0.0%
	District of Columbia	3,592	0.4%

Source: U.S. Bureau of the Census
  "State Population Totals Tables" (https://www.census.gov/programs-surveys/popest/data/data-sets.html)
*From July 1, 2017 to June 30, 2018. Net International Migration is the difference between migration to an area from outside the United States (immigration) and migration from the area to outside the United States (emigration) during the period. Includes legal immigration and estimates of undocumented immigration.

Percent of Population Foreign Born in 2017

National Percent = 13.7% of Population*

ALPHA ORDER

RANK ORDER

RANK	STATE	PERCENT	RANK	STATE	PERCENT
44	Alabama	3.5	1	California	26.9
24	Alaska	7.9	2	New York	22.9
14	Arizona	13.2	3	New Jersey	22.8
37	Arkansas	4.7	4	Florida	20.9
1	California	26.9	5	Nevada	19.9
19	Colorado	9.8	6	Hawaii	18.6
10	Connecticut	14.8	7	Texas	17.1
16	Delaware	10.2	8	Massachusetts	16.9
4	Florida	20.9	9	Maryland	15.3
16	Georgia	10.2	10	Connecticut	14.8
6	Hawaii	18.6	11	Illinois	14.3
30	Idaho	5.9	11	Washington	14.3
11	Illinois	14.3	13	Rhode Island	13.9
32	Indiana	5.3	14	Arizona	13.2
32	Iowa	5.3	15	Virginia	12.5
28	Kansas	6.9	16	Delaware	10.2
43	Kentucky	3.8	16	Georgia	10.2
41	Louisiana	4.1	18	Oregon	9.9
46	Maine	3.4	19	Colorado	9.8
9	Maryland	15.3	20	New Mexico	9.4
8	Massachusetts	16.9	21	Minnesota	8.7
26	Michigan	7.1	21	Utah	8.7
21	Minnesota	8.7	23	North Carolina	8.1
48	Mississippi	2.2	24	Alaska	7.9
40	Missouri	4.2	25	Nebraska	7.5
48	Montana	2.2	26	Michigan	7.1
25	Nebraska	7.5	27	Pennsylvania	7.0
5	Nevada	19.9	28	Kansas	6.9
29	New Hampshire	6.2	29	New Hampshire	6.2
3	New Jersey	22.8	30	Idaho	5.9
20	New Mexico	9.4	31	Oklahoma	5.7
2	New York	22.9	32	Indiana	5.3
23	North Carolina	8.1	32	Iowa	5.3
41	North Dakota	4.1	34	Tennessee	5.2
38	Ohio	4.5	35	Wisconsin	5.0
31	Oklahoma	5.7	36	South Carolina	4.9
18	Oregon	9.9	37	Arkansas	4.7
27	Pennsylvania	7.0	38	Ohio	4.5
13	Rhode Island	13.9	38	Vermont	4.5
36	South Carolina	4.9	40	Missouri	4.2
46	South Dakota	3.4	41	Louisiana	4.1
34	Tennessee	5.2	41	North Dakota	4.1
7	Texas	17.1	43	Kentucky	3.8
21	Utah	8.7	44	Alabama	3.5
38	Vermont	4.5	44	Wyoming	3.5
15	Virginia	12.5	46	Maine	3.4
11	Washington	14.3	46	South Dakota	3.4
50	West Virginia	1.6	48	Mississippi	2.2
35	Wisconsin	5.0	48	Montana	2.2
44	Wyoming	3.5	50	West Virginia	1.6

District of Columbia   14.7

Source: U.S. Bureau of the Census
   "2017 American Community Survey-Table R0501" (https://www.census.gov/programs-surveys/acs/)
*"Foreign born" are persons not born in the United States, Puerto Rico, a U.S. Island Area, or abroad of American parent or parents.

Percent of Population Speaking a Language
Other Than English at Home in 2017
National Percent = 21.8%*

ALPHA ORDER

RANK	STATE	PERCENT
47	Alabama	5.1
18	Alaska	15.9
8	Arizona	27.4
37	Arkansas	7.5
1	California	44.4
16	Colorado	16.9
13	Connecticut	22.4
22	Delaware	13.9
7	Florida	29.7
21	Georgia	14.1
9	Hawaii	25.8
28	Idaho	10.6
11	Illinois	23.5
31	Indiana	8.8
34	Iowa	8.1
23	Kansas	11.9
45	Kentucky	5.6
34	Louisiana	8.1
44	Maine	5.8
15	Maryland	19.1
10	Massachusetts	24.0
30	Michigan	9.9
23	Minnesota	11.9
49	Mississippi	3.7
42	Missouri	6.2
48	Montana	4.3
23	Nebraska	11.9
5	Nevada	31.1
36	New Hampshire	8.0
4	New Jersey	31.8
3	New Mexico	33.0
6	New York	30.9
26	North Carolina	11.8
43	North Dakota	5.9
38	Ohio	7.2
29	Oklahoma	10.2
20	Oregon	15.3
27	Pennsylvania	11.5
12	Rhode Island	22.9
38	South Carolina	7.2
41	South Dakota	6.4
40	Tennessee	7.1
2	Texas	35.6
19	Utah	15.6
45	Vermont	5.6
17	Virginia	16.5
14	Washington	19.6
50	West Virginia	2.4
32	Wisconsin	8.6
33	Wyoming	8.2

RANK ORDER

RANK	STATE	PERCENT
1	California	44.4
2	Texas	35.6
3	New Mexico	33.0
4	New Jersey	31.8
5	Nevada	31.1
6	New York	30.9
7	Florida	29.7
8	Arizona	27.4
9	Hawaii	25.8
10	Massachusetts	24.0
11	Illinois	23.5
12	Rhode Island	22.9
13	Connecticut	22.4
14	Washington	19.6
15	Maryland	19.1
16	Colorado	16.9
17	Virginia	16.5
18	Alaska	15.9
19	Utah	15.6
20	Oregon	15.3
21	Georgia	14.1
22	Delaware	13.9
23	Kansas	11.9
23	Minnesota	11.9
23	Nebraska	11.9
26	North Carolina	11.8
27	Pennsylvania	11.5
28	Idaho	10.6
29	Oklahoma	10.2
30	Michigan	9.9
31	Indiana	8.8
32	Wisconsin	8.6
33	Wyoming	8.2
34	Iowa	8.1
34	Louisiana	8.1
36	New Hampshire	8.0
37	Arkansas	7.5
38	Ohio	7.2
38	South Carolina	7.2
40	Tennessee	7.1
41	South Dakota	6.4
42	Missouri	6.2
43	North Dakota	5.9
44	Maine	5.8
45	Kentucky	5.6
45	Vermont	5.6
47	Alabama	5.1
48	Montana	4.3
49	Mississippi	3.7
50	West Virginia	2.4
	District of Columbia	17.6

Source: U.S. Bureau of the Census
   "2017 American Community Survey-Table CP02" (https://www.census.gov/programs-surveys/acs/)
*Population five years old and older.

Percent of Population Speaking Spanish at Home in 2017

National Percent = 13.4%*

ALPHA ORDER

RANK	STATE	PERCENT
36	Alabama	3.1
38	Alaska	2.9
6	Arizona	20.9
27	Arkansas	5.4
2	California	28.9
12	Colorado	11.6
11	Connecticut	12.2
23	Delaware	7.3
4	Florida	21.8
18	Georgia	8.1
42	Hawaii	2.3
19	Idaho	7.9
9	Illinois	13.6
29	Indiana	4.8
33	Iowa	3.9
20	Kansas	7.8
39	Kentucky	2.6
33	Louisiana	3.9
49	Maine	0.9
16	Maryland	8.5
14	Massachusetts	9.1
37	Michigan	3.0
35	Minnesota	3.8
44	Mississippi	2.2
39	Missouri	2.6
47	Montana	1.8
20	Nebraska	7.8
5	Nevada	21.6
42	New Hampshire	2.3
7	New Jersey	16.8
3	New Mexico	25.9
8	New York	15.2
22	North Carolina	7.6
44	North Dakota	2.2
41	Ohio	2.4
25	Oklahoma	7.1
15	Oregon	9.0
28	Pennsylvania	5.1
10	Rhode Island	12.3
30	South Carolina	4.6
44	South Dakota	2.2
32	Tennessee	4.0
1	Texas	29.4
13	Utah	10.5
48	Vermont	1.1
24	Virginia	7.2
17	Washington	8.4
49	West Virginia	0.9
31	Wisconsin	4.5
26	Wyoming	5.6

RANK ORDER

RANK	STATE	PERCENT
1	Texas	29.4
2	California	28.9
3	New Mexico	25.9
4	Florida	21.8
5	Nevada	21.6
6	Arizona	20.9
7	New Jersey	16.8
8	New York	15.2
9	Illinois	13.6
10	Rhode Island	12.3
11	Connecticut	12.2
12	Colorado	11.6
13	Utah	10.5
14	Massachusetts	9.1
15	Oregon	9.0
16	Maryland	8.5
17	Washington	8.4
18	Georgia	8.1
19	Idaho	7.9
20	Kansas	7.8
20	Nebraska	7.8
22	North Carolina	7.6
23	Delaware	7.3
24	Virginia	7.2
25	Oklahoma	7.1
26	Wyoming	5.6
27	Arkansas	5.4
28	Pennsylvania	5.1
29	Indiana	4.8
30	South Carolina	4.6
31	Wisconsin	4.5
32	Tennessee	4.0
33	Iowa	3.9
33	Louisiana	3.9
35	Minnesota	3.8
36	Alabama	3.1
37	Michigan	3.0
38	Alaska	2.9
39	Kentucky	2.6
39	Missouri	2.6
41	Ohio	2.4
42	Hawaii	2.3
42	New Hampshire	2.3
44	Mississippi	2.2
44	North Dakota	2.2
44	South Dakota	2.2
47	Montana	1.8
48	Vermont	1.1
49	Maine	0.9
49	West Virginia	0.9
	District of Columbia	9.4

Source: U.S. Bureau of the Census
   "2017 American Community Survey-Table CP02" (https://www.census.gov/programs-surveys/acs/)
*Population five years old and older.

Marriage Rate for Men in 2017

National Rate = 18.2 Marriages per 1,000 Men*

ALPHA ORDER

RANK	STATE	RATE
43	Alabama	15.9
2	Alaska	25.1
40	Arizona	16.3
3	Arkansas	22.5
30	California	17.3
4	Colorado	22.3
40	Connecticut	16.3
14	Delaware	20.1
29	Florida	17.5
19	Georgia	19.2
17	Hawaii	19.4
4	Idaho	22.3
39	Illinois	16.4
20	Indiana	19.0
25	Iowa	18.2
10	Kansas	20.7
4	Kentucky	22.3
44	Louisiana	15.8
49	Maine	13.6
21	Maryland	18.9
31	Massachusetts	16.9
31	Michigan	16.9
45	Minnesota	15.6
37	Mississippi	16.5
15	Missouri	19.6
42	Montana	16.2
28	Nebraska	17.7
12	Nevada	20.4
27	New Hampshire	17.8
47	New Jersey	14.7
49	New Mexico	13.6
31	New York	16.9
23	North Carolina	18.3
8	North Dakota	21.6
25	Ohio	18.2
12	Oklahoma	20.4
23	Oregon	18.3
36	Pennsylvania	16.6
48	Rhode Island	14.4
37	South Carolina	16.5
21	South Dakota	18.9
11	Tennessee	20.5
9	Texas	21.0
1	Utah	27.9
46	Vermont	15.4
17	Virginia	19.4
15	Washington	19.6
35	West Virginia	16.7
31	Wisconsin	16.9
4	Wyoming	22.3

RANK ORDER

RANK	STATE	RATE
1	Utah	27.9
2	Alaska	25.1
3	Arkansas	22.5
4	Colorado	22.3
4	Idaho	22.3
4	Kentucky	22.3
4	Wyoming	22.3
8	North Dakota	21.6
9	Texas	21.0
10	Kansas	20.7
11	Tennessee	20.5
12	Nevada	20.4
12	Oklahoma	20.4
14	Delaware	20.1
15	Missouri	19.6
15	Washington	19.6
17	Hawaii	19.4
17	Virginia	19.4
19	Georgia	19.2
20	Indiana	19.0
21	Maryland	18.9
21	South Dakota	18.9
23	North Carolina	18.3
23	Oregon	18.3
25	Iowa	18.2
25	Ohio	18.2
27	New Hampshire	17.8
28	Nebraska	17.7
29	Florida	17.5
30	California	17.3
31	Massachusetts	16.9
31	Michigan	16.9
31	New York	16.9
31	Wisconsin	16.9
35	West Virginia	16.7
36	Pennsylvania	16.6
37	Mississippi	16.5
37	South Carolina	16.5
39	Illinois	16.4
40	Arizona	16.3
40	Connecticut	16.3
42	Montana	16.2
43	Alabama	15.9
44	Louisiana	15.8
45	Minnesota	15.6
46	Vermont	15.4
47	New Jersey	14.7
48	Rhode Island	14.4
49	Maine	13.6
49	New Mexico	13.6
	District of Columbia	24.0

Source: U.S. Bureau of the Census
   "2017 American Community Survey-Table GCT1252" (https://www.census.gov/programs-surveys/acs/)
*Men age 15 and older. Marriages in the last year.

Estimated Median Age of Men at First Marriage in 2017

National Median = 29.9 Years*

ALPHA ORDER

RANK	STATE	YEARS
30	Alabama	29.3
39	Alaska	28.6
17	Arizona	29.9
48	Arkansas	27.3
3	California	30.9
17	Colorado	29.9
3	Connecticut	30.9
12	Delaware	30.3
7	Florida	30.6
28	Georgia	29.5
45	Hawaii	28.1
49	Idaho	26.7
7	Illinois	30.6
33	Indiana	29.0
37	Iowa	28.7
44	Kansas	28.3
46	Kentucky	28.0
22	Louisiana	29.8
14	Maine	30.1
13	Maryland	30.2
2	Massachusetts	31.2
15	Michigan	30.0
17	Minnesota	29.9
32	Mississippi	29.1
36	Missouri	28.9
22	Montana	29.8
41	Nebraska	28.5
25	Nevada	29.7
5	New Hampshire	30.7
5	New Jersey	30.7
22	New Mexico	29.8
1	New York	31.4
30	North Carolina	29.3
33	North Dakota	29.0
27	Ohio	29.6
47	Oklahoma	27.5
15	Oregon	30.0
11	Pennsylvania	30.4
7	Rhode Island	30.6
17	South Carolina	29.9
39	South Dakota	28.6
41	Tennessee	28.5
33	Texas	29.0
50	Utah	26.1
10	Vermont	30.5
25	Virginia	29.7
28	Washington	29.5
37	West Virginia	28.7
17	Wisconsin	29.9
41	Wyoming	28.5

RANK ORDER

RANK	STATE	YEARS
1	New York	31.4
2	Massachusetts	31.2
3	California	30.9
3	Connecticut	30.9
5	New Hampshire	30.7
5	New Jersey	30.7
7	Florida	30.6
7	Illinois	30.6
7	Rhode Island	30.6
10	Vermont	30.5
11	Pennsylvania	30.4
12	Delaware	30.3
13	Maryland	30.2
14	Maine	30.1
15	Michigan	30.0
15	Oregon	30.0
17	Arizona	29.9
17	Colorado	29.9
17	Minnesota	29.9
17	South Carolina	29.9
17	Wisconsin	29.9
22	Louisiana	29.8
22	Montana	29.8
22	New Mexico	29.8
25	Nevada	29.7
25	Virginia	29.7
27	Ohio	29.6
28	Georgia	29.5
28	Washington	29.5
30	Alabama	29.3
30	North Carolina	29.3
32	Mississippi	29.1
33	Indiana	29.0
33	North Dakota	29.0
33	Texas	29.0
36	Missouri	28.9
37	Iowa	28.7
37	West Virginia	28.7
39	Alaska	28.6
39	South Dakota	28.6
41	Nebraska	28.5
41	Tennessee	28.5
41	Wyoming	28.5
44	Kansas	28.3
45	Hawaii	28.1
46	Kentucky	28.0
47	Oklahoma	27.5
48	Arkansas	27.3
49	Idaho	26.7
50	Utah	26.1
	District of Columbia	30.7

Source: U.S. Bureau of the Census
    "2017 American Community Survey-Table R1204" (https://www.census.gov/programs-surveys/acs/)
*The median age at first marriage is calculated indirectly by estimating the proportion of young people who will marry during their lifetime, calculating one-half of this proportion, and determining the age (at the time of the survey) of people at this half-way mark. It does not represent the actual median age of the population who married during the calendar year.

Marriage Rate for Women in 2017

National Rate = 17.1 Marriages per 1,000 Women*

ALPHA ORDER			RANK ORDER		
RANK	STATE	RATE	RANK	STATE	RATE
44	Alabama	15.1	1	Utah	27.3
2	Alaska	25.3	2	Alaska	25.3
39	Arizona	15.6	3	Wyoming	24.2
7	Arkansas	21.6	4	North Dakota	23.0
29	California	16.2	5	Idaho	22.9
6	Colorado	22.0	6	Colorado	22.0
49	Connecticut	13.2	7	Arkansas	21.6
16	Delaware	18.2	8	Kentucky	21.2
36	Florida	15.7	9	Kansas	20.8
25	Georgia	17.3	10	Oklahoma	20.1
22	Hawaii	17.5	11	Texas	20.0
5	Idaho	22.9	12	Indiana	19.7
34	Illinois	15.9	13	Tennessee	19.6
12	Indiana	19.7	14	Nevada	18.6
21	Iowa	17.6	15	Missouri	18.5
9	Kansas	20.8	16	Delaware	18.2
8	Kentucky	21.2	17	South Dakota	18.0
46	Louisiana	14.2	18	Virginia	17.9
48	Maine	13.5	18	Washington	17.9
24	Maryland	17.4	20	Oregon	17.7
40	Massachusetts	15.5	21	Iowa	17.6
32	Michigan	16.1	22	Hawaii	17.5
41	Minnesota	15.4	22	Montana	17.5
28	Mississippi	16.3	24	Maryland	17.4
15	Missouri	18.5	25	Georgia	17.3
22	Montana	17.5	25	Ohio	17.3
29	Nebraska	16.2	27	North Carolina	17.2
14	Nevada	18.6	28	Mississippi	16.3
36	New Hampshire	15.7	29	California	16.2
47	New Jersey	13.8	29	Nebraska	16.2
43	New Mexico	15.2	29	South Carolina	16.2
42	New York	15.3	32	Michigan	16.1
27	North Carolina	17.2	32	Wisconsin	16.1
4	North Dakota	23.0	34	Illinois	15.9
25	Ohio	17.3	35	West Virginia	15.8
10	Oklahoma	20.1	36	Florida	15.7
20	Oregon	17.7	36	New Hampshire	15.7
36	Pennsylvania	15.7	36	Pennsylvania	15.7
50	Rhode Island	10.9	39	Arizona	15.6
29	South Carolina	16.2	40	Massachusetts	15.5
17	South Dakota	18.0	41	Minnesota	15.4
13	Tennessee	19.6	42	New York	15.3
11	Texas	20.0	43	New Mexico	15.2
1	Utah	27.3	44	Alabama	15.1
45	Vermont	14.9	45	Vermont	14.9
18	Virginia	17.9	46	Louisiana	14.2
18	Washington	17.9	47	New Jersey	13.8
35	West Virginia	15.8	48	Maine	13.5
32	Wisconsin	16.1	49	Connecticut	13.2
3	Wyoming	24.2	50	Rhode Island	10.9
				District of Columbia	20.4

Source: U.S. Bureau of the Census
  "2017 American Community Survey-Table GCT1251" (https://www.census.gov/programs-surveys/acs/)
*Women age 15 and older. Marriages in the last year.

Estimated Median Age of Women at First Marriage in 2017

National Median = 28.1 Years*

ALPHA ORDER				RANK ORDER		
RANK	STATE	YEARS		RANK	STATE	YEARS
39	Alabama	26.8		1	Massachusetts	30.1
44	Alaska	26.1		2	Connecticut	29.7
21	Arizona	27.9		2	New York	29.7
47	Arkansas	25.6		4	Rhode Island	29.3
8	California	29.0		5	Delaware	29.2
15	Colorado	28.2		6	New Hampshire	29.1
2	Connecticut	29.7		6	New Jersey	29.1
5	Delaware	29.2		8	California	29.0
8	Florida	29.0		8	Florida	29.0
17	Georgia	28.1		8	Illinois	29.0
15	Hawaii	28.2		8	Maryland	29.0
48	Idaho	25.2		12	Pennsylvania	28.9
8	Illinois	29.0		13	Louisiana	28.3
36	Indiana	27.0		13	Maine	28.3
33	Iowa	27.1		15	Colorado	28.2
45	Kansas	26.0		15	Hawaii	28.2
41	Kentucky	26.4		17	Georgia	28.1
13	Louisiana	28.3		17	Minnesota	28.1
13	Maine	28.3		19	Michigan	28.0
8	Maryland	29.0		19	Vermont	28.0
1	Massachusetts	30.1		21	Arizona	27.9
19	Michigan	28.0		21	New Mexico	27.9
17	Minnesota	28.1		21	Ohio	27.9
39	Mississippi	26.8		21	Virginia	27.9
31	Missouri	27.3		21	Wisconsin	27.9
37	Montana	26.9		26	Oregon	27.8
41	Nebraska	26.4		27	South Carolina	27.5
28	Nevada	27.4		28	Nevada	27.4
6	New Hampshire	29.1		28	North Carolina	27.4
6	New Jersey	29.1		28	South Dakota	27.4
21	New Mexico	27.9		31	Missouri	27.3
2	New York	29.7		31	Washington	27.3
28	North Carolina	27.4		33	Iowa	27.1
43	North Dakota	26.2		33	Texas	27.1
21	Ohio	27.9		33	West Virginia	27.1
46	Oklahoma	25.8		36	Indiana	27.0
26	Oregon	27.8		37	Montana	26.9
12	Pennsylvania	28.9		37	Tennessee	26.9
4	Rhode Island	29.3		39	Alabama	26.8
27	South Carolina	27.5		39	Mississippi	26.8
28	South Dakota	27.4		41	Kentucky	26.4
37	Tennessee	26.9		41	Nebraska	26.4
33	Texas	27.1		43	North Dakota	26.2
50	Utah	24.8		44	Alaska	26.1
19	Vermont	28.0		45	Kansas	26.0
21	Virginia	27.9		46	Oklahoma	25.8
31	Washington	27.3		47	Arkansas	25.6
33	West Virginia	27.1		48	Idaho	25.2
21	Wisconsin	27.9		49	Wyoming	25.0
49	Wyoming	25.0		50	Utah	24.8
					District of Columbia	30.4

Source: U.S. Bureau of the Census

"2017 American Community Survey-Table R1205" (https://www.census.gov/programs-surveys/acs/)

*The median age at first marriage is calculated indirectly by estimating the proportion of young people who will marry during their lifetime, calculating one-half of this proportion, and determining the age (at the time of the survey) of people at this half-way mark. It does not represent the actual median age of the population who married during the calendar year.

Ratio of Unmarried Men to Unmarried Women in 2017

National Ratio = 111.4 Unmarried Men for Every 100 Unmarried Women*

ALPHA ORDER

RANK	STATE	RATIO
49	Alabama	103.7
1	Alaska	137.7
14	Arizona	115.8
24	Arkansas	112.8
16	California	115.2
8	Colorado	118.5
42	Connecticut	106.6
48	Delaware	104.2
34	Florida	110.3
46	Georgia	104.8
4	Hawaii	125.7
6	Idaho	121.3
35	Illinois	110.2
27	Indiana	112.3
13	Iowa	116.0
7	Kansas	119.7
25	Kentucky	112.7
43	Louisiana	106.5
23	Maine	113.1
45	Maryland	105.4
46	Massachusetts	104.8
30	Michigan	111.1
18	Minnesota	114.8
44	Mississippi	105.7
32	Missouri	110.4
10	Montana	117.5
12	Nebraska	116.3
15	Nevada	115.5
37	New Hampshire	109.2
29	New Jersey	111.7
27	New Mexico	112.3
39	New York	107.4
40	North Carolina	107.2
2	North Dakota	134.3
36	Ohio	109.4
17	Oklahoma	115.0
19	Oregon	114.1
32	Pennsylvania	110.4
50	Rhode Island	102.0
38	South Carolina	108.3
5	South Dakota	124.1
40	Tennessee	107.2
22	Texas	113.3
11	Utah	116.7
21	Vermont	113.4
30	Virginia	111.1
9	Washington	118.2
19	West Virginia	114.1
26	Wisconsin	112.5
3	Wyoming	129.3

RANK ORDER

RANK	STATE	RATIO
1	Alaska	137.7
2	North Dakota	134.3
3	Wyoming	129.3
4	Hawaii	125.7
5	South Dakota	124.1
6	Idaho	121.3
7	Kansas	119.7
8	Colorado	118.5
9	Washington	118.2
10	Montana	117.5
11	Utah	116.7
12	Nebraska	116.3
13	Iowa	116.0
14	Arizona	115.8
15	Nevada	115.5
16	California	115.2
17	Oklahoma	115.0
18	Minnesota	114.8
19	Oregon	114.1
19	West Virginia	114.1
21	Vermont	113.4
22	Texas	113.3
23	Maine	113.1
24	Arkansas	112.8
25	Kentucky	112.7
26	Wisconsin	112.5
27	Indiana	112.3
27	New Mexico	112.3
29	New Jersey	111.7
30	Michigan	111.1
30	Virginia	111.1
32	Missouri	110.4
32	Pennsylvania	110.4
34	Florida	110.3
35	Illinois	110.2
36	Ohio	109.4
37	New Hampshire	109.2
38	South Carolina	108.3
39	New York	107.4
40	North Carolina	107.2
40	Tennessee	107.2
42	Connecticut	106.6
43	Louisiana	106.5
44	Mississippi	105.7
45	Maryland	105.4
46	Georgia	104.8
46	Massachusetts	104.8
48	Delaware	104.2
49	Alabama	103.7
50	Rhode Island	102.0
	District of Columbia	90.9

Source: U.S. Bureau of the Census
"2017 American Community Survey-Table R1203" (https://www.census.gov/programs-surveys/acs/)
*Population 15 to 44 years old.

Divorce Rate for Men in 2017

National Rate = 7.5 Divorces per 1,000 Men*

<table>
<tr><td colspan="3">ALPHA ORDER</td><td colspan="3">RANK ORDER</td></tr>
<tr><td>RANK</td><td>STATE</td><td>RATE</td><td>RANK</td><td>STATE</td><td>RATE</td></tr>
<tr><td>5</td><td>Alabama</td><td>9.7</td><td>1</td><td>Arkansas</td><td>11.4</td></tr>
<tr><td>14</td><td>Alaska</td><td>9.1</td><td>1</td><td>West Virginia</td><td>11.4</td></tr>
<tr><td>14</td><td>Arizona</td><td>9.1</td><td>3</td><td>South Dakota</td><td>11.1</td></tr>
<tr><td>1</td><td>Arkansas</td><td>11.4</td><td>4</td><td>Oklahoma</td><td>10.6</td></tr>
<tr><td>43</td><td>California</td><td>6.2</td><td>5</td><td>Alabama</td><td>9.7</td></tr>
<tr><td>20</td><td>Colorado</td><td>8.2</td><td>5</td><td>Utah</td><td>9.7</td></tr>
<tr><td>34</td><td>Connecticut</td><td>7.4</td><td>7</td><td>Kentucky</td><td>9.6</td></tr>
<tr><td>46</td><td>Delaware</td><td>5.4</td><td>7</td><td>Missouri</td><td>9.6</td></tr>
<tr><td>26</td><td>Florida</td><td>8.0</td><td>9</td><td>Georgia</td><td>9.4</td></tr>
<tr><td>9</td><td>Georgia</td><td>9.4</td><td>9</td><td>Idaho</td><td>9.4</td></tr>
<tr><td>50</td><td>Hawaii</td><td>5.1</td><td>9</td><td>Tennessee</td><td>9.4</td></tr>
<tr><td>9</td><td>Idaho</td><td>9.4</td><td>9</td><td>Wyoming</td><td>9.4</td></tr>
<tr><td>44</td><td>Illinois</td><td>5.9</td><td>13</td><td>New Mexico</td><td>9.3</td></tr>
<tr><td>14</td><td>Indiana</td><td>9.1</td><td>14</td><td>Alaska</td><td>9.1</td></tr>
<tr><td>38</td><td>Iowa</td><td>6.8</td><td>14</td><td>Arizona</td><td>9.1</td></tr>
<tr><td>20</td><td>Kansas</td><td>8.2</td><td>14</td><td>Indiana</td><td>9.1</td></tr>
<tr><td>7</td><td>Kentucky</td><td>9.6</td><td>17</td><td>Maine</td><td>8.6</td></tr>
<tr><td>26</td><td>Louisiana</td><td>8.0</td><td>18</td><td>Oregon</td><td>8.3</td></tr>
<tr><td>17</td><td>Maine</td><td>8.6</td><td>18</td><td>Virginia</td><td>8.3</td></tr>
<tr><td>40</td><td>Maryland</td><td>6.6</td><td>20</td><td>Colorado</td><td>8.2</td></tr>
<tr><td>45</td><td>Massachusetts</td><td>5.8</td><td>20</td><td>Kansas</td><td>8.2</td></tr>
<tr><td>31</td><td>Michigan</td><td>7.5</td><td>20</td><td>Montana</td><td>8.2</td></tr>
<tr><td>40</td><td>Minnesota</td><td>6.6</td><td>20</td><td>Washington</td><td>8.2</td></tr>
<tr><td>31</td><td>Mississippi</td><td>7.5</td><td>24</td><td>South Carolina</td><td>8.1</td></tr>
<tr><td>7</td><td>Missouri</td><td>9.6</td><td>24</td><td>Texas</td><td>8.1</td></tr>
<tr><td>20</td><td>Montana</td><td>8.2</td><td>26</td><td>Florida</td><td>8.0</td></tr>
<tr><td>31</td><td>Nebraska</td><td>7.5</td><td>26</td><td>Louisiana</td><td>8.0</td></tr>
<tr><td>29</td><td>Nevada</td><td>7.7</td><td>28</td><td>North Carolina</td><td>7.8</td></tr>
<tr><td>37</td><td>New Hampshire</td><td>6.9</td><td>29</td><td>Nevada</td><td>7.7</td></tr>
<tr><td>42</td><td>New Jersey</td><td>6.4</td><td>30</td><td>North Dakota</td><td>7.6</td></tr>
<tr><td>13</td><td>New Mexico</td><td>9.3</td><td>31</td><td>Michigan</td><td>7.5</td></tr>
<tr><td>48</td><td>New York</td><td>5.3</td><td>31</td><td>Mississippi</td><td>7.5</td></tr>
<tr><td>28</td><td>North Carolina</td><td>7.8</td><td>31</td><td>Nebraska</td><td>7.5</td></tr>
<tr><td>30</td><td>North Dakota</td><td>7.6</td><td>34</td><td>Connecticut</td><td>7.4</td></tr>
<tr><td>36</td><td>Ohio</td><td>7.0</td><td>35</td><td>Wisconsin</td><td>7.2</td></tr>
<tr><td>4</td><td>Oklahoma</td><td>10.6</td><td>36</td><td>Ohio</td><td>7.0</td></tr>
<tr><td>18</td><td>Oregon</td><td>8.3</td><td>37</td><td>New Hampshire</td><td>6.9</td></tr>
<tr><td>39</td><td>Pennsylvania</td><td>6.7</td><td>38</td><td>Iowa</td><td>6.8</td></tr>
<tr><td>46</td><td>Rhode Island</td><td>5.4</td><td>39</td><td>Pennsylvania</td><td>6.7</td></tr>
<tr><td>24</td><td>South Carolina</td><td>8.1</td><td>40</td><td>Maryland</td><td>6.6</td></tr>
<tr><td>3</td><td>South Dakota</td><td>11.1</td><td>40</td><td>Minnesota</td><td>6.6</td></tr>
<tr><td>9</td><td>Tennessee</td><td>9.4</td><td>42</td><td>New Jersey</td><td>6.4</td></tr>
<tr><td>24</td><td>Texas</td><td>8.1</td><td>43</td><td>California</td><td>6.2</td></tr>
<tr><td>5</td><td>Utah</td><td>9.7</td><td>44</td><td>Illinois</td><td>5.9</td></tr>
<tr><td>48</td><td>Vermont</td><td>5.3</td><td>45</td><td>Massachusetts</td><td>5.8</td></tr>
<tr><td>18</td><td>Virginia</td><td>8.3</td><td>46</td><td>Delaware</td><td>5.4</td></tr>
<tr><td>20</td><td>Washington</td><td>8.2</td><td>46</td><td>Rhode Island</td><td>5.4</td></tr>
<tr><td>1</td><td>West Virginia</td><td>11.4</td><td>48</td><td>New York</td><td>5.3</td></tr>
<tr><td>35</td><td>Wisconsin</td><td>7.2</td><td>48</td><td>Vermont</td><td>5.3</td></tr>
<tr><td>9</td><td>Wyoming</td><td>9.4</td><td>50</td><td>Hawaii</td><td>5.1</td></tr>
<tr><td></td><td></td><td></td><td></td><td>District of Columbia</td><td>5.1</td></tr>
</table>

Source: U.S. Bureau of the Census
   "2017 American Community Survey-Table GCT1254" (https://www.census.gov/programs-surveys/acs/)
*Men age 15 and older. Divorces in the last year.

Divorce Rate for Women in 2017

National Rate = 7.9 Divorces per 1,000 Women*

ALPHA ORDER

RANK	STATE	RATE
5	Alabama	10.9
35	Alaska	7.7
18	Arizona	8.4
1	Arkansas	13.3
43	California	6.9
7	Colorado	10.2
42	Connecticut	7.0
4	Delaware	11.4
24	Florida	8.2
12	Georgia	9.1
50	Hawaii	5.1
3	Idaho	11.5
47	Illinois	6.2
15	Indiana	8.9
33	Iowa	7.8
38	Kansas	7.5
2	Kentucky	11.7
27	Louisiana	8.0
9	Maine	10.1
22	Maryland	8.3
27	Massachusetts	8.0
36	Michigan	7.6
39	Minnesota	7.2
26	Mississippi	8.1
22	Missouri	8.3
46	Montana	6.5
18	Nebraska	8.4
10	Nevada	9.6
11	New Hampshire	9.5
47	New Jersey	6.2
32	New Mexico	7.9
49	New York	5.9
18	North Carolina	8.4
16	North Dakota	8.8
36	Ohio	7.6
6	Oklahoma	10.6
27	Oregon	8.0
43	Pennsylvania	6.9
39	Rhode Island	7.2
17	South Carolina	8.7
33	South Dakota	7.8
7	Tennessee	10.2
24	Texas	8.2
12	Utah	9.1
39	Vermont	7.2
27	Virginia	8.0
18	Washington	8.4
14	West Virginia	9.0
45	Wisconsin	6.7
27	Wyoming	8.0

RANK ORDER

RANK	STATE	RATE
1	Arkansas	13.3
2	Kentucky	11.7
3	Idaho	11.5
4	Delaware	11.4
5	Alabama	10.9
6	Oklahoma	10.6
7	Colorado	10.2
7	Tennessee	10.2
9	Maine	10.1
10	Nevada	9.6
11	New Hampshire	9.5
12	Georgia	9.1
12	Utah	9.1
14	West Virginia	9.0
15	Indiana	8.9
16	North Dakota	8.8
17	South Carolina	8.7
18	Arizona	8.4
18	Nebraska	8.4
18	North Carolina	8.4
18	Washington	8.4
22	Maryland	8.3
22	Missouri	8.3
24	Florida	8.2
24	Texas	8.2
26	Mississippi	8.1
27	Louisiana	8.0
27	Massachusetts	8.0
27	Oregon	8.0
27	Virginia	8.0
27	Wyoming	8.0
32	New Mexico	7.9
33	Iowa	7.8
33	South Dakota	7.8
35	Alaska	7.7
36	Michigan	7.6
36	Ohio	7.6
38	Kansas	7.5
39	Minnesota	7.2
39	Rhode Island	7.2
39	Vermont	7.2
42	Connecticut	7.0
43	California	6.9
43	Pennsylvania	6.9
45	Wisconsin	6.7
46	Montana	6.5
47	Illinois	6.2
47	New Jersey	6.2
49	New York	5.9
50	Hawaii	5.1
	District of Columbia	3.5

Source: U.S. Bureau of the Census
   "2017 American Community Survey-Table GCT1253" (https://www.census.gov/programs-surveys/acs/)
*Women age 15 and older. Divorces in the last year.

Average Family Size in 2017

National Average = 3.26 Persons per Family

ALPHA ORDER			RANK ORDER		
RANK	STATE	PERSONS	RANK	STATE	PERSONS
18	Alabama	3.23	1	Utah	3.63
5	Alaska	3.41	2	Hawaii	3.60
8	Arizona	3.32	3	California	3.57
25	Arkansas	3.14	4	Texas	3.49
3	California	3.57	5	Alaska	3.41
25	Colorado	3.14	5	New Mexico	3.41
23	Connecticut	3.18	7	Nevada	3.34
20	Delaware	3.20	8	Arizona	3.32
8	Florida	3.32	8	Florida	3.32
13	Georgia	3.31	8	Louisiana	3.32
2	Hawaii	3.60	8	New Jersey	3.32
15	Idaho	3.29	8	New York	3.32
17	Illinois	3.27	13	Georgia	3.31
28	Indiana	3.13	13	Mississippi	3.31
45	Iowa	3.01	15	Idaho	3.29
32	Kansas	3.10	15	Maryland	3.29
36	Kentucky	3.08	17	Illinois	3.27
8	Louisiana	3.32	18	Alabama	3.23
46	Maine	2.99	19	Oklahoma	3.21
15	Maryland	3.29	20	Delaware	3.20
25	Massachusetts	3.14	20	Virginia	3.20
39	Michigan	3.07	22	Rhode Island	3.19
32	Minnesota	3.10	23	Connecticut	3.18
13	Mississippi	3.31	24	South Carolina	3.17
35	Missouri	3.09	25	Arkansas	3.14
44	Montana	3.03	25	Colorado	3.14
39	Nebraska	3.07	25	Massachusetts	3.14
7	Nevada	3.34	28	Indiana	3.13
48	New Hampshire	2.97	29	North Carolina	3.12
8	New Jersey	3.32	29	Tennessee	3.12
5	New Mexico	3.41	31	Washington	3.11
8	New York	3.32	32	Kansas	3.10
29	North Carolina	3.12	32	Minnesota	3.10
49	North Dakota	2.94	32	Pennsylvania	3.10
43	Ohio	3.04	35	Missouri	3.09
19	Oklahoma	3.21	36	Kentucky	3.08
36	Oregon	3.08	36	Oregon	3.08
32	Pennsylvania	3.10	36	Wyoming	3.08
22	Rhode Island	3.19	39	Michigan	3.07
24	South Carolina	3.17	39	Nebraska	3.07
39	South Dakota	3.07	39	South Dakota	3.07
29	Tennessee	3.12	42	West Virginia	3.06
4	Texas	3.49	43	Ohio	3.04
1	Utah	3.63	44	Montana	3.03
50	Vermont	2.93	45	Iowa	3.01
20	Virginia	3.20	46	Maine	2.99
31	Washington	3.11	47	Wisconsin	2.98
42	West Virginia	3.06	48	New Hampshire	2.97
47	Wisconsin	2.98	49	North Dakota	2.94
36	Wyoming	3.08	50	Vermont	2.93
				District of Columbia	3.40

Source: U.S. Bureau of the Census
"2017 American Community Survey-Table CP02" (https://www.census.gov/programs-surveys/acs/)

Seats in the U.S. House of Representatives in 2019

National Total = 435 Seats*

ALPHA ORDER					RANK ORDER			
RANK	STATE		SEATS	% of USA	RANK	STATE	SEATS	% of USA
22	Alabama		7	1.6%	1	California	53	12.2%
44	Alaska		1	0.2%	2	Texas	36	8.3%
14	Arizona		9	2.1%	3	Florida	27	6.2%
30	Arkansas		4	0.9%	3	New York	27	6.2%
1	California		53	12.2%	5	Illinois	18	4.1%
22	Colorado		7	1.6%	5	Pennsylvania	18	4.1%
27	Connecticut		5	1.1%	7	Ohio	16	3.7%
44	Delaware		1	0.2%	8	Georgia	14	3.2%
3	Florida		27	6.2%	8	Michigan	14	3.2%
8	Georgia		14	3.2%	10	North Carolina	13	3.0%
39	Hawaii		2	0.5%	11	New Jersey	12	2.8%
39	Idaho		2	0.5%	12	Virginia	11	2.5%
5	Illinois		18	4.1%	13	Washington	10	2.3%
14	Indiana		9	2.1%	14	Arizona	9	2.1%
30	Iowa		4	0.9%	14	Indiana	9	2.1%
30	Kansas		4	0.9%	14	Massachusetts	9	2.1%
25	Kentucky		6	1.4%	14	Tennessee	9	2.1%
25	Louisiana		6	1.4%	18	Maryland	8	1.8%
39	Maine		2	0.5%	18	Minnesota	8	1.8%
18	Maryland		8	1.8%	18	Missouri	8	1.8%
14	Massachusetts		9	2.1%	18	Wisconsin	8	1.8%
8	Michigan		14	3.2%	22	Alabama	7	1.6%
18	Minnesota		8	1.8%	22	Colorado	7	1.6%
30	Mississippi		4	0.9%	22	South Carolina	7	1.6%
18	Missouri		8	1.8%	25	Kentucky	6	1.4%
44	Montana		1	0.2%	25	Louisiana	6	1.4%
36	Nebraska		3	0.7%	27	Connecticut	5	1.1%
30	Nevada		4	0.9%	27	Oklahoma	5	1.1%
39	New Hampshire		2	0.5%	27	Oregon	5	1.1%
11	New Jersey		12	2.8%	30	Arkansas	4	0.9%
36	New Mexico		3	0.7%	30	Iowa	4	0.9%
3	New York		27	6.2%	30	Kansas	4	0.9%
10	North Carolina		13	3.0%	30	Mississippi	4	0.9%
44	North Dakota		1	0.2%	30	Nevada	4	0.9%
7	Ohio		16	3.7%	30	Utah	4	0.9%
27	Oklahoma		5	1.1%	36	Nebraska	3	0.7%
27	Oregon		5	1.1%	36	New Mexico	3	0.7%
5	Pennsylvania		18	4.1%	36	West Virginia	3	0.7%
39	Rhode Island		2	0.5%	39	Hawaii	2	0.5%
22	South Carolina		7	1.6%	39	Idaho	2	0.5%
44	South Dakota		1	0.2%	39	Maine	2	0.5%
14	Tennessee		9	2.1%	39	New Hampshire	2	0.5%
2	Texas		36	8.3%	39	Rhode Island	2	0.5%
30	Utah		4	0.9%	44	Alaska	1	0.2%
44	Vermont		1	0.2%	44	Delaware	1	0.2%
12	Virginia		11	2.5%	44	Montana	1	0.2%
13	Washington		10	2.3%	44	North Dakota	1	0.2%
36	West Virginia		3	0.7%	44	South Dakota	1	0.2%
18	Wisconsin		8	1.8%	44	Vermont	1	0.2%
44	Wyoming		1	0.2%	44	Wyoming	1	0.2%
						District of Columbia**	0	0.0%

Source: U.S. Bureau of the Census

"Congressional Apportionment" (www.census.gov/topics/public-sector/congressional-apportionment.html)

*This table shows the number of seats after reapportionment of the 2010 Census. This apportionment became effective with the Congress elected in November 2012 and that took office in January 2013.

**The District of Columbia has one non-voting delegate. Each state has two members in the U.S. Senate.

Estimated Population per U.S. House Seat in 2019

National Rate = 750,494 Persons per House Member*

ALPHA ORDER			RANK ORDER		
RANK	STATE	RATE	RANK	STATE	RATE
43	Alabama	698,267	1	Montana	1,062,305
30	Alaska	737,438	2	Delaware	967,171
9	Arizona	796,850	3	South Dakota	882,235
22	Arkansas	753,456	4	Idaho	877,104
26	California	746,359	5	Oregon	838,143
6	Colorado	813,652	6	Colorado	813,652
36	Connecticut	714,533	7	North Carolina	798,740
2	Delaware	967,171	8	Texas	797,273
12	Florida	788,864	9	Arizona	796,850
24	Georgia	751,391	10	Utah	790,276
39	Hawaii	710,246	11	Iowa	789,036
4	Idaho	877,104	12	Florida	788,864
40	Illinois	707,838	13	Oklahoma	788,616
28	Indiana	743,542	14	Louisiana	776,663
11	Iowa	789,036	15	Virginia	774,335
32	Kansas	727,876	16	Massachusetts	766,905
27	Kentucky	744,734	17	Missouri	765,807
14	Louisiana	776,663	18	North Dakota	760,077
45	Maine	669,202	19	Nevada	758,598
20	Maryland	755,340	20	Maryland	755,340
16	Massachusetts	766,905	21	Washington	753,559
37	Michigan	713,994	22	Arkansas	753,456
41	Minnesota	701,397	23	Tennessee	752,223
25	Mississippi	746,633	24	Georgia	751,391
17	Missouri	765,807	25	Mississippi	746,633
1	Montana	1,062,305	26	California	746,359
46	Nebraska	643,089	27	Kentucky	744,734
19	Nevada	758,598	28	Indiana	743,542
44	New Hampshire	678,229	29	New Jersey	742,377
29	New Jersey	742,377	30	Alaska	737,438
42	New Mexico	698,476	31	Ohio	730,590
35	New York	723,786	32	Kansas	727,876
7	North Carolina	798,740	33	Wisconsin	726,696
18	North Dakota	760,077	34	South Carolina	726,304
31	Ohio	730,590	35	New York	723,786
13	Oklahoma	788,616	36	Connecticut	714,533
5	Oregon	838,143	37	Michigan	713,994
38	Pennsylvania	711,503	38	Pennsylvania	711,503
50	Rhode Island	528,658	39	Hawaii	710,246
34	South Carolina	726,304	40	Illinois	707,838
3	South Dakota	882,235	41	Minnesota	701,397
23	Tennessee	752,223	42	New Mexico	698,476
8	Texas	797,273	43	Alabama	698,267
10	Utah	790,276	44	New Hampshire	678,229
47	Vermont	626,299	45	Maine	669,202
15	Virginia	774,335	46	Nebraska	643,089
21	Washington	753,559	47	Vermont	626,299
48	West Virginia	601,944	48	West Virginia	601,944
33	Wisconsin	726,696	49	Wyoming	577,737
49	Wyoming	577,737	50	Rhode Island	528,658
				District of Columbia**	NA

Source: CQ Press using data from U.S. Bureau of the Census

"Congressional Apportionment" (www.census.gov/topics/public-sector/congressional-apportionment.html)
*Rates calculated using 2018 population estimates and do not include population of the District of Columbia. The District has one non-voting delegate. Each state has two members in the U.S. Senate. This table is based only on U.S. Representatives and not U.S. Senate members. This table reflects reapportionment resulting from the 2010 census and taking effect after the 2012 election. **Not applicable.

State Legislators in 2018

National Total = 7,383 Legislators*

<table>
<tr><td colspan="4">ALPHA ORDER</td><td colspan="4">RANK ORDER</td></tr>
<tr><th>RANK</th><th>STATE</th><th>LEGISLATORS</th><th>% of USA</th><th>RANK</th><th>STATE</th><th>LEGISLATORS</th><th>% of USA</th></tr>
<tr><td>27</td><td>Alabama</td><td>140</td><td>1.9%</td><td>1</td><td>New Hampshire</td><td>424</td><td>5.7%</td></tr>
<tr><td>49</td><td>Alaska</td><td>60</td><td>0.8%</td><td>2</td><td>Pennsylvania</td><td>253</td><td>3.4%</td></tr>
<tr><td>43</td><td>Arizona</td><td>90</td><td>1.2%</td><td>3</td><td>Georgia</td><td>236</td><td>3.2%</td></tr>
<tr><td>30</td><td>Arkansas</td><td>135</td><td>1.8%</td><td>4</td><td>New York</td><td>213</td><td>2.9%</td></tr>
<tr><td>35</td><td>California</td><td>120</td><td>1.6%</td><td>5</td><td>Minnesota</td><td>201</td><td>2.7%</td></tr>
<tr><td>42</td><td>Colorado</td><td>100</td><td>1.4%</td><td>6</td><td>Massachusetts</td><td>200</td><td>2.7%</td></tr>
<tr><td>9</td><td>Connecticut</td><td>187</td><td>2.5%</td><td>7</td><td>Missouri</td><td>197</td><td>2.7%</td></tr>
<tr><td>48</td><td>Delaware</td><td>62</td><td>0.8%</td><td>8</td><td>Maryland</td><td>188</td><td>2.5%</td></tr>
<tr><td>18</td><td>Florida</td><td>160</td><td>2.2%</td><td>9</td><td>Connecticut</td><td>187</td><td>2.5%</td></tr>
<tr><td>3</td><td>Georgia</td><td>236</td><td>3.2%</td><td>10</td><td>Maine</td><td>186</td><td>2.5%</td></tr>
<tr><td>46</td><td>Hawaii</td><td>76</td><td>1.0%</td><td>11</td><td>Texas</td><td>181</td><td>2.5%</td></tr>
<tr><td>39</td><td>Idaho</td><td>105</td><td>1.4%</td><td>12</td><td>Vermont</td><td>180</td><td>2.4%</td></tr>
<tr><td>13</td><td>Illinois</td><td>177</td><td>2.4%</td><td>13</td><td>Illinois</td><td>177</td><td>2.4%</td></tr>
<tr><td>19</td><td>Indiana</td><td>150</td><td>2.0%</td><td>14</td><td>Mississippi</td><td>174</td><td>2.4%</td></tr>
<tr><td>19</td><td>Iowa</td><td>150</td><td>2.0%</td><td>15</td><td>North Carolina</td><td>170</td><td>2.3%</td></tr>
<tr><td>17</td><td>Kansas</td><td>165</td><td>2.2%</td><td>15</td><td>South Carolina</td><td>170</td><td>2.3%</td></tr>
<tr><td>29</td><td>Kentucky</td><td>138</td><td>1.9%</td><td>17</td><td>Kansas</td><td>165</td><td>2.2%</td></tr>
<tr><td>25</td><td>Louisiana</td><td>144</td><td>2.0%</td><td>18</td><td>Florida</td><td>160</td><td>2.2%</td></tr>
<tr><td>10</td><td>Maine</td><td>186</td><td>2.5%</td><td>19</td><td>Indiana</td><td>150</td><td>2.0%</td></tr>
<tr><td>8</td><td>Maryland</td><td>188</td><td>2.5%</td><td>19</td><td>Iowa</td><td>150</td><td>2.0%</td></tr>
<tr><td>6</td><td>Massachusetts</td><td>200</td><td>2.7%</td><td>19</td><td>Montana</td><td>150</td><td>2.0%</td></tr>
<tr><td>23</td><td>Michigan</td><td>148</td><td>2.0%</td><td>22</td><td>Oklahoma</td><td>149</td><td>2.0%</td></tr>
<tr><td>5</td><td>Minnesota</td><td>201</td><td>2.7%</td><td>23</td><td>Michigan</td><td>148</td><td>2.0%</td></tr>
<tr><td>14</td><td>Mississippi</td><td>174</td><td>2.4%</td><td>24</td><td>Washington</td><td>147</td><td>2.0%</td></tr>
<tr><td>7</td><td>Missouri</td><td>197</td><td>2.7%</td><td>25</td><td>Louisiana</td><td>144</td><td>2.0%</td></tr>
<tr><td>19</td><td>Montana</td><td>150</td><td>2.0%</td><td>26</td><td>North Dakota</td><td>141</td><td>1.9%</td></tr>
<tr><td>50</td><td>Nebraska</td><td>49</td><td>0.7%</td><td>27</td><td>Alabama</td><td>140</td><td>1.9%</td></tr>
<tr><td>47</td><td>Nevada</td><td>63</td><td>0.9%</td><td>27</td><td>Virginia</td><td>140</td><td>1.9%</td></tr>
<tr><td>1</td><td>New Hampshire</td><td>424</td><td>5.7%</td><td>29</td><td>Kentucky</td><td>138</td><td>1.9%</td></tr>
<tr><td>35</td><td>New Jersey</td><td>120</td><td>1.6%</td><td>30</td><td>Arkansas</td><td>135</td><td>1.8%</td></tr>
<tr><td>38</td><td>New Mexico</td><td>112</td><td>1.5%</td><td>31</td><td>West Virginia</td><td>134</td><td>1.8%</td></tr>
<tr><td>4</td><td>New York</td><td>213</td><td>2.9%</td><td>32</td><td>Ohio</td><td>132</td><td>1.8%</td></tr>
<tr><td>15</td><td>North Carolina</td><td>170</td><td>2.3%</td><td>32</td><td>Tennessee</td><td>132</td><td>1.8%</td></tr>
<tr><td>26</td><td>North Dakota</td><td>141</td><td>1.9%</td><td>32</td><td>Wisconsin</td><td>132</td><td>1.8%</td></tr>
<tr><td>32</td><td>Ohio</td><td>132</td><td>1.8%</td><td>35</td><td>California</td><td>120</td><td>1.6%</td></tr>
<tr><td>22</td><td>Oklahoma</td><td>149</td><td>2.0%</td><td>35</td><td>New Jersey</td><td>120</td><td>1.6%</td></tr>
<tr><td>43</td><td>Oregon</td><td>90</td><td>1.2%</td><td>37</td><td>Rhode Island</td><td>113</td><td>1.5%</td></tr>
<tr><td>2</td><td>Pennsylvania</td><td>253</td><td>3.4%</td><td>38</td><td>New Mexico</td><td>112</td><td>1.5%</td></tr>
<tr><td>37</td><td>Rhode Island</td><td>113</td><td>1.5%</td><td>39</td><td>Idaho</td><td>105</td><td>1.4%</td></tr>
<tr><td>15</td><td>South Carolina</td><td>170</td><td>2.3%</td><td>39</td><td>South Dakota</td><td>105</td><td>1.4%</td></tr>
<tr><td>39</td><td>South Dakota</td><td>105</td><td>1.4%</td><td>41</td><td>Utah</td><td>104</td><td>1.4%</td></tr>
<tr><td>32</td><td>Tennessee</td><td>132</td><td>1.8%</td><td>42</td><td>Colorado</td><td>100</td><td>1.4%</td></tr>
<tr><td>11</td><td>Texas</td><td>181</td><td>2.5%</td><td>43</td><td>Arizona</td><td>90</td><td>1.2%</td></tr>
<tr><td>41</td><td>Utah</td><td>104</td><td>1.4%</td><td>43</td><td>Oregon</td><td>90</td><td>1.2%</td></tr>
<tr><td>12</td><td>Vermont</td><td>180</td><td>2.4%</td><td>43</td><td>Wyoming</td><td>90</td><td>1.2%</td></tr>
<tr><td>27</td><td>Virginia</td><td>140</td><td>1.9%</td><td>46</td><td>Hawaii</td><td>76</td><td>1.0%</td></tr>
<tr><td>24</td><td>Washington</td><td>147</td><td>2.0%</td><td>47</td><td>Nevada</td><td>63</td><td>0.9%</td></tr>
<tr><td>31</td><td>West Virginia</td><td>134</td><td>1.8%</td><td>48</td><td>Delaware</td><td>62</td><td>0.8%</td></tr>
<tr><td>32</td><td>Wisconsin</td><td>132</td><td>1.8%</td><td>49</td><td>Alaska</td><td>60</td><td>0.8%</td></tr>
<tr><td>43</td><td>Wyoming</td><td>90</td><td>1.2%</td><td>50</td><td>Nebraska</td><td>49</td><td>0.7%</td></tr>
<tr><td></td><td></td><td></td><td></td><td colspan="2">District of Columbia**</td><td>NA</td><td>NA</td></tr>
</table>

Source: National Conference of State Legislatures (Denver, CO)

"2018 Partisan Composition" (www.ncsl.org/research/about-state-legislatures/partisan-composition.aspx)

*There are 1,972 state senators (including Nebraska's 49 unicameral seats) and 5,411 state house members.

**Not applicable.

Population per State Legislator in 2018

National Rate = 44,218 Population per Legislator*

ALPHA ORDER			RANK ORDER		
RANK	STATE	RATE	RANK	STATE	RATE
22	Alabama	34,913	1	California	329,642
42	Alaska	12,291	2	Texas	158,574
6	Arizona	79,685	3	Florida	133,121
32	Arkansas	22,325	4	New York	91,747
1	California	329,642	5	Ohio	88,556
12	Colorado	56,956	6	Arizona	79,685
34	Connecticut	19,105	7	New Jersey	74,238
40	Delaware	15,600	8	Illinois	71,984
3	Florida	133,121	9	Michigan	67,540
19	Georgia	44,574	10	North Carolina	61,080
36	Hawaii	18,691	11	Virginia	60,841
39	Idaho	16,707	12	Colorado	56,956
8	Illinois	71,984	13	Tennessee	51,288
18	Indiana	44,613	14	Washington	51,263
33	Iowa	21,041	15	Pennsylvania	50,621
37	Kansas	17,645	16	Nevada	48,165
24	Kentucky	32,380	17	Oregon	46,563
25	Louisiana	32,361	18	Indiana	44,613
45	Maine	7,196	19	Georgia	44,574
26	Maryland	32,142	20	Wisconsin	44,042
23	Massachusetts	34,511	21	Nebraska	39,373
9	Michigan	67,540	22	Alabama	34,913
30	Minnesota	27,916	23	Massachusetts	34,511
38	Mississippi	17,164	24	Kentucky	32,380
27	Missouri	31,099	25	Louisiana	32,361
46	Montana	7,082	26	Maryland	32,142
21	Nebraska	39,373	27	Missouri	31,099
16	Nevada	48,165	28	Utah	30,395
50	New Hampshire	3,199	29	South Carolina	29,907
7	New Jersey	74,238	30	Minnesota	27,916
35	New Mexico	18,709	31	Oklahoma	26,464
4	New York	91,747	32	Arkansas	22,325
10	North Carolina	61,080	33	Iowa	21,041
48	North Dakota	5,391	34	Connecticut	19,105
5	Ohio	88,556	35	New Mexico	18,709
31	Oklahoma	26,464	36	Hawaii	18,691
17	Oregon	46,563	37	Kansas	17,645
15	Pennsylvania	50,621	38	Mississippi	17,164
43	Rhode Island	9,357	39	Idaho	16,707
29	South Carolina	29,907	40	Delaware	15,600
44	South Dakota	8,402	41	West Virginia	13,476
13	Tennessee	51,288	42	Alaska	12,291
2	Texas	158,574	43	Rhode Island	9,357
28	Utah	30,395	44	South Dakota	8,402
49	Vermont	3,479	45	Maine	7,196
11	Virginia	60,841	46	Montana	7,082
14	Washington	51,263	47	Wyoming	6,419
41	West Virginia	13,476	48	North Dakota	5,391
20	Wisconsin	44,042	49	Vermont	3,479
47	Wyoming	6,419	50	New Hampshire	3,199
				District of Columbia**	NA

Source: CQ Press using data from National Conference of State Legislatures (Denver, CO)

"2018 Partisan Composition" (www.ncsl.org/research/about-state-legislatures/partisan-composition.aspx)

*There are 1,972 state senators (including Nebraska's 49 unicameral seats) and 5,411 state house members. National rate does not include population for the District of Columbia. Calculated using 2018 population estimates.

**Not applicable.

Registered Voters in 2016

National Total = 157,596,000

ALPHA ORDER					RANK ORDER			
RANK	STATE	REGISTERED	% of USA		RANK	STATE	REGISTERED	% of USA
24	Alabama	2,526,000	1.6%		1	California	16,096,000	10.2%
48	Alaska	358,000	0.2%		2	Texas	11,724,000	7.4%
19	Arizona	3,145,000	2.0%		3	Florida	9,604,000	6.1%
32	Arkansas	1,456,000	0.9%		4	New York	9,142,000	5.8%
1	California	16,096,000	10.2%		5	Pennsylvania	6,909,000	4.4%
22	Colorado	2,893,000	1.8%		6	Illinois	6,665,000	4.2%
29	Connecticut	1,763,000	1.1%		7	Ohio	6,128,000	3.9%
45	Delaware	487,000	0.3%		8	Michigan	5,434,000	3.4%
3	Florida	9,604,000	6.1%		9	North Carolina	5,194,000	3.3%
10	Georgia	4,892,000	3.1%		10	Georgia	4,892,000	3.1%
44	Hawaii	530,000	0.3%		11	Virginia	4,399,000	2.8%
40	Idaho	790,000	0.5%		12	New Jersey	4,165,000	2.6%
6	Illinois	6,665,000	4.2%		13	Washington	3,906,000	2.5%
17	Indiana	3,298,000	2.1%		14	Massachusetts	3,660,000	2.3%
31	Iowa	1,657,000	1.1%		15	Missouri	3,333,000	2.1%
33	Kansas	1,438,000	0.9%		16	Wisconsin	3,323,000	2.1%
26	Kentucky	2,253,000	1.4%		17	Indiana	3,298,000	2.1%
25	Louisiana	2,446,000	1.6%		18	Tennessee	3,251,000	2.1%
39	Maine	830,000	0.5%		19	Arizona	3,145,000	2.0%
20	Maryland	3,114,000	2.0%		20	Maryland	3,114,000	2.0%
14	Massachusetts	3,660,000	2.3%		21	Minnesota	3,055,000	1.9%
8	Michigan	5,434,000	3.4%		22	Colorado	2,893,000	1.8%
21	Minnesota	3,055,000	1.9%		23	South Carolina	2,575,000	1.6%
30	Mississippi	1,725,000	1.1%		24	Alabama	2,526,000	1.6%
15	Missouri	3,333,000	2.1%		25	Louisiana	2,446,000	1.6%
42	Montana	581,000	0.4%		26	Kentucky	2,253,000	1.4%
36	Nebraska	1,008,000	0.6%		27	Oregon	2,147,000	1.4%
35	Nevada	1,371,000	0.9%		28	Oklahoma	1,861,000	1.2%
41	New Hampshire	763,000	0.5%		29	Connecticut	1,763,000	1.1%
12	New Jersey	4,165,000	2.6%		30	Mississippi	1,725,000	1.1%
37	New Mexico	916,000	0.6%		31	Iowa	1,657,000	1.1%
4	New York	9,142,000	5.8%		32	Arkansas	1,456,000	0.9%
9	North Carolina	5,194,000	3.3%		33	Kansas	1,438,000	0.9%
47	North Dakota	424,000	0.3%		34	Utah	1,398,000	0.9%
7	Ohio	6,128,000	3.9%		35	Nevada	1,371,000	0.9%
28	Oklahoma	1,861,000	1.2%		36	Nebraska	1,008,000	0.6%
27	Oregon	2,147,000	1.4%		37	New Mexico	916,000	0.6%
5	Pennsylvania	6,909,000	4.4%		38	West Virginia	913,000	0.6%
43	Rhode Island	538,000	0.3%		39	Maine	830,000	0.5%
23	South Carolina	2,575,000	1.6%		40	Idaho	790,000	0.5%
46	South Dakota	437,000	0.3%		41	New Hampshire	763,000	0.5%
18	Tennessee	3,251,000	2.1%		42	Montana	581,000	0.4%
2	Texas	11,724,000	7.4%		43	Rhode Island	538,000	0.3%
34	Utah	1,398,000	0.9%		44	Hawaii	530,000	0.3%
49	Vermont	351,000	0.2%		45	Delaware	487,000	0.3%
11	Virginia	4,399,000	2.8%		46	South Dakota	437,000	0.3%
13	Washington	3,906,000	2.5%		47	North Dakota	424,000	0.3%
38	West Virginia	913,000	0.6%		48	Alaska	358,000	0.2%
16	Wisconsin	3,323,000	2.1%		49	Vermont	351,000	0.2%
50	Wyoming	304,000	0.2%		50	Wyoming	304,000	0.2%
						District of Columbia	420,000	0.3%

Source: U.S. Bureau of the Census
"Voting and Registration" (Table 4a, http://www.census.gov/topics/public-sector/voting.html)

Percent of Eligible Voters Reported Registered in 2016

National Percent = 70.3%*

ALPHA ORDER

RANK	STATE	PERCENT
37	Alabama	69.2
27	Alaska	71.3
41	Arizona	68.6
38	Arkansas	68.8
48	California	64.7
12	Colorado	74.3
29	Connecticut	71.0
20	Delaware	72.8
45	Florida	66.6
34	Georgia	69.4
50	Hawaii	54.4
40	Idaho	68.7
12	Illinois	74.3
38	Indiana	68.8
21	Iowa	72.3
31	Kansas	70.9
34	Kentucky	69.4
19	Louisiana	73.0
1	Maine	80.0
10	Maryland	74.9
16	Massachusetts	73.7
15	Michigan	74.1
3	Minnesota	76.7
2	Mississippi	79.5
12	Missouri	74.3
17	Montana	73.5
6	Nebraska	75.5
34	Nevada	69.4
8	New Hampshire	75.4
33	New Jersey	69.9
47	New Mexico	65.6
46	New York	66.5
11	North Carolina	74.6
9	North Dakota	75.2
22	Ohio	72.1
42	Oklahoma	67.8
18	Oregon	73.3
23	Pennsylvania	72.0
32	Rhode Island	70.3
25	South Carolina	71.6
26	South Dakota	71.4
44	Tennessee	66.7
43	Texas	67.5
29	Utah	71.0
24	Vermont	71.9
6	Virginia	75.5
4	Washington	76.5
49	West Virginia	64.1
5	Wisconsin	76.3
28	Wyoming	71.1

RANK ORDER

RANK	STATE	PERCENT
1	Maine	80.0
2	Mississippi	79.5
3	Minnesota	76.7
4	Washington	76.5
5	Wisconsin	76.3
6	Nebraska	75.5
6	Virginia	75.5
8	New Hampshire	75.4
9	North Dakota	75.2
10	Maryland	74.9
11	North Carolina	74.6
12	Colorado	74.3
12	Illinois	74.3
12	Missouri	74.3
15	Michigan	74.1
16	Massachusetts	73.7
17	Montana	73.5
18	Oregon	73.3
19	Louisiana	73.0
20	Delaware	72.8
21	Iowa	72.3
22	Ohio	72.1
23	Pennsylvania	72.0
24	Vermont	71.9
25	South Carolina	71.6
26	South Dakota	71.4
27	Alaska	71.3
28	Wyoming	71.1
29	Connecticut	71.0
29	Utah	71.0
31	Kansas	70.9
32	Rhode Island	70.3
33	New Jersey	69.9
34	Georgia	69.4
34	Kentucky	69.4
34	Nevada	69.4
37	Alabama	69.2
38	Arkansas	68.8
38	Indiana	68.8
40	Idaho	68.7
41	Arizona	68.6
42	Oklahoma	67.8
43	Texas	67.5
44	Tennessee	66.7
45	Florida	66.6
46	New York	66.5
47	New Mexico	65.6
48	California	64.7
49	West Virginia	64.1
50	Hawaii	54.4
	District of Columbia	82.1

Source: U.S. Bureau of the Census
   "Voting and Registration" (Table 4a, http://www.census.gov/topics/public-sector/voting.html)
*As a percent of citizen population 18 and older.

Persons Voting in 2016

National Total = 137,537,000

ALPHA ORDER

RANK	STATE	VOTERS	% of USA
24	Alabama	2,095,000	1.5%
48	Alaska	308,000	0.2%
18	Arizona	2,769,000	2.0%
33	Arkansas	1,241,000	0.9%
1	California	14,416,000	10.5%
21	Colorado	2,707,000	2.0%
28	Connecticut	1,586,000	1.2%
45	Delaware	417,000	0.3%
3	Florida	8,578,000	6.2%
10	Georgia	4,246,000	3.1%
44	Hawaii	460,000	0.3%
40	Idaho	714,000	0.5%
6	Illinois	5,719,000	4.2%
17	Indiana	2,795,000	2.0%
31	Iowa	1,454,000	1.1%
32	Kansas	1,243,000	0.9%
27	Kentucky	1,850,000	1.3%
25	Louisiana	2,067,000	1.5%
38	Maine	754,000	0.5%
20	Maryland	2,737,000	2.0%
14	Massachusetts	3,315,000	2.4%
8	Michigan	4,713,000	3.4%
19	Minnesota	2,738,000	2.0%
30	Mississippi	1,470,000	1.1%
16	Missouri	2,906,000	2.1%
42	Montana	521,000	0.4%
36	Nebraska	893,000	0.6%
35	Nevada	1,195,000	0.9%
41	New Hampshire	698,000	0.5%
12	New Jersey	3,665,000	2.7%
37	New Mexico	765,000	0.6%
4	New York	7,869,000	5.7%
9	North Carolina	4,700,000	3.4%
46	North Dakota	362,000	0.3%
7	Ohio	5,408,000	3.9%
29	Oklahoma	1,555,000	1.1%
26	Oregon	1,942,000	1.4%
5	Pennsylvania	6,008,000	4.4%
43	Rhode Island	464,000	0.3%
23	South Carolina	2,233,000	1.6%
46	South Dakota	362,000	0.3%
22	Tennessee	2,630,000	1.9%
2	Texas	9,626,000	7.0%
34	Utah	1,234,000	0.9%
49	Vermont	305,000	0.2%
11	Virginia	3,973,000	2.9%
13	Washington	3,382,000	2.5%
39	West Virginia	723,000	0.5%
15	Wisconsin	3,068,000	2.2%
50	Wyoming	277,000	0.2%

RANK ORDER

RANK	STATE	VOTERS	% of USA
1	California	14,416,000	10.5%
2	Texas	9,626,000	7.0%
3	Florida	8,578,000	6.2%
4	New York	7,869,000	5.7%
5	Pennsylvania	6,008,000	4.4%
6	Illinois	5,719,000	4.2%
7	Ohio	5,408,000	3.9%
8	Michigan	4,713,000	3.4%
9	North Carolina	4,700,000	3.4%
10	Georgia	4,246,000	3.1%
11	Virginia	3,973,000	2.9%
12	New Jersey	3,665,000	2.7%
13	Washington	3,382,000	2.5%
14	Massachusetts	3,315,000	2.4%
15	Wisconsin	3,068,000	2.2%
16	Missouri	2,906,000	2.1%
17	Indiana	2,795,000	2.0%
18	Arizona	2,769,000	2.0%
19	Minnesota	2,738,000	2.0%
20	Maryland	2,737,000	2.0%
21	Colorado	2,707,000	2.0%
22	Tennessee	2,630,000	1.9%
23	South Carolina	2,233,000	1.6%
24	Alabama	2,095,000	1.5%
25	Louisiana	2,067,000	1.5%
26	Oregon	1,942,000	1.4%
27	Kentucky	1,850,000	1.3%
28	Connecticut	1,586,000	1.2%
29	Oklahoma	1,555,000	1.1%
30	Mississippi	1,470,000	1.1%
31	Iowa	1,454,000	1.1%
32	Kansas	1,243,000	0.9%
33	Arkansas	1,241,000	0.9%
34	Utah	1,234,000	0.9%
35	Nevada	1,195,000	0.9%
36	Nebraska	893,000	0.6%
37	New Mexico	765,000	0.6%
38	Maine	754,000	0.5%
39	West Virginia	723,000	0.5%
40	Idaho	714,000	0.5%
41	New Hampshire	698,000	0.5%
42	Montana	521,000	0.4%
43	Rhode Island	464,000	0.3%
44	Hawaii	460,000	0.3%
45	Delaware	417,000	0.3%
46	North Dakota	362,000	0.3%
46	South Dakota	362,000	0.3%
48	Alaska	308,000	0.2%
49	Vermont	305,000	0.2%
50	Wyoming	277,000	0.2%
	District of Columbia	380,000	0.3%

Source: U.S. Bureau of the Census
"Voting and Registration" (Table 4a, http://www.census.gov/topics/public-sector/voting.html)

Percent of Eligible Population Reported Voting in 2016

National Percent = 61.4%*

ALPHA ORDER			RANK ORDER		
RANK	STATE	PERCENT	RANK	STATE	PERCENT
42	Alabama	57.4	1	Maine	72.7
31	Alaska	61.3	2	Wisconsin	70.5
35	Arizona	60.4	3	Colorado	69.5
39	Arkansas	58.7	4	New Hampshire	69.0
41	California	57.9	5	Minnesota	68.7
3	Colorado	69.5	6	Virginia	68.2
19	Connecticut	63.9	7	Mississippi	67.7
26	Delaware	62.3	8	North Carolina	67.5
37	Florida	59.5	9	Nebraska	66.8
36	Georgia	60.2	10	Massachusetts	66.7
50	Hawaii	47.3	11	Oregon	66.3
27	Idaho	62.1	11	Washington	66.3
20	Illinois	63.8	13	Montana	65.9
40	Indiana	58.3	14	Maryland	65.8
22	Iowa	63.4	15	Missouri	64.8
31	Kansas	61.3	15	Wyoming	64.8
44	Kentucky	57.0	17	Michigan	64.3
29	Louisiana	61.6	18	North Dakota	64.2
1	Maine	72.7	19	Connecticut	63.9
14	Maryland	65.8	20	Illinois	63.8
10	Massachusetts	66.7	21	Ohio	63.6
17	Michigan	64.3	22	Iowa	63.4
5	Minnesota	68.7	23	Utah	62.7
7	Mississippi	67.7	24	Pennsylvania	62.6
15	Missouri	64.8	25	Vermont	62.5
13	Montana	65.9	26	Delaware	62.3
9	Nebraska	66.8	27	Idaho	62.1
34	Nevada	60.5	27	South Carolina	62.1
4	New Hampshire	69.0	29	Louisiana	61.6
30	New Jersey	61.5	30	New Jersey	61.5
47	New Mexico	54.8	31	Alaska	61.3
43	New York	57.2	31	Kansas	61.3
8	North Carolina	67.5	33	Rhode Island	60.6
18	North Dakota	64.2	34	Nevada	60.5
21	Ohio	63.6	35	Arizona	60.4
45	Oklahoma	56.6	36	Georgia	60.2
11	Oregon	66.3	37	Florida	59.5
24	Pennsylvania	62.6	38	South Dakota	59.1
33	Rhode Island	60.6	39	Arkansas	58.7
27	South Carolina	62.1	40	Indiana	58.3
38	South Dakota	59.1	41	California	57.9
48	Tennessee	54.0	42	Alabama	57.4
46	Texas	55.4	43	New York	57.2
23	Utah	62.7	44	Kentucky	57.0
25	Vermont	62.5	45	Oklahoma	56.6
6	Virginia	68.2	46	Texas	55.4
11	Washington	66.3	47	New Mexico	54.8
49	West Virginia	50.8	48	Tennessee	54.0
2	Wisconsin	70.5	49	West Virginia	50.8
15	Wyoming	64.8	50	Hawaii	47.3
				District of Columbia	74.3

Source: U.S. Bureau of the Census
  "Voting and Registration" (Table 4a, http://www.census.gov/topics/public-sector/voting.html)
*As a percent of citizen population 18 and older.

Percent of Registered Population Reported Voting in 2016

National Percent = 87.3%*

ALPHA ORDER				RANK ORDER		
RANK	STATE	PERCENT		RANK	STATE	PERCENT
45	Alabama	82.9		1	Colorado	93.6
35	Alaska	86.0		2	Wisconsin	92.3
19	Arizona	88.0		3	New Hampshire	91.5
39	Arkansas	85.2		4	Wyoming	91.1
13	California	89.6		5	Maine	90.8
1	Colorado	93.6		6	Massachusetts	90.6
11	Connecticut	90.0		7	North Carolina	90.5
37	Delaware	85.6		7	Oregon	90.5
15	Florida	89.3		9	Idaho	90.4
27	Georgia	86.8		10	Virginia	90.3
27	Hawaii	86.8		11	Connecticut	90.0
9	Idaho	90.4		12	Montana	89.7
36	Illinois	85.8		13	California	89.6
41	Indiana	84.7		13	Minnesota	89.6
22	Iowa	87.7		15	Florida	89.3
32	Kansas	86.4		16	Nebraska	88.6
47	Kentucky	82.1		17	Ohio	88.3
42	Louisiana	84.5		17	Utah	88.3
5	Maine	90.8		19	Arizona	88.0
21	Maryland	87.9		19	New Jersey	88.0
6	Massachusetts	90.6		21	Maryland	87.9
29	Michigan	86.7		22	Iowa	87.7
13	Minnesota	89.6		23	Missouri	87.2
39	Mississippi	85.2		23	Nevada	87.2
23	Missouri	87.2		25	Pennsylvania	87.0
12	Montana	89.7		26	Vermont	86.9
16	Nebraska	88.6		27	Georgia	86.8
23	Nevada	87.2		27	Hawaii	86.8
3	New Hampshire	91.5		29	Michigan	86.7
19	New Jersey	88.0		29	South Carolina	86.7
44	New Mexico	83.5		31	Washington	86.6
34	New York	86.1		32	Kansas	86.4
7	North Carolina	90.5		33	Rhode Island	86.2
38	North Dakota	85.4		34	New York	86.1
17	Ohio	88.3		35	Alaska	86.0
43	Oklahoma	83.6		36	Illinois	85.8
7	Oregon	90.5		37	Delaware	85.6
25	Pennsylvania	87.0		38	North Dakota	85.4
33	Rhode Island	86.2		39	Arkansas	85.2
29	South Carolina	86.7		39	Mississippi	85.2
46	South Dakota	82.8		41	Indiana	84.7
49	Tennessee	80.9		42	Louisiana	84.5
47	Texas	82.1		43	Oklahoma	83.6
17	Utah	88.3		44	New Mexico	83.5
26	Vermont	86.9		45	Alabama	82.9
10	Virginia	90.3		46	South Dakota	82.8
31	Washington	86.6		47	Kentucky	82.1
50	West Virginia	79.2		47	Texas	82.1
2	Wisconsin	92.3		49	Tennessee	80.9
4	Wyoming	91.1		50	West Virginia	79.2
					District of Columbia	90.5

Source: CQ Press using data from U.S. Bureau of the Census
  "Voting and Registration" (Table 4a, http://www.census.gov/topics/public-sector/voting.html)
*As a percent of citizen population 18 and older registered to vote.

XIV. Social Welfare

Poverty Rate in 2017

National Rate = 13.4% of Population in Poverty*

ALPHA ORDER				RANK ORDER		
RANK	STATE	PERCENT		RANK	STATE	PERCENT
6	Alabama	16.9		1	Mississippi	19.8
35	Alaska	11.1		2	Louisiana	19.7
11	Arizona	14.9		2	New Mexico	19.7
7	Arkansas	16.4		4	West Virginia	19.1
22	California	13.3		5	Kentucky	17.2
42	Colorado	10.3		6	Alabama	16.9
46	Connecticut	9.6		7	Arkansas	16.4
19	Delaware	13.6		8	Oklahoma	15.8
17	Florida	14.0		9	South Carolina	15.4
11	Georgia	14.9		10	Tennessee	15.0
47	Hawaii	9.5		11	Arizona	14.9
26	Idaho	12.8		11	Georgia	14.9
27	Illinois	12.6		13	North Carolina	14.7
20	Indiana	13.5		13	Texas	14.7
39	Iowa	10.7		15	Michigan	14.2
30	Kansas	11.9		16	New York	14.1
5	Kentucky	17.2		17	Florida	14.0
2	Louisiana	19.7		17	Ohio	14.0
35	Maine	11.1		19	Delaware	13.6
49	Maryland	9.3		20	Indiana	13.5
41	Massachusetts	10.5		21	Missouri	13.4
15	Michigan	14.2		22	California	13.3
47	Minnesota	9.5		23	Oregon	13.2
1	Mississippi	19.8		24	Nevada	13.0
21	Missouri	13.4		24	South Dakota	13.0
28	Montana	12.5		26	Idaho	12.8
38	Nebraska	10.8		27	Illinois	12.6
24	Nevada	13.0		28	Montana	12.5
50	New Hampshire	7.7		28	Pennsylvania	12.5
44	New Jersey	10.0		30	Kansas	11.9
2	New Mexico	19.7		31	Rhode Island	11.6
16	New York	14.1		32	Vermont	11.3
13	North Carolina	14.7		32	Wisconsin	11.3
42	North Dakota	10.3		32	Wyoming	11.3
17	Ohio	14.0		35	Alaska	11.1
8	Oklahoma	15.8		35	Maine	11.1
23	Oregon	13.2		37	Washington	11.0
28	Pennsylvania	12.5		38	Nebraska	10.8
31	Rhode Island	11.6		39	Iowa	10.7
9	South Carolina	15.4		40	Virginia	10.6
24	South Dakota	13.0		41	Massachusetts	10.5
10	Tennessee	15.0		42	Colorado	10.3
13	Texas	14.7		42	North Dakota	10.3
45	Utah	9.7		44	New Jersey	10.0
32	Vermont	11.3		45	Utah	9.7
40	Virginia	10.6		46	Connecticut	9.6
37	Washington	11.0		47	Hawaii	9.5
4	West Virginia	19.1		47	Minnesota	9.5
32	Wisconsin	11.3		49	Maryland	9.3
32	Wyoming	11.3		50	New Hampshire	7.7
					District of Columbia	16.6

Source: U.S. Bureau of the Census
"2017 American Community Survey-Table DP03" (https://www.census.gov/programs-surveys/acs/)
*This is a one-year figure. Census has discontinued three-year averages that had been used previously. The poverty threshold for a family of four (two children) in 2017 was $24,858.

Percent of Senior Citizens Living in Poverty in 2017

National Percent = 9.3%*

ALPHA ORDER

RANK	STATE	PERCENT
12	Alabama	9.9
40	Alaska	7.4
19	Arizona	9.0
7	Arkansas	10.2
7	California	10.2
36	Colorado	7.8
44	Connecticut	7.1
25	Delaware	8.5
7	Florida	10.2
11	Georgia	10.1
14	Hawaii	9.3
31	Idaho	8.1
24	Illinois	8.6
38	Indiana	7.7
48	Iowa	6.6
41	Kansas	7.3
6	Kentucky	10.3
3	Louisiana	12.0
31	Maine	8.1
35	Maryland	7.9
19	Massachusetts	9.0
25	Michigan	8.5
47	Minnesota	7.0
1	Mississippi	13.7
22	Missouri	8.7
42	Montana	7.2
42	Nebraska	7.2
25	Nevada	8.5
50	New Hampshire	5.8
29	New Jersey	8.4
2	New Mexico	12.2
4	New York	11.4
17	North Carolina	9.1
12	North Dakota	9.9
38	Ohio	7.7
17	Oklahoma	9.1
22	Oregon	8.7
25	Pennsylvania	8.5
19	Rhode Island	9.0
15	South Carolina	9.2
33	South Dakota	8.0
15	Tennessee	9.2
5	Texas	10.8
49	Utah	6.4
44	Vermont	7.1
44	Virginia	7.1
33	Washington	8.0
7	West Virginia	10.2
36	Wisconsin	7.8
29	Wyoming	8.4

RANK ORDER

RANK	STATE	PERCENT
1	Mississippi	13.7
2	New Mexico	12.2
3	Louisiana	12.0
4	New York	11.4
5	Texas	10.8
6	Kentucky	10.3
7	Arkansas	10.2
7	California	10.2
7	Florida	10.2
7	West Virginia	10.2
11	Georgia	10.1
12	Alabama	9.9
12	North Dakota	9.9
14	Hawaii	9.3
15	South Carolina	9.2
15	Tennessee	9.2
17	North Carolina	9.1
17	Oklahoma	9.1
19	Arizona	9.0
19	Massachusetts	9.0
19	Rhode Island	9.0
22	Missouri	8.7
22	Oregon	8.7
24	Illinois	8.6
25	Delaware	8.5
25	Michigan	8.5
25	Nevada	8.5
25	Pennsylvania	8.5
29	New Jersey	8.4
29	Wyoming	8.4
31	Idaho	8.1
31	Maine	8.1
33	South Dakota	8.0
33	Washington	8.0
35	Maryland	7.9
36	Colorado	7.8
36	Wisconsin	7.8
38	Indiana	7.7
38	Ohio	7.7
40	Alaska	7.4
41	Kansas	7.3
42	Montana	7.2
42	Nebraska	7.2
44	Connecticut	7.1
44	Vermont	7.1
44	Virginia	7.1
47	Minnesota	7.0
48	Iowa	6.6
49	Utah	6.4
50	New Hampshire	5.8
	District of Columbia	14.2

Source: U.S. Bureau of the Census
    "2017 American Community Survey-Table DP03" (https://www.census.gov/programs-surveys/acs/)
*People 65 years and older living with incomes below the poverty level.

Percent of Children Living in Poverty in 2017

National Percent = 18.4%*

ALPHA ORDER				RANK ORDER		
RANK	STATE	PERCENT		RANK	STATE	PERCENT
5	Alabama	24.6		1	Louisiana	28.0
30	Alaska	14.9		2	New Mexico	27.2
14	Arizona	20.8		3	Mississippi	26.9
7	Arkansas	22.5		4	West Virginia	25.9
23	California	18.1		5	Alabama	24.6
44	Colorado	12.0		6	South Carolina	22.6
42	Connecticut	12.6		7	Arkansas	22.5
20	Delaware	18.5		8	Kentucky	22.4
15	Florida	20.3		9	Oklahoma	21.5
12	Georgia	21.0		10	North Carolina	21.2
47	Hawaii	11.5		10	Tennessee	21.2
29	Idaho	15.3		12	Georgia	21.0
24	Illinois	17.0		13	Texas	20.9
22	Indiana	18.4		14	Arizona	20.8
43	Iowa	12.3		15	Florida	20.3
31	Kansas	14.8		16	Ohio	20.1
8	Kentucky	22.4		17	Michigan	19.7
1	Louisiana	28.0		17	New York	19.7
41	Maine	13.1		19	Missouri	18.6
44	Maryland	12.0		20	Delaware	18.5
39	Massachusetts	13.5		20	Nevada	18.5
17	Michigan	19.7		22	Indiana	18.4
46	Minnesota	11.8		23	California	18.1
3	Mississippi	26.9		24	Illinois	17.0
19	Missouri	18.6		24	Pennsylvania	17.0
32	Montana	14.7		26	Rhode Island	16.6
35	Nebraska	14.1		26	South Dakota	16.6
20	Nevada	18.5		28	Oregon	16.5
50	New Hampshire	10.3		29	Idaho	15.3
37	New Jersey	13.9		30	Alaska	14.9
2	New Mexico	27.2		31	Kansas	14.8
17	New York	19.7		32	Montana	14.7
10	North Carolina	21.2		33	Wisconsin	14.5
48	North Dakota	10.9		34	Washington	14.3
16	Ohio	20.1		35	Nebraska	14.1
9	Oklahoma	21.5		36	Virginia	14.0
28	Oregon	16.5		37	New Jersey	13.9
24	Pennsylvania	17.0		38	Vermont	13.8
26	Rhode Island	16.6		39	Massachusetts	13.5
6	South Carolina	22.6		40	Wyoming	13.3
26	South Dakota	16.6		41	Maine	13.1
10	Tennessee	21.2		42	Connecticut	12.6
13	Texas	20.9		43	Iowa	12.3
49	Utah	10.7		44	Colorado	12.0
38	Vermont	13.8		44	Maryland	12.0
36	Virginia	14.0		46	Minnesota	11.8
34	Washington	14.3		47	Hawaii	11.5
4	West Virginia	25.9		48	North Dakota	10.9
33	Wisconsin	14.5		49	Utah	10.7
40	Wyoming	13.3		50	New Hampshire	10.3
					District of Columbia	25.6

Source: U.S. Bureau of the Census
"2017 American Community Survey-Table DP03" (https://www.census.gov/programs-surveys/acs/)
*Children 17 and under living in families with incomes below the poverty level.

Percent of Families Living in Poverty in 2017

National Percent = 9.5%*

<table>
<thead>
<tr><th colspan="3">ALPHA ORDER</th><th colspan="3">RANK ORDER</th></tr>
<tr><th>RANK</th><th>STATE</th><th>PERCENT</th><th>RANK</th><th>STATE</th><th>PERCENT</th></tr>
</thead>
<tbody>
<tr><td>6</td><td>Alabama</td><td>12.8</td><td>1</td><td>New Mexico</td><td>15.2</td></tr>
<tr><td>33</td><td>Alaska</td><td>7.4</td><td>2</td><td>Mississippi</td><td>14.9</td></tr>
<tr><td>13</td><td>Arizona</td><td>10.7</td><td>3</td><td>Louisiana</td><td>14.7</td></tr>
<tr><td>7</td><td>Arkansas</td><td>11.6</td><td>4</td><td>West Virginia</td><td>14.1</td></tr>
<tr><td>19</td><td>California</td><td>9.6</td><td>5</td><td>Kentucky</td><td>12.9</td></tr>
<tr><td>42</td><td>Colorado</td><td>6.7</td><td>6</td><td>Alabama</td><td>12.8</td></tr>
<tr><td>45</td><td>Connecticut</td><td>6.4</td><td>7</td><td>Arkansas</td><td>11.6</td></tr>
<tr><td>20</td><td>Delaware</td><td>9.2</td><td>7</td><td>Oklahoma</td><td>11.6</td></tr>
<tr><td>16</td><td>Florida</td><td>10.1</td><td>9</td><td>South Carolina</td><td>11.3</td></tr>
<tr><td>11</td><td>Georgia</td><td>11.1</td><td>9</td><td>Texas</td><td>11.3</td></tr>
<tr><td>33</td><td>Hawaii</td><td>7.4</td><td>11</td><td>Georgia</td><td>11.1</td></tr>
<tr><td>26</td><td>Idaho</td><td>8.6</td><td>12</td><td>Tennessee</td><td>10.9</td></tr>
<tr><td>24</td><td>Illinois</td><td>9.0</td><td>13</td><td>Arizona</td><td>10.7</td></tr>
<tr><td>20</td><td>Indiana</td><td>9.2</td><td>14</td><td>North Carolina</td><td>10.6</td></tr>
<tr><td>42</td><td>Iowa</td><td>6.7</td><td>15</td><td>New York</td><td>10.4</td></tr>
<tr><td>29</td><td>Kansas</td><td>7.9</td><td>16</td><td>Florida</td><td>10.1</td></tr>
<tr><td>5</td><td>Kentucky</td><td>12.9</td><td>17</td><td>Ohio</td><td>9.8</td></tr>
<tr><td>3</td><td>Louisiana</td><td>14.7</td><td>18</td><td>Michigan</td><td>9.7</td></tr>
<tr><td>46</td><td>Maine</td><td>6.3</td><td>19</td><td>California</td><td>9.6</td></tr>
<tr><td>47</td><td>Maryland</td><td>6.2</td><td>20</td><td>Delaware</td><td>9.2</td></tr>
<tr><td>36</td><td>Massachusetts</td><td>7.2</td><td>20</td><td>Indiana</td><td>9.2</td></tr>
<tr><td>18</td><td>Michigan</td><td>9.7</td><td>20</td><td>Missouri</td><td>9.2</td></tr>
<tr><td>49</td><td>Minnesota</td><td>5.8</td><td>23</td><td>Nevada</td><td>9.1</td></tr>
<tr><td>2</td><td>Mississippi</td><td>14.9</td><td>24</td><td>Illinois</td><td>9.0</td></tr>
<tr><td>20</td><td>Missouri</td><td>9.2</td><td>25</td><td>Oregon</td><td>8.8</td></tr>
<tr><td>31</td><td>Montana</td><td>7.7</td><td>26</td><td>Idaho</td><td>8.6</td></tr>
<tr><td>36</td><td>Nebraska</td><td>7.2</td><td>27</td><td>South Dakota</td><td>8.4</td></tr>
<tr><td>23</td><td>Nevada</td><td>9.1</td><td>28</td><td>Pennsylvania</td><td>8.1</td></tr>
<tr><td>50</td><td>New Hampshire</td><td>4.9</td><td>29</td><td>Kansas</td><td>7.9</td></tr>
<tr><td>35</td><td>New Jersey</td><td>7.3</td><td>29</td><td>Rhode Island</td><td>7.9</td></tr>
<tr><td>1</td><td>New Mexico</td><td>15.2</td><td>31</td><td>Montana</td><td>7.7</td></tr>
<tr><td>15</td><td>New York</td><td>10.4</td><td>32</td><td>Wyoming</td><td>7.6</td></tr>
<tr><td>14</td><td>North Carolina</td><td>10.6</td><td>33</td><td>Alaska</td><td>7.4</td></tr>
<tr><td>48</td><td>North Dakota</td><td>6.1</td><td>33</td><td>Hawaii</td><td>7.4</td></tr>
<tr><td>17</td><td>Ohio</td><td>9.8</td><td>35</td><td>New Jersey</td><td>7.3</td></tr>
<tr><td>7</td><td>Oklahoma</td><td>11.6</td><td>36</td><td>Massachusetts</td><td>7.2</td></tr>
<tr><td>25</td><td>Oregon</td><td>8.8</td><td>36</td><td>Nebraska</td><td>7.2</td></tr>
<tr><td>28</td><td>Pennsylvania</td><td>8.1</td><td>38</td><td>Virginia</td><td>7.1</td></tr>
<tr><td>29</td><td>Rhode Island</td><td>7.9</td><td>38</td><td>Washington</td><td>7.1</td></tr>
<tr><td>9</td><td>South Carolina</td><td>11.3</td><td>38</td><td>Wisconsin</td><td>7.1</td></tr>
<tr><td>27</td><td>South Dakota</td><td>8.4</td><td>41</td><td>Vermont</td><td>7.0</td></tr>
<tr><td>12</td><td>Tennessee</td><td>10.9</td><td>42</td><td>Colorado</td><td>6.7</td></tr>
<tr><td>9</td><td>Texas</td><td>11.3</td><td>42</td><td>Iowa</td><td>6.7</td></tr>
<tr><td>42</td><td>Utah</td><td>6.7</td><td>42</td><td>Utah</td><td>6.7</td></tr>
<tr><td>41</td><td>Vermont</td><td>7.0</td><td>45</td><td>Connecticut</td><td>6.4</td></tr>
<tr><td>38</td><td>Virginia</td><td>7.1</td><td>46</td><td>Maine</td><td>6.3</td></tr>
<tr><td>38</td><td>Washington</td><td>7.1</td><td>47</td><td>Maryland</td><td>6.2</td></tr>
<tr><td>4</td><td>West Virginia</td><td>14.1</td><td>48</td><td>North Dakota</td><td>6.1</td></tr>
<tr><td>38</td><td>Wisconsin</td><td>7.1</td><td>49</td><td>Minnesota</td><td>5.8</td></tr>
<tr><td>32</td><td>Wyoming</td><td>7.6</td><td>50</td><td>New Hampshire</td><td>4.9</td></tr>
<tr><td></td><td></td><td></td><td></td><td>District of Columbia</td><td>13.3</td></tr>
</tbody>
</table>

Source: U.S. Bureau of the Census

"2017 American Community Survey-Table DP03" (https://www.census.gov/programs-surveys/acs/)

*Families living with incomes below the poverty level.

Percent of Female-Headed Families with Children Living in Poverty in 2017

National Percent = 35.7%*

ALPHA ORDER

RANK	STATE	PERCENT
4	Alabama	45.6
50	Alaska	23.5
25	Arizona	34.6
7	Arkansas	41.8
32	California	32.7
45	Colorado	28.6
47	Connecticut	27.5
41	Delaware	30.1
29	Florida	34.0
20	Georgia	36.0
44	Hawaii	29.5
10	Idaho	40.0
22	Illinois	35.2
15	Indiana	38.0
34	Iowa	31.7
24	Kansas	34.7
5	Kentucky	42.9
2	Louisiana	47.3
36	Maine	31.4
49	Maryland	24.5
31	Massachusetts	32.8
16	Michigan	37.7
48	Minnesota	27.2
3	Mississippi	46.1
19	Missouri	36.5
25	Montana	34.6
28	Nebraska	34.3
39	Nevada	31.0
46	New Hampshire	27.7
43	New Jersey	29.6
6	New Mexico	42.8
21	New York	35.8
13	North Carolina	38.3
33	North Dakota	32.4
12	Ohio	39.7
11	Oklahoma	39.9
27	Oregon	34.4
23	Pennsylvania	35.0
18	Rhode Island	37.5
8	South Carolina	41.1
14	South Dakota	38.2
9	Tennessee	40.7
17	Texas	37.6
42	Utah	30.0
37	Vermont	31.3
40	Virginia	30.9
38	Washington	31.2
1	West Virginia	52.1
34	Wisconsin	31.7
30	Wyoming	32.9

RANK ORDER

RANK	STATE	PERCENT
1	West Virginia	52.1
2	Louisiana	47.3
3	Mississippi	46.1
4	Alabama	45.6
5	Kentucky	42.9
6	New Mexico	42.8
7	Arkansas	41.8
8	South Carolina	41.1
9	Tennessee	40.7
10	Idaho	40.0
11	Oklahoma	39.9
12	Ohio	39.7
13	North Carolina	38.3
14	South Dakota	38.2
15	Indiana	38.0
16	Michigan	37.7
17	Texas	37.6
18	Rhode Island	37.5
19	Missouri	36.5
20	Georgia	36.0
21	New York	35.8
22	Illinois	35.2
23	Pennsylvania	35.0
24	Kansas	34.7
25	Arizona	34.6
25	Montana	34.6
27	Oregon	34.4
28	Nebraska	34.3
29	Florida	34.0
30	Wyoming	32.9
31	Massachusetts	32.8
32	California	32.7
33	North Dakota	32.4
34	Iowa	31.7
34	Wisconsin	31.7
36	Maine	31.4
37	Vermont	31.3
38	Washington	31.2
39	Nevada	31.0
40	Virginia	30.9
41	Delaware	30.1
42	Utah	30.0
43	New Jersey	29.6
44	Hawaii	29.5
45	Colorado	28.6
46	New Hampshire	27.7
47	Connecticut	27.5
48	Minnesota	27.2
49	Maryland	24.5
50	Alaska	23.5
	District of Columbia	41.6

Source: U.S. Bureau of the Census
   "2017 American Community Survey-Table DP03" (https://www.census.gov/programs-surveys/acs/)
*Households headed by females with own children under 18 years living with them with incomes below the poverty level as a percent of all such female-headed households.

State and Local Government Expenditures for Public Welfare Programs in 2016

National Total = $637,644,176,000*

ALPHA ORDER

ALPHA ORDER

RANK ORDER

RANK	STATE	EXPENDITURES	% of USA	RANK	STATE	EXPENDITURES	% of USA
28	Alabama	$7,158,421,000	1.1%	1	California	$98,459,084,000	15.4%
45	Alaska	2,233,832,000	0.4%	2	New York	65,607,574,000	10.3%
12	Arizona	14,021,170,000	2.2%	3	Texas	36,946,153,000	5.8%
29	Arkansas	6,996,132,000	1.1%	4	Pennsylvania	30,314,179,000	4.8%
1	California	98,459,084,000	15.4%	5	Florida	26,728,285,000	4.2%
25	Colorado	8,502,189,000	1.3%	6	Ohio	26,160,186,000	4.1%
26	Connecticut	7,516,618,000	1.2%	7	Illinois	20,180,604,000	3.2%
44	Delaware	2,447,242,000	0.4%	8	Massachusetts	19,970,612,000	3.1%
5	Florida	26,728,285,000	4.2%	9	New Jersey	17,716,379,000	2.8%
19	Georgia	11,743,010,000	1.8%	10	Michigan	16,875,727,000	2.6%
39	Hawaii	2,855,188,000	0.4%	11	Minnesota	15,639,601,000	2.5%
43	Idaho	2,455,950,000	0.4%	12	Arizona	14,021,170,000	2.2%
7	Illinois	20,180,604,000	3.2%	13	North Carolina	13,386,143,000	2.1%
15	Indiana	12,711,647,000	2.0%	14	Washington	12,852,765,000	2.0%
31	Iowa	6,463,373,000	1.0%	15	Indiana	12,711,647,000	2.0%
36	Kansas	4,182,882,000	0.7%	16	Wisconsin	12,271,135,000	1.9%
21	Kentucky	11,209,221,000	1.8%	17	Virginia	12,099,840,000	1.9%
24	Louisiana	8,699,827,000	1.4%	18	Maryland	12,087,917,000	1.9%
38	Maine	3,379,319,000	0.5%	19	Georgia	11,743,010,000	1.8%
18	Maryland	12,087,917,000	1.9%	20	Tennessee	11,544,591,000	1.8%
8	Massachusetts	19,970,612,000	3.1%	21	Kentucky	11,209,221,000	1.8%
10	Michigan	16,875,727,000	2.6%	22	Oregon	10,439,386,000	1.6%
11	Minnesota	15,639,601,000	2.5%	23	Missouri	8,928,192,000	1.4%
32	Mississippi	6,253,763,000	1.0%	24	Louisiana	8,699,827,000	1.4%
23	Missouri	8,928,192,000	1.4%	25	Colorado	8,502,189,000	1.3%
47	Montana	1,758,517,000	0.3%	26	Connecticut	7,516,618,000	1.2%
40	Nebraska	2,712,254,000	0.4%	27	South Carolina	7,360,229,000	1.2%
35	Nevada	4,229,286,000	0.7%	28	Alabama	7,158,421,000	1.1%
42	New Hampshire	2,550,988,000	0.4%	29	Arkansas	6,996,132,000	1.1%
9	New Jersey	17,716,379,000	2.8%	30	Oklahoma	6,563,401,000	1.0%
33	New Mexico	5,722,576,000	0.9%	31	Iowa	6,463,373,000	1.0%
2	New York	65,607,574,000	10.3%	32	Mississippi	6,253,763,000	1.0%
13	North Carolina	13,386,143,000	2.1%	33	New Mexico	5,722,576,000	0.9%
48	North Dakota	1,626,817,000	0.3%	34	West Virginia	4,435,575,000	0.7%
6	Ohio	26,160,186,000	4.1%	35	Nevada	4,229,286,000	0.7%
30	Oklahoma	6,563,401,000	1.0%	36	Kansas	4,182,882,000	0.7%
22	Oregon	10,439,386,000	1.6%	37	Utah	3,564,498,000	0.6%
4	Pennsylvania	30,314,179,000	4.8%	38	Maine	3,379,319,000	0.5%
41	Rhode Island	2,620,787,000	0.4%	39	Hawaii	2,855,188,000	0.4%
27	South Carolina	7,360,229,000	1.2%	40	Nebraska	2,712,254,000	0.4%
49	South Dakota	1,060,080,000	0.2%	41	Rhode Island	2,620,787,000	0.4%
20	Tennessee	11,544,591,000	1.8%	42	New Hampshire	2,550,988,000	0.4%
3	Texas	36,946,153,000	5.8%	43	Idaho	2,455,950,000	0.4%
37	Utah	3,564,498,000	0.6%	44	Delaware	2,447,242,000	0.4%
46	Vermont	1,772,358,000	0.3%	45	Alaska	2,233,832,000	0.4%
17	Virginia	12,099,840,000	1.9%	46	Vermont	1,772,358,000	0.3%
14	Washington	12,852,765,000	2.0%	47	Montana	1,758,517,000	0.3%
34	West Virginia	4,435,575,000	0.7%	48	North Dakota	1,626,817,000	0.3%
16	Wisconsin	12,271,135,000	1.9%	49	South Dakota	1,060,080,000	0.2%
50	Wyoming	843,210,000	0.1%	50	Wyoming	843,210,000	0.1%
					District of Columbia	3,785,463,000	0.6%

Source: U.S. Bureau of the Census, Governments Division
   "2016 State and Local Government Finances" (https://www.census.gov/programs-surveys/gov-finances.html)
*Direct general expenditures. Includes funds for cash assistance programs, medical and other vendor payments, welfare institutions, and other public welfare programs.

Per Capita State and Local Government Expenditures
for Public Welfare Programs in 2016
National Per Capita = $1,974*

ALPHA ORDER

RANK	STATE	PER CAPITA
37	Alabama	$1,471
2	Alaska	3,013
22	Arizona	2,019
15	Arkansas	2,340
11	California	2,511
35	Colorado	1,534
19	Connecticut	2,100
7	Delaware	2,578
47	Florida	1,296
50	Georgia	1,140
24	Hawaii	1,999
39	Idaho	1,459
34	Illinois	1,573
26	Indiana	1,916
21	Iowa	2,064
43	Kansas	1,437
10	Kentucky	2,526
28	Louisiana	1,860
9	Maine	2,538
23	Maryland	2,013
3	Massachusetts	2,926
31	Michigan	1,696
5	Minnesota	2,832
20	Mississippi	2,093
38	Missouri	1,467
32	Montana	1,689
44	Nebraska	1,423
40	Nevada	1,448
27	New Hampshire	1,900
25	New Jersey	1,996
6	New Mexico	2,734
1	New York	3,340
46	North Carolina	1,318
17	North Dakota	2,157
16	Ohio	2,248
33	Oklahoma	1,671
8	Oregon	2,552
14	Pennsylvania	2,371
12	Rhode Island	2,479
36	South Carolina	1,484
48	South Dakota	1,229
30	Tennessee	1,737
45	Texas	1,322
49	Utah	1,172
4	Vermont	2,842
42	Virginia	1,439
29	Washington	1,762
13	West Virginia	2,423
18	Wisconsin	2,126
41	Wyoming	1,443

RANK ORDER

RANK	STATE	PER CAPITA
1	New York	$3,340
2	Alaska	3,013
3	Massachusetts	2,926
4	Vermont	2,842
5	Minnesota	2,832
6	New Mexico	2,734
7	Delaware	2,578
8	Oregon	2,552
9	Maine	2,538
10	Kentucky	2,526
11	California	2,511
12	Rhode Island	2,479
13	West Virginia	2,423
14	Pennsylvania	2,371
15	Arkansas	2,340
16	Ohio	2,248
17	North Dakota	2,157
18	Wisconsin	2,126
19	Connecticut	2,100
20	Mississippi	2,093
21	Iowa	2,064
22	Arizona	2,019
23	Maryland	2,013
24	Hawaii	1,999
25	New Jersey	1,996
26	Indiana	1,916
27	New Hampshire	1,900
28	Louisiana	1,860
29	Washington	1,762
30	Tennessee	1,737
31	Michigan	1,696
32	Montana	1,689
33	Oklahoma	1,671
34	Illinois	1,573
35	Colorado	1,534
36	South Carolina	1,484
37	Alabama	1,471
38	Missouri	1,467
39	Idaho	1,459
40	Nevada	1,448
41	Wyoming	1,443
42	Virginia	1,439
43	Kansas	1,437
44	Nebraska	1,423
45	Texas	1,322
46	North Carolina	1,318
47	Florida	1,296
48	South Dakota	1,229
49	Utah	1,172
50	Georgia	1,140
	District of Columbia	5,514

Source: CQ Press using data from U.S. Bureau of the Census, Governments Division
"2016 State and Local Government Finances" (https://www.census.gov/programs-surveys/gov-finances.html)
*Direct general expenditures. Includes funds for cash assistance programs, medical and other vendor payments, welfare institutions, and other public welfare programs.

State and Local Government Spending for Public Welfare Programs as a Percent of All State and Local Government Expenditures in 2016

National Percent = 21.7%*

ALPHA ORDER				RANK ORDER		
RANK	STATE	PERCENT		RANK	STATE	PERCENT
34	Alabama	18.7		1	Arizona	28.8
46	Alaska	16.3		1	Arkansas	28.8
1	Arizona	28.8		1	Kentucky	28.8
1	Arkansas	28.8		4	Maine	28.7
20	California	23.0		5	New Mexico	27.9
37	Colorado	18.1		5	West Virginia	27.9
31	Connecticut	19.6		7	Minnesota	27.5
17	Delaware	24.2		8	Massachusetts	26.7
35	Florida	18.5		9	Tennessee	25.7
42	Georgia	17.1		10	Rhode Island	25.6
24	Hawaii	21.0		11	Ohio	25.3
23	Idaho	22.2		12	Oregon	25.2
37	Illinois	18.1		12	Vermont	25.2
15	Indiana	24.4		14	Pennsylvania	24.8
26	Iowa	20.9		15	Indiana	24.4
45	Kansas	16.6		15	New York	24.4
1	Kentucky	28.8		17	Delaware	24.2
24	Louisiana	21.0		18	Mississippi	24.0
4	Maine	28.7		18	Wisconsin	24.0
27	Maryland	20.6		20	California	23.0
8	Massachusetts	26.7		21	New Hampshire	22.9
29	Michigan	20.4		22	Oklahoma	22.5
7	Minnesota	27.5		23	Idaho	22.2
18	Mississippi	24.0		24	Hawaii	21.0
31	Missouri	19.6		24	Louisiana	21.0
30	Montana	20.0		26	Iowa	20.9
47	Nebraska	15.6		27	Maryland	20.6
27	Nevada	20.6		27	Nevada	20.6
21	New Hampshire	22.9		29	Michigan	20.4
33	New Jersey	19.2		30	Montana	20.0
5	New Mexico	27.9		31	Connecticut	19.6
15	New York	24.4		31	Missouri	19.6
40	North Carolina	17.3		33	New Jersey	19.2
44	North Dakota	17.0		34	Alabama	18.7
11	Ohio	25.3		35	Florida	18.5
22	Oklahoma	22.5		36	Washington	18.2
12	Oregon	25.2		37	Colorado	18.1
14	Pennsylvania	24.8		37	Illinois	18.1
10	Rhode Island	25.6		39	South Carolina	18.0
39	South Carolina	18.0		40	North Carolina	17.3
49	South Dakota	15.2		41	Texas	17.2
9	Tennessee	25.7		42	Georgia	17.1
41	Texas	17.2		42	Virginia	17.1
48	Utah	15.3		44	North Dakota	17.0
12	Vermont	25.2		45	Kansas	16.6
42	Virginia	17.1		46	Alaska	16.3
36	Washington	18.2		47	Nebraska	15.6
5	West Virginia	27.9		48	Utah	15.3
18	Wisconsin	24.0		49	South Dakota	15.2
50	Wyoming	9.6		50	Wyoming	9.6
					District of Columbia	29.6

Source: CQ Press using data from U.S. Bureau of the Census, Governments Division

"2016 State and Local Government Finances" (https://www.census.gov/programs-surveys/gov-finances.html)

*As a percent of direct general expenditures. Includes funds for cash assistance programs, medical and other vendor payments, welfare institutions, and other public welfare programs.

Social Security (OASDI) Payments in 2016

National Total = $911,132,000,000*

ALPHA ORDER

RANK	STATE	PAYMENTS	% of USA
21	Alabama	$16,336,000,000	1.8%
50	Alaska	1,352,000,000	0.1%
16	Arizona	19,462,000,000	2.1%
30	Arkansas	9,669,000,000	1.1%
1	California	85,057,000,000	9.3%
26	Colorado	12,512,000,000	1.4%
29	Connecticut	11,008,000,000	1.2%
44	Delaware	3,255,000,000	0.4%
2	Florida	66,293,000,000	7.3%
11	Georgia	25,782,000,000	2.8%
42	Hawaii	3,911,000,000	0.4%
39	Idaho	4,728,000,000	0.5%
8	Illinois	34,026,000,000	3.7%
14	Indiana	20,594,000,000	2.3%
31	Iowa	9,543,000,000	1.0%
33	Kansas	8,266,000,000	0.9%
24	Kentucky	13,865,000,000	1.5%
27	Louisiana	12,343,000,000	1.4%
40	Maine	4,676,000,000	0.5%
23	Maryland	15,286,000,000	1.7%
17	Massachusetts	19,077,000,000	2.1%
7	Michigan	34,440,000,000	3.8%
22	Minnesota	15,418,000,000	1.7%
32	Mississippi	9,139,000,000	1.0%
18	Missouri	18,795,000,000	2.1%
45	Montana	3,188,000,000	0.3%
38	Nebraska	5,035,000,000	0.6%
34	Nevada	7,561,000,000	0.8%
41	New Hampshire	4,611,000,000	0.5%
10	New Jersey	26,632,000,000	2.9%
37	New Mexico	5,824,000,000	0.6%
4	New York	55,182,000,000	6.1%
9	North Carolina	30,225,000,000	3.3%
48	North Dakota	1,852,000,000	0.2%
6	Ohio	34,540,000,000	3.8%
28	Oklahoma	11,206,000,000	1.2%
25	Oregon	12,632,000,000	1.4%
5	Pennsylvania	43,178,000,000	4.7%
43	Rhode Island	3,339,000,000	0.4%
20	South Carolina	16,371,000,000	1.8%
46	South Dakota	2,453,000,000	0.3%
13	Tennessee	20,823,000,000	2.3%
3	Texas	58,394,000,000	6.4%
36	Utah	5,826,000,000	0.6%
47	Vermont	2,157,000,000	0.2%
12	Virginia	22,497,000,000	2.5%
15	Washington	20,129,000,000	2.2%
35	West Virginia	6,966,000,000	0.8%
19	Wisconsin	18,358,000,000	2.0%
49	Wyoming	1,625,000,000	0.2%

RANK ORDER

RANK	STATE	PAYMENTS	% of USA
1	California	$85,057,000,000	9.3%
2	Florida	66,293,000,000	7.3%
3	Texas	58,394,000,000	6.4%
4	New York	55,182,000,000	6.1%
5	Pennsylvania	43,178,000,000	4.7%
6	Ohio	34,540,000,000	3.8%
7	Michigan	34,440,000,000	3.8%
8	Illinois	34,026,000,000	3.7%
9	North Carolina	30,225,000,000	3.3%
10	New Jersey	26,632,000,000	2.9%
11	Georgia	25,782,000,000	2.8%
12	Virginia	22,497,000,000	2.5%
13	Tennessee	20,823,000,000	2.3%
14	Indiana	20,594,000,000	2.3%
15	Washington	20,129,000,000	2.2%
16	Arizona	19,462,000,000	2.1%
17	Massachusetts	19,077,000,000	2.1%
18	Missouri	18,795,000,000	2.1%
19	Wisconsin	18,358,000,000	2.0%
20	South Carolina	16,371,000,000	1.8%
21	Alabama	16,336,000,000	1.8%
22	Minnesota	15,418,000,000	1.7%
23	Maryland	15,286,000,000	1.7%
24	Kentucky	13,865,000,000	1.5%
25	Oregon	12,632,000,000	1.4%
26	Colorado	12,512,000,000	1.4%
27	Louisiana	12,343,000,000	1.4%
28	Oklahoma	11,206,000,000	1.2%
29	Connecticut	11,008,000,000	1.2%
30	Arkansas	9,669,000,000	1.1%
31	Iowa	9,543,000,000	1.0%
32	Mississippi	9,139,000,000	1.0%
33	Kansas	8,266,000,000	0.9%
34	Nevada	7,561,000,000	0.8%
35	West Virginia	6,966,000,000	0.8%
36	Utah	5,826,000,000	0.6%
37	New Mexico	5,824,000,000	0.6%
38	Nebraska	5,035,000,000	0.6%
39	Idaho	4,728,000,000	0.5%
40	Maine	4,676,000,000	0.5%
41	New Hampshire	4,611,000,000	0.5%
42	Hawaii	3,911,000,000	0.4%
43	Rhode Island	3,339,000,000	0.4%
44	Delaware	3,255,000,000	0.4%
45	Montana	3,188,000,000	0.3%
46	South Dakota	2,453,000,000	0.3%
47	Vermont	2,157,000,000	0.2%
48	North Dakota	1,852,000,000	0.2%
49	Wyoming	1,625,000,000	0.2%
50	Alaska	1,352,000,000	0.1%
	District of Columbia	1,140,000,000	0.1%

Source: U.S. Department of Health and Human Services, Social Security Administration
"Social Security Bulletin, Annual Statistical Supplement 2017" (https://www.ssa.gov/policy/docs/statcomps/supplement/)
*"OASDI" is Old Age, Survivors and Disability Insurance. National total includes $14,555,000,000 in payments to recipients in U.S. territories and foreign countries.

Per Capita Social Security (OASDI) Payments in 2016

National Per Capita = $2,775*

<table>
<tr><td colspan="3">ALPHA ORDER</td><td colspan="3">RANK ORDER</td></tr>
<tr><td>RANK</td><td>STATE</td><td>PER CAPITA</td><td>RANK</td><td>STATE</td><td>PER CAPITA</td></tr>
<tr><td>8</td><td>Alabama</td><td>$3,358</td><td>1</td><td>West Virginia</td><td>$3,805</td></tr>
<tr><td>50</td><td>Alaska</td><td>1,823</td><td>2</td><td>Maine</td><td>3,512</td></tr>
<tr><td>31</td><td>Arizona</td><td>2,802</td><td>3</td><td>Michigan</td><td>3,461</td></tr>
<tr><td>10</td><td>Arkansas</td><td>3,233</td><td>4</td><td>Vermont</td><td>3,459</td></tr>
<tr><td>47</td><td>California</td><td>2,169</td><td>5</td><td>New Hampshire</td><td>3,435</td></tr>
<tr><td>46</td><td>Colorado</td><td>2,258</td><td>6</td><td>Delaware</td><td>3,429</td></tr>
<tr><td>19</td><td>Connecticut</td><td>3,076</td><td>7</td><td>Pennsylvania</td><td>3,378</td></tr>
<tr><td>6</td><td>Delaware</td><td>3,429</td><td>8</td><td>Alabama</td><td>3,358</td></tr>
<tr><td>11</td><td>Florida</td><td>3,213</td><td>9</td><td>South Carolina</td><td>3,302</td></tr>
<tr><td>44</td><td>Georgia</td><td>2,502</td><td>10</td><td>Arkansas</td><td>3,233</td></tr>
<tr><td>37</td><td>Hawaii</td><td>2,739</td><td>11</td><td>Florida</td><td>3,213</td></tr>
<tr><td>29</td><td>Idaho</td><td>2,809</td><td>12</td><td>Wisconsin</td><td>3,180</td></tr>
<tr><td>39</td><td>Illinois</td><td>2,653</td><td>13</td><td>Rhode Island</td><td>3,159</td></tr>
<tr><td>16</td><td>Indiana</td><td>3,105</td><td>14</td><td>Tennessee</td><td>3,134</td></tr>
<tr><td>22</td><td>Iowa</td><td>3,047</td><td>15</td><td>Kentucky</td><td>3,124</td></tr>
<tr><td>28</td><td>Kansas</td><td>2,839</td><td>16</td><td>Indiana</td><td>3,105</td></tr>
<tr><td>15</td><td>Kentucky</td><td>3,124</td><td>17</td><td>Missouri</td><td>3,088</td></tr>
<tr><td>41</td><td>Louisiana</td><td>2,638</td><td>18</td><td>Oregon</td><td>3,087</td></tr>
<tr><td>2</td><td>Maine</td><td>3,512</td><td>19</td><td>Connecticut</td><td>3,076</td></tr>
<tr><td>43</td><td>Maryland</td><td>2,546</td><td>20</td><td>Montana</td><td>3,063</td></tr>
<tr><td>32</td><td>Massachusetts</td><td>2,795</td><td>21</td><td>Mississippi</td><td>3,058</td></tr>
<tr><td>3</td><td>Michigan</td><td>3,461</td><td>22</td><td>Iowa</td><td>3,047</td></tr>
<tr><td>33</td><td>Minnesota</td><td>2,791</td><td>23</td><td>New Jersey</td><td>3,001</td></tr>
<tr><td>21</td><td>Mississippi</td><td>3,058</td><td>24</td><td>North Carolina</td><td>2,976</td></tr>
<tr><td>17</td><td>Missouri</td><td>3,088</td><td>25</td><td>Ohio</td><td>2,969</td></tr>
<tr><td>20</td><td>Montana</td><td>3,063</td><td>26</td><td>Oklahoma</td><td>2,854</td></tr>
<tr><td>40</td><td>Nebraska</td><td>2,642</td><td>27</td><td>South Dakota</td><td>2,843</td></tr>
<tr><td>42</td><td>Nevada</td><td>2,590</td><td>28</td><td>Kansas</td><td>2,839</td></tr>
<tr><td>5</td><td>New Hampshire</td><td>3,435</td><td>29</td><td>Idaho</td><td>2,809</td></tr>
<tr><td>23</td><td>New Jersey</td><td>3,001</td><td>29</td><td>New York</td><td>2,809</td></tr>
<tr><td>34</td><td>New Mexico</td><td>2,783</td><td>31</td><td>Arizona</td><td>2,802</td></tr>
<tr><td>29</td><td>New York</td><td>2,809</td><td>32</td><td>Massachusetts</td><td>2,795</td></tr>
<tr><td>24</td><td>North Carolina</td><td>2,976</td><td>33</td><td>Minnesota</td><td>2,791</td></tr>
<tr><td>45</td><td>North Dakota</td><td>2,455</td><td>34</td><td>New Mexico</td><td>2,783</td></tr>
<tr><td>25</td><td>Ohio</td><td>2,969</td><td>35</td><td>Wyoming</td><td>2,781</td></tr>
<tr><td>26</td><td>Oklahoma</td><td>2,854</td><td>36</td><td>Washington</td><td>2,759</td></tr>
<tr><td>18</td><td>Oregon</td><td>3,087</td><td>37</td><td>Hawaii</td><td>2,739</td></tr>
<tr><td>7</td><td>Pennsylvania</td><td>3,378</td><td>38</td><td>Virginia</td><td>2,675</td></tr>
<tr><td>13</td><td>Rhode Island</td><td>3,159</td><td>39</td><td>Illinois</td><td>2,653</td></tr>
<tr><td>9</td><td>South Carolina</td><td>3,302</td><td>40</td><td>Nebraska</td><td>2,642</td></tr>
<tr><td>27</td><td>South Dakota</td><td>2,843</td><td>41</td><td>Louisiana</td><td>2,638</td></tr>
<tr><td>14</td><td>Tennessee</td><td>3,134</td><td>42</td><td>Nevada</td><td>2,590</td></tr>
<tr><td>48</td><td>Texas</td><td>2,090</td><td>43</td><td>Maryland</td><td>2,546</td></tr>
<tr><td>49</td><td>Utah</td><td>1,915</td><td>44</td><td>Georgia</td><td>2,502</td></tr>
<tr><td>4</td><td>Vermont</td><td>3,459</td><td>45</td><td>North Dakota</td><td>2,455</td></tr>
<tr><td>38</td><td>Virginia</td><td>2,675</td><td>46</td><td>Colorado</td><td>2,258</td></tr>
<tr><td>36</td><td>Washington</td><td>2,759</td><td>47</td><td>California</td><td>2,169</td></tr>
<tr><td>1</td><td>West Virginia</td><td>3,805</td><td>48</td><td>Texas</td><td>2,090</td></tr>
<tr><td>12</td><td>Wisconsin</td><td>3,180</td><td>49</td><td>Utah</td><td>1,915</td></tr>
<tr><td>35</td><td>Wyoming</td><td>2,781</td><td>50</td><td>Alaska</td><td>1,823</td></tr>
<tr><td></td><td></td><td></td><td></td><td>District of Columbia</td><td>1,660</td></tr>
</table>

Source: CQ Press using data from U.S. Department of Health and Human Services, Social Security Administration
"Social Security Bulletin, Annual Statistical Supplement 2017" (https://www.ssa.gov/policy/docs/statcomps/supplement/)
*"OASDI" is Old Age, Survivors and Disability Insurance. National per capita does not include payments or population in U.S. territories and foreign countries.

Social Security (OASDI) Monthly Payments in 2016

National Total = $75,917,962,000*

RANK	STATE	PAYMENTS	% of USA
21	Alabama	$1,341,514,000	1.8%
50	Alaska	113,938,000	0.2%
16	Arizona	1,643,717,000	2.2%
31	Arkansas	795,729,000	1.0%
1	California	7,126,458,000	9.4%
26	Colorado	1,052,599,000	1.4%
29	Connecticut	922,735,000	1.2%
44	Delaware	274,916,000	0.4%
2	Florida	5,584,296,000	7.4%
11	Georgia	2,147,409,000	2.8%
42	Hawaii	331,474,000	0.4%
39	Idaho	398,558,000	0.5%
8	Illinois	2,823,703,000	3.7%
14	Indiana	1,706,346,000	2.2%
30	Iowa	795,782,000	1.0%
33	Kansas	689,743,000	0.9%
24	Kentucky	1,132,277,000	1.5%
27	Louisiana	1,001,883,000	1.3%
40	Maine	389,823,000	0.5%
23	Maryland	1,281,271,000	1.7%
17	Massachusetts	1,590,928,000	2.1%
6	Michigan	2,850,592,000	3.8%
22	Minnesota	1,296,913,000	1.7%
32	Mississippi	749,026,000	1.0%
18	Missouri	1,554,999,000	2.0%
45	Montana	268,148,000	0.4%
38	Nebraska	420,808,000	0.6%
34	Nevada	638,063,000	0.8%
41	New Hampshire	388,252,000	0.5%
10	New Jersey	2,225,451,000	2.9%
37	New Mexico	485,568,000	0.6%
4	New York	4,599,203,000	6.1%
9	North Carolina	2,530,940,000	3.3%
48	North Dakota	154,076,000	0.2%
7	Ohio	2,839,739,000	3.7%
28	Oklahoma	925,736,000	1.2%
25	Oregon	1,063,195,000	1.4%
5	Pennsylvania	3,581,701,000	4.7%
43	Rhode Island	279,187,000	0.4%
20	South Carolina	1,372,112,000	1.8%
46	South Dakota	205,702,000	0.3%
13	Tennessee	1,726,649,000	2.3%
3	Texas	4,854,798,000	6.4%
36	Utah	489,367,000	0.6%
47	Vermont	181,120,000	0.2%
12	Virginia	1,885,766,000	2.5%
15	Washington	1,696,167,000	2.2%
35	West Virginia	565,260,000	0.7%
19	Wisconsin	1,538,938,000	2.0%
49	Wyoming	137,056,000	0.2%

RANK	STATE	PAYMENTS	% of USA
1	California	$7,126,458,000	9.4%
2	Florida	5,584,296,000	7.4%
3	Texas	4,854,798,000	6.4%
4	New York	4,599,203,000	6.1%
5	Pennsylvania	3,581,701,000	4.7%
6	Michigan	2,850,592,000	3.8%
7	Ohio	2,839,739,000	3.7%
8	Illinois	2,823,703,000	3.7%
9	North Carolina	2,530,940,000	3.3%
10	New Jersey	2,225,451,000	2.9%
11	Georgia	2,147,409,000	2.8%
12	Virginia	1,885,766,000	2.5%
13	Tennessee	1,726,649,000	2.3%
14	Indiana	1,706,346,000	2.2%
15	Washington	1,696,167,000	2.2%
16	Arizona	1,643,717,000	2.2%
17	Massachusetts	1,590,928,000	2.1%
18	Missouri	1,554,999,000	2.0%
19	Wisconsin	1,538,938,000	2.0%
20	South Carolina	1,372,112,000	1.8%
21	Alabama	1,341,514,000	1.8%
22	Minnesota	1,296,913,000	1.7%
23	Maryland	1,281,271,000	1.7%
24	Kentucky	1,132,277,000	1.5%
25	Oregon	1,063,195,000	1.4%
26	Colorado	1,052,599,000	1.4%
27	Louisiana	1,001,883,000	1.3%
28	Oklahoma	925,736,000	1.2%
29	Connecticut	922,735,000	1.2%
30	Iowa	795,782,000	1.0%
31	Arkansas	795,729,000	1.0%
32	Mississippi	749,026,000	1.0%
33	Kansas	689,743,000	0.9%
34	Nevada	638,063,000	0.8%
35	West Virginia	565,260,000	0.7%
36	Utah	489,367,000	0.6%
37	New Mexico	485,568,000	0.6%
38	Nebraska	420,808,000	0.6%
39	Idaho	398,558,000	0.5%
40	Maine	389,823,000	0.5%
41	New Hampshire	388,252,000	0.5%
42	Hawaii	331,474,000	0.4%
43	Rhode Island	279,187,000	0.4%
44	Delaware	274,916,000	0.4%
45	Montana	268,148,000	0.4%
46	South Dakota	205,702,000	0.3%
47	Vermont	181,120,000	0.2%
48	North Dakota	154,076,000	0.2%
49	Wyoming	137,056,000	0.2%
50	Alaska	113,938,000	0.2%
	District of Columbia	95,379,000	0.1%

Source: U.S. Department of Health and Human Services, Social Security Administration

"Social Security Bulletin, Annual Statistical Supplement 2017" (https://www.ssa.gov/policy/docs/statcomps/supplement/)

*For December 2016. "OASDI" is Old Age, Survivors and Disability Insurance. National total includes $1,172,952,000 in payments to recipients in U.S. territories and foreign countries.

Social Security (OASDI) Beneficiaries in 2016

National Total = 59,373,422*

ALPHA ORDER

ALPHA ORDER

RANK	STATE	BENEFICIARIES	% of USA
20	Alabama	1,120,486	1.8%
50	Alaska	95,500	0.2%
16	Arizona	1,274,815	2.1%
29	Arkansas	685,361	1.1%
1	California	5,754,771	9.4%
27	Colorado	830,604	1.4%
30	Connecticut	664,688	1.1%
45	Delaware	201,748	0.3%
2	Florida	4,431,473	7.3%
10	Georgia	1,751,227	2.9%
42	Hawaii	261,513	0.4%
40	Idaho	325,247	0.5%
7	Illinois	2,196,032	3.6%
14	Indiana	1,318,046	2.2%
32	Iowa	630,014	1.0%
33	Kansas	535,673	0.9%
23	Kentucky	972,352	1.6%
25	Louisiana	882,185	1.4%
39	Maine	334,291	0.5%
24	Maryland	966,632	1.6%
18	Massachusetts	1,246,936	2.0%
8	Michigan	2,162,113	3.5%
22	Minnesota	994,806	1.6%
31	Mississippi	653,352	1.1%
17	Missouri	1,269,508	2.1%
43	Montana	223,401	0.4%
38	Nebraska	335,361	0.6%
34	Nevada	506,324	0.8%
41	New Hampshire	294,322	0.5%
11	New Jersey	1,597,052	2.6%
36	New Mexico	416,674	0.7%
4	New York	3,546,954	5.8%
9	North Carolina	2,020,386	3.3%
48	North Dakota	127,962	0.2%
6	Ohio	2,311,984	3.8%
28	Oklahoma	768,889	1.3%
26	Oregon	836,215	1.4%
5	Pennsylvania	2,768,956	4.5%
44	Rhode Island	220,420	0.4%
21	South Carolina	1,089,728	1.8%
46	South Dakota	171,594	0.3%
13	Tennessee	1,412,299	2.3%
3	Texas	4,024,516	6.6%
37	Utah	385,942	0.6%
47	Vermont	144,889	0.2%
12	Virginia	1,471,294	2.4%
15	Washington	1,291,198	2.1%
35	West Virginia	470,240	0.8%
19	Wisconsin	1,189,455	2.0%
49	Wyoming	106,720	0.2%

RANK ORDER

RANK	STATE	BENEFICIARIES	% of USA
1	California	5,754,771	9.4%
2	Florida	4,431,473	7.3%
3	Texas	4,024,516	6.6%
4	New York	3,546,954	5.8%
5	Pennsylvania	2,768,956	4.5%
6	Ohio	2,311,984	3.8%
7	Illinois	2,196,032	3.6%
8	Michigan	2,162,113	3.5%
9	North Carolina	2,020,386	3.3%
10	Georgia	1,751,227	2.9%
11	New Jersey	1,597,052	2.6%
12	Virginia	1,471,294	2.4%
13	Tennessee	1,412,299	2.3%
14	Indiana	1,318,046	2.2%
15	Washington	1,291,198	2.1%
16	Arizona	1,274,815	2.1%
17	Missouri	1,269,508	2.1%
18	Massachusetts	1,246,936	2.0%
19	Wisconsin	1,189,455	2.0%
20	Alabama	1,120,486	1.8%
21	South Carolina	1,089,728	1.8%
22	Minnesota	994,806	1.6%
23	Kentucky	972,352	1.6%
24	Maryland	966,632	1.6%
25	Louisiana	882,185	1.4%
26	Oregon	836,215	1.4%
27	Colorado	830,604	1.4%
28	Oklahoma	768,889	1.3%
29	Arkansas	685,361	1.1%
30	Connecticut	664,688	1.1%
31	Mississippi	653,352	1.1%
32	Iowa	630,014	1.0%
33	Kansas	535,673	0.9%
34	Nevada	506,324	0.8%
35	West Virginia	470,240	0.8%
36	New Mexico	416,674	0.7%
37	Utah	385,942	0.6%
38	Nebraska	335,361	0.6%
39	Maine	334,291	0.5%
40	Idaho	325,247	0.5%
41	New Hampshire	294,322	0.5%
42	Hawaii	261,513	0.4%
43	Montana	223,401	0.4%
44	Rhode Island	220,420	0.4%
45	Delaware	201,748	0.3%
46	South Dakota	171,594	0.3%
47	Vermont	144,889	0.2%
48	North Dakota	127,962	0.2%
49	Wyoming	106,720	0.2%
50	Alaska	95,500	0.2%
	District of Columbia	81,274	0.1%

Source: U.S. Department of Health and Human Services, Social Security Administration
   "Social Security Bulletin, Annual Statistical Supplement 2017" (https://www.ssa.gov/policy/docs/statcomps/supplement/)
*For December 2016. "OASDI" is Old Age, Survivors and Disability Insurance. National total includes 1,533,885 beneficiaries in U.S. territories and foreign countries.

Average Monthly Social Security (OASDI) Payment in 2016

National Average = $1,259 Each Month per Beneficiary*

ALPHA ORDER

RANK	STATE	PER BENEFICIARY
43	Alabama	$1,197
44	Alaska	1,193
13	Arizona	1,289
48	Arkansas	1,161
31	California	1,238
22	Colorado	1,267
2	Connecticut	1,388
3	Delaware	1,363
25	Florida	1,260
33	Georgia	1,226
20	Hawaii	1,268
34	Idaho	1,225
15	Illinois	1,286
10	Indiana	1,295
24	Iowa	1,263
14	Kansas	1,288
47	Kentucky	1,164
50	Louisiana	1,136
45	Maine	1,166
4	Maryland	1,326
18	Massachusetts	1,276
6	Michigan	1,318
8	Minnesota	1,304
49	Mississippi	1,146
34	Missouri	1,225
41	Montana	1,200
28	Nebraska	1,255
25	Nevada	1,260
5	New Hampshire	1,319
1	New Jersey	1,393
46	New Mexico	1,165
9	New York	1,297
29	North Carolina	1,253
38	North Dakota	1,204
32	Ohio	1,228
38	Oklahoma	1,204
19	Oregon	1,271
11	Pennsylvania	1,294
22	Rhode Island	1,267
27	South Carolina	1,259
42	South Dakota	1,199
36	Tennessee	1,223
37	Texas	1,206
20	Utah	1,268
30	Vermont	1,250
17	Virginia	1,282
7	Washington	1,314
40	West Virginia	1,202
11	Wisconsin	1,294
16	Wyoming	1,284

RANK ORDER

RANK	STATE	PER BENEFICIARY
1	New Jersey	$1,393
2	Connecticut	1,388
3	Delaware	1,363
4	Maryland	1,326
5	New Hampshire	1,319
6	Michigan	1,318
7	Washington	1,314
8	Minnesota	1,304
9	New York	1,297
10	Indiana	1,295
11	Pennsylvania	1,294
11	Wisconsin	1,294
13	Arizona	1,289
14	Kansas	1,288
15	Illinois	1,286
16	Wyoming	1,284
17	Virginia	1,282
18	Massachusetts	1,276
19	Oregon	1,271
20	Hawaii	1,268
20	Utah	1,268
22	Colorado	1,267
22	Rhode Island	1,267
24	Iowa	1,263
25	Florida	1,260
25	Nevada	1,260
27	South Carolina	1,259
28	Nebraska	1,255
29	North Carolina	1,253
30	Vermont	1,250
31	California	1,238
32	Ohio	1,228
33	Georgia	1,226
34	Idaho	1,225
34	Missouri	1,225
36	Tennessee	1,223
37	Texas	1,206
38	North Dakota	1,204
38	Oklahoma	1,204
40	West Virginia	1,202
41	Montana	1,200
42	South Dakota	1,199
43	Alabama	1,197
44	Alaska	1,193
45	Maine	1,166
46	New Mexico	1,165
47	Kentucky	1,164
48	Arkansas	1,161
49	Mississippi	1,146
50	Louisiana	1,136

| | District of Columbia | 1,174 |

Source: CQ Press using data from U.S. Department of Health and Human Services, Social Security Administration "Social Security Bulletin, Annual Statistical Supplement 2017" (https://www.ssa.gov/policy/docs/statcomps/supplement/)
*As of December 2016. "OASDI" is Old Age, Survivors and Disability Insurance. National average does not include beneficiaries or payments in U.S. territories or foreign countries.

Social Security Supplemental Security Income Beneficiaries in 2016

National Total = 8,251,161 Beneficiaries*

ALPHA ORDER

RANK	STATE	BENEFICIARIES	% of USA
16	Alabama	167,377	2.0%
48	Alaska	12,468	0.2%
23	Arizona	118,913	1.4%
26	Arkansas	108,596	1.3%
1	California	1,277,078	15.5%
31	Colorado	72,576	0.9%
32	Connecticut	64,607	0.8%
45	Delaware	16,884	0.2%
4	Florida	575,194	7.0%
9	Georgia	258,527	3.1%
42	Hawaii	24,221	0.3%
40	Idaho	30,712	0.4%
8	Illinois	272,247	3.3%
20	Indiana	128,340	1.6%
35	Iowa	50,958	0.6%
36	Kansas	48,064	0.6%
13	Kentucky	180,639	2.2%
15	Louisiana	177,526	2.2%
37	Maine	37,313	0.5%
22	Maryland	120,669	1.5%
11	Massachusetts	186,783	2.3%
7	Michigan	274,059	3.3%
28	Minnesota	93,806	1.1%
21	Mississippi	120,694	1.5%
19	Missouri	138,515	1.7%
44	Montana	18,287	0.2%
41	Nebraska	27,867	0.3%
34	Nevada	55,199	0.7%
43	New Hampshire	19,262	0.2%
12	New Jersey	182,381	2.2%
33	New Mexico	63,636	0.8%
3	New York	644,944	7.8%
10	North Carolina	233,263	2.8%
49	North Dakota	8,206	0.1%
6	Ohio	310,318	3.8%
27	Oklahoma	96,368	1.2%
29	Oregon	87,342	1.1%
5	Pennsylvania	363,371	4.4%
38	Rhode Island	33,228	0.4%
25	South Carolina	117,205	1.4%
47	South Dakota	14,718	0.2%
14	Tennessee	180,057	2.2%
2	Texas	657,595	8.0%
39	Utah	31,323	0.4%
46	Vermont	15,617	0.2%
17	Virginia	156,523	1.9%
18	Washington	150,570	1.8%
30	West Virginia	74,707	0.9%
24	Wisconsin	117,819	1.4%
50	Wyoming	6,702	0.1%

RANK ORDER

RANK	STATE	BENEFICIARIES	% of USA
1	California	1,277,078	15.5%
2	Texas	657,595	8.0%
3	New York	644,944	7.8%
4	Florida	575,194	7.0%
5	Pennsylvania	363,371	4.4%
6	Ohio	310,318	3.8%
7	Michigan	274,059	3.3%
8	Illinois	272,247	3.3%
9	Georgia	258,527	3.1%
10	North Carolina	233,263	2.8%
11	Massachusetts	186,783	2.3%
12	New Jersey	182,381	2.2%
13	Kentucky	180,639	2.2%
14	Tennessee	180,057	2.2%
15	Louisiana	177,526	2.2%
16	Alabama	167,377	2.0%
17	Virginia	156,523	1.9%
18	Washington	150,570	1.8%
19	Missouri	138,515	1.7%
20	Indiana	128,340	1.6%
21	Mississippi	120,694	1.5%
22	Maryland	120,669	1.5%
23	Arizona	118,913	1.4%
24	Wisconsin	117,819	1.4%
25	South Carolina	117,205	1.4%
26	Arkansas	108,596	1.3%
27	Oklahoma	96,368	1.2%
28	Minnesota	93,806	1.1%
29	Oregon	87,342	1.1%
30	West Virginia	74,707	0.9%
31	Colorado	72,576	0.9%
32	Connecticut	64,607	0.8%
33	New Mexico	63,636	0.8%
34	Nevada	55,199	0.7%
35	Iowa	50,958	0.6%
36	Kansas	48,064	0.6%
37	Maine	37,313	0.5%
38	Rhode Island	33,228	0.4%
39	Utah	31,323	0.4%
40	Idaho	30,712	0.4%
41	Nebraska	27,867	0.3%
42	Hawaii	24,221	0.3%
43	New Hampshire	19,262	0.2%
44	Montana	18,287	0.2%
45	Delaware	16,884	0.2%
46	Vermont	15,617	0.2%
47	South Dakota	14,718	0.2%
48	Alaska	12,468	0.2%
49	North Dakota	8,206	0.1%
50	Wyoming	6,702	0.1%
	District of Columbia	26,838	0.3%

Source: U.S. Department of Health and Human Services, Social Security Administration

"Social Security Bulletin, Annual Statistical Supplement 2017" (https://www.ssa.gov/policy/docs/statcomps/supplement/)

*For December 2016. National total includes1,049 beneficiaries in U.S. territories or otherwise not distributed by state. The SSI program provides income support to persons age 65 and older and blind or disabled adults and children.

Average Monthly Social Security
Supplemental Security Income Payment in 2016
National Average = $526.74 Each Month per Beneficiary*

ALPHA ORDER

RANK	STATE	AVERAGE BENEFIT
34	Alabama	$514.06
44	Alaska	504.41
11	Arizona	534.54
25	Arkansas	523.26
33	California	516.23
27	Colorado	522.48
15	Connecticut	532.10
12	Delaware	534.07
18	Florida	527.21
26	Georgia	522.61
29	Hawaii	521.25
30	Idaho	520.79
6	Illinois	547.14
9	Indiana	539.69
40	Iowa	507.22
22	Kansas	524.42
24	Kentucky	523.77
17	Louisiana	528.50
45	Maine	501.49
2	Maryland	551.78
20	Massachusetts	526.92
3	Michigan	551.25
7	Minnesota	543.45
38	Mississippi	508.76
32	Missouri	517.57
47	Montana	499.65
39	Nebraska	507.33
8	Nevada	540.48
42	New Hampshire	506.14
43	New Jersey	506.02
41	New Mexico	506.16
13	New York	533.90
35	North Carolina	513.08
50	North Dakota	482.92
5	Ohio	548.88
23	Oklahoma	523.94
14	Oregon	532.19
1	Pennsylvania	554.33
19	Rhode Island	527.17
36	South Carolina	512.95
49	South Dakota	497.68
31	Tennessee	519.38
37	Texas	508.81
21	Utah	525.62
46	Vermont	500.61
28	Virginia	521.71
4	Washington	549.54
16	West Virginia	530.03
10	Wisconsin	535.56
48	Wyoming	499.36

RANK ORDER

RANK	STATE	AVERAGE BENEFIT
1	Pennsylvania	$554.33
2	Maryland	551.78
3	Michigan	551.25
4	Washington	549.54
5	Ohio	548.88
6	Illinois	547.14
7	Minnesota	543.45
8	Nevada	540.48
9	Indiana	539.69
10	Wisconsin	535.56
11	Arizona	534.54
12	Delaware	534.07
13	New York	533.90
14	Oregon	532.19
15	Connecticut	532.10
16	West Virginia	530.03
17	Louisiana	528.50
18	Florida	527.21
19	Rhode Island	527.17
20	Massachusetts	526.92
21	Utah	525.62
22	Kansas	524.42
23	Oklahoma	523.94
24	Kentucky	523.77
25	Arkansas	523.26
26	Georgia	522.61
27	Colorado	522.48
28	Virginia	521.71
29	Hawaii	521.25
30	Idaho	520.79
31	Tennessee	519.38
32	Missouri	517.57
33	California	516.23
34	Alabama	514.06
35	North Carolina	513.08
36	South Carolina	512.95
37	Texas	508.81
38	Mississippi	508.76
39	Nebraska	507.33
40	Iowa	507.22
41	New Mexico	506.16
42	New Hampshire	506.14
43	New Jersey	506.02
44	Alaska	504.41
45	Maine	501.49
46	Vermont	500.61
47	Montana	499.65
48	Wyoming	499.36
49	South Dakota	497.68
50	North Dakota	482.92
	District of Columbia	569.60

Source: U.S. Department of Health and Human Services, Social Security Administration
"Social Security Bulletin, Annual Statistical Supplement 2017" (https://www.ssa.gov/policy/docs/statcomps/supplement/)
*As of December 2016. National average includes payments to beneficiaries in U.S. territories and foreign countries. The SSI program provides income support to persons age 65 and older and blind or disabled adults and children.

Medicare Enrollees in 2017

National Total = 58,457,244 Enrollees*

RANK	STATE	ENROLLEES	% of USA
20	Alabama	1,007,423	1.7%
50	Alaska	91,879	0.2%
16	Arizona	1,226,671	2.1%
30	Arkansas	616,231	1.1%
1	California	5,965,489	10.2%
25	Colorado	847,702	1.5%
29	Connecticut	654,718	1.1%
45	Delaware	193,585	0.3%
2	Florida	4,295,216	7.3%
10	Georgia	1,624,056	2.8%
42	Hawaii	259,408	0.4%
40	Idaho	306,390	0.5%
7	Illinois	2,149,620	3.7%
17	Indiana	1,204,903	2.1%
31	Iowa	598,167	1.0%
33	Kansas	509,925	0.9%
24	Kentucky	895,963	1.5%
26	Louisiana	828,719	1.4%
39	Maine	322,151	0.6%
22	Maryland	984,017	1.7%
15	Massachusetts	1,275,550	2.2%
8	Michigan	1,981,476	3.4%
23	Minnesota	967,270	1.7%
32	Mississippi	580,012	1.0%
18	Missouri	1,182,965	2.0%
43	Montana	215,492	0.4%
38	Nebraska	329,480	0.6%
34	Nevada	492,325	0.8%
41	New Hampshire	280,990	0.5%
11	New Jersey	1,553,278	2.7%
36	New Mexico	396,908	0.7%
4	New York	3,482,221	6.0%
9	North Carolina	1,877,420	3.2%
48	North Dakota	124,089	0.2%
6	Ohio	2,249,050	3.8%
28	Oklahoma	706,317	1.2%
27	Oregon	807,584	1.4%
5	Pennsylvania	2,629,753	4.5%
44	Rhode Island	211,664	0.4%
21	South Carolina	1,006,419	1.7%
46	South Dakota	165,403	0.3%
13	Tennessee	1,294,909	2.2%
3	Texas	3,883,588	6.6%
37	Utah	371,924	0.6%
47	Vermont	139,235	0.2%
12	Virginia	1,427,679	2.4%
14	Washington	1,277,421	2.2%
35	West Virginia	427,858	0.7%
19	Wisconsin	1,110,269	1.9%
49	Wyoming	101,935	0.2%

RANK	STATE	ENROLLEES	% of USA
1	California	5,965,489	10.2%
2	Florida	4,295,216	7.3%
3	Texas	3,883,588	6.6%
4	New York	3,482,221	6.0%
5	Pennsylvania	2,629,753	4.5%
6	Ohio	2,249,050	3.8%
7	Illinois	2,149,620	3.7%
8	Michigan	1,981,476	3.4%
9	North Carolina	1,877,420	3.2%
10	Georgia	1,624,056	2.8%
11	New Jersey	1,553,278	2.7%
12	Virginia	1,427,679	2.4%
13	Tennessee	1,294,909	2.2%
14	Washington	1,277,421	2.2%
15	Massachusetts	1,275,550	2.2%
16	Arizona	1,226,671	2.1%
17	Indiana	1,204,903	2.1%
18	Missouri	1,182,965	2.0%
19	Wisconsin	1,110,269	1.9%
20	Alabama	1,007,423	1.7%
21	South Carolina	1,006,419	1.7%
22	Maryland	984,017	1.7%
23	Minnesota	967,270	1.7%
24	Kentucky	895,963	1.5%
25	Colorado	847,702	1.5%
26	Louisiana	828,719	1.4%
27	Oregon	807,584	1.4%
28	Oklahoma	706,317	1.2%
29	Connecticut	654,718	1.1%
30	Arkansas	616,231	1.1%
31	Iowa	598,167	1.0%
32	Mississippi	580,012	1.0%
33	Kansas	509,925	0.9%
34	Nevada	492,325	0.8%
35	West Virginia	427,858	0.7%
36	New Mexico	396,908	0.7%
37	Utah	371,924	0.6%
38	Nebraska	329,480	0.6%
39	Maine	322,151	0.6%
40	Idaho	306,390	0.5%
41	New Hampshire	280,990	0.5%
42	Hawaii	259,408	0.4%
43	Montana	215,492	0.4%
44	Rhode Island	211,664	0.4%
45	Delaware	193,585	0.3%
46	South Dakota	165,403	0.3%
47	Vermont	139,235	0.2%
48	North Dakota	124,089	0.2%
49	Wyoming	101,935	0.2%
50	Alaska	91,879	0.2%
	District of Columbia	91,051	0.2%

Source: U.S. Department of Health and Human Services, Centers for Medicare and Medicaid Services
"Medicare Enrollment Dashboard"
(https://www.cms.gov/Research-Statistics-Data-and-Systems/Statistics-Trends-and-Reports/CMSProgramStatistics/Dashboard.html)
*Includes original Medicare, Medicare Advantage, and other Medicare health plans. Includes Aged and Disabled enrollees. Total includes 1,223,402 enrollees in Puerto Rico and other outlying areas, foreign countries, or whose address is unknown.

Percent of Population Enrolled in Medicare in 2017

National Percent = 17.6% of Population*

ALPHA ORDER			RANK ORDER		
RANK	STATE	PERCENT	RANK	STATE	PERCENT
5	Alabama	20.7	1	Maine	24.1
49	Alaska	12.4	2	West Virginia	23.5
36	Arizona	17.4	3	Vermont	22.3
7	Arkansas	20.5	4	New Hampshire	20.8
46	California	15.1	5	Alabama	20.7
46	Colorado	15.1	6	Pennsylvania	20.6
25	Connecticut	18.3	7	Arkansas	20.5
10	Delaware	20.2	7	Florida	20.5
7	Florida	20.5	7	Montana	20.5
45	Georgia	15.6	10	Delaware	20.2
27	Hawaii	18.2	11	Kentucky	20.1
30	Idaho	17.8	12	Rhode Island	20.0
41	Illinois	16.8	12	South Carolina	20.0
28	Indiana	18.1	14	Michigan	19.9
21	Iowa	19.0	15	Oregon	19.5
34	Kansas	17.5	16	Mississippi	19.4
11	Kentucky	20.1	16	Missouri	19.4
32	Louisiana	17.7	18	Ohio	19.3
1	Maine	24.1	18	Tennessee	19.3
44	Maryland	16.3	20	Wisconsin	19.2
24	Massachusetts	18.6	21	Iowa	19.0
14	Michigan	19.9	21	New Mexico	19.0
36	Minnesota	17.4	23	South Dakota	18.9
16	Mississippi	19.4	24	Massachusetts	18.6
16	Missouri	19.4	25	Connecticut	18.3
7	Montana	20.5	25	North Carolina	18.3
38	Nebraska	17.2	27	Hawaii	18.2
42	Nevada	16.6	28	Indiana	18.1
4	New Hampshire	20.8	29	Oklahoma	18.0
34	New Jersey	17.5	30	Idaho	17.8
21	New Mexico	19.0	30	New York	17.8
30	New York	17.8	32	Louisiana	17.7
25	North Carolina	18.3	33	Wyoming	17.6
43	North Dakota	16.4	34	Kansas	17.5
18	Ohio	19.3	34	New Jersey	17.5
29	Oklahoma	18.0	36	Arizona	17.4
15	Oregon	19.5	36	Minnesota	17.4
6	Pennsylvania	20.6	38	Nebraska	17.2
12	Rhode Island	20.0	38	Washington	17.2
12	South Carolina	20.0	40	Virginia	16.9
23	South Dakota	18.9	41	Illinois	16.8
18	Tennessee	19.3	42	Nevada	16.6
48	Texas	13.7	43	North Dakota	16.4
50	Utah	12.0	44	Maryland	16.3
3	Vermont	22.3	45	Georgia	15.6
40	Virginia	16.9	46	California	15.1
38	Washington	17.2	46	Colorado	15.1
2	West Virginia	23.5	48	Texas	13.7
20	Wisconsin	19.2	49	Alaska	12.4
33	Wyoming	17.6	50	Utah	12.0
				District of Columbia	13.1

Source: CQ Press using data from U.S. Department of Health and Human Services, Centers for Medicare and Medicaid Services
  "Medicare Enrollment Dashboard"
  (https://www.cms.gov/Research-Statistics-Data-and-Systems/Statistics-Trends-and-Reports/CMSProgramStatistics/Dashboard.html)
*Includes original Medicare, Medicare Advantage, and other Medicare health plans. Includes Aged and Disabled enrollees. National
rate does not include enrollees or population in Puerto Rico and other outlying areas, foreign countries, or whose address is
unknown.

Medicare Actual Costs in 2016

National Total = $342,275,929,819*

ALPHA ORDER

RANK	STATE	ACTUAL COSTS	% of USA
19	Alabama	$6,079,331,451	1.8%
50	Alaska	720,780,141	0.2%
21	Arizona	5,880,395,251	1.7%
28	Arkansas	3,888,284,756	1.1%
1	California	32,306,158,016	9.4%
29	Colorado	3,827,806,303	1.1%
26	Connecticut	4,795,156,739	1.4%
41	Delaware	1,638,806,007	0.5%
2	Florida	24,701,872,197	7.2%
13	Georgia	8,853,861,730	2.6%
47	Hawaii	823,928,005	0.2%
42	Idaho	1,485,801,930	0.4%
5	Illinois	15,282,221,317	4.5%
15	Indiana	7,963,871,666	2.3%
30	Iowa	3,800,614,979	1.1%
31	Kansas	3,638,215,093	1.1%
23	Kentucky	5,418,964,546	1.6%
22	Louisiana	5,451,272,168	1.6%
38	Maine	1,888,089,598	0.6%
14	Maryland	8,750,143,004	2.6%
11	Massachusetts	9,767,988,773	2.9%
8	Michigan	12,250,811,541	3.6%
32	Minnesota	3,269,867,024	1.0%
27	Mississippi	4,546,064,699	1.3%
16	Missouri	6,921,804,629	2.0%
43	Montana	1,211,269,133	0.4%
36	Nebraska	2,401,013,387	0.7%
34	Nevada	2,740,324,515	0.8%
37	New Hampshire	2,035,713,375	0.6%
7	New Jersey	13,355,807,378	3.9%
39	New Mexico	1,826,901,051	0.5%
4	New York	21,206,811,603	6.2%
10	North Carolina	10,785,884,211	3.2%
48	North Dakota	768,057,189	0.2%
9	Ohio	12,037,706,274	3.5%
25	Oklahoma	5,178,625,090	1.5%
33	Oregon	3,129,455,818	0.9%
6	Pennsylvania	13,944,708,908	4.1%
44	Rhode Island	1,058,252,360	0.3%
20	South Carolina	6,030,948,454	1.8%
46	South Dakota	994,917,311	0.3%
17	Tennessee	6,807,939,211	2.0%
3	Texas	24,627,249,015	7.2%
40	Utah	1,752,002,035	0.5%
45	Vermont	995,914,256	0.3%
12	Virginia	9,016,163,842	2.6%
18	Washington	6,601,562,909	1.9%
35	West Virginia	2,595,216,111	0.8%
24	Wisconsin	5,188,239,247	1.5%
49	Wyoming	766,567,161	0.2%

RANK ORDER

RANK	STATE	ACTUAL COSTS	% of USA
1	California	$32,306,158,016	9.4%
2	Florida	24,701,872,197	7.2%
3	Texas	24,627,249,015	7.2%
4	New York	21,206,811,603	6.2%
5	Illinois	15,282,221,317	4.5%
6	Pennsylvania	13,944,708,908	4.1%
7	New Jersey	13,355,807,378	3.9%
8	Michigan	12,250,811,541	3.6%
9	Ohio	12,037,706,274	3.5%
10	North Carolina	10,785,884,211	3.2%
11	Massachusetts	9,767,988,773	2.9%
12	Virginia	9,016,163,842	2.6%
13	Georgia	8,853,861,730	2.6%
14	Maryland	8,750,143,004	2.6%
15	Indiana	7,963,871,666	2.3%
16	Missouri	6,921,804,629	2.0%
17	Tennessee	6,807,939,211	2.0%
18	Washington	6,601,562,909	1.9%
19	Alabama	6,079,331,451	1.8%
20	South Carolina	6,030,948,454	1.8%
21	Arizona	5,880,395,251	1.7%
22	Louisiana	5,451,272,168	1.6%
23	Kentucky	5,418,964,546	1.6%
24	Wisconsin	5,188,239,247	1.5%
25	Oklahoma	5,178,625,090	1.5%
26	Connecticut	4,795,156,739	1.4%
27	Mississippi	4,546,064,699	1.3%
28	Arkansas	3,888,284,756	1.1%
29	Colorado	3,827,806,303	1.1%
30	Iowa	3,800,614,979	1.1%
31	Kansas	3,638,215,093	1.1%
32	Minnesota	3,269,867,024	1.0%
33	Oregon	3,129,455,818	0.9%
34	Nevada	2,740,324,515	0.8%
35	West Virginia	2,595,216,111	0.8%
36	Nebraska	2,401,013,387	0.7%
37	New Hampshire	2,035,713,375	0.6%
38	Maine	1,888,089,598	0.6%
39	New Mexico	1,826,901,051	0.5%
40	Utah	1,752,002,035	0.5%
41	Delaware	1,638,806,007	0.5%
42	Idaho	1,485,801,930	0.4%
43	Montana	1,211,269,133	0.4%
44	Rhode Island	1,058,252,360	0.3%
45	Vermont	995,914,256	0.3%
46	South Dakota	994,917,311	0.3%
47	Hawaii	823,928,005	0.2%
48	North Dakota	768,057,189	0.2%
49	Wyoming	766,567,161	0.2%
50	Alaska	720,780,141	0.2%
	District of Columbia	709,108,177	0.2%

Source: U.S. Department of Health and Human Services, Centers for Medicare and Medicaid Services
"Medicare Geographic Variation" (Public Use File)
(https://www.cms.gov/Research-Statistics-Data-and-Systems/Statistics-Trends-and-Reports/Medicare-Geographic-Variation/)
*Total actual costs not standardized for geographical variations. National figure includes payments to enrollees in Puerto Rico and other outlying areas.

Medicare Actual Costs per Beneficiary in 2016

National Rate = $6,409*

ALPHA ORDER

RANK	STATE	PER BENEFICIARY
27	Alabama	$6,389
4	Alaska	9,103
43	Arizona	5,273
22	Arkansas	6,659
35	California	6,054
46	Colorado	5,028
9	Connecticut	8,110
3	Delaware	9,187
32	Florida	6,125
36	Georgia	5,911
49	Hawaii	3,647
44	Idaho	5,251
13	Illinois	7,757
15	Indiana	7,016
20	Iowa	6,727
14	Kansas	7,663
25	Kentucky	6,424
16	Louisiana	6,999
29	Maine	6,310
1	Maryland	10,176
5	Massachusetts	8,515
23	Michigan	6,491
50	Minnesota	3,634
7	Mississippi	8,172
31	Missouri	6,236
33	Montana	6,083
11	Nebraska	7,870
30	Nevada	6,296
8	New Hampshire	8,126
2	New Jersey	9,553
45	New Mexico	5,097
19	New York	6,740
34	North Carolina	6,074
21	North Dakota	6,683
37	Ohio	5,747
10	Oklahoma	7,878
48	Oregon	4,209
39	Pennsylvania	5,698
40	Rhode Island	5,618
26	South Carolina	6,393
24	South Dakota	6,483
41	Tennessee	5,569
18	Texas	6,938
42	Utah	5,277
12	Vermont	7,804
17	Virginia	6,980
38	Washington	5,699
28	West Virginia	6,344
47	Wisconsin	4,963
6	Wyoming	8,191

RANK ORDER

RANK	STATE	PER BENEFICIARY
1	Maryland	$10,176
2	New Jersey	9,553
3	Delaware	9,187
4	Alaska	9,103
5	Massachusetts	8,515
6	Wyoming	8,191
7	Mississippi	8,172
8	New Hampshire	8,126
9	Connecticut	8,110
10	Oklahoma	7,878
11	Nebraska	7,870
12	Vermont	7,804
13	Illinois	7,757
14	Kansas	7,663
15	Indiana	7,016
16	Louisiana	6,999
17	Virginia	6,980
18	Texas	6,938
19	New York	6,740
20	Iowa	6,727
21	North Dakota	6,683
22	Arkansas	6,659
23	Michigan	6,491
24	South Dakota	6,483
25	Kentucky	6,424
26	South Carolina	6,393
27	Alabama	6,389
28	West Virginia	6,344
29	Maine	6,310
30	Nevada	6,296
31	Missouri	6,236
32	Florida	6,125
33	Montana	6,083
34	North Carolina	6,074
35	California	6,054
36	Georgia	5,911
37	Ohio	5,747
38	Washington	5,699
39	Pennsylvania	5,698
40	Rhode Island	5,618
41	Tennessee	5,569
42	Utah	5,277
43	Arizona	5,273
44	Idaho	5,251
45	New Mexico	5,097
46	Colorado	5,028
47	Wisconsin	4,963
48	Oregon	4,209
49	Hawaii	3,647
50	Minnesota	3,634
	District of Columbia	9,575

Source: CQ Press using data from U.S. Department of Health and Human Services, Centers for Medicare and Medicaid Services "Medicare Geographic Variation" (Public Use File)
(https://www.cms.gov/Research-Statistics-Data-and-Systems/Statistics-Trends-and-Reports/Medicare-Geographic-Variation/)
*Total actual costs not standardized for geographical variations. National figure includes payments and enrollees in Puerto Rico and other outlying areas.

Medicaid Enrollment in 2016

National Total = 80,184,501 Enrollees*

ALPHA ORDER

RANK	STATE	ENROLLEES	% of USA
26	Alabama	1,037,037	1.3%
47	Alaska	155,865	0.2%
12	Arizona	1,849,166	2.3%
30	Arkansas	799,488	1.0%
1	California	13,739,388	17.1%
19	Colorado	1,344,548	1.7%
29	Connecticut	860,758	1.1%
43	Delaware	221,229	0.3%
5	Florida	3,900,380	4.9%
10	Georgia	1,973,586	2.5%
37	Hawaii	358,302	0.4%
39	Idaho	295,267	0.4%
6	Illinois	3,230,870	4.0%
17	Indiana	1,421,696	1.8%
34	Iowa	624,973	0.8%
36	Kansas	435,850	0.5%
18	Kentucky	1,361,722	1.7%
16	Louisiana	1,504,333	1.9%
41	Maine	277,697	0.3%
20	Maryland	1,324,796	1.7%
11	Massachusetts	1,889,306	2.4%
3	Michigan	4,448,582	5.5%
25	Minnesota	1,088,610	1.4%
32	Mississippi	726,473	0.9%
27	Missouri	982,776	1.2%
44	Montana	207,340	0.3%
42	Nebraska	244,355	0.3%
33	Nevada	629,265	0.8%
45	New Hampshire	206,997	0.3%
15	New Jersey	1,679,572	2.1%
28	New Mexico	884,368	1.1%
2	New York	6,139,403	7.7%
9	North Carolina	2,028,935	2.5%
49	North Dakota	93,422	0.1%
7	Ohio	3,022,121	3.8%
31	Oklahoma	792,387	1.0%
24	Oregon	1,109,321	1.4%
8	Pennsylvania	2,753,618	3.4%
38	Rhode Island	325,177	0.4%
21	South Carolina	1,235,361	1.5%
48	South Dakota	125,395	0.2%
14	Tennessee	1,684,268	2.1%
4	Texas	4,051,664	5.1%
40	Utah	294,707	0.4%
46	Vermont	200,481	0.3%
23	Virginia	1,111,999	1.4%
13	Washington	1,820,084	2.3%
35	West Virginia	553,318	0.7%
22	Wisconsin	1,204,511	1.5%
50	Wyoming	64,442	0.1%

RANK ORDER

RANK	STATE	ENROLLEES	% of USA
1	California	13,739,388	17.1%
2	New York	6,139,403	7.7%
3	Michigan	4,448,582	5.5%
4	Texas	4,051,664	5.1%
5	Florida	3,900,380	4.9%
6	Illinois	3,230,870	4.0%
7	Ohio	3,022,121	3.8%
8	Pennsylvania	2,753,618	3.4%
9	North Carolina	2,028,935	2.5%
10	Georgia	1,973,586	2.5%
11	Massachusetts	1,889,306	2.4%
12	Arizona	1,849,166	2.3%
13	Washington	1,820,084	2.3%
14	Tennessee	1,684,268	2.1%
15	New Jersey	1,679,572	2.1%
16	Louisiana	1,504,333	1.9%
17	Indiana	1,421,696	1.8%
18	Kentucky	1,361,722	1.7%
19	Colorado	1,344,548	1.7%
20	Maryland	1,324,796	1.7%
21	South Carolina	1,235,361	1.5%
22	Wisconsin	1,204,511	1.5%
23	Virginia	1,111,999	1.4%
24	Oregon	1,109,321	1.4%
25	Minnesota	1,088,610	1.4%
26	Alabama	1,037,037	1.3%
27	Missouri	982,776	1.2%
28	New Mexico	884,368	1.1%
29	Connecticut	860,758	1.1%
30	Arkansas	799,488	1.0%
31	Oklahoma	792,387	1.0%
32	Mississippi	726,473	0.9%
33	Nevada	629,265	0.8%
34	Iowa	624,973	0.8%
35	West Virginia	553,318	0.7%
36	Kansas	435,850	0.5%
37	Hawaii	358,302	0.4%
38	Rhode Island	325,177	0.4%
39	Idaho	295,267	0.4%
40	Utah	294,707	0.4%
41	Maine	277,697	0.3%
42	Nebraska	244,355	0.3%
43	Delaware	221,229	0.3%
44	Montana	207,340	0.3%
45	New Hampshire	206,997	0.3%
46	Vermont	200,481	0.3%
47	Alaska	155,865	0.2%
48	South Dakota	125,395	0.2%
49	North Dakota	93,422	0.1%
50	Wyoming	64,442	0.1%
	District of Columbia	251,791	0.3%

Source: U.S. Department of Health and Human Services, Centers for Medicare and Medicaid Services
   "2016 Medicaid Managed Care Enrollment Report" (https://www.medicaid.gov/medicaid/managed-care/enrollment/index.html)
*Unduplicated enrollment as of July 1, 2016. National total includes 1,617,501 Medicaid enrollees in Puerto Rico.

Percent of Population Enrolled in Medicaid in 2016

National Percent = 24.3% of Population*

ALPHA ORDER			RANK ORDER		
RANK	STATE	PERCENT	RANK	STATE	PERCENT
28	Alabama	21.3	1	Michigan	44.7
29	Alaska	21.0	2	New Mexico	42.3
13	Arizona	26.6	3	California	35.0
12	Arkansas	26.7	4	Louisiana	32.2
3	California	35.0	5	Vermont	32.1
20	Colorado	24.3	6	New York	31.3
22	Connecticut	24.1	7	Rhode Island	30.8
23	Delaware	23.3	8	Kentucky	30.7
38	Florida	18.9	9	West Virginia	30.2
37	Georgia	19.2	10	Massachusetts	27.7
17	Hawaii	25.1	11	Oregon	27.1
40	Idaho	17.5	12	Arkansas	26.7
16	Illinois	25.2	13	Arizona	26.6
27	Indiana	21.4	14	Ohio	26.0
33	Iowa	20.0	15	Tennessee	25.3
43	Kansas	15.0	16	Illinois	25.2
8	Kentucky	30.7	17	Hawaii	25.1
4	Louisiana	32.2	18	Washington	25.0
30	Maine	20.9	19	South Carolina	24.9
24	Maryland	22.1	20	Colorado	24.3
10	Massachusetts	27.7	20	Mississippi	24.3
1	Michigan	44.7	22	Connecticut	24.1
36	Minnesota	19.7	23	Delaware	23.3
20	Mississippi	24.3	24	Maryland	22.1
41	Missouri	16.1	25	Nevada	21.6
35	Montana	19.9	26	Pennsylvania	21.5
47	Nebraska	12.8	27	Indiana	21.4
25	Nevada	21.6	28	Alabama	21.3
42	New Hampshire	15.4	29	Alaska	21.0
38	New Jersey	18.9	30	Maine	20.9
2	New Mexico	42.3	30	Wisconsin	20.9
6	New York	31.3	32	Oklahoma	20.2
33	North Carolina	20.0	33	Iowa	20.0
48	North Dakota	12.4	33	North Carolina	20.0
14	Ohio	26.0	35	Montana	19.9
32	Oklahoma	20.2	36	Minnesota	19.7
11	Oregon	27.1	37	Georgia	19.2
26	Pennsylvania	21.5	38	Florida	18.9
7	Rhode Island	30.8	38	New Jersey	18.9
19	South Carolina	24.9	40	Idaho	17.5
44	South Dakota	14.5	41	Missouri	16.1
15	Tennessee	25.3	42	New Hampshire	15.4
44	Texas	14.5	43	Kansas	15.0
50	Utah	9.7	44	South Dakota	14.5
5	Vermont	32.1	44	Texas	14.5
46	Virginia	13.2	46	Virginia	13.2
18	Washington	25.0	47	Nebraska	12.8
9	West Virginia	30.2	48	North Dakota	12.4
30	Wisconsin	20.9	49	Wyoming	11.0
49	Wyoming	11.0	50	Utah	9.7
				District of Columbia	36.7

Source: CQ Press using data from U.S. Department of Health and Human Services, Centers for Medicare and Medicaid Services "2016 Medicaid Managed Care Enrollment Report" (https://www.medicaid.gov/medicaid/managed-care/enrollment/index.html)
*Unduplicated enrollment as of July 1, 2016. National percent does not include recipients or population in U.S. territories.

Estimated Medicaid Expenditures in 2018

National Total = $603,166,000,000*

ALPHA ORDER

RANK	STATE	EXPENDITURES	% of USA
28	Alabama	$6,754,000,000	1.1%
40	Alaska	2,326,000,000	0.4%
13	Arizona	12,596,000,000	2.1%
27	Arkansas	7,105,000,000	1.2%
1	California	97,288,000,000	16.1%
22	Colorado	9,928,000,000	1.6%
26	Connecticut	8,080,000,000	1.3%
41	Delaware	2,274,000,000	0.4%
5	Florida	27,277,000,000	4.5%
20	Georgia	10,308,000,000	1.7%
45	Hawaii	2,140,000,000	0.4%
44	Idaho	2,147,000,000	0.4%
7	Illinois	23,799,000,000	3.9%
16	Indiana	11,613,000,000	1.9%
33	Iowa	4,971,000,000	0.8%
36	Kansas	3,481,000,000	0.6%
19	Kentucky	10,329,000,000	1.7%
18	Louisiana	11,205,000,000	1.9%
38	Maine	2,786,000,000	0.5%
17	Maryland	11,501,000,000	1.9%
9	Massachusetts	16,674,000,000	2.8%
8	Michigan	17,798,000,000	3.0%
12	Minnesota	12,656,000,000	2.1%
32	Mississippi	5,089,000,000	0.8%
21	Missouri	10,187,000,000	1.7%
46	Montana	1,834,000,000	0.3%
43	Nebraska	2,150,000,000	0.4%
35	Nevada	3,971,000,000	0.7%
42	New Hampshire	2,178,000,000	0.4%
10	New Jersey	15,142,000,000	2.5%
30	New Mexico	5,681,000,000	0.9%
2	New York	55,645,000,000	9.2%
11	North Carolina	13,948,000,000	2.3%
48	North Dakota	1,231,000,000	0.2%
6	Ohio	26,459,000,000	4.4%
31	Oklahoma	5,532,000,000	0.9%
25	Oregon	9,113,000,000	1.5%
4	Pennsylvania	31,887,000,000	5.3%
39	Rhode Island	2,740,000,000	0.5%
29	South Carolina	6,604,000,000	1.1%
49	South Dakota	912,000,000	0.2%
15	Tennessee	11,658,000,000	1.9%
3	Texas	34,688,000,000	5.8%
37	Utah	3,044,000,000	0.5%
47	Vermont	1,602,000,000	0.3%
23	Virginia	9,861,000,000	1.6%
14	Washington	12,344,000,000	2.0%
34	West Virginia	4,147,000,000	0.7%
24	Wisconsin	9,856,000,000	1.6%
50	Wyoming	627,000,000	0.1%

RANK ORDER

RANK	STATE	EXPENDITURES	% of USA
1	California	$97,288,000,000	16.1%
2	New York	55,645,000,000	9.2%
3	Texas	34,688,000,000	5.8%
4	Pennsylvania	31,887,000,000	5.3%
5	Florida	27,277,000,000	4.5%
6	Ohio	26,459,000,000	4.4%
7	Illinois	23,799,000,000	3.9%
8	Michigan	17,798,000,000	3.0%
9	Massachusetts	16,674,000,000	2.8%
10	New Jersey	15,142,000,000	2.5%
11	North Carolina	13,948,000,000	2.3%
12	Minnesota	12,656,000,000	2.1%
13	Arizona	12,596,000,000	2.1%
14	Washington	12,344,000,000	2.0%
15	Tennessee	11,658,000,000	1.9%
16	Indiana	11,613,000,000	1.9%
17	Maryland	11,501,000,000	1.9%
18	Louisiana	11,205,000,000	1.9%
19	Kentucky	10,329,000,000	1.7%
20	Georgia	10,308,000,000	1.7%
21	Missouri	10,187,000,000	1.7%
22	Colorado	9,928,000,000	1.6%
23	Virginia	9,861,000,000	1.6%
24	Wisconsin	9,856,000,000	1.6%
25	Oregon	9,113,000,000	1.5%
26	Connecticut	8,080,000,000	1.3%
27	Arkansas	7,105,000,000	1.2%
28	Alabama	6,754,000,000	1.1%
29	South Carolina	6,604,000,000	1.1%
30	New Mexico	5,681,000,000	0.9%
31	Oklahoma	5,532,000,000	0.9%
32	Mississippi	5,089,000,000	0.8%
33	Iowa	4,971,000,000	0.8%
34	West Virginia	4,147,000,000	0.7%
35	Nevada	3,971,000,000	0.7%
36	Kansas	3,481,000,000	0.6%
37	Utah	3,044,000,000	0.5%
38	Maine	2,786,000,000	0.5%
39	Rhode Island	2,740,000,000	0.5%
40	Alaska	2,326,000,000	0.4%
41	Delaware	2,274,000,000	0.4%
42	New Hampshire	2,178,000,000	0.4%
43	Nebraska	2,150,000,000	0.4%
44	Idaho	2,147,000,000	0.4%
45	Hawaii	2,140,000,000	0.4%
46	Montana	1,834,000,000	0.3%
47	Vermont	1,602,000,000	0.3%
48	North Dakota	1,231,000,000	0.2%
49	South Dakota	912,000,000	0.2%
50	Wyoming	627,000,000	0.1%
	District of Columbia**	NA	NA

Source: National Association of State Budget Officers
"State Expenditure Report" (www.nasbo.org)
*Estimates for fiscal year 2018.
**Not available.

Percent Change in Medicaid Expenditures: 2017 to 2018

National Percent Change = 7.3% Increase*

ALPHA ORDER				RANK ORDER		
RANK	STATE	PERCENT CHANGE		RANK	STATE	PERCENT CHANGE
28	Alabama	4.1		1	Illinois	49.3
2	Alaska	15.0		2	Alaska	15.0
17	Arizona	6.6		2	Colorado	15.0
46	Arkansas	(0.3)		4	Minnesota	14.7
13	California	8.5		5	Utah	14.3
2	Colorado	15.0		6	Nevada	11.7
10	Connecticut	9.2		7	Delaware	10.7
7	Delaware	10.7		7	North Dakota	10.7
15	Florida	7.9		9	Louisiana	10.4
40	Georgia	1.6		10	Connecticut	9.2
50	Hawaii	(3.6)		10	Idaho	9.2
10	Idaho	9.2		12	New York	8.7
1	Illinois	49.3		13	California	8.5
43	Indiana	0.5		14	Massachusetts	8.0
28	Iowa	4.1		15	Florida	7.9
21	Kansas	5.0		16	Pennsylvania	7.8
25	Kentucky	4.4		17	Arizona	6.6
9	Louisiana	10.4		17	Texas	6.6
24	Maine	4.6		19	Tennessee	5.3
38	Maryland	1.8		20	Virginia	5.1
14	Massachusetts	8.0		21	Kansas	5.0
23	Michigan	4.9		21	Missouri	5.0
4	Minnesota	14.7		23	Michigan	4.9
47	Mississippi	(1.3)		24	Maine	4.6
21	Missouri	5.0		25	Kentucky	4.4
26	Montana	4.3		26	Montana	4.3
31	Nebraska	3.8		26	New Jersey	4.3
6	Nevada	11.7		28	Alabama	4.1
44	New Hampshire	0.4		28	Iowa	4.1
26	New Jersey	4.3		30	Rhode Island	3.9
41	New Mexico	1.3		31	Nebraska	3.8
12	New York	8.7		31	Oklahoma	3.8
49	North Carolina	(1.6)		33	Wisconsin	3.6
7	North Dakota	10.7		34	Ohio	3.1
34	Ohio	3.1		35	Washington	2.8
31	Oklahoma	3.8		36	South Dakota	2.0
48	Oregon	(1.4)		36	Wyoming	2.0
16	Pennsylvania	7.8		38	Maryland	1.8
30	Rhode Island	3.9		39	West Virginia	1.7
42	South Carolina	0.7		40	Georgia	1.6
36	South Dakota	2.0		41	New Mexico	1.3
19	Tennessee	5.3		42	South Carolina	0.7
17	Texas	6.6		43	Indiana	0.5
5	Utah	14.3		44	New Hampshire	0.4
45	Vermont	0.2		45	Vermont	0.2
20	Virginia	5.1		46	Arkansas	(0.3)
35	Washington	2.8		47	Mississippi	(1.3)
39	West Virginia	1.7		48	Oregon	(1.4)
33	Wisconsin	3.6		49	North Carolina	(1.6)
36	Wyoming	2.0		50	Hawaii	(3.6)
				District of Columbia**		NA

Source: National Association of State Budget Officers
  "State Expenditure Report" (www.nasbo.org)
*Estimates for fiscal year 2018.
**Not available.

Percent of Population Receiving Public Aid in 2016

National Percent = 3.4% of Population*

<u>ALPHA ORDER</u>

RANK	STATE	PERCENT
9	Alabama	3.9
24	Alaska	2.8
43	Arizona	2.0
9	Arkansas	3.9
1	California	5.6
42	Colorado	2.1
35	Connecticut	2.4
20	Delaware	3.0
18	Florida	3.2
28	Georgia	2.7
24	Hawaii	2.8
43	Idaho	2.0
35	Illinois	2.4
41	Indiana	2.2
35	Iowa	2.4
43	Kansas	2.0
2	Kentucky	5.4
8	Louisiana	4.1
17	Maine	3.3
24	Maryland	2.8
13	Massachusetts	3.6
19	Michigan	3.1
34	Minnesota	2.5
6	Mississippi	4.4
28	Missouri	2.7
32	Montana	2.6
43	Nebraska	2.0
28	Nevada	2.7
47	New Hampshire	1.8
35	New Jersey	2.4
4	New Mexico	4.5
4	New York	4.5
15	North Carolina	3.4
48	North Dakota	1.4
13	Ohio	3.6
22	Oklahoma	2.9
20	Oregon	3.0
9	Pennsylvania	3.9
7	Rhode Island	4.2
24	South Carolina	2.8
35	South Dakota	2.4
12	Tennessee	3.7
32	Texas	2.6
50	Utah	1.3
15	Vermont	3.4
40	Virginia	2.3
22	Washington	2.9
3	West Virginia	4.9
28	Wisconsin	2.7
48	Wyoming	1.4

<u>RANK ORDER</u>

RANK	STATE	PERCENT
1	California	5.6
2	Kentucky	5.4
3	West Virginia	4.9
4	New Mexico	4.5
4	New York	4.5
6	Mississippi	4.4
7	Rhode Island	4.2
8	Louisiana	4.1
9	Alabama	3.9
9	Arkansas	3.9
9	Pennsylvania	3.9
12	Tennessee	3.7
13	Massachusetts	3.6
13	Ohio	3.6
15	North Carolina	3.4
15	Vermont	3.4
17	Maine	3.3
18	Florida	3.2
19	Michigan	3.1
20	Delaware	3.0
20	Oregon	3.0
22	Oklahoma	2.9
22	Washington	2.9
24	Alaska	2.8
24	Hawaii	2.8
24	Maryland	2.8
24	South Carolina	2.8
28	Georgia	2.7
28	Missouri	2.7
28	Nevada	2.7
28	Wisconsin	2.7
32	Montana	2.6
32	Texas	2.6
34	Minnesota	2.5
35	Connecticut	2.4
35	Illinois	2.4
35	Iowa	2.4
35	New Jersey	2.4
35	South Dakota	2.4
40	Virginia	2.3
41	Indiana	2.2
42	Colorado	2.1
43	Arizona	2.0
43	Idaho	2.0
43	Kansas	2.0
43	Nebraska	2.0
47	New Hampshire	1.8
48	North Dakota	1.4
48	Wyoming	1.4
50	Utah	1.3

	District of Columbia	5.9

Source: CQ Press using data from U.S. Department of Health and Human Services, Social Security Administration
"Social Security Bulletin, Annual Statistical Supplement 2017" (https://www.ssa.gov/policy/docs/statcomps/supplement/) and
U.S. Department of Health and Human Services, Administration for Children and Families
"TANF Caseload Data" (https://www.acf.hhs.gov/programs/ofa/programs/tanf/data-reports)
*As of December 2016. Includes recipients of Temporary Assistance to Needy Families (TANF) and/or Supplemental Security
Income payments.

Recipients of Temporary Assistance to Needy Families (TANF) Payments in 2018
National Total = 2,236,711 Monthly Recipients*

ALPHA ORDER

RANK	STATE	RECIPIENTS	% of USA
27	Alabama	17,643	0.7%
42	Alaska	7,511	0.3%
29	Arizona	14,498	0.6%
44	Arkansas	6,015	0.2%
1	California	768,932	30.9%
14	Colorado	36,129	1.5%
26	Connecticut	19,165	0.8%
35	Delaware	10,447	0.4%
6	Florida	65,565	2.6%
24	Georgia	21,197	0.9%
33	Hawaii	12,140	0.5%
48	Idaho	2,941	0.1%
22	Illinois	21,630	0.9%
34	Indiana	11,509	0.5%
25	Iowa	19,516	0.8%
47	Kansas	4,176	0.2%
13	Kentucky	38,707	1.6%
30	Louisiana	13,749	0.6%
41	Maine	7,531	0.3%
11	Maryland	43,412	1.7%
9	Massachusetts	51,632	2.1%
18	Michigan	29,830	1.2%
12	Minnesota	41,253	1.7%
39	Mississippi	8,519	0.3%
23	Missouri	21,262	0.9%
37	Montana	9,777	0.4%
36	Nebraska	9,952	0.4%
21	Nevada	23,398	0.9%
43	New Hampshire	6,703	0.3%
20	New Jersey	24,681	1.0%
19	New Mexico	24,788	1.0%
2	New York	202,557	8.1%
5	North Carolina	85,365	3.4%
49	North Dakota	2,518	0.1%
4	Ohio	85,574	3.4%
31	Oklahoma	13,690	0.6%
16	Oregon	32,387	1.3%
3	Pennsylvania	112,808	4.5%
38	Rhode Island	9,559	0.4%
28	South Carolina	17,165	0.7%
45	South Dakota	5,933	0.2%
10	Tennessee	47,029	1.9%
8	Texas	53,508	2.2%
40	Utah	8,245	0.3%
46	Vermont	4,938	0.2%
15	Virginia	33,592	1.4%
7	Washington	54,447	2.2%
32	West Virginia	12,758	0.5%
17	Wisconsin	31,585	1.3%
50	Wyoming	1,348	0.1%

RANK ORDER

RANK	STATE	RECIPIENTS	% of USA
1	California	768,932	30.9%
2	New York	202,557	8.1%
3	Pennsylvania	112,808	4.5%
4	Ohio	85,574	3.4%
5	North Carolina	85,365	3.4%
6	Florida	65,565	2.6%
7	Washington	54,447	2.2%
8	Texas	53,508	2.2%
9	Massachusetts	51,632	2.1%
10	Tennessee	47,029	1.9%
11	Maryland	43,412	1.7%
12	Minnesota	41,253	1.7%
13	Kentucky	38,707	1.6%
14	Colorado	36,129	1.5%
15	Virginia	33,592	1.4%
16	Oregon	32,387	1.3%
17	Wisconsin	31,585	1.3%
18	Michigan	29,830	1.2%
19	New Mexico	24,788	1.0%
20	New Jersey	24,681	1.0%
21	Nevada	23,398	0.9%
22	Illinois	21,630	0.9%
23	Missouri	21,262	0.9%
24	Georgia	21,197	0.9%
25	Iowa	19,516	0.8%
26	Connecticut	19,165	0.8%
27	Alabama	17,643	0.7%
28	South Carolina	17,165	0.7%
29	Arizona	14,498	0.6%
30	Louisiana	13,749	0.6%
31	Oklahoma	13,690	0.6%
32	West Virginia	12,758	0.5%
33	Hawaii	12,140	0.5%
34	Indiana	11,509	0.5%
35	Delaware	10,447	0.4%
36	Nebraska	9,952	0.4%
37	Montana	9,777	0.4%
38	Rhode Island	9,559	0.4%
39	Mississippi	8,519	0.3%
40	Utah	8,245	0.3%
41	Maine	7,531	0.3%
42	Alaska	7,511	0.3%
43	New Hampshire	6,703	0.3%
44	Arkansas	6,015	0.2%
45	South Dakota	5,933	0.2%
46	Vermont	4,938	0.2%
47	Kansas	4,176	0.2%
48	Idaho	2,941	0.1%
49	North Dakota	2,518	0.1%
50	Wyoming	1,348	0.1%
	District of Columbia	10,864	0.4%

Source: U.S. Department of Health and Human Services, Administration for Children and Families
"TANF Caseload Data" (https://www.acf.hhs.gov/programs/ofa/programs/tanf/data-reports)
*As of June 2018. National total includes 16,633 recipients in U.S. territories (14,972 in Puerto Rico).

Percent Change in TANF Recipients: 2017 to 2018

National Percent Change = 10.0% Decrease*

ALPHA ORDER				RANK ORDER		
RANK	STATE	PERCENT CHANGE		RANK	STATE	PERCENT CHANGE
44	Alabama	(15.1)		1	New Hampshire	45.1
40	Alaska	(13.7)		2	Georgia	43.1
47	Arizona	(16.7)		3	Louisiana	9.7
33	Arkansas	(11.6)		4	Maine	8.2
27	California	(10.3)		5	Idaho	4.0
36	Colorado	(12.4)		6	Wyoming	2.1
9	Connecticut	(1.2)		7	Nevada	(0.7)
13	Delaware	(5.3)		8	South Dakota	(1.0)
24	Florida	(9.2)		9	Connecticut	(1.2)
2	Georgia	43.1		10	Massachusetts	(1.7)
35	Hawaii	(12.3)		11	Oregon	(4.8)
5	Idaho	4.0		12	Nebraska	(5.0)
48	Illinois	(21.8)		13	Delaware	(5.3)
37	Indiana	(12.8)		14	North Dakota	(5.9)
39	Iowa	(13.3)		15	New Mexico	(6.3)
50	Kansas	(57.6)		16	Maryland	(6.4)
49	Kentucky	(31.7)		17	Washington	(6.6)
3	Louisiana	9.7		18	West Virginia	(7.3)
4	Maine	8.2		19	New York	(7.5)
16	Maryland	(6.4)		19	South Carolina	(7.5)
10	Massachusetts	(1.7)		21	Wisconsin	(7.6)
30	Michigan	(10.9)		22	Minnesota	(7.8)
22	Minnesota	(7.8)		23	Oklahoma	(9.0)
43	Mississippi	(14.9)		24	Florida	(9.2)
31	Missouri	(11.0)		24	Vermont	(9.2)
41	Montana	(14.0)		26	Virginia	(9.9)
12	Nebraska	(5.0)		27	California	(10.3)
7	Nevada	(0.7)		27	Texas	(10.3)
1	New Hampshire	45.1		29	Pennsylvania	(10.6)
45	New Jersey	(15.2)		30	Michigan	(10.9)
15	New Mexico	(6.3)		31	Missouri	(11.0)
19	New York	(7.5)		32	North Carolina	(11.5)
32	North Carolina	(11.5)		33	Arkansas	(11.6)
14	North Dakota	(5.9)		34	Rhode Island	(12.0)
42	Ohio	(14.6)		35	Hawaii	(12.3)
23	Oklahoma	(9.0)		36	Colorado	(12.4)
11	Oregon	(4.8)		37	Indiana	(12.8)
29	Pennsylvania	(10.6)		38	Utah	(12.9)
34	Rhode Island	(12.0)		39	Iowa	(13.3)
19	South Carolina	(7.5)		40	Alaska	(13.7)
8	South Dakota	(1.0)		41	Montana	(14.0)
46	Tennessee	(16.4)		42	Ohio	(14.6)
27	Texas	(10.3)		43	Mississippi	(14.9)
38	Utah	(12.9)		44	Alabama	(15.1)
24	Vermont	(9.2)		45	New Jersey	(15.2)
26	Virginia	(9.9)		46	Tennessee	(16.4)
17	Washington	(6.6)		47	Arizona	(16.7)
18	West Virginia	(7.3)		48	Illinois	(21.8)
21	Wisconsin	(7.6)		49	Kentucky	(31.7)
6	Wyoming	2.1		50	Kansas	(57.6)

District of Columbia   19.5

Source: CQ Press using data from U.S. Department of Health and Human Services, Administration for Children and Families
"TANF Caseload Data" (https://www.acf.hhs.gov/programs/ofa/programs/tanf/data-reports)
*June 2017 to June 2018. National percent includes recipients in U.S. territories.

TANF Work Participation Rates in 2017

National Rate = 54.3%*

ALPHA ORDER				RANK ORDER		
RANK	STATE	PERCENT		RANK	STATE	PERCENT
20	Alabama	50.1		1	Illinois	91.4
21	Alaska	49.4		2	Wyoming	84.5
45	Arizona	28.8		3	Idaho	79.6
31	Arkansas	43.2		4	Ohio	78.5
14	California	57.7		5	Maine	76.5
28	Colorado	46.0		6	New Hampshire	74.7
25	Connecticut	47.7		7	Wisconsin	72.8
42	Delaware	33.2		8	Oregon	69.1
34	Florida	40.1		9	Massachusetts	67.7
48	Georgia	27.6		10	Nebraska	63.4
22	Hawaii	49.1		11	Minnesota	60.8
3	Idaho	79.6		12	South Dakota	60.6
1	Illinois	91.4		13	Michigan	57.9
43	Indiana	31.6		14	California	57.7
17	Iowa	53.4		15	North Dakota	55.7
29	Kansas	45.0		16	Oklahoma	54.1
23	Kentucky	48.7		17	Iowa	53.4
47	Louisiana	28.1		18	West Virginia	53.0
5	Maine	76.5		19	Washington	52.1
41	Maryland	34.4		20	Alabama	50.1
9	Massachusetts	67.7		21	Alaska	49.4
13	Michigan	57.9		22	Hawaii	49.1
11	Minnesota	60.8		23	Kentucky	48.7
33	Mississippi	41.7		24	South Carolina	48.5
44	Missouri	29.7		25	Connecticut	47.7
36	Montana	39.7		26	Vermont	47.4
10	Nebraska	63.4		27	Nevada	47.3
27	Nevada	47.3		28	Colorado	46.0
6	New Hampshire	74.7		29	Kansas	45.0
40	New Jersey	35.3		30	New Mexico	44.0
30	New Mexico	44.0		31	Arkansas	43.2
32	New York	42.6		32	New York	42.6
45	North Carolina	28.8		33	Mississippi	41.7
15	North Dakota	55.7		34	Florida	40.1
4	Ohio	78.5		35	Tennessee	40.0
16	Oklahoma	54.1		36	Montana	39.7
8	Oregon	69.1		37	Virginia	37.1
39	Pennsylvania	36.0		38	Utah	36.9
50	Rhode Island	22.7		39	Pennsylvania	36.0
24	South Carolina	48.5		40	New Jersey	35.3
12	South Dakota	60.6		41	Maryland	34.4
35	Tennessee	40.0		42	Delaware	33.2
49	Texas	27.3		43	Indiana	31.6
38	Utah	36.9		44	Missouri	29.7
26	Vermont	47.4		45	Arizona	28.8
37	Virginia	37.1		45	North Carolina	28.8
19	Washington	52.1		47	Louisiana	28.1
18	West Virginia	53.0		48	Georgia	27.6
7	Wisconsin	72.8		49	Texas	27.3
2	Wyoming	84.5		50	Rhode Island	22.7
					District of Columbia	46.8

Source: U.S. Department of Health and Human Services, Administration for Children and Families
"Work Participation Rates - Fiscal Year 2017" (Table 6C) (https://www.acf.hhs.gov/ofa/programs/tanf/data-reports)
*For fiscal year 2017. Work-eligible individuals with hours of participation in various work and training activities. National average includes recipients in U.S. territories.

Average Monthly TANF Assistance per Family in 2017

National Average = $425*

ALPHA ORDER			RANK ORDER		
RANK	STATE	PER FAMILY	RANK	STATE	PER FAMILY
41	Alabama	$215	1	Alaska	$611
1	Alaska	611	2	New York	582
38	Arizona	244	3	Hawaii	575
47	Arkansas	151	4	New Hampshire	554
5	California	543	5	California	543
19	Colorado	371	6	Maryland	522
10	Connecticut	454	7	Montana	512
37	Delaware	245	8	Massachusetts	470
39	Florida	233	9	Vermont	455
NA	Georgia**	NA	10	Connecticut	454
3	Hawaii	575	11	Oregon	441
31	Idaho	298	12	Wyoming	440
44	Illinois	198	13	South Dakota	432
45	Indiana	197	14	Rhode Island	428
27	Iowa	315	15	Minnesota	406
35	Kansas	259	16	Washington	403
36	Kentucky	255	17	Utah	399
33	Louisiana	282	18	Wisconsin	373
22	Maine	351	19	Colorado	371
6	Maryland	522	20	Nebraska	358
8	Massachusetts	470	21	Ohio	357
25	Michigan	327	22	Maine	351
15	Minnesota	406	23	Nevada	342
48	Mississippi	138	24	New Mexico	331
40	Missouri	219	25	Michigan	327
7	Montana	512	26	Pennsylvania	317
20	Nebraska	358	27	Iowa	315
23	Nevada	342	28	Texas	309
4	New Hampshire	554	29	North Dakota	308
30	New Jersey	302	30	New Jersey	302
24	New Mexico	331	31	Idaho	298
2	New York	582	32	West Virginia	285
NA	North Carolina**	NA	33	Louisiana	282
29	North Dakota	308	34	Virginia	277
21	Ohio	357	35	Kansas	259
42	Oklahoma	212	36	Kentucky	255
11	Oregon	441	37	Delaware	245
26	Pennsylvania	317	38	Arizona	244
14	Rhode Island	428	39	Florida	233
43	South Carolina	207	40	Missouri	219
13	South Dakota	432	41	Alabama	215
46	Tennessee	167	42	Oklahoma	212
28	Texas	309	43	South Carolina	207
17	Utah	399	44	Illinois	198
9	Vermont	455	45	Indiana	197
34	Virginia	277	46	Tennessee	167
16	Washington	403	47	Arkansas	151
32	West Virginia	285	48	Mississippi	138
18	Wisconsin	373	NA	Georgia**	NA
12	Wyoming	440	NA	North Carolina**	NA
				District of Columbia	330

Source: U.S. Department of Health and Human Services, Administration for Children and Families
"Characteristics and Financial Circumstances of TANF Recipients, Fiscal Year 2017 " (Table 37)
(https://www.acf.hhs.gov/ofa/programs/tanf/data-reports)
*For fiscal year 2017. National average includes families in U.S. territories.
**Not available.

Percent of Households with Food Insecurity in 2017

National Percent = 12.3% of Households*

ALPHA ORDER			RANK ORDER		
RANK	STATE	PERCENT	RANK	STATE	PERCENT
5	Alabama	16.3	1	New Mexico	17.9
29	Alaska	11.6	2	Arkansas	17.4
18	Arizona	13.1	3	Louisiana	17.3
2	Arkansas	17.4	4	Mississippi	17.2
32	California	11.2	5	Alabama	16.3
47	Colorado	9.2	6	Oklahoma	15.0
25	Connecticut	12.2	7	West Virginia	14.9
34	Delaware	11.1	8	Kentucky	14.7
27	Florida	11.9	9	Maine	14.4
19	Georgia	13.0	9	North Carolina	14.4
50	Hawaii	7.4	11	Texas	14.0
35	Idaho	11.0	12	Ohio	13.7
32	Illinois	11.2	13	Indiana	13.6
13	Indiana	13.6	13	Michigan	13.6
39	Iowa	10.5	15	Nebraska	13.5
16	Kansas	13.3	16	Kansas	13.3
8	Kentucky	14.7	17	Wyoming	13.2
3	Louisiana	17.3	18	Arizona	13.1
9	Maine	14.4	19	Georgia	13.0
40	Maryland	10.4	20	Oregon	12.9
41	Massachusetts	10.2	20	Tennessee	12.9
13	Michigan	13.6	22	Missouri	12.8
45	Minnesota	9.5	23	Nevada	12.4
4	Mississippi	17.2	23	Rhode Island	12.4
22	Missouri	12.8	25	Connecticut	12.2
30	Montana	11.4	26	Pennsylvania	12.1
15	Nebraska	13.5	27	Florida	11.9
23	Nevada	12.4	28	South Carolina	11.7
46	New Hampshire	9.4	29	Alaska	11.6
49	New Jersey	8.6	30	Montana	11.4
1	New Mexico	17.9	30	South Dakota	11.4
36	New York	10.9	32	California	11.2
9	North Carolina	14.4	32	Illinois	11.2
48	North Dakota	9.0	34	Delaware	11.1
12	Ohio	13.7	35	Idaho	11.0
6	Oklahoma	15.0	36	New York	10.9
20	Oregon	12.9	37	Washington	10.8
26	Pennsylvania	12.1	38	Utah	10.7
23	Rhode Island	12.4	39	Iowa	10.5
28	South Carolina	11.7	40	Maryland	10.4
30	South Dakota	11.4	41	Massachusetts	10.2
20	Tennessee	12.9	42	Virginia	10.1
11	Texas	14.0	43	Wisconsin	10.0
38	Utah	10.7	44	Vermont	9.8
44	Vermont	9.8	45	Minnesota	9.5
42	Virginia	10.1	46	New Hampshire	9.4
37	Washington	10.8	47	Colorado	9.2
7	West Virginia	14.9	48	North Dakota	9.0
43	Wisconsin	10.0	49	New Jersey	8.6
17	Wyoming	13.2	50	Hawaii	7.4
				District of Columbia	11.2

Source: U.S. Department of Agriculture, Economic Research Service
"Household Food Security in the United States, 2017" (www.ers.usda.gov/topics/food-nutrition-assistance/food-security-in-the-us/)
*Three-year average for 2015-2017. Refers to households for which access to enough food is limited by a lack of money and other resources. About one-third of food-insecure households have very low food security, meaning that at times the food intake of some household members is reduced and their normal eating patterns are disrupted.

Supplemental Nutrition Assistance Program Benefits in 2018

National Total = $60,609,401,339*

ALPHA ORDER

RANK	STATE	BENEFITS	% of USA
16	Alabama	$1,084,563,290	1.8%
43	Alaska	187,357,117	0.3%
14	Arizona	1,210,429,898	2.0%
33	Arkansas	479,990,195	0.8%
1	California	6,332,750,403	10.4%
28	Colorado	668,610,833	1.1%
30	Connecticut	614,967,955	1.0%
42	Delaware	196,899,033	0.3%
2	Florida	5,763,762,595	9.5%
7	Georgia	2,336,788,286	3.9%
34	Hawaii	469,687,064	0.8%
41	Idaho	199,514,037	0.3%
5	Illinois	2,777,948,512	4.6%
23	Indiana	867,533,147	1.4%
35	Iowa	446,259,982	0.7%
37	Kansas	293,539,988	0.5%
24	Kentucky	853,986,982	1.4%
12	Louisiana	1,297,321,641	2.1%
40	Maine	218,506,978	0.4%
22	Maryland	910,098,604	1.5%
15	Massachusetts	1,159,118,508	1.9%
9	Michigan	1,894,036,767	3.1%
32	Minnesota	544,800,296	0.9%
27	Mississippi	680,119,008	1.1%
17	Missouri	1,061,334,229	1.8%
44	Montana	158,485,987	0.3%
39	Nebraska	229,206,174	0.4%
31	Nevada	614,241,936	1.0%
47	New Hampshire	101,517,491	0.2%
19	New Jersey	1,012,654,300	1.7%
29	New Mexico	638,421,821	1.1%
4	New York	4,526,970,964	7.5%
10	North Carolina	1,870,724,235	3.1%
48	North Dakota	75,391,175	0.1%
8	Ohio	2,078,237,006	3.4%
25	Oklahoma	832,653,493	1.4%
21	Oregon	937,798,988	1.5%
6	Pennsylvania	2,592,183,684	4.3%
NA	Rhode Island**	NA	NA
20	South Carolina	943,922,431	1.6%
45	South Dakota	131,112,641	0.2%
11	Tennessee	1,424,890,904	2.4%
3	Texas	5,525,177,455	9.1%
38	Utah	258,536,027	0.4%
46	Vermont	106,781,746	0.2%
18	Virginia	1,051,800,978	1.7%
13	Washington	1,268,734,555	2.1%
36	West Virginia	440,298,715	0.7%
26	Wisconsin	817,238,607	1.3%
49	Wyoming	40,676,283	0.1%

RANK ORDER

RANK	STATE	BENEFITS	% of USA
1	California	$6,332,750,403	10.4%
2	Florida	5,763,762,595	9.5%
3	Texas	5,525,177,455	9.1%
4	New York	4,526,970,964	7.5%
5	Illinois	2,777,948,512	4.6%
6	Pennsylvania	2,592,183,684	4.3%
7	Georgia	2,336,788,286	3.9%
8	Ohio	2,078,237,006	3.4%
9	Michigan	1,894,036,767	3.1%
10	North Carolina	1,870,724,235	3.1%
11	Tennessee	1,424,890,904	2.4%
12	Louisiana	1,297,321,641	2.1%
13	Washington	1,268,734,555	2.1%
14	Arizona	1,210,429,898	2.0%
15	Massachusetts	1,159,118,508	1.9%
16	Alabama	1,084,563,290	1.8%
17	Missouri	1,061,334,229	1.8%
18	Virginia	1,051,800,978	1.7%
19	New Jersey	1,012,654,300	1.7%
20	South Carolina	943,922,431	1.6%
21	Oregon	937,798,988	1.5%
22	Maryland	910,098,604	1.5%
23	Indiana	867,533,147	1.4%
24	Kentucky	853,986,982	1.4%
25	Oklahoma	832,653,493	1.4%
26	Wisconsin	817,238,607	1.3%
27	Mississippi	680,119,008	1.1%
28	Colorado	668,610,833	1.1%
29	New Mexico	638,421,821	1.1%
30	Connecticut	614,967,955	1.0%
31	Nevada	614,241,936	1.0%
32	Minnesota	544,800,296	0.9%
33	Arkansas	479,990,195	0.8%
34	Hawaii	469,687,064	0.8%
35	Iowa	446,259,982	0.7%
36	West Virginia	440,298,715	0.7%
37	Kansas	293,539,988	0.5%
38	Utah	258,536,027	0.4%
39	Nebraska	229,206,174	0.4%
40	Maine	218,506,978	0.4%
41	Idaho	199,514,037	0.3%
42	Delaware	196,899,033	0.3%
43	Alaska	187,357,117	0.3%
44	Montana	158,485,987	0.3%
45	South Dakota	131,112,641	0.2%
46	Vermont	106,781,746	0.2%
47	New Hampshire	101,517,491	0.2%
48	North Dakota	75,391,175	0.1%
49	Wyoming	40,676,283	0.1%
NA	Rhode Island**	NA	NA
	District of Columbia	188,433,398	0.3%

Source: U.S. Department of Agriculture, Food, Nutrition and Consumer Services
"Supplemental Nutrition Assistance Program" (https://www.fns.usda.gov/pd/supplemental-nutrition-assistance-program-snap)
*Preliminary data for fiscal year 2018. National total includes $193,384,997 to U.S. territories. Costs are for benefits only and exclude administrative expenditures. Program formerly called the Food Stamp Program.
**Not available.

Monthly Supplemental Nutrition Assistance Program Recipients in 2018

National Total = 40,324,454 Recipients*

ALPHA ORDER

RANK	STATE	RECIPIENTS	% of USA
16	Alabama	766,681	1.9%
44	Alaska	91,995	0.2%
14	Arizona	845,733	2.1%
33	Arkansas	372,451	0.9%
1	California	3,949,535	9.8%
29	Colorado	449,824	1.1%
32	Connecticut	387,329	1.0%
42	Delaware	140,298	0.3%
3	Florida	3,347,518	8.3%
7	Georgia	1,539,468	3.8%
40	Hawaii	163,618	0.4%
41	Idaho	157,858	0.4%
5	Illinois	1,826,011	4.5%
24	Indiana	617,032	1.5%
34	Iowa	345,406	0.9%
36	Kansas	217,420	0.5%
25	Kentucky	610,419	1.5%
13	Louisiana	867,342	2.2%
39	Maine	167,858	0.4%
22	Maryland	646,483	1.6%
15	Massachusetts	770,566	1.9%
9	Michigan	1,281,862	3.2%
31	Minnesota	428,986	1.1%
27	Mississippi	505,308	1.3%
18	Missouri	736,590	1.8%
43	Montana	115,223	0.3%
38	Nebraska	169,811	0.4%
30	Nevada	439,941	1.1%
46	New Hampshire	86,502	0.2%
17	New Jersey	760,303	1.9%
28	New Mexico	456,251	1.1%
4	New York	2,796,620	6.9%
10	North Carolina	1,075,037	2.7%
48	North Dakota	52,621	0.1%
8	Ohio	1,421,366	3.5%
26	Oklahoma	585,064	1.5%
23	Oregon	633,970	1.6%
6	Pennsylvania	1,818,589	4.5%
NA	Rhode Island**	NA	NA
20	South Carolina	658,119	1.6%
45	South Dakota	87,410	0.2%
11	Tennessee	970,875	2.4%
2	Texas	3,895,207	9.7%
37	Utah	189,093	0.5%
47	Vermont	73,058	0.2%
19	Virginia	736,221	1.8%
12	Washington	877,244	2.2%
35	West Virginia	321,009	0.8%
21	Wisconsin	652,885	1.6%
49	Wyoming	29,330	0.1%

RANK ORDER

RANK	STATE	RECIPIENTS	% of USA
1	California	3,949,535	9.8%
2	Texas	3,895,207	9.7%
3	Florida	3,347,518	8.3%
4	New York	2,796,620	6.9%
5	Illinois	1,826,011	4.5%
6	Pennsylvania	1,818,589	4.5%
7	Georgia	1,539,468	3.8%
8	Ohio	1,421,366	3.5%
9	Michigan	1,281,862	3.2%
10	North Carolina	1,075,037	2.7%
11	Tennessee	970,875	2.4%
12	Washington	877,244	2.2%
13	Louisiana	867,342	2.2%
14	Arizona	845,733	2.1%
15	Massachusetts	770,566	1.9%
16	Alabama	766,681	1.9%
17	New Jersey	760,303	1.9%
18	Missouri	736,590	1.8%
19	Virginia	736,221	1.8%
20	South Carolina	658,119	1.6%
21	Wisconsin	652,885	1.6%
22	Maryland	646,483	1.6%
23	Oregon	633,970	1.6%
24	Indiana	617,032	1.5%
25	Kentucky	610,419	1.5%
26	Oklahoma	585,064	1.5%
27	Mississippi	505,308	1.3%
28	New Mexico	456,251	1.1%
29	Colorado	449,824	1.1%
30	Nevada	439,941	1.1%
31	Minnesota	428,986	1.1%
32	Connecticut	387,329	1.0%
33	Arkansas	372,451	0.9%
34	Iowa	345,406	0.9%
35	West Virginia	321,009	0.8%
36	Kansas	217,420	0.5%
37	Utah	189,093	0.5%
38	Nebraska	169,811	0.4%
39	Maine	167,858	0.4%
40	Hawaii	163,618	0.4%
41	Idaho	157,858	0.4%
42	Delaware	140,298	0.3%
43	Montana	115,223	0.3%
44	Alaska	91,995	0.2%
45	South Dakota	87,410	0.2%
46	New Hampshire	86,502	0.2%
47	Vermont	73,058	0.2%
48	North Dakota	52,621	0.1%
49	Wyoming	29,330	0.1%
NA	Rhode Island**	NA	NA
	District of Columbia	111,312	0.3%

Source: U.S. Department of Agriculture, Food, Nutrition and Consumer Services
   "Supplemental Nutrition Assistance Program" (https://www.fns.usda.gov/pd/supplemental-nutrition-assistance-program-snap)
*Preliminary for fiscal year 2018. National total includes 77,807 recipients in U.S. territories. Program formerly called the Food
Stamp Program.
**Not available.

Average Monthly Supplemental Nutrition Assistance Program Benefit per Recipient in 2018
National Average = $125.25 per Recipient*

ALPHA ORDER

RANK	STATE	PER RECIPIENT
28	Alabama	$117.89
2	Alaska	169.72
23	Arizona	119.27
45	Arkansas	107.39
6	California	133.62
13	Colorado	123.87
7	Connecticut	132.31
31	Delaware	116.95
4	Florida	143.48
9	Georgia	126.49
1	Hawaii	239.22
47	Idaho	105.32
8	Illinois	126.78
30	Indiana	117.16
44	Iowa	107.67
39	Kansas	112.51
33	Kentucky	116.58
12	Louisiana	124.65
43	Maine	108.48
29	Maryland	117.31
10	Massachusetts	125.35
15	Michigan	123.13
46	Minnesota	105.83
41	Mississippi	112.16
20	Missouri	120.07
36	Montana	114.62
40	Nebraska	112.48
34	Nevada	116.35
49	New Hampshire	97.80
42	New Jersey	110.99
32	New Mexico	116.61
5	New York	134.89
3	North Carolina	145.01
22	North Dakota	119.39
17	Ohio	121.85
26	Oklahoma	118.60
14	Oregon	123.27
25	Pennsylvania	118.78
NA	Rhode Island**	NA
21	South Carolina	119.52
11	South Dakota	125.00
16	Tennessee	122.30
27	Texas	118.20
38	Utah	113.94
18	Vermont	121.80
24	Virginia	119.05
19	Washington	120.52
37	West Virginia	114.30
48	Wisconsin	104.31
35	Wyoming	115.57

RANK ORDER

RANK	STATE	PER RECIPIENT
1	Hawaii	$239.22
2	Alaska	169.72
3	North Carolina	145.01
4	Florida	143.48
5	New York	134.89
6	California	133.62
7	Connecticut	132.31
8	Illinois	126.78
9	Georgia	126.49
10	Massachusetts	125.35
11	South Dakota	125.00
12	Louisiana	124.65
13	Colorado	123.87
14	Oregon	123.27
15	Michigan	123.13
16	Tennessee	122.30
17	Ohio	121.85
18	Vermont	121.80
19	Washington	120.52
20	Missouri	120.07
21	South Carolina	119.52
22	North Dakota	119.39
23	Arizona	119.27
24	Virginia	119.05
25	Pennsylvania	118.78
26	Oklahoma	118.60
27	Texas	118.20
28	Alabama	117.89
29	Maryland	117.31
30	Indiana	117.16
31	Delaware	116.95
32	New Mexico	116.61
33	Kentucky	116.58
34	Nevada	116.35
35	Wyoming	115.57
36	Montana	114.62
37	West Virginia	114.30
38	Utah	113.94
39	Kansas	112.51
40	Nebraska	112.48
41	Mississippi	112.16
42	New Jersey	110.99
43	Maine	108.48
44	Iowa	107.67
45	Arkansas	107.39
46	Minnesota	105.83
47	Idaho	105.32
48	Wisconsin	104.31
49	New Hampshire	97.80
NA	Rhode Island**	NA
	District of Columbia	141.07

Source: U.S. Department of Agriculture, Food, Nutrition and Consumer Services
"Supplemental Nutrition Assistance Program" (https://www.fns.usda.gov/pd/supplemental-nutrition-assistance-program-snap)
*Preliminary for fiscal year 2018. National average includes recipients in U.S. territories. Program formerly called the Food Stamp Program.
**Not available.

Percent of Population Receiving
Supplemental Nutrition Assistance Program Benefits in 2018
National Percent = 12.3%*

ALPHA ORDER

RANK	STATE	PERCENT
5	Alabama	15.7
20	Alaska	12.5
25	Arizona	11.8
22	Arkansas	12.4
36	California	10.0
43	Colorado	7.9
32	Connecticut	10.8
10	Delaware	14.5
5	Florida	15.7
9	Georgia	14.6
28	Hawaii	11.5
39	Idaho	9.0
12	Illinois	14.3
38	Indiana	9.2
31	Iowa	10.9
45	Kansas	7.5
16	Kentucky	13.7
2	Louisiana	18.6
20	Maine	12.5
34	Maryland	10.7
29	Massachusetts	11.2
19	Michigan	12.8
44	Minnesota	7.6
4	Mississippi	16.9
24	Missouri	12.0
32	Montana	10.8
40	Nebraska	8.8
10	Nevada	14.5
47	New Hampshire	6.4
42	New Jersey	8.5
1	New Mexico	21.8
12	New York	14.3
35	North Carolina	10.4
46	North Dakota	6.9
23	Ohio	12.2
8	Oklahoma	14.8
7	Oregon	15.1
15	Pennsylvania	14.2
NA	Rhode Island**	NA
18	South Carolina	12.9
37	South Dakota	9.9
12	Tennessee	14.3
17	Texas	13.6
48	Utah	6.0
26	Vermont	11.7
41	Virginia	8.6
27	Washington	11.6
3	West Virginia	17.8
29	Wisconsin	11.2
49	Wyoming	5.1

RANK ORDER

RANK	STATE	PERCENT
1	New Mexico	21.8
2	Louisiana	18.6
3	West Virginia	17.8
4	Mississippi	16.9
5	Alabama	15.7
5	Florida	15.7
7	Oregon	15.1
8	Oklahoma	14.8
9	Georgia	14.6
10	Delaware	14.5
10	Nevada	14.5
12	Illinois	14.3
12	New York	14.3
12	Tennessee	14.3
15	Pennsylvania	14.2
16	Kentucky	13.7
17	Texas	13.6
18	South Carolina	12.9
19	Michigan	12.8
20	Alaska	12.5
20	Maine	12.5
22	Arkansas	12.4
23	Ohio	12.2
24	Missouri	12.0
25	Arizona	11.8
26	Vermont	11.7
27	Washington	11.6
28	Hawaii	11.5
29	Massachusetts	11.2
29	Wisconsin	11.2
31	Iowa	10.9
32	Connecticut	10.8
32	Montana	10.8
34	Maryland	10.7
35	North Carolina	10.4
36	California	10.0
37	South Dakota	9.9
38	Indiana	9.2
39	Idaho	9.0
40	Nebraska	8.8
41	Virginia	8.6
42	New Jersey	8.5
43	Colorado	7.9
44	Minnesota	7.6
45	Kansas	7.5
46	North Dakota	6.9
47	New Hampshire	6.4
48	Utah	6.0
49	Wyoming	5.1
NA	Rhode Island**	NA
	District of Columbia	15.8

Source: CQ Press using data from U.S. Department of Agriculture, Food, Nutrition and Consumer Services
"Supplemental Nutrition Assistance Program" (https://www.fns.usda.gov/pd/supplemental-nutrition-assistance-program-snap)
*Preliminary data for fiscal year 2018. National rate does not include recipients in U.S. territories. Program formerly called the Food Stamp Program.
**Not available.

Percent of Households Receiving
Supplemental Nutrition Assistance Program Benefits in 2018
National Percent = 16.7% of Households*

ALPHA ORDER

RANK	STATE	PERCENT
9	Alabama	19.6
24	Alaska	16.2
29	Arizona	15.2
33	Arkansas	14.3
31	California	15.0
42	Colorado	10.4
21	Connecticut	16.5
10	Delaware	19.2
5	Florida	22.7
10	Georgia	19.2
14	Hawaii	18.3
40	Idaho	11.2
12	Illinois	19.1
41	Indiana	10.8
36	Iowa	13.1
45	Kansas	9.0
23	Kentucky	16.4
2	Louisiana	23.2
21	Maine	16.5
27	Maryland	15.6
19	Massachusetts	17.3
18	Michigan	17.4
44	Minnesota	9.8
7	Mississippi	21.2
32	Missouri	14.4
35	Montana	13.2
43	Nebraska	10.1
8	Nevada	20.9
46	New Hampshire	8.2
37	New Jersey	11.8
1	New Mexico	28.7
6	New York	21.4
27	North Carolina	15.6
48	North Dakota	7.9
29	Ohio	15.2
14	Oklahoma	18.3
4	Oregon	22.8
12	Pennsylvania	19.1
NA	Rhode Island**	NA
24	South Carolina	16.2
38	South Dakota	11.6
16	Tennessee	18.2
20	Texas	17.0
47	Utah	8.0
26	Vermont	16.0
39	Virginia	11.3
17	Washington	17.7
3	West Virginia	23.1
34	Wisconsin	14.0
49	Wyoming	5.8

RANK ORDER

RANK	STATE	PERCENT
1	New Mexico	28.7
2	Louisiana	23.2
3	West Virginia	23.1
4	Oregon	22.8
5	Florida	22.7
6	New York	21.4
7	Mississippi	21.2
8	Nevada	20.9
9	Alabama	19.6
10	Delaware	19.2
10	Georgia	19.2
12	Illinois	19.1
12	Pennsylvania	19.1
14	Hawaii	18.3
14	Oklahoma	18.3
16	Tennessee	18.2
17	Washington	17.7
18	Michigan	17.4
19	Massachusetts	17.3
20	Texas	17.0
21	Connecticut	16.5
21	Maine	16.5
23	Kentucky	16.4
24	Alaska	16.2
24	South Carolina	16.2
26	Vermont	16.0
27	Maryland	15.6
27	North Carolina	15.6
29	Arizona	15.2
29	Ohio	15.2
31	California	15.0
32	Missouri	14.4
33	Arkansas	14.3
34	Wisconsin	14.0
35	Montana	13.2
36	Iowa	13.1
37	New Jersey	11.8
38	South Dakota	11.6
39	Virginia	11.3
40	Idaho	11.2
41	Indiana	10.8
42	Colorado	10.4
43	Nebraska	10.1
44	Minnesota	9.8
45	Kansas	9.0
46	New Hampshire	8.2
47	Utah	8.0
48	North Dakota	7.9
49	Wyoming	5.8
NA	Rhode Island**	NA

District of Columbia   23.0

Source: CQ Press using data from U.S. Department of Agriculture, Food, Nutrition and Consumer Services
"Supplemental Nutrition Assistance Program" (https://www.fns.usda.gov/pd/supplemental-nutrition-assistance-program-snap)
*Preliminary data for fiscal year 2018. Percent calculated using 2017 estimated total households. National percent excludes households in U.S. territories. Program formerly called the Food Stamp Program.
**Not available.

Average Monthly Participants in Women, Infants, and Children (WIC) Special Nutrition Program in 2018
National Total = 6,867,785 Participants*

ALPHA ORDER

RANK	STATE	PARTICIPANTS	% of USA
17	Alabama	120,605	1.8%
44	Alaska	17,089	0.2%
11	Arizona	149,513	2.2%
30	Arkansas	73,606	1.1%
1	California	1,009,868	14.7%
28	Colorado	85,258	1.2%
35	Connecticut	47,296	0.7%
45	Delaware	16,701	0.2%
3	Florida	449,157	6.5%
7	Georgia	217,574	3.2%
40	Hawaii	26,115	0.4%
39	Idaho	33,717	0.5%
10	Illinois	199,360	2.9%
13	Indiana	143,643	2.1%
32	Iowa	60,249	0.9%
33	Kansas	50,589	0.7%
23	Kentucky	101,743	1.5%
20	Louisiana	112,362	1.6%
42	Maine	18,323	0.3%
15	Maryland	128,535	1.9%
21	Massachusetts	108,631	1.6%
8	Michigan	213,964	3.1%
22	Minnesota	105,946	1.5%
29	Mississippi	85,246	1.2%
18	Missouri	114,323	1.7%
46	Montana	16,682	0.2%
37	Nebraska	35,835	0.5%
31	Nevada	62,500	0.9%
47	New Hampshire	12,332	0.2%
14	New Jersey	141,559	2.1%
36	New Mexico	46,165	0.7%
4	New York	415,661	6.1%
5	North Carolina	221,719	3.2%
48	North Dakota	12,313	0.2%
9	Ohio	208,955	3.0%
24	Oklahoma	98,532	1.4%
27	Oregon	85,774	1.2%
6	Pennsylvania	218,198	3.2%
41	Rhode Island	18,943	0.3%
26	South Carolina	92,153	1.3%
43	South Dakota	17,333	0.3%
16	Tennessee	128,121	1.9%
2	Texas	746,246	10.9%
34	Utah	48,989	0.7%
49	Vermont	11,427	0.2%
19	Virginia	113,952	1.7%
12	Washington	145,054	2.1%
38	West Virginia	35,412	0.5%
25	Wisconsin	92,443	1.3%
50	Wyoming	9,062	0.1%

RANK ORDER

RANK	STATE	PARTICIPANTS	% of USA
1	California	1,009,868	14.7%
2	Texas	746,246	10.9%
3	Florida	449,157	6.5%
4	New York	415,661	6.1%
5	North Carolina	221,719	3.2%
6	Pennsylvania	218,198	3.2%
7	Georgia	217,574	3.2%
8	Michigan	213,964	3.1%
9	Ohio	208,955	3.0%
10	Illinois	199,360	2.9%
11	Arizona	149,513	2.2%
12	Washington	145,054	2.1%
13	Indiana	143,643	2.1%
14	New Jersey	141,559	2.1%
15	Maryland	128,535	1.9%
16	Tennessee	128,121	1.9%
17	Alabama	120,605	1.8%
18	Missouri	114,323	1.7%
19	Virginia	113,952	1.7%
20	Louisiana	112,362	1.6%
21	Massachusetts	108,631	1.6%
22	Minnesota	105,946	1.5%
23	Kentucky	101,743	1.5%
24	Oklahoma	98,532	1.4%
25	Wisconsin	92,443	1.3%
26	South Carolina	92,153	1.3%
27	Oregon	85,774	1.2%
28	Colorado	85,258	1.2%
29	Mississippi	85,246	1.2%
30	Arkansas	73,606	1.1%
31	Nevada	62,500	0.9%
32	Iowa	60,249	0.9%
33	Kansas	50,589	0.7%
34	Utah	48,989	0.7%
35	Connecticut	47,296	0.7%
36	New Mexico	46,165	0.7%
37	Nebraska	35,835	0.5%
38	West Virginia	35,412	0.5%
39	Idaho	33,717	0.5%
40	Hawaii	26,115	0.4%
41	Rhode Island	18,943	0.3%
42	Maine	18,323	0.3%
43	South Dakota	17,333	0.3%
44	Alaska	17,089	0.2%
45	Delaware	16,701	0.2%
46	Montana	16,682	0.2%
47	New Hampshire	12,332	0.2%
48	North Dakota	12,313	0.2%
49	Vermont	11,427	0.2%
50	Wyoming	9,062	0.1%
	District of Columbia	12,423	0.2%

Source: U.S. Department of Agriculture, Food, Nutrition and Consumer Services
   "WIC Program (https://www.fns.usda.gov/pd/wicmain.htm)
*Preliminary data for fiscal year 2018. National total includes 130,594 participants in outlying areas not shown separately (Puerto Rico has 112,709 participants).

Average Monthly Benefit per Participant in Women, Infants, and Children (WIC) Special Nutrition Program in 2018
National Average = $40.83*

ALPHA ORDER

RANK	STATE	AVERAGE BENEFIT
9	Alabama	$44.92
2	Alaska	55.59
29	Arizona	38.47
16	Arkansas	43.33
17	California	43.14
34	Colorado	36.97
14	Connecticut	43.55
26	Delaware	38.94
13	Florida	43.57
25	Georgia	39.02
1	Hawaii	55.99
44	Idaho	33.43
6	Illinois	48.61
38	Indiana	35.54
47	Iowa	30.93
35	Kansas	36.68
32	Kentucky	38.01
8	Louisiana	46.57
24	Maine	39.28
27	Maryland	38.92
33	Massachusetts	37.33
36	Michigan	36.40
23	Minnesota	39.55
5	Mississippi	52.37
39	Missouri	34.97
41	Montana	34.58
19	Nebraska	41.40
40	Nevada	34.68
46	New Hampshire	31.55
3	New Jersey	55.49
30	New Mexico	38.06
4	New York	52.50
20	North Carolina	40.62
7	North Dakota	46.62
48	Ohio	30.87
43	Oklahoma	33.97
42	Oregon	34.28
12	Pennsylvania	44.01
15	Rhode Island	43.52
10	South Carolina	44.55
18	South Dakota	41.71
22	Tennessee	39.58
50	Texas	26.87
31	Utah	38.05
11	Vermont	44.52
49	Virginia	30.85
28	Washington	38.69
21	West Virginia	39.81
37	Wisconsin	36.35
45	Wyoming	32.22

RANK ORDER

RANK	STATE	AVERAGE BENEFIT
1	Hawaii	$55.99
2	Alaska	55.59
3	New Jersey	55.49
4	New York	52.50
5	Mississippi	52.37
6	Illinois	48.61
7	North Dakota	46.62
8	Louisiana	46.57
9	Alabama	44.92
10	South Carolina	44.55
11	Vermont	44.52
12	Pennsylvania	44.01
13	Florida	43.57
14	Connecticut	43.55
15	Rhode Island	43.52
16	Arkansas	43.33
17	California	43.14
18	South Dakota	41.71
19	Nebraska	41.40
20	North Carolina	40.62
21	West Virginia	39.81
22	Tennessee	39.58
23	Minnesota	39.55
24	Maine	39.28
25	Georgia	39.02
26	Delaware	38.94
27	Maryland	38.92
28	Washington	38.69
29	Arizona	38.47
30	New Mexico	38.06
31	Utah	38.05
32	Kentucky	38.01
33	Massachusetts	37.33
34	Colorado	36.97
35	Kansas	36.68
36	Michigan	36.40
37	Wisconsin	36.35
38	Indiana	35.54
39	Missouri	34.97
40	Nevada	34.68
41	Montana	34.58
42	Oregon	34.28
43	Oklahoma	33.97
44	Idaho	33.43
45	Wyoming	32.22
46	New Hampshire	31.55
47	Iowa	30.93
48	Ohio	30.87
49	Virginia	30.85
50	Texas	26.87
	District of Columbia	41.11

Source: U.S. Department of Agriculture, Food, Nutrition and Consumer Services
"WIC Program (https://www.fns.usda.gov/pd/wicmain.htm)
*Preliminary data for fiscal year 2018. National average includes outlying areas and Indian reservations not shown separately.

Percent of Public Elementary and Secondary School Students Eligible for Free or Reduced-Price Meals in 2017
National Percent = 51.6%*

ALPHA ORDER				RANK ORDER		
RANK	STATE	PERCENT		RANK	STATE	PERCENT
14	Alabama	51.7		1	Mississippi	75.0
29	Alaska	44.0		2	New Mexico	71.3
NA	Arizona**	NA		3	South Carolina	66.8
43	Arkansas	34.5		4	Louisiana	63.0
12	California	57.2		5	Oklahoma	62.3
32	Colorado	42.1		6	Georgia	62.0
42	Connecticut	35.3		7	Nevada	60.7
NA	Delaware**	NA		8	Texas	58.9
10	Florida	58.0		9	Kentucky	58.7
6	Georgia	62.0		10	Florida	58.0
19	Hawaii	47.6		11	North Carolina	57.4
23	Idaho	45.8		12	California	57.2
16	Illinois	49.8		13	New York	52.1
20	Indiana	47.2		14	Alabama	51.7
34	Iowa	40.2		15	Missouri	50.5
18	Kansas	47.7		16	Illinois	49.8
9	Kentucky	58.7		17	Oregon	48.2
4	Louisiana	63.0		18	Kansas	47.7
27	Maine	44.2		19	Hawaii	47.6
22	Maryland	46.7		20	Indiana	47.2
NA	Massachusetts**	NA		21	Rhode Island	47.1
27	Michigan	44.2		22	Maryland	46.7
37	Minnesota	37.6		23	Idaho	45.8
1	Mississippi	75.0		24	Montana	45.3
15	Missouri	50.5		25	Nebraska	44.7
24	Montana	45.3		26	West Virginia	44.6
25	Nebraska	44.7		27	Maine	44.2
7	Nevada	60.7		27	Michigan	44.2
45	New Hampshire	27.1		29	Alaska	44.0
39	New Jersey	36.9		30	Washington	43.6
2	New Mexico	71.3		31	Pennsylvania	43.3
13	New York	52.1		32	Colorado	42.1
11	North Carolina	57.4		33	Virginia	40.8
44	North Dakota	30.3		34	Iowa	40.2
NA	Ohio**	NA		35	Wyoming	38.6
5	Oklahoma	62.3		36	South Dakota	37.7
17	Oregon	48.2		37	Minnesota	37.6
31	Pennsylvania	43.3		38	Wisconsin	37.4
21	Rhode Island	47.1		39	New Jersey	36.9
3	South Carolina	66.8		40	Vermont	36.8
36	South Dakota	37.7		41	Utah	35.7
NA	Tennessee**	NA		42	Connecticut	35.3
8	Texas	58.9		43	Arkansas	34.5
41	Utah	35.7		44	North Dakota	30.3
40	Vermont	36.8		45	New Hampshire	27.1
33	Virginia	40.8		NA	Arizona**	NA
30	Washington	43.6		NA	Delaware**	NA
26	West Virginia	44.6		NA	Massachusetts**	NA
38	Wisconsin	37.4		NA	Ohio**	NA
35	Wyoming	38.6		NA	Tennessee**	NA
					District of Columbia**	NA

Source: CQ Press using data from U.S. Department of Education, National Center for Education Statistics "ElSi Table Generator" (https://nces.ed.gov/ccd/elsi/)

*For school year 2016-2017. National rate does not include states not shown separately.

**Not available.

Child Support Collections in 2017

National Total = $28,284,627,921*

ALPHA ORDER

ALPHA ORDER

RANK	STATE	COLLECTIONS	% of USA
26	Alabama	$320,472,376	1.1%
44	Alaska	91,580,013	0.3%
28	Arizona	310,751,664	1.1%
32	Arkansas	226,334,421	0.8%
2	California	2,339,598,869	8.3%
27	Colorado	318,001,995	1.1%
31	Connecticut	240,197,387	0.8%
46	Delaware	74,674,436	0.3%
5	Florida	1,474,661,220	5.2%
10	Georgia	695,453,588	2.5%
41	Hawaii	97,241,056	0.3%
38	Idaho	170,006,144	0.6%
9	Illinois	787,682,797	2.8%
19	Indiana	529,806,427	1.9%
29	Iowa	305,476,647	1.1%
36	Kansas	187,303,061	0.7%
22	Kentucky	367,103,526	1.3%
21	Louisiana	400,575,903	1.4%
40	Maine	97,795,280	0.3%
20	Maryland	528,767,756	1.9%
14	Massachusetts	626,795,847	2.2%
6	Michigan	1,309,828,824	4.6%
18	Minnesota	561,127,628	2.0%
25	Mississippi	327,399,379	1.2%
17	Missouri	580,321,575	2.1%
49	Montana	60,742,572	0.2%
34	Nebraska	204,462,116	0.7%
35	Nevada	187,677,416	0.7%
45	New Hampshire	74,828,643	0.3%
8	New Jersey	1,111,861,182	3.9%
39	New Mexico	121,914,934	0.4%
3	New York	1,716,965,360	6.1%
11	North Carolina	656,441,704	2.3%
42	North Dakota	95,775,243	0.3%
4	Ohio	1,612,205,996	5.7%
24	Oklahoma	336,207,183	1.2%
23	Oregon	355,411,282	1.3%
7	Pennsylvania	1,213,348,917	4.3%
47	Rhode Island	74,058,172	0.3%
30	South Carolina	289,376,633	1.0%
43	South Dakota	92,283,955	0.3%
16	Tennessee	598,990,132	2.1%
1	Texas	4,090,214,243	14.5%
33	Utah	211,549,807	0.7%
50	Vermont	42,203,355	0.1%
15	Virginia	602,399,240	2.1%
13	Washington	632,754,285	2.2%
37	West Virginia	178,978,477	0.6%
12	Wisconsin	646,836,291	2.3%
48	Wyoming	60,923,456	0.2%

RANK ORDER

RANK	STATE	COLLECTIONS	% of USA
1	Texas	$4,090,214,243	14.5%
2	California	2,339,598,869	8.3%
3	New York	1,716,965,360	6.1%
4	Ohio	1,612,205,996	5.7%
5	Florida	1,474,661,220	5.2%
6	Michigan	1,309,828,824	4.6%
7	Pennsylvania	1,213,348,917	4.3%
8	New Jersey	1,111,861,182	3.9%
9	Illinois	787,682,797	2.8%
10	Georgia	695,453,588	2.5%
11	North Carolina	656,441,704	2.3%
12	Wisconsin	646,836,291	2.3%
13	Washington	632,754,285	2.2%
14	Massachusetts	626,795,847	2.2%
15	Virginia	602,399,240	2.1%
16	Tennessee	598,990,132	2.1%
17	Missouri	580,321,575	2.1%
18	Minnesota	561,127,628	2.0%
19	Indiana	529,806,427	1.9%
20	Maryland	528,767,756	1.9%
21	Louisiana	400,575,903	1.4%
22	Kentucky	367,103,526	1.3%
23	Oregon	355,411,282	1.3%
24	Oklahoma	336,207,183	1.2%
25	Mississippi	327,399,379	1.2%
26	Alabama	320,472,376	1.1%
27	Colorado	318,001,995	1.1%
28	Arizona	310,751,664	1.1%
29	Iowa	305,476,647	1.1%
30	South Carolina	289,376,633	1.0%
31	Connecticut	240,197,387	0.8%
32	Arkansas	226,334,421	0.8%
33	Utah	211,549,807	0.7%
34	Nebraska	204,462,116	0.7%
35	Nevada	187,677,416	0.7%
36	Kansas	187,303,061	0.7%
37	West Virginia	178,978,477	0.6%
38	Idaho	170,006,144	0.6%
39	New Mexico	121,914,934	0.4%
40	Maine	97,795,280	0.3%
41	Hawaii	97,241,056	0.3%
42	North Dakota	95,775,243	0.3%
43	South Dakota	92,283,955	0.3%
44	Alaska	91,580,013	0.3%
45	New Hampshire	74,828,643	0.3%
46	Delaware	74,674,436	0.3%
47	Rhode Island	74,058,172	0.3%
48	Wyoming	60,923,456	0.2%
49	Montana	60,742,572	0.2%
50	Vermont	42,203,355	0.1%
	District of Columbia	47,259,508	0.2%

Source: U.S. Department of Health and Human Services, Office of Child Support Enforcement
"Child Support Enforcement Annual Report to Congress" (https://www.acf.hhs.gov/css/data)
*Preliminary data for fiscal year 2017. Total does not include $340,666,162 collected in U.S. territories.

XV. Transportation

Federal Highway Funding in 2018

National Total = $41,420,520,075*

ALPHA ORDER

RANK	STATE	FUNDS	% of USA
16	Alabama	$798,592,462	1.9%
30	Alaska	527,794,368	1.3%
18	Arizona	770,153,352	1.9%
28	Arkansas	544,979,392	1.3%
1	California	3,863,394,035	9.3%
27	Colorado	562,866,921	1.4%
29	Connecticut	528,685,798	1.3%
48	Delaware	178,058,011	0.4%
3	Florida	1,994,334,006	4.8%
8	Georgia	1,359,129,884	3.3%
49	Hawaii	178,031,957	0.4%
41	Idaho	301,068,202	0.7%
6	Illinois	1,496,539,901	3.6%
13	Indiana	1,002,977,210	2.4%
32	Iowa	517,312,715	1.2%
36	Kansas	397,776,344	1.0%
22	Kentucky	699,381,985	1.7%
19	Louisiana	738,774,269	1.8%
47	Maine	194,304,897	0.5%
26	Maryland	632,550,030	1.5%
25	Massachusetts	639,295,840	1.5%
9	Michigan	1,108,263,489	2.7%
23	Minnesota	686,384,758	1.7%
33	Mississippi	509,087,926	1.2%
14	Missouri	996,486,818	2.4%
35	Montana	431,879,254	1.0%
40	Nebraska	304,247,397	0.7%
38	Nevada	382,221,701	0.9%
50	New Hampshire	173,915,712	0.4%
12	New Jersey	1,050,984,021	2.5%
37	New Mexico	386,545,823	0.9%
4	New York	1,766,855,733	4.3%
10	North Carolina	1,097,816,127	2.7%
44	North Dakota	261,327,819	0.6%
7	Ohio	1,410,935,784	3.4%
24	Oklahoma	667,575,430	1.6%
31	Oregon	526,123,426	1.3%
5	Pennsylvania	1,727,056,799	4.2%
45	Rhode Island	230,202,826	0.6%
21	South Carolina	704,850,578	1.7%
42	South Dakota	296,847,082	0.7%
15	Tennessee	889,486,516	2.1%
2	Texas	3,831,926,012	9.3%
39	Utah	365,507,771	0.9%
46	Vermont	213,631,530	0.5%
11	Virginia	1,071,151,543	2.6%
20	Washington	713,575,916	1.7%
34	West Virginia	460,005,319	1.1%
17	Wisconsin	792,011,303	1.9%
43	Wyoming	269,660,722	0.7%

RANK ORDER

RANK	STATE	FUNDS	% of USA
1	California	$3,863,394,035	9.3%
2	Texas	3,831,926,012	9.3%
3	Florida	1,994,334,006	4.8%
4	New York	1,766,855,733	4.3%
5	Pennsylvania	1,727,056,799	4.2%
6	Illinois	1,496,539,901	3.6%
7	Ohio	1,410,935,784	3.4%
8	Georgia	1,359,129,884	3.3%
9	Michigan	1,108,263,489	2.7%
10	North Carolina	1,097,816,127	2.7%
11	Virginia	1,071,151,543	2.6%
12	New Jersey	1,050,984,021	2.5%
13	Indiana	1,002,977,210	2.4%
14	Missouri	996,486,818	2.4%
15	Tennessee	889,486,516	2.1%
16	Alabama	798,592,462	1.9%
17	Wisconsin	792,011,303	1.9%
18	Arizona	770,153,352	1.9%
19	Louisiana	738,774,269	1.8%
20	Washington	713,575,916	1.7%
21	South Carolina	704,850,578	1.7%
22	Kentucky	699,381,985	1.7%
23	Minnesota	686,384,758	1.7%
24	Oklahoma	667,575,430	1.6%
25	Massachusetts	639,295,840	1.5%
26	Maryland	632,550,030	1.5%
27	Colorado	562,866,921	1.4%
28	Arkansas	544,979,392	1.3%
29	Connecticut	528,685,798	1.3%
30	Alaska	527,794,368	1.3%
31	Oregon	526,123,426	1.3%
32	Iowa	517,312,715	1.2%
33	Mississippi	509,087,926	1.2%
34	West Virginia	460,005,319	1.1%
35	Montana	431,879,254	1.0%
36	Kansas	397,776,344	1.0%
37	New Mexico	386,545,823	0.9%
38	Nevada	382,221,701	0.9%
39	Utah	365,507,771	0.9%
40	Nebraska	304,247,397	0.7%
41	Idaho	301,068,202	0.7%
42	South Dakota	296,847,082	0.7%
43	Wyoming	269,660,722	0.7%
44	North Dakota	261,327,819	0.6%
45	Rhode Island	230,202,826	0.6%
46	Vermont	213,631,530	0.5%
47	Maine	194,304,897	0.5%
48	Delaware	178,058,011	0.4%
49	Hawaii	178,031,957	0.4%
50	New Hampshire	173,915,712	0.4%
	District of Columbia	167,953,361	0.4%

Source: U.S. Department of Transportation, Federal Highway Administration
"Highway Apportionments under the FAST Act" (https://www.fhwa.dot.gov/fastact/funding.cfm)
*Fiscal Year 2018. National total does not include federal funds for U.S. territories. Totals are before sequestration, penalties, and post-apportionment set-asides.

Per Capita Federal Highway Funding in 2018

National Per Capita = $127*

ALPHA ORDER				RANK ORDER		
RANK	STATE	PER CAPITA		RANK	STATE	PER CAPITA
16	Alabama	$163		1	Alaska	$716
1	Alaska	716		2	Wyoming	467
42	Arizona	107		3	Montana	407
11	Arkansas	181		4	North Dakota	344
46	California	98		5	Vermont	341
45	Colorado	99		6	South Dakota	336
22	Connecticut	148		7	West Virginia	255
9	Delaware	184		8	Rhode Island	218
48	Florida	94		9	Delaware	184
30	Georgia	129		9	New Mexico	184
35	Hawaii	125		11	Arkansas	181
12	Idaho	172		12	Idaho	172
39	Illinois	117		13	Mississippi	170
21	Indiana	150		14	Oklahoma	169
15	Iowa	164		15	Iowa	164
25	Kansas	137		16	Alabama	163
20	Kentucky	157		16	Missouri	163
18	Louisiana	159		18	Louisiana	159
23	Maine	145		19	Nebraska	158
44	Maryland	105		20	Kentucky	157
49	Massachusetts	93		21	Indiana	150
41	Michigan	111		22	Connecticut	148
36	Minnesota	122		23	Maine	145
13	Mississippi	170		24	South Carolina	139
16	Missouri	163		25	Kansas	137
3	Montana	407		26	Wisconsin	136
19	Nebraska	158		27	Pennsylvania	135
32	Nevada	126		28	Texas	134
31	New Hampshire	128		29	Tennessee	131
38	New Jersey	118		30	Georgia	129
9	New Mexico	184		31	New Hampshire	128
50	New York	90		32	Nevada	126
43	North Carolina	106		32	Oregon	126
4	North Dakota	344		32	Virginia	126
37	Ohio	121		35	Hawaii	125
14	Oklahoma	169		36	Minnesota	122
32	Oregon	126		37	Ohio	121
27	Pennsylvania	135		38	New Jersey	118
8	Rhode Island	218		39	Illinois	117
24	South Carolina	139		40	Utah	116
6	South Dakota	336		41	Michigan	111
29	Tennessee	131		42	Arizona	107
28	Texas	134		43	North Carolina	106
40	Utah	116		44	Maryland	105
5	Vermont	341		45	Colorado	99
32	Virginia	126		46	California	98
47	Washington	95		47	Washington	95
7	West Virginia	255		48	Florida	94
26	Wisconsin	136		49	Massachusetts	93
2	Wyoming	467		50	New York	90
					District of Columbia	239

Source: CQ Press using data from U.S. Department of Transportation, Federal Highway Administration
"Highway Apportionments under the FAST Act" (https://www.fhwa.dot.gov/fastact/funding.cfm)
*Fiscal Year 2018. National per capita does not include federal funds for U.S. territories. Totals are before sequestration, penalties, and post-apportionment set-asides.

Public Road and Street Mileage in 2017

National Total = 4,165,349 Miles*

ALPHA ORDER

RANK	STATE	MILES	% of USA
18	Alabama	101,097	2.4%
46	Alaska	15,535	0.4%
33	Arizona	66,558	1.6%
17	Arkansas	102,603	2.5%
2	California	176,214	4.2%
22	Colorado	88,818	2.1%
44	Connecticut	21,544	0.5%
48	Delaware	6,452	0.2%
9	Florida	122,848	2.9%
7	Georgia	128,355	3.1%
50	Hawaii	4,476	0.1%
35	Idaho	52,437	1.3%
3	Illinois	145,936	3.5%
19	Indiana	96,790	2.3%
13	Iowa	114,637	2.8%
4	Kansas	142,054	3.4%
26	Kentucky	80,054	1.9%
34	Louisiana	61,411	1.5%
43	Maine	22,860	0.5%
41	Maryland	32,211	0.8%
40	Massachusetts	36,723	0.9%
10	Michigan	122,036	2.9%
5	Minnesota	139,449	3.3%
28	Mississippi	77,445	1.9%
6	Missouri	131,879	3.2%
32	Montana	73,566	1.8%
21	Nebraska	95,163	2.3%
37	Nevada	48,234	1.2%
45	New Hampshire	16,156	0.4%
38	New Jersey	38,896	0.9%
30	New Mexico	77,205	1.9%
14	New York	113,559	2.7%
16	North Carolina	106,975	2.6%
23	North Dakota	87,688	2.1%
8	Ohio	122,987	3.0%
15	Oklahoma	112,865	2.7%
27	Oregon	79,275	1.9%
11	Pennsylvania	120,521	2.9%
49	Rhode Island	6,027	0.1%
29	South Carolina	77,364	1.9%
24	South Dakota	82,584	2.0%
20	Tennessee	95,986	2.3%
1	Texas	314,319	7.5%
36	Utah	49,290	1.2%
47	Vermont	14,255	0.3%
31	Virginia	75,238	1.8%
25	Washington	80,429	1.9%
39	West Virginia	38,854	0.9%
12	Wisconsin	115,547	2.8%
42	Wyoming	30,430	0.7%

RANK ORDER

RANK	STATE	MILES	% of USA
1	Texas	314,319	7.5%
2	California	176,214	4.2%
3	Illinois	145,936	3.5%
4	Kansas	142,054	3.4%
5	Minnesota	139,449	3.3%
6	Missouri	131,879	3.2%
7	Georgia	128,355	3.1%
8	Ohio	122,987	3.0%
9	Florida	122,848	2.9%
10	Michigan	122,036	2.9%
11	Pennsylvania	120,521	2.9%
12	Wisconsin	115,547	2.8%
13	Iowa	114,637	2.8%
14	New York	113,559	2.7%
15	Oklahoma	112,865	2.7%
16	North Carolina	106,975	2.6%
17	Arkansas	102,603	2.5%
18	Alabama	101,097	2.4%
19	Indiana	96,790	2.3%
20	Tennessee	95,986	2.3%
21	Nebraska	95,163	2.3%
22	Colorado	88,818	2.1%
23	North Dakota	87,688	2.1%
24	South Dakota	82,584	2.0%
25	Washington	80,429	1.9%
26	Kentucky	80,054	1.9%
27	Oregon	79,275	1.9%
28	Mississippi	77,445	1.9%
29	South Carolina	77,364	1.9%
30	New Mexico	77,205	1.9%
31	Virginia	75,238	1.8%
32	Montana	73,566	1.8%
33	Arizona	66,558	1.6%
34	Louisiana	61,411	1.5%
35	Idaho	52,437	1.3%
36	Utah	49,290	1.2%
37	Nevada	48,234	1.2%
38	New Jersey	38,896	0.9%
39	West Virginia	38,854	0.9%
40	Massachusetts	36,723	0.9%
41	Maryland	32,211	0.8%
42	Wyoming	30,430	0.7%
43	Maine	22,860	0.5%
44	Connecticut	21,544	0.5%
45	New Hampshire	16,156	0.4%
46	Alaska	15,535	0.4%
47	Vermont	14,255	0.3%
48	Delaware	6,452	0.2%
49	Rhode Island	6,027	0.1%
50	Hawaii	4,476	0.1%
	District of Columbia	1,514	0.0%

Source: U.S. Department of Transportation, Federal Highway Administration
"Highway Statistics 2017" (Table HM-20, https://www.fhwa.dot.gov/policyinformation/statistics/2016/)
*Does not include 18,359 miles of roads and streets in Puerto Rico.

Percent of Public Road and Street Mileage Federally Funded in 2017

National Percent = 24.6% of Public Road and Street Mileage*

ALPHA ORDER

RANK	STATE	PERCENT
17	Alabama	26.5
7	Alaska	29.0
43	Arizona	20.6
38	Arkansas	22.1
2	California	32.0
46	Colorado	19.8
5	Connecticut	29.4
23	Delaware	24.8
36	Florida	22.5
23	Georgia	24.8
1	Hawaii	35.0
37	Idaho	22.3
30	Illinois	23.7
21	Indiana	25.1
34	Iowa	22.9
26	Kansas	24.4
48	Kentucky	18.2
34	Louisiana	22.9
13	Maine	27.8
19	Maryland	25.4
3	Massachusetts	30.7
4	Michigan	30.0
30	Minnesota	23.7
10	Mississippi	28.4
33	Missouri	23.4
45	Montana	20.0
41	Nebraska	21.8
50	Nevada	15.9
40	New Hampshire	22.0
12	New Jersey	28.1
49	New Mexico	16.0
26	New York	24.4
38	North Carolina	22.1
42	North Dakota	21.5
25	Ohio	24.5
9	Oklahoma	28.6
32	Oregon	23.5
29	Pennsylvania	23.8
6	Rhode Island	29.2
15	South Carolina	27.5
28	South Dakota	24.1
44	Tennessee	20.5
8	Texas	28.7
47	Utah	19.7
14	Vermont	27.6
11	Virginia	28.2
20	Washington	25.3
16	West Virginia	27.1
22	Wisconsin	24.9
18	Wyoming	26.1

RANK ORDER

RANK	STATE	PERCENT
1	Hawaii	35.0
2	California	32.0
3	Massachusetts	30.7
4	Michigan	30.0
5	Connecticut	29.4
6	Rhode Island	29.2
7	Alaska	29.0
8	Texas	28.7
9	Oklahoma	28.6
10	Mississippi	28.4
11	Virginia	28.2
12	New Jersey	28.1
13	Maine	27.8
14	Vermont	27.6
15	South Carolina	27.5
16	West Virginia	27.1
17	Alabama	26.5
18	Wyoming	26.1
19	Maryland	25.4
20	Washington	25.3
21	Indiana	25.1
22	Wisconsin	24.9
23	Delaware	24.8
23	Georgia	24.8
25	Ohio	24.5
26	Kansas	24.4
26	New York	24.4
28	South Dakota	24.1
29	Pennsylvania	23.8
30	Illinois	23.7
30	Minnesota	23.7
32	Oregon	23.5
33	Missouri	23.4
34	Iowa	22.9
34	Louisiana	22.9
36	Florida	22.5
37	Idaho	22.3
38	Arkansas	22.1
38	North Carolina	22.1
40	New Hampshire	22.0
41	Nebraska	21.8
42	North Dakota	21.5
43	Arizona	20.6
44	Tennessee	20.5
45	Montana	20.0
46	Colorado	19.8
47	Utah	19.7
48	Kentucky	18.2
49	New Mexico	16.0
50	Nevada	15.9

	District of Columbia	30.0

Source: CQ Press using data from U.S. Department of Transportation, Federal Highway Administration
"Highway Statistics 2017" (Table HM-15, http://www.fhwa.dot.gov/policyinformation/statistics/2016/)
*National percent does not include federally-funded highway miles in Puerto Rico.

Average Number of Lanes Per Mile of Public Road and Street Mileage in 2016

National Average = 2.09 Lanes per Mile*

ALPHA ORDER

RANK	STATE	LANES PER MILE
26	Alabama	2.09
48	Alaska	2.03
5	Arizona	2.18
39	Arkansas	2.05
2	California	2.22
31	Colorado	2.08
10	Connecticut	2.13
8	Delaware	2.16
1	Florida	2.23
13	Georgia	2.12
4	Hawaii	2.19
39	Idaho	2.05
20	Illinois	2.10
26	Indiana	2.09
39	Iowa	2.05
45	Kansas	2.04
26	Kentucky	2.09
13	Louisiana	2.12
39	Maine	2.05
3	Maryland	2.20
17	Massachusetts	2.11
20	Michigan	2.10
36	Minnesota	2.06
26	Mississippi	2.09
20	Missouri	2.10
45	Montana	2.04
45	Nebraska	2.04
13	Nevada	2.12
36	New Hampshire	2.06
5	New Jersey	2.18
20	New Mexico	2.10
17	New York	2.11
10	North Carolina	2.13
48	North Dakota	2.03
10	Ohio	2.13
31	Oklahoma	2.08
39	Oregon	2.05
31	Pennsylvania	2.08
17	Rhode Island	2.11
20	South Carolina	2.10
48	South Dakota	2.03
13	Tennessee	2.12
8	Texas	2.16
20	Utah	2.10
39	Vermont	2.05
7	Virginia	2.17
31	Washington	2.08
36	West Virginia	2.06
35	Wisconsin	2.07
26	Wyoming	2.09

RANK ORDER

RANK	STATE	LANES PER MILE
1	Florida	2.23
2	California	2.22
3	Maryland	2.20
4	Hawaii	2.19
5	Arizona	2.18
5	New Jersey	2.18
7	Virginia	2.17
8	Delaware	2.16
8	Texas	2.16
10	Connecticut	2.13
10	North Carolina	2.13
10	Ohio	2.13
13	Georgia	2.12
13	Louisiana	2.12
13	Nevada	2.12
13	Tennessee	2.12
17	Massachusetts	2.11
17	New York	2.11
17	Rhode Island	2.11
20	Illinois	2.10
20	Michigan	2.10
20	Missouri	2.10
20	New Mexico	2.10
20	South Carolina	2.10
20	Utah	2.10
26	Alabama	2.09
26	Indiana	2.09
26	Kentucky	2.09
26	Mississippi	2.09
26	Wyoming	2.09
31	Colorado	2.08
31	Oklahoma	2.08
31	Pennsylvania	2.08
31	Washington	2.08
35	Wisconsin	2.07
36	Minnesota	2.06
36	New Hampshire	2.06
36	West Virginia	2.06
39	Arkansas	2.05
39	Idaho	2.05
39	Iowa	2.05
39	Maine	2.05
39	Oregon	2.05
39	Vermont	2.05
45	Kansas	2.04
45	Montana	2.04
45	Nebraska	2.04
48	Alaska	2.03
48	North Dakota	2.03
48	South Dakota	2.03

| | District of Columbia | 2.28 |

Source: CQ Press using data from U.S. Department of Transportation, Federal Highway Administration
   "Highway Statistics 2016" (Tables HM-20 and HM-48, https://www.fhwa.dot.gov/policyinformation/statistics/2016/)
*Lane-miles divided by public road and street mileage.

Interstate Highway Mileage in 2017

National Total = 48,254 Miles*

ALPHA ORDER

RANK	STATE	MILES	% of USA
18	Alabama	1,004	2.1%
17	Alaska	1,080	2.2%
15	Arizona	1,169	2.4%
33	Arkansas	749	1.6%
2	California	2,456	5.1%
20	Colorado	952	2.0%
45	Connecticut	346	0.7%
50	Delaware	41	0.1%
7	Florida	1,495	3.1%
12	Georgia	1,247	2.6%
49	Hawaii	55	0.1%
36	Idaho	611	1.3%
3	Illinois	2,185	4.5%
10	Indiana	1,262	2.6%
31	Iowa	786	1.6%
27	Kansas	874	1.8%
29	Kentucky	842	1.7%
21	Louisiana	938	1.9%
44	Maine	366	0.8%
42	Maryland	480	1.0%
38	Massachusetts	575	1.2%
11	Michigan	1,251	2.6%
24	Minnesota	913	1.9%
30	Mississippi	822	1.7%
8	Missouri	1,380	2.9%
14	Montana	1,192	2.5%
41	Nebraska	483	1.0%
37	Nevada	602	1.2%
47	New Hampshire	225	0.5%
43	New Jersey	432	0.9%
19	New Mexico	1,000	2.1%
5	New York	1,744	3.6%
9	North Carolina	1,272	2.6%
39	North Dakota	571	1.2%
6	Ohio	1,574	3.3%
23	Oklahoma	933	1.9%
34	Oregon	730	1.5%
4	Pennsylvania	1,861	3.9%
48	Rhode Island	70	0.1%
28	South Carolina	851	1.8%
35	South Dakota	679	1.4%
13	Tennessee	1,201	2.5%
1	Texas	3,459	7.2%
22	Utah	937	1.9%
46	Vermont	320	0.7%
16	Virginia	1,119	2.3%
32	Washington	764	1.6%
40	West Virginia	555	1.2%
26	Wisconsin	877	1.8%
24	Wyoming	913	1.9%

RANK ORDER

RANK	STATE	MILES	% of USA
1	Texas	3,459	7.2%
2	California	2,456	5.1%
3	Illinois	2,185	4.5%
4	Pennsylvania	1,861	3.9%
5	New York	1,744	3.6%
6	Ohio	1,574	3.3%
7	Florida	1,495	3.1%
8	Missouri	1,380	2.9%
9	North Carolina	1,272	2.6%
10	Indiana	1,262	2.6%
11	Michigan	1,251	2.6%
12	Georgia	1,247	2.6%
13	Tennessee	1,201	2.5%
14	Montana	1,192	2.5%
15	Arizona	1,169	2.4%
16	Virginia	1,119	2.3%
17	Alaska	1,080	2.2%
18	Alabama	1,004	2.1%
19	New Mexico	1,000	2.1%
20	Colorado	952	2.0%
21	Louisiana	938	1.9%
22	Utah	937	1.9%
23	Oklahoma	933	1.9%
24	Minnesota	913	1.9%
24	Wyoming	913	1.9%
26	Wisconsin	877	1.8%
27	Kansas	874	1.8%
28	South Carolina	851	1.8%
29	Kentucky	842	1.7%
30	Mississippi	822	1.7%
31	Iowa	786	1.6%
32	Washington	764	1.6%
33	Arkansas	749	1.6%
34	Oregon	730	1.5%
35	South Dakota	679	1.4%
36	Idaho	611	1.3%
37	Nevada	602	1.2%
38	Massachusetts	575	1.2%
39	North Dakota	571	1.2%
40	West Virginia	555	1.2%
41	Nebraska	483	1.0%
42	Maryland	480	1.0%
43	New Jersey	432	0.9%
44	Maine	366	0.8%
45	Connecticut	346	0.7%
46	Vermont	320	0.7%
47	New Hampshire	225	0.5%
48	Rhode Island	70	0.1%
49	Hawaii	55	0.1%
50	Delaware	41	0.1%
	District of Columbia	12	0.0%

Source: U.S. Department of Transportation, Federal Highway Administration
"Highway Statistics 2017" (Table HM-15, https://www.fhwa.dot.gov/policyinformation/statistics/2016/)
*Does not include 301 miles of highway in Puerto Rico that are part of the interstate system.

Rural Road and Street Mileage in 2017

National Total = 2,945,505 Rural Miles*

ALPHA ORDER				RANK ORDER			
RANK	STATE	MILES	% of USA	RANK	STATE	MILES	% of USA
17	Alabama	72,405	2.5%	1	Texas	205,503	7.0%
43	Alaska	12,681	0.4%	2	Kansas	127,820	4.3%
34	Arizona	40,200	1.4%	3	Minnesota	117,218	4.0%
10	Arkansas	85,422	2.9%	4	Missouri	107,531	3.7%
18	California	71,549	2.4%	5	Iowa	101,989	3.5%
20	Colorado	68,120	2.3%	6	Illinois	96,200	3.3%
46	Connecticut	5,691	0.2%	7	Oklahoma	94,467	3.2%
48	Delaware	2,804	0.1%	8	Wisconsin	91,695	3.1%
37	Florida	36,481	1.2%	9	Nebraska	87,284	3.0%
14	Georgia	76,091	2.6%	10	Arkansas	85,422	2.9%
49	Hawaii	1,666	0.1%	11	North Dakota	84,816	2.9%
32	Idaho	46,215	1.6%	12	Michigan	84,075	2.9%
6	Illinois	96,200	3.3%	13	South Dakota	79,163	2.7%
21	Indiana	66,685	2.3%	14	Georgia	76,091	2.6%
5	Iowa	101,989	3.5%	15	Ohio	75,498	2.6%
2	Kansas	127,820	4.3%	16	Pennsylvania	72,759	2.5%
24	Kentucky	64,958	2.2%	17	Alabama	72,405	2.5%
33	Louisiana	43,801	1.5%	18	California	71,549	2.4%
40	Maine	19,454	0.7%	19	Montana	69,337	2.4%
41	Maryland	13,571	0.5%	20	Colorado	68,120	2.3%
45	Massachusetts	6,193	0.2%	21	Indiana	66,685	2.3%
12	Michigan	84,075	2.9%	22	New Mexico	66,106	2.2%
3	Minnesota	117,218	4.0%	23	North Carolina	65,691	2.2%
25	Mississippi	64,397	2.2%	24	Kentucky	64,958	2.2%
4	Missouri	107,531	3.7%	25	Mississippi	64,397	2.2%
19	Montana	69,337	2.4%	26	Oregon	64,221	2.2%
9	Nebraska	87,284	3.0%	27	Tennessee	64,199	2.2%
36	Nevada	38,080	1.3%	28	New York	63,874	2.2%
44	New Hampshire	11,092	0.4%	29	Washington	56,250	1.9%
47	New Jersey	5,443	0.2%	30	South Carolina	56,042	1.9%
22	New Mexico	66,106	2.2%	31	Virginia	48,695	1.7%
28	New York	63,874	2.2%	32	Idaho	46,215	1.6%
23	North Carolina	65,691	2.2%	33	Louisiana	43,801	1.5%
11	North Dakota	84,816	2.9%	34	Arizona	40,200	1.4%
15	Ohio	75,498	2.6%	35	Utah	38,115	1.3%
7	Oklahoma	94,467	3.2%	36	Nevada	38,080	1.3%
26	Oregon	64,221	2.2%	37	Florida	36,481	1.2%
16	Pennsylvania	72,759	2.5%	38	West Virginia	32,202	1.1%
50	Rhode Island	1,342	0.0%	39	Wyoming	27,662	0.9%
30	South Carolina	56,042	1.9%	40	Maine	19,454	0.7%
13	South Dakota	79,163	2.7%	41	Maryland	13,571	0.5%
27	Tennessee	64,199	2.2%	42	Vermont	12,753	0.4%
1	Texas	205,503	7.0%	43	Alaska	12,681	0.4%
35	Utah	38,115	1.3%	44	New Hampshire	11,092	0.4%
42	Vermont	12,753	0.4%	45	Massachusetts	6,193	0.2%
31	Virginia	48,695	1.7%	46	Connecticut	5,691	0.2%
29	Washington	56,250	1.9%	47	New Jersey	5,443	0.2%
38	West Virginia	32,202	1.1%	48	Delaware	2,804	0.1%
8	Wisconsin	91,695	3.1%	49	Hawaii	1,666	0.1%
39	Wyoming	27,662	0.9%	50	Rhode Island	1,342	0.0%
					District of Columbia	0	0.0%

Source: U.S. Department of Transportation, Federal Highway Administration
"Highway Statistics 2017" (Table HM-20, https://www.fhwa.dot.gov/policyinformation/statistics/2016/)
*Does not include 3,191 miles of rural roads and streets in Puerto Rico.

Urban Road and Street Mileage in 2017

National Total = 1,219,844 Urban Miles*

ALPHA ORDER

ALPHA ORDER

RANK	STATE	MILES	% of USA
15	Alabama	28,692	2.4%
47	Alaska	2,854	0.2%
17	Arizona	26,358	2.2%
27	Arkansas	17,180	1.4%
2	California	104,665	8.6%
23	Colorado	20,698	1.7%
28	Connecticut	15,853	1.3%
43	Delaware	3,648	0.3%
3	Florida	86,368	7.1%
4	Georgia	52,264	4.3%
48	Hawaii	2,810	0.2%
39	Idaho	6,222	0.5%
5	Illinois	49,736	4.1%
14	Indiana	30,105	2.5%
33	Iowa	12,648	1.0%
31	Kansas	14,235	1.2%
29	Kentucky	15,096	1.2%
26	Louisiana	17,610	1.4%
45	Maine	3,406	0.3%
24	Maryland	18,640	1.5%
13	Massachusetts	30,529	2.5%
10	Michigan	37,962	3.1%
21	Minnesota	22,231	1.8%
32	Mississippi	13,048	1.1%
18	Missouri	24,348	2.0%
42	Montana	4,229	0.3%
37	Nebraska	7,879	0.6%
36	Nevada	10,154	0.8%
40	New Hampshire	5,064	0.4%
11	New Jersey	33,452	2.7%
35	New Mexico	11,099	0.9%
6	New York	49,686	4.1%
9	North Carolina	41,284	3.4%
46	North Dakota	2,873	0.2%
8	Ohio	47,489	3.9%
25	Oklahoma	18,398	1.5%
30	Oregon	15,054	1.2%
7	Pennsylvania	47,762	3.9%
41	Rhode Island	4,685	0.4%
22	South Carolina	21,322	1.7%
44	South Dakota	3,421	0.3%
12	Tennessee	31,788	2.6%
1	Texas	108,817	8.9%
34	Utah	11,175	0.9%
50	Vermont	1,501	0.1%
16	Virginia	26,543	2.2%
19	Washington	24,179	2.0%
38	West Virginia	6,652	0.5%
20	Wisconsin	23,852	2.0%
49	Wyoming	2,768	0.2%

RANK ORDER

RANK	STATE	MILES	% of USA
1	Texas	108,817	8.9%
2	California	104,665	8.6%
3	Florida	86,368	7.1%
4	Georgia	52,264	4.3%
5	Illinois	49,736	4.1%
6	New York	49,686	4.1%
7	Pennsylvania	47,762	3.9%
8	Ohio	47,489	3.9%
9	North Carolina	41,284	3.4%
10	Michigan	37,962	3.1%
11	New Jersey	33,452	2.7%
12	Tennessee	31,788	2.6%
13	Massachusetts	30,529	2.5%
14	Indiana	30,105	2.5%
15	Alabama	28,692	2.4%
16	Virginia	26,543	2.2%
17	Arizona	26,358	2.2%
18	Missouri	24,348	2.0%
19	Washington	24,179	2.0%
20	Wisconsin	23,852	2.0%
21	Minnesota	22,231	1.8%
22	South Carolina	21,322	1.7%
23	Colorado	20,698	1.7%
24	Maryland	18,640	1.5%
25	Oklahoma	18,398	1.5%
26	Louisiana	17,610	1.4%
27	Arkansas	17,180	1.4%
28	Connecticut	15,853	1.3%
29	Kentucky	15,096	1.2%
30	Oregon	15,054	1.2%
31	Kansas	14,235	1.2%
32	Mississippi	13,048	1.1%
33	Iowa	12,648	1.0%
34	Utah	11,175	0.9%
35	New Mexico	11,099	0.9%
36	Nevada	10,154	0.8%
37	Nebraska	7,879	0.6%
38	West Virginia	6,652	0.5%
39	Idaho	6,222	0.5%
40	New Hampshire	5,064	0.4%
41	Rhode Island	4,685	0.4%
42	Montana	4,229	0.3%
43	Delaware	3,648	0.3%
44	South Dakota	3,421	0.3%
45	Maine	3,406	0.3%
46	North Dakota	2,873	0.2%
47	Alaska	2,854	0.2%
48	Hawaii	2,810	0.2%
49	Wyoming	2,768	0.2%
50	Vermont	1,501	0.1%
	District of Columbia	1,514	0.1%

Source: U.S. Department of Transportation, Federal Highway Administration
   "Highway Statistics 2017" (Table HM-20, https://www.fhwa.dot.gov/policyinformation/statistics/2016/)
*Does not include 15,166 miles of urban roads and streets in Puerto Rico.

Bridges in 2017

National Total = 612,677 Bridges*

ALPHA ORDER

RANK	STATE	BRIDGES	% of USA
15	Alabama	16,129	2.6%
47	Alaska	1,569	0.3%
28	Arizona	8,289	1.4%
23	Arkansas	12,864	2.1%
4	California	25,657	4.2%
27	Colorado	8,717	1.4%
39	Connecticut	4,238	0.7%
49	Delaware	879	0.1%
24	Florida	12,355	2.0%
17	Georgia	14,863	2.4%
48	Hawaii	1,135	0.2%
37	Idaho	4,492	0.7%
3	Illinois	26,775	4.4%
11	Indiana	19,291	3.1%
7	Iowa	24,215	4.0%
5	Kansas	25,001	4.1%
18	Kentucky	14,280	2.3%
22	Louisiana	12,910	2.1%
45	Maine	2,458	0.4%
34	Maryland	5,335	0.9%
36	Massachusetts	5,192	0.8%
25	Michigan	11,180	1.8%
21	Minnesota	13,329	2.2%
14	Mississippi	17,072	2.8%
6	Missouri	24,487	4.0%
35	Montana	5,302	0.9%
16	Nebraska	15,330	2.5%
46	Nevada	1,944	0.3%
44	New Hampshire	2,479	0.4%
32	New Jersey	6,737	1.1%
40	New Mexico	3,999	0.7%
13	New York	17,456	2.8%
12	North Carolina	18,183	3.0%
38	North Dakota	4,377	0.7%
2	Ohio	27,345	4.5%
8	Oklahoma	23,071	3.8%
30	Oregon	8,147	1.3%
9	Pennsylvania	22,779	3.7%
50	Rhode Island	778	0.1%
26	South Carolina	9,341	1.5%
33	South Dakota	5,818	0.9%
10	Tennessee	20,169	3.3%
1	Texas	53,869	8.8%
42	Utah	3,051	0.5%
43	Vermont	2,772	0.5%
20	Virginia	13,932	2.3%
29	Washington	8,233	1.3%
31	West Virginia	7,228	1.2%
19	Wisconsin	14,253	2.3%
41	Wyoming	3,127	0.5%

RANK ORDER

RANK	STATE	BRIDGES	% of USA
1	Texas	53,869	8.8%
2	Ohio	27,345	4.5%
3	Illinois	26,775	4.4%
4	California	25,657	4.2%
5	Kansas	25,001	4.1%
6	Missouri	24,487	4.0%
7	Iowa	24,215	4.0%
8	Oklahoma	23,071	3.8%
9	Pennsylvania	22,779	3.7%
10	Tennessee	20,169	3.3%
11	Indiana	19,291	3.1%
12	North Carolina	18,183	3.0%
13	New York	17,456	2.8%
14	Mississippi	17,072	2.8%
15	Alabama	16,129	2.6%
16	Nebraska	15,330	2.5%
17	Georgia	14,863	2.4%
18	Kentucky	14,280	2.3%
19	Wisconsin	14,253	2.3%
20	Virginia	13,932	2.3%
21	Minnesota	13,329	2.2%
22	Louisiana	12,910	2.1%
23	Arkansas	12,864	2.1%
24	Florida	12,355	2.0%
25	Michigan	11,180	1.8%
26	South Carolina	9,341	1.5%
27	Colorado	8,717	1.4%
28	Arizona	8,289	1.4%
29	Washington	8,233	1.3%
30	Oregon	8,147	1.3%
31	West Virginia	7,228	1.2%
32	New Jersey	6,737	1.1%
33	South Dakota	5,818	0.9%
34	Maryland	5,335	0.9%
35	Montana	5,302	0.9%
36	Massachusetts	5,192	0.8%
37	Idaho	4,492	0.7%
38	North Dakota	4,377	0.7%
39	Connecticut	4,238	0.7%
40	New Mexico	3,999	0.7%
41	Wyoming	3,127	0.5%
42	Utah	3,051	0.5%
43	Vermont	2,772	0.5%
44	New Hampshire	2,479	0.4%
45	Maine	2,458	0.4%
46	Nevada	1,944	0.3%
47	Alaska	1,569	0.3%
48	Hawaii	1,135	0.2%
49	Delaware	879	0.1%
50	Rhode Island	778	0.1%
	District of Columbia	245	0.0%

Source: U.S. Department of Transportation, Federal Highway Administration
   "Deficient Bridges by State and Highway System, 2017" (https://www.fhwa.dot.gov/bridge/deficient.htm)
*As of December 2017. Includes federal-aid and nonfederal-aid system bridges. National total does not include 2,325 bridges in Puerto Rico.

Structurally Deficient Bridges in 2017

National Total = 54,259 Structurally Deficient Bridges*

ALPHA ORDER				RANK ORDER			
RANK	STATE	BRIDGES	% of USA	RANK	STATE	BRIDGES	% of USA
17	Alabama	1,200	2.2%	1	Iowa	5,067	9.3%
45	Alaska	165	0.3%	2	Pennsylvania	4,173	7.7%
43	Arizona	205	0.4%	3	Oklahoma	3,234	6.0%
25	Arkansas	765	1.4%	4	Missouri	3,086	5.7%
13	California	1,603	3.0%	5	Illinois	2,303	4.2%
31	Colorado	488	0.9%	6	Nebraska	2,258	4.2%
36	Connecticut	332	0.6%	7	Kansas	2,115	3.9%
49	Delaware	39	0.1%	8	Mississippi	2,008	3.7%
41	Florida	265	0.5%	9	North Carolina	1,854	3.4%
27	Georgia	692	1.3%	10	New York	1,837	3.4%
48	Hawaii	66	0.1%	11	Louisiana	1,821	3.4%
35	Idaho	393	0.7%	12	Ohio	1,653	3.0%
5	Illinois	2,303	4.2%	13	California	1,603	3.0%
14	Indiana	1,435	2.6%	14	Indiana	1,435	2.6%
1	Iowa	5,067	9.3%	15	West Virginia	1,372	2.5%
7	Kansas	2,115	3.9%	16	Wisconsin	1,245	2.3%
19	Kentucky	1,110	2.0%	17	Alabama	1,200	2.2%
11	Louisiana	1,821	3.4%	18	Michigan	1,175	2.2%
37	Maine	326	0.6%	19	Kentucky	1,110	2.0%
39	Maryland	300	0.6%	20	South Dakota	1,081	2.0%
32	Massachusetts	482	0.9%	21	Tennessee	953	1.8%
18	Michigan	1,175	2.2%	22	South Carolina	926	1.7%
26	Minnesota	709	1.3%	23	Texas	847	1.6%
8	Mississippi	2,008	3.7%	24	Virginia	825	1.5%
4	Missouri	3,086	5.7%	25	Arkansas	765	1.4%
30	Montana	515	0.9%	26	Minnesota	709	1.3%
6	Nebraska	2,258	4.2%	27	Georgia	692	1.3%
50	Nevada	31	0.1%	28	North Dakota	614	1.1%
40	New Hampshire	270	0.5%	29	New Jersey	596	1.1%
29	New Jersey	596	1.1%	30	Montana	515	0.9%
42	New Mexico	251	0.5%	31	Colorado	488	0.9%
10	New York	1,837	3.4%	32	Massachusetts	482	0.9%
9	North Carolina	1,854	3.4%	33	Oregon	444	0.8%
28	North Dakota	614	1.1%	34	Washington	399	0.7%
12	Ohio	1,653	3.0%	35	Idaho	393	0.7%
3	Oklahoma	3,234	6.0%	36	Connecticut	332	0.6%
33	Oregon	444	0.8%	37	Maine	326	0.6%
2	Pennsylvania	4,173	7.7%	38	Wyoming	310	0.6%
44	Rhode Island	181	0.3%	39	Maryland	300	0.6%
22	South Carolina	926	1.7%	40	New Hampshire	270	0.5%
20	South Dakota	1,081	2.0%	41	Florida	265	0.5%
21	Tennessee	953	1.8%	42	New Mexico	251	0.5%
23	Texas	847	1.6%	43	Arizona	205	0.4%
47	Utah	87	0.2%	44	Rhode Island	181	0.3%
46	Vermont	145	0.3%	45	Alaska	165	0.3%
24	Virginia	825	1.5%	46	Vermont	145	0.3%
34	Washington	399	0.7%	47	Utah	87	0.2%
15	West Virginia	1,372	2.5%	48	Hawaii	66	0.1%
16	Wisconsin	1,245	2.3%	49	Delaware	39	0.1%
38	Wyoming	310	0.6%	50	Nevada	31	0.1%
					District of Columbia	8	0.0%

Source: U.S. Department of Transportation, Federal Highway Administration

"Deficient Bridges by State and Highway System, 2017" (https://www.fhwa.dot.gov/bridge/deficient.htm)

*As of December 2017. Includes federal-aid and nonfederal-aid system bridges. National total does not include 301 structurally deficient bridges in Puerto Rico. Includes only bridges that are structurally deficient. Does not include bridges that are functionally obsolete.

Structurally Deficient Bridges as a Percent of Total Bridges in 2017

National Percent = 8.9% of Bridges Are Structurally Deficient*

ALPHA ORDER			RANK ORDER		
RANK	**STATE**	**PERCENT**	**RANK**	**STATE**	**PERCENT**
29	Alabama	7.4	1	Rhode Island	23.3
14	Alaska	10.5	2	Iowa	20.9
47	Arizona	2.5	3	West Virginia	19.0
34	Arkansas	5.9	4	South Dakota	18.6
32	California	6.2	5	Pennsylvania	18.3
37	Colorado	5.6	6	Nebraska	14.7
27	Connecticut	7.8	7	Louisiana	14.1
45	Delaware	4.4	8	North Dakota	14.0
48	Florida	2.1	8	Oklahoma	14.0
43	Georgia	4.7	10	Maine	13.3
36	Hawaii	5.8	11	Missouri	12.6
23	Idaho	8.7	12	Mississippi	11.8
25	Illinois	8.6	13	New Hampshire	10.9
29	Indiana	7.4	14	Alaska	10.5
2	Iowa	20.9	14	Michigan	10.5
26	Kansas	8.5	14	New York	10.5
27	Kentucky	7.8	17	North Carolina	10.2
7	Louisiana	14.1	18	South Carolina	9.9
10	Maine	13.3	18	Wyoming	9.9
37	Maryland	5.6	20	Montana	9.7
21	Massachusetts	9.3	21	Massachusetts	9.3
14	Michigan	10.5	22	New Jersey	8.8
40	Minnesota	5.3	23	Idaho	8.7
12	Mississippi	11.8	23	Wisconsin	8.7
11	Missouri	12.6	25	Illinois	8.6
20	Montana	9.7	26	Kansas	8.5
6	Nebraska	14.7	27	Connecticut	7.8
49	Nevada	1.6	27	Kentucky	7.8
13	New Hampshire	10.9	29	Alabama	7.4
22	New Jersey	8.8	29	Indiana	7.4
31	New Mexico	6.3	31	New Mexico	6.3
14	New York	10.5	32	California	6.2
17	North Carolina	10.2	33	Ohio	6.0
8	North Dakota	14.0	34	Arkansas	5.9
33	Ohio	6.0	34	Virginia	5.9
8	Oklahoma	14.0	36	Hawaii	5.8
39	Oregon	5.4	37	Colorado	5.6
5	Pennsylvania	18.3	37	Maryland	5.6
1	Rhode Island	23.3	39	Oregon	5.4
18	South Carolina	9.9	40	Minnesota	5.3
4	South Dakota	18.6	41	Vermont	5.2
43	Tennessee	4.7	42	Washington	4.8
49	Texas	1.6	43	Georgia	4.7
46	Utah	2.9	43	Tennessee	4.7
41	Vermont	5.2	45	Delaware	4.4
34	Virginia	5.9	46	Utah	2.9
42	Washington	4.8	47	Arizona	2.5
3	West Virginia	19.0	48	Florida	2.1
23	Wisconsin	8.7	49	Nevada	1.6
18	Wyoming	9.9	49	Texas	1.6
				District of Columbia	3.3

Source: CQ Press using data from U.S. Department of Transportation, Federal Highway Administration
"Deficient Bridges by State and Highway System, 2017" (https://www.fhwa.dot.gov/bridge/deficient.htm)
*As of December 2017. Includes federal-aid and nonfederal-aid system bridges. National figure does not include structurally deficient bridges in Puerto Rico. Includes only bridges that are structurally deficient. Does not include bridges that are functionally obsolete.

Vehicle-Miles of Travel in 2016

National Total = 3,174,407,958,000 Miles

ALPHA ORDER				RANK ORDER			
RANK	STATE	MILES	% of USA	RANK	STATE	MILES	% of USA
16	Alabama	69,226,971,000	2.2%	1	California	340,114,937,000	10.7%
50	Alaska	5,258,556,000	0.2%	2	Texas	271,262,838,000	8.5%
17	Arizona	65,785,730,000	2.1%	3	Florida	215,550,749,000	6.8%
30	Arkansas	35,754,797,000	1.1%	4	New York	122,929,969,000	3.9%
1	California	340,114,937,000	10.7%	5	Georgia	122,802,186,000	3.9%
24	Colorado	52,151,611,000	1.6%	6	Ohio	118,607,622,000	3.7%
33	Connecticut	31,638,569,000	1.0%	7	North Carolina	116,748,681,000	3.7%
44	Delaware	10,177,585,000	0.3%	8	Illinois	107,314,103,000	3.4%
3	Florida	215,550,749,000	6.8%	9	Pennsylvania	101,362,493,000	3.2%
5	Georgia	122,802,186,000	3.9%	10	Michigan	99,432,538,000	3.1%
43	Hawaii	10,635,428,000	0.3%	11	Virginia	84,462,672,000	2.7%
39	Idaho	17,198,715,000	0.5%	12	Indiana	83,182,776,000	2.6%
8	Illinois	107,314,103,000	3.4%	13	New Jersey	77,092,632,000	2.4%
12	Indiana	83,182,776,000	2.6%	14	Tennessee	76,883,747,000	2.4%
31	Iowa	33,336,972,000	1.1%	15	Missouri	74,018,576,000	2.3%
32	Kansas	32,102,610,000	1.0%	16	Alabama	69,226,971,000	2.2%
25	Kentucky	49,312,718,000	1.6%	17	Arizona	65,785,730,000	2.1%
26	Louisiana	49,155,613,000	1.5%	18	Wisconsin	64,046,407,000	2.0%
40	Maine	14,838,258,000	0.5%	19	Massachusetts	61,824,851,000	1.9%
21	Maryland	59,137,327,000	1.9%	20	Washington	61,017,811,000	1.9%
19	Massachusetts	61,824,851,000	1.9%	21	Maryland	59,137,327,000	1.9%
10	Michigan	99,432,538,000	3.1%	22	Minnesota	59,028,802,000	1.9%
22	Minnesota	59,028,802,000	1.9%	23	South Carolina	54,552,642,000	1.7%
28	Mississippi	40,754,709,000	1.3%	24	Colorado	52,151,611,000	1.6%
15	Missouri	74,018,576,000	2.3%	25	Kentucky	49,312,718,000	1.6%
42	Montana	12,598,723,000	0.4%	26	Louisiana	49,155,613,000	1.5%
37	Nebraska	20,699,916,000	0.7%	27	Oklahoma	49,013,278,000	1.5%
36	Nevada	26,787,988,000	0.8%	28	Mississippi	40,754,709,000	1.3%
41	New Hampshire	13,512,597,000	0.4%	29	Oregon	36,719,189,000	1.2%
13	New Jersey	77,092,632,000	2.4%	30	Arkansas	35,754,797,000	1.1%
35	New Mexico	27,885,521,000	0.9%	31	Iowa	33,336,972,000	1.1%
4	New York	122,929,969,000	3.9%	32	Kansas	32,102,610,000	1.0%
7	North Carolina	116,748,681,000	3.7%	33	Connecticut	31,638,569,000	1.0%
45	North Dakota	9,739,209,000	0.3%	34	Utah	31,448,897,000	1.0%
6	Ohio	118,607,622,000	3.7%	35	New Mexico	27,885,521,000	0.9%
27	Oklahoma	49,013,278,000	1.5%	36	Nevada	26,787,988,000	0.8%
29	Oregon	36,719,189,000	1.2%	37	Nebraska	20,699,916,000	0.7%
9	Pennsylvania	101,362,493,000	3.2%	38	West Virginia	19,539,443,000	0.6%
48	Rhode Island	7,927,071,000	0.2%	39	Idaho	17,198,715,000	0.5%
23	South Carolina	54,552,642,000	1.7%	40	Maine	14,838,258,000	0.5%
46	South Dakota	9,506,534,000	0.3%	41	New Hampshire	13,512,597,000	0.4%
14	Tennessee	76,883,747,000	2.4%	42	Montana	12,598,723,000	0.4%
2	Texas	271,262,838,000	8.5%	43	Hawaii	10,635,428,000	0.3%
34	Utah	31,448,897,000	1.0%	44	Delaware	10,177,585,000	0.3%
49	Vermont	7,381,890,000	0.2%	45	North Dakota	9,739,209,000	0.3%
11	Virginia	84,462,672,000	2.7%	46	South Dakota	9,506,534,000	0.3%
20	Washington	61,017,811,000	1.9%	47	Wyoming	9,322,542,000	0.3%
38	West Virginia	19,539,443,000	0.6%	48	Rhode Island	7,927,071,000	0.2%
18	Wisconsin	64,046,407,000	2.0%	49	Vermont	7,381,890,000	0.2%
47	Wyoming	9,322,542,000	0.3%	50	Alaska	5,258,556,000	0.2%
					District of Columbia	3,621,959,000	0.1%

Source: U.S. Department of Transportation, Federal Highway Administration
"Highway Statistics 2016" (Table VM-2, http://www.fhwa.dot.gov/policyinformation/statistics/2016/)

Highway Fatalities in 2016

National Total = 37,461 Fatalities

ALPHA ORDER

RANK	STATE	FATALITIES	% of USA
11	Alabama	1,038	2.8%
48	Alaska	84	0.2%
14	Arizona	962	2.6%
25	Arkansas	545	1.5%
2	California	3,623	9.7%
22	Colorado	608	1.6%
35	Connecticut	293	0.8%
44	Delaware	119	0.3%
3	Florida	3,174	8.5%
4	Georgia	1,554	4.1%
43	Hawaii	120	0.3%
38	Idaho	253	0.7%
8	Illinois	1,082	2.9%
17	Indiana	821	2.2%
30	Iowa	404	1.1%
29	Kansas	429	1.1%
16	Kentucky	834	2.2%
19	Louisiana	757	2.0%
41	Maine	161	0.4%
27	Maryland	505	1.3%
33	Massachusetts	389	1.0%
9	Michigan	1,064	2.8%
32	Minnesota	392	1.0%
20	Mississippi	690	1.8%
15	Missouri	945	2.5%
40	Montana	190	0.5%
39	Nebraska	218	0.6%
34	Nevada	328	0.9%
42	New Hampshire	136	0.4%
24	New Jersey	601	1.6%
31	New Mexico	402	1.1%
12	New York	1,025	2.7%
5	North Carolina	1,450	3.9%
46	North Dakota	113	0.3%
7	Ohio	1,132	3.0%
21	Oklahoma	683	1.8%
28	Oregon	495	1.3%
6	Pennsylvania	1,188	3.2%
50	Rhode Island	51	0.1%
13	South Carolina	1,015	2.7%
45	South Dakota	116	0.3%
10	Tennessee	1,041	2.8%
1	Texas	3,776	10.1%
36	Utah	281	0.8%
49	Vermont	62	0.2%
18	Virginia	760	2.0%
26	Washington	537	1.4%
37	West Virginia	269	0.7%
23	Wisconsin	607	1.6%
47	Wyoming	112	0.3%

RANK ORDER

RANK	STATE	FATALITIES	% of USA
1	Texas	3,776	10.1%
2	California	3,623	9.7%
3	Florida	3,174	8.5%
4	Georgia	1,554	4.1%
5	North Carolina	1,450	3.9%
6	Pennsylvania	1,188	3.2%
7	Ohio	1,132	3.0%
8	Illinois	1,082	2.9%
9	Michigan	1,064	2.8%
10	Tennessee	1,041	2.8%
11	Alabama	1,038	2.8%
12	New York	1,025	2.7%
13	South Carolina	1,015	2.7%
14	Arizona	962	2.6%
15	Missouri	945	2.5%
16	Kentucky	834	2.2%
17	Indiana	821	2.2%
18	Virginia	760	2.0%
19	Louisiana	757	2.0%
20	Mississippi	690	1.8%
21	Oklahoma	683	1.8%
22	Colorado	608	1.6%
23	Wisconsin	607	1.6%
24	New Jersey	601	1.6%
25	Arkansas	545	1.5%
26	Washington	537	1.4%
27	Maryland	505	1.3%
28	Oregon	495	1.3%
29	Kansas	429	1.1%
30	Iowa	404	1.1%
31	New Mexico	402	1.1%
32	Minnesota	392	1.0%
33	Massachusetts	389	1.0%
34	Nevada	328	0.9%
35	Connecticut	293	0.8%
36	Utah	281	0.8%
37	West Virginia	269	0.7%
38	Idaho	253	0.7%
39	Nebraska	218	0.6%
40	Montana	190	0.5%
41	Maine	161	0.4%
42	New Hampshire	136	0.4%
43	Hawaii	120	0.3%
44	Delaware	119	0.3%
45	South Dakota	116	0.3%
46	North Dakota	113	0.3%
47	Wyoming	112	0.3%
48	Alaska	84	0.2%
49	Vermont	62	0.2%
50	Rhode Island	51	0.1%
	District of Columbia	27	0.1%

Source: U.S. Department of Transportation, National Highway Traffic Safety Administration
"Traffic Safety Facts 2016" (https://crashstats.nhtsa.dot.gov/)

Highway Fatality Rate in 2016

National Rate = 1.18 Fatalities per 100 Million Vehicle-Miles of Travel

ALPHA ORDER

RANK	STATE	RATE
8	Alabama	1.50
4	Alaska	1.60
11	Arizona	1.46
6	Arkansas	1.52
32	California	1.07
26	Colorado	1.17
40	Connecticut	0.93
26	Delaware	1.17
9	Florida	1.47
20	Georgia	1.27
30	Hawaii	1.13
9	Idaho	1.47
35	Illinois	1.01
37	Indiana	0.99
24	Iowa	1.21
18	Kansas	1.34
2	Kentucky	1.69
5	Louisiana	1.54
31	Maine	1.09
44	Maryland	0.85
50	Massachusetts	0.63
32	Michigan	1.07
48	Minnesota	0.66
2	Mississippi	1.69
19	Missouri	1.28
7	Montana	1.51
34	Nebraska	1.05
22	Nevada	1.22
35	New Hampshire	1.01
47	New Jersey	0.78
12	New Mexico	1.44
46	New York	0.83
21	North Carolina	1.24
29	North Dakota	1.16
38	Ohio	0.95
13	Oklahoma	1.39
16	Oregon	1.35
26	Pennsylvania	1.17
49	Rhode Island	0.64
1	South Carolina	1.86
22	South Dakota	1.22
16	Tennessee	1.35
13	Texas	1.39
42	Utah	0.89
45	Vermont	0.84
41	Virginia	0.90
43	Washington	0.88
15	West Virginia	1.38
38	Wisconsin	0.95
25	Wyoming	1.20

RANK ORDER

RANK	STATE	RATE
1	South Carolina	1.86
2	Kentucky	1.69
2	Mississippi	1.69
4	Alaska	1.60
5	Louisiana	1.54
6	Arkansas	1.52
7	Montana	1.51
8	Alabama	1.50
9	Florida	1.47
9	Idaho	1.47
11	Arizona	1.46
12	New Mexico	1.44
13	Oklahoma	1.39
13	Texas	1.39
15	West Virginia	1.38
16	Oregon	1.35
16	Tennessee	1.35
18	Kansas	1.34
19	Missouri	1.28
20	Georgia	1.27
21	North Carolina	1.24
22	Nevada	1.22
22	South Dakota	1.22
24	Iowa	1.21
25	Wyoming	1.20
26	Colorado	1.17
26	Delaware	1.17
26	Pennsylvania	1.17
29	North Dakota	1.16
30	Hawaii	1.13
31	Maine	1.09
32	California	1.07
32	Michigan	1.07
34	Nebraska	1.05
35	Illinois	1.01
35	New Hampshire	1.01
37	Indiana	0.99
38	Ohio	0.95
38	Wisconsin	0.95
40	Connecticut	0.93
41	Virginia	0.90
42	Utah	0.89
43	Washington	0.88
44	Maryland	0.85
45	Vermont	0.84
46	New York	0.83
47	New Jersey	0.78
48	Minnesota	0.66
49	Rhode Island	0.64
50	Massachusetts	0.63
	District of Columbia	0.75

Source: U.S. Department of Transportation, National Highway Traffic Safety Administration
"Traffic Safety Facts 2016" (https://crashstats.nhtsa.dot.gov/)

Percent of Traffic Fatalities That Were Speeding-Related in 2016

National Percent = 27.0%*

ALPHA ORDER				RANK ORDER		
RANK	STATE	PERCENT		RANK	STATE	PERCENT
22	Alabama	30.5		1	New Hampshire	56.6
5	Alaska	42.9		2	Vermont	46.8
18	Arizona	32.3		3	Rhode Island	45.1
43	Arkansas	21.5		4	Hawaii	45.0
23	California	29.1		5	Alaska	42.9
14	Colorado	34.7		6	Pennsylvania	42.5
27	Connecticut	27.0		7	North Carolina	39.0
17	Delaware	32.8		8	Illinois	38.6
50	Florida	9.8		9	Nevada	38.1
46	Georgia	17.1		10	South Carolina	37.5
4	Hawaii	45.0		11	New Mexico	36.1
44	Idaho	21.3		12	Wisconsin	34.9
8	Illinois	38.6		13	Maine	34.8
30	Indiana	25.9		14	Colorado	34.7
34	Iowa	23.5		14	Missouri	34.7
33	Kansas	24.7		16	Virginia	33.8
47	Kentucky	16.5		17	Delaware	32.8
37	Louisiana	22.9		18	Arizona	32.3
13	Maine	34.8		19	Montana	32.1
32	Maryland	25.1		20	South Dakota	31.9
27	Massachusetts	27.0		21	New York	30.6
36	Michigan	23.0		22	Alabama	30.5
34	Minnesota	23.5		23	California	29.1
49	Mississippi	11.7		24	Oregon	28.7
14	Missouri	34.7		24	Washington	28.7
19	Montana	32.1		26	Texas	28.3
47	Nebraska	16.5		27	Connecticut	27.0
9	Nevada	38.1		27	Massachusetts	27.0
1	New Hampshire	56.6		29	Oklahoma	26.8
42	New Jersey	21.6		30	Indiana	25.9
11	New Mexico	36.1		31	Utah	25.6
21	New York	30.6		32	Maryland	25.1
7	North Carolina	39.0		33	Kansas	24.7
41	North Dakota	22.1		34	Iowa	23.5
38	Ohio	22.7		34	Minnesota	23.5
29	Oklahoma	26.8		36	Michigan	23.0
24	Oregon	28.7		37	Louisiana	22.9
6	Pennsylvania	42.5		38	Ohio	22.7
3	Rhode Island	45.1		39	West Virginia	22.3
10	South Carolina	37.5		39	Wyoming	22.3
20	South Dakota	31.9		41	North Dakota	22.1
45	Tennessee	17.6		42	New Jersey	21.6
26	Texas	28.3		43	Arkansas	21.5
31	Utah	25.6		44	Idaho	21.3
2	Vermont	46.8		45	Tennessee	17.6
16	Virginia	33.8		46	Georgia	17.1
24	Washington	28.7		47	Kentucky	16.5
39	West Virginia	22.3		47	Nebraska	16.5
12	Wisconsin	34.9		49	Mississippi	11.7
39	Wyoming	22.3		50	Florida	9.8
					District of Columbia	59.3

Source: CQ Press using data from U.S. Department of Transportation, National Highway Traffic Safety Administration
"Traffic Safety Facts 2016" (https://crashstats.nhtsa.dot.gov/)
*A speeding-related crash is if the driver was charged with a speeding-related offense or if an officer indicated that racing, driving too fast for conditions, or exceeding the posted speed limit was a contributing factor in the crash.

Percent of Vehicles Involved in Fatal Crashes That Were Large Trucks in 2016

National Percent = 8.1%*

ALPHA ORDER

RANK	STATE	PERCENT		RANK	STATE	PERCENT
14	Alabama	9.3		1	Wyoming	17.8
46	Alaska	4.6		2	Nebraska	14.8
40	Arizona	6.0		3	Oklahoma	13.4
19	Arkansas	8.5		4	Kansas	11.4
39	California	6.3		5	Idaho	10.8
9	Colorado	10.0		5	Iowa	10.8
33	Connecticut	7.4		7	Texas	10.2
44	Delaware	5.3		8	North Dakota	10.1
40	Florida	6.0		9	Colorado	10.0
19	Georgia	8.5		9	Pennsylvania	10.0
48	Hawaii	3.2		11	Illinois	9.5
5	Idaho	10.8		12	Indiana	9.4
11	Illinois	9.5		12	Montana	9.4
12	Indiana	9.4		14	Alabama	9.3
5	Iowa	10.8		15	Minnesota	9.1
4	Kansas	11.4		15	Vermont	9.1
24	Kentucky	8.0		17	Mississippi	8.7
25	Louisiana	7.9		18	Virginia	8.6
34	Maine	7.3		19	Arkansas	8.5
23	Maryland	8.2		19	Georgia	8.5
45	Massachusetts	5.0		21	Missouri	8.3
37	Michigan	6.8		21	West Virginia	8.3
15	Minnesota	9.1		23	Maryland	8.2
17	Mississippi	8.7		24	Kentucky	8.0
21	Missouri	8.3		25	Louisiana	7.9
12	Montana	9.4		26	Oregon	7.8
2	Nebraska	14.8		26	Tennessee	7.8
42	Nevada	5.8		28	Ohio	7.6
50	New Hampshire	2.9		28	Wisconsin	7.6
36	New Jersey	7.0		30	New Mexico	7.5
30	New Mexico	7.5		30	New York	7.5
30	New York	7.5		30	North Carolina	7.5
30	North Carolina	7.5		33	Connecticut	7.4
8	North Dakota	10.1		34	Maine	7.3
28	Ohio	7.6		35	South Carolina	7.1
3	Oklahoma	13.4		36	New Jersey	7.0
26	Oregon	7.8		37	Michigan	6.8
9	Pennsylvania	10.0		38	Washington	6.7
49	Rhode Island	3.0		39	California	6.3
35	South Carolina	7.1		40	Arizona	6.0
47	South Dakota	4.3		40	Florida	6.0
26	Tennessee	7.8		42	Nevada	5.8
7	Texas	10.2		43	Utah	5.5
43	Utah	5.5		44	Delaware	5.3
15	Vermont	9.1		45	Massachusetts	5.0
18	Virginia	8.6		46	Alaska	4.6
38	Washington	6.7		47	South Dakota	4.3
21	West Virginia	8.3		48	Hawaii	3.2
28	Wisconsin	7.6		49	Rhode Island	3.0
1	Wyoming	17.8		50	New Hampshire	2.9
					District of Columbia	0.0

Source: U.S. Department of Transportation, National Highway Traffic Safety Administration
   "Traffic Safety Facts: Large Trucks" (https://crashstats.nhtsa.dot.gov/)
*Large trucks are those with gross vehicle weight greater than 10,000 pounds. In 2016, 4,213 large trucks were involved in fatal crashes.

Lives Saved by Child Restraints, Seat Belts,
Air Bags, and Motorcycle Helmets in 2016
National Total = 19,611 Lives

ALPHA ORDER					RANK ORDER			
RANK	STATE		LIVES	% of USA	RANK	STATE	LIVES	% of USA
11	Alabama		533	2.7%	1	Texas	2,115	10.8%
49	Alaska		34	0.2%	2	California	2,035	10.4%
21	Arizona		357	1.8%	3	Florida	1,433	7.3%
26	Arkansas		294	1.5%	4	North Carolina	891	4.5%
2	California		2,035	10.4%	5	Georgia	864	4.4%
27	Colorado		278	1.4%	6	Michigan	641	3.3%
37	Connecticut		134	0.7%	7	Tennessee	624	3.2%
42	Delaware		65	0.3%	8	Illinois	593	3.0%
3	Florida		1,433	7.3%	9	Ohio	538	2.7%
5	Georgia		864	4.4%	10	New York	535	2.7%
43	Hawaii		48	0.2%	11	Alabama	533	2.7%
38	Idaho		117	0.6%	12	Pennsylvania	485	2.5%
8	Illinois		593	3.0%	13	South Carolina	466	2.4%
15	Indiana		443	2.3%	14	Missouri	461	2.4%
29	Iowa		251	1.3%	15	Indiana	443	2.3%
31	Kansas		239	1.2%	16	Kentucky	424	2.2%
16	Kentucky		424	2.2%	17	Louisiana	415	2.1%
17	Louisiana		415	2.1%	18	Mississippi	400	2.0%
40	Maine		96	0.5%	19	Oregon	370	1.9%
28	Maryland		261	1.3%	20	Virginia	364	1.9%
33	Massachusetts		170	0.9%	21	Arizona	357	1.8%
6	Michigan		641	3.3%	22	Oklahoma	352	1.8%
30	Minnesota		248	1.3%	23	Wisconsin	344	1.8%
18	Mississippi		400	2.0%	24	Washington	319	1.6%
14	Missouri		461	2.4%	25	New Jersey	298	1.5%
41	Montana		84	0.4%	26	Arkansas	294	1.5%
39	Nebraska		116	0.6%	27	Colorado	278	1.4%
34	Nevada		144	0.7%	28	Maryland	261	1.3%
43	New Hampshire		48	0.2%	29	Iowa	251	1.3%
25	New Jersey		298	1.5%	30	Minnesota	248	1.3%
32	New Mexico		206	1.1%	31	Kansas	239	1.2%
10	New York		535	2.7%	32	New Mexico	206	1.1%
4	North Carolina		891	4.5%	33	Massachusetts	170	0.9%
47	North Dakota		40	0.2%	34	Nevada	144	0.7%
9	Ohio		538	2.7%	35	West Virginia	142	0.7%
22	Oklahoma		352	1.8%	36	Utah	139	0.7%
19	Oregon		370	1.9%	37	Connecticut	134	0.7%
12	Pennsylvania		485	2.5%	38	Idaho	117	0.6%
50	Rhode Island		20	0.1%	39	Nebraska	116	0.6%
13	South Carolina		466	2.4%	40	Maine	96	0.5%
47	South Dakota		40	0.2%	41	Montana	84	0.4%
7	Tennessee		624	3.2%	42	Delaware	65	0.3%
1	Texas		2,115	10.8%	43	Hawaii	48	0.2%
36	Utah		139	0.7%	43	New Hampshire	48	0.2%
46	Vermont		43	0.2%	45	Wyoming	44	0.2%
20	Virginia		364	1.9%	46	Vermont	43	0.2%
24	Washington		319	1.6%	47	North Dakota	40	0.2%
35	West Virginia		142	0.7%	47	South Dakota	40	0.2%
23	Wisconsin		344	1.8%	49	Alaska	34	0.2%
45	Wyoming		44	0.2%	50	Rhode Island	20	0.1%
						District of Columbia	7	0.0%

Source: CQ Press using data from U.S. Department of Transportation, National Highway Traffic Safety Administration
"Traffic Safety Facts: Lives Saved in 2016" (https://crashstats.nhtsa.dot.gov/)

Safety Belt Usage Rate in 2017

National Rate = 89.7% Use Safety Belts

ALPHA ORDER				RANK ORDER		
RANK	STATE	PERCENT		RANK	STATE	PERCENT
11	Alabama	92.9		1	Georgia	97.1
23	Alaska	90.1		2	Hawaii	96.9
33	Arizona	86.1		3	Oregon	96.8
44	Arkansas	81.0		4	California	96.2
4	California	96.2		5	Washington	94.8
40	Colorado	83.8		6	Michigan	94.1
21	Connecticut	90.3		6	New Jersey	94.1
17	Delaware	91.4		8	Illinois	93.8
22	Florida	90.2		9	New York	93.4
1	Georgia	97.1		10	Indiana	93.0
2	Hawaii	96.9		11	Alabama	92.9
43	Idaho	81.2		12	South Carolina	92.3
8	Illinois	93.8		13	Maryland	92.1
10	Indiana	93.0		14	Minnesota	92.0
17	Iowa	91.4		15	Texas	91.9
42	Kansas	82.0		16	New Mexico	91.5
32	Kentucky	86.8		17	Delaware	91.4
30	Louisiana	87.1		17	Iowa	91.4
26	Maine	88.9		17	North Carolina	91.4
13	Maryland	92.1		20	Nevada	90.6
49	Massachusetts	73.7		21	Connecticut	90.3
6	Michigan	94.1		22	Florida	90.2
14	Minnesota	92.0		23	Alaska	90.1
46	Mississippi	78.8		24	West Virginia	89.7
39	Missouri	84.0		25	Wisconsin	89.4
47	Montana	78.0		26	Maine	88.9
34	Nebraska	85.9		27	Utah	88.8
20	Nevada	90.6		28	Tennessee	88.5
50	New Hampshire	67.6		29	Rhode Island	88.3
6	New Jersey	94.1		30	Louisiana	87.1
16	New Mexico	91.5		31	Oklahoma	86.9
9	New York	93.4		32	Kentucky	86.8
17	North Carolina	91.4		33	Arizona	86.1
45	North Dakota	79.3		34	Nebraska	85.9
41	Ohio	82.8		35	Pennsylvania	85.6
31	Oklahoma	86.9		36	Virginia	85.3
3	Oregon	96.8		37	Wyoming	84.8
35	Pennsylvania	85.6		38	Vermont	84.5
29	Rhode Island	88.3		39	Missouri	84.0
12	South Carolina	92.3		40	Colorado	83.8
48	South Dakota	74.8		41	Ohio	82.8
28	Tennessee	88.5		42	Kansas	82.0
15	Texas	91.9		43	Idaho	81.2
27	Utah	88.8		44	Arkansas	81.0
38	Vermont	84.5		45	North Dakota	79.3
36	Virginia	85.3		46	Mississippi	78.8
5	Washington	94.8		47	Montana	78.0
24	West Virginia	89.7		48	South Dakota	74.8
25	Wisconsin	89.4		49	Massachusetts	73.7
37	Wyoming	84.8		50	New Hampshire	67.6
					District of Columbia	93.6

Source: U.S. Department of Transportation, National Highway Traffic Safety Administration
"Traffic Safety Facts: Seat Belt Use in 2017" (https://crashstats.nhtsa.dot.gov/)

Percent of Passenger Car Occupant Fatalities
Where Victim Used a Seat Belt in 2016
National Percent = 48% of Passenger Car Occupant Fatalities*

ALPHA ORDER

RANK	STATE	PERCENT
38	Alabama	38
47	Alaska	29
36	Arizona	39
34	Arkansas	42
1	California	62
21	Colorado	46
32	Connecticut	43
15	Delaware	49
9	Florida	52
21	Georgia	46
40	Hawaii	35
40	Idaho	35
14	Illinois	51
28	Indiana	44
9	Iowa	52
21	Kansas	46
21	Kentucky	46
28	Louisiana	44
17	Maine	47
9	Maryland	52
45	Massachusetts	30
5	Michigan	54
2	Minnesota	58
25	Mississippi	45
40	Missouri	35
44	Montana	32
39	Nebraska	36
25	Nevada	45
49	New Hampshire	26
6	New Jersey	53
28	New Mexico	44
3	New York	56
6	North Carolina	53
48	North Dakota	27
28	Ohio	44
32	Oklahoma	43
3	Oregon	56
43	Pennsylvania	33
17	Rhode Island	47
25	South Carolina	45
50	South Dakota	25
17	Tennessee	47
9	Texas	52
16	Utah	48
6	Vermont	53
34	Virginia	42
9	Washington	52
36	West Virginia	39
17	Wisconsin	47
45	Wyoming	30

RANK ORDER

RANK	STATE	PERCENT
1	California	62
2	Minnesota	58
3	New York	56
3	Oregon	56
5	Michigan	54
6	New Jersey	53
6	North Carolina	53
6	Vermont	53
9	Florida	52
9	Iowa	52
9	Maryland	52
9	Texas	52
9	Washington	52
14	Illinois	51
15	Delaware	49
16	Utah	48
17	Maine	47
17	Rhode Island	47
17	Tennessee	47
17	Wisconsin	47
21	Colorado	46
21	Georgia	46
21	Kansas	46
21	Kentucky	46
25	Mississippi	45
25	Nevada	45
25	South Carolina	45
28	Indiana	44
28	Louisiana	44
28	New Mexico	44
28	Ohio	44
32	Connecticut	43
32	Oklahoma	43
34	Arkansas	42
34	Virginia	42
36	Arizona	39
36	West Virginia	39
38	Alabama	38
39	Nebraska	36
40	Hawaii	35
40	Idaho	35
40	Missouri	35
43	Pennsylvania	33
44	Montana	32
45	Massachusetts	30
45	Wyoming	30
47	Alaska	29
48	North Dakota	27
49	New Hampshire	26
50	South Dakota	25
	District of Columbia	17

Source: U.S. Department of Transportation, National Highway Traffic Safety Administration
   "Traffic Safety Facts: Occupant Protection" (https://crashstats.nhtsa.dot.gov/)
*Only those fatalities where seat belts are known to have been used are counted.

Fatalities in Alcohol-Related Crashes in 2017

National Total = 12,747 Fatalities*

ALPHA ORDER

RANK	STATE	FATALITIES	% of USA	RANK	STATE	FATALITIES	% of USA
13	Alabama	317	2.5%	1	Texas	1,715	13.5%
49	Alaska	24	0.2%	2	California	1,316	10.3%
12	Arizona	337	2.6%	3	Florida	974	7.6%
28	Arkansas	157	1.2%	4	North Carolina	477	3.7%
2	California	1,316	10.3%	5	Georgia	435	3.4%
22	Colorado	208	1.6%	6	Illinois	418	3.3%
31	Connecticut	134	1.1%	7	Ohio	381	3.0%
46	Delaware	37	0.3%	8	South Carolina	374	2.9%
3	Florida	974	7.6%	9	Michigan	371	2.9%
5	Georgia	435	3.4%	10	Pennsylvania	357	2.8%
42	Hawaii	50	0.4%	11	New York	342	2.7%
37	Idaho	74	0.6%	12	Arizona	337	2.6%
6	Illinois	418	3.3%	13	Alabama	317	2.5%
18	Indiana	256	2.0%	14	Tennessee	310	2.4%
34	Iowa	103	0.8%	15	Missouri	304	2.4%
32	Kansas	112	0.9%	16	Virginia	279	2.2%
20	Kentucky	213	1.7%	17	Louisiana	264	2.1%
17	Louisiana	264	2.1%	18	Indiana	256	2.0%
41	Maine	60	0.5%	19	Wisconsin	232	1.8%
23	Maryland	206	1.6%	20	Kentucky	213	1.7%
30	Massachusetts	136	1.1%	21	Washington	211	1.7%
9	Michigan	371	2.9%	22	Colorado	208	1.6%
33	Minnesota	104	0.8%	23	Maryland	206	1.6%
25	Mississippi	173	1.4%	24	Oklahoma	193	1.5%
15	Missouri	304	2.4%	25	Mississippi	173	1.4%
39	Montana	63	0.5%	26	New Jersey	165	1.3%
38	Nebraska	73	0.6%	27	Oregon	160	1.3%
35	Nevada	101	0.8%	28	Arkansas	157	1.2%
48	New Hampshire	32	0.3%	29	New Mexico	145	1.1%
26	New Jersey	165	1.3%	30	Massachusetts	136	1.1%
29	New Mexico	145	1.1%	31	Connecticut	134	1.1%
11	New York	342	2.7%	32	Kansas	112	0.9%
4	North Carolina	477	3.7%	33	Minnesota	104	0.8%
42	North Dakota	50	0.4%	34	Iowa	103	0.8%
7	Ohio	381	3.0%	35	Nevada	101	0.8%
24	Oklahoma	193	1.5%	36	West Virginia	85	0.7%
27	Oregon	160	1.3%	37	Idaho	74	0.6%
10	Pennsylvania	357	2.8%	38	Nebraska	73	0.6%
47	Rhode Island	35	0.3%	39	Montana	63	0.5%
8	South Carolina	374	2.9%	40	Utah	61	0.5%
44	South Dakota	47	0.4%	41	Maine	60	0.5%
14	Tennessee	310	2.4%	42	Hawaii	50	0.4%
1	Texas	1,715	13.5%	42	North Dakota	50	0.4%
40	Utah	61	0.5%	44	South Dakota	47	0.4%
50	Vermont	21	0.2%	45	Wyoming	45	0.4%
16	Virginia	279	2.2%	46	Delaware	37	0.3%
21	Washington	211	1.7%	47	Rhode Island	35	0.3%
36	West Virginia	85	0.7%	48	New Hampshire	32	0.3%
19	Wisconsin	232	1.8%	49	Alaska	24	0.2%
45	Wyoming	45	0.4%	50	Vermont	21	0.2%
					District of Columbia	16	0.1%

Source: U.S. Department of Transportation, National Highway Traffic Safety Administration
     "Traffic Safety Facts: Alcohol-Impaired Driving" (https://crashstats.nhtsa.dot.gov/)
*Drivers with Blood Alcohol Content (BAC) of .01 or more. "Legally Drunk" BAC differs from state to state but is often .08 or higher.

Fatalities in Alcohol-Related Crashes
as a Percent of All Highway Fatalities in 2017
National Percent = 34% of Highway Fatalities*

ALPHA ORDER

RANK	STATE	PERCENT
24	Alabama	33
38	Alaska	30
20	Arizona	34
28	Arkansas	32
11	California	37
28	Colorado	32
1	Connecticut	48
32	Delaware	31
32	Florida	31
43	Georgia	28
2	Hawaii	46
38	Idaho	30
7	Illinois	38
43	Indiana	28
32	Iowa	31
49	Kansas	24
46	Kentucky	27
18	Louisiana	35
18	Maine	35
11	Maryland	37
6	Massachusetts	39
15	Michigan	36
41	Minnesota	29
48	Mississippi	25
24	Missouri	33
20	Montana	34
28	Nebraska	32
24	Nevada	33
32	New Hampshire	31
47	New Jersey	26
7	New Mexico	38
20	New York	34
20	North Carolina	34
4	North Dakota	44
28	Ohio	32
41	Oklahoma	29
15	Oregon	36
32	Pennsylvania	31
5	Rhode Island	42
7	South Carolina	38
15	South Dakota	36
38	Tennessee	30
2	Texas	46
50	Utah	22
32	Vermont	31
24	Virginia	33
11	Washington	37
43	West Virginia	28
7	Wisconsin	38
11	Wyoming	37

RANK ORDER

RANK	STATE	PERCENT
1	Connecticut	48
2	Hawaii	46
2	Texas	46
4	North Dakota	44
5	Rhode Island	42
6	Massachusetts	39
7	Illinois	38
7	New Mexico	38
7	South Carolina	38
7	Wisconsin	38
11	California	37
11	Maryland	37
11	Washington	37
11	Wyoming	37
15	Michigan	36
15	Oregon	36
15	South Dakota	36
18	Louisiana	35
18	Maine	35
20	Arizona	34
20	Montana	34
20	New York	34
20	North Carolina	34
24	Alabama	33
24	Missouri	33
24	Nevada	33
24	Virginia	33
28	Arkansas	32
28	Colorado	32
28	Nebraska	32
28	Ohio	32
32	Delaware	31
32	Florida	31
32	Iowa	31
32	New Hampshire	31
32	Pennsylvania	31
32	Vermont	31
38	Alaska	30
38	Idaho	30
38	Tennessee	30
41	Minnesota	29
41	Oklahoma	29
43	Georgia	28
43	Indiana	28
43	West Virginia	28
46	Kentucky	27
47	New Jersey	26
48	Mississippi	25
49	Kansas	24
50	Utah	22
	District of Columbia	53

Source: U.S. Department of Transportation, National Highway Traffic Safety Administration
   "Traffic Safety Facts: Alcohol-Impaired Driving" (https://crashstats.nhtsa.dot.gov/)
*Drivers with Blood Alcohol Content (BAC) of .01 or more. "Legally Drunk" BAC differs from state to state but is often .08 or higher.

Percent of Fatal Traffic Accidents Involving Older Drivers in 2016

National Percent = 13.7%*

ALPHA ORDER

RANK	STATE	PERCENT	RANK	STATE	PERCENT
46	Alabama	11.2	1	Wisconsin	18.7
49	Alaska	10.2	2	Maine	18.0
37	Arizona	13.1	3	Kansas	17.3
28	Arkansas	14.4	4	Vermont	16.9
47	California	10.8	5	Minnesota	16.8
21	Colorado	14.9	6	Rhode Island	16.7
43	Connecticut	11.7	6	South Dakota	16.7
41	Delaware	12.4	8	Idaho	16.2
18	Florida	15.4	8	West Virginia	16.2
32	Georgia	13.9	10	New York	16.1
34	Hawaii	13.7	10	Pennsylvania	16.1
8	Idaho	16.2	12	Missouri	15.9
25	Illinois	14.6	12	New Jersey	15.9
35	Indiana	13.5	14	Massachusetts	15.8
22	Iowa	14.8	14	Tennessee	15.8
3	Kansas	17.3	16	Nebraska	15.6
29	Kentucky	14.3	16	Washington	15.6
48	Louisiana	10.5	18	Florida	15.4
2	Maine	18.0	19	Ohio	15.3
39	Maryland	12.7	20	New Hampshire	15.0
14	Massachusetts	15.8	21	Colorado	14.9
23	Michigan	14.7	22	Iowa	14.8
5	Minnesota	16.8	23	Michigan	14.7
27	Mississippi	14.5	23	Nevada	14.7
12	Missouri	15.9	25	Illinois	14.6
36	Montana	13.2	25	Oregon	14.6
16	Nebraska	15.6	27	Mississippi	14.5
23	Nevada	14.7	28	Arkansas	14.4
20	New Hampshire	15.0	29	Kentucky	14.3
12	New Jersey	15.9	30	North Carolina	14.2
44	New Mexico	11.6	31	Virginia	14.0
10	New York	16.1	32	Georgia	13.9
30	North Carolina	14.2	33	North Dakota	13.8
33	North Dakota	13.8	34	Hawaii	13.7
19	Ohio	15.3	35	Indiana	13.5
42	Oklahoma	11.8	36	Montana	13.2
25	Oregon	14.6	37	Arizona	13.1
10	Pennsylvania	16.1	38	Utah	12.9
6	Rhode Island	16.7	39	Maryland	12.7
45	South Carolina	11.5	40	Wyoming	12.6
6	South Dakota	16.7	41	Delaware	12.4
14	Tennessee	15.8	42	Oklahoma	11.8
50	Texas	10.0	43	Connecticut	11.7
38	Utah	12.9	44	New Mexico	11.6
4	Vermont	16.9	45	South Carolina	11.5
31	Virginia	14.0	46	Alabama	11.2
16	Washington	15.6	47	California	10.8
8	West Virginia	16.2	48	Louisiana	10.5
1	Wisconsin	18.7	49	Alaska	10.2
40	Wyoming	12.6	50	Texas	10.0

District of Columbia   2.6

Source: U.S. Department of Transportation, National Highway Traffic Safety Administration
"Traffic Safety Facts: Older Population" (https://crashstats.nhtsa.dot.gov/)
*Drivers 65 years old and older. People 65 or older make up 15 percent of the total U.S. population.

Percent of Highway Fatalities Who Were Young Drivers in 2016

National Percent = 5.1% of Fatalities*

ALPHA ORDER

RANK	STATE	PERCENT
5	Alabama	6.8
1	Alaska	8.3
38	Arizona	4.2
28	Arkansas	4.8
28	California	4.8
44	Colorado	3.8
44	Connecticut	3.8
49	Delaware	2.5
36	Florida	4.3
13	Georgia	5.9
14	Hawaii	5.8
42	Idaho	4.0
14	Illinois	5.8
19	Indiana	5.5
34	Iowa	4.5
8	Kansas	6.5
30	Kentucky	4.7
21	Louisiana	5.4
48	Maine	3.1
44	Maryland	3.8
40	Massachusetts	4.1
21	Michigan	5.4
36	Minnesota	4.3
24	Mississippi	5.1
11	Missouri	6.1
38	Montana	4.2
32	Nebraska	4.6
26	Nevada	4.9
6	New Hampshire	6.6
47	New Jersey	3.5
16	New Mexico	5.7
40	New York	4.1
10	North Carolina	6.2
4	North Dakota	7.1
16	Ohio	5.7
24	Oklahoma	5.1
19	Oregon	5.5
26	Pennsylvania	4.9
43	Rhode Island	3.9
32	South Carolina	4.6
3	South Dakota	7.8
16	Tennessee	5.7
30	Texas	4.7
23	Utah	5.3
50	Vermont	1.6
6	Virginia	6.6
11	Washington	6.1
34	West Virginia	4.5
9	Wisconsin	6.3
2	Wyoming	8.0

RANK ORDER

RANK	STATE	PERCENT
1	Alaska	8.3
2	Wyoming	8.0
3	South Dakota	7.8
4	North Dakota	7.1
5	Alabama	6.8
6	New Hampshire	6.6
6	Virginia	6.6
8	Kansas	6.5
9	Wisconsin	6.3
10	North Carolina	6.2
11	Missouri	6.1
11	Washington	6.1
13	Georgia	5.9
14	Hawaii	5.8
14	Illinois	5.8
16	New Mexico	5.7
16	Ohio	5.7
16	Tennessee	5.7
19	Indiana	5.5
19	Oregon	5.5
21	Louisiana	5.4
21	Michigan	5.4
23	Utah	5.3
24	Mississippi	5.1
24	Oklahoma	5.1
26	Nevada	4.9
26	Pennsylvania	4.9
28	Arkansas	4.8
28	California	4.8
30	Kentucky	4.7
30	Texas	4.7
32	Nebraska	4.6
32	South Carolina	4.6
34	Iowa	4.5
34	West Virginia	4.5
36	Florida	4.3
36	Minnesota	4.3
38	Arizona	4.2
38	Montana	4.2
40	Massachusetts	4.1
40	New York	4.1
42	Idaho	4.0
43	Rhode Island	3.9
44	Colorado	3.8
44	Connecticut	3.8
44	Maryland	3.8
47	New Jersey	3.5
48	Maine	3.1
49	Delaware	2.5
50	Vermont	1.6
	District of Columbia	0.0

Source: CQ Press using data from U.S. Department of Transportation, National Highway Traffic Safety Administration "Traffic Safety Facts: Young Drivers" (https://crashstats.nhtsa.dot.gov/)

*Drivers 15 to 20 years old. Based on 1,908 fatalities of young drivers. An additional 2,945 passengers, occupants in other vehicles, and nonoccupants were killed in crashes involving young drivers. Young drivers accounted for 5.4 percent of all drivers.

Licensed Drivers in 2016

National Total = 221,711,918 Licensed Drivers

<table>
<tr><td colspan="4">ALPHA ORDER</td><td colspan="4">RANK ORDER</td></tr>
<tr><td>RANK</td><td>STATE</td><td>DRIVERS</td><td>% of USA</td><td>RANK</td><td>STATE</td><td>DRIVERS</td><td>% of USA</td></tr>
<tr><td>22</td><td>Alabama</td><td>3,943,082</td><td>1.8%</td><td>1</td><td>California</td><td>26,199,436</td><td>11.8%</td></tr>
<tr><td>49</td><td>Alaska</td><td>534,585</td><td>0.2%</td><td>2</td><td>Texas</td><td>15,879,876</td><td>7.2%</td></tr>
<tr><td>15</td><td>Arizona</td><td>5,082,305</td><td>2.3%</td><td>3</td><td>Florida</td><td>14,675,160</td><td>6.6%</td></tr>
<tr><td>30</td><td>Arkansas</td><td>2,391,103</td><td>1.1%</td><td>4</td><td>New York</td><td>11,947,568</td><td>5.4%</td></tr>
<tr><td>1</td><td>California</td><td>26,199,436</td><td>11.8%</td><td>5</td><td>Pennsylvania</td><td>8,996,815</td><td>4.1%</td></tr>
<tr><td>21</td><td>Colorado</td><td>4,066,580</td><td>1.8%</td><td>6</td><td>Illinois</td><td>8,514,644</td><td>3.8%</td></tr>
<tr><td>28</td><td>Connecticut</td><td>2,611,007</td><td>1.2%</td><td>7</td><td>Ohio</td><td>7,974,951</td><td>3.6%</td></tr>
<tr><td>44</td><td>Delaware</td><td>756,328</td><td>0.3%</td><td>8</td><td>North Carolina</td><td>7,267,042</td><td>3.3%</td></tr>
<tr><td>3</td><td>Florida</td><td>14,675,160</td><td>6.6%</td><td>9</td><td>Michigan</td><td>7,074,674</td><td>3.2%</td></tr>
<tr><td>10</td><td>Georgia</td><td>6,975,900</td><td>3.1%</td><td>10</td><td>Georgia</td><td>6,975,900</td><td>3.1%</td></tr>
<tr><td>42</td><td>Hawaii</td><td>931,703</td><td>0.4%</td><td>11</td><td>New Jersey</td><td>6,238,436</td><td>2.8%</td></tr>
<tr><td>38</td><td>Idaho</td><td>1,160,922</td><td>0.5%</td><td>12</td><td>Virginia</td><td>5,912,048</td><td>2.7%</td></tr>
<tr><td>6</td><td>Illinois</td><td>8,514,644</td><td>3.8%</td><td>13</td><td>Washington</td><td>5,635,715</td><td>2.5%</td></tr>
<tr><td>17</td><td>Indiana</td><td>4,553,259</td><td>2.1%</td><td>14</td><td>Tennessee</td><td>5,197,904</td><td>2.3%</td></tr>
<tr><td>31</td><td>Iowa</td><td>2,245,640</td><td>1.0%</td><td>15</td><td>Arizona</td><td>5,082,305</td><td>2.3%</td></tr>
<tr><td>32</td><td>Kansas</td><td>2,030,025</td><td>0.9%</td><td>16</td><td>Massachusetts</td><td>5,040,662</td><td>2.3%</td></tr>
<tr><td>26</td><td>Kentucky</td><td>3,031,447</td><td>1.4%</td><td>17</td><td>Indiana</td><td>4,553,259</td><td>2.1%</td></tr>
<tr><td>24</td><td>Louisiana</td><td>3,395,095</td><td>1.5%</td><td>18</td><td>Maryland</td><td>4,264,875</td><td>1.9%</td></tr>
<tr><td>41</td><td>Maine</td><td>1,021,332</td><td>0.5%</td><td>19</td><td>Missouri</td><td>4,249,579</td><td>1.9%</td></tr>
<tr><td>18</td><td>Maryland</td><td>4,264,875</td><td>1.9%</td><td>20</td><td>Wisconsin</td><td>4,206,770</td><td>1.9%</td></tr>
<tr><td>16</td><td>Massachusetts</td><td>5,040,662</td><td>2.3%</td><td>21</td><td>Colorado</td><td>4,066,580</td><td>1.8%</td></tr>
<tr><td>9</td><td>Michigan</td><td>7,074,674</td><td>3.2%</td><td>22</td><td>Alabama</td><td>3,943,082</td><td>1.8%</td></tr>
<tr><td>25</td><td>Minnesota</td><td>3,377,910</td><td>1.5%</td><td>23</td><td>South Carolina</td><td>3,746,681</td><td>1.7%</td></tr>
<tr><td>33</td><td>Mississippi</td><td>2,018,862</td><td>0.9%</td><td>24</td><td>Louisiana</td><td>3,395,095</td><td>1.5%</td></tr>
<tr><td>19</td><td>Missouri</td><td>4,249,579</td><td>1.9%</td><td>25</td><td>Minnesota</td><td>3,377,910</td><td>1.5%</td></tr>
<tr><td>43</td><td>Montana</td><td>797,145</td><td>0.4%</td><td>26</td><td>Kentucky</td><td>3,031,447</td><td>1.4%</td></tr>
<tr><td>37</td><td>Nebraska</td><td>1,404,479</td><td>0.6%</td><td>27</td><td>Oregon</td><td>2,855,746</td><td>1.3%</td></tr>
<tr><td>35</td><td>Nevada</td><td>1,872,376</td><td>0.8%</td><td>28</td><td>Connecticut</td><td>2,611,007</td><td>1.2%</td></tr>
<tr><td>40</td><td>New Hampshire</td><td>1,096,234</td><td>0.5%</td><td>29</td><td>Oklahoma</td><td>2,498,178</td><td>1.1%</td></tr>
<tr><td>11</td><td>New Jersey</td><td>6,238,436</td><td>2.8%</td><td>30</td><td>Arkansas</td><td>2,391,103</td><td>1.1%</td></tr>
<tr><td>36</td><td>New Mexico</td><td>1,521,785</td><td>0.7%</td><td>31</td><td>Iowa</td><td>2,245,640</td><td>1.0%</td></tr>
<tr><td>4</td><td>New York</td><td>11,947,568</td><td>5.4%</td><td>32</td><td>Kansas</td><td>2,030,025</td><td>0.9%</td></tr>
<tr><td>8</td><td>North Carolina</td><td>7,267,042</td><td>3.3%</td><td>33</td><td>Mississippi</td><td>2,018,862</td><td>0.9%</td></tr>
<tr><td>47</td><td>North Dakota</td><td>555,935</td><td>0.3%</td><td>34</td><td>Utah</td><td>1,960,366</td><td>0.9%</td></tr>
<tr><td>7</td><td>Ohio</td><td>7,974,951</td><td>3.6%</td><td>35</td><td>Nevada</td><td>1,872,376</td><td>0.8%</td></tr>
<tr><td>29</td><td>Oklahoma</td><td>2,498,178</td><td>1.1%</td><td>36</td><td>New Mexico</td><td>1,521,785</td><td>0.7%</td></tr>
<tr><td>27</td><td>Oregon</td><td>2,855,746</td><td>1.3%</td><td>37</td><td>Nebraska</td><td>1,404,479</td><td>0.6%</td></tr>
<tr><td>5</td><td>Pennsylvania</td><td>8,996,815</td><td>4.1%</td><td>38</td><td>Idaho</td><td>1,160,922</td><td>0.5%</td></tr>
<tr><td>45</td><td>Rhode Island</td><td>753,143</td><td>0.3%</td><td>39</td><td>West Virginia</td><td>1,159,348</td><td>0.5%</td></tr>
<tr><td>23</td><td>South Carolina</td><td>3,746,681</td><td>1.7%</td><td>40</td><td>New Hampshire</td><td>1,096,234</td><td>0.5%</td></tr>
<tr><td>46</td><td>South Dakota</td><td>622,663</td><td>0.3%</td><td>41</td><td>Maine</td><td>1,021,332</td><td>0.5%</td></tr>
<tr><td>14</td><td>Tennessee</td><td>5,197,904</td><td>2.3%</td><td>42</td><td>Hawaii</td><td>931,703</td><td>0.4%</td></tr>
<tr><td>2</td><td>Texas</td><td>15,879,876</td><td>7.2%</td><td>43</td><td>Montana</td><td>797,145</td><td>0.4%</td></tr>
<tr><td>34</td><td>Utah</td><td>1,960,366</td><td>0.9%</td><td>44</td><td>Delaware</td><td>756,328</td><td>0.3%</td></tr>
<tr><td>48</td><td>Vermont</td><td>553,670</td><td>0.2%</td><td>45</td><td>Rhode Island</td><td>753,143</td><td>0.3%</td></tr>
<tr><td>12</td><td>Virginia</td><td>5,912,048</td><td>2.7%</td><td>46</td><td>South Dakota</td><td>622,663</td><td>0.3%</td></tr>
<tr><td>13</td><td>Washington</td><td>5,635,715</td><td>2.5%</td><td>47</td><td>North Dakota</td><td>555,935</td><td>0.3%</td></tr>
<tr><td>39</td><td>West Virginia</td><td>1,159,348</td><td>0.5%</td><td>48</td><td>Vermont</td><td>553,670</td><td>0.2%</td></tr>
<tr><td>20</td><td>Wisconsin</td><td>4,206,770</td><td>1.9%</td><td>49</td><td>Alaska</td><td>534,585</td><td>0.2%</td></tr>
<tr><td>50</td><td>Wyoming</td><td>421,098</td><td>0.2%</td><td>50</td><td>Wyoming</td><td>421,098</td><td>0.2%</td></tr>
<tr><td></td><td></td><td></td><td></td><td></td><td>District of Columbia</td><td>489,831</td><td>0.2%</td></tr>
</table>

Source: U.S. Department of Transportation, Federal Highway Administration
"Highway Statistics 2016" (Table DL-22, http://www.fhwa.dot.gov/policyinformation/statistics/2016/)

Licensed Drivers per 1,000 Driving Age Population in 2016

National Ratio = 859 Licensed Drivers

ALPHA ORDER

ALPHA ORDER

RANK	STATE	RATIO
2	Alabama	1,012
11	Alaska	930
13	Arizona	926
2	Arkansas	1,012
42	California	840
17	Colorado	920
25	Connecticut	894
5	Delaware	980
34	Florida	866
36	Georgia	862
45	Hawaii	809
23	Idaho	896
43	Illinois	833
32	Indiana	869
21	Iowa	903
26	Kansas	893
40	Kentucky	856
18	Louisiana	919
16	Maine	921
27	Maryland	884
22	Massachusetts	900
27	Michigan	884
48	Minnesota	772
38	Mississippi	859
31	Missouri	873
8	Montana	949
9	Nebraska	946
46	Nevada	801
4	New Hampshire	990
33	New Jersey	867
14	New Mexico	924
49	New York	744
23	North Carolina	896
12	North Dakota	928
40	Ohio	856
44	Oklahoma	814
38	Oregon	859
35	Pennsylvania	863
36	Rhode Island	862
10	South Carolina	939
15	South Dakota	923
6	Tennessee	977
50	Texas	743
29	Utah	880
1	Vermont	1,062
30	Virginia	875
7	Washington	965
47	West Virginia	773
20	Wisconsin	906
19	Wyoming	913

RANK ORDER

RANK	STATE	RATIO
1	Vermont	1,062
2	Alabama	1,012
2	Arkansas	1,012
4	New Hampshire	990
5	Delaware	980
6	Tennessee	977
7	Washington	965
8	Montana	949
9	Nebraska	946
10	South Carolina	939
11	Alaska	930
12	North Dakota	928
13	Arizona	926
14	New Mexico	924
15	South Dakota	923
16	Maine	921
17	Colorado	920
18	Louisiana	919
19	Wyoming	913
20	Wisconsin	906
21	Iowa	903
22	Massachusetts	900
23	Idaho	896
23	North Carolina	896
25	Connecticut	894
26	Kansas	893
27	Maryland	884
27	Michigan	884
29	Utah	880
30	Virginia	875
31	Missouri	873
32	Indiana	869
33	New Jersey	867
34	Florida	866
35	Pennsylvania	863
36	Georgia	862
36	Rhode Island	862
38	Mississippi	859
38	Oregon	859
40	Kentucky	856
40	Ohio	856
42	California	840
43	Illinois	833
44	Oklahoma	814
45	Hawaii	809
46	Nevada	801
47	West Virginia	773
48	Minnesota	772
49	New York	744
50	Texas	743
	District of Columbia	858

Source: CQ Press using data from U.S. Department of Transportation, Federal Highway Administration
"Highway Statistics 2016" (Table DL-22, http://www.fhwa.dot.gov/policyinformation/statistics/2016/)

Motor Vehicle Registrations in 2016

National Total = 266,799,083 Motor Vehicles*

ALPHA ORDER				RANK ORDER			
RANK	STATE	VEHICLES	% of USA	RANK	STATE	VEHICLES	% of USA
19	Alabama	5,468,301	2.0%	1	California	30,221,033	11.2%
49	Alaska	794,614	0.3%	2	Texas	21,766,166	8.1%
15	Arizona	5,786,891	2.2%	3	Florida	16,600,317	6.2%
31	Arkansas	2,808,138	1.0%	4	New York	11,122,392	4.1%
1	California	30,221,033	11.2%	5	Pennsylvania	10,748,822	4.0%
21	Colorado	5,116,341	1.9%	6	Ohio	10,686,057	4.0%
30	Connecticut	2,841,842	1.1%	7	Illinois	10,277,182	3.8%
45	Delaware	1,003,840	0.4%	8	Michigan	8,332,895	3.1%
3	Florida	16,600,317	6.2%	9	North Carolina	8,270,643	3.1%
10	Georgia	8,239,779	3.1%	10	Georgia	8,239,779	3.1%
43	Hawaii	1,231,728	0.5%	11	Virginia	7,301,081	2.7%
37	Idaho	1,842,245	0.7%	12	Washington	7,047,689	2.6%
7	Illinois	10,277,182	3.8%	13	Indiana	6,140,530	2.3%
13	Indiana	6,140,530	2.3%	14	New Jersey	5,940,997	2.2%
29	Iowa	3,676,290	1.4%	15	Arizona	5,786,891	2.2%
32	Kansas	2,649,736	1.0%	16	Tennessee	5,709,923	2.1%
24	Kentucky	4,224,788	1.6%	17	Missouri	5,684,525	2.1%
26	Louisiana	3,904,962	1.5%	18	Wisconsin	5,564,429	2.1%
44	Maine	1,107,674	0.4%	19	Alabama	5,468,301	2.0%
25	Maryland	4,178,873	1.6%	20	Minnesota	5,358,317	2.0%
22	Massachusetts	5,069,559	1.9%	21	Colorado	5,116,341	1.9%
8	Michigan	8,332,895	3.1%	22	Massachusetts	5,069,559	1.9%
20	Minnesota	5,358,317	2.0%	23	South Carolina	4,324,423	1.6%
35	Mississippi	2,067,222	0.8%	24	Kentucky	4,224,788	1.6%
17	Missouri	5,684,525	2.1%	25	Maryland	4,178,873	1.6%
39	Montana	1,794,732	0.7%	26	Louisiana	3,904,962	1.5%
36	Nebraska	1,951,766	0.7%	27	Oregon	3,811,706	1.4%
33	Nevada	2,398,659	0.9%	28	Oklahoma	3,737,405	1.4%
41	New Hampshire	1,322,682	0.5%	29	Iowa	3,676,290	1.4%
14	New Jersey	5,940,997	2.2%	30	Connecticut	2,841,842	1.1%
38	New Mexico	1,823,961	0.7%	31	Arkansas	2,808,138	1.0%
4	New York	11,122,392	4.1%	32	Kansas	2,649,736	1.0%
9	North Carolina	8,270,643	3.1%	33	Nevada	2,398,659	0.9%
46	North Dakota	894,954	0.3%	34	Utah	2,317,282	0.9%
6	Ohio	10,686,057	4.0%	35	Mississippi	2,067,222	0.8%
28	Oklahoma	3,737,405	1.4%	36	Nebraska	1,951,766	0.7%
27	Oregon	3,811,706	1.4%	37	Idaho	1,842,245	0.7%
5	Pennsylvania	10,748,822	4.0%	38	New Mexico	1,823,961	0.7%
47	Rhode Island	876,228	0.3%	39	Montana	1,794,732	0.7%
23	South Carolina	4,324,423	1.6%	40	West Virginia	1,704,825	0.6%
42	South Dakota	1,246,359	0.5%	41	New Hampshire	1,322,682	0.5%
16	Tennessee	5,709,923	2.1%	42	South Dakota	1,246,359	0.5%
2	Texas	21,766,166	8.1%	43	Hawaii	1,231,728	0.5%
34	Utah	2,317,282	0.9%	44	Maine	1,107,674	0.4%
50	Vermont	615,950	0.2%	45	Delaware	1,003,840	0.4%
11	Virginia	7,301,081	2.7%	46	North Dakota	894,954	0.3%
12	Washington	7,047,689	2.6%	47	Rhode Island	876,228	0.3%
40	West Virginia	1,704,825	0.6%	48	Wyoming	855,230	0.3%
18	Wisconsin	5,564,429	2.1%	49	Alaska	794,614	0.3%
48	Wyoming	855,230	0.3%	50	Vermont	615,950	0.2%
					District of Columbia	337,100	0.1%

Source: U.S. Department of Transportation, Federal Highway Administration
   "Highway Statistics 2016" (Table MV-1, http://www.fhwa.dot.gov/policyinformation/statistics/2016/)
*Includes automobiles, trucks and buses and motorcycles.

Motor Vehicles per Driving Age Population in 2016

National Rate = 1.04 Motor Vehicles*

ALPHA ORDER

RANK	STATE	RATE
7	Alabama	1.40
8	Alaska	1.38
32	Arizona	1.05
15	Arkansas	1.19
44	California	0.97
22	Colorado	1.16
44	Connecticut	0.97
10	Delaware	1.30
43	Florida	0.98
37	Georgia	1.02
29	Hawaii	1.07
6	Idaho	1.42
40	Illinois	1.01
19	Indiana	1.17
5	Iowa	1.48
19	Kansas	1.17
15	Kentucky	1.19
31	Louisiana	1.06
41	Maine	1.00
48	Maryland	0.87
46	Massachusetts	0.90
33	Michigan	1.04
11	Minnesota	1.22
47	Mississippi	0.88
19	Missouri	1.17
1	Montana	2.14
9	Nebraska	1.31
35	Nevada	1.03
15	New Hampshire	1.19
49	New Jersey	0.83
26	New Mexico	1.11
50	New York	0.69
37	North Carolina	1.02
4	North Dakota	1.49
23	Ohio	1.15
11	Oklahoma	1.22
23	Oregon	1.15
35	Pennsylvania	1.03
41	Rhode Island	1.00
27	South Carolina	1.08
2	South Dakota	1.85
29	Tennessee	1.07
37	Texas	1.02
33	Utah	1.04
18	Vermont	1.18
27	Virginia	1.08
13	Washington	1.21
25	West Virginia	1.14
14	Wisconsin	1.20
2	Wyoming	1.85

RANK ORDER

RANK	STATE	RATE
1	Montana	2.14
2	South Dakota	1.85
2	Wyoming	1.85
4	North Dakota	1.49
5	Iowa	1.48
6	Idaho	1.42
7	Alabama	1.40
8	Alaska	1.38
9	Nebraska	1.31
10	Delaware	1.30
11	Minnesota	1.22
11	Oklahoma	1.22
13	Washington	1.21
14	Wisconsin	1.20
15	Arkansas	1.19
15	Kentucky	1.19
15	New Hampshire	1.19
18	Vermont	1.18
19	Indiana	1.17
19	Kansas	1.17
19	Missouri	1.17
22	Colorado	1.16
23	Ohio	1.15
23	Oregon	1.15
25	West Virginia	1.14
26	New Mexico	1.11
27	South Carolina	1.08
27	Virginia	1.08
29	Hawaii	1.07
29	Tennessee	1.07
31	Louisiana	1.06
32	Arizona	1.05
33	Michigan	1.04
33	Utah	1.04
35	Nevada	1.03
35	Pennsylvania	1.03
37	Georgia	1.02
37	North Carolina	1.02
37	Texas	1.02
40	Illinois	1.01
41	Maine	1.00
41	Rhode Island	1.00
43	Florida	0.98
44	California	0.97
44	Connecticut	0.97
46	Massachusetts	0.90
47	Mississippi	0.88
48	Maryland	0.87
49	New Jersey	0.83
50	New York	0.69
	District of Columbia	0.59

Source: CQ Press using data from U.S. Department of Transportation, Federal Highway Administration
   "Highway Statistics 2016" (Table MV-1, http://www.fhwa.dot.gov/policyinformation/statistics/2016/)
*Persons age 16 and older. Motor Vehicles include automobiles, trucks, buses, and motorcycles.

Average Travel Time to Work in 2017

National Average = 26.9 Minutes*

ALPHA ORDER

RANK	STATE	MINUTES
25	Alabama	24.6
43	Alaska	19.6
19	Arizona	25.6
41	Arkansas	21.6
4	California	29.8
18	Colorado	25.9
16	Connecticut	26.4
14	Delaware	26.5
10	Florida	27.8
7	Georgia	28.8
13	Hawaii	27.0
42	Idaho	21.0
6	Illinois	29.1
33	Indiana	23.6
44	Iowa	19.4
45	Kansas	19.1
35	Kentucky	23.3
20	Louisiana	25.3
30	Maine	24.0
2	Maryland	33.3
4	Massachusetts	29.8
27	Michigan	24.3
31	Minnesota	23.8
23	Mississippi	24.9
32	Missouri	23.7
47	Montana	18.1
46	Nebraska	18.5
29	Nevada	24.2
11	New Hampshire	27.3
3	New Jersey	32.1
37	New Mexico	22.3
1	New York	33.7
23	North Carolina	24.9
50	North Dakota	16.5
33	Ohio	23.6
40	Oklahoma	21.9
27	Oregon	24.3
12	Pennsylvania	27.1
21	Rhode Island	25.1
25	South Carolina	24.6
49	South Dakota	17.3
21	Tennessee	25.1
14	Texas	26.5
39	Utah	22.0
36	Vermont	23.2
8	Virginia	28.6
9	Washington	27.9
17	West Virginia	26.0
38	Wisconsin	22.2
48	Wyoming	17.6

RANK ORDER

RANK	STATE	MINUTES
1	New York	33.7
2	Maryland	33.3
3	New Jersey	32.1
4	California	29.8
4	Massachusetts	29.8
6	Illinois	29.1
7	Georgia	28.8
8	Virginia	28.6
9	Washington	27.9
10	Florida	27.8
11	New Hampshire	27.3
12	Pennsylvania	27.1
13	Hawaii	27.0
14	Delaware	26.5
14	Texas	26.5
16	Connecticut	26.4
17	West Virginia	26.0
18	Colorado	25.9
19	Arizona	25.6
20	Louisiana	25.3
21	Rhode Island	25.1
21	Tennessee	25.1
23	Mississippi	24.9
23	North Carolina	24.9
25	Alabama	24.6
25	South Carolina	24.6
27	Michigan	24.3
27	Oregon	24.3
29	Nevada	24.2
30	Maine	24.0
31	Minnesota	23.8
32	Missouri	23.7
33	Indiana	23.6
33	Ohio	23.6
35	Kentucky	23.3
36	Vermont	23.2
37	New Mexico	22.3
38	Wisconsin	22.2
39	Utah	22.0
40	Oklahoma	21.9
41	Arkansas	21.6
42	Idaho	21.0
43	Alaska	19.6
44	Iowa	19.4
45	Kansas	19.1
46	Nebraska	18.5
47	Montana	18.1
48	Wyoming	17.6
49	South Dakota	17.3
50	North Dakota	16.5
	District of Columbia	30.8

Source: U.S. Bureau of the Census
"2017 American Community Survey-Table DP03" (https://www.census.gov/programs-surveys/acs/)
*Workers 16 and older not working at home.

Percent of Commuters Who Drive to Work Alone in 2017

National Percent = 76.4%*

ALPHA ORDER				RANK ORDER		
RANK	STATE	PERCENT		RANK	STATE	PERCENT
1	Alabama	85.7		1	Alabama	85.7
48	Alaska	69.3		2	Mississippi	85.5
35	Arizona	76.5		3	Arkansas	83.3
3	Arkansas	83.3		3	Ohio	83.3
41	California	73.9		5	Tennessee	83.2
39	Colorado	74.9		6	West Virginia	82.8
31	Connecticut	78.3		7	Louisiana	82.7
13	Delaware	82.0		8	Michigan	82.5
24	Florida	79.4		9	Indiana	82.4
28	Georgia	78.7		9	Kansas	82.4
49	Hawaii	67.6		11	Oklahoma	82.3
27	Idaho	79.1		12	Missouri	82.2
43	Illinois	73.0		13	Delaware	82.0
9	Indiana	82.4		13	Kentucky	82.0
18	Iowa	81.4		15	South Carolina	81.8
9	Kansas	82.4		16	Nebraska	81.7
13	Kentucky	82.0		17	North Dakota	81.6
7	Louisiana	82.7		18	Iowa	81.4
29	Maine	78.6		19	South Dakota	81.2
42	Maryland	73.7		20	North Carolina	81.1
47	Massachusetts	70.0		20	Wisconsin	81.1
8	Michigan	82.5		22	New Hampshire	80.9
32	Minnesota	78.0		23	Texas	80.6
2	Mississippi	85.5		24	Florida	79.4
12	Missouri	82.2		24	New Mexico	79.4
35	Montana	76.5		24	Rhode Island	79.4
16	Nebraska	81.7		27	Idaho	79.1
30	Nevada	78.5		28	Georgia	78.7
22	New Hampshire	80.9		29	Maine	78.6
46	New Jersey	71.0		30	Nevada	78.5
24	New Mexico	79.4		31	Connecticut	78.3
50	New York	53.1		32	Minnesota	78.0
20	North Carolina	81.1		33	Wyoming	77.9
17	North Dakota	81.6		34	Virginia	77.4
3	Ohio	83.3		35	Arizona	76.5
11	Oklahoma	82.3		35	Montana	76.5
44	Oregon	71.7		37	Pennsylvania	76.2
37	Pennsylvania	76.2		38	Utah	76.1
24	Rhode Island	79.4		39	Colorado	74.9
15	South Carolina	81.8		39	Vermont	74.9
19	South Dakota	81.2		41	California	73.9
5	Tennessee	83.2		42	Maryland	73.7
23	Texas	80.6		43	Illinois	73.0
38	Utah	76.1		44	Oregon	71.7
39	Vermont	74.9		44	Washington	71.7
34	Virginia	77.4		46	New Jersey	71.0
44	Washington	71.7		47	Massachusetts	70.0
6	West Virginia	82.8		48	Alaska	69.3
20	Wisconsin	81.1		49	Hawaii	67.6
33	Wyoming	77.9		50	New York	53.1
				District of Columbia		34.4

Source: U.S. Bureau of the Census
   "2017 American Community Survey-Table DP03" (https://www.census.gov/programs-surveys/acs/)
*Workers 16 and older who traveled to work by car, truck or van.

Percent of Commuters Who Drive to Work in Carpools in 2017

National Percent = 8.9%*

ALPHA ORDER			RANK ORDER		
RANK	STATE	PERCENT	RANK	STATE	PERCENT
35	Alabama	8.5	1	Hawaii	13.3
2	Alaska	11.8	2	Alaska	11.8
3	Arizona	11.0	3	Arizona	11.0
10	Arkansas	9.9	4	Utah	10.7
9	California	10.0	5	New Mexico	10.6
34	Colorado	8.6	6	Idaho	10.2
42	Connecticut	7.9	6	Washington	10.2
49	Delaware	7.1	6	Wyoming	10.2
22	Florida	9.1	9	California	10.0
10	Georgia	9.9	10	Arkansas	9.9
1	Hawaii	13.3	10	Georgia	9.9
6	Idaho	10.2	12	Nevada	9.8
44	Illinois	7.8	12	Oklahoma	9.8
30	Indiana	8.7	12	Texas	9.8
41	Iowa	8.0	15	Oregon	9.7
30	Kansas	8.7	16	South Carolina	9.5
17	Kentucky	9.4	17	Kentucky	9.4
20	Louisiana	9.2	17	Maine	9.4
17	Maine	9.4	17	Rhode Island	9.4
22	Maryland	9.1	20	Louisiana	9.2
48	Massachusetts	7.2	20	Vermont	9.2
30	Michigan	8.7	22	Florida	9.1
39	Minnesota	8.2	22	Maryland	9.1
22	Mississippi	9.1	22	Mississippi	9.1
37	Missouri	8.4	22	Nebraska	9.1
27	Montana	8.9	26	West Virginia	9.0
22	Nebraska	9.1	27	Montana	8.9
12	Nevada	9.8	27	North Carolina	8.9
38	New Hampshire	8.3	29	Tennessee	8.8
42	New Jersey	7.9	30	Indiana	8.7
5	New Mexico	10.6	30	Kansas	8.7
50	New York	6.3	30	Michigan	8.7
27	North Carolina	8.9	30	Virginia	8.7
39	North Dakota	8.2	34	Colorado	8.6
46	Ohio	7.7	35	Alabama	8.5
12	Oklahoma	9.8	35	Pennsylvania	8.5
15	Oregon	9.7	37	Missouri	8.4
35	Pennsylvania	8.5	38	New Hampshire	8.3
17	Rhode Island	9.4	39	Minnesota	8.2
16	South Carolina	9.5	39	North Dakota	8.2
44	South Dakota	7.8	41	Iowa	8.0
29	Tennessee	8.8	42	Connecticut	7.9
12	Texas	9.8	42	New Jersey	7.9
4	Utah	10.7	44	Illinois	7.8
20	Vermont	9.2	44	South Dakota	7.8
30	Virginia	8.7	46	Ohio	7.7
6	Washington	10.2	47	Wisconsin	7.6
26	West Virginia	9.0	48	Massachusetts	7.2
47	Wisconsin	7.6	49	Delaware	7.1
6	Wyoming	10.2	50	New York	6.3
				District of Columbia	5.2

Source: U.S. Bureau of the Census
    "2017 American Community Survey-Table DP03" (https://www.census.gov/programs-surveys/acs/)
*Workers 16 and older who traveled to work by car, truck or van.

Percent of Commuters Who Travel to Work by Public Transportation in 2017

National Percent = 5.0%*

ALPHA ORDER				RANK ORDER		
RANK	STATE	PERCENT		RANK	STATE	PERCENT
46	Alabama	0.4		1	New York	28.1
22	Alaska	1.7		2	New Jersey	11.8
20	Arizona	1.8		3	Massachusetts	10.4
48	Arkansas	0.3		4	Illinois	9.6
9	California	5.0		5	Maryland	8.5
14	Colorado	3.2		6	Washington	6.5
10	Connecticut	4.7		7	Hawaii	6.1
17	Delaware	2.2		8	Pennsylvania	5.3
22	Florida	1.7		9	California	5.0
19	Georgia	2.1		10	Connecticut	4.7
7	Hawaii	6.1		11	Oregon	4.5
40	Idaho	0.6		12	Virginia	4.2
4	Illinois	9.6		13	Minnesota	3.7
33	Indiana	0.9		14	Colorado	3.2
33	Iowa	0.9		15	Nevada	3.1
46	Kansas	0.4		16	Utah	2.3
29	Kentucky	1.1		17	Delaware	2.2
29	Louisiana	1.1		17	Rhode Island	2.2
40	Maine	0.6		19	Georgia	2.1
5	Maryland	8.5		20	Arizona	1.8
3	Massachusetts	10.4		20	Wisconsin	1.8
27	Michigan	1.3		22	Alaska	1.7
13	Minnesota	3.7		22	Florida	1.7
48	Mississippi	0.3		24	Ohio	1.5
27	Missouri	1.3		24	Vermont	1.5
36	Montana	0.8		26	Texas	1.4
37	Nebraska	0.7		27	Michigan	1.3
15	Nevada	3.1		27	Missouri	1.3
37	New Hampshire	0.7		29	Kentucky	1.1
2	New Jersey	11.8		29	Louisiana	1.1
29	New Mexico	1.1		29	New Mexico	1.1
1	New York	28.1		32	North Carolina	1.0
32	North Carolina	1.0		33	Indiana	0.9
44	North Dakota	0.5		33	Iowa	0.9
24	Ohio	1.5		33	West Virginia	0.9
48	Oklahoma	0.3		36	Montana	0.8
11	Oregon	4.5		37	Nebraska	0.7
8	Pennsylvania	5.3		37	New Hampshire	0.7
17	Rhode Island	2.2		37	South Dakota	0.7
44	South Carolina	0.5		40	Idaho	0.6
37	South Dakota	0.7		40	Maine	0.6
40	Tennessee	0.6		40	Tennessee	0.6
26	Texas	1.4		40	Wyoming	0.6
16	Utah	2.3		44	North Dakota	0.5
24	Vermont	1.5		44	South Carolina	0.5
12	Virginia	4.2		46	Alabama	0.4
6	Washington	6.5		46	Kansas	0.4
33	West Virginia	0.9		48	Arkansas	0.3
20	Wisconsin	1.8		48	Mississippi	0.3
40	Wyoming	0.6		48	Oklahoma	0.3
					District of Columbia	32.7

Source: U.S. Bureau of the Census
  "2017 American Community Survey-Table DP03" (https://www.census.gov/programs-surveys/acs/)
*Workers 16 and older.

Annual Miles per Vehicle in 2016

National Annual Average = 11,864 Miles*

ALPHA ORDER

RANK	STATE	MILES
15	Alabama	12,660
50	Alaska	6,618
27	Arizona	11,368
14	Arkansas	12,733
28	California	11,254
39	Colorado	10,193
30	Connecticut	11,133
40	Delaware	10,139
12	Florida	12,985
3	Georgia	14,904
47	Hawaii	8,635
43	Idaho	9,336
37	Illinois	10,442
7	Indiana	13,547
44	Iowa	9,068
20	Kansas	12,115
23	Kentucky	11,672
17	Louisiana	12,588
9	Maine	13,396
4	Maryland	14,152
19	Massachusetts	12,195
22	Michigan	11,933
33	Minnesota	11,016
1	Mississippi	19,715
11	Missouri	13,021
49	Montana	7,020
36	Nebraska	10,606
29	Nevada	11,168
38	New Hampshire	10,216
13	New Jersey	12,976
2	New Mexico	15,288
32	New York	11,052
5	North Carolina	14,116
35	North Dakota	10,882
31	Ohio	11,099
10	Oklahoma	13,114
41	Oregon	9,633
42	Pennsylvania	9,430
45	Rhode Island	9,047
16	South Carolina	12,615
48	South Dakota	7,627
8	Tennessee	13,465
18	Texas	12,463
6	Utah	13,571
21	Vermont	11,985
24	Virginia	11,569
46	Washington	8,658
26	West Virginia	11,461
25	Wisconsin	11,510
34	Wyoming	10,901

RANK ORDER

RANK	STATE	MILES
1	Mississippi	19,715
2	New Mexico	15,288
3	Georgia	14,904
4	Maryland	14,152
5	North Carolina	14,116
6	Utah	13,571
7	Indiana	13,547
8	Tennessee	13,465
9	Maine	13,396
10	Oklahoma	13,114
11	Missouri	13,021
12	Florida	12,985
13	New Jersey	12,976
14	Arkansas	12,733
15	Alabama	12,660
16	South Carolina	12,615
17	Louisiana	12,588
18	Texas	12,463
19	Massachusetts	12,195
20	Kansas	12,115
21	Vermont	11,985
22	Michigan	11,933
23	Kentucky	11,672
24	Virginia	11,569
25	Wisconsin	11,510
26	West Virginia	11,461
27	Arizona	11,368
28	California	11,254
29	Nevada	11,168
30	Connecticut	11,133
31	Ohio	11,099
32	New York	11,052
33	Minnesota	11,016
34	Wyoming	10,901
35	North Dakota	10,882
36	Nebraska	10,606
37	Illinois	10,442
38	New Hampshire	10,216
39	Colorado	10,193
40	Delaware	10,139
41	Oregon	9,633
42	Pennsylvania	9,430
43	Idaho	9,336
44	Iowa	9,068
45	Rhode Island	9,047
46	Washington	8,658
47	Hawaii	8,635
48	South Dakota	7,627
49	Montana	7,020
50	Alaska	6,618

District of Columbia — 10,744

Source: CQ Press using data from U.S. Department of Transportation, Federal Highway Administration
   "Highway Statistics 2016" (Tables MV-1 and VM-2, http://www.fhwa.dot.gov/policyinformation/statistics/2016/)
*Includes automobiles, trucks, buses and motorcycles.

Average Miles per Gallon in 2016

National Average = 17.9 Miles per Gallon*

ALPHA ORDER

RANK	STATE	MILES PER GALLON
7	Alabama	19.5
47	Alaska	14.2
17	Arizona	18.5
32	Arkansas	17.4
14	California	19.2
20	Colorado	18.3
18	Connecticut	18.4
10	Delaware	19.4
1	Florida	21.9
4	Georgia	20.8
2	Hawaii	21.5
37	Idaho	16.9
34	Illinois	17.3
12	Indiana	19.3
45	Iowa	14.3
20	Kansas	18.3
37	Kentucky	16.9
32	Louisiana	17.4
41	Maine	15.9
15	Maryland	18.7
7	Massachusetts	19.5
20	Michigan	18.3
26	Minnesota	18.1
35	Mississippi	17.2
27	Missouri	18.0
39	Montana	16.6
42	Nebraska	15.7
16	Nevada	18.6
30	New Hampshire	17.8
43	New Jersey	15.6
12	New Mexico	19.3
27	New York	18.0
3	North Carolina	20.9
49	North Dakota	13.9
18	Ohio	18.4
27	Oklahoma	18.0
30	Oregon	17.8
40	Pennsylvania	16.3
10	Rhode Island	19.4
44	South Carolina	15.5
49	South Dakota	13.9
25	Tennessee	18.2
45	Texas	14.3
7	Utah	19.5
5	Vermont	20.2
36	Virginia	17.1
20	Washington	18.3
20	West Virginia	18.3
6	Wisconsin	19.8
48	Wyoming	14.1

RANK ORDER

RANK	STATE	MILES PER GALLON
1	Florida	21.9
2	Hawaii	21.5
3	North Carolina	20.9
4	Georgia	20.8
5	Vermont	20.2
6	Wisconsin	19.8
7	Alabama	19.5
7	Massachusetts	19.5
7	Utah	19.5
10	Delaware	19.4
10	Rhode Island	19.4
12	Indiana	19.3
12	New Mexico	19.3
14	California	19.2
15	Maryland	18.7
16	Nevada	18.6
17	Arizona	18.5
18	Connecticut	18.4
18	Ohio	18.4
20	Colorado	18.3
20	Kansas	18.3
20	Michigan	18.3
20	Washington	18.3
20	West Virginia	18.3
25	Tennessee	18.2
26	Minnesota	18.1
27	Missouri	18.0
27	New York	18.0
27	Oklahoma	18.0
30	New Hampshire	17.8
30	Oregon	17.8
32	Arkansas	17.4
32	Louisiana	17.4
34	Illinois	17.3
35	Mississippi	17.2
36	Virginia	17.1
37	Idaho	16.9
37	Kentucky	16.9
39	Montana	16.6
40	Pennsylvania	16.3
41	Maine	15.9
42	Nebraska	15.7
43	New Jersey	15.6
44	South Carolina	15.5
45	Iowa	14.3
45	Texas	14.3
47	Alaska	14.2
48	Wyoming	14.1
49	North Dakota	13.9
49	South Dakota	13.9
	District of Columbia	27.8

Source: CQ Press using data from U.S. Department of Transportation, Federal Highway Administration
"Highway Statistics 2016" (Tables MF-21 and VM-2, https://www.fhwa.dot.gov/policyinformation/statistics/2016/)
*Total vehicle-miles for 2016 divided by total highway motor-fuel use. Includes gasoline, gasohol, diesel, and other "special fuels."

Percent of Traffic Fatalities That Were Pedestrians in 2016

National Percent = 16.0%*

ALPHA ORDER

RANK	STATE	PERCENT
32	Alabama	10.7
22	Alaska	14.3
11	Arizona	19.8
42	Arkansas	8.1
6	California	23.9
27	Colorado	13.0
12	Connecticut	18.4
7	Delaware	22.7
10	Florida	20.5
19	Georgia	14.9
5	Hawaii	24.2
43	Idaho	6.7
26	Illinois	13.7
34	Indiana	10.4
48	Iowa	5.4
37	Kansas	9.6
36	Kentucky	9.7
15	Louisiana	16.8
33	Maine	10.6
8	Maryland	20.6
8	Massachusetts	20.6
18	Michigan	15.2
20	Minnesota	14.8
40	Mississippi	8.4
35	Missouri	10.2
46	Montana	5.8
47	Nebraska	5.5
4	Nevada	24.4
29	New Hampshire	12.5
3	New Jersey	27.0
13	New Mexico	18.2
1	New York	29.7
25	North Carolina	13.8
45	North Dakota	6.2
31	Ohio	11.8
28	Oklahoma	12.7
21	Oregon	14.5
23	Pennsylvania	14.2
2	Rhode Island	27.5
23	South Carolina	14.2
49	South Dakota	5.2
38	Tennessee	9.3
14	Texas	17.8
29	Utah	12.5
44	Vermont	6.5
16	Virginia	16.1
17	Washington	15.6
39	West Virginia	8.9
40	Wisconsin	8.4
50	Wyoming	4.5

RANK ORDER

RANK	STATE	PERCENT
1	New York	29.7
2	Rhode Island	27.5
3	New Jersey	27.0
4	Nevada	24.4
5	Hawaii	24.2
6	California	23.9
7	Delaware	22.7
8	Maryland	20.6
8	Massachusetts	20.6
10	Florida	20.5
11	Arizona	19.8
12	Connecticut	18.4
13	New Mexico	18.2
14	Texas	17.8
15	Louisiana	16.8
16	Virginia	16.1
17	Washington	15.6
18	Michigan	15.2
19	Georgia	14.9
20	Minnesota	14.8
21	Oregon	14.5
22	Alaska	14.3
23	Pennsylvania	14.2
23	South Carolina	14.2
25	North Carolina	13.8
26	Illinois	13.7
27	Colorado	13.0
28	Oklahoma	12.7
29	New Hampshire	12.5
29	Utah	12.5
31	Ohio	11.8
32	Alabama	10.7
33	Maine	10.6
34	Indiana	10.4
35	Missouri	10.2
36	Kentucky	9.7
37	Kansas	9.6
38	Tennessee	9.3
39	West Virginia	8.9
40	Mississippi	8.4
40	Wisconsin	8.4
42	Arkansas	8.1
43	Idaho	6.7
44	Vermont	6.5
45	North Dakota	6.2
46	Montana	5.8
47	Nebraska	5.5
48	Iowa	5.4
49	South Dakota	5.2
50	Wyoming	4.5

	District of Columbia	29.6

Source: U.S. Department of Transportation, National Highway Traffic Safety Administration
   "Traffic Safety Facts: Pedestrians" (https://crashstats.nhtsa.dot.gov/)
*A pedestrian fatality is any person on foot, walking, running, jogging, hiking, sitting, or lying down who is involved in a motor vehicle traffic crash.

Percent of Traffic Fatalities That Were Bicyclists in 2016

National Percent = 2.2%*

ALPHA ORDER				RANK ORDER		
RANK	STATE	PERCENT		RANK	STATE	PERCENT
48	Alabama	0.2		1	Florida	4.3
35	Alaska	1.2		2	California	4.1
6	Arizona	3.2		3	Rhode Island	3.9
45	Arkansas	0.6		4	New York	3.7
2	California	4.1		5	Michigan	3.6
12	Colorado	2.6		6	Arizona	3.2
26	Connecticut	1.7		6	Maryland	3.2
26	Delaware	1.7		6	Washington	3.2
1	Florida	4.3		9	New Jersey	3.0
20	Georgia	1.9		10	Louisiana	2.9
49	Hawaii	0.0		11	North Dakota	2.7
16	Idaho	2.4		12	Colorado	2.6
21	Illinois	1.8		12	Massachusetts	2.6
17	Indiana	2.3		14	Maine	2.5
18	Iowa	2.0		14	South Carolina	2.5
35	Kansas	1.2		16	Idaho	2.4
38	Kentucky	1.1		17	Indiana	2.3
10	Louisiana	2.9		18	Iowa	2.0
14	Maine	2.5		18	Oregon	2.0
6	Maryland	3.2		20	Georgia	1.9
12	Massachusetts	2.6		21	Illinois	1.8
5	Michigan	3.6		21	Minnesota	1.8
21	Minnesota	1.8		21	Nevada	1.8
43	Mississippi	0.7		21	Utah	1.8
42	Missouri	0.8		21	Wisconsin	1.8
29	Montana	1.6		26	Connecticut	1.7
46	Nebraska	0.5		26	Delaware	1.7
21	Nevada	1.8		26	Texas	1.7
32	New Hampshire	1.5		29	Montana	1.6
9	New Jersey	3.0		29	Ohio	1.6
39	New Mexico	1.0		29	Vermont	1.6
4	New York	3.7		32	New Hampshire	1.5
35	North Carolina	1.2		33	Pennsylvania	1.3
11	North Dakota	2.7		33	Virginia	1.3
29	Ohio	1.6		35	Alaska	1.2
43	Oklahoma	0.7		35	Kansas	1.2
18	Oregon	2.0		35	North Carolina	1.2
33	Pennsylvania	1.3		38	Kentucky	1.1
3	Rhode Island	3.9		39	New Mexico	1.0
14	South Carolina	2.5		40	Tennessee	0.9
49	South Dakota	0.0		40	Wyoming	0.9
40	Tennessee	0.9		42	Missouri	0.8
26	Texas	1.7		43	Mississippi	0.7
21	Utah	1.8		43	Oklahoma	0.7
29	Vermont	1.6		45	Arkansas	0.6
33	Virginia	1.3		46	Nebraska	0.5
6	Washington	3.2		47	West Virginia	0.4
47	West Virginia	0.4		48	Alabama	0.2
21	Wisconsin	1.8		49	Hawaii	0.0
40	Wyoming	0.9		49	South Dakota	0.0
					District of Columbia	3.7

Source: U.S. Department of Transportation, National Highway Traffic Safety Administration
  "Traffic Safety Facts: Bicyclists and Other Cyclists" (https://crashstats.nhtsa.dot.gov/)
*A bicyclist fatality includes any person on a bicycle, tricycle, or unicycle powered solely by pedals that is involved in a vehicle traffic crash.

Percent of Recreational Boating Accidents Involving Alcohol in 2017

National Percent = 7.6% of Accidents*

RANK	STATE	PERCENT		RANK	STATE	PERCENT
12	Alabama	11.4		1	Vermont	33.3
33	Alaska	6.7		2	North Dakota	26.7
46	Arizona	1.6		3	Kentucky	17.1
35	Arkansas	6.3		4	West Virginia	16.7
42	California	4.0		5	Colorado	15.6
5	Colorado	15.6		6	Wisconsin	15.2
28	Connecticut	8.2		7	Kansas	13.8
10	Delaware	13.0		8	Minnesota	13.3
39	Florida	5.4		9	Oklahoma	13.2
18	Georgia	10.8		10	Delaware	13.0
48	Hawaii	0.0		11	Maine	12.2
16	Idaho	10.9		12	Alabama	11.4
26	Illinois	8.3		13	Montana	11.1
19	Indiana	10.5		13	Nebraska	11.1
22	Iowa	10.0		13	North Carolina	11.1
7	Kansas	13.8		16	Idaho	10.9
3	Kentucky	17.1		16	Maryland	10.9
21	Louisiana	10.4		18	Georgia	10.8
11	Maine	12.2		19	Indiana	10.5
16	Maryland	10.9		19	Missouri	10.5
40	Massachusetts	4.5		21	Louisiana	10.4
30	Michigan	7.8		22	Iowa	10.0
8	Minnesota	13.3		22	Wyoming	10.0
43	Mississippi	2.9		24	Tennessee	9.7
19	Missouri	10.5		25	Ohio	8.5
13	Montana	11.1		26	Illinois	8.3
13	Nebraska	11.1		26	Washington	8.3
38	Nevada	5.7		28	Connecticut	8.2
36	New Hampshire	6.1		29	South Carolina	7.9
47	New Jersey	0.9		30	Michigan	7.8
48	New Mexico	0.0		31	New York	7.2
31	New York	7.2		31	Pennsylvania	7.2
13	North Carolina	11.1		33	Alaska	6.7
2	North Dakota	26.7		34	Rhode Island	6.5
25	Ohio	8.5		35	Arkansas	6.3
9	Oklahoma	13.2		36	New Hampshire	6.1
44	Oregon	1.7		37	Texas	5.9
31	Pennsylvania	7.2		38	Nevada	5.7
34	Rhode Island	6.5		39	Florida	5.4
29	South Carolina	7.9		40	Massachusetts	4.5
48	South Dakota	0.0		41	Virginia	4.2
24	Tennessee	9.7		42	California	4.0
37	Texas	5.9		43	Mississippi	2.9
44	Utah	1.7		44	Oregon	1.7
1	Vermont	33.3		44	Utah	1.7
41	Virginia	4.2		46	Arizona	1.6
26	Washington	8.3		47	New Jersey	0.9
4	West Virginia	16.7		48	Hawaii	0.0
6	Wisconsin	15.2		48	New Mexico	0.0
22	Wyoming	10.0		48	South Dakota	0.0
					District of Columbia	0.0

Source: CQ Press using data from United States Coast Guard
   "Boating Statistics 2017" (www.uscgboating.org/statistics/accident_statistics.php)
*Alcohol involvement in a boating accident includes any accident in which alcoholic beverages are consumed in the boat and the investigating official has determined that the operator was impaired or affected while operating the boat.

Railroad Accidents and Incidents in 2017

National Total = 11,859*

ALPHA ORDER

RANK	STATE	ACCIDENTS	% of USA
13	Alabama	229	1.9%
43	Alaska	38	0.3%
30	Arizona	118	1.0%
27	Arkansas	138	1.2%
2	California	977	8.2%
17	Colorado	197	1.7%
18	Connecticut	191	1.6%
39	Delaware	84	0.7%
7	Florida	408	3.4%
8	Georgia	314	2.6%
50	Hawaii	0	0.0%
42	Idaho	48	0.4%
3	Illinois	855	7.2%
8	Indiana	314	2.6%
21	Iowa	179	1.5%
23	Kansas	173	1.5%
32	Kentucky	115	1.0%
11	Louisiana	275	2.3%
48	Maine	12	0.1%
25	Maryland	161	1.4%
15	Massachusetts	217	1.8%
25	Michigan	161	1.4%
16	Minnesota	202	1.7%
33	Mississippi	114	1.0%
19	Missouri	189	1.6%
35	Montana	106	0.9%
24	Nebraska	164	1.4%
47	Nevada	24	0.2%
49	New Hampshire	3	0.0%
5	New Jersey	710	6.0%
37	New Mexico	85	0.7%
1	New York	1,429	12.0%
19	North Carolina	189	1.6%
37	North Dakota	85	0.7%
10	Ohio	309	2.6%
31	Oklahoma	117	1.0%
28	Oregon	129	1.1%
6	Pennsylvania	640	5.4%
45	Rhode Island	32	0.3%
33	South Carolina	114	1.0%
44	South Dakota	37	0.3%
22	Tennessee	178	1.5%
4	Texas	772	6.5%
40	Utah	82	0.7%
45	Vermont	32	0.3%
14	Virginia	226	1.9%
12	Washington	273	2.3%
36	West Virginia	88	0.7%
29	Wisconsin	125	1.1%
41	Wyoming	60	0.5%

RANK ORDER

RANK	STATE	ACCIDENTS	% of USA
1	New York	1,429	12.0%
2	California	977	8.2%
3	Illinois	855	7.2%
4	Texas	772	6.5%
5	New Jersey	710	6.0%
6	Pennsylvania	640	5.4%
7	Florida	408	3.4%
8	Georgia	314	2.6%
8	Indiana	314	2.6%
10	Ohio	309	2.6%
11	Louisiana	275	2.3%
12	Washington	273	2.3%
13	Alabama	229	1.9%
14	Virginia	226	1.9%
15	Massachusetts	217	1.8%
16	Minnesota	202	1.7%
17	Colorado	197	1.7%
18	Connecticut	191	1.6%
19	Missouri	189	1.6%
19	North Carolina	189	1.6%
21	Iowa	179	1.5%
22	Tennessee	178	1.5%
23	Kansas	173	1.5%
24	Nebraska	164	1.4%
25	Maryland	161	1.4%
25	Michigan	161	1.4%
27	Arkansas	138	1.2%
28	Oregon	129	1.1%
29	Wisconsin	125	1.1%
30	Arizona	118	1.0%
31	Oklahoma	117	1.0%
32	Kentucky	115	1.0%
33	Mississippi	114	1.0%
33	South Carolina	114	1.0%
35	Montana	106	0.9%
36	West Virginia	88	0.7%
37	New Mexico	85	0.7%
37	North Dakota	85	0.7%
39	Delaware	84	0.7%
40	Utah	82	0.7%
41	Wyoming	60	0.5%
42	Idaho	48	0.4%
43	Alaska	38	0.3%
44	South Dakota	37	0.3%
45	Rhode Island	32	0.3%
45	Vermont	32	0.3%
47	Nevada	24	0.2%
48	Maine	12	0.1%
49	New Hampshire	3	0.0%
50	Hawaii	0	0.0%
	District of Columbia	141	1.2%

Source: U.S. Department of Transportation, Federal Railroad Administration, Office of Safety Analysis
   "Railroad Accidents and Incidents" (Table 1.12, https://safetydata.fra.dot.gov/OfficeofSafety/Default.aspx)
*Accidents or incidents include all events reportable to the U.S. Department of Transportation. These include train accidents causing damage above an established threshold; highway-rail grade crossing incidents involving impact between railroad equipment and highway users at crossings; and all other reportable incidents that cause a fatality or injury to any person or an occupational illness to a railroad employee. There were 823 fatalities involving railroads.

Railroad Mileage Operated in 2017

National Total = 136,898 Miles of Railroad*

ALPHA ORDER

RANK	STATE	MILES	% of USA
15	Alabama	3,272	2.4%
46	Alaska	506	0.4%
36	Arizona	1,820	1.3%
26	Arkansas	2,505	1.8%
5	California	4,828	3.5%
28	Colorado	2,427	1.8%
45	Connecticut	522	0.4%
48	Delaware	243	0.2%
23	Florida	2,851	2.1%
7	Georgia	4,607	3.4%
50	Hawaii	0	0.0%
37	Idaho	1,729	1.3%
2	Illinois	7,151	5.2%
11	Indiana	3,786	2.8%
10	Iowa	3,834	2.8%
6	Kansas	4,675	3.4%
24	Kentucky	2,624	1.9%
22	Louisiana	2,940	2.1%
40	Maine	1,077	0.8%
43	Maryland	769	0.6%
41	Massachusetts	1,057	0.8%
29	Michigan	2,417	1.8%
8	Minnesota	4,258	3.1%
27	Mississippi	2,455	1.8%
9	Missouri	3,862	2.8%
12	Montana	3,719	2.7%
20	Nebraska	3,117	2.3%
39	Nevada	1,193	0.9%
47	New Hampshire	354	0.3%
42	New Jersey	952	0.7%
35	New Mexico	1,879	1.4%
14	New York	3,279	2.4%
17	North Carolina	3,161	2.3%
13	North Dakota	3,287	2.4%
3	Ohio	5,132	3.7%
18	Oklahoma	3,158	2.3%
30	Oregon	2,382	1.7%
4	Pennsylvania	5,130	3.7%
49	Rhode Island	58	0.0%
31	South Carolina	2,278	1.7%
33	South Dakota	2,029	1.5%
25	Tennessee	2,552	1.9%
1	Texas	10,506	7.7%
38	Utah	1,386	1.0%
44	Vermont	578	0.4%
19	Virginia	3,141	2.3%
21	Washington	3,032	2.2%
32	West Virginia	2,214	1.6%
16	Wisconsin	3,253	2.4%
34	Wyoming	1,890	1.4%

RANK ORDER

RANK	STATE	MILES	% of USA
1	Texas	10,506	7.7%
2	Illinois	7,151	5.2%
3	Ohio	5,132	3.7%
4	Pennsylvania	5,130	3.7%
5	California	4,828	3.5%
6	Kansas	4,675	3.4%
7	Georgia	4,607	3.4%
8	Minnesota	4,258	3.1%
9	Missouri	3,862	2.8%
10	Iowa	3,834	2.8%
11	Indiana	3,786	2.8%
12	Montana	3,719	2.7%
13	North Dakota	3,287	2.4%
14	New York	3,279	2.4%
15	Alabama	3,272	2.4%
16	Wisconsin	3,253	2.4%
17	North Carolina	3,161	2.3%
18	Oklahoma	3,158	2.3%
19	Virginia	3,141	2.3%
20	Nebraska	3,117	2.3%
21	Washington	3,032	2.2%
22	Louisiana	2,940	2.1%
23	Florida	2,851	2.1%
24	Kentucky	2,624	1.9%
25	Tennessee	2,552	1.9%
26	Arkansas	2,505	1.8%
27	Mississippi	2,455	1.8%
28	Colorado	2,427	1.8%
29	Michigan	2,417	1.8%
30	Oregon	2,382	1.7%
31	South Carolina	2,278	1.7%
32	West Virginia	2,214	1.6%
33	South Dakota	2,029	1.5%
34	Wyoming	1,890	1.4%
35	New Mexico	1,879	1.4%
36	Arizona	1,820	1.3%
37	Idaho	1,729	1.3%
38	Utah	1,386	1.0%
39	Nevada	1,193	0.9%
40	Maine	1,077	0.8%
41	Massachusetts	1,057	0.8%
42	New Jersey	952	0.7%
43	Maryland	769	0.6%
44	Vermont	578	0.4%
45	Connecticut	522	0.4%
46	Alaska	506	0.4%
47	New Hampshire	354	0.3%
48	Delaware	243	0.2%
49	Rhode Island	58	0.0%
50	Hawaii	0	0.0%
	District of Columbia	22	0.0%

Source: Association of American Railroads
  "Railroads and States" (https://www.aar.org/data-center/railroads-states)
*Includes Class I and non-Class I miles. Excludes trackage rights. Synonymous with route-miles, so that a mile of single track is counted the same as a mile of double track.

Sources

ACT, Inc.
500 ACT Drive, P.O. Box 168
Iowa City, IA 52243-0168
319-337-1000
www.act.org

Administration for Children and Families
U.S. Department of Health and Human Services
330 C Street, SW
Washington, DC 20201
202-401-9215
www.acf.hhs.gov

American Cancer Society, Inc.
250 Williams Street, NW
Atlanta, GA 30303
800-227-2345
www.cancer.org

American Hospital Association
155 N. Wacker Drive
Chicago, IL 60606
312-422-3000
www.aha.org

Association of American Railroads
425 Third Street, SW, Suite 1000
Washington, DC 20024
202-639-2100
www.aar.org

Bureau of Economic Analysis
U.S. Department of Commerce
4600 Silver Hill Road
Washington, DC 20233
301-278-9004
www.bea.gov

Bureau of Justice Statistics
U.S. Department of Justice
810 Seventh Street, NW
Washington, DC 20531
202-307-0765
www.bjs.gov

Bureau of Labor Statistics
U.S. Department of Labor
2 Massachusetts Avenue, NE
Washington, DC 20212-0001
202-691-5200
www.bls.gov

Bureau of Transportation Statistics
U.S. Department of Transportation
1200 New Jersey Avenue, SE
Washington, DC 20590
800-853-1351
www.bts.gov

Census Bureau
4600 Silver Hill Road
Washington, DC 20233-0001
800-923-8282
www.census.gov

Centers for Disease Control and Prevention
1600 Clifton Road
Atlanta, GA 30329-4027
800-232-4636
www.cdc.gov

Centers for Medicare and Medicaid Services
7500 Security Boulevard
Baltimore, MD 21244-1850
877-267-2323
www.cms.gov

Economic Research Service
U.S. Department of Agriculture
1400 Independence Avenue, SW
Mail Stop 1800
Washington, DC 20250-0002
202-694-5139
www.ers.usda.gov

Energy Information Administration
U.S. Department of Energy
1000 Independence Avenue, SW
Washington, DC 20585
202-586-8800
www.eia.gov

Environmental Protection Agency
Ariel Rios Building
1200 Pennsylvania Avenue, NW
Washington, DC 20460
202-272-0167
www.epa.gov

Federal Bureau of Investigation
J Edgar Hoover Building
935 Pennsylvania Avenue, NW
Washington, DC 20535-0001
202-324-3000
www.fbi.gov

Federal Highway Administration
U.S. Department of Transportation
1200 New Jersey Avenue, SE
Washington, DC 20590
202-366-4000
www.fhwa.dot.gov

Federation of Tax Administrators
444 North Capitol Street, NW, Suite 348
Washington, DC 20001
202-624-5890
www.taxadmin.org

Food and Nutrition Service
U.S. Department of Agriculture
3101 Park Center Drive
Alexandria, VA 22302
703-305-2062
www.fns.usda.gov

General Services Administration
1800 F Street, NW
Washington, DC 20450
844-472-43111
www.gsa.gov

Health Resources and Services Administration
Division of Practitioner Data Banks
5600 Fishers Lane
Rockville, MD 20857
301-443-3376

Institute of Museum and Library Services
955 L'Enfant Plaza North, SW, Suite 4000
Washington, DC 20024-2135
202-653-4657
www.imls.gov

Internal Revenue Service
U.S. Department of the Treasury
1111 Constitution Avenue, NW
Washington, DC 20224
202-283-1710
www.irs.gov

Medical Expenditure Panel Survey
Agency for Healthcare Research and Quality
5600 Fishers Lane
Rockville, MD 20857
301-427-1364
www.meps.ahrq.gov

National Agricultural Statistics Service
1400 Independence Avenue, SW
Washington, DC 20250
800-727-9540
www.nass.usda.gov

National Assembly of State Arts Agencies
1200 18th Street, NW, Suite 1100
Washington, DC 20036
202-347-6352
www.nasaa-arts.org

National Center for Education Statistics
U.S. Department of Education
550 12th Street, SW
Washington, DC 20036
202-403-5551
https://nces.ed.gov/

National Center for Health Statistics
U.S. Department of Health and Human Services
3311 Toledo Road
Hyattsville, MD 20782
800-232-4636
www.cdc.gov/nchs/

National Conference of State Legislatures
7700 E. First Place
Denver, CO 80230
303-364-7700
www.ncsl.org

National Education Association
1201 16th Street, NW
Washington, DC 20036-3290
202-833-4000
www.nea.org

National Highway Traffic Safety Administration
1200 New Jersey Avenue, SE
Washington, DC 20590
888-327-4236
www.nhtsa.gov

National Institute on Alcohol Abuse and Alcoholism
5635 Fishers Lane, MSC 9304
Bethesda, MD 20892-9304
301-443-3860
www.niaaa.nih.gov

National Oceanic & Atmospheric Administration
U.S. Department of Commerce
1401 Constitution Avenue, NW, Room 5128
Washington, DC 20230
202-482-6090
www.noaa.gov

Office of Management and Budget
725 17th Street, NW
Washington, DC 20503
202-395-3080
www.USAspending.gov

Project on Student Debt
Institute for College Access and Success
405 14th Street, 11th Floor
Oakland, CA 94612
510-318-7900
https://ticas.org/posd/home

Social Security Administration
Office of Public Inquiries
1100 West High Rise
6401 Security Boulevard
Baltimore, MD 21235
800-772-1213 (information)
www.ssa.gov

Storm Prediction Center
National Weather Service
120 David Boren Boulevard
Norman, OK 73072
405-579-0771
www.spc.noaa.gov

Tax Foundation
1325 G Street, NW, Suite 950
Washington, DC 20005
202-464-6200
www.taxfoundation.org

U.S. Department of Defense
Directorate for Public Inquiry and Analysis
Room 2E565, The Pentagon
1400 Defense Pentagon
Washington, DC 20301-1400
703-571-3343
www.defense.gov

U.S. Department of Veterans Affairs
810 Vermont Avenue, NW
Washington, DC 20420
800-827-1000
www.va.gov

U.S. Geological Survey
12201 Sunrise Valley Drive
Reston, VA 20192
888-275-8747
www.usgs.gov

Index